Dietary Reference Intakes: RDA, AI*, (AMDR)

Life-Stage Group	Carbohydrate— Total Digestible (g/d)	Total Fiber (g/d)	Total Fat (g/d)	n-6 polyunsaturated fatty acids (linoleic acid) (g/d)	n-3 polyunsaturated fatty acids (α-linolenic acid) (g/d)	Protein and Amino Acids (g/d)[a]
Infants						
0–6 mo	60* (ND[b])[c]	ND	31*	4.4* (ND)	0.5* (ND)	9.1* (ND)
7–12 mo	95* (ND)	ND	30*	4.6* (ND)	0.5* (ND)	13.5 (ND)
Children						
1–3 y	130 (45–65)	19*	(30–40)	7* (5–10)	0.7* (0.6–1.2)	13 (5–20)
4–8 y	130 (45–65)	25*	(25–35)	10* (5–10)	0.9* (0.6–1.2)	19 (10–30)
Males						
9–13 y	130 (45–65)	31*	(25–35)	12* (5–10)	1.2* (0.6–1.2)	34 (10–30)
14–18 y	130 (45–65)	38*	(25–35)	16* (5–10)	1.6* (0.6–1.2)	52 (10–30)
19–30 y	130 (45–65)	38*	(20–35)	17* (5–10)	1.6* (0.6–1.2)	56 (10–35)
31–50 y	130 (45–65)	38*	(20–35)	17* (5–10)	1.6* (0.6–1.2)	56 (10–35)
51–70 y	130 (45–65)	30*	(20–35)	14* (5–10)	1.6* (0.6–1.2)	56 (10–35)
>70 y	130 (45–65)	30*	(20–35)	14* (5–10)	1.6* (0.6–1.2)	56 (10–35)
Females						
9–13 y	130 (45–65)	26*	(25–35)	10* (5–10)	1.0* (0.6–1.2)	34 (10–30)
14–18 y	130 (45–65)	26*	(25–35)	11* (5–10)	1.1* (0.6–1.2)	46 (10–30)
19–30 y	130 (45–65)	25*	(20–35)	12* (5–10)	1.1* (0.6–1.2)	46 (10–35)
31–50 y	130 (45–65)	25*	(20–35)	12* (5–10)	1.1* (0.6–1.2)	46 (10–35)
51–70 y	130 (45–65)	21*	(20–35)	11* (5–10)	1.1* (0.6–1.2)	46 (10–35)
>70 y	130 (45–65)	21*	(20–35)	11* (5–10)	1.1* (0.6–1.2)	46 (10–35)
Pregnancy						
≤18 y	175 (45–65)	28*	(20–35)	13* (5–10)	1.4* (0.6–1.2)	71 (10–35)
19–30 y	175 (45–65)	28*	(20–35)	13* (5–10)	1.4* (0.6–1.2)	71 (10–35)
31–50 y	175 (45–65)	28*	(20–35)	13* (5–10)	1.4* (0.6–1.2)	71 (10–35)
Lactation						
≤18 y	210 (45–65)	29*	(20–35)	13* (5–10)	1.3* (0.6–1.2)	71 (10–35)
19–30 y	210 (45–65)	29*	(20–35)	13* (5–10)	1.3* (0.6–1.2)	71 (10–35)
31–50 y	210 (45–65)	29*	(20–35)	13* (5–10)	1.3* (0.6–1.2)	71 (10–35)

Source: Reprinted with permission from "Dietary Reference Intakes for Energy, Carbohydrates, Fiber, Fat, Fatty Acids, Cholesterol, Protein, and Amino Acids (Macronutrients)," © 2002 by the National Academy of Sciences, courtesy of the National Academies Press, Washington, DC.

Note: This table is adapted from the DRI reports, see www.nap.edu. It lists Recommended Dietary Allowances (RDAs), with Adequate Intakes (AIs) indicated by an asterisk (*), and Acceptable Macronutrient Distribution Range (AMDR) data provided in parentheses. RDAs and AIs may both be used as goals for individual intake. RDAs are set to meet the needs of almost all (97% to 98%) individuals in a group. For healthy breastfed infants, the AI is the mean intake. The AI for other life stage and gender groups is believed to cover the needs of all individuals in the group, but lack of data prevent being able to specify with confidence the percentage of individuals covered by this intake.

[a] Based on 1.5 g/kg/day for infants, 1.1 g/kg/day for 1–3 y, 0.95 g/kg/day for 4–13 y, 0.85 g/kg/day for 14–18 y, 0.8 g/kg/day for adults, and 1.1 g/kg/day for pregnant (using pre-pregnancy weight) and lactating women.

[b] ND = Not determinable due to lack of data of adverse effects in this age group and concern with regard to lack of ability to handle excess amounts. Source of intake should be from food only to prevent high levels of intake.

[c] Data in parentheses are Acceptable Macronutrient Distribution Range (AMDR). This is the range of intake for a particular energy source that is associated with reduced risk of chronic disease while providing intakes of essential nutrients. If an individual consumes in excess of the AMDR, there is a potential of increasing the risk of chronic diseases and/or insufficient intakes of essential nutrients.

Dietary Reference Intakes: RDA, AI*

	Vitamins													
Life-Stage Group	Vitamin A (μg/d)[a]	Vitamin D (μg/d)[b]	Vitamin E (mg/d)[c]	Vitamin K (μg/d)	Thiamin (mg/d)	Riboflavin (mg/d)	Niacin (mg/d)[d]	Pantothenic Acid (mg/d)	Biotin (μg/d)	Vitamin B6 (mg/d)	Folate (μg/d)[e]	Vitamin B12 (μg/d)	Vitamin C (mg/d)	Choline (mg/d)
Infants														
0–6 mo	400*	5*	4*	2.0*	0.2*	0.3*	2*	1.7*	5*	0.1*	65*	0.4*	40*	125*
7–12 mo	500*	5*	5*	2.5*	0.3*	0.4*	4*	1.8*	6*	0.3*	80*	0.5*	50*	150*
Children														
1–3 y	300	5*	6	30*	0.5	0.5	6	2*	8*	0.5	150	0.9	15	200*
4–8 y	400	5*	7	55*	0.6	0.6	8	3*	12*	0.6	200	1.2	25	250*
Males														
9–13 y	600	5*	11	60*	0.9	0.9	12	4*	20*	1.0	300	1.8	45	375*
14–18 y	900	5*	15	75*	1.2	1.3	16	5*	25*	1.3	400	2.4	75	550*
19–30 y	900	5*	15	120*	1.2	1.3	16	5*	30*	1.3	400	2.4	90	550*
31–50 y	900	5*	15	120*	1.2	1.3	16	5*	30*	1.3	400	2.4	90	550*
51–70 y	900	10*	15	120*	1.2	1.3	16	5*	30*	1.7	400	2.4	90	550*
>70 y	900	15*	15	120*	1.2	1.3	16	5*	30*	1.7	400	2.4	90	550*
Females														
9–13 y	600	5*	11	60*	0.9	0.9	12	4*	20*	1.0	300	1.8	45	375*
14–18 y	700	5*	15	75*	1.0	1.0	14	5*	25*	1.2	400	2.4	65	400*
19–30 y	700	5*	15	90*	1.1	1.1	14	5*	30*	1.3	400	2.4	75	425*
31–50 y	700	5*	15	90*	1.1	1.1	14	5*	30*	1.3	400	2.4	75	425*
51–70 y	700	10*	15	90*	1.1	1.1	14	5*	30*	1.5	400	2.4	75	425*
>70 y	700	15*	15	90*	1.1	1.1	14	5*	30*	1.5	400	2.4	75	425*
Pregnancy														
≤18 y	750	5*	15	75*	1.4	1.4	18	6*	30*	1.9	600	2.6	80	450*
19–30 y	770	5*	15	90*	1.4	1.4	18	6*	30*	1.9	600	2.6	85	450*
31–50 y	770	5*	15	90*	1.4	1.4	18	6*	30*	1.9	600	2.6	85	450*
Lactation														
≤18 y	1200	5*	19	75*	1.4	1.4	17	7*	35*	2.0	500	2.8	115	550*
19–30 y	1300	5*	19	90*	1.4	1.4	17	7*	35*	2.0	500	2.8	120	550*
31–50 y	1300	5*	19	90*	1.4	1.4	17	7*	35*	2.0	500	2.8	120	550*

Sources: Reprinted with permission from the Dietary Reference Intakes series, National Academies Press. Copyright 1997, 1998, 2000, 2001, by the National Academy of Sciences. These reports may be accessed via www.nap.edu. Courtesy of the National Academies Press, Washington, DC.

Note: This table is adapted from the DRI reports; see www.nap.edu. It lists Recommended Dietary Allowances (RDAs), with Adequate Intakes (AIs) indicated by an asterisk (*). RDAs and AIs may both be used as goals for individual intake. RDAs are set to meet the needs of almost all (97 percent to 98 percent) individuals in a group. For healthy breastfed infants, the AI is the mean intake. The AI for other life stage and gender groups is believed to cover the needs of all individuals in the group, but lack of data prevent being able to specify with confidence the percentage of individuals covered by this intake.

[a] Given as retinal activity equivalents (RAE).
[b] Also known as calciferol. The DRI values are based on the absence of adequate exposure to sunlight.
[c] Also known as α-tocopherol.
[d] Given as niacin equivalents (NE), except for infants 0–6 months, which are expressed as preformed niacin.
[e] Given as dietary folate equivalents (DFE).

Make nutrition personal and practical for students

True or False?

1) **Students learn more when they apply course material to their own dietary behaviors.** T/F (see below)

2) **A good nutrition book should help improve students' critical thinking skills.** T/F (see below)

3) **Uniform presentation of concepts makes for more effective study and comprehension.** T/F (see page 2)

4) **Today's students are visual learners.** T/F (see page 2)

5) **Teaching tools are easier to use when gathered in one central location.** T/F (see page 6)

Self-Assessment

Are You at Risk for Osteoporosis?

There are several factors that increase your risk of osteoporosis and bone fractures. As with factors that affect your risk of hypertension, you can control some of these, but not others. Take the following Self-Assessment quiz to determine how many risk factors you have for osteoporosis. Shade in each part of the skeleton (on the next page) based on your answers.

1. **Gender:** Are you female?
   Yes ☐ **No** ☐ (If you answered no, shade in the left arm of the skeleton.)
   Females are at a higher risk for osteoporosis than males because they have smaller bones, and thus less bone mass. Also, bone mass is lost at a faster rate right after menopause due to the decline of estrogen in women's bodies. However, men can suffer from osteoporosis and can experience it at a fairly young age.[18]

2. **Ethnicity:** Are you a Caucasian or Asian-American female?
   Yes ☐ **No** ☐ (If no, shade in the right arm of the skeleton.)
   Caucasian and Asian women typically have lower bone mass than other women.

3. **Age:** Are you over 30 years of age?
   Yes ☐ **No** ☐ (If no, shade in the left hand of the skeleton.)
   You begin to lose bone mass after about age 30, which increases your risk of osteoporosis and fractures.

4. **Body Type:** Are you a small-boned or petite woman?
   Yes ☐ **No** ☐ (If no, shade in the right hand of the skeleton.)
   Thin women have lower bone mass and increased risk of fractures. A higher body weight puts more weight-bearing, mechanical stress on bones, helping them to stay healthy. A healthy body weight also means you'll have some padding should a fall occur. Also, since most of the estrogen

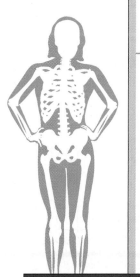

Assessment

Self Assessments in every chapter encourage students to think about their own health habits and how well they're meeting their needs for a healthy diet and lifestyle.

Critical Thinking

Two Points of View activities encourage students to think critically about both sides of controversial nutrition issues.

NUTRITION IN THE REAL WORLD

Two Points of View

Are Personal Trainers Reliable Sources of Credible Nutrition Information?

Many fitness advisors in gyms and other exercise facilities are happy to dispense nutrition advice, but is the advice always accurate?

Richard Cotton, MA
Exercise physiologist; Spokesman, American Council on Exercise

Richard Cotton, MA, has worked in the health and fitness industry for nearly 30 years, with a special focus on setting standards for fitness professionals and helping consumers find reliable exercise programs, trainers, and equipment. He has worked extensively with the American Council on Exercise (ACE), a major nonprofit fitness certifying organization and a consumer resource for reliable, ef-

Brenda Malinauskas, PhD, RD
East Carolina University

Brenda Malinauskas, PhD, RD, is an assistant professor and program coordinator for the graduate program in Nutrition at East Carolina University. Much of her research focuses on dieting behaviors, including dieting practices used by young women and male and female university athletes. She is an avid runner and cyclist and has worked with college athletes for over 10 years helping them

Consistency

Each nutrient in the Visual Summary Table is presented using the same categories (forms, functions, daily needs, food sources, toxicity and deficiency symptoms) and headings for a **consistent and easy-to-study format**.

Innovation

Eye-catching figures and photos are presented in a visual style that will capture student interest and help them remember key concepts in the chapter.

Sodium

What Are Sodium and Salt?

Sodium is an electrolyte in your body. Most sodium in your body is in your blood and in the fluid surrounding your cells.

About 90 percent of the sodium you consume is in the form of sodium chloride. Sodium chloride is commonly known as table salt.

Functions of Sodium

Sodium's chief role is regulation of fluid balance. Sodium also plays an important role in transporting substances such as amino acids across cell membranes.

Salt is frequently added to foods to enhance flavor and as a preservative. It is also added to yeast breads to help the dough rise and to reduce the growth of bacteria and mold in many bread products and luncheon meats. Sodium phosphate, sodium carbonate, and sodium bicarbonate (baking soda) are food additives and preservatives that perform similar functions in foods.

Monosodium glutamate (MSG) is a common additive in Asian cuisines that is used to intensify the flavor of foods.

Sodium Balance in Your Body

The amount of sodium in your body is maintained at a precise level. When your body needs more sodium, your kidneys reduce the amount that is excreted in your urine. Likewise, when you take in too much sodium, you excrete the excess. For example, when you eat salty pretzels or popcorn, your kidneys will excrete the extra sodium you take in from these snacks.

Smaller amounts of sodium are lost in your stool and through daily perspiration. The amount of sodium lost through perspiration depends upon the rate you are sweating, the amount of sodium you have consumed (the more sodium in your diet, the higher the loss), and the intensity of heat in the environment. As you get acclimated to environmental heat, less sodium will be lost over time in your sweat. This built-in protective mechanism helps to prevent the loss of too much sodium from your body.

Daily Needs

The penny shown below is covered with about 180 milligrams of sodium. This is the bare minimum you need daily. It is based on the amount of sodium needed by individuals who live in temperate climates and those who have become acclimated to hotter environments.[17]

Planning a balanced diet with this small an amount of sodium is virtually impossible, so the recommended sodium intake for adults up to 51 years of age is set at 1,500 milligrams daily. This sodium recommendation allows you to eat a variety of foods from all the food groups so that you can meet your other nutrient needs. It also covers any sodium that is lost in sweat by moderately active individuals, or those who are not acclimated to the environmental temperature. Those who are very physically active and/or not acclimated to the heat will likely need to consume a higher amount of sodium. This can easily be obtained in the diet.

Sodium is so widely available in foods that you don't have to go out of your way to meet your needs.

Milligrams of Sodium	
3,500	American adult daily consumption (>3,400 mg)
3,000	
2,500	Adult upper level (2,300 mg)
2,000	
1,500	Adult recommended daily (1,500 mg)
1,000	
500	
0	Adult needed daily (180 mg)

Americans are currently consuming more than double the recommended amount, or over 3,400 milligrams of sodium daily, on average.[18]

Food Sources

About 12 percent of Americans' consumption of sodium is from foods in which it occurs naturally, such as fruits, vegetables, milk, meat, fish, poultry, and legumes. Another 5 percent gets added during cooking and another 6 percent is used to season foods at the table.

Processed foods contribute a hefty 77 percent of the sodium in the diet of Americans. Comparing the amount of sodium in a fresh tomato (11 milligrams) to the amount found in a cup of canned tomatoes (355 milligrams) quickly illustrates just how much more sodium is found in processed foods.

Too Much or Too Little

There is a direct relationship between sodium and blood pressure in many people. In general, as a person's intake of sodium increases, so does their blood pressure. Blood pressure that becomes too high, known as **hypertension,** increases the risk for heart disease, stroke, and kidney disease (see the boxed feature "You and Your Blood Pressure" for more about hypertension.) Unfortunately, many Americans will develop hypertension sometime during their life. To help reduce the risk of hypertension, the upper level for adults for sodium is set at 2,300 milligrams. Recall from Chapter 2 that the current *Dietary Guidelines for Americans* also recommend that you limit your

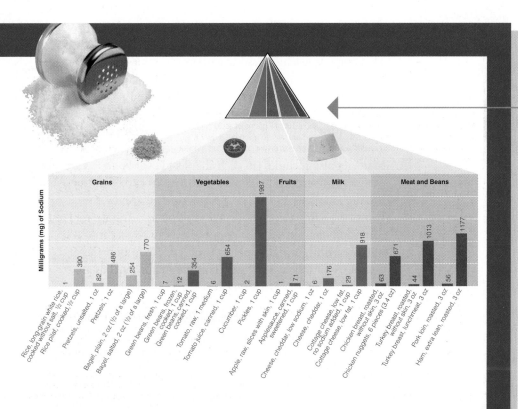

Nutrients-at-a-Glance

Food source diagrams found within each Visual Summary Table are tied to the new MyPyramid design. Students can immediately see how the food sources relate to the food groups of the pyramid, and determine the best food sources for each nutrient.

Milligrams (mg) of Sodium

Grains	Vegetables	Fruits	Milk	Meat and Beans

Grains:
- Rice, long-grain white rice cooked without salt, 1/2 cup: 1
- Rice pilaf, cooked, 1/2 cup: 390
- Pretzels, unsalted, 1 oz: 82
- Pretzels, 1 oz: 486
- Bagel, plain, 2 oz (1/2 of a large): 254
- Bagel, salted, 2 oz (1/2 of a large): 770

Vegetables:
- Green beans, fresh, 1 cup: 7
- Green beans, frozen cooked, 1 cup: 12
- Green beans, canned cooked, 1 cup: 354
- Tomato, raw, 1 medium: 6
- Tomato juice, canned, 1 cup: 654
- Cucumber, 1 cup: 2
- Pickles, 1 cup: 1987

Fruits:
- Apple, raw, slices with skin, 1 cup: 1
- Applesauce, canned sweetened, 1 cup: 71

Milk:
- Cheese, cheddar, low sodium, 1 oz: 6
- Cheese, cheddar, 1 oz: 176
- Cottage cheese, low fat, no sodium added, 1 cup: 29
- Cottage cheese, low fat, 1 cup: 918

Meat and Beans:
- Chicken breast, roasted without skin, 3 oz: 63
- Chicken nuggets, 6 pieces (3.4 oz): 671
- Turkey breast, roasted without skin, 3 oz: 44
- Turkey breast, lunchmeat, 3 oz: 1013
- Pork loin, roasted, 3 oz: 56
- Ham, extra lean, roasted, 3 oz: 1177

sodium intake for the same reason. Many Americans exceed this upper limit daily.

Because the majority of your sodium comes from processed foods, and a fair amount comes from the salt that you add to your foods, cutting back on these two sources is the best way to lower your intake.

When you buy processed foods, look for the terms "low," "reduced" or "sodium-free" on the labels to cut back on your sodium intake.

Bypass the salt shaker at the table. When cooking, season your foods with black pepper, Tabasco sauce, lemon juice, or a no-salt seasoning blend instead of salt.

Sodium deficiency is rare in healthy individuals consuming a balanced diet.

Table Tips
Shake Your Habit

Dilute and conquer. Combine a can of vegetable soup and a can of low-sodium vegetable soup for soup with less sodium. Add some cooked, frozen vegetables for an even healthier meal.

Keep your portions of deli meats to no more than 3 ounces and build a "meaty" sandwich by adding naturally low-sodium

tomatoes, lettuce, cucumbers, and shredded cabbage.

Nibble on low-sodium dried fruits (apricots, raisins) and unsalted walnut pieces for a sweet and crunchy snack.

Skip the salty french fries and enjoy the sodium-free baked potato at dinner.

Use olive oil and balsamic vinegar for a salad dressing with less sodium than is in bottled dressings. Or, dilute equal portions of regular salad dressing with vinegar to cut the sodium.

Real-Life Applications

Table Tips provide easy-to-follow suggestions that students can use to maximize the nutritional value of a meal.

Terms to Know
hypertension

Engage Students

With Interactive Media

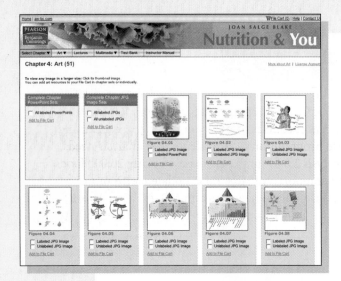

MEDIA MANAGER

This valuable teaching resource offers everything instructors need to create lecture presentations and other course materials, including JPEG and PowerPoint® files of all the art, tables, and selected photos from the text, and "stepped-out" art for selected figures from the text, as well as animations created from the ground up for the non-majors' nutrition course. The **Media Manager** also includes (in each chapter) PowerPoint lecture outlines with embedded links to animations and ABC News Lecture Launcher Videos, a *Jeopardy*-type quiz show, the Instructor Manual, Test Bank Word files and computerized test bank, and questions for Classroom Response Systems (CRS) in PowerPoint format, allowing professors to import these questions into their own CRS. This instructor tool has an easy-to-use interface that makes navigation simple.

ABC Video Clips

These 15 **video clips**, created in partnership with ABC News, range from 5–10 minutes in length and can be used to stimulate classroom discussion. Digital versions of the videos are integrated into the PowerPoint lecture outlines, and are available in a separate, full-screened format.

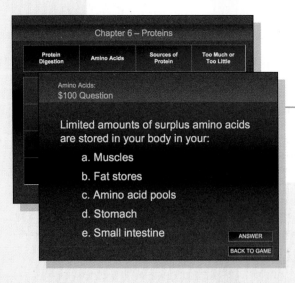

Quiz Show Game

Students look forward to going to class when you use these questions styled after the popular TV game show *Jeopardy*. Provided in PowerPoint format, you can use the questions to launch discussions of a topic, or to reinforce key concepts.

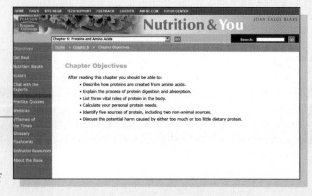

Companion Website

The **website** includes Chapter Quizzes, Cumulative Quizzes, web links, eThemes from the *New York Times*, flashcards, and a glossary. Students can complete the self assessments from the text in an interactive format, and expand their critical thinking with questions based on Two Points of View. The study questions help students prepare for exams, while other activities may be completed as homework or extra credit assignments.

www.aw-bc.com/blake

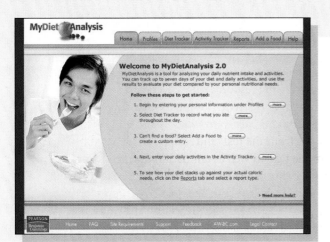

MYDIETANALYSIS 2.0

MyDietAnalysis 2.0 was developed by the nutrition database experts at ESHA Research, Inc. and is tailored for use in college nutrition courses. It offers an accurate, reliable, and easy-to-use program for your students' diet analysis needs. MyDietAnalysis 2.0 features a database of nearly 20,000 foods and multiple reports; version 2.0 is updated with more foods and functionality. Available on CD-ROM or online, the program allows students to track their diet and activity, and generate and submit reports electronically.

www.mydietanalysis.com

Assistance

The new profile wizard assists you with creating **up to three profiles** for analysis and is a detailed walkthrough of how to complete a profile, including a new activity level assessment. A Comparison Report is also available to compare intake between the three profiles.

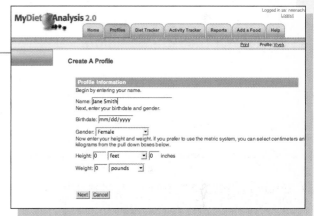

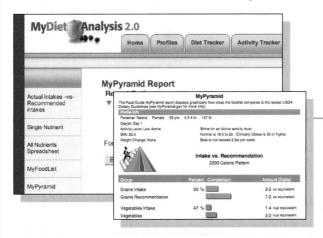

Reports

Updated reports incorporate the new 2005 Dietary Guidelines. MyDietAnalysis 2.0 features three new reports: My Food List, Energy Balance, and Comparison and an updated MyPyramid report. Reports can now be emailed or printed as a PDF, Excel, or HTML document.

Additional Access

MyDietAnalysis 2.0 is also available as a single sign-on to MyNutritionLab. Powered by CourseCompass, MyNutritionLab includes everything needed to teach introductory nutrition in one convenient place with content that can be customized for each course. Students and instructors can easily access animations, eThemes of *The New York Times*, study tools, an e-book, quizzes, gradebook, and much more.

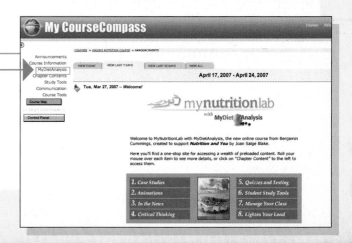

MYNUTRITIONLAB

MyNutritionLab, powered by CourseCompass,™ includes everything needed to teach introductory nutrition in one convenient place with content that can be customized for each course. Students and instructors can easily access animations, eThemes of *The New York Times*, study tools, an e-book, quizzes, grade book, Two Points of View activities, student study guide and much more. MyDietAnalysis 2.0 is available as a single sign-on to MyNutritionLab.

www.mynutritionlab.com

Course Management Tools

MyNutritionLab provides **course management tools,** including preloaded assignable quiz and test questions and a grade book that automatically records student progress on assigned tests. MyNutritionLab also provides access to an interactive e-book.

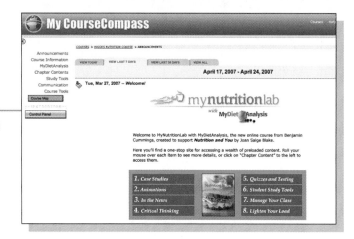

Video Clips

Engage students and spark classroom discussion with ABC News Lecture Launcher **video clips.**

Animations

Built from the ground up by Kathleen Munoz of Humboldt State University, longtime nutrition educator, these **26 new and dynamic animations** will be available to engage your students both in the classroom and on our MyNutritionLab course management site.

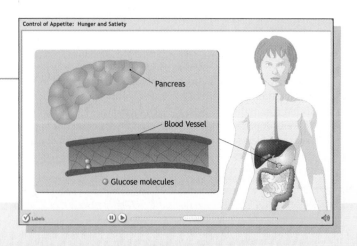

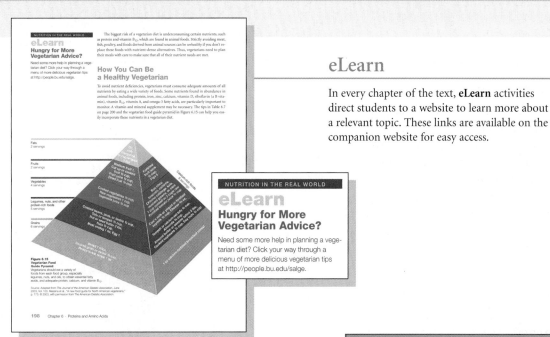

eLearn

In every chapter of the text, **eLearn** activities direct students to a website to learn more about a relevant topic. These links are available on the companion website for easy access.

Activities

Be a Nutrition Sleuth activities on the companion website are interactive exercises in which students use what they learned in each chapter to find and critically evaluate additional information about a particular scenario.

Application

Get Real! activities on the companion website help students apply what they have just learned to their own diets by asking them several questions about their eating patterns.

Teaching and Learning Solutions

For Successful Instructors and Students

For Instructors

Instructor Manual
978-0-321-49003-2 / 0-321-49003-7
This resource includes outlines that summarize each chapter, author-provided ideas for hands-on group assignments, key terms, teaching tips, suggested source materials, critical thinking questions, and topics for discussion.

Transparency Acetates
978-0-321-49780-2 / 0-321-49780-5
This set of full color transparency acetates features all the art and tables and selected disease photos from the text.

Media Manager CD-ROM
978-0-321-49005-6 / 0-321-49005-3
This valuable resource includes all figures, graphs, and illustrations from the book, as well as animations and ABC News Lecture Launcher videos. Selected disease photos from the book are also included.

Printed Test Bank
978-0-321-49801-4 / 0-321-49801-1
Computerized Test Bank
978-0-3214-9004-9 / 0-321-49004-5
These test banks provide multiple-choice, true/false, matching, short answer, and essay questions for each chapter of the text.

MyNutritionLab
Powered by CourseCompass, MyNutritionLab includes everything you need to teach introductory nutrition in one convenient place, with content that can be customized for each course. Students and instructors can access animations, ABC News video clips, eThemes of *The New York Times*, study tools, an e-book, quizzes, grade book, access to the Tutor Center, and much more. MyNutritionLab is also available with single sign-on to MyDietAnalysis 2.0.
www.mynutritionlab.com

WebCT
This open-access course management system contains preloaded content such as testing and assessment question pools.
www.aw-bc.com/webct

Blackboard
This open-access course management system contains preloaded content such as testing and assessment question pools.
www.aw-bc.com/blackboard

For Students

Study Guide
978-0-321-49803-8 / 0-321-49803-8
The Study Guide will help students get the best grade possible with key terms questions, text outlines, study questions, completion exercises, puzzles, and critical thinking questions for each section of each chapter.

Eat Right! Healthy Eating in College and Beyond
978-0-8053-8288-4
0-8053-8288-7
By Janet Anderson, et al.
This handy, full-color 80-page booklet provides practical guidelines, tips, shoppers' guides, and recipes so students can put healthy eating guidelines into action. Topics include: How to choose healthy foods in a cafeteria, dorm room, and fast food restaurant; eating on a budget; weight management tips; vegetarian alternatives; and guidelines on alcohol and health.

MyNutritionLab
www.mynutritionlab.com

MyDietAnalysis 2.0
MyDietAnalysis 2.0 offers an accurate, reliable and easy-to-use program for students to analyze their diets effectively. This ESHA-based diet analysis software includes nearly 20,000 foods including ethnic foods, name brand fast foods, convenience foods and supplements, and can be packaged with the text at a discount.
www.mydietanalysis.com

Companion Website
The companion website includes the Get Real! and Nutrition Sleuth exercises, links to eLearns, Chapter Quizzes, Cumulative Quizzes, web links, flashcards, and glossary. The multiple choice and essay questions help students prepare for exams, while other activities may be completed as homework or extra credit assignments.
www.aw-bc.com/blake

Nutrition & You

Joan Salge Blake, MS, RD, LDN
Boston University

PEARSON
Benjamin Cummings

San Francisco   Boston   New York
Cape Town   Hong Kong   London   Madrid   Mexico City
Montreal   Munich   Paris   Singapore   Sydney   Tokyo   Toronto

Acquisitions Editors: Sandra Lindelof, Deirdre Espinoza
Senior Project Editors: Susan Malloy, Barbara Yien
Development Manager: Claire Alexander
Development Editor: Cheryl Cechvala
Art Development Editor: Russell Chun
Assistant Editor: Emily Portwood
Editorial Assistants: Amy Yu, Joanna Nassar
Managing Editor: Deborah Cogan
Production Supervisor: Caroline Ayres
Production Management: The Left Coast Group
Copyeditor: Anna Reynolds Trabucco
Compositor: Thompson Type
Art Coordinators: Laura Murray, Chris Schabow

Interior Designer: Mark Ong
Cover Designer: Jeanne Calabrese
Illustrator: Precision Graphics
Photo Researcher: Kristin Piljay
Director, Image Resource Center: Melinda Patelli
Image Rights and Permissions Manager: Zina Arabia
Manufacturing Buyers: Stacy Jenson, Stacey Weinberger
Marketing Manager: Neena Chandra
Market Development Manager: Becky Ruden
Text Printer: Courier Kendallville
Cover Printer: Phoenix Color
Cover Photo Credit: StockFood Creative/Getty Images, Inc.

ISBN 10: 0-8053-5452-2 (Student edition)
ISBN 13: 978-08053-5452-2 (Student edition)
ISBN 10: 0-321-50158-6 (Professional copy)
ISBN 13: 978-0-321-50158-5 (Professional copy)

Library of Congress Cataloging-in-Publication Data
Blake, Joan Salge.
    Nutrition & you / Joan Salge Blake.
        p. cm.
    Includes bibliographical references and index.
    ISBN-13: 978-0-8053-5452-2 (student edition)
    ISBN-10: 0-8053-5452-2 (student edition)
    ISBN-13: 978-0-321-50158-5 (professional copy)
    ISBN-10: 0-321-50158-6 (professional copy)
1. Nutrition.   I. Title.   II. Title: Nutrition and you.
    RA784.B552 2008
    613.2—dc22
                            2007030164

2 3 4 5 6 7 8 9 10—CRK—12 11 10 09 08

PEARSON

Benjamin
Cummings   www.aw-bc.com

Brief Contents

Contents

4
Carbohydrates: Sugars, Starches, and Fiber   86

5
Fats, Oils, and Other Lipids   128

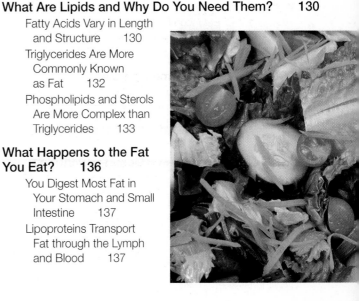

8
Minerals and Water 256

9
Alcohol 308

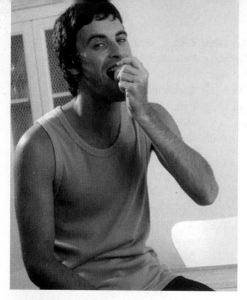

10
Weight Management   336

11
Nutrition and Fitness   382

12
Life Cycle Nutrition: Pregnancy through Infancy   416

13
Life Cycle Nutrition: Toddlers through the Later Years   454

14
Food Safety and Technology   488

15
Hunger at Home and Abroad   532

Appendices

Boxes

Feature Boxes

Self-Assessments

Two Points of View

About the Author

Joan Salge Blake is a clinical assistant professor and dietetics internship director at Boston University's Sargent College of Health and Rehabilitation Sciences. She teaches both graduate and undergraduate nutrition courses. She received her MS from Boston University.

Joan is a member of the American Dietetic Association (ADA) and the Massachusetts Dietetic Association (MDA). She has been a presenter and presiding officer at both the ADA Annual Meeting and the MDA Annual Convention and is a guest lecturer at the Boston University Goldman School of Dental Medicine. She was previously named the MDA's "Young Dietitian of the Year" and is the past MDA director of education and nominating committee chairperson. She has served on the MDA board for close to a decade.

Joan received the Whitney Powers Excellence in Teaching Award from Boston University and an Outstanding Dietetic Educator Award in 2007 from the ADA. She is also an ADA Media Spokesperson, responsible for representing the ADA in the media and promoting its initiatives.

In addition to teaching and writing, Joan has a private practice specializing in weight management and lifestyle changes. Joan is often asked to translate complex nutritional issues in popular terms, as a member of the ABC News Medical Expert Network and a contributor of articles to a variety of magazines. She has been featured in a monthly nutrition segment on Fox 25 television in Boston.

Why I Wrote *Nutrition & You*

"You'll probably finish this class with a whole new outlook on diet and exercise . . . and you'll probably be a lot healthier!"

"Professor Salge Blake makes the material seem like the most interesting material in the universe."

—Excerpts from student comments about my nutrition class at
Boston University, courtesy of ratemyprofessor.com

I wrote *Nutrition & You* for you. It is all about you. For more than a decade, I have taught an Introduction to Nutrition course to a packed classroom of almost 200 students, at the unseemly hour of 8 a.m. The students keep coming year after year because I not only deliver accurate nutrition science and information in an easy-to-understand, entertaining format, but more importantly, I personalize the information for them so that they can immediately apply it to their own lifestyles.

As a college student, you are exposed to a steady stream of nutrition and health information from the media, your family and friends, and the Internet. While you may think Google has the answer to your nutrition questions, I have seen students frequently fall victim to misinformation found via a quick Web search and a few glitzy websites. So I designed *Nutrition & You* to be as user friendly as possible, packed exclusively with sound nutrition information. The text goes beyond basic nutrition science and provides realistic advice and strategies to help you easily incorporate what you learn into your busy life. The text is written to meet *your* nutritional concerns and answer *your* questions.

As you read *Nutrition & You,* I want you to feel as though you are sitting in my class being entertained and informed. For this reason, I wrote the text in a conversational tone, and we designed it to visually communicate complex nutrition science and topics in an easy-to-understand way.

The information in this textbook is arranged in a deliberate **"What," Why,"** and **"How"** format. Each chapter will tell you:

"What" the nutrition concept is;
"Why" it is important and the role it plays in your body; and then, most importantly,
"How" to easily adjust your lifestyle based on what you just learned.

Let's start with the "What" part of *Nutrition & You.*

What Is the Nutrition Concept?

Each chapter begins with a **Campus Corner,** a short scenario about a college student who is experiencing a common nutrition-related situation pertinent to the chapter topic. Don't be surprised if the student reminds you of yourself, your roommate, or a relative! I want you to be able to immediately relate to the character in the scenario and his or her nutrition problem. As you read, you will learn how to apply the information in the chapter to this person's life situation (and yours) in a practical way.

The popular **Myths and Misperceptions Pretest** is a quiz that will help you recognize misperceptions that you may have about the chapter topic. The answers to these fun pretest questions are woven throughout the chapter with a complete explanation of the myth. You'll be smarter just by taking this pretest.

Why Is the Nutrition Concept Important to You?

Each chapter contains a **Self-Assessment** that will help you determine whether your current diet and lifestyle habits need a little fine tuning. The **Visual Summary Tables** are nutrition for your eyes. They visually summarize why each nutrient is invaluable to your health in a consistent and easy-to-study format. **The Top 10 Points to Remember** at the end of each chapter boils down the most important concepts of the entire chapter. Recurring visuals will accompany some of the points to remind you of the information that was initially discussed. Lastly, the **Putting It All Together** section at the end of each chapter builds upon all the chapters before it and shows you how the material learned in the current chapter fits in with the material learned in previous chapters.

How Can You Easily Adjust Your Lifestyle?

This book is filled with tools and tips to help you make positive diet and lifestyle changes. The **Food Source Diagrams** visually provide you with the most robust food sources of each nutrient and are based on the MyPyramid design. No need to memorize a boring list of food sources! The **Table Tips** are short and snappy lists of practical changes that will help you improve your diet.

The online **Nutrition in the Real World** activities will further allow you to apply what you have learned in a virtual environment. For example, a Build Your Own Pizza **eLearn** activity (cited in Chapter 5) allows you to create a virtual pizza, full of all your favorite toppings, and immediately see the nutritional effects of your choices. Other online, interactive Web tools such as **Get Real!** help you to make more real-life changes to your diet, while **Be a Nutrition Sleuth** will give you further strategies and tips to apply in the real world.

Finally, the **Two Points of View** at the end of each chapter contains questions and answers from two experts representing opposing viewpoints on a timely topic. This feature will encourage you to think critically about pro and con arguments on a given issue and decide for yourself which side you agree with. You will be applying the critical thinking skills that you learned in the chapter as you read each expert's point of view.

Remember, nutrition matters to *you!* What you eat today and tomorrow will affect you and your body for years to come.

I want to hear what you think of *Nutrition & You*. Feel free to e-mail me with any questions or comments at salge@bu.edu. Your feedback will help make future editions of *Nutrition & You* even better.

Acknowledgments

It takes a village, and then some, when it comes to writing a dynamic textbook. *Nutrition & You* is no exception. I personally want to thank all of those who passionately shared their expertise and support to make *Nutrition & You* better than I could have envisioned.

Beginning with the dynamic staff at Benjamin Cummings, I would like to thank Deirdre Espinoza and Sandy Lindelof, who helped make my vision for this textbook a reality. Cheryl Cechvala's on-the-mark developmental editing improved *Nutrition & You* and made it enjoyable to read. A special thanks to Claire Alexander for her second set of eyes, and for further lending thoughts and edits to the chapters. It takes a few project managers to make sure the village runs on a schedule, and both Susan Malloy and Barbara Yien kept me on track, especially when the FedEx packages were arriving daily. A textbook needs crackerjack supplements and assistant editor Emily Portwood worked diligently to obtain the best for *Nutrition & You*. Thanks also to editorial assistants Amy Yu and Joanna Nassar for all of their work, especially in commissioning reviewers during the developmental stages of this book.

A very special thanks to Caroline Ayres, production supervisor extraordinaire, and Chris Schabow, production coordinator at The Left Coast Group, for all of their hard work shepherding this book through to publication. My humble appreciation also goes to Russell Chun, art development editor, for turning my rudimentary stick figures into true pieces of art; to Kristin Piljay for obtaining the most vivid and unique photos available; to Mark Ong, whose design made the text, art, and photos all come alive; to art coordinator Laura Murray; and to Jeanne Calabrese and Marilyn Perry, whose efforts I must thank for the book's gorgeous cover.

Marketing takes energy, and that's exactly what marketing manager Neena Chandra and her energetic team seem to generate nonstop. My thoughtful thanks to Erin Joyce and Becky Ruden for their coordination of focus groups, market research, and the enlistment of class testers. The many instructors who reviewed and class-tested early versions of this book are listed on the following pages; I am grateful to all of them for helping to inform the development of *Nutrition & You*.

The village also included loyal contributors who lent their expertise to specific chapters. They are: LuAnn Soliah at Baylor University for solidifying the digestion and hunger chapters; Molly Michelman at the University of Nevada, Las Vegas for penning parts of the "lifecycle" chapters; and Tara Barber at East Carolina University for writing the nutrition and fitness chapter, as well as sharing her expertise on disordered eating in the weight management chapter. I also thank April Lynch for her work on the "Two Points of View" interviews.

A heartfelt thank you goes to my research assistant, Susan Bell, who went above and beyond the call of duty by helping to fact-check *Nutrition & You*. A warm thanks goes to Rob Duggan for his legal advice, and to my fellow Boston University colleagues for their exemplary expertise and patience: Roberta Durschlag, PhD, RD; Robert Jackman, PhD; Linda Bandini, PhD, RD; Susan Kandarian, PhD; Paula Quatromoni, ScD, RD; and Steve Borkin, MD.

Lastly, an endless thanks to my family, Adam, Brendan, and Craig, for their love and support when I was working more than I should have been.

Joan Salge Blake

Joan Salge Blake

Reviewers

Nancy Adamowicz
University of Arizona

Laurie Allen
University of North Carolina, Greensboro

Dawn Anderson
Winona State University

Francine Armenth-Brothers
Heartland Community College

Elizabeth Browne
Tidewater Community College

Nancy Buffum-Herman
Monroe Community College

Joanne Burke
University of New Hampshire

Thomas Castonguay
University of Maryland

Erin Caudill
Southeast Community College

Sai Chidambaram
Cansisius College

Janet Colson
Middle Tennessee State University

Priscilla Connor
University of North Texas

Nancy J. Correa-Matos
University of North Florida

Cathy Hix Cunningham
Tennessee Technological University

Eileen Daniel
State University of New York, Brockport

Carole Dupont
Springfield Technical Community College

Sally Feltner
Western Carolina University

Anna Marie Frank
DePaul University

Bernard Frye
University of Texas, Arlington

Mary Ellen Fydenkevez
Greenfield Community College

Christie Goodner
Winthrop University

Lisa Goodson
Prince George's Community College

Sue Grace
Monroe Community College, Brighton

Donna Hale
Southeastern Oklahoma State University

Charlene Harkins
University of Minnesota Duluth

Nancy Harris
Eastern Carolina University

Beverly Henry
Northern Illinois University

Chris Heuston
Front Range Community College

Thunder Jalili
University of Utah

Lori Kanauss
Western Illinois University

Judy Kaufman
Monroe Community College, Brighton

Danita Kelley
Western Kentucky University

Kathryn Kohel
Alfred University

Claire Kratz
Montgomery County Community College

Laura Kruskall
University of Nevada, Las Vegas

Melody Kyzer
University of North Carolina, Wilmington

Kris Levy
Columbus State Community College

Sue Linnenkohl
Marshall University

Jackie McClelland
North Carolina State University

Katherine Mellen
University of Iowa

Barbara Mercer
University of Louisville

Anna Miller
De Anza College

Kristin Moline
Lourdes College

Maria Montemagni
College of the Sequoias

Gina Marie Morris
Frank Phillips College

Ray Moss
Furman University

Rosemary Mueller
William Rainey Harper College

Katherine Musgrave
University of Maine, Orono

Rosemary O'Dea
Gloucester County College

Millie Owens
College of the Sequoias

Candi Possinger
State University of New York, Buffalo

Class Testers

Patricia Abraham
Arkansas State University

Laurie Allen
University of North Carolina, Greensboro

Francine Armenth-Brothers
Heartland Community College

Cassandra August
Baldwin Wallace College

Gregory Biren
Rowan University of New Jersey

Sally Black
St. Joseph's University

Joye Bond
Minnesota State University, Mankato

Nancy Buffum-Herman
Monroe Community College, Brighton

Nicole Ann Clark
Indiana University of Pennsylvania

Janet Colson
Middle Tennessee State University

Marsha Cummings
El Paso Community College

Bill Dress
Robert Morris University

Claudia Fajardo
California State University, Northridge

Sarah Folta
Tufts University

Heather Gibbs
Olivet Nazarene University

Nancy Gordon Harris
East Carolina University

Barbara Grossman
University of Georgia

Margaret Gunther
Palomar College

Rachelle Holmen
Carl Albert State College

Tawni Holmes
University of Central Oklahoma

Judith Ingle
Northwest State Community College

Thunder Jalili
University of Utah

Lydia Kloiber
Texas Tech University

Dauna Koval
Bellevue Community College

Karen Mason
Western Kentucky University

Kim Mattson
University of North Florida

Kathy Mellen
University of Iowa

Rhonda Meyers
Lower Columbia College

Gina Marie Morris
Frank Phillips College

Karen Myers
University of Central Oklahoma

Deb Murray
Ohio University

Millie Owens
College of the Sequioas

Anna Page
Johnson County Community College

Elizabeth Quintana
West Virginia University

Peggy Ramsey
Fullerton College

Linda Rankin
Idaho State University

Carol Reynolds
Fullerton College

Susan Rippy
Eastern Illinois University

Nidia Romer
Miami Dade Kendall Campus

Diane Rouse
Brazosport College

Tiffany Schinkle
University of Central Oklahoma

Doris Schomberg
Alamance Community College

Rich Seymour
Housatonic Community College

Denise Signorelli
Community College of Southern Nevada

Karen Smith
Washington College

Michelle Snyder
Grossmont College

Tammy Stephenson
University of Kentucky

Linda Vickers
Moorpark College

John Warber
Morehead State University

Annie Wetter
University of Wisconsin, Stevens Point

Margaret Wolson
Florida Community College, North Campus

Linda Wright
University of Wisconsin, Milwaukee

Ruth Young
Northern Essex Community College

I am nothing without
my ABCs.

Thanks.

1

What Is Nutrition?

1. Advertising is ineffective when it comes to influencing people's food choices. **T/F**

2. Heart disease is the leading cause of **death** in the United States. **T/F**

3. Carbohydrates, vitamins, and fat all provide you with **energy.** **T/F**

4. The energy in food is measured in **calories.** **T/F**

5. Water is an essential nutrient. **T/F**

6. As long as you take a **vitamin pill,** you don't have to worry about eating healthy foods. **T/F**

7. Meats, poultry, and fish contain a lot of **fiber.** **T/F**

8. Every year, Americans shell out more than **$5 billion** for supplements. **T/F**

9. The number of **obese** Americans is lower today than it was ten years ago. **T/F**

10. You can get good nutrition advice from anyone who calls himself a **nutritionist.** **T/F**

It's the night before the big biology exam, and Elizabeth, a junior, is in the midst of a down-to-the-wire cram session. She hasn't cracked open her textbook for weeks, so she is in high-stress mode. Elizabeth pours herself a very tall glass of caffeinated cola, opens up a family-size bag of rippled potato chips, and nervously plows through the bag and the book. She snacks and studies to the wee hours of the morning, stuffing as much information as possible into her head, and too many chips into her stomach. After a jittery 3 hours of sleep, Elizabeth heads to her 8 a.m. exam feeling tired, groggy, and still uncomfortably stuffed from her potato chip-and-soda cram session.

Would you be surprised to learn that Elizabeth did not do so well on her exam? Do you, like Elizabeth, sometimes eat snacks or other foods because you're stressed, rather than hungry? What other factors do you think influence your food choices, and how can you make sound nutritional decisions?

Answers

1. False. Companies spend an enormous amount of money on advertising to persuade you to purchase their food products and, whether you realize it or not, it often works. In fact, advertisers have been marketing their products to you since you were a child. To find out why, turn to page 6.
2. True. Heart disease is the leading cause of death among Americans. The good news is that your diet can play an important role in preventing it. For more information, turn to page 8.
3. False. Carbohydrates and fat provide energy, but vitamins are not an energy source. They do play important roles in helping your body use both carbohydrates and fat. To find out more, turn to page 10.
4. True. Calories are the measure of energy in foods. Turn to page 10 to find out which nutrients provide calories.
5. True. While water is often forgotten as an essential nutrient, it shouldn't be. To learn about the important roles water plays in your body, turn to page 11.
6. False. A supplement can augment a healthy diet, but it can't replace it. To find out why, turn to page 12.
7. False. Although lean meats, poultry, and fish are excellent sources of protein, they don't contain fiber. To find out how to get your fill of fiber, turn to page 12.
8. True. Shocked? Americans spend much more than that shopping for supplements. Turn to page 12 to find out more about supplements.
9. False. Currently, obesity is at epidemic proportions in the United States, and it isn't just affecting adults. Turn to page 13 for more information.
10. False. Anyone can call himself or herself a nutritionist. To find out whose advice you can trust, turn to page 18.

From the minute you were born, you began performing three automatic behaviors: you slept, you ate, and you expelled your waste products . . . often while you were sleeping. You didn't need to think about these actions, and you didn't have to decide to do them. You also didn't need to make choices about where to sleep, what to eat, or when to go to the bathroom. Life was so easy back then.

Now that you're older, these actions, particularly the eating part, are anything but automatic. You make numerous decisions every day about what to eat, and you make these decisions for reasons that you may not even be aware of. If your dietary advice comes from media sound bites, you may get constantly conflicting information. Yesterday's news flash announced that eating more protein would help you fight a bulging waist. Last week's headline boldly announced you should minimize *trans* fats in your diet to avoid a heart attack. This morning, the TV news lead was a health report advising you to eat more whole grains to live longer, but to hold the line on sodium, otherwise your blood pressure may go up.

Though you may find it frustrating that dietary advice seems to change with the daily news (though it actually doesn't), this bombardment of nutrition news is a positive thing. You are lucky to live in an era when so much is known and being discovered about what you eat and how it affects you. Today's research validates what nutrition professionals have known for decades: Nutrition plays an invaluable role in your health. As with any science, nutrition is not stagnant. Exciting discoveries will continue to be made about the roles that diet and foods play in keeping you healthy.

Let's find out more about nutrition, why it's so important to your health, and how you can identify sound sources of nutrition. We'll start with the basic concept of why you eat and how this impacts your nutrition.

What Drives Our Food Choices?

What did you have for dinner last night? Where did you eat it? Who were you with? How did you feel?

Do you ever think about what drives your food choices? Or are you on autopilot as you stand in line at the sub shop and squint at yet another lit menu board? Do you adore some foods and eat them often, while avoiding others with a vengeance?

Perhaps you have a grandparent who encourages you to eat more (and more!) of her traditional home cooking. You obviously need food to survive, but beyond your basic instinct to eat are many other factors that affect what goes into your stomach. Let's discuss some of these now.

We Need to Eat and Drink to Live

All creatures need fuel in order to function, and humans are no exception. We get our fuel from food in the form of chemical compounds that are collectively known as **nutrients.** These nutrients work together to provide energy, growth, and maintenance, and to regulate numerous body processes. Three of the six classes of nutrients—carbohydrates, fats (part of the larger class of lipids), and protein—provide energy in the form of **kilocalories.** Two other classes of nutrients, vitamins and minerals, help regulate many body processes, including **metabolism.** Some also play other supporting roles. The last class of nutrient, water, is found in all foods and beverages, and is so vital to life that you couldn't live more than a few days without it.

Foods also provide nonnutrient compounds like **phytochemicals** and other substances that help maintain and repair your body in order to keep it healthy. We will explore each of these nutrients in more depth later in this chapter, and in much more depth throughout the book.

Beyond the basic need to replenish our bodies with daily fuel are other factors that drive our food choices.

This isn't exactly what's meant by the phrase "You are what you eat," but it's close.

We Choose Foods for Many Other Reasons

You probably think your favorite foods are delicious, which is why they are your favorites. Certain foods are reminders of our culture and have become an intricate part of our social lives. Our food selections are determined by our times, influenced by media messages, and become an option based upon available time and accessibility. We sometimes eat not because we are hungry, but out of habit and in response to our emotions.

Taste and Culture

Research confirms that when it comes to making food choices, taste is the most important consideration.[1] This shouldn't be too much of a surprise, considering that there are at least 10,000 taste buds in your mouth, mainly on your tongue. Your taste buds tell you that chocolate cheesecake is sweet, fresh lemon juice is sour, and a pretzel is salty.

What you choose to put on your plate is often influenced by your culture. If you were a student in Mexico, you may be feasting on a dinner with corn tortillas and tamales, as maize (corn) is a staple of Mexican cuisine. In India, meals commonly include lentils and other legumes with rice and vegetables, whereas Native Americans often enjoy stews of mutton (sheep), corn, and other vegetables. In China, rice, a staple, would be front and center on your plate.

A culture's cuisine is greatly influenced by the environment. People tend to consume foods that are accessible and often have little experience eating foods that are scarce. For example, native Alaskans feast on fish because it is plentiful, but eat little fresh produce, which is difficult to grow locally.

nutrients Compounds in foods that sustain your body processes. There are six classes of nutrients: carbohydrates, fats (lipids), proteins, vitamins, minerals, and water.

kilocalories The measurement of energy in foods.

metabolism The numerous reactions that occur within the cell. The calories in foods are converted to energy in the cells of the body.

phytochemicals Nonnutritive compounds in plant foods that may play a role in fighting chronic diseases.

One in four Americans is of Hispanic, Native American, Asian, or African descent. Cultural food preferences often influence food choices.

Food, friends, and football . . . a way of life.

Social Reasons and Trends

Eating is an important way to bond with others. Every year, on the fourth Thursday in November, over 95 percent of Americans gather with family and friends to consume close to 700 million pounds of turkey as they celebrate Thanksgiving.[2] A person is likely to eat more on Thanksgiving than on any other Thursday, and this is partly because of all the other people eating with them. Eating dinner with others has been shown to increase the size of the meal by over 40 percent, and the more people present, the more you'll eat.[3] Enjoying your meals in the campus cafeteria also allows you to socialize with your classmates.

For many people, activities like watching a football game with fellow fans or going to a movie with friends often involve particular foods. More pizzas are sold on Super Bowl Sunday than any other day of the year.[4] Movie theatre owners bank on your buying popcorn, candy, and beverages at their concession stands before heading in to watch the picture. Revenue from these snack items can account for up to 50 percent of a theatre's profits. And if you're with a group of friends, you're even more likely to buy these snacks. Research shows that movie concession snacks are more often purchased when people are socializing in a group.[5]

Your food choices are also affected by popular trends. For instance, home cooks in the 1950s bought bags of newfangled frozen vegetables in order to provide healthy meals in less time. A few decades later, vegetables went upscale and consumers bought them as part of ready-to-heat stir-fry mixes. Today, shoppers pay a premium price for bags of fresh veggies, like carrots, that have been prewashed and peeled, sliced, or diced. As food manufacturers pour more money into research and development, who knows what tomorrow's trendy food item will be.

Advertising

Open a magazine or newspaper or switch on the television and you'll soon see or hear an advertisement for food. Manufacturers spend over $10 billion annually on food advertising, with over $700 million each spent on the marketing of breakfast cereals, candy, and gum. Another $500 million is spent on advertising carbonated soft drinks.[6] In comparison, when was the last time you saw an advertisement for broccoli? Have you ever seen an ad for broccoli?

Food companies know the enormous influence that advertisements have on people's food purchases and eating habits, especially on children and adolescents. American children view up to 40,000 television commercials annually. An estimated $200 billion of household purchases are influenced by children under the age of 12. On Saturday morning, more than half of the between-cartoon ads that children watch are for foods. Of these, over 40 percent are for sweets and treats such as candy, soft drinks, chips, and sugary breakfast cereals.[7] Consider this the next time you see a child asking for sweet sugar puffs in the cereal aisle of your local supermarket.

In contrast, commercials for fruits and vegetables are almost nonexistent, which is a shame because healthy foods can be successfully marketed. When the dairy industry noted a decline in milk consumption among Americans in 1994, it launched the *Got Milk?* ad campaign featuring celebrities wearing milk mustaches. This campaign strove to make drinking milk sexy and it worked. Milk sales increased by nearly 1.5 billion pounds, which is the equivalent of about 45 pounds of milk being sold for each advertising dollar spent.[8]

Cartoon characters are often used to advertise products to children.

> By the time you graduated from high school, you had likely viewed over 350,000 television advertisements.

Time and Convenience

When it comes to preparing food, time is often at a premium, and because of this, the foods that people choose have changed. Recent research shows that Americans, especially working women with families, want to spend less than 15 minutes preparing

One successful advertising campaign uses celebrities like Donovan McNabb (a quarterback for the Philadelphia Eagles football team) to promote and sell milk.

While brown rice is a healthy whole-grain addition to any meal, it takes close to an hour to cook. For time-strapped consumers, food manufacturers have developed instant brown rice that cooks in 10 minutes, and a precooked, microwavable variety that reheats in less than 2 minutes.

a meal.[9] Consequently, supermarkets have changed the types of foods they sell as well as how the food is presented.

If chicken is on the menu tonight, you can go to the poultry section in the store and buy it uncooked, or you can go to the take-out section of the store and buy it hot off the rotisserie, precooked and stuffed with bread crumbs, or grilled with teriyaki sauce. You can also probably get the cooked vegetables and rice side dishes to take home and reheat with the chicken.

Decades ago, the most convenient way to get a hot cup of coffee was to brew it yourself. Americans today are more likely to get their java from one of the 17,000 coffee shops, carts, and kiosks across the United States.[10] Coffee isn't the only food that people now obtain outside the home. In the 1970s, Americans spent about 25 percent of their household food budget on eating out compared with almost 45 percent today.[11]

Habits and Emotions

Your daily routine and habits will also affect what you eat. When you get home from work or school, do you head straight for the refrigerator, regardless of whether you're hungry? Do you always snack when you watch television at night? Habits often dictate not only when you eat, but what you eat. For example, many people are in the habit of starting their day with a bowl of cereal and a glass of orange juice. Ready-to-eat cereals are the number-one breakfast food choice among Americans, and citrus juice is the top juice choice of Americans in the morning.[12]

Emotions also influence your food choices. Recall that Elizabeth from earlier in the chapter nervously ate her way through a large bag of chips before her exam. Does this sound familiar? When the going gets tough, the tough often eat. For many, food is used as an emotional crutch during times of stress, sadness, or joy.

Happiness can also trigger eating. Many people celebrate their end-of-term good grades or a promotion at work with a celebratory meal with friends or family. On vacation, you likely reward yourself with fun, relaxation, and, of course, good food. No matter your mood, food is often part of how you express your emotions.

The Take-Home Message Food provides the nutrients that your body needs to function, and the foods that you choose are influenced by many factors. Taste is the primary reason why certain foods have become your favorites. The availability of certain foods has made them a part of your culture and a habitual part of your day. Advertising, food trends, limits on your time, convenience, and your emotions will also influence your food choices.

What Is Nutrition and Why Is Good Nutrition so Important?

Whereas food is the source of nutrients that your body needs, **nutrition** is about more than just food. Nutrition is the science that studies how the nutrients and compounds in foods nourish you, help you function, and affect your health.

Your body needs all the nutrients to function properly. A chronic deficiency of even one nutrient will impact your body's ability to function in the short term. Chronic deficiencies, excesses, and imbalances of many nutrients can also affect your long-term health.

Good nutrition plays a role in reducing the risk of four of the top ten leading causes of death in the United States, including the top three—heart disease, cancer, and stroke—as well as diabetes (Table 1.1). Nutrition also plays an important role in preventing other diseases and conditions that can impede your lifestyle. A healthy diet can help keep your bones strong and reduce your risk of osteoporosis. Eating right will help you better manage your body weight, which in turn will reduce your risk of developing obesity, diabetes mellitus, and high blood pressure.

Table 1.1		
Leading Causes of Death in the United States		
Disease/Cause of Death	**Nutrition Related**	**Other**
1. **Heart Disease**	X	
2. **Cancer**	X	
3. **Stroke**	X	
4. Respiratory Diseases		X
5. Accidents		X
6. **Diabetes**	X	
7. Influenza/Pneumonia		X
8. Alzheimer's Disease		X
9. Kidney Disease		X
10. Blood Poisoning		X

Source: Centers for Disease Control. 2006. "Leading Causes of Death in the United States." www.cdc.gov/nchs/fastats/lcod.htm.

nutrition The science that studies how the nutrients and compounds in foods that you eat nourish and affect your body functions and health.

As we learn more about nutrition from ongoing research, we are likely to find even more ways in which what we eat affects our personal health. One exciting area of research is **nutritional genomics.** Genomics is the study of genes, their functions in your body, and how the environment may influence **gene expression.** Your genes determine your inherited, specific traits. With the completion of the **Human Genome Project,** the complete sequencing of **deoxyribonucleic acid (DNA)** in your cells is now known. Your DNA contains the genetic instructions needed to develop and direct the activities of your body.

Nutritional genomics is concerned with how the specific components in foods that you eat interact on a cellular level with the expression of your genes. Certain dietary components can cause different effects on your genes, and thus, initiate a very specific response in your body that could be different than the response it initiates in another person. For example, nutritional genomics will help determine the specific dietary combination of types of fats that you should consume to lower your risk of heart disease based on your genetic makeup.[13] As more becomes known about the application of nutritional genomics, you will have more control over how your diet affects your long-term health.

You are a product of what you eat, what you *don't* eat, or what you may eat *too much* of. You want to eat the best combination of a variety of foods to meet your nutritional needs and to be healthy. To do that, you need to understand the roles of the essential nutrients in your body and which foods to eat to get them.

The Take-Home Message Nutrition is the scientific study of how the nutrients and compounds in foods nourish your body. Good nutrition plays a role in reducing the risk of many chronic diseases and conditions. Long-term imbalances of many nutrients will affect your health. Nutritional genomics is the study of how specific dietary components affect the expression of your genes and your health.

What Are the Essential Nutrients and Why Do You Need Them?

The classes of nutrients that we introduced earlier are all *essential* because you must have them in order to function. (Alcohol, in contrast, is a not an essential nutrient, because though it provides energy in the form of kilocalories, your body does not need it to function.)

Carbohydrates, lipids (fats), and proteins are called **macronutrients,** because you need higher amounts of them in your diet. Vitamins and minerals, though equally important to your health, are considered **micronutrients** because you need them in lesser amounts. You need to consume the final nutrient, water, in copious amounts daily so that you are well hydrated.

Kilocalories (commonly referred to as calories, which is the term we will use throughout this book) from the macronutrients are used as energy during the process of metabolism, and many vitamins and minerals are essential to this process. Vitamins and minerals are also needed for growth and reproduction and to help repair and maintain your body (Figure 1.1).

nutritional genomics A field of study that researches the relationship between nutrition and genomics (the study of genes and gene expression).

gene expression The processing of genetic information to create a specific protein.

Human Genome Project A project sponsored by the United States government to determine the complete set and sequencing of DNA in your cells and identify all human genes.

deoxyribonucleic acid (DNA) Contains the genetic instructions needed to develop and direct the activities of your body.

macronutrients The energy-containing essential nutrients that you need in higher amounts: carbohydrates, lipids (fats), and proteins.

micronutrients Essential nutrients you need in smaller amounts: vitamins and minerals.

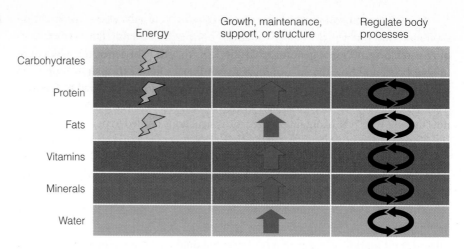

Although each nutrient is unique, they are all equally important, as they work together in numerous ways to keep you healthy. An imbalance of just one will affect your health. Let's take a closer look at the macro- and micronutrients, and water.

Carbohydrates, Fats, and Proteins Provide Energy

Carbohydrates, fats (lipids), and proteins are the energy-yielding nutrients, as they contain calories. Carbohydrates and protein provide four calories per gram, whereas fats provide nine calories per gram. One calorie equals the amount of energy needed to raise the temperature of one kilogram (a liter) of water one degree Celsius. The number of calories in a given food can be determined based on the weight, measured in grams, of each of the three nutrients in one serving of the food.

The amount of calories that you need daily to maintain your weight is estimated based on your age, gender, and activity level. However, you need these nutrients for many reasons beyond their providing energy. You must consume a healthy combination of carbohydrates, fats, and protein so that excesses, deficiencies, and imbalances don't occur that may increase your risk of chronic disease.

Carbohydrates supply the simple sugar, called glucose, that your cells use as the major energy source to fuel your body. Most of your daily calories should come from carbohydrates. Fats are another major fuel source. They also help cushion your organs to prevent damage and act as insulation under your skin to help maintain your body temperature. Proteins can be used as energy, but are better used to build and maintain your tissues, muscles, and organs. You also need protein to make most enzymes and some hormones, to help transport other nutrients, and for a healthy immune system. A healthy diet should provide adequate amounts of carbohydrates and fats for energy, and enough protein to maintain and repair your body.

Carbohydrates, fats, and proteins are all **organic** because they contain the element carbon. They also contain two other elements, hydrogen and oxygen. Proteins also contain nitrogen, while carbohydrates and fats do not.

Vitamins and Minerals Are Essential for Metabolism

You need vitamins and minerals to use carbohydrates, fats, and proteins and to sustain numerous chemical reactions. A deficiency of vitamins and minerals can cause ill effects ranging from fatigue to stunted growth, weak bones, and organ damage.

organic Containing carbon.

Many vitamins and minerals aid **enzymes,** which are substances that speed up reactions in your body. For example, many of the B vitamins function as coenzymes in the metabolism of carbohydrates and fats. Many minerals, such as calcium and phosphorus, work with protein-containing hormones and enzymes to maintain and strengthen your teeth and bones. The fate of carbohydrates, protein, and fats in your body is very much dependent upon your consuming enough vitamins and minerals in your daily diet.

Vitamins are organic compounds that usually need to be obtained from your foods. Your body is able to make some vitamins, such as vitamin D, but sometimes cannot make enough of it to maintain good health. In these situations, your diet has to supplement your body's efforts.

Minerals are **inorganic** substances that play a role in body processes and are key to the structure of some tissues, such as bone. A deficiency of any of the minerals can cause disease symptoms. Anyone who has ever suffered from iron-deficiency anemia can tell you that falling short of your daily iron needs, for example, can cause fatigue and interfere with your ability to function.

Water Is Vital for Many Processes in Your Body

Staying hydrated is an important part of staying healthy, as water is vital to key body functions. As part of the fluid medium inside your cells, water helps chemical reactions, such as those involved in the production of energy, take place. Water also bathes the outside of your cells, playing a key role in transporting vital nutrients and oxygen to, and removing waste products from, your cells. Water helps maintain your body temperature and acts as a lubricant for your joints, eyes, mouth, and intestinal tract. It surrounds your organs and cushions them from injury.

The Take-Home Message Your body needs carbohydrates, fats (lipids), protein, vitamins, minerals, and water to survive. These six classes of nutrients have specific roles in your body, and you need them in specific amounts for good health. While carbohydrates, fats, and protein provide energy, vitamins, minerals, and water are needed to use the energy-producing nutrients and to maintain good health. Water is part of the medium inside and outside your cells that carries nutrients to, and waste products from, your cells. Water also helps maintain your body temperature and acts as a lubricant and protective cushion.

How Should You Get These Important Nutrients?

There is no question that you need all six classes of nutrients to function properly. But is there an advantage to consuming them through food rather than taking them as supplements? Is there more to a healthy diet than just meeting your basic nutrient needs? Let's look at these questions in more detail.

enzymes Substances that speed up reactions in your body.

inorganic Not containing carbon. Inorganic compounds include minerals, water, and salts.

The Best Way to Meet Your Nutrient Needs Is with a Well-Balanced Diet

Many foods provide a variety of nutrients. For example, low-fat milk is high in carbohydrates and protein and provides a small amount of fat. Milk is also a good source of the vitamins A, D, and riboflavin, as well as the minerals potassium and calcium, and is approximately 90 percent water by weight. Whereas milk contains a substantial variety of all six classes of nutrients, a single food item doesn't have to provide all nutrients in order to be good for you. Rather, a well-balanced diet composed of a variety of foods can provide you with all of these important nutrients (Figure 1.2).

A well-balanced diet will also provide other dietary compounds such as phytochemicals and **fiber** that have been shown to help fight many diseases. At least 900 different phytochemicals have been identified in foods and more are likely to be discovered. Don't assume that these compounds can be extracted from foods, put in a pill, and still produce the same positive effect on your health. The disease-fighting properties of phytochemicals likely go beyond the compounds themselves, and work with fiber, nutrients, or unknown substances in foods to provide a synergistic, positive effect on your health.

Fiber is the portion of plant foods that isn't digested in the small intestine. Some foods, such as whole grains, fruits, and vegetables that are high in fiber are also phytochemical powerhouses. Studies have shown that diets rich in these foods fight disease.

Also, let's not forget some of the other wonderful elements of eating food. The delicious texture and aroma of foods coupled with the social interaction of meals are lost when you pop a pill to meet your nutrient needs. That said, some individuals *should* take a supplement if food alone can't meet their needs.

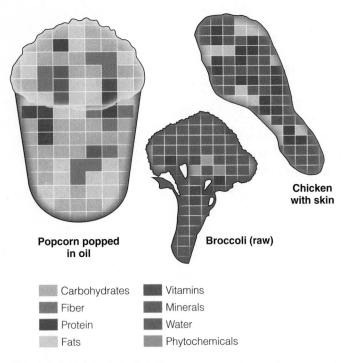

Chicken with skin

Popcorn popped in oil

Broccoli (raw)

- Carbohydrates
- Fiber
- Protein
- Fats
- Vitamins
- Minerals
- Water
- Phytochemicals

Figure 1.2 Nutrients in Foods
Foods provide more than calories. In addition to nutrients like carbohydrates, vitamins, and minerals, they contain nonnutritive compounds such as phytochemicals.

You Can Meet Some Nutrient Needs with a Supplement

Although many people can get all their nutrients through their diet, others have diet restrictions or higher nutrient needs such that they would benefit from taking a supplement in addition to consuming a healthy diet. For example, someone who is lactose intolerant (meaning they have difficulty digesting milk products) may have to meet his or her calcium needs from other sources. A calcium supplement could be an option for these individuals. Pregnant women should take an iron supplement because their increased need for this mineral is unlikely to be met through the diet alone. As you can see, a well-balanced diet and dietary supplements aren't mutually exclusive. In some situations, they should be partnered as the best nutritional strategy for good health.

Even with an abundance of foods and the availability of supplements for those who may need them, the diets of Americans aren't as healthy as they could be. Let's find out why this is the case.

fiber The portion of plant foods that isn't digested in the small intestine.

overweight Carrying extra weight on your body in relation to your height. (See Chapter 10 for the clinically defined weight range.)

obesity Carrying an excessive amount of body fat above the level of being overweight. (See Chapter 10 for the clinically defined level.)

Healthy People 2010 A set of disease prevention and health promotion objectives for Americans to meet during the first decade of the new millennium.

The Take-Home Message A well-balanced diet will likely meet all of your nutrient needs and also provide a variety of compounds that may help prevent chronic diseases. People who cannot meet their nutrient needs through food alone may benefit from taking a supplement.

How Does the Average American Diet Stack Up?

1991

Most Americans are not doing very well when it comes to meeting all their nutrient needs without exceeding their calorie needs. The average American diet is high in sodium, saturated fat, and calories, but low in vitamin E, calcium, and fiber.[14] As people take in more calories than they need and burn fewer calories because of sedentary lifestyles, they create a recipe for ill health.

Incidence of Overweight and Obesity Is on the Rise

1996

Americans have been battling the bathroom scale for the last two decades, and the scale is winning as conditions of **overweight** and **obesity** have become an epidemic in the United States (see Figure 1.3). Along with the weight gain have come higher rates of type 2 diabetes, particularly among children, and increased rates of heart disease, cancer, and stroke. Over 65 percent of American adults and 15 percent of children aged 6 to 19 are currently overweight.[15]

Improving Americans' Diets Is One Goal of *Healthy People 2010*

2004

The U.S. Surgeon General has issued calls for a nationwide health improvement program since 1979. The latest edition of this report is **Healthy People 2010**, which contains a set of health objectives for the nation to achieve over the first decade of the twenty-first century.

Healthy People 2010 focuses on two broad goals: (1) to help all Americans increase their life expectancy and improve their quality of life and (2) to eliminate health disparities among different segments of the population. There are 28 areas of focus in *Healthy People 2010*, ranging from ensuring that Americans have adequate access to medical care to improvements in their diets and physical activity. Objectives have been developed within each focus area.

For example, "Nutrition and Overweight" is one focus area; its goal is to promote good health and reduce the chronic diseases associated with diet and weight. There are numerous objectives developed within this focus area that, if fulfilled, will help Americans improve their diet and reduce their weight. See Table 1.2 on page 14 for the list of objectives in this area of focus.

As you can see from the table, though the first objective is for 60 percent of Americans to be at a healthy weight by 2010, only 42 percent of Americans met this objective in 2000, the start of *Healthy People 2010*.[16] Current research indicates that Americans' body weights are increasing rather than decreasing. When it comes to eating

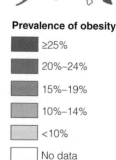

Prevalence of obesity

- ≥25%
- 20%–24%
- 15%–19%
- 10%–14%
- <10%
- No data

Figure 1.3 Obesity Trends Among U.S. Adults
Over the last two decades, rates of overweight and obesity have risen significantly in the United States.

Source: Centers for Disease Control. 2006. "Overweight and Obesity: Obesity Trends." www.cdc.gov/nccdphp/dnpa/obesity/trend/maps/index.htm.

Table 1.2

Healthy People 2010 Nutrition and Overweight Objectives

Objectives	Target for Americans (%)	Status of Americans (%)
Increase the proportion of adults who are at a healthy weight	60	42
Reduce the proportion of adults who are obese	15	23
Increase the proportion of persons aged 2 years and older who consume at least two daily servings of fruit	75	28
Increase the proportion of persons aged 2 years and older who consume at least three daily servings of vegetables, with at least one-third being dark green or deep yellow vegetables	50	3
Increase the proportion of persons aged 2 years and older who consume at least six daily servings of grain products, with at least three being whole grains	50	7

The incidence of overweight and obesity among adults and children is becoming more prevalent in the United States.

adequate amounts of fruits, vegetables, and whole grains, which are all beneficial to managing one's weight, Americans have plenty of room for improvement to meet the goal by the year 2010.

The Take-Home Message Rates of overweight and obese Americans are increasing, yet many people are falling short of some nutrient needs. *Healthy People 2010* is a set of health objectives for Americans for the first decade of the new millennium. The goals of *Healthy People 2010* are to help all Americans increase their life expectancy and improve their quality of life, and to eliminate health disparities among different segments of the population. Nutrition and overweight is one focus area of *Healthy People 2010*.

What's the Real Deal When It Comes to Nutrition Research and Advice?

consensus The opinion of a group of experts based on a collection of information.

scientific method A stepwise process used by scientists to generate sound research findings.

hypothesis An idea generated by scientists based on their observations.

If you "Google" the word *nutrition*, you will get a list of about 147,000,000 entries in less than .08 seconds. Obviously, the world is full of nutrition information.

Just ask anyone who is trying to lose weight and that person will probably tell you how hard it is to keep up with the latest diet advice—because it seems to keep changing. In the 1970s, waist watchers were told that carbohydrates were the bane of their existence and that a protein-rich, low-carbohydrate diet was the name of the game when it came to shrinking their waistline. A decade later, avoiding fat was the key to winning the battle of the bulge. By 2000, carbohydrates were being ousted yet again, and protein-rich diets were back in vogue. But now protein-heavy diets seem to be fading out of the limelight and high-carbohydrate diets are once again becoming the way to fight weight gain. So . . . are you frustrated yet?

Even though popular wisdom and trends seem to change with the wind, scientific knowledge about nutrition doesn't change this frequently. While the media publicizes results from studies deemed newsworthy, in reality it takes many, many affirming research studies before a **consensus** is reached about nutrition advice. News of the results of one study is just that: news. In contrast, advice from an authoritative health organization or committee, such as the American Heart Association or the Dietary Guidelines Committee, that is based on a consensus of research information is just that: authoritative advice. Headlines in newspapers, lead articles on websites, and the sound bites on television often report the results of a single, recent research study. The boxed feature "Evaluating Media Headlines with a Critical Eye" on page 16 discusses how to scrutinize information about current research findings and not get caught up in the media hype.

Nutrition-related research findings are often lead stories in newspapers and magazines, and on websites.

Sound Nutrition Research Begins with the Scientific Method

Research studies that generate enough information are based on a process called the **scientific method.** Scientists are like detectives. They observe something in the natural world, ask questions, come up with an idea (or **hypothesis**) based on their observations, test their hypothesis, and then see if their idea is correct. There are many steps in the scientific method and many adjustments made along the way before a scientist has gained enough information to support his or her hypothesis. In fact, the entire process can takes years to complete.

Let's walk through a nutrition-related study in which scientists used the scientific method to study rickets. Rickets is a disease in children in which the leg bones are so weakened that they are unable to hold up the child's body weight. The legs bow as a result. In the early 1800s, parents often relied on folklore medicine to treat diseases, and in the case of rickets, they used cod-liver oil because it provided a miraculous cure.

The first steps of the scientific method are to make an observation and ask questions. Originally, scientists were piqued by the cod-liver oil curing phenomenon. They asked themselves why cod-liver oil cured rickets (Figure 1.4). In the second step of the scientific method, a hypothesis is formulated. Because cod-liver oil is very rich in vitamin A, scientists initially thought that this vitamin must be the curative factor. To confirm this, scientists proceeded to the next step in the scientific method, which was to conduct an experiment.

The scientists altered the cod-liver oil to destroy all of its vitamin A. The altered oil was given to rats that had been fed a diet that caused rickets. Surprisingly, the rats were still cured of rickets. This disproved the scientists' original hypothesis that vitamin A was the curative factor. They then needed to modify their hypothesis, as it was obvious that there was something else in the cod-liver oil that cured rickets. They next

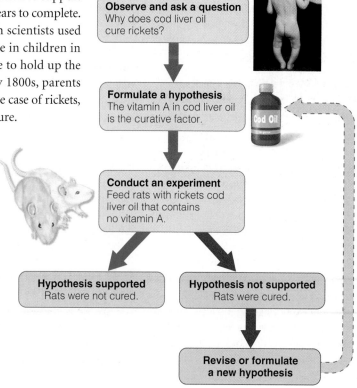

Observe and ask a question
Why does cod liver oil cure rickets?

Formulate a hypothesis
The vitamin A in cod liver oil is the curative factor.

Conduct an experiment
Feed rats with rickets cod liver oil that contains no vitamin A.

Hypothesis supported
Rats were not cured.

Hypothesis not supported
Rats were cured.

Revise or formulate a new hypothesis

Figure 1.4 Steps of the Scientific Method
The scientific method is used to conduct credible research in nutrition and other scientific fields.

Evaluating Media Headlines with a Critical Eye

Based on this headline, you may be tempted to toss out the apple and get yourself a couple of chocolate bars. However, you would be doing a disservice to your health if you didn't read below this tantalizing headline, which is designed to grab your attention but not necessarily tell you the whole story.

The media is routinely bombarded by press releases sent from medical journals, food companies, organizations, and universities about research being conducted and/or conferences being sponsored by these institutions. These releases are sent for one reason: to gain publicity. Reputable news organizations that report these findings will seek out independent experts in the field to weigh in on the research and, just as importantly, explain how these findings relate to the public. If you don't read beyond the headlines, you are probably missing important details of the story. Even worse, if you begin making dietary and lifestyle changes based on each news flash, you become a scientific guinea pig.

When a headline piques your interest, read the article with a critical eye, and ask yourself the following questions.

1. Was the research finding published in a peer-reviewed journal?

You can be confident that studies published in a peer-reviewed journal have been thoroughly reviewed by experts in this area of research. In most cases, the study does not get published. If the research isn't published in a peer-reviewed journal, you have no way of knowing if the study was conducted in an appropriate manner and whether the findings are accurate. A study about the possible virtues of chocolate in fighting heart disease that is published in the *New England Journal of Medicine* has more credibility than a similar article published in a baking magazine.

October 31, 2005

An Apple a Day for Health? Mars Recommends Two Bars of Chocolate

By Alexei Barrionuevo, *The New York Times*

---

2. Was the study done using animals or humans?

Animals are animals and humans are humans. Experiments with animals are often used to study how a particular substance affects a health outcome. But if the study is conducted in rats, it doesn't necessarily mean that the substance will have the same effect if consumed by humans. This doesn't mean that animal studies are frivolous. They are important stepping stones to designing and conducting similar experiments involving humans.

3. Do the study participants resemble me?

When you read or hear about studies involving humans, you always want to find out more information about the individuals who took part in the research. For example, were the people in the candy bar study college-aged subjects or older individuals with heart disease and high blood pressure? If older adults were studied, then would these findings be of any benefit to young adults who don't have high blood pressure or heart disease?

4. Is this the first time I've heard about this?

A single study in a specific area of research is a lonely entity in the scientific world. Is this the first study regarding the designer chocolate bars? If the media

article doesn't confirm that other studies have also supported these findings, this initial study may be the *only* study of its kind. Wait until you hear that these research findings are confirmed from a reputable health organization, such as the American Heart Association, before considering making any changes in your diet. These organizations will only change their advice based on a consensus of research findings.

In your lifetime, you are going to read thousands of newspaper and website headlines, as well as watch and listen to who-knows-how-many similar television and radio reports. Your critical thinking skills in evaluating the sources and information presented will be your best friend when it comes to deciding which blurbs to believe. These skills may also save you considerable money by helping you avoid nutrition gimmicks. When it comes to assessing nutrition information in the media, it's worth your time and effort to find out where it came from and why (or if) you should care.

Note: You can view the referenced article at www.nytimes.com.

hypothesized that it was the vitamin D that cured the rats, and conducted another experiment to confirm this hypothesis, which it did.

The next step in the scientific method involves sharing these findings with the scientific community. What good would it be to make this fabulous discovery if other scientists couldn't find out about it? To do this, scientists summarize and submit their research findings to a **peer-reviewed journal** (Figure 1.5). Other scientists (peers) then look at the researchers' findings to make sure that they are sound. If so, the research study is published in the journal. (If this relationship between vitamin D and rickets was discovered today, it would probably be the lead story on CNN.)

As more and more studies were done that confirmed that vitamin D can cure and prevent rickets, a theory developed. We now know with great certainty that vitamin D can prevent rickets and that a deficiency of vitamin D will cause this type of deformed bones in children. Because of this, there is a consensus among health professionals as to the importance of vitamin D in the diets of children.

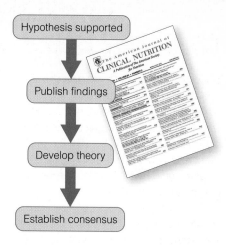

Figure 1.5 A Hypothesis Can Lead to a Scientific Consensus
When a hypothesis is supported by research, the results are published in peer-reviewed journals. Once a theory has been developed and supported by subsequent experiments, a consensus is reached in the scientific community.

Research Studies and Experiments Confirm Hypotheses

Scientists can use different types of experiments to test their hypothesis. The experiment above with the rats is called a **laboratory experiment,** as it was done in the confines of a lab. Research conducted with humans is usually **observational** or **experimental.** Observational research involves looking at factors in two or more groups of subjects to see if there is a relationship to a certain disease or other health outcome.

One type of observational research is **epidemiological research,** which looks at populations of people. For example, scientists may look at people who live in Norway and notice that there is a higher incidence of rickets among children there than in Australia. Through their observation, they may find a relationship between the lack of sun exposure in Norway and the high incidence of rickets there compared with sunny Australia. However, the scientists can't rule out that the difference in the incidence of rickets in these two populations may also be due to other factors in the subjects' diet or lifestyle.

Experimental research involves at least two groups of subjects. One group, the **experimental group,** is given a treatment, and another group, the **control group,** isn't. When scientists hypothesized that vitamin D cured rickets, they would have randomly assigned children with rickets to two groups. The scientist would have given the experimental group a vitamin D supplement but would have given the control group a sugar pill, also called a **placebo,** that looked just like the vitamin D supplement but contained only sugar. If neither of the two groups of subjects knew which pill they received, then the subjects were "blind" to the treatment. If the scientists who were giving the placebo and the vitamin D supplement also couldn't distinguish between the two treatments and didn't know which group received which treatment, this would be called a **double-blind placebo-controlled study.** The scientists would also have to make sure that all variables were the same or controlled for both groups during the experiment. For example, they couldn't let the control group go outside in the sunshine, which is known to be a source of vitamin D, and at the same time, keep the experimental group of subjects inside. The exposure to the sunshine would change the outcome of the experiment.

A double-blind, placebo-controlled study is considered the "gold standard" of research because all of the variables are the same and controlled for the groups of subjects, and neither the subjects nor the researcher are biased toward one group, as

peer-reviewed journal A research journal in which fellow scientists (peers) review studies to assess if they are accurate and sound before they are published.

laboratory experiment A scientific experiment conducted in a laboratory. Some laboratory experiments involve animals.

observational research Research that involves looking at factors in two or more groups of subjects to see if there is a relationship to certain outcomes.

experimental research Research involving at least two groups of subjects.

epidemiological research Research that looks at populations of people; it is often observational.

experimental group The group given a specific treatment.

control group The group given a placebo.

placebo A sugar pill that has no impact on the individual's health when ingested.

double-blind placebo-controlled study When the scientists in a research experiment can't distinguish between the treatment given to the subjects and don't know which group of subjects received which treatment.

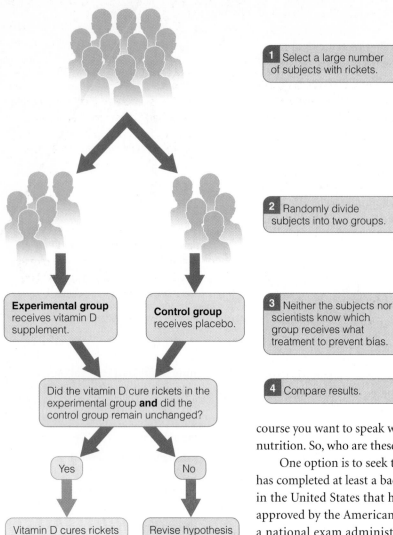

1 Select a large number of subjects with rickets.

2 Randomly divide subjects into two groups.

3 Neither the subjects nor scientists know which group receives what treatment to prevent bias.

4 Compare results.

Experimental group receives vitamin D supplement.

Control group receives placebo.

Did the vitamin D cure rickets in the experimental group **and** did the control group remain unchanged?

Yes

No

Vitamin D cures rickets

Revise hypothesis

Figure 1.6 Controlled Scientific Experiments Scientists use experimental research to test hypotheses.

registered dietitian (RD) A health professional who has completed at least a bachelor's degree in an accredited university or college in the United States, completed a supervised practice, and passed an exam administered by the American Dietetic Association (ADA).

medical nutrition therapy The integration of nutrition counseling and dietary changes based on an individual's medical and health needs to treat a patient's medical condition.

public health nutritionists An individual who may have an undergraduate degree in nutrition but isn't an RD.

they don't know which group received which treatment (Figure 1.6).

The beauty of science is that one discovery builds on another. Though this may seem frustrating when the findings of one research study dispute the results of another from just a few months before, these findings help scientists create new questions. Acting as detectives, scientists continually observe and keep asking questions about the world around them. Although many hypotheses fail along the way, a great many discoveries are also made.

You Can Trust the Advice of Nutrition Experts

If you want legal advice, you seek the expertise of a lawyer. If you need a knee operation, you should visit an orthopedic surgeon. If you want nutrition advice, to whom should you turn? Of course you want to speak with a credible expert who has training in the field of nutrition. So, who are these people and where do you find them?

One option is to seek the expertise of a **registered dietitian (RD).** The RD has completed at least a bachelor's degree at an accredited university or college in the United States that has incorporated specific coursework and has been approved by the American Dietetic Association (ADA). RDs have also passed a national exam administered by the ADA. They have an understanding of **medical nutrition therapy,** which is an integration of nutrition counseling and dietary changes based on an individual's medical history and current health needs to improve that person's health.

RDs work with their patients to make dietary changes that can help prevent diseases such as heart disease, diabetes, stroke, and obesity. Many physicians, based on the diagnosis of their patients, refer them to RDs for nutrition advice and guidance. RDs must participate in continuing professional education in order to remain current in the fast-changing world of nutrition, medicine, and health and maintain their registration. RDs work in hospitals and other health care facilities, private practice, universities, medical schools, professional athletic teams, food companies, and other nutrition-related businesses.

Individuals with advanced degrees in nutrition can also provide credible nutrition information. Sometimes physicians may have taken a nutrition course in medical school and gone on to get a master of science in public health (MPH), which involves some nutrition courses, or an MS in nutrition at an accredited university or college.

Some **public health nutritionists** may have an undergraduate degree in nutrition but didn't complete a supervised practice, so are not eligible to take the ADA exam. These individuals can work in the government organizing community outreach nutrition programs, such as programs for the elderly.

Quackwatchers

Consumers beware. The snake oil sales-people of yesteryear never left the building. They just left the oil behind and moved on to selling nutrition supplements and other products. These skilled salespeople introduce health fears into your mind and then try to sell services and products to allay these newly created fears. They make unrealistic promises and guarantees.

In order to avoid falling for one of their shady schemes, you should be leery of infomercials, magazine ads, and websites that try to convince you that:

- Most Americans are not adequately nourished.
- Everyone should take vitamin supplements.
- You need supplements to relieve stress or give you energy.

- You can lose a lot of weight in a short amount of time.
- Their products can produce amazing results and cure whatever ails you.
- Your behavior is caused by your diet.
- Herbs are safe because they are natural.
- Sugar will poison you.
- A hair sample can identify nutrient deficiencies.
- Your MD or RD is a quack to whom you should not listen.
- There is no risk, as there is a money-back guarantee. Good luck getting your money back!

Sources: S. Barrett, Signs of a 'Quacky' Web Site and Twenty-Five Ways to Spot Quacks and Vitamin Pushers. Available at http://quackwatch.org.

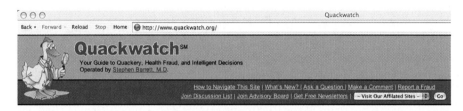

In order to protect the health of the public receiving nutrition information, over 30 states in the United States currently license nutrition professionals, who must meet specified educational and experience criteria to be considered experts in the field of nutrition. A person who meets these qualifications is a **licensed dietitian** (LD) and so will have the letters "LD" after his or her name. Because RDs have completed the rigorous standards set forth by the ADA, they automatically meet the criteria for LD and often will have both "RD" and "LD" after their names.

Be careful when taking nutrition advice from a trainer at the gym or the person who works at the local health food store. Whereas some of these people may be credible, many are not, and thus, less likely to give you information based on solid scientific evidence. Anyone who calls himself or herself a **nutritionist** may have taken few or no accredited courses in nutrition.

You also need to beware of individuals who specialize in health **quackery** or fraud. Such scammers will try to persuade you with false nutrition claims and anecdotal stories that aren't backed up by sound science and research. Americans spend billions of dollars annually on fraudulent health products, an injustice that Stephen Barrett, MD, a nationally known author and consumer advocate, has been trying to fight for decades. His website, quackwatch.org, helps consumers identify quackery and health fraud and make educated decisions about health-related information and products. Dr. Barrett's list of common deceptive statements made by health quacks is in the boxed feature "Quackwatchers."

Identifying quackery and fraud is important not only when you are seeking out an expert for advice, but also when you read about nutrition on the Internet. The Web is overflowing with nutrition information and *mis*information.

licensed dietitian (LD) An individual who has met specified educational and experience criteria deemed by a state licensing board necessary to be considered an expert in the field of nutrition. An RD would meet all the qualifications to be an LD.

nutritionist A generic term with no recognized legal or professional meaning. Some people may call themselves nutritionists without having any credible training in nutrition.

quackery The promotion and selling of health products and services of questionable validity. A quack is a person who promotes these products and services in order to make money.

You Can Obtain Accurate Nutrition Information on the Internet

Mark Twain once said, "Be careful about reading health books. You could die of a misprint." If he was alive today, he probably would have included websites that dole out health advice. Over 70 percent of American adult Internet users, or 117 million people, have surfed more than 3 million websites looking for health and medical information.[17]

Don't assume a slick website is a sound website. Although many websites, such as Shape Up America! (www.shapeup.org) and the Tufts Health & Nutrition Newsletter (www.healthletter.tufts.edu/) provide credible, reliable, up-to-date nutrition information, anyone with computer skills can put up a slick website. The National Institutes of Health (NIH) has developed ten questions that you should consider when viewing a nutrition- or health-related website:[18]

1. Who Runs the Site?

Credible websites are willing to show their credentials. For example, the National Center for Complementary and Alternative Medicine (www.nccam.nih.gov) provides information about its association with the NIH and its extensive ongoing research and educational programs. If you have to spend more than a minute trying to find out who runs the website, you should click to another site.

2. Who Pays for the Site?

Running a website is expensive, and finding out who's paying for a particular site will tell you something about the reliability of its content. Websites sponsored by the government (with urls ending in .gov), a nonprofit organization (ending in .org), or an academic institution (.edu) are more reliable than many commercial websites (.com or .net). Some commercial websites, such as *Web*MD, carry articles that can be reliable if they are written by credible health professionals, but other websites may be promoting information to suit a company's own purposes.

For example, if the funding source for the website is a vitamin and mineral supplement company, are all the articles geared toward supporting the use of supplements? Does the website have advertisers and do their products also influence the content on the website? You need to investigate if the website content may be biased based on the funding source.

3. What Is the Purpose of the Site?

After you answer the first two questions, look for the "About This Site" link. This will help you understand the website's purpose. For example, at Nutrition.gov, the purpose is to "provide easy access to the best food and nutrition information across the federal government." This website doesn't exist to sell you anything, but to help you find reliable information.

4. Where Does the Information Come From?

You should always know who wrote what you are reading. Is the author a qualified nutrition expert or did she or he interview qualified individuals? If the site obtained information from another source, was that source cited?

5. What Is the Basis of the Information?

Is the article's information based on medical facts and figures that have references? For example, any medical news items released on the American Heart Association website (www.americanheart.org) will include the medical journal from which the information came. In fact, the website will often include the opinion of experts regarding the news items.

6. How Is the Information Selected?

A physician who is a well-known medical expert for a major television network once commented that he spends most of his time not delivering medical advice, but trying to stop the networks from publicizing health news that isn't credible. Always look to see if the website has an editorial board of medical and health experts and if qualified individuals review or write the content before it is released.

7. How Current Is the Information?

Once a website is on the Internet, it will stay there until someone removes it. Consequently, the health information that you read may not be the most up-to-date. Always check to see when the content was written, and if it is over a year old, whether it has been updated.

8. How Does the Site Choose Links to Other Sites?

Some medical sites don't like to link to other sites as they don't have control over other sites' credibility and content. Others do link, if they are confident that these sites meet their criteria. Some sites receive financial reimbursement from the links that they post. Don't always assume that the link is credible.

9. What Information Is Collected About You and Why?

Websites track the pages that you click on in order to analyze their more popular topics. Sometimes, they elicit personal information such as your gender, age, and health concerns. After collecting data on your viewing selections and your personal information, they can sell this information to interested companies. These companies can create promotional materials about their goods and services targeted to your needs. Credible sites should tell you about their privacy policy and if they will or will not give this information to other sources. A website's privacy policy is often found in a link at the bottom of its screens.

10. How Does the Site Manage Interactions with Visitors?

You should always be able to easily find the contact information of the website's owners should you have any concerns or questions that you want answered. If the site has a chat room or ongoing discussion group, you should know how it is moderated. Read the discussion group dialogue before you jump in.

The Take-Home Message Sound nutrition advice is based on years of research using the scientific method. You should only take nutrition advice from a credible source such as a registered dietitian or other valid nutrition expert. When obtaining nutrition information from the Internet, you need to carefully peruse the site to make sure that it is credible, contains up-to-date information, and its content isn't influenced by those that fund and support the website.

Two Points of View

Food Advertisements: Help or Hindrance?

With so much money being spent on the advertising of foods, is it easy for the consumer to eat a healthy diet? Let's ask two experts to share their point of view on this issue.

Margo G. Wootan, DSc
Director of Nutrition Policy, Center for Science in the Public Interest

Margo Wootan, DSc, is the director of nutrition policy at the Center for Science in the Public Interest (CSPI), a health advocacy organization that specializes in nutrition and obesity. Dr. Wootan received her BS in nutrition from Cornell University and her doctorate in nutrition from Harvard University's School of Public Health. Dr. Wootan cofounded the National Alliance for Nutrition and Activity (NANA).

Q: Is the consumer pressured by food companies to buy more heavily advertised foods, such as sweetened beverages, cookies, candies, and snack items? Why or why not?

A: Yes, company practices have a big effect on people's food preferences and choices. While some experts are still scratching their heads and wondering why obesity rates have been skyrocketing in adults and children, all you have to do is look around to see why: The existing food environment is not supportive of healthy choices. There are many powerful forces—and powerful companies—working against Americans' efforts to eat well and maintain a healthy weight. They include advertising and marketing, large portion sizes, eating out, food everywhere, too many sugary soft drinks, and junk food in schools.

Q: Is there research to support your point of view?

A: There's no disputing the fact that the goal of food marketing is to influence children's food choices. Companies clearly believe that marketing works—or they wouldn't spend billions of dollars each year marketing to children. Also, studies demonstrate that food advertising gets children's attention and affects their food choices, food purchases, and what they ask their parents to purchase. A comprehensive study by the National Academies' Institute of Medicine strongly concluded that marketing works—it affects children's diets and health. Any parent can tell you that ads and cartoon characters on food packages affect not only which foods their children ask them to purchase, but which foods their kids are willing to eat.

Q: How can the food industry help consumers purchase and eat more fruits and vegetables?

A: Companies should market fruits and vegetables using television, print, and other ads, cartoon characters on packages or stickers on fruits and vegetables, Internet marketing,

(continued)

Radley Balko
Policy Analyst, Columnist

Radley Balko is a policy analyst for the Cato Institute, a non-profit public policy research foundation headquartered in Washington, D.C. He specializes in consumer choice issues, including alcohol and tobacco control, obesity, and civil liberties. He is a columnist for *FoxNews.com* and has been published in *TIME* magazine, the *Washington Post,* the *Los Angeles Times,* Canada's *National Post,* and several other publications. Balko has also appeared on CNN, CNBC, Fox News Channel, NPR, and MSNBC.

Q: Is the consumer pressured by food companies to buy more heavily advertised foods, such as sweetened beverages, cookies, candies, and snack items? Why or why not?

A: I doubt it. Advertising's two main purposes are to foster brand loyalty and to bump customers up to a higher (read: more expensive) line of product. Most people are smart enough to know that fruits and vegetables are better for them than cookies and chips. If you've made the conscious decision to eat healthy, television commercials aren't going to bring you back to pizza and donuts. If more Americans are skipping the produce section for the snack aisle, that's of course their prerogative. I don't blame the food companies for what ultimately is an exercise in personal choice.

Q: Is there research to support your point of view?

A: My point of view is driven primarily by philosophy—what we put into our mouths ought to be our own business, not the business of nutrition activists, government bureaucrats, or politicians. I don't think we need much research to prove the point that most of us know that produce is better for our health than ice cream. One thing that often gets lost in these debates is just how healthy America really is. Life expectancy continues to reach all-time highs in America. Deaths from heart disease, cancer, and stroke—the country's three biggest killers—have been in decline for 15 years. Our waistlines may be getting thicker, but it isn't clear that that poses any large-scale threat to our overall health.

Q: How can the food industry help consumers purchase and eat more fruits and vegetables?

A: It isn't so much what the food industry can do as what the government can do—or should stop doing. I do agree with the nutrition activists that government should stop

(continued)

Food Advertisements: Help or Hindrance?, continued

Margo G. Wootan, DSc, continued

and other marketing techniques now used mostly to market foods of poor nutritional quality. Marketing healthy foods can work. Sales of Darling clementines increased 25 percent after they put Nickelodeon's Dora the Explorer and SpongeBob SquarePants on the packs.

Food manufacturers and restaurants also should develop new products and reformulate existing products to add more fruits and vegetables. It is great that McDonald's has Apple Dippers, Fruit 'n Yogurt Parfaits, and salads, but that doesn't give people enough choices to find something that they really like. There are hundreds of other fruits and vegetables that could be added to the menu.

Q: What responsibility do food companies have to help Americans eat healthfully?

A: Of course, it is up to individuals to decide what they will eat. But, we need to recognize that it's not easy to exercise personal responsibility in our junk-food culture. While obesity rates have increased over the last 20 years, there's no evidence to show that over that time period willpower has declined or that parents love their children any less.

The CSPI is working to change policies and the "food environment" to make healthy eating easier. [Its efforts] include getting soda and junk food out of schools, stopping junk-food marketing to kids, and providing calorie labeling on fast-food menus. Such policies support personal responsibility, parental authority, and parents' ability to feed their children a healthy diet. For example, it's parents' responsibility to keep their children from playing in traffic, but that doesn't mean we don't need laws that prohibit people from recklessly driving 80 miles per hour through residential neighborhoods. Similarly, we need policies that make it possible for children—and adults—to eat well and achieve a healthy weight.

Radley Balko, continued

subsidizing corn, and should lift its tariffs on sugar. These policies create unnatural distortions in the food market. Another suggestion: *Access* seems to be the main problem when it comes to produce and low-income people. Big box stores such as Wal-Mart have figured out how to get inexpensive, high-quality produce to low-income consumers. We should be applauding when big box grocers open stores in urban areas, not chasing them out of town.

Q: What responsibility do food companies have to help Americans eat healthfully?

A: Individual Americans are responsible for their own diets, not food companies. A company's only real responsibility is to (1) make profits for its shareholders, and (2) be honest and forthright about what it's putting on the market. If a food company is misleading or untruthful about its product, then yes, it should be held accountable. But to offer one example, Baskin-Robbins makes ice cream. It has always made ice cream. I see no reason why a company that has always made a product meant to be consumed as an indulgence has any "responsibility" to help Americans "eat healthfully." If Americans truly want to eat healthy, companies that produce healthy foods will flourish. But I see no reason why a fast food company, for example, should take a loss or go out of business pushing health food no one wants to buy.

NUTRITION IN THE REAL WORLD

Be a Nutrition Sleuth

Spotting a Bogus Weight-Loss Product

When a miraculous weight-loss product sounds a little too good to be true, it probably is! Identify the signs of a bogus product at www.aw-bc.com/blake.

NUTRITION IN THE REAL WORLD

Get Real!

Find Online Information You Can Use

Don't know where to begin to find credible nutrition information on the Internet? Visit www.aw-bc.com/blake for a reliable starting point.

The Top Ten Points to Remember

1. Food choices are influenced by personal taste, culture, social life, advertising, accessibility, and time constraints. You eat out of habit, in response to your emotions, and, of course, because food is delicious.

2. There are six categories of nutrients: carbohydrates, lipids (fats), proteins, vitamins, minerals, and water. Your body needs a mixture of these nutrients in specific amounts to stay healthy.

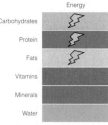

3. Nutrition plays an important role in preventing many of the leading causes of death in the United States, including heart disease, cancer, stroke, and a certain type of diabetes.

4. Nutrition is a science and new discoveries are continually made. Nutritional genomics is the integration of nutrition and genomics. Genomics is the study of genes, their functions in your body, and how the environment, including the foods and nutrients that you eat, influences the expression of your genes and, therefore, your health.

5. Carbohydrates, fats, and proteins provide the energy that your body needs. The majority of your daily calories should come from carbohydrates. You also need adequate amounts of both fats and proteins. Most of the proteins that you eat should be used to build and maintain your body tissues, muscles, and organs, rather than for energy.

6. Vitamins and minerals are important for metabolism and to properly utilize carbohydrates, fats, and protein. Many vitamins aid enzymes in your body.

7. Water is an essential nutrient that is vital for many functions. It bathes the inside and outside of your cells, helps maintain your body temperature, and acts as a lubricant and protective cushion.

8. Eating a well-balanced diet is the best way to meet your nutrient and health needs. Vitamin and mineral supplements can help complete a healthy diet but should not replace foods.

9. Sound nutrition information is the result of numerous scientific studies that are based on the scientific method. These research findings should be reviewed by and shared with the medical and scientific community. You should never change your diet or lifestyle based upon the findings of just one or a few studies.

10. Nutritional advice should come from credible sources. Individuals who call themselves nutritionists may or may not have a credible nutrition education. Always assess the source of the nutrition information to make sure that it is from a credible source.

Test Your Knowledge

1. Which of the following can influence your food choices?
   a. your ethnic background
   b. your busy schedule
   c. your emotions
   d. all of the above

2. Nutrition is
   a. the study of genes, how they function in your body, and how the environment can influence your genes.
   b. the study of how your body functions.
   c. the scientific study of how nutrients and compounds in foods that you eat nourish and affect your body functions and health.
   d. the study of hormones and how they function in your body.

3. The energy in foods is measured in carbohydrates.
   a. true
   b. false

4. The majority of your daily calories should come from
   a. fats.
   b. minerals.
   c. vitamins.
   d. carbohydrates.
   e. water.

5. Which nutrients may help enzymes function in your body?
   a. carbohydrates
   b. vitamins
   c. minerals
   d. all of the above
   e. b and c only

6. Everyone needs to take vitamin and mineral supplements to be healthy.
   a. true
   b. false

7. The two broad goals of *Healthy People 2010* are
   a. to help Americans increase their life expectancy and improve their quality of life.
   b. to increase the hours Americans sleep each night.

c. to eliminate health disparities among different segments of the population.

d. a and b only.

e. a and c only.

8. The first step in the scientific method is to

a. make observations and ask questions.

b. form a hypothesis.

c. do an experiment.

d. develop a theory.

9. You decide to have your diet assessed and be counseled by a nutrition professional because you want to lose weight. Which of the following individuals would be the most credible source of information?

a. an employee of your local health food store

b. your personal trainer at the gym

c. a licensed dietitian

d. your aunt

e. your roommate, who runs for the campus track team

10. When exploring a website that provides nutrition and health information, which of the following should you look at to assess its content?

a. who wrote it

b. when it was written

c. when it was last updated

d. a and b only

e. a, b, and c

Answers

1. (d) Your food choices are influenced by many factors, including your ethnic background, the limited time you may have to devote to food preparation, and your emotions.

2. (c) Nutrition is about how nutrients affect your body and health. The study of genes is called genomics. Physiology is the study of how your body functions. The study of hormones and their function in your body is called endocrinology.

3. (b) False. Carbohydrates are a source of energy in your foods. The energy in your foods is measured in units called calories.

4. (d) The majority of your daily calories should come from carbohydrates. Vitamins, minerals, and water don't provide calories. Fats do contain calories but these shouldn't be the main source of energy in your diet.

5. (e) Certain vitamins and minerals may aid enzymes in your body. Carbohydrates don't aid enzymes, but these nutrients need enzymes to be properly metabolized.

6. (b) False. Many people can meet their vitamin and mineral needs from a well-balanced diet. Those who can't should take a supplement in addition to eating a healthy diet.

7. (e) The two broad goals are increasing life expectancy and the quality of life, as well as reducing health disparities among Americans. Increasing the amount of hours Americans sleep isn't a goal of *Healthy People 2010*.

8. (a) The scientific method begins with scientists observing and asking questions. From this step, a hypothesis follows. The scientists will then test their hypothesis using an experiment. After many experiments confirm their hypothesis, a theory will be developed.

9. (c) Unless the salesperson, personal trainer, your aunt, and your roommate are licensed dietitians, they are not qualified to provide nutrition counseling.

10. (e) When reading nutrition and health information on the Internet, it is very important to make sure the source is qualified to provide this information. Because you also need to assess if the information is current, you should find out when it was written and if it has been or needs to be updated.

Web Support

Examples of reliable nutrition and health websites include:

- Agricultural Research Service: www.nal.usda.gov/fnic/foodcomp
- American Cancer Society: www.cancer.org
- American College of Sports Medicine: www.acsm.org
- American Diabetes Association: www.diabetes.org
- American Dietetic Association: www.eatright.org
- American Heart Association: www.amhrt.org
- American Institute for Cancer Research: www.aicr.org
- American Medical Association: www.ama.assn.org
- Centers for Disease Control: www.cdc.gov
- Center for Science in the Public Interest: www.cspinet.org
- Food Allergy Network: www.foodallergy.org
- Food and Drug Administration: www.fda.gov
- Food and Nutrition Information Center: www.nal.usda.gov/fnic
- National Cholesterol Education Program: http://www.nhlbi.nih.gov/about/ncep
- National Institutes of Health: www.nih.gov
- National High Blood Pressure Program: www.nhlbi.nih.gov/hbp
- National Osteoporosis Foundation: www.nof.org
- Shape Up America!: www.shapeup.org
- Tufts University Health & Nutrition Newsletter: www.healthletter.tufts.edu
- U.S. Department of Agriculture: www.nutrition.gov
- Vegetarian Resource Group: www.vrg.org
- Weight Control Information Network: www.win.niddk.nih.gov/index.htm

2

1. The current **Dietary Reference Intakes** for vitamins and minerals are set at the amount you should consume daily to prevent a nutrient deficiency. **T/F**

2. To be healthy, you should be **physically active** at least three times a week. **T/F**

3. The *Dietary Guidelines for Americans* apply only to individuals over the age of 18. **T/F**

4. If you follow the advice in the *Dietary Guidelines for Americans* you can reduce your risk of dying from **chronic diseases** such as heart disease, high blood pressure, and diabetes mellitus. **T/F**

5. According to the USDA, there are five basic **food groups.** **T/F**

6. All packaged foods must contain a **food label.** **T/F**

7. Food manufacturers decide what nutrients to list on the **Nutrition Facts panel** of a food label. **T/F**

8. A **nutrient claim** on the food label describes how much of that nutrient is in one serving of the food. **T/F**

9. A **health claim** on a label must state the beneficial component that the food contains and the disease or condition that it can improve. **T/F**

10. A **functional food** positively affects your health beyond providing basic nutrients. **T/F**

Tools for Healthy Eating

J essie, a 19-year-old biology major, has been told by her doctor to watch her sodium intake so as to keep her borderline high blood pressure from becoming full-fledged high blood pressure (hypertension). Although Jessie takes care to make sodium-conscious food choices at her meals, she also likes to microwave a mug of hot soup in her dorm room. If Jessie read the label on her soup, she might be surprised to discover that her frequent soup snacks are providing more sodium than her meals.

What Is Healthy Eating and What Tools Can Help?

Answers

1. False. They are set at a level higher than the minimum amount needed to prevent a deficiency. To find out why, turn to page 29.
2. False. You should be physically active for at least 30 minutes *daily.* To find out why, turn to page 32.
3. False. These guidelines are the latest recommendations for nutrition and physical activity for healthy Americans over 2 years of age. That means that they apply to you! To learn about these new guidelines, turn to page 33.
4. True. The latest *Dietary Guidelines* were designed to help reduce your risk of the leading causes of death in the United States. To learn more, turn to page 33.
5. True. The five basic food groups are grains, vegetables, fruit, milk, and meat and beans. Turn to page 35 to find out more about the food groups and how MyPyramid can help guide your food choices.
6. True. The FDA requires a food label on all packaged food items, and specific information must be included. To find out exactly what must be disclosed on the food label, turn to page 44.
7. False. There are strict guidelines about the nutrients that must be listed on the food label. To find out what these nutrients are, turn to page 44.
8. True. Specific descriptive terms approved by the FDA must be used. To find out what these terms are and what they mean, turn to page 48.
9. True. However, more than one type of health claim is allowed on a label. Turn to page 50 to learn about the types of claims that food manufacturers may use.
10. True. Eating functional foods helps lower a person's risk of heart disease and some cancers. To learn more about functional foods, turn to page 52.

Healthy eating involves the key principles of balance, variety, and moderation. As a student, you are probably familiar with these principles from other areas of your life. Think about how you balance your time between work, school, and your family and friends. You engage in a variety of activities to avoid being bored, and enjoy each in moderation, since spending too much time on one activity (like working) will disrupt the amount of time you can spend on others (like studying or socializing). A chronic imbalance of any one of these activities will affect the others. If you regularly forgo sleep in order to work extra hours at a job, your sleep deprivation would affect your ability to stay awake in class, which would hamper your studies. You may be too exhausted to study, exercise, or socialize. Your unbalanced life would soon become unhealthy and unhappy.

Likewise, your diet must be balanced, varied, and moderate in order to be healthy. You need to consume a variety of foods, some more moderately than others, and balance your food choices to meet your nutrient and health needs.

A diet that lacks variety and is unbalanced can cause **undernutrition,** a state whereby you are not meeting your nutrient needs. If you were to consume only grains like bread and rice, and avoid other foods such as milk products, fruits, vegetables, and meats, your body wouldn't get enough protein and other important nutrients. You would eventually become **malnourished.**

In contrast, **overnutrition** occurs when a diet provides too much of a nutrient such as iron, which can be toxic in high amounts, or too many calories, which can lead to obesity. A person who is overnourished can also be malnourished. For example, a person can be overweight on a diet laden with less nutritious sweets and treats—foods that should be eaten in moderation—because he or she is taking in more calories than needed. These foods often displace more nutrient-rich choices. Excess calories are causing this person to be overweight while also falling short of many key nutrients and thus malnourished.

There are several tools that help you avoid both under- and overnutrition. The Dietary Reference Intakes provide recommendations regarding your nutrient needs, while the *Dietary Guidelines for Americans* provide broad dietary and lifestyle advice. MyPyramid is a food guidance system that helps you implement the recommendations in the DRIs and the advice in the *Dietary Guidelines*. MyPyramid provides personalized food choices among a variety of food groups to help you create a balanced diet. Finally, the Daily Values on food labels help you decide which foods to buy. Together, these tools help you plan a varied, moderate, and balanced diet that meets your nutrient and health needs.

Let's look at each of these tools, beginning with the DRIs.

What Are the Dietary Reference Intakes?

The **Dietary Reference Intakes (DRIs)** are specific reference values for each nutrient issued by the United States' National Academy of Sciences' Institute of Medicine. The DRIs are the specific amounts of each nutrient that is needed to be consumed to maintain good health, prevent chronic diseases, and avoid unhealthy excesses.[1] The Institute of Medicine periodically organizes committees of U.S. and Canadian scientists and health experts to update these recommendations based on the latest scientific research.

DRIs Tell You How Much of Each Nutrient You Need

Since the 1940s, the Food and Nutrition Board, part of the Institute of Medicine, has recommended amounts of essential nutrients needed daily to prevent a deficiency and promote good health. Because nutrient needs change with age, and because needs are different for men and women, different sets of recommendations were developed for each nutrient based on an individual's age and gender. In other words, a teenager may need more of a specific nutrient than a 55-year-old (and vice versa) and women need more of certain nutrients during pregnancy and lactation, so they all have different DRIs. Since the 1940s the DRIs have been updated ten times.

In the 1990s, nutrition researchers identified expanded roles for many nutrients. Though nutrient deficiencies were still an important issue, research suggested that higher amounts of some nutrients could play a role in disease prevention. Also, as consumers began using more dietary supplements and fortified foods, committee members grew concerned that excessive consumption of some nutrients might be as unhealthy as, or even more dangerous than, not consuming enough. Hence, the Food and Nutrition Board convened a variety of committees between 1997 and 2004 to take on the enormous task of reviewing the research on vitamins, minerals, carbohydrates, fats, protein, water, and other substances such as fiber and developing the current DRI reference values for all the nutrients.

DRIs Encompass Several Reference Values

The DRIs comprise five reference values: Estimated Average Requirement (EAR), Recommended Dietary Allowance (RDA), Adequate Intake (AI), the Tolerable Upper Intake Level (UL), and the Acceptable Macronutrient Distribution Range (AMDR) (Figure 2.1). Each of these values is unique, and serves a different need in planning a healthy diet. It may seem like a lot to remember, but you will use only the RDA or

Healthy eating is a way of life.

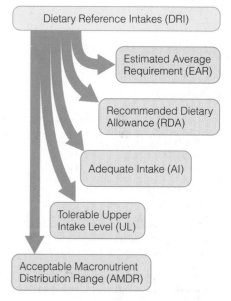

Figure 2.1 The Dietary Reference Intakes
When planning your diet, focus on the RDAs or AIs and the AMDR. Avoid consuming the UL of any nutrient.

undernutrition A state of inadequate nutrition whereby a person's nutrient and/or calorie needs aren't met through the diet.

malnourished The long-term outcome of consuming a diet that doesn't meet nutrient needs.

overnutrition A state of excess nutrients and calories in the diet.

Dietary Reference Intakes (DRIs) Reference values for the essential nutrients needed to maintain good health, to prevent chronic diseases, and to avoid unhealthy excesses.

Figure 2.2 The DRIs in Action
(a) The EAR is the average amount of a nutrient that is likely to meet the daily needs of half of the healthy individuals in a specific age and gender group. **(b)** The RDA, which is higher than the EAR, will meet the needs of approximately 97 to 98 percent of healthy individuals in a specific group. Consuming more than the RDA but less than the UL is safe for individuals. **(c)** The UL is the highest amount of a nutrient that is unlikely to pose any risk of adverse health effects even if consumed daily. As the intake of a nutrient increases above the UL, the risk of toxicity increases.

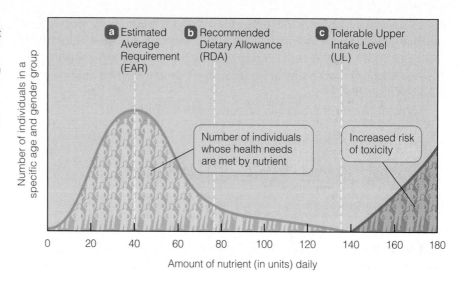

Estimated Average Requirement (EAR) The average amount of a nutrient that is known to meet the needs of 50 percent of the individuals in a similar age and gender group.

Recommended Dietary Allowance (RDA) The average amount of a nutrient that meets the needs of nearly all individuals (97 to 98 percent) in a similar age and gender group. The RDA is higher than the EAR.

Adequate Intake (AI) The *approximate* amount of a nutrient that groups of similar individuals are consuming to maintain good health.

Tolerable Upper Intake Level (UL) The highest amount of a nutrient that can be consumed daily without harm in a similar age and group of individuals.

toxicity The level at which exposure to a substance becomes harmful.

AI (not both), the AMDR, and the UL to assess whether your diet is meeting your nutrient needs.

The EAR is the starting point in the process of determining the other values. Let's look at how the values are determined.

The DRI committee members begin by reviewing a variety of research studies to determine the **Estimated Average Requirement (EAR)** for the nutrient. They may look at studies that investigate the consequences of eating a diet too low in the nutrient and the associated side effects or physical changes that develop, as well as how much of the nutrient should be consumed to correct the deficiency. They may also review studies that measure the amount a healthy individual absorbs, stores, and maintains daily. Additionally, they look at research studies that address the role the nutrient plays in reducing the risk of associated chronic diseases, such as heart disease. After a thorough review process, the EAR for the nutrient is determined.

The EAR is the average amount of a nutrient that is known to meet the needs of 50 percent of the individuals in a similar age and gender group (Figure 2.2). The EAR is a starting point to determine the amount of a nutrient individuals should consume daily for good health.

Let's use Figure 2.2 to locate the EAR for Nutrient X. As you can see from the figure, the EAR for Nutrient X is about 40 units. If the recommended reference value for Nutrient X was set at 40 units, then half of the individuals would be able to either meet or exceed their needs. However, the other 50 percent of the individuals would need more than the EAR to be healthy.

This is where the **Recommended Dietary Allowance (RDA)** comes in. The RDA is based on the EAR, but it is set higher; it represents the average amount of a nutrient that meets the needs of nearly all (97 to 98 percent) of the individuals in a similar group. The RDA for Nutrient X in Figure 2.2 is 75 units. So, by setting the reference value at 75 units, nearly all of the individuals in this group will meet their needs for this nutrient.

If there is insufficient scientific information to determine the EAR for a nutrient, the RDA can't be developed. When this happens, an **Adequate Intake (AI)** is determined instead. The AI is the next best scientific estimate of the amount of a nutrient that groups of similar individuals should consume to maintain good health.

Because consuming too much of some nutrients can be harmful, the committees developed the **Tolerable Upper Intake Level (UL).** The UL refers to the highest amount of a nutrient that is unlikely to cause harm if the amount is consumed daily. The higher the consumption above the UL, the higher the risk of **toxicity.** You should not try to

Table 2.1

The Do's and Don'ts of the DRIs

The Reference Values and Their Meaning	When Planning Your Diet
Estimated Average Requirement (EAR)	**Don't** use this amount.
Recommended Dietary Allowances (RDA)	**Do** aim for this amount!
Adequate Intake (AI)	**Do** aim for this amount if an RDA isn't available.
Tolerable Upper Intake Level (UL)	**Don't** exceed this amount on a daily basis.
Acceptable Macronutrient Distribution Range (AMDR)	**Do** follow these guidelines regarding the percentage of carbohydrates, protein, and fat in your diet.

Reprinted with permission from the National Academies Press, © 2003 National Academy of Sciences.

consume the UL of a nutrient. There isn't any known benefit from consuming a higher amount, and it may cause health problems.

The DRI committee also developed a range of intakes for the energy-containing nutrients, carbohydrates, proteins, and fats. These ranges are called the **Acceptable Macronutrient Distribution Ranges (AMDR)** and are as follows:

- Carbohydrates should comprise   45 to 65 percent of your daily calories
- Fat should comprise   20 to 35 percent of your daily calories
- Proteins should comprise   10 to 35 percent of your daily calories

Consuming these nutrient types in these ranges will ensure that you meet your calorie and nutrient needs, and reduce your risk of developing chronic diseases such as heart disease and obesity.

How to Use the DRIs

You can use the DRIs to select healthy food choices and plan a quality diet. To meet your needs, your goal should be to meet the RDA or the AI of all nutrients, but not exceed the UL. Table 2.1 summarizes the DRIs for you. On the inside cover of your textbook, you will find the DRIs for all the nutrients that you need daily.

Each chapter in this textbook will further explain what each nutrient is, why it is important, how much, based on the DRIs, you need to consume, and how to get enough, without consuming too much, in your diet.

Whereas the DRIs were released to prevent undernutrition, the *Dietary Guidelines for Americans* were developed out of concern over the incidence of overnutrition among Americans. Let's now look at the second tool that can help you obtain a healthy diet and lifestyle, the *Dietary Guidelines for Americans*.

The Take-Home Message The Dietary Reference Intakes (DRIs) are specific reference values that help you determine your daily nutrient needs to maintain good health, prevent chronic diseases, and avoid unhealthy excesses. The reference values include the EAR, RDA, AI, UL, and AMDR. Try to meet your RDA or AI and consume below the UL for each nutrient daily.

NUTRITION IN THE REAL WORLD

eLearn

Healthy Eating on a Budget

Healthy eating is not only better for your body, it's better for your wallet. According to the USDA, an individual between the ages of 20 and 50 can eat a healthy diet for as little as about $30 to $40 a week. If you want to learn how to eat healthfully and shop smart on a budget, visit www.aw-bc.com/blake.

Acceptable Macronutrient Distribution Range (AMDR) A healthy range of intakes for the energy-containing nutrients—carbohydrates, proteins, and fats—in your diet designed to meet your nutrient needs and help reduce the risk of chronic diseases.

The *Dietary Guidelines for Americans* at a Glance

The *Dietary Guidelines for Americans 2005* is divided into nine closely related, and often intertwined, categories that address various health concerns. Because of the vast amount of information in these guidelines, the following is only a short overview of each category and some supporting diet and lifestyle recommendations. Each chapter in this book elaborates on at least one of these guidelines and shows you how to easily make additional diet and lifestyle changes to improve your health. The complete guidelines and more information are available online at www.healthierus.gov/dietaryguidelines.

Adequate Nutrients within Calorie Needs

The Health Concern in a Nutshell: Many Americans are consuming more calories than they need, yet still falling short of receiving some important nutrients.

It's Recommended that You: Consume a variety of nutrient-dense foods and beverages within and among the basic food groups but be careful not to exceed the amount of daily calories you need to maintain a healthy weight.

Weight Management

The Health Concern in a Nutshell: Over 65 percent of Americans are overweight, and so are at an increased risk of heart disease, cancer, stroke, and diabetes mellitus—some of the major causes of death in the United States.

It's Recommended that You: Maintain a balance between the amount of calories that you consume daily and the amount you need to maintain a healthy weight. Daily physical activity will help, as it allows you to eat some additional calories while maintaining your weight. If you need to lose weight, take in fewer calories and increase your physical activity level.

Physical Activity

The Health Concern in a Nutshell: Even though being physically active reduces the risk of many chronic diseases, over half of American adults don't exercise enough to gain this protective effect. To make matters worse, 25 percent of Americans are considered "couch potatoes" because they don't move at all during their leisure time.

It's Recommended that You: Try to be physically active every day. You should spend at least 30 minutes a day in moderately intense physical activity, such as brisk walking, roller blading, or aerobic dancing. If you engage in more vigorous activities, such as jogging or a step aerobics class, you'll reap even more health benefits. If weight loss is your goal, increase your exercise to at least 60 minutes of a moderate-intensity activity throughout the day.

Food Groups to Encourage

The Health Concern in a Nutshell: Americans are falling short of the recommended amounts of whole grains, fat-free and low-fat milk products, whole fruits, and vegetables.

What Are the *Dietary Guidelines for Americans?*

By the 1970s, research had shown that Americans' overconsumption of foods rich in fat, saturated fat, cholesterol, and sodium was increasing their risk for chronic diseases, such as heart disease and stroke.[2] In 1977, the U.S. government released the *Dietary Goals for Americans,* which were designed to improve the nutritional quality of Americans' diets and to try to reduce the incidence of overnutrition and its associated health problems.[3]

Amid controversy over the scientific validity of the goals, the government asked scientists to lend credence to the goals and provide dietary guidance. Their work culminated in the 1980 *Dietary Guidelines for Americans,* which emphasized eating a variety of foods to obtain a nutritionally well-balanced daily diet. Since 1990, the U.S. Department of Agriculture (USDA) and the Department of Health and Human

It's Recommended that You: Eat more from these food groups on a daily basis. Remember this phrase: *"Give three two me, please."* Have at least *three* servings of whole grains and *three* servings of fat-free or low-fat milk products daily. Enjoy at least *two* cups of a variety of fruit and at least *two* and a half cups of colorful vegetables throughout the day.

Fats

The Health Concern in a Nutshell: While some fat is essential, too much saturated and *trans* fat, as well as dietary cholesterol, is unhealthy for your heart.

It's Recommended that You: Keep your dietary fat to between 20 to 35 percent of your daily calories and get mostly heart-healthy, unsaturated fats such as those found in vegetable oils, nuts, and fish. Consume less than 10 percent of your calories from saturated fat by choosing only lean meats, skinless poultry, and low-fat dairy foods. Eat fewer commercially made baked goods that are made with *trans* fats. Consume less than 300 milligrams of dietary cholesterol daily.

Carbohydrates

The Health Concern in a Nutshell: Although carbohydrate-rich foods such as whole grains, lean dairy foods, whole fruits, and vegetables are excellent sources of nutrients, foods high in sugary carbohydrates also tend to be high in calories. These less healthy carbohydrate sources may also displace more nutritious foods in your diet.

It's Recommended that You: Choose lean dairy products, whole grains, fruits, and vegetables more often than sugary soft drinks, candy, bakery items, and fruit drinks.

Sodium and Potassium

The Health Concern in a Nutshell: Most Americans will develop high blood pressure sometime in their life. A continually high blood pressure increases your risk of heart disease and stroke. Generally, as your intake of salt goes up, so does your blood pressure. Whereas potassium can help lower blood pressure, most individuals don't eat enough potassium-rich fruits and vegetables for this to be effective.

It's Recommended that You: Keep your sodium intake to less than 2,300 milligrams (approximately 1 teaspoon) of salt daily. Avoid salting your foods and choose processed foods made with less salt. Make sure that you consume plenty of fruits and vegetables daily.

Alcoholic Beverages

The Health Concern in a Nutshell: Though consuming alcohol in moderation may be heart-healthy for some individuals, it can be harmful to others depending upon their age, medical history, and lifestyle.

It's Recommended that You: Avoid alcohol if you are a woman of childbearing age who may become pregnant, a pregnant or lactating woman, under the age of 21, taking medications that can interact with alcohol, have a specific medical condition for which doctors advise against alcohol consumption, an alcoholic, or are driving or operating machinery—your judgment may be impaired by alcohol consumption.

Food Safety

The Health Concern in a Nutshell: Each year, over 70 million Americans suffer from food-borne illnesses, also known as food poisoning, from consuming foods contaminated with bacteria, parasites, and viruses.

It's Recommended that You: Properly clean, prepare, and store your foods.

Services (DHHS) have been mandated by law to update the guidelines every five years. The guidelines serve as one governmental voice to shape all federally funded nutrition programs in areas such as research and labeling, and to educate and guide consumers about healthy diet and lifestyle choices.[4]

The ***Dietary Guidelines for Americans 2005*** reflect the most current nutrition and physical activity recommendations for good health. They are designed to help individuals aged 2 and over improve the quality of their diet in order to lower their risk of chronic diseases and conditions, such as high blood pressure, high blood cholesterol levels, diabetes mellitus, heart disease, certain cancers, osteoporosis, and being overweight. Following these guidelines could reduce American adults' risk of dying of these conditions by as much as 9 to 16 percent.[5] The feature box "The *Dietary Guidelines for Americans* at a Glance" provides an overview of the guidelines and will help you incorporate these dietary and lifestyle recommendations into your life.

The final tool provided by the government to help you eat healthily is a food guidance system called MyPyramid.

Dietary Guidelines for Americans 2005 Guidelines published in 2005 that provide dietary and lifestyle advice to healthy individuals over the age of 2 to maintain good health and prevent chronic diseases.

food guidance systems Visual diagrams that provide a variety of food recommendations to help a person create a well-balanced diet.

MyPyramid A food guidance system that illustrates the recommendations in the *Dietary Guidelines for Americans 2005* and the Dietary Reference Intakes (DRIs) nutrient goals.

The Take-Home Message The *Dietary Guidelines for Americans 2005* provide dietary and lifestyle advice to healthy individuals over the age of 2. The goal of the guidelines is to help individuals maintain good health and prevent chronic diseases.

What Is a Food Guidance System?

With so many nutrient and dietary recommendations in the DRIs and the *Dietary Guidelines,* you may be wondering how to keep them straight and plan a diet that meets all of your nutritional needs. Luckily, there are several carefully designed **food guidance systems** to help you select the best foods for your diet. These illustrated systems picture healthy food choices from a variety of food groups from which you can choose, and show you how to proportion your food choices. Many countries have developed food guidance systems based on their food supply, cultural food preferences, and the nutritional needs of their population (Figure 2.3).[6]

Some researchers have also developed food guidance systems to help individuals reduce their risk of certain diseases. For example, the DASH (Dietary Approaches to Stop Hypertension) diet is based on an eating style that has been shown to significantly lower a person's blood pressure. High blood pressure is a risk factor for heart disease and stroke. The DASH diet will be discussed in Chapter 8.

MyPyramid is the most recent food guidance system released by the USDA for American eaters.

MyPyramid Is the USDA Food Guidance System

Released in 2005, MyPyramid visually depicts the recommendations in the *Dietary Guidelines for Americans 2005* (see Figure 2.4 on page 36). It recommends the number of servings you need to consume from each food group to meet the DRIs for your nutrient needs, based on your calorie needs. In essence, MyPyramid provides a personalized diet plan based on the latest nutrition and health recommendations.

MyPyramid replaced an earlier system, the Food Guide Pyramid, which was created in the early 1990s.

MyPyramid Emphasizes Physical Activity, Proportionality, Moderation, Variety, Personalization, and Gradual Improvement

In addition to showing a variety of foods that can make up a healthy diet, MyPyramid illustrates the diet and lifestyle themes of physical activity, proportionality, moderation, variety, personalization, and gradual improvement. See Figure 2.4 for explanations about how each of these themes is shown in the MyPyramid diagram. The silhouette climbing the pyramid reminds you to engage in physical activity. As you remember, the *Dietary Guidelines* recommend that you be physically active for at least 30 minutes daily. Being physically active helps you to stay fit and reduces your risk of chronic diseases such as heart disease and cancer. You can also eat more food without compromising your weight. The more physical activity you do, the more calories (food) you will need to consume to fuel those activities. This increased need

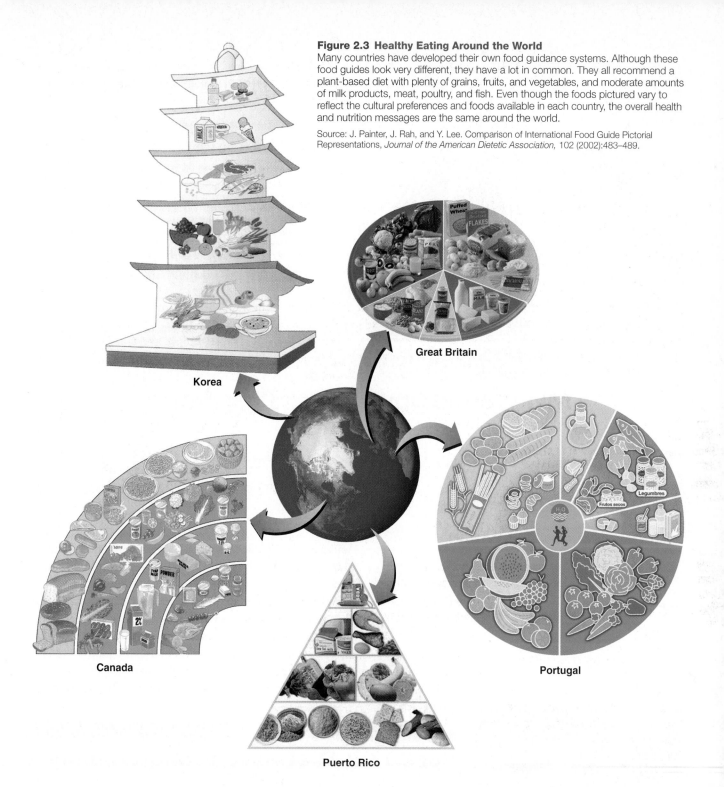

Figure 2.3 Healthy Eating Around the World
Many countries have developed their own food guidance systems. Although these food guides look very different, they have a lot in common. They all recommend a plant-based diet with plenty of grains, fruits, and vegetables, and moderate amounts of milk products, meat, poultry, and fish. Even though the foods pictured vary to reflect the cultural preferences and foods available in each country, the overall health and nutrition messages are the same around the world.

Source: J. Painter, J. Rah, and Y. Lee. Comparison of International Food Guide Pictorial Representations, *Journal of the American Dietetic Association,* 102 (2002):483–489.

Korea

Great Britain

Canada

Puerto Rico

Portugal

for calories allows you to eat a greater amount and variety of foods, which in turn means you are more likely to meet all of your nutrient needs.

The widths of the color bands in MyPyramid reinforce **proportionality,** or how much of your total diet should be eaten from each of five food groups. The colored bands represent the food groups: grains, vegetables, fruits, milk, and meat and beans. A sixth color band (the yellow one) represents oils. (Note that oils are not a food group.) The wider bands of the grains, vegetables, fruits, and lean milk groups tell you that these should provide the bulk of your diet. The comparatively thinner bands of oils

proportionality The relationship of one entity to another. Grains, fruits, and vegetables should be consumed in a higher proportion to oils and meats in the diet.

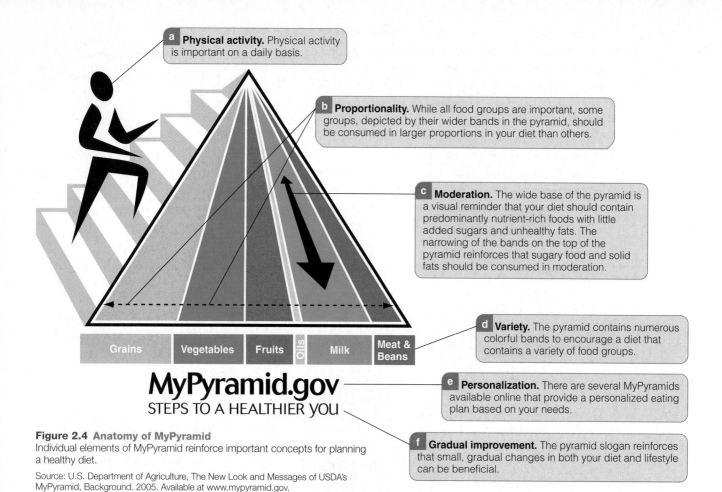

a **Physical activity.** Physical activity is important on a daily basis.

b **Proportionality.** While all food groups are important, some groups, depicted by their wider bands in the pyramid, should be consumed in larger proportions in your diet than others.

c **Moderation.** The wide base of the pyramid is a visual reminder that your diet should contain predominantly nutrient-rich foods with little added sugars and unhealthy fats. The narrowing of the bands on the top of the pyramid reinforces that sugary food and solid fats should be consumed in moderation.

Grains | Vegetables | Fruits | Oils | Milk | Meat & Beans

MyPyramid.gov
STEPS TO A HEALTHIER YOU

d **Variety.** The pyramid contains numerous colorful bands to encourage a diet that contains a variety of food groups.

e **Personalization.** There are several MyPyramids available online that provide a personalized eating plan based on your needs.

f **Gradual improvement.** The pyramid slogan reinforces that small, gradual changes in both your diet and lifestyle can be beneficial.

Figure 2.4 Anatomy of MyPyramid
Individual elements of MyPyramid reinforce important concepts for planning a healthy diet.

Source: U.S. Department of Agriculture, The New Look and Messages of USDA's MyPyramid, Background. 2005. Available at www.mypyramid.gov.

> Americans from 2 to 18 years of age spend an average of almost 5½ hours watching television and playing video games every day.

and meats mean that these should be eaten in lesser amounts. Take the Self-Assessment below to see how well-proportioned your diet is.

The narrowing of the pyramid from a wide base to a thin tip tells you to choose mostly **nutrient-dense** foods from each food group. Nutrient density refers to the amount of nutrients a food contains in relationship to the number of calories it contains. More nutrient-dense foods provide more nutrients per calorie (and in each bite) than less nutrient-dense foods, and so are a better choice for meeting your DRIs. The foundation of your diet

It's important to be physically active every day.

Self-Assessment

Does Your Diet Have Proportionality?

Answer yes or no to the following questions.

1. Are grains the main food choice at all your meals? Yes ☐ No ☐
2. Do you often forget to eat vegetables? Yes ☐ No ☐
3. Do you typically eat fewer than three pieces of fruit daily? Yes ☐ No ☐
4. Do you often have fewer than three cups of milk daily? Yes ☐ No ☐
5. Is the portion of meat, chicken or fish the largest item on your dinner plate? Yes ☐ No ☐

Answer

If you answered yes to three or more of these questions, it is very likely that your diet lacks proportionality. This section explains how to improve your diet.

should comprise nutrient-dense foods with little added sugar and solid fats. Foods near the tip of the MyPyramid, with added sugar and fats, should be eaten in **moderation** because they add fewer nutrient-dense calories to your diet.

Let's compare the nutrient density of two versions of the same food: a baked potato and potato chips. Both are in the vegetable group, but the baked version is more nutrient dense than the chips (Figure 2.5). Although a medium baked potato and one ounce of potato chips have about the same number of calories, the baked potato provides much more folate, potassium, and vitamin C than the deep-fried chips. If you routinely choose foods with a lot of added sugar and saturated fats, you will have to reduce your food intake elsewhere to compensate for the extra calories. This could cause you to displace healthier foods in your diet. If you don't adjust for these extra calories, but eat them in addition to your normal diet, you will soon experience weight gain. Figure 2.6 helps you identify some nutrient-dense and less healthy food choices in each food group.

Lastly, the multicolored bands in MyPyramid tell you to eat a **variety** of foods. Eating foods from each food group will increase your chances of consuming all 40 of the nutrients your body needs. Because no single food or food group provides all the nutrients, a varied diet of nutrient-dense foods is the savviest strategy. Figure 2.7 on page 38 provides tips on how to choose a variety of foods from each food group.

The interactive website component of MyPyramid is designed to help you plan a personalized diet based upon your dietary and lifestyle needs. We will discuss this in more detail later in the chapter.

Remember, "Rome wasn't built in a day." Adopting a healthier diet and lifestyle, and changing long-term eating habits, takes time. The slogan "Steps to a Healthier You" and the steps on the side of MyPyramid reinforce the need for **gradual improvement.** Taking small steps of improvement every day can be less overwhelming and will ultimately be beneficial to your health.

Let's next look at the foods of each food group, and why each group is uniquely important to you.

MyPyramid Emphasizes Whole Grains, Vegetables, Fruits, Lean Milk Products, and Meat and Beans

MyPyramid guides you in choosing a diet abundant in nutrient-dense whole grains, vegetables, fruits, and fat-free and low-fat milk products, along with some lean meat,

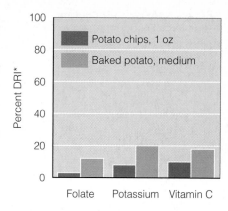

Figure 2.5 Which Is the Healthier Way to Enjoy Your Potatoes?
While one ounce of potato chips and one medium baked potato have similar amounts of calories, their nutrient content is worlds apart. A baked potato is more nutrient dense than potato chips.

*Note: Based on the percentage of the DRI for 19–50-year-old males. All these percentages apply to females in the same age range except for vitamin C. Females have lower vitamin C needs than males so a baked potato provides over 20 percent of the DRI for this vitamin for women.

nutrient density The amount of nutrients per calorie in a given food. Nutrient-dense foods provide more nutrients per calorie than less nutrient-dense foods.

moderation Consuming reasonable but not excessive amounts of foods.

variety Consuming different food groups and foods within each group.

gradual improvement Making small changes over time in order to realize long-term results.

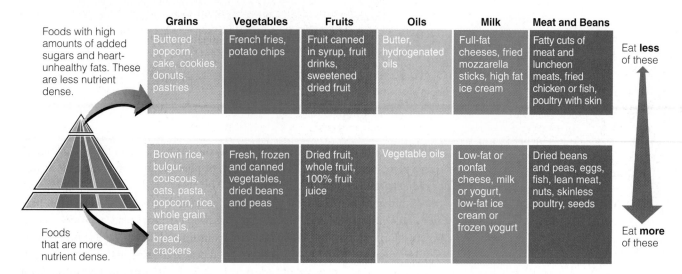

Figure 2.6 My Nutrient-Dense Pyramid
Nutrient-dense foods provide more nutrition per calorie. Choose nutrient-dense food more often to build a well-balanced diet.

Figure 2.7 Mix Up Your Choices Within Each Food Group

Source: USDA Consumer Brochure, Finding Your Way to a Healthier You. Based on the *Dietary Guidelines for Americans.*

Focus on fruits. Eat a variety of fruits—whether fresh, frozen, canned, or dried—rather than fruit juice for most of your fruit choices. For a 2,000 calorie diet, you will need 2 cups of fruit each day (for example, 1 small banana, 1 large orange, and ¼ cup of dried apricots or peaches).

Vary your veggies. Eat more dark green veggies, such as broccoli, kale, and other dark leafy greens; orange veggies, such as carrots, sweet potatoes, pumpkin, and winter squash; and beans and peas, such as pinto beans, kidney beans, black beans, garbanzo beans, split peas, and lentils.

Get your calcium-rich foods. Get 3 cups of low-fat or fat-free milk—or an equivalent amount of low-fat yogurt and/or low-fat cheese (1½ ounces of cheese equals 1 cup of milk)—every day. For kids aged 2 to 8, it's 2 cups of milk. If you don't or can't consume milk, choose lactose-free milk products and/or calcium-fortified foods and beverages.

Make half your grains whole. Eat at least 3 ounces of whole-grain cereals, breads, crackers, rice, or pasta every day. One ounce is about 1 slice of bread, 1 cup of breakfast cereal, or ½ cup of cooked rice or pasta. Look to see that grains such as wheat, rice, oats, or corn are referred to as "whole" in the list of ingredients.

Go lean with protein. Choose lean meats and poultry. Bake it, broil it, or grill it. And vary your protein choices—with more fish, beans, peas, nuts, and seeds.

Know the limits on fats, salt, and sugars. Read the Nutrition Facts label on foods. Look for foods low in saturated fats and *trans* fats.Choose and prepare foods and beverages with little salt (sodium) and/or added sugars (caloric sweeteners).

poultry, fish, and modest amounts of healthy oils. As you read in the *Dietary Guidelines,* a plant-based diet with some lean meats, poultry, and fish is the best strategy for reducing your risk of chronic diseases.

With that in mind, at least half of your grain servings should come from high-fiber whole grains such as whole-grain cereals, whole-wheat bread, and brown rice. A mix of colorful, high-fiber vegetables and fruits, including dark green broccoli and kale, deep orange carrots and cantaloupe, dried peas and beans, and starchy vegetables such as corn and potatoes, should adorn your plate. Fat-free or low-fat milk and milk products are excellent sources of bone-strengthening calcium, and lean meats, poultry, fish, and beans are all rich in protein.

The abundance of servings from the fruits, vegetables, and dairy group will also help you meet the DRI for potassium, and the use of vegetable oils as the primary source of fat will help you meet your vitamin E needs. Following the MyPyramid and choosing nutrient-dense foods within each food group enables you to eat a diet that provides well over 100 percent of the DRIs for many of the nutrients you need daily.[7]

The number-one source of saturated fat in the U.S. diet is cheese. Remember to choose part-skim, low-fat, or reduced-fat cheeses most often.

How to Use MyPyramid

You now know to eat a variety of nutrient-dense foods to be healthy, and that MyPyramid helps you select a diverse group of foods, but you may be wondering how much from each food group *you*, personally, should be eating. The MyPyramid interactive website at www.mypyramid.gov will give you the exact numbers of servings to eat from each food group based on your daily calorie needs.

Your calorie needs are based upon your age and gender (two factors beyond your control) and your activity level (a factor you can control). As you just read, the more active you are, the more calories you burn to fuel your activities, and the more calories you can (and need) to consume in foods.

At the website, you will enter your age, gender, and activity level. Based on this information your daily calorie needs will be determined and your personalized eating plan, specifying the exact number of servings from each of the MyPyramid food groups, will be provided. With this information, you can plan your meals and snacks for the day. If you cannot go to the website, you can obtain similar information by using Tables 2.2 and 2.3 in this chapter. Let's use the tables to obtain your MyPyramid recommendations.

The first step in creating your personalized MyPyramid is to figure out how many calories you should be eating daily. To do this, you need to find out how active you are. Use Table 2.2 to see some examples of moderate and vigorous activity; based on

Table 2.2
What Is Moderate and Vigorous Activity?

Do you know what exercise is moderate and what is vigorous? Check your assumptions below.

Moderate Activities Expend 3½ to 7 Calories a Minute	Vigorous Activities Expend More Than 7 Calories a Minute
Brisk walking	Jogging or running
Bicycling 5 to 9 mph	Bicycling more than 10 mph
Shooting hoops	Playing competitive sports like basketball, soccer, or lacrosse
Using free weights	Rowing on a machine vigorously
Yoga	Karate, judo, or tae kwon do
Walking a dog	Jumping rope

Adapted from Centers for Disease Control and Prevention, General Physical Activities Defined by Level of Intensity. Available at www.cdc.gov.

Table 2.3

How Many Calories Do You Need Daily?

The amount of calories that you need daily is based upon your age, gender, and activity level.*

	Males				Females		
		Moderately				**Moderately**	
Age	**Sedentary***	**Active**	**Active**	**Age**	**Sedentary**	**Active**	**Active**
16–18	2,400	2,800	3,200	**18**	1,800	2,000	2,400
19–20	2,600	2,800	3,000	**19–20**	2,000	2,200	2,400
21–25	2,400	2,800	3,000	**21–25**	2,000	2,200	2,400
26–30	2,400	2,600	3,000	**26–30**	1,800	2,000	2,400
31–35	2,400	2,600	3,000	**31–35**	1,800	2,000	2,200
36–40	2,400	2,600	2,800	**36–40**	1,800	2,000	2,200
41–45	2,200	2,600	2,800	**41–45**	1,800	2,000	2,200
46–50	2,200	2,400	2,800	**46–50**	1,800	2,000	2,200

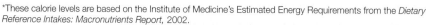

*These calorie levels are based on the Institute of Medicine's Estimated Energy Requirements from the *Dietary Reference Intakes: Macronutrients Report,* 2002.
Sedentary: Partaking in less than 30 minutes a day of moderate physical activity in addition to daily activities.
Moderately Active: Partaking in at least 30 minutes and up to 60 minutes a day of moderate physical activity in addition to daily activities.
Active: Partaking in 60 or more minutes a day of moderate physical activity in addition to daily activities.

Source: U.S. Department of Agriculture, MyPyramid. Available at www.mypyramid.gov.

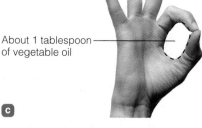

A woman's palm is approximately 3 ounces of cooked meat, chicken, or fish

a

A woman's fist is about 1 cup of pasta or vegetables (a man's fist is the size of about 2 cups)

b

About 1 tablespoon of vegetable oil

c

Figure 2.8 What's a Serving? Eat With Your Hands!
Your hands can guide you in estimating portion sizes.

discretionary calorie allowance
Calories left over in the diet once all nutrient needs have been met from the basic food groups.

these examples, do you think you are moderately or vigorously active? Next, look at Table 2.3 for the number of calories you need based on your activity level, age, and gender. When you know the number of calories you need daily, Table 2.4 will tell you how many servings from each food group you should consume to healthfully obtain those calories. This is the equivalent of *your* personalized MyPyramid.

Let's say that you are a moderately active female who needs 2,000 calories daily. To healthfully meet this level, you should consume:

- 6 servings from the grains group
- 2½ cups of dark green, orange, starchy, and other vegetables, and some legumes
- 2 cups of fruits
- 3 cups of fat-free or low-fat milk and yogurt
- 5½ ounces of lean meat, poultry, and fish or the equivalent in meat alternatives such as beans
- You should also add 3 tablespoons of vegetable oils to your diet over the course of the day.

If you are having difficulty figuring out what one cup of vegetables, three ounces of meat, or 1 tablespoon of salad dressing looks like, use Figure 2.8. It provides an easy way to eyeball your serving sizes.

If all of your food selections are low in fat and added sugar, the above menu will provide a total of about 1,740 calories. This means that, after meeting your nutrient requirements, you have about 260 of your 2,000 calories left. This is your **discretionary calorie allowance** (see Figure 2.9). You can "spend" these calories on extra servings of foods such as grains, fruits, and/or vegetables, or on occasion as an added fat, sweet, or dessert.

Table 2.4

How Much Should You Eat from Each Food Group?

The following are suggested amounts to consume daily from each of the basic food groups and the oils based on your daily calorie needs. Remember that most of your choices should be fat-free or low fat and contain little added sugar.

Calorie Level	Grains (oz eq)	Vegetables (cups)	Fruits (cups)	Oil (tsp)	Milk (cups)	Meat and Beans (oz eq)
1,400	5	1.5	1.5	4	2	4
1,600	5	2	1.5	5	3	5
1,800	6	2.5	1.5	5	3	5
2,000	6	2.5	2	6	3	5.5
2,200	7	3	2	6	3	6
2,400	8	3	2	7	3	6.5
2,600	9	3.5	2	8	3	6.5
2,800	10	3.5	2.5	8	3	7
3,000	10	4	2.5	10	3	7
3,200	10	4	2.5	11	3	7

Grains: Includes all foods made with wheat, rice, oats, cornmeal, or barley, such as bread, pasta, oatmeal, breakfast cereals, tortillas, and grits. In general, 1 slice of bread, 1 cup of ready-to-eat cereal, or ½ cup of cooked rice, pasta, or cooked cereal is considered 1 ounce equivalent (oz eq) from the grains group. *At least half of all grains consumed should be whole grains such as whole-wheat bread, oats, or brown rice.*

Vegetables: Includes all fresh, frozen, canned, and dried vegetables, and vegetable juices. In general, 1 cup of raw or cooked vegetables or vegetable juice, or 2 cups of raw leafy greens, is considered 1 cup from the vegetable group.

Fruits: Includes all fresh, frozen, canned, and dried fruits, and fruit juices. In general, 1 cup of fruit or 100% fruit juice, or ½ cup of dried fruit, is considered 1 cup from the fruit group.

Oils: Includes vegetable oils such as canola, corn, olive, soybean, and sunflower oil, fatty fish, nuts, avocadoes, mayonnaise, salad dressings made with oils, and soft margarine.

Milk: Includes all fat-free and low-fat milk, yogurt, and cheese. In general, 1 cup of milk or yogurt, 1½ ounces of natural cheese, or 2 ounces of processed cheese is considered 1 cup from the milk group.

Meat and Beans: In general, 1 ounce of lean meat, poultry, or fish, 1 egg, 1 tbs peanut butter, ¼ cup cooked dry beans, or ½ ounce of nuts or seeds is considered 1 ounce equivalent (oz eq) from the meat and beans group.

Source: U.S. Department of Agriculture, www.MyPyramid.com.

The calorie levels and distribution of food groups in MyPyramid are calculated using the leanest food choices with no added sugar. So if you pour whole milk (high in fat) over your sweetened cereal (added sugar) instead of using skim milk (fat free) to drench your shredded wheat (no added sugar), the extra fat and sugar have used up some of your discretionary calories. As you can see from Table 2.5 on page 42, these discretionary calories can be used up quickly depending on the foods you choose.

Let's now use these recommended amounts of servings from each food group and plan a 2,000-calorie menu. Figure 2.10 on page 42 shows how servings from the various food groups can create well-balanced meals and snacks throughout the day.

Although this particular menu is balanced and the foods are nutrient dense, it is unlikely that every day will be this ideal. The good news is that your nutrient needs

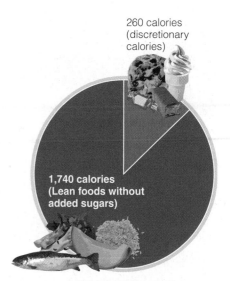

260 calories (discretionary calories)

1,740 calories (Lean foods without added sugars)

2,000 total daily calories

Figure 2.9 How Discretionary Calories Fit into a Balanced Diet
If you select mostly nutrient-dense, lean foods that don't contain added sugar, you may have leftover calories to "spend" on extra helpings or a sweet dessert.

Table 2.5

Using Discretion with Discretionary Calories

As you can see, your discretionary calories can be used up quickly depending on your food selections.

Choosing . . .	Over . . .	Will Cost You
Whole milk (1 cup)	Fat-free milk (1 cup)	65 discretionary calories
Roasted chicken thigh with skin (3 oz)	Roasted chicken breast, skinless (3 oz)	70 discretionary calories
Glazed donut, yeast type (3¾″ diameter)	English muffin (1 muffin)	165 discretionary calories
French fries (1 medium order)	Baked potato (1 medium)	299 discretionary calories
Regular soda (1 can, 12 fl oz)	Diet soda (1 can, 12 fl oz)	150 discretionary calories

Source: U.S. Department of Agriculture, MyPyramid, How Do I Count the Discretionary Calories I Eat? Available at www.mypyramid.gov.

Figure 2.10 Using MyPyramid to Plan a Healthy Diet
A variety of foods from each food group create a well-balanced diet.

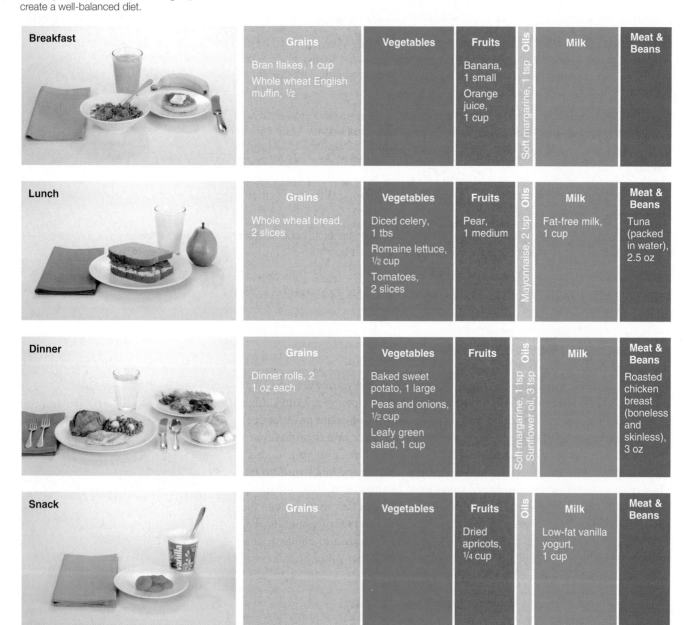

Breakfast	Grains	Vegetables	Fruits	Oils	Milk	Meat & Beans
	Bran flakes, 1 cup Whole wheat English muffin, ½		Banana, 1 small Orange juice, 1 cup	Soft margarine, 1 tsp		

Lunch	Grains	Vegetables	Fruits	Oils	Milk	Meat & Beans
	Whole wheat bread, 2 slices	Diced celery, 1 tbs Romaine lettuce, ½ cup Tomatoes, 2 slices	Pear, 1 medium	Mayonnaise, 2 tsp	Fat-free milk, 1 cup	Tuna (packed in water), 2.5 oz

Dinner	Grains	Vegetables	Fruits	Oils	Milk	Meat & Beans
	Dinner rolls, 2 1 oz each	Baked sweet potato, 1 large Peas and onions, ½ cup Leafy green salad, 1 cup		Soft margarine, 1 tsp Sunflower oil, 3 tsp		Roasted chicken breast (boneless and skinless), 3 oz

Snack	Grains	Vegetables	Fruits	Oils	Milk	Meat & Beans
			Dried apricots, ¼ cup		Low-fat vanilla yogurt, 1 cup	

Table 2.6

A Combination of Good Food

Many of the foods you eat are probably mixed dishes that contain servings from multiple food groups. The following list should help you estimate the servings from each food group for some popular food items. Because the preparation process can vary greatly among recipes, these are only estimates.

Food and Sample Portion	Grains Group (oz eq)	Vegetable Group (cups)	Fruit Group (cups)	Milk Group (cups)	Meat and Beans Group (oz eq)	Estimated Total Calories
Cheese pizza, thin crust (1 slice from medium pizza)	1	⅛	0	½	0	215
Macaroni and cheese (1 cup, made from packaged mix)	2	0	0	½	0	260
Bean and cheese burrito (1)	2½	⅛	0	1	2	445
Chicken fried rice (1 cup)	1½	¼	0	0	1	270
Large cheeseburger	2	0	0	⅓	3	500
Turkey sub sandwich (6″ sub)	2	½	0	¼	2	320
Peanut butter and jelly sandwich (1)	2	0	0	0	2	375
Apple pie (1 slice)	2	0	¼	0	0	280

Source: U.S. Department of Agriculture, Mixed Dishes in MyPyramid. Available at www.mypyramid.gov.

are averaged over several days, or a week, of eating. If one day you eat insufficient servings of one food group or a specific nutrient, you can make up for it the next day. For example, let's say that you don't eat enough fruit one day but do eat an extra serving of grains. The next day you can adjust your diet by cutting back on your grain servings and adding an extra serving of fruit.

If the foods at your meals are sometimes mixed dishes that contain a combination of foods, such as pizza, then they probably contribute servings to more than one food group. Table 2.6 provides examples of foods that contribute servings from multiple groups.

Now that you know what constitutes a healthy diet, the next step is to go food shopping. As you shop, you'll want to make sure you know the nutrient and calorie contents of the foods you buy. The food label will give you this information, and more.

The Take-Home Message MyPyramid is the latest food guidance system developed by the USDA. It is a personalized educational tool that helps you choose a well-balanced diet from all the food groups to meet your nutrient needs. It emphasizes daily physical activity, a varied diet rich in fruits, vegetables, whole grains, and lean dairy products, and only a moderate amount of foods high in saturated and *trans* fats, sugar, salt, and alcohol. MyPyramid encourages you to make gradual, small changes in your diet and lifestyle.

A Few Words About the Exchange Lists

The **Exchange Lists for Meal Planning** were designed in 1950 to give people with diabetes a structured eating plan; the lists are still in use. The Exchange Lists group foods together according to their carbohydrate, protein, and fat composition and provide specific portion sizes for each food. This assures that each food in the group contributes a similar amount of calories per serving.

Some weight-loss programs have adopted a similar meal planning tool to help their members manage their weight by controlling the number of calories that they consume. Because of the similarity of the foods within each group, foods can be exchanged or swapped with each other at meals and snacks. This flexible meal plan is a useful tool to control calorie, carbohydrate, protein, and fat intakes. Appendix C provides more information on the Exchange Lists.

What Is a Food Label and Why Is It Important?

Imagine walking down the supermarket aisle and finding that all the foods on the shelves are packaged in plain cardboard boxes and unmarked aluminum cans. How would you know if a brown box contained one pound of pasta or 100 dog biscuits? Do the blank cans hold chicken noodle soup or crushed pineapple? You rely on the food labels more than you think to make your food choices!

Cereal-box readers will read the information on the box as many as 12 times before they consume the last spoonful!

The Food Label Tells You What's in the Package

To help consumers make informed food choices, the Food and Drug Administration (FDA) regulates the labeling of all packaged foods in the United States.[8] Since the 1930s, the FDA has mandated that every packaged food be labeled with:

- The name of the food
- The net weight, which is the weight of the food in the package, excluding the weight of the package or packing material
- The name and address of the manufacturer or distributor
- A list of ingredients in descending order by weight, with the heaviest item listed first

Newer labeling laws have been enacted to further benefit the consumer. In 1990, the Nutrition Labeling and Education Act (NLEA) became law, mandating that labels include uniform nutrition information, serving sizes, and specific criteria for health claims.[9]

Because of this newer law, shoppers can be assured that labels now also show:

- Nutrition information, which lists total calories, calories from fat, total fat, saturated fat, *trans* fats, cholesterol, sodium, total carbohydrate, dietary fiber, sugars, vitamin A, vitamin C, calcium, and iron

Exchange Lists for Meal Planning A grouping of foods, in specific portions, according to their carbohydrate, protein, and fat composition to ensure that each food in the group contributes a similar amount of calories per serving.

Nutrition Facts panel The area on the food label that provides a uniform listing of specific nutrients obtained in one serving of the food.

- Serving sizes that are uniform among similar products, which allows for easier comparison shopping by the consumer
- An indication of how a serving of the food fits into an overall daily diet
- Uniform definitions for descriptive label terms such as "light" and "fat-free"
- Health claims that are accurate and science based, if made about the food or one of its nutrients

Very few foods are exempt from carrying a Nutrition Facts panel on the label. Such foods include plain coffee and tea; some spices, flavorings, and other foods that don't provide a significant amount of nutrients; deli items, bakery foods, and other ready-to-eat foods that are prepared and sold in retail establishments; restaurant meals; and foods produced by small businesses (companies that have total sales of less than $500,000).[10]

Compare the two food labels in Figure 2.11. Note that the amount and type of nutrition information on the 1925 box of cereal is vague and less informative than the more recent version, which meets the FDA's current labeling requirements. Whereas raw fruits and vegetables and fresh fish typically don't have a label, these foods fall under the FDA's voluntary, point-of-purchase nutrition information program. Under the guidelines of this program, at least 60 percent of a nationwide sample of grocery stores must post the nutrition information of the most commonly eaten fruits, vegetables, and fish near where the foods are sold. The FDA surveys a sample of nationwide grocery stores every two years. The latest findings show that over 70 percent of stores surveyed are in compliance with the program.[11]

Although a similar voluntary program is in place for meat and poultry, the USDA (which regulates meat and poultry) is considering mandating labels on these foods. This is because less than 60 percent of meat and poultry retailers and manufacturers have provided the information voluntarily.[12]

The Food Label Can Help You Make Healthy Food Choices

Suppose you're in the dairy aisle of a supermarket trying to select a carton of milk. You want to watch your fat intake, so you have narrowed your choices to reduced fat 2% milk or nonfat milk. How do they compare in terms of calories, fat, and other nutrients per serving? How do you decide which is more healthful? The answer is simple: Look at the labels. All the information that you need to make a smart choice is provided on one area of the label, the **Nutrition Facts panel.**

Figure 2.11 Out with the Old and In with the New
(a) A cereal box from the 1920s carried vague nutrition information. **(b)** Today, manufacturers must adhere to strict labeling requirements mandated by the FDA.

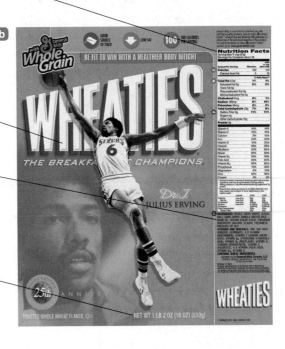

The **Nutrition Facts panel** lists standardized serving sizes, specific nutrients, and shows how a serving of the food fits into a healthy diet by stating its contribution to the percentage of the Daily Value for each nutrient. The old cereal box doesn't contain this information.

The **name** of the product must be displayed on the front label.

The **ingredients** must be listed in descending order by weight. This format is missing in the old box. Whole grain wheat is the predominant ingredient in the current cereal box.

The **net weight** of the food in the box must now be located at the bottom of the package.

On the Label: The Nutrition Facts Panel

The Nutrition Facts panel provides a nutritional snapshot of the food inside a package. By law, the panel must list amounts of calories, calories from fat, total fat, saturated fat, *trans* fat, cholesterol, sodium, total carbohydrate, dietary fiber, sugars, protein, vitamin A, vitamin C, calcium, and iron.[13] If an additional nutrient, such as vitamin E or vitamin B_{12}, has been added, or if the product makes a claim about a nutrient, then that nutrient must also be listed. Other nutrients, such as additional vitamins and minerals, can be listed by the manufacturer on a voluntary basis. The majority of the packaged foods you purchase will contain this nutrition information.

Let's learn how to decipher the Nutrition Facts panel (Figure 2.12). At the top of the panel is the serving size. By law, the serving size must be listed both by weight in grams (less useful to you) and in common household measures, such as cups and ounces (more useful to you). Because serving sizes are standardized among similar food products, you can compare one brand of macaroni and cheese with a different brand to assess which one better meets your needs.

The rest of the information on the panel is based on the listed serving size (in this case, one cup) of the food. For example, if you ate two servings (two cups) of this macaroni and cheese, which is the number of servings in the entire box, you would double the nutrient information on the label to calculate the calories as well as the fat and other nutrients. The servings per container are particularly useful for portion control.

Below the serving size is listed the calories per serving. The calories from fat give you an idea of what proportion of the food's calories comes from fat. In this box of macaroni and cheese, 110 out of a total of 250 calories—that is, nearly half—are from fat.

Next are the nutrients that you should limit or add to your diet. Americans typically eat too much fat, including saturated fat, *trans* fat, and cholesterol, and too much sodium. In contrast, they tend to fall short in dietary fiber, vitamins A and C, and iron. These are on the label to remind you to make sure to eat foods rich in these substances. The Nutrition Facts panel can be your best shopping guide when identifying and choosing foods that are low in the nutrients you want to limit (like saturated fat) and high in the nutrients that you need to eat in higher amounts (like fiber).

Are you wondering what determines if a food contains a "high" or "low" amount of a specific nutrient? That's where the Daily Values come into play.

On the Label: The Daily Values

Unlike the DRIs, which are precise recommended amounts you should eat of each nutrient, the **Daily Values (DV)** listed on the Nutrition Facts panel are general reference levels for the nutrients listed on the food label. The DVs give you a ballpark idea of how the nutrients in the foods you buy fit into your overall diet. The DVs are based on older reference levels and are not as current as the DRIs. For example, whereas the DRIs recommend an upper level of dietary sodium of no more than 2,300 milligrams (daily), the DVs use less than 2,400 mg as the reference level.

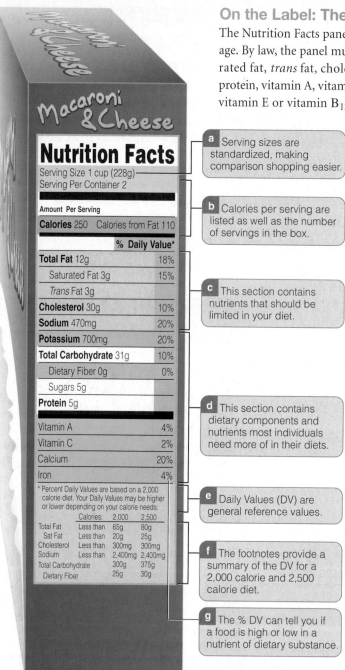

Figure 2.12 Understanding the Nutrition Facts Panel
Know how to read and understand the Nutrition Facts panel of a label.

Source: Center for Food Safety and Applied Nutrition. How to Understand and Use the Nutrition Facts Label. 2004.

Daily Values (DVs) Ballpark reference levels used only on the food label.

There are no DVs listed on the label for *trans* fat, sugars, and protein. This is because there isn't enough information available to set reference values for *trans* fat and sugars. Although there are reference values for protein, consuming adequate amounts of protein isn't a health concern for most Americans over age 4, so listing the percent of the DV for this nutrient isn't warranted on the label. The DV for protein will only be listed if the product is being marketed for children under the age of 4, such as a jar of baby food, or if a claim is made about the food, such as that it is "high in protein."[14]

The DVs on the food label are based on a 2,000-calorie diet. If you need more or fewer than 2,000 calories daily, some of your DV values may be higher or lower than are listed on the Nutrition Facts panel.

If a serving provides 20 percent or more of the DV, it is considered high in that nutrient. For example, a serving of this macaroni and cheese is high in sodium (not a healthy attribute) and is also high in calcium (a healthy attribute). If you eat this entrée for lunch, you'll need to eat less sodium during the rest of the day. However, the good news is that a serving of this pasta meal also provides 20 percent of the DV for calcium.

If a nutrient provides 5 percent or less of the DV, it is considered low in that nutrient. A serving of macaroni and cheese doesn't provide much fiber, vitamin A, vitamin C, or iron. You will need to add other foods to supply these nutrients to your diet on the days that you eat macaroni and cheese.

Lastly, depending on the size of the food package, there may be a footnote at the bottom of the label. This provides a summary of the DVs for a 2,000-calorie diet as well as a 2,500-calorie diet. This area of the panel provides you with a little "cheat sheet" to help you when you are shopping so that you don't have to memorize the values. As you can see from the footnote, you should try to keep your sodium intake to less than 2,400 milligrams daily. Since you know that this macaroni and cheese is high in sodium, providing 20 percent of the DV, or 470 milligrams, of sodium, you should try to keep the sodium in your remaining food choices during the day to under 2,000 milligrams.

Now that you know how to read the Nutrition Facts panel, let's return to the milk question posed at the beginning of this section and use what you've learned to compare the reduced fat 2% and nonfat milk labels in Figure 2.13.

Let's start at the top:

a. Both cartons have the same standardized one-cup serving, which makes the comparison easy.

b. The reduced fat milk has 50 percent more calories than the nonfat milk; almost half of the calories in the reduced fat milk are from fat.

c. Use the percent of the DV to assess whether the milk is considered "high" or "low" in a given nutrient. For instance, a serving of reduced fat milk provides more than 5 percent of the DV for both total and saturated fat (as well as cholesterol), so it isn't considered "low" in

Figure 2.13 Using the Nutrition Facts Panel to Comparison Shop
The Nutrition Facts panel makes comparison shopping between types and brands of foods easier for the consumer.

Source: U.S. Food and Drug Administration, Center for Food Safety and Applied Nutrition, *How to Understand and Use the Nutrition Facts Label.* (2004)

these nutrients. In fact, the saturated fat provides 15 percent of the DV, which is getting close to the definition of "high" (20 percent of the DV). In contrast, the nonfat milk doesn't contain any fat, saturated fat, or cholesterol, so it appears so far to be the healthier choice.

d. However, since being low in fat doesn't necessarily mean being healthier, let's make sure that the nonfat milk is as nutritious as the reduced fat variety. Comparing the remaining nutrients, especially calcium and vitamin D, confirms that the nonfat milk has all the vitamins and minerals that reduced fat milk does, but with fewer calories and less fat, saturated fat, and cholesterol. In fact, both milks provide a "high" amount of calcium and vitamin D. So, when it comes to choosing milk, the nonfat version is the smarter choice.

While the Nutrition Facts panel on the side or back of the package can help you make healthier food choices, some foods carry claims on their front labels that may also influence your decision to buy. Let's look at these next.

On the Label: Labeling Claims

In the 1980s, the savvy Kellogg Company ran an ad campaign for its fiber-rich All Bran cereal reminding the public of the National Cancer Institute's recommendation to eat low-fat, high-fiber foods, fresh fruits, and vegetables to maintain a healthy weight. According to the FDA, sales of high-fiber cereals increased over 35 percent within a year.[15] Manufacturers realized that putting nutrition and health claims on labels was effective in influencing consumer purchases. Supermarket shelves were soon crowded with products boasting various claims.

In a recent consumer survey, over 40 percent of respondents said they had purchased foods that claimed to reduce the risk of heart disease and over 25 percent had chosen items that claimed to reduce the risk of cancer. Health claims do influence food decisions.

So, can you feel confident that the jar of light mayonnaise is really lighter in calories and fat than regular mayonnaise? Yes, you can. The FDA mandates that all claims on labels follow strict guidelines.

Currently, the FDA allows the use of three types of claims on food products: (1) **nutrient content claims,** (2) **health claims,** and (3) **structure/function claims.** All foods displaying these claims on the label must meet specified criteria. Let's look at each of these claims closely.

Nutrient Content Claims

A food product can make a claim about the amount of a nutrient it contains (or doesn't contain) by using descriptive terms such as *free* (fat-free yogurt), *high* (high-fiber crackers), *low* (low saturated fat cereal), *reduced* (reduced sodium soup), and *extra lean* (extra lean ground beef) as long as it meets the strict criteria designated by the FDA. These terms can help you identify at a glance the food items that best meet your needs.

Jessie, the student with borderline high blood pressure from the beginning of this chapter, could look for low-sodium claims on labels to help limit the amount of sodium in her diet. As you may remember, Jessie enjoys a mug of hot soup during her late-night studying. But she's probably sipping more sodium than she thinks.

Look at the labels of the canned soups in Figure 2.14. Jessie should be looking for the "low sodium" label on her chicken soup, as that soup cannot contain more than 140 milligrams of sodium per serving. A next best choice would be the soup with the term "less sodium" on the label, which means that it must contain at least 25 percent less sodium than the regular variety. The classic can of chicken soup contains almost 900 milligrams for a serving, which is likely the same or even more sodium than Jessie consumed at dinner. Table 2.7 on page 50 provides some of the

nutrient content claims Claims on the label that describe the level or amount of a nutrient in a food product.

health claims Claims on the label that describe a relationship between a food or dietary compound and a disease or health-related condition.

structure/function claims Claims on the label that describe how a nutrient or dietary compound affects the structure or function of the human body.

Figure 2.14 Soup's On!
Nutrient claims on the food label can help you choose foods that meet your needs. **(a)** Because this can of chicken noodle soup displays the "low sodium" nutrient claim, it can't provide more than 140 milligrams of sodium in a serving. **(b)** This can of soup has more than 25 percent less sodium than the classic version, so the term "less" can be displayed on its label. **(c)** The classic variety of chicken noodle soup has the most sodium per serving.

most common nutrient claims on food labels, the specific criteria that each claim must meet as mandated by the FDA, and examples of food products that carry these nutrient claims.

Health Claims

Suppose you are sitting at your kitchen table eating a bowl of Cheerios in skim milk, and staring at the front of the cereal box. You notice a claim on the front of the box that's as big as a newspaper headline. The claim states: "The soluble fiber in Cheerios, as part of a heart healthy diet, can help you lower your cholesterol." Do you recognize this as a health claim that links Cheerios with better heart health?

Table 2.7

What Does That Labeling Term Mean?

Nutrient	Free	Low	Reduced/Less	Light
Calories	<5 calories (cal) per serving	≤40 cal per serving	At least 25% fewer calories per serving	If the food contains 50% or more of its calories from fat, then the fat must be reduced
Fat	<0.5 grams (g) per serving	≤3 g per serving	At least 25% less fat per serving	Same as above
Saturated fat	<0.5 g per serving	≤1 g per serving	At least 25% less saturated fat per serving	N/A
Cholesterol	<2 milligrams (mg) per serving	≤20 mg per serving	At least 25% less cholesterol per serving	N/A
Sodium	<5 mg per serving	<140 mg per serving	At least 25% less sodium per serving	If the food is reduced by at least 50% per serving
Sugars	<0.5 g	N/A	At least 25% less sugar per serving	N/A

Other Labeling Terms

Term	Definition
"High," "Rich in," or "Excellent source of"	The food contains 20% or more of the DV of the nutrient in a serving. Can be used to describe protein, vitamins, minerals, fiber, or potassium.
"Good source of"	A serving of the food provides 10–19% of the DV. Can be used to describe meals or main dishes.
"More," "Added," "Extra," or "Plus"	A serving of the food provides 10% of the DV. Can only be used to describe vitamins, minerals, protein, fiber, and potassium.
"Lean"	Can be used on seafood and meat that contains less than 10 g of fat, 4.5 g or less of saturated fat, and less than 95 mg of cholesterol per serving.
"Extra lean"	Can be used on seafood and meat that contains less than 5 g of fat, less than 2 g of saturated fat, and less than 95 mg of cholesterol per serving.

N/A = not applicable

A health claim must contain two important components: (1) a food or a dietary compound, such as fiber, and (2) a corresponding disease or health-related condition that is associated with the claim.[16] In the Cheerios example, the soluble fiber (the dietary compound) that naturally occurs in oats has been shown to lower blood cholesterol levels (the corresponding health-related condition), which can help reduce the risk of heart disease.

There are three types of health claims: (1) authorized health claims, (2) health claims based on authoritative statements, and (3) qualified health claims. The differences between them lie in the amount of supporting research and agreement among scientists about the strength of the relationship between the food or dietary ingredient and the disease or condition. See Table 2.8 for a definition of these claims and examples of each.

Table 2.8

Sorting Out the Label Claims

Type of Claim	Definition	Examples
Authorized health claims (well-established)	Claims based on a well-established relationship between the food or compound and the health benefit. Food manufacturers must submit a petition to the FDA and provide the scientific research that backs up the claim. If there is significant agreement among the supporting research and a consensus among numerous scientists and experts in the field that there is a relationship between the food or dietary ingredient and the disease or health condition, the FDA will allow an authorized health claim. Specified wording must be used. The FDA has approved 12 authorized health claims.	■ Calcium and osteoporosis ■ Sodium and hypertension ■ Dietary fat and cancer ■ Dietary saturated fat and cholesterol and risk of coronary heart disease ■ Fiber-containing grain products, fruits, and vegetables and cancer ■ Fruits, vegetables, and grain products that contain fiber, particularly soluble fiber, and the risk of coronary heart disease ■ Fruits and vegetables and cancer ■ Folate and neural tube defects ■ Dietary sugar, alcohol, and dental caries ■ Soluble fiber from certain foods and risk of coronary heart disease ■ Soy protein and risk of coronary heart disease ■ Plant sterol/stanol esters and risk of coronary heart disease
Health claims based on authoritative statements (well-established)	Claims based on statements made by a U.S. government agency, such as the Centers for Disease Control and Prevention (CDC) and the National Institutes of Health (NIH). If the FDA approves the claim submitted by the manufacturer, the wording of these claims must include "may," as in "whole grains may help reduce the risk of heart disease," to illustrate that other factors in addition to the food or dietary ingredient may play a role in the disease or condition. This type of health claim can only be used on food and cannot be used on dietary supplements.	■ Whole-grain foods and risk of heart disease and certain cancers ■ Potassium and the risk of high blood pressure ■ Flouridated water and the reduced risk of dental caries.
Qualified health claims (less well-established)	Claims based on evidence that is still emerging. However, the current evidence to support the claim is greater than the evidence suggesting that the claim isn't valid. These are allowed in order to expedite the communication of potential beneficial health information to the public. They must be accompanied by the statement "the evidence to support the claim is limited or not conclusive" or "some scientific evidence suggests. . . ." Many experts, including the American Dietetics Association, don't support this type of health claim, as it is based on emerging evidence. Qualified Health Claims can be used on dietary supplements if approved by the FDA.	■ Selenium and cancer ■ Antioxidant vitamins and cancer ■ Nuts and heart disease ■ Omega-3 fatty acids and coronary heart disease ■ B vitamins and vascular disease ■ Monounsaturated fatty acids from olive oil and coronary heart disease ■ Unsaturated fatty acids from canola oil and reduced risk of coronary heart disease.

Functional Foods: What Role Do They Play in Your Diet?

Have you ever snacked on baby carrots? Did you know at the time that you were eating a functional food? A **functional food** is one that has been shown to have a positive effect on your health beyond its basic nutrients. Baby carrots are a functional food because they are rich in beta-carotene, which, in addition to being a key source of vitamin A, helps protect your cells from damaging substances that can increase your risk of some chronic diseases, such as cancer. In other words, the beta-carotene's function goes beyond its basic nutritional role as a source of vitamin A, because it may also help fight cancer. Oats are another functional food because they contain the soluble fiber, beta-glucan, which has been shown to lower blood cholesterol levels. This can play a positive role in lowering the risk for heart disease.[1]

If the beneficial compound in the food is derived from plants, such as in the case of beta-carotene and beta-glucan, it is

functional foods Foods that have a positive effect on health beyond providing basic nutrients.

phytochemicals Plant chemicals that have been shown to reduce the risk of certain diseases such as cancer and heart disease. Beta-carotene is a phytochemical.

zoochemicals Compounds in animal food products that are beneficial to human health. Omega-3 fatty acids are an example of zoochemicals.

called a **phytochemical** (*phyto* = plant). If it is derived from animals it is called a **zoochemical** (*zoo* = animal). Heart-healthy, omega-3 fatty acids, found in fatty fish such as salmon and sardines, are considered zoochemicals. The accompanying table provides a list of currently known compounds in foods that have been shown to provide positive health benefits. Manufacturers are promoting foods containing naturally occurring phytochemicals and zoochemicals and have also begun fortifying other food products with these compounds. You can buy margarine with added plant sterols and a cereal with the soluble fiber, psyllium, which both help lower blood cholesterol levels, as well as pasta that has omega-3 fatty acids added to it (see table).

Are People Buying Functional Foods?

Yes, people are buying them. Americans spend an estimated $18 billion annually on functional foods, and the market is predicted to grow as more consumers take a self-care approach to their health. In a survey conducted in 2002 of over 1,000 Americans, over 70 percent of participants believed that food and nutrition play a key role in maintaining and improving their health.[2]

Baby boomers, the generation of people born between 1946 and 1964 and who are currently reaching age 50 at the rate of one every 7.7 seconds, are particularly interested in trying to hedge against the aging process and age-related diseases through their diets. With $150 bil-

lion in discretionary income, these adults can afford foods that are promoted as having a health advantage.[3]

What Are the Benefits of Functional Foods?

Functional foods are being used by health care professionals to thwart patients' chronic diseases and, in some situations, as an economical way to treat a disease. For example, many doctors send their patients to a registered dietitian for diet advice to treat specific medical conditions, such as an elevated blood cholesterol level, rather than automatically prescribing cholesterol-lowering medication. Eating a diet that contains a substantial amount of cholesterol-lowering oats or plant sterols is less expensive, and often more appealing, than taking costly prescription medication. Ideally, the registered dietitian, who is trained in the area of nutrition, can recommend the addition of functional foods to the diet based on the person's own medical history and nutritional needs.

However, problems can arise when consumers haphazardly add functional foods to their diets.

What Concerns Are Associated with Functional Foods?

With so many labeling claims now adorning products on supermarket shelves, consumers have an array of enhanced functional foods from which to choose. Having so many options can be confusing. Consumers often cannot tell if a pricey box of cereal with added "antioxidants to help support the immune system" is

Structure/Function Claims

The last type of label claim is the structure/function claim, which describes how a nutrient or dietary compound affects the structure or function of the human body (See Figure 2.15 on page 53).[17] The claims "calcium (nutrient) builds strong bones (body structure)" and "fiber (dietary compound) maintains bowel regularity (body function)" are examples of structure/function claims. Structure/function claims cannot state that the nutrient or dietary compound can be used to treat a disease or a condition.[18] These claims can be made on both foods and dietary supplements. Unlike

Your Guide to Functional Foods

This Functional Food/ Food Source	Contains This Compound	And May Have This Health Benefit	If Taken in This Amount Daily
Psyllium in Kellogg's All Bran	Soluble fiber	Lowers blood cholesterol	1 g daily
Soy in soy milk	Protein	Lowers blood cholesterol	25 g daily
Oats in oatmeal	Beta-glucan	Lowers blood cholesterol	3 g daily
Fortified margarines, like Benecol spreads	Plant sterol and stanol esters	Lowers blood cholesterol	1.3 g daily of sterols or 1.7 g daily of stanols
Cranberries in cranberry juice	Proanthocyanidins	Reduces urinary tract infections	1¼ c daily
Fatty fish like salmon and sardines	Omega-3 fatty acids	Reduces the risk of heart disease	2 fish meals weekly
Garlic	Organosulfur compounds	Lowers blood cholesterol	1 fresh clove daily
Tomatoes in processed tomato products, like sauce and paste	Lycopene	Reduces the risk of prostate cancer	½ cup daily
Active cultures in fermented dairy products such as yogurt	Probiotics	Supports intestinal health	Enjoy daily

Source: Adapted from: C. M. Hasler, A. S. Bloch, C. A. Thomson, E. Enrione, and C. Manning. 2004. Position of the American Dietetic Association: Functional Foods. 2004. *Journal of the American Dietetic Association* 104:814–826; C. M. Hasler, The Changing Face of Functional Foods, *Journal of the American College of Nutrition* 19 (2000): 499S–506S.

really better than an inexpensive breakfast of oatmeal and naturally antioxidant-rich orange juice. There is also a concern that by eating a bowl of this antioxidant-enhanced cereal, consumers may think they are "off the hook" about eating healthfully the rest of the day. Often, more than one serving of a functional food is needed to reap the beneficial effect of the food compound, but the consumer hasn't been educated appropriately about how much of such a food to consume.

As with most dietary substances, problems may arise if too much is consumed. For example, whereas consuming some omega-3 fatty acids can help reduce the risk of heart disease, consuming too much can be problematic for people on certain medications or for those at risk for a specific type of stroke.[4] A person can unknowingly overconsume a dietary compound if his or her diet contains many different functional foods enhanced with the same compound.[5]

How to Use Functional Foods

Although functional foods can be part of a healthy diet, consumers would benefit from more research, regulation, and education. For now, keep in mind that whole grains, fruits, vegetables, healthy vegetable oils, lean meat and dairy products, fish, and poultry all contain varying amounts of naturally occurring phytochemicals and zoochemicals and are the quintessential functional foods. If you consume other, packaged functional foods, take care not to overconsume any one compound. Look to a registered dietitian (RD) for sound nutrition advice on whether you would benefit from added functional foods, and, if so, how to balance them in your diet. Visit the ADA website at www.eatright.org to find an RD in your area.

the other health claims, structure/function claims don't need to be preapproved by the FDA. They do need to be truthful and not misleading, but the manufacturer is responsible for making sure that the claim is accurate. These claims can be a source of confusion. Shoppers can easily fall into the trap of assuming that one brand of a product with a structure/function claim on its label is superior to another product without the claim. For instance, a yogurt that says "calcium builds strong bones" on its label may be identical to another yogurt without the flashy label claim. The consumer has to recognize the difference between claims that are supported by a significant amount

Figure 2.15 A Structure/Function Label Claim

A structure/function claim describes how a nutrient or substance, such as the antioxidants that have been added to this cereal, support the immune system, which is a function in the body. The manufacturer can't claim that the food lowers a consumer's risk of a chronic disease or health condition.

of solid research and approved by the FDA, and structure/function claims that don't need prior approval for use.

If a dietary supplement such as a multivitamin is to contain a structure/function claim, its manufacturer must notify the FDA no later than 30 days after the product has been on the market. Dietary supplements that use structure/function claims must display a disclaimer on the label that the FDA did not evaluate the claim and that the dietary supplement is not intended to "diagnose, treat, cure or prevent any disease." Manufacturers of foods bearing structure/function claims do not have to display this disclaimer on the label, just on dietary supplements.

All foods that boast a health claim and/or a structure/function claim can also be marketed as "functional foods." The feature box "Functional Foods: What Role Should They Play in Your Diet?" discusses this trendy category of foods.

Although keeping the types of health and structure/function claims straight can be challenging, here's one way to remember them: Authorized Health Claims and Health Claims Based on Authoritative Statements are the strongest, as they are based on years of accumulated research or an authoritative statement. Qualified Health Claims are made on potentially healthful foods or dietary ingredients but because the evidence is still emerging, the claim has to be "qualified" as such. All health claims provide information on how the food or dietary ingredient can help you reduce your risk of a condition or a disease.

Structure/function claims are the weakest claims, as they are just statements or facts about the role the nutrient or dietary ingredient plays in your body. They can't claim how the food or dietary ingredient lowers your risk of developing a chronic disease such as heart disease or cancer. As you read the claims on the labels, you will quickly see that those with less established scientific evidence behind them have the weakest wording.

The Take-Home Message The FDA regulates the labeling on all packaged foods. Every food label must contain the name of the food, its net weight, the name and address of the manufacturer or distributor, a list of ingredients, and standardized nutrition information. The FDA allows and regulates the use of nutrient content claims, health claims, and structure/function claims on food labels. Any foods or dietary supplements displaying these claims on the label must meet specified criteria and be truthful.

Two Points of View

Are Super Size Portions a Super Problem for Americans?

Over the past several years, the portion sizes of meals served in restaurants have increased. Do larger meals at restaurants play a role in America's expanding waistlines?

Sheila R. Cohn, RD, LD
National Restaurant Association

Sheila R. Cohn, RD, LD, is the director of nutrition policy in the health and safety regulatory affairs department of the National Restaurant Association. Her department advises the association, senior industry executives, and membership on legislative and regulatory health and safety issues that affect the restaurant industry. Typical subjects include nutrition labeling, obesity, dietary guidelines for Americans, food allergies, public health and sanitation, security, and energy management.

Q: Why and how much have restaurant portion sizes increased over the years?

A: The restaurant industry is an industry of choice. Numerous studies have shown that customers want choice and flexibility in the foods they eat. For this reason, restaurants have always offered consumers a wide variety of venues, menu items, and portion sizes to accommodate any individual's dietary needs, tastes, and preferences. Serving several portion sizes (including appetizers, half-portions, and regular portions) has become prevalent across all types of restaurants, from casual to fine dining.

Q: How does portion size affect a person's consumption and appeal of a meal when dining at restaurants?

A: With approximately half of all table-service restaurateurs reporting that their customers are even more value-conscious today than they were just two years ago, it isn't surprising that most operators want consumers to choose portions that will satisfy them. Approximately half of table-service restaurants with per-person dinner checks of less than $25 made a practice of encouraging customers to order the size portion that was appropriate for them, and four out of 10 offered half-size portions at a reduced price.

Q: Is it the patron's or the restaurant's responsibility to control the portions of foods when dining out?

A: The responsibility of portion control is one that is shared between restaurants and their guests. As I mentioned earlier, restaurants provide many options (appetizers, shared portions, half-portions, regular portions) for their guests so that they make choices based on their individual needs and preferences. It is not, however, the responsibility of the restaurant to monitor or critique what their guests order or

(continued)

Barbara J. Rolls, PhD
Pennsylvania State University

Barbara J. Rolls, PhD, is professor of nutritional sciences and occupant of the Guthrie Chair in Nutrition. She is past-president of the North American Association for the Study of Obesity and in 2003 was awarded Honorary Membership in the American Dietetic Association. In 2006 she was elected a fellow of the American Association for the Advancement of Science. She is the author of five books, including *The Volumetrics Weight-Control Plan: Feel Full on Fewer Calories.*

Q: Why and how much have restaurant portion sizes increased over the years?

A: Portion sizes have increased as the restaurant industry has found that customers appreciate good value for their money, which translates into large portions at a low price. The cost of the food is only a small percentage of the overall costs of serving a meal at a restaurant. Therefore, from the restaurant's standpoint, increasing the portion size doesn't dramatically increase the overall cost of the meal, but it can increase the loyalty of the customer to that restaurant. Customers often frequent restaurants based on the perceived value.

While some portion sizes, such as sliced bread, haven't changed over the years, others have, especially those items are that are energy or calorie dense. For example, muffins can weigh as much as half a pound and bowls of pasta served in restaurants can hold more than 2 pounds. Hamburgers can be more than double the size they were years ago.

Q: How does portion size affect a person's consumption and appeal of a meal when dining at restaurants?

A: We have learned from our research that when you give individuals larger portions of food, they eat more at that meal. In one study, when we gave participants a serving of macaroni and cheese that was 50 percent larger than a standard portion, their caloric intake increased by 19 percent, and when we increased the portion size by 100 percent, they ate 30 percent more calories. Consumers appear to base the amount they eat on the amount that they are served. More disturbingly, our studies show that individuals don't make adjustments for this increased consumption

(continued)

Are Super Size Portions a Super Problem for Americans?, continued

Sheila R. Cohn, RD, LD, continued

consume. (How would you like it if your server commented that you were eating too much? Or that based on the fit of your pants, you should probably just have a salad today?)

Based on research conducted by the National Restaurant Association, nearly two-thirds of adults agreed that table-service restaurants make it easy for them to choose the portion size they want. In fact, 75 percent of restaurant operators indicate increased customization of menu items by their guests.

One popular way to meet the needs of consumers who have smaller appetites is to encourage them to choose an appetizer or several appetizers in lieu of an entrée. It is important to note that this relaxed attitude toward portion-size options is coupled with an increase over the past five years in the proportion of table-service menus offering appetizer selections.

Q: What changes can the restaurant industry make to help Americans enjoy their experience, but not overindulge, when dining out?

A: Our research also shows that 71 percent of adults agreed that there are enough portion sizes available at restaurants, so they can receive as much or as little as they want. Virtually all restaurants allow customers to customize their meals, whether it is food-preparation method or substitution of food items to meet their individual needs. Ninety-five percent of restaurants provide take-away containers for consumers that want to turn "tonight's dinner into tomorrow's lunch."

Americans eat out an average of four times a week, meaning there are approximately 17 other meals each week that comprise one's diet—not to mention other lifestyle choices, such as whether an individual exercises, and how much.

Barbara J. Rolls, PhD, continued

of calories at other meals, setting the stage for potential weight gain over time.

Q: Is it the patron's or the restaurant's responsibility to control the portions of foods when dining out?

A: Unfortunately, we are not a species that has a lot of restraint when it comes to pleasurable experiences such as eating. In the end it is the consumer's responsibility, but since people are unaware of how much they are eating, customers should have more choices. They need help from the restaurant industry.

Q: What changes can the restaurant industry make to help Americans enjoy their experience, but not overindulge, when dining out?

A: I would like to see restaurants offering a variety of portion sizes so that individuals have the option to order smaller portions. Restaurants could also reduce the energy or calorie density of the meal by using less fat and adding more vegetables, fruits, and whole grains. This will enable the portion size to remain ample but lower the calories at that meal. For example, a pizza could be made with whole-wheat flour and topped with less cheese and plenty of vegetables instead of fatty meats. We need cuisines with more creative flavors that please our palate but for fewer calories. The focus in restaurants should be on the quality of the food, not on the quantity.

NUTRITION IN THE REAL WORLD

Be a Nutrition Sleuth

Portion Distortion?

Years ago, a standard bagel could fit in the palm of your hand. Today, a typical bagel is likely larger than your entire hand. Today's supersized hamburger dwarfs the average burger of the 1950s. Over the last few decades, the portion sizes of many commercially prepared and fast foods have increased greatly, and so have the number of calories from a serving.

Can you guess the calorie differences between the servings of yesteryear and those of today? Go online at www.aw-bc.com/blake to find out.

Get Real!

MyPyramid: Planning YOUR Pyramid

How does your daily diet measure up to MyPyramid recommendations? Visit www.aw-bc.com/blake and learn how to use the MyPyramid Tracker to evaluate your daily food choices.

The Top Ten Points to Remember

1. The Dietary Reference Intakes (DRIs) are specific reference values, based on your age and gender, for the essential nutrients you need daily. The DRIs are designed to prevent nutrient deficiencies, maintain good health, prevent chronic diseases, and avoid unhealthy excesses. The DRIs consist of the Estimated Average Requirement, Recommended Dietary Allowance, Adequate Intake, Tolerable Upper Intake Level, and the Acceptable Macronutrient Distribution Ranges.

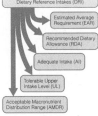

2. The *Dietary Guidelines for Americans 2005* is the current nutrition and physical activity recommendations for healthy Americans aged 2 and older. These guidelines are designed to help individuals improve their diet to lower their risk of chronic diseases and conditions such as diabetes mellitus, heart disease, certain cancers, osteoporosis, obesity, high blood pressure, and high blood cholesterol levels.

3. Food guidance systems are carefully designed visual recommendations of food groups that provide a variety of food choices for creating a well-balanced diet. Many countries have developed food guidance systems based on their food supply, cultural food preferences, and the specific nutritional needs of their citizens.

4. MyPyramid is the USDA's latest food guidance system. It visually represents many of the recommendations in the *Dietary Guidelines for Americans 2005* and helps you meet your daily DRIs for these

nutrients. MyPyramid recommends the number of servings that you should eat every day from each food group based on your calorie needs. There are five food groups: grains, vegetables, fruits, milk, and meat and beans. Oils are also shown on MyPyramid. MyPyramid emphasizes daily physical activity, proportionality between the foods groups and variety within the food groups, as well as moderation when consuming foods with unhealthy fats and added sugar. It provides a personalized eating plan based on your needs and encourages gradual improvements in your diet and lifestyle choices to improve your health.

5. The FDA regulates all packaged foods to ensure that they are accurately labeled. The Nutrition Facts panel on the food label must list the serving size of the food. It must also show the corresponding amount of calories, fat, saturated fat, *trans* fat, cholesterol, sodium, sugars, protein, vitamins A and C, calcium, and iron that are contained in a serving of the food. Other nutrients can be added by the manufacturer voluntarily. If a food product makes a claim about a nutrient, it must be listed in the Nutrition Facts panel.

6. The Daily Values are reference levels of intakes for the nutrients listed on the food label. Unlike the DRIs, they are not specific, individualized recommended intakes, but rather reference points that allow you to assess how the nutrients in the foods you buy can fit into your overall diet.

7. A food product label can carry a nutrient content claim about the amount of a nutrient the food contains by using descriptive terms such as free, high, low, reduced, and extra lean as long as it meets the strict criteria for each item designated by the FDA.

8. A health claim must contain a food compound or a dietary ingredient and a corresponding disease or health-related condition that is associated with the claim. All health claims must be approved by the FDA.

9. Structure/function claims describe how a food or dietary compound affects the structure or function of the body. These claims must be truthful and accurate and do not need FDA approval before being used. They cannot be tied to a disease or health-related condition.

10. Functional foods have been shown to have a positive effect on health beyond providing basic nutrients. Some foods are deliberately enhanced with compounds and marketed as functional foods.

Test Your Knowledge

1. The *Dietary Guidelines for Americans 2005* recommend that you
   a. consume adequate nutrients within your calorie needs and be physically active daily.
   b. stop smoking and walk daily.
   c. sleep eight hours a night and jog every other day.
   d. consume adequate nutrients within your calorie needs and stop smoking.

2. The Dietary Reference Intakes (DRIs) are reference values for nutrients and are designed to
   a. only prevent a nutritional deficiency.
   b. provide a ballpark range of your nutrient needs.
   c. prevent nutritional deficiencies by meeting your nutrient needs as well as prevent the consumption of excessive and dangerous amounts of nutrients.

3. The Estimated Average Intake (EAR) is
   a. the estimated amount of a nutrient that you should consume daily to be healthy.
   b. the amount of a nutrient that meets the average needs of 50 percent of individuals in a specific age and gender group.
   c. the maximum safe amount of a nutrient that you should consume daily.

4. MyPyramid is a food guidance system that
   a. can help you implement the recommendations in the DRIs.
   b. can help you use the advice in the *Dietary Guidelines for Americans.*
   c. provides personalized food choices among a variety of food groups to help you create a balanced diet.
   d. does all of the above.

5. Which of the following are the food groups in MyPyramid?
   a. grains, vegetables, milk, sweets, and meat and beans
   b. grains, fruits, alcohol, sweets, and meat and beans
   c. grains, vegetables, fruits, milk, and meat and beans
   d. grains, vegetables, sweets, milk, and meat and beans

6. Which of the following foods is most nutrient dense?
   a. an orange ice pop
   b. an orange
   c. orange-flavored punch
   d. orange sherbet

7. By law, which of the following MUST be listed on the food label?
   a. calories, fat, and potassium
   b. fat, saturated fat, and vitamin E
   c. calories, fat, and saturated fat
   d. calories, sodium, and vitamin D

8. The bran cereal that you eat in the morning carries a "high-fiber" claim on its label. This is an example of a
   a. nutrient claim.
   b. structure/function claim.
   c. health claim.

9. The yogurt that you enjoy as a morning snack states that a serving provides 30 percent of the Daily Value for calcium. Is this a high or low amount of calcium?
   a. high
   b. low

10. Oatmeal contains a soluble fiber that can help lower your cholesterol. Oatmeal is considered a functional food.
    a. true
    b. false

Answers

1. (a) The *Dietary Guidelines for Americans* recommend that you consume a balanced diet to meet your nutrient needs without overconsuming calories, and that you be physically active daily. Though the *Dietary Guidelines* do not specifically address stopping smoking, this is a habit worth kicking. Walking or jogging daily are wonderful ways to be physically active. Sleeping eight hours a night isn't mentioned in the *Dietary Guidelines* but is another terrific lifestyle habit.

2. (c) The DRIs tell you the amount of nutrients you need to prevent deficiencies, maintain good health, and avoid toxicity.

3. (b) The EAR is the amount of a nutrient that would meet the needs of half of the individuals in a specific age and gender group. The EAR is used to obtain the Recommended Dietary Allowance, which is the amount of a nutrient that you should be consuming daily to maintain good health. The Tolerable Upper Intake Level is the maximum amount of a nutrient that you can consume on a regular basis that is unlikely to cause harm.

4. (d) MyPyramid is a food guidance tool that helps you to create a balanced diet so that you can eat healthily. It is designed to help you meet the nutrient needs recommended in the DRIs and also implement the advice in the *Dietary Guidelines for Americans*.

5. (c) Grains, vegetables, fruit, milk, and meat and beans are the five basic food groups in MyPyramid. Sweets and alcohol are not food groups and should be limited in the diet.

6. (b) While an orange ice pop and orange sherbet may be refreshing treats on a hot day, the orange is by far the most nutrient-dense food among the choices. The orange-flavored punch is a sugary drink with orange flavoring.

7. (c) The Nutrition Facts panel on the package must contain the calories, fat, and saturated fat per serving. Vitamins E and D do not have to be listed unless they have been added to the food and/or the product makes a claim about them on the label.

8. (a) This high-fiber cereal label boasts a nutrient claim and is helping you meet your daily fiber needs.

9. (a) If you consume 20 percent or more of the Daily Value for a nutrient, it is considered "high" in that nutrient. If a nutrient provides 5 percent or less of the Daily Value, it is considered "low" in that nutrient.

10. (a) Functional foods go beyond providing basic nutrients and also provide other health benefits. Oats contain the soluble fiber, beta-glucan, which has been shown to help reduce blood cholesterol levels. Because of this, oatmeal is considered a functional food.

Web Support

- For more tips and resources for MyPyramid, visit www .MyPyramid.gov

3

The Basics of Digestion

1. You cannot fully enjoy food without your sense of **smell.** **T/F**

2. The **GI tract** is essentially a long tube. **T/F**

3. You absorb only **75 percent** of the nutrients in your food. **T/F**

4. Food enters your stomach from the **trachea.** **T/F**

5. Hydrochloric acid is produced in the **esophagus.** **T/F**

6. Protein, fat, and carbohydrates are all digested at the same **rate.** **T/F**

7. All nutrients are **absorbed** in the small intestine. **T/F**

8. **Stool** is mostly made up of food remnants and bacteria. **T/F**

9. Few people experience **heartburn.** **T/F**

10. Dietary **fiber** is useless. **T/F**

Twenty-one-year-old Rachel hadn't eaten breakfast and was getting antsy for lunch as she sat in her 11 a.m. nutrition class. In spite of her churning stomach and vague discomfort, she was paying close attention to her instructor's gripping lecture on digestive enzymes. Suddenly, a loud rumble emanated from her midsection. As the students near her glanced over, Rachel realized that the growling was heard throughout the room. Her initial mild embarrassment quickly turned into distress as the professor stopped talking about lipase and asked the class if they had all heard the growling stomach, and did they know what caused it?

Can you guess the reason for Rachel's belly rumblings? Would you know how to quiet your own noisy midsection if faced with a similar scenario? In this chapter, we'll explore the process of digestion and the organs involved, as well as some common ailments. Also, though a growling stomach isn't cause for concern, we'll discuss its causes and solutions as well.

Answers

1. True. Smell is a big part of taste. Turn to page 63 to find out more.
2. True. The gastrointestinal, or GI, tract runs through the body and connects the mouth to the anus. Turn to page 64 to find out more about the organs that make up the GI tract.
3. False. Your body is very efficient and absorbs over 90 percent of the nutrients in your food. To find out how this happens, turn to page 65.
4. False. The trachea is the windpipe. To find out what happens if food mistakenly enters it, turn to page 66.
5. False. Hydrochloric acid is only produced in the stomach. For more about digestive juices, turn to page 67.
6. False. Fats and protein take longer to digest than carbohydrates. Turn to page 67 to find out why.
7. False. Though most absorption does take place in the small intestine, some nutrients, particularly water, are absorbed in the large intestine. Turn to page 70 to learn more.
8. True. Stool (or feces) contains leftover food residue, nondigestible fibers, bacteria, gases, and sloughed-off intestinal cells. Turn to page 70 to find out more about the waste products of digestion.
9. False. Approximately 20 percent of adults experience heartburn everyday. Turn to page 76 to learn what causes it.
10. False. Fiber helps keep you "regular." To find out more, turn to page 77.

What Makes Eating So Enjoyable?

As much fun as it is to eat, you're not just taking in food for fun. Food satisfies a genuine physical need. Eating food and drinking fluids often begins with the sensation of either **hunger** or **thirst.** The amount of food that we eat and the timing of our meals are driven by physical needs. **Appetite** is another powerful drive, but it is often unreliable. Appetite is influenced by our food preferences and the psychological stimulation to eat. In other words, you can become interested in food, pursue food, and experience the desire to eat too much food without actually needing nourishment or being hungry.

Chapter 1 discussed many factors that affect how, when, and why you eat, so you know that everything from your social situation to your cultural heritage will impact what you put on your plate. But beyond these external factors, there are qualities in foods that affect your desire to eat them. *Taste* and *aroma* are two of these qualities.

We Develop a Taste for Certain Foods

Everyone enjoys eating food that tastes delicious, but what exactly *is* taste? There are five basic categories of taste: sweet, salty, sour, bitter, and savory ("umami"). Most taste buds are located on the tongue, but additional taste buds are found in the throat and elsewhere in the mouth. Food scientists estimate that each of us has at least 10,000 taste buds.

As you can see in Figure 3.1, the taste buds most sensitive to sweet flavors are on the tip of the tongue, sour and salty are on the sides, and the maximum bitter sensation is on the back of the tongue. The umami taste is distributed throughout the mouth. However, some people are not aware of, or are not sensitive to, this taste sensation.

Even though each of us has our own favorite foods, we share some taste traits. In general, we all have an innate preference for sweet, salty, and fatty foods. There is a scientific explanation for these preferences. Sugar seems to elicit universal pleasure

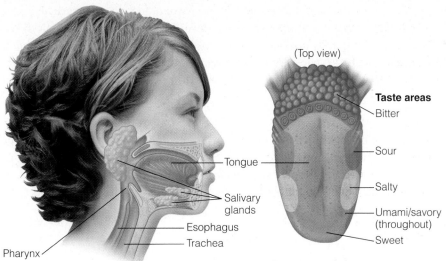

(Top view)

Taste areas
- Bitter
- Sour
- Salty
- Umami/savory (throughout)
- Sweet

Tongue

Salivary glands

Esophagus

Trachea

Pharynx

(even among infants), and the brain seeks pleasure.[1] Salt provides two important **electrolytes** (sodium and chloride) and can stimulate the appetite. High-fat foods have rich textures and aromas that round out the flavors of food.[2] Thus, we tend to enjoy rich sauces, gravies, salad dressings, and the like.

Sometimes, our food preferences and our nutritional needs conflict. We may eat too much because the food is so pleasurable. When there is a reason to change our food habits, such as a need to lose weight or reduce salt or fat intake, we realize how challenging it is to control our food choices.

How does the brain recognize taste? When food is consumed, portions of the food are dissolved in saliva. These fluids then make contact with the tongue's surface. The taste (gustatory) cells send a message to the brain. The brain then translates the nerve impulses into taste sensations that you recognize.

> The word *umami* means "delicious" in Japanese.

Aromas and Flavors Enhance the Pleasure of Eating

The sensing structures in the nose are also important to the ability to taste foods. The average person is capable of distinguishing 2,000 to 4,000 aromas.[3] We detect food aroma through the nose when we smell foods and, as we eat, when food odors enter the mouth and migrate to the back of the throat and into the nasal cavities.[4] The average person has about 10 million to 20 million olfactory cells (odor cells) in the nasal cavity. Therefore, both your mouth and your nose contribute to the tasting of foods. This explains why you lose interest in eating when you have a cold or experience other forms of nasal congestion: Food loses some of its appeal when you can't smell it.

Both the taste and aroma of a food contribute to its flavor. The term flavor also refers to the complete food experience. For example, when you eat a candy bar, you sense a sweet taste, but the flavor is chocolate.

The presence of fat tends to enhance the flavor of foods. When the fat content increases, the intensity of the flavor also increases as many aromatic compounds are

hunger The physical need for food.

thirst The physical need for water.

appetite The psychological desire to eat or drink.

electrolytes Charged particles (positive or negative ions). Vomiting and diarrhea cause the loss of electrolytes from your body.

The smell of food, such as freshly baked bread, often triggers the appetite. As you eat a piece of bread, its aroma will also contribute to its flavor.

soluble in fat. Increased fat content causes the flavor of food to last longer compared with flavor compounds dissolved in water. Flavors dissolved in water are quickly detected, but also quickly dissipated.[5] This explains why most people prefer premium ice cream over frozen popsicles. It also explains why several low-fat foods have an acceptable flavor, but they are not as delicious as their high-fat counterparts.

The Take-Home Message The five categories of taste are sweet, salty, sour, bitter, and savory (umami). Humans have an innate taste for salty, sugary, and fatty foods. The tastes and aromas of foods are a big part of what makes eating pleasurable. Flavor includes both taste and aroma. In general, the higher the fat content, the more intensely flavored the food.

What Is Digestion and Why Is It Important?

The simple definition of digestion is the breaking down of foods into absorbable components in the **gastrointestinal (GI) tract.** Through a multistep **digestive process,** food is softened with moisture and heat, and then broken down into smaller particles by chewing and exposing them to **enzymes.**

Digestion Occurs in the GI Tract

gastrointestinal (GI) tract Referring to the organs of the digestive tract. It extends from the mouth to the anus.

digestive process The breakdown of foods into absorbable components using mechanical and chemical means.

enzymes Substances that produce chemical changes or catalyze chemical reactions.

lumen The interior of the digestive tract, through which food passes.

mechanical digestion Breaking food down through chewing and grinding, or moving it through the GI tract with peristalsis.

peristalsis The forward, rhythmic motion that moves food through the digestive system. Peristalsis is a form of mechanical digestion because it influences motion, but it does not add chemical secretions.

chemical digestion Breaking down food with enzymes or digestive juices.

The GI tract consists of the mouth, esophagus, stomach, small intestine, large intestine, and other organs. The main roles of the GI tract are to (1) break food down into its smallest components; (2) absorb the nutrients; and (3) prevent microorganisms or other harmful compounds consumed with food from entering the tissues of the body.[6]

The GI tract is a tube about 23 feet long; stretched vertically, this would be about as high as a two-story building. The many circular folds, grooves, and projections in the stomach and intestines provide an extensive surface area over which absorption can occur. The cells lining your GI tract have a very brief life span. They function for three to five days and then they are shed into the **lumen** (interior of the intestinal tract) and are replaced with new, healthy cells.

Digestion Is Mechanical and Chemical

There are two forms of digestion: mechanical and chemical. **Mechanical digestion** involves chewing, grinding, and breaking food apart in the mouth so that it can be comfortably swallowed. The muscular activity and rhythmic contractions, or **peristalsis,** that move food through the GI tract and mix it with enzymes are also part of mechanical digestion.

Chemical digestion involves using digestive juices and enzymes to break down food into absorbable nutrients that are small enough to enter the cells of the GI tract, blood, or lymph tissue.

Digestion Allows Us to Absorb Nutrients from Foods

Digestion is the forerunner to **absorption.** Once the nutrients have been completely broken down, they are ready to be used by the cells of the body. In order to reach the cells, however, they have to leave the GI tract and move to the other parts of the body. To accomplish this, nutrients are absorbed through the walls of the intestines and into the body's two transport systems: the circulatory and lymph systems. They are then taken to the liver for processing before moving on to their destination.

The body is remarkably efficient when it comes to absorbing nutrients. Under normal conditions, you digest and absorb 92 to 97 percent of the nutrients from your food.[7]

The Take-Home Message Digestion is the chemical or mechanical breaking down of food into smaller units until it can be absorbed for use by the body. Digestion takes place in the gastrointestinal tract, which includes the mouth, esophagus, stomach, small intestine, large intestine, and other organs. Absorption is the process by which the digested nutrients move into your tissues. You absorb over 90 percent of the nutrients that you take in from foods.

What Happens in the Individual Organs of the GI Tract?

The organs of the GI tract each play a unique and crucial role in digestion. Before we examine the individual roles of the organs, take a look at Figure 3.2 on page 66 and refresh your memory of how organs are built from cells and tissues and how they work together in various body systems. Understanding how cells build tissues will help you understand how digestion and absorption happen in the body.

> You produce 1 to 1.5 liters of saliva every day.

You Begin Breaking Down Food in the Mouth

The process of digestion begins when you first see, smell, or think about a food that you want to eat. Glands in your mouth release **saliva,** a watery fluid that will help soften the food you are about to eat. Once you take a bite and begin to chew, your teeth, powered by your jaw muscles, cut and grind the food into smaller pieces and with your tongue mix it with saliva. Saliva helps dissolve small food particles and allows us to comfortably swallow dry food. In addition to water, saliva contains electrolytes, a few enzymes, and **mucus.** The mucus helps lubricate the food, helps it stick together, and protects the inside of the mouth. Once food has been adequately chewed, it's pushed to the back of the mouth and into the **pharynx** by the tongue.

Swallowing seems simple because we do it hundreds of times a day, but it is actually a complicated process. Pushing chewed food to the pharynx is a voluntary

absorption The process by which digested nutrients move into the tissues where they can be transported and used by the body's cells.

saliva Watery fluid secreted by the salivary glands in the mouth. Saliva moistens food and makes it easier to swallow.

mucus Viscous, slippery secretions found in saliva.

pharynx The throat. Passageway for the respiratory (air) and digestive tracts (food and beverages).

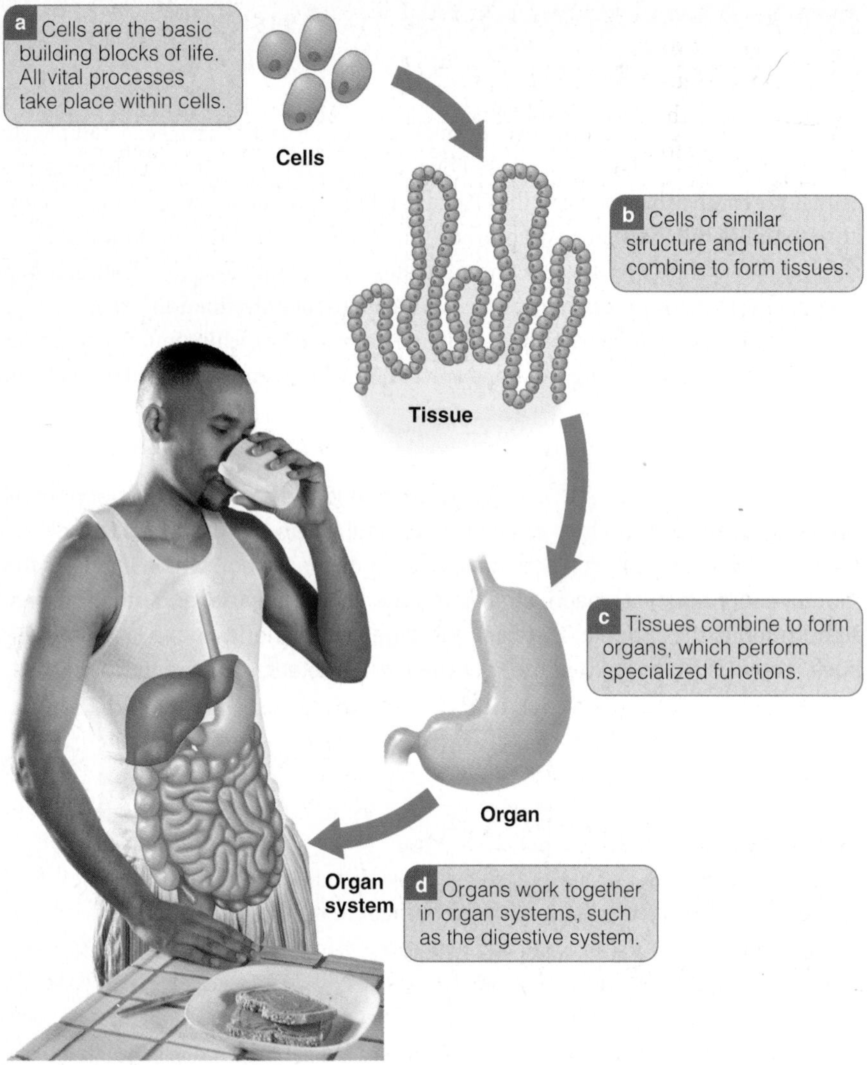

Figure 3.2 From Cells to Organs and Organ Systems

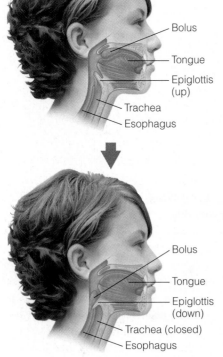

a Cells are the basic building blocks of life. All vital processes take place within cells.

Cells

b Cells of similar structure and function combine to form tissues.

Tissue

c Tissues combine to form organs, which perform specialized functions.

Organ

Organ system

d Organs work together in organ systems, such as the digestive system.

Figure 3.3 The Epiglottis
The epiglottis prevents food from entering the trachea when you swallow.

Bolus

Tongue

Epiglottis (up)

Trachea

Esophagus

Bolus

Tongue

Epiglottis (down)

Trachea (closed)

Esophagus

bolus Chewed mass of food.

epiglottis Flap of tissue that protects the trachea while swallowing.

esophagus Tube that extends from the throat to the stomach.

act—that is, you control it. Once the food mass (now called a **bolus**) enters the pharynx, the swallowing reflex kicks in, and you no longer control the action.

You have probably experienced an episode of "swallowing gone wrong" in which you've accidentally propelled food down the wrong pipe. When this happens (and you find yourself in a coughing fit trying to expel the item), it is because the normal mechanism that protects your trachea (or windpipe) didn't engage properly. Usually, a small flap called the **epiglottis** closes off your trachea during swallowing (Figure 3.3). The epiglottis ensures that food and drink go down the correct pipe—the **esophagus**—rather than down the windpipe. When the epiglottis doesn't work properly, food can get lodged in the trachea, and potentially result in choking.

The Esophagus Propels Food into the Stomach

Once swallowed, a bolus of food is pushed down your esophagus by *peristalsis* (Figure 3.4). When the bolus of food reaches the stomach, the lower part of the esophagus relaxes, allowing the bolus to enter the stomach. Solid or partially chewed food passes through the esophagus in about 8 seconds. Soft food and liquids pass through in about one to two seconds.[8]

The esophagus narrows at the bottom (just above the stomach) and ends at a sphincter, called the **lower esophageal sphincter (LES).** Under normal conditions, when we swallow food, the LES relaxes and allows food to pass into the stomach. The stomach also relaxes to comfortably receive the food.[9] After food enters the stomach, the LES should close. If it doesn't, hydrochloric acid from the stomach may flow back into the esophagus and irritate its lining. This is called *heartburn* because it causes a burning sensation in the middle of the chest.

Chronic heartburn and the reflux of stomach acids are symptoms of gastro-esophageal reflux disease (GERD). The condition, GERD, and the treatment for it will be discussed later in this chapter.

The Stomach Stores, Mixes, and Prepares Food for Digestion

The **stomach** continues mechanical digestion by churning and contracting to mix food with digestive juices. The food is continuously mixed for several hours. The stomach also has a role in chemical digestion in that it produces powerful digestive secretions. These secretions include **hydrochloric acid (HCl),** various enzymes, mucus, intrinsic factor (needed for vitamin B_{12} absorption), and the stomach hormone, **gastrin.** The swallowed bolus of food soon becomes **chyme,** a semi-liquid substance that contains digestive secretions plus the original food. The stomach can expand to hold 2 to 4 liters of chyme.

Hydrochloric acid has important digestive functions. These include activation of the protein-digesting enzyme **pepsin,** enhanced absorption of minerals, break-down of connective tissue in meat, and the destruction of some ingested microorganisms.[10] You might think that such a strong chemical would "digest" the stomach itself, but mucus produced in the stomach acts as a barrier between the HCl and the stomach lining, protecting the lining from irritation or damage.

Enzymes in the stomach including pepsin and gastric lipase, begin breaking down protein into polypeptides and a few triglycerides into shorter chain fatty acids. (The majority of triglycerides are broken down in the small intestine with the help of another enzyme.) The hormone gastrin stimulates the secretion of HCl, among other functions.

Have you ever noticed that some foods keep you feeling full longer than others? Foods high in carbohydrate exit the stomach faster, and therefore make you feel less full, than foods high in protein, fat, or fiber. Most liquids, carbohydrates, and low-fiber foods require minimal digestive activity, are easier to absorb, and have less surface area due to low fiber content.

Similarly, low-calorie foods exit the stomach faster than concentrated, high-calorie foods. This is because low-calorie foods frequently require minimal digestion. For example, a lightly sweetened cup of tea, a lower calorie beverage, requires less digestion than a higher calorie, nutrient dense milkshake. Digesting the tea involves only the breakdown of the sugar, sucrose, into fructose and glucose (you'll learn more about all of these sugars in Chapter 4). In contrast, digesting the milkshake involves breaking down fat, protein, and carbohydrates.

As digestion continues, peristaltic contractions push the chyme toward the lower part of the stomach. As the chyme accumulates near the **pyloric sphincter,** the muscular sphincter relaxes and the chyme gradually enters the small intestine. Approximately 1 to 5 ml (1 tsp) of chyme is released into the small intestine every 30 seconds

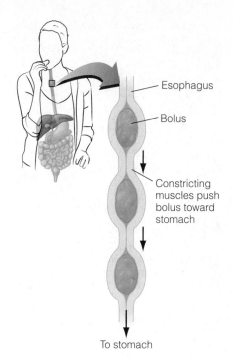

Figure 3.4 Peristalsis
Muscles around the organs of the GI tract constrict in a wavelike manner to help move food along.

Esophagus

Bolus

Constricting muscles push bolus toward stomach

To stomach

lower esophogeal sphincter (LES) A circular band of muscle between the esophagus and stomach that opens and closes to allow food to enter the stomach.

stomach Digestive organ that holds food after it's moved down the esophagus and before it is propelled into the small intestine.

hydrochloric acid (HCl) A powerful acid made in the stomach that has digestive functions. It also helps to kill microorganisms and lowers the pH in the stomach.

gastrin A digestive hormone produced in the stomach that stimulates digestive activities and increases motility and emptying.

chyme A liquid combination of partially digested food, water, HCl, and digestive enzymes.

pepsin A digestive enzyme produced in the stomach that breaks down protein.

pyloric sphincter Sphincter in the bottom of the stomach that separates the pylorus from the duodenum of the small intestine.

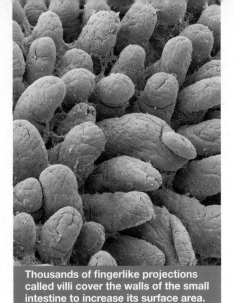

Thousands of fingerlike projections called villi cover the walls of the small intestine to increase its surface area.

during digestion.[11] The pyloric sphincter prevents chyme from exiting the stomach too soon, and it prevents intestinal contents from returning to the stomach.

Figure 3.5 provides an overview of the digestive process.

Most Digestion and Absorption Occur in the Small Intestine

The **small intestine** is a long, narrow, coiled chamber in the abdominal cavity. It consists of three segments—duodenum, jejunum, and ileum—and extends from the pyloric sphincter to the beginning of the large intestine. The first segment, the duodenum, is approximately 10 inches long. The second area, the jejunum, is about 8 feet long, and the final region, the ileum, is about 12 feet long. The "small" in "small intestine" refers to its diameter, not its extended length.

The small intestine is actually the primary organ for digestion and absorption within the human body. The small intestine has tremendous surface area compared with the stomach (Figure 3.6), and its digestive secretions do most of the work when it comes to breaking down food into absorbable nutrients.

The interior of the small intestine is covered with thousands of small projections called **villi.** The villi increase the surface area of the small intestine's lining and mix the partially digested chyme with intestinal secretions. Each individual villus is adjacent to a cluster of blood capillaries, lymph vessels, and nerve fibers.

The villi are covered by even smaller projections called **microvilli,** which provide additional surface area and maximize nutrient absorption. The lining of the small intestine is also arranged in unique, circular folds, which further increase the absorptive surface area. The circular folds cause the chyme to spiral forward through the small intestine, rather than merely move in a straight line.

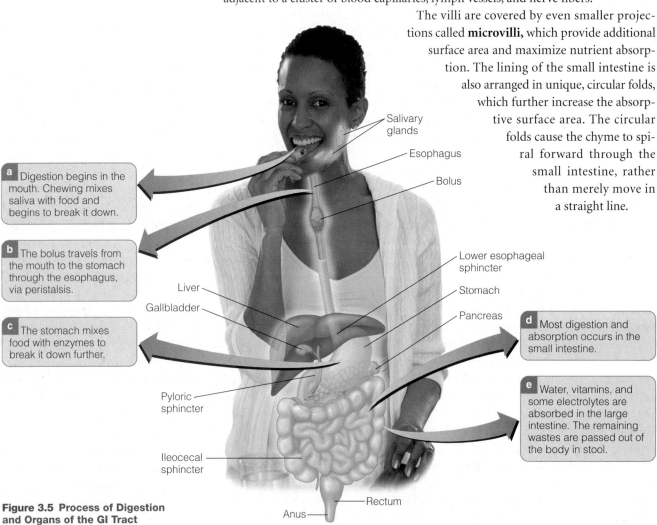

a Digestion begins in the mouth. Chewing mixes saliva with food and begins to break it down.

b The bolus travels from the mouth to the stomach through the esophagus, via peristalsis.

c The stomach mixes food with enzymes to break it down further.

d Most digestion and absorption occurs in the small intestine.

e Water, vitamins, and some electrolytes are absorbed in the large intestine. The remaining wastes are passed out of the body in stool.

Salivary glands
Esophagus
Bolus
Lower esophageal sphincter
Stomach
Pancreas
Liver
Gallbladder
Pyloric sphincter
Ileocecal sphincter
Rectum
Anus

Figure 3.5 Process of Digestion and Organs of the GI Tract

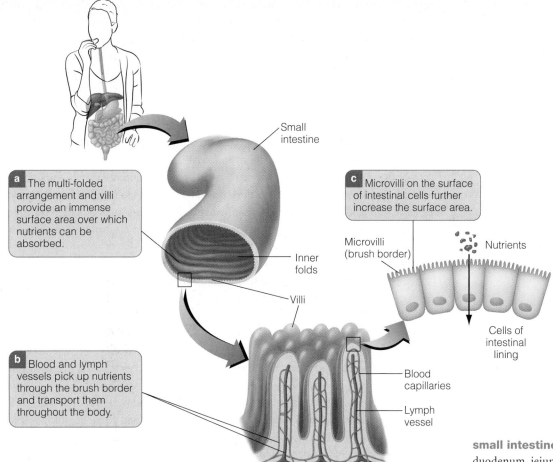

a The multi-folded arrangement and villi provide an immense surface area over which nutrients can be absorbed.

b Blood and lymph vessels pick up nutrients through the brush border and transport them throughout the body.

c Microvilli on the surface of intestinal cells further increase the surface area.

Small intestine

Inner folds

Villi

Microvilli (brush border)

Nutrients

Blood capillaries

Lymph vessel

Cells of intestinal lining

Figure 3.6 Surface Area in the Small Intestine

Both mechanical and chemical digestion occur in the small intestine. Mechanical digestion occurs through peristalsis, segmentation, and pendular movement. You already know that peristalsis is a mechanical, muscular movement that helps propel the contents through the GI tract. **Segmentation** is a "sloshing" motion that thoroughly mixes the chyme with the chemical secretions of the intestine. **Pendular movement** is a constrictive wave that involves both forward and reverse movements and enhances nutrient absorption. Together, these three actions move the chyme through the small intestine at a rate of 1 centimeter/minute.[12] Depending on the amount of food and the type of food consumed, the contact time in the small intestine is about three to ten hours.[13]

The Large Intestine Absorbs Water and Some Nutrients

Once the chyme has passed through the small intestine, it comes to the **ileocecal sphincter,** which serves as the gateway to its next digestive destination, the **large intestine.** The primary purpose of the ileocecal sphincter is to prevent backflow of fecal contents from the large intestine into the ileum. In general, this sphincter is quite strong and resists reverse pressure. About 750 ml (approximately 3 cups) of unabsorbed

small intestine Comprised of the duodenum, jejunum, and ileum. The longest part of the GI tract. Most of the digestion and absorption of food occurs in the small intestine.

villi Projections on the walls of the small intestine that increase the surface area over which nutrients can be absorbed. Villi are in turn covered with **microvilli,** which increase the surface area even more.

segmentation A "sloshing" motion that thoroughly mixes chyme with the chemical secretions of the intestine.

pendular movement A constrictive wave that involves both forward and reverse movements of chyme and enhances nutrient absorption.

ileocecal sphincter Gateway between the end of the small intestine and the beginning of the large intestine. The sphincter prevents backflow of fecal contents from the large intestine into the small intestine.

large intestine Final organ of the GI tract. It consists of the cecum, appendix, colons, and rectum.

residue enters the large intestine each day. The slow entry of this residue from the small to the large intestine enables the body to maximize nutrient absorption.[14]

By the time food enters the large intestine, it has been digested and the majority of the nutrients have been absorbed. But the large intestine serves some important functions, including the absorption of water, production of a few vitamins, absorption of important electrolytes, and the formation and storage of fecal material.

The large intestine is about 5 feet long and 2½ inches in diameter. It looks and acts much differently than the small intestine in that it does not contain villi or microvilli, and is not tightly coiled. Further, the large intestine does not secrete or use digestive enzymes and hormones. Rather, the chemical digestion that takes place in the large intestine is due to the efforts of bacteria. The large intestine produces mucus that protects the cells and acts as a lubricant for fecal matter. The cells of the large intestine absorb water and electrolytes much more efficiently than do the cells of the small intestine.

There are three segments of the large intestine: the cecum, colon, and rectum (Figure 3.7). The cecum is a small, pouchlike area that has the appendix hanging from one end. The middle section, or colon, is the largest portion of the large intestine. (Note that while the terms "colon" and "large intestine" are often used interchangeably, they're not technically the same thing.) The colon includes the ascending, transverse, descending, and sigmoid regions. These regions are relatively long and straight. Most of the vitamin production and absorption of water and electrolytes occur within the first half of the colon. The last half of the colon stores fecal matter.

The colon receives about l liter (about 1 quart) of fluid material each day from the cecum, consisting of water, undigested or unabsorbed food particles, indigestible residue, and bacteria. It slowly and gently mixes these intestinal contents and absorbs the majority of the fluids presented to it. The colon gradually produces a semi-solid material that is reduced to about 200 grams (about 7 ounces) of fecal matter (**stool, or feces**). The intestinal matter passes through the colon within 12 to 70 hours, depending on a person's age, health, diet, and fiber intake.[15]

Bacteria in the colon play a role in producing some vitamins, including the B vitamin, biotin, and vitamin K.[16] Bacteria also ferment some of the undigested and unabsorbed dietary carbohydrates into simpler compounds, methane gas, carbon dioxide, and hydrogen. Similarly, some of the colon's bacteria break down undigested fiber and produce various short-chain fatty acids. Amino acids that reach the colon are converted to hydrogen, sulfide, some fatty acids, and other chemical compounds.

As in the small intestine, the colon moves contents through via peristalsis and segmentation. Peristalsis occurs within the ascending colon, but the waves of contraction are quite slow. The mixing motion of segmentation allows the organ to progressively absorb fluids.[17]

The stool is propelled forward until it reaches the **rectum,** the final eight-inch portion of the large intestine, where it is stored. When stool distends the rectum, the action stimulates stretch receptors which in turn stimulate the defecation reflex. This causes nerve impulses of the rectum to communicate with the rectum's muscles. The end result is relaxation of the internal sphincter of the anus.

The **anus** is connected to the rectum and controlled by two sphincters: an internal and an external sphincter. Under normal conditions, the anal sphincters are closed. Periodically, the anal sphincters will relax, stool will enter the anal canal and defecation will occur. The final stage of defecation is under our voluntary control and influenced by age, diet, prescription medicines, health, and abdominal muscle tone.

Sausage casings were originally made from the intestinal lining of pigs.

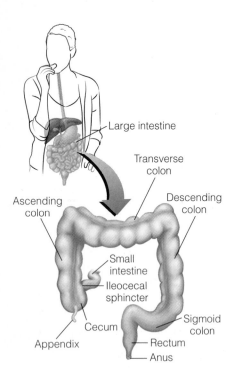

Figure 3.7 Anatomy of the Large Intestine
By the time chyme reaches the large intestine, most of its nutrients have been absorbed. However, water and some electrolytes are absorbed in the colon. The final waste products of digestion pass out of the body as stool through the anus.

stool (feces) Waste products that are stored in the large intestine and then excreted from the body. Stool consists mostly of bacteria, sloughed-off gastrointestinal cells, inorganic matter, water, unabsorbed nutrients, food residue, undigested fibers, fatty acids, mucus, and remnants of digestive fluids.

rectum The lowest part of the large intestine, continuous with the sigmoid colon and the **anus.**

Enzymes, Hormones, and Bile Aid Digestion

The complete digestion of chyme requires chemical secretions, including enzymes, hormones, and bile. Supportive digestive organs such as the pancreas, liver, and gallbladder contribute or concentrate many of these fluids. The stomach and small intestine also produce digestive enzymes.

The purpose of the enzymes is to break apart food particles into small, unbound, nutrients that can be efficiently absorbed. Enzymes are like workers on the assembly line in a factory: They do the work, but are directed by "supervisors," which are digestive hormones.

> There are more microorganisms than human cells in your body, and many of them are located in your large intestine.

There are several **hormones** such as *gastrin, insulin,* and *glucagon* that regulate digestion. Some hormones are produced in the stomach and the small intestine. Technically, hormones don't digest food, but they regulate the function of other cells, such as by controlling digestive secretions (gastric and pancreatic secretions) and regulating enzymes. They are stimulated by various dietary factors and their activity varies according to the digestive function required. Hormones influence gastrointestinal motility, stomach emptying, gallbladder contraction, insulin release, cell growth, intestinal absorption, and even hunger.

The hormone gastrin, for example, causes the release of gastric secretions that contain the enzyme gastric lipase. Gastric lipase contributes to the digestion of short- and medium-chain fatty acids, which are primarily found in human milk (consumed by infants) or in other dairy foods. These types of fatty acids are found less often in the diets of adults, as most of the dietary fats we consume contain long-chain fatty acids. Thus, gastric lipase is not a particularly important enzyme in adulthood. Gastrin also stimulates the secretion of HCl, increases gastric motility and emptying, and increases the tone of the LES.[18] Two other important hormones, insulin and glucagon, are produced in the pancreas and play important roles in your body. You will learn much more about these two hormones in Chapter 4.

Table 3.1 summarizes the functions of digestive secretions.

hormones Chemical substances that regulate, coordinate, or alter cellular activity.

Table 3.1
Functions of Digestive Secretions

Secretion	Secreted From	Function
Saliva	Glands in the mouth	Moistens food, eases swallowing, contains the enzyme salivary amylase
Mucus	Stomach, small and large intestines	Lubrication and coating of the internal mucosa to protect it from chemical or mechanical damage
Hydrochloric acid (HCl)	Stomach	Activation of enzymes that begin protein digestion
Bile	Liver (stored in the gallbladder)	Emulsifies fat in the small intestine
Bicarbonate	Pancreas	Raises pH and neutralizes stomach acid
Enzymes (amylases, proteases, and lipases)	Stomach, small intestine, pancreas	Chemicals that break down food into nutrient components that can be absorbed
Hormones (gastrin, secretin, cholecystokinin, and gastric inhibiting peptide)	Stomach, small intestine	Chemicals that regulate digestive activity, increase or decrease peristalsis, and stimulate various digestive secretions

bile A greenish yellow fluid made in the liver and concentrated and stored in the gallbladder. It helps emulsify fat and prepare it for digestion.

liver The largest gland of the body. The liver aids in digestive activity and is responsible for the metabolism of nutrients, detoxification of alcohol, and some nutrient storage.

pancreas Accessory organ for digestion that produces hormones and enzymes. It's connected to the duodenum via the bile duct.

The Liver, Gallbladder, and Pancreas Are Accessory Organs

Although food doesn't pass through the liver, gallbladder, or pancreas during digestion, these three accessory organs are still essential to the process. The liver, for example, makes **bile,** a greenish yellow liquid that is important for fat digestion, and the gallbladder concentrates and stores the bile. As mentioned, the pancreas makes the hormones insulin and glucagon, as well as some important digestive enzymes.

Weighing in at about three pounds, the **liver** is the largest gland in the body. It is so important that you couldn't survive without it. In addition to its key role of producing bile, the liver helps regulate the metabolism of carbohydrates, fats, and protein. The liver also stores several nutrients, including vitamins A, D, B_{12}, E, the minerals iron and copper, and the storage form of glucose in the body known as glycogen. The liver is also essential for processing and detoxifying alcohol. You'll learn about each of these functions in more depth in later chapters of this book. For our overview of digestion, we'll focus on the liver's role in bile production.

Bile has two main functions: fat breakdown and emulsification. Bile breaks up large fat globules into small, suspended fat droplets (about 1 millimeter in diameter).[19] This action enhances the absorption of fats because it increases the surface area exposed to fat-digesting enzymes (lipases). The breakdown of fat also increases the rate of fat digestion.

Bile also functions as an emulsifier. Emulsification is the dispersion of fat or the surrounding of fat with hydrophilic (water-soluble) and hydrophobic (fat-soluble) portions. This action is similar to the detergent activity of dishwashing soap on greasy dishes. Bile lowers the surface tension of the fat, thus allowing water-soluble enzymes to make contact with the fat and ultimately to proceed with fat digestion and absorption.

The liver produces about 500 to 1,000 ml (about 2 pints) of bile each day.[20] Bile consists of water, bile acids (and/or salts), cholesterol, phospholipids, pigments, and several ions. The salts and phospholipids in the bile are crucial for digestive function because of the role they play in fat emulsification. Bile salts also enhance the activity of digestive enzymes and the absorption of fatty acids, cholesterol, and fat-soluble vitamins. Bile is collected, drained, and released into the gallbladder.

The gallbladder is attached to the liver and stores approximately 30 to 50 ml (1 to 2 ounces) of concentrated bile at a time. Bile is released into the GI tract in response to the ingestion of fat. Bile aids in fat digestion but isn't digested itself. Whereas some compounds of bile leave the body in stool, the bile acids are reabsorbed and return to the liver to be reused in new bile.

The **pancreas** is an organ about the size and shape of your hand that produces hormones, including the two blood-regulating hormones, insulin and glucagon. It also produces digestive enzymes that are delivered into the duodenum. The pancreas has a duct that merges with the bile duct (from the gallbladder) and enters the duodenum through the common bile duct.

Sodium bicarbonate and several powerful, specific enzymes essential for the final stages of food digestion are produced in the pancreas. Sodium bicarbonate neutralizes the acidic chyme (raises the pH), creating a neutral environment. This protects certain enzymes that would otherwise become inactivated in an acidic environment.

Some of the most important enzymes produced by the pancreas are *amylase*, which digests carbohydrate; *lipase*, which digests fat; and *trypsin*, *chymotrypsin*, and

Table 3.2
Organs of the GI Tract and Their Functions

Organ	Function
Mouth	Begins breaking down food into smaller components through chewing
Esophagus	Transfers food from the mouth to the stomach
Stomach	Mixes food with digestive juices; breaks down some nutrients into smaller components
Small intestine	Completes digestion of food and absorbs nutrients through its walls
Large intestine	Absorbs water and some nutrients; passes waste products out of the body
Sphincters (LES, pyloric, ileocecal)	Keep swallowed food from returning to the esophagus, stomach, or small intestine
Accessory organs (liver, gallbladder, pancreas)	Release bile, enzymes, and hormones to help break down food or direct digestive activity

carboxypeptidase, which digest protein. The enzymes from the pancreas are responsible for the digestion of almost all (90 percent) of ingested fat, about half (50 percent) of all ingested protein, and half (50 percent) of all carbohydrates.[21]

Pancreatic secretion is regulated by various hormones. When acidic chyme enters the small intestine, the hormone secretin is produced by intestinal cells. Secretin stimulates the pancreas to secrete copious amounts of sodium bicarbonate and various digestive enzymes. When partially digested protein and fat enter the small intestine, the intestinal cells secrete the hormone cholecystokinin. This powerful hormone also stimulates the pancreas to secrete digestive enzymes, slows down gastric motility (which controls the pace of digestion), and contributes to meal satisfaction.

Table 3.2 summarizes the organs of the GI tract and their functions.

The Take-Home Message In the mouth, saliva mixes with food during chewing, moistening it and making it easier to swallow. Swallowed food that has mixed with digestive juices in the stomach becomes chyme. Maximum digestion and absorption occur through the villi and microvilli in the small intestine. Undigested residue next enters the large intestine, where additional absorption of water and electrolytes occurs. Eventually, the remnants of digestion reach the anus and exit the body in stool. Enzymes, hormones, and bile help break down food and regulate digestion. The liver, gallbladder, and pancreas are important accessory organs. The liver produces bile and the gallbladder concentrates and stores it. The pancreas produces enzymes and hormones.

What Other Body Systems Affect Your Use of Nutrients?

The human body is a well-coordinated organism. Each of us eats, drinks, sleeps, and lives a normal existence without too much thought to what we are consuming. We don't have to constantly worry about keeping ourselves nourished, or distributing nutrients to our cells, because numerous body systems are doing this work for us. Among the systems that remind us to eat, distribute nutrients in our bodies, and excrete waste products are the nervous system, the circulatory and lymphatic systems, and the excretory system.

The Nervous System Stimulates Your Appetite

The main role of the nervous system in keeping you nourished is to let you know when you need to eat and drink and when to stop. Your brain, with the help of hormones, has a central role in communicating and interpreting the message of hunger and encouraging you to seek food. For example, when your stomach is empty, the hormone ghrelin signals your brain to eat. If you ignore the signals of hunger or thirst sent by your nervous system, you may experience a headache, dizziness, or weakness. The nervous system helps each of us make daily decisions regarding what to eat, when to eat, where to eat, and, perhaps most important, when to stop eating.

The Circulatory System Distributes Nutrients through Your Blood

The blood is the body's primary transport system, shuttling oxygen, nutrients, hormones, and waste products throughout the body. The oxygen-rich blood that the heart receives from the lungs is pumped from the right side of the heart out to the body for its use (Figure 3.8). During digestion, the blood picks up nutrients through the capillary walls in the GI tract, transports them to your liver, and eventually to the cells of your body. Without the circulatory system, nutrients that you eat would not reach your cells. Equally important, the blood removes carbon dioxide, excess water, and waste products from the cells and brings these substances to the lungs (carbon dioxide) and kidneys (water, waste products) for excretion (see below).

The Lymphatic System Distributes Some Nutrients through Your Lymph

The lymphatic system is a complex network of capillaries, small vessels, valves, nodes, and ducts that helps maintain the internal fluid environment. Lymph contains white blood cells that aid your immune system. The lymph also transports digested fat-soluble vitamins and fat from the intestinal tract to your blood. The lymph eventually connects with the blood near the heart.

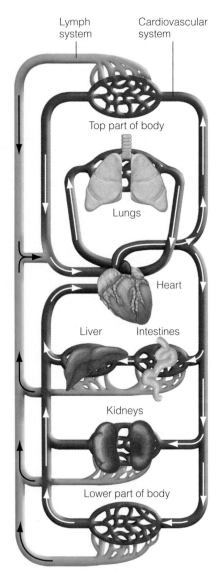

Lymph system

Cardiovascular system

Top part of body

Lungs

Heart

Liver

Intestines

Kidneys

Lower part of body

Figure 3.8 The Circulatory and Lymphatic Systems
Blood and lymph are fluids that circulate throughout the body. They both distribute nutrients to cells and blood also picks up waste products from cells and delivers them to the kidneys for eventual excretion.

The Excretory System Passes Urine Out of the Body

The excretory system eliminates wastes from the circulatory system. After the cells have gleaned the nutrients and other useful metabolic components they need, waste products accumulate. The kidneys filter the blood allowing the waste products to be excreted via urine and out of your body (Figure 3.9).

The Take-Home Message In addition to the digestive system, other body systems help us use the nutrients we take in from foods. The nervous system lets us know when we need to eat or drink, the blood and lymph systems deliver absorbed nutrients to cells, and the excretory system helps filter and eliminate waste products from the blood.

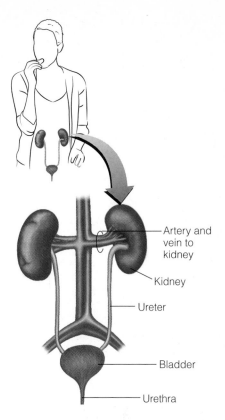

Figure 3.9 The Excretory System
Water and waste products from cells are filtered from your blood in the kidneys and expelled from your body in urine.

What Are Some Common Digestive Disorders?

Generally, the digestive tract works just fine. As a matter of fact, it doesn't usually require tinkering or medications to be healthy. But sometimes the digestive tract gets "off track" and the resulting symptoms can quickly catch your attention. Some of the problems are minor, like occasional heartburn or indigestion; other problems are very serious, like ulcers or colon cancer.

Disorders of the Mouth and Esophagus

Oral health involves healthy teeth, gums, and supporting tissue. Maintaining a healthy oral environment is important because these tissues are used to bite, chew, taste, speak, smile, swallow, and communicate through facial expressions. Properly nourishing yourself can be difficult if you have chronic oral disease or extensive dental problems. There are many oral diseases, but we will only review some of the most common ones in this section.

Gingivitis and Periodontal Disease

In addition to tooth decay, which we'll discuss in depth in Chapter 4, common oral health problems include gingivitis and periodontal disease. Gingivitis is an early form of periodontal disease that involves gum swelling, bleeding, and oral pain. Periodontal disease is an inflammation of the gums that leads to multiple dental diseases. It is caused by infections or by plaque that adheres to the surface of the teeth, and is a common problem for adults over age 35.[22] Periodontitis results in a gradual loss of teeth as they loosen or partially separate from the gums and jawbone. Even though these conditions are serious, they are treatable with various dental procedures, optimal food choices, and excellent oral hygiene.

Other oral health problems include dry mouth, inflamed oral tissue, cold sores, soft tissue ulceration, oral cancers, fungal infections, or various abnormalities of the tongue. Certain diseases such as diabetes, autoimmune conditions, AIDS, and various cancer therapies can also have a major impact on oral health. A range of treatment strategies, various dietary modifications, and dental specialists can provide care and/or specialized intervention strategies for these conditions.

Swallowing Problems

Under some circumstances the ability to swallow is compromised. Difficult swallowing, or **dysphagia,** can have mechanical causes such as tumors, scar tissue, obstruction, cancer, trauma, or other barriers in the throat. Dysphagia can also result from nerve damage or when individuals suffer from a stroke.

Swallowing problems can lead to malnutrition, respiratory problems, tooth decay, nasal regurgitation, and compromised health. Various health care professionals are trained to help a person overcome swallowing difficulties.

Esophageal Problems

Several esophageal problems can lead to annoying symptoms such as belching, hiccups, burning sensations, or uncomfortable feelings of fullness. Some serious esophageal problems include cancer, obstruction from tumors, faulty nerve impulses, severe inflammation, and abnormal sphincter function.

One of the most common problems involving the esophagus is **heartburn,** or *reflux disease.* About 7 percent of the population experience daily heartburn, about 20 percent of adults report frequent heartburn, and 25 to 35 percent of adults have occasional symptoms.[23] Collectively, this adds up to millions of people experiencing heartburn symptoms.

Heartburn, also known as indigestion or acid reflux, is caused by hydrochloric acid flowing from the stomach back into the esophagus or even the throat. The acid causes a lingering, unpleasant, sour taste in the mouth. Other symptoms include nausea, bloating, belching, a vague burning sensation, or an uncomfortable feeling of fullness. Chronic heartburn can lead to a condition called **gastroesophageal reflux disease,** or **GERD.**

A weak LES is often the culprit in HCl reflux, because it sometimes permits this backflow of stomach fluids into the esophagus. Certain foods, including chocolate, fried or fatty foods, coffee, soda, onions, and garlic, seem to be associated with this condition.[24] Lifestyle factors also play a role. For example, smoking cigarettes, drinking alcohol, wearing tight-fitting clothes, being overweight or obese, eating large evening meals, and reclining after eating tend to cause or worsen the condition. If dietary changes and behavior modification are insufficient to relieve the heartburn, over-the-counter antacids or prescription drugs may help. In rare circumstances, surgical intervention is required to treat severe, unrelenting heartburn.

Esophageal cancer is another medical condition that has serious consequences. According to the National Cancer Institute, esophageal cancer is one of the most common cancers of the digestive tract, and the seventh leading cause of cancer-related deaths worldwide. In the United States, this type of cancer is typically found among individuals older than 50 years, men, those who live in urban areas, long-term smokers, and heavy drinkers.[25] Treatments include surgery, radiation, and chemotherapy.

dysphagia Difficult swallowing.

heartburn A burning sensation originating in the esophagus. Heartburn is usually caused by the reflux of gastric contents from the stomach into the esophagus. Chronic heartburn can lead to **gastroesophageal reflux disease (GERD).**

Disorders of the Stomach

Stomach problems can range from the trivial, like an occasional stomachache, to life-threatening complications such as bleeding ulcers or stomach cancer.

At some point in time, everyone has had a stomachache. Common causes include overeating, gastric bloating, or eating too fast. Other possible causes include eating foods that are high in fat or fiber, lactose intolerance, or swallowing air while eating.

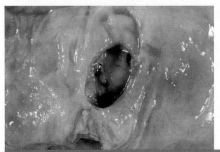 

(Left) An ulcer is created when the mucosal lining of the GI tract erodes or breaks. (Right) Gallstones result from the crystallization of salts and other compounds in bile. Luckily, most don't get this large.

More serious causes of a stomachache include the flu or consuming food or water that is contaminated with bacteria. Stomach flu or **gastroenteritis** is an inflammation of the stomach or intestines caused by a virus or bacteria. Flu symptoms include nausea, vomiting, diarrhea, and abdominal cramping. Sometimes the problem requires medical intervention, but usually rest, oral rehydration therapy, and a soft-food diet will help with the symptoms of this type of flu.

Peptic ulcers occur in the lower region of the stomach.[26] Ulcers are a sore or erosion in the stomach or intestinal lining caused by drugs, alcohol, or more often, a bacterium. Symptoms of an ulcer include abdominal pain, vomiting, fatigue, bleeding, and general weakness. Medical treatments may consist of prescription drugs and dietary recommendations, such as limiting alcohol and caffeine-containing beverages, and/or restricting spices and acidic foods.

Gallbladder Disease

One common problem of an unhealthy gallbladder is the presence of **gallstones.** Most people with gallstones have abnormally thick bile, and the bile is high in cholesterol and low in bile acids. Over an extended period of time, the high-cholesterol bile forms crystals, then sludge, and finally gallstones. Some individuals with gallstones experience no pain or mild pain. Others have severe pain accompanied by fever, nausea, vomiting, cramps, and obstruction of the bile duct.

Medical treatment for gallstones may involve surgery to remove the gallbladder, prescription medicine to dissolve the stones, shock-wave therapy (a type of ultrasound treatment) to break them up, or a combination of therapies. If surgery is required to remove the gallbladder, patients typically recover quickly. After gallbladder removal surgery, the anatomy of the biliary tract adapts. The liver continues to produce the bile and secrete it directly into the duodenum. Interestingly, the remaining bile duct dilates, forming a "simulated pouch" that works in a manner very similar to the original gallbladder.

Disorders of the Intestines

The rumbling stomach, or *borborygmus,* that Rachel experienced at the beginning of this chapter isn't really a disorder (though if it's accompanied by pain or vomiting, it can be a sign of a larger problem, such as a mechanical obstruction).[27] Rather, the gurgling is due to the gas and air pockets that form as stomach contents are pushed through

gastroenteritis Formal term for "stomach flu." Caused by virus or bacteria and results in inflammation of the stomach and/or intestines.

peptic ulcers Sores, erosions, or breaks in the mucosal lining of the stomach.

gallstones Small, hard, crystalline structures formed in the gallbladder or bile duct due to abnormally thick bile.

the GI tract. The best way to quiet the noise is to eat or drink something, or to apply mild pressure to the abdomen.

More serious small and large intestine problems tend to involve nutrient malabsorption, which can cause severe health consequences. Celiac disease, gastroenteritis, duodenal ulcers, intestinal enzyme deficiencies, and short bowel syndrome are all examples of intestinal disorders (see the boxed feature "Celiac Disease: An Issue of Absorption" on page 79). The symptoms of these diseases vary, but they include abdominal pain, nausea, vomiting, bloating, loss of appetite, diarrhea, anxiety, weight loss, and fatigue. The medical problems that have to be addressed include various anemias, gastrointestinal blockages, inflammation, malnutrition, growth failure, vitamin and mineral deficiencies, and other medically complicated challenges.

Disorders of the colon include constipation, diarrhea, and irritable bowel syndrome. **Constipation** is caused by excessively slow movements of the undigested residue through the colon, and is often due to insufficient fiber or water intake. Consuming an adequate amount of dietary fiber daily can help prevent constipation. Stress, inactivity, or various illnesses can also lead to constipation. It is usually treated with a high-fiber, high-liquid diet. Daily exercise, establishing eating and resting routines, and using over-the-counter stool softeners are usually recommended to treat this condition.

Diarrhea is the passage of frequent, watery, loose stools. It is considered more serious than constipation because of the loss of fluids and electrolytes. If the diarrhea continues for an extended period of time, you may malabsorb additional nutrients, which can lead to malnutrition. There are many causes of diarrhea, including contaminated water, various microorganisms, stress, or excessive fiber intake. Diarrhea is generally treated with fluid and electrolyte replacement. Most physicians identify the cause(s) of the diarrhea in addition to treating the symptoms.

Irritable bowel syndrome (IBS) is a functional disorder that involves changes in colon rhythm; it is not an actual disease. People with IBS do not have tissue damage, inflammation, or immunologic involvement of the colon.[28] They do, however, overrespond to colon stimuli. This results in alternating patterns of diarrhea, constipation, and abdominal pain. The exact cause of IBS is unknown, but low-fiber diets, stress, consumption of irritating foods, and intestinal motility disorders are all suspected factors.[29] Medical management includes dietary modification, stress management, and occasional use of prescription drugs.

Colon cancer is one of the leading forms of cancer and the second leading cause of cancer deaths. Fortunately, colon cancer is one of the most curable forms of cancer, if it is detected in the early stages.

Colon cancer often begins with polyps on the lining of the colon. They vary in size from that of a small pea to that of a mushroom or plum. The good news is that polyps can be removed surgically, and they are often small and benign. If the polyps are not removed or change to cancerous tumors, colon cancer can be difficult to cure.

Individuals diagnosed with colon cancer may require radiation therapy, chemotherapy, and surgery to remove part of the colon or the entire colon. After surgery, patients are given dietary advice regarding the foods that would be the most comfortable to eat. Survival rates vary depending on the individual's age, health, treatment response, and stage of cancer diagnosis.

Table 3.3 on page 80 summarizes these common digestive disorders.

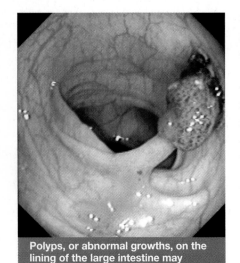
Polyps, or abnormal growths, on the lining of the large intestine may indicate early stages of colon cancer.

constipation Difficulty in passing stools.

diarrhea Frequent, loose, watery stools.

irritable bowel syndrome (IBS) A functional disorder that involves changes in colon rhythm.

Celiac Disease: An Issue of Absorption

One of the more serious malabsorption conditions to occur in the small intestine is **celiac disease.** A healthy small intestine contains the numerous villi and microvilli that efficiently and exhaustively absorb nutrients from food. In some people, the lining of the small intestine flattens out due to an autoimmune reaction to gluten, a protein found in wheat and other grains. This reduces the intestine's ability to absorb nutrients. The exact cause of celiac disease is unknown, but it is believed to be genetic, and the risk for the disease may be decreased by breast-feeding rather than bottle-feeding infants.

Celiac disease is more common among people of European descent. Since many Americans are descendants of European nationalities, this autoimmune disease afflicts many Americans. One out of 133 people is affected by celiac disease in the United States. This is a larger percentage than previously thought.

The classic celiac symptoms include reoccurring abdominal bloating, cramping, diarrhea, gas, fatty and foul-smelling stools, weight loss, anemia, fatigue, bone

celiac disease An illness of the small intestine that involves the inability to digest the protein gluten.

or joint pain, and even a painful skin rash. Depending on the length of time between symptom development and diagnosis, the complications from celiac disease can be serious. They include increased incidence of osteoporosis from poor calcium absorption, diminished growth because of nutrient malabsorption, and even seizures due to inadequate folate absorption.

Some people develop the symptoms of celiac disease in infancy or childhood. Others develop the disease later in life, after being misdiagnosed with irritable bowel syndrome or various food intolerances. Celiac disease is sometimes detected or caused by surgery, pregnancy, a viral infection, or severe emotional stress. Diagnosing celiac disease is sometimes difficult because it resembles other very similar malabsorption diseases.

The only treatment for celiac disease is a gluten-free diet. This should stop the symptoms from progressing, allow the intestines to heal, and prevent further damage. The symptoms often improve within a few days after beginning the gluten-free diet. Within three to six months, the absorption area of the intestinal tract often returns to normal status, if the diet is faithfully followed. Depending on the age at diagnosis and the severity of the

disease, there may be some permanent health problems such as delayed or stunted growth.

Adhering to a gluten-free diet, which means avoiding breads, pasta, and cereals, among other foods, can be challenging. However, there are many gluten-free foods to choose from, such as meat, milk, eggs, fruit, and vegetables. These foods are permissible in any quantity. Rice, potatoes, corn, and beans are also acceptable because they do not contain gluten. Specially formulated gluten-free breads, pasta, and cereal products are also available in many supermarkets.

The most problematic feature of the diet is avoiding the multiple foods that contain "latent," or hidden, sources of gluten. Individuals with celiac disease need to read food labels.

Celiac disease is a manageable condition. Individuals with celiac disease can live normal lives. They can learn about their condition by talking to health care professionals. Researchers are currently working to determine the exact component in gluten that causes celiac disease, and to develop enzymes that would destroy these immunotoxic peptides.

The Take-Home Message Gastrointestinal diseases and digestive disorders include less serious conditions, like heartburn (GERD), indigestion, and stomach flu, to more serious conditions, such as esophageal cancer and gastric ulcers. Disorders of the small intestine can be the most dangerous, as they may result in malabsorption and/or malnutrition. Constipation, diarrhea, and irritable bowel syndrome are all disorders of the large intestine. Colon cancer typically begins with polyps on the intestinal lining. If caught early, colon cancer is highly curable, but less so during its later stages.

Table 3.3

Common Digestive Disorders

Site	Disorder	Symptoms	Causes	Treatment
Esophagus and stomach	Gastrointestinal reflux disease (GERD)	Sore throat, burning sensation in the chest (heartburn)	Poor eating habits; overeating; other lifestyle choices	Eat smaller meals; eat more slowly; decrease fat and/or alcohol intake; quit smoking
Stomach or small intestine	Gastric and duodenal ulcers	Bleeding, pain, vomiting, fatigue, weakness	Multiple causes	Prescription drugs and an as-tolerated diet
Gallbladder	Gallstones	Cramps, bloating, intense abdominal pain, diarrhea	The concentration of high-cholesterol containing bile that crystallizes and forms stones in the duct.	Gallbladder removal, medication, or shock-wave therapy
Small intestine	Celiac disease	Malabsorption	Error of gluten metabolism	Gluten-free diet
Large intestine	Constipation	Cramping, bloated uncomfortable feeling in abdomen	Too little water or too little fiber; inactivity	More water, fiber, and exercise
Large intestine	Diarrhea	Too-frequent bowel movements	Multiple causes	Water and electrolyte replacement
Large intestine	Irritable bowel syndrome (IBS)	Diarrhea and constipation in alternating sequence; pain	Unknown cause(s); stress worsens the condition	Self-management with fiber therapy, stress relief, and good sleep habits
Large intestine	Colon cancer	Symptoms are often silent. May include weight loss, internal bleeding, iron-deficiency anemia, fatigue.	Multiple causes (genetics, various colon diseases, smoking, exposure to dietary carcinogens)	Radiation therapy, chemotherapy, surgery

Putting It All Together

You may be familiar with the saying, "Food is food, until you swallow it; then it becomes nutrition." Your digestive tract can only use the food you consume, and your body builds your health around the food choices you make.

You can use the guidelines you read about in Chapter 2, including the DRIs and MyPyramid, to make healthful food choices and ensure that you receive adequate amounts of the essential nutrients without taking in too many calories. Food choice, however, is a multifaceted effort. What we should eat, actually eat, and prefer to eat are sometimes conflicting decisions. Hopefully, the more you learn, the more healthful your choices will be.

In the next few chapters, you will learn more about the individual categories of nutrients that make up a healthy diet, and their functions in the body. As you read about carbohydrates, fat, proteins, vitamins, minerals, and water, keep in mind that they are all digested in your GI tract, distributed throughout your body by your blood and lymph, provide energy to your individual cells, and regulate numerous critical processes.

Two Points of View

How Effective Is the Weight-Loss Drug Orlistat?

The weight-loss drug orlistat (Xenical), which works by reducing fat absorption in the GI tract, is now available in a lower-dose, over-the-counter form. Is the drug effective? Are there risks to using it? Two experts share their views.

James Anderson, MD

Professor, Medicine and Clinical Nutrition, University of Kentucky

James Anderson, MD, teaches at the University of Kentucky and directs the university's Health Management Resources Weight Management Program. His research interests relate to diabetes, blood lipid disorders, obesity, and nutrition. Currently, he is investigating novel ways to reduce blood cholesterol, the use of soy protein in diabetes, new treatment approaches for obesity, and the role of antioxidants in atherosclerosis.

Q: What is the goal of orlistat and how does the drug work?

A: Orlistat works by limiting the body's absorption of dietary fat. It inhibits absorption of approximately 25 percent of the fat in the food that a person eats. Xenical, the brand name for orlistat, is available by prescription at 120 milligrams for recommended use three times daily before meals. An over-the-counter version, known as Alli, is available in low-dose 60 milligrams capsules.

The goal of Alli is to fill the void in over-the-counter options by providing a boost to weight-loss efforts that include a low-fat, reduced-calorie diet with physical activity. Orlistat helps people lose 50 percent more weight than dieting alone. Instead of losing 10 pounds by dieting, with the aid of orlistat, one can lose 15 pounds.

Q: What are the main benefits associated with orlistat?

A: Orlistat has a long history of safe and effective use, with more than 25 million patient treatments as a prescription medication in 145 countries. Alli is the only safe and effective over-the-counter weight-loss drug for adults (18 years or older). This is important because other over-the-counter weight-loss products are not approved by the FDA. The primary benefit of over-the-counter orlistat will be that it helps provide significantly more weight loss—up to 50 percent more—than a reduced-calorie diet alone. In addition, clinical data on orlistat use has shown improvements in conditions associated with being overweight, such as elevated cholesterol levels and blood pressure.

Q: What are the primary risks or side effects of orlistat?

A: Some people experience side effects or treatment effects which are associated with how the drug works—since the drug inhibits absorption of fat, the undigested fat must pass

(continued)

Madelyn Fernstrom, PhD, CNS

Founder and Director, University of Pittsburgh Medical Center, Weight Management Center

Madelyn Fernstrom, PhD, CNS, is associate director of the Center for Nutrition at the University of Pittsburgh Medical Center. She is also an associate professor of psychiatry, epidemiology, and surgery at the University of Pittsburgh School of Medicine. For more than 25 years, Dr. Fernstrom has devoted herself to clinical and laboratory work, studying and treating obesity and eating disorders.

Q: What is the goal of orlistat and how does the drug work?

A: Orlistat is a weight-loss medication that the FDA has approved for long-term (up to two years) use. Orlistat blocks fat absorption—up to one-third of the fat in the food that you ingest. The fat passes through the digestive tract and is eliminated. The goal of orlistat is to help people reduce their fat intake. Fat is the most dense of the "big three" nutrients, so the easy way to decrease the total number of calories you eat is to cut down on the fat. It's a sort of shortcut. If you eat in restaurants a lot, or can't recognize hidden fat in food, this can help you in some cases.

Q: What are the main benefits associated with orlistat?

A: In people for whom fat makes up more than 30 percent of their diet, orlistat may help lower fat intake and therefore aid in weight loss. Orlistat causes side effects that are meant to encourage you to eat less fat. If you eat a diet too high in fat, the results of that unabsorbed fat can be stomach cramping, bloating, diarrhea, and anal leakage. These effects last as long as you're taking the drug. They don't go away over time. The drug works as a negative reinforcer. I've seen dozens of patients come into the clinic and say, "I've got terrible diarrhea, and I can't tolerate this medication." They don't understand that it's supposed to work that way.

Q: What are the primary risks or side effects of orlistat?

A: The side effects are as I described earlier: stomach cramping, bloating, diarrhea, and anal leakage. Those aren't really "side effects," though. With this medication, the side effects are also the main effect. These physical effects let you know that you've been eating too much fat, and that the drug is working.

(continued)

How Effective Is the Weight-Loss Drug Orlistat?, continued

James Anderson, MD, continued

through the body. These effects, which were experienced by about half of subjects in clinical trials, may include bowel changes such as loose and more frequent stools, gas with oily spotting, and urgent bowel movements. The treatment effects are very manageable if users adhere to the recommended reduced-calorie, low-fat diet. In controlled clinical trials, only 3 percent of subjects stopped using orlistat due to treatment effects. Users often report that these treatment effects provide a signal that they had eaten too much fat and serve as a guide to consume less fat. In addition, according to data from clinical trials, patient satisfaction with weight loss from orlistat was significantly higher than in the group who lost weight from dieting alone.

Anyone who has had an organ transplant or is taking cyclosporine, has problems absorbing food, or is not overweight should *not* take orlistat. In addition, anyone taking warfarin, diabetes medications, or other weight-loss medications should talk to their doctor or pharmacist prior to taking orlistat. Since orlistat can reduce the absorption of some vitamins, it is recommended that individuals take a multivitamin daily when using orlistat.

Q: Is it safe to inhibit the absorption of fat in the way that orlistat does?

A: Yes, orlistat is the most comprehensively studied and best understood weight-loss medication ever. Its safety and efficacy have been well established through data from more than 100 clinical studies involving more than 30,000 patients. Unlike other products on the market that claim to have "fat-blocking" effects, orlistat works by limiting the body's absorption of dietary fat. Because most people don't seek or receive advice about weight control from their doctor, they often rely on weight-loss products that aren't proven safe or effective by the FDA. Many of these dietary supplements may act on the central nervous system (CNS) and are systemically absorbed through the bloodstream. They can be associated with CNS side effects (e.g., seizure, stroke, and anxiety) or systemic side effects (e.g., heart palpitations, elevated blood pressure, and heart problems). Orlistat, on the other hand, has no known effect on the CNS or the cardiovascular system.

Q: Overall, do the benefits of orlistat outweigh the risks? What special considerations should someone take into account before using orlistat?

A: The potential benefits of orlistat far exceed the potential risks. By limiting the absorption of dietary fat, orlistat provides significantly more weight loss than dieting alone. It also encourages users to modify their diet and behavior and to become more aware of fat and caloric contents in foods and reduce their intake.

Madelyn Fernstrom, PhD, CNS, continued

People with any kind of irritable bowel syndrome or any general GI tract disturbance should not take orlistat. But there are very few serious medical risks, because it's a very benign compound. That's why the FDA approved the sale of an over-the-counter version.

Q: Is it safe to inhibit the absorption of fat in the way that orlistat does?

A: Yes. There is a slight risk of decline in absorption of fat-soluble vitamins. But you can just take a vitamin and mineral supplement outside of the time you're taking orlistat. The drug only acts at the time of the meal you take it with, for about two hours. If you have gastrointestinal disturbance after taking the drug, you need to revisit your lifestyle and think about what you're eating. If you have diarrhea and stomach upset, that's a wake-up call that you're eating too much fat.

Q: Overall, do the benefits of orlistat outweigh the risks? What special considerations should someone take into account before using orlistat?

A: For people who struggle with keeping their fat intake below 30 percent, it can have some benefit. About 30 percent of those who use it may see increased weight loss of about 15 to 20 percent. But orlistat is not for everyone. From what we've seen in our clinical experience, people really don't like it. For many people, the drug won't be effective because too much fat in their diet isn't the problem—they've already cut their fat intake down. People tend to look for help with hunger and fullness regulation, not fat intake. Orlistat does nothing for feelings of hunger and fullness. And remember, it doesn't help with calories that don't come from fat. I spoke with one person who actually gained weight while taking orlistat, because she had just replaced her high-fat calories with calories from proteins and carbs.

There's also an issue of cost. Xenical (the brand name) is expensive and isn't typically covered by insurance. About 95 percent of the people who use it will experience 5 percent more weight loss, which isn't all that much. Imagine a 200-pound person going to 190 pounds. That may be considered clinically effective, but in a practical sense, it's really not, especially when you factor in the cost. The FDA's standard for "clinically effective" is 5 percent weight loss. But that's not significant enough for most people.

(continued)

How Effective Is the Weight-Loss Drug Orlistat?, continued

James Anderson, MD, continued

It's also important to note that one's readiness and commitment to lose weight is vital because dieting is hard work—there's no "quick fix." A low-fat/reduced-calorie diet and increased physical activity are critical to any weight-control program intended to sustain weight loss. One needs to have realistic expectations for weight loss, and one should also recognize the health benefit of even modest weight loss. Small steps make big progress.

Diving into Digestion

You just ate a hamburger on a whole-wheat bun for lunch. What happens to the food during the digestive process? Visit www.aw-bc.com/blake and trace the path of your meal through your digestive system!

How Do Your Eating Habits Stack Up?

What are your less-than-healthy eating habits? Visit www.aw-bc.com/blake and learn how your eating habits measure up.

The Top Ten Points to Remember

1. There are five categories of taste—sweet, salty, sour, bitter, and savory (umami)—but there are thousands of aromas and flavors. Hunger and thirst alert you to your basic physical need to take in food and fluid. Appetite is less about physical need and more about the psychological desire to take in foods.
2. Digestion is the process of breaking down food into absorbable nutrients. Digestion takes place in the organs of the GI tract—particularly in the stomach, small intestine, and large intestine.
3. There are both mechanical and chemical aspects of digestion. Mechanical digestion includes chewing and peristalsis. Chemical digestion involves mixing consumed food with enzymes and gastric juices to break it down.
4. Digestion begins in the mouth as chewing breaks down food and mixes it with saliva. Swallowing is a coordinated process that involves the mouth, throat, and esophagus. The stomach mixes food with enzymes and stores it before propelling it into the small intestine, where most digestion and absorption occurs. The walls of the small intestine are covered with villi, which greatly increase its surface area and facilitate absorption. The large intestine absorbs water and some nutrients, before pushing waste through the colon and out of the body via the anus. Several sphincters control entry and exit of food and chyme through the organs of the GI tract.

5. Hydrochloric acid, hormones, enzymes, bile, and bicarbonate are all necessary for efficient digestion. Hydrochloric acid is a gastric juice that helps prepare the food for further digestion. Hormones are chemical messengers that direct activities in the body. Hormones direct enzymes that do the actual work of facilitating reactions. Bile is produced in the liver and stored in the gallbladder and is particularly important for fat digestion.

6. In addition to producing bile, the liver processes and metabolizes several nutrients after they have been digested and absorbed. The liver also stores several nutrients, and plays an important role in detoxifying alcohol. The gallbladder stores concentrated forms of bile. The pancreas produces both hormones and enzymes that play roles in digestion.

7. Body systems other than the digestive system help you use the nutrients you eat. Your nervous system lets you know when you are hungry or thirsty. Your circulatory and lymph systems distribute nutrients to all your cells, and the excretory system filters waste products from the blood and passes them out of the body in urine.

8. Digestive disorders can range from the trivial, such as an occasional stomachache, to the serious conditions of ulcers and cancer. Heartburn is the layman's term for the uncomfortable sensation of stomach acid returning to the esophagus or throat. A primary cause of heartburn is poor eating habits and other lifestyle choices. Peptic ulcers are sores or breaks in the lining of the stomach, or upper part of the small intestine. Colon cancer begins with polyps on the intestinal lining and is very treatable if caught early.

9. Constipation is a generally benign condition of sluggish colon movements commonly caused by a low-fiber, low-fluid diet. Diarrhea is a potentially serious and distressing condition characterized by frequent, loose, and watery stools. It is often caused by exposure to microorganisms in food or water.

10. Celiac disease is a disorder of the small intestine that can be treated with a gluten-free diet. Those with irritable bowel syndrome experience difficulty establishing and sustaining a normal rhythm in their colon and often alternate between bouts of diarrhea and constipation.

Test Your Knowledge

1. The tastes you can perceive in your mouth are salty, sweet, bitter, savory (umami), and
   a. cold.
   b. sour.
   c. fruity.
   d. stony.

2. _____ is the process that breaks down food into absorbable units.
   a. Circulation
   b. Digestion
   c. Absorption
   d. Excretion

3. Digestion begins in the
   a. liver.
   b. stomach.
   c. mouth.
   d. colon.

4. The name of the protective tissue that covers the trachea when you swallow is the
   a. esophagus.
   b. tongue.
   c. pharynx.
   d. epiglottis.

5. What causes heartburn?
   a. improper relaxation of the lower esophageal sphincter
   b. improper contraction of the lower esophageal sphincter
   c. improper and rapid swallowing
   d. improper breathing and chest congestion

6. The name of the secretion produced in the stomach that helps break down protein and activates pepsin is
   a. hydrochloric acid.
   b. amylase.
   c. bile.
   d. gastrin.

7. The sphincter that separates the stomach from the duodenum is the
   a. lower esophageal sphincter.
   b. ileocecal sphincter.
   c. pyloric sphincter.
   d. colon sphincter.

8. The name of the fat-digesting enzyme produced in the pancreas is the
   a. amylase.
   b. protease.
   c. lipase.
   d. maltase.
9. What is the purpose of the gallbladder?
   a. to make bile
   b. to modify bile so it becomes liquid
   c. to digest bile
   d. to concentrate and store bile
10. Which of the following is true regarding the small intestine?
   a. The small intestine has a vast digestive surface area.
   b. The small intestine has minimal digestive surface area.
   c. The small intestine has access to lymph tissue, but not to the bloodstream.
   d. The small intestine is unimportant in the process of digestion.

Answers

1. (b) Sour is the fifth type of taste bud in your mouth. Cold, fruity, and stony are not categories of taste.
2. (b) Digestion. Circulation is the process of distributing blood or lymph throughout the body. Absorption is the process of pulling nutrients from the GI tract into the body. Excretion is the passing of waste products out of the body.
3. (c) Digestion begins in the mouth where chewing starts breaking food down and mixing it with saliva and enzymes. The liver is an accessory organ to digestion. The stomach and colon (part of the large intestine) are organs in the GI tract.
4. (d) Epiglottis. The esophagus is a tube that connects your mouth with your stomach. The tongue is a muscle that pushes food to the back of the mouth into the pharynx. The pharynx is a chamber that food passes through just before being swallowed.
5. (a) Heartburn occurs when the lower esophageal sphincter allows acid from the stomach back into the esophagus.
6. (a) Hydrochloric acid (HCl) is part of the gastric juices produced in the stomach that activates pepsin, breaks down connective tissue in meat, and destroys some ingested microorganisms. Amylase is an enzyme in the mouth that begins breaking down carbohydrates. Bile is made by the liver and emulsifies fat. Gastrin is a hormone in the stomach that stimulates digestive activity.
7. (c) The pyloric sphincter allows chyme to pass from the bottom of the stomach to the beginning of the duodenum, the first part of the small intestine. The ileocecal sphincter separates the ileum from the colon. The colon sphincter is also called the anal sphincter and it is the last part of the GI tract.
8. (c) Lipase. Amylase is a carbohydrate-digesting enzyme, protease is a protein-digesting enzyme, and maltase digests the sugar, maltose.
9. (d) Bile is concentrated and stored in the gallbladder. The liver makes the bile in dilute, liquid form. Bile is not digested; rather, it circulates through the digestive tract.
10. (a) With numerous villi and microvilli along its interior wall, the small intestine indeed has a vast surface area which enhances digestion. Nutrients are absorbed through these projections and are transported through the blood and lymph throughout the body. The small intestine is critical to the process of digestion.

Web Support

- To find out more about various conditions involving the GI tract, visit http://personalmd.com
- To find out more about colon cancer, go to http://colonsurgeryinfo.com
- To learn more about cancer and the various treatment options or to contact a cancer information specialist with questions about cancer, visit www.cancercenter.com
- To learn about numerous types of cancer, cancer treatments, and preparation for treatment, visit www.oncologychannel.com
- Go to www.medicinenet.com to learn more about GI concerns, disease, conditions, medicines, procedures, and treatments
- Visit the National Library of Medicine for an abundant Internet resource for health care professionals, the public, researchers, and librarians at www.nlm.nih.gov
- For more information about irritable bowel syndrome, go to www.ibs-research-update.org.uk/ibs/digestion1ie4.html
- To learn more about various digestive diseases, go to http://digestive.niddk.nih.gov

4

Carbo

1. You don't **need** to eat carbohydrates. T/F

2. People who are **lactose intolerant** need to avoid all dairy products. T/F

3. Carbohydrates make you **fat.** T/F

4. Sugar causes **cavities.** T/F

5. **Honey** is more nutritious than sugar. T/F

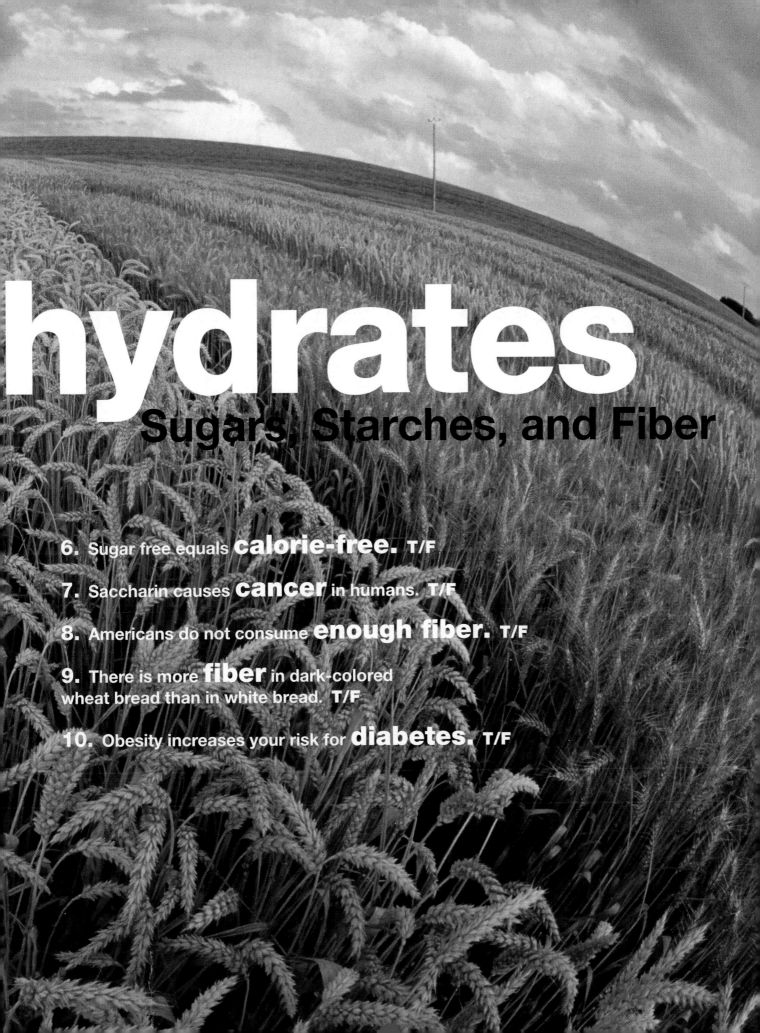

hydrates
Sugars, Starches, and Fiber

6. Sugar free equals **calorie-free.** T/F

7. Saccharin causes **cancer** in humans. T/F

8. Americans do not consume **enough fiber.** T/F

9. There is more **fiber** in dark-colored wheat bread than in white bread. T/F

10. Obesity increases your risk for **diabetes.** T/F

Adam is a star hockey center on his college team, and skates a minimum of two hours a day (and up to four hours daily when the team is in the throes of a hockey tournament). When not on the ice, Adam is in the library maintaining a 3.7 GPA. Besides being a hockey genius, Adam has been an insulin-dependent, type 1 diabetic ever since he laced up his first pair of skates at age two.

Adjusting his daily diet and insulin injections to his rigorous exercise schedule is no small feat. "Once when I was in a hockey league in high school, I buckled on the ice because I didn't eat enough before the game. I was taken to the hospital in an ambulance because my blood sugar dropped too low," recalls Adam. "Now, I work with the team trainer and the cam-pus dietitian to make sure my pregame snack covers my ice time. Ironically, because of my diabetes, I probably eat better than anyone else on the team and have the most energy. I can out-skate them all," he boasts proudly.

Diabetes is a condition related to blood glucose levels, which are affected by diet, particularly carbohydrate intake. In this chapter, you will learn the unique role that carbohydrates play in providing fuel for your body, the nutritional differences between simple and complex carbohydrates, the powerful role that high-fiber foods can play in fighting diseases such as obesity, heart disease, cancer, and, diabetes, and, most importantly, how to change your diet to take advantage of all the wonderful attributes of carbohydrates.

Answers

1. False. You need a *minimum* amount of carbohydrates daily to fuel your brain. See this page to find out how much you need to eat.
2. False. Many people who are lactose intolerant may still be able to enjoy some dairy products, especially if they are eaten with meals. In fact, dairy foods may be just what the doctor ordered. Turn to page 95 to learn why.
3. False. Calories, not carbs, are what you need to monitor to avoid weight gain. In fact, some high-fiber carbohydrates can actually help you lose weight. Turn to page 102 to find out why.
4. True. The more sugar you eat, the more likely you are to have tooth decay. Turn to page 103 to find out why this is the case.
5. False. Honey contains a small amount of nutrients but not enough to make it nutritionally superior to sugar. Turn to page 103 to learn more.
6. False. Foods that contain sugar alcohols, such as sorbitol, can be labeled "sugar free" because they are carbohydrates but not sugars. But they still provide calories. Turn to page 108 to learn more.
7. False. Though saccharin once bore the stigma of being a cancer causer, it's no longer thought to cause cancer in humans. Turn to page 110 to learn more about this turnaround.
8. True. The average American consumes about half the amount of fiber that's recommended daily. Turn to page 112 to learn more about the potential problems associated with this shortfall.
9. False. Dark bread doesn't necessarily have more fiber than white bread. Learn why on page 113.
10. True. Being overweight or obese can increase your chances of developing type 2 diabetes. Turn to page 115 to learn more.

What Are Carbohydrates and Why Do You Need Them?

Carbohydrates are essential nutrients that make up the foundation of diets the world over. They are predominant in plant-based foods such as grains (rice and pasta), fruits, vegetables, nuts, and legumes (dry beans and peas). These foods are staples in cuisines from Asia to Latin America, the United States to the Mediterranean. In Asia, rice accounts for 80 percent of people's daily calories. In Latin America, carbohydrate-laden bananas, chilies, beans, tubers, and nuts adorn most dinner plates. In the Mediterranean, grain-based pastas, breads, and couscous are plentiful, and here in the United States, many people consume the good old potato on a daily basis.[1]

You need carbohydrates because they are the most desirable source of energy for your body. Their main role is to supply fuel, primarily in the form of **glucose** (*ose* = carbohydrate), the predominant sugar in high-carbohydrate foods, to your cells. Your brain in particular relies on glucose to function, as do your red blood cells. With such important roles as these in the body, it isn't surprising that foods high in carbohydrates are a big part of the diet, no matter what continent you live on.

The Take-Home Message Carbohydrates are found primarily in plant-based foods and are needed by your cells, including brain cells and red blood cells, for energy. Numerous cultures around the world rely on carbohydrate-based foods as staples in their diets.

Where Do Carbohydrates Come From?

The carbohydrates we eat come mostly from plant foods. Plants make carbohydrates to store energy and to build their root and stem structures. Animals, including humans, also store energy as carbohydrates, but in limited amounts. The storage form of carbohydrates in animals breaks down when the animal dies, so eating meat and poultry will not supply carbohydrates to our diets.

Plants Convert the Sun's Energy into Glucose

Plants form the basic carbohydrate, glucose, in a process called **photosynthesis** (Figure 4.1). During photosynthesis, plants use the **chlorophyll** in their leaves to absorb the energy in sunlight. The absorbed energy splits water in the plant into its

Foods high in carbohydrates are staples in many of the world's cuisines.

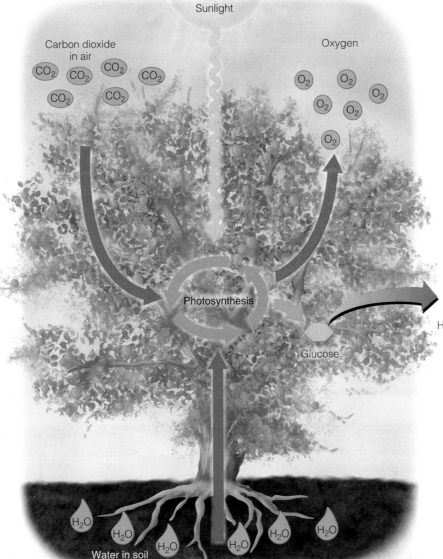

Figure 4.1 Photosynthesis: How Glucose Is Made
During photosynthesis, the leaves of green plants absorb the energy from sunlight. This energy splits six molecules of water (H_2O) into hydrogen and oxygen. The hydrogen joins with carbon dioxide in the plant to create glucose. In this process, six molecules of oxygen are released into the air. Glucose is the most abundant sugar in nature and the optimal fuel for your body.

glucose The most abundant sugar in foods and the energy source for your body.

photosynthesis A process by which green plants create carbohydrates using the energy from sunlight.

chlorophyll The green pigment in plants that absorbs energy from sunlight to begin the process of photosynthesis.

component parts of hydrogen and oxygen. Glucose is formed when the hydrogen joins with carbon dioxide that the plant has taken in from the air. The oxygen is released as a waste product.

Glucose is the most abundant carbohydrate in nature, and plants use it as energy, or combine it with minerals from the soil to make other compounds, such as protein and vitamins. They also link glucose units together and store them in the form of starch. Plants synthesize an estimated 140 billion tons of carbohydrates a year. This equals about 20 tons per person in the world.[2]

The Take-Home Message Glucose is created in plants through the process of photosynthesis, and is the most abundant carbohydrate in nature.

What Are Simple and Complex Carbohydrates?

Carbohydrates are divided into two categories based on the number of units that are joined together. **Simple carbohydrates** include **monosaccharides** (*mono* = one, *saccharide* = sugar) and **disaccharides** (*di* = two), and **complex carbohydrates** include **polysaccharides** (*poly* = many).

Monosaccharides and Disaccharides Are Simple Carbohydrates

There are three monosaccharides found in foods. In addition to glucose, there are **fructose** and **galactose** (Figure 4.2). Fructose is the sweetest of the simple sugars and is found abundantly in fruit. For this reason, it is often referred to as fruit sugar. Galactose is found in dairy foods. From these three sugars, the other simple and complex carbohydrates can be created.

When two glucose units join together, the disaccharide **maltose** is created. Maltose is the sugar found in grains. When glucose and fructose join together, the disaccharide **sucrose,** or table sugar, is formed. Galactose is joined with glucose to create **lactose** (often called milk sugar, as it is found in dairy foods).

Polysaccharides Are Complex Carbohydrates

Polysaccharides consist of long chains and branches of sugars linked together, so it makes sense that they are called complex carbohydrates. **Starch, fiber,** and **glycogen** are all polysaccharides.

Starch Is the Storage Form in Plants
Plants can store thousands of straight or branched glucose units strung together as starch. The straight chains of glucose units in starch are called amylose, whereas the branched chains of glucose units are called amylopectin. Pasta, rice, bread, and potatoes are excellent sources of starch.

a Monosaccharides

Fructose   Glucose   Galactose

b Disaccharides

Sucrose   Maltose   Lactose
(glucose and   (glucose and   (glucose and
fructose)   glucose)   galactose)

c Polysaccharides (starch)

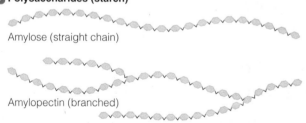

Amylose (straight chain)

Amylopectin (branched)

Figure 4.2 Creating Monosaccharides, Dissaccharides, and Polysaccharides
(a) Fructose, glucose, and galactose are the three monosaccharides that are found in nature. **(b)** The disaccharides sucrose, maltose, and lactose are created from the monosaccharides. **(c)** The polysaccharide, starch, is composed of many glucose units joined together. These glucose units can be joined in a straight chain (amylose) or have branches of glucose units (amylopectin).

simple carbohydrates A category of carbohydrates that contain a single sugar unit or two sugar units combined. Monosaccharides and disaccharides are simple carbohydrates.

monosaccharides One sugar unit. There are three monosaccharides: glucose, fructose, and galactose.

Fiber Is Nondigestible but Important

Humans lack the digestive enzyme needed to break down fiber, so for the most part, fiber is the part of the plant that we eat but cannot digest. Plant components like cellulose, hemicellulose, lignins, gums, and pectin are all types of fibers. **Dietary fiber** is found naturally in foods and **functional fiber** is added to food for a specific, beneficial effect. For example, the fiber psyllium is sometimes added to ready-to-eat cereals because of its laxative effect. Together, dietary and functional fibers account for the *total fiber* that you eat.

Many compounds can be classified as both dietary fiber and functional fiber, depending on how they are used. For example, pectin occurs naturally in foods such as apples and citrus fruits and would be considered a source of dietary fiber. However, pectin can also be isolated and added to foods, such as nonfat yogurt, to add texture. In this situation, pectin is considered a functional fiber.

Fiber is sometimes also classified according to its affinity for water. **Soluble fiber** dissolves in water, while **insoluble fiber** does not. In general, viscous, soluble fiber found in foods such as oats and beans is fermented (or digested) by bacteria in the large intestine (though not all soluble fibers are viscous), whereas insoluble fiber, found in foods such as bran flakes, is not viscous and is fermented less readily by bacteria. A viscous fiber has gummy or thickening properties. For example, the viscous soluble fiber in oats thickens cooked oatmeal.

A fiber's solubility affects how quickly it moves through the digestive tract. This classification system isn't exact, as most foods typically contain both types of fiber and some fibers can have multiple effects in your body. In general, insoluble fibers include cellulose, hemicellulose, and lignins and are found in the bran portion of whole grains, cereal fiber, seeds, and in many fruits and vegetables (see the boxed feature "Grains, Glorious Whole Grains"). They typically move more quickly through your intestinal tract, so can have a laxative effect. Soluble fiber, like pectin in fruits and vegetables, beta-glucan in oats and barley, gums in legumes, and psyllium, is more viscous and moves slowly through your digestive system. Meat and dairy products do not contain fiber. Even though fiber is mostly nondigestible, it can have powerful health effects in your body. We will discuss some of its effects in depth later in the chapter.

Glycogen Is the Storage Form in Animals

Glycogen is the storage form of glucose in humans and animals and is found in the liver and in muscle cells. Glycogen is branched glucose similar to amylopectin. Humans store only limited amounts of glycogen in their bodies, but it can be an important source of glucose for the blood.

The Take-Home Message Carbohydrates are divided into two categories: simple and complex. Simple carbohydrates include the monosaccharides and disaccharides; complex carbohydrates include polysaccharides. Glucose, fructose, and galactose are the three monosaccharides. Sucrose, lactose, and maltose are the three disaccharides. Starch, fiber, and glycogen are all polysaccharides. Dietary fiber occurs naturally in plant-based foods. Functional fiber has been added to foods because it has been shown to have a specific, functional effect. The total fiber in your diet is a combination of dietary and functional fiber. Viscous, soluble fiber has thickening properties and can be fermented by intestinal bacteria and moves slowly through your intestinal tract. Insoluble fiber typically moves more quickly through your digestive system so can have a laxative effect.

Unripe fruit tastes more starchy than sweet. As fruit ripens, its complex carbohydrates are broken down into simple sugars, including fructose. The more it ripens, the more fructose it has.

---

disaccharides Two sugar units combined. There are three disaccharides: sucrose, lactose, and maltose.

complex carbohydrates A category of carbohydrates that contain many sugar units combined. A polysaccharide is a complex carbohydrate.

polysaccharides Many sugar units combined. Starch, glycogen, and fiber are all polysaccharides.

fructose The sweetest of all the monosaccharides; also known as fruit sugar.

galactose A monosaccharide that links with glucose to create the sugar found in dairy foods.

maltose A disaccharide composed of two glucose units joined together.

sucrose A disaccharide composed of glucose and fructose. Also known as table sugar.

lactose A disaccharide composed of glucose and galactose; also known as milk sugar.

starch The storage form of glucose in plants.

fiber A nondigestible polysaccharide.

glycogen The storage form of glucose in humans and animals.

dietary fiber Nondigestible polysaccharides found in foods.

functional fiber The nondigestible polysaccharides that are added to foods because of a specific desired effect on human health.

soluble fiber A type of fiber that dissolves in water and is fermented by intestinal bacteria. Many soluble fibers are viscous and have gummy or thickening properties.

insoluble fiber A type of fiber that doesn't dissolve in water or fermented by intestinal bacteria.

Grains, Glorious Whole Grains

Grains are not only an important staple in the diet but also a wonderful source of nutrition. Americans' consumption of wheat, corn, oats, barley, and rye products has increased by nearly 50 percent since the 1970s. The consumption of starchy flour and cereal products is estimated to be approximately 140 pounds per person each year.[1]

There are three edible parts in a kernel of grain: the bran, the endosperm, and the germ (see figure). The **bran** or outer shell of the wheat kernel is rich in fiber, B vitamins, phytochemicals, and trace minerals such as chromium and zinc. The **germ** or seed of the kernel is a nutritional powerhouse providing vitamin E, heart-healthy fats, phytochemicals, and plenty of B vitamins. The **endosperm,** or starchy component of the grain, contains protein, B vitamins, and some fiber, although not as much as the bran.

Depending upon which parts of the kernel are used, grain products can be divided into two main categories: **refined grains** and **whole grains.** In refined grains, such as wheat or white bread and white rice, the grain kernel goes through a milling process that strips out the bran and germ, leaving only the endosperm of the kernel in the end product. As a result, some, though not all, of the B vitamins, iron, phytochemicals, and dietary fiber are removed.

To restore some of the nutrition lost from refined grains, **enriched grains** have folic acid, thiamin, niacin, riboflavin, and iron added to them. This improves their nutritional quality somewhat, but the fiber and the phytochemicals are lost. Though refined grains can still be a good source of complex carbohydrates, you can think of *refined* as having left some of the nutrition *behind*. From a health standpoint, what was left behind may end up being the most important part of the kernel.

Whole-grain foods, such as whole-wheat bread, brown rice, and oatmeal, contain all three parts of the kernel. Whole grains are potential disease-fighting allies in the diet.[2] Research has shown that as little as one serving of whole grains daily may help lower the risk of dying from heart disease or cancer and reduce the risk of stroke.[3] Several research studies have also shown that the fiber in whole grains may help reduce the risk of diabetes.[4] Because whole grains are abundant in vitamins, minerals, fiber, and phytochemicals, it is uncertain which of these substances are the disease-fighting heroes in these grains or if some or all of them work in a complementary fashion to provide the protection.[5]

Over 80 percent of Americans' grain choices are not whole grains, but refined grains. Whereas the current recommendation is to consume at least three servings of whole-grain products every day, Americans eat only one serving of whole grains daily, on average.[6]

The good news is that it's easy to incorporate more grains into your diet. When it comes to whole grain, you have a lot of choices:

- Brown rice
- Bulgur (cracked wheat)
- Graham flour
- Oatmeal
- Popcorn
- Pearl barley
- Whole-grain cornmeal
- Whole oats
- Whole rye
- Whole wheat

bran The indigestible outer shell of the grain kernel.

germ The seed of the grain kernel.

endosperm The starchy part of the grain kernel.

refined grains Grain foods that are made with only the endosperm of the kernel. The bran and germ are not included.

whole grains Grain foods that are made with the entire edible grain kernel: the bran, the endosperm, and the germ.

enriched grains Refined grain foods that have folic acid, thiamin, niacin, riboflavin, and iron added.

What Happens to the Carbohydrates You Eat?

When you eat plant foods, your body breaks down the carbohydrates for energy. Let's look at how your body digests a meal of pasta (starch), milk (lactose), and a handful of cherries (sucrose and fiber).

Ways to Enjoy Whole Grains

Choose whole-grain cereal such as shredded wheat, bran flakes, raisin bran, and oatmeal in the morning.

Combine a 100% whole-wheat English muffin and low-fat cheddar cheese for a hearty breakfast cheese melt.

Enjoy your lunchtime sandwich made with a whole-wheat pita or 100% whole-grain bread.

Try instant brown rice for a quick whole grain at dinner.

Snack on popcorn or 100% whole-wheat crackers for a high-fiber filler in the afternoon.

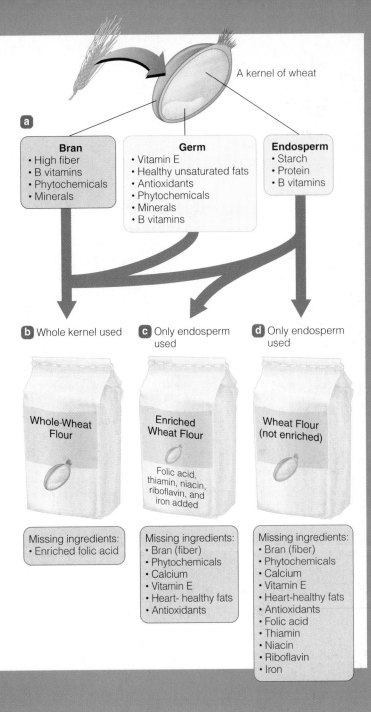

From Wheat Kernel to Flour
(a) The wheat grain kernel has three parts: the bran, endosperm, and germ. **(b)** Whole-wheat flour is made using the entire grain kernel. It is not enriched. **(c)** Enriched wheat flour doesn't contain the bran and germ, so it is missing nutrients and phytochemicals. The nutrients, including folic acid, thiamin, niacin, riboflavin, and iron, are added back to the flour during an enrichment process. **(d)** Wheat flour that is not enriched lacks not only the bran and germ, but also many nutrients and phytochemicals.

You Digest Carbohydrates in Your Mouth and Intestines

The digestion of carbohydrates starts in your mouth (Figure 4.3 on page 94). The act of chewing mixes the saliva in your mouth with the food. Your saliva delivers a powerful enzyme called amylase (*ase* = enzyme), which starts breaking down the starch, specifically the amylose and amylopectin, in the pasta into smaller starch units. Some of the starch is broken down to the disaccharide, maltose.

This mixture of starch and amylase, along with the disaccharides maltose, lactose (in the milk), and sucrose (in the cherries), and the fiber (in the cherries) travels

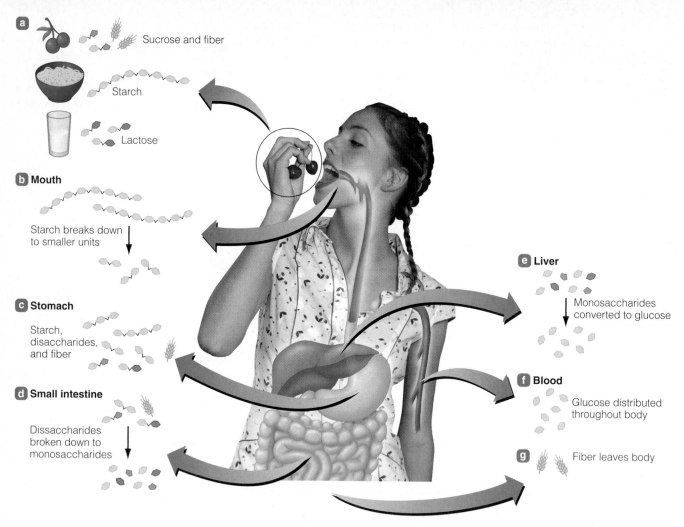

Figure 4.3 From Carbohydrates to Glucose in Your Body
(a) Cherries, pasta, and milk are all sources of glucose. **(b)** The digestion of carbohydrates begins in the mouth. Amylase in the saliva breaks down the starch into smaller units, including maltose. **(c)** The starch, maltose, sucrose, lactose, and fiber travel down to the stomach and on to the small intestine. Once in the small intestine, the remaining starch units are broken down into maltose. **(d)** All disaccharides are broken down to the monosaccharides glucose, fructose, and galactose with the help of enzymes located in the lining of your digestive tract. **(e)** The monosaccharides travel in the blood to your liver. **(f)** The monosaccharides are converted to glucose in the liver and travel in your blood to your cells. **(g)** The fiber travels down to the colon and then most of it is eliminated from your body.

down to your stomach. The amylase continues to break down the starch until your stomach acids deactivate this enzyme. Once the food leaves your stomach, it moves through your small intestine. The arrival of the food in the small intestine signals the pancreas to release another enzyme, pancreatic amylase. The pancreatic amylase breaks down the remaining starch units into maltose.

All the disaccharides—maltose, lactose, and sucrose—are absorbed in your small intestine. The disaccharides brush up against the lining of your digestive tract. A variety of enzymes such as maltase, lactase, and sucrase, called brush border enzymes, are housed in the microvilli in your small intestine. These enzymes break down the disaccharides into monosaccharides, specifically glucose, fructose, and galactose. The monosaccharides are now ready to be absorbed into the blood.

These absorbed monosaccharides travel in your blood to the liver. There the fructose and galactose are converted to glucose. The glucose is either stored in the liver or shipped back out into the blood for delivery to your cells.

The fiber continues down to the large intestine, where some of it is metabolized by bacteria in your colon. However, the majority of the fiber is eliminated from your body in stool.

Some People Cannot Digest Milk Sugar

Lactose, or milk sugar, is the principal carbohydrate found in dairy products such as milk, yogurt, and cheese. People with a deficiency of the brush border enzyme lactase cannot properly digest lactose.

Lactose maldigestion is a natural part of the aging process. In fact, as soon as a child stops nursing, his body makes less lactase. An estimated 25 percent of Americans, and 75 percent of adults around the world, maldigest lactose. Some lucky individuals of specific ethnic origins, such as those from northern Europe, central Africa, and the Middle East, aren't as prone to developing lactose maldigestion. They appear to have a genetic predisposition to maintaining higher levels of lactase throughout their adult life.[3]

Though the term lactose maldigestion may sound serious, it doesn't mean that dairy foods have to be eliminated from the diet. In fact, many people continue to eat milk, yogurt, and cheese throughout their lives without any problems or unpleasant side effects.[4] This is good news, as dairy products provide over 70 percent of the calcium in the diet.[5]

However, in some individuals the amount of lactase in the digestive tract decreases so much that they start to experience distressing symptoms. The undigested lactose draws water into the digestive tract, causing diarrhea. To make matters worse, once the lactose reaches the colon, the bacteria that normally live in the colon ferment this sugar and produce various gases. For some lactose-sensitive individuals, bloating, flatulence (gassiness), and cramps can sometimes be an unpleasant reminder that they ate lactose-containing foods. When these symptoms occur within two hours after eating or drinking foods that contain lactose, these people may be **lactose intolerant.**[6]

Lactose intolerance is not the same as having an allergy to milk. A milk allergy is a response by your immune system to one or more of the proteins in cow's milk. This condition typically affects only about 1 to 3 percent of children, and it rarely occurs in adults.[7] We talk more about food allergies in Chapter 12.

You should never self-diagnose lactose intolerance, or any other medical condition that you may be experiencing. This could not only cause you to inflict unnecessary dietary restrictions on yourself if your diagnosis is incorrect, it could delay you from receiving an accurate diagnosis of a potentially more serious medical condition. There are many documented cases of individuals who thought that they were lactose intolerant but discovered they weren't once the proper testing was done.[8] It is best to leave medical diagnosis to your physician.

People with lactose intolerance have varying thresholds for tolerating lactose-containing foods and beverages (Table 4.1). These thresholds can be raised depending upon how much of a lactose-containing food one eats at a time. Consuming smaller amounts of dairy foods throughout the day can be better tolerated than having a large amount at one time. Eating these foods with a meal or snack, rather than by themselves, can also influence how much can be tolerated.[9]

Including dairy foods regularly in your diet may also improve your tolerance, as the continuous exposure to undigested lactose promotes an acidic environment created by the fermenting of lactose by the bacteria in the colon, which inhibits further fermentation. Also, the constant presence of lactose in the colon perpetuates an

Table 4.1
How Much Lactose Is in Your Foods?

Food	Amount	Lactose (grams)
Milk, whole, 1%, or skim	1 cup	11
Lactaid milk,	1 cup	<1
Soy milk	1 cup	0
Ice cream	½ cup	6
Yogurt, low fat	1 cup	5
Sherbet	½ cup	2
Cottage cheese	½ cup	2
Swiss, Blue, Cheddar, Parmesan cheese	1 oz	1
Cream cheese	1 oz	1

Don't Forget These Hidden Sources of Lactose

Baked goods

Baking mixes for pancakes, biscuits, and cookies

Bread

Breakfast drinks

Candies

Cereals, processed

Instant potatoes

Lunch meats (other than kosher meats)

Margarine

Salad dressings

Soups

Source: Adapted from the American Dietetic Association, Manual of Clinical Dietetics 2000; food manufacturers; and the National Digestive Diseases Information Clearinghouse. 2002. *Lactose Intolerance.* National Institutes of Health Publication No. 02-2751.

lactose maldigestion The inability to digest lactose in foods due to low levels of the enzyme lactase.

lactose intolerant When maldigestion of lactose results in symptoms such as nausea, cramps, bloating, flatulence, and diarrhea.

Many products are available to help those who are lactose intolerant enjoy dairy foods.

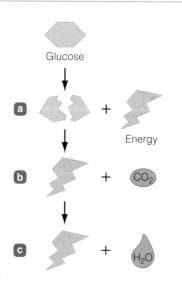

Figure 4.4 Generating Energy from Glucose
When your body needs to break down glucose for energy, it begins a three-step process in your cells. **(a)** First, glucose is broken down to two sets of a three-carbon compound, which generates the first release of energy. **(b)** Then the three-carbon compounds are further broken down for another release of energy. **(c)** Lastly, the most abundant amount of energy is released from these remnants of glucose.

increase in the growth of nongaseous bacteria and subsequent displacement of the gas-producing bacteria.[10]

People tend to respond differently to various dairy foods.[11] Whole milk tends to be better tolerated than skim milk. Cheese typically has less lactose than milk so is better tolerated. Hard, aged cheeses are especially well tolerated, as the amount of lactose remaining after the aging process is negligible. Yogurts that contain active cultures are better tolerated than skim or low-fat milk.

For those who want to enjoy dairy foods without worrying about developing the unpleasant side effects, there are lactose-reduced dairy products such as milk, cottage cheese, ice cream, and other items available in many supermarkets. Lactase pills are available that can be consumed with meals that contain lactose. See Table Tips for some more ideas on how to develop a tolerance for lactose.

The Take-Home Message The digestion of carbohydrates begins in your mouth and continues in your stomach and small intestine. Enzymes help break down the carbohydrates into disaccharides and then monosaccharides so that they can be absorbed. All the monosaccharides are converted to glucose in your liver to be used as energy by your cells, or stored as glycogen or fat. Fiber travels to your colon and then most of it is eliminated from your body. Lactose maldigestion is the inability to properly absorb the milk sugar lactose due to a decrease in the amount of lactase in your digestive tract.

How Does Your Body Use Carbohydrates?

Your body uses carbohydrates—specifically glucose—for energy, and there are chemical messengers called **hormones** that regulate the amount of glucose in your blood. Hormones are like traffic cops, directing specific actions in your body. After you eat a carbohydrate-heavy meal, your blood is flooded with glucose. To lower your blood glucose level, your pancreas releases the hormone **insulin** into the blood. Insulin helps direct the uptake of glucose by your cells and also determines whether it will be used immediately as energy or stored for later use.

Insulin Regulates Glucose in Your Blood

When your cells need fuel, insulin stimulates the conversion of glucose to energy (Figure 4.4). If the amount of glucose in your blood exceeds your body's immediate energy needs, insulin directs it to be stored for later use.

As mentioned, the surplus of glucose is stored in long, branched chains called glycogen. (Recall that plants store glucose as starch. Animals and humans store glucose as glycogen.) This process of generating glycogen for later use is call **glycogenesis** (*glyco* = sugar/sweet, *genesis* = origin) (Figure 4.5a). Glycogenesis occurs only in your liver and muscle cells. Whereas plants have an unlimited capacity to store glucose as starch, you can't squirrel away unlimited extra energy in the form of glycogen.

However, your body can store energy in another form: fat! Insulin can direct the conversion of the excess glucose to fat. In fact, most of the energy stored in your body is in the form of fat. Very little of it is in the form of glycogen. Fat is covered in detail in Chapter 5.

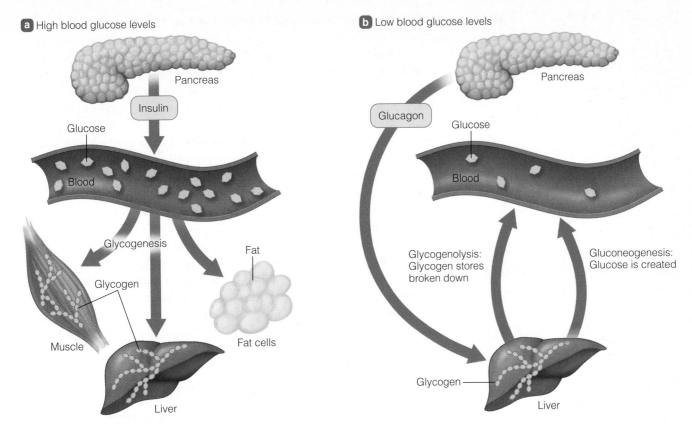

a High blood glucose levels

Pancreas

Insulin

Glucose

Blood

Glycogenesis

Glycogen

Muscle

Fat

Fat cells

Liver

b Low blood glucose levels

Pancreas

Glucagon

Glucose

Blood

Glycogenolysis: Glycogen stores broken down

Gluconeogenesis: Glucose is created

Glycogen

Liver

Figure 4.5 Insulin Directs Excess Glucose into Storage
(a) When your blood glucose levels are too high, the pancreas releases the hormone insulin into your blood to direct glucose. Excess glucose will be stored in your muscles and liver as glycogen and in your fat cells as fat. **(b)** When your blood glucose levels drop too low, the pancreas releases the hormone glucagon, which directs the release of glucose from stored glycogen and the creation of glucose from gluconeogenesis in your liver.

Carbohydrates Fuel Your Body Between Meals

As mentioned, both glycogen and fat are important sources of stored fuel that meet your body's energy needs. These storage forms come in handy between meals when you aren't eating but your body continues to need fuel. Remember, your red blood cells and your brain, as well as the rest of your nervous system, rely on a steady supply of glucose to function properly. When your blood glucose level dips too low, such as if it has been longer than four hours since your last meal, your body calls upon its glycogen reserves to supply glucose to your blood. The glycogen in your liver is used to maintain your blood glucose level, and your muscle glycogen is used exclusively by the muscles for fuel. During this time, your body will also break down your fat stores to provide the energy for your tissues, such as your muscles.

For example, let's say that your nutrition class is at 8 a.m. and that you overslept and didn't eat breakfast. The last time you ate was at dinner last night—over 12 hours ago. As your blood glucose level begins to drop, your pancreas releases another hormone, **glucagon,** which directs the release of glucose from the stored glycogen in your liver to help raise your blood glucose level. This breakdown of glycogen is called **glycogenolysis** (*lysis* = loosening) (Figure 4.5b). In addition to directing the breakdown of glycogen, glucagon signals the liver to start **gluconeogenesis** (*gluco* = sugar/sweet, *neo* = new, *genesis* = origin). This is the creation of glucose from noncarbohydrate sources, mostly from protein. Gluconeogenesis can only occur in your liver and

hormones Chemical messengers in your body that initiate or direct specific actions.

insulin The hormone that directs the glucose from your blood into your cells. Insulin is produced in and released from the pancreas.

glycogenesis The process of converting excess glucose into glycogen in your liver and muscle.

glucagon The hormone that directs glycogenolysis and gluconeogenesis to increase glucose in the blood. Glucagon is produced in and released from the pancreas.

glycogenolysis The breakdown of glycogen to release glucose.

gluconeogenesis The creation of glucose from noncarbohydrate sources, predominantly protein.

kidneys, as these are the only organs that have all the enzymes needed. Most of the time, this glucose-generating process occurs in your liver. Gluconeogenesis kicks in from the kidney only after long periods of fasting. In times of deprivation, your body dismantles protein, using specific remnants (amino acids, which we will discuss in Chapter 6) to generate the glucose that it needs. If you don't feed your blood with glucose, your body will attempt to feed it. Once your blood glucose returns to normal, glucagon will no longer be released.

In addition to glucagon, other hormones can increase your blood glucose level. Epinephrine, also known as adrenaline, acts on the liver and muscle cells to stimulate glycogenolysis to quickly flood your blood with glucose. Emotional and physical forms of stress, such as fear, excitement, and bleeding, will increase your body's output of epinephrine. For example, if a ferocious dog was chasing you down the street, your body would be pumping out epinephrine to help provide the fuel you need to run. For this reason, epinephrine is also referred to as the "fight or flight" hormone.

A low blood glucose level can also trigger the release of epinephrine. In fact, some of the symptoms that you may experience when your blood glucose level dips too low, such as anxiety, rapid heart beat, turning pale, and shakiness, are caused by the release of epinephrine.

Carbohydrates Fuel Your Body During Fasting

Skipping breakfast is one thing. Fasting, or not eating for long periods of time, is quite another. After about 18 hours of fasting, your liver's glycogen stores are depleted. Your body continues to break down fat stores for fuel. However, to burn fat thoroughly, you need some carbohydrate. Without adequate amounts of glucose, **ketone bodies,** by-products of the incomplete breakdown of fat, are created and spill out into your blood. Ketone bodies can cause your blood to become slightly acidic. After about two days of fasting, the number of ketone bodies in your blood is at least doubled, and you are in a state of **ketosis.** Individuals who follow low-carbohydrate diets are often in ketosis because they consume inadequate amounts of carbohydrates.

While your body continues to break down fat for fuel, it uses protein to generate glucose. You can't store extra protein for this situation, so protein from your muscles and organs will be broken down to make glucose. To preserve these tissues and lessen the demand for glucose, after a few days of fasting some parts of your brain switch over to using ketone bodies as fuel. This reduces the need to generate glucose from internal protein sources. If you continue to fast, your body's protein reserves will reach a dangerously low level, and you will die.

The Take-Home Message After a meal, when your blood glucose level begins to rise, the hormone insulin is released from the pancreas, directing glucose into your cells to be used for energy. Excess glucose is stored as glycogen or as fat. When your blood glucose drops too low, the hormone glucagon directs the release of glucose from glycogen in your liver to increase the glucose in your blood. Glucagon will also signal the start of gluconeogenesis in the liver, which is the creation of glucose from noncarbohydrate sources, such as protein. Epinephrine also plays a role in increasing your blood glucose level. When you fast, stored fat and ketone bodies become the primary source of energy to fuel your body. This spares your protein-rich tissues by reducing the amount of protein that needs to be broken down to generate glucose. If the fasting continues, death is inevitable.

ketone bodies The by-products of the incomplete breakdown of fat.

ketosis The condition of increased ketone bodies in the blood.

How Much Carbohydrate Do You Need and What Are Its Food Sources?

Although your body has mechanisms in place to provide the energy it needs on demand, you have to feed it the proper fuel to keep it running efficiently. Consequently, the question of how much carbohydrate you should consume daily has two answers. The first refers to the minimum amount of carbohydrates that you should eat to provide adequate fuel for your body, specifically your brain, to function efficiently. The longer, and more challenging, answer relates to the best type and source of carbohydrates that you should eat daily for long-term health. First, let's look at the minimum amount of carbohydrates that you should eat daily.

You Need a Minimum Amount of Carbohydrates Daily

The latest Dietary Reference Intakes (DRIs) for carbohydrates recommend that adults and children consume a minimum of 130 grams daily.[12] This is based on the estimated minimum amount of glucose your brain needs to function efficiently. This may sound like a lot, but 130 grams is less than the amount you would consume by eating the minimum recommended daily servings for each food group in MyPyramid, that is, 6 servings from the grain group, 3 servings each from the vegetable and dairy groups, and 2 servings from the fruit group.

If your diet is well balanced, feeding your brain should be a no-brainer. In the United States, adult males consume, on average, 220 grams to 330 grams of carbohydrates daily, whereas adult females eat 180 grams to 230 grams daily, well over the minimum DRI.

Recall from Chapter 2 that the AMDR for carbohydrates is 45 to 65 percent of your total daily calories. Adults in the United States consume about half of their calories from carbohydrate-rich foods, so they are easily meeting this optimal range.

Scientists, dietitians, doctors, and especially diet book authors, have a variety of opinions about the best type of carbohydrates you should eat to ensure long-term health. You need to understand all the facts and obtain your nutrition information from reliable and credible sources.

The Best Carbohydrates Are Found in These Foods

As with other nutrients, it's important to know that all carbohydrate-laden foods are not created equal. Excess calories from foods high in carbohydrates and saturated fat can not only lead to weight gain, they can also be unhealthy for your heart. Likewise, eating high-sugar foods that don't contain many other nutrients will provide a lot of calories but not much else. Therefore, you should choose your carbohydrates from a range of nutrient-dense, low saturated fat foods whenever possible. In general, the best strategy for long-term health is to consume a diet with low to moderate amounts of simple carbohydrates and higher amounts of fiber and other complex carbohydrates.

An orange has four times the fiber of six ounces of orange juice.

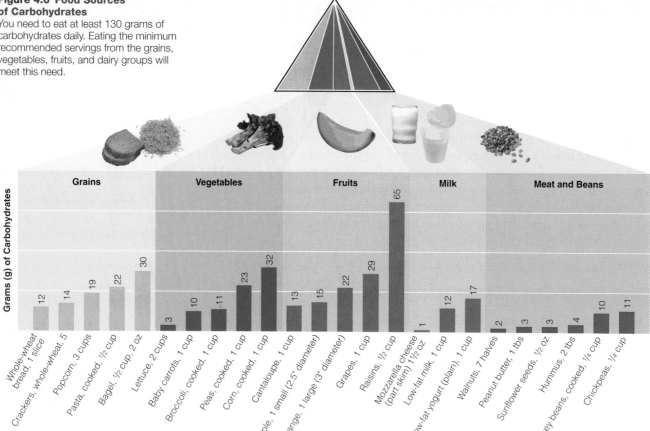

Figure 4.6 Food Sources of Carbohydrates
You need to eat at least 130 grams of carbohydrates daily. Eating the minimum recommended servings from the grains, vegetables, fruits, and dairy groups will meet this need.

Simple carbohydrates are found naturally in fruits, vegetables, and dairy foods (Figure 4.6). Though you can also get simple sugars from processed foods and sweets, the higher calorie and lower nutrient levels in these foods make them a less healthy option (you'll learn more about the pros and cons of natural and added sugars in the next section).

Complex carbohydrates, including starch and fiber, are found abundantly in grains, whole fruits, and vegetables. Starch is the primary complex carbohydrate found in grains and potatoes, while fiber is found in whole grains, whole fruits, vegetables, legumes, nuts, and seeds.

Filling Up on Fiber

Fiber plays many important roles in your body, so the current DRIs recommend that you consume 14 grams of fiber for every 1,000 calories you eat to promote heart health.[13] For example, individuals who need 2,000 calories daily to maintain their weight should consume 28 grams of fiber daily. Because few people know the exact number of calories they consume daily, the recommendations for fiber are categorized by both age and gender so that your estimated needs can be determined (Table 4.2). Unfortunately, most Americans fall short of this goal and consume only a little over 15 grams of fiber a day, on average.

Whole grains, fruits, vegetables, legumes, nuts, and seeds are fiber powerhouses. These foods should be included at your meals and snacks to meet your daily needs (Figure 4.7). See the High Five! Table Tips for some ways to add fiber to your diet.

A word of caution: Initially, a high-fiber diet can have negative side effects (flatulence). Gradually increasing the fiber in your diet, rather than suddenly adding large

Table 4.2

What Are Your Fiber Needs?

	Grams of Fiber Daily*	
	Males	Females
14 through 18 years old	38	36
19 through 50 years old	38	25
51 through 70+ years old	30	21
Pregnancy		28
Lactation		29

*Based on an Adequate Intake (AI) for fiber.

Source: Institute of Medicine. 2002. *Dietary Reference Intakes for Energy, Carbohydrate, Fiber, Fat, Fatty Acids, Cholesterol, Protein, and Amino Acids.* Washington, D.C.: The National Academies Press.

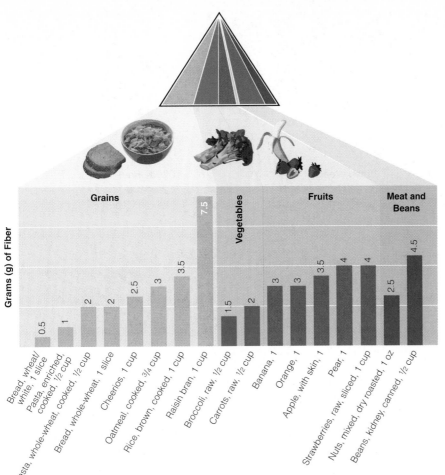

Figure 4.7 Food Sources of Fiber
Adults need to consume about 20 to 38 grams of fiber daily.

Source: Position of the American Dietetic Association, Health Implications of Dietary Fiber, *Journal of the American Dietetic Association* 102 (2002): 993–1000; USDA National Nutrient Database for Standard Reference, www.nal.usda.gov/fnic.

Grams (g) of Fiber

Grains | Vegetables | Fruits | Meat and Beans

0.5 — Bread, wheat/white, 1 slice
1 — Pasta, enriched, cooked, ½ cup
2 — Pasta, whole-wheat, cooked, ½ cup
2 — Bread, whole-wheat, 1 slice
2.5 — Cheerios, 1 cup
3 — Oatmeal, cooked, ¾ cup
3.5 — Rice, brown, cooked, 1 cup
7.5 — Raisin bran, 1 cup
1.5 — Broccoli, raw, ½ cup
2 — Carrots, raw, ½ cup
3 — Banana, 1
3 — Orange, 1
3.5 — Apple, with skin, 1
4 — Pear, 1
4 — Strawberries, raw, sliced, 1 cup
2.5 — Nuts, mixed, dry roasted, 1 oz
4.5 — Beans, kidney, canned, ½ cup

amounts, will allow your body to adjust to the increased amount of fiber and minimize the side effects. A small, steady increase of fiber will be easier on your colon and on those around you. As you add more fiber to your diet, you should also drink more fluids.

The Take-Home Message You need to consume a minimum of 130 grams of carbohydrates daily to provide adequate glucose for your brain; it is recommended that 45 to 65 percent of your daily calories come from carbohydrates. Whole fruits and vegetables, whole grains, legumes, and lean dairy products are the best food sources of carbohydrates. You should consume 14 grams of fiber for every 1,000 calories you eat. Whole grains, fruits, vegetables, legumes, nuts, and seeds are excellent sources of fiber.

What's the Difference Between Natural and Added Sugars?

Finding the taste of sweet foods pleasurable is an innate response. A child being fed puréed applesauce for the first time will probably show his pleasure with a big smile. You're not likely to see the same smile when Junior is eating plain oatmeal.

Table Tips

High Five! Five Ways to Increase Fiber Daily

Choose only whole-grain cereals for breakfast.

Eat two pieces of whole fruit daily as snacks.

Use only 100% whole-wheat bread for your lunchtime sandwich.

Layer lettuce, tomatoes, or other vegetables on your sandwich.

Eat a large salad with dinner nightly.

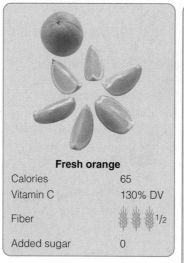

Fresh orange

Calories	65
Vitamin C	130% DV
Fiber	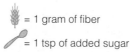 1/2
Added sugar	0

Candy orange

Calories	300
Vitamin C	0% DV
Fiber	0
Added sugar	

= 1 gram of fiber

= 1 tsp of added sugar

You don't have to fight this taste for sweetness. A modest amount of sweet foods can easily be part of a well-balanced diet. However, some sources of sugar provide more nutrition than others.

Your taste buds can't distinguish between **naturally occurring sugars,** which are found in foods such as fruit and dairy products, and **added sugars,** which are added by manufacturers to foods such as soda or candy. From a nutritional standpoint, however, there is a big difference between these sugar sources. Foods that contain naturally occurring sugar tend to be nutrient dense and thus provide more nutrition per bite. In contrast, foods that contain a lot of added sugar tend to give little else. The calories in sugar-laden foods are often called **empty calories** because they provide so little nutrition.

Many Foods Naturally Contain Sugar

Just one bite into a ripe peach, a crisp apple, or some chilled grapes will confirm that fruit can taste sweet, and not surprisingly, can contain more than 15 percent sugar by weight. There are many nutritional advantages of satisfying your sweet tooth with fruit rather than sweets with added sugar. Let's compare slices from a fresh navel orange with candy orange slices (Figure 4.8).

Six slices of a navel orange provides about 65 calories, over 100 percent of the daily value for vitamin C, and 3.5 grams of fiber, which is more than 10 percent of the amount of fiber that many adults should consume daily. These juicy slices also provide fluid. In fact, over 85 percent of the weight of the orange is water. The hefty amounts of fiber and water make whole fruits such as oranges a hearty, sweet snack that provides bulk. This bulk can increase eating satisfaction, or satiation. When you eat fruit, you not only satisfy your urge for a sweet, but you will also feel full before you overeat.

In contrast, six candy orange slices provide 300 calories of added sugar and little else. The candy is quite energy dense: It provides more than four times as many calories as the fresh orange. However, as it provides no fiber and only negligible amounts of water, it contains a concentrated amount of calories in relationship to the volume of food in the serving. You wouldn't likely feel satiated after consuming six candy

naturally occurring sugars Sugars such as fructose and lactose that are found naturally in fruit and dairy foods.

added sugars Sugars that are added to processed foods and sweets.

empty calories Calories that come with little nutrition. Jelly beans are an example of a food that provides lots of calories from sugar but few nutrients.

orange slices. To consume close to the 300 calories found in the six pieces of candy, you would have to eat more than four oranges. It would be easier to overeat candy orange slices than fresh oranges.

Fiber-abundant whole fruits (and vegetables, for that matter) are not only very nutritious, but they are also kind to your waist, as their bulk tends to fill you up before they fill you out. In other words, it is more difficult to overconsume calories from fruits and vegetables because you will feel full and stop eating before you take in too many calories. In fact, researchers at the USDA recently reviewed the diets of Americans and found that adults who ate more fruit had healthier body weights. According to the researchers, this finding may be due to lower calorie fruit being substituted for higher calorie cake or other sweets on the dessert plates of Americans.[14]

Processed Foods and Sweets Often Contain Added Sugars

Between 1980 and 2000, our yearly consumption of added sugars increased by more than 20 percent.[15] Sugars are added to foods for many reasons. In baked goods, they can hold onto water, which helps keep the product moist and soft. They help provide a golden brown color to the finished product. Sugars function as preservatives and thickeners in foods such as sauces. Fermenting sugars in dough produce the carbon dioxide that makes yeast breads rise. And of course, sugars make foods taste sweet.

Are Added Sugars Bad for You?

Although sugar has been blamed for everything from hyperactive children to diabetes, many of these claims are myths. Adults often point to sugary foods as the culprit behind the overly excited behavior of children at parties and holidays; however, research does not support the theory that sugar makes kids hyperactive.[16] The excitable behavior in the kids is more likely due to the festivities of the day than the sweets being consumed. Too much sugar can contribute to dental caries but so can other sources of carbohydrates. (See the boxed feature "Avoiding a Trip to the Dentist" on page 105.) Contrary to popular thought, sugar doesn't cause diabetes mellitus, as discussed in the section, "What Is Diabetes Mellitus?" Though these claims are sugar myths, a high-sugar diet has been associated with some real potential health problems.

Too much sugar in the diet can increase the blood level of triglycerides, the primary form of fat in your body, and lower the "good" HDL cholesterol, which may increase your risk for heart disease.[17] Luckily, a reduction in the amount of sugar coupled with an increase in fiber in one's diet can typically alleviate this problem. (This will be discussed in detail in Chapter 5.) Consuming calories from sugar won't cause you to gain weight as long as you do not exceed the amount of total calories that you need daily. However, it is easy to overeat high-calorie, sugary foods and quickly add excess calories to your diet. This can make weight management challenging. Moderation and balance are essential when it comes to added sugars.

Finding the Added Sugars in Your Foods

While sucrose and fructose are the most common added sugars in our foods, sugars can appear on the food label under numerous different names. Figure 4.9 includes some of the most common added sugars in foods.

Over the years, some of these forms of added sugar, such as honey and fructose, have been publicized in the popular press as being more nutritious than table sugar. This is an exaggeration.

Honey should never be given to children younger than one year of age, as it may contain spores of *Clostridium botulinum*. These spores can germinate in the immature digestive tracts of babies and cause deadly botulism. Adults do not face this risk.

ⓐ The many aliases of added sugar

SUGAR

Corn sweetener   Corn syrup
Dextrose Sucrose Brown sugar
Fructose Lactose Honey Syrup
High-fructose corn syrup
Fruit juice concentrate
Invert sugar   Raw sugar
Malt syrup Maltose
Molasses

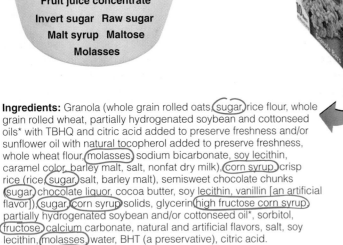

ⓑ

Nutrition Facts
Serving Size 1 Bar (24g)
Servings Per Container 10

Amount Per Serving		
Calories 90	Calories from Fat 20	
		% Daily Value*
Total Fat 2g		3%
Saturated Fat 0.5g		3%
Trans Fat 0g		
Sodium 80 mg		3%
Total Carbohydrate 19g		6%
Dietary Fiber 1g		3%
Sugars 7g		
Protein 1g		

Calcium	8%	• Iron	4%

Not a significant source of Cholesterol, Vitamin A, Vitamin C

* Percent Daily Values are based on a 2,000 calorie diet. Your Daily Values may be higher or lower depending on your calorie needs:

		Calories:	2,000	2,500
Total Fat	Less than		65g	80g
Sat Fat	Less than		20g	25g
Cholesterol	Less than		300mg	300mg
Sodium	Less than		2,400mg	2,400mg
Total Carbohydrate			300g	375g
Dietary Fiber			25g	30g

Ingredients: Granola (whole grain rolled oats, sugar, rice flour, whole grain rolled wheat, partially hydrogenated soybean and cottonseed oils* with TBHQ and citric acid added to preserve freshness and/or sunflower oil with natural tocopherol added to preserve freshness, whole wheat flour, molasses, sodium bicarbonate, soy lecithin, caramel color, barley malt, salt, nonfat dry milk), corn syrup, crisp rice (rice, sugar, salt, barley malt), semisweet chocolate chunks (sugar, chocolate liquor, cocoa butter, soy lecithin, vanillin [an artificial flavor]), sugar, corn syrup solids, glycerin, high fructose corn syrup, partially hydrogenated soybean and/or cottonseed oil*, sorbitol, fructose, calcium carbonate, natural and artificial flavors, salt, soy lecithin, molasses, water, BHT (a preservative), citric acid.

* Adds a dietarily insignificant amount of *trans* fat.

Figure 4.9 Finding Added Sugars on the Label
(a) Sugar can be called a number of different names on ingredients lists and labels. **(b)** A food is likely to contain a large amount of sugar if added sugars appear first or second on the ingredients list and/or if there are many varieties of added sugars listed. You can also look on the Nutrition Facts panel to see the total grams of sugar.

Honey provides a negligible amount of potassium, and it actually has more calories than sugar. A teaspoon of honey contains 21 calories. The same amount of sugar provides only 16 calories.

Consuming 20 grams or more of fructose can have a laxative effect on the body. That may seem like a generous amount, but keep in mind that a 12-ounce can of soda or 8 ounces of apple juice can have 14 to 22 grams of fructose.[18] Though honey and fructose may have been glamorized in the media, these added sugars aren't nutritionally superior to sucrose.

To find the amount and type of added sugars in the foods that you eat, read the ingredients on the food label. If added sugars appear first or second on the list or if the product contains many varieties of added sugars, it is likely to be high in sugar.

The Nutrition Facts panel that is currently used on food labels doesn't distinguish between naturally occurring and added sugars. For example, the nutrition labels on ready-to-eat cereals such as raisin bran and dairy products such as milk list 21 grams of sugars for raisin bran and 12 grams for low-fat milk. This can be misleading, as the grams of sugars listed for the raisin bran cereal include both the amount of naturally occurring sugars from the raisins and the sugars added to sweeten the cereal. For the milk, the sugar listed on the Nutrition Facts panel includes the naturally occurring sugar, lactose. With the growing concern about the rising levels of added sugars in the diets of Americans, various health professionals and organizations have pressured the FDA to require that all *added* sugars be disclosed on the food label. A final decision by the FDA is pending.

A super-large soda at the movie theatre can be as large as 64 ounces! This giant beverage contains over 800 calories and over 50 teaspoons of added sugars.

Avoiding a Trip to the Dentist

Carbohydrates play a role in the formation of dental caries. Over the past 30 years, the incidence of **dental caries** (tooth decay) in the United States has decreased as the use of fluoride has increased.[7] (The mineral fluoride will be covered in more detail in Chapter 8.) Though things are improving in the world of dental health, an estimated 20 percent of children from age 2 to 4 still have dental caries, and by the time these children reach age 17, almost 80 percent will have experienced a cavity, the later stage of dental caries. Dental caries are the cause of tooth loss in over two-thirds of adults age 35 to 44 years.[8] In order to avoid dental caries, you need to understand the role your diet plays in tooth decay.

Feeding into Dental Caries

If you constantly eat carbohydrate-heavy foods, such as cookies, candy, and crackers, you are continually providing a buffet of easily fermentable sugars and starches to the bacteria bathing your teeth. A recent study of American diets revealed that adults who drank sugary sodas three or more times daily had 60 percent more dental caries than those who didn't drink any soda. To make matters worse, soft drinks often contain phosphoric acid and citric acid, which can also erode teeth if consumed over a prolonged time.[9]

Eating three balanced meals daily is best for minimizing tooth decay. Snacks should be kept to a minimum, and you should choose fruit or vegetables over candies or pastries. Whole fruits and raw vegetables tend not to cause tooth decay, so snack on these to your teeth's content.[10]

Sticky foods like dried fruits, such as raisins and figs, can adhere to your teeth, so their fermentable sugars hang onto the tooth for longer periods. The longer the carbohydrate is in contact with your tooth, the more opportunity there is for the acids to do damage. Eating sticky foods in combination with other foods will discourage their adherence to your teeth. Drinking water after you eat will help by rinsing your teeth.

Fruit juice, even unsweetened juices, may be a problem for teeth, especially in small children. A child who routinely falls asleep with a bottle in his mouth that contains carbohydrate-containing beverages is at risk for developing **baby bottle tooth decay** because the baby's teeth are continually exposed to fermentable sugars during sleep.[11] Children need adequate amounts of fluids, such as water, but they should not be given a continual supply of sweetened beverages.

Foods That Fight Dental Caries

There are actually some foods that may help reduce this risk of acid attacks on your teeth. The texture of cheese stimulates the release of cleansing saliva. Cheese is also rich in protein, calcium, and phosphorus, all of which can help buffer the acids in your mouth following a meal or snack. The calcium can also assist in **remineralization** of your teeth. Eating as little as half an ounce of cheese after a snack, or eating cheese with a meal, has been shown to protect your teeth.[12] Chewing sugarless gum can also be a healthy ending to a meal or snack if you can't brush your teeth. It encourages the production of saliva and provides a postmeal bath for your teeth. Xylitol, a sugar substitute often found in sugarless chewing gum, may even help with remineralization.[13]

With regular visits to your dentist, good dental hygiene, and a healthy diet, you can reduce the risk of dental caries. Follow these Do's and Don'ts to keep your teeth healthy:

DO eat three solid meals but keep snacks to a minimum.

DON'T graze all day long!

DO snack, if necessary, on whole fruit, raw vegetables, and low-fat cheese, which tend to be friendlier to your teeth.

DON'T munch on sugary foods such as candy, cookies, and other sweets.

DO drink plenty of water.

DON'T drink a lot of sugar-sweetened beverages. Not only are the calories hefty, but this constant flow of sugar can provide a continual meal for the acid-producing bacteria in your mouth.

DO chew sugarless gum or eat a piece of low-fat cheese after meals and snacks when you can't brush your teeth.

DON'T think that sugarless gum and cheese can replace a routine of brushing and flossing.

DO brush your teeth at least twice a day and floss daily.

DON'T forget this!

---

dental caries The decay or erosion of your teeth.

baby bottle tooth decay The decay of baby teeth in children due to continual exposure to fermentable sugary liquids.

remineralization The repairing of teeth by adding back the minerals lost during tooth decay. Your saliva can help remineralize teeth.

As you know, added sugars come from many sources and are found in many products. In fact, most Americans don't eat the majority of the added sugars in their diets—they drink them. The number-one source of added sugars in the United States

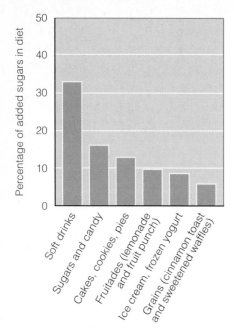

Figure 4.10 Where Are All These Added Sugars Coming From?
Soft drinks are the number-one source of added sugars in the diets of Americans. Sugar, candy, bakery items, fruitades, dairy desserts, and some grains are also sources of added sugars.

is sweetened soft drinks (Figure 4.10). Fruitades and sugary fruit drinks are also major sources. This fact isn't too surprising when you look at the size of the sweetened beverages that Americans consume. A classic (and rare) 8-ounce bottle of cola provides almost 7 teaspoons of added sugars. In today's vending machine, you are more likely to find a 12-ounce can or a 20-ounce bottle. Because people typically consume the entire can or bottle, regardless of its size, they consume more sugar (Figure 4.11). In addition to beverages, added sugars are hidden in many other foods (Table 4.3).

How Much Added Sugar Is Too Much?

The latest DRI recommends that you keep your intake of added sugars to no more than 25 percent of your daily calories.[19] This may be too generous for many Americans, especially for most women, sedentary individuals, and older adults who have lower daily calorie needs. These individuals need to make sure that they are getting a substantial amount of nutrition from each bite of food.

The World Health Organization and the Food and Agriculture Organization recently commissioned an expert report which recommends that individuals lead an active lifestyle and consume a diet that is abundant in fruits and vegetables and low in saturated fat, sugar, and energy-dense foods. The report recommends keeping calories from added sugars* to less than 10 percent of the diet. These two agencies maintain that this type of diet is among the best strategies to fight chronic diseases such as heart disease, diabetes, and obesity.[20]

This more conservative limit for consumption of sugars would mean that a person who consumes 2,200 calories (about the number of calories needed daily for active women) should keep added sugar to about 8 teaspoons daily or 9 percent of total calories. Those consuming 2,800 calories daily (approximately the amount of calories needed daily for active men) should consume no more than about 18 teaspoons of added sugar daily, or 10 percent of total calories.

Americans currently consume over 30 teaspoons of added sugars daily.[21] Eating this much added sugar can have a major impact on daily nutrition and is one of the many reasons Americans are overweight. The Table Tips can help you trim some added sugars from your diet.

The Take-Home Message Your taste buds can't distinguish between naturally occurring and added sugars. Foods with naturally occurring sugars, such as whole fruit, tend to provide more nutrition and satiation than empty-calorie sweets such as candy. Sugar can contribute to dental caries, an elevated level of fat in your blood, and a lowering of the "good" HDL cholesterol. Foods with added sugars may displace more nutritious foods and quickly add excess calories to your diet. The current recommendation is to keep added sugars to no more than 25 percent of your daily calories, but this amount may be too high for individuals with lower daily calorie needs.

Figure 4.11 The Many Sizes of Soft Drinks
A bottle or can of soda can provide from 6 to 17 teaspoons of added sugars, depending upon the size of the container.

*This report includes the sugars that naturally occur in fruit juice as "added sugars." The 2005 *Dietary Guidelines for Americans* do not include fruit juice sugars in the category of added sugars.

Table 4.3

Sugar Smacked!

Food Groups	Teaspoons of Added Sugar
Bread, Cereal, Rice, Pasta	
Bread, 1 slice	0
Cookies, 2 medium	(1 teaspoon)
Doughnut, 1 medium	(1 teaspoon)
Cake, frosted, 1/16 average	(10 teaspoons)
Pie, fruit, 2 crust, 1/8, 8″ pie	(10 teaspoons)
Fruit	
Fruit, canned in juice, 1/2 cup	0
Fruit, canned in heavy syrup, 1/2 cup	(4 teaspoons)
Milk, Yogurt, and Cheese	
Milk, plain, 1 cup	0
Chocolate milk, 2% fat, 1 cup	(3 teaspoons)
Yogurt, low fat, plain, 8 oz	0
Yogurt, fruit, sweetened, 8 oz	(8 teaspoons)
Chocolate shake, 10 fl oz	(9 teaspoons)
Other	
Chocolate bar, 2 oz	(6 teaspoons)
Fruit drink, ade, 12 fl oz	(12 teaspoons)

= 1 teaspoon of sugar

Source: USDA. 2000. *Dietary Guidelines for Americans.* 5th ed. Home and Garden Bulletin No. 232.

Lowering Your Added Sugars

Mix chocolate milk with an equal amount of regular low-fat milk.

Mix equal amounts of sweetened cereal with an unsweetened variety for a breakfast cereal with half the added sugar.

Drink water rather than soda or sweetened beverages throughout the day.

Buy sweets such as candy and cookies in individual serving size pouches rather than large packages. The less you buy, the less you'll eat.

Mix an ounce of 100% fruit juice with 10 ounces of sparkling water for a no-sugar-added "fruit" drink.

What Are Sugar Substitutes and What Forms Can They Take?

Because eating too much sugar can be unhealthy, what's a person with a sweet tooth to do? Americans have looked to sugar-free beverages and foods over the years to limit their sugar intake while satisfying their yen for sugar (Figure 4.12 on page 108). Such items contain **sugar substitutes** that are as sweet, or sweeter, than sugar but contain fewer calories.

All sugar substitutes must be approved by the FDA and deemed safe for consumption before they are allowed in food products sold in the United States.[22] There are several sugar substitutes presently available to consumers, including polyols, saccharin, aspartame, acesulfame-K, sucralose, and neotame. Alitame and cyclamate are two other sugar substitutes that are not yet approved for use in the United States but are on the horizon. Polyols don't promote dental caries and cause a slower rise in blood glucose than sugar does. Saccharin, aspartame, acesulfame-K, sucralose, and neotame also won't promote dental caries and have the added advantage of not affecting blood

sugar substitutes Alternatives to table sugar that sweeten foods for fewer calories.

Figure 4.12 Growing Interest in Sugar-Free Foods and Beverages
The use of sugar-free products has more than doubled since 1984.

Source: Calorie Control Council, Popularity of Low-Calorie, Sugar-Free Foods and Beverages. 2003. www.caloriecontrol.org.

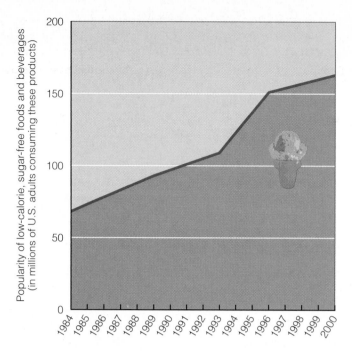

A variety of sugar substitutes are available to the consumer.

glucose levels. These sugar substitutes are a plus for people with diabetes, who have a more challenging time managing their blood glucose levels. All these sugar substitutes are either reduced in calories or are calorie free. See Table 4.4 for a comparison of available sweeteners.

Polyols Are Sugar Alcohols

Polyols are often called sugar alcohols because they have the chemical structure of sugar with an alcohol component added. Whereas polyols such as sorbitol, mannitol, and xylitol are found naturally in plants, they are also produced synthetically and are used as sweeteners in foods such as chewing gum and candies. They can be used tablespoon for tablespoon to substitute for sucrose. Sorbitol and mannitol are also less likely to promote dental caries because the bacteria on your teeth metabolize them so slowly. (Humans lack the enzyme needed to ferment xylitol.) Their slower absorption means that they do not produce a spike in blood glucose, which is a benefit for those with diabetes.

Chewing gums and candies that contain sugar alcohols can be labeled "sugar free" and boast that they don't promote tooth decay. Keep in mind, though, that even though these products are sugar free, they are not necessarily calorie free. Even more importantly, because polyols are incompletely absorbed in your digestive tract, they can cause diarrhea. For this reason, they should be used in moderation.

Another type of polyol is hydrogenated starch hydrolysates (HSH), which are made by partially breaking down corn, wheat, or potato starch into smaller pieces and then adding hydrogen to these pieces. The end product is a wide range of polyols, including those that can be strung together and used commercially. HSH adds sweetness, texture, and bulk to many sugarless products such as baked goods and candies.[23]

Saccharin Is the Oldest Sugar Substitute

Saccharin was first discovered in 1879, and during the two World Wars, when sugar was being rationed, saccharin was used as a sugar substitute in the United States and Europe. Today, you probably know saccharin as those little pink packets often found on

Table 4.4

Oh So Sweet!

Sweetener	Calories/Gram	Trade Names	Sweetening Power	The Facts
Sucrose	4	Table Sugar	—	Sweetens food, enhances flavor, tenderizes, and contributes browning properties to baked goods
Reduced-Calorie Sweeteners				
Polyols (Sugar Alcohols)				
Sorbitol	2.6	Sorbitol	50 to 70% as sweet as sucrose	Found in foods such as sugarless chewing gum, jams, baked goods, and candy. May cause diarrhea when ≥50 grams (about 15 sugar-free candies) are consumed.
Mannitol	1.6	Mannitol	50 to 70% as sweet as sucrose	Found in foods such as chewing gum, jams, and as a bulking agent in powdered foods. Excessive amounts may cause diarrhea.
Xylitol	2.4	Xylitol	Equally sweet as sucrose	Found in foods such as chewing gum, candies; also in pharmaceuticals and hygiene products
Hydrogenated starch hydrolysates (HSH)	3.0	HSH	50 to 70% as sweet as sucrose	Found in confections and can be used as a bulking agent
Calorie-Free Sweeteners				
Saccharin	0	Sweet'N Low	200 to 700% sweeter than sucrose	Retains its sweetening power at high temperatures such as baking
Aspartame	4*	Nutrasweet, Equal	Approximately 200% sweeter than sucrose	Sweetening power is reduced at high temperatures such as baking. Can be added at end stages of recipes such as cooked puddings if removed from heat source. Individuals with PKU need to monitor all dietary sources of phenylalanine, including aspartame.
Acesulfame-K	0	Sunette	200% sweeter than sucrose	Retains its sweetening power at high temperatures
Sucralose	0	Splenda	600% sweeter than sucrose	Retains its sweetening power at high temperatures
Neotame	0	Neotame	7,000 to 13,000% sweeter than sucrose	Retains its sweetening power at high temperatures

*Since so little aspartame is needed to sweeten foods, it provides negligible calories.

coffee shop counters or diner tables. It has been used in foods, beverages, vitamins, and pharmaceuticals. Because saccharin is not metabolized in your body, it doesn't provide any calories.

In 1977, the FDA banned saccharin due to reports from the research community that it could cause bladder cancer in rats. Congress immediately implemented an 18-month moratorium on this ban through the Saccharin Study and Labeling Act. This allowed the continued commercial use of saccharin, but required that any saccharin-containing products bear a warning label stating that saccharin was potentially hazardous to your health as it caused cancer in laboratory animals.

In 2000, the National Toxicology Program (NTP) removed saccharin from the list of substances that could potentially cause cancer. After extensive review, the NTP determined that the observed bladder tumors in rats were actually from a mechanism that wasn't relevant to humans.[24] The lesson learned from this is that though you can safely consume saccharin in moderation, you shouldn't feed it to your pet rat. Saccharin is used in over 100 countries in the world today.

Aspartame Is Derived from Amino Acids

In 1965, a scientist named James Schlatter was conducting research on amino acids in his quest to find a treatment for ulcers. To pick up a piece of paper in his laboratory, he licked his finger and stumbled upon a sweet-tasting compound.[25] It was the "lick" that was soon to be "tasted" around the world. Schlatter had just discovered aspartame, a substance that would change the world of sugar substitutes.

Aspartame is composed of two amino acids: a modified aspartic acid and phenylalanine. Enzymes in your digestive tract break down aspartame into its components, and the amino acids are absorbed, providing 4 calories per gram. Consequently, aspartame has the potential to provide calories to foods as an added sweetener. However, as aspartame is 200 times sweeter than sucrose, only a small amount is needed to sweeten a food.

In 1981, the FDA approved aspartame for use in tabletop sweeteners such as Equal and Nutrasweet, and for various other uses, such as to sweeten breakfast cereals, chewing gums, and carbonated beverages. The majority of the aspartame that is consumed in the United States is in soft drinks. In 1996, the FDA gave the food industry carte blanche to use aspartame in all types of foods and beverages. It is currently used as a sweetener in over 100 countries, and can now be found in over 6,000 foods, as well as pharmaceuticals and personal care products, sold in the United States.

Aspartame has undergone continual, vigorous reviews to ensure that it is safe for human consumption. The FDA considers it one of the most thoroughly studied and tested food additives approved by the agency. The FDA has reevaluated the safety of aspartame more than 25 times since it first came on the market and each time has concluded that it is safe to consume.[26]

Although aspartame has undergone intense evaluation, it has been, and still is, blamed for ailments ranging from headaches to Gulf War Syndrome. Major health organizations such as the American Dietetic Association, the American Medical Association, and the American Diabetes Association all support aspartame's use by healthy adults, children, and pregnant women in moderation as part of a well-balanced diet.[27] The FDA has set an acceptable daily intake (ADI) for aspartame at 50 milligrams per kilogram (mg/kg) of body weight. To exceed this ADI, a 150-pound person would need to consume almost sixteen 12-ounce cans of a "diet" (aspartame-containing) soda daily for a lifetime. Currently the general public consumes an estimated 4 to 7 percent of the ADI, or 2 to 3.5 mg/kg body weight daily.[28]

Individuals with a rare, inherited disorder known as phenylketonuria (PKU) are unable to metabolize one of the amino acids in aspartame, phenylalanine, and must adhere to a special diet. PKU affects about 1 out of every 15,000 infants in the United States. It is usually the result of a deficiency of phenylalanine hydroxylase, an enzyme needed to properly metabolize phenylalanine.[29]

People with PKU need to control all dietary sources of this amino acid, including aspartame as well as protein-rich foods such as meat, milk, eggs, and nuts. These individuals do not necessarily have to avoid aspartame, but they need to monitor it as

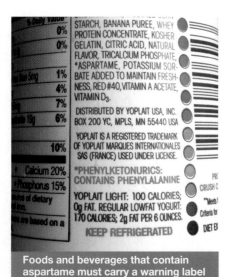

Foods and beverages that contain aspartame must carry a warning label that says phenylalanine is present.

an additional source of phenylalanine in their diet. Because of the seriousness of this disorder, the FDA mandates that all food products that contain phenylalanine carry a label declaring its content.

Acesulfame-K Contains Potassium

While less than sweet sounding, acesulfame-K (the K refers to the potassium component) is about 200 times sweeter than sucrose. It is available as a tabletop sweetener, called Sunette, and is currently used in chewing gum, candy, desserts, yogurt, and alcoholic beverages. Your body does not metabolize acesulfame-K.

Sucralose Is Made from Sucrose

Sucralose was developed in 1976 by slightly changing the structure of the sucrose molecule. Unlike sucrose, sucralose isn't absorbed by your body—it is excreted in your urine. In 1998, sucralose was approved as a tabletop sweetener, and it's available commercially as Splenda.

> Substituting sweeteners for sugar isn't shaving off the pounds. Although the consumption of low-calorie sweeteners has tripled since 1980, the prevalence of overweight and obese Americans has increased by 60 percent.

Neotame Is Also Derived from Amino Acids

The newest addition to the world of sugar substitutes is neotame. The FDA approved neotame in 2002. Neotame comprises the same two amino acids—aspartic acid and phenylalanine—as aspartame, but they are joined together in such a way that the body cannot break them apart. So, individuals with PKU can use neotame without concern. Neotame is completely eliminated in either the urine or stool. It has been approved as a sweetener and for a variety of uses, such as chewing gum, frostings, frozen desserts, puddings, fruit juices, and syrups.[30]

The Take-Home Message Millions of Americans consume reduced-calorie or calorie-free sugar substitutes. The FDA has approved polyols, saccharin, aspartame, acesulfame-K, potassium, sucralose, and neotame to be used in a variety of foods. These sugar substitutes do not promote dental caries and can benefit those with diabetes who are trying to manage their blood glucose.

Why Is Fiber so Important?

Even though fiber is a nondigestible substance that is resistant to being broken down in your small intestine, it can have many powerful health effects in your body. Fiber has been shown to help lower your risk of developing constipation, diverticulosis, obesity, heart disease, cancer, and diabetes mellitus (Table 4.5). Let's look closely at how this works.

Table 4.5

Table 4.5
Type-Casting Fiber

Type	Found in	Can Help Reduce the Risk of
Insoluble fiber Cellulose Hemicellulose Lignins	Whole grains, whole-grain cereals, bran, oats, fruit, and vegetables	Constipation Diverticulosis Certain cancers Heart disease Obesity
Soluble, viscous fibers Pectin Beta-glucan Gums Psyllium	Citrus fruits, prunes, legumes, oats, barley, brussels sprouts, carrots	Constipation Heart disease Diabetes mellitus Obesity

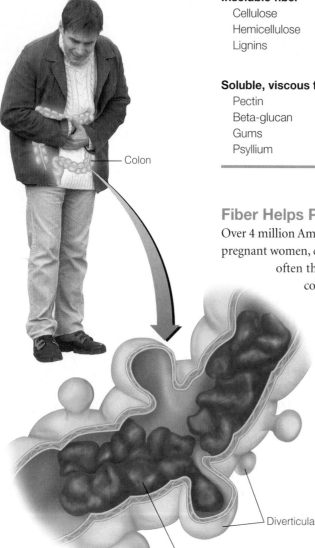

— Colon

— Diverticula

— Stool

Figure 4.13 Diverticula
Diverticula are small pouches that can occur along your colon. When stool gets trapped in them, they can become inflamed, and this can lead to diverticulitis.

diverticulosis The existence of diverticula in the lining of your intestine.

diverticula Small bulges at weak spots in the colon wall.

Fiber Helps Prevent Constipation and Diverticulosis

Over 4 million Americans complain about being constipated, with women, especially pregnant women, children, and adults 65 years of age and older experiencing it more often than others. The uncomfortable, bloated, and sluggish feelings of constipation compel Americans to spend over $700 million each year on laxative products.[31] Because a diet lacking sufficient high-fiber whole grains, fruits, and vegetables and abounding in cheese, eggs, and meats is a recipe for constipation, many people would be better off spending time in the produce and whole-grain aisles of the supermarket than shopping for laxatives.

A diet plentiful in insoluble fibers such as bran, whole grains, and many fruits and vegetables will help keep things moving along in your digestive tract and decrease your likelihood of becoming constipated. As remnants of food move through your colon, water is absorbed, which causes the formation of solid waste products (stool). The contractions of the muscles in your colon push the stool toward your rectum to be eliminated. If these muscle contractions are sluggish, the stool may linger too long in your colon, which can cause too much water to be reabsorbed. This can create hard, dry stools that are more difficult and painful to expel. (Note: Some soluble fibers, such as psyllium, can also be an aid in constipation, as its water-attracting capability allows the stool to increase in bulk and form a gel-like, soft texture, which makes it easier to pass.)

Constipation can become more frequent during different stages of your life. During pregnancy, hormonal changes as well as the pressure of the growing baby on the intestine can make regular bowel movements more difficult. As you age, your metabolism slows, which results in a slower moving digestive tract as well as loss of intestinal muscle tone. Unfortunately, abusing laxatives can damage the nerve cells in the colon and disrupt the colon's natural movements. This can cause you to depend on laxatives in order to bring on a normal bowel movement.[32]

Long-term constipation can lead to a disorder called **diverticulosis** (*osis* = condition). Constipation is the main cause of increased pressure in the colon and may cause the weak spots along your colon wall to bulge out, forming **diverticula** (Figure 4.13).

Infection of the diverticula, a condition known as **diverticulitis** (*itis* = inflamation), can lead to stomach pain, fever, nausea, vomiting, cramping, and chills. Though not proven, it is believed that the stool and its bacteria in the colon may get stuck in the diverticula and cause the infection. Approximately 50 percent of Americans age 60 to 80 and the majority of individuals over 80 years of age have diverticulosis.[33] The disorder is more common in developed countries, such as the United States and England, and is rarely found in areas where high-fiber diets are more commonplace, such as Asia and Africa. Consuming a diet with adequate fiber may reduce the symptoms associated with diverticulosis. The best way to prevent both diverticulosis and diverticulitis is to eat a diet that is generous in fiber to avoid constipation and to keep things moving through your system.

Fiber Helps Prevent Obesity

A fiber-rich diet can also be kind to your waist. As mentioned earlier, high-fiber foods, such as whole grains, fruits, and vegetables, can add to satiation so that fewer calories need to be eaten to feel full. Research studies have shown that obese men and women tend to have lower amounts of dietary fiber daily than their leaner counterparts. This lends credence to the concept that fiber plays a role in weight management.[34] Whereas some weight-loss diets restrict carbohydrates, these plans would work better if they *increased* high-fiber carbohydrates.

Fiber Helps Prevent Heart Disease, Diabetes, and Cancer

Viscous, soluble fibers have been shown to help lower elevated blood cholesterol levels. A high blood cholesterol level can increase the risk of heart disease. It is believed that viscous fiber interferes with the reabsorption of bile acids in the intestines. Bile acids are high in cholesterol and are released into your intestine by your gallbladder to help with the digestion of fat. The bile acids are likely "grabbed" by the fiber before they can be reabsorbed by the body. They then end up being excreted along with the fiber in your waste products. Your body replaces these lost bile acids by removing cholesterol from the blood to generate new bile acids in the liver. Blood cholesterol levels are lowered as a result.

Slow-moving, viscous, soluble fibers may reduce the rate at which fat and carbohydrates are absorbed from your meals. Delayed absorption can lower the surge of fat in your blood after a meal, and may help improve sensitivity to the hormone, insulin. Both high levels of fat in the blood and a decreased sensitivity to insulin are considered risk factors for heart disease.

Viscous, soluble fiber may not be the only type of fiber that can promote heart health. Several research studies have shown that cereal and grains, which contain insoluble fiber, may help to lower the risk of heart disease.[35] A study looking at the dietary habits of over 65,000 women for a period of 10 years found that the risk of developing heart disease was over 30 percent lower in those consuming the highest amount of cereal fiber.[36]

Viscous, soluble fibers have also been shown to help individuals with diabetes mellitus. They slow the release of food from your stomach, and thus, slow down the digestion and absorption of glucose. This could help avoid a large spike in blood glucose after eating and help diabetics improve the long-term control of their blood glucose level.[37] Fiber may also play a role in preventing diabetes. Research studies involving both men and women have shown that a higher consumption of fiber from cereals helped reduce the risk of a certain type of diabetes.[38]

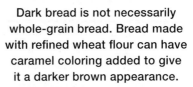

Dark bread is not necessarily whole-grain bread. Bread made with refined wheat flour can have caramel coloring added to give it a darker brown appearance.

diverticulitis Infection of the diverticula.

Fiber is thought to have many positive and protective effects in the fight against certain cancers. Fiber from cereals has been shown to help lower the risk of breast cancer.[39] Research also suggests that as fiber consumption increases, the incidence of colorectal cancer is reduced.

As mentioned earlier, fiber increases the bulk of stool, which can dilute cancer-promoting substances in the colon. Fiber helps keeps things moving through the digestive tract so that potential cancer-promoting substances spend less time in contact with the intestinal lining. Fiber encourages the growth of friendly bacteria in the colon and their fermentation by-products, both of which may have cancer-fighting potential. Because an increased amount of bile acids in the colon is thought to be associated with colon and rectal cancer, fiber's ability to reduce the concentration of these acids is viewed as a cancer deterrent.[40]

Over the years, some studies have challenged fiber's protective role against colorectal cancer. Several short-term research studies failed to show an anticancer effect of fiber. These findings may have been due to several factors. The amount of fiber consumed in the studies may not have been large enough to make a difference; the studies may have been too short in length to show an effect; and the fiber that was used in these studies wasn't from a variety of sources.[41]

Current research supports the cancer-fighting potential of fiber. A large research study involving over 500,000 individuals recruited from ten European countries showed that individuals who consumed the most fiber (35 grams of fiber, on average), compared with those eating the least amount of fiber daily (15 grams, on average), reduced their risk of colorectal cancer by about 40 percent.[42] The dietary sources of fiber were varied among the countries and included fiber from cereal, vegetables, fruits, and legumes.

Because this large study was done with high-fiber foods and not fiber supplements, it is difficult to tease out if the potential cancer-fighting substance in these foods is only the fiber, or the other nutrients and phytochemicals in these plant-based foods operating in concert with the fiber. Once again, the best advice is to eat a varied, balanced, plant-based diet rich in whole grains, fruits, vegetables, and legumes.

The Take-Home Message Fiber is an nondigestible substance that can help reduce your risk of constipation, diverticulosis, heart disease, obesity, diabetes mellitus, and certain cancers.

What Is Diabetes Mellitus and Why Is It an Epidemic?

Diabetes mellitus, or *diabetes,* is becoming so common that it would be rare if you *didn't* know someone who has it. An estimated 21 million American adults—over 7 percent of the population—have diabetes. Another 7 million have the disease, but don't know it yet.[43]

Recall that the hormone insulin directs glucose into the cells to be used as immediate energy or stored in another form for later use. Individuals develop diabetes because they aren't producing enough insulin and/or they have developed **insulin resistance,** such that their cells do not respond to the insulin when it arrives.[44] In essence, insulin is available in the blood, but the cells' decreased sensitivity interferes

diabetes mellitus A medical condition whereby an individual either doesn't have enough insulin or is resistant to the insulin available. This will cause the blood glucose level to rise. Diabetes mellitus is often called diabetes.

insulin resistance The inability of the cells to respond to insulin.

with its ability to work properly. Hence, the bloodstream is flooded with glucose that can't get into the cells. In this situation, the body thinks that it must be fasting and shifts into fasting mode. The liver begins the process of breaking down its glycogen stores (glycogenolysis) and making glucose from noncarbohydrate sources (gluconeogenesis) in an attempt to provide the glucose for its cells. This floods the blood with even more glucose. Eventually, the level of glucose builds up in the blood and some of it spills over into the urine and leaves the body.

Mellitus is Latin for "honey-sweet," which is what the blood and urine of a person with diabetes might be, due to the increased amount of glucose.

At the same time, the body has called on its energy reserve, fat, to be used as fuel. The body needs glucose in order to thoroughly burn fat; otherwise, it makes ketone bodies. In poorly managed diabetes, when glucose is unable to get into the cells, acidic ketone bodies build up in the blood to dangerous levels, causing **ketoacidosis.** Diabetic ketoacidosis can cause nausea and confusion, and in some cases, if left untreated, could result in coma or death. (Note: Although ketosis can develop in individuals who are fasting or consuming a low-carbohydrate diet, ketoacidosis only occurs when insulin is lacking in the body. Ketosis is not the same as diabetic ketoacidosis nor is it life-threatening.)

There Are Several Forms of Diabetes

All forms of diabetes involve insulin and unregulated blood glucose levels. Some are due to insulin resistance, as just described, and others are due to a lack of insulin production. Still another form occurs only during pregnancy. Let's discuss some of these forms specifically.

Type 1 and Type 2 Diabetes

The most prevalent types of diabetes are type 1 and type 2. Type 1 diabetes is considered an autoimmune disease and is the rarer of the two forms. Type 2 is the more common form and is seen in people who have because insulin resistant.

Type 1 diabetes usually begins in childhood and the early adult years and is found in 5 to 10 percent of the individuals with diabetes in the United States.[45] The immune system of type 1 diabetics actually destroys the insulin-producing cells in the pancreas. Symptoms such as increased thirst, frequent urination, constant blurred vision, hunger, weight loss, and fatigue are common, as the glucose can't get into the cells of the body. If not treated with insulin, the person is susceptible to the dangers of ketoacidosis. Individuals with type 1 diabetes must inject insulin every day in order to live a normal life.

Type 2 diabetes accounts for 90 to 95 percent of diagnoses of the disease and being overweight increases the risk of type 2 diabetes.[46] People with type 2 diabetes typically produce insulin but have become insulin resistant. After several years of exhausting their insulin-producing cells in the pancreas, their production of insulin decreases to the point where they have to take medication and/or insulin to manage their blood glucose level.

One of the major problems with type 2 diabetes is that this condition can go undiagnosed for some time. While some people may have symptoms such as increased thirst, others may not. Consequently, diabetes can silently damage a person's vital organs without their awareness. Because of this, the American Diabetes Association (ADA) recommends that everyone 45 years of age and older undergo testing for diabetes. However, if a person is at a higher risk for developing diabetes, he or she shouldn't wait until age 45 to be tested. Take the Self-Assessment on the next page to see if you are at risk.

There are many ways for an individual to monitor his or her blood glucose levels.

ketoacidosis The buildup of ketone bodies to dangerous levels, which can result in coma or death.

Are You at Risk for Type 2 Diabetes?

Take the following quiz to assess if you are at a higher risk for developing type 2 diabetes. Whereas this list contains the presently known risk factors for type 2 diabetes, there may be others. If you have questions or doubts, check with your doctor.

Do you have a body mass index (BMI) of 25 or higher*?　　　　**Yes** ☐　**No** ☐

If you answered no, you don't need to continue. If you answered yes, continue.

1. Does your mom, dad, brother, or sister have diabetes?　　**Yes** ☐　**No** ☐
2. Do you typically get little exercise?　　　　　　　　　　**Yes** ☐　**No** ☐
3. Are you of African-American, Alaska Native, Native American, Asian-American, Hispanic-American, or Pacific Islander-American descent?　　　　　　　　　　　　　　　**Yes** ☐　**No** ☐
4. Have you ever delivered a baby that weighed more than 9 pounds at birth?　　　　　　　　　　　　　　**Yes** ☐　**No** ☐
5. Have you ever had diabetes during pregnancy?　　　　**Yes** ☐　**No** ☐
6. Do you have a blood pressure of 140/90 millimeters of mercury (mmHg) or higher?　　　　　　　　　　**Yes** ☐　**No** ☐
7. Have you been told by your doctor that you have too much fatty triglycerides (fat) in your blood (more than 250 mg/dl) or too little of the "good" HDL cholesterol (less than 35 mg/dl)?　**Yes** ☐　**No** ☐
8. Have you ever had blood glucose test results that were higher than normal?　　　　　　　　　　　　　　**Yes** ☐　**No** ☐
9. Have you ever been told that you have vascular disease or problems with your blood vessels?　　　　　　**Yes** ☐　**No** ☐
10. Do you have polycystic ovary syndrome[†]?　　　　**Yes** ☐　**No** ☐

Answers

If you are overweight and answered yes to any of the above questions, you could benefit from speaking with your doctor.

*BMI is a measure of your weight in relationship to your height. See Chapter 10 for a chart to determine your BMI.

[†]Polycystic ovary syndrome is a disorder in women due to an abnormal level of hormones, including insulin. This disorder increases your risk of diabetes as well as heart disease and high blood pressure.

Because the hormone insulin is derived from the components of protein, it can't be taken orally, as it would be broken down in the same manner that other protein-containing foods are digested. Therefore, most individuals have to inject themselves with insulin using a syringe. Researchers are continually testing alternative ways for those with diabetes to self-administer insulin. New methods include insulin pens, insulin jet injectors, and insulin pumps. Researchers hope that someday those with diabetes will no longer have to use needles to obtain the insulin they critically need.

Prediabetes

A simple blood test at a physician's office can reveal if a person's blood glucose is higher than normal and whether he or she has **impaired glucose intolerance,** or *prediabetes.* The blood is typically drawn first thing in the morning after fasting overnight for 8 to 12 hours. A fasting blood glucose level of under 100 milligrams per deciliter (mg/dl) is considered "negative" and a fasting blood glucose of 126 mg/dl or higher is considered a "positive" test for diabetes (Table 4.6). A reading between 100 mg/dl and 126 mg/dl

impaired glucose intolerance
A condition whereby a fasting blood glucose level is higher than normal (>100 mg/dl), but not high enough (≤126 mg/dl) to be classified as having diabetes mellitus. Also called prediabetes.

is classified as prediabetes. Individuals with prediabetes have a blood glucose level that is higher than it should be but not yet high enough to be classified as diabetic. About 16 million people over the age of 40 have prediabetes and are at a higher risk of developing not only diabetes, but also heart disease.[47] When a person is in this prediabetic state, damage may already be occurring to the heart and circulatory system.

Diabetes Can Result in Long-Term Damage

Constant exposure to high blood glucose levels can damage vital organs over time. Diabetes, especially if it is poorly managed, increases the likelihood of a multitude of dire effects such as nerve damage, leg and foot amputations, eye diseases, including blindness, tooth loss, gum problems, kidney disease, and heart disease.[48]

Nerve damage occurs in an estimated 50 percent of individuals with diabetes, and the longer the person has diabetes, the greater the risk for the damage. Numbness in the toes, feet, legs, and hands, as well as changes in bowel, bladder, and sexual function are all signs of damage to nerves. This nerve damage can affect the ability to feel a change in temperature or pain in the legs and feet. A cut or sore on the foot could go unnoticed until it becomes infected. The poor blood circulation common in those with diabetes can also make it harder for sores or infections to heal. The infection could infiltrate the bone, causing the need for an amputation.

Diabetes can also damage the tiny blood vessels in the retina of the eye, which can cause bleeding and cloudy vision, and eventually destroy the retina and cause blindness. A high blood glucose level can cause tooth and gum problems, including the loss of teeth, and damage to the kidneys. If the kidneys are damaged, protein can leak out into the urine, and at the same time, cause a backup of wastes in the blood. Kidney failure could result.

Diabetes is a risk factor for heart disease. The excess amount of fat often seen in the blood in poorly managed diabetes is most probably an important factor in the increased risk of heart disease in those with diabetes. Fortunately, good nutrition habits play a key role in both the prevention and management of diabetes.

Control Is Key

For years, people with diabetes have been advised to keep their blood glucose level under control. In the early 1990s, the research community finally gathered the evidence to back up that advice. The groundbreaking Diabetes Control and Complications Trial (DCCT), conducted from 1983 to 1993, involved over 1,400 people with type 1 diabetes. It showed that controlling the level of blood glucose with an intense regimen of diet, insulin, and exercise, along with monitoring blood sugar levels and routinely visiting health care professionals, slowed the onset of some of the complications of diabetes. In this study, it was shown that reducing high blood glucose helped lower the risk of eye disease by 76 percent and the risk of kidney and nerve disease by at least 50 percent. However, because some of the individuals in this study experienced bouts of hypoglycemia, this type of intense regimen is not recommended for children under age 13, people with heart disease or advanced complications of heart disease, older people, and those prone to frequent bouts of severe hypoglycemia.[49] For all others, diligent and conscientious management of their blood glucose can minimize the devastating complications of diabetes often seen later in life.

The nutrition and lifestyle goals for individuals with type 1 or 2 diabetes are the same: to minimize the complications of diabetes by adopting a healthy, well-balanced diet and participating in regular physical activity that maintains a blood glucose level in a normal or close to normal range. The ADA recommends that individuals with

Table 4.6

Interpreting Blood Glucose Levels

If a Fasting Blood Glucose Level Is	The Level Is Considered
<100 mg/dl	Normal
100 to 125 mg/dl	Prediabetic
≥126 mg/dl*	Diabetic

*There must be two "positive" tests, done on separate days, for an official diagnosis of diabetes.

Source: American Diabetes Association, Diagnosis and Classification of Diabetes Mellitus, *Diabetes Care* 29 (2006): S43–S48.

The Glycemic Index of Foods

Foods	GI*
Rice, low amylose	126
Potato, baked	121
Cornflakes	119
Jelly beans	114
Green peas	107
Cheerios	106
Puffed wheat	105
Bagel, plain	103
Carrots	101
White bread	100
Angel food cake	95
Ice cream	87
Bran muffin	85
Rice, long grain rice†	80
Brown rice	79
Oatmeal	79
Popcorn	79
Corn	78
Banana, overripe	74
Carrots	71
Chocolate	70
Baked beans	69
Sponge cake	66
Pear, canned in juice	63
Custard	61
Spaghetti	59
Rice, long grain‡	58
Apple	52
Pear	47
Banana, underripe	43
Kidney beans	42
Whole milk	39
Peanuts	21

*GI = Glycemic Index
†Boiled for 25 minutes.
‡Boiled for 5 minutes.

Figure 4.14 The Glycemic Index of Commonly Eaten Foods

diabetes consume a diet that includes a combination of predominantly high-fiber carbohydrates from whole grains, fruits, and vegetables, along with low-fat milk, adequate amounts of lean protein sources, and unsaturated fats.[50]

The glycemic index (GI) and glycemic load (GL) can be used to classify the effects of carbohydrate-containing foods on blood glucose. The GI refers to the measured upward rise, peak, and eventual fall of blood glucose following the consumption of a carbohydrate-intense food. Some foods cause a sharp spike and rapid fall in blood glucose levels compared with others that cause less of a spike and a more gradual decline.[51] The index ranks high-carbohydrate foods according to their effect on blood glucose levels compared with that of an equal amount of white bread or pure glucose.

If a carbohydrate-rich food causes your blood glucose level to produce a curve with a larger area than the standard curve of white bread, the food is considered a high-GI food. A carbohydrate-containing food that produces a smaller blood glucose level curve than that of white bread would be considered a low-GI food. For example, 50 grams of white bread have a glycemic index of 100. A 50-gram portion of kidney beans has a GI of 42, whereas the same amount of puffed wheat cereal has a GI of 105. Consequently, the kidney beans are considered a low-GI food compared with the white bread, while puffed wheat is considered a high-GI food (Figure 4.14). The problem with use of the GI is that 50 grams of puffed wheat would be over 4 cups of cereal, an amount that is unlikely to be eaten in one sitting. The glycemic load (GL) adjusts the GI to take into account the amount of carbohydrate consumed in a typical serving of a food, and in the case of puffed wheat cereal would lower its effect on blood glucose dramatically.

Other factors can also affect the GI of a food. Overripe fruits have more easily digested sugar and a higher GI than underripe ones. Both cooking and food processing change the structure of foods and make them more easily digested, increasing the GI compared with raw, unprocessed equivalents. Larger chunks or bigger particle sizes of food contribute to slower digestion and lower GI than the same foods chopped into smaller pieces. Foods with viscous, soluble fiber tend to be absorbed more slowly so will have a lower GI than refined carbohydrates. In general, whole grains, vegetables, whole fruit, and legumes tend to have a low GI.[52] Lastly, eating carbohydrate-heavy foods with protein and/or fat can also lower the GI.[53]

Whereas the overall amount of carbohydrate within a healthy diet along with weight management are key factors in managing diabetes, the GI and GL may also help those with diabetes, according to the American Diabetes Association. The ADA recommends that individuals with diabetes consume a diet that includes a combination of predominantly high-fiber carbohydrates from whole grains, fruits, and vegetables, along with low-fat milk, monounsaturated fat, and adequate amounts of lean protein sources, which also help control GI.[54]

Though sugar was once thought of as a "diabetic no-no" it can now be part of a diabetic's diet. Research has found that eating sucrose doesn't cause a rise in a person's blood glucose level to any greater extent than does starch, so avoidance of sugar isn't necessary. However, because weight management is often a concern, especially for type 2 diabetics, there's little room for a lot of sweets and treats in a diabetic diet (or *anyone's* diet, for that matter).

Cases of Diabetes Are on the Rise

The incidence of adults being diagnosed with diabetes in the United States has more than doubled since the early 1990s.[55] In fact, diabetes is expected to afflict about 9 percent of American adults in the year 2025.[56]

Over 200,000 Americans die from diabetic complications annually, and diabetes is the sixth leading cause of death in the United States. Diabetes is not only a deadly disease but also an extremely costly one. Disability insurance payments, time lost from employment, and the medical costs associated with diabetes cost the United States almost $100 billion annually.[57]

The number of people who have diabetes is not only strikingly high, it's rising, particularly among children. Whereas the disease used to be common only in adults, in the last couple of decades there's been a steady increase among those under age 20.

Children and Diabetes

The rising incidence of overweight and obesity is happening among younger and younger children.[58] Approximately 15 percent (almost 9 million) of American children and teens age 6 to 19 are overweight, which is more than double the percentage in the 1970s. Obesity increases the risk factor for type 2 diabetes in children.

Type 1 diabetes used to be the only prevalent type of diabetes in children. In fact, in 1990, less than 4 percent of diabetic children had type 2 diabetes. However, up to 45 percent of the new cases of diabetes in children is the type 2 variety, and of those children, as many as 85 percent are also overweight or obese.[59] This explosion in the incidence of type 2 diabetes in children is most likely a combination of increased obesity and physical inactivity. Sedentary indoor activities such as surfing the Web and playing video games have replaced the active biking and outdoor games of yesteryear.

Developing diabetes at a younger age means longer exposure to the disease and its medical complications. Early detection is important for effective treatment, and all children who are at risk for developing type 2 diabetes should be screened (Table 4.7).

Preventing Type 2 Diabetes

Recent research has suggested that shedding some excess weight, exercising regularly, and eating a balanced, high-fiber, healthy diet may be the best strategy to lower the risk of developing diabetes. A landmark study by the Diabetes Prevention Program

Table 4.7

Red Flags for Type 2 Diabetes in Children and Adolescents

The following risk factors may increase the risk of childhood type 2 diabetes in children and adolescents:

 Being overweight

AND any two of the following:

🏴 Having a parent or grandparent with type 2 diabetes

🏴 Being of American Indian, African-American, Hispanic-American, Asian-American, or Pacific Islander descent

🏴 Showing signs of being resistant to insulin or having conditions associated with insulin resistance such as high blood pressure or too much fat and/or cholesterol in the blood, and polycystic ovary syndrome

of over 3,000 individuals with prediabetes showed that those who made changes in their lifestyle, such as losing weight, exercising 2.5 hours a week, eating a plant-based, heart-healthy diet, and meeting with a health professional for ongoing support and education, were 58 percent less likely to develop type 2 diabetes than those who did not partake in such intervention.[60] When it comes to winning the battle against diabetes, a healthful diet and lifestyle is the best game plan.

The Take-Home Message Diabetes is a condition involving inadequate regulation of blood glucose levels. Individuals with type 1 diabetes produce inadequate amounts of insulin. Those with type 2 diabetes have developed insulin resistance. Chronic high blood glucose levels can damage the vital organs of the body, including the heart. Individuals with diabetes need to take medications and/or insulin to manage their blood glucose. A high-fiber diet and routine exercise play important roles in managing and preventing diabetes. Diabetes is becoming more common in children, especially those who are overweight and inactive.

What Is Hypoglycemia?

Whereas a high level of glucose in your blood on a regular basis isn't healthy, a blood glucose level that is too low, or **hypoglycemia,** can be unpleasant for many of us and downright dangerous for some with diabetes. Individuals who experience hypoglycemia may feel hungry, nervous, dizzy, light-headed, confused, weak, shaky, and even begin to sweat. Eating or drinking carbohydrate-rich foods, such as hard candies, juice, or soda, can relieve these symptoms quickly and raise the blood glucose level to a normal range.

Those with diabetes who need to use insulin and/or blood glucose-lowering medications daily are at risk of hypoglycemia if they skip meals and snacks or if they don't eat enough to cover the effects of the medication. If these individuals ignore their symptoms, their blood glucose level can drop so low that they could faint, or slip into a coma.[61] Those with diabetes need to eat regularly to maintain blood glucose levels that coincide with their medication. A change in their activities or exercise level can also lower the blood glucose level. Diabetics need to check their blood glucose level before they exercise to determine if a snack is needed.

Though not common, people without diabetes may also experience bouts of hypoglycemia after meals, better known as reactive hypoglycemia, which may be hormone related. This can occur within four hours after a meal and cause the similar hypoglycemic symptoms: shakiness, dizziness, hunger, and perspiration. A doctor can diagnose this condition by testing a person's blood glucose level while they are having these symptoms. Though the cause of reactive hypoglycemia is not known, one thought is that some people may be overly sensitive to epinephrine, one of the hormones normally released when the blood glucose level begins to drop. The hormone glucagon may also play a role. Eating smaller, well-balanced meals throughout the day can help avoid hypoglycemia.

Drinking juice can help restore blood glucose level to a normal range.

hypoglycemia A blood glucose level that drops to lower than 70 mg/dl. Hunger, shakiness, dizziness, perspiration, and light-headedness are some signs of hypoglycemia.

Another type of hypoglycemia, called fasting hypoglycemia, can occur in the morning, after fasting throughout the night. It can also occur during long stretches between meals or after exercise. Some medications, illnesses, certain tumors, hormone imbalances, or drinking too much alcohol may cause this type of hypoglycemia.

The Take-Home Message Symptoms of hypoglycemia include feeling hungry, nervous, light-headed, shaky, and sweaty. Those who take medication and/or insulin to manage their diabetes but don't eat properly are at a greater risk of experiencing hypoglycemia. Individuals without diabetes may experience reactive hypoglycemia several hours after a meal. Fasting hypoglycemia can occur in the morning upon awakening and can be caused by some medications, illnesses, hormone imbalances, or excessive consumption of alcohol.

Putting It All Together

Carbohydrates are an important part of a healthy diet. Whole grains, fruits, vegetables, and lean dairy products provide carbohydrates along with vitamins and minerals and should be the predominant source of carbohydrates in your diet. Whole grains, fruits, and vegetables are also good sources of fiber and phytochemicals. A diet that contains plenty of these foods can help prevent many chronic diseases. Sugary foods also provide carbohydrates but are less nutrient dense, so should be used in moderation.

Carbohydrates

What Are Carbohydrates?

Carbohydrates are essential nutrients that are predominant in plant-based foods, and they make up the foundation of many diets around the world. You need carbohydrates on a daily basis because they are the most desirable source of energy for your body. Their main role is to supply fuel, primarily in the form of **glucose** (*ose* = carbohydrate), the predominant sugar in carbohydrate-rich foods, to your cells. Plants form glucose in a process called **photosynthesis.**

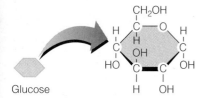

Glucose

Simple and Complex Carbohydrates

Carbohydrates are divided into two categories based on the number of sugar units that are joined together. **Simple carbohydrates,** or sugars, include **monosaccharides** (*mono* = one, *saccharide* = sugar) and **disaccharides** (*di* = two), and **complex carbohydrates** include **polysaccharides** (*poly* = many).

There are three monosaccharides that are found in foods: glucose, **fructose,** and

ⓐ Monosaccharides

Fructose   Glucose   Galactose

ⓑ Disaccharides

Sucrose
(glucose and
fructose)

Maltose
(glucose and
glucose)

Lactose
(glucose and
galactose)

ⓒ Polysaccharides (starch)

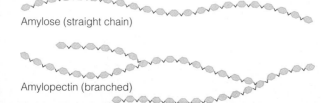

Amylose (straight chain)

Amylopectin (branched)

galactose. Fructose is the sweetest of the simple sugars and is found abundantly in fruit. For this reason, it is often referred to as fruit sugar. Galactose is found in dairy foods. From these three sugars, the other simple and complex carbohydrates can be created.

When two glucose units join together, the disaccharide **maltose** is created. Maltose is the sugar found in grains. When glucose and fructose pair up, the disaccharide **sucrose,** or table sugar, is formed. Galactose is joined with glucose to create lactose (often called milk sugar, as it is found in dairy foods).

Polysaccharides contain the most sugars so it makes sense that they are called complex carbohydrates. **Starch, fiber,** and **glycogen** are all polysaccharides.

Functions of Carbohydrates

Your body uses carbohydrates, specifically glucose, for energy, and there are chemical messengers called **hormones** that regulate the amount of glucose in your blood. To lower your blood glucose level, your pancreas releases the hormone **insulin** into the blood.

Surplus glucose is stored in long chains of glycogen. The process of generating glycogen for later use is call **glycogenesis** (*glyco* = sugar/sweet, *genesis* = origin). Glycogenesis occurs only in your liver and muscle cells. You can't squirrel away unlimited extra energy reserves in the form of glycogen. However, you can store excess energy in the form of fat.

Your pancreas releases another hormone, **glucagon,** when the body needs to direct the release of glucose from the stored glycogen in your liver to help raise your blood glucose level. This breakdown of glycogen is called **glycogenolysis** (*lysis* = loosening).

Fiber Has Many Health Benefits

Fiber has been shown to help lower your risk of developing constipation, diverticulosis, obesity, heart disease, cancer, and diabetes mellitus.

Meals high in fiber are typically digested more slowly, which allows the absorption of the nutrients to be extended over a longer period of time. Foods high in fiber, such as whole grains, fruits, and vegetables, can add to satiation so that fewer calories need to be eaten to feel full.

Viscous, soluble fibers have been shown to help lower elevated blood cholesterol levels. A high blood cholesterol level can increase the risk of heart disease.

Daily Needs

The latest Dietary Reference Intakes (DRIs) for carbohydrates recommend that adults and children consume a minimum of 130 grams daily. This is based on the estimated minimum amount of glucose your brain needs to function efficiently. A quick look at MyPyramid shows that 130 grams is less than the amount you would consume by eating the minimum recommended daily servings from the grain group (6 servings), vegetable group (3 servings), fruit group (2 servings), and dairy group (3 servings).

In the United States, adult males consume, on average, 220 grams to 330 grams of carbohydrates daily, whereas adult females eat 180 grams to 230 grams daily, well over the minimum DRI.

According to the latest DRIs, 45 to 65 percent of your total daily calories should come from carbohydrates. Adults in the United States consume about half of their calories from carbohydrate-laden foods, so they are easily meeting this optimal range.

Food Sources

In general, you want your diet to contain low to moderate amounts of simple carbohydrates and be high in fiber and other complex carbohydrates. This is the best strategy for long-term health.

Simple carbohydrates are found naturally in fruits, vegetables, and dairy foods.

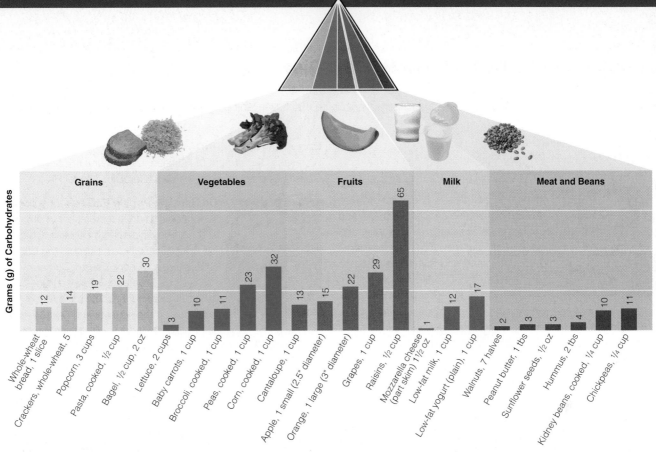

Grams (g) of Carbohydrates

Food	Grams
Grains	
Whole-wheat bread, 1 slice	12
Crackers, whole-wheat, 5	14
Popcorn, 3 cups	19
Pasta, cooked, 1/2 cup	22
Bagel, 1/2 cup, 2 oz	30
Vegetables	
Lettuce, 2 cups	3
Baby carrots, 1 cup	10
Broccoli, cooked, 1 cup	11
Peas, cooked, 1 cup	23
Corn, cooked, 1 cup	32
Fruits	
Cantaloupe, 1 cup	13
Apple, 1 small (2.5" diameter)	15
Orange, 1 large (3" diameter)	22
Grapes, 1 cup	29
Raisins, 1/2 cup	65
Milk	
Mozzarella cheese (part skim) 1 1/2 oz	1
Low-fat milk, 1 cup	12
Low-fat yogurt (plain), 1 cup	17
Meat and Beans	
Walnuts, 7 halves	2
Peanut butter, 1 tbs	3
Sunflower seeds, 1/2 oz	3
Hummus, 2 tbs	4
Kidney beans, cooked, 1/4 cup	10
Chickpeas, 1/4 cup	11

Though you can also get simple sugars from processed foods and sweets, the higher calorie and lower nutrient levels in these foods make them a less healthy option.

Complex carbohydrates, including starch and fiber, are found abundantly in grains, whole fruits, and vegetables. Starch is the primary complex carbohydrate found in grains and potatoes, while fiber is found in whole grains, whole fruits, vegetables, legumes, nuts, and seeds.

Too Much or Too Little?

Adding too much carbohydrates in the diet can displace other essential nutrients, whereas consuming too little carbohydrates can create a diet that falls short of many vitamins, minerals, fiber, and phytochemicals. Both extremes will produce an unbalanced diet. Individuals with diabetes need to monitor their carbohydrate intake to maintain a healthy blood glucose level. Chronic, poor regulation of blood glucose levels can damage the body.

What Is Diabetes?

Individuals develop **diabetes** because they aren't producing enough insulin (type 1 diabetes) and/or they have developed **insulin resistance,** such that their cells do not respond to the insulin when it arrives (type 2 diabetes).

Type 1 diabetes is considered an autoimmune disease and is the rarer of the two forms. Type 2 is the more common form and is seen in people who have become insulin resistant. Type 2 diabetes accounts for 90 to 95 percent of diagnoses of the disease.

Diabetes, especially if it is poorly managed, increases the likelihood of a multitude of dire effects such as nerve damage, leg and foot amputations, eye diseases, including blindness, tooth loss, gum problems, kidney disease, and heart disease. Diabetes can also damage the tiny blood vessels in the retina of the eye, which can cause bleeding and cloudy vision, and eventually destroy the retina and cause blindness.

Good nutrition habits play a key role in both the prevention and management of diabetes. The ADA (American Diabetes Association) recommends that individuals with diabetes consume a diet that includes a combination of predominantly high-fiber carbohydrates from whole grains, fruits, and vegetables, along with low-fat milk, adequate amounts of lean protein sources, and unsaturated fats.

Terms to Know

glucose ■ photosynthesis ■ simple carbohydrates ■ monosaccharides ■ disaccharides ■ complex carbohydrates ■ polysaccharides ■ fructose ■ galactose ■ maltose ■ sucrose ■ starch ■ fiber ■ glycogen ■ hormones ■ insulin ■ glycogenesis ■ glucagon ■ glycogenolysis ■ diabetes ■ insulin resistance

Two Points of View

Can Soft Drinks Be Part of a Healthy Diet?

From sodas to fruit drinks and sports drinks, two experts weigh in on Americans' soft drink consumption and its ramifications for public health.

Robert Earl, MPH, RD
Senior Director, Nutrition Policy, Food Products Association

Robert Earl MPH, RD, directs nutrition and health policy activities for the Food Products Association, the principal scientific and technical trade association representing the food products industry. Earl provides food industry leadership and technical assistance for the Washington, D.C.-based group, focusing on dietary and food guidance, food and nutrition programs, nutrition requirements, and nutrition and health claims in food labeling. A registered dietitian, Earl holds a master's degree in public health nutrition from the University of North Carolina at Chapel Hill.

Q: Has Americans' soft drink consumption changed over time? If so, how has it changed and why?

A: Just looking at traditional soft drinks such as sodas—not newer products such as fruit drinks or sports drinks—consumption had been going up. But that has changed in the last couple of years. Consumption now appears to be leveling off or dropping.

Why is this the case? The variety of caloric and non-caloric beverages has changed, so there are more choices. It is becoming clearer that Americans understand the "calories count" message. They are understanding that to manage weight or lose weight, they need to think about overall calorie consumption and their level of physical activity. That is factoring into their beverage choices. People understand that beverages are a part of their calorie intake.

Q: How has the change in soft drink consumption affected the health of Americans?

A: That depends on what individuals consume, their overall diet, and their level of physical activity. One has to look at whether a consumer is drinking caloric soft drinks or calorie-free soft drinks. And those choices have to be factored into total dietary patterns and physical activity patterns.

Q: How can soft drinks be part of a healthy diet?

A: Any individual has room to consume soft drinks, particularly non-caloric soft drinks, as part of a healthful diet. Beverages that have no calories are useful in fulfilling an individual's hydration needs. While many beverages—milk, juice, soft drinks—can come with a contribution of calories, if someone is active and eats a wide variety of foods, a caloric soft drink could fit within their caloric needs. It's all about balance,

(continued)

Barry M. Popkin, PhD
Professor, Department of Nutrition; Director, Interdisciplinary Obesity Center University of North Carolina, Chapel Hill

Dr. Barry M. Popkin PhD has a doctorate in economics and is a professor of nutrition at the University of North Carolina, Chapel Hill (UNC-CH), where he directs the UNC-CH's Interdisciplinary Obesity Center. He initiated the Beverage Guidance Panel, a group of prominent scholars that offers guidance on the benefits and risks of various beverage choices. Popkin conducts a wide range of U.S. and international research on diet, health, and obesity solutions.

Q: Has Americans' soft drink consumption changed over time? If so, how has it changed and why?

A: Today, the average American gets about 21 percent of his or her calories from beverages. Most age and gender groups are consuming about 150 to 300 more calories than they did, and about half of that increase comes from soft drinks and fruit drinks. From the 1970s to the present, we experienced three trends of equal importance: per capita intake of soft drinks and fruit drinks went up; the number of times per day that people consumed caloric, sweetened beverages went up; and the portion size went up. In the late '70s, we used to get just under 3 percent of our daily calories from soft drinks. By the late '90s, that figure went up to 7 percent. Interestingly, the average American adult consumes 227 more calories per day from beverages in 2002 than he or she did in 1965.

A principal driver behind this change is how drink manufacturers are working to make us drink more and more of their products. And that's not just soft drinks. We are getting more of our calories from fruit drinks compared to the late 1970s, and more from alcohol.

Q: How has the change in soft drink consumption affected the health of Americans?

A: The evidence isn't perfect that soft drinks will increase your weight or lead to obesity or diabetes or tooth decay, but it's pretty solid. Soft drinks and fruit drinks are clearly a bigger culprit than any other beverage for 10- to 35-year-olds. But other beverages have contributed too. Some groups of adults have tripled their daily alcohol intake. Others have started having a smoothie a day.

People need to remember that beverages are much less satiating than solid foods. When you consume calories

(continued)

Can Soft Drinks Be Part of a Healthy Diet?, continued

Robert Earl, MPH, RD, continued

variety, and moderation. One has to look at one's food and beverage choices, and factor in physical activity to get the total picture.

Q: What can the soft drink industry do (or what is it doing) to help improve public health?

A: The soft drink and beverage industry has introduced a wide variety of options for the consumer. Those options aren't limited to the range of regular, mid-calorie, and calorie-free versions of soft drinks now available. There are so many other beverage alternatives from these companies, and one benefit to the public is this incredible variety. Most large traditional soft drink companies now also sell sports drinks, calorie-free beverages, juice, and water. Some even have dairy-based products. And look at water. While this isn't a benefit exclusively driven by soft drink companies, never before has water been so available to consumers in portable form.

The soft drink industry is also being very active in promoting responsible beverage consumption to children, adolescents, and adults. The industry is working with schools, promoting both nutrition and hydration, as well as providing support for improved physical activity. They are working to expand the range of options in vending machines and cafeterias in schools and in workplaces. Nutrition education and physical activity programs are also being funded.

Barry M. Popkin, PhD, continued

from beverages, you don't compensate by eating less food later on. Liquid calories don't register with our appetite controls.

Q: How can soft drinks be part of a healthy diet?

A: I don't see a way soft drinks can be part of a healthy diet unless you are an athlete or very physically active. Otherwise, they lead to weight gain. Non-diet soft drinks have zero benefits and major costs. If you have a 12-ounce serving of soft drinks or fruit drinks, you've got to compensate for the 160 calories you get from it.

I am also very cautious about saying that you can consume a lot of diet drinks. Some studies suggest that these beverages condition children and adults to have a high preference for sweetness. Moreover they suggest we adjust over time, so we need more and more sweetness to be satisfied. That may drive up overall consumption of sweet or sweetened foods, which also leads to weight gain. Our (beverage) panel is monitoring some of this new research closely.

Q: What can the soft drink industry do (or what is it doing) to help improve public health?

A: They could promote water and unsweetened, unflavored low-fat or skim milk. They could also change their messages about how we need to be drinking beverages all the time to stay hydrated. That messaging is not only incorrect but it is rather misleading—people already know how to follow their thirst and consume enough liquids. The messages only serve to drive up consumption of calorically-sweetened beverages.

Be a Nutrition Sleuth

Sweet on Sweets

Go to www.aw-bc.com/blake to see one student's typical daily diet—high in added sugars and low in fiber. Use Table 4.3 and Figure 4.7 to see if you can come up with healthier choices that will satisfy a sweet tooth and provide the fiber this student needs.

Get Real!

How Much Fiber Are You Eating?

Do you think you have enough fiber in your diet? You may be surprised. Go to www.aw-bc.com/blake and fill out the daily food record. Use Appendix A or the MyDietAnalysis program to complete the record and see how you are really doing!

The Top Ten Points to Remember

1. Glucose, fructose, and galactose are monosaccharides. Glucose is the most abundant monosaccharide and the preferred fuel for your nervous system, including your brain, and red blood cells. When two monosaccharides are joined, a disaccharide is formed. The best-known disaccharide, sucrose (table sugar), is made of fructose and glucose. Lactose, or milk sugar, is made up of glucose and galactose. Maltose is two glucose units joined together. When many glucose units are joined together, starch, a polysaccharide, is formed. Glycogen is the polysaccharide storage form of glucose in your body. Fiber is a nondigestible polysaccharide.

   a Monosaccharides
   Fructose Glucose Galactose

2. Your blood glucose level is maintained in a healthy range with the help of hormones. Insulin directs glucose into your cells. When your blood glucose level drops too low, the hormone glucagon is released to increase your blood glucose level. When your diet is deficient in carbohydrates, your body will not be able to break down fat completely. Ketone bodies are created.

3. A minimum of 130 grams of dietary carbohydrates is needed daily. It's recommended that 45 to 65 percent of your daily calories come from carbohydrates. Adults should consume 20 to 35 grams of fiber daily, depending on their age and gender.

4. Your body can't distinguish between naturally occurring and added sugar. Food sources of naturally occurring sugars tend to be more nutritious than foods with a lot of added sugar. The major source of dietary added sugar is soft drinks. Sugary foods contain calories but little else and can crowd out more nutritious food choices in the diet.

5. Polyols, saccharin, aspartame, acesulfame-K, sucralose, and neotame are sugar substitutes currently deemed safe by the FDA. Because aspartame contains the amino acid phenylalanine, individuals with phenylketonuria must limit all dietary sources of this amino acid.

6. Frequently exposing your teeth to starch and sugary foods, especially sticky foods, can increase your risk of dental caries.

7. Whole grains contain vitamins, minerals, fiber, and phytochemicals. Whereas refined grains can be "enriched" with some of the vitamins and minerals that were lost during processing, the fiber and phytochemicals are not added back. At least half of your daily servings of grains should be whole grains.

8. Carbohydrates themselves don't cause weight gain. Consuming excess calories from any source on a regular basis is the culprit behind gaining weight. Meals containing whole grains, fruits, and vegetables tend to be higher in bulk and are processed more slowly in your body than low-fiber meals, which may help you feel satiated and cause you to eat less.

9. Diabetes mellitus, particularly type 2 diabetes, is becoming more prevalent in the United States, especially among children. Those with diabetes should consume a well-balanced diet and exercise regularly to help maintain a blood glucose level within a healthy range. Medication and/or insulin as well as regular blood tests may also be needed to manage blood glucose.

10. Hypoglycemia or low blood sugar can occur in individuals with diabetes, especially if they are taking medication and/or insulin and are not eating properly. Individuals without diabetes can also experience hypoglycemia, but the incidence is less common.

Test Your Knowledge

1. _____ is the storage form of glucose in your body.
   a. Glucagon
   b. Glycogen
   c. Gluconeogenesis
   d. Glucose

2. Sucrose is a
   a. monosaccharide.
   b. disaccharide.
   c. polysaccharide.
   d. starch.

3. The hormone that directs the breakdown of glycogen is
   a. galactose.
   b. glucagon.
   c. insulin.
   d. none of the above.

4. The minimum amount of carbohydrates needed daily is
   a. 75 grams.
   b. 100 grams.
   c. 120 grams.
   d. 130 grams.
   e. 150 grams.

5. Which of the following can help someone who's lactose intolerant enjoy dairy products?
   a. drinking Lactaid milk
   b. pouring milk over a cup of bran cereal
   c. enjoying cheese a little at a time, and building up to larger servings
   d. all of the above
   e. none of the above

6. Reducing consumption of which item would have the biggest impact on decreasing the amount of added sugars that Americans consume?
   a. watermelon
   b. candy
   c. soft drinks
   d. apples

7. Your blood cholesterol level is too high so you would like to eat additional viscous, soluble high-fiber foods to help lower it. A good choice would be
   a. low-fat milk.
   b. chocolate chip cookies.
   c. bananas.
   d. oatmeal.

8. Which of the following nutrients are added to enriched grains?
   a. folic acid, thiamin, B_{12}, niacin, and calcium
   b. folic acid, thiamin, riboflavin, B_{12}, and iron
   c. fiber, thiamin, riboflavin, niacin, and iron
   d. folic acid, thiamin, riboflavin, niacin, and iron

9. The small bulging pouches that are sometimes found along the intestinal lining are called
   a. diverticulosis.
   b. diverticulitis.
   c. diverticula.
   d. diabetes.

10. Which of the following can help reduce your risk of type 2 diabetes?
    a. avoiding sugar
    b. eating a high-fiber, plant-based diet
    c. exercising regularly
    d. all of the above
    e. b and c only

Answers

1. (b) glycogen. Glycogen is stored in your liver and muscles and provides a ready-to-use form of glucose for your body. Glucagon is the hormone that directs the release of glucose from the stored glycogen. Gluconeogenesis is the creation of glucose from non-carbohydrate sources.

2. (b) Sucrose contains the two monosaccharides glucose and fructose, and is therefore a disaccharide. Starch contains many units of glucose linked together and is therefore a polysaccharide.

3. (b) When your blood glucose level drops too low, glucagon is released from your pancreas to direct the breakdown of glycogen in your liver to raise your blood level of glucose. Insulin is a hormone that directs the uptake of glucose by your cells. Galactose is a monosaccharide found in dairy foods.

4. (d) You should consume at least 130 grams of carbohydrates daily to supply your body, particularly your brain, with the glucose needed to function effectively.

5. (d) All of these can help improve lactose absorption. The Lactaid milk is pretreated to facilitate the breakdown of the lactose in the milk. Consuming lactose-containing foods, such as milk, with a meal or snack will improve the digestion of lactose. Gradually adding dairy foods to the diet will lessen the symptoms of lactose intolerance.

6. (c) Soft drinks are the number-one source of added sugars in the American diet, so reducing the intake of these sugary beverages would go a long way in reducing the amount of added sugars that Americans consume. Reducing the amount of candy that Americans consume would also help reduce the added sugars in the diet but not as much as soft drinks. Watermelon and apples contain naturally occurring sugars.

7. (d) oatmeal. Oatmeal is rich in beta-glucan, a viscous fiber that can help lower your cholesterol when eaten as part of a heart-healthy diet. While nutrient dense, the bananas and milk do not contain fiber. Cookies won't help lower your cholesterol.

8. (d) These nutrients are added to enriched grains.

9. (c) Diverticula are a condition of diverticulosis. When these pouches become inflamed, diverticulitis occurs. Diabetes is a chronic disease that results from poor regulation of blood glucose.

10. (e) Eating a high-fiber, plant-based diet and getting regular exercise, both of which will help you maintain a healthy weight, is the best approach, at present, to help reduce your risk of developing type 2 diabetes. Eating sugar doesn't cause diabetes.

Web Support

- For more on fiber, visit the American Heart Association at www.americanheart.org
- For more on diabetes, visit the FDA's Diabetes Information site at www.fda.gov/diabetes/
- For more on lactose intolerance, visit the National Institute of Diabetes and Digestive and Kidney Disease (NIDDK) at http://digestive.niddk.nih.gov/ddiseases/pubs/lactoseintolerance

5

1. You need to eat **cholesterol** daily to meet your needs. **T/F**

2. A healthy diet is very low in **fat.** **T/F**

3. Only commercially made products such as fried foods, baked goods, and snack items contain ***trans* fats.** **T/F**

4. You can eat as many fat-free **cookies** as you want without gaining weight. **T/F**

5. A high amount of **HDL** cholesterol in your blood is good for you. **T/F**

Fats, Oils, and Other Lipids

6. Saturated fat is a major dietary culprit behind an elevated blood cholesterol level. **T/F**

7. Butter is better for you than **margarine.** **T/F**

8. Peanut butter is high in cholesterol. **T/F**

9. If you don't eat **fish,** you should take a fish oil supplement. **T/F**

10. Vegetarian baked beans can help lower your cholesterol. **T/F**

Brian and Jim are college sophomores who both play for their school's baseball team. One afternoon, they're sitting on a bleacher waiting for their turns at bat. As usual with their late afternoon practices, they're both starving and in need of a quick snack to tide them over until they have time for a full meal. Luckily, Brian has brought along a package of light potato chips, and he's willing to share. As he pulls apart the top of the package, Jim notices a big bright icon that says "Olean." He watches with horror as his friend reaches in to grab a handful.

"What are you doing," he asks, "don't you know those things give you the runs? Do you want to end up in the bathroom all night?" Brian stops with his hand in mid-air. "Huh?" he replies in confusion. "These are good for me. Look, it says right here, they're fat-free. How can they be bad?"

Who do you think has his facts straight, Brian or Jim? Have you heard rumors that some fat substitutes cause digestive problems? Do you know what fats are, how they affect your heart, and the roles they play in your overall health? In this chapter, we answer these questions as well as debunk some popular myths about fat and fat substitutes. We'll also discuss the different types of fats, the foods in which they're found, and which of them you should aim to eat during meals and snacks.

What Are Lipids and Why Do You Need Them?

Answers

1. False. Your body *does* need cholesterol for important functions. However, you don't need to eat any to meet your needs. Turn to page 135 to find out why.
2. False. Whereas too much dietary fat may cause you to gain weight, eating too little isn't healthy either. A diet low in fat but high in added sugars may increase the level of fat in your blood. To find out more, read page 142.
3. False. Though the majority of *trans* fats are made from hydrogenated oils that are found in commercially prepared, processed foods, *trans* fats also occur naturally in meat and dairy foods. Turn to page 147 to learn more.
4. False. Fat-free foods are not necessarily calorie free. Find out more on page 150.
5. True. High levels of HDL cholesterol can help reduce your risk of heart disease. Turn to page 153 to find out how.
6. True. A diet high in saturated fat can raise your cholesterol. To find out how to lower your saturated fat intake, turn to page 155.
7. False. Although stick margarines can contain heart-unhealthy *trans* fats, butter has more total cholesterol-raising fats than margarine, and so is ultimately less healthy. Find out more on page 158.
8. False. Because peanut butter doesn't come from an animal, it does not contain cholesterol. Turn to page 158 to learn more.
9. False. Consuming too much fish oil can be unhealthy. Find out more on page 159.
10. True. The viscous, soluble fiber found in beans and other foods can lower your blood cholesterol. Turn to page 159 to find out more.

When you think of the word **lipid,** you may think it's a synonym for fat. That's not entirely correct. Whereas "lipo" means *fatty,* lipids actually refer to a category of carbon, oxygen, and hydrogen compounds that are all **hydrophobic** (*hydro* = water, *phobic* = fear). In other words, they don't dissolve in water. If you were to drop lipids like butter or olive oil into a glass of water, you would see these substances rise to the top and sit on the water's surface. This repelling of water allows lipids to play a unique role in foods and in your body.

Lipids can perform a variety of functions in cooking, including giving flaky texture to pie crusts and other baked goods, and making meat tender. The flavors and aromas that lipids provide can make your mouth water as you eye crispy fried chicken or smell doughnuts frying. Foods that are higher in lipids contribute to satiety, that feeling of fullness you experience after eating.

In your body, lipids are essential for energy storage and insulation, and they play a key role in transporting proteins in your blood. One type of lipid makes up a large part of your cell membranes.

There are three types of lipids: triglycerides, phospholipids, and sterols. Two of these, triglycerides and phospholipids, are built from a basic unit called a fatty acid. Let's start our discussion of lipids with the fatty acids.

Fatty Acids Vary in Length and Structure

All **fatty acids** (Figure 5.1) consist of a chain of carbon and hydrogen atoms, with an acid group (COOH) at one end. There are over 20 different fatty acids. They can vary by (1) the length of the chain, (2) whether or not the carbons have a single or a double bond between them (C—C or C=C), and (3) the total number of double bonds.

If carbons have single bonds with other carbons in a fatty acid, that means they are also bonded to hydrogen. When all of the carbons on a fatty acid are bound with hydrogen, it is called a **saturated fatty acid.** In contrast, if a fatty acid has carbons that are not bound to hydrogen, but rather to each other so that one or more double bonds are created, it is called an **unsaturated fatty acid.** Let's take a look at some specific fatty acids.

The fatty acid stearic acid (Figure 5.2a) has 18 carbons, all of which are bound, or saturated, with hydrogen; therefore, it is a saturated fatty acid. Saturated fatty acids have no double bonds. Long fatty acids, such as stearic acid, are strongly attracted to one another so are able to pack tightly together in food, and thus are solid at room temperature. Stearic acid can be found in cocoa butter (in chocolate) and in the fatty part of meat. Shorter saturated fatty acids (with fewer than 12 carbons) have a weaker attraction to one another

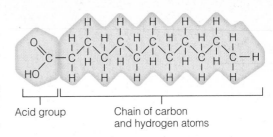

Acid group   Chain of carbon and hydrogen atoms

Figure 5.1 Structure of a Fatty Acid
Fatty acids are the building blocks of some lipids.

a Stearic acid, a saturated fatty acid

b Oleic acid, a monounsaturated fatty acid

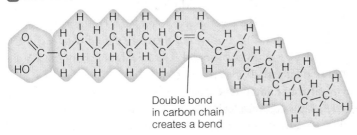

Double bond in carbon chain creates a bend

c Linoleic acid, a polyunsaturated fatty acid

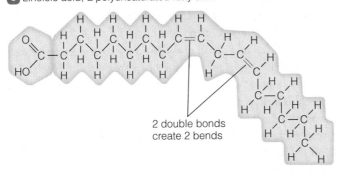

2 double bonds create 2 bends

d Alpha-linolenic acid, a polyunsaturated, omega-3 fatty acid

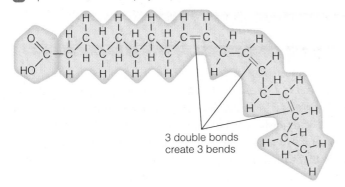

3 double bonds create 3 bends

Figure 5.2 Saturated and Unsaturated Fatty Acids
Fatty acids differ by the length of the fatty acid chain, whether or not there are double bonds between the carbons, and (if there are double bonds) how many double bonds they contain.

lipid A category of carbon, hydrogen, and oxygen compounds that are insoluble in water.

hydrophobic Having an aversion to water.

fatty acid The most basic unit of triglyercides and phospholipids.

saturated fatty acid A fatty acid that has all of its carbons bound with hydrogen.

unsaturated fatty acid A fatty acid that has one or more double bonds between carbons.

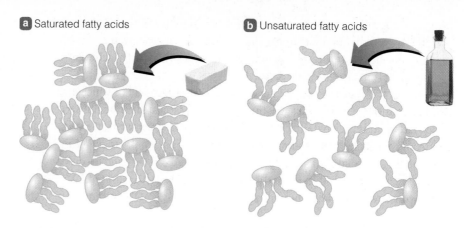

a Saturated fatty acids   **b** Unsaturated fatty acids

Figure 5.3 Saturated and Unsaturated Fatty Acids Help Shape Foods
Saturated fatty acids are able to pack tightly together and are solid at room temperature. The double bonds in unsaturated fatty acids cause kinks in their shape and prevent them from packing tightly together, so they tend to be liquid at room temperature.

Cocoa butter melts at body temperature. This is why solid milk chocolate melts in your mouth.

---

monounsaturated fatty acid (MUFA) A fatty acid that has one double bond.

polyunsaturated fatty acid (PUFA) A fatty acid with two or more double bonds.

oils Lipids that are liquid at room temperature.

essential fatty acids The two polyunsaturated fatty acids that the body cannot make and therefore must be eaten in foods: linoleic acid and alpha-linolenic acid.

linoleic acid A polyunsaturated essential fatty acid; part of the omega-6 fatty acid family.

alpha-linolenic acid A polyunsaturated essential fatty acid; part of the omega-3 fatty acid family.

glycerol The three-carbon backbone of a triglyceride.

triglyceride Three fatty acids that are attached to a glycerol backbone. Also known as **fat**.

so do not pack tightly together. Because of this, foods that contain them are liquid at room temperature. Whole milk contains short-chain fatty acids.

Like stearic acid, oleic acid contains 18 carbons (Figure 5.2b), but two of them are paired with each other rather than hydrogen, so it has one double bond. This one double bond makes oleic acid a **monounsaturated fatty acid** (*mono* = one).

A **polyunsaturated fatty acid** (*poly* = many) contains more than one double bond and is less saturated with hydrogen. Double bonds cause a kink in the chain of the fatty acid. This also inhibits these fatty acids from packing together tightly. Thus, unsaturated fatty acids are liquid at room temperature. (Lipids that are liquid at room temperature are called **oils.**) The monounsaturated fatty acid oleic acid is found in olive oil, and the polyunsaturated fatty acids, linoleic acid and alpha-linolenic acid, are found in soybean oil (Figures 5.2c and 5.2d).

The length of the fatty acid chain and the presence of double bonds between carbons will also determine the melting point, or temperature at which a fat changes from a solid to liquid (Figure 5.3). In general, a long-chain saturated fatty acid has a higher melting point. The lower melting points of shorter chain and unsaturated fatty acids mean they tend to be liquid at room temperature.

Your body can make most of the fatty acids it needs, but there are two that it cannot make, so you must consume them in your diet. These two **essential fatty acids** are **linoleic acid** and **alpha-linolenic acid,** and we'll discuss them later in the chapter.

Triglycerides Are More Commonly Known as Fat

Three fatty acids connected to a **glycerol** (*glyc* = sweet; *ol* = alcohol) backbone create a **triglyceride** (*tri* = three), which is the most common lipid found in foods and in your body. Glycerol is a three-carbon compound that contains three alcohol (OH) groups. The fatty acids join to each of the alcohol groups (Figure 5.4).

The more common name for triglycerides is **fat,** and this is the term we'll use throughout this chapter and the rest of the book. Most of the lipids that you eat and

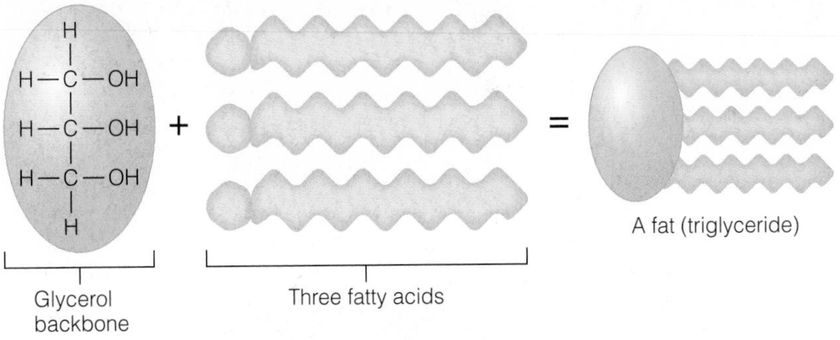

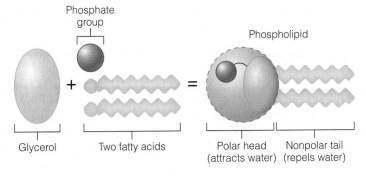

Figure 5.4 Structure of a Triglyceride
A triglyceride consists of three fatty acids attached to a glycerol backbone.

Glycerol backbone

Three fatty acids

A fat (triglyceride)

that are in your body are in the form of fat. Fats that are made up of mostly saturated fatty acids are called **saturated fats,** whereas those that contain mostly unsaturated fatty acids are **unsaturated fats.**

The Take-Home Message Lipids are hydrophobic compounds made up of carbon, hydrogen, and oxygen. The three types of lipids are triglycerides, phospholipids, and sterols. Fatty acids, which consist of a carbon and hydrogen chain and an alcohol group, are the basic structural units of triglycerides and phospholipids. Triglycerides are formed from three fatty acids connected to a glycerol backbone and are the most prevalent lipids in your food and body. Saturated fats tend to be solid at room temperature. Unsaturated fats tend to be liquid at room temperature. A saturated fat contains predominantly saturated fatty acids, whereas an unsaturated fat contains mostly unsaturated fatty acids.

Phospholipids and Sterols Are More Complex than Triglycerides

Phospholipids and sterols are more complex in structure than fats. Like fats, **phospholipids** contain a glycerol backbone, but instead of being made up of three fatty acids, they contain two fatty acids and a phosphorus group (Figure 5.5). The phosphorus-containing head is polar, which attracts charged particles, such as water, and the fatty

Phosphate group

Phospholipid

Glycerol

Two fatty acids

Polar head (attracts water)

Nonpolar tail (repels water)

Figure 5.5 Structure of a Phospholipid
Phospholipids are similar to triglycerides but they have only two fatty acids and a phosphorus group connected to the glycerol backbone. This configuration allows phospholipids, such as lecithin, to be attracted to both water and fat.

saturated fats Fats that contain mostly saturated fatty acids.

unsaturated fats Fats that contain mostly unsaturated fatty acids.

phospholipids Lipids made up of two fatty acids and a phosphorus-containing group attached to a glycerol backbone.

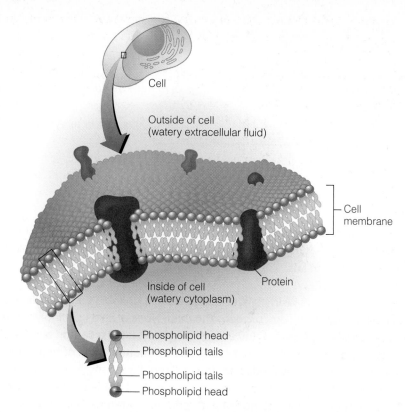

Cell

Outside of cell
(watery extracellular fluid)

Cell
membrane

Inside of cell
(watery cytoplasm)

Protein

Phospholipid head
Phospholipid tails

Phospholipid tails
Phospholipid head

Figure 5.6 Phospholipids' Role in Your Cell Membranes
Because the phosphorus-containing head is polar, it attracts charged particles, such as water located both outside and inside your cells. Its fatty acid–containing tail is nonpolar, so it mingles and lines up with other nonpolar molecules such as the fatty acid–containing ends of other phospholipids. This creates a two-layer membrane that surrounds the cell and acts as a barrier, allowing certain substances to enter the cell but keeping others from leaving.

acid–containing tail is nonpolar, so it mingles with other nonpolar molecules such as fats. In other words, one end of the phospholipid is hydrophilic (*philic* = loving) and the other end is hydrophobic (*phobic* = fear).

Phospholipids make up the phospholipid bilayer in cell membranes. Their water-loving heads face outward to the watery areas both outside and inside your cells, and their fat-loving tails line up with each other in the center, creating a phospholipid membrane that surrounds the cell and acts as a barrier (Figure 5.6). The cell membrane allows certain substances, such as water, to enter the cell but keeps others, like protein, from leaking out. You can visualize this phospholipid layer as being like a picket fence, acting as a barrier and surrounding your cells, as a picket fence would surround the property of a home.

The major phospholipid in your cell membranes is lecithin. Even though lecithin plays an important role in your body, you don't have to worry about eating large amounts of lecithin in foods. As with all phospholipids, your body is able to make all the lecithin that it needs.

Because of its unique water- and fat-loving attributes, lecithin is used in many foods as an **emulsifier,** which helps keep incompatible substances, such as water and

emulsifier A compound that keeps two incompatible substances, such as oil and water, mixed together.

oil, mixed together. For example, an emulsifier is sometimes added to commercially made salad dressings to prevent the fat from separating and rising to the top of the dressing (Figure 5.7). The emulsifier's nonpolar, fat-attracting tail surrounds the droplets of fat, which orients the polar, water-attracting head of the emulsifier toward the watery solution of the dressing. This keeps the fat droplet suspended in the dressing and allows these two incompatible substances to stay blended together. We'll see the process of emulsification again when we discuss how the body uses fat.

Unlike phospholipids, **sterols** do not contain glycerol or fatty acids. Sterols are comprised mainly of four connecting rings of carbon and hydrogen (Figure 5.8). The best known sterol is cholesterol. Though cholesterol's association with heart disease has blemished its reputation, it plays an important role in your cell membranes and is the **precursor** of some very important compounds in your body. As with lecithin, don't be concerned about meeting your daily need for this important substance through your diet. Your tissues manufacture all the cholesterol you need.

Figure 5.9 summarizes the structures of the three types of lipids.

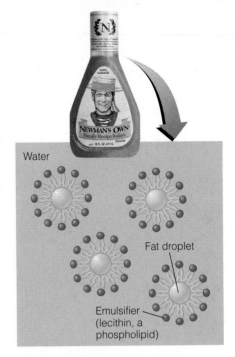

Figure 5.7 Keeping a Salad Dressing Blended
To prevent the fat from separating out in a salad dressing, an emulsifier is added. The emulsifier's fat-attracting tails surround the droplets of fat, whereas the water-attracting heads remain oriented toward the watery portion of the solution or dressing. This allows the fat droplet to stay suspended and blended in the dressing.

Lipid	Structure	Examples
Triglycerides	Glycerol — Fatty acids	Saturated fat, Unsaturated fat, *Trans* fat
Phospholipids	Phosphate head — Fatty acids	Lecithin
Sterols	HO	Cholesterol

Figure 5.9 Three Types of Lipids
The three types of lipids vary in structure. Triglycerides and phospholipids are built from fatty acids, while sterols are composed of carbon rings.

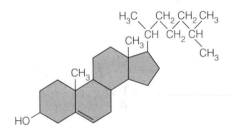

Figure 5.8 Structure of a Sterol
Rather than being made from fatty acids attached to a glycerol backbone, sterols have a carbon ring configuration with hydrogens and an oxygen attached. Cholesterol is the best-known sterol.

The Take-Home Message Phospholipids are made of two fatty acids and a phosphorous-containing group attached to a glycerol backbone. Phospholipids are an important part of the structure of cell membranes. The phospholipid lecithin has unique water- and fat-loving properties, which allow it to play important roles in your cell membranes and as an emulsifier in foods. Cholesterol is an important sterol in your cell membranes and is the precursor to other essential compounds.

sterol A lipid that contains four connecting rings of carbon and hydrogen.

precursor A substance that is converted into or leads to the formation of another substance.

What Happens to the Fat You Eat?

As with all nutrients, the digestion of fat begins in your mouth. Chewing mechanically breaks down the food, and the enzyme lingual lipase plays a minor role in breaking down some fat (Figure 5.10a). Once the food is swallowed, the stomach breaks fat down further. Let's follow fat through the rest of the GI tract.

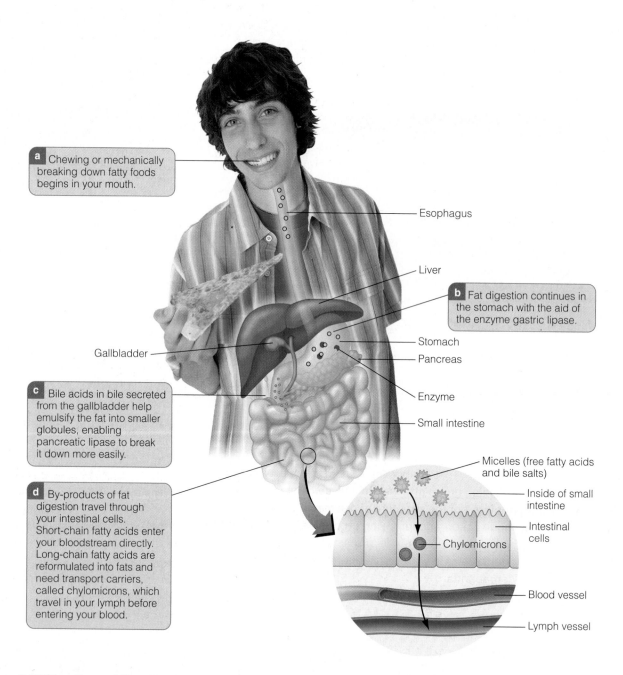

a Chewing or mechanically breaking down fatty foods begins in your mouth.

Esophagus

Liver

b Fat digestion continues in the stomach with the aid of the enzyme gastric lipase.

Gallbladder

Stomach

Pancreas

Enzyme

Small intestine

c Bile acids in bile secreted from the gallbladder help emulsify the fat into smaller globules, enabling pancreatic lipase to break it down more easily.

d By-products of fat digestion travel through your intestinal cells. Short-chain fatty acids enter your bloodstream directly. Long-chain fatty acids are reformulated into fats and need transport carriers, called chylomicrons, which travel in your lymph before entering your blood.

Micelles (free fatty acids and bile salts)

Inside of small intestine

Intestinal cells

Chylomicrons

Blood vessel

Lymph vessel

Figure 5.10 Digesting and Absorbing Fat

You Digest Most Fat in Your Stomach and Small Intestine

In the stomach, fat mixes with gastric lipase, an enzyme that breaks down some of it into a fatty acid and a **diglyceride** (the remnant of fat digestion when only two fatty acids are left joined to the glycerol backbone) (Figure 5.10b).

The majority of fat digestion occurs in your small intestine. Once in your small intestine, an enzyme released from your pancreas, pancreatic lipase, continues to break down the fat into two fatty acids and a **monoglyceride** (the remnant of fat digestion when only one fatty acid is left joined to the glycerol backbone).

Just as oil and water don't mix, fat can't mix with the watery fluids in your digestive tract. The fat globules tend to cluster together rather than disperse throughout the fluids. Mixing fats with watery fluids requires the addition of **bile,** which is made in your liver and stored in your gallbladder. When fat arrives in your intestines, your gallbladder releases bile. Bile contains bile acids that help to emulsify the fat into smaller globules within the watery digestive solution (Figure 5.10c). This keeps the smaller fat globules dispersed throughout the fluids, and provides more surface area so that the pancreatic lipase can more easily break down the fat.

Monoglycerides and fatty acids are next packaged with lecithin, which is in the bile, and other substances to create **micelles** (small transport carriers). Once close to the mucosa of your small intestine, micelles travel through your intestinal cells.

The length of the fatty acid chain determines what happens next. Short-chain fatty acids will enter your bloodstream and go directly to your liver. The long-chain fatty acids can't enter your bloodstream directly. They enter your **lymph** and need transport carriers (Figure 5.10d).

Lipoproteins Transport Fat through the Lymph and Blood

Long-chain fatty acids are reformulated into a fat within the wall of your intestines as they are absorbed. These fats (as well as other lipids, such as cholesterol) are not soluble in your watery blood. They need to be packaged inside protein-containing carriers called **lipoproteins.** Think of lipoproteins as capsule-shaped transport carriers that have an outer shell high in protein and phospholipids and an inner compartment that carries the insoluble fat, as well as cholesterol, through your lymph and bloodstream. One example of a lipoprotein carrier that transports these lipids is a **chylomicron** (Figure 5.11).

Chylomicrons are too large to be absorbed directly into your bloodstream, so they travel through your lymph system first and then enter your blood. Once in the blood, the fat is broken down into fatty acids and glycerol with the help of the enzyme lipoprotein lipase, which is located in the walls of the capillaries.

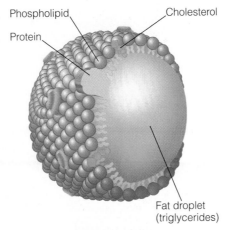

Phospholipid
Cholesterol
Protein
Fat droplet (triglycerides)

Figure 5.11 Chylomicron
Chylomicrons are one type of lipoprotein.

diglyceride A glycerol with only two attached fatty acids.

monoglyceride A glycerol with only one attached fatty acid.

bile A secretion that's squirted into the small intestine to emulsify fat into smaller globules, which allows enzymes to break the fat down. Bile is made in the liver and stored in the gallbladder.

micelles Small transport carriers in the intestine that enable fatty acids and other compounds to be absorbed.

lymph Watery fluid that circulates through the body in lymph vessels and eventually enters the blood.

lipoproteins Capsule-shaped transport carriers that enable fat and cholesterol to travel through the lymph and blood.

chylomicron A type of lipoprotein that carries digested fat and other lipids through the lymph system into the blood.

Figure 5.12 Lipoproteins
The various types of lipoproteins and their composition.

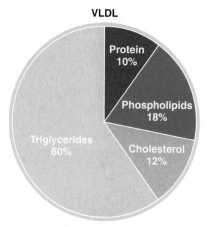

VLDL

- Protein 10%
- Phospholipids 18%
- Cholesterol 12%
- Triglycerides 60%

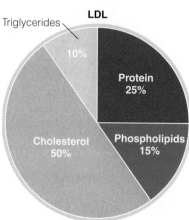

LDL

- Triglycerides 10%
- Protein 25%
- Cholesterol 50%
- Phospholipids 15%

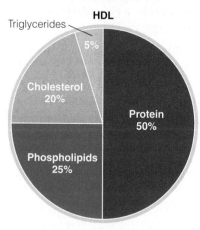

HDL

- Triglycerides 5%
- Cholesterol 20%
- Protein 50%
- Phospholipids 25%

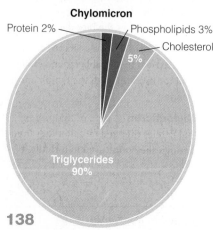

Chylomicron

- Protein 2%
- Phospholipids 3%
- Cholesterol 5%
- Triglycerides 90%

Fatty acids are used by your heart and muscles as energy or stored as an energy reserve in your fat cells. After the fat is removed from the chylomicrons, the remnants of these lipoproteins go to your liver to be dismantled.

The liver produces other lipoproteins with different roles in your body. There are three other types of lipoproteins: **very low-density lipoprotein (VLDL)**, **low-density lipoprotein (LDL),** and **high-density lipoprotein (HDL).** Though all lipoproteins contain fat, phospholipids, cholesterol, and protein, the proportion of the protein in these transport carriers determines their overall density (Figure 5.12).

The greater the amount of protein in the lipoprotein, the higher the density of the transport carrier. For example, VLDLs are composed mostly of triglycerides and have the least amount of protein of the three lipoproteins, so they are considered to be of very low density. The LDLs, which are mostly made of cholesterol and protein, have more protein than the VLDLs but are still of low density compared with the HDLs, which have the highest density. The protein in the lipoproteins helps them to perform their functions in your body. For example, the high protein content in HDLs not only helps remove cholesterol from your cells, but also enables the carrier to expand and contract, depending upon the amount of fat and cholesterol it is carrying.

Why is the proportion of protein in a lipoprotein carrier important? Each lipoprotein has a different role. The main role of the VLDLs is to deliver fat that is made in the liver to your tissues. Once the fat is delivered, the VLDL remnants are converted into LDLs. The LDLs deliver cholesterol to your cells and are often referred to as the "*bad*" cholesterol carriers because they deposit cholesterol in the walls of your arteries, which can lead to heart disease. To help you remember this, you may want to think of the "**L**" in LDL as being of "Little" health benefit.

The HDLs, as mentioned above, are mostly protein and remove cholesterol from your cells. HDLs deliver cholesterol to your liver to be used to make bile and to be excreted from your body. The HDLs are often referred to as the "*good*" cholesterol carriers, as they help remove cholesterol from your arteries. An easy way to remember this is to think of the "**H**" in HDL as referring to "**H**ealthy" (Figure 5.13).

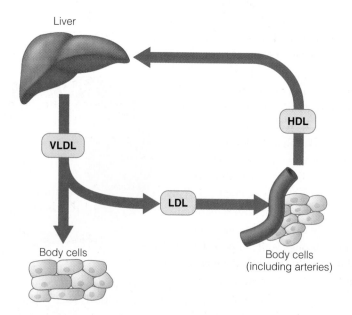

Figure 5.13 Roles of Lipoproteins
(a) VLDLs deliver fat made in your liver to your cells; **(b)** LDLs deposit cholesterol in the walls of your arteries; **(c)** HDLs remove cholesterol from your body and deliver it to the liver.

The Take-Home Message The digestion of fat begins in your mouth, and with the help of enzymes and emulsifying bile acids, most of it is digested and then absorbed in your small intestine. Fat is generally packaged as part of a chylomicron lipoprotein carrier, and travels in the lymph before entering your bloodstream. The other lipoproteins are VLDLs, LDLs, and HDLs. The VLDLs are converted to the "bad" LDL cholesterol carriers, which can deposit cholesterol in the walls of your arteries. The "good" HDL cholesterol carriers remove cholesterol from your arteries and deliver it to your liver to be excreted from your body.

How Does Your Body Use Fat and Cholesterol?

Fat is an important source of energy, and helps the absorption of some compounds. Fat also insulates your body and cushions your major organs.

Fat Is Used as Energy, to Help Absorb Certain Compounds, and to Insulate the Body

At 9 calories per gram, compared with 4 calories per gram for both carbohydrates and protein, fat is a major fuel source for your body. Your body has an *unlimited* ability to store excess energy (calories) as fat. In fact, your fat reserves have the capacity to enlarge as much as 1,000 times their original size, as more fat is added. If your cells fill to capacity, your body can add more fat cells.

Remember from Chapter 4 that your body only has a limited ability to store glucose, which is needed for the brain and red blood cells to function. When your blood glucose level begins to decline, the hormone glucagon promotes the release of glucose from the liver in order to supply the blood with glucose. Glucagon simultaneously promotes the release of fat from fat cells to provide additional energy for your body. Your heart, liver, and resting muscles prefer fat as their fuel source, which spares glucose to be used for your nervous system and red blood cells. In fact, fat is your main source of energy throughout the day. This fat stored in your fat cells provides a backup source of energy between meals. In a famine situation, some individuals could last months without eating, depending upon the extent of their fat stores and the availability of adequate fluids. Fat allows you to absorb the fat-soluble vitamins A, D, E, and K, as well as carotenoids, compounds that can have antioxidant properties in your body.[1]

The fat that is located just under your skin helps to insulate your body and maintain your body temperature. Fat also acts as a protective cushion for your bones, organs, and nerves.

There are differences among the types of fat that you eat. Different fats can have different effects on your health, specifically your heart. Let's look at the essential and nonessential fatty acids and the roles these play in your body.

very low-density lipoprotein (VLDL) A lipoprotein that delivers fat made in the liver to the tissues. VLDL remnants are converted into LDLs.

low-density lipoprotein (LDL) A lipoprotein that deposits cholesterol in the walls of the arteries. Because this can lead to heart disease, LDL is referred to as the *bad* cholesterol carrier.

high-density lipoprotein (HDL) A lipoprotein that removes cholesterol from the tissues and delivers it to the liver to be used as part of bile and/or to be excreted from the body. Because of this, it is known as the *good* cholesterol carrier.

Essential Fatty Acids Make Eicosanoids and Help Keep Cell Membranes Healthy

Fat provides fatty acids that are important to your health. Two polyunsaturated fatty acids, linoleic acid and alpha-linolenic acid, are essential, which means that your body can't make them so you need to obtain them from your diet. In fact, a deficiency of these essential fatty acids can interfere with normal cell membranes and growth and result in scaly skin. Vegetable oils and nuts are good sources of these essential fatty acids (Figure 5.14). Essential fatty acids are also necessary to make other substances your body needs. Linoleic acid is used to make another polyunsaturated fatty acid, called arachidonic acid. This fatty acid is important for your cells and for making **eicosanoids.** Among other roles, eicosanoids help with inflammation, blood clotting, and raising blood pressure.

Alpha-linolenic acid is also referred to as an omega-3 fatty acid. If this sounds Greek to you, it should. The letters of the Greek alphabet help identify the placement of the carbons in fatty acids. Omega is the last letter of the Greek alphabet. Because the numbering of the carbons in a fatty acid starts from the acid end and is counted outward, the omega carbon is the *last* carbon of the fatty acid. In alpha-linolenic acid, the first double bond occurs at the third carbon from the omega end. Hence, it is referred to as an omega-3 fatty acid (Figure 5.2d).

A limited amount of alpha-linolenic acid can be converted to two other important omega-3 fatty acids: **eicosapentaenoic acid (EPA)** and **docosahexaenoic acid (DHA).**[2] All fish contain EPA and DHA, although fatty fish such as salmon, herring, and sardines are especially rich sources (Figure 5.15). Cod-liver oil is abundant in EPA and DHA, but also in the fat-soluble vitamins A and D, which can both be toxic if consumed in high amounts. Eating fish is a safer way to obtain EPA and DHA, and it can also be very healthy for your heart.

Figure 5.14 Food Sources of the Essential Fatty Acids
Many oils and nuts contain high amounts of the two essential fatty acids that you need to obtain in your diet.

eicosanoids Hormonelike substances in the body. Prostaglandins, thromboxanes, and leukotrienes are all eicosanoids.

eicosapentaenoic acid (EPA) and **docosahexaenoic acid (DHA)** Two omega-3 fatty acids that are heart healthy. Fatty fish such as salmon are good sources.

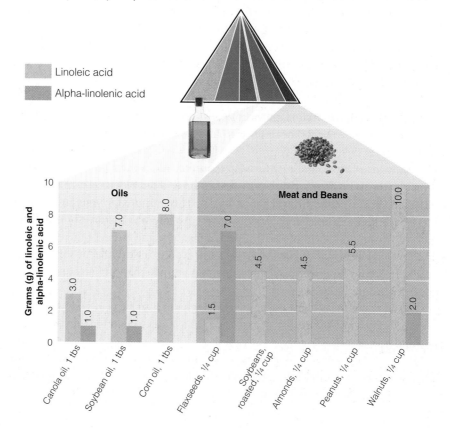

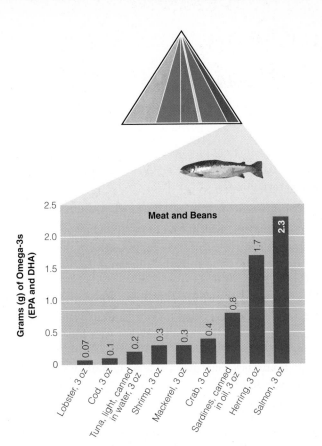

Cholesterol Has Many Important Roles

Your body needs cholesterol both as a part of your cell membranes and as the precursor for vitamin D and bile acids. Cholesterol is also the precursor for the sex hormones such as estrogen and testosterone, which help to determine our sexual characteristics.

The confusion over cholesterol persists. Though dietary cholesterol has been proclaimed as unhealthy, the cholesterol in your blood can be either "good" or "bad" cholesterol. How can one substance be both Dr. Jekyll and Mr. Hyde? Later in this chapter, we will look at the health effects of cholesterol, and try to unravel this confusion. During the discussion keep in mind that the cholesterol in your diet isn't the only factor that determines the levels of cholesterol in your blood.

The Take-Home Message Fat contains 9 calories per gram and is an energy-dense source of fuel for your body. Fat cushions and protects your bones, organs, and nerves and insulates you to help maintain your body temperature. Fat also provides essential fatty acids and is needed for the absorption of fat-soluble vitamins and carotenoids. A limited amount of alpha-linolenic acid can be converted to two other omega-3 fatty acids, EPA and DHA, which are also found in fish. Cholesterol is part of your cell membranes and is needed to make vitamin D, bile acids, and sex hormones.

How Much (and What Types of) Fat Should You Eat?

We've discussed many different types of lipids so far, but which should you eat, and which should you try to limit in your diet? The following should help summarize what you have learned thus far:

- **DO** be sure to get enough of the two heart-healthy essential fatty acids, linoleic acid and alpha-linolenic acid, in your foods by adding plenty of polyunsaturated fats in your daily diet (see Figure 5.14 for examples of these).
- **DON'T** worry about eating enough cholesterol, because your body makes all that it needs.
- **DO** choose mono- and polyunsaturated fats over saturated fats when possible, as these unsaturated fats are better for you. Saturated fats should be kept to a dietary minimum, because they aren't good for your heart or your blood cholesterol levels.
- **DON'T** add *trans* fats to your diet. These are unhealthy for your heart and blood cholesterol levels and should be consumed as little as possible (we'll talk about *trans* fats at length in a subsequent section).

Over the years, Americans' fat intake appears to have been on a roller-coaster ride. In the 1930s, Americans were consuming about 34 percent of their calories from fat, which climbed to 40 to 42 percent in the mid 1960s. The fat in the American diet started a gradual descent to 36 percent of total calories in 1984 and is currently at an all-time low of about 33 percent of calories.[3] Though this reduction is more in line with the current recommendations, we can't break out the hot fudge sundaes just yet. Measuring fat consumption only as a percentage of total calories, and not including the absolute grams of fat, can be misleading.

When researchers looked at the latest patterns of food intake by Americans, they reported that the grams of fat we consume daily have not only increased about 4 percent since the early 1990s, but the amount of *calories* has also increased about 10 percent.[4] In other words, Americans are eating more of both calories and fat, and the reason that the percentage of fat in their diets has gone down is because the number of calories has gone up. The main source of this increase in calories is soft drinks, which are high in refined carbohydrates.

As you can see, the overall consumption of fat (and calories) in the United States is higher than it should be. But dietary fat is still essential for health. So, how much should you eat?

You Need to Consume Some Fat Daily

The current AMDR (Acceptable Macronutrient Distribution Range) recommendation is that 20 to 35 percent of your daily calories should come from fat. For some individuals, especially sedentary, overweight folks, a very low-fat diet (providing less than 20 percent of daily calories from fat) that is consequently high in carbohydrates may cause an increase in fat in the blood and a lowering of the good HDL cholesterol—not exactly a healthy combination for the heart. For others, consuming more than 35 percent of their total daily calories from fat could perpetuate obesity, which is a risk factor for heart disease.[5]

Table 5.1

Capping Your Fat Intake

If You Need This Many Calories to Maintain Your Weight	You Should Eat No More Than This Much	
	Fat (grams) (20% to 35% of total calories)	Saturated Fat and Trans Fat (grams) (<10% of total calories)
1,600	36–62	18
1,700	38–66	19
1,800	40–70	20
1,900	42–74	21
2,000	44–78	22
2,100	47–82	23
2,200	49–86	24
2,300	51–89	26
2,400	53–93	27
2,500	56–97	28
2,600	58–101	29
2,700	60–105	30
2,800	62–109	31

Sedentary women consume approximately 1,600 calories daily. Teenage girls, active women, and many sedentary men need approximately 2,200 calories daily. Teenage boys, many active men, and some very active women need about 2,800 calories daily.

The percentage of calories from fat and the corresponding grams of fat can be calculated by multiplying your number of daily calories by 20 percent and 35 percent and then dividing those numbers by 9. (Fat provides 9 calories per gram.) To determine the amount of calories you should be eating daily, turn to Table 2.3 in Chapter 2.

For example, if you consume 2,000 calories daily:

$$2,000 \times 0.20 \text{ (20 percent)} = 400 \text{ calories} \div 9 = 44 \text{ grams}$$

$$2,000 \times 0.35 \text{ (35 percent)} = 700 \text{ calories} \div 9 = 78 \text{ grams}$$

Your range of fat intake should be 44 to 78 grams daily.

To find the maximum grams of saturated and *trans* fats that you should be consuming daily, repeat the process:

$$2,000 \times 0.10 \text{ (10 percent)} = 200 \text{ calories} \div 9 = 22 \text{ grams}$$

The total amount of saturated fat and *trans* fat intake should be no more than 22 grams daily.

Though consuming fat won't increase your weight unless you consistently consume more calories than you need, remember that dietary fat has more than twice the calories per gram of carbohydrates or protein. Therefore, eating too many fatty foods could perpetuate a weight management problem. Numerous research studies have shown that reducing dietary fat can also reduce dietary calories, which can result in weight loss.[6] Consequently, controlling one's fat intake may help control one's weight.

According to the AMDR recommendation, if you need 2,000 calories daily to maintain your weight, you can consume between 44 and 74 grams of fat daily (Table 5.1). For your heart health, you should consume no more than 10 percent of your calories, or 22 grams, from a *combination* of saturated fats and *trans* fats. (*Trans* fats are discussed later in this chapter.)

Table 5.2
How Much Cholesterol Is in Your Foods?

	Cholesterol (mg)
Liver, 3 oz	324
Breakfast biscuit with egg and sausage, 1	302
Egg, 1 large	212
Shrimp, 3 oz, canned	147
Fast-food hamburger, large, double patty	122
Ice cream, soft serve, vanilla, ½ cup	78
Beef, ground, cooked, 3 oz	77
Salmon, cooked, 3 oz	74
Chicken or turkey, breast, cooked, 3 oz	72
Lobster, cooked, 3 oz	61
Turkey, light meat, cooked, 3 oz	59
Egg noodles, 1 cup	53
Butter, 1 tbs	31
Cheddar cheese, 1 oz	30
Frankfurter, beef, 1	24
Milk, whole, 1 cup	24
Cheddar cheese, low fat, 1 oz	6
Milk, skim, 1 cup	4

Source: USDA National Nutrient Database for Standard Reference, Release 16. Available at www.ars.usda.gov. Accessed August 2003.

To ensure that you are consuming enough linoleic acid and alpha-linolenic acid, a recommended amount has been set for each of these important nutrients. A minimum of 5 percent and up to 10 percent of the total calories in your diet should come from linoleic acid, and alpha-linolenic acid should make up 0.6 percent to 1.2 percent of your total calories.[7] These recommended amounts are based on the estimated daily caloric needs according to your gender and age. For example, men aged 19 to 50 need 17 grams of linoleic acid daily, and women aged 19 to 50 who aren't pregnant or lactating need 12 grams daily. For alpha-linolenic acid, men aged 14 to 70 need 1.6 grams daily whereas women of the same age need 1.1 grams daily.

Linoleic and alpha-linolenic acids must also be consumed in the proper ratio. Too much linoleic acid in relationship to alpha-linolenic acid can inhibit the conversion of alpha-linolenic acid to DHA, while the inverse (too much alpha-linolenic acid and not enough linoleic acid) can inhibit the conversion of linoleic acid to arachidonic acid.

As mentioned earlier, your body can make all the cholesterol that it needs. Therefore, you do not need to consume it in your diet, and in fact, you should limit the amount of cholesterol you take in for the sake of your heart and arteries. Healthy individuals over the age of 2 are advised to limit their dietary cholesterol to under 300 milligrams (mg) daily, on average.[8] Adult males in the United States currently consume about 330 milligrams daily, whereas adult females eat slightly over 210 milligrams of cholesterol daily, on average. Table 5.2 lists a variety of foods and their cholesterol content.

Self-Assessment

How Much Fat Is in Your Diet?

Is your diet too overloaded with fat, saturated fat, and/or *trans* fat? Use a diet analysis program, the food tables in Appendix A, or food labels to track your fat consumption for a day. How does your actual intake compare to the amount recommended for you in Table 5.1?

Food Log

	Food/Drink	Amount	Fat (g)	Saturated Fat (g)	*Trans* Fat (g)
Breakfast					
Snack					
Lunch					
Snack					
Dinner					
Snack					
Total					

When it comes to keeping track of your fat intake, counting grams of fat in your foods is the best strategy. Table 5.1 provided you with a healthy range of recommended fat intake based on your daily caloric needs. (To figure out your approximate daily caloric needs, see Chapter 2.) Use the Self-Assessment to estimate how much fat, saturated fat, and *trans* fat you consume daily.

The Take-Home Message You need to consume some fat in your diet, particularly the essential fatty acids, but you should limit other fats, like saturated fats and *trans* fats. Your fat intake should range from 20 to 35 percent of your total calories. To meet your essential fatty acid needs, 5 to 10 percent of your calories should come from linoleic acid and 0.6 to 1.2 percent of your daily calories should come from alpha-linolenic acid. No more than 10 percent of your fat intake should come from saturated and *trans* fats. You do not need to eat cholesterol in foods, as your body makes all that it needs.

What Are the Best Food Sources of Fats?

Foods that contain unsaturated fats are better for your health than foods high in saturated fat, cholesterol, and/or *trans* fat. (*Trans* fats will be discussed in the next section.) So, where can you find the healthier fats in foods?

Unsaturated fats are abundant in vegetable oils, such as soybean, corn, and canola oils, as well as soybeans, walnuts, flaxseeds, and wheat germ. All the foods listed in Figure 5.14 are excellent sources of both unsaturated fats and essential fatty acids.

> The cheddar cheese on the top of a cheeseburger has more fat and saturated fat per ounce than the burger.

Foods high in saturated fat should be limited in your diet. Most saturated fat in the diet comes from animal foods such as fatty cuts of meat, whole-milk dairy products, like cheese, butter, and ice cream, and the skin on poultry (Figure 5.16 on page 146). Choosing lean meats and dairy foods, skinless poultry and oil-based spreads will help you minimize the saturated fat in your diet. Certain vegetable oils, such as coconut, palm, and palm kernel oils, are very high in saturated fat. Although food manufacturers now use these highly saturated tropical oils less often, they may still be found in foods such as candies, commercially made baked goods, and gourmet ice cream. Checking the ingredient label on food packages is the best way to find out if these oils are in the foods that you eat.

Because all fats and oils are a combination of fatty acids, however, it's not only impossible to eliminate saturated fat entirely from your diet, it is unhealthy for you to do so. Extreme trimming of fats and oils could lead to the unnecessary elimination of certain foods, such as soybean and canola oils, lean meats, fish, poultry, and low-fat dairy foods, which could cause you to fall short of important nutrients such as essential fatty acids, protein, and calcium. Rather, your goal should be to keep your dietary intake of saturated fat to less than 10 percent of your daily total calories.

Americans currently consume about 11 to 12 percent of their daily calories from saturated fat, so it's likely that you need to reduce your intake. You can use Figure 5.16 to make low-saturated-fat food choices at some of your meals and snacks.

Figure 5.16 Where's the Saturated Fat in Your Foods?

Choosing less-saturated-fat versions of some of your favorite foods at meals and snacks can dramatically lower the amount of "sat" fat you consume in your diet.

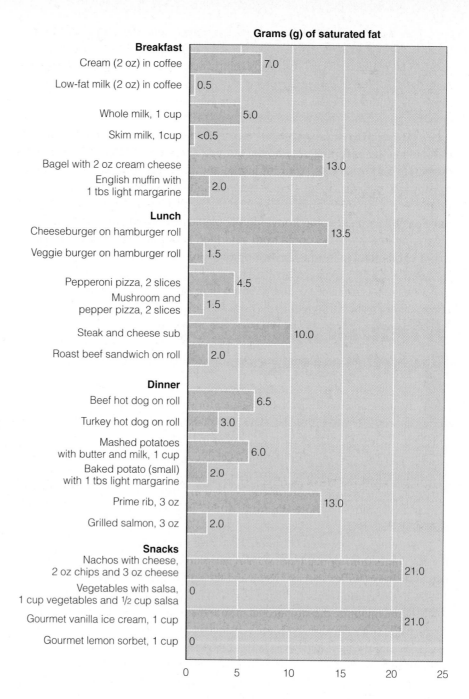

Grams (g) of saturated fat

Breakfast
- Cream (2 oz) in coffee — 7.0
- Low-fat milk (2 oz) in coffee — 0.5
- Whole milk, 1 cup — 5.0
- Skim milk, 1cup — <0.5
- Bagel with 2 oz cream cheese — 13.0
- English muffin with 1 tbs light margarine — 2.0

Lunch
- Cheeseburger on hamburger roll — 13.5
- Veggie burger on hamburger roll — 1.5
- Pepperoni pizza, 2 slices — 4.5
- Mushroom and pepper pizza, 2 slices — 1.5
- Steak and cheese sub — 10.0
- Roast beef sandwich on roll — 2.0

Dinner
- Beef hot dog on roll — 6.5
- Turkey hot dog on roll — 3.0
- Mashed potatoes with butter and milk, 1 cup — 6.0
- Baked potato (small) with 1 tbs light margarine — 2.0
- Prime rib, 3 oz — 13.0
- Grilled salmon, 3 oz — 2.0

Snacks
- Nachos with cheese, 2 oz chips and 3 oz cheese — 21.0
- Vegetables with salsa, 1 cup vegetables and ½ cup salsa — 0
- Gourmet vanilla ice cream, 1 cup — 21.0
- Gourmet lemon sorbet, 1 cup — 0

(x-axis: 0, 5, 10, 15, 20, 25)

The Take-Home Message Eating lean meats, skinless poultry, lean dairy products, and vegetable oils while limiting commercially prepared baked goods and snack items is a good strategy for overall good health. These foods will provide you with enough healthy unsaturated fats with plenty of essential fatty acids while limiting your intake of unhealthy, saturated fats.

What Is *Trans* Fat and Where Do You Find It?

At one time, saturated fats from animal sources, like lard, and highly saturated tropical plant oils, like coconut and palm oils, were staples in home cooking and commercial food preparation. These saturated fats work well in commercial food products because they provide a rich, flaky texture to baked goods and are more resistant to **rancidity** than the unsaturated fats found in oils. (The double bonds in unsaturated fats make them more susceptible to being damaged by oxygen, and thus, becoming rancid.) Then, in the early twentieth century, a German chemist discovered the technique of **hydrogenation** of oils, which caused the unsaturated fatty acids in the oils to become more saturated. *Trans* fats were born.

The process of hydrogenation involves heating an oil and exposing it to hydrogen gas, which causes some of the double bonds in the unsaturated fatty acid to become saturated with hydrogen. Typically, the hydrogens of a double bond are lined up in a *cis* (*cis* = same) configuration, that is, they are all on the same side of the carbon chain in the fatty acid. During hydrogenation, some hydrogens cross to the opposite side of the carbon chain, resulting in a *trans* (*trans* = cross) configuration (Figure 5.17). The newly configured fatty acid is now a **trans fatty acid.**

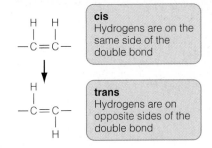

cis Hydrogens are on the same side of the double bond

trans Hydrogens are on opposite sides of the double bond

Figure 5.17 Creating *Trans* Fatty Acids Hydrogenating, or adding hydrogen to an unsaturated fatty acid, will create a more saturated fatty acid. This process will also cause some of the double bonds to twist from a *cis* position to a *trans* position. This creates a *trans* fatty acid.

Trans Fats Are Found in Many Processed Foods

Trans fats provide a richer texture, a longer shelf life, and better resistance to rancidity than unsaturated fats, so food manufacturers use them in many commercially made food products. The first partially hydrogenated shortening, Crisco, was made from cottonseed oil, and became available in 1911.

Trans fats came into even more widespread commercial use when saturated fat fell out of favor in the 1980s. Research had confirmed that saturated fat played a role in increased risk of heart disease, so food manufacturers reformulated many of their products to contain less saturated fat. The easiest solution was to replace the saturated fat with *trans* fats. Everything from cookies, cakes, and crackers to fried chips and doughnuts used *trans* fats to maintain their texture and shelf life. *Trans* fats were also frequently used for frying at fast-food restaurants.

We now know that *trans* fats are actually worse for heart health than saturated fat because they not only raise the LDL cholesterol levels, but they also lower HDL cholesterol in the body. *Trans* fat currently provides an estimated 2.5 percent of the daily calories in the diets of adults in the United States. Of this amount, about 25 percent of them are coming from naturally occurring *trans* fats that are found in meat and dairy foods.[9] We don't yet know if the naturally occurring *trans* fats have the same heart-unhealthy effects as do those that are created through hydrogenation. *Trans* fats should be kept as low as possible in the diet.

The major sources of *trans* fats are commercially prepared baked goods, margarines, fried potatoes, snacks, shortenings, and salad dressings (Figure 5.18).[10] Whole grains, fruits, and vegetables don't contain any *trans* fats, so consuming a plant-based diet with minimal commercially prepared foods will go a long way toward preventing *trans* fat (and saturated fat) from overpowering your diet.

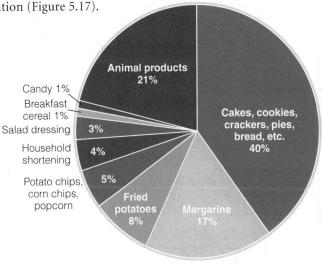

Animal products 21%

Candy 1%
Breakfast cereal 1%
Salad dressing 3%
Household shortening 4%
Potato chips, corn chips, popcorn 5%
Fried potatoes 8%
Margarine 17%
Cakes, cookies, crackers, pies, bread, etc. 40%

Figure 5.18 Major Food Sources of *Trans* Fat for U.S. Adults Commercially made baked goods and snack items are the major contributors of *trans* fat in the diet.

Source: FDA, Questions and Answers About *Trans* Fat Nutrition Labeling, 2003.

rancidity The decomposition, or spoiling, of fats through oxidation.

hydrogenation Adding hydrogen to an unsaturated fatty acid to make it more saturated and solid at room temperature.

trans fat Substance that contains mostly **trans fatty acids**, which result from the hydrogenating of an unsaturated fatty acid, causing a reconfiguring of some of its double bonds. A small amount of *trans* fatty acids occur naturally in animal foods.

Trans Fat Must Be Listed on Food Labels

Commercially made peanut butter doesn't have any detectable levels of *trans* fatty acids. Even though partially hydrogenated oil is used as a stabilizer in many peanut butter brands, the amount is so small that it is insignificant.

To make consumers more aware of *trans* fat, the FDA mandated in 2006 that most foods, and even some dietary supplements such as energy bars, list the grams of *trans* fats per serving on the Nutrition Facts panel on the food label. The FDA estimates that providing this information to consumers to help them make healthier food choices will save between $900 million and $1.8 billion annually in reduced medical care costs, lost productivity, and pain and suffering.[11] The label allows you to quickly add up the saturated and *trans* fats listed and makes it easier for you to monitor the amount of these fats that you consume.

The Take-Home Message *Trans* fats are made by heating oil and adding hydrogen gas to saturate the carbons of the fatty acids with hydrogen. *Trans* fats are heart unhealthy because they raise the levels of the "bad" LDL cholesterol and lower the blood levels of the "good" HDL cholesterol. *Trans* fats are found in many commercially prepared foods and must be listed on the food label.

What Are Fat Substitutes and How Can They Be Part of a Healthy Diet?

If you adore the taste and texture of creamy foods but don't adore the extra fat in your diet, you're not alone. A survey conducted in 2000 found that over 160 million Americans (79 percent of the adults in the United States) chose lower-fat foods and beverages. Respondents cited their health as the major reason they were actively shopping for these foods.[12] To meet this demand, food manufacturers introduced more than 1,000 reduced-fat or low-fat products, from margarine to potato chips, each year during the 1990s.[13] Today, with few exceptions you will probably find a lower-fat alternative for almost any high-fat food on the grocery store shelves. The keys to these products' containing less fat than their counterparts are **fat substitutes.**

Fat substitutes are designed to provide all the creamy properties of fat for fewer calories and total fat grams. Because fat has more than double the calories per gram of carbohydrates or protein, fat substitutes have the potential to reduce calories from fat by more than 50 percent without sacrificing taste and texture.

Fat Substitutes Can Be Carbohydrate, Protein, or Fat Based

fat substitutes Substances that replace added fat in foods by providing the creamy properties of fat for fewer calories and fewer total fat grams.

No single substitute works in all foods and with all cooking preparations, so there are several types of fat substitutes. They fall into three categories depending on their primary ingredient: (1) carbohydrate-based substitutes, (2) protein-based substitutes, and (3) fat-based substitutes.[14] Table 5.3 lists all three types of fat substitutes and their uses in foods.

Table 5.3

The Lighter Side of Fat: Fat Substitutes

Name (trade names)	Calories per gram	Properties	How It's Used
Carbohydrate Based			
Fibers from grains (Betatrim)	1–4	Gelling, thickener	Baked goods, meats, spreads
Fibers, cellulose (Cellulose gel)	0	Water retention, texture, mouthfeel	Sauces, dairy products, frozen desserts, salad dressings
Gums	0	Thickener, texture, mouthfeel, water retention	Salad dressings, processed meats
Polydextrose (Litesse)	1	Water retention, adds bulk	Baked goods, dairy products, salad dressings, cookies, and gum
Modified food starch (Sta Slim)	1–4	Thickener, gelling, texture	Processed meats, salad dressings, frostings, fillings, frozen desserts
Protein Based			
Microparticulated protein (Simplesse)	1–4	Mouthfeel	Dairy products, salad dressings, spreads
Fat Based			
Mono- or diglycerides (Dur-Lo)	9*	Mouthfeel, moisture retention	Baked goods
Short-chain fatty acids (Salatrim)	5	Mouthfeel	Confections, baked goods
Olestra (Olean)	0	Mouthfeel	Savory snacks

*Less of this fat substitute is needed to create the same effect as fat, so the calories are reduced in foods using this product.

Source: R. D. Mattes. Fat Replacers. 1998. *Journal of the American Dietetic Association* 98: 463–468; J. Wylie-Rosett. 2002. Fat Substitutes and Health: An Advisory from the Nutrition Committee of the American Heart Association. *Circulation* 105: 2800–2804.

The majority of fat substitutes are carbohydrate-based that use plant polysaccharides such as fiber, starches, gums, and cellulose to help retain moisture and provide a fatlike texture.[15] For example, low-fat muffins might have fiber added to them to help retain the moisture that is lost when fat is reduced. Carbohydrate-based fat substitutes have been used for years and work well under heat preparations other than frying.

Protein-based fat substitutes are created from the protein in eggs and milk. The protein is heated and broken down into microscopic balls that tumble over each other when you eat them, providing a creamy mouthfeel that's similar to that of fat. Because protein-based substitutes are derived from protein, they break down under high temperatures and lose their creamy properties. Therefore, they are not suitable for frying and baking.[16]

Fat-based substitutes are fats that have been modified to either provide the physical attributes of fat for fewer calories or interfere with the absorption of fat.[17] Mono- and diglycerides are used as emulsifiers in products such as baked goods and icings to provide moistness and mouthfeel. Though these remnants of fat have the same amount of calories per gram as fat, less of them are needed to create the same effect, so that the total amount of calories and fat is reduced in the food product.[18] One fat substitute, olestra (also known as Olean), is a mixture of sucrose and long-chain fatty acids. Unlike fat, which contains three fatty acids connected to a glycerol backbone, olestra contains six to eight fatty acids connected to sucrose. The enzymes that normally break apart fatty acids from their glycerol backbones during digestion cannot disconnect the fatty acids in olestra. Instead, olestra moves through your gastrointestinal tract intact and unabsorbed. Thus, it doesn't provide calories. Olestra is very heat stable, so it can be used in baked and fried foods.

In 1996, the FDA approved olestra's use in salty snacks such as potato and corn chips. An ounce of potato chips made with olestra can trim half the calories and all the fat from regular chips. Because of its inability to be absorbed, there was concern about olestra's interference with the absorption of fat-soluble vitamins and carotenoids.[19] (Absorption of water-soluble vitamins is not affected by olestra.) Consequently, the FDA has mandated that fat-soluble vitamins be added to olestra to offset these losses. Because olestra travels through your digestive tract untouched, there was also a concern that it may cause stomach cramps and loose stools. Though there have been anecdotal studies of individuals experiencing bouts of diarrhea and cramps after consuming olestra-containing products, controlled research studies don't seem to support this phenomenon.[20] In a study of over 3,000 individuals, there wasn't any significant difference in gastrointestinal complaints between the group that consumed olestra-containing snacks and the individuals who ate regular snacks. Ironically, those who consumed the largest amount of *regular* chips actually complained *more* of loose stools and more frequent bowel movements than those consuming the olestra-containing chips.[21] Brian, the baseball player from the beginning of the chapter, can probably eat his light potato chips without developing the runs, though he should be concerned about consuming too many empty calories.

Whereas the FDA used to require that all olestra-containing foods disclose on their label the interaction with fat-soluble vitamins and carotenoids and the potential gastrointestinal issues, it concluded, based on scientific review of numerous research studies and further investigation, that this warning label was no longer warranted based on the "real-life" consumption of olestra-containing products. However, the fat-soluble vitamins will continue to be added.[22]

Reduced-Fat Products Aren't Calorie Free

The use of fat substitutes doesn't seem to be helping Americans curb their calories or weight, and one reason for this may be people's overeating of low-fat and fat-free foods. Research indicates that people who snack on olestra-containing products may be reducing their overall fat intake, but not their overall intake of calories.[23] As with sugar substitutes, consumers need to recognize that using reduced-fat or fat-free products does not write a blank check for eating unlimited amounts of those foods. The foods still contain calories, and overconsuming calories leads to weight gain.

Also, some fat-free foods, especially baked goods, may have reduced fat content but added carbohydrates, which will add back some calories. Consequently, the savings in fat calories isn't always much of a savings in total calories (Table 5.4). Consumers should be careful not to assume that fat-free foods are healthy, because they often aren't. Jelly beans are fat free, but they don't provide the vitamins and minerals found in, for example, naturally fat-free green beans.

Whereas snacking on 4 ounces of fat-free chips will provide half of the 600 calories found in the same amount of regular chips, the real problem is that the fat-free chips are displacing 300 calories of more nutritious foods, such as fruits, vegetables, and whole grains, elsewhere in your diet. If you want chips, enjoy a handful rather than a large bag full, alongside your whole-grain sandwich and large salad at lunch.

Foods made with fat substitutes aren't calorie free.

Table 5.4

Fat Free Doesn't Equal Calorie Free

	Serving Size (g)	Calories	Fat (g)	Carbohydrates (g)	Calories Saved
Fig Newtons (Nabisco)	2 (31 g)	110	2.5	20	
Fat-Free Fig Newtons (Nabisco)	2 (29 g)	90	0	22	20
Oatmeal Raisin Cookies (Archway)	1 (29 g)	110	4	19	
Fat-Free Oatmeal Raisin Cookies (Archway)	1 (31g)	110	0	25	0
Fudgsicle Pop (Popsicle)	1 (1.65 fl oz)	60	1.5	12	
Fat-Free Fudgsicle Bar (Popsicle)	1 (1.75 fl oz)	70*	0	14	0

*Note: These contain *more* calories than the regular variety.

Source: Food manufacturers.

Fats impact more than your weight and waistline. They also impact the health of your heart. Let's take a closer look at how lipids in your diet can affect your risk for heart disease.

The Take-Home Message Fat substitutes are used in foods to provide the properties of fat for fewer calories and grams of fat. Fat substitutes can be carbohydrate based, protein based, or fat based. Though some fat substitutes provide fewer calories and fat grams than regular fat, others, such as olestra, aren't absorbed so are fat and calorie free. Reduced-fat or fat-free foods may help reduce the calories and fat in some foods, but shouldn't displace naturally low-fat and healthy foods such as fruits and vegetables in your diet.

What Is Heart Disease and What Increases Your Risk?

Cardiovascular disease has been the number-one killer of adults in the United States since 1918. Though it was once believed to be more of a danger to males than females, heart disease actually takes the lives of more women than men. More than half a million American women die each year—about one every minute—from heart disease, whereas about 440,000 men lose their lives to heart disease annually.[24] Let's look at how heart disease develops, and the types of lipids that can accelerate it.

> One in every 30 American women dies each year of breast cancer, but one in every two female adult deaths is from either heart disease or stroke.

Heart Disease Begins with a Buildup in the Arteries

Heart disease develops when the coronary arteries, the large blood vessels that lead to the heart, accumulate a buildup of substances such as fat and cholesterol along their walls. As the artery gets narrower, blood flow is impeded, and less oxygen and

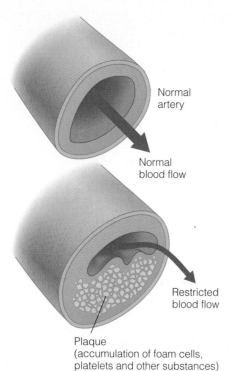

Normal artery

Normal blood flow

Restricted blood flow

Plaque (accumulation of foam cells, platelets and other substances)

Figure 5.19 Atherosclerosis
When plaque builds up in the coronary arteries, it narrows the passageway and causes a decreased flow of oxygen-rich blood to the heart. A blood clot, traveling in the blood, can partially or totally block the arteries to the heart, leading to a heart attack.

heart attack Permanent damage to the heart muscle that results from a sudden lack of oxygen-rich blood.

stroke A condition caused by a lack of oxygen to the brain that could result in paralysis and possibly death.

atherosclerosis Narrowing of the coronary arteries due to buildup of debris along the artery walls.

plaque The hardened buildup of cholesterol-laden foam cells, platelets, cellular waste products, and calcium in the arteries that results in atherosclerosis.

nutrients are delivered to the heart. If the heart doesn't receive enough oxygen, chest pains can result.

A narrowed artery also increases the likelihood that a normal blood clot (many of which form and dissolve harmlessly in the body every day) can get stuck and block the vessel, leading to a **heart attack.** If the artery leads to the brain, a **stroke** can occur. Over 6 million Americans experience chest pains, and over 7 million suffer a heart attack every year.

The exact cause of the narrowed arteries, also known as **atherosclerosis** (*athero* = past, *sclera* = hardness, *sis* = condition), is unknown, but researchers think it begins with an injury to the lining of the arteries. High blood levels of cholesterol and fat, high blood pressure, and smoking likely contribute to this damage.

Over time, LDLs and other substances are deposited along an injured artery wall.[25] The LDLs that accumulate become oxidized and attract macrophages (white blood cells), which become enlarged with cholesterol-laden LDL and develop into foam cells. The foam cells stick to the walls of the artery and build up, along with platelets (fragments of cells in the blood) and other substances, into **plaque.** The plaque narrows the passageway of the artery (Figure 5.19).

Risk Factors for Heart Disease

While the primary risk factor for heart disease is an elevated LDL cholesterol level there are many other risk factors for heart disease (Table 5.5). Unfortunately, you have control over some, but not all, of these risk factors.

Risk Factors You Can't Control

As your blood cholesterol increases, so does your risk of developing heart disease and experiencing a heart attack. Your blood cholesterol level tends to rise with age until it stabilizes around the age of 65. Your gender will also play a role. Up until menopause, which is around the age of 50, women tend to have a lower blood cholesterol level than men and a reduced risk of heart disease. After menopause, the blood cholesterol level in women tends to catch up and even surpass that of a man of the same age.[26] About one in eight American women between 45 and 64 years of age has heart disease, but this jumps to one out of every three women over the age of 65. The decrease in the level of the hormone estrogen in postmenopausal women plays a part in the increased risk of heart disease that occurs in older women.[27]

Because high blood cholesterol levels can be partly determined by your genes, such levels can sometimes run in families.[28] If your father or brother had early signs of heart disease before age 55, or your mother or sister had them before the age of 65, then you are at a greater risk of getting heart disease. Having diabetes increases the risk of heart disease. Though the less common form of diabetes, type 1, is not preventable, the more prevalent form, type 2 diabetes, can be controlled.

Risk Factors You Can Control

Controlling diabetes can help dramatically lower the risk of heart disease for those with this condition.[29] Type 2 diabetes can be managed, and as you read in the last chapter, possibly even prevented, through diet and lifestyle changes. Sometimes, the use of doctor-prescribed medication is also needed to control type 2 diabetes. Diseases of the heart and blood vessels are the cause of death of an estimated 75 percent of adults with diabetes.

Table 5.5
Risk Factors for Heart Disease

Factors You Cannot Control	Factors You Can Control
Your age and gender	Type 2 diabetes mellitus
Your family history of heart disease	High blood pressure
Type 1 diabetes mellitus	Smoking
	Physical inactivity
	Excess weight
	A low HDL "good" cholesterol level
	A high LDL "bad" cholesterol level

Chronic high blood pressure can damage your arteries. Blood pressure is the force of your blood against the walls of your arteries. A **normal blood pressure** is considered less than 120 millimeters mercury (Hg) for the systolic pressure (the top number in your blood pressure reading) and less than 80 millimeters Hg for the diastolic pressure (the bottom number). A blood pressure reading of 140/90 or higher is considered **hypertension,** or high blood pressure.

Individuals with chronic high blood pressure constantly have a higher than normal force pushing against the walls of their arteries. This thickens and "stiffens" the arteries, which accelerates the buildup of plaque. Chronic high blood pressure also causes the heart to work harder than normal and can lead to an enlarged heart. (Chapter 8 contains a detailed discussion of hypertension and how a healthy diet can help lower high blood pressure.)

Smoking damages the walls of the arteries and accelerates atherosclerosis and heart disease. In fact, women smokers are two to six times more likely to have a heart attack than female nonsmokers. Male smokers also increase their risk for heart disease.[30]

Because regular exercise can help lower your LDL cholesterol and raise your good HDL cholesterol, being inactive is a risk factor for heart disease.

Because high HDL cholesterol can help protect you from heart disease, having an HDL level of less than 40 milligrams per deciliter (mg/dl) increases your risk of heart disease, as you don't have enough of this "good" cholesterol carrier in your body. In contrast, having a high level of HDL cholesterol, 60 mg/dl or higher, is considered a "negative" risk factor. In other words, there is so much of this "good" cholesterol in your body helping to protect against heart disease that it allows you to "erase" a risk factor from your list.

In addition to regular exercising, losing excess weight and quitting smoking can help increase your HDL cholesterol. Exercise can also help you better manage your weight. Being overweight can raise your LDL cholesterol and increase your risk of heart disease.

Whereas drinking modest amounts of alcohol has also been shown to raise HDL cholesterol, other problems can outweigh this benefit. In fact, for some individuals, drinking alcohol is not advised.[31]

You can find out more about diet and lifestyle habits that may lead to lower risk for heart disease in the boxed feature "The Traditional Mediterranean Diet" on page 156.

Every pack of cigarettes smoked in the United States costs the nation about $7.18 in medical care and lost job productivity. Whereas the average pack of cigarettes may cost $5, it costs 1½ times that to keep the smoker healthy and productive.

normal blood pressure Less than 120 mm Hg (systolic—the top number) and less than 80 mm Hg (diastolic—the bottom number). Referred to as 120/80.

hypertension High blood pressure.

Other Potential Risk Factors

There are some individuals who don't have an elevated level of LDL cholesterol in their blood, yet still experience a heart attack and heart disease, which points to other factors that must be affecting their heart health. These other potential risk factors are referred to as emerging risk factors.

Researchers are continually searching for clues or "markers" in the blood, other than cholesterol levels, that are signs of the presence of heart disease. For example, high amounts of the amino acid homocysteine may injure the arteries, decrease their flexibility, and increase the likelihood of blood clots. The presence of *chlamydia pneumoniae,* a bacterium that can cause pneumonia and respiratory infections, in the blood may also damage or inflame the vessel walls. Another lipoprotein, Lp(a) protein, is being investigated for its role in causing excessive blood clotting and exacerbating inflammation. Lastly, high blood levels of C-reactive protein can indicate that there is inflammation in the walls of the arteries.[32]

Though the name sounds mysterious, Syndrome X, also called metabolic syndrome, refers to a cluster of risk factors that put some people at risk for heart disease regardless of their level of LDL cholesterol. The risk factors include abdominal obesity (too much weight around the middle), high blood pressure, elevated blood levels of triglycerides and the slower clearance of this fat from the blood, a low level of HDL cholesterol, smaller and more dense LDL cholesterol particles, the higher likelihood of forming and maintaining blood clots, too much insulin, and, possibly, too much glucose in the blood.

The culprit behind this syndrome appears to be the resistance of the cells in the body to insulin. Being overweight and inactive increases the risk for insulin resistance. Exercise and weight reduction can help reduce all of the risk factors associated with this syndrome.[33]

The Take-Home Message Heart disease, the leading cause of death in the United States, develops when atherosclerosis causes a narrowing of the coronary arteries and a decreased flow of nutrient-rich blood to the heart. An elevated blood LDL cholesterol level is the major risk factor for heart disease. Risk factors that you can't control are your age, gender, family history of heart disease, and having type 1 diabetes. Risk factors that you can control include preventing and controlling type 2 diabetes, high blood pressure, smoking, physical inactivity, excess weight, a low HDL cholesterol level, and an elevated LDL cholesterol level. A low HDL cholesterol level may be raised by losing excess weight, getting regular exercise, and quitting smoking. Syndrome X is a group of risk factors that collectively increase the risk of heart disease.

What Is High Blood Cholesterol and What Can You Do to Lower It?

Numerous research studies have shown that reducing the amount of LDL cholesterol in your blood will reduce your risk for heart disease.[34] Starting at age 20, you should have your blood tested at least once every five years to obtain your "lipoprotein

Table 5.6

What Your Cholesterol Level* Can Tell You

If Your Total Cholesterol Level Is	That Is Considered
<200	Fabulous! Keep up the good work!
200–239	Borderline high
≥240	High

If Your LDL Cholesterol Level Is	That Is Considered
<100	Fabulous! Congratulations!
100–129	Near or above optimal
130–159	Borderline high
160–189	High
190	Much too high!

If Your HDL Cholesterol Is	That Is Considered
≥60	Fabulous!
40–60	Good
<40	Too low

*All lipoprotein levels are measured in milligrams of cholesterol per deciliter of blood (mg/dl).

Source: Detection, Evaluation, and Treatment of High Blood Cholesterol in Adults (Adult Treatment Panel III). May 2001. National Cholesterol Education Program. National Institutes of Health Publication No. 01-3290.

profile." This shows the total cholesterol, LDL cholesterol, and HDL cholesterol levels in your blood. Table 5.6 provides the recommended goals for total cholesterol, LDL cholesterol, and HDL cholesterol.

The good news is that there are several diet and lifestyle changes you can make to help lower your LDL cholesterol level. In this section we'll discuss limiting saturated fat, *trans* fat, and dietary cholesterol, as well as adding foods to your diet that may help lower LDL cholesterol levels. Other dietary and lifestyle factors can affect both your LDL and HDL cholesterol levels.

Minimize Saturated Fats, *Trans* Fats, and Cholesterol in Your Diet

In general, saturated fats raise your LDL cholesterol level, while unsaturated fats, when they replace saturated fats in your diet, will have a cholesterol-lowering effect. (Note that saturated fats in your diet will raise your blood cholesterol level more than cholesterol in your diet will.) Typically, the higher your consumption of saturated fats, the higher the LDL cholesterol levels in your blood.[35] Figure 5.16 shows how to choose lower saturated fat foods during the day.

Americans consume about five times more saturated fat than *trans* fat. A food that is low in *trans* fats can still be heart unhealthy if it is high in saturated fat. For example, years ago, some consumers switched from using stick margarine, which is high in *trans* fat, to butter, thinking that butter was better for their blood cholesterol.

Spreads and soft-gel tablets containing plant sterols and stanols can be used as part of a heart-healthy diet to lower LDL cholesterol.

The Traditional Mediterranean Diet: What Do People Living in the Mediterranean Do Differently?

The Mediterranean diet doesn't refer to the diet of a specific country but to the dietary patterns found in several areas of the Mediterranean region, specifically Crete (a Greek island), other areas of Greece, and southern Italy, circa 1960. Researchers were drawn to these areas because the adults living there had very low rates of chronic diseases, such as heart disease and cancer, and a very long life expectancy. For example, the natives of Greece had a rate of heart disease that was 90 percent lower than that of Americans at that time.[1] Ironically, the people in Crete, in particular, were less educated and affluent, and less likely to obtain good medical care than were Americans, so their health successes could not be explained by education level, financial status, or a superior health care system.

Researchers found that compared with the diets of affluent Americans, the Cretans' diet was dramatically lower in foods from animal sources such as meat, eggs, and dairy products and higher in fat (mostly from olive oil and olives) and inexpensive grains, fruits, and vegetables.

Current research continues to support the benefits of a Mediterranean-style diet. A study in Greece showed that greater adherence to a traditional Mediterranean diet was associated with greater longevity. In another study, individuals who had experienced a heart attack, and then adopted a Mediterranean-style diet, had a 50 to 70 percent lower risk of recurrent heart disease compared with those following a more classic low-saturated-fat, low-cholesterol diet.[2]

The Traditional Healthy Mediterranean Diet Pyramid was designed to reflect these dietary patterns and lifestyle habits (see figure).[3] Let's look a little closer at this pyramid, the dietary and lifestyle changes that augment it, and some potential changes that you can make in your diet and lifestyle to reap similar benefits.

The Mediterranean Lifestyle

First, notice that there are no portion recommendations in the Traditional Healthy Mediterranean Diet Pyramid. This purposeful omission portrays the relative importance and frequency of each grouping of foods as it contributes to the whole diet, rather than to a strict diet plan. It was designed to provide an overview of healthy food choices rather than dictate rigid amounts from each food group.[4]

Next, note that physical activity is front and center, at the base of this pyramid, reflecting the foundation for the Mediterranean way of life. This is an important concept, as the Mediterranean residents

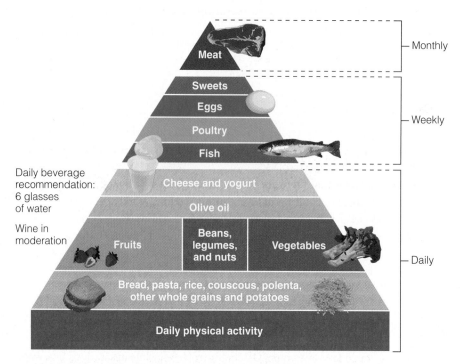

The Traditional Healthy Mediterranean Diet Pyramid
A plant-based diet with minimal amounts of high saturated fat, high-sugar foods, coupled with daily physical activity, reflects the healthy habits of the Mediterranean lifestyle.

in the 1960s were very active, and not surprisingly, much leaner than Americans at that time. In addition to exercise, Mediterranean citizens enjoyed other lifestyle habits that have been known to promote good mental and physical health. They had a supportive community of family and friends, long relaxing family meals, and afternoon siestas (naps).[5] Exercising daily, resting, and relaxing with family and friends is good health advice for all, no matter what food pyramid you follow.

A Plant-Based Diet Seasoned with Olive Oil and Dairy Foods

Plant-based foods such as whole grains, fruits, vegetables, legumes, and nuts are the focus of the Mediterranean diet. In fact, over 60 percent of the calories of the Cretans' diets in the 1960s were supplied by these high-fiber, nutritionally dense plant foods. In traditional Mediterranean-style eating, a combination of plant foods, such as vegetables and legumes ladled over couscous or pasta, was the focus of the meal.[6] Fresh bread, without margarine or butter, often accompanied the meal, and fruit was served as dessert.

Over 75 percent of the fat in the diets of the Cretans was supplied by olives and olive oil.[7] As previously discussed, vegetable oils are low in saturated fat, and olive oil in particular is high in monounsaturated fat.

Nonfat milk and yogurt, and low- or reduced-fat cheeses can be enjoyed on a daily basis when eating a Mediterranean-style diet. A small amount of grated parmesan cheese sprinkled over vegetables and a grain-based meal can provide a distinct Mediterranean flavor.

Occasional Fish, Poultry, Eggs, and Meat

Foods from animal sources were limited in the Cretan diet; they consumed less than 2 ounces of meat, fish, and poultry daily.[8] No more than four eggs were eaten weekly, which included those that were used in cooking and baking. Following this trend, the Traditional Healthy Mediterranean Diet Pyramid suggests eating fish, poultry, and eggs weekly, but relegates red meat to just monthly consumption.

Sweets, Water, and Wine

Historically, sweets were more prevalent during the holidays and fruit was the standard daily dessert.[9] Consequently, this pyramid recommends that consumption of honey- or sugar-based sweets remain modest. Water is recommended daily; the Cretans drank it all day long and with their meals. They also drank low to moderate amounts of wine, typically only with meals. Sometimes the wine was mixed with water, and many times women did not consume any alcohol. Though the pyramid depicts wine on a daily basis, it is actually considered optional and based on personal preferences, family and medical history, and social situations.

eLearn
A Virtual Trip to the Mediterranean

Do you want your diet to have more of a Mediterranean flavor? Visit an interactive guide to the Traditional Healthy Mediterranean Diet Pyramid at http://people.bu.edu/salge/pyramid/mediterranean to learn how.

How Does the Mediterranean Diet Pyramid Compare with MyPyramid?

There are many food similarities between the Traditional Healthy Mediterranean Diet Pyramid and MyPyramid. Both emphasize the importance of regular physical activity, and both encourage a plant-based diet rich in grains, fruits, and vegetables, and daily consumption of dairy products. Mediterranean-style eating encourages the use of olive oil, a fat source that is rich in heart-healthy, unsaturated fat. Vegetable oils are also encouraged on MyPyramid, but more modestly. Whereas fish, poultry, eggs, and meat are recommended more modestly in the Traditional Healthy Mediterranean Diet Pyramid than in MyPyramid, both advise minimizing intake of sweets. Both pyramids can be used as a foundation for a healthy diet. The key is to stick to the recommendations.

Table 5.7

The Cholesterol-Raising Effects of Popular Foods

Food	Total Fat	Saturated Fat	*Trans* Fat	Total Cholesterol-Raising Fats (Saturated fats + *trans* fats)
Spreads				
Butter, 1 tbs	**11**	**7.0**	0.5	7.5
Margarine (stick), 1 tbs	**11**	**2.0**	3.0	5.0
Margarine (tub), 1 tbs	**6.5**	**1.0**	0.5	1.5
Commercially Prepared Foods and Snacks				
French fries, medium (fast food)	**27**	**6.5**	8.0	14.5
Doughnut, 1	**18**	**4.5**	5.0	9.5
Potato chips, small bag	**11**	**2.0**	3.0	5.0
Cookies, 3	**6**	**1.0**	2.0	3.0

Source: Adapted from Center for Food Safety and Applied Nutrition. Updated 2006. Questions and Answers about *Trans* Fat Nutrition Labeling. CFSAN Office of Nutritional Products, Labeling and Dietary Supplements. Available at www.cfsan.fda.gov/~dams/qatrans2.html. Accessed 2006; U.S. Department of Agriculture. 2002. National Nutrient Database for Standard Reference, Release 15. Available at www.nal.usda.gov/fnic/foodcomp/search.

As shown in Table 5.7, while butter has less *trans* fat than stick margarine, if you combine both the saturated fat and *trans* fat in each spread, margarine would still be better for your blood cholesterol. Decreasing the *trans* fats in your diet at the expense of increasing the saturated fat won't be healthy for your heart.[36] When it comes to lowering your LDL cholesterol level, both types of fats need to be limited in your diet. For your heart's sake, cholesterol-raising saturated and *trans* fat combined should contribute no more than 10 percent of your daily calories.[37]

Dietary cholesterol raises your LDL cholesterol level, although saturated fats and *trans* fats will raise it more.[38] The less cholesterol in your diet, the better for your heart.

Dietary cholesterol is found only in foods from animal sources, with egg yolks being a significant contributor in the diet.[39] Limiting the amount of these foods and choosing low-fat dairy products will cut down fat and trim dietary cholesterol.

The cholesterol in an egg is contained entirely in the yolk—the egg white is cholesterol-free. Because egg yolks tend to be a significant source of cholesterol in Americans' diets, the National Institutes of Health (NIH) recommends consuming no more than four egg yolks per week to help prevent heart disease. However, research now suggests that consuming up to an egg daily may not be associated with an increased risk of heart disease. Given that eggs are also a source of many healthy nutrients, such as protein and vitamin B_{12}, some health professionals have suggested lifting the weekly cap on egg yolks for healthy individuals and focusing on keeping dietary cholesterol to no more than 300 milligrams daily, regardless of the source.[40] Hence, egg yolks can be eaten more often if the other sources of dietary cholesterol are low. (However, if you eat an egg a day, you don't have a lot a leeway in your diet.)

Some shellfish, such as shrimp, are also high in cholesterol; however, these are very low in saturated fat and contain some heart healthy omega-3 fatty acids. Lobster has less than one-third the amount of cholesterol of shrimp and is also very low in total fat. Unfortunately, the high price of shrimp and lobster limits their consumption for many people.

Because cholesterol is not found in foods from plant sources, you won't find it in vegetables, fruits, pasta, nuts, peanut butter, or vegetable oils. The best way to minimize dietary cholesterol intake is to keep your portions of lean meat, skinless poultry, and fish to about 6 ounces daily, use only low-fat or nonfat dairy foods, use vegetable oils more often than butter, keep the consumption of baked goods to a minimum, and fill up on cholesterol-free fruits, vegetables, and whole grains.

Eat More Fish and Plant Foods

Over a decade ago, researchers suggested that the Greenland Eskimos' regular consumption of fatty fish (approximately 14 ounces a day), which is rich in EPA and DHA, played a key role in their low incidences of dying from heart disease.[41] Ongoing research continues to support the protective roles EPA and DHA may play in reducing the risk of heart disease and stroke. These omega-3 fatty acids may prevent irregular heart beats, reduce atherosclerosis, mildly lower blood pressure, decrease the clustering or clumping of platelets, lower the level of fat in the blood, and modestly increase the amount of good HDL cholesterol in the blood, to name a few protective actions.[42] In fact, research studies have shown that eating a little over an ounce or more of fish daily may help to reduce your risk of dying from heart disease, and that consuming even one fish meal per week may help reduce your risk of heart attack.[43]

The American Heart Association (AHA) recommends that you consume at least two servings of fish (especially fatty fish such as salmon, sardines, or herring) per week to obtain these omega-3 fatty acids.[44] However, don't try to meet this quota at the fast food drive-through. Fried fish that is commercially prepared tends to have few of these fatty acids and is often fried in unhealthy fat. Note some cautions regarding fish consumption in the boxed feature "Mercury and Fish" on page 160.

In addition to fish, the AHA also recommends that you consume foods such as soybean and canola oils, walnuts, and flaxseeds that are high in alpha-linolenic acid.[45] As mentioned, some alpha-linolenic is converted in the body to these heart-healthy omega-3 fatty acids.

Though consuming some omega-3 fatty acids is good, more may not be better. Because EPA and DHA interfere with blood clotting, consuming more than three grams, which typically only happens by taking supplements, could raise both blood glucose and LDL cholesterol levels, increase the risk of excessive bleeding, and cause other related problems such as hemorrhagic stroke (*hemo* = blood, *rhagic* = ruptured flow) in certain people.[46] Because of these potential adverse side effects, omega-3 fatty acid supplements (fish oil supplements) should only be consumed with the advice and guidance of a doctor. (Consuming large amounts of fish oil supplements can also leave a less-than-appealing fishy aftertaste in your mouth.) However, eating approximately one gram of EPA and DHA daily from fish may provide some protection against heart disease without any known adverse risks.[47]

Americans are currently consuming only about 0.1 to 0.2 grams of EPA and DHA daily.[48] Figure 5.15 listed the omega-3 fatty acid content of some popular fish, and the Table Tips on this page provide a few quick ways to add fish to your diet. Think of fish as food for your heart.

Eating more plant foods high in viscous, soluble fiber may be one of the easiest ways to decrease your LDL cholesterol level. In reviewing over 65 studies, researchers found that each gram of viscous, soluble fiber consumed, in the range of 2 to 10 grams daily, from oatmeal, oat bran, legumes such as dried beans, psyllium, and/or pectin, lowered LDL cholesterol levels over 2.0 mg/dl on average.[49] While the DRI for fiber

Flake canned salmon over your lunch or dinner salad.

Add tuna to cooked pasta and vegetables and toss with a light salad dressing for a quick pasta salad meal.

Order baked, broiled, or grilled fish when dining out.

Try a shrimp cocktail on your next restaurant visit.

Grind whole flaxseeds before eating them to best reap their nutritional benefits. Whole flaxseeds can pass through your gastrointestinal tract intact, keeping their essential fatty acids and vitamin E enclosed in the shell.

Mercury and Fish

Although the health benefits of eating fish are well established, not everyone should be eating unlimited amounts of *all* types of fish. In fact, pregnant and nursing women, women of childbearing age who may become pregnant, and young children should avoid certain types of seafood that may contain high amounts of methylmercury. This form of mercury can be harmful to the nervous system of unborn children, especially during the first trimester of pregnancy, a time when women may not even realize that they are pregnant.[10]

Though mercury occurs naturally in nature, it is also a by-product of industrial processes and pollution. The airborne form of mercury accumulates on the surface of streams and oceans and is transformed by the bacteria in the water into the toxic form of methylmercury.[11] The fish absorb the methylmercury from the water, or get it by eating the organisms that live in the water. Because the ingested methylmercury accumulates over time, larger fish, such as swordfish, shark, king mackerel, and tilefish (golden bass or golden snapper), will have the highest concentration of methylmercury as they have a longer life span and feed on other, smaller fish.

The Food and Drug Administration (FDA) recommends that women of childbearing age and young children avoid eating these four types of fish. Pregnant women and women of childbearing age can eat up to 12 ounces weekly of other types of cooked fish, including shellfish, and should choose from a variety of fish. Luckily, the ten most popular types of seafood (canned *light* tuna, shrimp, pollock, salmon, cod, catfish, clams, flatfish, crabs, and scallops) contain only low amounts of methylmercury. Canned albacore (white) tuna has more mercury than the light variety, so should be limited to no more than 6 ounces weekly.[12]

While the FDA regulates all commercial fish, the Environmental Protection Agency (EPA) oversees all freshwater fish caught recreationally, such as by family members and friends. This agency recommends that all women who are or may become pregnant, nursing mothers, and young children should limit their consumption of freshwater fish to six ounces of cooked fish weekly for adults and two ounces of cooked fish weekly for children. If you eat noncommercial fish from local waters, you should always check with your state or local health department for specific advice, as there could be additional fish consumption advisories based on your local waters. The EPA recommends that if you want to eat coastal and ocean fish that is caught recreationally, you should check with your local or state health department and follow the FDA advice provided above.[13]

Large fish such as swordfish, sharks, and tilefish are likely to contain high levels of methylmercury.

---

ranges from consuming 20 to 38 grams daily, consuming about half of this amount, or 10 to 25 grams of viscous, soluble fiber, can help decrease high LDL cholesterol levels.[50] Increasing the soy in your diet may also help reduce the risk of heart disease. In a review of over 35 studies, researchers found that soy protein lowered total cholesterol, LDL cholesterol, and triglycerides by approximately 10 percent each, on average.[51]

Although all plant foods are cholesterol free, they do contain **phytosterols,** which are plant sterols similar to cholesterol that are found in the plant's cell membranes. Plant sterols can help lower LDL cholesterol levels by competing with cholesterol for absorption in the intestinal tract.[52] With less cholesterol being absorbed, there will be less in the blood. Plant sterols occur naturally in soybean oil, many fruits, vegetables, legumes, sesame seeds, nuts, cereals, and other plant foods.[53]

In a study of over 150 individuals with mildly high cholesterol levels, a margarine containing a plant sterol was shown to reduce LDL cholesterol levels by approximately 14 percent after one year of use.[54] Products such as margarines and soft-gel tablets that contain plant sterols are now available.

phytosterols Naturally occurring sterols found in plants. Phytosterols lower LDL cholesterol levels by competing with cholesterol for absorption in the intestinal tract.

Load Up on Antioxidants and Phytochemicals

You might think that a substance that starts with the prefix "anti" couldn't be good for you. However, the antioxidants vitamins C and E and beta-carotene appear to be "pro" heart health. Antioxidants appear to protect LDL cholesterol from being oxidized by inhibiting the formation of oxidants, intercepting them once they are created, or helping to repair any injury to cells due to these substances. Antioxidants may help LDL cholesterol become more resistant to oxidants.[55] However, when there are more oxidants than antioxidant defense mechanisms occurring in the body, an imbalance occurs. This can cause adverse effects, such as heart disease.

Antioxidant-rich foods contain many other vitamins and minerals, which are not only healthy for your heart in their own right, but may also work with antioxidants. These foods are naturally low in saturated fat and *trans* fat and are cholesterol free, so they can displace heart-unhealthy foods in your diet. Plant foods are also full of fiber, particularly soluble fiber. For all of these reasons, your heart will benefit if you eat plant foods high in antioxidants at each meal.

Nuts are one type of food that is rich in antioxidants, and they can have a positive effect on LDL cholesterol levels for other reasons. Research involving healthy men showed that a diet with 20 percent of the calories coming from walnuts lowered LDL cholesterol by a little over 15 percent. A study of over 80,000 women showed that those who ate nuts frequently—an ounce of nuts at least five times a week—had approximately a 35 percent reduction in the risk of heart disease compared with women who hardly ever ate nuts.[56] Because nuts are from plants, they are free of dietary cholesterol and very low in saturated fat, which is a healthy combination for lowering LDL cholesterol levels.[57]

There are other protective substances in nuts that may prove to be healthy for your heart. Nuts are high in fiber, and they contain plant sterols. Nuts also contain the B vitamin, folic acid, which has been shown to help reduce homocysteine, an emerging risk factor for heart disease. The FDA now allows the food label on certain nuts and nut products to claim that the product potentially helps fight heart disease.[58]

The only downside to nuts is that they're high in calories. A mere ounce of nuts (about 24 almonds or 28 peanuts) can contribute a hefty 160 to 200 calories to your diet. Routinely sitting down with a jar of peanuts while studying can quickly have you overconsuming calories. Without adjusting for these calories elsewhere, your weight may also be adjusted, upward, over the semester. Excess weight can increase your risk for heart disease. The Table Tips on this page provide ideas on how to enjoy a modest amount of nuts in your diet.

There are other substances that may provide an extra boost to your heart health. Whereas garlic may not be perfume to your breath, it may be slightly protective for your heart. Although not definite, garlic has been found in some studies to reduce high blood cholesterol levels by inhibiting cholesterol synthesis in the body, decreasing the clustering of platelets, interfering with blood clotting, and helping to lower blood pressure. Sulfur-containing compounds, specifically allicin, that are abundant in garlic are believed to be the protective factor.[59]

However, a more recent review of clinical studies questions whether adding garlic as part of a low-fat, low-cholesterol diet has a substantial cholesterol-lowering benefit.[60] Until more is known about garlic, your best bet is to enjoy it as part of your heart-healthy meals.

Tea may also reduce your risk of heart disease. Black and green tea are high in **flavonoids,** phytochemicals similar to antioxidants that are believed to prevent LDL

Though high in calories, nuts are an excellent source of antioxidants, have zero cholesterol, and are low in saturated fat.

Table Tips
Nuts About Nuts?

Toss some nuts in your mealtime salad. Use less oil or salad dressing and more nonfat vinegar to adjust for the added calories.

Swap nuts for meat, like chicken or beef, in meals such as stir-fries. A third of a cup of nuts is equal to an ounce of red meat or chicken.

Add a tablespoon of nuts to your morning cereal, and use skim rather than reduced-fat milk to offset some of the extra calories.

Add a tablespoon of chopped nuts to your afternoon yogurt.

Add a handful of peanuts to your air-popped popcorn the next time you need a snack.

flavonoids A phytochemical found in fruits, vegetables, tea, nuts, and seeds.

cholesterol from becoming oxidized in the body. In a study of over 800 elderly men, those who consumed the most flavonoids, predominantly from tea, cut their risk of dying from heart disease by about half compared with those who had low flavonoid consumption.[61] Drinking tea may be beneficial even if a person has had a heart attack. In a study of 1,900 heart attack victims, researchers found that those who consumed large amounts of tea (>14 cups weekly) had a 44 percent lower risk of dying from a heart attack during the 3½-year follow-up period compared with those who didn't consume any tea. Even those who drank moderate amounts of tea (<2 cups weekly) fared better than the tea abstainers, reducing their risk by 28 percent.[62]

Get Plenty of Exercise and Manage Your Weight

Routine exercise can help reduce LDL cholesterol levels, high blood pressure, insulin resistance, and excess weight, and improve HDL cholesterol levels.[63] A review of over 50 studies involving more than 4,500 people found that exercise training for more than 12 weeks increased HDL cholesterol levels by about 4.5 percent. Currently, the AHA recommends that healthy individuals partake in 30 minutes or more of moderate exercise, such as brisk walking, on most days, if not every day.[64] This amount of physical activity is considered sufficient to help reduce the risk of heart disease, but exercising longer than 30 minutes or at higher intensity could offer greater protection, especially when it comes to maintaining a healthy body weight.[65]

Regular physical activity can also help accelerate weight loss. Losing excess weight can help not only to lower LDL cholesterol levels, high blood pressure, and the risk of developing type 2 diabetes, but also to raise HDL cholesterol levels. Hence, sedentary individuals should "move" and sedentary, overweight individuals should "move and lose" to lower their risk of heart disease. Table 5.8 summarizes the diet and lifestyle changes you can make to reduce your LDL cholesterol and risk for heart disease.

A Word About the Protective Effects of Red Wine

Drinking alcohol in moderate amounts can reduce the risk of heart disease.[66] Alcohol can increase the level of the heart-protective HDL cholesterol. In fact, approximately 50 percent of alcohol's heart-protective effect is probably due to this positive effect on HDL cholesterol. Studies have also suggested that alcohol may decrease blood clotting by affecting the coagulation of platelets or by helping the blood to break up clots.[67]

Other studies have suggested that the antioxidants in wine as well as dark beer also contribute to the heart-protective aspects of alcohol.[68] However, these heart-health benefits of alcohol consumption are reaped only by middle-aged and older adults. We will talk more about alcohol in Chapter 9. Though some alcohol may be good, more is definitely not better. Individuals who consume three or more drinks per day *increase* their risk of dying prematurely.[69]

When it comes to reducing the risk of heart disease, the whole diet may be greater than the sum of its parts. A study of over 45 adults with elevated total and LDL cholesterol levels illustrated that a diet "portfolio" consisting of a diet low in saturated fat and cholesterol that was also high in soluble fiber, soy protein, plant sterols, and nuts lowered LDL cholesterol levels by almost 30 percent. This impressive reduction was

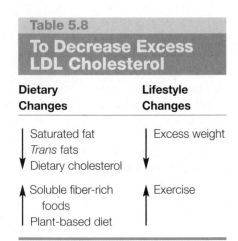

Table 5.8

To Decrease Excess LDL Cholesterol

Dietary Changes	Lifestyle Changes
↓ Saturated fat *Trans* fats ↓ Dietary cholesterol	↓ Excess weight
↑ Soluble fiber-rich foods ↓ Plant-based diet	↑ Exercise

similar to that observed in the group that was given a cholesterol-lowering drug but was limiting *only* the saturated fat and cholesterol in their diet. The latter group's diet did not include the other items in the portfolio diet.[70] Hence, a dietary portfolio approach to eating may be a viable way for individuals to lower high cholesterol levels and avoid taking medication that could have potential side effects.[71] The Table Tips on this page provide eating tips for a heart-healthy diet.

The Take-Home Message Limiting saturated fat, cholesterol, and *trans* fat, and increasing antioxidant-rich fruits, vegetables, whole grains and nuts are associated with a reduction in the risk of heart disease. Regular exercise and weight loss can also help lower LDL cholesterol levels and raise HDL cholesterol levels. Drinking a moderate amount of alcohol may help reduce the risk of heart disease. Some individuals should avoid alcoholic beverages.

Putting It All Together

How do lipids fit in with carbohydrates and the healthy eating tools you are familiar with when it comes to creating an overall healthy diet? As mentioned in the last chapter, your diet should include a proper balance of all nutrients, especially carbohydrates and fat, to meet your daily needs and for optimal long-term health.

As with carbohydrates, there are different types of lipids, and you need to know the best types to consume in your foods. You should aim to eat mostly unsaturated fats and limit the amount of saturated and *trans* fats. You can use the MyPyramid diagram and the DRIs to plan menus that are laden with complex carbohydrates, fiber, and the right types of lipids. A plant-based diet that includes lots of whole grains, fruits, and vegetables, with some low-fat dairy and lean meat, poultry, fish, and vegetable oils will be high in fiber, lower in saturated fats, *trans* fats and dietary cholesterol and be healthy for your heart.

Table Tips

Eating for a Healthy Heart

Choose only lean meats (round, sirloin, and tenderloin cuts) and skinless poultry and keep your portions of meat to about 6 ounces daily. Eat fish at least twice a week.

Use two egg whites in place of one whole egg when baking.

Use reduced-fat or nonfat dairy products, such as low-fat or skim milk, reduced-fat cheese, and low-fat or nonfat ice cream. Sprinkle cheese on top of your food rather than mix it in so you use less. Be sure to keep ice cream servings small.

Substitute cooked beans for half the meat in chili, soups, and casseroles.

Use canola, olive, soybean, or corn oil, and *trans* fat–free margarine instead of butter or shortening.

Lipids

What Are Lipids?

Lipids refer to a category of carbon, oxygen, and hydrogen compounds that are all **hydrophobic** (*hydro* = water, *phobic* = fear). In other words, they don't dissolve in water. There are three types of lipids: triglycerides, phospholipids, and sterols. Two of these, triglycerides and phospholipids, are built from a basic unit called a fatty acid.

Fatty Acids Vary in Length and Structure

All **fatty acids** consist of a chain of carbon and hydrogen atoms, with an acid group (OH) at one end. There are over 20 different fatty acids. They can vary by (1) the length of the chain, (2) whether or not the carbons have a single or double bond between them (C—C or C=C), and (3) the total number of double bonds.

If all the carbons have single bonds between each other in a fatty acid, they are also all bonded to hydrogen. When all of the carbons on a fatty acid are bound with hydrogen, it is called a **saturated fatty acid.** In contrast, if a fatty acid has carbons that are not bound to hydrogen, but rather to each other, which creates a double bond, it is called an **unsaturated fatty acid.**

Triglycerides Are More Commonly Known as Fat

Three fatty acids connected to a **glycerol** backbone create a **triglyceride,** which is the most common lipid found in foods and in your body. Glycerol is a three-carbon compound that contains three alcohol (OH) groups. The fatty acids join to each of the alcohol groups. The more common name for triglycerides is **fat.**

Phospholipids and Sterols Are More Complex

Like fats, **phospholipids** contain a glycerol backbone, but instead of being made up of three fatty acids, they contain two fatty acids and a phosphorus group. The phosphate-containing head is polar, which attracts charged particles, such as water, and the fatty acid–containing tail is nonpolar, so it mingles with other nonpolar molecules such as fats.

Unlike phospholipids, **sterols** do not contain glycerol or fatty acids. Sterols are comprised mainly of four connecting rings of carbon and hydrogen. The best known sterol is cholesterol.

Functions of Lipids

Fat provides fatty acids that are essential to your health and also allows you to absorb the fat-soluble vitamins, A, D, E, and K. Fat is also an important source of energy, helps insulate you, keeps you at a constant body temperature, and cushions your major organs.

Phospholipids make up the phospholipid bilayer in cell membranes. Lipoproteins, made of protein and phospholipids, are transport carriers that shuttle insoluble fat and cholesterol through your bloodstream and lymph to be used throughout the body.

Cholesterol is also an important part of your cell membranes. It is a precursor for vitamin D, bile acids, and sex hormones, such as estrogen and testosterone.

Daily Needs

The current AMDR recommendation is for 20 to 35 percent of your daily calories to come from fat. For some individuals, especially sedentary, overweight folks, a very low-fat diet (providing less than 20 percent of daily calories from fat) that's high in carbohydrates may cause an increase in fat in the blood and a lowering of the good HDL cholesterol. For others, consuming more than 35 percent of their total daily calories from fat could perpetuate obesity, which is a risk factor for heart disease.[72]

You Need to Consume the Essential Fatty Acids, Linoleic Acid and Alpha-Linolenic Acids, in Foods

A minimum of 5 percent and up to 10 percent of the total calories in your diet should come from linoleic acid, and alpha-linolenic acid should make up 0.6 percent to 1.2 percent of your total calories.[73]

Men aged 19 to 50 need 17 grams and women aged 19 to 50 who aren't pregnant or lactating need 12 grams of linoleic acid daily. For alpha-linolenic acid, men aged 14 to 70 need 1.6 grams daily, and women of the same age need 1.1 grams daily.

Linoleic and alpha-linolenic acids must also be consumed in the proper ratio. Too much linoleic acid in relationship to alpha-linolenic acid can inhibit the conversion of alpha-linolenic acid to DHA, while the inverse (too much alpha-linolenic acid and not enough linoleic acid) can inhibit the conversion of linoleic acid to arachidonic acid.

You Do Not Need to Consume Cholesterol or *Trans* Fat

Your body can make all the cholesterol that it needs, so you do not need to consume it in your diet, and you should limit your cholesterol intake for the sake of your heart and arteries. Healthy individuals over the age of 2 are advised to limit their dietary cholesterol to under 300 milligrams daily, on average.[74]

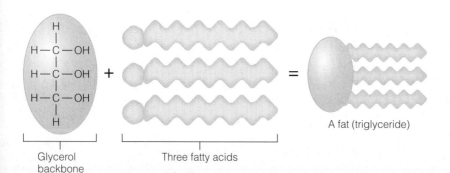

Glycerol backbone   Three fatty acids   A fat (triglyceride)

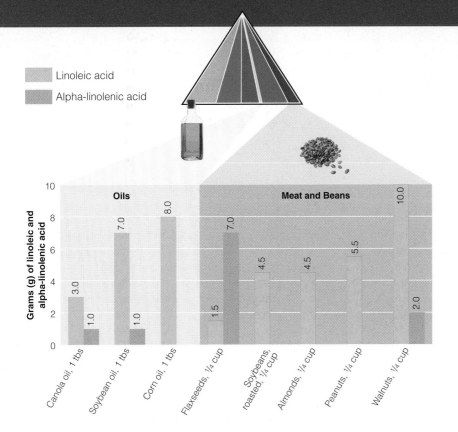

Linoleic acid
Alpha-linolenic acid

Oils | **Meat and Beans**

Grams (g) of linoleic and alpha-linolenic acid

Canola oil, 1 tbs: 3.0, 1.0
Soybean oil, 1 tbs: 7.0, 1.0
Corn oil, 1 tbs: 8.0
Flaxseeds, 1/4 cup: 7.0, 1.5
Soybeans, roasted, 1/4 cup: 4.5
Almonds, 1/4 cup: 4.5
Peanuts, 1/4 cup: 5.5
Walnuts, 1/4 cup: 10.0, 2.0

Trans fats are worse for heart health than saturated fat because they not only raise the LDL cholesterol levels, but they also lower HDL cholesterol in the blood. Therefore, *trans* fats should be limited in foods.

Food Sources

Unsaturated fats are abundant in vegetable oils, such as soybean, corn, and canola oils, as well as soybeans, walnuts, flaxseeds, and wheat germ, and these are also all good sources of essential fatty acids.

Foods high in cholesterol and saturated fat should be limited. Dietary cholesterol is found only in foods from animal sources, with egg yolks being a significant contributor. Because cholesterol is not found in foods from plant sources, you won't find it in vegetables, fruits, pasta, nuts, peanut butter, or vegetable oils.

Most saturated fat in the diet comes from animal foods such as fatty cuts of meat, whole-milk dairy products like cheese, butter, and ice cream, and the skin on poultry. Certain vegetable oils, such as coconut, palm, and palm kernel oils, are very high in saturated fat. Although food manufacturers now use these oils less often, they may still be found in foods such as candies, commercially made baked goods, and gourmet ice cream.

The best way to minimize both dietary cholesterol and saturated fat intake is to keep your portions of lean meat, skinless poultry, and fish to about 6 ounces daily, use only low-fat or nonfat dairy foods, use vegetable oils more often than butter, keep consumption of baked goods to a minimum, and fill up on fruits, vegetables and whole grains.

Too Much or Too Little

Overweight and Obesity

Your body has an *unlimited* ability to store excess energy (calories) as fat. In fact, your fat reserves have the capacity to enlarge as much as 1,000 times their original size, as more fat is added. If your cells fill to capacity, you can add more fat cells.

Heart Disease

Blood cholesterol levels are one of several factors that can affect your risk of heart disease. Eating foods low in saturated fat, dietary cholesterol, and *trans* fat, exercising regularly, and maintaining a healthy weight can help control your blood cholesterol levels and reduce your risk of heart disease. Quitting smoking, lowering high blood pressure, and controlling diabetes (if you have it) can also reduce your risk of heart disease.

In general, you want to lower your "bad" LDL cholesterol levels and raise your "good" HDL cholesterol levels. Having an LDL level of less than 100 milligrams per deciliter (mg/dl) is optimal. An HDL level less than 40 mg/dl increases your risk of heart disease, while a high level of HDL cholesterol, 60 mg/dl or higher, is considered a "negative" risk factor.

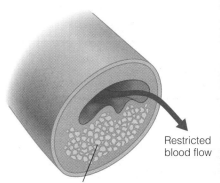

Restricted blood flow

Plaque (accumulation of foam cells, platelets and other substances)

Too Little of the Essential Fatty Acids Can Result in These Symptoms

A deficiency of the essential fatty acids can interfere with normal cell membranes and growth and result in scaly skin.

Terms to Know

hydrophobic ■ fatty acids ■ saturated fatty acid ■ unsaturated fatty acid ■ glycerol ■ triglyceride ■ fat ■ phospholipids ■ sterols

Two Points of View

Farmed Salmon vs Wild Salmon: Is One Healthier Than the Other?

Are there nutritional differences between farmed salmon and wild salmon? What does the research reveal? Two experts weigh in.

David O. Carpenter, MD
Professor; Director, Institute for Health and the Environment, University of Albany

 **Dr. David O. Carpenter, MD,** is director of the Institute for Health and the Environment at the University of Albany. He was the founding dean of the university's School of Public Health, and has particular interest in the areas of disease prevention, reducing exposure to harmful chemicals, and healthy diets. He has participated in several major studies of contaminants in salmon.

Q: Is there a nutritional difference between farmed and wild salmon? Is there a difference in methylmercury levels between the two?

A: We found that farmed salmon do have more of the omega-3 fatty acids. That's because they carry more fat. In farmed salmon, about 15 percent of total body weight is fat, compared to about 5 percent for wild salmon. But there is no strong evidence that excessive consumption of omega-3s provides any additional benefit.

Neither type has elevated levels of mercury. But there are other contaminants to consider that have risks similar to those of mercury.

Q: What other differences exist between farmed and wild salmon, if any, and why?

A: The major findings of our research were that farmed salmon have much higher levels of toxic chemicals such as PCBs (polychlorinated biphenyls, a toxic chemical) and certain pesticides. If a fish was higher in one contaminant, it was higher in all of them.

The contamination source in farmed fish is clearly fish oil and fishmeal in their feed. Salmon feed is made from small fish, and it's usually produced locally. Farmed salmon from northern Europe are more contaminated than those from North America, and North America is worse than South America. That tracks with human activity. Northern European waters have been subject to industrial pollution longer than North America, and North American waters longer than South America.

Our original paper in the journal *Science* in 2004 demonstrated that the levels of contaminants in farmed salmon were high enough to yield the following advisory: To prevent a higher risk of cancer, one should not eat more than one meal of farmed salmon every two months.

Alex Trent
Executive Director, Salmon of the Americas

Alex Trent is executive director of Salmon of the Americas, a trade association representing salmon farmers in Canada, the United States, and Chile. The New Jersey-based group works with scientists and nutrition experts to offer consumers information on the safety, health benefits, and nutritional value of farmed salmon. Fish farms now provide most of the salmon served in the United States.

Q: Is there a nutritional difference between farmed and wild salmon? Is there a difference in methylmercury levels between the two?

A: There are some nutritional differences, but none large enough to be significant. Farmed and wild varieties are both low in saturated fat and calories. Farmed Atlantic salmon has less than 200 calories per serving. Both are high in protein. And both are excellent sources of omega-3 fatty acids. There is some variety of omega-3 content between salmon species, but not enough for anyone to worry about it.

Salmon is a fish that does not have mercury problems. But we have a lot of confusion from consumers because they hear so much about other fish, like tuna or shark. The life cycle of salmon is really different from those fish, and doesn't allow mercury to accumulate. In salmon, mercury concerns are so small as to be negligible.

Q: What other differences exist between farmed and wild salmon, if any, and why?

A: PCBs (polychlorinated biphenyls, a toxic chemical) have been a big question for consumers. In the beginning of 2004, a Pew-funded study came out and said that farmed salmon had PCB levels 10 times as high as wild salmon. But those levels were still very low, well below what the Food and Drug Administration says are safe. The levels in farmed salmon samples from North and South America were lower than in other regions, and farmed salmon from the Americas makes up almost all the farmed salmon sold in the United States. And since then, PCB levels in farmed salmon have come down quite a bit. In the Pew study, some of the farmed salmon samples from the Americas had PCB levels of about 20 to 30 parts per billion. In industry-sponsored studies in 2004, the level was down to 14 parts per billion, and in 2005, it was 12 parts per billion.

David O. Carpenter, MD, continued

In our 2006 paper, published in the journal *Environmental Research*, we developed a cancer risk advisory based on more chemicals. We found that for northern European fish, one shouldn't eat more than one meal of farmed salmon every five months. For farmed salmon from North America, it was one meal every three months. For Chilean farmed salmon, it was one meal every month.

Q: Are any of these issues likely to change in the future?

A: I hope they are. The solution to the problem is that the industry has to stop feeding the salmon concentrated fish oil and fishmeal.

In our 2006 paper, we found that PCB levels hadn't come down much. What we did find was that levels did vary greatly from farm to farm, which shows the feed does have an effect.

Q: How can consumers make the most healthful choices when it comes to eating fish?

A: Be cautious. I'm increasingly of the opinion that benefits of fish have been oversold. Many of the risks have not been adequately addressed by the nutrition community. Know where your fish comes from. Wild salmon carry fewer contaminants, but they still have some.

Keep in mind when you need omega-3s most. The best evidence for their benefits is that they appear to reduce the chance you'll die if you have a heart attack. But many people aren't at the age where they are at risk of a heart attack. For men, it's after 45. For women, it's after 55. Omega-3s don't stay around in your body, but the contaminants in fish do. You can get omega-3s when you need them.

Alex Trent, continued

In 2006, the decreased levels in farmed salmon from the Americas were confirmed by a new, independent study published in the *Journal of Environmental Science and Technology*.

Q: Are any of these issues likely to change in the future?

A: You'll continue to see changes in how fish are fed, which affects levels of substances in their bodies. You'll probably see numbers like the PCB numbers come down a little more. But they won't disappear entirely. There's a certain level that remains in nature. You see PCBs in wild salmon, too.

Q: How can consumers make the most healthful choices when it comes to eating fish?

A: There are a lot of good, healthful fish. They don't all contain levels of omega-3s as high as salmon, but many varieties of fish are high in protein, low in calories, and low in saturated fat. You'll see more farmed cod and farmed halibut. The prices will be reasonable, so fish will remain a good choice. If you want omega-3s, look at salmon, trout, and mackerel. Wild Chinook salmon or farmed Atlantic salmon have about 2 grams of omega-3s per serving. Fresh yellowfin tuna fish has roughly 0.2 grams. Swordfish has about 0.6 grams.

NUTRITION IN THE REAL WORLD

Be a Nutrition Sleuth

Assessing the Fat Content of Fast Foods

What's got more saturated fat: a chocolate doughnut or a bagel with cream cheese? How much heart unhealthy fat is in a large mocha coffee? Visit www.aw-bc.com/blake to test your assumptions—the answers may surprise you!

NUTRITION IN THE REAL WORLD

Get Real!

Eating Right and Light

Your challenge: Plan a lower-fat fast-food meal (from restaurants like McDonald's, Taco Bell, and KFC) that will include at least one serving from four out of five food groups found in MyPyramid. Can it be done? Visit www.aw-bc.com/blake to find out.

The Top Ten Points to Remember

1. A fatty acid is a carbon and hydrogen chain with an acid group at one end. A triglyceride, also known as a fat, contains three fatty acids joined to a glycerol backbone and is the most abundant type of lipid in your body and in foods. A fatty acid without any double bonds is called a saturated fatty acid. If one or more double bonds is present, it is called an unsaturated fatty acid. A saturated fat contains mostly saturated fatty acids and tends to be solid at room temperature. An unsaturated fat has mostly unsaturated fatty acids, is liquid at room temperature, and is also known as an oil.

   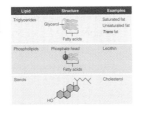

2. Phospholipids contain two fatty acids at their tail end and a phosphorus containing head. Their polar heads and nonpolar tails cause them to be attracted to both water and fat. Lecithin is the major phospholipid in your cell membranes. Lecithin is often used as an emulsifier in foods. Cholesterol is the major sterol in your body and in foods. Cholesterol is the precursor of vitamin D, bile acids, and sex hormones. Your body makes all the cholesterol that it needs.

3. The majority of fat in your diet is digested and absorbed in your small intestine with the help of bile acids and pancreatic lipase. The digested fat is predominantly packaged in protein- and phosphorus-containing lipoproteins called chylomicrons, which travel in your lymph to your bloodstream.

4. Other lipoproteins include the "bad" LDL cholesterol carrier and the "good" HDL cholesterol carrier. LDL cholesterol deposits cholesterol along your artery walls and contributes to atherosclerosis. HDL removes cholesterol from your body and brings it to your liver to be used or excreted from your body.

5. In your body, fat is used as a protective cushion for your bones, organs, and nerves and as insulation to maintain your body temperature. In food, fat provides texture and flavor, and contributes to satiety. Fat in food also aids in the absorption of fat-soluble vitamins.

6. Fat provides the essential fatty acids, linoleic and alpha-linolenic acid. A minimum of 5 percent and up to 10 percent of your total calories should be from linoleic acid and 0.6 percent to 1.2 percent of your total calories should be from alpha-linolenic acid. Soybean oil, walnuts, flaxseeds, and flaxseed oil are good sources of these essential fatty acids. A limited amount of alpha-linolenic acid can be converted to the omega-3 fatty acids, eicosapentaenoic acid (EPA) and docosahexaenoic acid (DHA), which have been shown to reduce the risk of heart disease and stroke. Because fish, especially fatty fish, are good sources of EPA and DHA, you should consume at least two servings of fish weekly.

7. Approximately 20 to 35 percent of your total calories should come from fat. Saturated fat, which raises LDL cholesterol, and *trans* fatty acids, which are created by hydrogenating unsaturated fatty acids, should be limited in your diet. Your intake of both saturated fat and *trans* fat should be no more than 10 percent of your total calories.

8. Eating a well-balanced plant-based diet that contains lean meats and dairy foods with moderate amounts of heart-healthy unsaturated fat is the best strategy to lower your LDL cholesterol level and your risk of heart disease. Commercially prepared baked goods, snack items, and fried foods should be limited to decrease *trans* fats. Your diet should contain no more than 300 milligrams of cholesterol daily, on average. Soluble fiber-containing foods such as oats, legumes, and psyllium-containing cereal, soy protein, and plant sterols can also help lower your LDL cholesterol level. Exercising and losing excess weight can help lower your LDL cholesterol level and increase your HDL cholesterol level.

9. Heart disease occurs when atherosclerosis causes narrowing of the passageways of the coronary arteries. A high level of LDL cholesterol is the major risk factor for heart disease. A high level of HDL cholesterol is protective against heart disease. A family history of heart disease, being a man or a postmenopausal woman, having diabetes, smoking, being physically inactive, having high blood pressure, being overweight, and having a low HDL cholesterol level can all increase the risk of heart disease.

10. Fat substitutes are designed to provide all the properties of fat but for fewer calories. Fat substitutes can reduce calories from fat in a food by more than 50 percent. Some fat-free foods, especially baked goods, may have reduced fat content but not necessarily a reduction in calories, as carbohydrates have been added to these foods. Consequently, fat-free foods may not be lower in calories.

Test Your Knowledge

1. The primary lipid in your body is
   a. cholesterol.
   b. lecithin.
   c. triglycerides.
   d. chylomicrons.
2. Fat provides
   a. flavor.
   b. calories.
   c. fat-soluble vitamins.
   d. all of the above.
3. The type of lipoprotein that carries absorbed fat and other lipids through your lymph system is called
   a. VLDL.
   b. LDL.
   c. bile acid.
   d. a chylomicron.
4. To obtain heart-healthy omega-3 fatty acids you could eat
   a. a tuna fish sandwich at lunch and a Burger King fish sandwich for dinner.
   b. shrimp for lunch and salmon for dinner.
   c. fish and chips for lunch and flounder at dinner.
   d. fried fish sticks at lunch and steamed lobster for dinner.
5. Which of following does not provide dietary cholesterol?
   a. steak
   b. skinless chicken
   c. low-fat milk
   d. margarine
6. You should keep your dietary fat intake between
   a. 8 and 10 percent of your daily calories.
   b. 20 and 35 percent of your daily calories.
   c. 35 and 40 percent of your daily calories.
   d. under 300 milligrams to 500 milligrams daily.
7. The major dietary component that raises your LDL cholesterol is
   a. viscous soluble fiber.
   b. dietary cholesterol.
   c. saturated fat.
   d. plant sterols.
8. Which of the following are good sources of the essential fatty acids linoleic acid and alpha-linolenic acid?
   a. flaxseeds
   b. walnuts
   c. soybean oil
   d. all of the above
9. To raise your level of HDL cholesterol, you can
   a. increase the viscous, soluble fiber in your diet.
   b. exercise more.
   c. lose excess weight.
   d. do b and c only.
10. *Trans* fats are unhealthy for your heart because they
    a. lower LDL cholesterol levels.
    b. raise HDL and LDL cholesterol levels.
    c. raise LDL cholesterol and lower HDL cholesterol levels.
    d. have no effect on LDL cholesterol.

Answers

1. (c) The major lipid in your body is triglycerides, also known as fat. Cholesterol is another type of lipid but is not as abundant as fat. Lecithin is a phospholipid found in your cell membranes and is used as an emulsifier in some foods. Chylomicrons are lipoproteins that transport fat and other lipids to your liver.
2. (d) Fat provides flavor, calories, and fat-soluble vitamins.
3. (d) Chylomicrons enable insoluble fat as well as cholesterol and phospholipids to travel through the lymph system. Bile acids help emulsify fat in your GI tract. VLDLs and LDLs transport fat and other lipids through your blood.
4. (b) Though tuna fish is a wonderful way to enjoy fish at lunch, the commercially prepared fried fish sandwich, fish and chips, and fish sticks have little of the omega-3 fatty acids. Shrimp and salmon are much better choices.
5. (d) Because dietary cholesterol can only be found in foods from animal sources, margarine, which is made from vegetable oils, is free of dietary cholesterol.
6. (b) Your daily fat intake should be between 20 and 35 percent of your daily calories.
7. (c) Whereas dietary cholesterol raises LDL cholesterol, saturated fat is the bigger culprit behind an elevated LDL cholesterol in the blood. Viscous, soluble fiber and plant sterols can help lower LDL cholesterol.
8. (d) Flaxseeds, walnuts, and soybean oil are all good sources of essential fatty acids.
9. (d) Increasing your exercise and losing excess weight can help increase your HDL cholesterol level. Increasing soluble fiber does not affect your level of HDL cholesterol.
10. (c) *Trans* fats provide a double whammy for your heart because they raise the "bad" LDL cholesterol and lower the "good" HDL cholesterol in your body.

Web Support

To learn more about heart disease and how to lower your risk, visit the

- National Cholesterol Education Program at www.nhlbi.nih.gov/chd
- American Heart Association at www.americanheart.org
- Centers for Disease Control and Prevention, at www.cdc.gov/nccdphp/dnpa/physical/index.htm

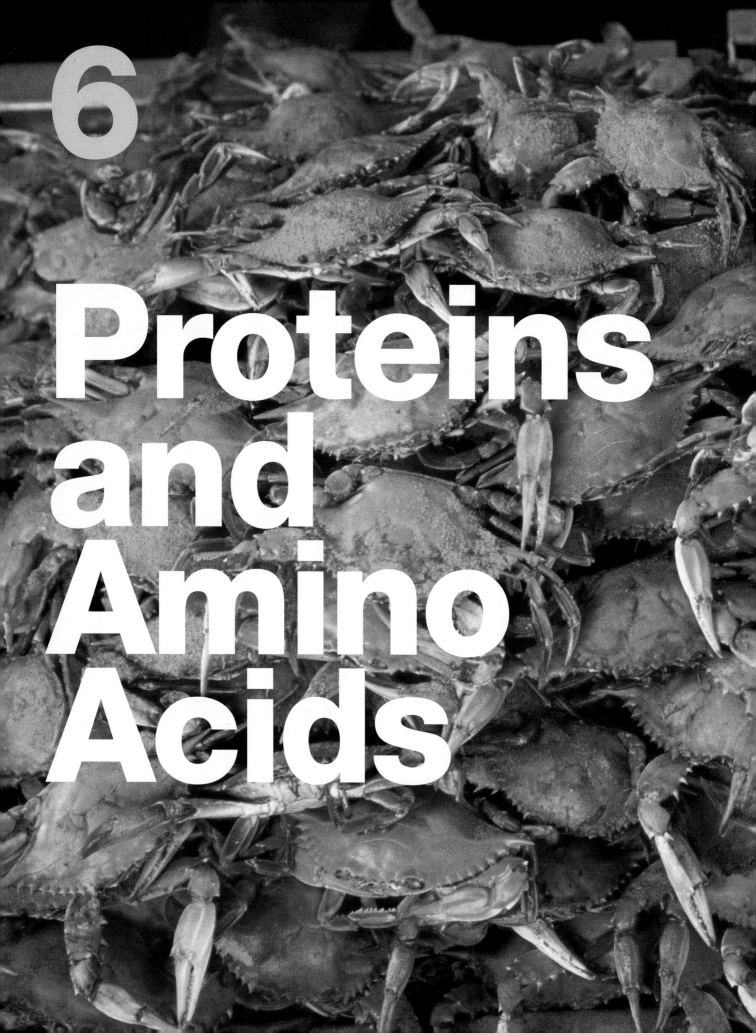

6

Proteins and Amino Acids

1. Your body can make all the **protein** that it needs. **T/F**

2. Proteins provide **structural** support in your body. **T/F**

3. Most **enzymes** in your body are proteins. **T/F**

4. Your body can use protein as an **energy source. T/F**

5. Your body can digest the protein in **pasta** as easily as the protein in a **chicken breast. T/F**

6. Approximately **one-half** of your daily calories should come from dietary protein. **T/F**

7. Consuming too much protein may be **unhealthy** for your heart. **T/F**

8. Active people need to eat **protein bars** to meet their daily protein needs. **T/F**

9. **Vegetarian** diets are always healthier than non-vegetarian diets. **T/F**

10. **Soy** is a good source of protein in the diet. **T/F**

Melissa Cone, a 35-year-old college student, started struggling with her weight when she went back to school and had to juggle class time and homework with her family's needs. She often found herself eating on the run between classes or family errands. After reading an article in a health magazine that said a high-protein diet would help her lose weight, Melissa cut back on eating grains, fruits, and vegetables and started eating more hamburgers, steaks, cheese, and fried foods. While she dropped a few pounds in the first week,

the bathroom scale didn't budge much thereafter. After about eight weeks of eating high-protein foods, she began to have stomach pains. When she visited her family doctor, a blood test revealed that she had higher than normal levels of some substances in her blood. Can you guess what problems Melissa was having as a result of her high-protein diet? In this chapter, we will discuss why Melissa's steady menu of fatty beef, cheese, and fried foods is unhealthy for both her bowels and her heart.

Answers

1. True. If you make the correct food choices, your body can extract all the building materials it needs to create all of the proteins that it needs. For more on how your body builds proteins, turn to page 174.
2. True. Protein also has other important roles in your body. Turn to page 180 to learn why.
3. True. There are thousands of unique enzymes in your body and the majority are made of protein. Turn to page 180 to discover why you need so many specialized enzymes.
4. True. However, burning proteins, rather than carbohydrates or fat, for energy is an inefficient way to use this precious nutrient. To learn why, turn to page 183.
5. False. While both pasta and chicken can contribute to your daily protein needs, the protein in poultry is more easily digested than the protein found in grains. Turn to page 183 to learn why.
6. False. While proteins play a vital role in your body, a little can go a long way. For most healthy adults, less than one-fifth of their daily calories should come from dietary protein. For more on how to meet your protein needs, see page 186.
7. True. A high-protein diet that contains artery-clogging saturated fat and low amounts of whole grains, fruits, and vegetables is not heart-friendly. To learn more, turn to page 189.
8. False. Even an extremely active person or competitive athlete can easily meet his or her protein needs through a well-balanced diet. To learn more about protein bars, turn to page 190.
9. False. While a well-planned vegetarian diet is quite healthy, one that isn't well balanced can lack nutrients. To learn about vegetarian diets, turn to page 194.
10. True. Soy foods are excellent sources of protein, and soy foods help fight certain chronic diseases. Turn to page 196 and find out more.

What Are Proteins?

Proteins are the predominant structural and functional materials in every cell, and you have thousands of unique proteins in your body. Your protein-rich muscles enable you to swim, jog, walk, stand, and hold your head up so you can read this textbook. Without adequate protein, your immune system wouldn't be able to fight off infections, your hair wouldn't grow, your fingernails would be mere stubs, and you wouldn't digest your food. In fact, proteins are involved in most of your body's functions and life processes, and without them, you wouldn't survive.[1]

While proteins are critical for your existence, protein-rich foods don't need to be the focus of your diet to meet your daily needs. In fact, too much protein, particularly at the expense of other nutrients, can be unhealthy for your heart, kidneys, and bones.

In this chapter, you will learn about the building blocks of proteins, the vital roles that proteins play in your body, how your body uses this precious nutrient, and where to find healthy sources of protein in your diet. Let's begin by exploring what proteins are and what they are made of.

The Building Blocks of Proteins Are Amino Acids

Proteins are made of important units called **amino acids.** The amino acids act like the digits (the numbers 0 to 9) in a long number. Your phone number, your Social Security number, and your bank pin number are all made up of the same digits arranged in different sequences of varying lengths (Figure 6.1). Each of these numbers has a specific purpose. Amino acids are like digits because they can be linked together to make unique sequences of varying lengths. Each amino acid sequence represents a unique protein that has a specific function in the human body.

Figure 6.1 Amino Acids Are Like Digits
They link together to form unique sequences with a specific purpose.

Table 6.1
The Mighty Twenty

Essential Amino Acids	Nonessential Amino Acids
Histidine (His)[a]	Alanine (Ala)
Isoleucine (Ile)	Arginine (Arg)[b]
Leucine (Leu)	Aspartic acid (Asp)
Lysine (Lys)	Asparagine (Asn)
Methionine (Met)	Cysteine (Cys)[b]
Phenylalanine (Phe)	Glutamic acid (Glu)
Threonine (Thr)	Glutamine (Gln)[b]
Tryptophan (Trp)	Glycine (Gly)[b]
Valine (Val)	Proline (Pro)[b]
	Serine (Ser)
	Tyrosine (Tyr)[b]

a. Histidine was once thought to be essential only for infants. It is now known that small amounts are also needed for adults.
b. These amino acids can be "conditionally essential" if there are either inadequate precursors or inadequate enzymes available to create these in the body. This can happen in certain illnesses and in premature infants.

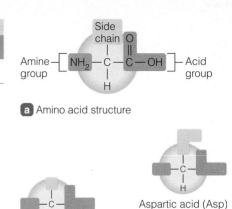

a Amino acid structure

Aspartic acid (Asp)

Glycine (Gly)

Phenylalanine (Phe)

b Different amino acids, showing their unique side chains

Figure 6.2 Amino Acid Structure
(a) All amino acids contain carbon, hydrogen, and oxygen, similar to carbohydrates and fat. They also contain a nitrogen-containing amine group and an acid group. **(b)** A unique side chain (shown in yellow) distinguishes the various amino acids.

As with carbohydrates and fats, amino acids contain carbon, hydrogen, and oxygen (Figure 6.2). Unlike carbohydrates and fats, amino acids also contain nitrogen.

Every amino acid has an **acid group** (COOH), which is why it is called an amino "acid"; an **amine group** (NH₂) that contains the nitrogen; and a unique **side chain.** The side chain gives each amino acid its distinguishing qualities. The side chain can be as simple as a single hydrogen atom, as in the amino acid glycine; or it can be a collection of atoms, as in aspartic acid and phenylalanine (see Figure 6.2b). (Do these last two amino acids sound familiar? Recall that they are the major components of the sugar substitute aspartame, which we discussed in Chapter 4.)

There are a total of 20 amino acids (thus 20 different side chains), which your body combines to make all the proteins that it needs. As you can see in Table 6.1, amino acids are categorized as either essential or nonessential. Let's take a closer look at the differences between these types of amino acids.

Essential and Nonessential Amino Acids

There are 9 amino acids that your body cannot make and that you must therefore obtain from foods. These are the **essential amino acids,** and you can find them in foods such as meat and milk. It is *essential* that you obtain them from your diet.

The remaining 11 amino acids are **nonessential amino acids** because they can be synthesized, or created, in your body. It is *not essential* that you consume them in your diet. Your body creates nonessential amino acids as needed by adding nitrogen to a carbon-containing structure. Some nonessential amino acids can also be made from other amino acids. This process occurs primarily in your liver.

Under some circumstances, certain nonessential amino acids, such as arginine, glutamine, and tyrosine, cannot be made by the body because of illness, or because the body lacks the **precursors** or possibly the enzymes necessary to make them. In such situations, they are conditionally essential amino acids and must be consumed in food. For example, premature infants may not be able to make enough of the enzymes needed to create arginine, so they need to get this amino acid in their diet.[2] Now let's look at how amino acids are used to build proteins.

proteins Compounds in your body that consist of numerous amino acids and are found in all living cells.

amino acids The building blocks of protein. Amino acids contain carbon, hydrogen, oxygen, and nitrogen. All amino acids are composed of an acid group, an amine group, and a unique side chain.

acid group The COOH group that is part of every amino acid.

amine group The nitrogen-containing part (NH₂) of an amino acid.

side chain The side group of an amino acid that provides it with its unique qualities.

essential amino acids The 9 amino acids that the body cannot synthesize; they must be obtained through dietary sources.

nonessential amino acids The 11 amino acids that the body can synthesize.

precursors Substances that precede a step or reaction. A precursor is a substance that is converted to another substance in your body.

Building Proteins from Amino Acids

Amino acids are joined to each other by **peptide bonds** to build proteins. A peptide bond is created when the acid group (COOH) of one amino acid is joined with the amine group (NH_2) of another amino acid. Two joined amino acids form a dipeptide; three amino acids joined together form a tripeptide; and a polypeptide chain is many amino acids joined together (Figure 6.3). Proteins typically contain between 100 and 10,000 amino acids in a sequence. The protein that forms the hemoglobin in your red blood cells, for example, consists of close to 300 amino acids.

The unique nature of each amino acid side chain prevents a protein from remaining in an orderly straight line. Rather, each polypeptide folds into a precise three-dimensional shape, such as a coil, based on the interactions of its amino acids side chains with each other and the environment. Some side chains are attracted to other side chains; some are neutral; and some repel each other.

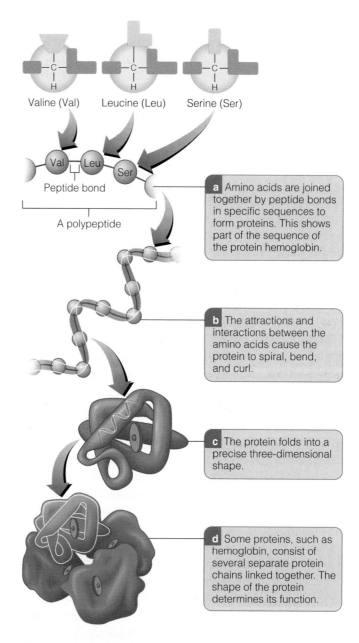

Valine (Val) Leucine (Leu) Serine (Ser)

Peptide bond

A polypeptide

a Amino acids are joined together by peptide bonds in specific sequences to form proteins. This shows part of the sequence of the protein hemoglobin.

b The attractions and interactions between the amino acids cause the protein to spiral, bend, and curl.

c The protein folds into a precise three-dimensional shape.

d Some proteins, such as hemoglobin, consist of several separate protein chains linked together. The shape of the protein determines its function.

peptide bonds The bonds that connect amino acids, created when the acid group of one amino acid is joined with the nitrogen-containing amine group of another amino acid.

Figure 6.3 The Making of a Protein

Additionally, side chains can be *hydrophilic* ("water-loving") or *hydrophobic* ("water-fearing"), and this affects how they react with their environment. The hydrophobic side chains tend to cluster together in the interior of the protein, causing the protein to be globular in shape. The hydrophilic side chains assemble on the outside surface of the protein, closer to the watery environments of blood and other body fluids. The shape of a protein determines its function in your body. Therefore, anything that alters the bonds between the side chains will alter its shape and thus its function.

Protein Function Is Altered by Denaturation

Proteins can be **denatured,** or unfolded, by heat, acids, bases, or salts (Figure 6.4). Denaturation doesn't alter the sequence of amino acids in the protein strand, but does change the shape of the protein. Changing the protein's shape will alter its function, sometimes permanently.

When you fry a raw egg, which is high in protein, the heat will denature the protein to create a firmer, better-tasting egg. This happens because heat disrupts the bonds between the amino acid side chains, causing the protein in the egg to uncoil. New bonds then form between the amino acid side chains, changing the shape of the protein and the structure and texture of the egg. (This solidifying attribute is why eggs are a key ingredient in custards, puddings, and cakes.[3])

Salt and acids can also denature proteins. When you marinate a chicken or steak before cooking it, you might use salt or acid to denature its protein. The end result is a juicer, more tender meat.[4] Your acidic stomach juices help denature and untangle proteins during digestion so that digestive enzymes can break down and prepare proteins for absorption in your intestinal tract.

The Take-Home Message An amino acid is made up of carbon, oxygen, hydrogen, a nitrogen-containing amine group, and a unique side chain. There are 20 side chains and so 20 unique amino acids. While all 20 amino acids are needed to make proteins, 11 of these can be synthesized in your body and are thus nonessential. The remaining 9 amino acids are the essential amino acids that your body cannot synthesize. Essential amino acids need to be obtained in your diet. Amino acids are joined together by peptide bonds to create proteins. The attractions and interactions between the side chains cause the protein to fold into a precise three-dimensional shape. The protein's shape determines its function. Heat, acids, bases, and salts can break, or denature, a protein and alter its shape and function.

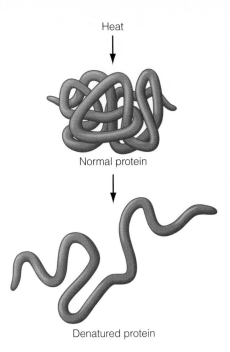

Heat

Normal protein

Denatured protein

Figure 6.4 Denaturing a Protein
A protein can be denatured, or unfolded, by exposure to heat, acids, bases, or salts. Any change in a protein's shape will alter its function.

Cooking, a form of protein denaturation, will often improve the quality, structure, and texture of the protein-rich foods you eat. Raw eggs, meat, and poultry are basically inedible, but cooking these foods greatly increases their palatability.

What Happens to the Protein You Eat?

When you enjoy a tasty peanut butter sandwich, what happens to the protein from the peanut butter once it's in your body? How is the protein in the peanuts broken down so that the valuable amino acids can be efficiently digested, absorbed, and used to synthesize other proteins?

denatured The alteration of a protein's shape, which changes the structure and function of the protein.

You Digest and Absorb Dietary Proteins in Your Stomach and Small Intestine

Protein digestion begins after chewed food enters your stomach (Figure 6.5). Stomach acids denature the protein strands, untangling their bonds. This allows the digestive enzyme pepsin, which is produced in your stomach lining and activated by its acidic environment, to begin breaking the proteins down and preparing them for absorption. Pepsin splits the protein into shorter polypeptide strands, and these strands are propelled into the small intestine.

In the small intestine, other enzymes further break down the strands into tripeptides and dipeptides as well as some amino acids. The protein remnants are then absorbed into the cells of the small intestine lining, where the remaining tripeptides and dipeptides are broken down into single amino acids, which enter the blood and travel to the liver.

How the liver uses these amino acids depends on the needs of your body. For example, they might be used to make new proteins or, if necessary, as an energy source. They can also be converted to glucose if you are not getting enough carbohydrate in your diet. Some of these amino acids also travel back out to the blood to be picked up and used by your cells.

Your Body Degrades and Synthesizes Proteins

amino acid pools A limited supply of amino acids stored in your blood and cells and used to build new proteins.

Your diet provides essential and nonessential amino acids. Your body stockpiles a limited amount of all these in **amino acid pools** in your blood and inside your cells

Figure 6.5 Digesting and Absorbing Proteins

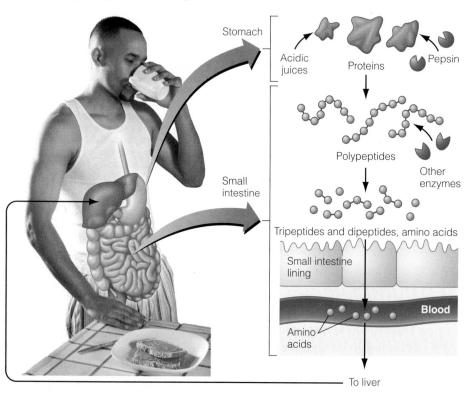

Stomach

Acidic juices

Proteins

Pepsin

Small intestine

Polypeptides

Other enzymes

Tripeptides and dipeptides, amino acids

Small intestine lining

Blood

Amino acids

To liver

1 In the stomach, acidic juices denature the protein and activate the enzyme pepsin, which breaks the protein into shorter strands.

2 These strands enter the small intestine. Pepsin is inactivated. Other enzymes further break down the polypeptide strands into tripeptides and dipeptides and single amino acids.

3 These protein remnants are absorbed through the small intestine lining. They are further broken down to single amino acids, which enter the blood and travel directly to the liver.

4 The liver uses some of the amino acids to make new proteins, or glucose or for other purposes. Other amino acids will pass through the liver and return to the blood to be picked up and used by the cells.

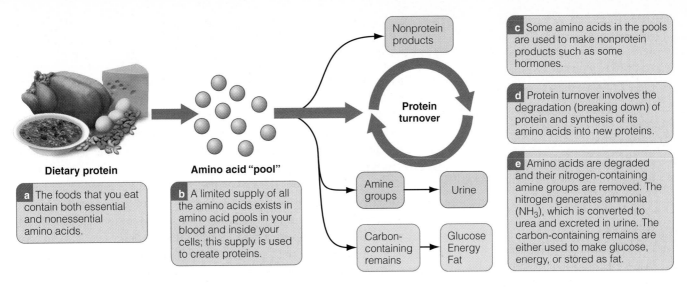

Figure 6.6 The Fate of Amino Acids in Your Body

Nonprotein products

Protein turnover

Amine groups → Urine

Carbon-containing remains → Glucose Energy Fat

Dietary protein

a The foods that you eat contain both essential and nonessential amino acids.

Amino acid "pool"

b A limited supply of all the amino acids exists in amino acid pools in your blood and inside your cells; this supply is used to create proteins.

c Some amino acids in the pools are used to make nonprotein products such as some hormones.

d Protein turnover involves the degradation (breaking down) of protein and synthesis of its amino acids into new proteins.

e Amino acids are degraded and their nitrogen-containing amine groups are removed. The nitrogen generates ammonia (NH_3), which is converted to urea and excreted in urine. The carbon-containing remains are either used to make glucose, energy, or stored as fat.

(Figure 6.6). Because your body can't make the essential amino acids, the pools need to be constantly restocked.

Your body is also constantly degrading its proteins, that is, breaking them down into their component parts, to synthesize other needed proteins. Hence, amino acids are continually being removed from your amino acid pools to create proteins on demand. This process of continually degrading and synthesizing protein is called **protein turnover** (Figure 6.6). In fact, over 200 grams of protein are turned over daily. The proteins in your intestines and liver—two active areas in your body—account for as much as 50 percent of this turnover.[5] The cells that make up the lining of your intestines are continually being sloughed off and replaced. The proteins in these sloughed-off cells are degraded, and most of the resulting amino acids are absorbed and recycled in your body, although some are lost in your stool and urine. Proteins and amino acids are also lost daily through sloughed-off skin, hair, and nails. Replacements for these proteins need to be synthesized, and the amino acid pools provide the building materials to do this. Some of the amino acids in the pools are used to synthesize nonprotein substances, including thyroid hormones and melanin, the pigment that gives color to dark skin and hair.

Amino acids are also broken down into their component parts for other uses or stored in another form. To begin the breakdown process, the amino acids lose their amine groups. The nitrogen in the amine groups forms ammonia (NH_2), which can be toxic to your cells in high amounts. Your liver converts the ammonia to **urea,** a waste product that is excreted in your urine via the kidneys.

The carbon-containing remnants of the amino acids are then converted to glucose, used as energy, or stored as fat, depending on the needs of your body. When your diet is too low in carbohydrates, the amino acids will be used to make glucose. When calories are inadequate, the amino acids can be sacrificed for energy. Surplus amino acids (beyond what is needed in the amino acid pools) from excess dietary protein can't be stored as protein in your body and so must be stored predominantly as fat. Hence, as you know from the last two chapters, *all* excess calories—whether from carbohydrates, proteins, or fats—will be stored as fat in your body.

Proteins don't have a mind of their own. How does your body know when to create or synthesize more proteins? Let's look at how proteins are synthesized in your body.

protein turnover The continual process of degrading and synthesizing protein. When the daily amount of degraded protein is equivalent to the amount that is synthesized, you are in protein balance.

urea A nitrogen-containing waste product that is excreted in your urine.

DNA The blueprint in cells that stores all genetic information. DNA remains in the nucleus of the cell and directs the synthesis of proteins.

gene A DNA segment that codes for a specific protein.

RNA A molecule \ that carries out the orders of DNA.

messenger RNA (mRNA) A type of RNA that copies the genetic information encoded in DNA and carries it out of the nucleus of the cell to synthesize the protein.

transfer RNA (tRNA) A type of RNA that collects the amino acids within the cell that are needed to make a specific protein.

DNA Directs the Synthesis of New Proteins

Protein synthesis is directed by a molecule in the nucleus of your cells called **DNA** (**d**eoxyribo**n**ucleic **a**cid). DNA is the blueprint for every cell in your body.

Each DNA molecule carries the code to synthesize every protein that you need. However, your cells specialize in their protein-producing capabilities. For example, only cells in the pancreas make the hormone insulin, because no other cell in the body expresses the **gene** (a DNA segment that codes for a specific protein) to make insulin. Several hormones prompt DNA to synthesize proteins as needed.

As with any blueprint, DNA doesn't do the actual building or synthesizing; it only provides the instructions. DNA can't leave the nucleus of the cell, so it directs another important molecule within the cell, called **RNA** (**ribon**ucleic **a**cid), to carry out its instructions for building a protein. There are two specialized RNAs, called **messenger RNA (mRNA)** and **transfer RNA (tRNA),** which perform very specific roles during protein synthesis. See Figure 6.7 to view how protein synthesis takes place in a cell.

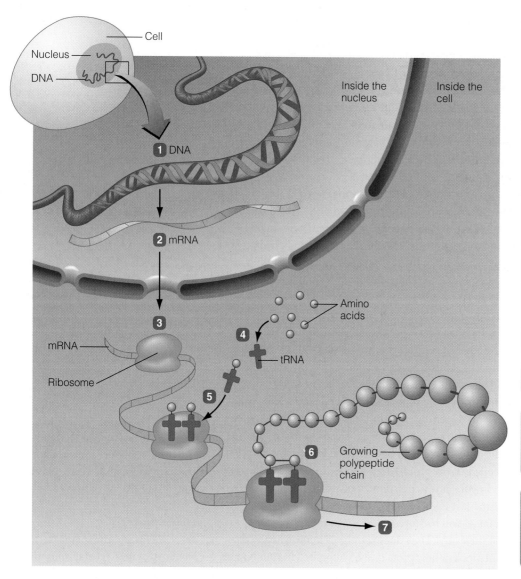

1 Each strand of DNA holds the information or code to create specific proteins. Since the DNA can't leave the nucleus of the cell, a copy of the code, called messenger RNA (mRNA) is made.

2 The mRNA takes this information outside the nucleus and brings it to the ribosome.

3 The ribosome moves along the mRNA, reading the code.

4 Another type of RNA called transfer RNA (tRNA) collects the specific amino acids that are needed to make the protein. There are 20 different tRNAs, one for each amino acid.

5 The tRNA brings the amino acid to the ribosome.

6 The ribosome then builds a chain of amino acids (the protein) in the proper sequence, based on the code in the mRNA.

7 The ribosome continues to move down the mRNA strand until all the appropriate amino acids are added and the protein is complete.

Figure 6.7 Protein Synthesis

When abnormalities occur during protein synthesis, a serious medical condition can result. One such condition is **sickle-cell anemia.** The most common inherited blood disorder in the United States, sickle-cell anemia is caused by the abnormal formation of the protein hemoglobin. According to the National Institutes of Health (NIH), approximately one in 12 African-Americans and one in 100 Hispanic Americans are carriers of the mutated gene that causes the disease.[6]

The mutation in the gene causes a change in the amino acid sequence in the hemoglobin molecule. In sickle-cell anemia, there is a displacement of just *one* amino acid, glutamine, with another amino acid, valine, in the polypeptide chains of hemoglobin. This causes the chains to stick to one another and form crescent-shaped structures rather than the normal globular ones. While red blood cells with normal hemoglobin are smooth and round, those with this mutation are stiff and form a sickle or half-moon shape under certain conditions, such as after vigorous exercise, when oxygen levels in the blood are low. These abnormal sickle cells are easily destroyed, which can lead to anemia, and they can build up in blood vessels, causing painful blockages and damage to tissues and organs.

Another rare genetic disorder, phenylketonuria (PKU), is caused by the body's inability to properly degrade phenylalanine, causing a buildup of this amino acid in the blood. If not identified and treated early in life, PKU can cause mental retardation. To prevent this, infants are screened for PKU at birth.

Red blood cells with normal hemoglobin, like the three similar ones, are smooth and round. A person with sickle-cell anemia has red blood cells like the one on the right; these cells are stiff and form a sickle (half-moon) shape when blood oxygen levels are low.

The Take-Home Message With the help of gastric juices and enzymes in your stomach and small intestine, proteins are broken down into amino acids and absorbed into your blood to be used by your cells. A limited supply of amino acids exists in pools in your body, which act as a reservoir for the synthesis of proteins as needed. Surplus amino acids are broken down, and the carbon-containing remains can be used for glucose, energy, or can be stored as fat, depending on your body's needs. The nitrogen in the amine groups is eventually converted to the waste product urea and excreted in your urine. Amino acids can be used to create nonprotein substances, including certain hormones. The synthesis of proteins is directed in the cell nucleus by DNA, which carries the code for the amino acid sequences necessary to build the proteins that you need.

How Does Your Body Use Proteins?

Without adequate amounts of proteins, you wouldn't be able to breathe, fight infections, or maintain your vital organs. This is because proteins play so many important roles, from providing structural and mechanical support and maintaining your body's tissue to creating enzymes and hormones and helping maintain acid-base and fluid balance. They also transport nutrients, assist your immune system, and, when necessary, are a source of energy.

sickle-cell anemia A blood disorder caused by a genetic defect in the development of hemoglobin. Sickle-cell anemia causes the red blood cells to distort into a sickle shape and can damage organs and tissues.

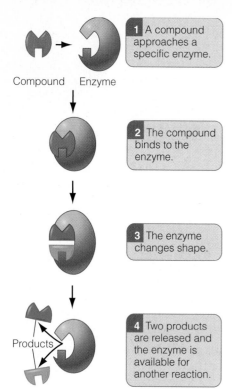

1 A compound approaches a specific enzyme.

Compound   Enzyme

2 The compound binds to the enzyme.

3 The enzyme changes shape.

Products

4 Two products are released and the enzyme is available for another reaction.

Figure 6.8 An Enzyme in Action
Enzymes speed up reactions in your body, yet they aren't changed, damaged, or used up in the process.

Proteins Provide Structural and Mechanical Support and Help Maintain Body Tissues

Proteins provide much of the structural and mechanical support that keeps you upright, moving, and flexible. Just as wood, nails, and plaster are the behind-the-scenes materials holding up the room around you, several fibrous proteins in your bones, muscles, and other tissues help hold up your body.

Collagen, the most abundant protein in your body, is found in all of your **connective tissues,** including the bones, tendons, and ligaments, that support and connect your joints and other body parts. Two other proteins, actin and myosin, provide mechanical support by helping your muscles contract so that you can run, walk, sit, and lay down.

The daily wear and tear on your body causes the breakdown of hundreds of grams of proteins each day. For example, the protein-rich cells of your skin are constantly sloughing off, and proteins help create a new layer of outer skin every 25 to 45 days.[7] Because your red blood cells have a short life span—only about 120 days—new red blood cells need to be continually regenerated. The cells that line the inner surfaces of your organs, such as your lungs and intestines, are also constantly sloughed off, excreted, and replaced.

In addition to regular maintenance, extra protein is sometimes needed for "emergency repairs." Protein is essential in healing, and a person with extensive wounds, such as severe burns, may have dietary protein needs that are more than triple his or her normal needs.

Proteins Build Most Enzymes and Many Hormones

When your body needs a reaction to take place promptly, such as breaking down carbohydrates after a meal, it calls upon **enzymes,** biological **catalysts** that speed up reactions. Without enzymes, reactions would occur so slowly that you couldn't survive. Most enzymes are proteins, although some may also have a **coenzyme,** such as a vitamin, that aids in initiating a reaction.

Each of the thousands of enzymes in your body catalyzes a specific reaction. Some enzymes, such as digestive enzymes, break compounds apart. (Recall from Chapter 4 that the enzyme lactase is needed to break down the milk sugar lactose.) Other enzymes, such as those used to synthesize proteins, help compounds combine. Enzymes aren't changed, damaged, or used up in the process of speeding up a particular reaction. Figure 6.8 shows how an enzyme breaks apart two compounds, yet isn't changed in the process. Thus, the enzyme is available to catalyze additional reactions.

While enzymes expedite reactions, hormones direct them. Many **hormones** are proteins that direct or signal an activity, often by turning on or shutting off enzymes. (Recall from Chapter 5 that some hormones can also be lipids.) Hormones are released from tissues and organs and travel to target cells in another part of your body to direct an activity. There are over 70 trillion cells in your body, and all of these cells interact with at least one of over 50 known hormones.[8]

Let's consider an example of one hormone in action. When your blood glucose level rises after a meal or snack, your pancreas (an organ) releases insulin (a hormone) into your blood, which in turn directs the uptake of glucose in your cells (the activity). If your blood glucose level drops too low, such as between meals, your pancreas

collagen A ropelike, fibrous protein that is the most abundant protein in your body.

connective tissues The most abundant tissue in the body. Made up primarily of collagen, it supports and connects body parts as well as providing protection and insulation.

enzymes Substances that act as catalysts and speed up reactions in the body.

catalysts Substances that aid and speed up reactions in your body without being changed, damaged, or used up in the process.

coenzyme Substances, often vitamins, that are needed by enzymes to perform many chemical reactions in your body.

hormones Protein- or lipid-based chemical messengers that initiate or direct a specific action. Insulin, glucagon, and estrogen are examples of hormones in your body.

(an organ) releases glucagon (a hormone), which promotes the release of glucose from the glycogen stored in your liver (the activity), which in turn raises your blood glucose level.

Proteins Help Maintain Fluid Balance

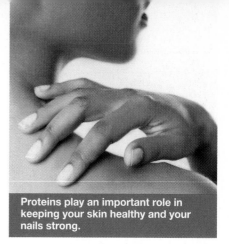

Proteins play an important role in keeping your skin healthy and your nails strong.

Your body is made up predominantly of water, which is distributed throughout various body compartments. Proteins help ensure that all this water is dispersed evenly, keeping you in a state of **fluid balance.**

Normally, your blood pressure forces the nutrient- and oxygen-rich fluids out of your capillaries and into the spaces between your cells. While fluids can flow easily in these spaces, proteins can't, because they are too big to cross the cell membranes. Proteins attract water, so the proteins remaining in the capillaries eventually draw the fluids back into the capillaries. Hence, protein plays an important role in the movement of fluids and in keeping the fluids balanced among these compartments. (Note: The mineral sodium also plays a major role in fluid balance.)

Certain hair conditioners deposit protein on damaged hair to give it extra strength. The protein is washed away during the next shampoo, so a new coating has to be applied to the hair.

When fewer proteins are available to draw the fluid from between the cells back into the bloodstream, as during severe malnutrition, a fluid imbalance results. The spaces between the cell become bloated and the body tissue swells, a condition known as **edema** (Figure 6.9).

Proteins Help Maintain Acid-Base Balance

Proteins can alter the pH (the concentration of hydrogen ions) of your body fluids. Normally, your blood has a pH of about 7.4, and the fluid in your cells has a pH of about 7.0. Even a small change in the pH of your blood in either direction can be harmful or even fatal. With a blood pH below 7.35, a condition called acidosis sets in, which can result in a coma. A blood pH above 7.45, known as alkalosis, can result in convulsions.

Proteins act as **buffers** and minimize the changes in acid-base levels by picking up or donating hydrogen ions in the blood. Should your blood become too acidic, some of the amino acid side chains in the proteins will pick up excess hydrogen ions. Other side chains can donate hydrogen ions to your blood if it becomes too basic.

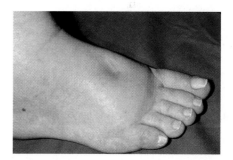

Figure 6.9 Edema
Inadequate protein in the blood can cause edema.

fluid balance The equal distribution of water throughout your body and within and between cells.

edema The accumulation of excess water in the spaces surrounding your cells, which causes swelling of the body tissue.

buffers Substances that help maintain the proper pH in a solution by attracting or donating hydrogen ions.

transport proteins Proteins that carry lipids (fat and cholesterol), oxygen, waste products, and vitamins through your blood to your various organs and tissues. Proteins can also act as channels through which some substances enter your cells.

Proteins Transport Substances throughout the Body

Transport proteins shuttle oxygen, waste products, lipids, some vitamins, and sodium and potassium through your blood and into and out of cells through cell membranes. Hemoglobin acts as a transport protein that carries oxygen to cells from the lungs. Hemoglobin also picks up carbon dioxide waste products from cells for transport to your lungs to be exhaled from your body. Once in your blood, vitamin A travels to your liver and is bound to yet another protein to be transported to your cells.

Transport proteins in cell membranes form a "doorway" that allows substances such as sodium and potassium to pass in and out of cells (Figure 6.10). Substances

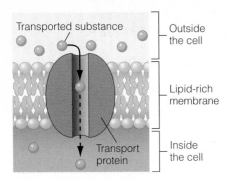

Figure 6.10 Protein Transport
Transport proteins form a channel, or doorway, through which substances such as sodium and potassium can move from one side of the cell membrane to the other.

that are not lipid-soluble or that are simply too big to pass through the lipid-rich membrane have to enter the cell through a protein channel.

Proteins Are Needed for Antibodies and the Immune Response

Your immune system works like an army to protect your body from foreign invaders, such as disease-causing bacteria and viruses. Specialized protein "soldiers" called **antibodies** eliminate these potentially harmful substances.

Once your body knows how to create antibodies against a specific invader, such as a virus, it stores that information and you have an **immunity** to that pathogen. The next time the invader enters your body, you can respond very quickly (producing up to 2,000 precise antibodies per second!) to fight it. When this rapid immune response works efficiently, it prevents the virus or other invader from multiplying to levels high enough to make you sick.

Sometimes, your body incorrectly perceives a nonthreatening substance as an invader and attacks it. This perceived invader is called an allergen. Food allergens are proteins in a food that are resistant to being broken down by heat during cooking or by the gastric juice and enzymes in the body.[9] Individuals who react to these allergens are diagnosed with food allergies. You will learn more about food allergies in Chapter 12.

Table 6.2	
The Many Roles of Proteins	
Role of Protein	**How It Works**
Structural and mechanical support and maintenance	Proteins are your body's building materials, providing strength and flexibility to your tissues, tendons, ligaments, muscles, organs, bones, nails, hair, and skin. Proteins are needed for the ongoing maintenance of your body.
Enzymes and hormones	Proteins are needed to make most enzymes that speed up reactions in your body and many hormones that direct specific activities, such as regulating your blood glucose level.
Fluid balance	Proteins play a major role in ensuring that your body fluids are evenly dispersed in your blood and inside and outside your cells.
Acid-base balance	Proteins act as buffers to help keep the pH of your body fluids balanced within a tight range. A drop in pH will cause your body fluids to become too acidic, whereas a rise in pH can make them too basic.
Transport	Proteins shuttle substances such as oxygen, waste products, and nutrients (such as sodium and potassium) through your blood and into and out of your cells.
Antibodies and the immune response	Proteins create specialized antibodies that attack pathogens in your body that can make you sick.
Energy	Because proteins provide 4 calories per gram, they can be used as fuel or energy in your body.

antibodies Proteins made by your body to bind to and neutralize foreign invaders, such as harmful bacteria, fungi, and viruses, as part of the body's immune response.

immunity The state of having built up antibodies to a particular foreign substance so that when particles of the substance enter the body, they are destroyed by the antibodies.

Proteins Can Provide Energy

Because proteins provide 4 calories per gram, they can be used as an energy source. However, the last thing you want to do is use this valuable nutrient, which plays so many important roles in your body, as a regular source of fuel, especially since carbohydrates and fats are far better suited for providing energy. When your diet contains adequate amounts of calories from carbohydrates and fat, proteins are used for their other important roles.

When your diet doesn't provide adequate amounts of calories—for example, in times of starvation—your body begins to break down its protein, mainly from muscles, into its amino acid components. The carbon skeletons of the amino acids are used for energy and for gluconeogenesis, the creation of glucose from noncarbohydrate sources. (Remember that your brain and nervous system need a minimum amount of glucose to function properly.) However, when proteins are used for energy, they create waste products that must be eliminated from your body, which is particularly burdensome for your liver and kidneys.

The best plan is to eat enough protein daily to meet your body's needs, along with a combination of carbohydrates and fats to keep the protein from being used as energy. Next, we will discuss what your daily protein needs are and how you can easily meet them with a balanced diet. Table 6.2 summarizes the many roles that proteins play in your body.

How Much Protein Do You Need and What Are Protein-Rich Food Sources?

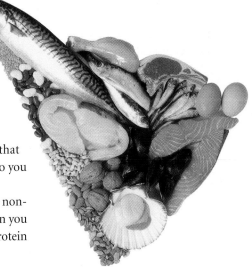

Now that you understand the key roles that proteins play in your body and that amino acids need to be continually available to synthesize these proteins, how do you make sure that you are meeting your protein needs?

You need to eat foods with enough of the essential amino acids and some nonessential amino acids every day. But before you can determine how much protein you need to eat to obtain these amino acids, you need to look at the quality of the protein that you consume. All protein sources are not the same.

Protein Quality Varies Among Food Sources

Protein quality is determined by two factors: your body's ability to digest the protein (the protein's **digestibility**) and the types and amounts of amino acids (essential, nonessential, or both) that the protein contains. Proteins that are more easily digested and that contain both essential and nonessential amino acids are of higher quality.

Digestibility

The **digestibility** of proteins varies, depending on their source. In general, animal proteins are more digestible than plant proteins. Some of the plant proteins, especially when consumed raw, are protected by the plant's cell walls and cannot be broken

protein quality The measure of a protein's digestibility and how its amino acid pattern compares with your body's needs. Proteins that are more easily digested and have a complete set of amino acids are of higher quality.

digestibility A food's capacity to be broken down so that it can be absorbed.

down by the enzymes in your intestinal tract. While 90 to 99 percent of the proteins from animal sources (cheese and other dairy foods, meat, poultry, and eggs) are digestible, only 70 to 90 percent of plant proteins, such as from chickpeas and other legumes, are typically digestible.[10]

Amino Acid Profile

The second factor that affects protein quality concerns the types and amounts of amino acids that the protein contains, or its **amino acid profile.** A protein that provides all 9 of the essential amino acids, along with some of the 11 nonessential amino acids, is considered a **complete protein.** A protein that is low in one or more of the essential amino acids is considered an **incomplete protein.** A complete protein is considered of higher quality than an incomplete protein. Protein from animal sources is typically complete protein, whereas protein from plant foods tends to be incomplete.

Two exceptions to this generalization are gelatin and soy. Gelatin, an animal protein, is not a complete protein because it is missing the amino acid tryptophan. Soy, a plant protein, has an amino acid profile that resembles the protein needs in your body, making it a complete protein.

Any protein chain is only as strong as its weakest amino acid link. If a single essential amino acid is in low supply in your diet, and thus in your body, your ability to synthesize the proteins that you need will be limited. The amino acid that is in the shortest supply in an incomplete protein is known as the **limiting amino acid.**

Imagine a jeweler trying to create a necklace. If the jeweler attempts to make a necklace using a diamond-ruby-emerald pattern with unlimited numbers of diamonds and rubies but only three emeralds, the emeralds are the limiting jewels in the pattern. After the third round of sequencing, the jeweler has run out of emeralds, and the necklace can't be completed as designed. Because the full chain can't be completed, the jewels have to be dismantled.

Similarly, when proteins are being synthesized in your body, all the amino acids have to be available at the same time to complete the protein. A half-synthesized protein can't wait for the needed amino acids to come along to complete the process. Rather, the unfinished protein will be degraded, and the amino acids will be used to make glucose, used as energy, or be stored as fat (see Figure 6.6).

Does that mean that plant proteins are of less value in the diet? Absolutely not. When incomplete proteins are coupled with modest amounts of animal proteins or soy, which have all the essential amino acids, or combined with other plant proteins that are rich in the incomplete protein's limiting amino acids, the incomplete protein is **complemented.** In other words, its amino acid profile is upgraded to a complete protein. You don't have to eat the two food sources of the complementing plant proteins at the same meal to improve the quality of the protein source. As long as the foods are consumed in the same day, all the essential amino acids will be provided to meet your daily needs.

Once the digestibility and the amino acid profile of a protein are known, the quality of a protein can be determined. Let's look at how this is done.

Protein Scoring

The **protein digestibility corrected amino acid score (PDCAAS),** which is measured as a percentage, takes into account both the amino acid profile and digestibility of a protein to give a good indication of its quality. Milk protein, which is easily digested and meets essential amino acid requirements, has a PDCAAS of 100 percent. In comparison, chickpeas garner a PDCAAS of 87 percent, and wheat has a score of only 44 percent. If your only dietary source of protein is wheat, you are not meeting your essential amino acid needs.

Chickpeas are short of the limiting amino acid methionine. The addition of sesame seed paste, which has an abundance of methionine, completes the protein. Add garlic and lemon as seasonings for a completely delicious hummus.

amino acid profile The composition of amino acids in a protein.

complete protein A protein that provides all the essential amino acids that your body needs, along with some nonessential amino acids. Soy protein and protein from animal sources, in general, are complete.

incomplete protein A protein that is low in one or more of the essential amino acids. Protein from plant sources tend to be incomplete.

limiting amino acid The amino acid that is in the shortest supply in an incomplete protein.

complemented proteins Incomplete proteins that are combined with modest amounts of animal or soy proteins or with other plant proteins that are rich in the limiting amino acids to create a complete protein.

protein digestibility corrected amino acid score (PDCAAS) A score measured as a percentage that takes into account both digestibility and amino acid profile and gives a good indication of the quality of a protein.

The Food and Drug Administration (FDA) uses the PDCAAS to assess the quality of dietary proteins. On a food label, when protein is listed as a percentage of the daily value, this percentage is determined based on its PDCAAS.

You Can Determine Your Personal Protein Needs

For healthy adults, the amount of dietary protein (amino acids) consumed every day should equal the amount of protein used. Because amino acids contain nitrogen, a person's nitrogen levels can be measured to determine the amount of protein in the body. Nitrogen balance studies, which measure nitrogen consumed against nitrogen excreted, have been used to find out how much dietary protein people need daily. If the nitrogen intake from dietary protein is equivalent to the amount of nitrogen excreted as urea in the urine, then the person is in nitrogen balance. Such an individual is consuming a balanced diet with adequate amounts of protein and excreting an equally balanced amount of nitrogen. Healthy adults are typically in nitrogen balance.

A body that retains more nitrogen than it excretes is in positive nitrogen balance. When you were a rapidly growing baby, child, and teenager, you were in positive nitrogen balance. Your body excreted less nitrogen than it took in because nitrogen was being used to aid your growth, build your muscles, and expand your supply of red blood cells. When your mother was pregnant with you, she, too, was in positive nitrogen balance because she was building a robust baby.

Individuals who are healing from a serious injury, fighting a fever caused by infection, or experiencing severe trauma, such as the burn victim mentioned earlier, are often in negative nitrogen balance. These situations all increase the body's need for both calories and protein. If the calories and protein in the diet are inadequate to cover these increased demands, then proteins from tissues are broken down to meet its needs. Figure 6.11 summarizes some of the situations that contribute to nitrogen balance or imbalance in your body.

Figure 6.11 Nitrogen Balance and Imbalance
(a) Pregnant women, growing children and adolescents, and some athletes tend to be in positive nitrogen balance. **(b)** A healthy adult is typically in nitrogen balance. **(c)** An individual who is experiencing a medical trauma or not eating a healthy diet is often in negative nitrogen balance.

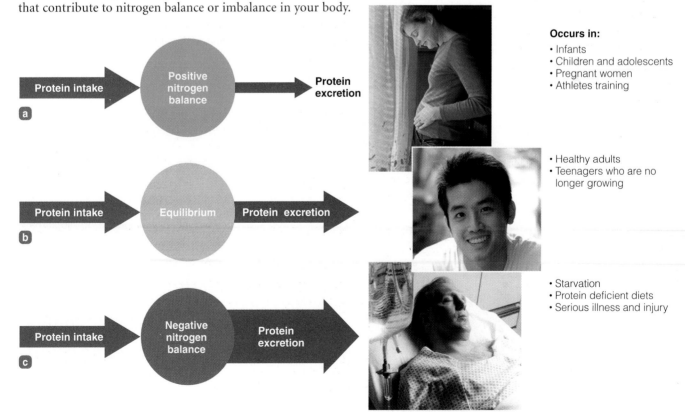

Occurs in:
- Infants
- Children and adolescents
- Pregnant women
- Athletes training

- Healthy adults
- Teenagers who are no longer growing

- Starvation
- Protein deficient diets
- Serious illness and injury

Do You Have a Protein-Friendly Diet?

Take this brief self-assessment to see if you have adequate amounts of protein-rich foods in your diet.

1. Do you eat at least 5 to 7 ounces of meat, fish, and/or poultry on most days of the week?
   Yes ☐ **No** ☐

2. Do you have at least 2 to 3 cups of milk, yogurt, soy milk, and/or soy yogurt daily?
   Yes ☐ **No** ☐

3. Do you enjoy at least 6 ounces of grains every day? (An ounce is considered 1 slice of bread, 1 cup of ready-to-eat cereal, or ½ cup of pasta or rice.)
   Yes ☐ **No** ☐

4. Do you eat at least 1 ounce of cheese or soy cheese daily?
   Yes ☐ **No** ☐

5. Do you eat at least 1 tablespoon of peanuts daily?
   Yes ☐ **No** ☐

6. Do you eat at least ½ cup of dried beans or peas, such as kidney beans or chickpeas, every day?
   Yes ☐ **No** ☐

7. Do you eat soy-based foods such as soy burgers and tofu daily?
   Yes ☐ **No** ☐

Answers

If you answered yes to at least the first three questions and are also meeting your calorie needs on a daily basis, you have a *very* protein-friendly diet! If you answered no to question 1 but yes to most of the other questions, you are also likely meeting your protein needs if your daily calories are adequate. If you have more no than yes answers, your diet may be in need of a protein makeover. Read on in the chapter to learn how you can easily add healthy sources of protein to your diet.

There are two ways to measure protein intake in the diet. It can be measured as a percentage of total calories or as grams of protein eaten per day. The latest dietary recommendation, based on data from numerous nitrogen balance studies, is to consume from 10 to 35 percent of your total daily calories from protein. Currently, adults in the United States consume about 15 percent of their daily calories from protein, which falls within this range.[11]

The current recommendation for the grams of protein that you need daily is based on your age and your weight (Table 6.3). Adults age 19 and older should consume 0.8 gram (g) of protein for each kilogram (kg) of body weight. For example, a person who weighs 176 pounds (lb) would weigh 80 kg (176 lb ÷ 2.2 = 80 kg) and should consume 80 kg 3 0.8 g, or 64 g of protein a day. A person who weighs 130 lb should consume approximately 47 g of protein daily (130 lb ÷ 2.2 = 59 kg × 0.8 g = 47). In the United States, men typically consume from 71 to 101 g of protein daily, while women on average consume 55 to 62 g. Americans are typically meeting, and even exceeding, their dietary protein needs.

Even though most Americans are consuming more protein than they need, their percentage of daily calories contributed by protein (approximately 15 percent) falls within the recommended range. This is because Americans are consuming an abundant amount of calories from carbohydrates and fats, which lowers the percentage of their total calories coming from protein.

An overweight individual's protein needs are not much greater than those of a normal-weight person of similar height. This is because the Recommended Dietary Allowance (RDA) for dietary protein is based on a person's need to maintain protein-dependent tissues like lean muscle and organs and to perform protein-dependent body functions. Because most overweight people carry their extra body weight predominantly as fat, not muscle, they do not need to consume significantly more protein than normal-weight people.

The American College of Sports Medicine, the American Dietetic Association, and other experts have advocated an increase of 50 to 100 percent more protein for competitive athletes participating in endurance exercise (marathon runners) or resistance exercise (weight lifters) to maintain their needs.[12] However, because of their active lifestyles, athletes typically have a higher intake of food and thus already consume higher amounts of both calories and protein.

Table 6.3

Calculating Your Daily Protein Needs

If You Are	You Need
14–18 years old	0.85 g/kg
≥19 years old	0.80 g/kg

To calculate your needs, first convert your body weight from pounds (lb) to kilograms (kg) by dividing by 2.2, like this:

Your weight in pounds: _____ lbs ÷ 2.2 = _____ kg

Then, multiply your weight in kilograms by 0.8 or 0.85:

Your weight in kilograms: _____ kg × 0.8 g = _____ g/day

Source: Institute of Medicine, National Academy of Science, *Dietary Reference Intake for Energy, Carbohydrate, Fiber, Fat, Fatty Acids, Cholesterol, Protein, and Amino Acids* (Washington, DC: The National Academy Press, 2002).

Now let's look at how you can meet your daily protein needs through a well-balanced diet.

Protein Is Found in These Foods

Do you think your diet is adequate in protein? Before you read this section, take the Self-Assessment quiz to find out.

While some amount of protein is found in many foods, it is particularly abundant in dairy foods, meat, fish, poultry, and meat alternatives such as dried beans, peanut butter, nuts, and soy (Figure 6.12). A 3-ounce serving of cooked meat, poultry, or fish provides approximately 21 to 25 grams of protein, or about 7 grams per ounce. This serving size, which is about the size of a woman's palm or a deck of cards, is plenty of protein for one meal. Grains and vegetables are less robust protein sources providing about 3 to 4 grams per serving, but as part of a varied, balanced diet, they can aid significantly in meeting your daily needs.

> More than half of the protein in an egg is in the white. In fact, two egg whites provide 7 grams of protein, compared with only 6 grams in a whole egg.

Eating a wide variety of foods is the best approach to meeting your protein needs. A diet that consists of the recommended servings from the MyPyramid food guidance system based on 1,600 calories, which is far less than most adults consume daily, will supply the protein needs for adult women and most adult men (see Table 6.4 on page 188). In fact, many people meet their daily protein needs before they even sit down to dinner!

Though most Americans are getting plenty of protein in their diets, there has recently been a boom in the consumption of high-protein energy bars. Are these a bargain? Are they necessary? The boxed feature "Protein Bars: Are They a Health Bargain?" elsewhere in this chapter takes a look at this hot topic.

Figure 6.12 Food Sources of Protein
Food choices from the meat, poultry, fish, meat alternative, and milk groups are the most abundant sources of dietary protein. Grains and vegetables provide less protein per serving but as part of a varied, balanced diet can add significantly to your daily needs.

Source: USDA National Nutrient Database for Standard Reference (www.nal.usda.gov/fnic).

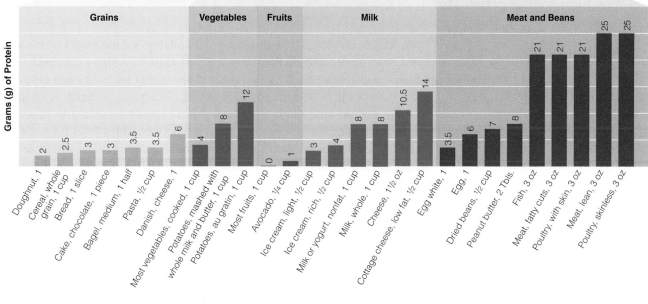

Table 6.4
A Typical Day in the Life

Food	Amount	Calories	Protein (g)	Grain Group (servings)	Vegetable Group (servings)	Fruit Group (servings)	Oil Group (tsp)	Milk Group (servings)	Meat Group (oz)
Breakfast									
Bran flakes	2 cups	256	7.5	2					
Milk, nonfat	1 cup	86	8					1	
Orange juice	8 oz	112	2			1			
Lunch									
Turkey and cheese sandwich:									
Turkey breast	2 oz	94	11						2
Cheese, low fat	2 oz	98	14					1	
Whole-wheat bread	2 slices	138	5	2					
Tossed salad	3 cups	30	2		1.5				
Italian dressing	1 tbs	69	0				3		
Snack									
Yogurt, vanilla	8 oz	160	8			1			
Banana	1	109	1			1			
Dinner									
Chicken breast, skinless	3 oz	189	25						3
Brown rice	1 cup	216	5	2					
Broccoli, cooked	1 cup	52	6		1				
Margarine	2 tsp	68	0				2		
Totals:		1,677	94.5	6	2.5	2	5	3	5

Note: A 140-pound adult needs 51 g of protein daily. A 180-pound adult needs 65 g of protein daily.

Source: MyPyramid.gov; J. Pennington and J. S. Douglass, *Bowes & Church's Food Values of Portions Commonly Used,* 18th ed (New York: Lippincott Williams & Wilkins, 2005).

The Take-Home Message Protein quality is determined by the protein's digestibility and by the types and amounts of amino acids (essential versus nonessential) it contains. Protein from animal foods is more easily digested than protein from plant foods. A complete protein, which is typically found in animal foods and soy, provides a complete set of the essential amino acids along with some nonessential amino acids. Plant proteins are typically incomplete, as they are missing one or more of the essential amino acids. Plant proteins can be complemented with protein from other plant sources or animal food sources to improve their protein quality. A well-balanced diet can easily meet your daily protein needs. Adults should consume 0.8 gram of protein for each kilogram of body weight. In the United States, men typically consume from 71 to 101 grams of protein daily, while women are consuming 55 to 62 grams—in both cases, far more than is needed.

What Happens if You Eat Too Much or Too Little Protein?

While protein is essential to health and normal body function, eating too much or too little can be unhealthy. Let's look at what happens to the human body when it gets too much or too little protein.

Eating Too Much Protein Can Be Harmful

As you read in the beginning of the chapter, Melissa, the college student, had switched to a high-protein diet to help her slim down. Unfortunately, her steady diet of low-fiber, fat-rich cheeses, hamburgers, and fried foods was affecting her health. The lack of fiber-rich whole grains, fruits, and vegetables was causing her to become extremely constipated and giving her bellyaches. As you remember from Chapter 5, a diet high in saturated fat can raise the LDL ("bad") cholesterol level in the blood. Before Melissa switched to a high-protein diet, her LDL cholesterol was in the healthy range. But, her steady diet of fatty foods caused her LDL cholesterol to climb into the dangerously high range. Her doctor sent her to a registered dietitian (RD), who advised her to trim the fatty foods from her diet and add back the fiber-rich whole grains, fruits, and vegetables. Melissa's cholesterol dropped to a healthy level within months, and the high-fiber foods helped to "keep things moving" in her intestinal tract and eliminate the constipation. The RD also recommended that Melissa walk on campus between classes daily to help her better manage her weight.

While consuming protein is a key to good health, eating more is not necessarily eating better. In fact, a diet that is too high in protein may increase the risk of heart disease, kidney stones, osteoporosis (thinning of the bones), and some types of cancer. Consuming too much protein, to the point where it replaces other essential nutrients, also leads to an unbalanced diet. This is important to remember if you are thinking about following a high-protein fad diet. We will talk more about high-protein diets in Chapter 10.

Depending on your food choices, a high-protein diet may have you overloading on heart-unhealthy saturated fat. While lean meats and skinless poultry contain less saturated fat than some other cuts of meat, they are not completely free of saturated fat. Hence, a high-protein diet can make keeping your diet low in saturated fat a challenge. As you read in Chapter 5, lowering the saturated fat in your diet is important in lowering your risk of heart disease.

A high-protein diet may also increase the risk of kidney stones, which commonly contain calcium. Over 10 percent of Americans will likely suffer from a kidney stone at least once in their lives.[13]

Though still a controversial issue, numerous research studies have shown that bones lose calcium when a person's diet is too high in protein. The loss seems to occur because calcium is taken from bone to act as a buffer, offsetting the acid generated when specific amino acids are broken down. In fact, in a study of individuals on a low-carbohydrate, high-protein diet, researchers observed a 50 percent loss of calcium in the subjects' urine. The calcium loss was not observed when these individuals were on a lower-protein diet, so it was concluded that it was due to the buffering effect.[14]

Protein Bars: Are They a Health Bargain?

The sales of protein and energy bars have skyrocketed over the last decade, fueling an industry that now generates over a billion dollars annually.[1] There are bars advertised for women, bars for men, bars for the elderly, and junior bars for children. When they emerged in the 1980s, these bars were marketed as a portable snack to keep athletes fueled for long-distance or endurance outings. Manufacturers often claim that the bars are needed to fuel daily activities and build strong muscles or that they serve as a quick meal in a cellophane wrapper.

As you learned from the previous two chapters, all foods provide calories and therefore energy. Whether your calories come from a balanced meal or a "balanced bar," your body will either use them as fuel or store them if they're not immediately needed. You also just learned that you can easily meet your daily protein needs by making wise food choices. Given this knowledge, what advantage, if any, do you think protein and energy bars provide?

If convenience and portability is the main attraction of protein and energy bars, then consider another classic, convenient, and portable food, the peanut butter sandwich. It can be made in a

Bar Hopping

Product	Price	Calories	Protein (g)	Total Carb (g)	Total Fat (g)	Sat. Fat (g)	Sugars (tsp)	Fiber (g)
Peanut butter (1 tbs) on 2 slices whole-wheat bread	**$0.22**	**234**	**9**	**29**	**11**	**2**	**<1 (5%)***	**5**
Dr Soy Double Chocolate	1.40	180	12	27	3	2.5	2.5 ½ (22%)	1
Balance Chocolate	1.28	200	14	22	6	3.5	4.5 ½ (36%)	<1
Zoneperfect Chocolate Peanut Butter	1.31	210	16	20	7	3	3.5 ½ (25%)	1
EAS AdvantEdge Chocolate Peanut Crisp	1.10	220	13	32	6	3	5 (26%)	1
Atkins Advantage Chocolate Decadence	2.29	220	17	25	11	7	0	11
Genisoy Ultimate Chocolate Fudge Brownie	1.15	230	14	33	4.5	3	7 (49%)	2
Carb Solutions Creamy Chocolate Peanut Butter	2.24	240	24	14	10	3.5	0.5 (3%)	1

snap, and since it doesn't need to be refrigerated, it can travel anywhere. The table below let's us do some comparison shopping to see how a peanut butter sandwich stacks up to a protein bar.

From a price standpoint, a peanut butter sandwich is a bargain compared with bars that can cost more than $2.50 each, or ten times as much as the sandwich. While the calories and protein content of the sandwich are similar to that in many bars, the saturated fat and sugar contents are not. Some bars provide up to 7 grams of saturated fat, which is about one-third of the upper limit recommended for many adults daily. In contrast, the sandwich contains less saturated fat than all the bars listed. Since these bars can contain up to 7 teaspoons of sugar, which supplies up to 50 percent of the calories in the bar, much of the "energy" in an energy bar is simply sugar. The bars with the most sugar tend to have the least amount of fiber. Ironically, the average consumer needs more fiber in their diet. Because the peanut butter sandwich has lower amounts of sugar and a higher amount of fiber than almost all of the bars, it's actually the healthier food choice.

Product	Price	Calories	Protein (g)	Total Carb (g)	Total Fat (g)	Sat. Fat (g)	Sugars (tsp)	Fiber (g)
PowerBar ProteinPlus Chocolate Fudge Brownie	1.99	270	24	36	5	3	5 (38%)	2
Met-Rx Protein Plus Chocolate Roasted Peanut	2.57	320	31	29	9	4.5	0.5 (3%)	1
PowerBar Pria Double Chocolate Cookie	0.94	110	5	16	3	2.5	2.5 ½ (36%)	0
Clif Luna Nutz Over Chocolate	1.40	180	10	24	4.5	2.5	3 (27%)	2
Kellogg's Krave Chocolate Delight	0.53	200	7	31	6	3.5	5.5 (44%)	2
Slim-Fast Meal Options Rich Chocolate Brownie	1.02	220	8	35	5	3	6 (44%)	2
Ensure Chewy Chocolate Peanut	1.13	230	9	35	6	4	6 (42%)	1

Key: ✎ = 1 tsp sugar

🌾 = 1 g fiber

* = % of calories

Source: Adapted from *Consumer Reports* 68 (June 2003): 19–21.

Other research has been done to determine if calcium loss leads to osteoporosis when there is an adequate amount of calcium in a high-protein diet. In fact, a higher dietary protein intake, especially if it is coming from foods such as low-fat milk, yogurt, and cheese, can add calcium to the diet.[15] Unfortunately, many American adults are falling short of their recommended calcium intake, and if their diets are also high in protein, this isn't a healthy combination for their bones.

The relationship between high-protein diets and cancer is another less-than-clear association. While large amounts of meat, especially red and processed meats, may increase the risk for colon cancer, research doesn't necessarily support a connection between high amounts of total protein and increased colon cancer risk.[16]

An important health concern surrounding a high-protein diet is the displacement of other foods. If your diet is overloaded with protein-rich foods such as meat, fish, and poultry, these will likely displace, or crowd out, other nutrient- and fiber-rich foods. As you know, a diet that contains high fiber and nutrient-rich foods can help you to reduce your risk of several chronic diseases, such as cancer, heart disease, diabetes, and stroke. If you fill up on meat and milk at meals and snacks, you could be shortchanging yourself on foods such as whole grains, fruits, and vegetables that contain disease-fighting compounds.

While many individuals have the luxury of worrying about consuming too much protein, others are desperately trying to meet their daily needs. Let's look at the serious health implications of chronically eating too little dietary protein.

Eating Too Little Protein Can Be Harmful

Eating too little protein can lead to many health problems, including compromised bone health. In fact, eating too little protein has been shown to lead to loss of bone mass. A study of over 500 women over age 55 showed that higher dietary protein consumption was associated with more dense bone. Another study of over 2,000 males and females ranging in age from 50 to 89 showed that those under the age of 70 who had a diet higher in protein had 65 percent fewer hip fractures compared with those with the lowest protein intake. When it comes to our bones, too much protein or too little can both be unhealthy for your bones.[17]

Protein Energy Malnutrition

Every day, almost 17,000 children around the world—approximately 6 million annually—die because they don't have access to enough food.[18] These children's diets are inadequate in either protein or calories or both, a condition known as **protein-energy malnutrition (PEM).** When calories and protein are inadequate, dietary protein is used for energy rather than reserved for its numerous other roles in the body. Moreover, other important nutrients, such as vitamins and minerals, also tend to be in short supply, which further compounds PEM.

Many factors can lead to PEM, including poverty, poor food quality, insufficient food intake, unsanitary living conditions, ignorance regarding the proper feeding of children, and stopping lactation (nursing) too early.[19] Because they are growing, infants and children have higher nutritional needs for their size than adults. They are also dependent on others to provide them with food. For these reasons, PEM is more frequently seen in infants and children than in adults.

Because protein is needed for so many functions in the body, it isn't surprising that a chronic protein deficiency can lead to many health problems. For example, without adequate dietary protein, the cells in the lining of the gastrointestinal tract aren't

protein-energy malnutrition (PEM) A lack of sufficient dietary protein and/or calories.

adequately replaced when they are routinely sloughed off. The inability to regenerate these cells inhibits their function. Absorption of the little amount of food that may be available is reduced, and bacteria that normally stay in the intestines can get into the blood and poison it, causing septicemia. Malnourished individuals frequently have a compromised immune system, which can make fighting even a minor infection, such as a respiratory infection or diarrhea, impossible. Malnourished children have died after exposure to measles as well as after bouts of diarrhea.[20]

While deficiencies of both calories and protein often occur simultaneously, sometimes one may be more prevalent than the other. A severe deficiency of protein is called **kwashiorkor,** whereas a severe deficiency of calories is called **marasmus.** A condition that is caused by a chronic deficiency of both calories and protein is called marasmic kwashiorkor. Let's look at each of these PEM conditions a little more closely.

Kwashiorkor

Kwashiorkor was first observed in the 1930s in tribes in Ghana (a republic of West Africa) when the firstborn child became sick when a new sibling became part of the family. Typically, the newborn displaced the first child, usually around 18 months of age, from his or her lactating mother and her nutritionally balanced breast milk. The first child was then relegated to an inadequate and unbalanced diet high in carbohydrate-rich grains but severely deficient in protein. This sets the stage for serious medical complications.

A classic symptom of severe kwashiorkor is edema in the legs, feet, and stomach (see Figure 6.13). As we discussed earlier, protein plays an important role in maintaining fluid balance in the blood and around the cells. With protein deficiency, fluid accumulates in the spaces surrounding the cells, causing swelling. The body wastes away as the muscle proteins are broken down to generate the amino acids needed to synthesize other proteins. Consequently, muscle tone and strength diminish. Those with kwashiorkor often have skin that is dry and peeling. Rashes or lesions can also develop. Their hair is often brittle and can be easily pulled out. These children often appear pale, have facial expressions that display sadness and apathy, and cry easily. They are prone to infections, rapid heart beats, excess fluid in the lungs, pneumonia, septicemia, and water and electrolyte imbalances—all of which can be deadly.[21]

Marasmus and Marasmic Kwashiorkor

The bloating seen in kwashiorkor is the opposite of the frail, emaciated appearance of marasmus (Figure 6.14). Because they are not consuming enough calories, marasmic individuals literally look as though they are starving. They are often not even at 60 percent of their desirable body weight. These children's bodies use all available calories to stay alive; thus, growth is interrupted. Marasmic children are weakened and appear apathetic. Many can't stand without support. They look old beyond their years, as the loss of fat in their face—one of the last places that the body loses fat during starvation—causes the disappearance of a robust childlike appearance. Their hair is thin and dry and lacks the sheen found in healthy children. Their body temperature and blood pressure are both low, and they are prone to dehydration, infections, and unnecessary blood clotting.[22]

Individuals with marasmic kwashiorkor have the worst of both conditions. They often have edema in their legs and arms, yet have a "skin and bones" appearance in other parts of the body. When these individuals are provided with medical and nutritional treatment, such as receiving adequate protein, the edema subsides and their clinical symptoms more closely resemble that of a person with marasmus.

Figure 6.13 Kwashiorkor
The edema in this child's belly is a classic sign of kwashiorkor.

kwashiorkor A state of PEM where there is a severe deficiency of dietary protein.

marasmus A state of PEM where there is a severe deficiency of calories that perpetuates wasting; also called starvation.

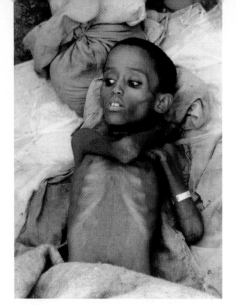

Figure 6.14 Marasmus
The emaciated appearance of this child is a symptom of marasmus.

Appropriate medical care and treatment can dramatically reduce the 20 to 30 percent mortality rate seen among children with severe PEM worldwide.[23] The treatment for PEM should be carefully and slowly implemented using a three-step approach.

The first step addresses the life-threatening factors, such as severe dehydration and fluid and nutrient imbalances. The second step is to restore the individual's depleted tissues by gradually providing nutritionally dense calories and high-quality protein. The third step involves transitioning the person to foods and introducing physical activity. The only successful way to cure PEM is to eradicate it.[24]

The Take-Home Message A high-protein diet may play a role in increasing the risk of heart disease, kidney problems, and calcium loss from bone. Consuming too much protein from animal sources can increase the amount of heart-unhealthy saturated fat in your diet. Too many protein-rich foods in the diet can displace whole grains, fruits, and vegetables, which have been shown to help reduce many chronic diseases. A low-protein diet has also been shown to lead to loss of bone mass. PEM is caused by an inadequate amount of protein and/or calories in the diet. A severe deficiency of protein is called kwashiorkor; a deficiency of calories is called marasmus. These conditions can be improved with proper food and treatment.

How Do Vegetarians Meet Their Protein Needs?

What do spaghetti topped with marinara sauce, cheese pizza, and macaroni and cheese all have in common? These common, classic **vegetarian** meals all lack meat, and you've probably eaten one or more of them—maybe even on a regular basis. From meal to meal, you may be eating like a vegetarian without realizing it. Does this mean that you are a vegetarian?

For many people, being a vegetarian is a lifestyle choice made for a particular reason. While some vegetarians avoid foods from animal sources for ethical, religious, or environmental reasons, others choose a vegetarian lifestyle for health reasons.[25]

Because vegetarians avoid meat, which is high in protein, they need to be sure to get adequate protein from other food sources. Vegetarians can meet their daily protein needs by consuming a varied plant-based diet that contains protein-rich meat alternatives such as soy, dried beans and other legumes, and nuts. Some vegetarians include protein-rich eggs, dairy foods, and fish as part of their diet. There are several types of vegetarians and associated ranges of acceptable foods. See Table 6.5 for a description of vegetarian diets and the foods associated with each.

An estimated 3 percent of American adults, or about 6 million people, follow a vegetarian diet. In the United States, the vegetarian food market has grown to an over $1.5 billion industry as manufacturers accommodate this growing consumer demand with an array of new vegetarian products each year.[26]

The supermarket is not the only place you can get a vegetarian meal. Over 70 percent of restaurants with table service offer a vegetarian entrée on their menus. Even some fast-food restaurants have added a veggie burger to the menu. Vegetarianism is also appearing on the college campus as universities offer vegetarian options to meet growing student demand.[27]

vegetarian A person who doesn't eat meat, fish, or poultry or (sometimes) foods made from these animal sources.

Table 6.5
The Many Types of Vegetarians

Type	Diet Restrictions	
	Does Eat	**Doesn't Eat**
Lacto-vegetarian	Grains, vegetables, fruits, legumes, nuts, dairy foods	Meat, fish, poultry, and eggs
Lacto-ovo-vegetarian	Grains, vegetables, fruits, legumes, seeds, nuts, dairy foods, eggs	Meat, fish, and poultry
Ovo-vegetarian	Grains, vegetables, fruits, legumes, seeds, nuts, eggs	Meat, fish, poultry, dairy foods
Vegan	Grains, vegetables, fruits, legumes, seeds, nuts	Any animal foods, meat, fish, poultry, dairy foods, eggs
Semivegetarian	A vegetarian diet that occasionally includes meat, fish, and poultry	Meat, fish, and poultry on occasion

The Potential Benefits and Risks of a Vegetarian Diet

A plant-based vegetarian diet can be rich in high-fiber whole grains, vegetables, fruits, legumes, and nuts, and thus, naturally lower in saturated fat and cholesterol-containing animal foods. Such a diet contains the fundamentals for reducing the risk of heart disease, high blood pressure, diabetes, cancer, stroke, and obesity.

Vegetarian food staples such as soy, nuts, and soluble fiber–rich foods such as beans and oats have all been shown to reduce blood cholesterol levels. Research collected from numerous studies have shown that deaths from heart disease are about 25 percent lower among vegetarians than among nonvegetarians.[28]

Vegetarians also tend to have lower blood pressure. The incidence of high blood pressure has been shown to be over two times higher in nonvegetarians.[29] High blood pressure is a risk factor not only for heart disease but also for stroke.

Since you know from Chapter 4 that a plant-based diet can help reduce the risk of type 2 diabetes, it won't surprise you that vegetarians tend to have a lower risk of diabetes. Diabetes mellitus is also a risk for heart disease. For those with diabetes, the predominance of foods rich in fiber and low in saturated fat and cholesterol makes a vegetarian diet a viable eating strategy to better manage this disease.[30]

Vegetarian diets have been shown to reduce the risk of both prostate and colon cancer. Respected health organizations, such as the American Institute for Cancer Research and the American Cancer Society, advocate a plant-based diet to reduce the risk of cancer.[31]

Also, a plant-based diet that contains mostly fiber-rich whole grains and low-calorie, nutrient-dense vegetables and fruits tends to be one that "fills you up before it fills you out," which means that you are likely to eat fewer overall calories. Consequently, the plant-based foods of a vegetarian diet can be a healthy and satisfying strategy for those fighting the battle against obesity.

The Joy of Soy

Soy has been used as a dietary staple for centuries in Asia. Soy consumption in the United States, in foods ranging from soy milk to soy burgers, has been increasing since the 1990s. According to the United Soybean Board, the number of consumers who use soy milk on a regular basis increased to 17 percent in 2003, up from 14 percent in 2002. One in six Americans consumes soy foods at least once a week, and the sales of soy bars, yogurt, chips, and cookies are propelling a $4 billion industry.[2]

The popularity of soy foods is increasing among many age-groups and ethnic groups, including baby boomers, who are more interested in good health and longevity than their parents' generation; Asian populations in the United States looking for traditional soy-based foods; and young adults with an increasing interest in vegetarian diets.[3]

Soy is a high-quality protein source that is low in saturated fat and that contains **isoflavones,** which are naturally occurring phytoestrogens (*phyto* = plant). These plant estrogens have a chemical structure similar to human **estrogen,** a female sex hormone. While they are considered weak estrogens (they have less than a thousandth of the potential activity of estrogen), they may interfere with or mimic some of estrogen's activities in certain cells in the body.[4] While isoflavones can also be found in other plant foods, such as grains, vegetables, and legumes, soybeans contain the largest amount found in food.

Soy and Your Health

Epidemiological studies, which look at health and disease in populations, have suggested that isoflavones may reduce the risk of chronic diseases, including heart disease and certain cancers. Some other studies suggest that isoflavones may help relieve menopausal symptoms.[5] At the same time, because isoflavones act as weak estrogens in the body, some concern exists that they may be harmful for diseases such as breast cancer.

Eating soy protein as part of a heart-healthy diet may reduce the risk of heart

isoflavones Naturally occurring phytoestrogens, or weak plant estrogens, which function in a similar fashion to the hormone estrogen in the human body.

estrogen The hormone responsible for female sex characteristics.

What's on the Soy Menu?

Tofu ▶
Cooked, pureed soybeans that are processed into a silken, soft, or firm texture; has a neutral flavor, which allows it to blend well
Use the silken version in dips, soups, and cream pies. Use the firm variety in stir-fries, on salads, or marinate it and then bake or grill it.

Soy milk ▲
A soy beverage made from a mixture of ground soybeans and water
Use it in place of cow's milk. Combine soy milk with ice and fruit in a blender for a soy shake.

Edamame ▲
Tender young soybeans; can be purchased fresh, frozen, or canned
Use in salads, grain dishes, stir-fries, and casseroles.

Soy flour ▲
Made from ground, roasted soybeans
Use it in baked goods such as pancakes, muffins, and cookies. It can also substitute for eggs in baked goods: Use 1 tbs soy flour combined with 1 tbs of water for each whole egg.

196

disease by lowering cholesterol levels. A review of over 35 research studies showed that soy protein lowered total cholesterol, the "bad" LDL cholesterol, and triglycerides all by about 10 percent. Originally, researchers theorized that isoflavones might play a major role in soy's cholesterol-lowering capabilities. However, a review of numerous research studies has questioned isoflavones' effect on cholesterol and concluded that if it does play a role, it is probably a minor one in comparison to the soy protein.[6]

Interest in soy as a cancer fighter was sparked after researchers observed that Asian countries had lower rates of breast cancer than Western countries, including the United States. Numerous studies suggest that the isoflavones in soy may help reduce the risk of cancer, as these weak estrogens may have anticancer functions in the body. One of the functions of isoflavones is that they compete with the hormone estrogen for its binding site on specific cells. The isoflavone latches onto the cell and blocks the binding of the hormone. Since estrogen may increase the risk of breast cancer, inhibiting or blocking the actions of estrogen may help reduce the risk.[7]

Timing may be an important part in the preventive role that soy plays in breast cancer. A study of Chinese women revealed that those who ate the most soy during their adolescent years had a reduced risk of breast cancer in adulthood. The early exposure of soy foods may be protective by stimulating the growth of cells in the breast, enhancing the rate at which the glands mature, and altering the tissues in a beneficial way.

However, this anticancer role of isoflavones may also be a detriment.[8] There is some concern that once the isoflavones are bound to the estrogen receptors, they can initiate the production of cancer cells, which can *raise* the risk of breast cancer. A recent review of over 200 research studies supports the safety of soy isoflavones when consumed as soy and soy products. However, this issue of potentially increasing the risk of breast cancer, especially for those who are at high risk of developing or who presently have breast cancer, isn't resolved as yet. The American Cancer Society advises women with breast cancer to avoid eating large amounts of soy without discussing it first with their doctor. If they do eat soy foods, they should limit consumption to no more than three servings daily.[9]

Soy can be an inexpensive, heart-healthy protein source that may also help lower your blood cholesterol. While soy may help lower the risk of certain cancers, it is currently unclear if it is beneficial or harmful for individuals at high risk of developing breast cancer.

Tempeh ▶
Made from cooked whole soybeans that are condensed into a solid block
Can be seasoned and used as a meat substitute.

Textured soy protein ▲
Created from defatted soy flour that has been compressed and dehydrated
Use it as a meat substitute in foods such as meatballs, meatloaf, chili, tacos, and spaghetti sauce.

Miso ▲
A flavorful paste of fermented soybeans used to season foods
Use in soups, stews, and sauces.

Soy meat analogs ▲
Products such as hot dogs, sausages, burgers, cold cuts, yogurts, and cheese that are made using soy
Use as a meat substitute at meals and snacks.

Source: Adapted from J. Henkel, Soy Health Claims for Soy Protein, Questions about Other Components, *FDA Consumer Magazine.* Available at www.cfsan.fda.gov/~dms/fdsoypr.html. Accessed July 2004.

eLearn
Hungry for More Vegetarian Advice?

Need some more help in planning a vegetarian diet? Click your way through a menu of more delicious vegetarian tips at http://people.bu.edu/salge.

The biggest risk of a vegetarian diet is underconsuming certain nutrients, such as protein and vitamin B_{12}, which are found in animal foods. Strictly avoiding meat, fish, poultry, and foods derived from animal sources can be *unhealthy* if you don't replace these foods with nutrient-dense alternatives. Thus, vegetarians need to plan their meals with care to make sure that all of their nutrient needs are met.

How You Can Be a Healthy Vegetarian

To avoid nutrient deficiencies, vegetarians must consume adequate amounts of all nutrients by eating a wide variety of foods. Some nutrients found in abundance in animal foods, including protein, iron, zinc, calcium, vitamin D, riboflavin (a B vitamin), vitamin B_{12}, vitamin A, and omega-3 fatty acids, are particularly important to monitor. A vitamin and mineral supplement may be necessary. The tips in Table 6.7 on page 200 and the vegetarian food guide pyramid in Figure 6.15 can help you easily incorporate these nutrients in a vegetarian diet.

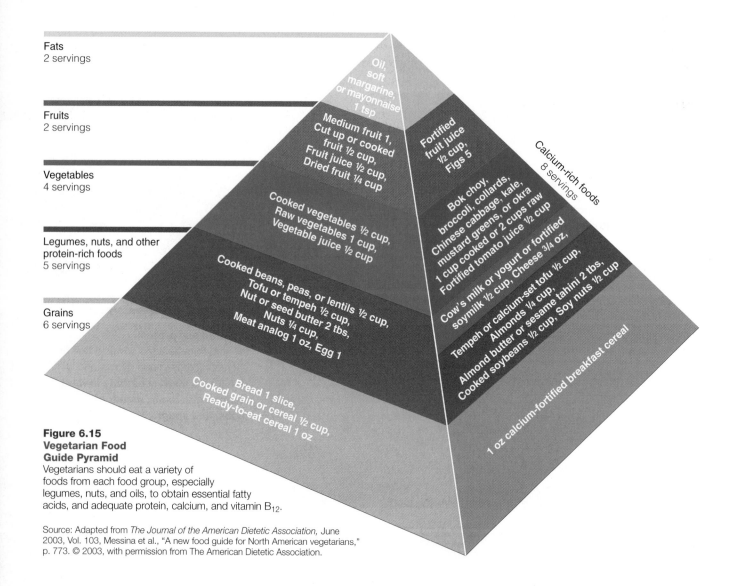

Figure 6.15
Vegetarian Food Guide Pyramid
Vegetarians should eat a variety of foods from each food group, especially legumes, nuts, and oils, to obtain essential fatty acids, and adequate protein, calcium, and vitamin B_{12}.

Source: Adapted from *The Journal of the American Dietetic Association,* June 2003, Vol. 103, Messina et al., "A new food guide for North American vegetarians," p. 773. © 2003, with permission from The American Dietetic Association.

The Take-Home Message Vegetarian diets can be a healthy eating style that may help reduce the risk of some chronic diseases. Some vegetarians abstain from all animal foods, while others may eat animal foods such as eggs and dairy products in limited amounts. All vegetarians must take care in planning a varied diet that meets their nutrient needs, especially for protein, iron, zinc, calcium, vitamin D, riboflavin (a B vitamin), vitamin B₁₂, vitamin A, and omega-3 fatty acids.

Putting It All Together

Table 6.6 provides a recap of the three energy or calorie-providing nutrients that we have discussed and their recommended contribution to your diet. The majority of your daily calories should come from carbohydrate-rich foods; your fat intake should be no more than about one-third of your daily calories; and protein should provide the rest. Figure 6.16 puts together information from the last three chapters to show you how to include healthy amounts of carbohydrates, fats, and proteins in your diet. Eat an abundance of grains (with at least half coming from whole grains), vegetables, and fruits. Eat only modest amounts of commercially made bakery and snack items, vegetables with creamy sauces or added butter, and sweets. Choose low fat dairy products and lean meat, poultry, and fish to minimize the intake of heart-unhealthy saturated fat.

Table 6.6
Makeup of Your Diet

Nutrient	Current Adult Dietary Intake Recommendations*
Carbohydrates	45–65
Fats	20–35
Proteins	10–35

Nutrient	Example of a Healthy Diet*
Carbohydrates	55
Fats	30
Proteins	15
Total	100

*Percent of total calories

Figure 6.16 Where's the Protein and Saturated Fat in Your Foods?
While many foods, in particular dairy foods and meats, can provide a hefty amount of protein, they can also provide a large amount of saturated fat. Choose nonfat and low-fat dairy foods and lean sources of meats and skinless poultry to enjoy your protein without consuming too much saturated fat.

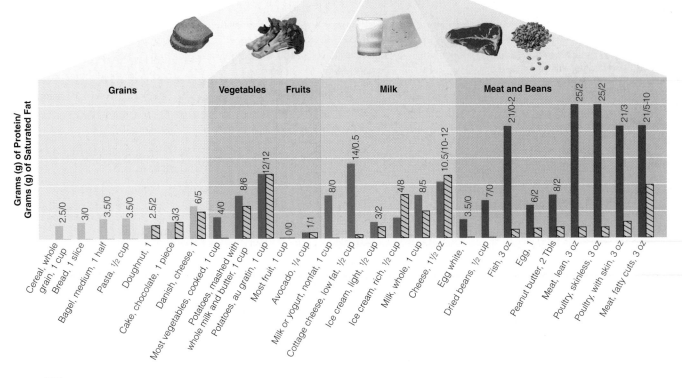

Grams (g) of Protein/Grams (g) of Saturated Fat

Grains — Cereal, whole grain, 1 cup 2.5/0; Bread, 1 slice 3/0; Bagel, medium, 1 half 3.5/0; Pasta, 1/2 cup 3.5/0; Doughnut, 1 2.5/2; Cake, chocolate, 1 piece 3/3; Danish, cheese, 1 6/5

Vegetables — Most vegetables, cooked, 1 cup 4/0; Potatoes, mashed with whole milk and butter, 1 cup 8/6; Potatoes, au gratin, 1 cup 12/12

Fruits — Most fruit, 1 cup 0/0; Avocado, 1/4 cup 1/1

Milk — Milk or yogurt, nonfat, 1 cup 8/0; Cottage cheese, low fat, 1/2 cup 14/0.5; Ice cream, light, 1/2 cup 3/2; Ice cream, rich, 1/2 cup 4/8; Milk, whole, 1 cup 8/5; Cheese, 1½ oz 10.5/10–12

Meat and Beans — Egg white, 1 3.5/0; Dried beans, 1/2 cup 7/0; Fish, 3 oz 21/0–2; Egg, 1 6/2; Peanut butter, 2 Tbls 8/2; Meat, lean, 3 oz 25/2; Poultry, skinless, 3 oz 25/2; Poultry, with skin, 3 oz 21/3; Meat, fatty cuts, 3 oz 21/5–10

⬚ = Saturated Fat

Table 6.7

Nutrients That Could Be MIA (Missing in Action) in a Vegetarian Diet

Vegetarians need to take care in planning a diet that meets all their nutritional needs. Here are the nutrients that vegetarians could fall short of in their diet, some vegetarian food sources for these nutrients, and tips on how to enjoy these foods as part of a balanced diet.

Nutrient	Risks	Vegetarian Food Sources	Table Tips
Protein	A vegetarian's protein needs can be met by consuming a *variety* of plant foods. A combination of protein-rich soy foods, legumes, nuts, and/or seeds should be eaten daily.	Soybeans, soy burgers, tofu, tempeh, nuts, peanuts, peanut butter, legumes, sunflower seeds, milk, soy milk, yogurt, cheese	■ Add nuts to your morning cereal. ■ Add beans to your salads, soups, and main entrées. ■ Have a soy burger for lunch. ■ Use tofu in stir-fries, rice and pasta dishes, and casseroles. ■ Snack on a soy milk and banana or berry shake.
Iron	The form of iron in plants is not as easily absorbed as the type in meat, milk, and poultry. Also, phytate in grains and rice and polyphenols in tea and coffee can inhibit iron absorption. The iron needs of vegetarians are about 1½ times higher than those of nonvegetarians. Vitamin C enhances the absorption of the iron in plant foods.	Iron-fortified cereals, enriched grains, pasta, bread, oatmeal, potatoes, wheat germ, cashews and other nuts, sunflower seeds, legumes, soybeans, tofu, bok choy, broccoli, mushrooms, dried fruits	■ Make sure your morning cereal is iron fortified. ■ Add soybeans to your lunchtime salad. ■ Eat bread with your salad lunch or make a sandwich. ■ Pack a trail mix of dried fruits and nuts for a snack. ■ Add vitamin C–rich foods (broccoli, tomatoes, citrus fruits) to all your meals.
Zinc	The absorption of zinc is enhanced by animal protein. Eating a vegetarian diet means that you lose out on this benefit and are more likely to develop a deficiency. Phytate also binds zinc, making it unavailable to your body. A vegan's zinc needs may be as much as 50 percent higher than a nonvegetarian's.	Soybeans, soy milk, tofu, tempeh, fortified soy burgers, legumes, nuts, sunflower seeds, wheat germ, fortified ready-to-eat cereals, mushrooms and low-fat or nonfat milk, yogurt, and cheese	■ Douse your morning cereal with low-fat milk. ■ Add low-fat cheese and soybeans to your lunchtime salad. ■ Snack on sunflower seeds. ■ Top an afternoon yogurt with wheat germ. ■ Add soybeans to your dinner rice.
Calcium	Calcium is abundant in lean dairy foods such as nonfat or low-fat milk, yogurt, and cheese, so obtaining adequate amounts shouldn't be difficult if you consume these foods. Calcium-fortified soy milk and orange juice as well as tofu can provide about the same amount of calcium per serving as is found in dairy foods.	Low-fat or nonfat milk, yogurt, and cheese, fortified soy milk, soy yogurt, and soy cheese, calcium-fortified orange juice, legumes, sesame tahini, tofu processed with calcium, bok choy, broccoli, kale, collard greens, mustard greens, okra.	■ Add milk to your morning cereal and coffee. ■ Have at least one yogurt a day. ■ Have a glass of calcium-fortified orange juice with lunch. ■ Snack on low-fat cheese or yogurt in the afternoon. ■ Eat green vegetables often at dinner.

Nutrients That Could Be MIA (Missing in Action) in a Vegetarian Diet

Nutrient	Risks	Vegetarian Food Sources	Table Tips
Vitamin D	Some vegetarians will need to consume vitamin D–fortified milk or soy products.	Low-fat or nonfat milk, egg yolk, fortified yogurt, soy milk, soy yogurt, ready-to-eat cereals; a vitamin supplement	■ Have a glass of milk or soy milk at breakfast every day. ■ Make sure your morning cereal is vitamin D fortified. ■ Use fortified evaporated skim milk as a base for cream sauces. ■ Snack on fortified cereals. ■ Have a fortified yogurt each day.
Vitamin B_{12}	Animal foods are the only naturally occurring food source of B_{12}, so it is extremely important that vegetarians, especially strict vegans, look to fortified cereals and soy milk or a supplement to meet their daily needs.	Low-fat and nonfat milk, yogurt, or cheese, eggs, fortified soy milk, ready-to-eat cereals, soy burgers, egg substitutes; vitamin supplement	■ Make sure your morning cereal is fortified with vitamin B_{12}. ■ Drink a cup of milk or fortified soy milk with your meals. ■ Top an afternoon yogurt snack with a fortified cereal. ■ Try an egg substitute omelet for lunch. ■ Use fortified soy "meat" alternatives at dinner.
Vitamin A	Vitamin A is found only in animal foods. However, vegetarians can meet their needs by consuming the vitamin A precursor, beta-carotene.	Fortified low-fat or nonfat milk and soy milk, apricots, cantaloupe, mangoes, pumpkin, kale, spinach	■ Enjoy a slice or bowl of cantaloupe in the morning. ■ Snack on dried apricots. ■ Add spinach to your lunchtime salad. ■ Drink a glass of fortified milk or soy milk with dinner. ■ Try mangoes for a sweet dessert.
Omega-3 fatty acids	If your vegetarian diet doesn't include fish, you may not be consuming enough of the essential omega-3 fatty acid called alpha-linolenic acid.	Fish, especially fatty fish such as salmon and sardines, walnuts, flaxseed and flaxseed oil, soybean and canola oil	■ Add walnuts to baked breads and muffins. ■ Try canned salmon on top of your lunchtime salad. ■ Top your yogurt with ground flaxseeds. ■ Have fish regularly for dinner. ■ Cook with canola and flaxseed oil.

Protein

What Are Proteins?

Proteins are the predominant structural and functional materials in every cell in your body. Proteins are made up of **amino acids.**

As with carbohydrates and fats, amino acids are made up of carbon, hydrogen, and oxygen atoms. Unlike carbohydrates and fats, amino acid molecules also contain nitrogen.

The atoms that make up every amino acid molecule are clustered into three groups. The **acid group** contains carbon, hydrogen, and oxygen atoms (COOH), which is why it is called an amino "acid." The **amine group** (NH$_2$) contains the nitrogen. These two groups are the same for every amino acid. The third group, a unique **side chain,** varies from amino acid to amino acid and gives each its distinguishing qualities.

There are 20 different amino acids, 9 of which are **essential** and 11 of which are **nonessential.** Essential amino acids are not made in the body and need to be obtained through foods. Nonessential amino acids are synthesized in the body.

Proteins Are Built with Amino Acids

Amino acids are joined to each other by **peptide bonds** to build proteins.

Two amino acids joined together form a **dipeptide.** Three amino acids joined together form a **tripeptide.** And a polypeptide consists of many amino acids joined together.

The shape of a protein determines its function.

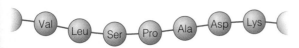

Shapes of Proteins Are Altered by Denaturation

The weak bonds between the side chains on the amino acids can be **denatured,** or broken apart, by temperature change or acids, bases, or salts. Although denaturation doesn't alter the sequence of amino acids in the protein strand, changing the protein's shape can alter its function, sometimes permanently.

Functions of Protein

- Proteins provide structural and mechanical support and help maintain body tissues.
- Proteins build enzymes and hormones.
- Proteins help maintain acid-base balance.
- Proteins transport substances throughout the body and act as channels in membranes.
- Proteins are needed for antibodies and the immune response.
- Proteins can provide energy.

Daily Needs

If you are 14 to 18 years old, you need 0.85 gram of protein per kilogram of body weight (g/kg) per day. If you are 19 years of age or older, you need 0.80 gram per kilogram daily.

Not all proteins are created equal. **Protein quality** is determined by two factors: your body's ability to digest the protein, which is unique to each person, and the types of amino acids (essential, nonessential, or both) that the protein contains.

Proteins that are more easily digested and that contain both essential and nonessential amino acids are of higher quality.

Food Sources

Protein is particularly abundant in meat, fish, poultry, dairy foods, and meat alternatives such as peanut butter and soy. A 3-ounce serving of cooked meat, poultry, or fish provides approximately 21 to 25 grams of protein, or about 7 grams per ounce.

Nonmeat protein sources are also abundant and particularly important for vegetarians. Half a cup of cooked dried beans provides 7 grams of protein, whereas an egg or 2 tablespoons of peanut butter each provides 8 grams of protein.

Too Much or Too Little

A diet that is too high in protein has been linked to health problems such as cardiovascular disease, kidney stones, osteoporosis, and some types of

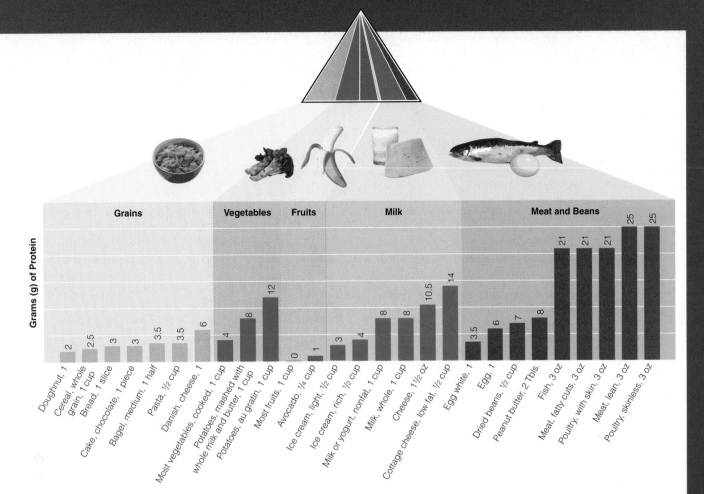

Grams (g) of Protein

Grains	Vegetables	Fruits	Milk	Meat and Beans

Grains:
- Doughnut, 1 — 2
- Cereal, whole grain, 1 cup — 2.5
- Bread, 1 slice — 3
- Cake, chocolate, 1 piece — 3
- Bagel, medium, 1 half — 3.5
- Pasta, 1/2 cup — 3.5
- Danish, cheese, 1 — 6

Vegetables:
- Most vegetables, cooked, 1 cup — 4
- Potatoes, mashed with whole milk and butter, 1 cup — 8
- Potatoes, au gratin, 1 cup — 12

Fruits:
- Most fruits, 1 cup — 0
- Avocado, 1/4 cup — 1

Milk:
- Ice cream, light, 1/2 cup — 3
- Ice cream, rich, 1/2 cup — 4
- Milk or yogurt, nonfat, 1 cup — 8
- Milk, whole, 1 cup — 8
- Cheese, 1 1/2 oz — 10.5
- Cottage cheese, low fat, 1/2 cup — 14

Meat and Beans:
- Egg white, 1 — 3.5
- Egg, 1 — 6
- Dried beans, 1/2 cup — 7
- Peanut butter, 2 Tbls. — 8
- Fish, 3 oz — 21
- Meat, fatty cuts, 3 oz — 21
- Poultry, with skin, 3 oz — 21
- Meat, lean, 3 oz — 25
- Poultry, skinless, 3 oz — 25

cancer. Eating too little protein can also lead to compromised bone health.

Diets that are inadequate in protein, calories, or both lead to **protein-energy malnutrition (PEM).** Two forms of PEM are marasmus and kwashiorkor.

Marasmus is a disease caused by insufficient intake of dietary protein. Marasmic individuals literally look as though they are starving and are often not even

at 60 percent of their desirable body weight for their height.

Kwashiorkor occurs when a person consumes sufficient calories but not suffi-

cient protein. A classic symptom of severe kwashiorkor is edema in the legs, feet, and stomach. Other symptoms include dry and peeling skin, rashes or lesions, and brittle hair that can be easily pulled out.

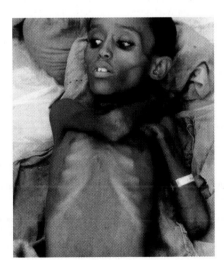

Swollen belly characteristic of kwashiorkor.

Child with marasmus.

Terms to Know

amino acid ■ acid group ■ amine group ■ side chain ■ essential amino acid ■ nonessential amino acid ■ peptide bonds ■ dipeptide ■ tripeptide ■ polypeptide ■ denatured ■ protein quality ■ protein-energy malnutrition (PEM)

Two Points of View

Do You Need to Eat Meat to Compete?

Two renowned sport nutritionists share their expertise about the protein needs, facts, and fallacies of professional, competitive, and recreational athletes.

Nancy Clark, MS, RD

Author of *Nancy Clark's Sports Nutrition Guidebook*

 **Nancy Clark, MS, RD,** is an internationally known sports nutritionist whose clients include the Boston Red Sox and many collegiate, elite, and Olympic athletes from a variety of sports. She is the author of the best-selling sports nutrition reference *Nancy Clark's Sports Nutrition Guidebook* and the nutrition columnist for *New England Runner, Adventure Cycling,* and *Rugby.*

Q: Is protein-rich meat, chicken, and/or fish, a dietary must for athletes to keep their competitive edge?

A: Meat, chicken, and fish are not a must for athletes; however, the nutrients in these foods are! Vegetarians—especially strict vegetarians or vegans—need to make sure that they consume alternative sources of protein, such as beans and tofu, and not just become a "nonmeat eater" who lives on bagels and pasta. The latter will be an athlete who falls short of his or her protein and nutrient needs.

Q: Do some sports warrant more dietary protein, especially from animal foods, than others?

A: Bodybuilders will claim that they need more protein—especially animal protein—but, currently, there isn't adequate research to support this. The sports with the highest protein needs are those that impose a calorie deficit, such as lightweight wrestling, crew, and figure skating. These athletes are often dieting and restrict calorie intake. Any athlete (or person) who has a calorie deficit will have higher protein needs than do those who take in adequate calories. Individuals with calorie-deficient diets will be using some of their dietary protein as energy rather than building and maintaining their bodies and muscle mass. Thus, they need to eat more protein.

Q: Have you ever worked with an athlete who was a vegetarian? Was he or she able to be as competitive as his or her peers? Were any dietary adjustments made in order for this athlete to perform competitively?

A: Anecdotes are not science, but one bodybuilder comes to mind who claimed she couldn't achieve her desired muscular gains unless she included fish in her otherwise vegan diet.

(continued)

Joan Buchbinder, MS, RD, FADA

 For over 15 years, **Joan Buchbinder, MS, RD, FADA,** has worked with recreational, collegiate, and professional athletes, including the Boston Celtics basketball team, the New England Patriots football team, the Boston Bruins hockey team, the New England Revolution soccer team, and the U.S. Olympic Committee's Sports Nutrition Program.

Q: Is protein-rich meat, chicken, and/or fish, a dietary must for athletes to keep their competitive edge?

A: *Theoretically,* to be competitive, athletes do not necessarily *have to* eat meat, chicken, and/or fish to fulfill their protein and nutrients needs. *Realistically,* however, it is much easier to meet nutrient needs if athletes include these animal products in their training diet. Vegetarian athletes need to add alternative protein foods (soybeans, soy products, and legumes), to obtain the nine essential amino acids that the body requires. Realistically this may be difficult for professional athletes to do daily.

Q: Do some sports warrant more dietary protein, especially from animal foods, than others?

A: Bodybuilders, football players, and other power athletes who focus on strength-training activities *believe* that their diets should be significantly higher in protein. Athletes who meet their caloric requirements obtain adequate protein, if not more, than they need. Any athlete who has not met his or her energy needs from carbohydrates will sacrifice some protein intake to energy use.

Q: Have you ever worked with an athlete who was a vegetarian? Was he or she able to be as competitive as his or her peers? Were any dietary adjustments made in order for this athlete to perform competitively?

A: As the nutritionist for the New England Patriots for 17 years, I encountered one lacto-ovo-vegetarian, who was on the lighter, leaner side (he was not a lineman!). I made sure that he had egg white cheese omelets, yogurt, protein shakes, soy burgers, cheese, tofu, and legumes. I had a Pro Bowl player who did not eat red meat. At team meals, I always had a nonmeat entrée for him. When working with athletes, it is essential to do a thorough assessment of their daily diet to assess potential deficiencies.

(continued)

Do You Need to Eat Meat to Compete?, continued

Nancy Clark, MS, RD, continued

Q: Vegetarians are at risk of being deficient in both iron and zinc, which are abundant in meat, poultry, and fish. Athletes, in general, are also commonly deficient in minerals. Why are these important in athletes' diets, and what challenges do these pose for vegetarian athletes?

A: Iron is very important as it is a part hemoglobin, bringing oxygen to working muscles. Studies have shown 30 to 50 percent of some varsity college female athletes (soccer, volleyball) suffer from iron deficiency and needless fatigue upon exertion. I encourage them to eat iron-fortified breakfast cereals. If they are not getting iron in fortified foods, then I encourage a daily multivitamin and mineral pill. Zinc is also very important because it is involved in nearly every metabolic process and enhances immune function and the healing of injuries. Sick and injured athletes who sit on the bench are a disadvantage to their team! Every time athletes exercise, they damage their muscles slightly. Zinc helps with the repair process.

Q: What about vitamin B_{12}, an important nutrient that is found naturally only in animal foods? Are athletes at risk of falling short of their daily vitamin B_{12} needs if they eliminate meat, fish, and/or poultry from their diets?

A: Vegan athletes must pay attention to their dietary vitamin B_{12} intake. While athletes who eat animal products may have surplus B_{12} that their body can store for years, the athlete who converts to a vegan diet can become depleted over the course of time. Among my clients, the percentage of vegan athletes is low compared to lacto-ovo-vegetarians, who can easily meet their needs through yogurt, cheese, eggs, or fortified breakfast cereals. But with the vegans, I actively encourage them to include Redstar nutritional yeast as well some fortified grains, soy milk, and commercial vegetarian products.

Joan Buchbinder, MS, RD, FADA, continued

Q: Vegetarians are at risk of being deficient in both iron and zinc, which are abundant in meat, poultry, and fish. Athletes, in general, are also commonly deficient in them. Why are these important in athletes' diets, and what challenges do these pose for vegetarian athletes?

A: When iron stores are low, the muscles do not receive as much oxygen. Inadequate diet as well as strenuous training, can lead to anemia. Vegetarian athletes most susceptible to iron-deficiency anemia include those who train at high altitude; are on low-calorie or fad diets; are going through a growth spurt; or experiencing heavy menstrual losses. Since iron-deficiency anemia adversely affects athletic performance, prevention is key. Zinc is a component of several enzymes involved in energy metabolism, protein synthesis, wound healing, and immune functions. A multivitamin with adequate minerals is essential for top athletic performance in vegetarians.

Q: What about vitamin B_{12}, an important nutrient that is found naturally only in animal foods? Are athletes at risk of falling short of their daily vitamin B_{12} needs if they eliminate meat, fish, and/or poultry from their diets?

A: As a vegetarian of 26 years, I can unfortunately address this question from personal experience. I became a vegetarian during my freshman year of college. In graduate school I developed "tingling" in my fingertips. My B_{12} levels were low and my doctor instructed me to take a supplement. Throughout the years, my compliance was poor. I assumed adding cottage cheese, yogurt, egg whites, and cheese to my diet would be adequate. When training for marathons in my 30s, I developed tingling and numbing in my toes. I was diagnosed with peripheral neuropathy, a neurological defect caused by vitamin B_{12} deficiency. A recent MRI revealed spinal cord damage that may not be reversible. The doctor informed me that the long-term effects could be dementia and ending up in a wheelchair. Diligent attention is needed when following a vegetarian diet.

NUTRITION IN THE REAL WORLD

Be a Nutrition Sleuth

Where's the Protein?

After reading this chapter, let's see if you can accurately guess how much protein is in the foods that you eat. Go to www.aw-bc.com/blake to match the foods with the amount of protein that they provide.

Get Real!

The Real Deal When It Comes to Dietary Protein

Go to www.aw-bc.com/blake to plan a realistic day of food choices that will allow you to meet your protein needs without exceeding your upper limits for saturated fat.

(Note: You can use Appendix A or the MyDietAnalysis program to help you plan your meals.)

The Top Ten Points to Remember

1. Proteins are made of amino acids, which contain an acid group, an amine group, and a unique side chain. Each group is made of carbon, hydrogen, oxygen, and, in the case of the amine group, nitrogen. There are 20 unique side chains and therefore 20 unique amino acids. Amino acids are joined together by peptide bonds to form proteins.

2. The interactions between the amino acids cause individual proteins to fold into precise three-dimensional shapes. The shape of a protein determines its function. Heat, acids, bases, and salts denature these bonds and disrupt the shape and function of a protein.

3. Of the 20 amino acids, 9 are essential, so you need to obtain them through your diet. Your body can synthesize the remaining 11 amino acids (see Table 6.1), so they are nonessential.

4. With the help of stomach juices and enzymes, your body digests and breaks down proteins into amino acids to make them available for use. A limited amount of amino acids exists in pools in your body. The DNA in your cells directs the synthesis of proteins. Excess amino acids are also broken down and either stored in another form or used as energy, depending on your needs. The nitrogen is converted to the waste product urea and excreted in your urine.

5. Proteins play many roles in your body. They provide structural and mechanical support, supply materials for ongoing maintenance, form enzymes and hormones, maintain acid-base and fluid balance, transport nutrients, and aid your immune system. Proteins can provide energy, be used to make glucose, or be stored as fat.

6. Protein quality is determined by a protein's digestibility corrected amino acid score (PDCAAS), which is based on the protein's digestibility and its amino acid profile. Protein from animal foods is more easily digested than protein from plant foods. Proteins from animal foods and soy are typically complete proteins and provide all of the essential amino acids along with some nonessential amino acids. Plant proteins are typically incomplete, as they are missing one or more essential amino acids.

7. Adults should consume 0.8 gram of protein for each kilogram of body weight. A varied diet provides most Americans with far more protein than they need.

8. Consuming too much protein from animal sources can increase the amount of heart-unhealthy saturated fat in your diet. A high-protein diet has been associated with the loss of calcium from the body and the development of kidney stones. An excess of protein-rich foods in the diet can displace whole grains, fruits, and vegetables.

9. Protein-energy malnutrition (PEM) is caused by an inadequate amount of protein and/or calories in the diet. Kwashiorkor is a severe deficiency of protein; marasmus is a severe deficiency of calories. A deficiency of both calories and protein is known as marasmic kwashiorkor.

10. Healthy vegetarian diets can reduce the risk of certain chronic diseases. Some vegetarians abstain from all animal foods, while others may eat a limited amount. All vegetarians must take care to eat a varied diet that meets all of their nutrient needs.

Test Your Knowledge

1. A protein's shape, and therefore its function in your body, is determined by the interactions of amino acids in the protein with each other and their environment.
   a. true
   b. false
2. Essential amino acids can be made by the body.
   a. true
   b. false
3. Which of the following will *not* denature a protein?
   a. grilling a chicken breast
   b. frying an egg
   c. marinating a steak in red wine
   d. refrigerating milk

4. Limited amounts of surplus amino acids are stored in your body in your
   a. muscles.
   b. fat stores.
   c. amino acid pools.
   d. stomach.
5. Proteins play important roles in your body, such as
   a. helping you fight the flu.
   b. allowing you to lie in a hammock.
   c. aiding in digesting the pizza that you ate for lunch.
   d. transporting fat and cholesterol through your blood.
   e. all of the above.
6. Proteins can be used to make glucose.
   a. true
   b. false
7. Protein is found abundantly in the
   a. milk group and the fat group.
   b. meat and beans group and the fruit group.
   c. fruit group and the milk group.
   d. milk group and the meat and beans group.
   e. vegetable group and the fruit group.
8. Which of the following is a source of complete protein?
   a. kidney beans
   b. peanut butter
   c. soy milk
   d. pasta
9. Kwashiorkor is a type of PEM that develops when
   a. there is a severe deficiency of protein in the diet but an adequate amount of calories.
   b. there are inadequate amounts of both protein and calories in the diet.
   c. there is inadequate amount of animal protein in the diet.
   d. there are adequate amounts of both protein and calories in the diet.
   e. there is an imbalance of animal and plant proteins in the diet.
10. A lacto-ovo-vegetarian is coming to your house for dinner. You need to make a meal that she will enjoy. An acceptable entrée would be
    a. stir-fry tofu and vegetables over brown rice.
    b. a cheese and broccoli omelet.
    c. baked ziti with ricotta cheese, spinach, and tomato sauce.
    d. a mushroom pizza.
    e. all of the above.

Answers

1. (a) The interactions of the amino acids with each other and with their environment determines the shape, and thus the function, of the proteins in your body.

2. (b) Essential amino acids cannot be made in the body and need to be obtained from foods.
3. (d) Heat and acids will denature proteins. Refrigeration does not alter the bonds between the amino acid side chains and so does not denature proteins.
4. (c) Limited amounts of all the amino acids exist in amino acid pools in your blood and inside your cells, not your stomach. Your muscles contain protein but don't store surplus amino acid. Your fat stores are the result of excess calories from carbohydrates, proteins, and/or fats.
5. (e) You need adequate amounts of protein to fight infections such as the flu, to provide structural and mechanical support when you're lying down, to build enzymes that help you digest your foods, and to transport substances such as fat and cholesterol through your blood.
6. (a) If you don't eat an adequate amount of carbohydrates, your body can break down proteins to create glucose.
7. (d) Both the milk group and the meat and beans group are full of protein-rich food sources. While there is some protein in vegetables, there is little in fruits. Fats do not contain protein.
8. (c) Soy foods such as soy milk provide all the essential amino acids that you need along with some nonessential amino acids and thus are a source of complete protein. Kidney beans, peanut butter, and pasta are missing adequate amounts of the essential amino acids.
9. (a) Kwashiorkor occurs when protein is deficient in the diet even though calories may be adequate. Marasmus occurs when calories are inadequate in a person's diet and thus he or she is starving. Protein from animal sources is not necessary because people can meet their protein needs from a combination of plant proteins, such as soy, legumes, grains, and vegetables as part of a well-balanced diet. There doesn't need to be a balance between animal and plant proteins.
10. (e) Because a lacto-ovo-vegetarian avoids meat, poultry, and fish but eats a predominantly plant-based diet with dairy foods and eggs, the tofu stir-fry, cheese omelet, baked ziti, and pizza with any vegetable topping are all fine.

Web Support

- For information on specific genetic disorders, including those that affect protein use in the body, visit the National Human Genome Research Institute at www.nhgri.nih.gov
- For more information on protein bars and supplements, visit the Center for Science in the Public Interest at www.cspinet.org/nah/12_00/barexam.html
- For more information on vegetarian diets, visit the Vegetarian Research Group at www.vrg.org
- For more information on soy foods, visit the United Soy Board at www.talksoy.com

7

Vitamins

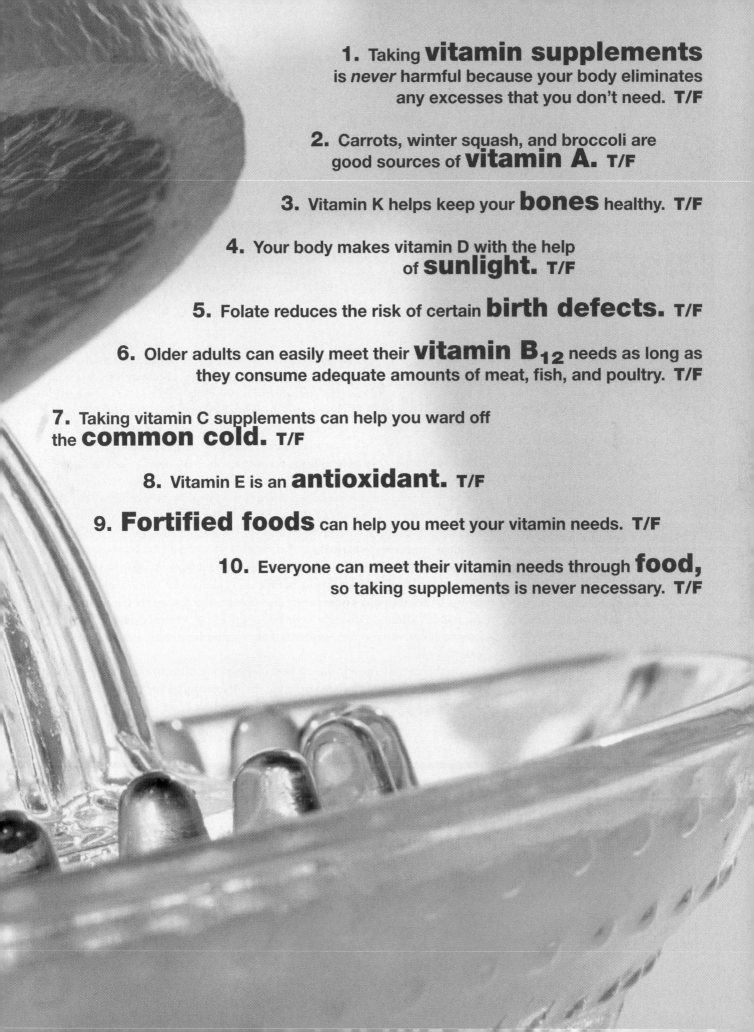

1. Taking **vitamin supplements** is *never* harmful because your body eliminates any excesses that you don't need. **T/F**

2. Carrots, winter squash, and broccoli are good sources of **vitamin A. T/F**

3. Vitamin K helps keep your **bones** healthy. **T/F**

4. Your body makes vitamin D with the help of **sunlight. T/F**

5. Folate reduces the risk of certain **birth defects. T/F**

6. Older adults can easily meet their **vitamin B$_{12}$** needs as long as they consume adequate amounts of meat, fish, and poultry. **T/F**

7. Taking vitamin C supplements can help you ward off the **common cold. T/F**

8. Vitamin E is an **antioxidant. T/F**

9. **Fortified foods** can help you meet your vitamin needs. **T/F**

10. Everyone can meet their vitamin needs through **food,** so taking supplements is never necessary. **T/F**

rendan Gardner is a college fresh-man and future track star at a state university. In addition to carrying a full course load and working part-time at the campus bookstore, Brendan works out at least 2 hours a day on the outdoor track. Within the first few weeks of school, Brendan caught a cold and had a stuffy nose and headache for a few days. As soon as he recovered, a second cold set in and lingered for more than a week.

Hoping to ward off another bout of illness, Brendan went online to find out what he could do to build up his immune system. He found websites that claimed that vitamin C would help protect against colds. After a visit to his local health food store, Brendan began to take vitamin C tablets, and soon his daily intake was 3,500 milligrams, about 100 times his daily needs. Within a week, his long train-ing runs were interrupted with bouts of diarrhea. He visited the student health center and complained to the staff doc-tor that the only training he was getting was running to the bathroom. The doctor recognized Brendan's symptoms as com-mon in runners who take particular sup-plements. Can you guess what caused Brendan's intestinal discomforts?

Answers

1. False. Some vitamins are stored in the body and can build up to toxic levels if taken in excess. To find out more, turn to page 212.
2. True. Deep orange vegetables and some green vegetables are good sources of the vitamin A precursor beta-carotene, which is converted to vitamin A in your body. To find out more about beta-carotene and vitamin A, turn to page 214.
3. True. Vitamin K helps a protein in your bones bind with the bone-strengthening mineral calcium. To learn about other functions of vitamin K, turn to page 220.
4. True. However, some people are unable to meet their vitamin D needs through sun-light exposure alone. To find out if you are at risk, turn to page 222.
5. True. Folate can lower the risk of some birth defects during pregnancy. However, timing is everything. To find out when a pregnant woman needs to be taking this B vitamin, turn to page 234.
6. False. While foods from animal sources usually contain vitamin B_{12}, some older adults have difficulty absorbing this vitamin from meat, poultry, and fish. To find out why, turn to page 236.
7. False. There is no clear evidence that vita-min C supplements protect you from the common cold. To find out what role it does play in combating colds, turn to page 241.
8. True. Vitamin E functions as an antioxidant in your body. To learn more about antioxi-dants, turn to page 243.
9. True. However, fortified foods are not al-ways healthy foods. To find out how to tell the difference, turn to page 246.
10. False. While foods are an excellent source of vitamins, some individuals may need extra vitamin support from a supplement. To find out who would benefit from a sup-plement, turn to page 248.

W hile vitamins (*vita* = vital) have always been in foods, they remained nameless and undiscovered substances as recently as 100 years ago. If you were to flash back to the early part of the twentieth century, you would find scientists hard at work searching for substances to cure diseases such as beriberi, scurvy, and rickets.[1] These may sound like the names of rock bands to you, but they're actually the devastating diseases caused by deficiencies of thiamin (for beriberi), vitamin C (for scurvy), and vitamin D (for rickets). Through-out the twentieth century, scientists received Nobel Prizes for their discoveries of the vitamins that cured these and other diseases. By the 1940s, the U.S. government mandated that specific vitamins be added to grains and milk to improve the nation's health by improving people's diet.

Now flash forward to the latter part of the twentieth century, when an improved diet meant that vitamin deficiencies became less of an issue for most Americans. Sci-entists shifted their focus from curing diseases with vitamins and began researching the role of vitamins in disease prevention. Today, research is being done to find out how vitamins impact and prevent everything from birth defects to heart disease and cancer.

In this chapter, we will look at how each vitamin functions in the body, how much of each vitamin you need to be healthy, in what foods you can find the vita-min, and the effects of consuming too much or too little of any of these nutrients in your diet.

What Are Vitamins?

Vitamins are tasteless organic compounds that you need in small amounts for growth, reproduction, and overall good health. They are essential nutrients for your well-being, and a deficiency of any one will cause physiological symptoms. There are 13 vit-amins, and you get most of them from foods, though the vitamins D, K, niacin, and biotin can also be synthesized in your body or by microorganisms in the intestinal tract.

A chronic deficiency of any of the essential vitamins can cause a cascade of symptoms from scaly skin to blindness. However, consuming too much of some vitamins can also cause adverse effects that can be as damaging as consuming too little. Balance is always your best bet when it comes to meeting your vitamin needs.

Vitamins Are Either Fat-Soluble or Water-Soluble

A vitamin is either fat-soluble or water-soluble, depending on how it is absorbed and handled in your body. Fat-soluble vitamins need dietary fat to be properly absorbed, while water-soluble vitamins are absorbed with water. Vitamins A, D, E, and K are fat-soluble, whereas the B vitamins and vitamin C are water-soluble (Figure 7.1).

The fat-soluble vitamins are absorbed at the beginning of your small intestine (Figure 7.2). They are packaged with fatty acids and bile in micelles, small transport carriers that shuttle them close to the intestinal mucosa or wall. Once there, the fat-soluble vitamins travel through the cells in the intestinal wall and are packaged with fat and other lipids in chylomicrons (one of the lipoprotein carriers discussed in Chapter 5). The vitamins then travel through your lymph system before they enter your bloodstream.

Fat-soluble vitamins are stored in your body and used as needed when your dietary intake falls short. Your liver is the main storage depot for vitamin A and to a lesser extent vitamins K and E, whereas vitamin D is mainly stored in your fat and muscle tissues. Because they are stored in the body, large quantities of some of the

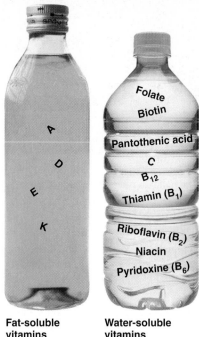

Fat-soluble vitamins **Water-soluble vitamins**

Figure 7.1 Categorizing the Vitamins: Fat-Soluble and Water-Soluble
Fat-soluble vitamins need dietary fat to be properly absorbed, while water-soluble vitamins are absorbed with water.

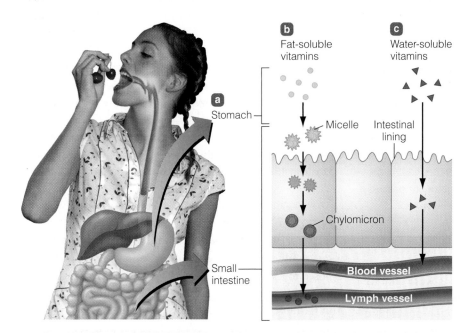

Figure 7.2 Digesting and Absorbing Vitamins
(a) Vitamins are absorbed at the beginning of the small intestine. Vitamin B_{12} is absorbed in the lower portion of the small intestine. **(b)** In the small intestine, the fat-soluble vitamins are packaged with fatty acids and bile in micelles that transport them to the intestinal wall. The fat-soluble vitamins travel through the cells in the intestinal wall and are packaged with fat and other lipids in chylomicrons. The chylomicrons travel through the lymph system and into the bloodstream.
(c) The water-soluble vitamins are absorbed directly into the bloodstream from the small intestine.

vitamins Essential nutrients that your body needs in small amounts to grow, reproduce, and maintain good health.

Vitamins were originally called vitamines. Casimir Funk, a chemist and early vitamin researcher, believed that vitamins were vital to life (he was correct) and were probably also a nitrogen-containing amine (he was incorrect). When later discoveries found that an amine wasn't present, the "e" was dropped from the word.

toxicity The accumulation of a substance to the level of being poisonous.

fat-soluble vitamins, particularly A and D, can build up to the point of **toxicity**, causing harmful symptoms and conditions.

Water-soluble vitamins are absorbed with water and enter your bloodstream directly. Most water-soluble vitamins are absorbed in the upper portion of your small intestine, although vitamin B_{12} is absorbed in the lower part of your small intestine. Water-soluble vitamins are not stored in your body, and excess amounts are excreted, so it's important to consume adequate amounts of them every day. Note that even though most water-soluble vitamins aren't stored, dietary excesses can still be harmful.

Vitamins Can Be Destroyed by Air, Water, or Heat

Water-soluble vitamins can be destroyed by exposure to air, water, or heat. In fact, vegetables and fruits begin to lose their vitamins almost immediately after being harvested, and some preparation and storage methods can accelerate vitamin loss. While the fat-soluble vitamins tend to be more stable than water-soluble vitamins, some food preparation techniques can cause the loss of these vitamins as well.

Don't Expose Your Produce to Air

Air (oxygen) exposure can destroy the water-soluble vitamins and the fat-soluble vitamins A, E, and K. For this reason, fresh vegetables and fruits should be stored in air-tight, covered containers and used soon after being purchased. Cutting vegetables and fruits increases the amount of surface exposed to air, so cut your produce close to the cooking and serving time to minimize vitamin loss.

A Little Water Is Enough

When you toss out the water that cooks your vegetables, you are also tossing out some water-soluble vitamins. Soaking foods will cause water-soluble vitamins to leech out of the food and into the liquid. To reduce vitamin loss, cook vegetables in a minimal amount of liquid—just enough to prevent the pot from scorching and to keep your vegetables crisp.

In contrast, cooking rice in water doesn't diminish its nutrient content, because the water is absorbed by the grain rather than discarded. However, washing the rice before cooking it will wash away the B vitamins that were sprayed on during the enrichment process.[2]

Reduce Cooking Time

Heat, especially prolonged heat from cooking, will also destroy water-soluble vitamins, especially vitamin C. Because they are exposed to less heat, vegetables cooked by microwaving, steaming, or stir-frying can have approximately 1½ times more vitamin C after cooking than if they were boiled, which involves longer heat exposure.[3] The first three cooking methods are faster than boiling, reducing the length of time the food is in direct contact with the heat, and they all use less added water. (Stir-frying typically uses only oil.) Cooking vegetables until "just tender" is best, as it reduces the cooking time and heat exposure and preserves the vitamins. If you find yourself with a plate full of limp and soggy vegetables, this is a sure sign that vitamins have been lost.

Keep Your Food Cool

While heat causes foods to lose vitamins, cooler temperatures help preserve them. For this reason, produce should be stored in your refrigerator rather than on a counter or in a pantry. A package of fresh spinach left at room temperature will lose over half of its folate, a B vitamin, after four days. Keeping the spinach in the refrigerator delays that loss until eight days.[4] See Table Tips for ways to preserve the vitamins in your foods.

Before we begin our discussion of the individual vitamins, take the Self-Assessment to see if your diet is rich in foods containing fat-soluble vitamins.

The Take-Home Message Vitamins are essential nutrients needed in small amounts for growth, reproduction, and overall good health. All vitamins are either fat-soluble or water-soluble. The fat-soluble vitamins, A, D, E, and K, need fat to be absorbed and are stored in your body. For this reason, chronic dietary excesses of some fat-soluble vitamins can be toxic. The water-soluble B and C vitamins are absorbed with water. Excess water-soluble vitamins are excreted from your body, and surplus amounts generally aren't stored. Many vitamins in foods can be destroyed or lost by exposure to air, water, and heat.

Self-Assessment

Are You Getting Enough Fat-Soluble Vitamins in Your Diet?

Take this brief self-assessment to see if your diet contains enough food sources of the four fat-soluble vitamins.

1. Do you eat at least 1 cup of deep yellow or orange vegetables, such as carrots and sweet potatoes, or dark green vegetables, such as spinach, every day?
   Yes ☐ **No** ☐
2. Do you consume at least 2 glasses (8 ounces each) of milk daily?
   Yes ☐ **No** ☐
3. Do you eat a tablespoon of vegetable oil, such as corn or olive oil, daily? (Tip: Salad dressings, unless they are fat-free, count!)
   Yes ☐ **No** ☐
4. Do you eat at least 1 cup of leafy green vegetables in your salad and/or put lettuce in your sandwich every day?
   Yes ☐ **No** ☐

Answers

If you answered yes to all four questions, you are on your way to acing your fat-soluble vitamins needs! If you answered no to any one of the questions, your diet needs some fine-tuning. Deep orange and dark green vegetables are excellent sources of vitamin A, and milk is an excellent choice for vitamin D. Vegetable oils provide vitamin E, and if you put them on top of your vitamin K–rich leafy green salad, you'll hit the vitamin jackpot. Continue reading this section to find out other ways to improve your diet.

Vitamin A

What Is Vitamin A?

Vitamin A is actually a family of substances called **retinoids** that includes **retinol, retinal,** and **retinoic acid.** These are called **preformed Vitamin A** because they are in a form that your body readily uses. Retinol is the most usable of the three forms and can be converted to both retinal and retinoic acid in your body.[5]

Preformed vitamin A is found only in foods from animal sources, such as liver and eggs, and is added to all processed milk.

Plant food sources do not contain preformed vitamin A, but some do contain **provitamin A carotenoids,** which can be converted to retinol in your body. Carotenoids are the yellow-red pigments that give carrots, butternut squash, and cantaloupe their vibrant, deep orange color.

There are over 600 different carotenoids, but only 3—beta-carotene (β-carotene), beta-cryptoxanthin (β-cryptoxanthin), and alpha carotene (α-carotene)—can be converted to vitamin A. These three provide approximately 25 to 35 percent of the dietary vitamin A consumed by adults in the United States, with the majority of it coming from beta-carotene.[6]

Functions of Vitamin A

Vitamin A Is Essential for Healthy Eyes

Rays of light are bouncing off this page. For you to read this sentence, your eyes receive this reflection of light and begin the process of translating the light into visible images.

The light enters your eye through your cornea and travels to the back of your eye to the macula and retina, as shown in the figure (a).

Vitamin A is a component of two light-sensitive proteins in your retina that are essential for vision. The two proteins, **rhodopsin** and **iodopsin,** are in the tips of light-absorbing cells in the retina called **rods** and **cones,** respectively (b).

As rhodopsin absorbs incoming light, the shape of vitamin A is altered, and it detaches from its protein. This causes a cascade of events that transmits visual

Light

a

Cornea
Light
Lens
Macula
Retina
Optic nerve
(signal to brain)

Retina

b

Light

Rod responsible for black and white vision (contains rhodopsin)

Cone responsible for color vision (contains iodopsin)

messages through your optic nerve to your brain. This change in rhodopsin is called **bleaching.** While the breakdown of iodopsin is similar, rhodopsin is more sensitive to light than iodopsin and is more likely to become bleached.

After bleaching, the vitamin A returns to its original shape and becomes part of the protein again, regenerating the eye's light-absorbing capabilities. This regeneration process can take a few moments.

Have you ever been outside on a sunny day without sunglasses and then entered a dark building? Was it difficult for you to initially see the objects in the room as your eyes adjusted to the dimmer light? The adjustment period happened because much of your rhodopsin had been bleached in the bright outdoor sun and

your eyes needed to regenerate it once you were in the dark room. Luckily, there is a pool of vitamin A in your retina to immediately help with this regeneration.

Vitamin A Is Involved in Cell Differentiation, Reproduction, and Immunity

Vitamin A plays an important role in cell division and **cell differentiation,** the processes that determines what a cell becomes in your body.[7]

Vitamin A impacts cell division by prompting gene expression, a process that uses genetic information to make the proteins needed to begin the process of cell division. As cells divide and cluster together, changes occur that cause them to become different from their initiating cells. This differentiation determines what they become in your body. For immature skin cells to differentiate into mature skin cells, for example, vitamin A acts as a signal to turn on the genes to create the proteins needed to make healthy skin.

This role of vitamin A is one reason dermatologists prescribe retinoid-containing medicines, such at Retin A or Accutane, to treat acne, such as shown in the photo. Retin-A is a topical medication that works by enhancing the turnover of skin cells and inhibiting the formation of acne. Accutane is a medication taken orally that manipulates cell differentiation through gene expression of acne-producing cells to alter their development in the skin.[8]

During the early stages of pregnancy, vitamin A signals cells to differentiate into tissues that form the baby's body.

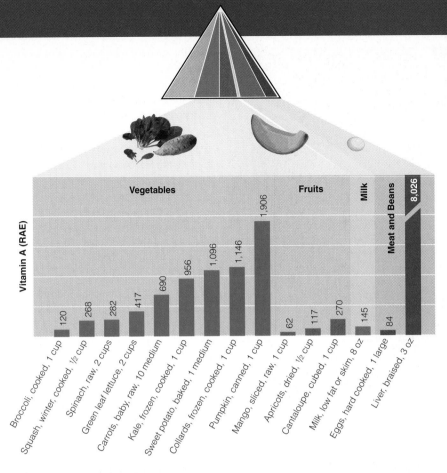

Vegetables | Fruits | Milk | Meat and Beans

Vitamin A (RAE)

- Broccoli, cooked, 1 cup — 120
- Squash, winter, cooked, 1/2 cup — 268
- Spinach, raw, 2 cups — 282
- Green leaf lettuce, 2 cups — 417
- Carrots, baby, raw, 10 medium — 690
- Kale, frozen, cooked, 1 cup — 956
- Sweet potato, baked, 1 medium — 1,096
- Collards, frozen, cooked, 1 cup — 1,146
- Pumpkin, canned, 1 cup — 1,906
- Mango, sliced, raw, 1 cup — 62
- Apricots, dried, 1/2 cup — 117
- Cantaloupe, cubed, 1 cup — 270
- Milk, low fat or skim, 8 oz — 145
- Eggs, hard cooked, 1 large — 84
- Liver, braised, 3 oz — 8,026

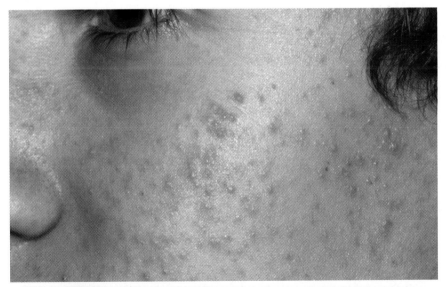

Vitamin A can aid in the treatment of acne.

Vitamin A plays a particularly important role in the development of the limbs, heart, eyes, and ears.[9]

Vitamin A may help regulate the cells involved in bone growth through gene expression. Too much vitamin A, however, can negatively affect healthy bones.

Vitamin A is important for keeping your skin and the mucous membranes of your lungs, intestinal tract, and kidneys healthy and structurally sound. If these linings are weakened or damaged, bacteria and viruses can infiltrate your body and make you sick.

Vitamin A helps keep your skin, which acts as another barrier to infections, healthy to prevent harmful bacteria from entering your body. Vitamin A also works with your immune system to create white blood cells that fight these foreign invaders should they enter your bloodstream.

Daily Needs

Vitamin A in foods and supplements can be measured in two ways: in micrograms (μg) of **retinol activity equivalents (RAE)** and in **international units (IU).**

Because retinol is the most usable form of vitamin A and because provitamin A carotenoids can be converted to retinol, the preferred way to measure vitamin A in foods is its conversion to RAE. However, some vitamin supplements and food labels use the older measure, IU, on their products. (One RAE in micrograms is the equivalent of 3.3 IU.)

Adult females need 700 μg RAE of vitamin A daily, whereas adult males need 900 μg RAE daily. This is the average amount needed to maintain adequate stores in your body to keep it healthy.[10]*

A daily recommendation for beta-carotene hasn't been established, but the Institute of Medicine suggests consuming 3 to 6 milligrams of beta-carotene every day from foods.[11] (Beta-carotene is measured in milligrams.) You can obtain this easily by eating five or more servings of fruits and vegetables. This amount of beta-carotene will also provide about 50 percent of the recommended vitamin A intake. Hence, choosing beta-carotene-rich foods will not only add antioxidants to your diet but also vitamin A.

Vegetarians who eat no animal foods, including vitamin A–rich milk and eggs, need to be especially conscientious about eating carotenoids and beta-carotene rich foods to meet their daily vitamin A needs.

Food Sources

Organ meats (liver), milk, cereals, cheese, and eggs are the most popular sources of preformed vitamin A in the U.S. diet.

Carrots, spinach, and sweet potatoes are American favorites for provitamin A carotenoids, including beta-carotene. Similar to vitamin A and other fat-soluble

*Throughout this book, the amount of each nutrient that is needed daily is based on adults age 19 and older. If you are younger than 19, your needs may be different. See the inside cover of this textbook for the specific amount of each nutrient you need daily based on your age and gender.

vitamins, carotenoids are absorbed more efficiently when fat is present in your intestinal tract. Adding as little as 1 tablespoon of vegetable oil to your diet can increase the absorption of carotenoids by as much as 25 percent.[12]

Too Much or Too Little

Because vitamin A is stored in your body, excessive amounts of preformed vitamin A can accumulate to toxic levels. The upper level for adults has been set at 3,000 milligrams of preformed vitamin A daily.

Overconsumption of preformed vitamin A is usually due to taking supplements and is less likely to occur from overeating vitamin A in foods. Consuming more than 15,000 micrograms of preformed vitamin A at one time or over a short period of time can lead to nausea, vomiting, headaches, dizziness, and blurred vision.[13]

Chronic daily consumption of more than 30,000 micrograms of vitamin A (more than 300 times the amount that adults need daily) can lead to **hypervitaminosis A** (*hyper* = over, *osis* = condition), an extremely serious condition in which the liver accumulates toxic levels of vitamin A. Hypervitaminosis A can lead to deterioration and scarring of the liver and even death.[14]

High intake of preformed vitamin A during pregnancy, particularly in the first trimester, can cause birth defects in the face and skull and damage the child's central nervous system. All women of childbearing age who are using retinoids for acne or other skin conditions should take the proper steps to avoid becoming pregnant.[15]

While vitamin A is needed for bone health, some research suggests that consuming too much may lead to **osteoporosis** (*osteo* = bone, *porosis* = porous), or thinning of the bone, which in turn increases the risk of fractures. Osteoporosis-related hip fractures appear to be prevalent in Swedes and Norwegians, who tend to have high consumption of vitamin-A-rich cod liver oil and specialty dairy products which have been heavily fortified with vitamin A.[16]

Additional studies involving both women and men have shown similar associations between high vitamin A intake and increased risks of fractures. As little as 1,500 micrograms (3,000 IU) of retinol, which is slightly more than twice the RDA recommended for women, can be unhealthy for bones.[17] This amount can be quickly reached when taking a supplement and eating a diet rich in vitamin A fortified foods. (The Daily Value [DV] for vitamin A used on food labels is 5,000 IU. Consuming a food that provides a large percentage of the DV for vitamin A may mean consuming more than the upper level.)

The upper level applies *only* to preformed vitamin A from foods, fortified

foods, and supplements. Provitamin A carotenoids in foods are not toxic and do not pose serious health problems. Your body has a built-in safeguard to prevent provitamin A carotenoids from contributing to vitamin A toxicity, birth defects, or bone damage. If you consume more carotenoids than you need to meet your vitamin A needs, your body will decrease their conversion to retinol. Extra amounts of carotenoids are stored in your liver and in the fat under your skin.[18]

Eating too many carotenoids can cause a nonthreatening condition called **carotenodermia** (*caroten* = carotene, *dermia* = skin), which results in orange-tinged skin, particularly on the palms of the hands and soles of the feet. Because these areas are cushioned with fat, they become more concentrated with the pigments and more visibly orange in color (right hand in photo). Cutting back on carotenoid-rich foods will reverse carotenodermia.

While a diet abundant in carotenoid-rich foods is not dangerous, carotenoid supplements may be. In a study of adult male smokers, those who consumed beta-carotene supplements were shown to have significantly higher rates of lung cancer than those who didn't take the supplements. However, when these research findings were further analyzed, it appeared that only the men in the study who drank one alcoholic drink daily and consumed the beta-carotene supplement experienced the higher incidences of lung cancer.[19]

There is no known benefit associated with taking beta-carotene supplements. Eating a variety of fruits and vegetables is the safest and most healthful way to meet your vitamin A needs.

A chronic vitamin A deficiency can lead to an inability to regenerate rhodopsin, causing **night blindness.** Individuals with night blindness have difficulty seeing at dusk, since they can't adjust from daylight to dark, and may not be able to drive a car during this time of the day. If diagnosed early, night blindness can be reversed by taking vitamin A.

A prolonged vitamin A deficiency can also lead to dryness and permanent damage to the cornea, a condition called **xerophthalmia** (*xero* = dry, *ophthalm* = eye). Up to 10 million children, mostly in developing countries,

suffer from xerophthalmia annually, and as many as 500,000 of these children go blind every year because they don't consume enough vitamin A. Vitamin A deficiency is the number one cause of preventable blindness in children.[20]

A deficiency of vitamin A is also associated with **stunting** of bones.

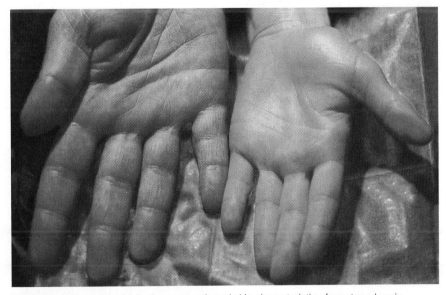

The hand on the right exhibits the orange-tinged skin characteristic of carotenodermia.

Terms to Know

retinoids ■ retinol ■ retinal ■ retinoic acid ■ preformed vitamin A ■ provitamin A carotenoids ■ rhodopsin ■ iodopsin ■ rods ■ cones ■ bleaching ■ cell differentiation ■ retinol activity equivalents (RAE) ■ international units (IU) ■ hypervitaminosis A ■ osteoporosis ■ carotenodermia ■ night blindness ■ xerophthalmia ■ stunting

Vitamin E

What Is Vitamin E?

Vitamin E is sometimes referred to as a vitamin in need of a disease to cure. For almost 40 years after its discovery, scientists searched unsuccessfully for a curative role for vitamin E. They now have shifted their focus and begun valuing the vitamin's importance as an effective antioxidant.[21]

There are eight different forms of naturally occurring vitamin E, but one form, **alpha-tocopherol (α-tocopherol),** is most active in your body. The synthetic form of vitamin E found in dietary supplements is only half as active as the natural form.[22]

Functions of Vitamin E

Vitamin E as an Antioxidant

Vitamin E's nutritional claim to fame is its role as a powerful antioxidant. This role is extremely important in protecting cell membranes and preventing oxidation of the "bad" LDL cholesterol carrier.

As you recall from Chapter 5, phospholipids (lipids that contain phosphorus and two fatty acids) are critical components of cell membranes. Many phospholipids contain unsaturated fatty acids, which are vulnerable to the damaging effects of free radicals. Free radicals and how antioxidants combat them, will be discussed later on in the chapter. Vitamin E neutralizes free radicals before they can harm cell membranes (see figure below).

When the bad LDL cholesterol carrier is oxidized, it contributes to the buildup of artery-clogging plaque. Antioxidants, including vitamin E, help protect the LDL cholesterol carrier from being oxidized and reduce the risk of this buildup in the arteries, called atherosclerosis.[23]

Other Functions of Vitamin E

Vitamin E is an **anticoagulant** (*anti* = against, *coagulant* = causes clotting), which means that it inhibits platelets (fragments of cells used in blood clotting) from unnecessarily clumping together and creating a damaging clot in your bloodstream. Vitamin E also alters the stickiness of the cells that line your lymph and blood vessels. This decreases the ability of blood components to stick to these walls and clog these passageways.

Studies are still under way to assess if the long-term use of vitamin E supplements could play a protective role against heart disease.[24]

Daily Needs

Adults need to consume 15 milligrams of vitamin E daily. Because alpha-tocopherol is the most active form of vitamin E in your body, your vitamin E needs are in alpha-tocopherol equivalents.

Researchers speculate that healthy Americans and Canadians, on average, are consuming more than the recommended 15 milligrams of vitamin E daily.[25]

Food Sources

Because vitamin E is fat-soluble, vegetable oils, foods that contain these oils, nuts, and seeds are good sources. The *Dietary Guidelines for Americans 2005* specifically recommend consuming vegetable oils daily to meet your vitamin E needs. Some green leafy vegetables and fortified cereals can also contribute to your daily needs.

Too Much or Too Little

There isn't any known risk of consuming too much vitamin E from natural food sources.

Overconsumption of the synthetic form that is found in supplements and/or fortified foods could pose risks.

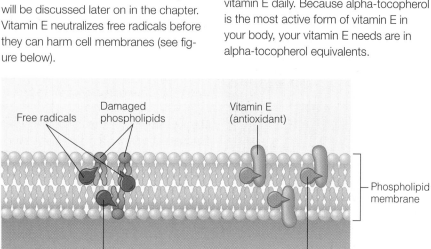

Free radicals

Damaged phospholipids

Vitamin E (antioxidant)

Phospholipid membrane

Free radicals damage phospholipids, essential components of the cell membrane

Vitamin E in cell membranes can neutralize free radicals, preventing them from damaging phospholipids

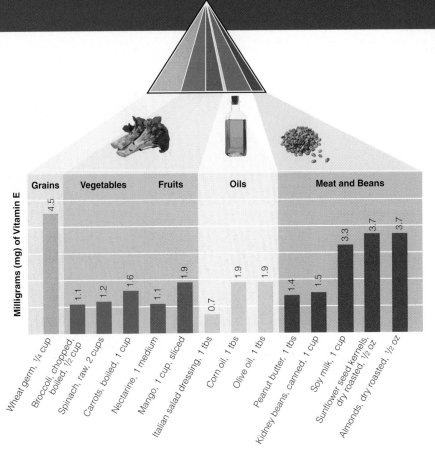

	Grains	Vegetables		Fruits		Oils			Meat and Beans			

Milligrams (mg) of Vitamin E

- Wheat germ, 1/4 cup — 4.5
- Broccoli, chopped, boiled, 1/2 cup — 1.1
- Spinach, raw, 2 cups — 1.2
- Carrots, boiled, 1 cup — 1.6
- Nectarine, 1 medium — 1.1
- Mango, 1 cup, sliced — 1.9
- Italian salad dressing, 1 tbs — 0.7
- Corn oil, 1 tbs — 1.9
- Olive oil, 1 tbs — 1.9
- Peanut butter, 1 tbs — 1.4
- Kidney beans, canned, 1 cup — 1.5
- Soy milk, 1 cup — 3.3
- Sunflower seed kernels, dry roasted, 1/2 oz — 3.7
- Almonds, dry roasted, 1/2 oz — 3.7

Because vitamin E can act as an anticoagulant and interfere with blood clotting, excess amounts in your body increase the risk of **hemorrhage.** Because of this, the upper level from supplements and/or fortified foods is 1,000 milligrams for adults. This applies only to healthy individuals consuming adequate amounts of vitamin K. (Vitamin K also plays a role in blood clotting. A deficiency of vitamin K can exacerbate the anticoagulant effects of vitamin E.) Individuals taking anticoagulant medication and vitamin E supplements should be monitored by their physician to avoid the serious situation in which the blood can't clot quickly enough to stop the bleeding from a wound.

While the upper level of 1,000 milligrams was set to keep you safe, it may actually be too high. A recent study showed that those at risk of heart disease who took 400 IU (265 milligrams) or more of vitamin E daily for at least one year had an overall higher risk of dying. One theory is that too much vitamin E may disrupt the balance of other antioxidants in the body, causing more harm than good.[26]

Though rare, a chronic deficiency can cause nerve problems, muscle weakness, and uncontrolled movement of body parts. Because vitamin E is an antioxidant and is found in the membranes of red blood cells, a deficiency can also increase the susceptibility of cell membranes to damage by free radicals.

Individuals who can't absorb fat properly may fall short of their vitamin E needs.

Table Tips
Enjoying Your Es

Add fresh spinach and broccoli to your lunch salad.

Add a slice of avocado or use guacamole as a spread on sandwiches.

Spread peanut butter on apple slices for a sweet treat.

Top low-fat yogurt with wheat germ for a healthy snack.

Pack a handful of almonds in a zip-closed bag for a midafternoon snack.

Terms to Know

alpha-tocopherol (α-tocopherol) ■ anticoagulant ■ hemorrhage

Vitamin K

What Is Vitamin K?

There are two forms of vitamin K: **mena-quinone** and **phylloquinone.** Mena-quinone is synthesized by the bacteria that exist naturally in your intestinal tract. Phylloquinone is found in green plants, which is the primary source of vitamin K in your diet.

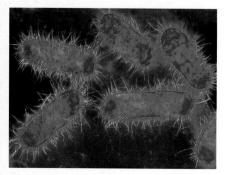

Bacteria in your GI tract synthesize one form of vitamin K.

Functions of Vitamin K

Vitamin K Is Essential for Blood Clotting

An easy way to remember vitamin K's major function is to associate the letter *K* with "klotting."

Vitamin K plays a major role in blood **coagulation,** or clotting. Blood clotting is a complex chain of events involving substances in your blood, many of which are proteins called clotting factors. Vitamin K plays a role in synthesizing four of these **clotting factors.** Without vitamin K, a simple cut on your finger would cause uncontrollable bleeding.

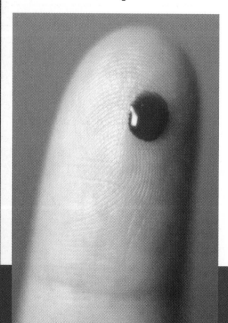

Vitamin K Is Important to Bone Health

Acting as a coenzyme, vitamin K aids an enzyme that alters the bone protein **osteocalcin.** Vitamin K enables osteocalcin to bind with the bone-strengthening mineral calcium.

Chronic inadequate amounts of dietary vitamin K may be a factor in osteoporosis. In a study of women over a ten-year period, researchers found that a low dietary intake of vitamin K was associated with an increased risk of hip fractures.[27]

Research continues in the area of vitamin K and bone health.

Daily Needs

Currently, it is not known how much of the vitamin K made from bacteria in your intestinal tract truly contributes to meeting your daily needs. Because of this, it is hard to pinpoint the exact amount you need to consume daily in your foods. Therefore, the recommendation for dietary vitamin K is based on the current amount that is consumed, on average, by healthy Americans.[28]

Adult women need 90 micrograms of vitamin K per day, and men need 120 micrograms daily.

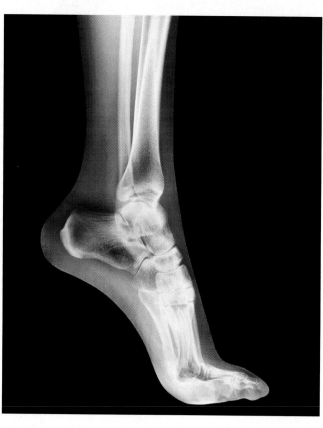

Food Sources

When it comes to meeting your vitamin K needs, think green. Vegetables like broccoli, asparagus, spinach, salad greens, brussels sprouts, and cabbage are all rich in vitamin K. Vegetable oils and margarine are the second largest source of vitamin K in the diet. A green salad with oil and vinegar dressing at lunch and ¾ cup broccoli at dinner will meet your vitamin K needs for the entire day.

Too Much or Too Little

There are no known adverse effects of consuming too much vitamin K from foods or supplements, so an upper intake level hasn't been set for healthy people.

Individuals taking anticoagulant (anti-clotting) medications such as **warfarin** (also known as Coumadin) need to keep

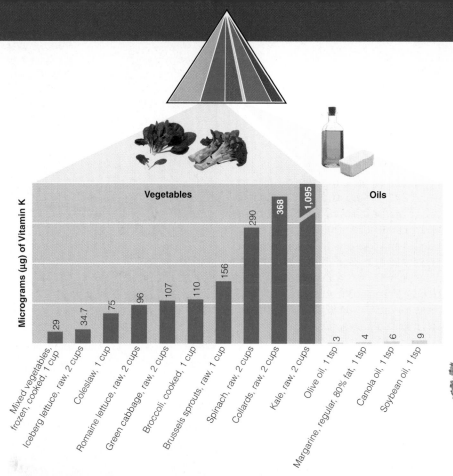

Micrograms (µg) of Vitamin K

Vegetables

Food	µg
Mixed vegetables, frozen, cooked, 1 cup	29
Iceberg lettuce, raw, 2 cups	34.7
Coleslaw, 1 cup	75
Romaine lettuce, raw, 2 cups	96
Green cabbage, raw, 2 cups	107
Broccoli, cooked, 1 cup	110
Brussels sprouts, raw, 1 cup	156
Spinach, raw, 2 cups	290
Collards, raw, 2 cups	368
Kale, raw, 2 cups	1,095

Oils

Food	µg
Olive oil, 1 tsp	3
Margarine, regular, 80% fat, 1 tsp	4
Canola oil, 1 tsp	6
Soybean oil, 1 tsp	9

a consistent intake of vitamin K. This medication decreases the activity of vitamin K and prolongs the time it takes for blood to clot (compare normally clotted blood with blood treated with warfarin, in the photos below). If these individuals suddenly increase the vitamin K in their diets, the vitamin can override the effect of the drug, enabling the blood to clot too quickly. In contrast, a sudden

decline in dietary vitamin K can enhance the effectiveness of the drug.[29]

A vitamin K deficiency severe enough to affect blood clotting is extremely rare in healthy individuals.[30] People with illnesses affecting absorption of fat in the intestinal tract, which is necessary to absorb fat-soluble vitamin K, may be at risk for not meeting their vitamin K needs.

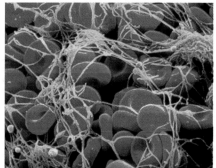

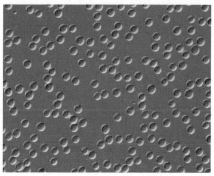

The photo at top shows normally clotted blood. The photo at bottom shows blood treated with warfarin.

Table Tips

Getting Your Ks

Have a green salad daily.

Cook with soybean oil.

Add shredded cabbage to your salad, or top it with a scoop of coleslaw.

Add a tad of margarine to your steamed spinach. Both will provide some vitamin K.

Dunk raw broccoli florets in salad dressing for two sources of vitamin K.

Terms to Know

menaquinone ■ phylloquinone ■ coagulation ■ clotting factors ■ osteocalcin ■ warfarin

Vitamin D

What Is Vitamin D?

Vitamin D is called the "sunshine vitamin" because it is made in your body with the help of **ultraviolet (UV) rays** from sunlight. In fact, most healthy people can synthesize all the vitamin D they need as long as they receive adequate sun exposure.[31] People who don't obtain enough sun exposure must meet their needs through their diets.

Whether from food or sunlight, vitamin D enters your body in an inactive form. The ultraviolet rays of the sun convert a cholesterol-containing compound in your skin to previtamin D, which is then converted to an inactive form of vitamin D in your blood. The vitamin D in your foods is also in this inactive form.

This inactive form travels in your blood to your liver, where it is changed into a circulating form of vitamin D and is released back into your blood. Once in your kidneys, it is converted to an active form of vitamin D.

Functions of Vitamin D

Vitamin D Helps Bone Health by Regulating Calcium and Phosphorus

Once in an active form, vitamin D acts as a hormone and regulates two important bone minerals, calcium and phosphorus. Vitamin D stimulates the absorption of calcium and phosphorus in your intestinal tract, helping to keep the levels of these minerals within a healthy range in your blood. Because of its role in regulating these minerals, vitamin D helps to build and maintain your bones.

While phosphorus deficiency is very rare, dietary calcium deficiencies do occur, causing blood levels of calcium to drop. When this happens, vitamin D and **parathyroid hormone** cause calcium to leave your bones to maintain the necessary levels in your blood. Vitamin D then signals your kidneys to decrease the amount of calcium excreted in the urine. All of these actions help to regulate the amount of calcium in your blood.

Vitamin D May Prevent Diabetes and Some Cancers

Research studies have shown that breast, colon, and prostate cancers are more prominent in individuals living in sun-poor areas of the world than in those living in sunny regions. Vitamin D helps regulate the growth and differentiation of certain cells. Researchers speculate that an inadequate amount of vitamin D in the body may reduce the proliferation of the healthy cells, and allow cancer cells to flourish.[32]

Vitamin D may also help prevent diabetes mellitus. Many individuals with type 2 diabetes mellitus have low blood levels of vitamin D. One study revealed that insulin resistance, the inability of the cells to effectively use insulin in the blood, was greater among those with low blood levels of vitamin D, suggesting that the vitamin plays a role in insulin sensitivity.[33]

With this expanded understanding of the role of vitamin D in disease prevention, in particular in osteoporosis and certain cancers, some researchers have

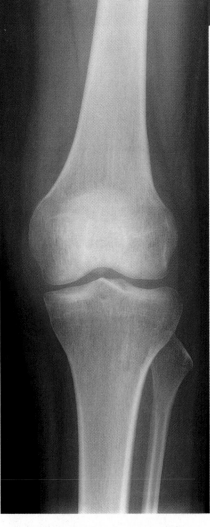

suggested that the U.S. government consider adding calcium and vitamin D to cereal and grain products as part of its food fortification program.[34]

Daily Needs

Not everyone can rely on the sun to meet their daily vitamin D needs.

During the winter months in areas above latitudes of approximately 40 degrees north (Boston, Toronto, Salt Lake City) and below approximately 40 degrees south (Melbourne, Australia), sun exposure isn't strong enough to synthesize vitamin D in the skin.

Individuals with darker skin, such as African-Americans, have a higher amount of the skin pigment melanin, which reduces vitamin D production from sunlight. These individuals need a longer period of sun exposure, compared to a person with less melanin, to derive the same amount of vitamin D. The use of sunscreen can also block the body's ability to synthesize vitamin D by more than 95 percent.[35]

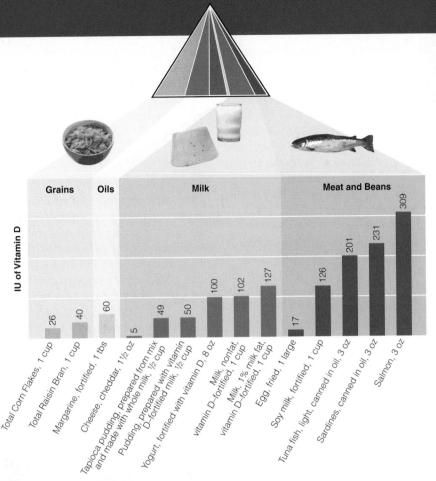

IU of Vitamin D

| Grains | Oils | Milk | Meat and Beans |

- Total Corn Flakes, 1 cup — 26
- Total Raisin Bran, 1 cup — 40
- Margarine, fortified, 1 tbs — 60
- Cheese, cheddar, 1½ oz — 5
- Tapioca pudding, prepared from mix and made with whole milk, ½ cup — 49
- Pudding, prepared with vitamin D-fortified milk, ½ cup — 50
- Yogurt, fortified with vitamin D, 8 oz — 100
- Milk, nonfat, vitamin D-fortified, 1 cup — 102
- Milk, 1% milk fat, vitamin D-fortified, 1 cup — 127
- Egg, fried, 1 large — 17
- Soy milk, fortified, 1 cup — 126
- Tuna fish, light, canned in oil, 3 oz — 201
- Sardines, canned in oil, 3 oz — 231
- Salmon, 3 oz — 309

Because of these variables involving sun exposure, your daily vitamin D needs are based on the amount you would need to eat in foods and are not based on the synthesis of vitamin D in your skin from sunlight.

Adults need 5 to 15 micrograms (200 to 600 IU) of vitamin D daily, depending on their age. When you are reading labels to assess the amount of vitamin D in your foods, keep in mind that the Daily Value (DV) on the Nutrition Facts panel is set at 400 IU, twice the amount recommended for children, teenagers, and many adults.

Food Sources

One of the easiest ways to get your vitamin D from food is to drink fortified milk, which provides 100 IU, or 2.5 micrograms, of vitamin D per cup. Other than fortified milk, breakfast cereals and yogurt, and fatty fish (such as sardines and salmon), very few foods provide ample amounts of vitamin D. With this scarcity of naturally occurring vitamin D–rich sources, it isn't surprising that many Americans are not meeting their daily vitamin D needs.[36]

Too Much or Too Little

Consuming too much vitamin D can cause loss of appetite, nausea, vomiting, and constipation. The upper level for vitamin D has been set at 2,000 IU (50 micrograms) or over three to ten times higher than recommended daily.

As with the other fat-soluble vitamins, excess amounts of vitamin D are stored in the fat cells, and an accumulation can reach toxic levels, causing **hypervitaminosis D.** This condition causes overabsorption of calcium from the intestines as well as calcium loss from bones. When both of these symptoms occur, blood calcium levels can become dangerously high.

A chronically high amount of calcium in the blood, or **hypercalcemia** (*hyper* = over, *calc* = calcium, *emia* = blood), can cause damaging calcium deposits in the tissues of your kidneys, lungs, blood vessels, and heart. Excess vitamin D can also affect your nervous system and cause severe depression.[37]

The good news is that it is highly unlikely that you will get hypervitaminosis D from foods, even fortified foods. The only exception is fish oils, specifically cod-liver oil, which provides 1,360 IU of vitamin D per tablespoon. Luckily, the less-than-pleasant taste of this oil is a safeguard against overconsumption. A more likely culprit behind hypervitaminosis D is the overuse of vitamin D supplements.

Sun worshippers don't have to worry about getting hypervitaminosis D from the sun (although they should be concerned about the risk of skin cancer). Overexposing the skin to UV rays will eventually destroy the inactive form of vitamin D in the skin, causing the body to shut down production of vitamin D.

Rickets on the Rise

Rickets is a vitamin D deficiency disease that occurs in children. The bones of children with rickets aren't adequately mineralized with calcium and phosphorus, and this causes them to weaken. Because of their "soft bones," these children develop bowed legs as they are unable to hold up their own body weight when they are standing upright.[38]

Since milk became fortified with vitamin D in the 1930s, rickets has been considered a rare disease among children in the United States. Recently, the disease has once again become a public health concern. In the late 1990s, a review of hospital records in Georgia suggested that as many as five out of every 1 million children between 6 months and 5 years of age were hospitalized with rickets associated with a vitamin D deficiency. This probably underestimates the prevalence of rickets in the state, as only

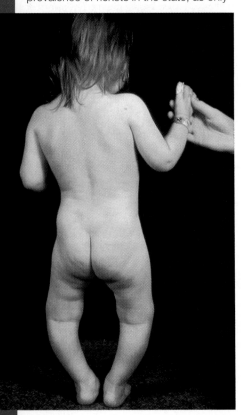

Child with rickets.

hospitalized children were investigated. Similarly, more than 20 percent of over 300 adolescents at a Boston-based hospital clinic were recently found to be deficient in vitamin D.[39]

Changes in the diets and lifestyles of children provide clues as to why rickets is on the rise in America. One factor may be the increased consumption of soft drinks. A U.S. Department of Agriculture (USDA) report found that the number of children who drank soft drinks, in and outside of school, has more than doubled over a 20-year period. During 1977–1978, 22 percent of 14- to 17-year-old-girls in the United States drank milk daily; this dropped to only 9 percent during 1994–1998.[40] This displacement of milk (a good source of vitamin D) with soft drinks (a poor source) is causing many children to come up short in their vitamin D intake.

Increased concern over skin cancer may be another factor. Skin cancer is the most common form of cancer in the United States, and childhood sun exposure appears to increase the risk of skin cancer in later years. Because of this, organizations such as the Centers for Disease Control and the American Cancer Society have run campaigns that recommend limiting exposure to ultraviolet light. People are encouraged to use sunscreen, wear protective clothing when outdoors, and minimize activities in the sun. The American Association of Pediatricians also recommends that infants younger than 6 months not be exposed to direct sunlight.[41] With less exposure to UV light, many children aren't able to synthesize vitamin D in adequate amounts to meet their needs, thereby increasing their risk of developing rickets.

The increased use of child day-care facilities, which may limit outdoor activities during the day, may also play a role in this increased prevalence of rickets.[42]

Finally, air pollution reduces the ultraviolet rays of the sun by as much as 60 percent—another factor limiting the production of vitamin D in the skin. In fact, children living in an industrial, polluted region of India were shown to have less vitamin D in their blood than children living in a less polluted area of the country.[43]

Other Vitamin D Deficiency Disorders

Osteomalacia is the adult equivalent of rickets and can cause muscle and bone weakness and pain. The bones can't mineralize properly because there isn't enough calcium and phosphorus available in the blood.[44] Although there may be adequate amounts of these minerals in the diet, the deficiency of vitamin D hampers their absorption.

Vitamin D deficiency and its subsequent effect on decreased calcium absorption can lead to **osteoporosis,** a condition in which the bones can mineralize properly, but there isn't enough calcium in the diet to maximize the bone density, or mass.

Table Tips
Dynamite Ways to Get Vitamin D

Use low-fat milk, not cream, in your hot or iced coffee. Some commercially made large lattes add more than 1 cup of milk per serving!

Buy vitamin D–fortified yogurts and have one daily as a snack. Top it with a vitamin D–fortified cereal for another boost of "D."

Start your morning with cereal, and douse it with plenty of low-fat or skim milk.

Flake canned salmon over your lunchtime salad.

Make instant hot cocoa with hot milk rather than water.

Terms to Know
ultraviolet (UV) rays ■ parathyroid hormone ■ hypervitaminosis D ■ hypercalcemia ■ rickets ■ osteomalacia ■ osteoporosis

The B Vitamins and Vitamin C Are Water-Soluble

Before we to move on to the water-soluble vitamins, take the Self-Assessment to see if you are consuming foods that are rich in the B vitamins and vitamin C.

In contrast to fat-soluble vitamins, which can be stored in your body, excess water-soluble vitamins are excreted in your urine. Consumers who take large amounts of water-soluble vitamins in an attempt to "beef up" their vitamin stores literally end up flushing their vitamins, and their money, down the toilet.

Though water-soluble vitamins aren't stored in your body, routine intakes of excessive amounts can be harmful. In fact, Brendan Gardner's illness, described at the beginning of the chapter, wasn't due to a vitamin deficiency but to overconsumption of the water-soluble vitamin C.

When initially discovered in the early 1900s, the "water-soluble B" was thought to be one vitamin. After years of research, it became apparent that this was not a single substance but rather many vitamins, known collectively as the B vitamins. These B vitamins—thiamin, riboflavin, niacin, vitamin B_6, folate, vitamin B_{12}, pantothenic acid, and biotin—share a common role as **coenzymes,** helping numerous enzymes produce reactions in your cells. Without the B vitamins, many enzymes wouldn't be able to function properly, and their reactions couldn't occur. As shown in Figure 7.3, this enzyme needs the help of a coenzyme (a B vitamin) for the reaction to occur. Once the coenzyme is present, the reaction can proceed and a new product can be released.

Although vitamins don't provide calories and thus aren't a source of energy, you need many of the B vitamins to use the three energy-yielding nutrients: carbohydrates, proteins, and fat. The roles of the B vitamins don't end here. Each vitamin has other important functions in your body (see the boxed feature "B Vitamins for Your Heart" on page 242). Vitamin C plays important roles in the immune system and in bone health, in addition to its other functions.

Store vitamin B–rich whole-wheat flour in an airtight container in your refrigerator or freezer. Because whole-wheat flour contains the germ of the wheat kernel, which is rich in unsaturated fatty acids, it is more susceptible to becoming rancid than refined white flour.

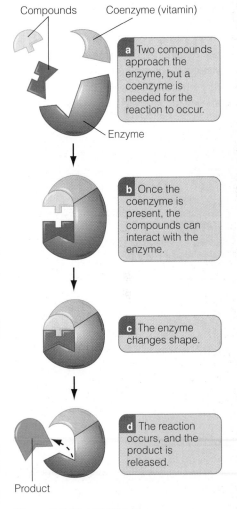

Figure 7.3 How B Vitamins Function as Coenzymes

a Two compounds approach the enzyme, but a coenzyme is needed for the reaction to occur.

b Once the coenzyme is present, the compounds can interact with the enzyme.

c The enzyme changes shape.

d The reaction occurs, and the product is released.

coenzymes Substances needed by enzymes to perform many chemical reactions in your body. Many vitamins act as coenzymes.

Thiamin (B₁)

What Is Thiamin?

Thiamin, or vitamin B₁, was the first B vitamin to be discovered. The path to its discovery began in the 1890s in East Asia. A Dutch doctor, Christiann Eijkman, noticed that chickens and pigeons that ate polished rice (rice with the nutrient- and thiamin-rich outer layer and germ stripped away) developed **polyneuritis** (*poly* = many, *neur* = nerves, *itis* = inflammation). This debilitating nerve condition resulted in the birds not being able to fly or stand up. Eijkman noted that polyneuritis was also a symptom of beriberi, a similar disease that had been observed in humans.

When Eijkman changed the birds' diet to unpolished rice, with the outer layer and germ intact, the birds were cured.[45] While Eijkman realized that the unpolished rice eliminated the symptoms, he didn't know why. Finally, in 1911, Casimir Funk

identified thiamin as the curative factor in the unpolished rice.

Functions of Thiamin

Thiamin Is Needed for Nerve Function and Energy Metabolism

Thiamin plays a role in the transmission of nerve impulses and so helps keep nerves healthy and functioning properly.

You also need thiamin for the metabolism of carbohydrates and certain amino acids. Thiamin also plays a role in breaking down alcohol in the body.

Daily Needs

The RDA for thiamin for adults is 1.1 milligrams for women and 1.2 milligrams for men. Currently, adult American men consume close to 2 milligrams of thiamin daily, whereas women, on average, eat approximately 1.2 milligrams daily, so both groups are meeting their daily needs.[46]

Food Sources

Enriched and whole-grain foods, such as bread and bread products, ready-to-eat cereals, pasta, and rice, and combined foods, such as sandwiches, are the biggest contributors of thiamin in the American diet. A medium-size bowl of

ready-to-eat cereal in the morning and a sandwich at lunch will just about meet your daily thiamin requirement.

Pork is the richest source of naturally occurring thiamin.

Too Much or Too Little

There are no known toxicity symptoms from consuming too much thiamin from food or supplements, so no upper level has been set.

The disease that occurs in humans who are deficient in thiamin is **beriberi.** Symptoms of beriberi include loss of appetite and weight loss, memory loss, and confusion.

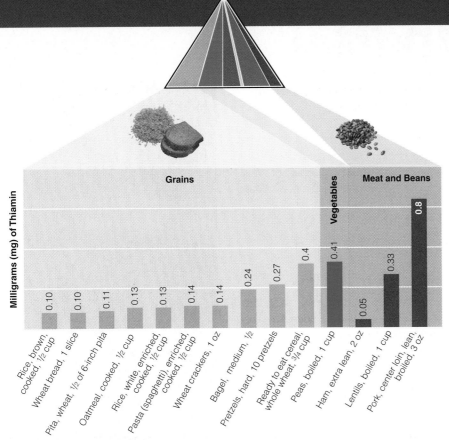

Grains

Vegetables

Meat and Beans

Milligrams (mg) of Thiamin

Rice, brown, cooked, 1/2 cup	0.10
Wheat bread, 1 slice	0.10
Pita, wheat, 1/2 of 6-inch pita	0.11
Oatmeal, cooked, 1/2 cup	0.13
Rice, white, enriched, cooked, 1/2 cup	0.13
Pasta (spaghetti), enriched, cooked, 1/2 cup	0.14
Wheat crackers, 1 oz	0.14
Bagel, medium, 1/2	0.24
Pretzels, hard, 10 pretzels	0.27
Ready to eat cereal, whole wheat, 3/4 cup	0.4
Peas, boiled, 1 cup	0.41
Ham, extra lean, 2 oz	0.05
Lentils, boiled, 1 cup	0.33
Pork, center loin, lean, broiled, 3 oz	0.8

In the United States, refined grains are enriched with thiamin, so instances of beriberi are rare. (Recall that enriched grains have the B vitamins thiamin, riboflavin, niacin, and folic acid, as well as the mineral iron, added to them.)

The populations of poor countries with an inadequate food supply rely heavily on refined grains that are not enriched. These people are more susceptible to a thiamin deficiency and the side effects of beriberi.

Americans, however, are not completely immune to thiamin deficiencies. Those who chronically abuse alcohol tend to have a poor diet that is probably deficient in thiamin. Alcohol consumption also interferes with the absorption of the small amounts of thiamin that may be in the diet, accelerating its loss from the body. Alcoholics may find themselves battling a thiamin deficiency, that can cause beriberi, and chronic alcohol abuse can lead to an advanced form of thiamin deficiency called **Wernicke-Korsakoff syndrome.** The syndrome is a progressively damaging brain disorder that can cause mental confusion and memory loss, difficulty seeing clearly, low blood pressure, uncontrolled movement of the arms and legs, and even coma. While some of these symptoms can be reversed after the person is medically treated with thiamin, some of the memory loss may be permanent.[47]

Terms to Know
polyneuritis ■ beriberi ■ Wernicke-Korsakoff syndrome

Riboflavin (B₂)

What Is Riboflavin?

Riboflavin, also known as vitamin B_2, is a light-sensitive B vitamin that is abundant in milk. One of the reasons that milk is packaged in opaque bottles or cardboard containers is to preserve its riboflavin content from being destroyed by light.

Not so long ago, milk made its way to a household not via the grocery store cooler, but by way of a daily visit from a milkman in the early hours of the morning. At each delivery, the milkman placed the clear glass milk bottles inside a covered "milk box" outside the home. The milk box helped protect the light-sensitive riboflavin in the milk from being destroyed by the morning sunlight. Sunlight destroys riboflavin quickly. In fact, just 30 minutes of midday summer sun will destroy over 30 percent of the riboflavin in glass-bottled milk.[48]

Functions of Riboflavin

Riboflavin Is Important for Energy Metabolism

Your body needs riboflavin to turn the carbohydrates, proteins, and fats that you eat into energy, and to keep the cells in your body healthy.[49] Riboflavin also enhances the functions of other B vitamins, such as niacin and B_{12}.

Daily Needs

You need to consume a little over 1 milligram of riboflavin daily to be healthy. Adult males should consume 1.3 milligrams and females, 1.1 milligrams of riboflavin every day.

Food Sources

Milk and yogurt are the most popular sources of riboflavin in the diets of American adults, followed by enriched cereals and grains. A breakfast of cereal and milk and a lunchtime pita sandwich and yogurt will provide your riboflavin needs for the day.

Too Much or Too Little

Your body has a limited ability to absorb riboflavin, so excessive amounts are excreted in urine. In fact, because riboflavin is a bright yellow compound, consuming large amounts through supplements will turn urine as yellow as a school bus. While this isn't dangerous to your health, it isn't beneficial either, so you should skip

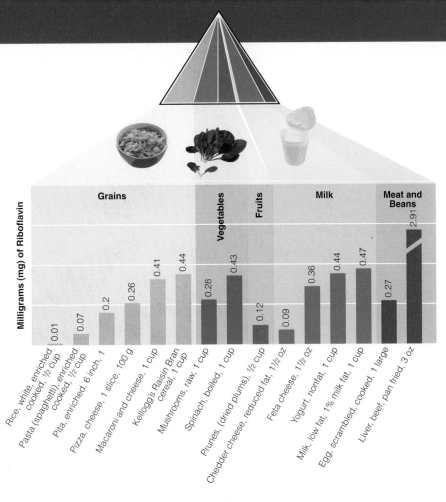

Milligrams (mg) of Riboflavin

Group	Food	mg
Grains	Rice, white, enriched cooked, 1/2 cup	0.01
Grains	Pasta (spaghetti), enriched cooked, 1/2 cup	0.07
Grains	Pita, enriched, 6 inch, 1	0.2
Grains	Pizza, cheese, 1 slice, 100 g	0.26
Grains	Macaroni and cheese, 1 cup	0.41
Grains	Kellogg's Raisin Bran cereal, 1 cup	0.44
Vegetables	Mushrooms, raw, 1 cup	0.28
Vegetables	Spinach, boiled, 1 cup	0.43
Fruits	Prunes, (dried plums), 1/2 cup	0.12
Milk	Chedder cheese, reduced fat, 1 1/2 oz	0.09
Milk	Feta cheese, 1 1/2 oz	0.36
Milk	Yogurt, nonfat, 1 cup	0.44
Milk	Milk, low fat, 1% milk fat, 1 cup	0.47
Meat and Beans	Egg, scrambled, cooked, 1 large	0.27
Meat and Beans	Liver, beef, pan fried, 3 oz	2.91

the supplements and pour yourself a glass of milk instead. No upper level for riboflavin has been determined.

If you don't consume enough of this B vitamin, the cells in the tissues that line your throat, mouth, tongue, and lips will be the first to signal a deficiency. Your throat would be sore, the inside of your mouth would swell, your tongue would be inflamed and look purplish red, and your lips will be dry and scaly. Deficiencies are rarely seen in healthy individuals who eat a balanced diet.

Table Tips

Rally Your Riboflavin

Have a glass of milk with your meals.

A yogurt snack is a riboflavin snack.

Pizza is a good source of riboflavin.

Enriched pasta will enrich your meal with riboflavin.

Macaroni and cheese provides a double source of riboflavin from the pasta and cheese.

Niacin (B₃)

What Is Niacin?

Niacin, or vitamin B_3, is the generic term for **nicotinic acid** and **nicotinamide,** which are the two active forms of niacin that are derived from foods.

Functions of Niacin

Niacin Is Needed to Use the Energy in Your Food

Niacin is another nutrient your body needs to use carbohydrates, proteins, and fats. Without niacin, you wouldn't be able to create energy from the foods that you eat. Niacin is also needed to synthesize fat and cholesterol.

Other Functions of Niacin

Niacin is needed to keep your skin cells healthy and your digestive system functioning properly.

Niacin has been shown to lower the total amount of cholesterol in the blood and the "bad" LDL cholesterol carrier. It can also lower high levels of fat (triglycerides) in the blood and simultaneously raise the level of the "good" HDL cholesterol carrier. The nicotinic acid form of niacin is sometimes prescribed by physicians for patients with high blood cholesterol levels. When niacin is used to treat high blood cholesterol, it is considered a drug. The amount prescribed by a physician is often more than 40 times the upper level for niacin. Note that you should *never* consume high amounts of niacin unless a physician is monitoring you.

Daily Needs

The recommended daily amount for adults is 14 milligrams for women and 16 milligrams for men, an amount set to prevent the deficiency disease pellagra. American adults, on average, far exceed their daily niacin needs.[50]

While niacin is found in many foods, it can also be synthesized in the body from the amino acid **tryptophan.** For this reason, your daily niacin needs are measured in **niacin equivalents (NE).** It is estimated that 60 milligrams of tryptophan can be converted to 1 milligram of niacin or 1 milligram NE.

Food Sources

Niacin is found in meat, fish, poultry, enriched whole-grain breads and bread products, and fortified cereals. Protein-rich foods, particularly animal foods such as meat, are good sources of tryptophan and thus of niacin. However, if you are falling short of both your dietary protein and niacin, tryptophan will first be used to make protein in your body, at the expense of your niacin needs.[51]

As with thiamin, your niacin needs are probably met after you eat your breakfast and lunch, especially since similar foods contain both vitamins.

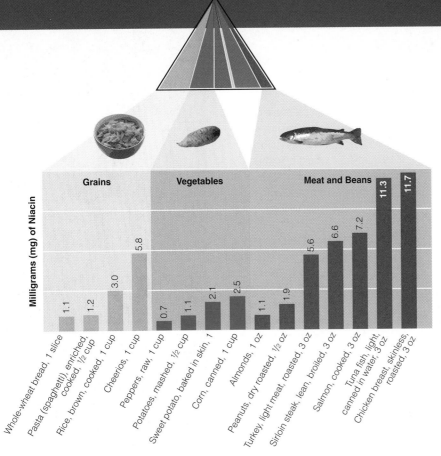

Grains				Vegetables				Meat and Beans					

Milligrams (mg) of Niacin

Values shown on bars:
- Whole-wheat bread, 1 slice: 1.1
- Pasta (spaghetti), enriched, cooked, 1/2 cup: 1.2
- Rice, brown, cooked, 1 cup: 3.0
- Cheerios, 1 cup: 5.8
- Peppers, raw, 1 cup: 0.7
- Potatoes, mashed, 1/2 cup: 1.1
- Sweet potato, baked in skin, 1: 2.1
- Corn, canned, 1 cup: 2.5
- Almonds, 1 oz: 1.1
- Peanuts, dry roasted, 1/2 oz: 1.9
- Turkey, light meat, roasted, 3 oz: 5.6
- Sirloin steak, lean, broiled, 3 oz: 6.6
- Salmon, cooked, 3 oz: 7.2
- Tuna fish, light, canned in water, 3 oz: 11.3
- Chicken breast, skinless, roasted, 3 oz: 11.7

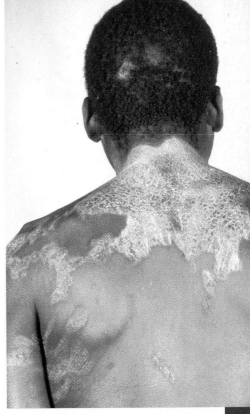

Inflamed skin (dermatitis) can result from pellagra.

Too Much or Too Little

As with most water-soluble vitamins, there isn't any known danger of consuming too much niacin from foods such as meat and enriched grains. However, overconsuming niacin by taking supplements or eating too many overly fortified foods can cause **flushing,** a reddish coloring of the face, arms, and chest. Too much niacin consumption can also cause nausea and vomiting, be toxic to your liver, and raise your blood glucose levels.

The upper level for niacin for adults is 35 milligrams to prevent flushing, the first side effect to be observed when too much niacin is consumed. This upper level applies only to healthy individuals; it may be too high for those with certain medical conditions, such as diabetes mellitus and liver disease.[52]

Too little niacin in the diet can result in the deficiency disease called **pellagra.** In the early 1900s, pellagra was widespread among the poor living in the southern United States, where people relied on corn—a poor source of niacin—as a dietary staple. The symptoms of pellagra—**dermatitis** (inflammation or irritation of the skin), **dementia** (loss of memory along with confusion and disorientation), and **d**iarrhea—led to its being known as the disease of the three Ds. A fourth D, **d**eath, was often associated with the disease.

Once other cereal grains were available, pellagra disappeared as a widespread disease in the United States. The niacin in the grains was later identified as the curative factor for pellagra. Although no longer common in the United States, pellagra does occur among individuals who abuse alcohol and have a very poor diet.

Terms to Know

nicotinic acid ■ nicotinamide ■ tryptophan ■ niacin equivalents (NE) ■ flushing ■ pellagra ■ dermatitis ■ dementia

Vitamin B₆

What Is Vitamin B₆?

Vitamin B₆ is a collective name for several related compounds, including **pyridoxine,** the major form found in plant foods and the form used in supplements and fortified foods.[53] Two other forms, **pyridoxal** and **pyridoxamine,** are found in animal food sources such as chicken and meat.

Functions of Vitamin B₆

Vitamin B₆ Is an Active Coenzyme

Vitamin B₆ acts as a coenzyme with over 100 enzymes involved in the metabolism of proteins. It is needed to create nonessential amino acids and to convert the amino acid tryptophan to niacin.[54] Vitamin B₆ also helps your body metabolize fats and carbohydrates and break down glycogen, the storage form of glucose.

Other Functions of B₆

Vitamin B₆ is needed to make the oxygen-carrying hemoglobin in your red blood cells and to keep your immune and nervous systems healthy.[55]

Finally, recent research indicates that vitamin B₆, along with two other water-soluble vitamins, folate and vitamin B₁₂, may help reduce the risk of heart disease (see the "B Vitamins for Your Heart" feature box on page 242).

Daily Needs

Adult women need 1.3 to 1.5 milligrams and men need 1.3 to 1.7 milligrams of vitamin B₆ daily depending on their age.

Food Sources

Because vitamin B₆ is found in so many foods, including ready-to-eat cereals, meat, fish, poultry, many vegetables and fruits, nuts, peanut butter, and other legumes, Americans on average easily meet their daily needs.

Too Much or Too Little

To protect against potential nerve damage, the upper level for vitamin B₆ is set at 100 milligrams daily for adults over the age of 19. Luckily, it would be extremely difficult to take in a dangerous level of vitamin B₆ from food alone.

However, taking vitamin B₆ in supplement form can be harmful. Over the years, vitamin B₆ has been touted to aid a variety of ailments, including **carpal tunnel syndrome** and **premenstrual syndrome (PMS).**

But research studies have failed to show any significant clinical benefit for taking vitamin B₆ supplements for either of these syndromes.

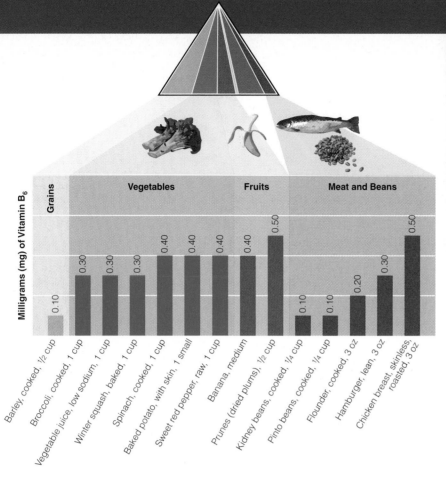

	Grains	Vegetables						Fruits		Meat and Beans				

Milligrams (mg) of Vitamin B$_6$

- Barley, cooked, 1/2 cup — 0.10
- Broccoli, cooked, 1 cup — 0.30
- Vegetable juice, low sodium, 1 cup — 0.30
- Winter squash, baked, 1 cup — 0.30
- Spinach, cooked, 1 cup — 0.40
- Baked potato, with skin, 1 small — 0.40
- Sweet red pepper, raw, 1 cup — 0.40
- Banana, medium — 0.40
- Prunes (dried plums), 1/2 cup — 0.50
- Kidney beans, cooked, 1/4 cup — 0.10
- Pinto beans, cooked, 1/4 cup — 0.10
- Flounder, cooked 3 oz — 0.20
- Hamburger, lean, 3 oz — 0.30
- Chicken breast, skinless, roasted, 3 oz — 0.50

In fact, taking large amounts of vitamin B$_6$ through supplements may be associated with a variety of ill effects, including nerve damage. Individuals taking as little as 500 milligrams and as much as 6,000 milligrams of vitamin B$_6$ daily for two months experienced difficulty walking and tingling sensations in their legs and feet. These symptoms subsided once supplement consumption stopped.[56]

The telltale signs of a vitamin B$_6$ deficiency are a sore tongue, inflammation of the skin, depression, confusion, and possibly **anemia.**

Those who consume too much alcohol are more likely to fall short of their needs. Not only does alcohol cause your body to lose vitamin B$_6$, but those suffering from alcoholism are likely to have an unbalanced diet, with little variety.

Table Tips
Beam with B$_6$

Have a stuffed baked potato with steamed broccoli and grilled chicken for lunch.

Grab a banana for a midmorning snack.

Add cooked barley to your soup.

Snack on prunes.

Add kidney beans to your chili or salad.

Terms to Know

pyridoxine ▪ pyridoxal ▪ pyridoxamine ▪ carpal tunnel syndrome ▪ premenstrual syndrome (PMS) ▪ anemia

Folate

What Is Folate?

There are two forms of the vitamin **folate:** the naturally occurring folate in foods and the synthetic form, **folic acid,** which is added to foods (such as ready-to-eat cereals and grains) and found in supplements. (A very small amount of folic acid can occur naturally in foods. But, for practical purposes in this book, folic acid will always refer to the synthetic variety.)

Functions of Folate

Folate Is Vital for DNA Synthesis

Folate is vital to making the DNA in your cells. If the synthesis of DNA is disrupted, your body's ability to create and maintain new cells is impaired.[57] For this reason, folate plays many important roles, from maintaining healthy blood cells and preventing birth defects to fighting cancer and heart disease. Folate also helps your body use amino acids and is needed to help red blood cells divide and increase in adequate numbers.

Folate Prevents Birth Defects

Folate plays an extremely important role during pregnancy, particularly in the first few weeks after conception, often before the mother knows she is pregnant. Folate is needed to create new cells so that the baby can grow and develop.

A folate deficiency during pregnancy can result in birth defects called **neural tube defects.** The neural tube forms the baby's spine, brain, and skull. If the neural

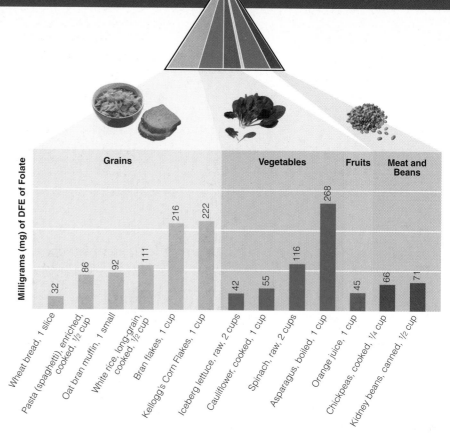

tube doesn't develop properly, two common birth defects, **anencephaly** and **spina bifida,** can occur. In anencephaly, the brain doesn't completely form so the baby can't move, hear, think, or function. An infant with anencephaly dies soon after birth. In spina bifida (see photo), the baby's spinal cord and backbone aren't properly developed, causing learning and physical disabilities, such as the inability to walk.[58]

Folic acid reduces the risk of these birth defects by 50 to 70 percent if consumed at least the month prior to conception and during the early part of pregnancy.[59]

Research studies to date suggest that synthetic folic acid has a stronger protective effect than the folate found

naturally in foods. Since 1998, the FDA has mandated that folic acid be added to all enriched grains and cereal products. This enrichment program has reduced the incidence of neural tube defects by over 25 percent.[60]

Infant with spina bifida.

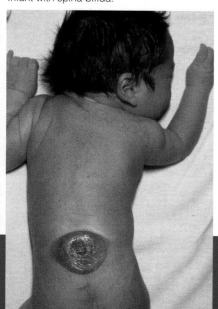

Folate Reduces Some Cancer Risks

Folate has been shown to help reduce the risk of certain cancers, specifically colon cancer. Studies show that men and women taking a multivitamin supplement or otherwise consuming their recommended amounts of folate have a lower risk of developing colon cancer. Other studies show an association between diets low in folate and an increased risk of breast and pancreatic cancers. Inadequate amounts of folate in the body can disrupt the cell's DNA, potentially triggering the development of cancer.[61]

Daily Needs

Your body absorbs the synthetic folic acid more easily than it absorbs naturally occurring folate. In fact, synthetic folic acid, which is added to enriched grains and cereals, is absorbed 1.7 times more efficiently than folate that is found in foods such as orange juice.[62] Because of this, your folate needs are measured in **dietary folate equivalents (DFE).** Most adults should consume 400 micrograms DFE of folate daily.

While the foods in your diet analysis program database list the micrograms of folate as DFE, the Nutrition Facts panel on the food label doesn't make this distinction. To convert the micrograms of folic acid found on the food labels of foods with folic acid added, such as enriched pasta, rice, cereals, and bread, to dietary folate equivalents, multiply the amount listed on the label by 1.7:

$$100 \ \mu g \times 1.7 = 170 \ \mu g \ DFE$$

Because 50 percent of pregnancies in the United States are unplanned, women at risk of becoming pregnant should consume 400 micrograms of synthetic folic acid daily from fortified foods or supplements, along with a diet high in naturally occurring folate. Women with a family history of neural tube defects should, under the guidance of their physicians, take even larger amounts.[63]

Food Sources

Enriched pasta, rice, breads and cereals, legumes (dried peas and beans), leafy green vegetables (spinach, lettuce, collards), broccoli, and asparagus are all good sources of this vitamin.

Too Much or Too Little

There isn't any danger in consuming excessive amounts of naturally occurring folate in foods. However, consuming too much folic acid, either through supplements or fortified foods, can be harmful for individuals who are deficient in vitamin B_{12}. A vitamin B_{12} deficiency can cause anemia and, more dangerous, crippling and irreversible nerve damage. Too much folate in the diet masks the symptoms of B_{12} deficiency anemia. Though the folate can correct anemia, the nerve damage due to the vitamin B_{12} deficiency persists. This delays a proper diagnosis and corrective therapy with vitamin B_{12}. By the time the person is given the vitamin B_{12}, irreversible nerve damage may have occurred.[64]

A folate deficiency can also result in abnormally large and immature cells known as **megaloblasts** (*megalo* = large). These megaloblasts develop into abnormally large red blood cells, or **macrocytes,** that have a diminished oxygen-carrying capacity. Eventually, **macrocytic anemia** causes a person to feel tired, weak, and irritable and to experience shortness of breath. Because folate needs vitamin B_{12} to produce healthy red blood cells, a deficiency of either vitamin can lead to macrocytic anemia.

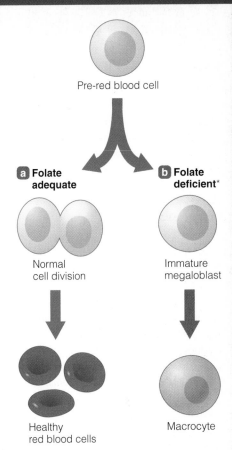

Pre-red blood cell

a Folate adequate

Normal cell division

Healthy red blood cells

b Folate deficient*

Immature megaloblast

Macrocyte

*A vitamin B_{12} deficiency can also cause the formation of macrocytes

An upper level of 1,000 micrograms has been set for folic acid from enriched and fortified foods and supplements to safeguard those who may be unknowingly deficient in vitamin B_{12}.

Table Tips
Fulfill Your Folate Needs

Have a bowl of cereal in the morning.

Add chickpeas to your salad.

Enjoy a tossed salad with your lunch.

Add fresh spinach leaves to your sandwich.

Have a handful of crackers as a late-afternoon snack.

Terms to Know

folate ■ folic acid ■ neural tube defects ■ anacephaly ■ spina bifida ■ dietary folate equivalents (DFE) ■ megaloblasts ■ macrocytes ■ macrocytic anemia

Vitamin B$_{12}$

What Is Vitamin B$_{12}$?

The family of compounds referred to as vitamin B$_{12}$ is also called cobalamin because it contains the metal cobalt.[65]

Vitamin B$_{12}$ is the only water-soluble vitamin that can be stored in your body, primarily in your liver.

B$_{12}$ Needs Intrinsic Factor to be Absorbed

A protein produced in your stomach called **intrinsic factor** is needed to promote vitamin B$_{12}$ absorption. Intrinsic factor binds with vitamin B$_{12}$ in your small intestine, where the vitamin is absorbed. Individuals who cannot produce intrinsic factor are unable to absorb vitamin B$_{12}$ and are diagnosed with **pernicious anemia** (*pernicious* = harmful). Individuals with this condition, must be given regular shots of vitamin B$_{12}$, which injects the vitamin directly into the blood, bypassing the intestine.

Because your body stores plenty of vitamin B$_{12}$ in the liver, the symptoms of pernicious anemia can take years to develop.

Functions of Vitamin B$_{12}$

Vitamin B$_{12}$ Is Vital for Healthy Nerves and Red Blood Cells

Your body needs vitamin B$_{12}$ to use certain fatty acids and amino acids and to make the DNA in your cells. Vitamin B$_{12}$ is also needed for healthy nerves and tissues. Like folate, vitamin B$_{12}$ plays an important role in keeping your cells, particularly your red blood cells, healthy.[66] It is also one of the three B vitamins that collectively could be heart-healthy (see "B Vitamins for Your Heart" feature box later in this chapter).

Daily Needs

Adults needs 2.4 micrograms of vitamin B$_{12}$ daily. American adults, on average, are consuming over 4 micrograms daily.

The body's ability to absorb naturally occurring vitamin B$_{12}$ from foods diminishes with age. This decline appears to be due to a reduction in the acidic juices in the stomach, which are needed to break the bonds that bind the B$_{12}$ to the proteins in food. If the bonds aren't broken, the vitamin can't be released. Up to 30 percent of individuals over the age of 50 experience this decline in acidic juices in their stomachs. Not surprisingly, the pernicious anemia associated with a vitamin B$_{12}$

deficiency occurs in about 2 percent of individuals over the age of 60.[67]

With less acid juice present, the bacteria normally found in the intestines aren't properly destroyed and so tend to overgrow. This abundance of bacteria feed on vitamin B$_{12}$, diminishing the amount of the vitamin that may be available. Luckily, the synthetic form of vitamin B$_{12}$ that is used in fortified foods and supplements isn't bound to a protein, so it doesn't depend on your stomach secretions to be absorbed. (Synthetic vitamin B$_{12}$ still needs intrinsic factor to be absorbed.)

Because the synthetic variety is a more reliable source, individuals over the age of 50 should meet their vitamin B$_{12}$

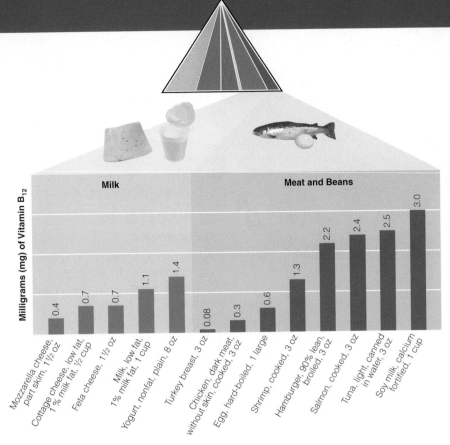

Milligrams (mg) of Vitamin B_{12}

Milk

- Mozzarella cheese, part skim, 1½ oz: 0.4
- Cottage cheese, low fat, 1% milk fat, ½ cup: 0.7
- Feta cheese, 1½ oz: 0.7
- Milk, low fat, 1% milk fat, 1 cup: 1.1
- Yogurt, nonfat, plain, 8 oz: 1.4

Meat and Beans

- Turkey breast, 3 oz: 0.08
- Chicken, dark meat, without skin, cooked, 3 oz: 0.3
- Egg, hard-boiled, 1 large: 0.6
- Shrimp, cooked, 3 oz: 1.3
- Hamburger, 90% lean, broiled, 3 oz: 2.2
- Salmon, cooked, 3 oz: 2.4
- Tuna, light, canned in water, 3 oz: 2.5
- Soy milk, calcium fortified, 1 cup: 3.0

needs primarily from fortified foods or a supplement.[68]

Food Sources

Naturally occurring vitamin B_{12} is found only in foods from animal sources, such as meat, fish, poultry, and dairy products. A varied diet including the minimum recommended servings of these food groups will easily meet your daily needs.

Synthetic vitamin B_{12} is found in fortified soy milk and some ready-to-eat cereals, which are ideal sources for older adults and strict vegetarians, who avoid all foods from animal sources.

If you are relying solely on fortified foods to meet your vitamin B_{12} needs, continually check the labels on these products to make sure they haven't suddenly been reformulated to exclude the vitamin.

Too Much or Too Little

At present, there are no known risks of consuming too much vitamin B_{12} from foods, fortified foods, or supplements, and no upper level has been set. There is also no known benefit from taking B_{12} supplements if your diet contains foods from animal sources and/or fortified foods.

A Vitamin B_{12} Deficiency Can Cause Macrocytic Anemia

Because vitamin B_{12} and folate work closely together to make healthy red blood cells, a vitamin B_{12} deficiency can cause macrocytic anemia, the same type of anemia caused by a folate deficiency. In macrocytic anemia due to a vitamin B_{12} deficiency, there is enough folate available for red blood cells to divide but the folate can't be utilized properly because there isn't enough vitamin B_{12} available. In fact, the true cause of macrocytic anemia is more likely a B_{12} deficiency than a folate deficiency.

Because pernicious anemia (caused by a lack of intrinsic factor) is a type of macrocytic anemia, its initial symptoms are the same as those seen in a folate deficiency: fatigue and shortness of breath.

Vitamin B_{12} is needed to protect nerve cells, including those in your brain and spine, so one long-term consequence of pernicious anemia is nerve damage marked by tingling and numbness in the arms and legs and problems walking. If diagnosed early enough, these symptoms can be reversed with treatments of vitamin B_{12}.

Table Tips

Boost Your B_{12}

Enjoy heart-healthy fish at least twice a week.

Sprinkle your steamed vegetables with reduced-fat shredded cheese.

Drink milk or fortified soy milk.

Try a cottage cheese and fruit snack in the afternoon.

Enjoy a grilled chicken breast on a bun for lunch.

Terms to Know

intrinsic factor ■ pernicious anemia

Vitamin C

You don't have to go out of your way to ensure that your dog's daily chow contains enough vitamin C. Dogs and many other animals possess an enzyme that can synthesize vitamin C from glucose. Humans, however, lack the necessary enzyme for this conversion, and have to rely on food to meet their daily vitamin C needs.[69]

Functions of Vitamin C

Vitamin C Acts as a Coenzyme

Vitamin C, also known as **ascorbic acid**, acts as a coenzyme that is needed to synthesize and use certain amino acids. In particular, vitamin C is needed to make collagen, the most abundant protein in your body. Collagen is plentiful in your connective tissue, which supports and connects all your body parts, so this protein is needed for healthy bones, teeth, skin, and blood vessels.[70] Thus, a vitamin C deficient diet would affect your entire body.

Vitamin C Acts as an Antioxidant

Like beta-carotene and vitamin E, vitamin C acts an antioxidant that may help reduce the risk of chronic diseases such as heart disease and cancer (you will learn more about antioxidants later in the chapter). It also helps you absorb the iron in plant foods such as grains and cereals and break down histamine, the component behind the inflammation seen in many allergic reactions.[71]

fight infections, and this immune-boosting role has fostered the belief that high doses of vitamin C can cure the common cold. (The "Gesundheit! Myths and Facts about the Common Cold" box takes a look at this theory.)

Daily Needs

Women need to consume 75 milligrams of vitamin C daily, and men need to consume 90 milligrams daily to meet their needs.

Smoking accelerates the breakdown and elimination of vitamin C from the body, so smokers need to consume an additional 35 milligrams of vitamin C every day to make up for these losses.[72]

Food Sources

Americans meet about 90 percent of their vitamin C needs by consuming fruits and vegetables, with orange and/or grapefruit juice being the most popular source in the diet. One serving of either juice will just about meet an adult's daily needs. Tomatoes, peppers, potatoes, broccoli, oranges, and cantaloupe are also excellent sources.

Too Much or Too Little

Brendan Gardner, the track athlete introduced at the beginning of this chapter, attempted to ward off a cold by taking vitamin C supplements. His attempt to solve one medical dilemma created another one that impeded his training more than his sniffling and sneezing.

While excessive amounts of vitamin C aren't known to be toxic, consuming over 3,000 milligrams daily

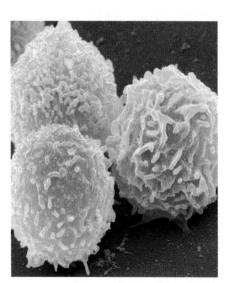

White blood cells.

Vitamin C Boosts Your Immune System

Vitamin C helps keep your immune system healthy by enabling your body to make white blood cells, like the ones shown in the photo above. These blood cells

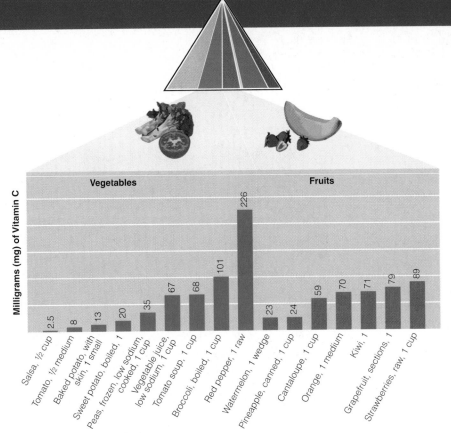

Milligrams (mg) of Vitamin C

Vegetables

Salsa, 1/2 cup	2.5
Tomato, 1/2 medium	8
Baked potato, with skin, 1 small	13
Sweet potato, boiled, 1	20
Peas, frozen, low sodium, cooked, 1 cup	35
Vegetable juice, low sodium, 1 cup	67
Tomato soup, 1 cup	68
Broccoli, boiled, 1 cup	101
Red pepper, 1 raw	226

Fruits

Food	mg
Watermelon, 1 wedge	23
Pineapple, canned, 1 cup	24
Cantaloupe, 1 cup	59
Orange, 1 medium	70
Kiwi, 1	71
Grapefruit, sections, 1	79
Strawberries, raw, 1 cup	89

damage many organs in your body, including the liver and heart.

For centuries, **scurvy,** the disease of a vitamin C deficiency, was the affliction of sailors on long voyages. After many weeks at sea, sailors would run out of vitamin C–rich produce and then develop the telltale signs of scurvy: swollen and bleeding gums, a rough rash on the skin,

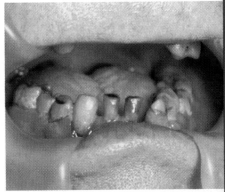

Swollen gums characteristic of scurvy.

coiled or curly arm hairs, and wounds that wouldn't heal.

In 1753, a British naval surgeon discovered that orange and lemon juice prevented scurvy. Decades later, the British government added lemon or lime juice to their standard rations for their sailors to thwart scurvy. In 1919, vitamin C was discovered as the curative factor in these juices.[73]

through the use of supplements has been shown to cause nausea, stomach cramps, and diarrhea. Brendan can attribute the diarrhea he experienced to his daily 3,500-milligrams supplement of vitamin C. Once he stopped taking the supplement, his diarrhea ceased.

The upper level for vitamin C for adults is set at 2,000 milligrams to avoid the intestinal discomfort that excessive amounts of the vitamin can cause. Too much vitamin C can also lead to the formation of kidney stones in individuals with a history of kidney disease.

Because vitamin C helps to absorb the form of iron found in plant foods, those with a rare disorder called **hemochromatosis** (*hemo* = blood; *chroma* = color; *osis* = condition), which causes the body to store too much iron, should avoid excessive amounts of vitamin C. Iron toxicity is extremely dangerous and can

Table Tips

Juicy Ways to Get Vitamin C

Have a least one citrus fruit (such as an orange or grapefruit) daily.

Put sliced tomatoes on your sandwich.

Enjoy a fruit cup for dessert.

Drink low-sodium vegetable juice for an afternoon refresher.

Add strawberries to your low-fat frozen yogurt.

Terms to Know

ascorbic acid ■ hemochromatosis ■ scurvy

Pantothenic Acid and Biotin

What Are Pantothenic Acid and Biotin?

Pantothenic acid and biotin are B vitamins.

Functions of Pantothenic Acid and Biotin

Pantothenic acid and biotin aid in the metabolism of the nutrients that provide you with energy—carbohydrates, proteins, and fats.

Daily Needs

Adults need 5 milligrams of pantothenic acid and 30 micrograms of biotin daily.

Food Sources

Both pantothenic acid and biotin are widely available in foods, including whole grains and whole-grain cereals, nuts and legumes, peanut butter, meat, milk, and eggs. Most Americans easily meet their needs.[74]

Biotin deficiency is so rare that an accurate list of the amount in foods is hard to find.

In addition to its abundance in foods, biotin can be synthesized by the bacteria in your intestinal tract, providing yet another avenue to meet your needs.

Eating a healthy diet to meet all of your other B vitamin needs will ensure that you meet your needs for pantothenic acid and biotin.

Too Much or Too Little

Like many of the other B vitamins, there are no known adverse effects from consuming too much pantothenic acid or biotin. An upper level has not been determined for either of these vitamins.

Although a pantothenic acid deficiency is rare, if you do fall short of your needs, your symptoms might include fatigue, nausea, vomiting, numbness, muscle cramps, and difficulties walking.

During World War II, prisoners of war in Asia experienced a "burning feet" syndrome. The symptoms ranged from heat

sensations and tingling on the soles of their feet to a painful burning intense enough to disrupt sleep. Their diet consisted predominantly of nutrient-poor polished rice. A doctor in India who was studying an identical phenomenon in his patients discovered that when he gave them supplements of pantothenic acid, the condition stopped.[75] In both cases, the syndrome was later attributed to a diet deficient in pantothenic acid.

Consuming inadequate amounts of biotin can cause hair loss, skin rash, and feelings of depression, fatigue, and nausea.[76]

While deficiencies are rare, it can occur if you eat a lot of raw egg whites. The protein avidin, found in egg whites, binds with biotin and blocks it from being absorbed in your intestine. Cooking the egg denatures and inactivates the protein, eliminating the problem.[77]

Gesundheit! Myths and Facts about the Common Cold

You probably know the symptoms well. Your nose runs like a leaky faucet and turns beet red from constant wiping. Your head seems stuffed with cotton, and it feels like someone is playing bongo drums under your scalp. Between coughing and sneezing, you can't catch the rest you need to relieve what feels like constant fatigue. The diagnosis? At least one of the more than 200 varieties of cold virus has invaded your body, and you have a cold that could last as long as two weeks.

You're never alone if you have a case of the common cold. Colds are the leading cause of doctor visits in the United States, and Americans will suffer a billion of them this year alone. Students miss over 20 million school days every year battling the common cold.

The Truth about Catching a Cold

Contrary to popular belief, you can't catch a cold from being outside on a cold day without a coat or hat. Rather, the only way to catch a cold is to come into contact with a cold virus. Contact can be direct, such as when you hug or shake hands with someone who is carrying the virus, or indirect, as when you touch an object like a keyboard or telephone contaminated with a cold virus. The next time you touch your nose or rub your eyes, you transfer these germs from your hands into your body. You can also catch a cold virus by inhaling virus-carrying droplets from a cough or sneeze of someone with the cold.

The increased frequency of colds during the fall and winter is likely due to people spending more time indoors in the close quarters of classrooms, dorm rooms, and the workplace, which makes the sharing of germs easier. The low humidity of the winter air can also cause the inside of your nose to be drier and more permeable to the invasion of these viruses.

Vitamin C and the Common Cold

In the 1970s, a scientist named Linus Pauling theorized that consuming at least 1,000 milligrams of vitamin C would prevent the common cold. Since then, study after study has shown that megadoses of vitamin C are not effective in preventing colds. However, some research has suggested that vitamin C may help reduce the duration and severity of a cold in some individuals once it is contracted. This may be due to the antihistamine effect that vitamin C can have in the body when taken at large doses.[1]

Other Cold Remedies: The Jury Is Still Out

Recently, other dietary substances, such as the herb echinacea and the mineral zinc, have emerged as popular treatment strategies for the common cold. Echinacea had been used centuries ago by some Native American populations to treat coughs and sore throats. Recent studies have shown that the herb comes up short in preventing or affecting the duration or severity of a cold and may contribute to side effects such as a rash and intestinal discomfort. The results of a recent review of over 300 studies using echinacea were inconclusive. More research needs to be done to establish whether echinacea can help prevent or treat the common cold.[2]

Studies of zinc have also had mixed results. Too much zinc can be toxic and can actually suppress your immune system. You will learn more about zinc and its role in the immune system in the next chapter.

What You Can Do

One of the best ways to reduce your chances of catching a cold is to wash your hands frequently with soap and water. This will lower the likelihood of your transmitting germs from your hands to your mouth, nose, or eyes. One study found that children who washed their hands four times a day had over 20 percent fewer sick days from school than those who washed their hands less frequently. When soap and water aren't available, gel sanitizers or disposable alcohol-containing hand wipes can be an effective alternative.[3] Covering your mouth and nose when you cough or sneeze and then immediately washing your hands will help you keep from contaminating the people around you.

Finally, the Centers for Disease Control recommends the following steps to take if you do get a cold:

- Get plenty of rest.
- Drink plenty of fluids. (Chicken soup and juices are considered fluids.)
- Gargle with warm salt water or use throat lozenges for a sore throat.
- Dab petroleum jelly on a raw nose to relieve irritation.
- Take aspirin* or acetaminophen (Tylenol) for headache or fever.

*The American Academy of Pediatrics recommends that children and teenagers avoid consuming aspirin or medicine containing aspirin when they have a viral illness, as it can lead to a rare but serious illness called Reye's syndrome. This syndrome can cause brain damage or death.

B Vitamins for Your Heart

In the late 1970s, researchers made a curious discovery. They noticed that individuals with a very rare genetic disorder, whereby they have too much of the amino acid homocysteine in their blood, suffer from a higher than average incidence of heart disease. Since then, approximately 80 research studies have found an association between high levels of homocysteine and the increased risk for heart disease. While it isn't known exactly how this amino acid contributes to heart disease, it may be that excessive amounts of homocysteine injure the arteries, decrease the flexibility of the blood vessels, or increase the likelihood of clots forming in the blood. Since vitamin B_6, folate, and vitamin B_{12} are all involved in breaking down homocysteine in the body, researchers began studying the effect of these vitamins on this amino acid.[4]

Numerous studies have suggested that low blood levels of these B vitamins, especially folate, are associated with an increased level of homocysteine in the body. In fact, the mandatory addition of folic acid to enriched grains and grain products that began in the late 1990s to prevent certain birth defects may also be fighting heart disease. In a study of over 1,000 individuals, the average blood level of folate was higher and the level of the amino acid homocysteine lower in individuals seen in the time period after the implementation of the folic acid enrichment program as compared to before the program began.[5]

Studies are currently under way to determine if taking supplements of these B vitamins will lower the risk of heart disease. Until more is known, you should eat a diet that is naturally rich in these B vitamins.

Are There Other Important Nutrients?

Choline Is an Essential Nutrient

Choline is an essential nutrient that your body needs for healthy cells and nerves, but it is not classified as a vitamin. Although your body can synthesize it, a study has shown that males given choline-deficient diets weren't able to synthesize enough of it to meet their needs and experienced liver damage. Research has not yet determined whether this would occur in women, infants, children, and older adults.[78] To be safe, the current recommendation of 425 milligrams for women and 550 milligrams for men is based on the amount needed to protect your liver.

Choline is so widely available in foods, especially milk, liver, eggs, and peanuts, that it unlikely that your intake would ever fall short. However, too much choline from supplements can cause sweating and vomiting as well as **hypotension** (*hypo* = low), or low blood pressure. Too much choline can also cause a person to emit an unpleasant fishy odor as the body tries to get rid of the excess. The upper level of 3,500 milligrams for choline has been set to prevent your blood pressure from dropping too low and to keep you from smelling like a fish.

Carnitine, Lipoic Acid, and Inositol Are Vitamin-like Substances

Certain vitamin-like substances are needed for overall health and important body functions, but they are not considered essential nutrients because your body can synthesize them in adequate amounts without consuming them in foods, and deficiency symptoms are not known to occur in humans.

choline A vitamin-like substance needed for healthy cells and nerves.

hypotension Low blood pressure.

Carnitine (*carnus* = flesh) is needed to properly utilize fat. It is abundant in foods from animal sources, such as meat and dairy products. Although there is no research to support the claim, carnitine supplements are sometimes advertised to promote weight loss and help athletes improve their performance.[79]

Similar to many B vitamins, **lipoic acid** helps your cells generate energy, and it was in fact initially thought to be a vitamin.[80] Lipoic acid is also being studied for its potential role as an antioxidant that could help reduce the risk of certain chronic diseases, such as diabetes mellitus and cataracts.

Lastly, **inositol** is needed to keep cell membranes healthy. Inositol can be found in foods from plant sources. As with the other important vitamin-like substances, healthy individuals can synthesize enough inositol to meet their needs, so supplements are not necessary.

The Take-Home Message Choline is an essential nutrient that is needed for healthy cells and nerves. Carnitine, lipoic acid, and inositol are needed for important body functions and overall health, but are not essential nutrients. Your body can synthesize these substances in adequate amounts, and there are no known deficiency symptoms.

What Are Antioxidants?

Antioxidants (*anti* = against; *oxidants* = oxygen-containing substances) are a group of compounds that include vitamins E and C, the mineral selenium, **flavonoids** (colorful pigments found in fruits and vegetables), and carotenoids (such as beta-carotene, zeaxanthin, lutein, and lycopene). Just as their name implies, antioxidants counteract the **oxidation** that takes place in your cells.

During oxidation harmful oxygen-containing molecules called **free radicals** damage your cells by altering their structure, their proteins, and even their DNA.[81] Free radicals are the by-products of your body's metabolic reactions when you create energy from food. Free radicals can also result from exposure to chemicals in the environment (such as cigarette smoke and air pollution) and from the damaging effects of the sun's ultraviolet rays on unprotected skin.

Free radicals have an unpaired **electron,** which makes them very unstable. These restless molecules act like thieves on the prowl, looking to steal an electron from another molecule in order to become more stable. Once such a robbery takes place, a new free radical is created and becomes a thief in pursuit of another molecule to attack. A free radical can also become stable by dumping its unpaired electron onto another molecule. This causes the molecule that takes on the electron to become a new free radical. Antioxidants are part of your body's natural defense system to harness free radicals and stop them from damaging cells.

If free radicals accumulate faster than your body can neutralize them, a condition known as **oxidative stress,** their damaging effects can contribute to various chronic diseases and conditions, including heart disease, cancer, aging, diabetes mellitus, arthritis, Parkinson's disease and Alzheimer's disease.[82] Figure 7.4 on page 244 illustrates free radicals in action in your body.

Free radicals can also be damaging to your eyes, contributing to **age-related macular degeneration (AMD)** and cataracts. AMD results from damage to the macula, a tiny area of the eye that is needed for central vision (the ability to see things that are directly in front of you). The macula is shown in the eye illustrated in

carnitine A vitamin-like substance needed to properly utilize fat.

lipoic acid A vitamin-like substance in your body needed in energy production; it may also act as an antioxidant.

inositol A substance synthesized in your body that helps to keep your cells and their membranes healthy.

antioxidants Substances that neutralize free radicals that can cause cell damage. Vitamins A, C, and E and beta-carotene are antioxidants.

flavonoids A food pigment that acts as an antioxidant in many fruits, vegetables, tea, and wine that may help reduce the risk of chronic diseases.

oxidation The process during which oxygen combines with other molecules.

free radicals Unstable oxygen-containing molecules that can damage the cells of the body and possibly contribute to the increased risk of chronic diseases.

electron The negatively charged particles in an atom, which is the smallest unit of all matter. Electrons determine how atoms interact with one another.

oxidative stress A condition whereby the production of harmful free radicals overwhelms the ability of the body's natural defense system to keep them at bay.

age-related macular degeneration (AMD) A disease that affects the macula of the retina, causing blurry vision.

Figure 7.4 Free Radicals
(a) Free radicals are the by-products of normal reactions in your body as well as exposure to chemicals in the environment and the damaging effects of the sun's ultraviolet rays. Free radicals can damage cells and tissues and lead to chronic diseases. **(b)** Antioxidants help neutralize free radicals, limiting the damage that free radicals cause and helping to reduce the risk of many chronic diseases.

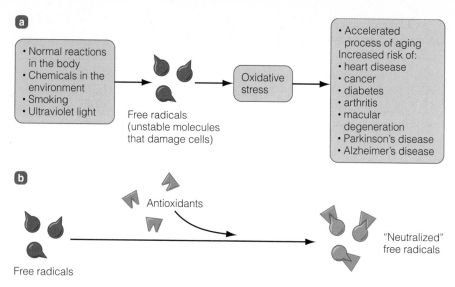

a
- Normal reactions in the body
- Chemicals in the environment
- Smoking
- Ultraviolet light

Free radicals (unstable molecules that damage cells)

Oxidative stress

- Accelerated process of aging Increased risk of:
- heart disease
- cancer
- diabetes
- arthritis
- macular degeneration
- Parkinson's disease
- Alzheimer's disease

b
Antioxidants

Free radicals

"Neutralized" free radicals

a Normal vision

b Age-related macular degeneration

c Cataract

Figure 7.5 Normal and Impaired Vision
(a) Normal vision and the ability to clearly see the world around you is often taken for granted. **(b)** People with age-related macular degeneration (AMD) have difficulty seeing things directly in front of them. **(c)** Cataracts cause vision to become cloudy.

Source: National Institutes of Health, National Eye Institute

the Vitamin A section. AMD can make activities such as reading, driving, and watching television impossible (Figure 7.5). AMD is usually the culprit when Americans 60 years of age and older experience blindness.[83]

A study conducted by the National Eye Institute (NEI), a branch of the National Institutes of Health (NIH), discovered that supplements containing large amounts of antioxidants (vitamin C, Vitamin E, and beta-carotene) along with the minerals zinc and copper were effective in reducing the risk of AMD as well as the loss of vision in individuals with advanced stages of AMD. Some studies have also suggested that specific antioxidants—namely vitamins C and E and the carotenoids lutein and zeaxanthin—may help lower the risk of cataracts.[84]

A **cataract** is a common eye condition among older adults where the lens of the eye becomes cloudy, resulting in blurred vision, as shown in Figure 7.5. More than half of all Americans have experienced cataracts by the time they reach 80 years of age, and many undergo surgery to remove them. NEI recommends consuming antioxidant- and carotenoid-rich vegetables and fruits, such as citrus fruits, broccoli, and dark leafy green vegetables for the health of your eyes.[85]

There is no question that antioxidants play an important role in your body and that diets high in antioxidant-rich fruits, vegetables, and whole grains are associated with lower incidences of some diseases. However, these foods may provide protection beyond what these antioxidants offer. Other compounds may work with antioxidants to provide protection.

For example, **phytochemicals** (*phyto* = plant), naturally occurring plant compounds that give fruits and vegetables their vibrant colors, have many beneficial functions in the body, such as acting as antioxidants, stimulating the immune system, and interacting with hormones that may help prevent certain cancers.[86] Carotenoids and flavonoids are considered phytochemicals that have antioxidant properties. Table 7.1 emphasizes the importance of a colorful diet in getting your share of phytochemicals.

Fruits, vegetables, and whole grains are also rich in disease-fighting fiber, vitamins and minerals, and they are low in heart-unhealthy saturated fat. It is likely that all of these attributes work together with the phytochemicals to provide protection from chronic diseases, in particular, heart disease and cancer.

The big question that remains is if antioxidant *supplements* provide the same health protection as antioxidants consumed in foods. Studies are currently under way exploring the role of antioxidant supplements in fighting disease. At this time,

Table 7.1

The Phytochemical Color Guide

The National Cancer Institute recommends eating a variety of colorful fruits and vegetables daily to provide your body with valuable vitamins, minerals, fiber, and disease-fighting phytochemicals. Whole grains also have phytochemicals and have been added to this list.

Color	Phytochemical	Found In
Red	Anthocyanins	Apples, beets, cabbage, cherries, cranberries, red cabbage, red onion, red beans
Yellow/Orange	β-Carotene	Apricots, butternut squash, cantaloupe, carrots, mangoes, peaches, pumpkin, sweet potatoes
	Flavonoids	Apricots, clementines, grapefruits, lemons, papaya, pears, pineapple, yellow raisins
White	Alliums/allicin	Chives, garlic, leeks, onions, scallions
Green	Lutein, zeaxanthin	Broccoli, collard greens, honeydew melon, kale, kiwi, lettuce, mustard greens, peas, spinach
	Indoles	Arugula, broccoli, bok choy, brussels sprouts, cabbage, cauliflower, kale, Swiss chard, turnips
Blue/Purple	Anthocyanins	Blackberries, black currants, elderberries, purple grapes
	Phenolics	Eggplant, plums, prunes, raisins
Brown	β-gluton, lignans, phenols, plant sterols, phytoestrogens, saponins, tocotrienols	Barley, brown rice, oats, oatmeal, whole grains, whole-grain cereals, whole wheat

Source: Adapted from the National Institute of Health, National Cancer Institute's The Color Guide. Available at www.5aday.gov/color.

the American Heart Association, National Cancer Institute, and United States Preventive Services Task Force do not advocate taking supplements to reduce the risk of specific diseases, but encourage eating a phytochemical- and antioxidant-rich well-balanced diet.[87] Filling your plate with a colorful variety of plant-based foods is currently one of the best-known strategies to fight chronic diseases.

The Take-Home Message Antioxidants, such as vitamins E and C, the mineral selenium, flavonoids, and carotenoids help counteract the damaging effects of oxygen-containing molecules called free radicals. If free radicals accumulate faster than your body can neutralize them, their damaging effects can contribute to chronic diseases and conditions. Fruits, vegetables, and whole grains are wonderful sources of antioxidants.

cataract A common eye disorder that occurs when the lens of the eye becomes cloudy.

phytochemicals Naturally occurring substances in fruits, vegetables, and whole grains that protect against certain chronic diseases.

NUTRITION IN THE REAL WORLD

eLearn

Salad Bar Savvy

A trip to your local salad bar can be a wonderful way to add vitamin-rich vegetables to your diet. However, some of the food choices at a salad bar may also be high in heart-unhealthy saturated fat. To learn how to build a heart-friendly, vitamin-rich salad at the salad bar, visit www.aw-bc.com/blake.

How Should You Get Your Vitamins?

Natural food sources, like fruits and vegetables, have long been advocated as an excellent way to get your vitamins. With advances in fortified foods and supplements, new options became available for meeting your nutrient needs. Let's look at the pros and cons of each of these next.

Foods Are Still the Best Way to Meet Your Vitamin Needs

Because foods provide more than just vitamins (many are also rich in disease-fighting phytochemicals, antioxidants, and fiber), they are the best way to meet your vitamin needs. The substances and nutrients in foods all work together to keep you healthy. For example, the fat in your salad dressing helps you absorb the carotenoids in the carrots in your salad. The vitamin-C rich tomatoes on your sandwich help you absorb the iron in the wheat bread. The whole is indeed greater than the sum of its parts when it comes to eating a balanced diet to meet your vitamin needs.

The *Dietary Guidelines for Americans* 2005 recommends eating a wide variety of foods from each food group and has increased the amount of fruits, vegetables, whole grains, and dairy foods in the recommended diet, as compared to previous years. These changes are reflected in MyPyramid and increase the opportunity to meet your daily vitamin needs. Figure 7.6 illustrates each food group and the vitamins that they contribute to your diet.

Table 7.2 shows the estimated intake for each nutrient that a 2,000-calorie diet based on the *Dietary Guidelines* will provide. As you can see from the table, vitamin E is the only nutrient that may be a challenge to meet.[88] However, adding some margarine on your morning toast, a few nuts to your yogurt, and a little salad dressing to your dinner salad would likely do the trick. Refer to the Table Tips for Vitamin E for more suggestions on meeting your vitamin needs for the day.

If you are falling short of some vitamins in your diet, fortified foods can help make up the difference.

Figure 7.6 Vitamins Found Widely in MyPyramid
Eating a wide variety of foods from all food groups will ensure that you meet your vitamin needs.

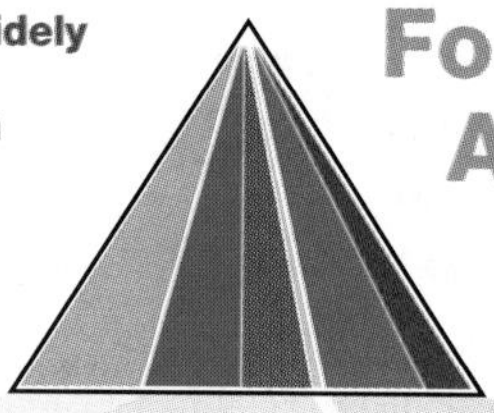

Grains	Vegetables	Fruit	Milk	Meat and Beans
Folic acid	Folate	Folate	Riboflavin	Niacin
Niacin	Vitamin A	Vitamin C	Vitamin A	Thiamin
Vitamin B_6	Vitamin C		Vitamin B_{12}	Vitamin B_6
Vitamin B_{12} (if fortified)	Vitamin E		Vitamin D	Vitamin B_{12}
Riboflavin				
Thiamin				

Fortified Foods Can Provide Additional Nutrients

When you pour your morning glass of orange juice, you know that you are getting a significant splash of vitamin C. However, depending on the brand of orange juice, you may also be meeting your vitamin E and vitamin D needs—two nutrients that are not (and never have been) naturally found in oranges. Welcome to the world of fortified foods.

Fortified foods are becoming more popular with the American consumer. Sales have tripled since 1997, with sales topping $18 billion in 2001 and expected to continue to grow.[89]

Table 7.2

You Can Meet Your Vitamin Needs with Healthy Food Choices

Nutrient	USDA Food Intake Pattern, 2,000 calories*	Institute of Medicine Recommendations RDA/AI
Vitamin A, μ RAE	1,057	900
Vitamin E, mg AT	9.0	15
Thiamin, mg	2.1	1.2
Riboflavin, mg	3.0	1.3
Niacin, mg	23	16.0
Vitamin B_6, mg	2.4	1.3
Vitamin B_{12}, μg	7.9	2.4
Folate, μg	610	400
Vitamin C, mg	174	90

*The highest intake level for young adult men or women is stated
Note: RDA = Recommended Dietary Allowance; AI = Adequate Intakes; RAE = retinol activity equivalents; AT = α-tocopherol; mg = milligrams; μg = micrograms

Source: U.S. Department of Agriculture. 2005. *Report of the Dietary Guidelines Advisory Committee on the Dietary Guidelines for Americans.* Available at www.health.gov/dietaryguidelines/dga2005/report. Accessed February 2005.

Fortified foods—that is, foods that have nutrients added to them—can be a valuable option for individuals whose diet fall short of some nutrients. For instance, someone who doesn't drink milk, such as a strict vegetarian or an individual who is lactose intolerant, would benefit from drinking vitamin D- and calcium-fortified soy milk. Older adults who are inactive and thus have lower calorie needs may choose fortified foods to add nutrients, such as vitamins B_{12} and E, to their limited dietary selections. Women in their childbearing years may look to folic acid-fortified cereals to help them meet their daily needs of this B vitamin.

However, fortified foods can do a disservice in the diet if they displace other vitamin- and mineral-rich foods. For example, a sugary orange drink that has vitamin C added to it should not replace vitamin C–rich orange juice. While the vitamin C content of the two beverages may be the same, the orange-flavored drink doesn't compare to the juice when it comes to providing other nutrients and phytochemicals. As you can see from Figure 7.7 on the next page, the orange drink is basically orange-flavored water sweetened with 7 teaspoons of sugar and enriched with vitamin C.

A diet containing numerous fortified foods can put you at risk of overconsuming some nutrients. If a heavily fortified food, like some cereals, snack bars, and beverages, claims to contain "100% of the vitamins needed daily," then eating several servings of the food or a combination of several fortified foods is similar to taking several multivitamin supplements. You are more likely to overconsume vitamins from fortified foods than from whole foods.

Fortified foods can give your diet a vitamin boost.

Vitamin Supplements Are Not a Substitute for Healthy Eating

An estimated 40 percent of Americans spend over $1 billion a year on vitamin and mineral supplements. In a survey in the United States, the most popular reason for taking supplements was for good "health" and because they are "good for you." Vitamin

fortified foods Foods with added nutrients.

Figure 7.7 What Are You Pouring in Your Glass?
While both of these beverages are a good source of vitamin C, they are worlds apart in their nutrition. **(a)** Pure orange juice is also an excellent source of the mineral potassium and doesn't contain any added sugar. **(b)** Orange drink is basically sugar water with vitamin C added to it. A glass will contain the equivalent of 7 teaspoons of added sugar.

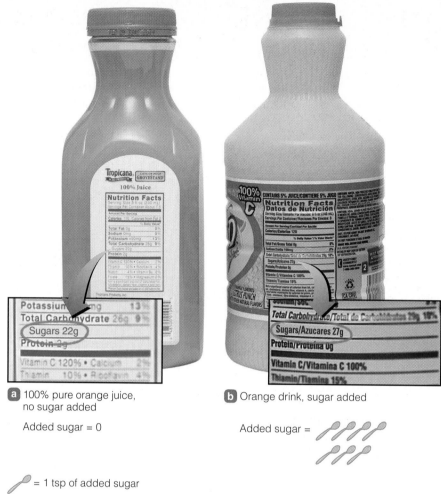

a 100% pure orange juice, no sugar added

Added sugar = 0

b Orange drink, sugar added

Added sugar =

= 1 tsp of added sugar

and mineral supplements are the third most popular over-the counter drug category that Americans buy.[90]

Vitamin supplements are called supplements for a reason: A vitamin pill or a combined multivitamin and mineral pill may be used to *supplement* your diet. Supplements should never be used to replace a healthy diet. A consistent diet of nonnutritious foods followed by a daily supplement won't transform your less-than-desirable eating habits into a healthy diet. The disease-fighting phytochemicals, fiber, and other substances that your body needs are all missing from a bottle of supplements.

Who Might Benefit from a Supplement?

Supplements are useful for people who cannot meet their nutrient needs through a regular, varied diet. Among those who may benefit from taking a dietary supplement are:[91]

- Women of childbearing age who may become pregnant, as they need to consume adequate amounts of folic acid to prevent certain birth defects
- Pregnant and lactating women who can't meet their increased nutrient needs with foods
- Older individuals, who need adequate amounts of synthetic vitamin B_{12}
- Individuals who do not drink enough milk and/or do not have adequate sun exposure to meet their vitamin D needs
- Individuals on low-calorie diets that limit the amount of vitamin and minerals they can consume through food

NUTRITION IN THE REAL WORLD

eLearn
Do I Shake the Cantaloupe to Tell If It's Ripe?

Fruits are loaded with vitamins and antioxidants, but how do you spot Mother Nature's tastiest gems? To learn how to find the ripest fruit at the supermarket, visit www.aw-bc.com/blake.

Foods, Fortified Foods, and Supplements

There are a variety of ways to meet your vitamin needs. Consider the pros and cons to find out the best combination for you.

◄ **Foods**
Pros: Sources of other nutrients and energy; can supply phytochemicals, antioxidants, and fiber; delicious and satisfying
Cons: Need to shop and prepare for meals; need to plan for in diet

Supplements ►
Pros: Easy to obtain; no planning or preparation involved
Cons: Can be expensive; risk of overconsumption of nutrients; lack of antioxidants, phytochemicals, and fiber found naturally in foods; not satisfying

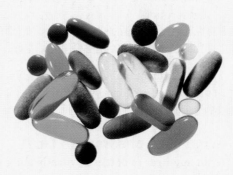

Fortified Foods ▲
Pros: Easy to obtain a specific nutrient; can be delicious and satisfying
Cons: Often more expensive than regular variety; risk of overconsumption of nutrients; can displace a more nutrient-dense food

- Strict vegetarians, who have limited dietary options for vitamins B_{12} and D and other nutrients
- Individuals with food allergies or a lactose intolerance that limits food choices
- Individuals who abuse alcohol, have medical conditions such as intestinal disorders, or are taking medications that may increase their need of certain vitamins

Always talk to your health care professional or a registered dietitian before taking a vitamin or mineral supplement to make sure it is appropriate based on your medical history. Supplements can interact or interfere with certain medications, so you will also need to check with your doctor if you are taking prescription medications. If you regularly eat many fortified foods, the addition of a supplement could cause you to overconsume some nutrients. A meeting with a registered dietitian for a diet "checkup" can help you decide if a supplement is needed.

Who's Minding the Vitamin Store?

Dietary supplements, a category that includes vitamins, minerals, and herbs, are regulated less stringently by the Food and Drug Administration (FDA) than drugs. In 1994, Congress passed the Dietary Supplement Health and Education Act which shifted the responsibility for determining the quality, effectiveness, and safety of the dietary supplements from the FDA to the manufacturers. Unlike drugs, dietary supplements do not need approval from the FDA before they can be marketed to the public unless they contain a new ingredient that hadn't been used prior to 1994. Recall from Chapter 2 that supplement manufacturers are legally permitted to make a structure/function claim on the labels of dietary supplements. The FDA cannot remove a

supplement from the marketplace unless it has been shown to be unsafe or harmful to the consumer.[92]

The FDA is trying to tighten its regulation of dietary supplements to better safeguard the public against harmful products and misleading claims. One way it plans to do this is to improve the criteria that it uses to make enforcement decisions about dietary supplements. The FDA is also trying to improve its process for evaluating potential safety concerns and adverse reports that may arise from a variety of sources including consumers, media reports, consumer groups, and experts.

There is an organization that provides some guidance for consumers when it comes to labeling dietary supplements. The **U.S. Pharmacopoeia (USP)** is a nonprofit organization that sets standards for dietary supplements.[93] While they do *not* endorse or validate health claims that the supplement manufacturers make, they will test the supplement to ensure that it

- contains the ingredients in the amounts stated on the label
- will disintegrate and dissolve in a reasonable amount of time in the body for proper absorption
- is free of contaminants
- has been manufactured using safe and sanitary procedures

Supplement manufacturers can voluntarily submit their products to the USP's staff of scientists for review. Products that meet the preceding criteria can display USP's seal on their labels.

What's a Consumer to Do?

With hundreds of bottles of vitamin and mineral supplements available on the store shelves, you could get dizzy trying to find one that's right for you. The best place to start when picking a supplement is to carefully read the label. The FDA has strict guidelines for the information that must appear on any supplement label. For example, the term "high potency" can only be used if at least two-thirds of the nutrients in the supplement contain at least 100 percent of the daily value (Figure 7.8). The label must also clearly identify the contents of the bottle. While a supplement may have

Figure 7.8 Supplement Smarts
The FDA has strict guidelines for the information that must appear on any supplement label. **(a)** The FDA allows the term "high potency" to be used as long as at least two-thirds of the nutrients contain at least 100 percent of the daily value. **(b)** All supplements must clearly identify what is in the bottle. **(c)** Always look for the USP seal of approval for quality and purity. Choose the cheapest supplement with the seal to save you a few dollars. **(d)** The FDA disclaimer is a reminder that this doesn't have the FDA seal of approval for effectiveness. **(e)** The structure/function claim explains that vitamin C is beneficial for your immune system. **(f)** The net quantity of contents must be listed. The Nutrition Facts Panel lists the serving size, the vitamins in the supplement, and the amount of the vitamin in each capsule. **(g)** The amount of each supplement is also given as a percentage of the daily value. Remember, the daily value may be higher than you actually need. **(h)** All the ingredients must be listed in descending order by weight. **(i)** The name and address of the manufacturer or distributor must be provided.

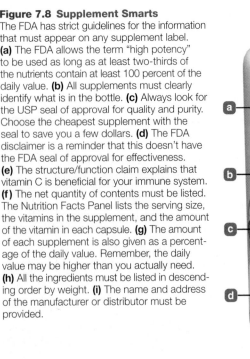

When you need to perform your best, take vitamin C. It's a smart choice to help your immune system.

DIRECTIONS FOR USE: Take one capsule daily.

Supplement Facts

Serving Size 1 Capsule		%DV
Amount Per Capsule		
Vitamin C	60mg	100%

Other ingredients: Gelatin, water, and ascorbic acid.

XYZ Company
Some Place, NJ 00001

U.S. Pharmacopeia (USP) A nonprofit organization that sets purity and reliability standards for dietary supplements.

the USP seal of approval for quality and purity, it doesn't have the FDA's approval, even if it makes a claim. Supplements must contain a panel that lists the serving size, the number of tablets in the bottle, the amount of the vitamin in each capsule, and the percentage of the daily value. All the ingredients must also be listed.

The Take-Home Message A well-balanced diet that provides adequate calories can meet most individuals' daily vitamin needs. Fortified foods, as part of a healthy diet, can provide extra nutrients for those whose diets fall short. A vitamin supplement is another option for individuals unable to meet their daily vitamin needs. The consumer needs to take care when selecting a dietary supplement and should seek advice and guidance from a qualified health professional.

Putting It All Together

You have learned thus far that your diet needs to be adequate in carbohydrates, proteins, healthy fats, and now vitamins for your body to function properly. A diet rich in whole grains, fruits, and vegetables and adequate in lean dairy foods and meats, poultry, fish, and healthy oils can help provide these nutrients in the proper balance for good health.

Two Points of View

Can Some Sun Exposure Be a Good Thing?

While skin cancer is the most common form of cancer in the United States and exposure to the sun's ultraviolet (UV) rays increases the risk for this cancer, sun exposure is also a major source of vitamin D for your body. Can some sun exposure be a good thing for overall good health? Let's discuss this hot topic with two skin and cancer experts.

Michael Holick, MD, PhD
Author of *The UV Advantage*

 **Dr. Michael Holick, MD, PhD,** is professor of medicine, physiology, and dermatology and chief of endocrinology, metabolism, and nutrition at Boston University School of Medicine. Dr. Holick is a renowned researcher and expert on vitamin D and the author of *The UV Advantage.* Dr. Holick advocates that some sun exposure is beneficial, as it decreases the risk of many chronic diseases, such as osteoporosis, certain cancers, high blood pressure, type 1 diabetes, multiple sclerosis (MS), and depression.

(continued)

Robert A. Smith, PhD
Director, Cancer Screening, American Cancer Society

 **Robert A. Smith, PhD,** is the director of cancer screening at the American Cancer Society's National Home Office. He is a cancer epidemiologist and an adjunct professor of epidemiology at Rollins School of Public Health at Emory University School of Medicine. He has served on national and federal advisory committees and workgroups, and is co-chair of the National Colorectal Cancer Roundtable.

(continued)

Can Some Sun Exposure Be a Good Thing?, continued

Michael Holick, MD, PhD, continued

Q: Many Americans are falling short of their daily dietary needs of vitamin D. What are your feelings about skin exposure to sunlight in order to obtain vitamin D, an essential nutrient?

A: Chronic, excessive exposure to sunlight and sunburn occurrences during childhood and young adult life significantly increases the risk of certain types of skin cancer. However, for most humans the sun is the major source of vitamin D in their body. Individuals need only a *minimum* amount of sun exposure to satisfy their vitamin D needs.

Q: Why do you feel so strongly about this issue?

A: Every cell and tissue in your body requires vitamin D for maximal function and to be healthy. Therefore, to maintain good health it's essential that you get an adequate source of vitamin D either from sun exposure or from supplements.

Q: The American Cancer Society recommends that individuals protect their skin from sun exposure by covering their bodies with clothing, including long-sleeve shirts and full-length pants, wearing a broad-brim hat, and applying sunscreen before going outdoors. Is there an amount of sun exposure that is considered healthy and safe?

A: Yes. Some sensible exposure of your skin to the sun for several minutes every day could meet your daily vitamin D needs without significantly increasing the risk of skin cancer.

Q: Some research suggests that sensible sun exposure—exposing the arms and legs or hands, arms, and face, to the sun for 5 to 15 minutes, two to three times per week, between 10 a.m. and 3 p.m. without sunscreen protection—is a reasonable approach to meeting a person's vitamin D needs. What do you think of this recommendation? Would this amount of sun exposure increase the risk of skin cancer?

A: This amount of sensible sun exposure in the spring, summer, and autumn would create enough vitamin D to last through the winter for those living in higher latitudes, such as the Northeast, when the sun isn't strong enough during this season, so little vitamin D is made in the body. This amount of sensible sun exposure isn't of the magnitude to significantly increase the risk of skin cancer. However, after the recommended time, you should apply a broad-spectrum sunscreen (one that blocks UVA and UVB rays) with a high-SPF of 15 or more. Follow the directions on the sunscreen label to make sure that you apply it correctly.

Q: Research suggests that a vitamin D deficiency may be associated with an increased risk of certain cancers. What do you think about this association and the possible protective role that vitamin D could play?

Robert A. Smith, PhD, continued

Q: Many Americans are falling short of their daily dietary needs of vitamin D. What are your feelings about skin exposure to sunlight in order to obtain vitamin D, an essential nutrient?

A: Exposure to sunlight is clearly an easy, often rapid, and "free" way for the body to obtain vitamin D. However, exposure to sunlight—even in small amounts—also results in damage to the skin and an increase in risk of skin cancer. Direct exposure to the sun for vitamin D may be practical for individuals in some geographic areas, but for the majority of individuals in North America, it is unlikely to be an effective strategy.

Q: Why do you feel so strongly about this issue?

A: First, the duration of sun exposure will vary based on an individual's skin tone, age, location, the season of the year, the time of day, and the weather. Second, it simply isn't clear how much vitamin D a person needs in order to lower the risks for various cancers. Therefore, a recommendation that involves reducing one risk by raising another isn't practical. Thus, while a younger, light-skinned individual living in the southern latitudes might obtain sufficient vitamin D with 10 to 15 minutes of exposure to the hands, arms, and face three days per week, people with dark skin, the elderly, people living in northern latitudes, or in parts of the country with a greater average number of overcast days, would require longer exposures to ultraviolet light, with higher risks of skin damage.

Q: The American Cancer Society recommends that individuals protect their skin from sun exposure by covering their bodies with clothing, including long-sleeve shirts and full-length pants, wearing a broad-brim hat, and applying sunscreen before going outdoors. Is there an amount of sun exposure that is considered healthy and safe?

A: This is a fair question. Certainly some exposure to the sun has healthy benefits (such as the synthesis of vitamin D), but unprotected exposure to UV radiation can begin to cause damage to the skin within several minutes. It is important to understand that over the course of a *lifetime* we accumulate skin damage from UV radiation. These current recommendations for sun protection are intended to minimize damage to the skin caused by UV radiation and reduce risk of skin cancer. The recommendations are practical and intended to balance daily activities with appropriate skin protection.

Q: Some research suggests that sensible sun exposure—exposing the arms and legs or hands, arms, and face, to the sun for 5 to 15 minutes, two to three times per week, between 10 a.m. and 3 p.m. without sunscreen protection—is a reasonable approach to meeting a person's vitamin D

(continued)

(continued)

Can Some Sun Exposure Be a Good Thing?, continued

Michael Holick, MD, PhD, continued

A: For over 60 years, we have recognized an association between living at a higher latitude in the United States—which means less sun exposure and lower levels of vitamin D in the body—and the increased risk of dying from colon, breast, ovarian, and prostate cancers. Living in a higher latitude is also associated with an increased risk of developing multiple sclerosis, heart disease, hypertension, and type 2 diabetes. Meeting your vitamin D is important for good health.

Q: How should Americans meet their daily vitamin D needs?

A: Americans can meet their needs through the use of a supplement or, if they take the necessary precautions discussed above, through sensible sun exposure. It is difficult for some individuals to meet their current daily recommendation for vitamin D need with diet alone. In fact, some experts, including myself, think that the current daily recommendation for vitamin D is too low, which would make it even more challenging to meets one's needs through diet alone.

Robert A. Smith, PhD, continued

needs. What do you think of this recommendation? Would this amount of sun exposure increase the risk of skin cancer?

A: Even though this amount of sun exposure seems modest, it would result in damage to the skin, and would increase the risk of skin cancer albeit that increase in risk would be small overall, and would vary by the individual characteristics described above.

Q: Research suggests that a vitamin D deficiency may be associated with an increased risk of certain cancers. What do you think about this association and the possible protective role that vitamin D could play?

A: The findings are compelling and further research must become a high priority. If simply raising average vitamin D levels in the body could reduce cancer risk, this would be an exciting discovery for the public.

Q: How should Americans meet their daily vitamin D needs?

A: While diet can be a source of some vitamin D, it is very difficult to meet the current daily recommendation for vitamin D just through diet. Dietary supplements can be tailored to individual needs, and do not result in the trade-offs between the skin damage from unprotected sun exposure and your daily need for vitamin D. However, Americans should first consult their doctors before increasing vitamin D intake and also should watch for a change in the official recommendation.

NUTRITION IN THE REAL WORLD

Be a Nutrition Sleuth

Deciphering the Food Label

As mentioned in Chapter 2, the current Daily Values (DV) for vitamins and minerals that appear on the food label are based on reference values introduced in the 1970s! Consequently, these values may be higher or lower than the *latest* amounts recommended for each vitamin that you read about in this chapter.

Go to www.aw-bc.com/blake to see if you can figure out how much of vitamins A, D, and C are in typical breakfast cereals and milk. You may be surprised!

NUTRITION IN THE REAL WORLD

Get Real!

Are You Meeting Your Vitamin Needs?

Let's get real and find out if you are getting an adequate amount of vitamins in your diet. Go to www.aw-bc.com/blake and use the food chart to enter a typical daily diet. Don't forget to put in any vitamin supplements or fortified foods that you consume.

Use Appendix A or the MyDietAnalysis program to complete the chart to see how you fare with these specific vitamins. You may discover that there are vitamins you are getting too much or too little of in your diet.

The Top Ten Points to Remember

1. Vitamins are essential nutrients needed by your body to grow, reproduce, and maintain good health. They are found naturally in foods, added to foods, or in pill form in dietary supplements.

2. Fat-soluble vitamins are stored in your body and need fat to be absorbed. They can accumulate to the point of toxicity if your intake is excessive. Water-soluble vitamins are absorbed with water and typically aren't stored for extended periods. Excess amounts of water-soluble vitamins do not accumulate to toxic levels, but can be harmful if you routinely consume too much.

3. Vitamin A is needed for strong vision, reproduction, and healthy fetal development. Carotenoids are yellow-reddish pigments that give some fruits and vegetables their vibrant yellow-red color. One carotenoid, beta-carotene, is a provitamin that can be converted to vitamin A in your body. Two other carotenoids, lutein and zeaxanthin, are being investigated for their potential role in eye health.

4. Vitamin D is necessary for absorption of calcium and phosphorus. Although vitamin D can be made in your body with the help of ultraviolet rays from the sun, some individuals are not exposed to enough sunlight to meet their needs. A deficiency of vitamin D can cause rickets in children and osteomalacia in adults. Milk and fortified yogurts are excellent sources of vitamin D.

5. Vitamin E is an antioxidant that protects your cells' membranes. It plays an important role in helping prevent the "bad" LDL cholesterol carrier from being oxidized. High levels of artery-clogging, oxidized LDL cholesterol are a risk factor for heart disease. Vitamin K helps your blood to clot and to synthesize proteins that keep bones healthy.

6. The B vitamins thiamin, riboflavin, niacin, vitamin B_6, pantothenic acid, and biotin are all coenzymes that help numerous energy-producing reactions.

7. The B vitamins folate and vitamin B_{12} are needed for healthy red blood cells. A deficiency of either can cause macrocytic anemia. Adequate amounts of folic acid can reduce the risk of certain birth defects. A prolonged vitamin B_{12} deficiency can cause nerve damage.

8. Vitamin C is needed for healthy bones, teeth, skin, and blood vessels, and for a healthy immune system. Excessive amounts can cause intestinal discomfort. Vitamin C doesn't prevent the common cold but may reduce the duration and severity of a cold in some people once it is contracted.

9. Antioxidants, such as vitamins E and C and beta-carotene suppress harmful oxygen-containing molecules called free radicals that can damage cells. Free radicals can contribute to chronic diseases such as cancer and heart disease and accelerate the aging process. Diets rich in antioxidant-rich fruits, vegetables, and whole grains are associated with a lower incidence of many diseases.

10. Fortified foods and vitamin supplements can help individuals with inadequate diets to meet their nutrient needs. However, supplements should never replace a healthy diet. The U.S. Pharmacopoeia (USP) seal on a supplement label indicates that the supplement has been tested and meets the criteria for purity and accuracy.

Test Your Knowledge

1. Which of the following vitamins are water-soluble? (Circle all that apply.)
   a. vitamin A
   b. vitamin C
   c. vitamin B_6
   d. vitamin K
   e. folic acid

2. The most usable form of vitamin A in your body is
   a. retinol.
   b. retinal.
   c. retinoic acid.
   d. retinoids.
   e. none of the above.

3. Vitamin D is
   a. a hormone.
   b. made in your body with the help of sunlight.
   c. found in fortified milk.
   d. all of the above.
   e. a and b only.

4. You are enjoying a salad bar lunch (good choice!). You want to top your greens with vitamin E–rich foods. You could choose
   a. olive oil and vinegar.
   b. chopped nuts.
   c. avocado slices.
   d. all of the above.
   e. none of the above.

5. A deficiency of thiamin can cause
   a. rickets.
   b. beriberi.
   c. scurvy.
   d. osteomalacia.
6. Which of the following are considered antioxidants?
   a. vitamin E
   b. vitamin K
   c. beta-carotene
   d. all of the above
   e. a and c only
7. Adam Craig is 55 years old. Which of the following might his body have difficulty absorbing?
   a. The vitamin B_{12} in a piece of steak.
   b. The vitamin B_6 in liver.
   c. The folate in spinach.
   d. The riboflavin in milk.
   e. The thiamin in bread.
8. You are enjoying a lovely breakfast of raisin bran cereal doused in skim milk and a glass of orange juice. The vitamin C in the orange juice will enhance the absorption of
   a. the calcium in milk.
   b. the vitamin D in fortified milk.
   c. the iron in the cereal.
   d. none of the above.
   e. a and b only.
9. Folic acid can help reduce the risk of
   a. acne.
   b. neural tube defects.
   c. night blindness.
   d. pellagra.
   e. none of the above.
10. The USP seal on the vitamin label means that the dietary supplement has been tested and shown to
   a. be free of any contaminants.
   b. be manufactured using safe and sanitary procedures.
   c. contain the amount of the substance that is stated on the label.
   d. all of the above.
   e. a and b only.

Answers

1. (b, c, e) Vitamins C, B_6, and folic acid are water-soluble, whereas vitamins A and K are fat-soluble.
2. (b) Retinol is the most usable form of vitamin A in your body. Retinoids includes all three forms of preformed vitamin A: retinol, retinal, and retinoic acid.
3. (d) Vitamin D is a hormone and can be made in your body with the help of adequate exposure to the sun's ultraviolet rays. You can also obtain it by drinking fortified milk.
4. (d) Go for all of them. Vegetables, nuts, and avocados are all excellent sources of vitamin E.
5. (b) A chronic deficiency of thiamin can cause beriberi. A vitamin D deficiency can cause rickets in children and osteomalacia in adults. Scurvy is the result of a vitamin C deficiency.
6. (e) Both vitamin E and beta-carotene function as antioxidants in your body. While vitamin K isn't an antioxidant, it helps your blood clot.
7. (a) Approximately 10 to 30 percent of adults over the age of 50 have reduced secretions of acidic stomach juices, which affects the absorption of the vitamin B_{12} that is found naturally in food. The other B vitamins should be absorbed regardless of Adam's age.
8. (c) Vitamin C will help your body absorb the iron in grain products and cereals. Vitamin C does not affect the absorption of calcium or vitamin D. However, the vitamin D in the milk will help you absorb the mineral calcium.
9. (b) If consumed prior to and during the first several weeks of pregnancy, adequate amounts of folic acid can reduce the risk of neural tube defects, a birth defect that can occur early in pregnancy. Vitamin A–containing medication may be used to treat acne. Vitamin A can also help prevent night blindness. Consuming adequate amounts of niacin prevents pellagra.
10. (d) Manufacturers of dietary supplements can voluntarily have their products tested for all of the above. The U.S. Pharmacopoeia (USP) seal also signifies that the supplement has been tested for its ability to dissolve in a reasonable amount of time in your body so that it can be properly absorbed.

Web Support

- To learn more about phytochemicals, visit www.5aday.com/html/phytochem/pic_home.php
- For more information on the disease-fighting capabilities of fruits and vegetables, visit www.5aday.gov
- To find out the latest recommendations for vitamins, visit http://ods.od.nih.gov/Health_Information/Vitamin_and_Mineral_Supplement_Fact_Sheets.aspx
- To learn more about preparing and cooking vitamin-rich foods and vegetables, visit www.cdc.gov/nccdphp/dnpa/5aday/month/index.htm

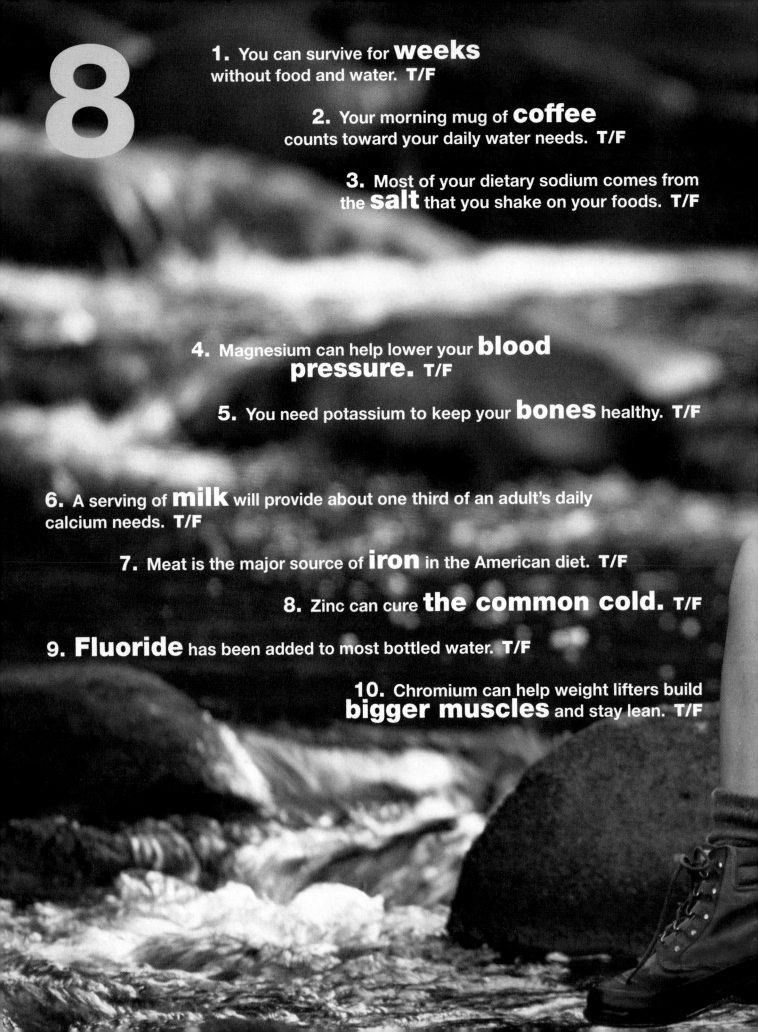

8

1. You can survive for **weeks** without food and water. **T/F**

2. Your morning mug of **coffee** counts toward your daily water needs. **T/F**

3. Most of your dietary sodium comes from the **salt** that you shake on your foods. **T/F**

4. Magnesium can help lower your **blood pressure**. **T/F**

5. You need potassium to keep your **bones** healthy. **T/F**

6. A serving of **milk** will provide about one third of an adult's daily calcium needs. **T/F**

7. Meat is the major source of **iron** in the American diet. **T/F**

8. Zinc can cure **the common cold.** **T/F**

9. **Fluoride** has been added to most bottled water. **T/F**

10. Chromium can help weight lifters build **bigger muscles** and stay lean. **T/F**

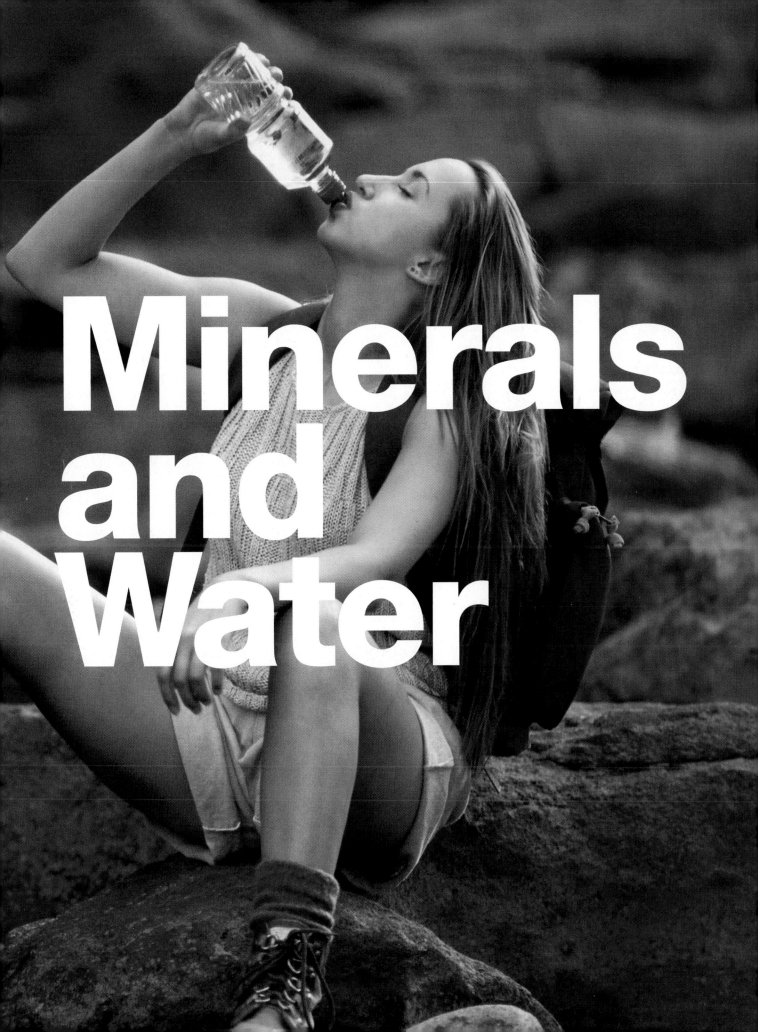

Minerals and Water

Desiree Kegan, a college sophomore, stops off at the campus convenience store every morning to buy a bottle of water to take to her classes and her part-time job. Later in the day, she purchases another bottle before heading for the gym. Her mother sent her a reusable water bottle that she could fill at numerous on-campus water fountains, but Desiree scoffed at her mom's suggestion to drink tap water instead of bottled water. Desiree believes that bottled water is pure and safer to drink than tap water. But if Desiree does a little homework, she will find that her assumptions about the quality of the campus tap water are incorrect, and her daily bottled water buys are burning an unnecessary hole in her wallet.

Everyone needs water to live, but is there really any benefit to drinking bottled water instead of tap water? This is one of several common questions we will answer as we explore the world of water and minerals.

Answers

1. False. You may be able to survive weeks without food but you couldn't live more than a few days without water. See this page to learn more.
2. True. Your mug of java does contribute to your daily water needs, even though it may contain caffeine, a diuretic. Turn to page 265 to find out why.
3. False. Although seasoning your food with salt adds sodium, it is not the major culprit in sodium overload. Turn to page 271 to find out what is.
4. True. Magnesium, along with calcium and potassium, is part of a diet that has been shown to substantially lower blood pressure. To find out more, turn to page 272.
5. True. A potassium-rich diet plays a key role in keeping your bones healthy and strong. However, that's not the only role of potassium in your body. Turn to page 274 to find out how important this mineral is.
6. True. In fact, the recommended three servings of milk, yogurt, and/or cheese will almost nail your calcium needs for the day. Unfortunately, most Americans' diets fall short of this food group. To find out how to meet your needs, turn to page 276.
7. False. While meat, fish, and poultry are fabulous sources of iron, they are not the main sources in Americans' diets. Turn to page 287 to find out what contributes the most iron to our diets.
8. False. Zinc lozenges are unlikely to clear up your runny nose and stuffy head. They could, however, cause some uncomfortable problems. Turn to page 290 to find out more.
9. False. Most bottled water sold in the United States doesn't contain fluoride. Turn to page 295 to find out why this could be bad news for your teeth.
10. False. Dream on. Turn to page 296 to learn the truth.

What do a cast-iron skillet, the salt on an icy road, and the copper pipes in some houses all have in common? They're made from some of the same **minerals** that play essential roles in your body. From iron to sodium to copper, these rocky substances occur as part of the earthen world around you and are necessary for your day-to-day functioning. Along with another essential nutrient, water, minerals help chemical reactions take place in your cells, help your muscles contract, and keep your heart beating. They are essential to your overall health and well-being.

In this chapter, we will explore the myriad roles that water and minerals play in your body. We will also find out how to make sure that you are meeting your daily needs for each of these nutrients and, equally important, how to avoid consuming toxic amounts.

What Is Water and Why Is It so Important?

Water is the most abundant substance in your body and, as such, is one of the most important. The average healthy adult is about 60 percent water. However, the amount of water in your body depends upon your age, gender, and the amount of fat and muscle tissue you carry (Figure 8.1). Muscle tissue is approximately 65 percent water, whereas fat tissue is only 10 to 40 percent water.[1] Males have a higher percentage of muscle mass and a lower percentage of fat tissue than females of the same age, so males will have more body water. For the same reason, muscular athletes will have a higher percentage of body water than sedentary individuals.

You could survive for weeks without food, but only a few days without water. This is in part because of water's role in allowing chemical reactions, including those that provide you with energy, to take place within your cells. Water is also part of your blood and the fluid that bathes your trillions of cells. It plays a key part in carrying nutrients to and removing wastes from your cells.

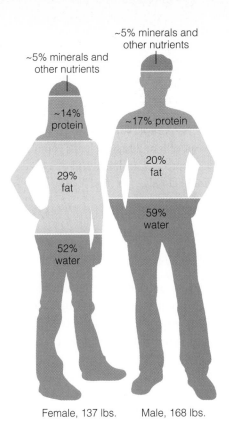

~5% minerals and other nutrients

~5% minerals and other nutrients

~14% protein

~17% protein

29% fat

20% fat

52% water

59% water

Female, 137 lbs.   Male, 168 lbs.

Figure 8.1 The Composition of Your Body
Your body is mostly water. Protein, fat, and minerals make up most of the rest of you.

Water is vital for many body functions, but it isn't stored in the body, so it's important to take in enough water every day.

As part of your body fluid, water is essential for maintaining fluid balance. You learned in Chapter 6 that fluid balance refers to the equal distribution of fluid among several compartments in your body. The fluid inside your cells is in the **intracellular fluid compartment,** whereas the fluid in the space outside your cells is in the **extracellular fluid compartment.** The extracellular fluids are further broken down into (1) **interstitial fluids,** which are in the space immediately outside your cells, and (2) the fluids in your blood (see Figure 8.2 on page 260). The interstitial fluids act as an area of exchange between your blood fluids and your cells. Maintaining the equal distribution of all this fluid is crucial to health, and your body has several mechanisms for this purpose.

Some minerals play an important role in balancing fluids between these compartments by acting as **electrolytes** (*electro* = electricity; *lytes* = soluble), or charged ions, in the body. For example, when the minerals sodium (Na) and chloride (Cl) dissolve in the watery solution of your blood, they become electrolytes because they break up into the charged ions of Na^+ and Cl^-. As electrolytes, the minerals potassium, phosphate, magnesium, calcium, and chloride play a role in attracting water into and out of blood and cells. However, sodium is the major electrolyte in your blood, and so has a greater effect than these other minerals. We will talk about minerals in greater depth later in this chapter.

The Take-Home Message Your body is mostly water. Muscle tissue has more water than fat tissue. The water in your body fluids is balanced among several compartments. Your intracellular fluids are inside your cells, whereas your extracellular fluids, comprised of interstitial fluid and fluid in the blood, are outside the cells and in your blood. Electrolytes help you maintain fluid balance.

minerals Inorganic elements essential to the nutrition of humans.

intracellular fluid compartment The fluid located inside your cells.

extracellular fluid compartment The fluid located outside your cells. Interstitial fluids and fluids in the blood are extracellular fluids.

interstitial fluids Fluids located between cells.

electrolytes Charged ions that conduct an electrical current in a solvent such as water. Sodium, potassium, and chloride are examples of electrolytes in the body.

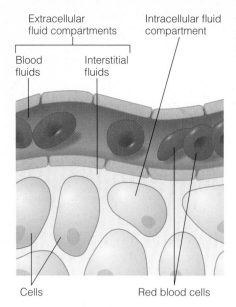

Extracellular fluid compartments | Intracellular fluid compartment

Blood fluids | Interstitial fluids

Cells | Red blood cells

Figure 8.2 Water Inside and Outside Your Cells
Water is a key component of the fluid compartments both inside and outside cells.

What Does Water Do in Your Body?

What are some of the essential roles that water plays in your body? For starters, it is a medium in which other substances can dissolve. As part of blood and other fluids, it also transports nutrients and substances between cells and tissues, helps you maintain a constant temperature, and lubricates and protects your joints and other areas. Let's explore each of these functions of water more closely.

Water Is the Universal Solvent and a Transport Medium

Water is a wonderful **solvent,** a liquid in which substances dissolve. In fact, water is commonly known as the universal solvent. As a solvent, water is part of the medium in which molecules come into contact with each other. This contact between molecules allows chemical reactions to take place. For example, the combining of specific amino acids to synthesize a protein occurs in the watery medium inside your cells.

Only about 45 percent of your blood is red blood cells; most of the rest is water. As part of blood, water helps transport oxygen, nutrients, and hormones to your cells. As part of interstitial fluid, water also helps transport waste products away from cells to be excreted in urine and stool.

Water Helps Maintain Body Temperature

The water in your blood is like the coolant that runs through a car. They both absorb, carry, and ultimately release heat in order to keep a running machine from overheating. In the case of the car, the coolant absorbs the heat from a running engine and carries it to the radiator for release. In your body, the water in your circulating blood absorbs the heat from your internal core and carries it to the skin for release (Figure 8.3). Water works so well as a coolant in both your car and your body because it has a unique ability to absorb and release a tremendous amount of heat.

Sometimes, your body's core may get too hot and this cooling mechanism is not enough to maintain a safe temperature. If you decided to go jogging on a hot summer day, the enormous amount of internal heat generated by this exercise would likely tax the heat-absorbing capacity of your body's water. The increasing heat breaks apart the hydrogen (H_2O) bonds of the water, transforming it from a liquid (sweat) to a vapor. The evaporation of sweat from your skin releases the heat and cools you down, thus maintaining a safe body temperature.

Water Is a Lubricant and a Protective Cushion

Water, combined with other molecules, acts as a lubricant for your joints and eyes. Water is also part of the saliva that moistens your mouth and foods and the mucus that lubricates your intestinal tract. Water is the main part of the fluid that surrounds certain organs, including your brain, and thus acts as a cushion to protect

solvent A liquid that acts as a medium in which substances dissolve. Water is considered the universal solvent.

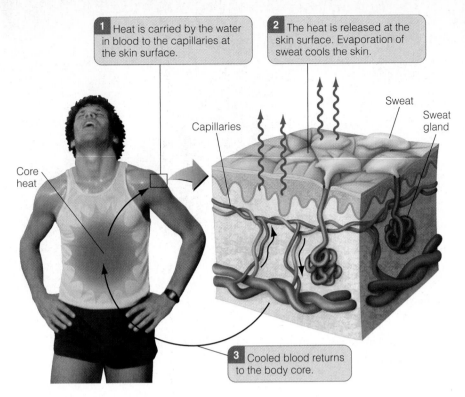

Figure 8.3 Water Helps Regulate Your Body Temperature

1 Heat is carried by the water in blood to the capillaries at the skin surface.

2 The heat is released at the skin surface. Evaporation of sweat cools the skin.

Sweat

Sweat gland

Capillaries

Core heat

3 Cooled blood returns to the body core.

them from injury during a fall or other trauma. During pregnancy, a developing fetus is surrounded by a sac of watery amniotic fluid, which helps protect it from any physical harm.

The Take-Home Message Water is a universal solvent that helps transport oxygen and nutrients throughout your body, absorbs and releases heat to regulate your body temperature, acts as a lubricant through saliva and mucus, and provides a protective cushion for your brain and other organs.

A developing fetus is cushioned in a sac of watery amniotic fluid to protect it from physical harm during pregnancy.

What Is Water Balance and How Do You Maintain It?

When the amount of water that you consume is equal to the amount that you lose daily, you are in **water balance.** When you are not in water balance—that is, having too much or too little water in your system—there can be negative effects. Thus, maintaining water balance is very important. There are several ways in which water is lost from your body and several mechanisms that help you replenish those losses. Let's look at how the whole process works.

You Take in Water through Beverages and Food

The first aspect of being in water balance is consuming enough water. You get most of your daily water from beverages such as tap or bottled water, milk, juices, and soft drinks. You also get some water from the foods that you eat, although much less in

water balance The state whereby an equal amount of water is lost and replenished daily in the body.

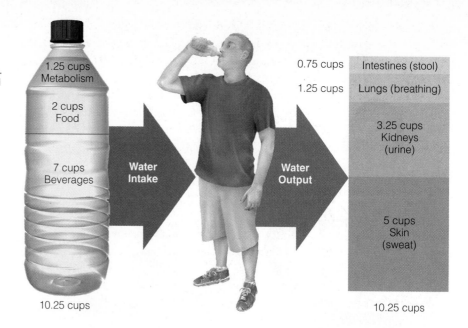

Figure 8.4 Water Intake and Water Output
You get most of your water from foods and beverages, though a small amount is also generated through the process of metabolism. You lose water in your urine, stool, sweat, and exhaled breath. The amount of water that you take in is balanced with the amount that you excrete every day.

comparison (Figure 8.4). Even the driest foods, like oatmeal and bread, provide some water. A small amount of water is also generated during metabolism.

You Lose Water through Your Kidneys, Large Intestine, Lungs, and Skin

The other aspect of water balance is excreting excess water so that you don't have too much in your body. You lose water daily through four routes: your kidneys, your intestinal tract, your lungs, and your skin. You lose much water via your kidneys in the form of urine, and some water is also lost through intestinal fluids in your stool. The water lost in your stool is normally a small amount unless you are experiencing diarrhea. The water that evaporates when you exhale and the water lost through your skin when you release the heat generated during normal reactions is called **insensible water loss,** as it occurs without your noticing it. An individual living in a moderate or temperate climate and doing little physical activity loses between one-half and one quart of water daily through insensible water loss.[2]

Insensible water loss doesn't include the water lost in sweat. Sweating is your body's way of releasing a higher than normal amount of heat. The amount of water lost during sweating varies greatly and depends upon many environmental factors, such as the temperature, the humidity, the wind, the sun's intensity, clothing worn, and the amount of physical activity you are doing.[3] For example, if you jump rope in the noontime sun on a summer day wearing a winter coat, you'll soon be losing a lot of water as sweat. In contrast, little or no sweat will leave your body if you sit under a shady tree on a dry, cool day wearing a light tee shirt and slacks.

Losing Too Much Water Can Cause Dehydration

Dehydration is a state in which you've lost too much, or aren't taking in enough, water. Dehydration can result from not drinking enough fluids and/or from conditions that

insensible water loss The water that is lost from the body daily through routine respiration and evaporation off the skin.

dehydration The state whereby there is too little water in the body due to too much water being lost, too little being consumed, or a combination of both.

diuretics Substances such as alcohol and some medications that cause the body to lose water.

thirst mechanism Various bodily reactions caused by dehydration that signal you to drink fluids.

osmosis The movement of a solvent, such as water, from an area of lower concentration of solutes across a membrane to an area of higher concentration of solutes. Osmosis balances the concentration of solutes between the compartments.

antidiuretic hormone (ADH) A hormone that directs the kidneys to concentrate and reduce the volume of urine produced in order to reduce water loss from the body.

result in too much water (and sodium) being lost from the body, such as diarrhea, vomiting, high fever, and the use of **diuretics.** If dehydration persists, a person can experience weight loss, dizziness, and confusion, as well as impairment of the ability to perform physical activity, and, in extreme situations, death.[4]

Have you ever been outside for a while on a hot day and noticed that your mouth was as dry as the Sahara Desert? The dry mouth is part of your **thirst mechanism,** and is your body's way of telling you to find a water source—you are on the road to dehydration. The thirst mechanism plays an important role in helping you avoid dehydration and restore the water balance in your body.

Your Thirst Mechanism Signals Dehydration

The dry mouth that makes you thirsty when you are dehydrated is due to the increased concentration of electrolytes in your blood. As the concentration of these minerals increases, less water is available to your salivary glands to make saliva.[5] Thus, your mouth feels very dry.

When you are dehydrated, the fluid volume in your blood decreases, resulting in a higher concentration of sodium in the blood. In order to restore balance, the fluid inside your cells will move through the membrane to the outside of the cell and into your blood to balance the concentration of sodium between these compartments. This movement of water across the cell membrane is called **osmosis** (see Figure 8.5).

Your brain detects the increased concentration of sodium in your blood and triggers your thirst mechanism, reminding you to drink fluids. Your brain will also trigger the secretion of **antidiuretic hormone (ADH)** from the pituitary gland. ADH causes your kidneys to decrease further loss of water and thus concentrate your urine.[6] These mechanisms work together to keep your body in water balance.

Other Ways to Tell if You Are Dehydrated

Just quenching your thirst will not typically provide enough fluids to remedy dehydration. This isn't a concern for moderately active individuals eating a balanced diet, as fluids from beverages and food throughout the day will eventually restore water balance.[7] However, elderly people, and individuals who are very physically active and/or who have vigorous jobs, such as fire fighters, are at higher risk of dehydration because they don't take in enough fluid, or they lose body water copiously through sweating. These individuals need to take additional steps to ensure that they are properly hydrated.

One way to monitor hydration is the cornerstone method, which involves measuring body weight before and after long bouts of high physical activity or labor and noting any changes. If a person weighs less after an activity than before, the weight change is due to loss of body water, and that water must be replenished. (Alternatively, if a weight gain is noted, overhydration is likely, and you need to drink less before your next activity.)

Urine color can also be used to assess hydration. When you are dehydrated, you produce less urine due to the release of ADH. The urine you do produce is more concentrated, as it contains a higher proportion of compounds to the smaller volume of water. This causes the urine to be darker in color.[8] The National Athletic Trainers Association has created a chart to help individuals assess if they are drinking enough fluids to offset the amount of water lost through sweating (see Figure 8.6).[9] If you are very physically active and the color of your urine darkens during the day, to the point where it resembles the shade of a "yield" sign or darker, you likely need to increase the amount of fluids in your diet. (Note: Other factors, such as consuming excessive amounts of the B vitamin, riboflavin, and certain medications can also affect the color of urine.)

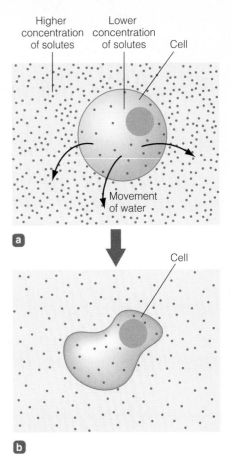

Figure 8.5 Osmosis
(a) Osmosis is the process whereby water moves through a membrane from an area of lower concentration of solutes to one that has a higher concentration of solutes. **(b)** This restores balance to the concentration of solutes on both sides of the membrane.

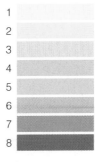

Figure 8.6 What the Color of Your Urine Can Tell
The color of your urine can help you determine if you are drinking enough fluids to avoid dehydration. If you collect your urine in a cup and it looks like the color of 1 through 3 on the chart, you are well hydrated. If it resembles color 7 or is darker, you are dehydrated and need to drink more fluids.

Consuming Too Much Water Can Cause Hyponatremia

For healthy individuals who consume a balanced diet, it's hard to consume too much water, because the body will just produce more urine to eliminate the excess. However, some individuals have experienced water toxicity in certain circumstances, particularly soldiers during military training and athletes who participate in endurance events such as marathons.[10]

In April 2002, 28-year-old Cynthia Lucero was running the Boston Marathon. About five miles from the finish line, Lucero began to feel wobbly and mentioned to a friend that she felt dehydrated even though she had been consuming fluids throughout her run. She suddenly collapsed and was taken to a nearby hospital. She died the next day, not of dehydration, but of overhydration. The cause of death was swelling of the brain brought on by too low a level of sodium in the blood, or **hyponatremia** (*hypo* = under, *natrium* = sodium, *emia* = blood), caused by overconsumption of fluids.[11]

When swelling occurs in the brain, the person can experience symptoms similar to those of dehydration—fatigue, confusion, and disorientation.[12] Mistakenly treating these symptoms by consuming more fluids will only make matters worse.

Even though dehydration is more common and a bigger challenge to physically active individuals than overhydration, the seriousness of overhydration has prompted the USA Track & Field association to revise its hydration guidelines for long-distance and marathon runners to avoid hyponatremia. Chapter 11 will provide these guidelines and show you how to calculate how much fluid you need during exercise.

How Much Water Do You Need and What Are the Best Sources?

Your daily water requirements may be different from those of your grandparents, parents, siblings, and even the classmate sitting next to you. The amount of water a person needs depends on his or her physical activity, environmental factors such as air temperature, and diet. (Recall from Chapter 4 that increasing the fiber in your diet should be accompanied by an increase in water consumption.)

The current recommendation for the amount of water you should consume daily is based on the reported total water intake (from both beverages and food) of healthy Americans.[13] Currently, healthy female adults consume about 12 cups, whereas men consume about 16 cups of water daily. About 80 percent of this intake is from beverages. Therefore, adult women should ingest about 9 cups (~80 percent of 12 cups), and adult males, approximately 13 cups (~80 percent of 16 cups) of beverages daily. People who are very active will have higher water requirements because they lose more water by sweating.

If you think that sounds like a lot, keep in mind that a well-balanced, 2,200-calorie diet that includes beverages at all meals and snacks will provide about 12 cups of water.[14] Drinking water, either from the tap or from a bottle, milk, and juices throughout the day can help you meet your needs. The feature box "Tap Water or Bottled Water: Is Bottled Better?" discusses the differences and similarities between tap water and bottled water on page 266.

hyponatremia A condition of too little sodium in the blood.

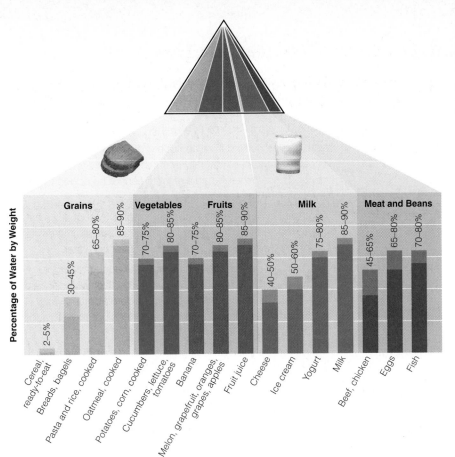

Figure 8.7 Water Content of Foods
Approximately 20 percent of the water you consume comes from foods. Cooked grains, fruits, and vegetables all contain a high percentage of water by weight.

Source: A. Grandjean and S. Campbell, *Hydration: Fluids for Life.* (Washington, D.C.: ILSI Press, 2004). Available at www.ilsi.org.

The remaining 20 percent of your water can come from foods. All foods contain some water. Cooked hot cereals and many fruits and vegetables are robust sources of water (see Figure 8.7).

Contrary to popular belief, beverages like caffeinated coffee, tea, and soft drinks will contribute to your daily water needs. Caffeine is a diuretic, so it causes water to be excreted, but the water loss it causes is short lived. In other words, the caffeine doesn't cause a significant loss of body water over the course of a day compared with noncaffeinated beverages. In fact, research suggests that individuals who routinely consume caffeinated beverages actually develop a tolerance to its diuretic effect and experience less water loss over time.[15]

Even though caffeinated beverages can count as a water source, this doesn't mean you should start guzzling caffeinated colas and other soft drinks. Their high calorie and sugar contents can quickly have you drinking your way into a very unbalanced, high-calorie diet. These soft drinks also contain acids that can contribute to erosion of tooth enamel.

The Take-Home Message
You lose water daily through your kidneys, intestinal tract, lungs, and skin. If you lose more water than you take in, you will become dehydrated. Your thirst mechanism reminds you to drink fluids. Though rare, hyponatremia can occur and can be fatal. Adult women should ingest about 9 cups of water daily, whereas adult males should drink about 13 cups daily. Those who are very active will need more water to avoid dehydration. Foods and caffeinated beverages do contribute to your daily water needs.

Table Tips

Bottoms Up

Drink low-fat or skim milk with each meal to add calcium as you meet your fluid needs.

Freeze grapes for a juicy and refreshing snack.

Add a vegetable soup to your lunch for a fluid-packed meal.

Cool down with a sweet treat by spooning slightly thawed frozen strawberries onto low-fat vanilla ice cream. Look for packaged berries in the frozen food section of your supermarket.

Add zip to your water by adding a slice of fresh lemon or lime to your mealtime glass of water.

Tap Water or Bottled Water: Is Bottled Better?

What items do you *have* to have when you walk out the door in the morning? Your keys? Your student ID? Your wallet? What about a bottle of water? Would you never leave home without it? Are you one of the many individuals, like Desiree Kegan from the beginning of this chapter, who drinks *only* bottled water because you think it is the only pure water? If you are, you're certainly not alone. But is bottled water really better or safer for you than tap water?

Desiree is wrong in her assumption that her bottled water is "pure." In fact, drinking 100 percent *pure* water is impossible. Whether you fill your reusable water bottle from the tap or purchase bottled water, the water will contain some impurities. However, this does not mean that the water is unsafe for most individuals to drink. (Note that individuals with a weakened immune system, such as those with HIV/AIDS, undergoing chemotherapy, and/or taking steroids, should speak with their health care provider prior to drinking any water. These individuals may need to take precautions such as boiling their water—no matter the source—before consuming it.[1])

The source of any water, whether tap or bottled, will vary from faucet to faucet and bottle to bottle, so it is virtually impossible to make a direct comparison. There are some basic points to understand about each type, though. Let's look at how tap and bottled water compare in terms of regulation, cost, and safety.

Turn On the Tap

Most Americans obtain their drinking water from a community water system. The source of this municipal water can be underground wells or springs, or rivers, lakes, or reservoirs. Regardless of the source, all municipal water is sent to a treatment plant where any dirt and debris are filtered out, bacteria are killed, and other contaminants are removed. The Environmental Protection Agency (EPA) oversees the safety of public drinking water with national standards that set limits for more than 80 contaminants, either naturally occurring ones, such as bacteria, or manmade ones, such as chemicals, that may find their way into your drinking water. Hundreds of billions of dollars have been invested in these treatment systems to ensure that the public water is safe to drink.[2]

Each year, the water supplier in your community must provide you with an annual report about the quality and source of your tap water. In fact, many of these regional reports can be accessed online at www.epa.gov.

Many municipalities add fluoride to their water. About two-thirds of Americans who drink from public systems have fluoride in their water.[3] Fluoridation of public water has had a positive impact on the nation's dental health, reducing the incidence of dental caries.

Lastly, tap water costs less than a penny a gallon, making it a very affordable way to stay hydrated.

Bottling Boom

Bottled water is second only to carbonated soft drinks in popularity among

A Well of Sources for Bottled Water

Water can be classified according to its source or how it is treated prior to bottling.

Mineral water	Water that is derived from an underground source that contains a specific amount of naturally occurring minerals and trace elements. These minerals and elements cannot be added to the water after it has been bottled.
Spring water	Water that is obtained from underground water that flows naturally to the surface. The water is collected at the spring or the site of the well purposefully drilled to obtain this water.
Sparkling water	Spring water that has carbon dioxide gas added to supply "bubbles" before it is bottled. Also called seltzer water or club soda. Note: This is not technically considered bottled water but rather a soft drink. Sparkling water does not have to adhere to FDA regulations for bottled water.
Distilled water	Water that has been boiled and processed to remove most, but not all, contaminants.
Flavored water	Water that has a flavor such as lemon or lime added. It may also contain added sugars and calories.
Vitamin water	Water that has vitamins added to it. Such water may also contain added sugars and calories.

Source: A. Bullers, Bottled Water: Better Than Tap? *FDA Consumer Magazine,* Food and Drug Administration; Center for Science in the Public Interest, Water, Water . . . Everywhere. In *Nutrition Action Health Letter* (June 2000).

Americans. The per capita consumption of bottled water has doubled in the last decade and is expected to rise even more in the years to come.

Bottled water that is sold through interstate commerce is regulated by the FDA. Thus, as with other food products, manufacturers must adhere to specific FDA regulations, such as standards of identity. In other words, if the label on the bottle states that it is "spring water," the manufacturer must derive the water from a very specific source (see table). Interestingly, some bottled water may actually be from a municipal water source. (In fact, Desiree may be drinking municipal water in the bottled water that she purchases daily.) The bottled water must also adhere to a standard of quality set forth by the FDA, which specifies the maximum amount of contaminants that can be in the water and it still be considered safe for consumption. The FDA sets

its standards for bottled water based on the EPA's standards for public drinking water. However, water that is bottled and sold in the same state is not regulated by the FDA.[4]

The price of bottled water can be hefty, ranging from $1 to $4 a gallon. Desiree has a very expensive bottled water habit. She pays $1.50 per bottle and buys two bottles daily, so Desiree is shelling out over $20 a week and more than $80 monthly buying bottled water. Over the course of her nine months at college, she is spending over $750 on a beverage that she can get free from the campus water fountain. Finally, many bottled waters are not fluoridated, so you may be losing out on this important cavity

fighter if this is your predominant source of drinking water.[5]

Keep in mind that reusing the bottles from bottled water is not advised. The plastic containers cannot withstand repeated washing and the plastic can actually break down, causing chemicals to leach into the water. Sturdier water bottles that are designed for reuse must be thoroughly cleaned with hot soapy water after each use to kill germs.

The bottom line is that both tap water and bottled water can be safe to drink. Your choice is likely to come down to personal preference and costs. The table Bottled vs Tap Water summarizes the similarities and differences between the two types of water.

Bottled vs Tap Water: A Summary

Bottled Water

Cost to Consumers

- About $1.00–$4.00 per gallon

Safety

- Bottled water is generally safe.
- Some bottled water is not tested for contaminants.
- Only bottled water sold across state lines is regulated by the FDA.
- Bottled water not sold across state lines is regulated by state and local guidelines.

Benefits to Consumers

- The packaging of bottled water may make it more convenient than tap water.
- Bottled water may taste better than tap water.

Tap Water

- About $0.003 per gallon

- Municipal water is regulated by EPA, state, and local regulations.
- EPA guidelines require that the public have access to water quality reports and that it be notified if water quality is outside established bounds.

- Tap water is available at the faucet.
- Tap water often contains fluoride, which helps to prevent tooth decay.

What Are Minerals and Why Do You Need Them?

Minerals are **inorganic** elements that your body needs in relatively small amounts. Like vitamins, minerals don't provide calories so they aren't a source of energy themselves, but they work with other nutrients, such as protein and carbohydrates, to enable your body to function properly.

You already read that the electrolytes (minerals that are charged ions in your body fluids) help maintain fluid balance. Minerals can also, like vitamins, be part of enzymes, work with your immune system, and play an invaluable role in structural growth. Minerals are found in both plant and animal foods, but the best food sources, as you will soon see, tend to be vegetables, legumes, milk, and meats.

Absorption of minerals from your foods can vary depending upon their **bioavailability.** The mineral content of plants reflects the soil in which they are grown, as plants must derive nutrients from the soil through their roots. Some minerals also compete with each other for absorption in your intestinal tract, and too much of one can cause an imbalance of another. For example, too much zinc in your diet can decrease the absorption of copper. Minerals are also sometimes bound to other substances and your body cannot absorb them (they are eliminated from your body in your stool). An example of this is the calcium in spinach. Spinach is technically high in calcium, but is a poor source of this nutrient because it contains oxalates, which bind with the calcium and render most of it unavailable for absorption. Recall from Chapter 6 that the phytates in plant foods and the polyphenols in tea and coffee can inhibit your body's absorption of iron. In contrast, vitamin C will enhance the absorption of iron that is found in plant foods. Protein from animal foods will enhance the absorption of zinc, while the phytates in plant foods bind with this mineral and prevent its absorption. All these factors affect the bioavailability of these nutrients.

Minerals are categorized into two groups, depending on how much of them you need. The **major minerals,** known also as macrominerals, are needed in amounts greater than 100 milligrams per day, and the **trace minerals,** known also as microminerals, are needed in amounts less than 20 milligrams per day. Let's look at these separately.

You Need Major Minerals in Larger Amounts

The major minerals are major because you need more of them in your body, and thus, you need more of them in your diet (Figure 8.8).[16] Your daily needs for the major minerals ranges from hundreds of milligrams daily to over a thousand. The major minerals include sodium, chloride, potassium, calcium, phosphorus, magnesium, and sulfur.

inorganic Compounds that do not contain carbon and are not formed by living things.

bioavailability The degree to which a nutrient from foods is available for absorption by the body.

major minerals Minerals needed from your diet and in your body in amounts greater than 100 milligrams per day. These include sodium, chloride, potassium, calcium, phosphorus, magnesium, and sulfur.

trace minerals Minerals needed from your diet and in your body in small amounts, less than 20 milligrams daily. These include iron, zinc, selenium, fluoride, chromium, copper, manganese, and molybdenum.

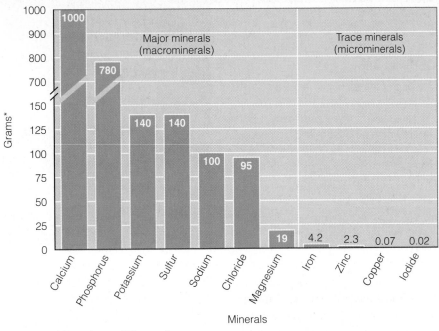

* Based on a 154 pound person

Figure 8.8 The Minerals in Your Body
The major minerals are present in larger amounts than the trace minerals. However, all are equally important to your health.

Many of these minerals work closely together to perform major body functions. For example, the sodium and chloride located mainly outside your cells, and the potassium, calcium, magnesium, and sulfur, which are mostly inside your cells, all play a key role in maintaining fluid balance. Calcium, phosphorus, and magnesium work together to strengthen your bones and teeth.

The following pages contain visual summaries of the major minerals you need to stay healthy.

Sodium

What Are Sodium and Salt?

Sodium is an electrolyte in your body. Most sodium in your body is in your blood and in the fluid surrounding your cells.

About 90 percent of the sodium you consume is in the form of sodium chloride. Sodium chloride is commonly known as table salt.

Functions of Sodium

Sodium's chief role is regulation of fluid balance. Sodium also plays an important role in transporting substances such as amino acids across cell membranes.

Salt is frequently added to foods to enhance flavor and as a preservative. It is also added to yeast breads to help the dough rise and to reduce the growth of bacteria and mold in many bread products and luncheon meats. Sodium phosphate, sodium carbonate, and sodium bicarbonate (baking soda) are food additives and preservatives that perform similar functions in foods.

Monosodium glutamate (MSG) is a common additive in Asian cuisines that is used to intensify the flavor of foods.

Sodium Balance in Your Body

The amount of sodium in your body is maintained at a precise level. When your body needs more sodium, your kidneys reduce the amount that is excreted in your urine. Likewise, when you take in too much sodium, you excrete the excess. For example, when you eat salty pretzels or popcorn, your kidneys will excrete the extra sodium you take in from these snacks.

Smaller amounts of sodium are lost in your stool and through daily perspiration. The amount of sodium lost through perspiration depends upon the rate you are sweating, the amount of sodium you have consumed (the more sodium in your diet, the higher the loss), and the intensity of heat in the environment. As you get acclimated to environmental heat, less sodium will be lost over time in your sweat. This built-in protective mechanism helps to prevent the loss of too much sodium from your body.

Daily Needs

The penny shown below is covered with about 180 milligrams of sodium. This is the bare minimum you need daily. It is based on the amount of sodium needed by individuals who live in temperate climates and those who have become acclimated to hotter environments.[17]

Planning a balanced diet with this small an amount of sodium is virtually impossible, so the recommended sodium intake for adults up to 51 years of age is set at 1,500 milligrams daily. This sodium recommendation allows you to eat a variety of foods from all the food groups so that you can meet your other nutrient needs. It also covers any sodium that is lost in sweat by moderately active individuals, or those who are not acclimated to the environmental temperature. Those who are very physically active and/or not acclimated to the heat will likely need to consume a higher amount of sodium. This can easily be obtained in the diet.

Sodium is so widely available in foods that you don't have to go out of your way to meet your needs.

Milligrams of Sodium

- 3,500 —
- 3,000 —
- 2,500 — American adult daily consumption (>3,400 mg)
- 2,000 — Adult upper level (2,300 mg)
- 1,500 —
- 1,000 — Adult recommended daily (1,500 mg)
- 500 —
- 0 — Adult needed daily (180 mg)

Americans are currently consuming more than double the recommended amount, or over 3,400 milligrams of sodium daily, on average.[18]

Food Sources

About 12 percent of Americans' consumption of sodium is from foods in which it occurs naturally, such as fruits, vegetables, milk, meat, fish, poultry, and legumes. Another 5 percent gets added during cooking and another 6 percent is used to season foods at the table.

Processed foods contribute a hefty 77 percent of the sodium in the diet of Americans. Comparing the amount of sodium in a fresh tomato (11 milligrams) to the amount found in a cup of canned tomatoes (355 milligrams) quickly illustrates just how much more sodium is found in processed foods.

Too Much or Too Little

There is a direct relationship between sodium and blood pressure in many people. In general, as a person's intake of sodium increases, so does their blood pressure. Blood pressure that becomes too high, known as **hypertension,** increases the risk for heart disease, stroke, and kidney disease (see the boxed feature "You and Your Blood Pressure" for more about hypertension.) Unfortunately, many Americans will develop hypertension sometime during their life. To help reduce the risk of hypertension, the upper level for adults for sodium is set at 2,300 milligrams. Recall from Chapter 2 that the current *Dietary Guidelines for Americans* also recommend that you limit your

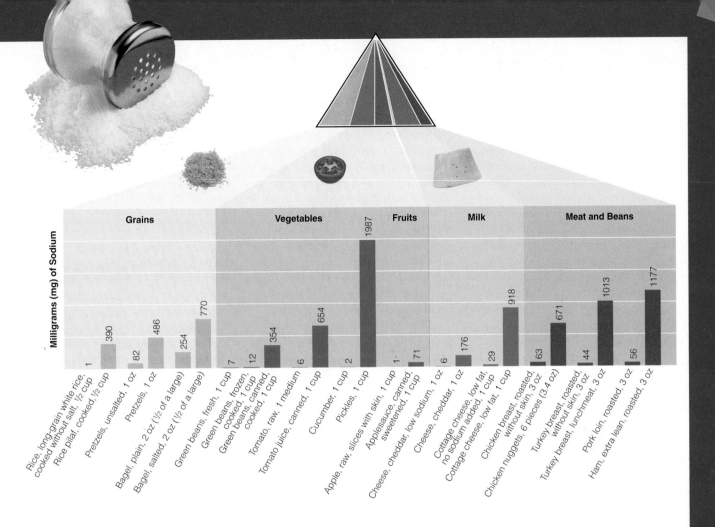

Milligrams (mg) of Sodium

Grains	Vegetables	Fruits	Milk	Meat and Beans

Grains:
- Rice, long-grain white rice, cooked without salt, 1/2 cup: 1
- Rice pilaf, cooked, 1/2 cup: 390
- Pretzels, unsalted, 1 oz: 82
- Pretzels, 1 oz: 486
- Bagel, plain, 2 oz (1/2 of a large): 254
- Bagel, salted, 2 oz (1/2 of a large): 770

Vegetables:
- Green beans, fresh, 1 cup: 7
- Green beans, frozen, cooked, 1 cup: 12
- Green beans, canned, cooked, 1 cup: 354
- Tomato, raw, 1 medium: 6
- Tomato juice, canned, 1 cup: 654
- Cucumber, 1 cup: 2
- Pickles, 1 cup: 1987

Fruits:
- Apple, raw, slices with skin, 1 cup: 1
- Applesauce, canned, sweetened, 1 cup: 71

Milk:
- Cheese, cheddar, low sodium, 1 oz: 6
- Cheese, cheddar, 1 oz: 176
- Cottage cheese, low fat, no sodium added, 1 cup: 29
- Cottage cheese, low fat, 1 cup: 918

Meat and Beans:
- Chicken breast, roasted, without skin, 3 oz: 63
- Chicken nuggets, 6 pieces (3.4 oz): 671
- Turkey breast, roasted, without skin, 3 oz: 44
- Turkey breast, lunchmeat, 3 oz: 1013
- Pork loin, roasted, 3 oz: 56
- Ham, extra lean, roasted, 3 oz: 1177

sodium intake for the same reason. Many Americans exceed this upper limit daily.

Because the majority of your sodium comes from processed foods, and a fair amount comes from the salt that you add to your foods, cutting back on these two sources is the best way to lower your intake.

When you buy processed foods, look for the terms "low," "reduced" or "sodium-free" on the labels to cut back on your sodium intake.

Bypass the salt shaker at the table. When cooking, season your foods with black pepper, Tabasco sauce, lemon juice, or a no-salt seasoning blend instead of salt.

Sodium deficiency is rare in healthy individuals consuming a balanced diet.

Table Tips
Shake Your Habit

Dilute and conquer. Combine a can of vegetable soup and a can of low-sodium vegetable soup for soup with less sodium. Add some cooked, frozen vegetables for an even healthier meal.

Keep your portions of deli meats to no more than 3 ounces and build a "meaty" sandwich by adding naturally low-sodium

tomatoes, lettuce, cucumbers, and shredded cabbage.

Nibble on low-sodium dried fruits (apricots, raisins) and unsalted walnut pieces for a sweet and crunchy snack.

Skip the salty french fries and enjoy the sodium-free baked potato at dinner.

Use olive oil and balsamic vinegar for a salad dressing with less sodium than is in bottled dressings. Or, dilute equal portions of regular salad dressing with vinegar to cut the sodium.

Terms to Know
hypertension

You and Your Blood Pressure

High blood pressure, or **hypertension,** is an increasing problem in the United States. In fact, if you were sitting in a room with three other adults, there is a good chance that one of you would have high blood pressure. High blood pressure increases the risk of heart disease, stroke, and kidney damage.[6] Up to 30 percent of individuals with high blood pressure have "white coat hypertension." This refers to the phenomenon whereby an individual's blood pressure measurement is elevated when taken at a doctor's office or clinic by a staff person (a person typically wearing a white lab coat) but the pressure is normal when taken elsewhere. This isn't the same as constant high blood pressure.

What Is Blood Pressure?

Your blood pressure is a measure of the force your blood exerts against the walls of your arteries. With every beat, your heart pumps blood into your arteries, and thus to all the areas in your body. Blood pressure is highest at the moment of the heart beat. This is known as your **systolic pressure.** Pressure is lower when your heart is at rest between beats. This is called your **diastolic pressure.** Your blood pressure is expressed using these two measurements: the systolic pressure/ diastolic pressure. Blood pressure of less than 120/80 mm Hg (millimeters of mercury) is considered normal. Your blood pressure rises naturally as you age, which is believed to be due in part to the increased stiffness of the arteries.[7] However, if it rises too much, serious medical problems may occur.

Why Is Hypertension a Silent Killer?

Hypertension happens gradually. As blood pressure begins to rise above normal—

hypertension High blood pressure.

systolic pressure The force of your blood against the artery walls when your heart beats.

diastolic pressure The pressure of your blood against the artery walls when the heart is at rest between beats.

that is, systolic is 120 or above and diastolic is 80 or above—it is classified as prehypertension. Many individuals with prehypertension will develop hypertension if they don't lower their blood pressure. A blood pressure of 140/90 mm Hg or above is called hypertension.

Hypertension is referred to as the "silent killer" because there aren't any outward symptoms that your pressure is dangerously elevated and people can have it for years without knowing it. The only way to be sure you don't have it is to have your blood pressure checked regularly.

Individuals with chronic high blood pressure have a higher than normal force pounding against the walls of their arteries, which makes the walls thicker and stiffer, and contributes to atherosclerosis. The heart becomes enlarged and weakened as it has to work harder to pump enough oxygen- and nutrient-laden blood throughout the body. This can lead to fatigue, shortness of breath, and possibly heart attack. Hypertension can also damage the arteries leading to the brain, kidneys, and legs, which increases the risk of stroke, kidney failure, and partial amputation of a leg.[8]

Can You Control Your Hypertension?

There are factors that increase the chances of developing hypertension, some of which you can control and others you cannot.

Your family history, the aging process, and your race can all impact the likelihood that you will develop high blood pressure. These are the risk factors that you can't control. If your parents, siblings, and/or grandparents have or had hypertension, you are at a higher risk of developing it yourself. Typically, the risk of hypertension increases with age. It is more likely to occur after the age of 35 for men, and women generally experience it after menopause. Hypertension is more prevalent in African-Americans, and tends to occur earlier and be more severe than in Caucasians.[9]

The good news is that there are more risk factors that you *can* control than those that you can't. You can change several dietary and lifestyle habits to help reduce your risk. Among these are your weight and your physical activity level. Individuals who are obese are twice as likely to have hypertension as those at a healthy weight. Even a modest weight loss can have an impact. Losing as little as 10 pounds can reduce a person's blood pressure, and may actually prevent hypertension in overweight individuals even if they haven't yet reached a healthy weight. Additional weight loss can have an even more dramatic effect on blood pressure. Regular physical activity can lower blood pressure even if weight loss hasn't occurred.[10]

You can also control your alcohol

Sweets
(5 or less per week)

Beans, nuts, seeds
(4–5 per week)

Oils, salad dressing, mayonnaise
(2–3 per day)

Low-fat dairy
(2–3 per day)

Seafood, poultry, lean meat
(0–2 per day)

Grains (preferably whole)
(7–8 per day)

Vegetables and fruit
(8–10 per day)

The DASH diet, which is rich in whole grains, fruits, vegetables, and low-fat dairy foods, can help lower blood pressure.

consumption, which affects your risk of developing high blood pressure. Studies have shown that drinkers who consumed 3 to 6 drinks daily and then reduced their alcohol consumption by 67 percent, on average, were able to reduce their systolic pressure by over 3 mm Hg and their diastolic pressure by 2 mm Hg.[11] Less drinking and more physical activity is the name of the game when it comes to keeping high blood pressure at bay.

Lastly, eating a balanced diet is a proven strategy to lower your blood pressure. A large research study, called the DASH (Dietary Approaches to Stop Hypertension) study, followed individuals on three different diets. One diet was a typical American diet: low in fruits, vegetables, and dairy products and high in fat, saturated fat, and cholesterol. A second was rich in just fruits and vegetables, and a third, the DASH diet, was a balanced diet that was lower in fat, saturated fat, cholesterol, and sweets, and high in whole grains, fruits, vegetables, and low-fat dairy products. In fact, the DASH diet was very similar to the recommended diet of MyPyramid (see figure).

The individuals in the study who followed the DASH diet experienced a significant reduction in blood pressure compared with those who followed the other two diets. Because the sodium content of all three diets was the same, about 3,000 milligrams, which is the approximate amount that Americans consume daily, on average, the blood pressure lowering effect was attributed to some other substance, or a combination of nutrients working together. For example, due to its abundance of fruits and vegetables, the DASH diet provides healthy doses of potassium and magnesium, and because of its numerous servings of dairy foods, it is also rich in calcium. Dietary potassium, magnesium, and calcium can all play a role in lowering blood pressure.[12]

A follow-up to the DASH study, called the DASH-Sodium study, went one step further and investigated whether reducing the amount of dietary sodium in each of the three diets could also help lower blood pressure. Not surprisingly, it did. We know that, in general, as a person's sodium intake increases, so will their blood pressure. While the result of this study showed that reducing dietary sodium from about 3,300 milligrams to 2,400 milligrams daily lowered blood pressure, the biggest reduction occurred when sodium intake was limited to only 1,500 milligrams daily. Most importantly, the overall best diet combination for lowering blood pressure was the DASH diet plus consuming only 1,500 milligrams of sodium daily.[13] This study not only reinforced sodium's role in blood pressure but also showed that the DASH diet, along with a reduction of sodium, is the best dietary combination to fight hypertension.

The table shows how effective each of these changes can be once you decide to take charge of your diet and lifestyle.

Take Charge of Your Blood Pressure!

Diet and lifestyle changes help reduce blood pressure and help prevent hypertension.

If You	By	Your Systolic Blood Pressure[*] May Be Reduced By
Reduce your sodium intake	Keeping dietary sodium consumption to no more than 2,400 mg daily	8–14 mm Hg
Lose excess weight	An amount that allows you to maintain a normal, healthy body weight	5–20 mm Hg for every 22 lbs of weight loss
Stay physically active	Partaking in 30 minutes of aerobic activity (brisk walking) on most days of the week	4–9 mm Hg
Drink alcohol moderately	Limiting consumption to no more than 2 drinks daily for men and 1 drink daily for women	2–4 mm Hg
Follow the DASH diet	Consuming a heart-healthy DASH diet that is abundant in fruits and vegetables and low-fat dairy products	8–14 mm Hg

[*]Controlling the systolic pressure is more difficult than controlling the diastolic pressure, especially for individuals 50 years of age and older. Therefore, it is the primary focus for lowering blood pressure. Typically, as systolic pressure goes down with diet and lifestyle changes, the diastolic pressure will follow.

Source: Adapted from A.V. Chobanian, et al., The Seventh Report of the Joint National Committee on Prevention, Detection, Evaluation, and Treatment of High Blood Pressure, Journal of the American Medical Association, 289 (2003): 2560–2572.

Potassium

What Is Potassium?

Potassium is an important mineral with numerous functions in your body. Luckily, it is also found in numerous foods, so it's not difficult to meet your needs for it.

Functions of Potassium

Potassium Is Needed for Fluid Balance and as a Blood Buffer

Over 95 percent of the potassium in your body is inside your cells, with the remainder in the fluids outside your cells, including your blood. As with other electrolytes, potassium helps maintain fluid balance and keeps your blood pH and acid-base balance correct.

Potassium Is Needed for Muscle Contraction and Nerve Impulse Conduction

Potassium plays a role in the contraction of your muscles, including your heart, and the conduction of nerve impulses. Because of this, a dramatic increase of potassium in your body can lead to irregular heart beats or heart attack, while dangerously low levels could cause paralysis. Thus, potassium is tightly controlled and balanced in your body with the help of your kidneys.

Potassium Can Help Lower High Blood Pressure

A diet with plentiful potassium has been shown to help lower blood pressure, especially in salt-sensitive individuals who respond more intensely to sodium's blood pressure-raising capabilities. Potassium causes the kidneys to excrete excess sodium from the body, and keeping sodium levels low can help lower blood pressure. The DASH diet is abundant in foods with potassium.

Potassium Aids in Bone Health and Reduces Kidney Stones

Because potassium plays a buffering role in your blood, it helps keep the bone-strengthening minerals, calcium and phosphorus, from being lost from the bones and kidneys.[19] Numerous studies suggest

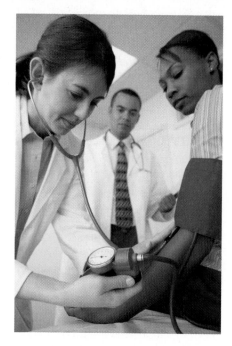

that having plenty of potassium in your diet helps increase the density, and thus the strength, of your bones.

Potassium also helps reduce the risk of kidney stones by causing the body to excrete citrate, a compound that binds with calcium to form kidney stones, shown in the photo below.

Kidney stone

Daily Needs

Adults should consume 4,700 milligrams of potassium daily. This amount is recommended to help those with sodium sensitivity reduce their risk of high blood pressure. It is also beneficial to all Americans, in general, to lower their risk of

developing kidney stones and preserve bone health.

Because Americans fall short of their servings of fruits and vegetables, adult females are consuming only about 2,200 to 2,500 milligrams of potassium, and adult males are consuming only 3,300–3,400 milligrams daily, on average.

Food Sources

Both the *Dietary Guidelines for Americans* and MyPyramid recommend consuming an abundance of fruits and vegetables in order to meet your potassium needs. A diet rich in at least 7 servings of fruits and vegetables, especially leafy greens, which is the *minimum* amount you should be consuming daily, can easily meet your potassium needs. Dairy foods, nuts, and legumes are also good sources (see figure).

Too Much or Too Little

There isn't any known danger from consuming too much potassium that occurs naturally in foods. These excesses will be excreted in your urine. However, consuming too much from supplements or salt substitutes (the sodium in some salt substitutes is replaced with potassium) can cause **hyperkalemia** (*hyper* = too much; *kalemia* = potassium in blood) for some individuals. Hyperkalemia can cause irregular heartbeats, damage the heart, and be life-threatening.

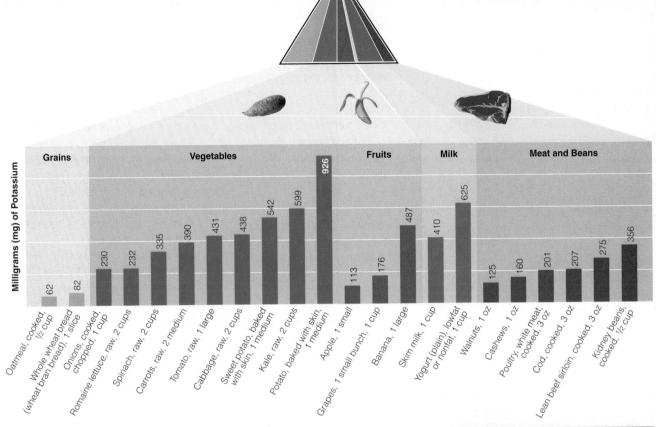

Milligrams (mg) of Potassium

Grains

Oatmeal, cooked, ½ cup	62
Whole wheat bread (wheat bran bread), 1 slice	82

Vegetables

Onions, cooked, chopped, 1 cup	230
Romaine lettuce, raw, 2 cups	232
Spinach, raw, 2 cups	335
Carrots, raw, 2 medium	390
Tomato, raw, 1 large	431
Cabbage, raw, 2 cups	438
Sweet potato, baked with skin, 1 medium	542
Kale, raw, 2 cups	599
Potato, baked with skin, 1 medium	926

Fruits

Apple, 1 small	113
Grapes, 1 small bunch, 1 cup	176
Banana, 1 large	487

Milk

Skim milk, 1 cup	410
Yogurt (plain), lowfat or nonfat, 1 cup	625

Meat and Beans

Walnuts, 1 oz	125
Cashews, 1 oz	160
Poultry, white meat, cooked, 3 oz	201
Cod, cooked, 3 oz	207
Lean beef sirloin, cooked, 3 oz	275
Kidney beans, cooked, ½ cup	356

Those at a higher risk for hyperkalemia include individuals with impaired kidneys, such as people with type 1 diabetes mellitus, those with kidney disease, and individuals taking medications for heart disease or diuretics that cause the kidneys to block the excretion of potassium. These individuals may also need to consume less than the recommended amount of potassium daily as advised by their health care professional.

Although a deficiency of dietary potassium is rare, too little potassium can cause **hypokalemia.** This may occur during bouts of vomiting and/or diarrhea. It has been seen in individuals who suffer with anorexia and/or bulimia.

Hypokalemia can cause muscle weakness, cramps, and, in severe situations, irregular heartbeats and paralysis.[20]

Individuals who consume high-protein diets that contain few fruits and vegetables may be depriving themselves of the buffering actions of potassium. The breakdown of excessive amounts of dietary protein causes the formation of acids that are balanced by the buffering action of potassium. A diet too low in fruits and vegetables is setting the stage for an imbalance of acids and bases in the blood and the increased risk of kidney stones, loss of bone mass, and high blood pressure.

Terms to Know
hyperkalemia ■ hypokalemia

Calcium

What Is Calcium?

Calcium is one of the most abundant minerals in nature and is found in everything from pearls to seashells to eggshells. Calcium is also the most abundant mineral in your body. Over 99 percent of your body's calcium is located in your bones and teeth.

Functions of Calcium

Calcium Helps Build Strong Bones and Teeth

Calcium couples with phosphorus to form hydroxyapatite, providing strength and structure in your bones and the enamel on your teeth. Adequate dietary calcium is needed to build and maintain bone mass. Calcium makes up almost 40 percent of the weight of your bones.[21]

Calcium Plays a Role in Your Muscles, Nerves, and Blood

The remaining 1 percent of calcium is in your blood, in the fluids that surround your cells, in your muscles, and in other tissues. Calcium is needed to contract your muscles, dilate and contract your blood vessels, help your blood clot, secrete hormones and enzymes, and help your nervous system transmit messages. It must be maintained at a constant level for your body to function properly.[22]

Calcium May Help Lower High Blood Pressure

Studies have shown that a heart-healthy diet rich in calcium, potassium, magnesium, fruits, vegetables, and low-fat dairy products can help lower blood pressure. One example of such a diet, the DASH diet, contains three servings of lean dairy foods, the minimum amount of servings recommended to obtain this protective effect[23] (see the boxed feature "You and Your Blood Pressure" on page 272).

Calcium May Fight Colon Cancer

A diet with plenty of calcium has been shown to help reduce the risk of developing benign tumors in the colon that may eventually lead to cancer. Calcium may protect the lining of the colon from damaging bile acids and cancer-promoting substances.[24]

Calcium May Reduce the Risk of Kidney Stones

Approximately 2 million American adults visit their doctors annually with **kidney stones.** The majority of these stones are composed mainly of calcium oxalate.[25] Although health professionals in the past often warned those who suffer with kidney stones to minimize their dietary calcium, this advice has since been reversed. Research has shown that a balanced diet, along with adequate amounts of calcium, may actually reduce the risk of developing kidney stones. Calcium binds with the oxalates in foods in the intestines and prevents their absorption. With fewer oxalates filtering through the kidneys, fewer stones are formed.[26]

Calcium May Reduce the Risk of Obesity

Some preliminary research suggests that low-calcium diets may trigger several responses that stimulate fat production and its storage in cells, which increases the risk for obesity.[27] When dietary calcium is inadequate, the active form of vitamin D increases in the body in order to enhance calcium absorption from the diet. Parathyroid hormone is also increased, which causes less calcium to be lost from the body. These hormone responses may also cause a shift of calcium into fat cells, which is the mechanism that stimulates fat production and storage.[28]

Daily Needs

Adults need 1,000 to 1,200 milligrams of calcium daily, depending upon their age. Americans 20 years of age and older are consuming, on average, less than 800 milligrams of calcium daily.[29]

Food Sources

Milk, yogurt, and cheese are the major sources of calcium in the American diet. Each serving from the dairy group will provide approximately 300 milligrams of calcium. (Choose only nonfat and low-fat milk and yogurt and reduced fat or skim milk cheeses to reduce the amount of saturated fat in these foods.) Although three servings of dairy foods will just about meet many adults' daily needs, Americans consume only 1½ servings of dairy daily, on average.[30]

Broccoli, kale, canned salmon with bones (the calcium is in the bones), and tofu that is processed with calcium can also add calcium to the diet. Calcium-fortified foods, such as juices and cereals, are also excellent sources.

Too Much or Too Little

The upper level for calcium has been set at 2,500 milligrams daily to avoid **hypercalcemia,** or too much calcium in the blood, subsequent impaired kidneys, and calcium deposits in the body. Too much dietary calcium can also cause constipation and interfere with the absorption of other minerals, such as iron, zinc, magnesium, and phosphorus.

If your diet is low in calcium, calcium leaves your bones in order to maintain a constant level in your blood. A chronic deficiency of dietary calcium can lead to less dense, weakened, and brittle bones and increased risk for **osteoporosis** and bone fractures[31]

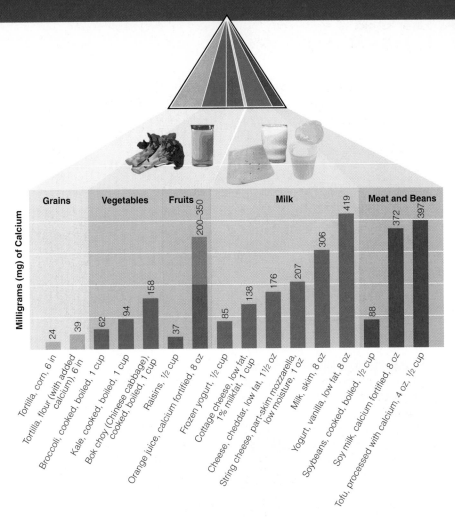

Milligrams (mg) of Calcium

| Grains | Vegetables | Fruits | Milk | Meat and Beans |

Grains:
- Tortilla, corn, 6 in — 24
- Tortilla, flour (with added calcium), 6 in — 39

Vegetables:
- Broccoli, cooked, boiled, 1 cup — 62
- Kale, cooked, boiled, 1 cup — 94
- Bok choy (Chinese cabbage), cooked, boiled, 1 cup — 158

Fruits:
- Raisins, ½ cup — 37
- Orange juice, calcium fortified, 8 oz — 200–350

Milk:
- Frozen yogurt, ½ cup — 85
- Cottage cheese, low fat, 1% milkfat, 1 cup — 138
- Cheese, cheddar, low fat, 1½ oz — 176
- String cheese, part-skim mozzarella, low moisture, 1 oz — 207
- Milk, skim, 8 oz — 306
- Yogurt, vanilla, low fat, 8 oz — 419

Meat and Beans:
- Soybeans, cooked, boiled, ½ cup — 88
- Soy milk, calcium fortified, 8 oz — 372
- Tofu, processed with calcium, 4 oz, ½ cup — 397

(compare healthy bone, left in photo, with weakened bone at right). See the boxed feature "Osteoporosis" on page 283 for greater detail.

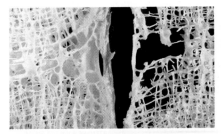

Healthy bone (left) vs weakened bone (right)

Calcium Supplements

Some individuals, based on their diet and/or medical history, are advised by their health care provider to take a calcium supplement. The calcium in these supplements is part of a compound, typically either calcium carbonate or calcium citrate. Calcium carbonate tends to be the least expensive and the most common form of calcium purchased. It is most effective when consumed with a meal, as the acidic juices in your stomach help with its absorption.[32] Calcium citrate can be taken any time throughout the day, as it doesn't need the help of acidic juices to be absorbed. Calcium citrate is a plus for those age 50 and older who may be producing less stomach acid as they age.

Regardless of the form, all calcium, whether from supplements or from fortified or naturally occurring foods, should be consumed in doses of 500 milligrams or less, as this is the maximum that your body can absorb efficiently at one time.[33] In other words, if a person has been advised to take 1,000 milligrams of calcium daily, 500 milligrams should be consumed in the morning and the other 500 milligrams in the afternoon or evening.

Calcium from unrefined oyster shell, bone meal, or dolomite (a rock rich in calcium) may also contain lead and other toxic metals. Supplements from these sources should state on the label that they are "purified" or carry the USP symbol to ensure purity. Because calcium can interfere with and reduce the absorption of iron, a calcium supplement shouldn't be taken along with an iron supplement.

Calcium supplements can sometimes cause constipation and flatulence (gas), especially when large amounts are taken. Increasing the fiber in the diet can help avoid these less-than-pleasurable side effects. There is an upper level set on the daily dosage of calcium; be cautious about adding a calcium supplement to your diet if you are already consuming plenty of lean dairy foods and/or calcium-fortified foods.

Table Tips

Calcium Counts!

Make cereal doused with skim or low-fat milk a morning habit.

Spoon a few chunks of tofu onto your salad bar lunch for extra calcium.

Use low-fat pudding or yogurt to satisfy a sweet tooth and obtain tooth-friendly calcium to boot.

Top your calcium-rich cheese pizza with calcium-rich broccoli for a pizza with calcium pizzazz.

Mozzarella string cheese sticks are an easy grab-as-you-go calcium snack.

Terms to Know
kidney stones ■ hypercalcemia ■ osteoporosis

Phosphorus

What Is Phosphorus?

Phosphorus is the second most abundant mineral in your body. The majority of phosphorus—about 85 percent—is in your bones. The remainder is in your cells and fluids outside your cells, including your blood.

Functions of Phosphorus

Phosphorus Is Needed for Bones and Teeth and Is an Important Component of Cells

As mentioned, phosphorus combines with calcium to form hydroxyapatite, the strengthening material found in bones and teeth.

Phosphorus is part of phospholipids, which give your cell membranes their structure (see figure). Phospholipids act as a barrier to keep specific substances out of the cells, while letting others in.

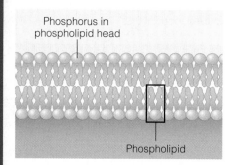

Phosphorus in phospholipid head

Phospholipid

Phosphorus Is Needed during Metabolism

Phosphorus helps store, for later use, energy generated from the metabolism of carbohydrates, protein, and fat from food. Your body can draw upon these stores as needed.

Phosphorus Acts as a Buffer and Is Part of the DNA and RNA of Every Cell

If your blood becomes too acidic or too basic, phosphorus can act as a buffer to help return your blood pH to normal. Your blood pH must stay within a very narrow range to prevent damage to your tissues.

Phosphorus is part of your DNA and RNA. The instructions for your genes are coded in your DNA and transcribed in your RNA to make the proteins needed in your body.

Daily Needs

Adults, both male and female, need 700 milligrams of phosphorus daily. Americans, on average, are consuming over 1,000 milligrams of phosphorus daily.[34]

Food Sources

A balanced, varied diet will easily meet your phosphorus needs. Foods from animal sources such as meat, fish, poultry, and dairy products are excellent sources of phosphorus. Phosphorus is also part of many food additives.

Too Much or Too Little

Typically, consuming too much dietary phosphorus and its subsequent effect, **hyperphosphatemia** (*hyper* = over; *phosphat* = phosphate; *emia* = blood), is only an issue for individuals with kidney problems who cannot excrete excess phosphorus.

Constantly high phosphorus and low calcium intake can cause the loss of calcium from your bones and a subsequent decrease in bone mass. Loss of bone mass increases the risk of osteoporosis. Hyperphosphatemia can also lead to calcification of tissues in the body. To protect against this, the upper level for phosphorus has been set

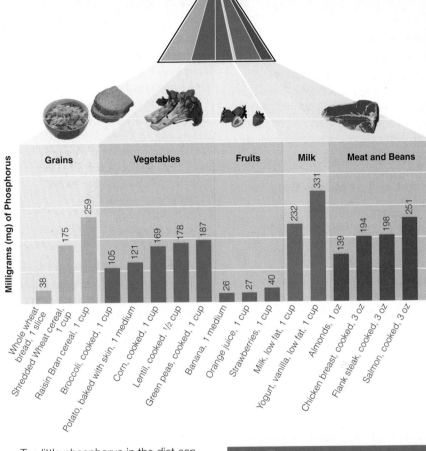

	Grains			Vegetables					Fruits			Milk		Meat and Beans			

Milligrams (mg) of Phosphorus

- Whole wheat bread, 1 slice: 38
- Shredded Wheat cereal, 1 cup: 175
- Raisin Bran cereal, 1 cup: 259
- Broccoli, cooked, 1 cup: 105
- Potato, baked with skin, 1 medium: 121
- Corn, cooked, 1 cup: 169
- Lentil, cooked, 1/2 cup: 178
- Green peas, cooked, 1 cup: 187
- Banana, 1 medium: 26
- Orange juice, 1 cup: 27
- Strawberries, 1 cup: 40
- Milk, low fat, 1 cup: 232
- Yogurt, vanilla, low fat, 1 cup: 331
- Almonds, 1 oz: 139
- Chicken breast, cooked, 3 oz: 194
- Flank steak, cooked, 3 oz: 198
- Salmon, cooked, 3 oz: 251

at 4,000 milligrams daily for adults age 19 to 50 and 3,000 milligrams for those 50 years of age and older.

Too little phosphorus in the diet can cause its level in your blood to drop dangerously low and result in muscle weakness, bone pain, rickets, confusion, and, at the extreme, death. Because phosphorus is so abundant in the diet, a deficiency is rare. In fact, a person would have to be in a state of near starvation before experiencing a phosphorus deficiency.[35]

Terms to Know
hyperphosphatemia

Magnesium

What Is Magnesium?

Magnesium is another abundant mineral in your body. While about half of the magnesium is in your bones, most of the remaining magnesium is inside the cells. A mere 1 percent is found in your blood and, like calcium, this amount must be maintained at a constant level.

Functions of Magnesium

Magnesium Is Needed for Metabolism and to Maintain Healthy Muscles, Nerves, Bones, and Heart

Magnesium helps over 300 enzymes produce reactions inside your cells. It is needed for the metabolism of carbohydrates, proteins, and fats. Magnesium is used during the synthesis of protein and to help your muscles and nerves function properly. It is also needed to help you maintain healthy bones and a regular heart beat.[36]

Magnesium May Help Lower High Blood Pressure

Studies have shown that magnesium may help regulate blood pressure and that a plant-based diet abundant in fruits and vegetables, which are rich in magnesium as well as other minerals, lowered blood pressure.[37]

The blood-pressure-lowering DASH diet, which has been clinically proven to lower blood pressure, is rich in magnesium as well as calcium and potassium (see the feature box "You and Your Blood Pressure" on page 272).[38]

Magnesium May Help Reduce the Risk of Diabetes Mellitus

Some studies suggest that a diet abundant in magnesium may help decrease the risk of type 2 diabetes. Low blood levels of magnesium, which often occurs in individuals with type 2 diabetes mellitus, may impair the release of insulin, one of the hormones that regulates blood glucose. This may lead to elevated blood glucose levels in those with preexisting diabetes, and may contribute to higher than normal blood glucose levels in those at risk for type 2 diabetes.[39]

Daily Needs

Adult females age 19 to 30 need 310 milligrams of magnesium, whereas men of the same age need 400 milligrams daily. Females age 31 and  over need 320 milligrams while men of this age need 420 milligrams of magnesium daily.

Currently, many Americans fall short of their magnesium needs. Females consume only about 70 percent of their needs, or about 220 milligrams daily, on average. Males consume approximately 320 milligrams daily, on average, which is only about 80 percent of the amount recommended daily. Because older adults tend to consume fewer calories, and thus less dietary magnesium, elders are at an even higher risk of falling short of their needs.

Food Sources

The biggest contributors of magnesium in Americans' diets are vegetables, whole grains, nuts, and fruits. Milk, yogurt, meat,

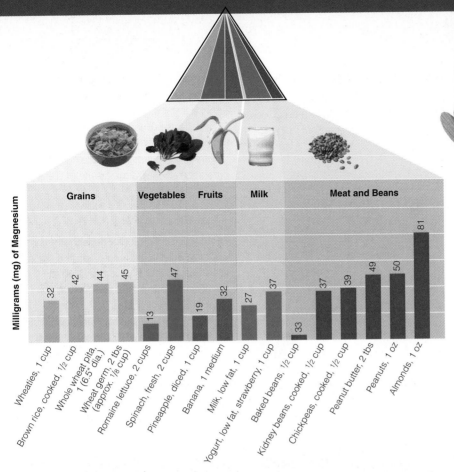

Milligrams (mg) of Magnesium

Grains				Vegetables		Fruits		Milk		Meat and Beans					

- Wheaties, 1 cup — 32
- Brown rice, cooked, 1/2 cup — 42
- Whole wheat pita, 1 (6.5" dia.) — 44
- Wheat germ, 2 tbs (approx. 1/8 cup) — 45
- Romaine lettuce, 2 cups — 13
- Spinach, fresh, 2 cups — 47
- Pineapple, diced, 1 cup — 19
- Banana, 1 medium — 32
- Milk, low fat, 1 cup — 27
- Yogurt, low fat, strawberry, 1 cup — 37
- Baked beans, 1/2 cup — 33
- Kidney beans, cooked, 1/2 cup — 37
- Chickpeas, cooked, 1/2 cup — 39
- Peanut butter, 2 tbs — 49
- Peanuts, 1 oz — 50
- Almonds, 1 oz — 81

and eggs are also good sources. Because the majority of the magnesium is in the bran and germ of the grain kernel, products made with refined grains, such as white flour, are poor sources.

It's not difficult to meet your magnesium needs. A peanut butter sandwich on whole-wheat bread, chased with a glass of low-fat milk and a banana, will provide over 200 milligrams, or about half of an adult's daily needs.

Too Much or Too Little

There isn't any known risk in consuming too much magnesium from food sources. However, consuming large amounts from supplements has been shown to cause intestinal problems such as diarrhea, cramps, and nausea. In fact, some laxatives purposefully contain magnesium because of its known cathartic effect. Because of this distress on the intestinal system, the upper level for magnesium from supplements, not foods, is set at 350 milligrams for adults. This level is to prevent diarrhea, the first symptom that typically arises when too much magnesium is consumed.[40]

Even though many Americans don't meet their magnesium needs, deficiencies are rare in healthy individuals because the kidneys compensate for low magnesium intake by excreting less of it.

However, some medications may cause magnesium deficiency. Certain diuretics can cause the body to lose too much magnesium, and some antibiotics, such as tetracycline, can inhibit the absorption of magnesium, both of which can lead to a deficiency. Individuals with poorly controlled diabetes or who abuse alcohol can experience excessive losses of magnesium in the urine, which could also cause a deficiency.

A severe magnesium deficiency can cause muscle weakness, seizures, fatigue, depression, and irregular heart beats.

Table Tips
Magnificent Magnesium

Sprinkle chopped almonds over your morning whole-grain cereal for two crunchy sources of magnesium.

Add baby spinach to your salad.

Add rinsed, canned black beans to salsa for a veggie dip with a magnesium punch.

Spread peanut butter on whole-wheat crackers for a satisfying afternoon snack.

Try precooked brown rice for an easy way to add whole grains to your dinner!

Chloride

What Is Chloride?

Chloride is a form of chlorine, a mineral you've surely smelled in bleach. Chlorine is a powerful disinfectant that if inhaled or ingested can be poisonous.

Fortunately, most of the chlorine in your body is in the nontoxic form of chloride (Cl^-). Chloride is part of hydrochloric acid, a strong acid in your stomach that enhances protein digestion and kills harmful bacteria that may be consumed with your foods.

Functions of Chloride

Chloride Helps Maintain Fluid Balance and Acid-Base Balance

Sodium and chloride are the major electrolytes outside your cells and in your blood. They help maintain fluid balance between these two compartments.

Chloride also acts as a buffer to help keep your blood at a normal pH.

Daily Needs and Food Sources

Adults aged 19 to 50 should consume 2,300 milligrams of chloride a day. Sodium chloride, which is 60 percent chloride, is

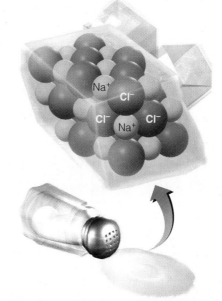

the main source of chloride in your diet, so the food sources for it are the same as those for sodium.

Because Americans consume plenty of salt, it is estimated that they are consuming, on average, 3,400 milligrams to just over 7,000 milligrams of dietary chloride daily.

Too Much or Too Little

Because sodium chloride is the major source of chloride in the diet, the upper level for adults for chloride is set at 3,600 milligrams to coincide with the upper level of sodium.[41]

A chloride deficiency rarely occurs in healthy individuals. Individuals who experience significant bouts of vomiting and diarrhea may become deficient as chloride is lost from the body.

Sulfur

What Is Sulfur?

Sulfur is typically found in your body as part of other compounds. For example, sulfur is part of vitamins, thiamin, biotin, and pantothenic acid.

Functions of Sulfur

Sulfur Helps Shape Some Amino Acids

The amino acids methionine and cysteine both contain sulfur. The sulfur part of these amino acids helps give some proteins their three-dimensional shape. This enables these proteins to perform effectively as enzymes and hormones.[42]

Sulfites Are Preservatives

Sulfur-based substances called sulfites are often used as a preservative by food manufacturers. They help prevent food spoilage and discoloration. We discuss sulfites further in Chapter 14.

Food Sources

Foods that contain the two amino acids mentioned above are the major dietary sources of sulfur. A varied diet that contains meat, poultry, fish, eggs, legumes, dairy foods, fruits, and vegetables will provide sulfur.

Daily Needs and Too Much or Too Little

There isn't any set recommended amount of sulfur to be consumed daily, nor are there any known toxicity or deficiency symptoms. Most people get plenty of sulfur in their diet.

Osteoporosis: Not Just Your Grandmother's Problem

If you are fortunate enough to have elders, such as grandparents, in your life, you may have heard them comment that they are "shrinking as they age." Of course, they aren't really shrinking. But they may be losing height as the vertebrae in their backbone collapse, causing curvature of the spine, which affects their posture (see figure). This outward sign means that their backbone has lost bone mass over the years, and has become unsturdy to the point that it can't hold up their body weight. As older individuals begin to hunch over, they can lose as much as a foot in height.[14]

Bones Are Constantly Changing

Bones are a dynamic, living tissue. Older layers of bones are constantly removed, and new bone is constantly added. In fact, your entire skeleton is replaced with new bone about every decade. During childhood and adolescence, more bone is added than removed, as the bones are growing in length and in mass. Although growth of bone length typically ceases during the teenage years, bone mass will continue to accumulate into the early years of young adulthood. **Peak bone mass,** which is the genetically determined maximum amount of bone mass an individual can build up, typically occurs when a person is in his or her 20s. Some additional bone mass can be added when an individual is in his or her 30s. After peak bone mass is reached, the loss of bone mass begins to slowly exceed the rate at which new bone is added.[15]

As bones lose mass they become porous and **osteoporosis** (*osteo* = bone; *porosis* = porous) can develop. The weakened, fragile bones are prone to fractures. A minor stumble while walking can result in a broken ankle, rib cage, or arm bone as the result of an ensuing fall. Shopping for groceries, showering, dressing, and even brushing one's teeth become challenges for many older people with osteoporosis.

Hip fractures can be devastating because they often render a person immobile, which quickly affects quality of life. Feelings of helplessness and depression often ensue. Up to two-thirds of all individuals with hip fractures are never able to regain the quality of life they had prior to the injury and about 20 percent will die within a year due to complications from the injury.[16] It is estimated that by the year 2020, one out of every two Americans will either have or be at risk for hip fractures due to osteoporosis and even more will be at risk for fractures of other bones.[17]

Adults can have a bone test done by their doctors to assess how their **bone mineral density (BMD)** compares with that of a healthy 30-year-old. BMD refers to the amount of minerals, in particular calcium, per volume in an individual's bone. The more dense the bones, the stronger the bones. A low test score indicates **osteopenia** (*penia* = poverty), which signals low bone mass. A very low test score indicates osteoporosis.

Ironically, though osteoporosis is often thought of as a condition of the elderly, it has its roots in childhood and must be prevented throughout adulthood. Saving up bone mass is like saving money for retirement. The more you save when you are young and preserve throughout your adulthood, the more you will have for your later years. Conversely, if you don't save enough early in life, you may end up with little to fall back on when you need it later. If children don't reach their maximum bone mass by young adulthood, they will not have adequate bone mass stored for their later years. If an adult doesn't have a healthy diet and lifestyle that includes regular exercise, he or she may experience accelerated bone loss after age 30.

It's never too late to try to reduce your risk of osteoporosis. To take a look at the risk factors involved, see the Self-Assessment on the next page.

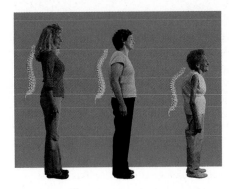

Weak bones cause the spine to collapse over time.

In your early years, more bone mass is added than lost in your body. In their mid-30s, women begin to slowly lose bone mass until menopause, when the rate of loss is accelerated for several years. Bone loss continues after age 60 but at a slower rate. Bone loss also occurs in men as they age.

(Bone growth/loss chart) Active growth · Slow loss · Rapid loss · Less rapid loss · Age in years: 10 20 30 40 50 60 70 80 90

peak bone mass The genetically determined maximum amount of bone mass an individual can build up.

osteoporosis A condition whereby the bones are less dense, increasing the risk of fractures.

bone mineral density (BMD) The amount of minerals, in particular calcium, per volume in an individual's bone. The denser the bones, the stronger the bones.

osteopenia Low bone mass.

Are You at Risk for Osteoporosis?

There are several factors that increase your risk of osteoporosis and bone fractures. As with factors that affect your risk of hypertension, you can control some of these, but not others. Take the following Self-Assessment quiz to determine how many risk factors you have for osteoporosis. Shade in each part of the skeleton (on the next page) based on your answers.

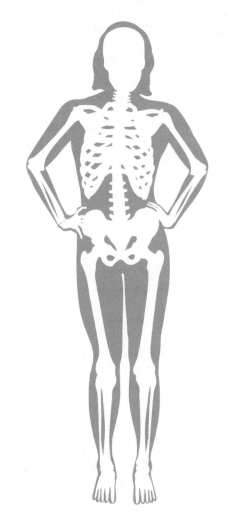

1. **Gender:** Are you female?
   Yes ☐ **No** ☐ (If you answered no, shade in the left arm of the skeleton.)
   Females are at a higher risk for osteoporosis than males because they have smaller bones, and thus less bone mass. Also, bone mass is lost at a faster rate right after menopause due to the decline of estrogen in women's bodies. However, men can suffer from osteoporosis and can experience it at a fairly young age.[18]

2. **Ethnicity:** Are you a Caucasian or Asian-American female?
   Yes ☐ **No** ☐ (If no, shade in the right arm of the skeleton.)
   Caucasian and Asian women typically have lower bone mass than other women.

3. **Age:** Are you over 30 years of age?
   Yes ☐ **No** ☐ (If no, shade in the left hand of the skeleton.)
   You begin to lose bone mass after about age 30, which increases your risk of osteoporosis and fractures.

4. **Body Type:** Are you a small-boned or petite woman?
   Yes ☐ **No** ☐ (If no, shade in the right hand of the skeleton.)
   Thin women have lower bone mass and increased risk of fractures. A higher body weight puts more weight-bearing, mechanical stress on bones, helping them to stay healthy. A healthy body weight also means you'll have some padding should a fall occur. Also, since most of the estrogen

After you have completed the self-assessment, look at the skeleton. If it has mostly shaded areas, you have fewer risk factors for osteoporosis, while the more risk factors you have, the higher your risk of developing osteoporosis. Many of these risk factors can be reduced by a healthy diet and lifestyle.

Although you cannot control the first five risk factors (your gender, ethnicity, age, body type, and family history), you can control the remaining six risk factors. If your sex hormone levels are lower than they should be and/or if you are taking medications that may increase your risk of osteoporosis, talk to your doctor. Quitting smoking, exercising regularly, and limiting or avoiding alcohol will help reduce your risk. Lastly, make sure that you are consuming adequate amounts of vitamin D (Chapter 7) and calcium (see Visual Summary Table on page 276) to meet your needs. If you can't meet your calcium needs through food, a supplement may be necessary.

produced in menopausal women's bodies is formed in fat tissue, thinner women have less bone-protecting estrogen.[19]

5. **Family History of Fractures:** Have your parents or grandparents ever experienced any bone fractures in their golden years?
Yes ☐ **No** ☐ (If no, shade in the left leg of the skeleton.) A family history of bone fractures in your relatives' later years increases your risk of osteoporosis.

6. **Level of Sex Hormones:** Are you a premenonpausal woman who has stopped menstruating, a menopausal woman (have low estrogen levels), or a male with low testosterone levels?
Yes ☐ **No** ☐ (If no, shade in the right leg of area of the skeleton.) Women with amenorrhea (the absence of menstrual periods) experience hormonal imbalances especially if they are at a dangerously low body weight.[20] Menopausal women, or men with low levels of sex hormones, which are protective against bone loss, are also at a higher risk.

7. **Medications:** Are you taking certain medications such as glucocorticoids (prednisone), antiseizure medications (pheytoin), aluminum-containing antacids, and/or excessive amounts of thyroid replacement hormones?
Yes ☐ **No** ☐ (If no, shade in the torso of the skeleton.) The long-term use of glucocorticoids, antiseizure medicines, certain antacids, or too much thyroid hormone-replacing medication can lead to a loss of bone mass and increase the risk of fractures.[21] Certain cancer treatments can also cause bone loss. Though you shouldn't stop taking any prescribed medications, you should speak to your doctor regarding your bone health.

8. **Smoking:** Do you smoke?
Yes ☐ **No** ☐ (If no, shade in the left foot of the skeleton.)

Smokers absorb less calcium than do nonsmokers. Women smokers have lower levels of estrogen in their bodies and begin menopause earlier than do nonsmokers.

9. **Physical Activity:** Do you spend less than 30 minutes exercising daily?
Yes ☐ **No** ☐ (If no, shade in the left hip of the skeleton.) Regular physical activity not only contributes to higher peak bone mass in a person's early years, but strength and weight-bearing activities such as walking, hiking, and tennis help maintain bone mass during adulthood. These activities cause you to work against gravity, which helps your bones become stronger. Regular exercise also helps you maintain healthy muscles and improves your coordination and balance, which can help you prevent falls.[22]

10. **Alcohol:** Do you consume more than one alcoholic drink a day if you are a woman or consume more than two alcoholic drinks daily if you are a man?
Yes ☐ **No** ☐ (If no, shade in the right hip of the skeleton.) Heavy consumption of alcohol can reduce bone mass by inhibiting the formation of new bone, preventing the activation of vitamin D, and increasing the loss of calcium. It can also increase the risk of stumbling and falling.[23]

11. **Inadequate Amounts of Calcium and Vitamin D:** Do you consume less than 3 cups daily of milk or yogurt that has been fortified with vitamin D?
Yes ☐ **No** ☐ (If no, shade in the right foot of the skeleton.) Because calcium is needed to build and maintain bone mass, and vitamin D is needed for your body to absorb this mineral, having inadequate amounts of either or both of these nutrients increases your risk of low bone mass, bone loss, and bone fractures.

The Trace Minerals Are Needed in Small Amounts

The trace minerals—iron, zinc, selenium, fluoride, chromium, copper, iodine, manganese, and molybdenum—are needed in much smaller amounts, less than 20 milligrams daily, compared with the major minerals. There are even smaller amounts of trace minerals in your body.[43] However, don't assume that this diminishes their importance. Trace minerals play essential roles that are as important as those of the major minerals. Some (chromium, iodine) help certain hormones, such as insulin and thyroid hormones, function. They are indispensable for maintaining healthy red blood cells (iron) and protecting your teeth (fluoride), and can be cofactors (iron, zinc, copper, manganese, and molybdenum) that work with enzymes to ensure that numerous critical reactions occur. Let's look at each of these essential trace minerals.

Iron

What Is Iron?

Iron is the most abundant mineral on Earth, and the most abundant trace mineral in your body. A 130-pound female has over 2,300 milligrams of iron in her body—about the weight of a dime—whereas a 165-pound male will have 4,000 milligrams of iron in his body—slightly less than two dimes.[43]

As a key component of blood, iron is highly valuable to the body and is treated accordingly. For the most part, iron is not excreted in the urine or stool, so once absorbed very little of it leaves the body. Approximately 95 percent of your iron is recycled and reused.[44] Whereas some iron is shed in hair, skin, and sloughed-off intestinal cells, most iron loss is due to bleeding.

Iron Occurs in Two Forms: Heme and Non-Heme

Foods from animal sources, such as meat, poultry, and fish, provide heme iron in your diet. Heme iron (see figure) is part of the protein **hemoglobin** in your red blood cells and the protein **myoglobin**

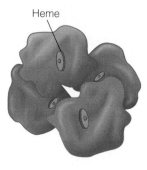

Heme

in your muscles. Heme iron is easily absorbed by your body.

Plant foods such as grains and vegetables are the main sources of non-heme iron in your diet. Non-heme iron is not as easily absorbed as heme iron. This is because other compounds in foods, such as phytates in legumes, rice, and grains, the polyphenols in tea, and the protein in soy products, all inhibit its absorption.

In general, your body absorbs only about 10–15 percent of the iron you eat.

However, if your body stores are low, the amount you absorb from foods will increase.

You can enhance your non-heme iron absorption by eating a food that's high in vitamin C along with iron-rich foods. Vitamin C and the acids in your stomach change the configuration of non-heme iron, which improves its absorption. As little as 25 milligrams of vitamin C—the amount in about one-quarter cup of orange juice—can double the amount of non-heme iron you absorb from your meal and 50 milligrams of vitamin C can increase the amount absorbed by about sixfold. Keep this in mind when you make your next peanut butter-on-whole-wheat sandwich and have an orange for dessert.

Another way to enhance non-heme iron absorption from foods is to eat meat, fish, or poultry at the same meal. The peptides (joined amino acids) in these animal-derived foods are thought to be

the enhancing factors. The meat in your next turkey sandwich will help enhance the absorption of the non-heme iron in whole-wheat bread.

Functions of Iron

Hemoglobin and Myoglobin Transport Oxygen

Approximately two-thirds of the iron in your body is in hemoglobin, the oxygen-carrying transport protein in your red blood cells. The iron-containing heme

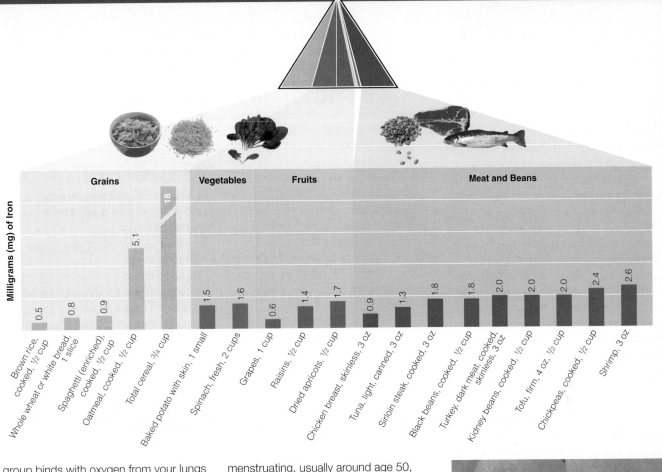

Milligrams (mg) of Iron

Grains	Vegetables	Fruits	Meat and Beans

- Brown rice, cooked, 1/2 cup — 0.5
- Whole wheat or white bread, 1 slice — 0.8
- Spaghetti (enriched), cooked, 1/2 cup — 0.9
- Oatmeal, cooked, 1/2 cup — 5.1
- Total cereal, 3/4 cup — 18
- Baked potato with skin, 1 small — 1.5
- Spinach, fresh, 2 cups — 1.6
- Grapes, 1 cup — 0.6
- Raisins, 1/2 cup — 1.4
- Dried apricots, 1/2 cup — 1.7
- Chicken breast, skinless, 3 oz — 0.9
- Tuna, light, canned, 3 oz — 1.3
- Sirloin steak, cooked, 3 oz — 1.8
- Black beans, cooked, 1/2 cup — 1.8
- Turkey, dark meat, cooked, skinless, 3 oz — 2.0
- Kidney beans, cooked, 1/2 cup — 2.0
- Tofu, firm, 4 oz, 1/2 cup — 2.0
- Chickpeas, cooked, 1/2 cup — 2.4
- Shrimp, 3 oz — 2.6

group binds with oxygen from your lungs and is transported to your tissues for their use. Hemoglobin also picks up carbon dioxide waste products from your cells and brings them to your lungs to be exhaled from your body.

Similarly, iron is part of the myoglobin that transports and stores oxygen in your muscles.

Iron Is Needed for Brain Function

Iron helps enzymes that are involved in the synthesis of neurotransmitters in your brain send messages to the rest of your body. A deficiency of iron in children can impact their ability to learn and retain information. Studies have shown that children with iron deficiency anemia in their early years can have persistent, decreased cognitive ability during their later school years.[45]

Daily Needs

Adult females, age 19 to 50, need 18 milligrams daily to cover the iron lost during menstruation. After a woman stops

menstruating, usually around age 50, her daily iron needs drop to 8 milligrams because she is no longer losing blood monthly.

Adult males need 8 milligrams of dietary iron daily. These recommendations for women and men take into account a typical American diet, which includes both heme and non-heme iron sources.

Adult men consume more than twice their recommended iron needs—over 16 milligrams, on average, daily. Adult premenopausal women consume only about 70 percent of their daily need, or approximately 13 milligrams, on average. Postmenopausal women are consuming slightly over 12 milligrams of iron daily, so, like men, they are meeting their needs.

The iron needs of vegetarians are 1.8 times higher than those of nonvegetarians due to components in plant foods that inhibit iron absorption.[46]

Food Sources

About half of Americans' dietary iron intake comes from iron-enriched bread and other grain foods such as cereals. Heme

iron in meat, fish, and poultry contributes only 12 percent of the dietary iron needs of males and females. Cooking foods in iron pans and skillets can increase their non-heme iron content, as foods absorb iron from the pan.[47]

Too Much or Too Little

Consuming too much iron from supplements can cause constipation, nausea, vomiting, and diarrhea. The upper level for iron for adults is set at 45 milligrams daily, as this level is slightly less than the amount known to cause these intestinal symptoms. This upper level doesn't apply to individuals with liver disease or other diseases, such as hemochromatosis (see below), which can affect iron stores in the body; it is too high for these individuals.

In the United States the accidental consumption of supplements containing iron is the leading cause of poisoning deaths in children under age 6. Ingestion of as little as 200 milligrams of iron has been shown to be fatal. Children who swallow iron supplements can experience symptoms such as nausea, vomiting, and diarrhea within minutes. Intestinal bleeding can also occur, which can lead to shock, coma, and even death. The FDA has mandated that a warning statement about the risk of iron poisoning in small children be put on every iron supplement label and that pills that contain 30 milligrams or more of iron must be individually wrapped.[48]

Undetected excessive storing of iron in the body over several years is called iron overload and can damage a person's tissues and organs, including the heart, kidneys, liver, and nervous system. **Hemochromatosis,** a genetic disorder in which individuals absorb too much dietary iron, can cause iron overload. Though this condition is congenital, its symptoms often aren't manifested until adulthood. If not diagnosed and treated early enough, organ damage can occur. These individuals need to avoid iron supplements throughout their lives, as well as large amounts of vitamin C supplements, which enhance iron absorption.

Iron overload from consuming too much dietary iron has occurred in South Africans and Zimbabwean natives who consume large amounts of beer. The iron content in the particular beer that they are drinking is high: 80 milligrams per liter. However, these individuals may also have a genetic disorder that contributes to excessive iron storage in the body. It is not known if excessive amounts of dietary iron alone in healthy individuals could cause iron overload.

The jury is still out about the role of iron in heart disease. Some studies suggest that iron can stimulate free radical production in the body, which can damage the arteries leading to the heart. Though this association is not definite, unless you are medically diagnosed with iron deficiency, it doesn't make any sense to consume excessive amounts of iron.

Iron deficiency is the most common nutritional disorder in the world. If your

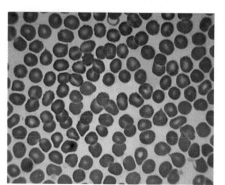
Normal red blood cells.

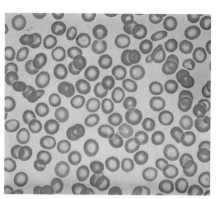
Blood cells affected by anemia.

diet is deficient in iron, your body stores will be slowly depleted so as to keep your blood hemoglobin in a normal range. **Iron-deficiency anemia** occurs when your stores are so depleted that your hemoglobin levels decrease. This will diminish the delivery of oxygen through the body, causing fatigue and weakness. Premenopausal females, pregnant women, preterm and low-birth-weight infants, and older infants and toddlers are at risk of developing iron-deficiency anemia because they often fall short of the recommended dietary amounts. This will be discussed further in Chapters 12 and 13.

Pregnant women (because of their increased iron needs), menstruating women, and teenage girls, especially those with heavy blood losses, as well as older infants and toddlers are often not meeting their iron needs and are at risk of becoming deficient.[49]

Terms to Know

hemoglobin ■ myoglobin ■ hemochromatosis ■ iron-deficiency anemia

Copper

What Is Copper?

Copper may bring to mind ancient tools, great sculptures, or American pennies (although pennies are no longer made of solid copper), but it is also associated with several key body functions.

Functions of Copper

Copper is part of many enzymes and proteins. It is important for iron absorption and transfer and the synthesis of hemoglobin and red blood cells.

Copper helps generate energy in your cells, synthesize melanin (the dark pigment found in skin), and link the proteins collagen and elastin together in connective tissue. It works with enzymes to protect your cells from free radicals.

Copper also plays an important role in blood clotting and in maintaining a healthy immune system.[50]

Daily Needs

Both adult women and men need 900 micrograms of copper daily. American women consume 1,000 to 1,100 micrograms, whereas men consume 1,300 to 1,500 micrograms daily, on average.

Food Sources

Organ meats such as liver, seafood, nuts, and seeds are abundant in copper. Bran cereals, whole-grain products, and cocoa are also good sources. Whereas potatoes, milk, and chicken are low in copper, they are consumed in such abundant amounts that they contribute a fair amount of copper to Americans' diets.

Too Much or Too Little

Too much copper can cause stomach pains and cramps, nausea, diarrhea, vomiting, and even liver damage. The upper level for copper for adults is set at 10,000 micrograms daily.

Copper deficiency is rare in the United States. It has occurred in premature babies fed milk formulas, malnourished infants fed cow's milk, and individuals given intravenous feedings that lacked adequate amounts of copper.

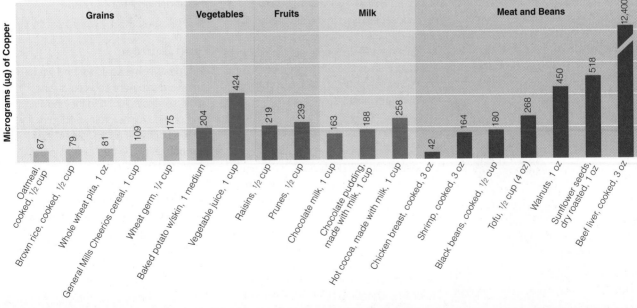

Microgram (µg) of Copper

| Grains | Vegetables | Fruits | Milk | Meat and Beans |

- Oatmeal, cooked, 1/2 cup: 67
- Brown rice, cooked, 1/2 cup: 79
- Whole wheat pita, 1 oz: 81
- General Mills Cheerios cereal, 1 cup: 109
- Wheat germ, 1/4 cup: 175
- Baked potato w/skin, 1 medium: 204
- Vegetable juice, 1 cup: 424
- Raisins, 1/2 cup: 219
- Prunes, 1/2 cup: 239
- Chocolate milk, 1 cup: 163
- Chocolate pudding, made with milk, 1 cup: 188
- Hot cocoa, made with milk, 1 cup: 258
- Chicken breast, cooked, 3 oz: 42
- Shrimp, cooked, 3 oz: 164
- Black beans, cooked, 1/2 cup: 180
- Tofu, 1/2 cup (4 oz): 268
- Walnuts, 1 oz: 450
- Sunflower seeds, dry roasted, 1 oz: 518
- Beef liver, cooked, 3 oz: 12,400

Zinc

What Is Zinc?

Zinc is found in almost every cell of your body. It is involved in the function of more than 100 enzymes, including those used for protein synthesis. As important as it is, it was not considered an essential nutrient until 1974.

Functions of Zinc

Zinc Is Needed for DNA Synthesis and Growth and Development

Zinc plays a role in the structure of both RNA and DNA in your cells and in gene expression.

Zinc is needed for adequate growth in developing infants and throughout the adolescent years.[51]

Zinc Helps Keep Your Immune System Healthy and Helps Wounds Heal

Zinc is needed for production of white blood cells, so it helps keep your immune system healthy.

Zinc helps reduce the inflammation that can accompany skin wounds. Zinc also helps in wound healing by being part of enzymes and proteins that repair and enhance the proliferation of skin cells.[52]

Zinc Brings Out the Best in Your Taste Buds

One lick of a chocolate ice cream cone or a forkful of cherry cheesecake will make you appreciate the role that zinc plays in taste acuity, which is the ability to savor the flavors of your foods. A deficiency

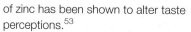

of zinc has been shown to alter taste perceptions.[53]

The Truth about Zinc and the Common Cold

Zinc lozenges are sometimes advertised to help you reduce the severity and duration of the common cold. Unfortunately, the metallic taste of zinc may have cold sufferers fooled into thinking, as a team of researchers put it, ". . . anything tasting as bad as zinc and with as much aftertaste as zinc must be good medicine."[54] Don't let zinc's medicinal taste fool you.

Whereas a few studies have suggested that zinc intake, at high doses, may help fight against colds, a review of numerous studies has failed to find that it has any effect on sniffles and sneezes. In fact, the high dosages used in the studies often exceeded the recommended upper level. If consumed for too long, doses this high could put an individual at risk of more uncomfortable, medically worse problems than a stuffy nose.[55]

Zinc Plays a Role in Fighting AMD Disease

Research studies do support the assertion that zinc may play a role in reducing the risk of age-related macular degeneration (AMD), a condition that hampers central vision. Zinc may work with an enzyme in your eyes that's needed to properly utilize vitamin A for vision. Zinc may also help mobilize vitamin A from the liver to ensure adequate blood levels of this

vitamin. Supplements that contain antioxidants along with zinc have been shown to reduce the risk of AMD. (See the section on antioxidants in Chapter 7.)

Daily Needs

Adult males need 11 milligrams of zinc, whereas women need 8 milligrams daily. American adults, on average, are meeting their daily zinc needs. Men are consuming from 11 milligrams to over 14 milligrams and women are consuming 8 to 9 milligrams of zinc daily, on average.

Vegetarians, especially strict vegetarians, can have as much as a 50 percent higher need for zinc. Phytates in plant foods such as grains and legumes, which are staples of vegan diets, can bind with zinc, reducing its absorption in the intestinal tract.

Food Sources

Red meat, some seafood, and whole grains are excellent sources of zinc. Because zinc is found in the germ and bran portion of the grain, refined grains stripped of these components have as much as 80 percent less zinc than whole grains.

Too Much or Too Little

The upper level for zinc in food and/or supplements for adults is set at 40 milligrams daily. Consuming too much zinc, as little as 50 milligrams, can cause stomach pains, nausea, vomiting, and diarrhea. Approximately 60 milligrams of zinc

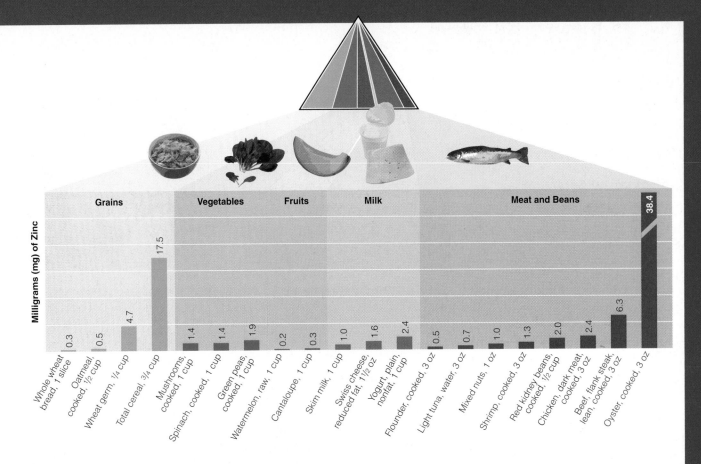

Milligrams (mg) of Zinc

Food	mg of Zinc
Grains	
Whole wheat bread, 1 slice	0.3
Oatmeal, cooked, ½ cup	0.5
Wheat germ, ¼ cup	4.7
Total cereal, ¾ cup	17.5
Vegetables	
Mushrooms, cooked, 1 cup	1.4
Spinach, cooked, 1 cup	1.4
Green peas, cooked, 1 cup	1.9
Fruits	
Watermelon, raw, 1 cup	0.2
Cantaloupe, 1 cup	0.3
Milk	
Skim milk, 1 cup	1.0
Swiss cheese, reduced fat, 1½ oz	1.6
Yogurt, plain, nonfat, 1 cup	2.4
Meat and Beans	
Flounder, cooked, 3 oz	0.5
Light tuna, water, 3 oz	0.7
Mixed nuts, 1 oz	1.0
Shrimp, cooked, 3 oz	1.3
Red kidney beans, cooked, ½ cup	2.0
Chicken, dark meat, cooked, 3 oz	2.4
Beef, flank steak, lean, cooked, 3 oz	6.3
Oyster, cooked, 3 oz	38.4

daily has been shown to lower the level of copper in your body by competing with this mineral for absorption in the intestinal tract. This is an excellent example of how the overconsumption of one mineral can compromise the benefits of another.

Excessive amounts, such as 300 milligrams of zinc daily, have been shown to suppress the immune system and lower the HDL ("good") cholesterol.

A deficiency of zinc can cause hair loss, loss of appetite, impaired taste of foods, diarrhea, and delayed sexual maturation, as well as impotence and skin rashes.

Because zinc is needed during development, a deficiency can slow and impair growth. Classic studies of groups of people in the Middle East showed that people who consumed a diet mainly of

unleavened bread, which is high in zinc-binding phytates, experienced impaired growth and dwarfism.[56]

Table Tips

Zapping Your Zinc Needs!

Enjoy a tuna fish sandwich on whole-wheat bread at lunch for a double serving (fish and bread) of zinc.

Add kidney beans to your cup of soup. (These beans are often at cafeteria salad bars, so add a spoonful to your soup and salad lunch.)

Pack a small handful of mixed nuts and raisins in a zip-closed bag for a snack on the run.

Make your breakfast oatmeal with milk for two servings of zinc in one bowl!

Add cooked green peas to casseroles, stews, soups, and salads.

Selenium

What Is Selenium?

The mineral selenium is part of a class of proteins called selenoproteins, many of which are enzymes. Selenoproteins have important functions in your body.

Functions of Selenium

Selenium Is Needed by Your Thyroid

Selenium-containing enzymes help regulate thyroid hormones in your body.

Selenium Plays an Antioxidant Role

Selenoproteins can also function as antioxidants that protect your cells from free radicals. (See the section on antioxidants in Chapter 7.) As you recall, free radicals are natural by-products of metabolism and can also result from exposure to chemicals in the environment. If free radicals accumulate faster than your body can neutralize them, their damaging effects can contribute to chronic diseases, such as heart disease.[57]

Selenium May Help Fight Cancer

Research studies have suggested that deaths from cancers, such as lung, colon, and prostate cancers, are lower in groups of people that consume more selenium. Selenium's antioxidant capabilities, and its ability to potentially slow the growth of tumors, are thought to be the mechanism behind its anticancer effects.

The FDA now allows a Qualified Health Claim on food labels and dietary supplements that states that "selenium may reduce the risk of certain cancers but the evidence is limited and not conclusive to date."[58]

A National Institutes of Health (NIH) study is currently under way to see if selenium alone or with vitamin E will reduce the risk of prostate cancer in men. The study is scheduled to end in 2013.

Daily Needs

Both adult females and males need 55 micrograms of selenium daily. American adults are more than meeting their needs—they consume about 80 micrograms to 160 micrograms daily, on average.

Food Sources

Meat, seafood, cereal, grains, dairy foods, and fruits and vegetables can all contribute to dietary selenium. However, the amount of selenium in the foods that you eat depends upon the soil where the plants were grown and the animals grazed.

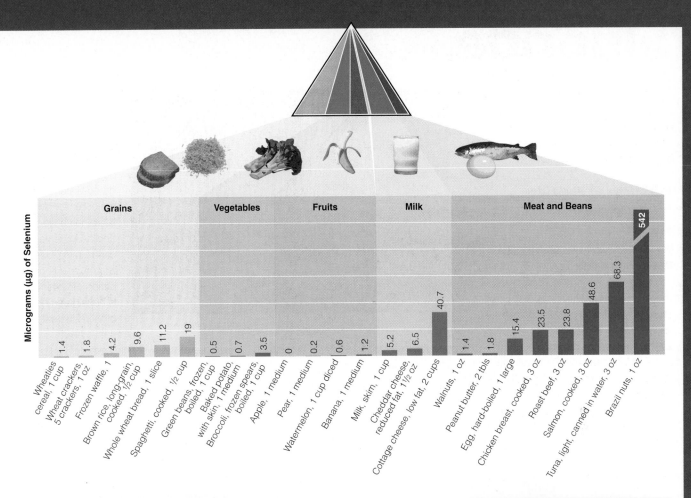

Micrograms (µg) of Selenium

Category	Food	µg
Grains	Wheaties cereal, 1 cup	1.4
	Wheat crackers, 5 crackers, 1 oz	1.8
	Frozen waffle, 1	4.2
	Brown rice, long-grain, cooked, ½ cup	9.6
	Whole wheat bread, 1 slice	11.2
	Spaghetti, cooked, ½ cup	19
Vegetables	Green beans, frozen, boiled, 1 cup	0.5
	Baked potato, with skin, 1 medium	0.7
	Broccoli, frozen spears, boiled, 1 cup	3.5
Fruits	Apple, 1 medium	0
	Pear, 1 medium	0.2
	Watermelon, 1 cup diced	0.6
	Banana, 1 medium	1.2
Milk	Milk, skim, 1 cup	5.2
	Cheddar cheese, reduced fat, 1½ oz	6.5
	Cottage cheese, low fat, 2 cups	40.7
Meat and Beans	Walnuts, 1 oz	1.4
	Peanut butter, 2 tbls	1.8
	Egg, hard-boiled, 1 large	15.4
	Chicken breast, cooked, 3 oz	23.5
	Roast beef, 3 oz	23.8
	Salmon, cooked, 3 oz	48.6
	Tuna, light, canned in water, 3 oz	68.3
	Brazil nuts, 1 oz	542

For example, wheat grown in selenium-rich soil can have more than a tenfold higher amount of the mineral than an identical wheat grown in selenium-poor soil.

Too Much or Too Little

Too much selenium can cause toxicity and a condition called **selenosis.** A person with selenosis will have brittle nails and hair, both of which may fall out. Other symptoms include stomach and intestinal discomfort, a skin rash, garlicky breath, fatigue, and damage to the nervous system. The upper level for selenium for adults is set at 400 micrograms to prevent the loss and brittleness of nails and hair, which is the most common symptom of selenosis.

While rare in the United States, a selenium deficiency can cause **Keshan disease,** which damages the heart. This disease typically only occurs in children who live in rural areas that have selenium-poor soil. However, some researchers speculate that selenium deficiency alone may not cause Keshan disease, but the selenium-deficient individual may also be exposed to a virus, which, together with the selenium deficiency, leads to the damaged heart.[59]

Terms to Know
selenosis ■ Keshan disease

Seeking Out Selenium

Top a toasted whole-wheat bagel with a slice of reduced fat cheddar cheese for a hot way to start the day.

Spread peanut butter on whole-wheat crackers and top with a slice of banana.

Top your dinner pasta with broccoli for a selenium-smart meal.

Zap sliced apples, sprinkled with a little apple juice and cinnamon, in the microwave and top with vanilla yogurt.

Spoon a serving of low-fat cottage cheese into a bowl and top with canned sliced peaches and almonds for a fabulous dessert.

Fluoride

What Is Fluoride?

Fluoride is the safe ion form of fluorine, a poisonous gas. Calcium fluoride is the form that is found in your bones and teeth.

Functions of Fluoride

Fluoride Protects Against Dental Caries

The best known function of fluoride is its role in keeping teeth healthy. Your teeth have an outer layer called enamel (see the figure below), which can become eroded over time by acids and result in dental caries. The acids are produced by the bacteria in your mouth when they feast on the carbohydrates that you eat. Continual exposure of your teeth to these acids can cause erosion and create a cavity.

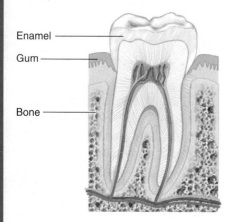

Fluoride from food, beverages, and dental products, such as toothpaste, helps protect your teeth in several ways. It helps to repair the enamel that has already started to erode.

Fluoride also interferes with the ability of the bacteria to metabolize carbohydrates, thus reducing the amount of acid they produce.

Finally, fluoride provides a protective barrier between your tooth and the destructive acids. As a component of saliva, it provides a continual fluoride bath to your teeth's surfaces.[60]

Consuming adequate amounts of fluoride is extremely important during infancy and childhood, when teeth are developing,

and for maintenance of healthy teeth throughout your life.

Fluoride in Drinking Water Has Improved the Nation's Dental Health

In the 1930s, scientists noticed lower rates of dental caries among individuals whose community water systems contained significant amounts of fluoride. Studies confirmed that the fluoride was the protective factor in the water that helped fight dental decay. Since 1945, most communities have fluoridated their water, and today, 67 percent of Americans live in communities that have a fluoridated water supply.

The increase in access to fluoridated water is the major reason why there has been a decline in dental caries in the United States, and fluoridation of water is considered one of the ten greatest public health advances of the twentieth century.[61]

To find out if your community water is fluoridated and how much fluoride is added, visit the Centers for Disease Control and Prevention's website, My Water's Fluoride, at: http://apps.nccd.cdc.gov/MWF/Index.asp.

Daily Needs

Adult men should consume 3.8 milligrams and women 3.1 milligrams of fluoride daily to meet their needs. If the tap water in your community is fluoridated at 1 milligram/liter, you would have to consume at least 13 cups of water daily,

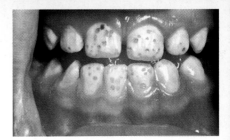

Teeth pitted by fluorosis

If you shy away from tap water and drink and cook predominantly with bottled water, you may be robbing yourself of some cavity protection. Most bottled waters sold in the United States have less than the optimal amount of fluoride. It is difficult to determine the fluoride content of many bottled waters because currently, the amount of fluoride in bottled water only has to be listed on the label if fluoride has been specifically added. Check the label to see if your bottled water contains added fluoride. For more information about the differences between bottled and tap water, and their advantages and disadvantages, see the boxed feature "Tap Water or Bottled Water: Is Bottled Better?" on page 266.

through either beverages or cooking, to meet your fluoride needs (1 liter = 4.2 cups).

Currently, adults are consuming 1.4 to 3.4 milligrams of fluoride daily if they are living in communities with fluoridated water. That number drops to only 0.3 to 1.0 milligrams consumed daily if the water isn't fluoridated.[62]

Food Sources

Foods in general are not a good source of fluoride. The best sources are fluoridated water and beverages and foods made with this water, such as coffee, tea, and soups. Another source of flouride can be juices made from concentrate using fluoridated tap water (remember, not all tap water contains fluoride).

Water and processed beverages, such as soft drinks, account for up to 75 percent of Americans' fluoride intake.

Tea is also a good source of fluoride, as tea leaves accumulate fluoride. Note that decaffeinated tea has twice the amount of fluoride as the caffeinated variety.[63]

Too Much or Too Little

Because of fluroide's protective qualities, too little exposure to or consumption of fluoride increases the risk of dental caries.

Having some fluoride is important for healthy teeth, but too much can cause fluorosis, a condition whereby the teeth become mottled (pitted) and develop white patches or stains on the surface. Fluorosis creates teeth that are extremely resistant to caries but cosmetically unappealing (see photo).

Fluorosis occurs when teeth are forming, so only infants and children up to 8 years of age are at risk. Once teeth break through the gums, fluorosis can't occur. Fluorosis results from overfluorida- tion of water, swallowing toothpaste, or excessive use of dental products that contain fluoride. Some research suggests that fluorosis may be reversable but more studies are needed to determine this.

Skeletal fluorosis can occur in bones when a person consumes at least 10 milligrams of fluoride daily for 10 or more years. This is a rare situation when water is mistakenly overly fluoridated. This can cause bone concentrations of fluoride that are up to 5 times higher than normal and result in stiffness or pain in joints, osteoporosis, and calcification of the ligaments.

The upper level for adults has been set at 10 milligrams to reduce the risk of fluorosis in the bones. (Note, however, that the upper level for infants and children is much lower, to prevent fluorosis in teeth. See the inside cover of the textbook for this upper level.)

Table Tips
Fabulous Ways to Get Fluoride

Pour orange juice into ice cube trays and pop a couple of frozen cubes into a glass of tap water for a refreshing and flavorful beverage.

Use tap water when making coffee, tea, or juice from concentrate, and for food preparation.

Brew a mug of flavored decaffeinated tea, such as French vanilla or gingerbread, to keep you warm while you're hitting the books.

Terms to Know
fluorosis

Chromium

What Is Chromium?

The most recent mineral to be found necessary in humans, chromium was identified as an essential mineral in 1977, although researchers have had an interest in chromium and its roles in the metabolism of glucose since the 1950s.[64]

Functions of Chromium

Chromium Helps Insulin in Your Body

The main function of this mineral is to increase insulin's effectiveness in cells. The hormone insulin plays an important role in the metabolism and storage of carbohydrates, fats, and protein in your body. Individuals who were intravenously fed a chromium-free diet experienced high blood levels of glucose, weight loss, and nerve problems—all telltale signs of uncontrolled diabetes and poor blood glucose control. The problems were corrected when chromium was provided.[65]

Chromium May Reduce Pre-Diabetes

Because it works with insulin, some researchers think that chromium may help individuals who have diabetes mellitus or pre-diabetes (glucose intolerance) improve their blood glucose control. There has yet to be a large research study in the United States that confirms this theory.

One small study suggests that a chromium supplement may reduce the risk of insulin resistance, and therefore, favorably affect the handling of glucose in the body. Improving the body's sensitivity to insulin and maintaining a normal blood glucose level can possibly lower the incidence of type 2 diabetes in individuals at risk.

Based on this one study, the FDA has allowed a Qualified Health Claim on chromium supplements. However, the supplement label must state that the evidence regarding the relationship between chromium supplements and either insulin resistance or type 2 diabetes is not certain at this time.[66]

Chromium Does Not Help Build Muscle Mass

Although advertisements have sometimes touted chromium supplements as an aid to losing weight and building lean muscle, the research doesn't support the claim. A review of over 20 research studies didn't find any benefits from taking up to 1,000 micrograms of chromium daily.[67]

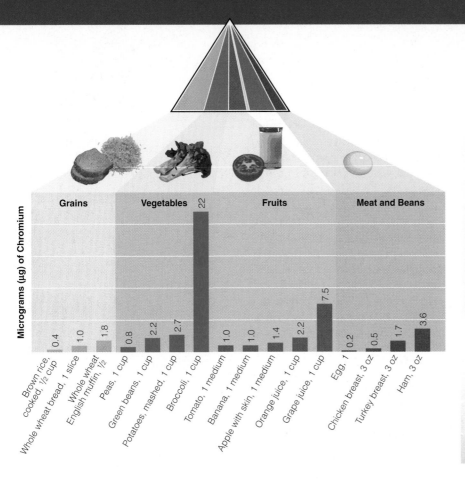

Micrograms (µg) of Chromium

Grains			Vegetables				Fruits					Meat and Beans			

Brown rice, cooked, 1/2 cup — 0.4
Whole wheat bread, 1 slice — 1.0
Whole wheat English muffin, 1/2 — 1.8
Peas, 1 cup — 0.8
Green beans, 1 cup — 2.2
Potatoes, mashed, 1 cup — 2.7
Broccoli, 1 cup — 22
Tomato, 1 medium — 1.0
Banana, 1 medium — 1.0
Apple with skin, 1 medium — 1.4
Orange juice, 1 cup — 2.2
Grape juice, 1 cup — 7.5
Egg, 1 — 0.2
Chicken breast, 3 oz — 0.5
Turkey breast, 3 oz — 1.7
Ham, 3 oz — 3.6

If you are trying to become lean and mean, taking chromium supplements isn't going to help.

Daily Needs

Adult men aged 19 to 50 need 30 to 35 micrograms of chromium daily, whereas women of the same age need 20 to 25 micrograms daily, on average, depending upon their age. It is estimated that American men consume 33 micrograms of chromium from foods, and women consume 25 micrograms, on average, daily.[68]

Food Sources

Grains are good sources of chromium. Meat, fish, and poultry and some fruits and vegetables can also provide chromium, whereas dairy foods are low in the mineral.

Too Much or Too Little

As yet, there is no known risk from consuming excessive amounts of chromium from food or supplements, so no upper level has been set.

A chromium deficiency is very rare in the United States. However, a study in China, where chromium deficiency has been shown to exist, determined that individuals with type 2 diabetes experienced lower blood glucose levels and less insulin resistance when they were given chromium supplements. Again, it is not clear if individuals with diabetes who did

not have a chromium deficiency would benefit by taking a supplement.[69]

Table Tips
Cram in the Chromium

Toast a whole-wheat English muffin and top it with a slice of lean ham for a meaty, chromium-laden breakfast.

Add broccoli florets to your salad for a chromium-packed lunch.

Try an afternoon glass of cold grape juice for a refreshing break. Add an apple for a double dose of chromium.

Combine mashed potatoes and peas for a sweet and starchy addition to your dinner plate and your chromium count.

Split a firm banana in half, lengthwise, and spread a small amount of peanut butter on each side.

Iodine

What Is Iodine?

Like the fluoridation of community drinking water, the iodization of salt was a significant advance for public health in the United States. Prior to the 1920s, many Americans suffered from the iodine deficiency disease, goiter.

Once salt manufacturers began adding iodine to their product, incidence of the disease dropped. Today, rates of the disease are very low in the United States, though not in other parts of the world.

Functions of Iodine

Iodine is an essential mineral for your thyroid, a butterfly-shaped gland located in your neck. The thyroid needs iodine to make some essential hormones. In fact, approximately 60 percent of your thyroid hormones are comprised of iodine.

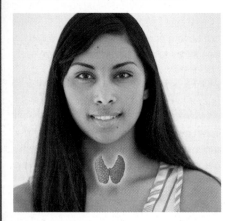

Thyroid hormones affect the majority of your cells, regulate your metabolic rate, and help your heart, nerves, muscles, and intestines function properly. Children need thyroid hormones for normal growth of bones and brain development.[70]

Daily Needs

Adult men and women need 150 micrograms of iodine daily to meet their needs. Americans are currently consuming 230 micrograms to 410 micrograms of iodine daily, on average, depending upon their age and gender.

Food Sources

The amount of iodine that occurs naturally in foods is typically low, approximately 3 to 75 micrograms in a serving, and is influenced by the amount of iodine in the soil, water, and fertilizers used to grow foods.

Fish can provide higher amounts of iodine, as they concentrate it from seawater. Iodized salt provides 400 micrograms of iodine per teaspoon. Note that not all salt has added iodine. Kosher salt, for example, has no additives, including iodine. Processed foods that use iodized salt or iodine-containing preservatives are also a source.

Too Much or Too Little

Consuming too much iodine can challenge the thyroid, impairing its function and reducing the synthesis and release of thyroid hormones. Because of this, the upper level for adults for iodine is 1,100 micrograms.

An early sign of iodine deficiency is **goiter,** which is an enlarged thyroid gland (see photo below). An iodine-deficient thyroid has to work harder to make the thyroid hormones, causing it to become enlarged.[71] A goiter epidemic in the midwestern United States is what prompted the campaign for mandatory iodization of salt. Based on the success of the campaign, the use of iodized salt spread rapidly throughout the United States.

A deficiency of iodine during the early stages of fetal development can damage the brain of the developing baby, causing mental retardation. Inadequate iodine during this critical time can cause lower IQ scores. Depending upon the severity of the iodine deficiency, **cretinism,** also known as **congenital hypothyroidism** (*congenital* = born with; *hypo* = under; *ism* = condition), can occur. Individuals with cretinism can experience abnormal sexual development, mental retardation, and dwarfism (see photo below).

Early detection of an iodine deficiency and treatment in children is critical to avoiding irreversible damage.

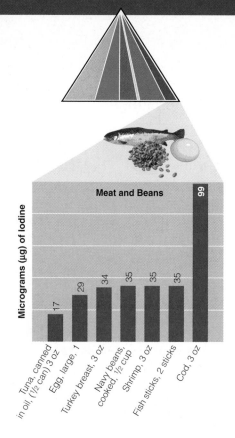

Meat and Beans

Micrograms (μg) of Iodine

17 — Tuna, canned in oil, (1/2 can) 3 oz
29 — Egg, large, 1
34 — Turkey breast, 3 oz
35 — Navy beans, cooked, 1/2 cup
35 — Shrimp, 3 oz
35 — Fish sticks, 2 sticks
99 — Cod, 3 oz

Cretinism

Terms to Know
goiter ■ cretinism (congenital hypothyroidism)

Goiter

Manganese

What Is Manganese?

Manganese is either part of, or activates, many enzymes in your body.

Functions of Manganese

Manganese Is Needed in Metabolism and for Healthy Bones

This mineral is involved in the metabolism of carbohydrates, fats, and amino acids. Manganese is needed for the formation of bone.

Daily Needs

Adult women need 1.8 milligrams, whereas men need 2.3 milligrams, of manganese daily. Americans are easily meeting their manganese needs. Adult women are consuming over 2 milligrams of manganese daily, and adult men are consuming over 2.8 milligrams daily, on average, from the foods in their diet.[72]

Food Sources

When it comes to meeting your manganese needs, look to whole grains, nuts, legumes, tea, vegetables, and fruits such as pineapples, strawberries, and bananas. A teaspoon of ground cinnamon provides just under 0.5 milligram of manganese.

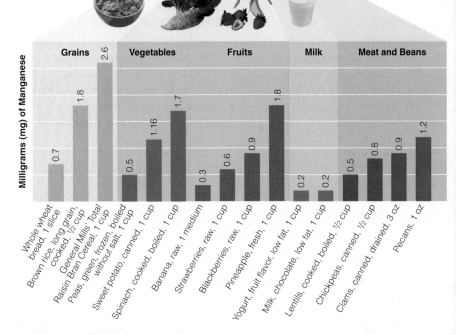

Milligrams (mg) of Manganese

Grains			Vegetables			Fruits			Milk		Meat and Beans		
Whole wheat bread, 1 slice	Brown rice, long grain, cooked, ½ cup	General Mills' Total Raisin Bran Cereal, 1 cup	Peas, green, frozen, boiled without salt, 1 cup	Sweet potato, canned, 1 cup	Spinach, cooked, boiled, 1 cup	Banana, raw, 1 medium	Strawberries, raw, 1 cup	Blackberries, raw, 1 cup	Pineapple, fresh, 1 cup	Yogurt, fruit flavor, low fat, 1 cup	Milk, chocolate, low fat, 1 cup	Lentils, cooked, boiled, ½ cup	Chickpeas, canned, ½ cup	Clams, canned, drained, 3 oz	Pecans, 1 oz
0.7	1.8	2.6	0.5	1.16	1.7	0.3	0.6	0.9	1.8	0.2	0.2	0.5	0.8	0.9	1.2

Too Much or Too Little

Manganese toxicity, which has occurred in miners who have inhaled manganese dust, can cause damage to the nervous system and symptoms that resemble Parkinson's disease.[73]

A study of individuals who drank water with high levels of manganese showed that they also experienced Parkinson's disease-like symptoms.

To protect against this toxicity, the upper level has been set at 11 milligrams daily.

A deficiency of manganese is rare in healthy individuals who have a balanced diet. Individuals fed a manganese-deficient diet developed a rash and scaly skin.

Table Tips
Managing Your Manganese

Sprinkle your whole-wheat toast with a dusting of cinnamon to spice up your morning.

Combine cooked brown rice, canned and rinsed lentils, and chickpeas for a dinner in a snap.

Spoon vanilla yogurt over canned crushed pineapples and sliced bananas for a tropical snack.

Molybdenum

What Is Molybdenum?

Molybdenum is part of several enzymes involved in the breakdown of certain amino acids and other compounds.

Daily Needs

Adult men and women need to consume 45 micrograms of molybdenum daily. American women currently consume 76 micrograms and men consume 109 micrograms of molybdenum daily, on average.

Food Sources

Legumes are excellent sources of molybdenum. Grains and nuts are also good sources.[74]

Too Much or Too Little

There is limited research on the adverse effects of too much dietary molybdenum in humans. In animal studies, too much molybdenum can cause reproductive problems. Because of this finding in animals, the upper level for molybdenum in humans has been set at 2 milligrams for adults.

A deficiency of molybdenum has not been seen in healthy individuals. However, a deficiency was observed in an individual who was fed intravenously for years and developed symptoms that included rapid heart beats, headaches, and night blindness.

Other Minerals: Arsenic, Boron, Nickel, Silicon, and Vanadium

A few other minerals exist in your body but their nutritional importance in humans has not yet been established. These minerals include arsenic, boron, nickel, silicon, and vanadium. While limited research suggests that these may have a function in animals, there isn't enough data to confirm an essential role in humans.[75]

Table 8.1 summarizes these minerals, their potential role in animal health, their food sources, and the levels of deficiency and toxicity, if known, in humans.

Table 8.1
Additional Minerals

Mineral	Potential Role and Deficiency Symptoms	Food Sources	Potential Toxicity
Arsenic	May be needed in the metabolism of a specific amino acid in rats. A deficiency may impair growth and reproduction in animals.	Dairy products, meat, poultry, fish, grains, and cereal products	No known adverse effect in humans from the organic form of arsenic found in foods. The inorganic form is poisonous for humans.
Boron	A deficiency may be associated with reproduction abnormalities in certain fish and frogs, which suggests a possible role in normal development in animals.	Grape juice, legumes, potatoes, pecans, peanut butter, apples, and milk	No known adverse effect from boron in food. Some research suggests that high amounts of boron may cause reproductive and developmental problems in animals. Because of this, the upper limit for human adults has been set at 20 mg daily, which is more than 10 times the amount American adults are consuming daily, on average.
Nickel	May be needed by specific enzymes in the body. It is considered an essential mineral in animals.	Grains and grain products, vegetables, legumes, nuts, and chocolate	No known toxicity of nickel in humans when consuming a normal diet. In rats, large exposure to nickel salts can cause toxicity, with symptoms such as lethargy, irregular breathing, and a lower than normal weight gain. Because of this, the upper limit for adults is set at 1 mg daily for nickel salts.
Silicon	May be needed for bone formation in animals.	Grains, grain products, and vegetables	No known risk of silicon toxicity in humans from food sources.
Vanadium	In animals, vanadium has insulin-like actions and a deficiency increases the risk of abortion.	Mushrooms, shellfish, parsley and black pepper	No known risk of toxicity in humans from vanadium in foods. Too much has been shown to cause kidney damage in animals. Vanadium can be purchased as supplements. Because of the known toxicity in animals, the upper limit for adults is set at 1.8 mg daily.

Source: Institute of Medicine. *Dietary Reference Intakes: Vitamin A, Vitamin K, Arsenic, Boron, Chromium, Copper, Iodine, Iron, Manganese, Molybdenum, Nickel, Silicon, Vanadium, and Zinc.* (Washington, D.C.: The National Academies Press, 2001). Available at www.nap.edu.

Putting It All Together

Water and minerals round out the list of essential nutrients that your body needs to maintain good health. Water is the universal solvent, and the main component of the fluids in which all reactions involving the energy-producing nutrients (carbohydrates, protein, and fats) take place in your body. Vitamins and minerals aid in these chemical reactions. All of these nutrients work together to keep you functioning properly. Currently Americans, on average, are meeting many of their nutrient needs but, as Table 8.2 shows, could use a little dietary fine-tuning to meet all of the recommendations for a healthy diet.

Consuming a wide variety of foods from all the food groups, with an emphasis on whole grains, whole fruits, and vegetables along with adequate amounts of lean dairy and meat, poultry, and plenty of fluids, is the best diet prescription to meet your needs for carbohydrates, protein, fat, vitamins, minerals, and water.

Table 8.2
Putting It All Together: Making Better Choices

American Adults Typically *Consume Enough:*	But Could Fine-Tune Their Dietary Choices to *Include More:*
Saturated fat	Unsaturated fat in place of saturated fat
Carbohydrates	Fiber-rich foods and less added sugars
Vitamins A, E, and K	Vitamin D if not exposed to adequate sunlight
B vitamins and vitamin C	Synthetic folic acid (premenopausal women only)
	(Synthetic vitamin B_{12} (individuals 51+ years only; vegans)
Sodium, phosphorus, zinc, selenium, chromium, copper, iodine, manganese, molybdenum	Potassium, calcium, magnesium, iron (premenopausal women only; vegans) zinc (vegans), fluoride (if not consuming fluoridated water)
Fluids with added sugar	Fluids (water)

Two Points of View

Shaking the Habit

How realistic is the current recommendation for adults to consume a mere 1,500 milligrams of sodium daily? Let's talk with two experts in the field of sodium and hypertension to find out if Americans can really shake the salt habit.

Tom Moore, MD
Boston University School of Medicine
Author, DASH Diet

Stella Volpe, PhD, RD, LDN, FACSM
University of Pennsylvania

Tom Moore, MD, is a professor of medicine at Boston University School of Medicine. He is the chairman of the steering committee of the DASH Trial, a large National Institutes of Health–funded research study involving the use of nutritional approaches to prevent and treat hypertension, which culminated in the DASH diet. He is the lead author of *The DASH Diet for Hypertension.* He has studied the blood pressure effects of foods and salt intake for over 20 years.

Q: While the current DRI for sodium is set at 1,500 milligrams daily for young adults, Americans, on average, are currently consuming over 3,000 milligrams of sodium daily. Is this DRI for sodium a realistic level for Americans, especially college students, to obtain? Why or why not?

A: It would not be easy for any American, young or old, to limit his or her sodium intake to 1,500 milligrams per day in our current U.S. food environment. Most of the sodium we consume is "hidden" in prepared foods such as chips, soup, sausage, and bread. There seems to be no harm from limiting sodium intake to this level and no advantage (for young healthy people) to consuming a higher sodium intake. So maybe holding the 1,500 milligram target is a goal; not expecting people to absolutely achieve that goal is appropriate.

Q: How important is it for young, healthy college students at this stage of their life to limit their daily sodium intake to 1,500 milligrams?

A: High blood pressure is the most well-documented medical complication of a liberal sodium intake. This is not a common problem in Americans below the age of 25. However, if people are going to adjust their sodium intake, the sooner in life they do it the better. College students, with their meal plans dictated by the universities and food services, might be a particularly well-positioned group to convince intellectually (and their taste buds) that a lower sodium intake might be wise for them to follow.

Q: How important are other nutrients in the diet, or the diet as a whole, when it comes to lowering high blood pressure or preventing it?

A: This issue is, of course, what the DASH study (Dietary Approaches to Stop Hypertension) was meant to assess. And,

Stella Volpe, PhD, RD, LDN, FACSM, is a faculty member at the University of Pennsylvania and is the Miriam Stirl Term Endowed Chair of Nutrition. She is also assistant director for integrative research of the Institute for Diabetes, Obesity, and Metabolism in the School of Medicine.
Dr. Volpe is an associated faculty member of the Center for Health Disparities in the School of Nursing, an associate scholar in the Center for Clinical Epidemiology and Biostatistics, an associate faculty member in the Graduate Program in Public Health, and a co-Director in Excellence in Partnerships for Community Outreach, Research on Health Disparities, and Training (EXPORT) all in the School of Medicine. She served on the Institute of Medicine's Panel on Dietary Reference Intakes (DRI) for Electrolytes and Water.

Q: While the current DRI for sodium is set at 1,500 milligrams daily for young adults, Americans, on average, are currently consuming over 3,000 milligrams of sodium daily. Is this DRI for sodium a realistic level for Americans, especially college students, to obtain? Why or why not?

A: This is a realistic goal for Americans to achieve, but it is a goal that they will have to make a conscious effort to accomplish. It literally takes two weeks for people to lose their "salt taste." Thus, by slowly decreasing the sodium in their diets, people will soon realize that 1,500 milligrams/day is just fine for their taste buds. Nonetheless, for athletes, higher sodium recommendations are typically suggested. This helps them maintain their hydration status, and also helps prevent cramping in some athletes. Therefore, for active individuals, the 1,500 milligrams/day recommendation may be too low, unless they have a medical reason to lower the sodium content in their diets.

Q: How important is it for young, healthy college students at this stage of their life to limit their daily sodium intake to 1,500 milligrams?

A: In general, for a person with healthy kidneys, the 1,500 milligrams/day sodium requirement is still one to strive for; however, one does not need to be so specific in exactly achieving this goal. Nonetheless, heart disease and hypertension do not start when someone is 55 years of age, but when they are in their teens, which is why cardiovascular

(continued)

(continued)

Shaking the Habit, continued

Tom Moore, MD, continued

although I know that the DASH diet lowers blood pressure, I do not know why. By this I mean we do not know if there are particularly active components of the DASH diet that lower blood pressure. We also know from the results of the DASH-sodium trial that the DASH diet plus sodium reduction lowers blood pressure more effectively than either intervention alone. However, from the point of view of a college student, the same argument in the answer above is also applicable here. College students by and large do not have high blood pressure. However, I would propose that there is a lot more to the health benefits of a well-balanced diet than just its effect on blood pressure levels. Diets like the DASH diet, well-balanced among all the healthy food groups, would surely be something we should encourage all Americans to eat—and the younger the better.

Q: Are you involved in or know of any research on the horizon that may uncover any new dietary changes that may help prevent and/or lower high blood pressure?

A: A recent study tested two variants of the DASH diet—one higher in protein, largely from vegetable protein, and one higher in mono- and polyunsaturated fats. The study reported that both alternatives were effective at lowering blood pressure and were also successful at improving lipid levels. While this study, called OmniHeart, is promising, there is no indication which patient population would be better suited for DASH versus either of the two DASH variants. The Mediterranean diet is also getting attention from many different angles. These are the kinds of dietary approaches currently being looked at for their blood-pressure lowering (and other cardiac-risk-factor lowering) effects.

Stella Volpe, PhD, RD, LDN, FACSM, continued

disease is a chronic disease. Thus, if college students practice healthy eating, including lowering their daily sodium intake to 1,500 milligrams, they may prevent disease. They will not need to make drastic changes in their diets when they get older, because they will already be accustomed to a lower sodium diet.

Q: How important are other nutrients in the diet, or the diet as a whole, when it comes to lowering high blood pressure or preventing it?

A: Our nutrient intake for overall health is important. When it comes to preventing high blood pressure, sodium, potassium, and calcium play key roles. Lowering sodium intake and increasing potassium and calcium intakes has been shown to help decrease blood pressure. This has been especially true for potassium.

Q: Are you involved in or know of any research on the horizon that may uncover any new dietary changes that may help prevent and/or lower high blood pressure?

A: A key study that has been published called "Dietary Approaches to Stop Hypertension (DASH), has shown that increased fruit and vegetable intake, along with increased low-fat or non-fat dairy intake, helped to lower blood pressure in a large group of individuals. One of the key nutrients in fruit and vegetables is potassium; in dairy products it is calcium. This study is a landmark study for dietary intake in the prevention of hypertension.

NUTRITION IN THE REAL WORLD

Be a Nutrition Sleuth

Where's the Sodium in Your Foods?

Go online to www.aw-bc.com/blake and take a virtual trip down the supermarket aisle to find the sodium content of some of your favorite foods. (Beware: If you're a ramen fan, click with caution.)

NUTRITION IN THE REAL WORLD

Get Real!

Calcium Counter

Are you falling short of your calcium needs? Or are you enjoying too many calcium-fortified food products, possibly exceeding the upper limit? Visit the Calcium Counter at www.aw-bc.com/blake and get a ballpark estimate of your current calcium intake.

The Top Ten Points to Remember

1. Water is an important solvent that helps transport oxygen, nutrients, and substances throughout your body and waste products away from your cells. It helps regulate your body temperature and cushion your organs. Combined with other substances to form saliva and mucus, it acts as a lubricant in your mouth and intestines. Adult women should consume 9 cups of water, and adult men should drink approximately 13 cups of water, daily. Caffeinated beverages, juices, and milk can all count toward meeting your water needs.

2. Minerals are micronutrients that play many roles in the body. Many are part of enzymes. Minerals help maintain fluid and acid-base balance, play a role in nerve transmission and muscle contractions, help strengthen bones, teeth, and your immune system, and are involved in growth. Minerals are found in both plant and animal foods.

3. Sodium plays an important role in balancing the fluid between your blood and cells. Americans currently consume more than double the sodium recommended daily, predominantly as sodium chloride (table salt). Processed foods are the major source of sodium chloride in the diet. Reducing dietary sodium and following the DASH diet, which is abundant in foods rich in potassium, magnesium, and calcium, can help lower blood pressure. Losing excess weight, being physically active, and limiting alcohol can also lower blood pressure.

4. Potassium helps keep your heart, muscles, nerves, and bones healthy. The current recommendations to increase the fruits and vegetables in your diet will help you meet your potassium needs.

5. Calcium, along with phosphorus, provides your bones and teeth with strength and structure. A diet adequate in protein, vitamin K, calcium, and vitamin D, along with regular physical activity, is needed to build and maintain healthy bones. Dairy foods can be a good source of both nutrients. Osteoporosis is a condition caused by frail bones. A chronic deficiency of dietary calcium and/or vitamin D, excess alcohol consumption, and smoking can all increase the risk of osteoporosis.

6. Iron is part of the oxygen-carrying transport proteins—hemoglobin in your red blood cells and myoglobin in your muscles. Heme iron is found in meat, poultry, and fish. Non-heme iron is found in plant foods, such as grains and vegetables. Non-heme iron is the predominant source of the iron in your diet but isn't absorbed as readily as heme iron. A deficiency of iron in children can impact their ability to learn and retain information. Iron-deficiency anemia can cause fatigue and weakness.

7. Over 100 enzymes in your cells need zinc to function properly. Zinc plays a role in the structure of both RNA and DNA, in your taste acuity, and in helping fight age-related macular degeneration (AMD). Meat, fish, and whole grains are good sources of zinc. Research studies to date have failed to confirm that zinc can help fight the common cold.

8. Selenium acts as an antioxidant in your body and may help fight cancer. Chromium helps the hormone, insulin, function but has not been proven to enhance weight loss or build muscle mass during exercise. Iodine is essential to make thyroid hormones, which affect the majority of the cells and help regulate metabolic rate.

9. Copper is part of many enzymes and proteins that are involved in the absorption and transfer of iron and the synthesis of hemoglobin and red blood cells. Both manganese and molybdenum also help enzymes function in your body.

10. Both tap and bottled waters can be safe to drink. Fluoride is often added to water that comes from the tap, whereas bottled water typically does not contain added fluoride. In the United States, bottled water is not safer or more pure than tap water.

Test Your Knowledge

1. The most abundant substance in your body is
   a. magnesium.
   b. hemoglobin.
   c. sodium.
   d. water.
2. All bottled water is regulated by the FDA.
   a. true
   b. false

3. In your body, minerals can
   a. help maintain fluid balance.
   b. be part of enzymes.
   c. work with your immune system.
   d. do all of the above.
4. The recommendation for dietary sodium intake daily for adults up to age 51 is
   a. 3,400 milligrams.
   b. 2,300 milligrams.
   c. 1,500 milligrams.
   d. 180 milligrams.
5. How many servings of fruits and vegetables would you have to eat daily to meet your potassium needs?
   a. 3
   b. 4
   c. 5
   d. 7
6. Which of the following can increase the risk for hypertension?
   a. a family history of high blood pressure
   b. consuming excessive amounts of alcohol
   c. being inactive
   d. all of the above
7. One cup of skim milk, 8 ounces of low-fat yogurt, and 1½ ounces of reduced fat cheddar cheese EACH provide
   a. 100 milligrams of calcium.
   b. 200 milligrams of calcium.
   c. 300 milligrams of calcium.
   d. 400 milligrams of calcium.
8. You are having pasta for dinner. You want to enhance the absorption of the non-heme iron in the pasta. To do that you could top your spaghetti with
   a. butter.
   b. olive oil.
   c. tomato sauce.
   d. nothing; eat it plain.
9. Chromium increases the effectiveness of
   a. thyroid hormones.
   b. the hormone insulin.
   c. antidiuretic hormone (ADH).
10. Fluoride will help strengthen and repair the enamel on your teeth. What other mineral strengthens your teeth?
   a. chloride
   b. phosphorus
   c. sulfur
   d. zinc

Answers

1. (d) Your body is 60 percent water. Water bathes the trillions of cells in your body and is part of the fluid inside your cells where reactions take place. Iron, while part of hemoglobin, is a trace mineral so you only have small amounts in your body. Both magnesium and sodium are major minerals in your body but are not as abundant as water.
2. (b) False. The FDA only regulates bottled water that is sold through interstate commerce. Bottled water that is manufactured and sold within the same state is not regulated by the FDA.
3. (d) Although you need only small amounts of minerals in your diet, they play enormously important roles in your body, such as helping to maintain fluid balance, being part of enzymes, and working with your immune system to keep you healthy.
4. (b) The daily recommended amount of sodium for these adults is 1,500 milligrams. The upper level for sodium daily is 2,300 milligrams, whereas the absolute minimum that should be consumed is 180 milligrams per day. Unfortunately, Americans far exceed these recommendations and consume over 3,400 milligrams of sodium daily.
5. (d) Seven servings of fruits and vegetables daily will enable you to meet your potassium needs.
6. (d) They all can increase the risk of hypertension. People can't change their family history, but they can become more physically active, lose excess weight, and limit their alcohol consumption, all of which will help them to better manage their blood pressure.
7. (c) Each of these servings of dairy foods provides 300 milligrams of calcium. Consuming the recommended 3 servings of lean dairy products daily will just about meet the amount recommended daily (1,000 milligrams) for many adults.
8. (c) Ladle the tomato sauce on your pasta—the vitamin C in it can enhance non-heme iron absorption. Though the butter and olive oil will give your spaghetti flavor, they won't help you absorb iron.
9. (b) Chromium increases insulin's effectiveness in your cells. Iodine is needed to make thyroid hormones, and ADH is the hormone that directs kidneys to minimize water loss and concentrate urine.

10. (b) Phosphorus, along with calcium, forms hydroxyapatite, which is the strengthening material found in your teeth. Chloride is one of the electrolytes in your blood that helps maintain fluid and acid-base balance. Sulfur plays an important role as part of many compounds in your body, such as certain amino acids. Zinc helps with wound healing and maintaining a healthy immune system.

Web Support

■ For more on the DASH diet, visit DASH for Health at www.dashforhealth.com

■ For more on osteoporosis, visit The National Osteoporosis Foundation at www.nof.org

■ For more on high blood pressure, visit www.nhlbi.nih.gov/hbp/index.html

9

1. Alcohol is an **essential** nutrient. **T/F**

2. A shot of **whiskey** contains more alcohol than a can of **beer.** **T/F**

3. Red wine contains **phytochemicals** that are good for your heart. **T/F**

4. **Women** feel the effects of alcohol sooner than **men.** **T/F**

5. Your body can metabolize **two** alcoholic beverages per hour. **T/F**

6. The best way to cure a **hangover** is to drink a Bloody Mary (tomato juice and vodka). **T/F**

7. Alcohol provides **7 calories** per gram. **T/F**

8. Drinking too much alcohol can lead to **malnutrition.** **T/F**

9. Some states in the United States have lowered the **legal age** to consume and purchase alcohol to 18. **T/F**

10. Alcoholism can be cured through counseling. **T/F**

Alcohol

Twenty-one-year-old Leah has a brother, Steve, who craves alcohol. Steve says he needs to have "a few" drinks daily to relax. When he arrives home from work, he is often anxious or grouchy but becomes "human" again, as Leah puts it, after several beers. Sometimes he drinks his dinner, eating very little food, making a meal out of a second six-pack. His girlfriend broke up with him because he drank too much. Steve has tried to cut back on the amount of beer he drinks, but once he gets started he can't seem to stop. When he tried to give up drinking cold turkey, he became anxious, shaky, and nauseous, and broke out in cold sweats. He has become dependent upon alcohol to "steady his nerves." Leah knows these symptoms all too well, as Steve's drinking patterns and behaviors mimic her father's, who died of cirrhosis of the liver when he was 62, and her grandfather's, who "drank himself to his grave," according to her mother.

Though Leah doesn't consider herself a heavy drinker, she does have a beer after dinner on most nights of the week. She is afraid that the beer that she consumes on weeknights as well as her weekend partying with friends is becoming a habit that she can't stop.

Leah is right to be worried—her brother exhibits the four classic symptoms of a drinking problem, and she is at a higher risk of following in her brother's footsteps. Do you know what the four symptoms are and why she should be concerned about her alcohol intake? In this chapter, we will discuss some forms of alcohol use and abuse, as well as its potential health effects.

Answers

1. False. Although alcohol provides calories, it's not an essential nutrient. See this page to find out why.
2. False. A straight shot of liquor may look and taste more potent than a can of beer, but it isn't. To learn more, turn to page 309.
3. True. Red wine does contain heart-healthy compounds. To find out more about them, turn to page 310.
4. True. Women respond more quickly to the narcotic effects of alcohol than do men. To find out why, turn to page 311.
5. False. In general, your body can only metabolize about one drink per 1½ hours. To find out what factors play a role in this, turn to page 312.
6. False. Drinking more alcohol isn't going to take away the ill effects of a hangover. To find out what will, turn to page 316.
7. True. However, not all alcoholic beverages contain equal amounts of calories. For an eye-opener as to the amount of calories in some common alcoholic drinks, turn to page 317.
8. True. You're darn right it can. If you're puzzled as to how that can happen, turn to page 318.
9. False. Decades ago, some states lowered their legal drinking age, but today you have to be 21 to legally purchase and consume alcohol in the United States. You may be surprised as to why this age was selected. Turn to page 326 to learn more.
10. False. Although counseling is an important component of alcoholism recovery, it will not cure it. Page 327 explains why.

Your body doesn't need alcohol to survive. Therefore, alcohol is not an essential nutrient. You don't gain any nutrition from drinking it, other than calories. Ounce for ounce, it can cost 100 times more than bottled water. It's legally sold in the United States, but supposedly off limits to those who aren't adults, even though teenagers often feel under social pressure to consume it. Some medical reports say that in moderation, it can be good for you, while others tell you that drinking too much of it can kill you.

What's the real story about alcohol? Let's find out.

What Is Alcohol and How Is It Made?

What is the first image that comes to your mind when you hear the word **alcohol?** Do you envision a bottle of beer, a glass of wine, or a rum and coke? Technically, these beverages aren't alcohol by themselves, but they all contain a type of alcohol called **ethanol.**

Ethanol is one of three similar compounds in the chemical category of alcohol. The other two compounds, methanol (used in antifreeze) and isopropanol (used in rubbing alcohol) are both poisonous when ingested. Ethanol is considered safe for consumption, but it is not harmless. Consuming excessive amounts of ethanol can be toxic and damage your body. Too much can even kill you.

Ethanol is made through the **fermentation** of yeast and the natural sugars in grains (glucose and maltose) and fruits (fructose and glucose). The yeast breaks down the sugar into ethanol and carbon dioxide. The carbon dioxide evaporates, leaving an alcohol-containing beverage. Grapes provide the sugar for making wine, whereas the starch from grains provides the sugar when producing beer.

Liquors, such as rum, scotch, and whiskey, are made through a process called **distillation** and are more accurately called distilled spirits.[1] In this process, an alcoholic beverage is heated, causing the ethanol to vaporize. The vapor is collected, cooled, and condensed into a very concentrated liquid called liquor.

Although ethanol is the scientific name for the alcohol found in beverages, we will use the more common term "alcohol" throughout this chapter.

The Take-Home Message Ethanol is the type of alcohol consumed in alcoholic beverages. Alcoholic beverages are made by the processes of fermentation or distillation.

Beer is made from the fermentation of yeast and the natural sugars from grains.

Why Do People Drink Alcohol?

People around the world drink alcohol in many different forms and for many different reasons. The sake (rice wine) of Japan is used during tea and Shinto ceremonies, while the dark beer of the Irish is consumed when many pub patrons celebrate their favorite sport. The vodka of Russia and the chardonnay of Napa Valley are consumed in the pursuit of relaxation and pleasure. Globally, wine is part of many religious traditions, including the Catholic Mass and the Jewish Sabbath, and in some cultures, it's the beverage of choice during the main meal of the day. For parts of human history, wine and beer were safer to drink than water.

In the United States, more than half of adults consume at least one alcoholic beverage per month.[2] Americans drink alcohol for many of the same reasons people in other parts of the world do. We use it to relax, celebrate, and socialize. Lately, we have also found that it may provide health benefits. Let's explore these motives for drinking alcohol more closely.

People Drink to Relax, Celebrate, and Socialize

Alcohol is a drug that alters your conscious mind. Within minutes of sipping an alcoholic beverage, a person will feel more relaxed. After a few more sips, a mild, pleasant euphoria sets in and inhibitions begin to loosen. By the end of the first or second drink, a person will often feel more outgoing, happy, and social. This anxiety-reducing, upbeat initial effect is why people seek out and continue to drink alcohol.[3]

Having a drink with another person symbolizes social bonding.[4] When it comes to mingling with others or celebrating a special occasion, whether it's with friends, coworkers, or even strangers, pubs and parties are common gathering spots, and alcoholic drinks are commonly served.

Alcohol May Have Health Benefits

Some studies have suggested that moderate alcohol consumption may reduce the risk of heart disease, and the risk of dying in general, for middle-aged and older adults.[5] **Moderate alcohol consumption** is considered to be up to one standard drink for adult women and up to two drinks daily for adult men. A standard drink is a 12-ounce serving of beer, a 1.5-ounce shot of liquor, or a 5-ounce glass of wine, as each

alcohol A chemical class of substances that contain ethanol, methanol, and isopropanol. Ethanol is often referred to as "alcohol."

ethanol The type of alcohol in alcoholic beverages such as wine, beer, and liquor.

fermentation The process by which yeast converts sugars in grains or fruits into ethanol and carbon dioxide, resulting in an alcoholic beverage.

distillation The evaporation and then collection of a liquid by condensation. Liquors are made using distillation.

moderate alcohol consumption Consuming no more than one alcoholic drink daily for adult women and no more than two drinks daily for men.

Figure 9.1 What Is a Standard Drink?
One standard drink of beer (12 ounces), liquor (1½ ounces), or wine (5 ounces) contains the same amount of alcohol.

of these contain about half an ounce of alcohol (Figure 9.1). Recall from Chapter 5 that alcohol can increase the level of the heart-protective HDL cholesterol and may also help make blood platelets less "sticky" and less likely to create unwanted blood clots that can lead to heart attack and stroke.

On November 17, 1991, the television news show *60 Minutes* aired a segment called "The French Paradox," touting the benefits of modest amounts of red wine to help reduce the risk of heart disease. The French Paradox is so called because the people of France have lower rates of heart disease even though their saturated fat intake mimics that of Americans. They also drink more red wine than Americans do, which is thought to be the differentiating factor. (However, the French also consume fewer *trans* fats and have a less stressful lifestyle and better developed social networks, which can also contribute to their impressively lower risk of heart disease.) In the four weeks after the segment was aired, sales of red wine increased by about 45 percent.[6] Suddenly, instead of thinking that "an apple a day keeps the doctor away" people were hoping that "a drink a day keeps the cardiologist at bay." Were these people on the right track?

Red wine contains resveratrol, a flavonoid and type of phytochemical, which acts as an antioxidant. (Dark beer also contains flavonoids.) Antioxidants help prevent the LDL "bad" cholesterol from becoming oxidized, which leads to their accumulation in the artery wall and atherosclerosis. Flavonoids also help inhibit the stickiness of platelets in the blood. Because of these potential heart-healthy attributes, red wine has been in the media limelight since the 1990s.

There isn't enough evidence to support the theory that wine, whether red, white, or rosé, has any health superiority over beer and distilled spirits. In fact, some studies comparing various alcohol sources have found the majority of heart-protective effects are attributable to the alcohol content regardless of the source.[7] In other words, a beer, a glass of cabernet, or a shot of scotch all appear to have similar heart-protective effects. When it comes to the health benefits of alcohol, the source is unlikely to make much of a difference.

But before you crack open a beer to celebrate, be aware that the people who gain the health benefits from moderate alcohol consumption are women age 55 and older and men age 45 and older. Alcohol consumption by younger people has not been shown to provide many—if any—health benefits. In fact, drinking alcohol during your younger years increases the risk of injuries and violent, traumatic deaths, which offsets any possible health benefits from the alcohol.[8]

The Take-Home Message People drink alcohol to relax, celebrate, and socialize. Moderate alcohol consumption may provide health benefits in some older adults.

What Happens to Alcohol in the Body?

Your body treats alcohol differently from any other substance you consume. Unlike the other energy-containing nutrients, such as carbohydrates and fats, your body cannot store alcohol. Because alcohol is a toxin, the body quickly works to metabolize and eliminate it.

Many factors, including your gender, your body type, the amount of food in your stomach, and the amount of alcohol you drink, will affect how quickly you absorb and metabolize it.[9] Alcohol travels through the body in the blood, and is distributed throughout the watery tissues, including the brain. Let's follow a swallow of beer through your digestive system and see how it's handled along the way (Figure 9.2).

You Absorb Alcohol in Your Stomach and Small Intestine

Within seconds of the first sip of the beer, alcohol will be in your blood. This is because alcohol is one of those rare substances that can be absorbed through the stomach directly into your blood. Some alcohol is also metabolized in the stomach by an enzyme called **alcohol dehydrogenase** before it is absorbed. About 20 percent of the alcohol you consume is absorbed in your stomach. (The majority of alcohol, about 80 percent, is absorbed in the small intestine.)

Women Are More Susceptible to the Effects of Alcohol Than Men

Women have about 20 to 30 percent less alcohol dehydrogenase in their stomach than men, so more alcohol will enter the blood immediately through women's stomachs.[10] In essence, every alcoholic beverage that a male consumes is the equivalent to about 1⅓ alcoholic beverages for a woman. Women also have less muscle mass, and thus less body water, than men. (Recall from the last chapter that muscle tissue has a higher percentage of water than fat.) Because alcohol mixes in water, muscular individuals are able to distribute more of the alcohol throughout their body than those who have more fat tissue and, consequently, less body water. So even if a woman is the same height and weight as a man, the female, drinking the same amount of alcohol, will have a higher concentration of alcohol in her blood than the male.

Because of these factors—less stomach alcohol dehydrogenase and less body water in which to distribute the ingested alcohol—women will feel alcohol's narcotic effects sooner than men. Women take note: When socializing, females can't keep up, drink for drink, with their male friends. A woman will begin to feel the effects of alcohol long before a man will.

Food in the Stomach Affects Absorption

The amount and type of food in the stomach determines how long alcohol lingers there before entering the small intestine. If your swallow of beer chases a bacon

alcohol dehydrogenase One of the alcohol-metabolizing enzymes in the body.

Figure 9.2 The Metabolism of Alcohol

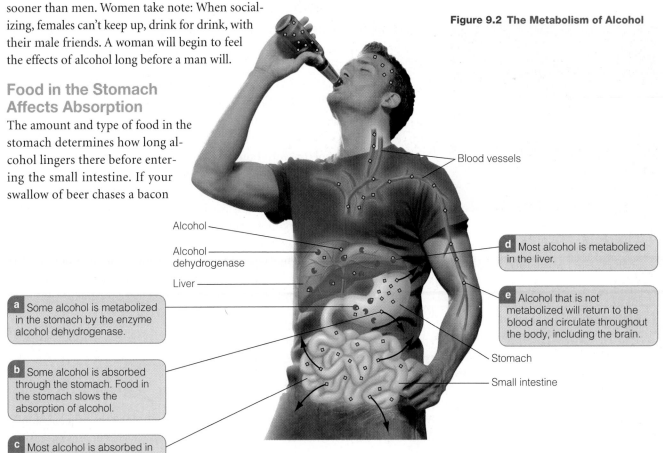

Blood vessels

Alcohol

Alcohol dehydrogenase

Liver

a Some alcohol is metabolized in the stomach by the enzyme alcohol dehydrogenase.

b Some alcohol is absorbed through the stomach. Food in the stomach slows the absorption of alcohol.

c Most alcohol is absorbed in the small intestine.

d Most alcohol is metabolized in the liver.

e Alcohol that is not metabolized will return to the blood and circulate throughout the body, including the brain.

Stomach

Small intestine

eLearn
How Much Alcohol Is Too Much?

If you drink alcohol, take the short, 10-question survey based on the World Health Organization's Alcohol Use Disorders Identification Test (AUDIT), which will help you analyze your current drinking habits and provide information on what to do if you drink too much. To access the survey, log on to www.alcoholscreening.org/index.asp.

cheeseburger and fries, the alcohol will take longer to leave the stomach and enter the small intestine than if the beer was consumed on an empty stomach. Fat also slows down the departure of food from the stomach, so the large amount of fat in this burger meal will help delay the arrival of the alcohol into the small intestine.

Here lies the logic behind advice to avoid drinking alcohol on an empty stomach. Without food in the stomach, alcohol rapidly leaves the stomach, moves into and is absorbed through the intestine, and enters the blood. In fact, a study showed that an alcoholic drink consumed after a meal was absorbed about three times more slowly than if it was consumed on an empty stomach.[11] Keep in mind, however, that while a full stomach will delay the arrival of alcohol in the small intestine, the alcohol will still eventually arrive there. If a person drinks several glasses of beer with dinner, the alcohol will be absorbed once the stomach starts emptying. Intoxication could be an unexpected postdinner surprise.

You Metabolize Alcohol Primarily in Your Liver

Once in your blood, alcohol travels to the liver, where the majority of it is metabolized. Enzymes in the liver, most importantly alcohol dehydrogenase, convert the alcohol to **acetaldehyde,** which is eventually metabolized to carbon dioxide and water.[12] A healthy liver can metabolize about one alcoholic drink in about 1½ to 2 hours. Regardless of the amount consumed, the metabolism of alcohol occurs at a steady rate in your body.

There is a second major enzyme system in the liver that metabolizes alcohol: the **microsomal ethanol-oxidizing system (MEOS).** Individuals who consume a lot of alcohol will have a somewhat higher level of MEOS because this system is revved up when chronically high levels of alcohol are present in the liver.

Alcohol Circulates in Your Blood

If your liver cannot handle the amount of alcohol all at once, some of the alcohol enters the blood and is distributed in the watery tissues in your body. Though the liver will eventually metabolize most of the alcohol that is consumed, a small amount will leave your body intact through your breath and urine.

Your **blood alcohol concentration (BAC)** is the amount of alcohol in your blood, measured in grams of alcohol per deciliter of blood, usually expressed as a percentage.[13] Table 9.1 gives you a ballpark idea of how your BAC is affected by the number of alcoholic beverages you consume. As you can see, the more you drink, the higher your BAC. Because alcohol infiltrates your brain, as your BAC increases so does your level of mental impairment and intoxication.

The amount of alcohol in your breath correlates with the amount of alcohol in your blood. For this reason, a Breathalyzer test can be used to measure a person's BAC. A Breathalyzer may be used by police officers who suspect that a person has consumed too much alcohol.

A Breathalyzer is used to measure a person's blood alcohol concentration (BAC).

acetaldehyde An intermediary by-product of the breakdown of ethanol in the liver.

microsomal ethanol-oxidizing system (MEOS) The other major enzyme system in the liver that metabolizes alcohol.

blood alcohol concentration (BAC) The measurement of the amount of alcohol in your blood. BAC is measured in grams of alcohol per deciliter of blood, usually expressed as a percentage.

The Effects of Alcohol on Your Brain

Alcohol is a depressant of the central nervous system. It slows the transmission of nerve impulses. Your brain is part of the central nervous system and is very sensitive

Table 9.1
Blood Alcohol Concentration Tables

For Women

Body Weight in Pounds

Drinks per hour	100	120	140	160	180	200
1	0.05	0.04	0.03	0.03	0.03	0.02
2	0.09	0.08	0.07	0.06	0.05	0.05
3	0.14	0.11	0.10	0.09	0.08	0.07
4	0.18	0.15	0.13	0.11	0.10	0.09
5	0.23	0.19	0.16	0.14	0.13	0.11
6	0.27	0.23	0.19	0.17	0.15	0.14
7	0.32	0.27	0.23	0.20	0.18	0.16
8	0.36	0.30	0.26	0.23	0.20	0.18
9	0.41	0.34	0.29	0.26	0.30	0.20
10	0.45	0.38	0.32	0.28	0.25	0.23

For Men

Body Weight in Pounds

Drinks per hour	100	120	140	160	180	200
1	0.04	0.03	0.03	0.02	0.02	0.02
2	0.08	0.06	0.05	0.05	0.04	0.04
3	0.11	0.09	0.08	0.07	0.06	0.06
4	0.15	0.12	0.11	0.09	0.08	0.08
5	0.19	0.16	0.13	0.12	0.11	0.09
6	0.23	0.19	0.16	0.14	0.13	0.11
7	0.26	0.22	0.19	0.16	0.15	0.13
8	0.30	0.25	0.21	0.19	0.17	0.15
9	0.34	0.28	0.24	0.21	0.19	0.17
10	0.38	0.31	0.27	0.23	0.21	0.19

Notes: Shaded area indicates legal intoxication.
Blood alcohol concentrations are expressed as percent, meaning grams of alcohol per 10 milliliters (per deciliter) of blood. Tables are adapted from those of the Pennsylvania Liquor Control Board, Harrisburg.

to alcohol. The depressant effect of alcohol on the brain is what slows down a person's reaction time to stimuli (such as a car coming toward you on the road) after drinking. Because the brain controls your thoughts, actions, and behavior, alcohol impairs all of these.

The more you drink, the more areas of the brain are affected. Look at Table 9.2 and Figure 9.3 on the next page to see how increasing BAC levels impact the specific areas of the brain, and how body movements and behaviors will thus be affected. (Note: A person's BAC can continue to rise even after unconsciousness.) If enough alcohol has been consumed, the activities of the brain stem, which controls breathing and circulation, can be suppressed, impairing breathing and heart rate and ultimately causing death.

Coffee will not sober you up. An intoxicated person who drinks coffee will end up being a stimulated drunk. It takes time to sober up because your liver has to metabolize all the alcohol that you consumed.

Table 9.2

Progressive Effects of Alcohol

Blood Alcohol Concentration	Changes in Feelings and Personality	Brain Regions Affected	Impaired Functions (continuum)
0.01–0.05	Relaxation, sense of well-being, loss of inhibition	Cerebral cortex	Alertness; judgment
0.06–0.10	Pleasure, numbing of feelings, nausea, sleepiness, emotional arousal	Cerebral cortex and forebrain	Coordination (especially fine motor skills); visual tracking
0.11–0.20	Mood swings, anger, sadness, mania	Cerebral cortex, forebrain, and cerebellum	Reasoning and depth perception; appropriate social behavior
0.21–0.30	Aggression, reduced sensations, depression, stupor	Cerebral cortex, forebrain, cerebellum, and brain stem	Speech; balance; temperature regulation
0.31–0.40	Unconsciousness, coma, death possible	Entire brain	Bladder control; breathing
0.41 and greater	Death		Heart rate

Source: National Institute on Alcohol Abuse and Alcoholism. 2003. Understanding Alcohol: Investigations into Biology and Behavior. Available at http://science.education.nih.gov/supplements/nih3/alcohol/default.htm.

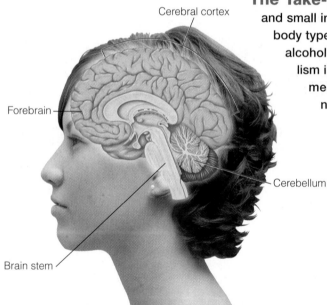

Figure 9.3 The Brain and Alcohol
As you consume more alcohol, additional areas of your brain are affected. Your cerebral cortex is affected first, followed by your forebrain, cerebellum, and brain stem. The greater the alcohol intake, the greater the physical and behavioral changes in your body.

The Take-Home Message Alcohol is absorbed in the stomach and small intestine and is metabolized primarily in the liver. Your sex, body type, the amount of food in your stomach, and the quantity of alcohol consumed will affect the rate of absorption and metabolism in your body. The blood alcohol concentration (BAC) is the measurement of alcohol in your blood. Alcohol is a central nervous system depressant. Because your brain is sensitive to alcohol, alcohol affects your behavior.

How Can Alcohol Be Harmful?

Although alcohol is often advertised in magazines, billboards, and television commercials as a trendy and sexy way to relax and socialize (see the boxed feature "Alcohol and Advertising"), it can cause a number of problems for those who abuse it. Some of these problems merely cause temporary discomfort, but other long-term effects can be extremely damaging to health.

Alcohol Can Disrupt Sleep and Cause Hangovers

Many people wrongly think that a drink before bed will help them sleep better, but it will actually have the opposite effect. Whereas having a drink within an hour before bed may help you to fall asleep sooner, it will disrupt your sleep cycle, cause you to awaken in the middle of the night, and make returning to sleep a challenge.[14] You will

Alcohol and Advertising

Advertising for alcoholic beverages is pervasive and persuasive. You need only drive down a major highway or turn on your television to see billboards and commercials for a beer or liquor brand. In some media, including popular magazines like *Rolling Stone* and *Sports Illustrated*, alcohol ads can outnumber nonalcohol ads by almost 3 to 1.[1]

Companies that make alcoholic beverages pay large sums of money to create and show these ads for one reason: They work. Studies have shown that advertisements for alcoholic beverages are associated with an increase of drinking among adolescents. Many ads tend to emphasize sexual and social stereotypes. When targeted to underage drinkers, this type of message has been shown to increase adolescents' desire to emulate those portrayed in the advertisements.[2]

Alcohol ads need to be viewed with caution, as the messages in them are often misleading and in some cases blatantly false. Let's take a look at the messages and realities in a typical alcohol advertisement that might appear in a magazine.

This Photo Says: "When I Drink, I Feel More Powerful and Manly"
Reality: Alcohol will increase fantasies of being more masculine, strong, and powerful. However, excessive alcohol consumption causes a reduction in male sex hormones along with changes that include breast development and testicle shrinkage.

This Photo Says: "Have a Drink.... You'll Be Relaxed and Happy"
Reality: While initially you may feel relaxed, consuming a few drinks will actually make you feel anxious and depressed.

This Photo Says: "When I Drink, I Am More Feminine and Attractive"
Reality: As with males, too much alcohol will interfere with a woman's sex hormones and cause sexual, menstrual, and infertility problems.

This Photo Says: "When I Drink, I Am VERY Sexy"
Reality: Alcohol will actually *reduce* sexual arousal. The more alcohol consumed, the worse the problem. Chronic drinking will decrease the level of sexual hormones in the body and sexual desire.

This Photo Says: "I Am Successful and Hang Out with Successful People"
Reality: Anyone can obtain and drink alcohol. It isn't a beverage tied to social class.

Source: Text courtesy of Dr. William R. Miller, University of New Mexico Center on Alcoholism, Substance Abuse and Addictions (CASAA).

feel tired the next morning, which will make it harder for you to pay attention to what you are learning in class, and you may doze off by the end of the lecture. Even a moderate amount of alcohol consumed at dinner or even late in the afternoon during happy hour can disrupt that evening's sleep.

If you have a bad night's sleep, it's a bad idea to drink alcohol the next day. Studies have shown that a night of sleep disruption followed by even small amounts of alcohol the next day reduces the reaction time and alertness in individuals performing a simulated driving test. Being tired and then drinking alcohol exacerbates alcohol's sedating effect.[15]

A **hangover** is your body's way of saying, "don't do that to me again." After a bout of heavy drinking, individuals can experience hangover symptoms ranging from a pounding headache, fatigue, nausea, and increased thirst to a rapid heart beat, tremors, sweating, dizziness, depression, anxiety, and irritability. A hangover begins within hours of your last drink, as your BAC begins to drop. The symptoms will appear in full force once all the alcohol is gone from your blood, and these symptoms can linger for up to an additional 24 hours.[16] In other words, a few hours of excessive alcohol consumption on a Saturday night can not only ruin your entire Sunday but even disrupt part of your Monday morning.

There are several ways that alcohol contributes to the symptoms of a hangover. Alcohol is a diuretic, so it can cause dehydration, and thus, electrolyte imbalances. It inhibits the release of antidiuretic hormone from your pituitary gland, which in turn causes your kidneys to excrete water, as well as electrolytes, in your urine. Vomiting and sweating during or after excessive drinking will further contribute to dehydration and electrolyte loss. Dehydration also increases your thirst and can make you feel light-headed, dizzy, and weak. Increased acid production in the stomach and secretions from the pancreas and intestines can cause stomach pain, nausea, and vomiting.

Lastly, alcoholic beverages often contain compounds called **congeners,** which enhance their taste and appearance but may contribute to hangover symptoms. Congeners can be produced during the fermentation process or be added during production of the alcoholic beverages. The large number of congeners in red wine can cause headaches in some people.[17]

Forget the old wives' tale of consuming an alcoholic beverage to "cure" a hangover. Drinking more alcohol, even if it is mixed with tomato or orange juice, during a hangover only prolongs the recovery time. In fact, time is the only true remedy for hangover symptoms. Whereas aspirin and other nonsteroidal anti-inflammatory medications, such as ibuprofen, can ease a headache, these medications can also contribute to stomachache and nausea. Taking acetaminophen (Tylenol) during and after alcohol consumption, when the alcohol is being metabolized, has been shown to intensify this pain reliever's toxicity to the liver and may cause liver damage in some cases.[18] The best strategy for dealing with a hangover is to avoid it by limiting the amount of alcohol consumed.

Alcohol Can Interact with Hormones

Many individuals who overindulge in alcohol tend not to eat enough while they are drinking, which causes their body's glucose stores to become depleted and their blood glucose levels to fall. Typically, the hormones insulin and glucagon would automatically be released to make glucose, but alcohol interferes with this process. Because the brain needs glucose to function properly, a low blood glucose level can contribute to the feelings of fatigue, weakness, mood changes, irritability, and anxiety often experienced during a hangover.[19]

In addition to the hormones that regulate your blood glucose level, alcohol can interfere with other hormones. Alcohol negatively affects parathyroid hormone and other bone-strengthening hormones, which can increase the risk of osteoporosis.[20] Alcohol can also increase estrogen levels in women, which may increase the risk of

hangover A collective term for the unpleasant symptoms, such as a headache and dizziness, that occur after drinking an excessive amount of alcohol.

congeners Compounds in alcohol that enhance the taste but may contribute to hangover symptoms.

Beer
Serving size: 12 oz
Alcohol serving: 1
Calories per drink: 150

Light beer
Serving size: 12 oz
Alcohol serving: 1
Calories per drink: 110

**Distilled spirits
(whiskey, vodka, gin, rum)**
Serving size: 1.5 oz
Alcohol serving: 1
Calories per drink: 100

Red or white wine
Serving size: 5 oz
Alcohol serving: 1
Calories per drink: 100–105

Cosmopolitan
Serving size: 2.5 oz
Alcohol servings: 1.7
Calories per drink: 131

Mudslide
Serving size: 12 oz
Alcohol servings: 4
Calories per drink: 820

Margarita ▶
Serving size: 6.3 oz
Alcohol servings: 3
Calories per drink: 327

◀ **Bloody Mary**
Serving size: 5.5 oz
Alcohol serving: 1
Calories per drink: 97

◀ **Rum and Coke**
Serving size: 12 oz
Alcohol servings: 2.7
Calories per drink: 361

Note: Alcohol servings are per beverage.

Source: U.S. Department of Agriculture. 2005. 2005 Report of the Dietary Guidelines Advisory Committee. Available at www.health.gov/dietaryguidelines/dga2005/report/. Accessed January 2006.

breast cancer.[21] Drinking alcohol can affect reproductive hormones and is associated with both male and female sexual dysfunction.

Alcohol May Lead to Overnutrition and Malnutrition

At 7 calories per gram, alcohol provides fewer calories than fat (9 calories per gram) but more than either carbohydrates or protein (4 calories per gram each). However, unless you are drinking a straight shot of liquor, your alcoholic beverages will contain additional calories (see above). For example, a rum and coke contains the calories from both the rum and the coke, making the drink more than three times as high in calories as the rum itself. Depending on the mixers and ingredients added to your beverage, the calorie count in your drink can escalate to that of a meal. A mudslide, made with vodka, Irish cream, coffee liqueur, ice cream, and cream, should be ordered from the dessert menu and served with a spoon.

Dinner 1

4 oz grilled chicken breast
3/4 cup mashed potatoes
1 1/2 cup steamed carrots
2 oz whole wheat dinner roll
4 tsp soft margarine
1 cup fat-free milk

Calories	724
Total fat (g)	28
Saturated fat (g)	8
Cholesterol (mg)	89
Fiber (g)	11
Sodium (mg)	1,764
Vitamin A RE (mcg)	1,264
Vitamin C (mg)	13
Calcium (mg)	456

Dinner 2

5 12-oz beers
1 large serving nachos with cheese
8 BBQ chicken wings
1 handful goldfish crackers

Calories	1,719
Total fat (g)	51
Saturated fat (g)	16
Cholesterol (mg)	154
Fiber (g)	1
Sodium (mg)	2,131
Vitamin A RE (mcg)	92
Vitamin C (mg)	1
Calcium (mg)	376

Figure 9.4 Too Much Alcohol Costs You Good Nutrition
A dinner of several alcoholic beverages and bar foods not only adds calories, fat, and saturated fat to your diet, but displaces healthier foods that would provide better nutrition.

If you consistently add extra calories from alcoholic beverages—or any food or beverage source—to a diet that is already meeting your daily calorie needs, you will gain weight. Excessive consumption of alcohol has also been shown to increase fat and weight around the stomach. Though this is usually referred to as a "beer" belly, extra calories from any type of alcoholic beverage can contribute to a paunch. If high-calorie "bar foods" are consumed with the drinks, the calories can add up rapidly (Figure 9.4).

Compensating for calories in alcoholic beverages by cutting out more nutritious foods will cause you to fall short of your nutrient needs. If you drink a daily glass of beer instead of an equal amount of low-fat milk, your waist may not suffer, but your bones could. You will rob yourself of an excellent source of calcium and vitamin D that the milk, but not the beer, provides. A chronic substitution of excessive amounts of alcohol for nutritious foods in the diet can lead to malnutrition.

Individuals who drink excessively often eat diets inadequate in nutrients, especially vitamins and minerals. Often, they drink too much and don't eat enough. Those who consume more than 30 percent of their daily calories from alcohol tend to consume less protein, fiber, vitamins A, C, D, riboflavin, and thiamin, and the minerals calcium and iron.[22] This isn't surprising once you consider that if a person consuming 2,000 calories daily devotes 600 (30 percent) of these calories to alcohol, there would only be 1,400 calories left to meet all of his or her nutrient needs. When you're routinely limited to a diet of 1,400 calories daily, you're bound to have nutrient deficiencies.

Excessive alcohol consumption can also affect how the body handles the essential nutrients it actually gets. Routinely drinking too much alcohol can interfere with the absorption and/or use of protein, zinc, magnesium, the B vitamins thiamin, folate, and B_{12}, and the fat-soluble vitamins A, D, E, and K. As you have read from the

Figure 9.5 The Stages of
Alcoholic Liver Disease

Normal liver

Fatty liver
A fatty liver can occur
after just a few days
of overconsumption.

Cirrhosis
By the cirrhosis stage, permanent
damage is done and scar tissue
has developed.

previous chapters, a chronic deficiency of nutrients can cause a cascade of ill health
conditions and diseases. In particular, a thiamin deficiency can affect brain function,
including memory loss, and increase the risk of Wernicke-Korsakoff syndrome, which
includes mental confusion and uncontrolled muscle movement (see Chapter 7).

Alcohol Can Harm Your Digestive Organs, Heart, and Liver

Chronically drinking too much alcohol can lead to an inflamed esophagus. Alcohol
inhibits the ability of the esophagus to contract. This enables the acid juices in the
stomach to flow back up into the esophagus, causing inflammation. Chronic inflammation can be a stepping stone to esophageal cancer. If you smoke when you drink,
your chances of developing esophageal cancer, as well as mouth and throat cancer,
are even higher, as the alcohol enhances the ability of cigarettes to promote cancer.[23]
Individuals who are heavy drinkers also have increased incidences of **gastritis**
(*gastr* = stomach, *itis* = inflammation) and stomach ulcers.[24]

Excessive amounts of alcohol can also affect the beating and rhythm of the heart,
which likely plays a role in the sudden deaths of some alcoholics.[25] It can damage heart
tissue and increase the risk of hypertension. Hypertension is a risk factor for both heart
disease and stroke.

Alcohol can also damage your liver and cause **alcohol liver disease.** The disease
develops in three stages, although some stages can occur simultaneously (Figure 9.5).
The first stage of the disease is **fatty liver,** which can result from just a weekend or a
few days of excessive drinking. Because alcohol metabolism takes top priority in the
liver, the metabolism of other nutrients, including fats, will take a back seat to alcohol. Thus, the liver isn't able to metabolize all the fat that arrives in the liver, causing
a buildup in this organ. Simultaneously, the liver uses some of the by-products of alcohol metabolism to make even more fat. The net effect is a liver that has cells that are
full of fat.[26] A fatty liver can reverse itself *if* the alcohol consumption is stopped.

gastritis Inflammation of the stomach.

alcohol liver disease A degenerative liver condition that occurs in three
stages: (1) fatty liver, (2) alcohol hepatitis, and (3) cirrhosis.

fatty liver Stage 1 of alcohol liver
disease.

Hangovers

Blurred vision

Brain damage, addiction, and stroke

Slurred speech

Heart disease, irregular heart beat

Breathing may stop

Liver disease, liver failure

Malnutrition, overnutrition

Infertility (in women), impotence (in men)

Osteoporosis

Figure 9.6 Effects of Alcohol on the Body

If the drinking doesn't stop, the second stage of liver disease, **alcoholic hepatitis,** can develop. In alcoholic hepatitis, the liver basically becomes irritated by various by-products of alcohol metabolism. Some by-products, namely acetaldehyde, are toxic to the liver. Free radicals, another by-product of alcohol metabolism, react with the proteins, lipids, and DNA in your cells, causing damage. Nausea, vomiting, fever, jaundice, and loss of appetite are signs of alcoholic hepatitis. Chronic, excessive amounts of alcohol may also impair your immune system, which can contribute to liver damage and increase the susceptibility to pneumonia and other infectious diseases.

Heavy drinking can also cause the increased passage of destructive **endotoxin,** which is released from bacteria in your intestines into your blood. Once endotoxin arrives in your liver, it can cause the release of substances called *cytokines* that further damage healthy liver cells and perpetuate scarring.[27]

As bouts of heavy drinking continue, chronic inflammation further injures the liver cells and can cause scarring. **Cirrhosis** is the third and final stage of alcohol liver disease. In cirrhosis, the cells of the liver die and form scars, which prevent this organ from performing critical metabolic roles, such as filtering toxins and waste products in the blood and out of the body. If these toxins and waste products build up, it can lead to mental confusion, nausea, tremors or shakiness, and even coma.

As many as 70 percent of individuals with alcoholic hepatitis end up developing cirrhosis.[28] More than 12,000 die from alcohol liver disease each year.[29] Figure 9.6 summarizes the many harmful effects of excessive drinking.

Alcohol Can Put a Healthy Pregnancy at Risk

Over 30 years ago, Drs. David Smith and Kenneth Jones noticed an interesting trait among children in their clinic at the University of Washington School of Medicine. Some children looked alike even though they weren't related. Many had facial abnormalities such as eyes with very small openings and thin upper lips (Figure 9.7). These children also weren't physically growing as normally as other children their age, and they seemed to have some mental and behavioral difficulties, such as reduced attention span and memory, and learning disabilities. The scientists discovered that these children were all born to women who drank alcohol during their pregnancy. The doctors coined the term "fetal alcohol syndrome" (FAS) to describe these physical, mental, and behavioral abnormalities.[30]

When a pregnant woman drinks, she is never drinking alone—her fetus becomes her drinking partner. Because the baby is developing, the alcohol isn't broken down as quickly as in the mother's body. The baby's BAC can become higher and stay higher longer than the mother's, causing serious damage to its central nervous system, particularly the brain. FAS is the leading cause of mental retardation and birth

alcohol hepatitis Stage 2 of alcohol liver disease; due to chronic inflammation.

endotoxin A damaging product produced by intestinal bacteria that travels in the blood to the liver and initiates the release of cytokines that damage liver cells, leading to scarring.

cirrhosis Stage 3 of alcohol liver disease in which liver cells die, causing severe scarring.

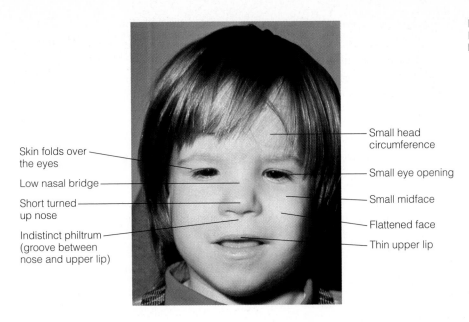

Figure 9.7 Fetal Alcohol Syndrome
Individuals with Fetal Alcohol Syndrome often have facial abnormalities.

Skin folds over the eyes

Low nasal bridge

Short turned up nose

Indistinct philtrum (groove between nose and upper lip)

Small head circumference

Small eye opening

Small midface

Flattened face

Thin upper lip

defects in the United States. Children with FAS often have problems in school and interacting socially with others, poor coordination, low IQ, and problems with everyday living.[31] Approximately 4 million infants each year in the United States experienced prenatal exposure to alcohol, and it is estimated that up to 6,000 babies are born with FAS.

Recently a newer term, **fetal alcohol spectrum disorders (FASDs)**, which includes FAS, has been adopted by major health organizations to describe a wide range of conditions that can occur in children exposed to alcohol prenatally. For example, not all children exposed to alcohol during pregnancy may experience *all* of the physical, mental, and behavioral abnormalities seen in FAS, which is the severe end of the FASDs. However, no matter the degree of abnormalities, FASDs are permanent. The only proven, safe amount of alcohol a pregnant woman can consume is *none*. Women should avoid alcohol if they think they are, or could become, pregnant.

The Take-Home Message Excessive drinking can disrupt your sleep, cause hangovers, and add extra calories to your diet, which can lead to weight gain. Drinking too much alcohol can also cause hormone imbalances, lead to malnutrition, harm your digestive organs, heart, and liver, and cause irreversible damage to a developing fetus during pregnancy. Individuals with alcohol liver disease can experience a fatty liver and deterioration of the liver that develops into alcohol-related hepatitis and cirrhosis.

What Are Alcohol Abuse and Alcoholism?

When people choose not to drink alcohol responsibly, they often end up abusing alcohol, or suffering from a full-blown addiction. **Alcohol abuse** begins when a person allows alcohol to interfere with his or her life. He may have to call in sick to work or school due to a hangover, or he may have blank spots in his memory due to intoxication.

fetal alcohol spectrum disorders (FASDs) A range of conditions that can occur in children who are exposed to alcohol in utero. Fetal alcohol syndrome (FAS) is the most severe of the FASDs; children with FAS will display physical, mental, and behavioral abnormalities.

alcohol abuse The continuation of alcohol consumption even though this behavior has created social, legal, and/or health problems.

At the extreme end of the spectrum is the disease of **alcoholism.** By the time a person is addicted to alcohol, she is no longer in control of her drinking habits and is at serious risk of suffering long-term health damage. Approximately 17 percent of regular drinkers either abuse or are addicted to alcohol.[32]

Let's take a closer look at both of these categories of alcohol dysfunction.

Binge Drinking, Drinking and Driving, and Underage Drinking Are Forms of Alcohol Abuse

When people continue to consume alcohol even though the behavior has created social, legal, and/or health problems for them, they are abusing alcohol. Binge drinking and drunk driving are situations in which alcohol is being abused. Because 21 is the legal drinking age in the United States, anyone under this age who consumes alcohol is abusing it.

Binge Drinking

Binge drinking occurs when a male consumes 5 or more drinks and when a woman consumes 4 or more drinks in a very short time. Approximately 1 in 3 American adults who drink alcohol have fallen into this category during the last month. College students who binge drink are more likely to miss classes, have hangovers, experience unintentional injuries, such as falling, motor vehicle accidents, and drowning, and may even die (Figure 9.8). In 2005, a 21-year-old junior at Fairleigh Dickinson University in New Jersey died when, after an evening of drinking with friends, he fell four stories out of his dorm room window.[33]

Research also indicates that binge drinkers engage in more unplanned sexual activity and fail to use safe sex strategies more frequently than non–binge drinkers.[34] Sexual aggression and assaults on campus increase when drinking enters the picture. Alcohol is involved with over 70 percent of the reported rapes on college campuses; victims are often too drunk to consent to or refuse the actions of the other person.

Binge drinking is associated with many other health problems, such as hypertension, heart attack, sexually transmitted disease, suicide, homicide, and child abuse.[35] Binge drinking can also cause **blackouts,** which are periods of time that a person cannot remember, even though he or she may have been conscious. A research study of over 700 college students found that more than half of them had blacked out at least once in their lives, and many found out after the fact that they had taken part in activities such as vandalism, unprotected sex, and driving a motor vehicle during the blackout period.[36]

Research shows that college students often have exaggerated perceptions of the amount of alcohol their peers consume. Many college-age binge drinkers think that everyone is drinking all the time, but this isn't always the case. Binge drinking was found to occur at rates ranging from almost never to nearly 70 percent of the students on a college campus.[37] Those who think binge drinking is just a normal part of the college experience often have a circle of like-minded buddies who reinforce their misperceptions.

Drinking in groups is associated with an increased intake of alcohol. Joining a fraternity or sorority tends to increase alcohol consumption among college students and frequenting frat parties raises the bar as to what is the normal amount and frequency of alcohol consumed during college life. The boxed feature "Smashed: Story of a Drunken Girlhood" describes the true story of Koren Zailckas, a recent college graduate, and her struggles with alcohol abuse. The Self-Assessment will help you recognize some red flags of alcohol abuse.

Number of college students, 18–24, per year

696,000

599,000

97,000

1,700

Deaths | Sexual assaults | Injuries | Assaults

Figure 9.8 Consequences of College Binge Drinking
Alcohol use by college students results in numerous assaults, injuries, and deaths each year.

Source: National Institute on Alcohol Abuse and Alcoholism, based on information from Hingson, R. et al. 2005. Magnitude of Alcohol-Related Mortality and Morbidity Among U.S. College Students Ages 18–24: Changes from 1998 to 2001. *Annual Review of Public Health* 26: 259–279.

alcoholism Also referred to as **alcohol dependence,** a chronic disease with genetic, psychological, and environmental components. Alcoholics crave alcohol, can't control their intake, and develop a higher tolerance for it. Alcoholics also exhibit a dependency on alcohol, as abstaining from drinking will cause withdrawal symptoms.

binge drinking The consumption of 5 or more alcoholic drinks by men, or 4 or more drinks by women, in a very short time.

blackouts Periods of time when an intoxicated person cannot recall part or all of an event.

Smashed: Story of a Drunken Girlhood

Koren Zailckas was a shy, meek, insecure girl raised in an upscale town in the Boston suburbs. She started drinking at the age of 14, and almost from her first sip, there was no turning back. During a socially awkward adolescence, Koren found it difficult to be at ease around other people, particularly girls her own age. When she drank, she became assertive and friendly. She bonded with other girls and met tons of guys. Throughout her high school and college years, alcohol was her crutch and best pal.

Koren didn't think of herself as an alcoholic, but she was a binge drinker. She drank herself into her first blackout with a thermos full of vodka at the age of 16. She woke up in her bedroom wearing a hospital Johnny and a pink plastic bracelet on her wrist that said "Zailckas, Koren." The bracelet was compliments of her local hospital emergency room. The Johnny had replaced her vomit-covered clothes the night before. Her stomach had been pumped. Her parents had carried her from the back seat of the family car to her bedroom in the middle of the night. They were devastated.

As a freshman entering college, Koren used beer and liquor to make friends and be accepted. She pledged a sorority for the sole purpose of sisterhood and booze. She frequently drank herself into a steady state of numbness and allowed sorority sisters and male mates to make many of her decisions. She was often the last girl to leave the party because she was too drunk to know that she should have left an hour before.

After college graduation, Koren continued her drunken lifestyle in the fast-paced mecca of New York City. She worked hard during the day and drank hard at night. One morning she woke up in a strange bed, in a strange condo, next to a stranger from the cab ride the night before. For Koren, this was rock bottom. She realized that her chronic drinking was a magnet for like-

minded people who similarly abused alcohol and were as damaged in life as she. But she wanted a good life. She wanted sound friendships and self-confidence, and she recognized that she wasn't going to achieve these goals with alcohol. At that moment, she decided to get help.

Through guidance from an addiction counselor and her own drive to quit drinking, Koren stopped her destructive behavior and began surrounding herself with a healthier circle of friends. Today, she is in her mid-20s and sober, and has a new lease on life.

You can read more about Koren's struggles and triumphs in her best-selling book, *Smashed* (Penguin, 2006), and on her website, www.korenzailckas.com.

Self-Assessment

Red Flags for Alcohol Abuse

Complete the following self-assessment to see if you may be at increased risk for alcohol abuse.

1. Do you fail to fulfill major work, school, or home responsibilities because of your consumption of alcohol?   **Yes** ☐   **No** ☐

2. Do you drink in situations that are potentially dangerous, such as while driving a car or operating heavy machinery?   **Yes** ☐   **No** ☐

3. Do you experience repeated alcohol-related legal problems, such as being arrested for driving while intoxicated?   **Yes** ☐   **No** ☐

4. Do you have relationship problems that are caused or made worse by alcohol?   **Yes** ☐   **No** ☐

Answers

If you answered yes to any of these questions, you should speak with your health care provider for insight and guidance.

Source: Adapted from National Institute on Alcohol Abuse and Alcoholism. 2003. Understanding alcohol: Investigations into Biology and Behavior. Available at http://science.education.nih.gov/supplements/nih3/alcohol/default.htm. Accessed December 2005; U.S. Department of Health and Human Services. 1997. Ninth Special Report of the U.S. Congress on Alcohol and Health. Bethesda, MD: National Institute on Alcohol Abuse and Alcoholism.

Table 9.3

The CAGE Screening Tool

C Have you ever felt that you should **c**ut down on your drinking?

A Have people **a**nnoyed you by criticizing your drinking?

G Have you ever felt **g**uilty about your drinking?

E Have you ever had a drink first thing in the morning (**e**ye opener) to steady your nerves or get rid of a hangover?

Source: National Institute on Alcohol Abuse and Alcoholism. 2003. Understanding Alcohol: Investigations into Biology and Behavior. Available at http://science .education.nih.gov/supplements/nih3/alcohol/default .htm. Accessed December 2005.

Binge drinking can lead to **alcohol poisoning.** Freya, a college student and binge drinker, is drinking her way to alcohol poisoning (Figure 9.9). Her BAC has risen to such a high level that her central nervous system is affected. Because alcohol depresses the nerves involved in numerous actions in the body, such as breathing and heart rate (see Table 9.2), Freya has passed out, yet the alcohol in her stomach and intestine will continue to be absorbed and her BAC will continue to rise as she sleeps. She could have stopped breathing, and ultimately died, if her friends hadn't gotten medical help.

Chronic drinking can lead to **alcohol tolerance,** which occurs over time as the body adjusts to long-term alcohol use. As the brain becomes less sensitive to alcohol, more is needed to get the same intoxicating effect.[38] People who've developed an alcohol tolerance should not think they can drink more without damaging the body. The harmful effects that you read about in the last section still occur.

Many health professionals use a four-question screening tool called CAGE to assess if their patients have a problem controlling their alcohol consumption (Table 9.3). If a person is experiencing two or more of the responses, this is a sign that alcohol abuse may be a problem for that individual.

Drinking and Driving

If you have spent any time behind a steering wheel, you know that you can't *just* drive. You have to drive defensively. Driving involves multitasking: You need to keep the car within your lane, stay within the speed limit, make constant quick decisions, and, of course, maneuver the car based on these decisions. Alcohol intake impairs all of these skills. It is illegal to drive in the United States with a BAC of 0.08 (some states in the United States have set their legal limit even lower), but the level of alcohol in the blood doesn't need to get that high to impair your driving. As we saw in Table 9.1, even the lowest level of BAC, the level that occurs after one alcoholic beverage, will impair alertness, judgment, and coordination. In 2004, over 16,000 people died in automobile accidents that involved a driver with a BAC of .01 or higher.[39]

> As the price of beer goes up, the number of people involved in fatal traffic accidents goes down.

alcohol poisoning When the BAC rises to such an extreme level that a person's central nervous system is affected and his or her breathing and heart rate are interrupted.

alcohol tolerance When the body adjusts to long-term alcohol use by becoming less sensitive to the alcohol. More alcohol needs to be consumed in order to get the same effect.

Drinking and driving can be deadly.

Freya goes to a party after having a few drinks at home to "warm up."

BAC = 0.01–0.05

She doesn't bother eating before she goes. As soon as she arrives she gets handed a glass of homemade punch—it tastes horrible, but makes her feel confident. She's chatty and having a good laugh with her friends.

Figure 9.9 Freya's Night of Binge Drinking

Source: At-Bristol. Available at www.at-bristol.org.uk/Alcoholandyou/effects/freya.html.

BAC = 0.06–0.10

The first drinks have affected her judgment, Freya's friends are now having trouble talking to her. She's saying things without thinking, stopping mid-conversation, and disappearing or trying to drag people onto the dance floor.

BAC = 0.11–0.20

After a few more drinks, Freya is having trouble understanding and remembering things so conversation with her is even harder. Her reactions are slow and she's bumping into people. All her movements are uncoordinated and when she tries to dance she keeps losing her balance. She's having trouble recognizing people, and her vision is blurry.

BAC = 0.21–0.30

Freya has stopped drinking, but she's getting drunker as the last few drinks are absorbed into her body. She's sleepy and confused and unsure as to where she is or what she's doing. Freya is emotional and doesn't know whether to laugh or cry. Her vision has gotten worse and she's slurring her words so badly no one can understand her.

BAC = 0.31–0.40

Freya feels terrible, the room is spinning, and she feels sick. She's not sure what time it is as she keeps falling asleep.

BAC ≥ 0.40

Freya is unconscious. Her skin feels cooler than normal; her breathing has slowed and is shallower than normal. Her friends give up trying to wake her and call an ambulance.

When it arrives, the EMTs tell them they did the right thing. She has poisoned herself by drinking too much alcohol and is taken to the hospital.

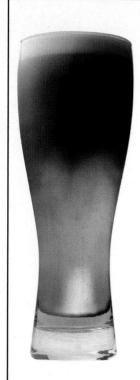

**The "It's Only Another Beer"
Black and Tan**

8 oz. pilsner lager
8 oz. stout lager
1 frosty mug
1 icy road
1 pick-up truck
1 10-hour day
1 tired worker
A few rounds with the guys

Mix ingredients.
Add 1 totalled vehicle.

**Never underestimate 'just a few.'
Buzzed driving is drunk driving.**

U.S. Department of Transportation

"Buzzed driving is drunk driving" was a successful ad campaign that underscored the dangers of drinking and driving.

The latest data, collected in 2002 regarding the alcohol intake of Americans, reports that over 2 percent of adults in the United States admitted to driving while alcohol impaired within the last 30 days. Even more astounding, 1.4 million Americans were arrested for driving under the influence (DUI) of alcohol or drugs. This translates to 1 out of every 137 licensed drivers being arrested for DUI and putting your life at risk if you are on the road at the same time with them.[40] Legal penalties for DUI can be severe, ranging from stiff fines and loss of license to jail time in some states.

People who ride with drunk drivers put themselves at high risk of being involved in an accident. To educate the public about the risks of drinking and driving, the Ad Council and the United States Department of Transportation launched a campaign in the early 1980s to promote the Designated Driver Program. The concept of the program was to designate a sober driver at social gatherings to ensure that people who choose to drink have a safe ride home. The "Friends Don't Let Friends Drive Drunk" tagline has been instrumental in reducing the annual number of alcohol-related automobile fatalities since its inception in 1983. Unfortunately, many people think they can still drive safely as long as they consume "only a few" drinks. But because even one alcoholic beverage can affect the skills needed when driving, the only sober driver is one who abstains from drinking alcohol.

Another campaign, entitled "Buzzed Driving Is Drunk Driving" has been launched to reinforce the concept that the designated driver shouldn't be the least drunk member of the group, but rather the one who hasn't consumed any alcohol.

Underage Drinking

The average age of the first drink for Americans from 12 to 20 years of age is 14 years old.[41] That means that many American youth are drinking alcohol when they are not even tall enough to see over the bar. By high school, over 30 percent of teenagers are binge drinking at least one time a month.[42] Underage drinking not only increases the risk of violence, injuries, and other health risks as discussed above, but alcohol consumption at this age can also interfere with brain development and lead to permanent cognitive and memory damage in teenagers.

Underage drinking, coupled with driving, is a disaster waiting to happen. Adolescent drivers are inexperienced behind the wheel to begin with, so it isn't surprising that automobile accidents are the number-one cause of death of young people between the ages of 15 and 20. Those between the ages of 16 and 20 who drink and drive are twice as likely to die in automobile accidents as those 21 years of age and older who drink before getting behind the wheel.[43] In fact, this is why the minimum legal drinking age in the United States is 21. Studies conducted between 1970 and 1975, when several states had lowered the legal drinking age to under 21, showed that the rate of motor vehicle crashes and fatalities increased among teenagers.[44] Since 1984, all states have adopted 21 as the minimum legal drinking age and prohibited the sale of alcohol to underage individuals.

There is another danger in consuming alcohol at a young age. The earlier in life a person starts drinking, the higher the chances that alcohol will become a problem later in life. A person who starts drinking at age 15 is four times more likely to suffer from alcoholism than an individual who doesn't start drinking until age 20.[45]

Alcoholism Is a Disease

In the beginning of the chapter, you read that Leah is concerned about her daily alcohol habit. Her brother Steve currently suffers from alcoholism, which is often referred to as alcohol dependence. Her father and grandfather both died of cirrhosis due to alcoholism.

Steve exhibits the four classic symptoms of alcoholism: (1) he craves alcohol; (2) he has developed a higher tolerance for it; (3) he can't control or limit his intake once he starts drinking; and (4) he has developed a dependency on alcohol because, if he stops drinking, his body reacts to the withdrawal. An alcoholic's craving, loss of control, and physical dependency distinguishes him or her as an "alcoholic" rather than a person who abuses alcohol but doesn't have these three other characteristics.[46]

Because the disease runs in her family, Leah is at a higher than average risk for alcoholism. Research has shown that approximately 50 percent of the risk for alcoholism is determined genetically.[47] However, this genetic risk alone will not destine Leah to become an alcoholic. Her risk for alcoholism is also influenced by her environment. Her home life, the drinking habits of her family and friends, social pressures, and access to alcohol will all impact whether she develops the disease. If Leah's roommate and friends drink heavily, and she works part-time as a bartender, she will be at greater risk of developing alcoholism. If she chooses to surround herself with friends and a lifestyle that don't focus on alcohol, she can reduce her risk of following in her brother's footsteps.

There is no cure for alcoholism. However, it can be treated using a physical and psychological approach. The physical symptoms, such as the severe craving for alcohol, can be treated with medication that helps reduce the craving. Psychologically, self-help therapies and support groups can be invaluable to an alcoholic on the road to recovery. Because alcoholics can't limit their consumption once they start drinking, reducing the amount of alcohol consumed will not work for them. They must eliminate alcohol entirely from their lifestyle in order to have a successful recovery.

Alcoholics Anonymous (AA), the first support group devoted to helping those who suffer with alcoholism, was created in 1935 by Bill Wilson, a stockbroker, and Dr. Robert Smith, a surgeon, who together declared themselves hopeless drunks. They founded AA to help themselves and others stay sober. With over 2 million members in 150 countries, AA is a worldwide fellowship of men and women with various backgrounds, lifestyles, and educational levels who meet, bond, and support each other, with the sole purpose of remaining sober. AA's 12 steps for recovery and supportive group meetings help individuals maintain sobriety.[48]

If you are interested in learning more about AA or finding a group in your area, look in your local telephone directory or online at www.alcoholics-anonymous.org. Everyone is welcomed at their meetings, including family members, friends, and coworkers.

Alcohol abusers and alcoholics should avoid alcohol. But they're not the only ones. Let's find out who else needs to abstain from drinking.

The Take-Home Message Individuals who abuse alcohol by binge drinking, drinking and driving, and underage drinking are putting themselves and others at risk of injuries, violence, and even death. Alcoholism is a disease that can't be cured, but it can be treated with medical help and psychological support.

Table Tips

Keeping Your Drinking to a Moderate Amount

Never drink on an empty stomach. The alcohol will be absorbed too quickly, which will impair your judgment and lower your willpower to decline the next drink.

Make your first—and even your second—drink at a party a tall glass of water. This will allow you to pace yourself and eliminate the chance that you will guzzle your first alcoholic drink because you are thirsty. Also, have a glass of water before you have a second alcoholic drink. By the time you drink all this water, it will be time to go home.

Drink fun nonalcoholic drinks. Try a Virgin Mary (a Bloody Mary without the vodka), a tame frozen margarita (use the mix and don't add the tequila), or a Tom Collins without the gin (club soda, lemon, and sugar).

Be an alcohol snob. Rather than consume excessive amounts of cheap beer or jug wine at parties, wait until you get home and have a better quality microbrewed beer or a glass of nice wine. Don't drink a lot of junk; drink a little of the good stuff.

Become the standing Designated Driver among your friends and make your passengers reimburse you for the cost of the gasoline. You'll be everyone's best friend and have the money to buy and drink the good stuff.

Who Should Avoid Alcohol and What Is Moderate Drinking?

12 oz
(1 drink)

16 oz
(1⅓ drink)

5 oz
(1 drink)

8 oz
(1½ drink)

Figure 9.10 When a Drink Is More Than a Drink. . . .
Depending on the size, one drink may actually be the equivalent of 1⅓ to 1½ drinks.

According to the latest *Dietary Guidelines for Americans*, the following people should abstain from alcohol:[49]

- Women of childbearing age who may become pregnant
- Pregnant and lactating women
- Children and adolescents
- Those taking medications that can interact with alcohol, which include prescription and over-the-counter medications
- Those with specific medical conditions, such as stomach ulcers
- Those engaging in activities that require attention, skill, or coordination, such as driving or operating machinery
- Those who cannot restrict their alcohol intake

For these individuals, abstinence is the best option, as even modest amounts of alcohol can have detrimental health effects.

No one needs to drink alcohol, but for those who choose to do so, moderate drinking is the only sensible approach. As a moderate drinker, you need to watch out for (1) the size of your drinks and (2) the frequency of your drinking.

Recall that a standard drink, whether it's a bottle of beer, a shot of liquor, or a glass of wine, contains about ½ ounce of alcohol. Sometimes, the drink you order at your local bar or restaurant is a standard drink, but often it's more than that. If your 8-ounce wine glass gets filled to the brim, or you chug an oversize mug of beer, you could consume close to two standard drinks in one glass or mug (Figure 9.10). Mixed drinks have also expanded in their portion size and alcohol content. One rum and coke could provide the equivalent of over 2½ alcoholic drinks.

Another very important point to remember about drinking in moderation is that abstaining from drinking for six days and then overdrinking on the seventh day does not count as moderate drinking. There isn't any "banking" allowed when it comes to alcohol. Drinking seven drinks on a Friday night after not drinking the rest of the week is binge drinking.

Light beer has about the same amount of alcohol as regular beer.

The Take-Home Message Many people, depending on their age, medical history, and lifestyle, would benefit from abstaining from alcohol. Many drinks served at bars and restaurants contain more than one serving of alcohol. Abstaining from alcohol for several days and then drinking a lot of it at once is binge drinking, not moderate drinking.

Putting It All Together

Unlike carbohydrates, protein, fat, vitamins, minerals and water, alcohol is not an essential nutrient, but it will contribute calories to your diet. Alcohol can displace essential nutrients and contribute to weight gain. For some older adults, alcohol in moderation may help reduce the risk of certain diseases, such as heart disease. Excessive amounts of alcohol will do more harm than good in your body. If you drink alcohol, you need to drink responsibly.

Two Points of View

Are There Health Benefits to Drinking Alcohol?

Is it true that alcohol consumption can have health benefits? If so, are the benefits worth the risks associated with alcohol use? Two experts present views on this controversial topic.

David Anderson, PhD
Professor; Director, Center for the Advancement of Public Health, George Mason University

 **David Anderson, PhD,** is a professor of education and human development at George Mason University. He coauthors two national surveys on college drug and alcohol prevention efforts, including the *College Alcohol Survey,* conducted every three years since 1979. He has worked with organizations and agencies on strategic planning and evaluation initiatives in issues of health promotion, substance abuse prevention, and related health issues for over 30 years.

Q: Are there health benefits to drinking alcohol?

A: For some people, some of the time, there can be some health benefits. But that does not translate into a wise motivator for choosing alcohol. The primary question one should ask is "What do I want to achieve by my decision to choose alcohol?" If I'm looking for health benefits and considering alcohol, can I get those benefits another way? For many people, alcohol has negative consequences from a safety, ethical, and/or legal perspective. Antioxidants in red wine might help my heart, but the drinking might promote me to become addicted. Do I want something healthful for the heart, or the whole body? We need to look at the whole story.

Q: How have these risks become apparent?

A: We've conducted the *College Alcohol Survey,* a survey of 330 colleges and universities across the country, since 1979. So much of society's emphasis is on addiction and drunk driving. But we've found that plenty of problems have nothing to do with those issues. We've found that alcohol is often involved with 50 percent or more of various campus problems, including property damage, violent behavior, diminished academic performance, and acquaintance rape.

(continued)

Charles Bamforth, PhD, DSc
Chair, Department of Food Science and Technology, University of California at Davis

 **Charles Bamforth, PhD, DSc,** is Chair of the Department of Food Science and Technology and Anheuser-Busch Endowed Professor of Malting and Brewing Sciences at the University of California, Davis. He is also a Special Professor in the School of Biosciences at the University of Nottingham, England; a Fellow of the Institute of Brewing and Distilling; and a Fellow of the Institute of Biology. Bamforth has published numerous papers, articles, and books on beer and brewing, including *Beer: Health and Nutrition* (Blackwell Publishing).

Q: Are there health benefits to drinking alcohol?

A: In moderation, yes. There is now ample evidence to show that a daily intake of either beer or wine reduces the risk of atherosclerosis (narrowing of the arteries). There are a number of other potential benefits of moderate alcohol consumption. These include fewer gallstones, fewer kidney stones, and improved cognitive function in the elderly. Other studies have shown that people with modest intake of alcohol are happier and more content.

Q: How have such benefits become apparent?

A: This type of study involves the investigation of the dietary habits of large numbers of people over lengthy periods of time. In these studies, people who showed some benefit engaged in regular, moderate alcohol consumption. The gallstone study, for example, followed a group of men for 10 years, tracking their alcohol intake and checking to see if they developed gallstones. The study, conducted by nutrition researchers affiliated with the Harvard University School of Public Health and published in 1999, found that men in the study who drank regular, moderate amounts of alcohol faced lower risk of developing gallstones than nondrinkers.

(continued)

Are There Health Benefits to Drinking Alcohol?, continued

David Anderson, PhD, continued

These issues aren't addiction or drunk driving, but they are still serious. Without alcohol as a factor in those instances, we'd be so much better off.

Q: Are some drinking choices more healthful than others?

A: Yes. We forget that when we talk about college students, most people most of the time make healthy choices. When we look at college students over the last 25 years, more are abstaining from alcohol. In 1980, 20 percent of students hadn't had a drink in the last 30 days. In 2004, that figure went up to 30 percent. The drinking age law is very clear—you have to be 21. The law is there for good reasons. For most people, the brain is not fully developed until the early twenties. If you are under 21, alcohol can compromise the development of the brain. And you are more likely to become dependent if you start drinking earlier. Abstention is a healthful choice.

Q: What special considerations should students keep in mind when it comes to drinking?

A: It's important that each individual makes his or her own informed choice. Ask, "How do my decisions about alcohol help me get to my goals, and how do they get in my way?" This isn't about not using alcohol. It's about responsible choices.

When I make a choice and you make a choice, I need to respect your choice. If you say "No," I should respect that. If I see someone getting in a danger zone, I'm going to talk to them about that. So much of this is non-conversation right now. It needs to be talked about. And if you're worried about peer pressure, remember that people around you may not be drinking as much as you think. If you think everyone is doing it, you are more likely to use too.

Charles Bamforth, PhD, DSc, continued

Many researchers have conducted studies that relate the risk of death to the consumption of alcohol. It would appear that one or two 12-ounce servings of beer or glasses of wine equates to the lowest risk. Excessive consumption of alcohol causes the risk of mortality to increase, not least because it leads to increased risk of accidents.

Q: Are some drinking choices more healthful than others?

A: There is much about the relative merits of different beverages. But there is no conclusive evidence that one type of drink is better than another. For example, red wine contains more antioxidants than does beer. But beer contains more vitamins than wine.

Some popular views about the health risks of certain drinks are incorrect. Beer, for example, has gained a reputation as a beverage high in unhealthful carbohydrates. But that isn't accurate. Beer, in moderation, can be part of a "low-carb" diet and potentially a good source of soluble fiber and other substances that promote digestion. Beer is not comprised merely of empty calories. Rather, it can contain significant levels of vitamins, antioxidants, minerals, and fiber. Furthermore, alcoholic drinks that contain mixers such as ginger ale, cola, tonic, and tomato juice are far more charged with carbohydrate than is beer.

Q: What special considerations should students keep in mind when it comes to drinking?

A: Absolutely avoid excess. It is illegal to drink alcohol before the permitted age in any given country. Once a person is of legal age, they should be restrained in their intake. Students should avoid binge drinking and should absolutely avoid irresponsible behavior such as drinking games. Alcohol is best consumed in moderation alongside food. It should be treated as another normal component of the diet. Nothing on a dinner plate or in a glass should be overindulged in.

Be a Nutrition Sleuth

Is Your Friend Too Drunk to Drive?

You be the judge. Go to www.aw-bc.com/blake to view two driving simulations, one through the eyes of a sober driver, the other through the eyes of a driver who has consumed alcohol.

You'll see the impairment caused by alcohol, which the affected driver may not even recognize.

Get Real!
Step Up to the Virtual Bar

Go to www.aw-bc.com/blake to learn how drinking a variety of beverages will affect *your* blood alcohol concentration (BAC). You can see how your BAC changes based on your gender, weight, type of drink, speed at which you're drinking, and food you have eaten.

The Top Ten Points to Remember

1. Ethanol is the type of alcohol in alcoholic beverages. Unlike other types of alcohol, ethanol isn't poisonous when ingested. However, it can be toxic if too much is consumed. Alcohol is not an essential nutrient.

2. Alcohol produces an initial euphoric, pleasurable state of mind. For adults who choose to drink, moderate alcohol consumption is considered up to one drink for women daily and up to two drinks a day for men. A standard drink is 12 ounces of beer, 5 ounces of wine, or 1.5 ounces of liquor. Drinking alcohol in moderation may help reduce the risk of heart disease in older adults.

3. Alcohol is one of the rare substances that is absorbed in the stomach. Alcohol dehydrogenase begins metabolizing some of the alcohol in the stomach before it reaches your blood. Women have less of this enzyme in their stomachs than men. Alcohol mixes with water and is distributed in the watery tissues of the body. Women have less body water than men. Both of these factors cause women to feel the narcotic effects of alcohol sooner than men do.

4. The presence of food will slow the departure of alcohol from your stomach to your intestines, where the majority of the alcohol is absorbed. This is why drinking on an empty stomach is not a good idea.

5. The majority of the alcohol you consume is metabolized in your liver. Some alcohol is lost from your body in your breath and urine. Your liver can only metabolize about one standard drink per 1½ hours. As you drink more alcohol, your BAC goes up, as does your level of impairment and intoxication.

6. Whereas alcohol is often thought of as a stimulant, it is actually a central nervous system depressant. Your brain is sensitive to the effects of alcohol, and depending on the amount you consume, alcohol can cause numerous mental, behavioral, and physical changes in your body. Your alertness, judgment, and coordination will initially be affected. As you drink more alcohol, your vision, speech, reasoning, and balance will be altered. An excessive amount of alcohol can interfere with your breathing and heart rate.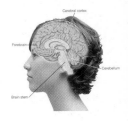

7. Alcohol can disrupt your sleep, cause hangovers, interfere with hormones, and add excess calories and/or displace healthier food choices from your diet. Chronically consuming excessive amounts of alcohol can harm your digestive organs, heart, and liver. The three stages of alcohol liver disease are fatty liver, alcoholic hepatitis, and cirrhosis. Many individuals die annually of alcohol-related liver disease. Alcohol can put a fetus at risk for fetal alcohol spectrum disorders.

8. Alcohol abuse occurs when people continue to consume alcohol even though this behavior negatively affects their lives. Binge drinking, underage drinking, and drinking and driving are examples of alcohol abuse. Individuals who binge drink, many of whom are also underage, are at risk for blackouts and alcohol poisoning. Individuals who chronically drink alcohol often develop alcohol tolerance, which occurs when the brain becomes less sensitive to alcohol. Because alcohol affects alertness and judgment, the only safe amount of alcohol to consume when driving is none.

9. Alcoholism, also called alcohol dependence, is a disease characterized by four symptoms, which include a craving for alcohol, a higher tolerance for alcohol, the inability to control or limit its intake, and a physical dependence on it. Genetics plays a role in increasing

the risk of certain people developing alcoholism. Though alcoholism can't be cured, it can be treated with medical and psychological support.

10. Alcohol should be avoided by: women of childbearing age who may become pregnant, or are pregnant or lactating; anyone under the age of 21; those taking certain medications or with specific medical conditions; those engaging in activities that would be impaired with alcohol consumption; and those who cannot restrict or limit their intake of alcohol.

Test Your Knowledge

1. Alcohol provides
   a. 9 calories per gram.
   b. 7 calories per gram.
   c. 4 calories per gram.
   d. 0 calories per gram.
   e. none of the above.
2. A standard drink is considered
   a. a 12-oz can of beer.
   b. a 5-oz glass of white wine.
   c. a shot (1.5 oz) of liquor.
   d. any of the above.
   e. none of the above.
3. The major site of alcohol metabolism in your body is your
   a. kidneys.
   b. lungs.
   c. liver.
   d. stomach.
   e. none of the above
4. Which of the following factors affect(s) your rate of absorption and the metabolism of alcohol?
   a. whether you're male or female
   b. the amount of food in your stomach
   c. the time of day you drink
   d. the individuals you are drinking with
   e. a and b only
5. Blood alcohol concentration (BAC) is the
   a. minimum amount of alcohol needed in your blood daily.
   b. amount of alcohol in your blood, measured in grams of alcohol per deciliter of blood.
   c. number of drinks you consumed in an hour.
   d. grams of alcohol per liter of beverage.
   e. none of the above
6. The *best* cure for a hangover is
   a. chicken soup.
   b. a light beer.
   c. time and abstinence.

   d. taking acetaminophen (Tylenol).
   e. none of the above.
7. Individuals who chronically drink excessively are at increased risk for
   a. malnutrition.
   b. gastritis.
   c. inflammation of the esophagus.
   d. fatty liver.
   e. all of the above.
8. The four characteristics of alcoholism are (1) a craving for alcohol, (2) the development of a higher tolerance to alcohol, (3) the inability to control or limit the intake of alcohol, and (4) _____.
   a. the inability to keep a stable job
   b. the inability to maintain social relationships
   c. the tendency to become violent
   d. the development of a dependency on alcohol
   e. the revoking of the person's driver's license
9. Of the following list, who shouldn't drink alcohol?
   a. your pregnant aunt
   b. your high school–aged brother
   c. your uncle who has a stomach ulcer
   d. your father while he is riding the lawn mower
   e. all of the above
10. Drinking 4 to 5 alcoholic beverages on one occasion in a very short time is called
    a. alcoholism.
    b. drunk driving.
    c. blackout.
    d. binge drinking.
    e. none of the above.

Answers

1. (b) Alcohol serves up 7 calories per gram, which is less than fat at 9 calories per gram, and more than carbohydrates and protein, which each provide 4 calories per gram. Alcohol isn't an essential nutrient—your body doesn't need it to survive—and it's not calorie free.
2. (d) All of these drinks contain ½ ounce of alcohol, so each is considered a standard drink.
3. (c) Most alcohol in the body is metabolized in the liver. A small amount of alcohol is lost in your urine (kidneys) and in your breath (your lungs). Some alcohol is also metabolized in your stomach, though substantially less than in your liver.
4. (e) Both your sex and the amount of food in your stomach will affect the rate of absorption and the metabolism of alcohol. Women have less of the enzyme alcohol dehydrogenase in their stomachs, which means they metabolize

less alcohol in the stomach and more alcohol will be absorbed into the blood. Drinking on a full stomach will delay the arrival of alcohol in your small intestine, which is the primary site of absorption. The time of day doesn't have any effect on the absorption and metabolism of alcohol. Your drinking partners also won't alter the absorption and metabolism of alcohol. Of course, they could influence the *amount* of alcohol you consume.

5. (b) Your BAC is the concentration of alcohol in your blood. It is measured in grams of alcohol per deciliter of blood. Your body doesn't need a minimum intake of alcohol daily. The number of drinks that you consume in an hour will affect your BAC; the more you drink, the higher the concentration of alcohol in your blood will be. BAC has nothing to do with the concentration of alcohol in a drink.

6. (c) The best cure is to stop drinking and let your body have the time it needs to recover from consuming too much alcohol. A warm bowl of chicken soup won't cure the fatigue or the other ill effects of drinking alcohol. Taking acetaminophen is not recommended as its toxicity to your liver is enhanced if it is consumed while alcohol is being metabolized. The worst thing you can do for a hangover is to have another alcoholic beverage.

7. (e) All of the above. When too much alcohol is chronically consumed, more nutritious foods are often displaced in the diet, increasing the risk of malnutrition. A constant intake of alcohol will not only cause irritation and inflammation of the esophagus but also your stomach. A fatty liver can occur after only a few days of excessive drinking.

8. (d) The last characteristic of alcoholism is the development of a dependency on alcohol, such that a withdrawal will cause symptoms in the body. Although alcoholism can have financial consequences such as job instability, interfere with personal relationships, and increase the risk of violence, not all individuals with alcoholism have these experiences.

9. (e) All pregnant women should avoid alcohol, as drinking during pregnancy will increase the risk of fetal alcohol spectrum disorders (FASD) in their newborn baby. Unless your brother is 21 years old, he shouldn't be drinking alcohol. Because alcohol causes gastritis, your uncle would benefit from avoiding alcohol. Your father should wait until he has finished mowing the lawn before having a drink, as this chore involves operating machinery that requires attention, skill, and coordination.

10. (d) Consuming that much alcohol in a very short time is considered binge drinking. Binge drinking can lead to alcoholism. Individuals who binge drink may experience blackouts or may drive while drunk.

Web Support

- For more information about drinking at college, visit www.collegedrinkingprevention.gov/
- For more information about alcohol and your health, visit the National Institute on Alcohol Abuse and Alcoholism (NIAAA) at www.niaaa.nih.gov/
- For more information about alcohol consumption and its consequences, visit the National Center for Chronic Disease Prevention and Health Promotion, Alcohol and Public Health, at www.cdc.gov/alcohol/index.htm

10

Weight

Manage

1. Overweight people have a harder time sleeping. **T/F**

2. Being **skinny** is always healthy. **T/F**

3. One of the best ways to tell if you are at a **healthy weight** is to compare yourself to celebrities. **T/F**

ment

4. Fat around the hips is as unhealthy as fat stored around the waist. **T/F**

5. The number of **calories** you burn daily is affected by your body size, genes, and sex. **T/F**

6. Your body weight is affected by your genes and your **environment.** **T/F**

7. Eating *more* **vegetables** and fruits can help you lose weight. **T/F**

8. The nutrient that has the most effect on **satiety** is fat. **T/F**

9. Disordered eating and eating disorders are the same thing. **T/F**

10. Eating disorders can be **fatal.** **T/F**

Eighteen-year-old Hannah is more nervous about the "freshman 15" than about her course load during her first year at college. After struggling with her weight for years, she was able to maintain a healthy 130 pounds during her senior year of high school by changing her eating habits and walking daily. Being away from home and being surrounded by unhealthy foods makes her anxious. Her dorm mate, Jenna, tends to skip breakfast and is a nervous snacker, especially in the evening. Han-

nah is afraid of becoming another freshman statistic: the student who gains 15 pounds by the end of the first year of college.

Hannah may be surprised to learn that the "freshman 15" is not as common as she thinks. However, Jenna has some habits that will make weight management more difficult. Later on in the chapter, you will learn why these habits are less than healthful, as well as strategies that college students can use to avoid unnecessary weight gain.

Answers

1. True. Overweight people can suffer from a condition called sleep apnea. To find out what this is and why being overweight contributes to it, turn to page 339.
2. False. Being underweight due to a poor diet can have serious health risks. Turn to page 339 to find out why.
3. False. Celebrities in magazine photos may reflect social trends, but they often don't reflect a healthy body weight. Turn to page 340 to find out more.
4. False. Fat around the belly puts a person at a higher health risk than fat stored on the hips and thighs. To find out why, turn to page 342.
5. True. But these aren't the only factors. Turn to page 345 to find out the others.
6. True. To find out why and how these factors interact with each other, turn to page 350.
7. True. Surprising as it may be, eating *more* of certain foods can help you lose weight. To find out why, turn to page 355.
8. False. Whereas fat makes food stay in the stomach longer, which slows its digestion and absorption, it isn't the nutrient that provides the greatest level of satiety. You may be surprised to learn what is. Turn to page 355 to find out.
9. False. Technically, disordered eating describes abnormal eating behaviors, while eating disorders are clinically diagnosed illnesses. Turn to page 369 to learn more about these behaviors and illnesses.
10. True. Some eating disorders can be life-threatening. Turn to page 371 to learn about the health effects of eating disorders.

Flip through a magazine, watch a little television, or surf the Internet, and before long you'll find someone talking about weight loss. You may be used to so much coverage of weight management, but it hasn't always been that way. In the early 1960s, fewer than 32 percent of Americans were overweight, so weight didn't receive much media attention. Today, about 65 percent of Americans are overweight, so it's a much hotter topic.[1] In fact, in 2005, obesity was the most frequently covered health story in the media.[2]

Americans' expanding girths are shrinking their wallets. Americans currently spend over $45 billion—the highest amount ever—on everything from over-the-counter diet pills to books, magazines, online support groups, and commercial dieting centers to help shed their excess weight. Unfortunately, they aren't having much success, and the U.S. health care system bears over $92 billion in costs of treating the medical complications associated with being overweight.[3] No matter what you weigh, some of your tax dollars are supporting these costs. Despite spending so much money on the battle of the bulge, we are not winning the war on weight control.

What is causing this trend and how unhealthy is it? What does it mean to manage your weight, and what are the best strategies for doing so? Lastly, should we strive to be thin at all costs—or can this be equally unhealthy?

Let's try to figure this all out.

What Is Weight Management and Why Is It Important?

Weight management means maintaining your weight within a healthy range. Either extreme—being very overweight or very underweight—can be unhealthy, a red flag for undernutrition of some nutrients, overnutrition of others, and impending health problems. So what, exactly, is a healthy weight?

A **healthy weight** is considered a body weight that doesn't increase the risk of developing weight-related health problems or diseases.[4] In contrast, being **overweight** means that a person weighs about 10 to 15 pounds more than a healthy weight.[5] Although 10 pounds may not sound like a lot, try this exercise: The next time you are in a supermarket, head to the produce aisle and pick up two 5-pound bags of potatoes. Try walking around with them for a while. Before long, your arms will probably be tired and you'll be ready to sit down for a rest. Can you imagine carrying this extra weight around every minute of your day?

Being overweight is also a stepping stone for developing **obesity.** A person with 25 to 40 or more pounds of weight (the equivalent of carrying around a toddler or young child all day) above his or her healthy weight is considered obese. Currently, 32 percent of Americans are obese.[6]

Being overweight leads to numerous health problems. In addition to potentially leading to obesity, being overweight can increase your risk of:

- Hypertension and stroke
- Heart disease
- Gallbladder disease
- Type 2 diabetes
- Osteoarthritis
- Some cancers
- Sleep apnea

The obesity trend is now such a hot topic in the United States that it is frequently covered by the mainstream media.

Generally, as a person's weight increases, so does his or her blood pressure. Overweight individuals can experience increased retention of sodium, which causes both increased blood volume and resistance in the blood vessels. This and additional demands on the heart all likely contribute to high blood pressure.[7] High blood pressure increases the risk of stroke and heart disease. Overweight people also tend to have high blood levels of both fat and the "bad" LDL cholesterol, and less of the "good" HDL cholesterol, which is an unhealthy combination for the heart. High blood cholesterol levels also increase the risk for gallstones and gallbladder disease. They are also more likely to contribute to an enlarged gallbladder, impeding its function.

American people aren't the only ones getting bigger—American pets are also putting on pounds. According to the National Academy of Sciences, there has been an epidemic of obesity among pet dogs and cats.

Over 80 percent of those with type 2 diabetes are overweight. Excess weight causes the body's cells to become insulin resistant. Over time, this resistance causes the pancreas to work harder to produce more insulin and can eventually cause the pancreas to stop producing it altogether. Incidences of cancers of the colon, uterus, and breast (in postmenopausal women) are also higher. Excess weight means extra stress on joints, especially in the knees, hips, and lower back, and contributes to osteoarthritis. Sleep apnea, a condition in which breathing stops for brief periods during sleep, disrupts a person's ability to obtain a restful slumber. The fat stored around the neck, as well as fat-induced inflammation in that area, may contribute to a smaller airway and interfere with breathing.[8]

Although being overweight can lead to many unhealthy conditions and diseases, the good news is that losing as little as 10 to 20 pounds can reduce a person's risk of all these conditions.[9]

For some, being very slender is their natural, healthy body shape, but for others, it's a sign of malnutrition. Being **underweight** means that a person doesn't have enough weight on his or her body for his or her height. An underlying medical condition such as cancer or an intestinal disorder, excessive calorie restriction and/or physical activity, or emotional stress can often cause someone to be underweight.[10] Undernourished elderly people, in particular, are at risk for low body protein and fat stores and a depressed immune system, which makes it more difficult to fight infections. Injuries, wounds, and illnesses that would normally abate in healthy individuals can cause serious medical complications, including death, in these individuals.[11]

weight management Maintaining your weight within a healthy range.

healthy weight A body weight in relationship to your height that doesn't increase the risk of developing any weight-related health problems or diseases.

overweight Weighing about 10 to 15 pounds more than a healthy weight for your height.

obesity Having an unhealthy amount of body fat.

underweight Weighing too little for your height.

The Take-Home Message Weight management means maintaining a healthy weight in order to reduce your risk of specific health problems. Being either overweight or underweight can be unhealthy.

How Do You Know if You're at a Healthy Weight?

Over the years, varying body shapes have trended in and out of the media spotlight. In the 1980s, fashion models were 8 percent thinner than the average woman. Today, the typical cover girl is over 20 percent thinner. The male physique is being held up to a similarly unattainable standard. Witness the change from scrawny to beefy in toy action figures over the years.[12] Although models, celebrities, and dolls may reflect the "in" look, they don't necessarily correlate with good health, nor should they be your reference for the body weight that *you* should strive to obtain.

So, how can you determine if your body weight is within a healthy range? Below are a few methods you can use.

Measure Your BMI

One of the easiest ways to assess if you are at a healthy weight is to measure your **body mass index (BMI).** The BMI is a calculation of your weight in relationship to your height. It is calculated using the following formula:

$$BMI = \frac{weight\ (pounds) \times 703}{height\ squared\ (inches^2)}$$

Over the years, the idealized model look has gone from curvy to stick thin to sporty and back to waiflike again. Today, superslender women are the norm in magazines and movies.

The male physique depicted in popular action figures in the 1970s, like Luke Skywalker and Han Solo from *Star Wars*, was more realistic than the bulked-up versions of the late 1990s.

Figure 10.1 shows you how to interpret the BMI number. A BMI of 18.5 to 24.9 is considered healthy. As your BMI increases from 25 and up to 29.9 (overweight), so does the risk of dying from diseases, although research shows that the risk is modest until a person reaches a BMI of 30 (obese).[13] Obese individuals have a 50 to 100 percent higher risk of dying prematurely compared with those at a healthy weight.[14]

Figure 10.1 also shows your approximate BMI using your weight and height. Your BMI can help you determine if your weight is putting you at risk for health problems. Figure 10.2 on page 342 shows you what various BMIs would look like.

As with any screening tool, the BMI may not be accurate for everyone. The BMI is not a *direct* measure of your percentage of body fat. It doesn't assess if your body weight is predominantly muscle or fat. Therefore, athletes and people with a high percentage of muscle mass may have a BMI over 25 yet have a low percentage of body fat.

Although these individuals are overweight based on their BMI, they are not "overfat" and unhealthy, and their muscular weight doesn't increase their health risk. In contrast, an elderly person may be in a healthy weight range, but may have been steadily losing weight due to an unbalanced diet or poor health. This chronic weight loss is a sign of loss of muscle mass and the depletion of nutrient stores in the body, which increases health risks even though the BMI seems healthy. Lastly, because height is factored into the BMI, individuals who are very short—under 5 feet—may have a high BMI, but, similarly to athletes, may not be unhealthy.[15]

Athletes with a high percentage of muscle mass will have higher body weights. NBA player Shaquille O'Neal has a BMI of over 30 (obese). But though his BMI is high, his weight doesn't put him at an increased health risk.

NUTRITION IN THE REAL WORLD

eLearn
Determining Your BMI

Want to know your exact BMI based on your height and weight? Use the BMI calculator at www.nhlbisupport.com/bmi/bmicalc.htm.

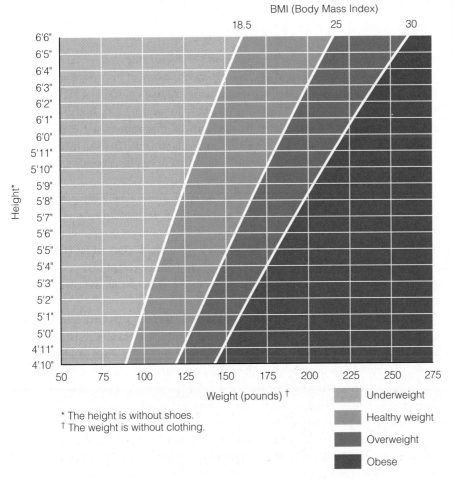

BMI (Body Mass Index)

* The height is without shoes.
† The weight is without clothing.

Underweight

Healthy weight

Overweight

Obese

Figure 10.1 What's Your BMI?
As your BMI increases, you are more likely to be overweight or obese. A BMI between 18.5 and 25 is considered healthy. A BMI over 25 is considered overweight, and a BMI over 30 is obese. A BMI under 18.5 is considered underweight, and can also be unhealthy.

body mass index (BMI) A calculation of your weight in relationship to your height. A BMI between 18.5 and 24.9 is considered healthy.

Figure 10.2 The Many Sizes of BMIs
People who look overweight or obese are likely to have a higher BMI.

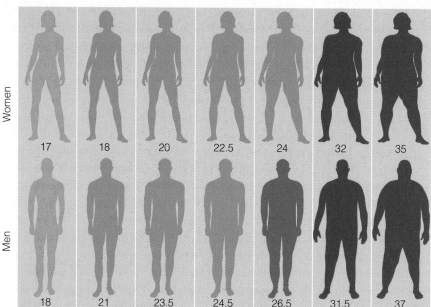

BMI (Body Mass Index)

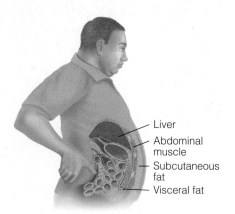

Figure 10.3 Visceral and Subcutaneous Fat Storage in the Body
Visceral fat stored around the waist is more likely to lead to health problems than subcutaneous fat stored elsewhere in the body.

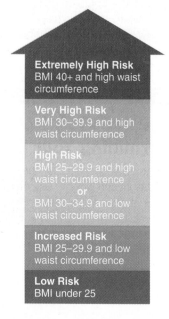

Extremely High Risk
BMI 40+ and high waist circumference

Very High Risk
BMI 30–39.9 and high waist circumference

High Risk
BMI 25–29.9 and high waist circumference
or
BMI 30–34.9 and low waist circumference

Increased Risk
BMI 25–29.9 and low waist circumference

Low Risk
BMI under 25

Figure 10.4 How at Risk Are You?
Considering both your BMI and your waist circumference can give you a good idea of your level of risk for health problems.

central obesity An excess storage of visceral fat in the abdominal area, which increases the risk of heart disease, diabetes, and hypertension.

visceral fat The fat stored in the abdominal area.

subcutaneous fat The fat located under the skin and between the muscles.

Measure Your Body Fat and Its Location

According to the American College of Sports Medicine, the average healthy adult male between the ages of 20 and 49 carries 16 to 21 percent of his weight as body fat. The average woman of the same age range carries 22 to 26 percent of her weight as body fat. There are several techniques you can use to measure total body fat, including skinfold thickness measurements, bioelectrical impedance, dual-energy X-ray absorptiometry, underwater weighing, and air displacement. These methods need to be conducted by trained technicians and some of them can be expensive. Table 10.1 describes the ways to measure body fat.

How much fat you carry isn't the only determinant of health risk—where you carry it also matters. Carrying excess fat around the waist versus carrying it around the hip and thighs has been shown to increase the risk of heart disease, diabetes, and hypertension.[16] **Central obesity** is due to storing too much **visceral fat** (the fat that surrounds organs in your chest and stomach and above your hips) around your waist. (Another type of fat, called **subcutaneous fat,** is the fat sandwiched between your skin and your muscles.) (See Figure 10.3.)

Because visceral fat is located near the liver, it is believed that fatty acids released from the fat storage area travel to the liver and can lead to insulin resistance, high levels of fat, low levels of the good HDL cholesterol, and high levels of LDL cholesterol in the blood, which all increase the risk of heart disease and diabetes. Insulin resistance also increases the risk for hypertension. Men, postmenopausal women, and obese people tend to have more visceral fat than young adults and lean individuals.

Measuring a person's waist circumference can quickly reveal whether he or she is at risk. A woman with a waist measurement of more than 35 inches or a man with a belly that's more than 40 inches around is at a higher health risk than people with slimmer middles. Carrying extra fat around your waist can increase health risks even if you are not overweight. In other words, a person who may be at a healthy weight according to BMI, but who has excess fat around the middle, is at a higher health risk. A person who has both a BMI ≥ 25 and a large waist circumference is considered at a higher risk for health problems than if he or she only had a high BMI (Figure 10.4).[17]

Table 10.1 Ways to Measure Percentage of Body Fat

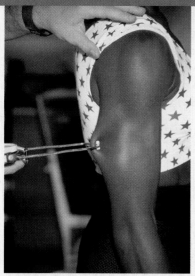

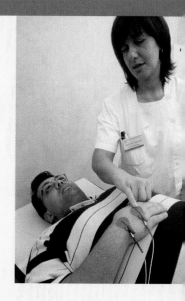

Bioelectrical Impedance ▶
How It Is Done: An electric current flows through the body and its resistance is measured. Lean tissue is highly conductive and less resistant than fat mass. Based on the current flow, the volume of lean tissue can be estimated. From this information, the percentage of body fat can be determined.
Cost: $

▲ **Skinfold Thickness Measurements**
How It Is Done: Calipers are used to measure the thickness of fat that is located just under the skin in the arm, in the back, on the upper thigh, and in the waist area. From these measurements, percent body fat can be determined.
Cost: $

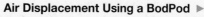

◀ **Dual-Energy X-Ray Absorptiometry (DXA)**
How It Is Done: A beam of energy is used to measure bone, fat, and lean tissue. The type of tissue that the beam passes through will absorb different amounts of energy. The amount of energy lost will allow the percentage of body fat to be determined.
Cost: $$$

Air Displacement Using a BodPod ▶
How It Is Done: A person's body volume is determined by measuring air displacement from a chamber. The person sits in a special chamber (called the BodPod) and the air displacement in the chamber is measured. From this measurement, the percentage of body fat can be estimated.
Cost: $$$

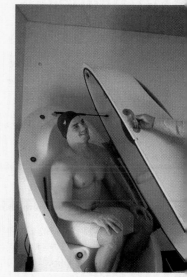

▲ **Underwater Weighing**
How It Is Done: A person is weighed on land and also suspended in a water tank. This is done to determine the density of the body. Fat is less dense and weighs less than muscle mass and will be reflected as such when the person is weighed in the water. The difference of a person's weight in water and on land is then used to calculate the percentage of body fat.
Cost: $$

$ = very affordable
$$ = less affordable
$$$ = expensive

Your waist circumference should be measured just above your hip bone, as shown by the dashed line.

The Take-Home Message The body mass index (BMI) is a calculation of your weight in relationship to your height and can be used to assess if your weight increases your health risks. It is not a direct measure of body fat and may be inaccurate for people who are muscular or frail due to illness. Skinfold thickness measurements using calipers, bioelectrical impedance, dual-energy X-ray absorptiometry, underwater weighing, and air displacement are all techniques that can be used to measure the percentage of body fat. Excess fat around the middle increases the risk of several chronic diseases, regardless of BMI.

What Is Energy Balance and What Determines Energy Needs?

In order to maintain your weight, you need to make sure that you don't consume more calories than you expend daily. Spending as many calories as you take in is the concept behind energy balance.

Energy Balance Is Calories In versus Calories Out

Energy balance is the state at which your energy intake and your energy expenditure, both measured in calories, are equal (Figure 10.5a). When you consume more calories than you expend, you are in **positive energy balance** (Figure 10.5b). Routinely eating more calories than you expend will cause the storage of fat. When your calorie intake falls short of your needs, you are in **negative energy balance** (Figure 10.5c). Imbalances that occur over a long time period, such as weeks and months, are what change body weight.

You can determine whether you are in positive or negative energy balance by comparing the number of calories you take in to the number of calories you expend on a given day. Figuring out how many calories you take in is fairly straightforward. You can use the food label or a diet analysis program (like the one available with this book) to find out how many calories are in the foods and beverages you eat and drink.

You can also use the grams of macronutrients in foods to calculate the number of total calories they contain. Recall from Chapter 1 that carbohydrates and protein each contain 4 calories/gram and fat contains 9 calories/gram. (Note that alcohol, at 7 calories/gram, can also contribute calories.) Multiplying the number of grams of carbohydrates, protein, or fat by the calories per gram and then adding up these numbers will provide the total amount of calories in the food.

Calculating the number of calories you expend daily is a little more complicated.

Energy Needs Are Different for Everyone

Your energy needs are different from those of your 80-year-old grandparents, your 50-year-old parents, and even your marathon-running roommate. Your energy needs are comprised of your basal metabolism, the thermic effect of food (TEF), and, lastly,

energy balance The state at which energy (calorie) intake and energy (calorie) output in the body are equal.

positive energy balance The state whereby you store more energy than you expend. Over time, this results in weight gain.

negative energy balance The state whereby you expend more energy than you consume. Over time, this results in weight loss.

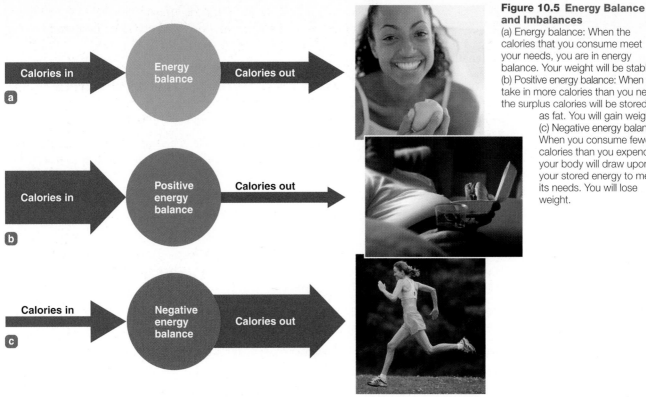

Figure 10.5 Energy Balance and Imbalances
(a) Energy balance: When the calories that you consume meet your needs, you are in energy balance. Your weight will be stable. (b) Positive energy balance: When you take in more calories than you need, the surplus calories will be stored as fat. You will gain weight. (c) Negative energy balance: When you consume fewer calories than you expend, your body will draw upon your stored energy to meet its needs. You will lose weight.

the calories needed to fuel your physical activities. (See Figure 10.6.)

Figure 10.6 The Three Components of Your Energy Needs
The "calories out" side of the energy balance equation includes your BMR, the thermic effect of food (TEF), and the energy you use to fuel your physical activity.

BMR 50–70%

Physical activity ~20–35%

TEF 10%

Your BMR Will Increase Your Energy Needs

Even when you're not at the gym or sprinting to class, your body is using energy. Pumping your blood, expanding your lungs, and using your brain all require energy every moment of your life. The **basal metabolism** is the amount of energy expended to meet the basic physiological needs that enable your organs and cells to function. Also referred to as your **basal metabolism rate (BMR),** it is the minimum energy needed to keep you alive.

Approximately 60 percent of your daily energy needs is determined by your BMR. The factor that most affects your BMR is your **lean body mass** (about 70 percent of your BMR). Age, gender, body size, genes, ethnicity, emotional and physical stress, thyroid hormone, nutritional state, and environmental temperature, as well as your caffeine and nicotine intake, affect your BMR. Table 10.2 on page 346 explains each of these factors.

The Thermic Effect of Food Affects Your Energy Needs

Your body uses energy to extract the calories from the foods that you consume. The **thermic effect of food (TEF)** is the amount of calories you expend to digest, absorb, and process your food. Approximately 10 percent of calories in the food consumed is used for TEF. In other words, if you eat a 100-calorie cookie, about 10 calories will be used to process the cookie.

basal metabolism The amount of energy the body expends to meet its basic physiological needs. Also referred to as **basal metabolism rate (BMR).**

lean body mass The body mass once the fat mass has been subtracted. It contains mostly muscle but also organs and fluids. Lean body mass is the metabolically active tissue in the body.

thermic effect of food (TEF) The amount of calories the body uses to digest, absorb, and process food.

Table 10.2

Factors That Affect Your Basal Metabolism Rate

Factor	Explanation
Lean body mass	Lean body mass, which is mostly muscle mass, is more metabolically active than fat tissue, so more calories are needed to maintain it. Athletes who have a large percentage of lean body mass due to their increased muscle mass will have a higher BMR than individuals who aren't athletic.
Age	For adults, BMR declines about 1 to 2 percent per decade after the early adult years but it increases by 15 percent during pregnancy. For children, BMR increases during times of rapid growth such as infancy and adolescence.
Gender	Women have less lean body mass, and typically have a higher percentage of body fat than men. This results in women having up to a 10 percent lower BMR. Women also tend to have a smaller body size. (See below.)
Body size	Taller individuals will have a higher BMR due to increased surface area compared with shorter individuals. More surface area means more heat lost from the body, which causes the metabolism rate to increase to maintain the body's temperature.
Genes	Research suggests that genes may affect BMR, as individuals within families have similar metabolic rates.
Ethnicity	African Americans have BMRs that are about 10 percent lower than of Caucasians.
Stress	Hormones such as epinephrine, which are released during emotional stress, increase BMR. Physiological stress on the body caused by injury, fever, burns, and infections also causes the release of hormones that raise BMR. Heat lost from the body through wounds, as well as the response of the immune system during infection, increases BMR.
Hormones	An increase in thyroid hormone increases BMR, whereas too little of this hormone lowers BMR. Hormone fluctuations during a woman's menstrual cycle lower BMR during the phase before ovulation.
Starvation	Starvation and fasting for more than about 48 hours lower BMR.
Environmental temperature	Being very cold or very hot can increase BMR but the change is minimal if you make adjustments in your clothing or in the temperature of your surroundings.
Caffeine	Caffeine can raise BMR but only slightly when consumed regularly in moderate amounts.
Drugs	Nicotine may increase BMR. Drugs such as amphetamine and ephedrine increase BMR.

*Note: Smoking is not a weight management strategy. Some people may think that replacing snacks with cigarettes helps them stay slim, but the health risks associated with smoking, such as lung cancer, heart disease, and stroke, make it a foolish habit. Anyone concerned about weight gain when quitting smoking can minimize the chances of this with exercise (plus, you'll be able to run farther and faster with your cleaner lungs!).

Source: Institute of Medicine. 2002. *Dietary Reference Intakes for Energy, Carbohydrate, Fiber, Fat, Fatty Acids, Cholesterol, Protein, and Amino Acids*. Available at www.iom.edu.

Physical Activity Will Increase Your Energy Needs

If you are very physically active, you're going to need more energy than someone who is sedentary. For sedentary people, the amount of energy expended in physical activity is less than half of their BMR. For very physically active individuals, such as athletes, it can be as much as double their BMR. The more physical activity you routinely incorporate into your day, the more calories you will need to eat to meet your energy needs.

The amount of energy expended during physical activity goes beyond the activity itself. Exercise causes a small increase in energy expenditure for some time after the activity has stopped.[18]

Calculating Your Energy Needs

Recall Table 2.3 from Chapter 2, which helped you estimate your energy needs. This table was derived from the DRIs' **estimated energy requirement (EER).** The EER is the average calorie intake that is estimated to maintain energy balance based on a person's gender, age, height, body weight, and level of physical activity. (The physical activity levels are separated into categories ranging from sedentary to very active.) While Table 2.3 used a reference height and weight for each age grouping, you can calculate your own EER using your specific height and weight with the Self-Assessment "What's Your Estimated Energy Expenditure (EER)?"

The Take-Home Message **Energy balance is the relationship between your energy intake and your energy expenditure, which are both measured in calories. Your basal metabolism, the thermic effect of food (TEF), and your physical activities all determine your daily energy needs.**

NUTRITION IN THE REAL WORLD

eLearn

An Estimated Energy Requirement Online Tool

To calculate a more precise EER, you need to record all of your daily physical activity. Visit the MyPyramid Tracker at www.mypyramidtracker.gov and enter your gender, height, weight, age, and all the activities you do in a 24-hour period. The Tracker will then calculate your EER.

Self-Assessment

What's Your Estimated Energy Expenditure (EER)?

Calculating your EER is a two-step process.

1. First, complete the information below.

   a. My age is [ ]

   b. My physical activity during the day based on the chart below is [ ]

Physical Activity	Male	Female
Sedentary (no exercise)	1.00	1.00
Low active (walks about 2 miles daily at 3–4 mph)	1.11	1.12
Active (walks about 7 miles daily at 3–4 mph)	1.26	1.27
Very active (walks about 17 miles daily at 3–4 mph)	1.48	1.45

   c. My weight in pounds is ______ divided by 2.2 = [ ] kg

   d. My height in inches is ______ divided by 39.4 = [ ] meters

2. Using your answers in each box in step 1, complete the following calculation based on your gender and age.

Males, 19+ years old, use this calculation:

$662 - (9.53 \times \underset{\mathbf{a}}{\underline{\qquad}}) + \underset{\mathbf{b}}{\underline{\qquad}} \times (15.91 \times \underset{\mathbf{c}}{\underline{\qquad}} + 539.6 \times \underset{\mathbf{d}}{\underline{\qquad}})$

$= \underset{\mathbf{EER}}{\underline{\qquad}}$

Females, 19+ years old, use this calculation:

$354 - (6.91 \times \underset{\mathbf{a}}{\underline{\qquad}}) + \underset{\mathbf{b}}{\underline{\qquad}} \times (9.36 \times \underset{\mathbf{c}}{\underline{\qquad}} + 726 \times \underset{\mathbf{d}}{\underline{\qquad}})$

$= \underset{\mathbf{EER}}{\underline{\qquad}}$

estimated energy requirement (EER) The average calorie intake that is estimated to maintain energy balance based on a person's gender, age, height, body weight, and level of physical activity.

What Are the Effects of an Energy Imbalance?

The handful of cheese curls that Pam eats every night while watching television is adding about 100 more calories than she needs. After three months, she's gained a little over two pounds. Bryan, on the other hand, is so busy juggling studying with tennis practice that he consumes about 50 calories fewer daily than he expends. After four months, he has dropped about 1½ pounds from his already light frame. Over time, a chronic energy imbalance results in a change in body weight. Let's look at what is happening inside your body when an energy imbalance occurs.

Too Few Calories Can Cause Underweight

Consuming fewer calories than you need daily will cause your body to draw upon its energy stores to overcome the deficit. Like Bryan, you will lose weight. In Chapter 4, you learned that when you don't eat, glycogen and fat are used as fuel sources to meet your body's glucose and energy needs until the next time you eat. Amino acids from the breakdown of body protein, particularly muscle, can also be used to make glucose.

In prolonged fasting, all of the glycogen in your liver is depleted. The breakdown of body fat contributes to your energy needs, while the breakdown of muscle provides materials to meet your glucose needs. Ketone bodies are also generated through the incomplete breakdown of fat, and these are used as an energy source. People at a healthy weight can't live much beyond 60 days of fasting, as their fat stores, as well as about one-third of their lean tissue mass, will be depleted by this time.[19]

Too Many Calories Can Cause Overweight

Eating more calories than you need, regardless of the foods they come from, will result in your body storing the excess as fat. Recall from Chapters 4 and 6 that you have limited capacity to store glucose as glycogen and that you can't store extra protein. However, you have unlimited capacity to store fat.

Your body contains about 35 billion fat cells, which can expand to accommodate a surplus of calories.

Although the relationship between eating too many calories and gaining weight appears straightforward, this isn't necessarily the case. The causes of overweight and obesity and the ability to prevent them can be complex, as there is more to eating than just nourishing the body. Let's look at this next.

The Take-Home Message When you don't eat enough calories to meet your needs, your glycogen and fat stores, as well as muscle mass, will be broken down for fuel. A chronic deficit of calories will produce weight loss. When you chronically consume too many calories, the excess will be stored as fat, and weight gain will occur.

What Factors Are Likely to Affect Body Weight?

There are numerous factors that impact weight management, starting with what and how often you eat. Physiology, genetics, and your environment also play a role. Let's look at how each of these can affect your body weight.

Hunger and Appetite Affect What You Eat

Recall from Chapter 3 that there is a difference between your physiological need for food (or hunger) and the psychological factors that prompt you to eat (your appetite.) Hunger is the physical need for nourishment that drives you to consume food. Once you start eating, hunger will subside as the feeling of **satiation** begins to set in. Satiation will determine how long and how much you eat. **Satiety** is the sensation that you feel when you have had enough to eat. Satiety determines the length of time between eating episodes.[20] An increase in satiety will delay the start of your next eating episode.

Your appetite is affected by hunger, as well as environmental factors, like seeing or smelling something that you think will taste good, your social setting, your stress level, and so forth. Hunger, in turn, is affected by many physiological mechanisms, as well as genetics. Both hunger and appetite ultimately affect what you eat.

Physiological Mechanisms Help Regulate Hunger

Being sleep deprived can increase your appetite by lowering the levels of leptin and increasing the amount of ghrelin in your body.

Various physiologic feedback mechanisms involving the mouth, stomach, intestines, and brain all work together to increase or decrease your hunger. For example, many hormones play a role. When your stomach is empty, the hormone, **ghrelin,** which is produced mainly in the stomach, signals your brain that you need to take in food. Your body produces more ghrelin during fasting (such as between meals) in order to stimulate hunger, and it produces less after food is consumed. Another hormone, **leptin,** which is produced in fat tissue, helps regulate your body fat by affecting hunger. As your fat stores increase, leptin signals the brain to decrease your level of hunger and food intake.

Once food enters your mouth, sensory signals are sent to the brain that tell you whether or not to continue eating. The feedback mechanism is very much affected by your prior experience of tasting that food.[21] For example, a spoonful of your favorite ice cream is a pleasant stimulus, and your brain would encourage you to keep eating it. However, if you took a sip of sour milk, this stimulus would be unacceptable to the brain, especially if the last time you drank sour milk it made you sick. Your brain will instruct you to spit out the sour milk so that you don't swallow it.

Once food is in your stomach, other factors, such as the size of the meal, come into play. After you eat a large meal, your stomach becomes distended. This will signal the brain to decrease your hunger, and you will stop eating. A distended stomach also causes the release of **cholecystokinin,** a hormone that is associated with the feeling of satiation. Cholecystokinin will also decrease your hunger.[22]

satiation The feeling during eating that determines how long and how much you eat.

satiety The sensation that you feel when you have had enough to eat. It determines how long you will go between meals and/or snacks.

ghrelin A hormone produced mainly in the stomach that increases hunger.

leptin A hormone produced in fat tissue that helps regulate body fat by signaling the reduction of food intake in the brain and interfering with the storage of fat in the cells.

cholecystokinin A hormone released when the stomach is distended. It is associated with the feeling of satiation.

When the food reaches your small intestine, the nutrients, protein, fatty acids, and monosaccharides all stimulate feedback to the brain to decrease your hunger. Once these nutrients are absorbed, the hormone insulin is released, which also causes the brain to decrease your hunger.[23]

In a perfect world, all these physiologic mechanisms would keep you in perfect energy balance. When you are hungry, you eat and when you are satiated, you stop. The reality, however, is that many people override these mechanisms and end up in energy imbalance. Factors like genetics and the environment also affect how much energy you consume and expend.

Genetics Play a Role in Determining Body Weight

Genetics has such a strong influence on your body weight that if your mother and father are overweight (BMI >25), your risk of becoming obese approximately doubles, and your risk triples if they are obese (BMI >30). If your parents are severely obese (BMI >40), your risk increases fivefold.[24] Studies on separated identical twins raised in different home environments confirm this, as both twins showed similar weight gain and body fat distribution.[25]

Research suggests that genetic differences in the level or the functioning of some hormones can influence a person's body weight and appetite. For example, genetically high levels of ghrelin may cause some people to overeat and become obese.[26] Individuals who are genetically prone to being leptin deficient become massively obese, yet when they are given leptin, their appetite decreases and their weight falls to within a healthy range.[27] Ironically, many obese people have adequate amounts of leptin but the brain has developed a resistance to it, rendering its appetite control ineffective.[28] For these individuals, other mechanisms are coming into play that prevent leptin from functioning as a regulator of their appetite.

Genetics may also affect how calories are expended in the body by affecting **thermogenesis** (*thermo* = heat, *genesis* = origin), which is the production of heat in body cells. Genes may cause different rates of **nonexercise-associated thermogenesis (NEAT),** which is the energy you expend during fidgeting, standing, chewing gum, getting up and turning off the television, and other nonexercise movement throughout the day. When some individuals overeat, they are able to rev up their NEAT to expend some of the excess calories and are thus better able to manage their energy balance.[29] Many overweight individuals don't appear to have this compensatory mechanism.

Some researchers have described a genetic "set point" that determines body weight. This theory holds that the body fights to remain at a specific body weight and opposes attempts at weight loss. The body may even enable very easy weight gain in order to get back to this "set point" when weight is lost. In other words, a person's weight remains fairly constant because the body "has a mind of its own." Given that the weight of Americans has disproportionately increased over the last few decades relative to previous decades, this theory either isn't true or the set point can be overridden.[30]

If a person's lifestyle stays the same, his or her weight should remain fairly stable. However, if the environment shifts to make it easier to gain weight, the body will also shift, but it will shift upward. For example, rats, who should genetically be able to maintain a healthy body weight, were shown in research to overeat and become fat when they had access to unlimited fatty foods and sweets.[31]

The Pima Indians of the southwestern United States genetically have a high rate of obesity. Research comparing their ancestors in Mexico to Pimas currently living in Arizona revealed that the environment can impact weight-susceptible populations. The

thermogenesis The production of heat in body cells.

nonexercise-associated thermogenesis (NEAT) The energy expenditure that occurs during nonexercise movements, such as fidgeting, standing, and chewing gum.

physically active traditional Mexican Pimas lived an active lifestyle and ate a diet both rich in complex carbohydrates and lower in animal fats than that of the "Americanized" Pimas living in Arizona, who had a more sedentary lifestyle and fatty diet. The overweight Mexican Pimas, on average, had a BMI of about 25, compared with the obese Arizona Pimas who had, on average, a BMI of over 33.[32] The traditional Pimas had a better chance of avoiding obesity because they lived in a healthier environment.

Environmental Factors Can Increase Appetite and Decrease Physical Activity

How many times have you eaten a satisfying meal before going to the movies, but bought a bucket of popcorn at the theater anyway? You didn't buy the popcorn because you were hungry. You just couldn't resist the buttery smell and the allure of munching during the film.

There are many stimuli in the environment that can drive your appetite. In addition to aromas and certain venues such as movie theatres, events such as holidays and sporting events, people such as your friends and family, and even the convenience of obtaining food can all encourage you to eat even when you're not hungry.

Over the past few decades, the environment around us has changed in ways that have made it easier for many of us to incur an energy imbalance and a propensity to gain weight. Take the Self-Assessment "Does Your Environment Impact Your Energy Balance?" to reflect upon how your environment may impact the lifestyle decisions that you make throughout your day.

An environment in which people can easily and cheaply obtain endless amounts of energy-dense food may be one of the biggest culprits in the current obesity epidemic. Referred to as a **gene-environment interaction,** those with a genetic propensity to become overweight will experience greater challenges to preventing obesity in an environment that is conducive to gaining weight. Whereas both genes and the environment play a role in weight management, researchers have used the analogy that genes load the gun but an obesity-promoting environment pulls the trigger to explain how these two entities interact with each other.[33]

Let's look at some environmental issues that are feeding Americans' energy imbalance.

We Work More and Cook Less

One reason Americans are getting larger is that they're not eating at home as much. Research shows that adults today spend more time traveling to work and devote more of their daily hours to work than in previous decades.[34] This longer workday means there is less time to devote to everyday activities, such as food preparation.

Today, almost one-third of Americans' daily calories come from ready-to-eat foods that are prepared outside the home.[35] Between 1972 and 1995, the prevalence of eating out in the United States increased by almost 90 percent, a trend that is expected to increase steadily to the year 2020.[36] To accommodate this demand, the number of eateries in the United States has almost doubled, to nearly 900,000 food service establishments, during the last three decades.[37]

Dining out frequently is associated with a higher BMI.[38] The top three foods selected when eating out, especially among college-aged diners, are energy-dense french fries, hamburgers, and pizza. Less energy-dense, waist-friendly vegetables, fruits, and

The average weight gain between Thanksgiving and New Year's Day is about a pound. But many people don't lose this extra weight during the year and add to it every year.

gene-environment interaction The interaction of both genetics and the environment that increases the risk of obesity in some people.

salads didn't even make the top five choices on the list among college-aged diners. For many people, dining out often is harming their diet by making energy-dense foods too readily available and displacing less energy-dense vegetables and fruits.

We Eat More (and More)

In the United States food is easy to get, there's a lot to choose from, and portion sizes are generous. All of these factors are associated with consuming too many calories.[39]

> Research has shown that women who dine out five or more times weekly consume close to 300 calories more on dining-out days than do women who eat at home.

Years ago, people went to a bookstore for the sole purpose of buying a book. Now they go to a bookstore to sip a mocha latte and nibble on biscotti while they ponder which book to buy. Americans can grab breakfast at a hamburger drive-through, lunch at a museum, a sub sandwich at many gas stations, and a three-course meal of nachos, pizza, and ice cream at a movie theater. At any given moment of your day, you can probably easily find a bundle of calories to consume.

This access to a variety of foods is problematic for weight-conscious individuals. While the appeal of a food diminishes as it continues to be eaten (that is, the first bite will taste the best but each subsequent bite loses some of that initial pleasure), having a variety of foods available allows the eater to move on to another food once boredom sets in.[40] The more good-tasting foods that are available, the more a person will eat. For example, during that three-course meal at the movie theater, once you're tired of the nachos, you can move on to the pizza, and when that loses its appeal, you can dig into the ice cream. If the pizza and ice cream weren't available, you would have stopped after the nachos and consumed fewer calories.

As you learned from Chapter 2, the portion sizes of many foods, such as french fries and sodas, have doubled, if not tripled, compared with the portions listed on food labels. Because the "supersized" portions often cost only slightly more than the regular size, they are perceived as bargains by the consumer. From the restaurant's point of view, the cost of increasing the portion size is outweighed by the extra money the consumer pays for the larger size. Hence, at many restaurants, movie theaters, and elsewhere, supersizing is common. Research shows that people tend to eat more of a food, and thus more calories, when larger portions are served. [41]

When serving yourself at home, the size of the serving bowl or package of food influences the amount of the food you put on your plate. Serving yourself from a large bowl or package has been shown to increase the serving size by more than 20 percent.[42] This means that you are more likely to scoop out (and eat) a bigger serving of ice cream from a half-gallon container than from a pint container. To make matters worse, most people don't compensate for these extra calories by reducing the portions at the next meal.[43]

We Sit More and Move Less

Americans are not only eating more calories—about 300 calories more daily since 1985—but they are expending less energy during their day.[44] The resulting increase in "calories in" and decrease in "calories out" is a recipe for an energy imbalance and weight gain. Compared to years past, Americans are expending less energy both at work and during their leisure time.

When your great grandparents went to work in the morning, chances are good they headed out to the fields or off to the factory. Your parents and older siblings, though, are more likely to head off to an office and sit in front of a computer, and you yourself probably sit at a desk for much of your day. This shift in work from jobs that required manual labor to jobs that are more sedentary has been shown to increase the risk of becoming overweight or obese.[45] One study found that men who sit for more than 6 hours during their workday are at higher risk of being overweight than those who sit for less than an hour daily.[46]

Technology in the workplace now allows us to communicate with everyone without having to leave our desks. This means that people no longer have to get up and walk to see the colleague down the hall or the client across town. Researchers have estimated that a 145-pound person expends 3.9 calories for each minute of walking, compared with 1.8 calories per minute sitting. Thus, walking 10 minutes during each workday to communicate in person with coworkers would expend 10,000 calories annually, yet only about 5,000 calories would be expended if the person sat in the office sending e-mails or calling colleagues on the phone.[47]

Labor-saving devices have also affected energy expenditure outside of work. Driving short distances is now the norm, while walking and biking have decreased over the years.[48] Many Americans have stopped pushing lawn mowers and are riding them instead to cut the grass. Dishes aren't washed by hand but are stacked in a dishwasher.[49]

All of these labor-saving devices add up, and the cumulative daily savings of energy expenditure can be more than 100 calories (about the amount in that handful of cheese curls Pam likes to eat.).[50] As technology continues to advance and allows you to become more energy efficient in your work and lifestyle habits, you need to offset this conservation of energy with *planned* physical activity at another time of the day.

More than half of Americans do not accumulate even the recommended minimum of 30 minutes of moderate-intensity activity on most days weekly.[51] In fact, over 20 percent of Americans report no leisure-time physical activity daily, due partly to the fact that leisure and social activities have become more sedentary.[52] Currently, 98 percent of homes in the United States own at least one television and over 40 percent have three or more televisions.[53] With so many TVs in the house, everyone can retreat to watch shows for hours on end. Other sedentary activities, such as playing video games and surfing the Web, have also increased. Research shows that those aged 2 to 18 years old spend over 5 hours daily, on average on a combination of "screen time" activities. These include watching TV, playing video games, and spending nonwork/school-related computer time—even though experts have suggested limiting screen time to 2 hours daily.[54]

We are moving less during both work and play. With less energy being expended, weight gain is becoming easier and the need for weight loss even greater. Combine this with an environment that is conducive to eating and with the genetic makeup of most Americans, and it's not difficult to see why many people are becoming overweight or obese. Many Americans have to begin making conscious diet and lifestyle changes that will help them lose weight, or at the very least, prevent further weight gain.

Let's look at what is a realistic amount of weight to lose and how to do it healthfully.

The Take-Home Message Your appetite is your desire to eat and is affected by hunger, satiation, and satiety. It is influenced by physiologic mechanisms, your genes, and your environment. Physiological mechanisms, such as hormones, signal your brain to increase your hunger when you are hungry and decrease it after you have eaten. Genetics can make it more difficult for some individuals to manage their weight. The current environment—which provides easy access to a variety of excessive amounts of energy-dense foods and at the same time decreases energy expenditure—encourages obesity.

Many of our leisure-time activities involve sitting in front of a screen rather than being physically active.

What Is a Reasonable Rate of Weight Loss?

There are more than 3,000 diet books on the market, written by everyone from popular TV show therapists to celebrity advisers and self-proclaimed experts with credible credentials. Many of these plans promise quick, dramatic results, but the reality is that few are based on legitimate science and some, such as those that encourage severe calorie restriction, can even put your health at risk. (See the feature box, "Fad Diets Are the Latest Fad," on page 358 for more on how the various diet plans compare).

According to the National Institutes of Health, overweight individuals should aim to lose about 10 percent of their body weight over a six-month period.[55] This means that the goal for an overweight, 180-pound person would be to shed 18 pounds over 6 months, which would be about 3 pounds a month or ¾ pound weekly.

Because a person must have an energy deficit of approximately 3,500 calories over time to lose a pound of fat, a deficit of 250 to 500 calories daily will result in a reasonable weight loss of about ½ to 1 pound weekly.

How Can You Lose Weight Healthfully?

Though there is no single diet approach that has been universally embraced, many health experts agree that a person needs to adjust three areas of life for successful, long-term weight loss. These three areas are diet, physical activity, and behavior changes (Figure 10.7). Let's start with the diet.

Eat Smart, Because Calories Count

When it comes to losing weight, there are two important words that need to be remembered: calories count—no matter where they come from. Because an energy imbalance of too many calories in and not enough calories out causes weight gain, reversing the imbalance will cause the opposite. That is, taking in fewer calories and burning off more will result in weight loss.

However, cutting back too drastically on calories often results in a failed weight-loss attempt. If a person skips meals or isn't satiated at each meal because of skimpy portions, the person will experience hunger between meals and be more inclined to snack on energy-dense foods.

Thus a key strategy during the weight-loss process is for the person to eat a healthy, balanced diet that is not only lower in calories, but is also *satisfying*. One way you can add heft and satiation to your lower calorie meals is by including higher volume foods.

Eat More Vegetables, Fruit, and Fiber

People tend to eat the same amount of food regardless of its energy density—that is, the amount of calories in the meal.[56] In other words, you need a certain volume of food in order to feel full. As you learned in Chapter 4, it is very easy to overeat energy-dense, low-volume foods such as candy, which can easily fill you *out* before they fill

HEALTHY WEIGHT

Healthy diet

Physical activity

Behavior modification

Figure 10.7 Three Pieces of the Long-Term Weight Loss Puzzle
Diet, physical activity, and behavior modification are all necessary for long-term weight management.

you *up*. You'll overeat them before you become satiated. The reverse of this—eating high-volume, low-energy-density foods that fill you up before they fill you out—can help in weight management. High-volume foods include fruits and vegetables, which are bulked up because of their water content, and whole grains, which contain a lot of fiber. These foods are also low in fat (which contains 9 calories/gram) and high in carbohydrate (which contains only 4 calories/gram.) Research shows that these foods are associated with increased satiety and reduced feelings of hunger and calorie intake.[57]

In fact, consuming a large, high-volume, low-energy-density salad before a meal can reduce the calories eaten at that meal by more than 10 percent.[58] Adding vegetables to sandwiches and soups will increase both the volume of food consumed and meal satisfaction and help displace higher calorie items (Figure 10.8 on page 356). If you are full after eating a sandwich loaded with vegetables, you'll eat less from the bag of energy-dense chips. This is important because you don't need to eliminate chips from your diet if you enjoy them. Any food—from chocolate to chips—can be modest in calories if you eat modest amounts. Table 10.3 on page 356 provides examples of low-, moderate-, and high-energy-density foods. See the Table Tips for ways to increase the volume of foods you consume, while decreasing your overall caloric intake.

Fiber also contributes to the bulk of vegetables and fruits and their ability to prolong satiety.[59] Overweight individuals have been shown to consume less dietary fiber and fruit than normal weight people.[60] For these reasons, high-fiber foods, such as vegetables, fruit, and whole grains, are a key part of a weight-loss diet.

Include Some Protein and Fat in Your Meals

Of all the dietary substances that increase satiety, protein will have the most dramatic effect. Even though the mechanism is unknown, this is likely one of the reasons why high-protein diets tend to reduce hunger and can help in weight loss.[61] Because fat slows the movement of food out of the stomach into the intestines, it can also prolong satiety. Therefore, including some lean protein and fat in all meals and even with snacks can help increase satiety between meals.

Table Tips

Eat More to Weigh Less

Eat more whole fruit and drink less juice at breakfast. The orange will have more fiber and bulk than the OJ.

Make the vegetable portions on your dinner plate twice the size of your meat portion.

Have a side salad with low-fat dressing with your lunchtime sandwich instead of a snack bag of chips.

Order your next pizza with less pepperoni and more peppers, onions, and tomatoes. A veggie pizza can have 25 percent fewer calories and about 50 percent less fat and saturated fat than a meat pie.

Cook up a whole-wheat blend pasta instead of enriched pasta for your next Italian dinner. Ladle on plenty of tomato sauce and don't forget the big tossed salad as the appetizer.

Sandwich	Calories
Whole-wheat bread, 2 slices	138
Ham, 4 oz	125
American cheese, 2 oz	213
Total	**476**

Soup	Calories
Chicken broth, 3/4 cup	29
Chicken (white meat), 1/2 cup	106
Noodles, 1 cup	212
Total	**347**

. . . to high-volume

Sandwich	Calories
Whole-wheat bread, 2 slices	138
Ham, 2 oz	63
American cheese, 1 oz	106
Tomato, 2 slices	7
Romaine lettuce, 2 leaves	10
Total	**324**

. . . to high-volume

Soup	Calories
Chicken broth, 3/4 cup	29
Chicken (white meat), 1/2 cup	106
Noodles, 1/2 cup	106
Mixed vegetables, 1/2 cup	59
Total	**300**

Figure 10.8 Adding Volume to Your Meals
Adding high-volume foods like fruits and vegetables to your sandwiches, soups, and meals can add to satiety and displace higher calorie foods, two factors that can help in weight management.

Table 10.3 The Energy Density of Foods

Low

These foods provide 0.7 to 1.5 calories per gram and are high in water and fiber. Examples include most vegetables and fruits—tomatoes, cantaloupe, strawberries, broccoli, cauliflower, broth-based soups, fat-free yogurt and cottage cheese.

Medium

These foods have 1.5 to 4 calories per gram and contain less water. They include bagels, hard-cooked eggs, dried fruits, lean sirloin steak, hummus, whole-wheat bread, and part-skim mozzarella cheese.

High

These foods provide 4 to 9 calories per gram, are low in moisture, and include chips, cookies, crackers, cakes, pastries, butter, oil, and bacon.

Source: Adapted from the Centers for Disease Control and Prevention, Can Eating Fruits and Vegetables Help People to Manage Their Weight? 2005. Available at www.cdc.gov/nccdphp/dnpa/nutrition/pdf/rtp_practitioner_10_07.pdf. Accessed July 2006.

However, you don't want to add high-saturated-fat foods such as whole-milk cheese, whole milk, fatty cuts of meat, and butter because eating these foods to feel full will come at the expense of your heart. It would be better to add lean meat, skinless chicken, fish, nuts, and oils, which are kinder to a person's waist and heart. (Note: Unsaturated fat still contains 9 calories per gram, so excessive amounts of nuts and oils, even though these are heart healthy, can quickly add excess calories to the diet.)

Look at the difference between the foods shown in Figure 10.9. The snack and dinner on the left are low in volume, but high in calories. The foods on the right are high in volume but have almost 500 fewer calories combined! These higher volume foods will be more satisfying for fewer calories.

Use MyPyramid as a Weight-Loss Guide

Meals that contain a high volume of fruits and vegetables, whole grains, some lean protein, and modest amounts of fat are a smart combination for weight loss, so a diet that contains all the food groups in MyPyramid can be used to lose weight. Most importantly, this type of diet is well balanced and will meet your daily nutrient needs.

Reducing caloric intake a little at a time can add up to healthy weight loss. A 180-pound, overweight person who consumes 2,800 calories daily can reduce his or her intake to 2,400 to 2,600 calories for a calorie deficit of 200–400 calories per day. He or she will then lose 10 pounds in about three months. Small changes, like switching from full fat to nonfat dairy products or replacing the afternoon soda with a glass of water, will contribute to this calorie reduction. Following the recommendations in MyPyramid to eat a variety of foods, but replacing higher calorie foods with lower calorie options within each food group, results in a satisfying diet while losing weight.

Low-volume, high-calorie meals

Snack	Calories
Dunkin Donuts Coffee Coolata® with cream, 16 oz	350
Dunkin Donuts chocolate chunk cookie, 1 cookie	110
Total	**460**

High-volume, low-calorie meals

Snack	Calories
Dunkin Donuts Hot Latte Lite (made with skim milk)	70
Pop Secret Snack popcorn, 94% fat free, butter	110
Total	**180**

Dinner	Calories
Pizza Hut Pepperoni Lover's Pizza (hand-tossed), 2 slices, large pizza	570
Cheese breadstick, 1 stick	320
Total	**890**

Dinner	Calories
Pizza Hut Veggie Lover's Pizza (hand tossed), 3 slices, large pizza	610
Romaine lettuce, 1 cup	8
Cherry tomatoes, 1/2 cup	13
Sliced cucumber, 1/2 cup	7
Light ranch dressing, 1 tbsp	38
Total	**676**

Figure 10.9 The Volume of Food You Eat
Low-volume, high-calorie foods can be much less satisfying than higher volume, lower calorie foods.

Fad Diets Are the Latest Fad

Americans spend over $30 billion annually on weight-loss programs, products, and pills and are more than willing to keep reaching into their wallets for the next quick diet fix.[1] Though it may seem that there is a new fad diet around every corner, many of these diets have actually been around for years.

The low-carbohydrate, high-protein and -fat diets of the 1970s (Dr. Atkins' Diet Revolution) were replaced by the very high-carbohydrate and very low-fat diets of the 1980s (Pritikin diets) and continued into the early 1990s (Dr. Ornish's diet). These diets led the way to the more carbohydrate-restricted, moderate protein and fat diets of the late 1990s (The Zone diet), only to flip back to the low-carbohydrate, high-protein and -fat diets in the early 2000s (Dr. Atkins' New Diet Revolution, South Beach). The tables "What's in the Fad Diets?" and "Battle of the Diet Books" on page 360 summarize how these diets compare with the DRIs, and how they compare with each other.

After four decades of clashing diet books, does one emerge as the clear winner in the battle of the bulge? The answer is no. Researchers who analyzed close to 200 weight-loss studies using a variety of these diets concluded that it's the calories, not the composition of the diet, that count when it comes to losing weight.[2] In fact, a study comparing the Atkins, Ornish, Weight Watchers, and Zone diets showed that no matter what diet the individuals followed, they all lost about the same amount of weight, on average, by the end of one year. Whereas each of these diets provides a different percentage of carbohydrates, protein, and fat, they all had one important thing in common: They all reduced calories.

A very interesting point emerged from this study: People who were most diligent about adhering to the diet—no matter which one—experienced the most weight loss. However, over 20 percent of the diet-ers called it quits only two months into the study and more than 40 percent of them dropped out after one year. The highest dropout rates occurred among followers of the Atkins or Ornish diets. The researchers speculate that the rigidity of these extreme diets may have caused the higher dropout rates.[3]

Some extreme diets may also be unhealthy in the long term. In fact, the high drop out rate for some fad diets has probably protected many individuals from serious ill health effects and long-term nutrient deficiencies.

The problem with many fad diets is that people give up on them long before they meet their weight-loss goals. A fad diet doesn't fix anything long term. If it did, there wouldn't be new (or recycled) fad diets continually appearing on the market. The two major points of this research are that 1) any diet can result in weight loss as long as calories are reduced, and 2) the more realistic and doable the diet, the more likely people will stick with it long enough to lose weight.

Marketers often make sensational claims about fad diets and weight-loss products. These red flags can often tell you if a diet is questionable.

Red Flags for Diet Hype

🚩 It's the Carbs, Not the Calories, That Make You Fat!

Many fad diet ads claim that you can eat as much protein and fat as you want as long as you keep away from the carbs. These diets claim that your consumption of pasta, breads, rice, and many fruits and vegetables should be limited, but fatty meats such as ribs, salami, bologna, and poultry with skin, as well as butter, bacon, and cheeses should be on the menu often.

The Truth Behind the Hype

Diets that severely limit carbohydrates (<100 grams daily) eliminate so many foods, as well as sweets and treats, that it is impossible for a person not to consume at least 500 fewer calories daily. This will theoretically produce about one pound of

What's in the Fad Diets?

Type of Diet	Percent of Calories from		
	Carbohydrates	Protein	Fat
Low carbohydrate, higher protein, high fat Example: Atkins diet, South Beach diet	<20	25–30	55–65
Very high carbohydrate, moderate protein, very low fat Example: Dr. Ornish's diet, Pritikin diet	>65	10–20	<10–19
Carbohydrate-restricted, higher protein, moderate fat Example: The Zone diet	40	30	30
Compared to DRI Dietary Recommendations	**45–65**	**10–35**	**20–35**

Source: Adapted from M. Freedman, J. King, and E. Kennedy, Popular Diets: A Scientific Review, *Obesity Research* 9 (2001): 1S–40S.

weight loss per week.[4] When you curtail the carbohydrates, you likely will also be cutting back on fat.[5] When you stop eating the bagel (carbs), you'll also eliminate the cream cheese (fat) you slather on each half. Also, the monotonous nature of these diets causes people to become "bored" with eating, so they stop. Because the bread, mashed potatoes, and corn are off limits at dinner, the dieter is limited to fatty steak and not much else. Most people can only eat so much of this before it loses its appeal, so they're likely to stop eating sooner. As always, putting down the fork will cut calorie consumption.

Buyer Beware

A diet high in saturated fat and low in fiber and phytochemicals because it is low in whole grains, fruits, and vegetables is a recipe for heart disease, cancer, constipation, elevated blood cholesterol levels, and deficiencies in many vitamins and minerals, such as vitamins A, E, and B_6, folate, calcium, iron, zinc, and potassium.[6] So each time you follow a diet low in whole grains, fruits, and vegetables and high in animal fats, you are robbing your body of the protection of plant foods and overfeeding it the wrong type of fat. The high protein content of these diets may also cause the loss of calcium, and thus increase the risk of osteoporosis, as well as kidney stones (see Chapter 6).

Lose Seven Pounds in One Week!

Many diets guarantee rapid weight loss. This may happen on a low-carbohydrate diet—but only during the first few days, and only temporarily.

The Truth Behind the Hype

The 4- to 7-pound weight loss during the first week of low-carbohydrate dieting is due to loss of body water that results from two physiological processes. First, because the reduced amount of carbohy-

drates can't support the body's need for glucose, the stored glycogen in the liver and muscle will be broken down. Each gram of glycogen removed from storage causes the loss of 2 grams of water with it. Because you store about 500 grams of glycogen in your body, you can expect to lose approximately 2 pounds of water weight during the first week of a low-carbohydrate diet. Secondly, the ketone bodies generated by the breakdown of fat are lost from the body through the kidneys. This will also cause the body to lose sodium. As you know from Chapter 8, where sodium goes, water follows. Therefore, the ketone bodies that cause you to lose sodium will also cause you to lose water.[7]

Buyer Beware

Though water weight may be lost during the first week, the rate of weight loss after that will be determined by the energy imbalance in the body, as in any calorie-reducing diet. As soon as carbohydrates are added back to the diet, the body will retain water and some water weight will come back on. When it comes to shedding weight, quick loss usually means quick regain.

Celebrity-Endorsed Miracle Weight-Loss Products with a Money-Back Guarantee!

Just because a celebrity tries to sell you a product doesn't mean that the product is valid. It just means that the celebrity is being paid to do what he or she does best: act.

The Truth Behind the Hype

No cream, shake, or potion will magically melt away body fat. The Federal Trade Commission (FTC) has charged many firms that sell dubious products with public deception and have fined them as much as $10 million.[8]

Buyer Beware

Forget about getting your money back. The FTC has received numerous complaints from dissatisfied customers who have unsuccessfully tried to get a refund. The more miraculous the claim, the more likely you are to lose (money, that is, not weight).

Naturally Occurring Plants, Herbs, and Other Substances Will Help You Lose Weight Without Risk!

"Natural" substances, such as glucomannan, guar gum, chitosan, and bitter orange are not necessarily safer or more effective for weight loss.

The Truth Behind the Hype

Glucomannan is a compound found in the root of the starchy konjac plant, and guar gum is a type of dietary fiber found in a specific bean. Both are ineffective in weight loss. Chitosan is produced from a substance found in shellfish. Though the claim is that these substances decrease the absorption of fat in the body, research doesn't back up the claim. Bitter orange is a plant that is being touted as a substitute for ephedra (see the medications listed in the box "Extreme Measures for Extreme Obesity" on page 366), yet the research is not definitive on its ability to stimulate weight loss.[9]

Buyer Beware

Guar gum has been shown to cause diarrhea, flatulence, and gastrointestinal disturbances. Chitosan may cause nausea and flatulence.[10] Bitter orange can increase blood pressure and interfere with the metabolism of other drugs in the body.[11] Naturally occurring substances are not necessarily safe to consume, and there's no evidence that they help you lose weight.

(continued)

Fad Diets Are the Latest Fad, continued

Battle of the Diet Books

Name	Claim	What You Eat
The South Beach Diet by Arthur Agatson	Switching to good carbs stops insulin resistance, cures cravings, and causes weight loss. Good fats protect the heart and prevent hunger.	Yes: Seafood, chicken breast, lean meat, low-fat cheese, most veggies, nuts, oils; (later) whole grains, most fruits, low-fat milk or yogurt, beans Less: Fatty meats, full-fat cheese, refined grains, sweets, juice, potatoes
The Ultimate Weight Solution by Phil McGraw	Foods that take time to prepare and chew lead to weight loss. Other "Keys to Weight Freedom" include "no-fail environment," "right thinking," "healing feelings," and "circle of support."	Yes: Seafood, poultry, meat, low-fat dairy, whole grains, most veggies, fruits, oils (limited) Less: Fatty meats, refined grains, full-fat dairy, microwaveable entrees, fried foods
Dr. Atkins' New Diet Revolution by Robert C. Atkins	A low-carb diet is the key to weight loss (and good health) because carbs cause high insulin levels.	Yes: Seafood, poultry, meat, eggs, cheese, salad veggies, oils, butter, cream; (later) limited amounts of nuts, fruits, wine, beans, veggies, whole grains Less: Sweets, refined grains, milk, yogurt
Enter the Zone by Barry Sears	Eating the right mix of the right fats, carbs, and protein keeps you trim and healthy by lowering insulin.	Yes: Seafood, poultry, lean meat, fruits, most veggies, low-fat dairy, nuts Less: Fatty meats, full-fat dairy, butter, shortening, grains (limited), sweets, potatoes, carrots, bananas
Eat More, Weigh Less by Dean Ornish	Slashing fat is the key to weight loss.	Yes: Beans, fruits, veggies, grains, nonfat dairy (limited) Less: Meat, seafood, poultry, oils, nuts, butter, dairy (except nonfat), sweets, alcohol

Source: D. Schardt. Adapted from *Nutrition Action Healthletter* (January/February 2004): 6–7.

Is the Science Solid?	Is the Diet Healthy?	Worst Feature	Most Preposterous Claim
Healthy version of Atkins diet that's backed by solid evidence on fats and heart disease.	Pro: Mostly healthy foods.	Restricts carrots, bananas, pineapple, and watermelon.	You won't ever be hungry (despite menus that average just 1,200 calories a day).
Tough-love manual that relies more on Dr. Phil's opinion than science.	Pro: Mostly healthy foods. Con: Gives no menus, recipes, or advice on how much of what to eat.	Readers may buy Dr. Phil's expensive, questionable supplements, bars, and shakes.	"Each of these nutrients [in his supplements] has solid clinical evidence (and a record of safety) behind it."
Low-carb "bible" overstates the results of weak studies and the evidence on supplements. (However, in recent small studies, people lost more weight after 6—but not 12—months on Atkins than on a typical diet.)	Con: Too much red meat may raise risk of colon or prostate cancer. Con: Lack of fiber, vegetables, and fruits may raise risk of heart disease, stroke, cancer, diverticulosis, and constipation.	Long-term safety not established.	"Only by doing Atkins can you lose weight eating the same number of calories on which you used to gain weight."
Exaggerates evidence that the Zone diet is the key to weight loss and implies that the diet can cure virtually every disease.	Pro: Mostly healthy foods. Con: Few recipes or menus.	May convince people to use the diet to treat cancer, AIDS, chronic pain, impotence, depression, and arthritis.	"I believe that the hormonal benefits gained from a Zone-favorable diet will be considered the primary treatment for all chronic disease states, with drugs being used as secondary backup."
Diet worked (when combined with exercise and stress reduction) in a small but long-term study.	Pro: Mostly healthy foods. Con: Too many carbs may raise triglycerides and lower HDL ("good") cholesterol if people don't exercise, lose weight, and reduce stress.	Unnecessarily restricts seafood, turkey and chicken breast, oils, nuts, and fat-free dairy.	Eating a very low-fat vegetarian diet is easy.

If this person added some extra physical activity, he or she could further increase that daily calorie deficit. Let's now look at the other side of the energy equation: energy expenditure.

Move to Lose

Research shows that regular physical activity is associated with a healthier body weight, and devoting up to 60 minutes daily to moderate-intensity activities can help prevent those at a healthy weight from becoming overweight, and aid in weight loss for those who need to lose weight.[62] Moderately intense physical activity would be the equivalent of walking 3.5 miles per hour (Table 10.4).

Regular physical activity can not only add to the daily energy deficit needed for weight loss, but can also displace sedentary activity such as watching television, which often leads to mindless snacking on energy-dense foods.[63] Going for a walk and expending calories rather than watching television while snacking on a bag of chips will provide caloric benefits beyond the exercise alone.

A way to assess if you are incorporating enough physical activity into your day is to count your steps (such as with a pedometer). Research suggests that accumulating 10,000 steps daily, which is the equivalent of walking 5 miles, can help reduce the risk of becoming overweight.[64] Americans, on average, accumulate only 900 to 3,000 steps daily.[65] To reach 10,000 steps, a conscious effort is needed by most people to keep moving. See the Table Tips for some ideas for fun ways to expend more energy during the day.

Break Bad Habits

Hannah, the freshman you read about at the beginning of the chapter, will be relieved to find out that a 15-pound weight gain is not inevitable for college freshmen. In fact, research to support the "freshman 15" is rather slim. Some research has found that weight gain didn't occur at all or didn't occur in the majority of the students during the first semester (the length of the study) or the entire first year.[66] Other studies found

Table 10.4
Calories Used During Activities

Moderate Physical Activity	Approximate Calories/Hour for a 154-lb Person*	Vigorous Physical Activity	Approximate Calories/Hour for a 154-lb Person*
Hiking	370	Running/jogging (5 mph)	590
Light gardening/yard work	330	Bicycling (>10 mph)	590
Dancing	330	Swimming (slow freestyle laps)	510
Golf (walking and carrying clubs)	330	Aerobics	480
Bicycling (<10mph)	290	Walking (4.5 mph)	460
Walking (3.5 mph)	280	Heavy yard work (chopping wood)	440
Weight lifting (general light workout)	220	Weight lifting (vigorous effort)	440
Stretching	180	Basketball (vigorous)	440

*Calories burned per hour will be higher for persons who weigh more than 154 lbs (70 kg) and lower for persons who weigh less.

Source: Adapted from Centers for Disease Control and Prevention, Dietary Guidelines for Americans 2005.

that students gained less than 5 pounds, on average, and one of these studies showed that certain behaviors such as snacking in the evening, consumption of junk foods, and the number of meals eaten on weekends were associated with weight gain.[67]

While Hannah can rest assured that as long as she continues her good eating habits, she won't pack on those extra pounds, her roommate Jenna is another story. If Jenna continues with her habits, she may find weight management during her freshman year to be an uphill struggle. Jenna would benefit from some behavior modification.

Behavior modification focuses on changing the behaviors that contribute to weight gain or impede weight loss. Several behavior modification techniques can be used to identify and change poor eating behaviors. These techniques include self-monitoring the behaviors by keeping a food log, controlling environmental cues that trigger eating when not hungry, and learning how to better manage stress.[68]

Do you really know when, why, and what you eat? Understanding the habits and emotions that drive your eating patterns can help you change your less-than-healthy behaviors. Keeping a food log is one way to track the kinds of foods you eat during the day, when and where you eat them, your moods, and hunger ratings. You can use this information to minimize or eliminate the eating behaviors that interfere with weight management.

For example, if Jenna was to keep a food record, a typical day's log may be similar to the one in Figure 10.10. Jenna has habits that are common to people who struggle

Figure 10.10 Food Log
Keeping track of when, where, and what you eat, as well as why you ate it, can yield some surprising information. Do you think you sometimes eat out of boredom or stress, rather than because you're hungry?

Food Log

For: Jenna

Date: Monday, September 6

Food and drink	Time eaten	What I ate/ Where I ate it	Hunger level*	Mood †
Breakfast		Skipped it	3	G
Snack	11 a.m.	Oreo cookies, PowerAde from vending machine during morning class.	5	E
Lunch	1:30 p.m.	Ham and cheese sandwich, 2 large M&M cookies in student union cafeteria.	4	B
Snack				
Dinner	6:30 p.m.	Hamburger, French fries, salad at kitchen table	4	F
Snack	7 p.m. to 10 p.m.	Large bag of tortilla chips and entire bag of Pepperidge Farm Milano cookies while studying at kitchen table	1	I

*Hunger levels (1–5): 1 = not hungry; 5 = super hungry

† **Moods:**
A = Happy; B = Content; C = Bored; D = Depressed; E = Rushed; F = Stressed; G = Tired; H = Lonely; I = Anxious; J = Angry

behavior modification Changing behaviors to improve health. Identifying and altering eating patterns that contribute to weight gain or impede weight loss is behavior modification.

Adopt Some Healthy Habits

Don't eat out of boredom; go for a jog instead. If we ate only when hungry, we would probably be a lot leaner.

Food shop with a full stomach and a grocery list. Walking around aimlessly while hungry means you are more likely to grab items on a whim.

When you feel wound up or stressed, lace up those sneakers and go for a walk.

The next time you pass a difficult course, or get that long-awaited raise, celebrate without a plate. Replace the traditional restaurant dinner with a no-calorie reward such as a new music download or the latest best seller.

Declare a vending machine–free day at least once a week and stop the impulsive snacking. On that day, pack two pieces of fruit as satisfying snacks.

with their weight. She skips breakfast daily, which causes her to be very hungry in the late morning and increases her impulsive snacking on energy-dense, low-nutrition foods from the vending machine. A study of overweight women who typically skipped breakfast showed that once they started consuming cereal for breakfast, they indulged in less impulsive snacking.[69] Eating a bowl of high-fiber whole-grain cereal (approximately 200 calories) will likely appease Jenna's morning hunger and help her bypass her 11 a.m. vending machine snack of 270-calorie cookies and a 210-calorie sports drink. This one behavior change would not only save her 280 calories in the morning, but reduce her added sugar intake and add more nutrition to her day. Similarly, adding a less-energy-dense salad at lunch could help increase her satiety and displace at least one of the cookies that she often eats with her sandwich.

Because studying for exams stresses her out and causes her to munch even though she isn't hungry, Jenna shouldn't study in her dorm, where she is surrounded by snacks, but should go to the campus library, where eating is prohibited. Exercising before or after studying would be a healthier way to relieve her stress than eating her way through a bag of snacks.

Changing behaviors that have become unhealthy habits is another important piece of improving weight management. Individuals who eat "out of habit" and in response to their emotions need to replace this unnecessary eating to better manage their weight. The Table Tips lists some healthy behaviors that can easily be incorporated into your life.

The Take-Home Message For successful, long-term weight loss, people need to reduce their daily calorie intake, increase their physical activity, and change their behavior. Adding low-energy-density high volume vegetables, fruit, and fiber along with some lean protein and healthy oils to the diet can help in satiety and reduce unplanned snacking. Incorporating approximately 60 minutes of physical activity daily can help with weight loss. Changing unhealthy habits by restructuring the environment to minimize or eliminate the eating behaviors that interfere with weight loss can also help shed extra pounds.

How Can You Maintain Weight Loss?

You, or someone you know, may be familiar with the typical fad diet experience: the triumphant rush associated with the dropping of ten pounds, the disappointment that sets in when fifteen pounds is regained, then a new round of hope when ten of them are re-shed. An estimated 90 to 95 percent of individuals who lose weight regain it within several years.[70] This fluctuation is known as **weight cycling,** and some research suggests that it can lead to problems such as hypertension, gallbladder disease, and elevated blood cholesterol levels, not to mention depression and feelings of frustration.[71]

Recent research suggests that weight cycling may not be as common as previously thought. A study of 800 people who lost weight showed that they were able to keep off at least 30 pounds for five years. These people were successful because they

weight cycling The repeated gain and loss of body weight.

maintained their physical activity habits and positive behavior changes after they reached their weight goal.[72] They commonly limited the intake of fatty foods, monitored their calorie intake, and ate nearly five times a day, on average. (For many people, eating smaller meals allows them to avoid becoming ravenous and overeating at the next meal.) The majority of them weighed themselves weekly and maintained a high level of daily physical activity, expending the energy equivalent of walking four miles a day.[73] This suggests that weight loss can be maintained as long as the individual doesn't abandon the healthy habits that promoted the weight loss and revert to the unhealthy habits that caused the excess weight in the first place.

Physical activity can also help those who've lost weight close the **"energy gap."** After weight loss, a person will have lower overall energy needs, as there is less body weight to maintain. The energy gap is the difference in daily calories that are needed for weight maintenance before and after weight loss.[74] Researchers have estimated that the energy gap is about 8 calories per pound of lost weight.[75]

For example, someone who lost 30 pounds would need approximately 240 fewer calories a day to maintain the new, lower body weight. This person can either eat 240 fewer calories, expend this amount of calories through added physical activity, or do a combination of both. Because the environment we live in seems to encourage eating more than discourage it, researchers feel that increasing daily physical activity is likely the easier way to close the energy gap.[76] *Adding* something (physical activity) to your lifestyle is often easier than *removing* something (calories). Individuals who lose weight are advised to engage in 60 to 90 minutes of moderate physical activity daily in order to maintain their weight loss.[77]

Some individuals are candidates for extreme treatment to help them shed their unhealthy excess weight. The feature box "Extreme Measures for Extreme Obesity" on page 366 discusses treatment options for those with BMIs of greater than 40.

The Take-Home Message People who lose weight are most likely to keep it off if they maintain the positive diet and lifestyle habits that helped them lose the weight. Eating less and/or exercising more will help close the energy gap after weight loss.

How Can You Gain Weight Healthfully?

For people who are underweight, weight gain can be as challenging and frustrating as losing weight is for an overweight individual. The major difference is that the thin person rarely gets sympathy from others. Like overweight individuals, those who are underweight experience an energy imbalance. In their case, however, they consume fewer calories than they expend.

People who want to gain weight need to do the opposite of those who are trying to lose weight. Whereas waist watchers hunt for the lower calorie foods, individuals seeking to gain weight should make each bite more energy dense. These individuals need to add at least 500 calories to their daily energy intake. This will enable them to add about a pound of extra body weight weekly.

Of course, someone who wants to gain weight should not just load up on high-fat, high-calorie foods. The quality of the extra calories is very important. Snacking

energy gap The difference between the number of calories needed to maintain weight before and after weight loss.

Extreme Measures for Extreme Obesity

People with a BMI greater than 40 fall into the category of **extreme obesity.** They are at such a high risk for conditions such as heart disease and stroke, and even of dying, that an aggressive weight-loss treatment is necessary. Treatments that go beyond eating less and exercising more, such as a very low-calorie diet, medications, and/or surgery, are often recommended. Let's look at each of these.

A Very Low-Calorie Diet

On her television show in 1988, a very petite Oprah Winfrey beamed with joy after having lost 67 pounds using a **very low-calorie diet.** Oprah achieved her weight loss by consuming a liquid protein diet or **protein-sparing modified fast.** Such protein-rich diets provide less than 800 calories daily, are very low in or devoid of carbohydrates, and have minimal amounts of fat. They are designed to help individuals at high risk of disease drop a substantial amount of weight in a short amount of time. However, they are not a long-term solution. After consuming the diet for 12 to 16 weeks, the dieter is switched over to a well-balanced, low-calorie diet.

Very low-calorie diets have to be supplemented with vitamins and minerals

> **extreme obesity** Having a BMI >40.
>
> **very low-calorie diet** or **protein-sparing modified fast** A diet of fewer than 800 calories per day and high in protein. These diets are very low in or devoid of carbohydrates and have a minimal amount of fat.
>
> **gastric bypass surgeries** Surgical procedures that reduce the functional volume of the stomach so that less food is eaten. Such surgeries are sometimes used to treat extreme obesity.
>
> **gastric banding** A type of gastric surgery that uses a silicon band to reduce the size of the stomach so that less food is needed to feel full.

and must be medically supervised by a doctor, as they can cause dangerous electrolyte imbalances as well as gallstones, constipation, fatigue, hair loss, and other side effects. The National Institutes of Health doesn't recommend very low-calorie diets because well-balanced low-calorie diets are just as effective in producing a similar amount of weight loss after one year and are less dangerous.[12]

After all that effort, Oprah ultimately regretted her very low-calorie diet. "I had literally starved myself for four months—not a morsel of food—to get into a pair of size 10 Calvin Klein jeans," claims Oprah. "Two hours after that show, I started eating to celebrate—of course, within two days those jeans no longer fit!"[13] In 2006, Oprah is at her goal weight of approximately 150 pounds.

Medication

Some prescription medications can help a person lose weight. The drugs either suppress the appetite or inhibit the absorption of fat in the intestinal tract. For example, the drug sibutramine (trade name Meridia) reduces hunger and increases thermogenesis, which increases energy expenditure. The drug can also increase a person's heart rate and blood pressure. Therefore, it may not be appropriate for those who have hypertension, which tends to occur often in overweight individuals. In fact, because all drugs have side effects, their use must be monitored by a doctor.

Orlistat (trade name Xenical; recall that this drug is discussed in the Chapter 3 Two Points of View) inhibits an intestinal enzyme that is needed to break down fat. If it isn't broken down, the fat (and calories) will not be absorbed by the body. Up to about one-third of the dietary fat will be blocked and expelled in the stool. Orlistat needs to be taken at each meal and should accompany a diet that provides no more than about 30 percent of its calories from fat. Because fat is lost in the stool, the drug can cause oily and more frequent stools, flatulence, and oily dis-

Oprah Winfrey after she lost 67 pounds (the amount of fat in the wagon) by consuming a very low-calorie, liquid protein diet.

charge.[14] Ironically, these side effects may help an individual adhere to a low-fat diet, as these effects are more pronounced if a high-fat meal is consumed.

Sometimes the side effects of weight-loss medications can be so serious that the medication must be withdrawn from the market. For instance, the FDA has prohibited the sale of supplements that contain ephedra (also called Ma huang), the plant source for ephedrine. Ephedrine has been shown to cause chest pains, palpitations, hypertension, and an accelerated heart rate. In 2003, baseball player Steve Bechler died at age 23 after taking a weight-loss supplement containing ephedrine during spring training. Ephedrine was determined to have contributed to his death.[15]

Whereas individuals who take prescription medications to lose weight have been shown to lose as much as 20 pounds, these drugs should be coupled with, and can't replace, a lower calorie diet, regular physical activity, and behavior modification for long-term weight loss.

Surgery

In 1998, approximately 13,000 obese patients went under the knife to reduce the size of their stomachs. Four years later, more than five times as many **gastric bypass surgeries,** or over 71,000, were done.[16] During this surgery, the majority of the stomach is stapled shut. This reduces the size of the stomach so that it holds about ¼ cup of fluid. Food consumed leaves the small stomach pouch through a surgically added intestinal loop that bypasses the original stomach and attaches directly to the small intestine. After the surgery, these individuals need to consume small, frequent meals because the stomach pouch can only expand to a maximum of about 5 ounces, the size of a woman's fist. Individuals not only eat less because of their smaller stomachs, but have higher levels of satiety and lower levels of hunger after the surgery. This effect on their appetite is thought to be associated with lower levels of ghrelin due to the loss of stomach area after the surgery.[17]

Because both the majority of the stomach and the upper part of the small

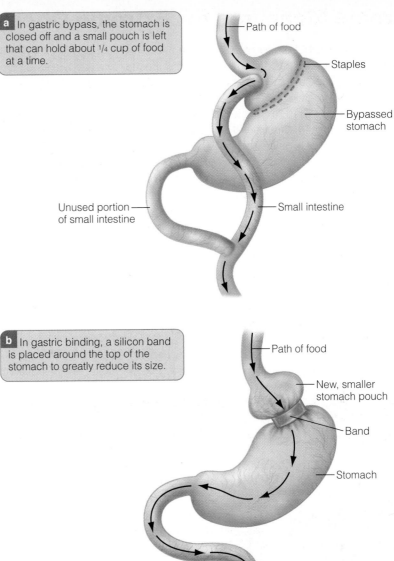

a In gastric bypass, the stomach is closed off and a small pouch is left that can hold about ¼ cup of food at a time.

Path of food
Staples
Bypassed stomach
Unused portion of small intestine
Small intestine

b In gastric binding, a silicon band is placed around the top of the stomach to greatly reduce its size.

Path of food
New, smaller stomach pouch
Band
Stomach

Gastric bypass and gastric binding.

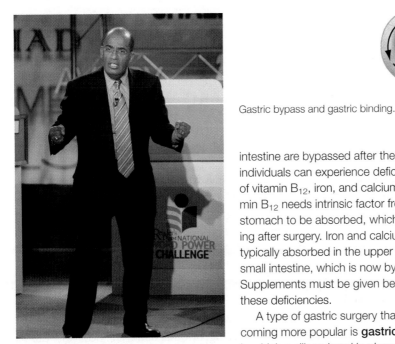

Al Roker, NBC's *Today Show* weather man, lost almost 100 pounds after gastric bypass surgery.

intestine are bypassed after the surgery, individuals can experience deficiencies of vitamin B_{12}, iron, and calcium. (Vitamin B_{12} needs intrinsic factor from the stomach to be absorbed, which is missing after surgery. Iron and calcium are typically absorbed in the upper part of the small intestine, which is now bypassed.) Supplements must be given because of these deficiencies.

A type of gastric surgery that's becoming more popular is **gastric banding,** in which a silicon band is placed around the top of the stomach to create a small pouch with a very narrow opening at the bottom for the food to pass through. This delays the emptying of the stomach contents so that a person will feel fuller longer. The doctor can adjust the opening of the pouch by inflating or deflating the band.

Although dramatic amounts of weight loss can occur and research has shown that incidences of hypertension, diabetes, high blood cholesterol levels, and sleep apnea have been reduced among people who've had the surgery, there are also risks involved. About 10 percent of those undergoing gastric bypass surgery experience complications such as gallstones,

(continued)

Extreme Measures for Extreme Obesity, continued

ulcers, and bleeding in the stomach and intestines. Approximately 1 to 2 percent die.[18] After surgery, individuals need to be monitored long term by their doctor and nutrition professionals to ensure that they remain healthy and meet their nutritional needs. (See the Two Points of View at the end of this chapter for more on the pros and cons of bariatric surgery.)

liposuction The surgical removal of subcutaneous fat with a penlike instrument. Usually performed on the abdomen, hips, and thighs, and/or other areas of the body.

cellulite A non-medical term that refers to fat cells under the skin that give it a ripplelike appearance. Contrary to popular belief, cellulite is no different from other fat in the body.

Another type of surgery, **liposuction,** is less about health and more about physical appearance. During liposuction, a doctor removes subcutaneous fat from the abdomen, hips, or thighs (and sometimes other areas of the body) by suctioning it out with a penlike instrument. People often undergo liposuction to get rid of **cellulite,** which isn't a medical term, but refers to the fat cells that give the skin a dimpled appearance. Complications such as infections, scars, and swelling can arise after liposuction. Fat can also reappear at

Liposuction is a surgical procedure that removes subcutaneous fat. Unlike gastric banding or bypass surgeries, liposuction is purely cosmetic and does not result in health benefits.

the site where it was removed, so the results of liposuction may not be permanent.

Very low-calorie diets, medications, and surgery may be viable options for those with extreme obesity, but they are not without risks. For those who are overweight, the safest route to a healthy weight is to make incremental diet and lifestyle changes to take in fewer calories and expend more. Of course, the best overall strategy for weight management is to avoid becoming overweight in the first place.

Healthy Snacks for Healthy Weight Gain

For healthy snacks that travel well and don't need refrigeration try this: Stash an 8-ounce can or box of 100 percent fruit juice (about 100 calories) in your bag along with one of the 150-calorie snacks listed below for a quick 250-calorie snack (food and juice combined) between meals.

Graham crackers, 5 crackers (2½″ square)

Mixed nuts, 1 oz

Fig bars, 2-oz package

Pudding, individual serving sizes, 4 oz

Peanut butter on whole-wheat crackers (1 tbs peanut butter on 6 crackers)

on an extra 500 calories of jelly beans will add 500 calories of sugar and little nutrition. Rather, these individuals should make energy-dense, nutritious choices from a variety of foods within each food group. For example, instead of eating a slice of toast in the morning they should choose a waffle. Adding coleslaw rather than cabbage will increase the calories in a salad bar lunch more than tenfold. Figure 10.11 contrasts more- and less-energy-dense foods within each food group. Eating snacks during the day will also add calories. The Table Tips provides easy and portable snack ideas.

The Take-Home Message People who want to gain weight need to add energy-dense foods to their diet so that they take in more energy than they expend. Adding nutrient-dense snacks between meals is an easy way to increase the number of calories consumed daily.

Attaining a healthy weight, whether it means gaining or losing a few pounds, is a worthwhile goal that can result in lowered risk of disease and a more productive life. However, it's important to maintain your weight in a healthy way. Patterns of eating that involve severe calorie restriction, purging, or other abnormal behaviors can be severely damaging to health. Whereas disordered eating and eating disorders are sometimes thought of as psychological rather than nutrition-related topics, it's important to be aware of them and recognize their symptoms. We'll discuss these next.

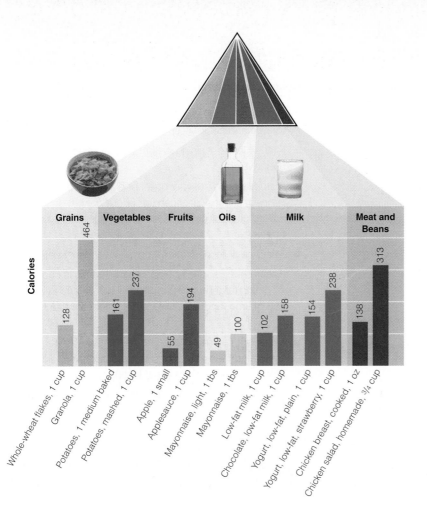

Figure 10.11 More- and Less-Energy-Dense Food Choices, by Food Group Choosing more energy-dense, but still nutritious, foods can help those who are underweight gain weight.

What Is Disordered Eating and How Can You Identify It?

The term **disordered eating** is used to describe a variety of eating patterns considered abnormal and potentially harmful. Refusing to eat, compulsive eating, binge eating, restrictive eating, vomiting after eating, and abusing diet pills, laxatives, or diuretics are all examples of disordered eating behaviors. **Eating disorders,** in contrast, are diagnosed by meeting specific criteria that include disordered eating behaviors as well as other factors (see Table 10.5 on page 370). It is possible for someone to engage in disordered eating patterns without having an actual eating disorder.

There are several different types of eating disorders that someone could develop, including anorexia nervosa, bulimia nervosa, binge eating disorder, and night eating syndrome. In the United States, approximately 11 million people struggle with eating disorders.[78] Adolescent and young adult females in predominantly white upper-middle- and middle-class families are the population with highest prevalence. However, eating disorders and disordered eating among males, minorities, and other age groups are increasing.[79] Anyone can develop one of these conditions regardless of gender, age, race, ethnicity, or social status.

disordered eating Abnormal and potentially harmful eating behaviors that do not meet specific criteria for anorexia nervosa or bulimia nervosa.

eating disorders The term used to describe psychological illnesses that involve specific abnormal eating behaviors: anorexia nervosa (self-starvation) and bulimia nervosa (bingeing and purging).

Table 10.5

Diagnostic Criteria for Eating Disorders

Eating Disorder	Diagnostic Criteria
Anorexia nervosa	■ Consistent body weight under the minimally normal weight for age and height (less than 85% of expected)
	■ Intense fear of gaining weight or becoming fat, even though underweight
	■ Disturbance in the way one's body weight or shape is experienced, excessive influence of body weight or shape on self-esteem, or denial of the seriousness of the current low body weight
	■ Absence of at least three consecutive menstrual cycles
Bulimia nervosa	■ Recurrent episodes of binge eating, which is characterized by eating larger than normal amounts of food in a short period of time, and a lack of control over eating during the binge
	■ Recurrent purging in order to prevent weight gain, such as by self-induced vomiting, misuse of laxatives, diuretics, enemas, or other medications; fasting; or excessive exercise
	■ The binging and purging occurs, on average, at least twice a week for three months
	■ Persistent overconcern with body shape and weight, which may influence self-esteem
Eating disorder not otherwise specified	■ Disordered eating behaviors that do not meet the criteria for anorexia nervosa or bulimia nervosa, including binge eating disorder and night eating syndrome.

Source: Adapted from American Psychiatric Association. 1994. *Diagnostic and Statistical Manual of Mental Disorders,* 4th ed. Washington, DC: American Psychiatric Association.

Most disordered eating patterns occur in females, which likely is a result of societal pressure to be thin and have a "perfect" figure. Images of models and celebrities with abnormally low body weights are portrayed as ideal, which frequently leads to body dissatisfaction among "normal" people. Thinness is too often associated with beauty, success, and happiness in our society, and therefore many people believe that they are not beautiful, successful, or happy unless they are thin. Many females will try to achieve this perfect figure at any cost, including plastic surgery, liposuction, and engaging in disordered eating behaviors. Many do not realize that pictures found in magazines and on billboards have been digitally enhanced or airbrushed and are not true images at all.

About 10 percent of all cases of anorexia nervosa and bulimia nervosa occur in men. This may be an underestimate though, as many men, as well as women, feel ashamed or embarrassed and may hide their problem. In fact, the prevalence of eating disorders among both males and females is probably higher than reported. Researchers have found that men diagnosed with eating disorders have higher rates of other psychiatric illness like depression and anxiety disorders compared with men who do not have eating disorders.[80]

Let's take a look at each type of disorder, and the specific criteria that make each one unique.

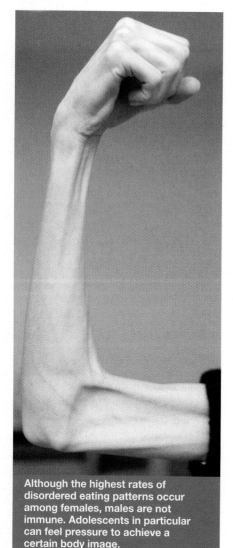

Although the highest rates of disordered eating patterns occur among females, males are not immune. Adolescents in particular can feel pressure to achieve a certain body image.

Anorexia Nervosa Results from Severe Calorie Restriction

Anorexia nervosa is a serious, potentially life-threatening eating disorder that is characterized by self-starvation and excessive weight loss. People who suffer from anorexia nervosa have an intense fear of gaining weight or being "fat." This fear causes them to control their food intake by restricting the amount of food they consume, resulting in significant weight loss.

Many people with anorexia nervosa have a distorted sense of body image and usually see themselves as fat even though they are underweight. This misperception of body size contributes to the behavior of restricting food intake in order to lose (more) weight. For instance, someone with anorexia nervosa might eat only a piece of fruit and a small container of yogurt during an entire day. They may also have a fear of eating certain foods, such as those that contain fat and sugar. They believe that these foods will make them fat, regardless of how much they eat. Some may also exercise excessively as a means of controlling their weight.

There are numerous health consequences that can occur with anorexia nervosa and some can be fatal. One of the most serious health effects is an electrolyte imbalance, specifically low blood potassium, which can occur if someone with anorexia nervosa also engages in episodes of purging. An electrolyte imbalance can lead to an irregular heart rhythm, which can be fatal. Someone who's lost an extreme amount of body fat may experience a drop in body temperature and feel cold even when it is hot outside. In an effort to regulate body temperature, their body may begin to grow **lanugo** (downy hair), particularly on the face and arms.

Because someone with anorexia nervosa is not getting enough calories, the body begins to slow or shut down some processes in an effort to conserve energy for its most vital functions. The person may experience a decrease in heart rate and blood pressure, overall weakness and fatigue, and hair loss. The digestive process also slows down, which often results in constipation, bloating, and delayed gastric emptying. Dehydration, iron deficiency, and osteoporosis are also negative health effects caused by anorexia nervosa.

Bulimia Nervosa Involves Cycles of Binge Eating and Purging

Bulimia nervosa is another type of eating disorder that can be life-threatening. During times of binge eating, the person lacks control over eating and consumes larger than normal amounts of food in a short period of time. Following the binge, the person counters the binge with some type of purging. Many people assume that bulimics purge by vomiting, but self-induced vomiting is only one form. Purging can be described as any behavior that assists in "getting rid" of food to prevent weight gain or to promote weight loss. This can include excessive exercise, abuse of diet pills, laxatives, or diuretics, and strict dieting or fasting.

Most of the health consequences that occur with bulimia nervosa are associated with self-induced vomiting, such as tears in the esophagus, swollen parotid glands, tooth decay and gum disease (due to stomach acid), and broken blood vessels in the eyes (due to pressure from vomiting). Electrolyte imbalance also occurs with bulimia nervosa and can be fatal. People with bulimia nervosa may also experience dehydration and constipation due to frequent episodes of binge eating and purging.

lanugo Very fine, soft hair on the face and arms of people with anorexia nervosa.

People with binge eating disorder often eat in secret.

Laxative abuse can also cause serious medical complications depending on the type, amount, and length of time the person has used them. Laxatives used repeatedly can cause constipation, dehydration due to fluid loss in the intestines, electrolyte imbalances, fluid retention, bloody stools, and impaired bowel function.

Binge Eating Disorder Involves Compulsive Overeating

Binge eating disorder is characterized by recurrent episodes of binge eating without purging. People who have binge eating disorder eat without regard to physiological cues. They may eat for emotional reasons, and feel out-of-control while eating. The overeating results in physical and psychological discomfort. Many people who struggle with this type of eating disorder will often eat in secret and feel ashamed about their behaviors.

The health effects of binge eating disorder are commonly those that are associated with obesity because most people who struggle with binge eating disorder are of normal or heavier-than-average weight. Health effects may include high blood pressure, high cholesterol levels, heart disease, type 2 diabetes, and gallbladder disease.

Binge eating disorder has specific signs and symptoms; however, it does not have its own diagnostic criteria like anorexia nervosa and bulimia nervosa. Because binge eating disorder does not meet the diagnostic criteria for anorexia or bulimia, but still requires treatment, it falls into the diagnostic category of "Eating Disorders Not Otherwise Specified." Other behaviors in this category include purging without bingeing, restrictive eating by people who are in a normal weight range despite having significant weight loss, binging and purging but not frequently enough to meet criteria for bulimia, and chewing and spitting out food instead of swallowing it.

Night Eating Syndrome Is a Type of Eating, Sleeping, and Mood Disorder

People with night eating syndrome may consume more than half their day's calories between 8 p.m. and 6 a.m.

Night eating syndrome is described as an abnormal eating pattern in which a person consumes the majority of daily calories after the evening meal, as well as wakes up during the night, possibly even several times, to eat. In addition, the person typically does not have an appetite during the morning hours and consumes very little throughout the day. One study found that people with night eating syndrome consume 56 percent of their 24-hour calorie intake between the hours of 8:00 p.m. and 6:00 a.m. This study also found that people with night eating syndrome generally do not binge eat with each awakening; rather, they eat smaller portions of food on several occasions throughout the night.[81] This disorder is most common among obese individuals, though people of normal weight can also develop night eating syndrome.[82]

Night eating syndrome appears to be a unique combination of disordered eating, a sleep disorder, and a mood disorder (see Table 10.6).[83] Research has shown that night eating syndrome is associated with low self-esteem, depression, reduced daytime hunger, and less weight loss among obese patients.[84] Stress also appears to be a contributing factor in the development and continuation of night eating syndrome.[85] Someone may feel guilty, ashamed, or embarrassed while they are eating during the night, as well as the next morning.

Table 10.6

Signs of Night Eating Syndrome

Sign	Explanation/Example
Morning anorexia	Not hungry in the morning, even if breakfast is eaten; eats very minimal amounts during morning and early afternoon hours
Eating during the night	Awakens to eat at least once a night, at least three nights a week, for at least three months; frequently consumes high-calorie snacks during awakenings
Eating after the last evening meal	At least 50% of the daily caloric intake is consumed in snacks after last evening meal

There Are Some Common Signs of Disordered Eating

Many people may know someone with an eating disorder, but may not know how to help them. Learning about eating disorders will help you understand why a friend or loved one can have destructive eating behaviors and be seemingly unaware of the damage, pain, or danger they can cause. You also need to know the warning signs so you can identify disordered eating behaviors that could progress into more serious eating disorders (Table 10.7 on page 374).

There are both physical and behavioral warning signs of eating disorders and disordered eating. Hair loss is very common among people with anorexia nervosa and bulimia nervosa, as the body does not receive adequate nutrients for hair maintenance and growth. You may also notice significant weight changes, such as sudden weight loss in anorexia nervosa, and sudden weight gain in bulimia nervosa, binge eating disorder, or night eating syndrome. *Russell's sign,* which is scar tissue on the knuckles of fingers used to induce vomiting, is one indicator of bulimia nervosa. This is caused by scraping the knuckles when removing the fingers from the mouth during purging.

People with disordered eating often avoid social situations because they know food will be present and do not feel comfortable eating around others. Preoccupation with food and body weight is also present among people with eating disorders, such as weighing several times each day or severely limiting calorie intake. They may also deny unusual eating behaviors if confronted about them.

Although there is typically no one cause of disordered eating and eating disorders, there are certain factors that may increase one's risk for developing these conditions. One common trait of people with eating disorders is perfectionism. Unrealistic standards can lead to a sense of failure and lowered self-worth. Many people who struggle with eating disorders are trying to gain some control in their lives. When external factors feel out of control, the person with an eating disorder gets a sense of security from being able to control personal food and weight issues. Depression, low self-esteem, and history of physical or sexual abuse, also occur among people who have eating disorders.

If you are concerned about someone, find a good time and place to gently express your concerns without criticism or judgment. Realize that you may be rejected or your friend may deny the problem. Be supportive and let the person know that you are available if they want to talk to you at another time. You should also realize that there are many things that you cannot do to help a loved one or friend get better. You cannot force an anorexic to eat, keep a bulimic from purging, or make a binge

Table 10.7
Warning Signs for Eating Disorders

Symptom	Explanation/Example
Weight is below 85% of ideal body weight	Refusal to accept and maintain body weight (even if it is within normal range)
Exercises excessively	Often exercises daily for long periods of time to burn calories and prevent weight gain. May skip work or class to exercise.
Preoccupation with food, weight, and diet	Constantly worries about amount and type of food eaten. May weigh themselves daily or several times per day.
Distorted body image	Do not see themselves as they truly are. May comment on being fat even if underweight.
Refusing to eat	Will avoid food in order to lose weight or prevent weight gain. May avoid only certain foods, such as those with fat and sugar.
Loss of menstrual period	Periods become irregular or completely absent.
Diet pill use or laxative use	Evidence of pill bottles, boxes, or packaging.
Changes in mood	May become more withdrawn, depressed, or anxious, especially around food.
Hair loss	Hair become thinner and falls out in large quantities.
Avoids eating around others	Wants to eat alone. Makes excuses to avoid eating with others.

eater stop overeating. It is up to the individual to decide when he or she is ready to deal with the issues in life that led to the eating disorder.

The best thing you can do is learn to listen. Find out about resources in your area for treating eating disorders so that you can refer someone there when that person is ready to get help. Some web-based resources are listed on page 381.

How Are Disordered Eating Behaviors Treated?

The most effective treatment for eating disorders is a multidisciplinary team approach including psychological, medical, and nutrition professionals. All members of the team must be knowledgeable and experienced with eating disorders because it is a complex area that some health care professionals do not feel comfortable treating. A psychologist can help the person deal with emotional and other psychological issues that may be contributing to the eating disorder. Anyone who struggles with an eating disorder should be closely monitored by a physician or other medical professional, as some eating disorders can be life-threatening. A registered dietitian can help someone with an eating disorder establish normal eating behaviors.

Are You at Risk for an Eating Disorder?

Check the appropriate box in the following statements to help you find out.

1. I constantly think about eating, weight, and body size. Yes ☐ No ☐
2. I'm terrified about being overweight. Yes ☐ No ☐
3. I binge eat and can't stop until I feel sick. Yes ☐ No ☐
4. I weigh myself several times each day. Yes ☐ No ☐
5. I exercise too much or get very rigid about my exercise plan. Yes ☐ No ☐
6. I have taken laxatives or forced myself to vomit after eating. Yes ☐ No ☐
7. I believe food controls my life. Yes ☐ No ☐
8. I feel extremely guilty after eating. Yes ☐ No ☐
9. I eat when I am nervous, anxious, lonely, or depressed. Yes ☐ No ☐
10. I believe my weight controls what I do. Yes ☐ No ☐

Answer

These statements are designed to help you identify potentially problematic eating behavior. These statements do *not* tell you if you have an eating disorder. Look carefully at any statement you marked as yes and decide if this behavior prevents you from enjoying life or makes you unhealthy. Changing these behaviors should be done gradually, making small changes one at a time. Contact your student health services center or your health care provider if you suspect you need help.

Some nutritional approaches to eating disorders include identifying binge triggers, safe and unsafe foods, and hunger and fullness cues. Food journals are often helpful to identify eating patterns, food choices, moods, eating disorder triggers, eating cues, and timing of meals and snacks. Meals plans are also used in some instances to ensure intake of adequate calories and nutrients among those with anorexia nervosa, and to help avoid overeating among those with bulimia nervosa or binge eating disorder.

Most people can recover from eating disorders and may not have to struggle with it for the rest of their lives. When treatment is sought in the early stages, there is a better chance that the person will recover fully and have a shorter recovery process than someone who begins treatment after many years. Some people continue to have the desire to engage in disordered eating behaviors; however, they are able to refrain from actually doing these behaviors. Unfortunately, some individuals may never fully recover from an eating disorder. Caregivers must recognize that recovery is a process that often takes years and has no "quick fix."

Putting It All Together

Managing your weight within a healthy range involves eating a well-balanced diet that includes all the food groups in MyPyramid. The diet needed to manage your weight is the same one you should be eating to maintain good health. It is a diet rich in complex carbohydrates such as whole grains, vegetables, and fruits that provide fiber, vitamins, and minerals. Lean meats, poultry, and fish, calcium-rich dairy foods, and healthy oils need to be included to provide protein, minerals, vitamins, and essential fats. This type of diet enables you to meet your nutrient needs, provides satiety, and should be coupled with adequate amounts of daily physical activity and healthy eating behaviors.

Two Points of View

Weighing the Pros and Cons of Gastric Bypass Surgery

What are the risks and benefits of gastric bypass surgery? Does the surgery result in successful weight loss? Two experts share their views.

Joanne Ikeda, MA, RD

Lecturer, Department of Nutritional Sciences; founding codirector of the Center for Weight and Health, University of California at Berkeley

Joanne Ikeda, MA, RD, is a cooperative extension nutrition education specialist and a founder of the Center for Weight and Health at the University of California, Berkeley. She has been a leader in designing approaches to the prevention and treatment of obesity that focus on helping children adopt healthier lifestyles. She is an advocate of community empowerment for the purpose of improving environments so that they are more supportive of healthy lifestyles in children and their families.

Q: Who is the typical patient for gastric bypass surgery and what qualifications must he or she meet?

A: I don't consult with potential surgery patients or help advise them on the qualifications, so this particular point is not my area of specialty.

Q: What are the benefits of the surgery?

A: I can understand why people whose mobility is impaired would see a benefit to the procedure. Once someone weighs over 300 pounds, they really are not able to exercise or walk briskly. Surgery is the only way they'll permanently lose weight and the only way they'll regain their mobility. By the time most people weigh 300 pounds or more, they've been on numerous diets and the dieting has contributed to their increasing weight gain over time. That leaves them looking for other options.

Q: What are the risks?

A: You are permanently altering your digestive tract, and you're doing it in a way that's not going to give you a normal digestive tract. Consequently, we see a large range of nutritional deficiencies. We're seeing some cases of beriberi— a serious neurological ailment caused by a deficiency of the B vitamin, thiamin. We've also seen copper deficiency and zinc deficiency. We can't tell in advance which of the nutrients surgery patients will be at risk of becoming deficient in. It appears that different nutrients are problems in different

(continued)

Shelley Kirk, PhD, RD, LD

Assistant Professor of Clinical Pediatrics, College of Medicine, University of Cincinnati

Shelley Kirk, PhD, RD, LD, has worked as a clinical dietitian in the field of pediatric obesity for the past 22 years. For the past eight years, she has served as center director for Health Works!, a family-based, behavioral weight program for overweight and obese youth at Cincinnati Children's Hospital Medical Center. She also has served for the past four years as the lead dietitian for the Comprehensive Weight Management Program, the bariatric surgery program for severely obese adolescents, at Cincinnati Children's Hospital.

Q: Who is the typical patient for gastric bypass surgery and what qualifications must he or she meet?

A: There are very specific criteria for extremely obese adolescents who would be considered. The guidelines were published in the journal *Pediatrics* in 2004. Adolescents being considered for bariatric surgery should have failed 6 months of organized attempts at weight management; have attained or nearly attained physiologic maturity; be very severely obese (with a BMI greater than 40) with serious obesity-related health problems, or have a BMI of greater than 50 with less severe health problems; demonstrate commitment to comprehensive medical and psychologic evaluations both before and after surgery; agree to avoid pregnancy for at least 1 year after the surgery; be capable of and willing to adhere to nutritional guidelines after the surgery; provide informed consent to surgical treatment; demonstrate decisional capacity; have a supportive family environment. We screen patients very closely to see that they meet those guidelines. For example, we have them start a nutrition and exercise program before surgery with similar behavioral tools to those they would use after surgery, and watch the results. These kids have significant disease and have failed with more conservative approaches.

Q: What are the benefits of the surgery?

A: The benefits are clear. There is considerable improvement of weight-related medical conditions. If someone has a

(continued)

Weighing the Pros and Cons of Gastric Bypass Surgery, continued

Joanne Ikeda, MA, RD, continued

people. And taking extra supplements isn't necessarily the answer. If the surgery leaves you unable to absorb the nutrient, you're not going to get the nutrient from food or from a vitamin pill. You're probably looking at having to get supplement injections.

A substantial number of patients have to have the surgery redone. Once you have the surgery, you'll never be able to eat "normally" again. The stomach size and GI tract size is so reduced that you'll be very dependent on eating small amounts of food at a time. There have also been deaths associated with gastric bypass surgery. It's a major surgery.

Q: Do people typically attain their desired weight after the surgery? Why or why not?

A: Only about half of all patients achieve a healthy body mass index. The other half lose weight but still have BMIs of over 30. Some patients start to regain the weight. Some surgeons have said this may occur because patients who nibble on food throughout the day restretch the stomach pouch and regain some of the weight. But we're still not entirely sure why this happens. This procedure is still fairly new. A couple of years ago it became very apparent that there were no standard recommendations for dietary intake after bariatric surgery. Now a group of registered dieticians who work closely with surgery patients is putting a list of recommendations together.

Q: Are there special considerations for younger patients considering the surgery, and if so, what are they?

A: Assuming that this surgery is easy or safer for younger people is a very naïve view. We really have no data on the long-term consequences of making these major alterations to the digestive tract. There have been a few studies that have followed patients in Scandinavia over about a ten-year period, and they appeared to be doing OK. But that's a very limited set of results. And many of these patients had experienced complications along the way—it wasn't as if they'd had a smooth ride.

Surgeons say that bariatric patients are patients for life because there are so many complications and problems down the road. What's going to happen after 20 or 25 or 30 years to a younger person? You're subjecting yourself to many unknowns.

If your mobility isn't impaired and you're still able to be physically active, you have many choices besides surgery. There are a number of people who we'd classify as obese but who are metabolically healthy. Those individuals have

(continued)

Shelley Kirk, PhD, RD, LD, continued

condition such as hypertension, or diabetes, or obstructive sleep apnea, there is usually either complete resolution or improvement. For most patients, there is considerable weight loss. In a study of adolescent patients, one group reported a long-term loss of 63 to 66 percent of excess weight.

Q: What are the risks?

A: About 15 percent of surgery patients do regain the weight. That can be due to lack of adherence to the guidelines we put out for eating behaviors, food choices, and physical activity. In some cases, there is enlargement of the stomach opening that allows more food to travel through more easily. The frequency of eating is also a factor. If you can't eat large volumes, but you're eating 10 to 12 times a day, this "grazing" pattern can lead to weight regain. Patients also are at risk for vitamin and mineral deficiencies, especially if they are not compliant with the vitamin and mineral regimen they have to follow for the rest of their lives. Postsurgical diets really focus on protein, but if a patient has trouble getting enough, significant hair loss results. They're also at risk for intestinal obstructions, which require additional surgery for some people. And finally, you are limited not only in the volume of food you can eat, but in the types of food. Patients need to be especially careful about foods that are high in sugar or fat. These can cause problems like vomiting and diarrhea.

Q: Do people typically attain their desired weight after the surgery? Why or why not?

A: There is no question there is a health benefit. Most patients do become healthier. But whether they reach their ideal weight—whether they can pose for some magazine—is a different question. How do you determine success? With surgery, there is this idea you'll achieve this perfect body weight. But even after losing 60 or 70 percent of excess weight, patients are still overweight or obese. They have lost so much, but some choose not to focus on that success. Instead, they focus on what they haven't achieved. Once these kids plateau, we should really talk about what they've achieved, really cheer them on, and not focus so much on what is a cosmetic concern.

There is also an issue of excess skin. If you're a young person at 400 or 500 pounds, and you lose 200 or 300 pounds, there's still that extra skin. It doesn't go away. Removing it requires more surgery. The procedure is usually considered cosmetic, so it's not covered by insurance. The excess skin can be quite disfiguring, and it can also affect their overall satisfaction with the surgery.

(continued)

Weighing the Pros and Cons of Gastric Bypass Surgery, continued

Joanne Ikeda, MA, RD, continued

a very hard time accepting that they just ended up at the larger end of the human spectrum when it comes to body shape. If you have high blood pressure, or if you already have type 2 diabetes or a whole host of health problems, then concern is justified. But if you don't have any of those problems, why would you subject yourself to the risk of surgery?

Shelley Kirk, PhD, RD, LD, continued

Q: Are there special considerations for younger patients considering the surgery, and if so, what are they?

A: You have to look carefully at physical and psychological maturity. They really have to understand the surgery. They have to understand what changes they have to make to their eating habits, and how does that fit into the rest of their lives. They're not going to be able to eat the same foods at the same volume. They really have to understand how this is going to affect their lives. And is the family environment supportive? This is not an eating plan someone else can follow. At the beginning, the eating plan is 500 to 600 calories a day. The family can help by having acceptable food and drink in the house and adjusting to new eating patterns. Additionally, there are important psychological issues. These kids may have been overweight so long that they haven't gone through some of the same developmental stages as other adolescents. If eating has been a source of comfort, and they can't do that any more, what do they do now? How do they manage stress? Those are important areas where they need to make a change.

NUTRITION IN THE REAL WORLD

Be a Nutrition Sleuth

Which Snacks Are the Highest in Calories?

Do you know how to avoid high-calorie snacks when you need a quick bite to eat? Go to www.aw-bc.com/blake to learn about a variety of satisfying snacks that are kind to your waist.

NUTRITION IN THE REAL WORLD

Get Real!

How to Order Healthy Food at a Restaurant

Visit the Nutrition and You Virtual Restaurant Menu at www .aw-bc.com/blake and learn how to order a complete healthy meal, from appetizer to dessert. No tipping necessary!

The Top Ten Points to Remember

1. A healthy body weight is considered a body weight that doesn't increase the risk of developing any weight-related health problems. Being very underweight increases the risk of nutritional deficiencies and related health problems. Being overweight increases the risk of chronic diseases such as heart disease, cancer, and type 2 diabetes.

2. To assess if you are at a healthy weight, you can measure your BMI, which is your weight in relationship to your height. A BMI of 18.5 to 24.9 is considered healthy. If your BMI is 25 or up to 29.9, you are considered overweight. A BMI of 30 or higher is considered obese. As your BMI increases above 25, so does your risk of dying from many chronic diseases. Some individuals, such as athletes, may have a high BMI but their weight doesn't put them at a health risk because they are not overfat. In contrast, some individuals who have unintentionally lost weight may have a healthy BMI but be at nutrition risk. Excess weight around the middle, measured by your waist circumference, could put you at a higher health risk, regardless of your BMI.

3. When your energy intake equals your energy expenditure, you are in energy balance. When you consume more energy (calories) than you expend, you are in positive energy balance and weight gain occurs. When your calories fall short of your needs and/or you expend more energy, you are in negative energy balance and lose weight. Your basal metabolism rate (BMR), the thermic effect of food (TEF), and your physical activities all factor into your daily energy needs. Your BMR is influenced mainly by your lean body mass but also by your age, gender, body size, genes, ethnicity, emotional and physical stress, thyroid hormone, nutritional state, and environmental temperature. Your caffeine intake and use of nicotine can also affect your BMR.

4. Appetite is your psychological desire for food and is affected by hunger, satiety, and satiation, as well as your emotions and your environment. Hunger prompts you to eat, and it will subside as the feeling of satiation sets in after you start eating. Satiety is the feeling you experience when you have had enough to eat and determines the length of time between meals or snacks. Physiological mechanisms such as hormones, sensory signals, and a distended stomach, as well as the size of the meal and the nutrients in your foods, all impact your appetite. Genetics and your environment also play a role in your appetite and weight. If your parents were overweight, you are at a higher risk of developing obesity. An environment that enables easy access to a variety of large portions of foods, and encourages you to be sedentary, will also promote obesity.

5. Losing 10 percent of your body weight over a six-month period is considered a reasonable rate of weight loss. Losing weight rapidly can cause a person to fall short of meeting nutrient needs. Many fad diets promise quick results but can be unhealthy for the long term.

6. When it comes to losing weight, calories count. Eating more low-energy-density, high-volume foods, such as vegetables and fruit, can help you lose weight because you will feel full for fewer calories. Fiber also promotes satiation. Because protein has the most dramatic effect on satiety, eating high-protein lean meats, chicken, and fish at meals can help reduce hunger between meals. Because fat slows the movement of food out of the stomach into the intestines, it can also prolong satiety.

7. Routine physical activity can add to the daily energy deficit needed for weight loss. To aid in weight loss, overweight individuals should partake in 60 minutes of moderate-intensity exercise daily and continue at least this amount of activity daily to maintain the weight loss.

8. Changing the eating behaviors that contribute to weight gain or impede weight loss is necessary for long-term weight-loss success. Self-monitoring of these behaviors by keeping a food record, controlling environmental cues that trigger eating when not hungry, and learning how to better manage stress are all behavior modification techniques that can be used by individuals who eat "out of habit" and in response to their environment.

9. Disordered eating describes a variety of abnormal eating patterns, such as restrictive eating, binge eating, vomiting after eating, and abusing laxatives or diet pills. Eating disorders are diagnosed by meeting specific criteria that include disordered eating behaviors. Anorexia nervosa is characterized by self-starvation and excessive weight loss. Bulimia nervosa involves repeated cycles of binge eating and purging. Binge eating disorders are characterized by binge eating without

purging. Night eating syndrome is described as excessive calorie intake in the evening and waking up during the night to eat.

10. Numerous health consequences can occur with eating disorders, such as hair loss, digestive problems, electrolyte imbalances, changes in heart rate and blood pressure, dehydration, and nutrient deficiencies. The most effective treatment for eating disorders involves a multidisciplinary team approach including psychological, nutrition, and medical professionals.

Test Your Knowledge

1. Being overweight can increase your risk of
   a. heart disease.
   b. osteoarthritis.
   c. gallbladder disease.
   d. all of the above.
2. Kyle has a BMI of 27. He is considered
   a. underweight.
   b. overweight.
   c. at a healthy weight.
   d. obese.
3. Central obesity refers to
   a. the accumulation of excess fat in your hips and thighs.
   b. the accumulation of excess fat in your stomach area.
   c. the accumulation of excess fat in your arms and legs.
   d. none of these.
4. Your basal metabolism rate (BMR) refers to
   a. the amount of energy you expend during physical activity.
   b. the amount of energy you expend digesting your food.
   c. the amount of energy (calories) that you consume daily.
   d. the amount of energy expended to meet your basic physiological needs that enables your organs and cells to function.
5. You just ate a large plate of pasta and tomato sauce, so your stomach is rather full and quite distended. Which hormone is released because of the distention of your stomach?
   a. cholecystokinin
   b. insulin
   c. thyroid hormone
   d. none of the above
6. Which of the following can increase your risk of becoming overweight?
   a. having a mother who is overweight
   b. having a father who is obese
   c. having a sedentary lifestyle

   d. living on your own away from home
   e. a, b, and c only
7. Which are examples of low-energy-density, high-volume foods that can aid in weight loss?
   a. raw vegetables and salsa
   b. tomato soup
   c. olive oil
   d. fruit salad
   e. a, b, and d only
8. Mary Ellen was obese and lost 30 pounds during the last year by eating a well-balanced, calorie-reduced diet and being physically active daily. To maintain her weight loss, she should continue to eat a healthy diet, monitor her eating behaviors, and
   a. accumulate 30 minutes of physical activity daily.
   b. accumulate 45 minutes of physical activity daily.
   c. accumulate 60 to 90 minutes of physical activity daily.
   d. do none of the above.
9. A form of purging in bulimia nervosa includes
   a. self-induced vomiting.
   b. fasting.
   c. exercise.
   d. all of the above.
10. Lanugo, or downy hair growth, is common in what type of eating disorder?
    a. anorexia nervosa
    b. bulimia nervosa
    c. binge eating disorder
    d. night eating syndrome

Answers

1. (d) Being overweight increases your risk of all these diseases and conditions as well as type 2 diabetes, some cancers, and sleep apnea.
2. (b) Because Kyle's BMI falls between 25 and 29.9, he is considered overweight. If his BMI was under 18.5, he would be underweight, whereas a BMI of 18.5 to 24.9 would put him in the healthy weight category. A BMI of 30 and higher is considered obese.
3. (b) Central obesity refers to the accumulation of excess fat in the stomach area and can be determined by measuring a person's waist circumference. Central obesity increases the risk of heart disease, diabetes, and hypertension.
4. (d) Your BMR refers to the bare minimum amount of energy (calories) needed to keep your blood circulating and lungs breathing so that you can stay alive. The amount of energy or calories that you expend during physical activity

is not factored into your BMR. The energy that you expend digesting, absorbing, and processing food is called the thermic effect of food (TEF) and is also not part of your BMR. The amount of energy or calories that you consume daily doesn't factor into your BMR.

5. (a) A distended stomach causes the release of cholecysto-kinin, which is associated with the feeling of satiation and the ending of eating. Insulin will be released once this carbohydrate-heavy meal is digested and absorbed into the blood. Thyroid hormone affects your BMR and is not associated with your stomach being distended.

6. (e) Having parents who are overweight and/or obese and not engaging in regular physical activity can all increase your risk of becoming overweight. Moving out of your home and living on your own won't necessarily cause you to gain weight unless you consume more calories than you need daily.

7. (e) Vegetables, including salsa and vegetable soups, and fruit are all low-energy-density, high-volume foods. These foods will increase satiation, contain few calories per bite, and can displace more energy-dense foods in the diet, all of which can help promote weight loss. Even though olive oil is a good source of heart-healthy unsaturated fat, it is very energy dense.

8. (c) If Mary Ellen would like to keep the weight off, she should try to accumulate 60 to 90 minutes of physical activity daily.

9. (d) Self-induced vomiting, fasting, and exercise are all forms of purging, as they assist in "getting rid" of food.

10. (a) Lanugo grows typically on the face and arms of people with anorexia nervosa as a way of regulating body temperature.

Web Support

- For more on overweight and obesity, visit the Centers For Disease Control and Prevention at www.cdc.gov/nccdphp/dnpa/obesity/index.htm
- For more information on weight control and physical activity, visit the Weight-control Information Network (WIN) at http://win.niddk.nih.gov/index.htm
- For more weight-loss shopping tips, recipes, and menu makeovers, visit the USDA's Nutrition and Weight Management website at www.nutrition.gov
- For more on eating disorders, visit the National Eating Disorder Association at www.nationaleatingdisorders.org

11

Nutrition and Fitness

1. Most people in the United States are physically **fit. T/F**

2. As little as 30 minutes of physical **activity** per day is enough to provide health benefits. **T/F**

3. Carbohydrate, fat, and protein provide **energy** during exercise. **T/F**

4. The better trained you are, the better your **endurance. T/F**

5. Athletes should eat immediately after training. **T/F**

6. Vitamin and mineral **supplements** always improve athletic performance. **T/F**

7. Many athletes are at risk for **iron** deficiency. **T/F**

8. Everyone who **exercises** should consume sports drinks. **T/F**

9. You can never drink too much **water. T/F**

10. The National Collegiate Athletic Association (NCAA) classifies **caffeine** as a banned substance when consumed in high amounts. **T/F**

reg Harper, a college junior, is the starting point guard for the men's basketball team. Greg starts his day very early in the morning with one hour of basketball practice before heading off to his 9 a.m. class. Because he likes to get as much sleep as possible, Greg usually doesn't eat breakfast before practice, but sometimes finds an energy bar in his book bag to eat on his way to class. He finishes his last class at 2 p.m. and then goes to practice again for another 2 to 3 hours. Greg has difficulty finding time in his busy schedule to eat anything, much less healthy foods, so he usually grabs a fast-food burger and fries before the afternoon practice. Despite the fact that he's in great shape, and considers himself to be healthy, Greg is often tired and cranky by the time he gets home in the evening.

What Greg doesn't realize is that his poor eating habits, including irregular meals and the types of foods that he is eating, are compromising his athletic performance. Do you think your eating habits have a significant impact on your level of fitness? We will explore this question, as well as other aspects of nutrition and how it relates to physical fitness and athletic performance, in this chapter.

Answers

1. False. Less than half of all Americans met recommendations for physical activity. Check out the potential drawbacks of this on page 385.
2. True. You don't have to be an Olympian to enjoy the health benefits of exercise. With just 30 minutes each day, you can burn more calories and lower your risk of certain diseases. Turn to page 388 for more information.
3. True. The body does use carbohydrate, fat, and protein for energy during exercise, but the amount that is used partly depends on the intensity of the exercise. Turn to page 390 to learn about energy sources during exercise.
4. True. Muscles adapt to training by storing more glycogen and using more body fat as fuel, which can increase endurance. Turn to page 393 to learn more.
5. True. Consumption of nutrients immediately after stopping exercise will improve recovery. Find out more on page 398.
6. False. Taking vitamin and/or mineral supplements will only improve performance if you're deficient in vitamins or minerals in the first place. Turn to page 399 to learn more about the roles of vitamins and minerals during exercise.
7. True. Female and vegetarian athletes are at higher risk for iron deficiency. Turn to page 401 to find out why this is the case.
8. False. Sports drinks are generally beneficial only when you exercise for longer than one hour. Find out more about fluid needs during exercise on page 404.
9. False. Drinking too much water can dilute your blood and alter the delicate fluid and electrolyte balance of your body. Turn to page 405 to learn more about proper hydration during exercise.
10. True. You may be surprised to learn that just a few cups of coffee can supply excessive amounts of caffeine. To learn more, turn to page 407.

What Is Fitness and Why Is It Important?

Physical fitness is simply defined as good health or physical condition, primarily as the result of exercise and proper nutrition. Some people think of exercise and physical activity as the same thing, but this isn't technically the case. **Physical activity** refers to body movement that results in expending calories. Activities such as gardening, walking the dog, and playing with children can all be regarded as physical activity. **Exercise** is defined as formalized training or structured activity, like step aerobics, running, or weight lifting. For the purpose of this chapter, the terms exercise and physical activity are used interchangeably.

Being physically active and consuming a healthy diet are the two most important components of overall health and fitness. You will not achieve optimal fitness if you ignore either of these areas.

Fitness Has Five Basic Components

The five basic components of fitness include cardiorespiratory endurance, muscular strength, muscular endurance, flexibility, and body composition. Most strength training programs blend muscular strength and muscular endurance, which is generally referred to as muscular fitness. To be physically fit, one must consider all five variables.

Cardiorespiratory endurance is the ability to sustain cardiorespiratory exercise, such as running and biking, for an extended length of time. This requires that the body's cardiovascular and respiratory systems provide enough oxygen and energy to the working muscles. Someone who can run a leisurely mile without being too out of breath to talk has good cardiorespiratory endurance. Someone who is out of breath after climbing one flight of stairs, on the other hand, does not.

Muscle strength is the ability to produce force for a brief period of time, while **muscle endurance** is the ability to exert force over a long period of time without fatigue. Increasing muscle strength and muscle endurance is best achieved with **weight training.** You probably associate muscle strength with bodybuilders or weight lifters, and it's true that these people train to be particularly strong. However, other athletes, such as cheerleaders and ballet dancers, also work hard to strengthen their muscles. Consider the strength it takes to lift another person above your head. If you could hold the person up for several minutes or an hour, that would show exceptional muscle endurance.

Flexibility is the range of motion around a joint and is improved with stretching. Athletic performance and joint and muscular function are all enhanced with improved flexibility, which also reduces the likelihood of injury. A gymnast exhibits high flexibility when performing stunts and dance routines. In contrast, someone with low flexibility would not be able to bend over and touch his toes from a standing or sitting position.

Finally, **body composition** is the proportion of muscle, fat, water, and other tissues in the body. Together, these make up your total body weight. Your body composition can change without your total body weight changing, due to the fact that muscle takes up less space (per pound) than does body fat. This is why you can lose inches on your body without losing pounds of weight when you increase your lean muscle mass and decrease body fat.

Running is a great way to improve cardiorespiratory fitness.

Fitness Provides Numerous Benefits

We have long heard that eating a balanced diet and exercising regularly helps prevent diseases and maintain health. We also know that any amount of exercise will provide health benefits, and the more you exercise, the more fit you'll be. You have to be cautious however, not to overexercise and increase your risk of injury.

So how does physical activity improve health? In addition to reducing the risk of developing several diseases, being physically fit can improve overall health in other ways, like helping you get restful sleep and reducing stress. Table 11.1 on page 386 lists some of the numerous health benefits that result from being physically active on a regular basis.

Despite knowing the benefits that exercise brings, over half of adults living in the United States do not meet the recommendations for regular physical activity.[1] In an effort to increase physical activity among adults and children in the United States, *Healthy People 2010* lists physical activity as a leading health indicator. Living a sedentary lifestyle raises your risk of developing chronic diseases like type 2 diabetes and cardiovascular disease.

The Take-Home Message Physical fitness is the state of being in good physical condition through proper nutrition and regular physical activity. The five components of physical fitness are cardiorespiratory endurance, muscular strength, muscular endurance, flexibility, and body composition. To achieve optimal fitness, all five components must be considered. The numerous health benefits of physical activity include reduced risk of several chronic diseases and better overall physical fitness.

What Does a Fitness Program Look Like?

Sarah is a college freshman and has always enjoyed being active. She wants to do well in her first year at college, so she spends most of her time studying and going to class. As a result, she has put aside exercise to make time for her school work, which has left

physical fitness The ability to perform physical activities requiring cardiorespiratory endurance, muscle endurance, and strength and/or flexibility; physical fitness is acquired through physical activity and adequate nutrition.

physical activity Voluntary movement that results in energy expenditure (burning calories).

exercise Any type of structured or planned physical activity.

cardiorespiratory endurance The body's ability to sustain prolonged exercise.

muscle strength The greatest amount of force exerted by the muscle at one time.

muscle endurance The ability of the muscle to produce prolonged effort.

weight training Exercising with weights to build, strengthen, and tone muscle to improve or maintain overall fitness; also called resistance training.

flexibility The joints' ability to move freely through a full and normal range of motion.

body composition The relative proportion of muscle, fat, water, and other tissues in the body.

Table 11.1 The Benefits of Physical Fitness

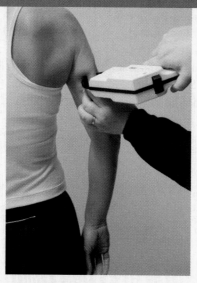

Reduced Risk of Cardiovascular Disease ▲

How It Works: Research has shown that moderate physical activity lowers blood pressure.[1] In addition, exercise is positively associated with high-density lipoprotein cholesterol (HDL).[2]

Improved Body Composition ▲

How It Works: Individuals with moderate cardiorespiratory fitness have less total fat and abdominal fat compared with people with low cardiorespiratory fitness.[3]

Reduced Risk of Type 2 Diabetes ▲

How It Works: Exercise helps control blood glucose levels by increasing insulin sensitivity.[4] This not only reduces risk for type 2 diabetes, but also improves blood glucose control for those who have been diagnosed with type 2 diabetes.

Improved Bone Health ▲

How It Works: Bone density has been shown to improve with weight-bearing exercise and resistance training, thereby reducing the risk for osteoporosis.[5]

Improved Immune System ▲

How It Works: Regular exercise can enhance the immune system, which may result in fewer colds and other infectious diseases.[6]

Improved Sleep ▲

How It Works: People who engage in regular exercise often have better quality of sleep. This is especially true for older adults.[7]

her feeling out of shape. She has recently noticed an increase in her weight and realizes the importance of physical activity to help her maintain a healthy weight and physical fitness. She seeks out a trainer in her school's fitness center and asks for exercise advice. The trainer recommends a fitness program that incorporates cardiorespiratory exercise, weight training, and stretching.

Cardiorespiratory Exercise Can Improve Cardiorespiratory Endurance and Body Composition

Cardiorespiratory exercise often involves continuous activities that use large muscle groups, such as high-impact aerobics, stair climbing, and brisk walking. This type of exercise is predominantly **aerobic** because it uses oxygen. During cardiorespiratory exercise, your heart beats faster and more oxygen-carrying blood is delivered to your tissues. How does this work? As you begin to exercise, your body requires more oxygen to break down nutrients for energy, so it increases blood flow (volume) to the working muscles. It accomplishes this by increasing your heart rate and **stroke volume.** Your body also redistributes blood from your internal organs to maximize the volume of blood that is delivered to the muscles during exercise.

> Between birth and old age, you will walk about 70,000 miles. Walking is one of the best activities you can do to improve cardiovascular health and maintain a healthy weight. Plus, it's free!

Cardiorespiratory exercise provides the most benefits to your cardiovascular system (heart, blood, and blood vessels), which improves your cardiorespiratory endurance. In addition, it reduces stress, and lowers your risk of heart disease by maintaining normal cholesterol levels, heart rate, and blood pressure. Cardiorespiratory exercise also helps you maintain a healthy weight and improve your body composition by reducing body fat.

Weight Training Can Improve Muscle Strength, Muscle Endurance, and Body Composition

Weight training has long been associated with gaining muscle mass, strength, and endurance. Maintaining adequate muscle mass and strength is important for everyone, and just because you weight train does not mean that you will develop large, bulky muscles. Many females, as well as males, use weight training to tone and define their muscles to improve their physical appearance and body composition.

In order to increase muscle strength, you should perform a low number of repetitions using heavy weights. If you want to increase muscle endurance, you should perform a high number of repetitions using lighter weights. However, heavier weights can also be used to improve muscle endurance by allowing short rest intervals between repetition sets.

Rest periods between sets of an exercise and between workouts are important so that you do not overwork your muscles and increase your risk of muscle strains or other injury. If you don't allow time for your muscles to rest, your muscles may break down and not recover, leading to a loss of muscle mass. The amount of rest depends on your fitness goals and level of conditioning. If increasing strength is your goal, you should allow long rest periods of 2 to 3 minutes between sets. If increasing muscle endurance is your goal, shorter rest periods of 30 seconds or less are recommended.

Weight training improves muscle strength and endurance.

aerobic With oxygen.

stroke volume The amount of blood pumped by the heart with each heart beat.

The general guideline for rest periods between workouts is two days, or a total of 48 hours, between workouts that use the same muscle groups. However, strength training can be done daily as long as different muscles are used on consecutive days.

Stretching Can Improve Flexibility

When you think about your degree of flexibility, you are likely referring to how far you can stretch in a particular way without feeling pain or discomfort. Stretching is the most common exercise used to improve your flexibility, or range of motion. Improving flexibility can reduce muscle soreness and your risk of injury, as well as improve balance, posture, and circulation of blood and nutrients throughout your body.

There are several types of stretching. The most common form among athletes and in general is static stretching, which consists of relaxing a muscle, then extending it to a point of mild discomfort for about 10 to 30 seconds, and then relaxing it again. You can use static stretching exercises to stretch one muscle at a time, or you can stretch more than one muscle or muscle group at the same time. If you are performing these stretches for the first time, you'll need to consult a qualified trainer, coach, or physician on proper techniques to reduce your risk of injury.

Other less common forms of stretching are types that involve a partner or machine to create the force needed to stretch the muscle, and controlled stretches that use momentum to create the force needed to extend the muscle.

Improving your flexibility can help you reduce muscle soreness and lower your risk of injury.

The FITT Principle Can Help You Design a Fitness Program

Do you feel like you don't have a 30-minute block of time to exercise? The good news is that you don't have to do an activity for 30 consecutive minutes to get health benefits. You can break this time up into three 10-minute bouts of activity and still receive the same benefits as if you were to do it all at one time.

Now that you know the components needed for fitness, you may be wondering how to create a program that ensures that you become physically fit. One easy way to do this is to follow the FITT principle. FITT is an acronym for frequency, intensity, time, and type. Let's take a closer look at each of these components of a well-rounded fitness program.

Frequency is how often you do the activity, such as the number of times per week. **Intensity** refers to the degree of difficulty at which you perform the activity. Common terms used to describe intensity are low, moderate, and vigorous (high). One measure of intensity for cardiorespiratory exercise is **rate of perceived exertion (RPE),** in which the person performing the activity self-assesses the level of intensity (see Table 11.2). For weight training, intensity is referred to as **repetitions of maximum (RM).** For example, 1 RM is the maximum amount of weight that can be lifted at one time. Time, or **duration,** is how long you performed the activity, such as a 30-minute run. And lastly, type means the specific activity that you are doing.

The frequency, intensity, time (duration), and type of exercise that is right for you depend partly on what goal you are trying to achieve. For moderate health benefits, the *Dietary Guidelines for Americans 2005* suggests at least 30 minutes of moderate-intensity physical activity, such as brisk walking or dancing, most days of the week. Engaging in more vigorous-intensity activities, such as jogging or fast-paced swimming, for longer duration will result in even greater health benefits.

To maintain your body weight and prevent gradual weight gain, you should participate in approximately 60 minutes of moderate- to vigorous-intensity activity on most days of the week while not consuming excess calories. To lose weight effectively,

intensity The level of difficulty of an activity.

rate of perceived exertion (RPE) A subjective measure of the intensity level of an activity using a numerical scale.

repetitions of maximum (RM) The maximum amount of weight that can be lifted for a specified number of repetitions.

duration The length of time of performing an activity.

Table 11.2

Rating of Perceived Exertion (RPE)

Scale	Perceived Exertion	Physical Signs
6 7	Very, very light	No perceptible sign
8 9	Very light	No perceptible sign
10 11	Fairly light	Feeling of motion
12 13	Somewhat hard	Warmth on a cool day, slight sweat on warm days
14 15	Hard	Sweating, but can still talk without difficulty
16 17	Very hard	Heavy sweating, difficulty talking
18 19 20	Very, very hard	Feeling of near exhaustion

Source: G. V. Borg, Psychophysical Bases of Perceived Exertion. *Medicine & Science in Sports & Exercise* 14 (1982): 377–381. Used by permission of Lippincott Williams & Wilkins.

you should participate in at least 60 to 90 minutes of daily moderate-intensity physical activity and make calorie adjustments to your diet. You can use the Physical Activity Pyramid to help you become more physically active or improve your current level of fitness (Figure 11.1). People with diabetes, high blood pressure, and other types of heart disease should consult with a health care provider before participating in any exercise program, especially one to be performed at a vigorous intensity.

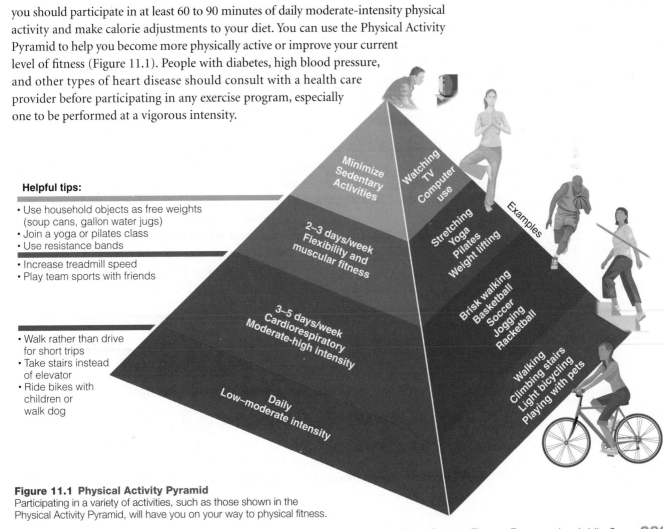

Helpful tips:

- Use household objects as free weights (soup cans, gallon water jugs)
- Join a yoga or pilates class
- Use resistance bands

- Increase treadmill speed
- Play team sports with friends

- Walk rather than drive for short trips
- Take stairs instead of elevator
- Ride bikes with children or walk dog

Minimize Sedentary Activities — Watching TV Computer use

2–3 days/week Flexibility and muscular fitness — Stretching Yoga Pilates Weight lifting

3–5 days/week Cardiorespiratory Moderate-high intensity — Brisk walking Basketball Soccer Jogging Racketball

Daily Low–moderate intensity — Walking Climbing stairs Light bicycling Playing with pets

Examples

Figure 11.1 Physical Activity Pyramid
Participating in a variety of activities, such as those shown in the Physical Activity Pyramid, will have you on your way to physical fitness.

Table 11.3

Using FITT to Improve fitness

	Cardiorespiratory Fitness	Muscular Fitness	Flexibility
Frequency	3–5 days per week	2–3 days per week	2–3 days per week
Intensity	55–90% of maximum heart rate	8–12 RM	Enough to develop and maintain range of motion
Time	20–60 minutes, continuous or intermittent (minimum of 10-minute bouts)	8–10 different exercises performed in 1–3 sets	At least 4 repetitions for each muscle group; hold static stretch for 10–30 seconds
Type	Brisk walking, jogging, biking, step aerobics	Weight training	Stretching

Source: Adapted from American College of Sports Medicine. Position Stand: The Recommended Quantity and Quality of Exercise for Developing and Maintaining Cardio-respiratory and Muscular Fitness, and Flexibility in Healthy Adults. *Medicine & Science in Sports & Exercise* 30 no. 6 (June 1998). Used by permission of Lippincott Williams & Wilkins.

e-Learn
Small Steps for Big Gains

You have numerous opportunities every day to be physically active. Go to www.smallstep.gov to see how you can incorporate little changes into your daily routine to attain the health benefits of physical activity.

The key to being physically active is to find activities that you enjoy so that you continue to do them on a regular basis. If you don't like jogging, you don't have to do it! Just find other activities that you like. Maybe you enjoy playing basketball, going for a walk, or hiking. It doesn't really matter what the activity is, as long as you take pleasure in what you are doing and do it regularly.

You can use the FITT approach to meet the American College of Sports Medicine's guidelines for cardiorespiratory endurance, muscular fitness, and flexibility for healthy adults, which are summarized in Table 11.3. For example, on your FITT program, you may want to jog three days a week for 30 minutes on Tuesday, Thursday, and Friday to attain your cardiorespiratory fitness. On Monday and Wednesday, you may want to lift weights for muscular fitness and make sure that you stretch beforehand to improve your flexibility.

The Take-Home Message Cardiorespiratory exercise improves cardio-respiratory endurance and body composition. Weight training can improve muscle strength and endurance as well as body composition. Flexibility can be enhanced by stretching. An effective training program can be designed using the FITT principle, which stands for frequency, intensity, time, and type of activity. Most people should aim for 30 minutes of moderate activity most days of the week for health, while greater amounts of exercise are needed for weight management and to improve physical fitness.

How Are Carbohydrate, Fat, and Protein Used during Exercise?

In addition to regular physical activity, you need the right foods and fluids in order to be physically fit. When you eat and drink, you meet your nutrient needs for physical activity in two ways. You supply the energy, particularly from carbohydrate and fat, that your body needs for the activity. And you provide the nutrients, particularly carbohydrate and protein, that will help you recover properly so that you can repeat the activity.

We mentioned earlier in the chapter that much energy production during cardiorespiratory exercise is aerobic because it uses oxygen. On the flip side, energy production can also be **anaerobic,** or without oxygen. During the first few minutes of physical activity the body relies heavily on anaerobic production of energy from two high-energy molecules in the cell: **adenosine triphosphate (ATP)** and **creatine phosphate.** The amount of ATP (energy) in cells is limited, and can support only a few seconds of intense exercise.

ATP is composed of a nucleoside, called adenosine, and a "tail" of three phosphates. ATP is converted into energy by removing one phosphate, leaving adenosine diphosphate (ADP) (see Figure 11.2). ADP gets recycled to ATP in the cell when a phosphate is donated from creatine phosphate. Creatine phosphate has a dual role in energy production: Direct energy production occurs by removal of the phosphate group from the creatine phosphate molecule, and indirect energy production occurs from donation of the phosphate to ADP, thereby regenerating ATP.

The amount of creatine that can be stored in the muscles is very limited and becomes depleted after about 10 seconds of maximum-intensity activity. Your body produces creatine with the help of the liver and kidneys and stores it in skeletal muscle and other tissues. Your body also obtains a small amount of creatine from foods that you eat, including meat and fish.

As you continue exercising beyond a few minutes, you will breathe more heavily and take in an increased amount of oxygen. At this point your body begins to rely more on aerobic energy production because the amount of ATP needed to support your activity cannot be generated fast enough by anaerobic energy production to meet the energy demands. In order to supply your body with the energy it needs, you begin to metabolize carbohydrate (glucose) and fat (fatty acids) to produce glucose in a manner that requires oxygen. The energy generated is then later converted to ATP.

Your body relies on carbohydrate, fat, and protein for energy during exercise, but the type and amount of energy that is used depends highly on the intensity and duration of the exercise, your nutritional status, and your level of physical fitness. Carbohydrate and fat contribute most of the energy needed for activity, while protein is best used to promote muscle growth and recovery. The following section discusses the roles of carbohydrate, fat, and protein during exercise.

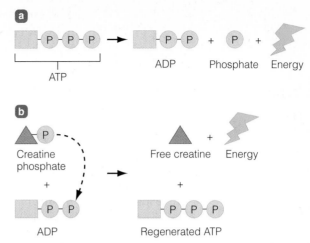

Figure 11.2 Energy Metabolism
During anaerobic metabolism, energy is derived from the breakdown of ATP and creatine phosphate.

Carbohydrate Is the Primary Energy Source during High-Intensity Exercise

During exercise, you obtain energy from carbohydrate through blood glucose and stored glycogen in the muscles and the liver. In an average-sized man, about 525 grams of glycogen are stored in the muscle and 25 grams of glucose in the blood. In addition, the liver stores about 100 grams of glycogen, which is also broken down into glucose and released into the blood to be used by the body. More discussion of this follows.

anaerobic Without oxygen.

adenosine triphosphate (ATP) A compound that is broken down to produce energy for working muscles and other tissues.

creatine phosphate A compound stored in the muscles that is broken down to replenish ATP stores.

The total amount of energy stored as carbohydrate in the body is about 2,600 calories, of which 2,000 calories can be used. This is enough energy to perform about 2 hours of moderate exercise, and then glycogen stores are almost completely depleted.

Glycogen stores are continuously being depleted and replenished. If you exercise often, eating carbohydrate-rich foods on a regular basis is important so that you provide your muscles with adequate glycogen. When glycogen stores are inadequate, the muscles no longer have the energy to support the activity, which has been shown to reduce athletic performance and promote fatigue.[2] Does this mean that if you eat a large amount of carbohydrates every day you will have more energy? Not exactly. The glycogen storage capacity of both the muscles and the liver is limited. Once your muscles and liver have stored all of the glycogen possible, any excess glucose will be stored in the form of body fat.

> One of the first athletic shoe ideas came from waffles. The cofounder of the company Nike poured rubber into his waffle iron to create ridges for the bottom of shoes that would increase traction and improve athletic performance, especially among runners.

Research has shown that the amount of glycogen that the muscles can hold can be affected by training.[3] When muscles are well trained, they have the ability to store 20 to 50 percent more glycogen than untrained muscles. More stored glycogen means more fuel for working muscles to use, which means you can exercise for a longer period of time and increase your endurance. Just eating a high-carbohydrate meal before competition will not help you perform at your best; you need to train your muscles *and* eat a high-carbohydrate diet regularly to improve endurance.

Though glucose derived from stored muscle glycogen is the preferred carbohydrate source for energy during exercise, liver glycogen stores are just as important to your body during activity. Glycogen provided by the liver is converted into glucose and delivered to the bloodstream in order to maintain normal blood glucose levels, both during times of activity and while you are at rest.

Whereas muscle glycogen provides energy for the muscles during activity, blood glucose is the energy source for your brain. If you are not supplying your brain with the energy it needs, you may feel a lack of coordination or lack of concentration—two things you especially *don't* want to experience during exercise or a sport competition.

When glucose is broken down at a very high rate, the muscles produce a by-product called **lactic acid.** Muscles effectively use lactic acid as an energy source when it is produced at a low rate. For example, during low-intensity exercise, the body is able to oxidize the lactic acid that is produced by the muscle for energy and therefore lactic acid does not accumulate in the working muscle tissue.

As exercise intensity increases, your body relies more heavily on breaking down glucose as an energy source (and therefore more lactic acid is formed) and the body shuttles the excess lactic acid to other tissues, such as the brain, heart, and liver. The good news is that the ability of your muscles to effectively use and shuttle lactic acid to other tissues improves with training. For many years, lactic acid "buildup" in muscles was thought to be a cause of muscle fatigue, but now scientists are finding that lactic acid can also be an important fuel during exercise.[4]

Intensity Affects How Much Glucose and Glycogen You Use

Your muscles will use carbohydrates for energy no matter how intense the exercise. However, the *amount* of carbohydrate used is affected by intensity, as well as your level of fitness, initial muscle glycogen stores, and whether you're consuming carbohydrates during exercise. Research shows that as the intensity of exercise increases, so does the use of glucose and glycogen for energy.[5] At very high intensities, most of the

lactic acid A by-product of rapid glucose metabolism.

energy is supplied by carbohydrates in the form of muscle glycogen. Although carbohydrates are not the main energy source during exercise of low to moderate intensity, they still provide some energy for the working muscles.

How Much Carbohydrate Do I Need for Exercise?

The amount of carbohydrate needed per day to fuel activity depends greatly on the duration of the activity. The best types of carbohydrates to eat during and/or after exercise are carbohydrates-rich foods such as baked potatoes, bagels, or corn flakes that are absorbed and enter the bloodstream quickly and therefore can be used immediately for energy (glucose) or to replenish glycogen stores. Carbohydrate-rich foods such as rice, oatmeal, pasta, and corn are ideal a couple of hours before exercise as their carbohydrate content enters the bloodstream much more slowly and provide a sustained source of energy.

You will learn more about timing your nutrient intake in a later section of this chapter. Table 11.4 shows the amount of carbohydrate needed for different durations of physical activity.[6] Carbohydrate loading is one training strategy that athletes use to build up muscle glycogen stores before a competition (see the feature box "Carbohydrate Loading" on the next page).

Table 11.4	
Carbohydrate Needs for Activity	
Duration of Activity (per Day)	**Grams Carbohydrate/Kg Body Weight (per Day)**
1 hour	6–7
2 hours	8
3 hours	10
4 hours or more	12–13

Source: C. Rosenbloom, ed. *Sports Nutrition: A Guide for the Professional Working with Active People.* 3rd ed. (Chicago: The American Dietetic Association, 2000), 16. © 2000 American Dietetic Association. Adapted with permission.

Fat Is the Primary Energy Source during Low- to Moderate-Intensity Exercise

Fat supplies nearly all of the energy required during low- to moderate-intensity activity. Even at rest, your body uses fat as its main energy source. Unlike glycogen, fat does not contain water, so the amount of energy stored in the form of body fat is far greater, and more concentrated, than the amount of energy that is stored as glycogen.

Fat is supplied as an energy source in two forms: fatty acids in adipose tissue and fatty acids in muscle tissue (in the form of triglycerides). When the body uses stored fat for energy, it is broken down into fatty acids and then supplied to the muscles via the bloodstream, where it is converted into energy. The process of converting fatty acids into energy is quite slow, which is why fat is the preferred energy source during activities that are of low to moderate intensity. In addition, your body requires more oxygen to convert fat into energy compared with carbohydrate, which creates more stress for the cardiovascular system.

Endurance training increases your body's utilization of fat for energy, which spares glycogen. When you use more fat for energy, you then "save" your glycogen stores for later energy use.

Intensity and Training Affect How Much Fat You Use

The intensity and duration of exercise affects how much fat is used for energy. Oxidation of fat for energy typically occurs after 15 to 20 minutes of aerobic exercise. For low-intensity exercise, your body uses mostly fat from adipose tissue, as well as any free fatty acids in the blood, for energy. During moderate exercise, your body begins to use fatty acids from muscle triglycerides (fat) in addition to the fatty acids from adipose tissue. At high levels of activity, fatty acids cannot be converted into energy fast enough to meet the demand; therefore, fat use decreases and carbohydrates become the preferred energy source.

Your level of training can affect how much fat your body will use for energy. Muscles that are well trained will burn more fat than muscles that are not as well trained. This is thought to be caused by an increase in enzymes that are necessary to burn fat

Carbohydrate Loading

The goal of **carbohydrate loading** before an endurance event is to maximize the storage capacity of muscle glycogen. Increasing the amount of stored muscle glycogen can improve an athlete's endurance performance by giving the energy to fuel activity at an optimal pace for a longer period of time.

Not all athletes or physically active people will have improved performance with carbohydrate loading. The people who are likely to benefit the most from this strategy are those who participate in endurance events or exercise that lasts more than 90 minutes. Examples of endurance events include marathons, triathlons, cross-country skiing, and long-distance cycling and swimming. If you exercise or train for less than 90 minutes, you should follow the standard recommendations for carbohydrate intake for athletes to ensure that you have adequate

carbohydrate loading A diet and training strategy that maximizes glycogen stores in the body before an endurance event.

muscle glycogen stores. Research has also shown that women are less likely than men to have improved performance with carbohydrate loading because women oxidize significantly more fat and less carbohydrate and protein compared with men during endurance exercise.[1]

So how do athletes start carbohydrate loading? When this concept was first recognized by athletes, they began by training very hard for three to four days in addition to eating a low-carbohydrate diet (less than 5 to 10 percent of total calories). This period was called the depletion phase and was thought to be necessary to increase glycogen stores during the next phase, called the loading phase. The loading phase involved three to four days

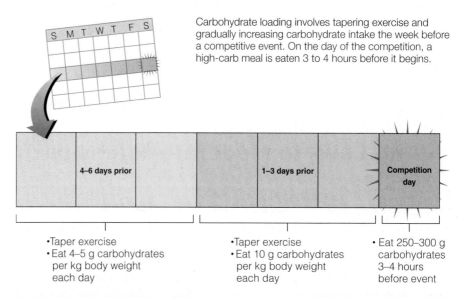

Carbohydrate loading involves tapering exercise and gradually increasing carbohydrate intake the week before a competitive event. On the day of the competition, a high-carb meal is eaten 3 to 4 hours before it begins.

4–6 days prior

- Taper exercise
- Eat 4–5 g carbohydrates per kg body weight each day

1–3 days prior

- Taper exercise
- Eat 10 g carbohydrates per kg body weight each day

Competition day

- Eat 250–300 g carbohydrates 3–4 hours before event

for energy. As a result, the body uses less glycogen for energy and more fat, thereby having the potential to increase endurance. So, if you are trying to lose weight and body fat, should you reduce the intensity of your workout? The feature box "The Truth about the Fat-Burning Zone" on page 396 discusses this interesting issue.

How Much Fat Do I Need for Exercise?

Dietary recommendations for fat intake are generally the same for active people as for the average adult population, with 25 to 30 percent of calories coming from fat.[7] Recall from Chapter 5 that high intakes of saturated and *trans* fats have been linked to high cholesterol levels and heart disease. Physically active people sometimes assume that because they're in shape, they don't have to worry about these diseases. While it is true that physical activity grants some protection against heart disease, athletes and other fit people can also have high cholesterol, heart attacks, and strokes. Everyone, regardless of activity level, should limit saturated fat to no more than 10 percent of total calories, and consume unsaturated fats in foods to meet the body's need for dietary fat.[8]

of minimal or no training while eating a diet high in carbohydrates. This resulted in higher muscle glycogen stores and better endurance performance.

Many people found the depletion phase hard to endure and would often experience irritability, hypoglycemia, and fatigue. In fact, today, many endurance athletes have modified this training strategy to exclude the depletion phase. Research has shown that depleting muscle glycogen stores is not necessary to increase the amount of stored muscle glycogen. However there will be greater increases in muscle glycogen by initially depleting muscle glycogen stores.[2]

To begin a modified carbohydrate loading regimen, you should taper your exercise about seven days prior to the event by doing a little bit less activity each day. This is often the hardest recommendation to follow because many athletes feel that they will be out of shape if they stop training before competition. But tapering your exercise is necessary to increase muscle glycogen; otherwise, you will continue to burn glycogen for fuel rather than storing it to be used for energy during the upcoming event. One study showed that you can decrease your training by 70 percent of your normal training schedule about one week prior to an endurance event without negatively affecting your performance.[3]

In addition to tapering your exercise, you should eat a high-carbohydrate diet that provides about 4 to 5 grams of carbohydrate per kilogram of body weight for the first three to four days. During the last three days of tapering exercise, increase your intake of carbohydrates to 10 grams per kilogram of body weight. Lastly, a meal that is high in carbohydrate (providing about 250 to 300 grams of carbohydrate), moderate in protein, and low in fat should be consumed about 3 to 4 hours prior to the start of the event to further maximize glycogen stores.

With the emphasis on carbohydrates, you do not want to compromise your intake of protein and fat by eating too much carbohydrate. Remember to include at least 0.8 grams of protein per kilogram of body weight (some athletes may require more protein) in your training diet, as well as about 20 to 25 percent of calories coming from fat, preferably unsaturated fats. The following is a sample one-day menu that is high in carbohydrate, adequate in protein, and low in fat.

Breakfast	Lunch	Dinner	Snack
1 cup orange juice	2 slices oatmeal bread	3 cups spaghetti (6 ounces uncooked)	1 cup vanilla yogurt
½ cup Grape-Nuts			6 fig bars
1 medium banana	3 oz turkey breast with lettuce, tomato	1 cup tomato sauce	
1 cup 2% milk		2 oz ground turkey	
1 English muffin	8 oz apple juice	¼ loaf multigrain bread (4 ounces)	
1 tbs jelly	1 cup frozen yogurt		
750 calories	750 calories	1,300 calories	500 calories
85% carbohydrates	65% carbohydrates	70% carbohydrates	80% carbohydrates

Total: 3,300 calories: 75% carbohydrates (610 g), 15% protein (125 g), 10% fat (40 g)

Source: N. Clark, *Nancy Clark's Sports Nutrition Guidebook,* 3rd ed. (Champaign, IL: Human Kinetics, 2003).

Some athletes, such as endurance runners and those in sports where low body weight is important, like gymnasts and figure skaters, may feel they can benefit from a very low-fat diet (less than 20 percent). Though consuming too much dietary fat is a concern, you don't want to limit your fat intake too much. When you consume less than adequate amounts of fat, you are more likely at risk for consuming inadequate calories, essential fatty acids, and fat-soluble vitamins, which can negatively affect exercise performance.[9]

Protein Is Primarily Needed to Build and Repair Muscle

Amino acids obtained from protein are the main nutrients needed to promote muscle growth and recovery. Muscle damage is one of the most significant physiological effects of exercise, especially in weight or strength training. You need to supply your

The Truth about the Fat-Burning Zone

Many people recognize the importance of exercise, especially of the cardiovascular system, for weight loss. They head off to the gym and jump on an exercise machine to start their workout. Once on the machine, they hook up to a device that monitors their heart rate, which lets them know if they are in the fat-burning zone (65 to 73 percent of one's maximum heart rate) or the "cardio" zone (more than 73 percent of one's maximum heart rate). Because most people seek to lose body fat, they exercise in the fat-burning zone because they believe that this is the most effective way to lose weight. After all, it is true that the body will burn more fat at lower intensities and will burn more carbohydrate as the intensity increases. So, is staying in the fat-burning zone the best advice to follow if you are trying to lose weight? The simple answer is no. Let's look at some calculations to better understand why.

If you are trying to lose weight, you need to burn more calories than you consume. Working out is an excellent way to do this, but you need to be aware of how many calories you are burning, and aim to work off as many as possible. In the fat-burning zone at 65 percent of maximum heart rate, a moderately fit person will burn an average of 220 calories during 30 minutes of exercise. Also at this same intensity, fat supplies about 50 percent of the total calories burned for energy. This means that the person is burning an average of 110 fat calories (50 percent of 220). As the intensity increases to about 85 percent of maximum heart rate, this same person burns an average of 330 calories during 30 minutes of exercise, with fat supplying only about 33 percent of the total calories burned. Guess what? The person still burns the same number of fat calories (33 percent of 330), but is burning more total calories (330 calories) at a higher intensity, which will help meet the weight loss goal sooner than exercising at a lower intensity (burning 220 calories).

The bottom line is, you don't need to stay in the fat-burning zone to effectively lose body fat. You just need to burn calories so that there is an overall calorie deficit.

If you prefer not to exercise at a high intensity, there is an advantage to exercising at a lower intensity. If you have time for a long workout, you can probably exercise at a lower intensity for a longer period of time without getting tired. In other words, if you are jogging (high intensity) you may get tired after you cover 3 miles. However, if you are walking briskly (lower intensity), you may be able to cover 4 miles because you aren't as fatigued. Covering that extra mile will allow you to expend more overall calories during your outing. But if you have a busy lifestyle and feel pressed for time to exercise, don't be afraid to go out of the fat-burning zone to get the most out of your workout and effectively lose weight!

muscles with protein so that this muscle damage does not result in decreased muscle mass and strength. Not all muscle damage is bad, however. It can stimulate remodeling of the muscle cells, which increases muscle strength and mass.

The Body Can Use Protein for Energy

Your body prefers to use carbohydrate and fat as its main energy sources during exercise (see Figure 11.3). Small amounts of protein are used for energy as well but only when calorie intake and carbohydrate stores are insufficient. If the body has to use a significant amount of protein for energy, that protein is not available to build and repair tissues. If this occurs too often, a loss of muscle mass will likely result.

Muscle protein is converted into energy by being broken down into amino acids that are then released into the bloodstream. The amino acids are carried to the liver where they get converted into glucose, which supplies the working muscles with energy.

How Much Protein Do I Need for Exercise?

Many athletes and exercisers assume that they need substantially more protein than non-exercisers. It is true that those who are fit and physically active need more protein than those who are sedentary, but those needs are not significantly higher. Recall from Chapter 6 that the RDA for protein for most healthy adults is 0.8 gram per kilogram of body weight per day, and most people, including athletes, far exceed this.

People who are recreational exercisers can meet their needs for protein with a balanced diet. The increased protein needs of competitive and elite athletes, as well as bodybuilders, can also be met with a balanced diet. Endurance athletes are advised to consume 1.2 to 1.4 grams of protein per kilogram of body weight. People who primarily participate in resistance and strength activities may need to consume as much as 1.6 to 1.7 grams per kilogram of body weight.[10]

Timing Affects Fitness and Athletic Performance

Timing the foods that you eat around exercise has a significant impact on energy levels and recovery time. Recall from Chapter 6 that inadequate calorie intake leads to muscles being broken down for energy. This in turn can lead to loss of muscle mass and strength, and lack of energy, which can negatively affect exercise performance.

During exercise, especially weight training, muscles are under a great deal of stress, which can result in overstretching and tearing of proteins and potential inflammation. After exercise, the body is in a catabolic (breaking down) state: Muscle and liver glycogen stores are low or depleted, muscle protein is broken down, and the immune system is suppressed. Therefore, supplying the body with the nutrients needed to reverse this catabolic state into an anabolic state (building up) is crucial and necessary for optimal fitness.

What Should I Eat Before Exercise?

You need to eat before exercise or a competition so that you have enough energy for optimal performance. However, one of the most important considerations about eating before exercise is allowing sufficient time for the food to digest so that it doesn't negatively affect your performance. In general, larger meals (making you feel quite full) may take 3 to 4 hours to digest, whereas smaller meals (making you feel satisfied but not overly full) may take only 2 to 3 hours to digest. If you are drinking a liquid supplement or having a small snack, you should allow about 30 minutes to 1 hour for digestion. These are general guidelines and may not apply to everyone, so be sure that you experiment with your own eating and exercise schedule well before a workout or competition so that you know how long you need to wait before starting your activity.

You just learned that carbohydrates are one of the main sources of energy during exercise; thus your preexercise meal should contain adequate amounts of carbohydrate so that you maximize muscle and liver glycogen stores and maintain normal blood glucose levels. In general, your preexercise meal should contain 1 to 4.5 grams of carbohydrate per kilogram of body weight and be consumed 1 to 4 hours prior to exercise.

Consuming carbohydrate immediately before exercise (about 15 to 30 minutes prior to the start) provides an advantage because it gives your muscles an immediate source of energy (glucose) and spares your glycogen stores so that you can exercise for a longer period or at a higher intensity without becoming tired as quickly.[11] Carbohydrate intake prior to the start of exercise can also help reduce muscle damage by causing the release of insulin, which promotes muscle protein synthesis.

Just as your body needs a continuous supply of carbohydrate, it also needs moderate amounts of protein throughout the day. Timing your protein intake around activity will have a significant impact on muscle preservation, growth, and recovery.

The consumption of both protein *and* carbohydrate before exercise benefits the body by causing a greater increase in muscle glycogen synthesis than consuming carbohydrate alone. With more glycogen in your muscles, you can increase endurance.

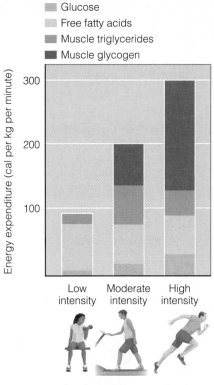

■ Glucose
■ Free fatty acids
■ Muscle triglycerides
■ Muscle glycogen

Figure 11.3 Energy Use during Varying Intensities of Exercise
During exercise, your body prefers to use carbohydrate and fat for energy. The intensity of the exercise will determine how much of these is used.

Source: Adapted from J. A. Romijn et al., Regulation of Endogenous Fat and Carbohydrate Metabolism in Relation to Exercise Intensity and Duration, *American Journal of Physiology-Endocrinology and Metabolism* 265 (September 1993): E380–E391.

A preexercise meal must contain adequate amounts of carbohydrate.

Another benefit of consuming both protein and carbohydrate before exercise is that it results in greater protein synthesis after the exercise is over compared with either protein or carbohydrate alone.[12] The making of new proteins, including muscles, is necessary for optimal fitness and muscle preservation, repair, and growth.

Foods with a higher fat content take longer to digest than foods that are higher in carbohydrate and protein. For this reason, high-fat foods should generally be avoided several hours before exercise. If you eat high-fat foods before exercise, you may feel sluggish or have stomach discomfort, which can impair your performance. Of course this is a general guideline, and not all active people have difficulty during exercise by consuming higher fat foods prior to the start. But eating a high-fat fast-food meal before basketball practice was probably the reason Greg, the basketball player, was feeling tired and cranky afterward.

What Should I Eat during Exercise?

For exercise lasting longer than 1 hour, carbohydrate intake should begin shortly after the start of exercise and continue at 15–20 minute intervals throughout. For long-lasting endurance activities, a total of 30 to 60 grams of carbohydrate should be consumed per hour to prevent early fatigue. Sports drinks and gels are one way to take in carbohydrate immediately before and/or during activity, but foods such as crackers and sports bars are also commonly eaten.

The best types of carbohydrate to consume during exercise are glucose, sucrose, and maltodextrin because they are absorbed by the body more quickly than other carbohydrates. Fructose, the sugar found in fruit and fruit juice, should generally be avoided because it may cause gastrointestinal problems or stomach discomfort.

Many sports drinks and gels contain only carbohydrate and electrolytes; others also contain protein. For endurance athletes, consuming both carbohydrate and protein during exercise has been shown to improve net protein balance at rest as well as during exercise and postexercise recovery.[13] This will, in turn, have an effect on muscle maintenance and growth.

What Should I Eat after Exercise?

What you eat after exercise will affect how fast you recover, which in turn may affect how soon you're ready for your next workout or training session. This is especially important for competitive athletes who may train more than once per day. Some people who load up on high-fat foods after a workout or competition experience fatigue that often results in less-than-optimal performance during the next workout.

Consuming carbohydrate after exercise will help replenish muscle and liver glycogen stores and stimulate muscle protein synthesis. The muscles are most receptive to storing new glycogen within the first 30 to 45 minutes after you have finished exercising, so this is a crucial time period in which to provide the body with carbohydrate.[14] Research shows that consuming carbohydrate immediately after exercise also results in a more positive body protein balance.[15]

Consuming protein and carbohydrate after exercise results in increased muscle protein synthesis. In addition, protein intake immediately after exercise rather than several hours later results in greater muscle protein synthesis. Research studies have shown that the addition of protein with carbohydrate causes an even greater increase in glycogen synthesis than carbohydrate or protein alone, and therefore both nutrients should be consumed after exercise.[16]

You can see that you recover more quickly after exercise when you consume carbohydrate and protein before, during, and/or after exercise. So now you might be thinking, "What is the best way to get these two nutrients?" Studies have shown that consumption of carbohydrate and protein in a ratio of approximately 3:1 (in grams)

Sports drinks can be a good source of carbohydrate during exercise.

is ideal to promote muscle glycogen synthesis, protein synthesis, and faster recovery time.[17] Whey protein (such as in milk) is the preferred protein source because it is rapidly absorbed and contains all of the essential amino acids that your body needs. Most athletes and regular exercisers prefer to use a liquid supplement that contains carbohydrate and protein rather than solid foods immediately after exercising. You can use commercial shakes and drinks, but those can be expensive. A cheaper alternative is low-fat chocolate milk, which will provide you with adequate amounts of carbohydrate and protein to assist in recovery after exercise.[18] If you consume a liquid supplement or small snack after exercise, this should be followed by a high-carbohydrate, moderate-protein, low-fat meal within the next 2 hours.

If you are a competitive athlete, always experiment with timing nutrient intake and consuming new foods and beverages during practice and not on the day of competition. You don't want to be unpleasantly surprised to find that a particular food doesn't agree with you a few hours before an important race or event.

In addition to consuming adequate protein and carbohydrate, drinking adequate fluids is important for exercise performance and recovery. You will learn more about hydration in a later section of this chapter.

Low-fat chocolate milk is a low-cost option for providing the whey protein and carbohydrate that help with muscle and glycogen synthesis after exercise.

The Take-Home Message Carbohydrate and fat are the primary sources of fuel during exercise. Carbohydrates provide energy in the form of blood glucose and muscle and liver glycogen, and are the main energy source during high-intensity exercise. Fat is the main energy source during low-intensity exercise. Protein provides amino acids that are necessary to promote muscle growth and repair muscle damage caused by exercise. Consuming the right balance of nutrients at the right time can improve exercise performance and recovery time.

What Vitamins and Minerals Are Important for Fitness?

Vitamins and minerals play a major role in the metabolism of carbohydrate, fat, and protein for energy during exercise. Many athletes mistakenly believe that vitamins and minerals themselves supply energy, and often consume extra vitamins and minerals so that they can perform better. In fact, studies have shown that multivitamin and mineral supplements are the most commonly used supplements by college athletes.[19] Can taking these supplements really improve athletic performance? The answer is: not unless you are experiencing a deficiency. For people who consume enough vitamins and minerals in their diet, taking more than the RDA will not result in improved performance during exercise.[20]

Active people generally do not need more vitamins than sedentary people because vitamins can be used repeatedly in metabolic reactions. Everyone, not just athletes, should obtain vitamins and minerals through nutrient-dense foods before considering the use of supplements. Eating a wide variety of foods that meets your calorie needs will likely provide your body with plenty of vitamins and minerals; thus it is probably a waste of money to use vitamin and mineral supplements.

Antioxidants and Cellular Damage Caused by Exercise

Your muscles use more oxygen during exercise than while you are at rest. Because of this, your body increases its production of free radicals that damage cells, especially during intense, prolonged exercise. Antioxidants, such as vitamins E and C, are known to protect cells from the damage of free radicals. Vitamin C also assists in the production of collagen, which provides most of the structure of connective tissues like bone, tendons, and ligaments. This, in turn, can affect your likelihood of developing strains, sprains, and fractures that may occur as a result of exercise.

Research has not proven that supplementation with vitamins E or C improves athletic performance, nor that it decreases oxidative stress in highly trained athletes.[21] Therefore, you do not need to consume more than the RDA for these vitamins, but you do need to be sure to consume adequate amounts from foods like nuts, vegetable oils, broccoli, and citrus fruits to meet your needs.

Minerals of Concern in Highly Active People

You learned in Chapter 8 that minerals have important roles in normal body functions and health. Minerals are also essential to physical fitness and athletic performance. Though active people do not need more minerals than less active individuals, there are two minerals that they must be careful to consume in adequate amounts.

Iron

Iron is important to exercise because it is necessary for energy metabolism and transporting oxygen throughout the body and within muscle cells. Iron is a structural component of hemoglobin and myoglobin, two proteins that carry and store oxygen in the blood and muscle, respectively. If iron levels are low, hemoglobin levels can also fall, diminishing the blood's ability to carry oxygen to the cells. If this occurs during exercise, you will experience early fatigue. (You can also feel tired if iron levels are low and you are not exercising.) Iron supplementation can improve aerobic performance for people with depleted iron stores.[22]

Many athletes and physically fit people are prone to iron-deficiency anemia. Although iron-deficiency anemia can occur in both females and males, female athletes are at a greater risk. Long-distance runners, as well as athletes in sports where they must "make weight" have also been noted to be at higher risk for iron-deficiency anemia. Athletes in other sports such as basketball, tennis, softball, and swimming also have been shown to have suboptimal iron status.[23]

Low iron levels can be a result of poor dietary intake or increased iron losses. Women can lose a lot of iron during menstruation, depending on their iron status and menstrual blood flow. Iron is also lost in sweat, but not in amounts significant enough to lead to iron deficiency.

Another effect of exercise on iron is intravascular hemolysis (*hemo* = blood, *lysis* = breaking down), which is the bursting of red blood cells. This happens when you are running and your feet repeatedly hit the ground (a hard surface), causing red blood cells to burst and release iron. This iron is recycled by the body and not lost, and therefore does not typically contribute to iron deficiency.

Some people experience decreased levels of hemoglobin because of training, especially when the training is quite strenuous. During exercise your blood volume increases, which in turn causes lower concentrations of hemoglobin in the blood. This is often referred to as sports anemia, or pseudoanemia, and is not the same as iron-deficiency anemia. Iron-deficiency anemia typically has to be treated with iron supplementation. Sports anemia can be corrected on its own because the body can adapt to training and produce more red blood cells, which restores normal hemoglobin levels.

Whether you exercise or not, you can maintain your iron status by consuming adequate amounts of iron-rich foods, and supplements if necessary. However, many female athletes do not consume enough iron to meet their needs, which often leads to low iron levels. Vegetarian athletes are especially susceptible to iron deficiency and need to plan their diets appropriately so they consume adequate amounts of foods plentiful in iron.

Calcium

Most people know about the importance of calcium to maintain bone health, but athletes are particularly susceptible to broken bones and fractures. Therefore, they need to consume enough calcium in their diets to reduce their risk of developing these types of injuries. Calcium affects both skeletal and heart muscle contraction, and hormone and neurotransmitter activity during exercise. It also assists in blood clotting when you have a cut or other minor hemorrhage, which may occur during exercise or competition.

Many people may not be aware that calcium is lost in sweat, and the more you sweat the more calcium you lose. One study concluded that bone loss is related to dietary calcium, and that exercise can increase bone mineral content (the mass of all minerals in bone) only when calcium intake is sufficient to compensate for what is lost through sweating.[24]

Calcium supplements are not recommended unless your intake from food and beverages is inadequate and you are not meeting your daily needs. Choosing foods that are high in calcium, including fortified foods, can ensure that athletes meet their needs for calcium.

The Take-Home Message Athletes need to pay special attention to their intakes of iron and calcium. Iron is important because of its role in transporting oxygen in blood and muscle, and deficiency is prevalent among athletes, especially females and vegetarians. Calcium intake is important for bone health and muscle contraction. Antioxidants such as vitamins E and C are not needed in excessive amounts, as they have not been proven to reduce oxidative damage to cells from exercise. Adequate amounts of all nutrients can be consumed in foods so supplements are not usually necessary.

How Does Fluid Intake Affect Fitness?

As basic as it sounds, water is one of the most important nutrients during physical activity. When you drink too little fluid, or you lose too much fluid and electrolytes through sweating, this causes physiological changes that can negatively affect exercise performance and health. You may experience early fatigue or weakness when your body doesn't have sufficient amounts of water. Consuming adequate fluids on a regular basis, as well as monitoring fluid losses during physical activity, are key to maintaining optimal performance and preventing **dehydration** and electrolyte imbalance.

dehydration Loss of water in the body as a result of inadequate fluid intake or excess fluid loss, such as through sweating.

Fluid and Electrolyte Balance and Body Temperature Are Affected by Exercise

Staying hydrated during physical activity is important to maintain electrolyte balance and help regulate body temperature.

You learned in Chapter 8 that water and some electrolytes are necessary to maintain the fluid balance in your body. When you are physically active, your body will lose more water via sweat and exhalation of water vapor than when you are less active, so you need to replace water lost during exercise to maintain normal fluid balance.

Sodium and chloride are the two primary electrolytes that are lost in sweat. Potassium is also lost in sweat, but to a lesser extent than sodium and chloride. An electrolyte imbalance can cause heat cramps, as well as nausea, lowered blood pressure, and edema in the hands and feet, all of which can hinder your performance. When electrolyte losses are within the range of normal daily dietary intake, they can easily be replaced by a balanced meal consumed within 24 hours after exercise. Electrolytes can also be replaced by beverages that contain them, such as sports drinks, if food is not available.

The sweat you produce during exercise releases heat and helps keep your body temperature normal. The amount of fluid lost through sweating depends on the type, intensity, and duration of exercise and varies from person to person. Some people sweat heavily, while others may sweat very little. Regardless of how much you sweat, it is important that you don't allow your body to lose too much fluid without replacing it with water or other beverages.

Exercising in hot, humid weather results in more fluid being lost in breathing in addition to sweating, which will increase your body's need for fluids. However, if the air outside is very humid (that is, it contains a lot of water), sweat may not evaporate off the skin, and the body won't cool down. This can cause heat to build up in your body, placing you at risk for heat exhaustion or heat stroke. One significant warning sign of heat stroke is if you are *not* sweating when you should be. This happens when you are extremely dehydrated and cannot produce sweat, which prevents the release of heat and causes your body temperature to rise. Other warnings signs of heat exhaustion and heat stroke are shown in Table 11.5.

You Need Fluids Before, During, and After Exercise

Many active people are aware that it's important to stay hydrated during exercise, but your need for water doesn't begin with your first sit-up or lap around the track. Meeting your fluid needs before and after activity is also important to maintain fluid and electrolyte balance and optimize performance.

You should consume adequate fluid every day. Recall from Chapter 8 that most healthy adult women need approximately 9 cups of beverages daily, while most healthy adult men need about 13 cups. This is a general guideline to follow for adequate hydration. Another way to determine your estimated daily fluid needs is to divide your body weight by 2. This tells you the number of ounces of fluid you need (8 ounces = 1 cup) on a daily basis, not including the additional needs associated with exercising.

Preexercise hydration is essential to replace sweat losses. As you learned in Chapter 8, you can determine your fluid needs during exercise by weighing yourself both before and after an activity. Because the amount of weight that is lost is mainly due to losses in body water, you should consume 16 to 24 fluid ounces (about 2 to 3 cups)

Table 11.5

Warning Signs of Heat Exhaustion and Heat Stroke

Heat Exhaustion	Heat Stroke
Profuse sweating	Extremely high body temperature
Fatigue	(above 103°F [39.4°C], orally)
Thirst	Red, hot, and dry skin (no sweating)
Muscle cramps	Rapid, strong pulse
Headache	Rapid, shallow breathing
Dizziness or light-headedness	Throbbing headache
Weakness	Dizziness
Nausea and vomiting	Nausea
Cool, moist skin	Extreme confusion
	Unconsciousness

Table 11.6

ACSM Hydration Recommendations

When?	How Much?
2 to 3 hours before exercise	14–22 fluid ounces (2–3 cups)
5 to 10 minutes before exercise	4–8 fluid ounces (½–1 cup) as tolerated
At 15- to 20-minute intervals after exercise has begun	6–12 fluid ounces (¾–1½ cups)

of fluid for every pound of body weight lost.[25] The American College of Sports Medicine (ACSM) has specific recommendations for how much fluid to drink before and during exercise. See Table 11.6 for these recommendations.

Some Beverages Are Better than Others

Beverages like tea, coffee, soft drinks, fruit juice, and, of course, water contribute to your daily fluid needs. But what is the best type of fluid for preventing dehydration prior to and during activity? What about for rehydrating your body after activity? For these purposes, not all beverages are equal.

Sports drinks are popular in the fitness world and are often marketed as tasty beverages to all groups of people, not just athletes. They typically contain 6 to 8 percent carbohydrate as well as sodium and potassium, two electrolytes that are critical in muscle contraction and maintaining fluid balance. One purpose of sports drinks is to replace fluid and electrolytes that are lost through sweating. These drinks have been shown to be superior to water for rehydration, mostly because their flavor causes people to drink more than they would of just plain water.[26]

Sports drinks also provide additional carbohydrate to prevent glycogen depletion. This is beneficial if you engage in long endurance events or exercise when glycogen stores may be running low. When you consume a sports drink during exercise, you provide your body with glucose to be used as an immediate energy source and prevent further decline in muscle glycogen stores.

Fluids such as milk and fruit and vegetable juices can help meet your daily water needs. Whole fruits and many other foods are also good sources of water.

However, not everyone actually needs sports drinks in order to stay adequately hydrated. For exercise that lasts less than 60 minutes, water is sufficient to replace fluids lost through sweating and food consumption following exercise will adequately replace electrolytes. A sports drink is most appropriate when physical activity lasts longer than 60 minutes.[27]

Sports drinks should be avoided as a regular daily beverage, as one study has shown that sports drinks may cause irreversible damage to tooth enamel that could result in tooth decay,[28] which may be from the additives and organic acids that are in these drinks. This damage was noted to be 3 to 11 times greater than that from cola-based drinks. Sports beverages provide approximately 60 calories for each 8-ounce cup, so remember that they can be a source of unwanted extra calories.

Other beverages may be suboptimal for hydration during physical activity. Fruit juice and juice drinks contain a larger concentration of carbohydrate and do not hydrate the body as quickly as beverages with a lower concentration of carbohydrates (like sports drinks). Carbonated drinks contain a large amount of water; however, the air bubbles from the carbonation can cause stomach bloating and may limit the amount of fluid consumed.

Though alcohol may seem like an unlikely choice for rehydration, some people may drink alcoholic beverages, such as beer, in order to quench thirst. But because alcohol is a diuretic, it can actually contribute to dehydration. Alcohol during performance can also impair your judgment and reasoning, which can lead to injuries not only for you, but for those around you.

Another diuretic, the caffeine found in coffee and some soft drinks, should only be consumed in moderate amounts, because excessive intake can cause increased heart rate, nausea, vomiting, excessive urination, restlessness, anxiety, and difficulty sleeping. Moderate caffeine intake is about 250 milligrams (amount found in about three cups of coffee) per day.[29]

Consuming Too Little or Too Much Fluid Can Be Harmful

As your body loses fluid through sweating and exhalation during physical activity, it will let you know that you need to replace these fluids by sending a signal of thirst. However, by the time you're thirsty, you may already be dehydrated. Figure 11.4 shows the effect of dehydration on exercise performance. As you can see from the figure, thirst is not a good indicator of fluid needs for most athletes and physically active people. Knowing the warning signs of dehydration so that you can respond by drinking adequate fluids will help prevent health consequences and impaired exercise performance.

If you become dehydrated over a short period of time, such as during a single exercise session or sport competition, **acute dehydration** may set in. Acute dehydration most commonly occurs if you are not adequately hydrated before beginning a hard exercise session, especially if you have been sick, if it is extremely hot and humid, or if the temperature is significantly different from what you are used to. To prevent acute dehydration, follow a regimented hydration schedule using water or sports drinks to hydrate before, during, and after exercise sessions and/or competition.

Chronic dehydration refers to when you are not adequately hydrated over an extended period of time, such as during several sport practices or games. The most common warning signs of chronic dehydration include fatigue, muscle soreness, poor recovery from a workout, headaches, and nausea. If your urine is very dark and you are not needing to go to the bathroom every 3 or 4 hours, then you could be experienc-

acute dehydration Dehydration starting after a short period of time.

chronic dehydration Dehydration over a long period of time.

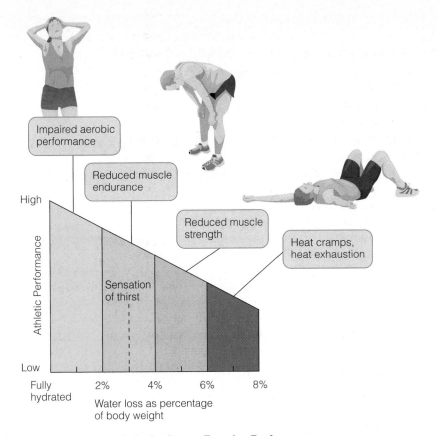

Figure 11.4 Effects of Dehydration on Exercise Performance
Failing to stay hydrated during exercise or competition can result in fatigue and cramps and, in extreme cases, heat exhaustion. Because the thirst mechanism doesn't kick in until after dehydration has begun, replacing fluids throughout physical activity is important.

Source: Adapted from E. Burke and J. Berning, *Training Nutrition.* (Travers City, MI: Cooper Publishing Group, 1996).

ing chronic dehydration. As with acute dehydration, following a regimented hydration schedule throughout the day will help prevent chronic dehydration.

When speaking of hydration and physical activity, we are usually concerned about consuming *enough* fluids so that we do not become dehydrated. As you recall from Chapter 8, consuming too much fluid can also be harmful. Taking in too much water without sufficient electrolytes can result in **hyponatremia.** Symptoms of severe hyponatremia may include rapid weight gain, bloated stomach, nausea, vomiting, swollen hands and feet, headache, dizziness, confusion, disorientation, and lack of coordination. Hyponatremia is more likely to occur in those who participate in endurance sports or prolonged exercise periods (greater than 4 hours), in which fluid and sodium loss is more likely.

Drinking as much fluid as possible and "staying ahead of thirst" has been the recommendation for hydration among long-distance runners for quite some time. Due to the growing concern about overhydration and hyponatremia, USA Track & Field (USATF) revised its guidelines on hydration in order to lower the risk of hyponatremia among long-distance runners. The USATF recommends consuming 100 percent of fluids lost due to sweat while exercising, and to be sensitive to the onset of thirst as the signal to drink, rather than "staying ahead of thirst."

If you are a distance runner, take the Self-Assessment to determine your fluid needs during long-distance races.[30] Keep in mind that you should perform this hydration test well before a competition or event, and perform the test again if your level of fitness improves or if the climate changes from when you initially determined your fluid needs.

hyponatremia Dangerously low levels of sodium in the blood.

Calculating Your Fluid Needs for Endurance Exercise

The next time you take a 1-hour training run, use the following process to determine your fluid needs.

1. Make sure that you are properly hydrated before the workout. Your urine should be clear.
2. Do a warm-up run to the point where you start to sweat, then stop. Urinate if necessary.
3. Weigh yourself on an accurate scale.
4. Run for one hour at an intensity similar to your targeted race.
5. Drink a measured amount of a beverage of your choice during the run to quench your thirst. Be sure to keep track of how much you drink.
6. Do not urinate during the run.
7. After you have finished the run, weigh yourself again on the same scale you used in step 3.
8. Calculate your fluid needs using the following formula:
   a. Enter your body weight from step 3 in pounds   _____
   b. Enter your body weight from step 7 in pounds   − _____
   c. Subtract B from A   = _____
                                                         ×   15.3
   d. Convert the pounds of weight in C to fluid ounces
      by multiplying by 15.3   _____
   e. Enter the amount of fluid you consumed during
      the run in ounces   + _____
   f. Add e to d   = _____

The final figure is the number of ounces of fluid that you must consume per hour to remain well hydrated.

Source: Adapted from D. Casa. *USA Track & Field Self-Testing Program for Optimal Hydration for Distance Running.* Available at www.usatf.org/groups/coaches/library/hydration/USATFselfTestingProgramForOptimalHydration.pdf

The Take-Home Message Being adequately hydrated before, during, and after exercise is important to sustain fluid and electrolyte balance and a normal body temperature. Inadequate hydration can impair performance. Water is the preferred beverage for hydration, but sports drinks can be beneficial during moderate- or vigorous-intensity exercise that lasts longer than 60 minutes.

Can Dietary Supplements Contribute to Fitness?

Competitive athletes are always looking for an edge, and many turn to supplements in the hopes of improving their performance. The pill and powder manufacturers may claim that their products enhance immunity, boost metabolism, improve memory, or provide some other physical advancement. Because dietary supplements are not strictly regulated by the Food and Drug Administration, their manufacturers do not have to prove the safety or efficacy of any of these claims. As a result, many athletes risk their health and, in some cases, eligibility for competition by taking supplements that can be ineffective or even dangerous.

Dietary Supplements and Ergogenic Aids May Improve Performance, But Can Have Side Effects

The term **ergogenic aid** describes any substance used to improve athletic performance, including dietary supplements. Although the makers of dietary supplements do not have to prove their effectiveness, researchers have examined several supplements and their effects on athletic performance. Studies have indicated that some dietary supplements have a positive effect on performance, while others do not. Further, some ergogenic aids cause serious side effects. Let's take a closer look at some of the most popular dietary supplements and ergogenic aids in the fitness industry.

Creatine

Creatine is one of the most well-known dietary supplements in the fitness industry today. In the early 1990s, research revealed that creatine supplementation increased creatine stores in the muscles (in the form of creatine phosphate), which increased the amount of ATP generated and improved performance during high-intensity, short-duration exercise.[31]

Athletes sometimes take supplements, such as creatine phosphate or caffeine, to enhance their athletic performance. Supplements are not strictly regulated by the FDA, so their quality and effectiveness can vary widely.

However, the data on whether creatine enhances performance is mixed. Studies have supported that creatine supplementation improves athletic performance in high-intensity, short-duration activities such as weight training, when the body relies on anaerobic energy metabolism. Creatine supplementation has been shown to increase muscle strength and muscle mass. But research has shown mixed results in creatine supplementation improving sprint running performance, with some studies showing improvement and others showing no benefit.[32]

To date, creatine has not been found to have negative effects on blood pressure, or kidney, or liver function among healthy people.[33] In fact, one case of kidney problems following the use of creatine has been documented, but it is unclear if this person had kidney problems prior to taking the supplement.[34] Anyone considering taking creatine supplements should check with a health care provider first.

Caffeine

Caffeine used to be known mostly in the context of its negative effect on hydration (recall that caffeine is a diuretic). Today, caffeine has gained popularity as an ergogenic aid among athletes, trainers, and coaches. Caffeine may decrease perception of effort by stimulating the central nervous system, directly affect the breakdown of muscle glycogen, and may increase the availability of fatty acids during exercise, therefore sparing glycogen stores. Studies on the effects of caffeine on exercise have shown that caffeine does enhance athletic performance, mostly during endurance events.[35] However, research has not proven that caffeine provides any benefit during short-duration activities, such as sprinting.[36] Caffeine is considered a banned substance by some athletic associations when consumed in high amounts. For example, the National Collegiate Athletic Association (NCAA) classifies caffeine as a banned substance when urine concentrations exceed 15 micrograms per milliliter. This would be the equivalent of drinking four or five cups of coffee.

ergogenic aid A substance, such as a dietary supplement, used to enhance athletic performance.

Anabolic Steroids

Anabolic steroids (anabolic = to stimulate growth) are testosterone-based substances designed to mimic the body-building traits of testosterone. There are two primary effects of anabolic steroids. The anabolic effect, which is the one users are seeking, results in the promotion of protein growth and muscle development, which leads to bigger muscles and greater strength. Most athletes want to be stronger and will often turn to anabolic steroids to build up muscle to a level that's not naturally possible.

The other, undesirable effect of anabolic steroids is the androgenic effect (*andro* = testosterone promoting). Taking in testosterone causes the body to decrease its own production of the hormone, leading to a hormone imbalance. In men, this can cause shrinkage of the testicles, decreased sperm production, impotence, painful urination, severe acne (especially on the back), and changes in hair growth (an increase in facial hair and a decrease in hair on the head). They may also experience psychiatric side effects such as extreme mood swings and aggressiveness, which can lead to violence.

Women who use anabolic steroids also experience androgenic effects. Just as with men using anabolic steroids, women experience severe acne, increased facial and body hair, and loss of hair on the head. Additionally, women may experience a lower voice, increased aggressiveness, **amenorrhea,** and increased sex drive.

Although anabolic steroids can increase muscle mass and strength, their use among collegiate and professional athletes is prohibited by most agencies. Abusing anabolic steroids, whether to improve performance or physical appearance, can lead to severe health consequences such as liver and kidney tumors, liver cancer, high blood pressure, trembling, and increases in LDL cholesterol.

Growth Hormone

Growth hormone has been promoted with claims of increasing muscle mass and strength and decreasing body fat, thereby improving performance. Some competitive athletes use growth hormone instead of anabolic steroids to build muscles because they believe it is less likely to be detected through current testing methods.

Growth hormone is naturally produced by the pituitary gland to stimulate growth in children. Synthetic, or man-made, growth hormone was originally created for children with growth hormone deficiency to enable them to grow to their full height. It targets numerous tissues, including bones, skeletal muscle, fat cells, immune cells, and liver cells. Growth hormone increases protein synthesis by increasing amino acid transport across cell membranes, causing an increase in muscle mass but not strength. This increased muscle mass but not strength could actually impair performance by reducing one's power, speed, and endurance.

Growth hormone also decreases glycogen synthesis and the use of glucose for energy, causing an increase in fat breakdown and the use of fatty acids for energy. This, in turn, can improve body composition by decreasing body fat. For these reasons, many people assume they can improve their performance with the use of growth hormone.

Little research exists on the effectiveness of growth hormone on improving fitness and athletic performance, and the results of studies that have been done are mixed. Growth hormone has been shown to reduce body fat and increase fat-free mass in well-trained adults.[37] However, other studies show that it does not improve muscle strength or lean body mass in healthy adult athletes or the elderly.[38] It also appears to have no positive effect on cardiovascular performance in adults with growth hormone deficiency.[39]

Abuse of growth hormone can have serious health effects, including the development of diabetes, atherosclerosis (hardening of the arteries), and hypertension. Excess growth hormone can also cause **acromegaly,** a condition in which tissues, bones, and internal organs grow abnormally large.

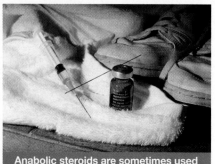

Anabolic steroids are sometimes used by athletes seeking to bulk up. Because they are testosterone based, they can have unique effects on the body for both men and women.

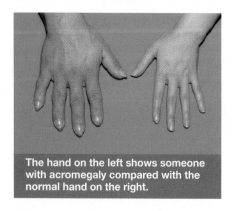

The hand on the left shows someone with acromegaly compared with the normal hand on the right.

amenorrhea Absence of menstruation.

acromegaly A condition caused by excess growth hormone in which tissues, bones, and internal organs grow abnormally large.

Erythropoietin and Blood Doping

Erythropoietin is a hormone produced by the kidneys when there is a decrease in blood oxygen levels. The hormone travels to the bone marrow and stimulates the formation of red blood cells, which carries oxygen to tissues. Synthetic versions of erythropoietin are used as ergogenic aids by athletes because increasing the number of red blood cells increases the oxygen-carrying capacity of the blood. This results in the athlete's being able to train at a higher intensity without becoming fatigued as quickly,[40] thereby having the potential to improve performance and overall physical fitness. Despite its popularity among competitive athletes, synthetic erythropoietin is a banned substance in most athletic organizations.

Before synthetic erythropoietin was discovered, the most common way to increase the oxygen-carrying capacity of the blood was blood doping. Blood doping, or red blood cell reinfusion, involves removing 250 to 500 milliliters of an athlete's own blood, extracting the red blood cells, and storing them for a few weeks prior to competition. The stored red blood cells are reinfused as the competition day approaches, so that the athlete has a higher than normal number of blood cells in his or her body. This results in an increase in the amount of oxygen in the blood, which can increase aerobic endurance.

Synthetic erythropoietin and blood doping can be dangerous because they increase blood viscosity (thickness). If the blood becomes too thick, it moves slowly and can clog capillaries. If this occurs in the brain, it results in a stroke. If there is a blood clot in the heart, it causes a heart attack. Both of these can be life-threatening. Erythropoietin may also cause sudden death during sleep, which is believed to have been a contributing factor in numerous deaths among professional European cyclists in recent years.

Sports Bars, Shakes, and Meal Replacers May Provide Benefits

Sports bars and shakes are not considered dietary supplements because they are more like food and contain one or more macronutrient. If you're a supremely busy person, such as Greg the basketball player, these products may be a convenient alternative to meals or snacks prepared at home. However, keep in mind that these items are often expensive. An energy bar may be trendy and easy to stash in your book bag, but an old-fashioned peanut butter sandwich on whole-grain bread would cost less and be just as easy to carry.

The main energy source in most sports bars and shakes is carbohydrate, with protein and fat contributing smaller amounts of energy. The ratio of the macronutrients in these foods varies depending on the purpose. Bars and shakes that are intended to provide energy for and recovery from exercise have a greater proportion of energy supplied by carbohydrates. Those that are promoted for muscle protein synthesis typically contain more protein than carbohydrate and fat. Bars and shakes that are high in protein are often used by vegetarians and some athletes who need additional sources of protein in their diet. Most bars and shakes also contain a variety of vitamins and minerals. Of course, these vitamins and minerals may not be necessary if you are consuming balanced meals regularly or taking a daily multivitamin.

The Take-Home Message Dietary supplements and ergogenic aids, such as creatine, caffeine, anabolic steroids, growth hormone, erythropoietin, and blood doping, may enhance performance, but can have serious health effects. Sports bars and shakes are convenient sources of energy, but are more expensive than whole foods and should only be included as a minor part of an overall healthy diet.

What Is the Female Athlete Triad?

Christy Henrich joined the U.S. gymnastics team in 1986 weighing 95 pounds at 4 feet, 11 inches tall. Christy soon succeeded as a gymnast, but after a judge told her she needed to lose weight, she developed anorexia nervosa. Sadly, her weight plummeted to 47 pounds, and she died from multiple organ failure at the age of 22.

The anorexia that Christy battled is one part of the *female athlete triad,* a combination of disordered eating, amenorrhea, and osteoporosis. Female athletes are often pressured to reach or maintain an unrealistically low body weight and/or level of body fat. This pressure contributes to the development of disordered eating, which helps to initiate the triad. Of major concern with this disorder is that it not only reduces the performance of the athlete, but may have serious medical and psychological consequences later in life.

The major components of the triad are discussed below.

Disordered Eating

Athletes who have disordered eating may engage in abnormal, and often harmful, eating behaviors in order to lose weight or maintain a low body weight. At one extreme are those who fulfill the diagnostic criteria for anorexia nervosa or bulimia nervosa. At the other are those who unintentionally take in fewer calories than they need. They may appear to be eating a healthy diet—one that would be adequate for a sedentary individual—but their caloric needs are higher due to their level of physical activity. Many athletes mistakenly believe that losing weight by any method enhances performance, and that disordered eating is harmless. Disordered eating is most common among athletes in sports where appearance is important, such as figure skating, gymnastics, and ballet, but can occur in athletes in all types of sports.

Amenorrhea

Amenorrhea, the absence of three to six consecutive menstrual cycles, is the most recognizable component of the triad. This menstrual disorder is caused by a failure to consume enough energy to compensate for the "energy cost" of the exercise. Unfortunately, many females welcome the convenience of not menstruating and do not report it; however, this may put them at risk for reduced bone mass and a faster rate of bone loss caused by decreased levels of estrogen in the body.

Female athletes for whom body size or appearance is an issue, such as dancers, gymnasts, and skaters, are often particularly vulnerable to the femal athlete triad.

Osteoporosis

Osteoporosis is the loss of bone mineral density and the inadequate formation of bone. Premature osteoporosis, which is perpetuated by poor nutrition and amenorrhea, puts the athlete at risk for stress fractures, hip and vertebral fractures, and the loss of bone mass, which may be irreplaceable.

All individuals, including friends, teachers, and coaches, involved with such athletes should be aware of the warning signs because the triad components are very often not recognized, not reported, or denied. Warning signs include menstrual changes, weight changes, disordered eating patterns, cardiac arrhythmia, depression, and stress fractures. People working with these athletes should provide a training environment in which athletes are not pressured to lose weight and should be able to recommend appropriate nutritional, medical, and/or psychological resources if needed.

Putting It All Together

Being physically active is as important to your overall health as consuming adequate amounts of the macro- and micronutrients that you read about in previous chapters. Using MyPyramid to make nutrient-dense food choices and understanding which foods provide the most energy will help you consume adequate energy for exercise without consuming too many calories. Consuming adequate fluid is an important goal for everyone, and athletes need to be particularly aware of their hydration levels during exercise and competition.

You can use the FITT principle and the Physical Activity Pyramid to help develop an exercise program to meet your health and fitness goals. Incorporating even modest amounts of physical activity into your day will help provide some of the same benefits of a healthful diet. Maintaining a healthy weight will help reduce your risk of obesity and diabetes, and physical fitness can also ensure that your "good" blood cholesterol levels are normal, which will be another risk reducer when it comes to heart disease.

Two Points of View

Are Personal Trainers Reliable Sources of Credible Nutrition Information?

Many fitness advisors in gyms and other exercise facilities are happy to dispense nutrition advice, but is the advice always accurate?

Richard Cotton, MA
Exercise physiologist; Spokesman, American Council on Exercise

Richard Cotton, MA, has worked in the health and fitness industry for nearly 30 years, with a special focus on setting standards for fitness professionals and helping consumers find reliable exercise programs, trainers, and equipment. He has worked extensively with the American Council on Exercise (ACE), a major nonprofit fitness certifying organization and a consumer resource for reliable, effective health and fitness information.

Q: What is a personal trainer and how is she or he trained and certified?

A: A personal trainer works with people in a one-on-one program of exercise assessment, design, and support. Trainers work with clients to help them shape and reach their exercise goals, based on the motivation of the client. Some clients are focused on improving their appearance, some on fitness, and some on health. So if the focus of the training is appearance, a trainer and a client can start there, knowing that exercise will also bring plenty of health benefits.

Qualified trainers receive their education in a variety of ways. Some get most of their training on the job, and some take special classes through a community college or university extension course. Others have college degrees in areas like physiology, exercise science, or health promotion. Building the knowledge needed to be a trainer takes time. If someone is a lifelong exerciser and has real passion and knowledge, he or she could take the necessary courses and be ready to take a certification exam in six months. If someone is coming from a sedentary lifestyle and suddenly gets an exercise bug and decides this is the right field, he or she might need a couple of years to get ready for the exam.

(continued)

Brenda Malinauskas, PhD, RD
East Carolina University

Brenda Malinauskas, PhD, RD, is an assistant professor and program coordinator for the graduate program in Nutrition at East Carolina University. Much of her research focuses on dieting behaviors, including dieting practices used by young women and male and female university athletes. She is an avid runner and cyclist and has worked with college athletes for over 10 years helping them to optimize their health and sports performance through nutrition.

Q: Are personal trainers reliable resources for credible nutrition information? Why or why not?

A: Although personal trainers may be very knowledgeable in the area of nutrition, the information they provide may or may not be correct. Basically, they haven't undergone the structured instruction that's required to be a reliable nutrition information resource. Their knowledge base isn't as in-depth as that of a Registered Dietitian (RD). The training program for an RD involves coursework not only in nutrition, but also nutritional biochemistry, anatomy, and physiology. RDs also learn about disease processes. Personal trainers may have had some of those courses, but they may also not have. When you're working with people on nutrition and health issues, it's essential to have all that information. RDs are also required to do a 9- to 12-month internship that is accredited by the American Dietetic Association, and pass a national exam. It's a very rigorous program. That's why RDs are considered the nutrition experts. We have the education and professional experience that qualifies us to provide the most up-to-date evidence-based nutrition recommendations.

(continued)

Are Personal Trainers Reliable Sources of Credible Nutrition Information?, continued

Richard Cotton, MA, continued

Qualified personal trainers are certified by groups like the ACE by passing a certification exam. To qualify for ACE certification, a personal trainer has to pass an intensive three hour, 150-question exam and written simulation that covers exercise science and programming knowledge, including anatomy, kinesiology, health screening, basic nutrition and instructional methods. The National Commission for Certifying Agencies (NCCA) accredits ACE's certification programs. ACE is one of a few select certifying organizations in the fitness industry whose programs have been accredited.

Q: What should a person look for when seeking out a personal trainer?

A: They should look for certification first, and that certification should come from a nationally recognized certifying organization. That's important, because it provides assurance that you're working with a trainer who can offer you a safe, effective workout.

Ask for references, including the names and phone numbers of other clients with goals similar to yours, and call them to see if they were pleased with their results. Make sure the trainer has liability insurance and provides business policies, like fees and cancellation policies, in writing. Look for a trainer who can assist you with your special goals and needs, and has you fill out a health history questionnaire. The right trainer should motivate you by positive, not negative, reinforcement.

Q: Are personal trainers trained in the area of nutrition?

A: That area is a delicate one, because there have been some tensions between trainers and nutritionists. Many trainers have some basic knowledge of nutrition. But nutrition expertise is a specialized field that requires a license or at least registration in most states. It's a separate practice, and a trainer needs to adhere to that fact and respect the distinction. Personal trainers who are not Registered Dietitians can provide basic nutrition information, but they shouldn't be providing personalized meal plans. But there are also lots of trainers who have gotten degrees or licenses in nutrition, and they are well qualified to talk to their clients about nutrition. There are also plenty of Registered Dietitians who have branched into physical fitness.

Q: Where should my personal trainer refer me for nutrition information?

A: Many trainers think the ADA website, www.eatright.org, is a great place to start. It's a trainer's responsibility to acquire his or her own network of nutrition and health professionals to help clients. Some trainers will refer clients to a local hospital or medical practice. But there are very good licensed

(continued)

Brenda Malinauskas, PhD, RD, continued

Q: Some personal trainers feel that they are credible when it comes to dispensing nutrition advice. How do you respond to this?

A: I would only agree with this statement if they were also a Registered Dietitian. An RD is trained to look at the whole picture and consider the health implications. For example, if you came to me with the question, "Should I take this supplement?" I'd look into whether that supplement was going to be harmful, either short term or long term, and then I'd provide that advice to you. I'd want to find out why you want to take the supplement. I would review the available scientific literature to see if there is any evidence-based information that shows that the supplement produces the results you're looking for. Many athletes and bodybuilders have questions about a supplement called creatine, which sometimes carries claims that it boosts strength, muscle mass, and energy. If I review the scientific literature on creatine and find that it increases muscle, then it might be a good fit for you. But if the evidence shows that creatine just increases overall body weight by increasing the water in the cells, then you'll gain weight but not muscle, and it's not a good fit. This process of answering nutrition-related questions, including sports-related nutrition questions, goes way beyond the sort of anecdotal advice ("Well, my cousin Frank took this and it worked for him") that is more common in people with less training.

I'd also talk to you about ways to change your diet so that you can achieve what you want without a supplement. It's not that supplements are necessarily bad. When it comes to herbs, for example, I'd often prefer someone take a supplement instead. With herbs, the active element may change based on how the herb has been harvested. In those cases, a supplement may be the better choice because the active ingredients are more controlled. But a person may also not need supplements at all. An RD will start by looking at a person's diet, and then look at other products. For example, if someone wanted to boost their immune system, they might be interested in probiotics. You can take a probiotic supplement. But there are also good levels of probiotics in yogurt. You can start there before trying a supplement. These are all considerations personal trainers may not take into account unless they are also Registered Dietitians.

Q: Where can a student go to obtain scientifically sound information about what to eat to maximize athletic performance, or to improve overall fitness?

(continued)

Are Personal Trainers Reliable Sources of Credible Nutrition Information?, continued

Richard Cotton, MA, continued

nutrition experts working the way trainers do. They go into people's kitchens and really help them assess their eating habits and develop a healthier nutrition plan. Qualified trainers should be helping their clients find qualified nutrition experts that fit their needs and lifestyle.

Brenda Malinauskas, PhD, RD, continued

A: A great start would be to take an undergraduate nutrition course that is taught within the Nutrition Department in their university. This course provides a sound scientific base for a student to better understand and evaluate nutrition information. If a student is interested in more specific guidance regarding his or her own diet or how to interpret the scientific literature, [my advice is to] seek out the services of an RD. Many universities employ dietitians to work with students (through student health services) and with student athletes (through the Athletics Department).

NUTRITION IN THE REAL WORLD

Be a Nutrition Sleuth

Stay Hydrated for Fitness

How much fluid should you drink before, during, and after your workout? Go to www.aw-bc.com/blake to find out.

NUTRITION IN THE REAL WORLD

Get Real!

Get Ready to Get FITT!

Are you ready to incorporate more "FITTness" into your physical activity program? Go to www.aw-bc.com/blake and use the FITT worksheet to assess your regular physical activities for frequency, intensity, time, and type. Track your activities for a week, and see where you need to make adjustments to optimize your workouts.

The Top Ten Points to Remember

1. Physical fitness is defined as good health or physical condition, especially as the result of exercise and proper nutrition. There are five basic components of fitness: cardiorespiratory endurance, muscle strength, muscle endurance, flexibility, and body composition.

2. Engaging in regular physical activity provides several health benefits, such as reducing the risk of chronic diseases like cardiovascular disease and type 2 diabetes; and improving body composition, immunity, and bone health. Thirty minutes of moderately intense activity most days of the week will give you health benefits, with more activity providing greater benefits.

3. The source of energy needed to fuel exercise depends on the intensity of the activity. Carbohydrate, specifically muscle glycogen, is the main energy source for high-intensity activity. Fat is the preferred source of energy during low- to moderate-intensity activity.

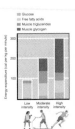

4. Protein is important to fitness because it functions to maintain, build, and repair tissues, including muscle tissue. Only small amounts of protein are used for energy during exercise.

5. Vitamins and minerals assist in energy metabolism and are necessary for fitness. Athletes do not have greater needs for vitamins and minerals than do nonathletes, and intakes of vitamins and minerals above the RDA do not improve athletic performance.

6. Female and vegetarian athletes are at greater risk of developing iron deficiency and should consume iron-rich foods regularly. Athletes also need to be sure their calcium intake is adequate to help reduce their risk of bone fractures during physical activity.

7. Being adequately hydrated before, during, and after exercise is important to both health and athletic performance. Staying hydrated helps maintain fluid and electrolyte balance and normal body temperature. Water is the best fluid for hydration during exercise, though sports drinks can be beneficial for moderate- to vigorous-intensity exercise that lasts longer than 60 minutes.

8. Dietary supplements are not strictly regulated for their safety and efficacy; those who choose to use them may be placing their health at risk. Some dietary supplements are used as ergogenic aids to improve athletic performance.

9. Creatine has been shown to increase both muscle strength and mass but research is mixed on it's role in athletic performance. Caffeine has been shown to improve endurance performance, but has not shown any benefit in activities of short duration. Anabolic steroids can increase muscle mass and strength, but will also cause undesirable androgenic side effects for both men and women. Growth hormone may increase muscle mass and decrease body fat, but also has serious health effects. Synthetic erythropoietin and blood doping can improve endurance, but can also thicken the blood, which may lead to a stroke or heart attack.

10. All athletes and physically active people must consume adequate calories, carbohydrate, protein, fat, vitamins, and minerals in order to achieve optimal fitness and athletic performance. Well-balanced meals and snacks consisting of whole foods should be the basis of an athlete's diet, with sports bars, shakes, and other supplements used only when necessary.

Test Your Knowledge

1. Which of the following is *not* a component of physical fitness?
   a. muscle strength
   b. cardiorespiratory endurance
   c. stress
   d. body composition

2. If you are able to do 100 consecutive push-ups without taking a break, you are exhibiting great
   a. cardiorespiratory endurance.
   b. muscle endurance.
   c. flexibility.
   d. muscle strength.

3. Well-trained muscles have the ability to store an unlimited amount of glycogen.
   a. True
   b. False

4. Your body obtains most of its energy from ____ during low-intensity activity from
   a. muscle glycogen.
   b. liver glycogen.
   c. muscle protein.
   d. fatty acids.

5. Under what conditions will the body use significant amounts of protein for energy during exercise?
   a. inadequate calorie intake
   b. inadequate carbohydrate stores
   c. inadequate fluid intake
   d. both A and B

6. A pregame meal should be
   a. high in carbohydrate, low in fat.
   b. high in carbohydrate and high in fat.
   c. low in carbohydrate, high in fat.
   d. low in protein, high in fat.

7. A condition that occurs when too much water is consumed or too much sodium is lost in sweating, resulting in abnormally low levels of sodium in the blood, is called
   a. acute dehydration.
   b. chronic dehydration.
   c. hyponatremia.

8. A commercial sports drink might be beneficial after 60 minutes or more of exercise because it
   a. contributes to hydration.
   b. provides electrolytes.
   c. provides carbohydrate.
   d. does all of the above.

9. An appropriate exercise recovery beverage would be
   a. a soft drink.
   b. coffee.
   c. low-fat chocolate milk.
   d. orange juice.
10. Acromegaly can be caused by abuse of which ergogenic aid?
   a. creatine.
   b. growth hormone.
   c. anabolic steroids.
   d. erythropoietin.

Answers

1. (c) Muscle strength, cardiorespiratory endurance, and body composition, along with muscle endurance and flexibility, are the five basic components of physical fitness. Stress is not a component of physical fitness.
2. (b) Performing 100 consecutive push-ups without resting shows great muscle endurance because you are able to exert the force needed to push yourself up over a long period of time without getting tired.
3. (b) Muscles that are well trained have the ability to store about 20 to 50 percent more glycogen than normal; however, the storage capacity of muscle glycogen is limited.
4. (d) Fatty acids are the main source of energy during low-intensity activity. As the intensity increases, the body will use less fatty acids and more glycogen for energy.
5. (d) The body will use larger amounts of protein for energy if overall calorie intake is inadequate and if carbohydrate stores are low.
6. (a) A meal before a game or workout should be high in carbohydrate to maximize glycogen stores and low in fat to prevent feelings of fatigue or discomfort.

7. (c) Hyponatremia occurs when blood levels of sodium become abnormally low as a result of drinking too much water or not replacing sodium lost through sweating. Long-distance runners are at higher risk for developing hyponatremia.
8. (d) Sports drinks supply fluids to rehydrate the body during and after exercise, electrolytes to replace those lost during sweating, and carbohydrate, which acts as an immediate source of energy that can potentially improve performance.
9. (c) Low-fat chocolate milk is a good exercise recovery beverage because it contains an appropriate ratio of carbohydrate and protein that is necessary for optimal recovery. Soft drinks, coffee, and orange juice will provide your body with fluids, but lack other nutrients that are ideal for recovery after exercise.
10. (b) Abusing growth hormone causes acromegaly, a disease in which tissues, bones, and internal organs grow abnormally large in size.

Web Support

For more on nutrition and fitness, visit:

- The President's Council on Physical Fitness and Sports, www.fitness.gov
- American Council on Exercise, www.acefitness.org
- American College of Sports Medicine, www.acsm.org
- American Dietetic Association, www.eatright.org
- Sports, Cardiovascular, and Wellness Nutritionists: A Dietetics Practice Group of the American Dietetic Association, www.scandpg.org
- Gatorade Sports Science Institute, www.gssiweb.org

12

Life Cycle Nutrition

Pregnancy through Infancy

1. A **father's** health has no impact on the health of a developing fetus. **T/F**

2. Drinking **red wine** is fine during pregnancy. **T/F**

3. **Morning sickness** only happens between 8 a.m. and noon during the first trimester. **T/F**

4. Pregnant women shouldn't **exercise.** **T/F**

5. **Formula** is better for babies than breast milk. **T/F**

6. Breast milk helps boost a baby's **immune** system. **T/F**

7. Chubby babies should be put on **diets.** **T/F**

8. Infants never need **supplements.** **T/F**

9. Commercially sold **baby food** is always less healthy than homemade. **T/F**

10. **Raw carrots** are a great way for an infant to get vitamin A. **T/F**

Kathy is 28 years old and in the midst of a career change. Though she enjoys her job in social work, she's decided that technology is more exciting and has enrolled in several computer science classes at her local community college. Kathy and her husband had expected to start their family once she finished her degree, but were thrilled when she unexpectedly became pregnant. She delivered her bouncing baby boy during the middle of spring semester.

Kathy wants to finish the semester so that she can get a part-time job in a high-tech company. She also wants to breast-feed while attending morning classes on campus. How can Kathy ensure that her newborn will receive adequate nutrition? How can she overcome the challenges of nursing while attending classes? In this chapter, we will discuss the nutrition needs of infants, as well as of parents and parents-to-be.

Answers

1. False. Fathers need to eat healthy diets and avoid certain substances to help produce a healthy baby. Turn to page 420 to find out why this is the case.
2. False. Any type of alcohol, including red wine, can harm a growing fetus. To find out what other substances can be harmful during pregnancy, turn to page 423.
3. False. Though it's called morning sickness, nausea during the first trimester can happen at any time of day. To learn more about conditions during pregnancy, turn to page 424.
4. False. Physical activity can be good for mothers-to-be, though some activities need to be avoided. To find out which activities are safe, turn to page 428.
5. False. Formula can be a healthy alternative, but breast milk is best for a baby. Turn to page 432 to find out why.
6. True. Antibodies in breast milk are passed from the mother to the baby, giving the baby an immunity boost. To learn about the other benefits of breast milk, turn to page 434.
7. False. Infants should never be put on a weight-loss diet. Babies need calories and fat to support their rapid growth and development. To find out more about the demands of infant growth, turn to page 440.
8. False. Most infants receive an injection of vitamin K at birth, and there are other nutrients that infants may need to supplement their diet. Find out why this is the case on page 440.
9. False. While there's probably nothing as delicious as fresh and homemade, certain brands of jarred baby foods are just as healthy. Read more about commercially made versus homemade baby foods on page 443.
10. False. Although they're a good source of vitamin A, raw carrots are a potential choking hazard for an infant. For more on potentially dangerous foods, turn to page 443.

Why Is Good Nutrition Essential for a Healthy Pregnancy?

When a woman is pregnant, her diet must not only maintain her own health, but also foster and maintain the health of her baby. Similarly, her lifestyle habits will affect both her health and the health of her growing child. In essence, she is breathing, eating, and living for two.

Before we explore the specific nutrient needs and lifestyle factors that help ensure a healthy pregnancy, let's examine how a pregnancy begins, and how the developing child obtains nutrients from the mother.

How Does a Baby Begin Developing?

As soon as a sperm fertilizes an egg, a woman is on her way to delivering a bundle of trillions of cells. A full-term pregnancy is approximately 40 weeks long and is divided into **trimesters.** The initial two weeks after **conception** is called the preembryo period, during which the fertilized egg, or **zygote,** travels down the fallopian tube to embed itself in the lining of the woman's uterus (Figure 12.1). Once attached, it immediately begins obtaining nutrients from the mother. This enables both the fertilized egg (soon to be called an **embryo**) and the placenta to develop. The **placenta** is the site of common tissue between the mother and the embryo where nutrients, oxygen, and waste products are exchanged through the **umbilical cord** (Figure 12.2). The placenta allows the embryo to use the mother's mature organ systems while it is developing.

After the eighth week of pregnancy, the developing embryo is called a **fetus.** As the fetus develops, the mother's diet and lifestyle habits are critical in supporting and nurturing it.

Next, let's look at the specific factors that can affect the health of a developing baby.

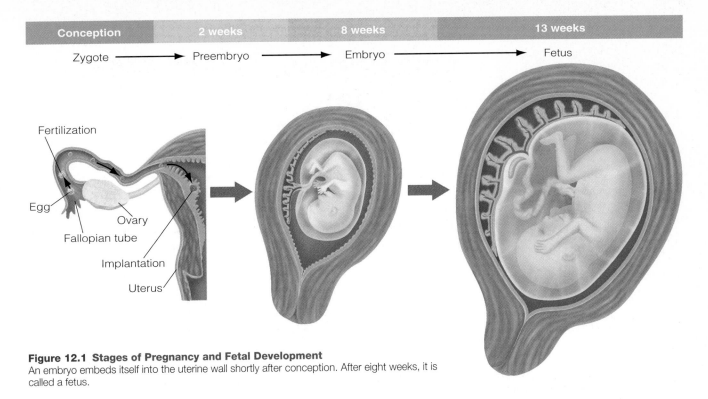

Conception	2 weeks	8 weeks	13 weeks

Zygote → Preembryo → Embryo → Fetus

Fertilization

Egg

Fallopian tube

Ovary

Implantation

Uterus

Figure 12.1 Stages of Pregnancy and Fetal Development
An embryo embeds itself into the uterine wall shortly after conception. After eight weeks, it is called a fetus.

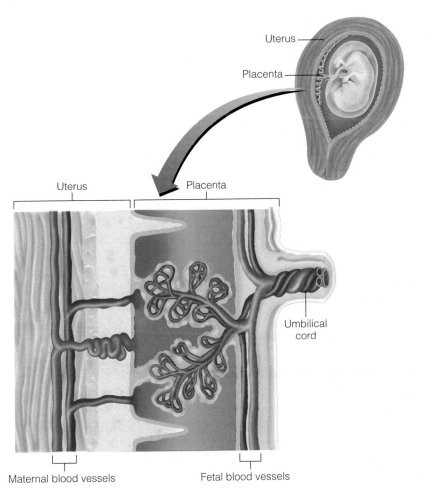

Uterus

Placenta

Uterus   Placenta

Umbilical cord

Maternal blood vessels   Fetal blood vessels

Figure 12.2 The Placenta
The placenta is the site of common tissue between the mother and the embryo where nutrients, oxygen, and waste products are exchanged.

trimesters The three time periods of pregnancy.

conception The moment when a sperm fertilizes an egg.

zygote Term that refers to a fertilized egg for the first two weeks after conception.

embryo Term that refers to a fertilized egg during the third through the eighth week of pregnancy. After the eighth week, the developing baby is called a fetus.

placenta The site of common tissue between the mother and growing embryo. The placenta is attached to the fetus with the **umbilical cord.**

fetus A developing embryo that is at least eight weeks old.

How Does a Baby Begin Developing?   **419**

What Nutrients and Behaviors Are Most Important for a Healthy Pregnancy?

Are You Nutritionally Ready for a Healthy Pregnancy?

Both males and females should have healthy habits before becoming parents. Take the following self-assessment to see if you need some diet and lifestyle fine tuning before trying to get pregnant.

For Both Men and Women

1. Are you overweight?
   Yes ☐ **No** ☐
2. Do you smoke?
   Yes ☐ **No** ☐
3. Do you abuse alcohol?
   Yes ☐ **No** ☐
4. Do you consume less than 400 micrograms of folic acid daily?
   Yes ☐ **No** ☐
5. Do you use any illicit drugs such as marijuana, cocaine, and/or Ecstasy?
   Yes ☐ **No** ☐

Additional Questions for Women Only

1. Do you drink alcohol?
   Yes ☐ **No** ☐
2. Do you take herbs or use herbal teas?
   Yes ☐ **No** ☐
3. Do you drink more than 12 ounce of caffeinated coffee or energy drinks or four cans of caffeinated soft drinks daily?
   Yes ☐ **No** ☐
4. Do you eat albacore tuna, swordfish, mackerel, tilefish, and/or shark?
   Yes ☐ **No** ☐

Answers

If you answered yes to any of these questions, read on to find out how these diet and lifestyle habits can impact a pregnancy.

Some of the dietary and lifestyle changes that need to be made before a woman gets pregnant, and during the pregnancy itself, are obvious. For instance, you probably know that women who smoke or drink alcohol while pregnant are gambling with their child's health. However, there are other changes that should be adopted, including some by the father-to-be, in order to support a healthy pregnancy. Let's review these now.

Before Conception, Fathers-to-Be Need to Eat Well for Healthy Sperm

The woman is not the only person who should consider dietary and lifestyle changes to improve the outcome of a pregnancy. Men take note: The male's lifestyle and diet habits may affect his success in fathering a child. Smoking, alcohol and drug abuse, and obesity have been associated with the decreased production and function of sperm.[1] In contrast, zinc and folate have both been associated with the production of healthy sperm and antioxidants, such as vitamins E and C and carotenoids, may help protect sperm from damage by free radicals.[2] Stopping smoking, abstaining from alcohol or drinking only in moderation, and striving for a healthy body weight are all beneficial.

Men should make sure that they consume a well-balanced diet that contains adequate amounts of fruits and vegetables (antioxidants and folate), as well as whole grains, lean meats and dairy foods, legumes, and nuts (zinc).[3] A healthy baby is the product of two healthy parents, so fathers-to-be who make appropriate diet and lifestyle changes prior to conception help ensure the health of their offspring.

Before Conception, Mothers Need to Adopt a Healthy Lifestyle

If you have ever run a marathon or know someone who has, you know that there is a tremendous amount of effort and diligence that goes into training for the event. Your commitment doesn't begin on the day of the race, but as far as a year in advance. In fact, the more time and effort the runner puts into preparing for the race, the better the results are likely to be.

Ask any woman who has had a baby and she will tell you that planning, carrying, and delivering a healthy child was the marathon of her life. The commitment to eat a healthy diet and change not-so-healthy lifestyle habits is an extremely important part of the prepregnancy and pregnancy periods.

Let's look at the nutritional and lifestyle adjustments a woman needs to make to improve the chances of delivering a healthy baby.

Attain a Healthy Weight

Women who want to get pregnant should strive for a healthy weight *before* conception. Women who begin pregnancy at a healthy weight are likely to conceive more easily, have an uncomplicated pregnancy, and have an easier time nursing the baby.[4]

In contrast, women who are obese may have a harder time getting pregnant, possibly due to irregular menstrual cycles. When they do become pregnant, they are at increased risk of hypertension or gestational diabetes.[5] They also have a greater chance of requiring an induced labor and a cesarean section.[6] Hypertension during pregnancy increases the risk of dying for both mother and baby.[7] Children born to obese women are at greater risk of being born larger than normal, having more difficulties breathing, having a slower heart rate, and potential heart defects and certain birth defects. These babies are also at a higher risk of developing childhood obesity.[8]

Obese women should consider shedding some excess weight prior to conception to improve the chances of a healthier pregnancy and baby. Once an obese woman becomes pregnant, she should focus on moderating her weight gain, rather than trying to lose weight. A woman, whether at a healthy weight, overweight, or obese, should never try to lose weight during pregnancy.

Underweight women also need to strive for a healthy weight before getting pregnant. A woman who is underweight has a lighter weight placenta, which can interfere with her body's ability to deliver nutrients to the developing baby. With less nutrition available, there is an increased risk of delivering a **low birth weight baby,** one weighing less than 5½ pounds. A low birth weight baby is at a higher risk of both health problems and dying within the first year of life than infants born at a healthy weight.

Get Plenty of Folic Acid

Folic acid is needed to create new cells and help the baby grow and develop properly. Consuming adequate folic acid has been shown to reduce the risk of neural tube birth defects in infants if consumed by the mother at least one month prior to conception and during the early weeks of pregnancy. These birth defects occur very early in the pregnancy, typically three to four weeks after conception—a time when few women even know that they are pregnant. For this reason, women who are capable of becoming pregnant and planning to conceive should consume 400 micrograms of folic acid through supplements or fortified foods (see Chapter 7). Women who have previously delivered a baby with a neural tube defect should consult with their health care provider, as they may benefit from an even higher dose of the vitamin.

Moderate Fish and Caffeine Consumption

As you recall from Chapter 5, the Food and Drug Administration (FDA) recommends that women of childbearing age who may become pregnant, those pregnant and nursing, and young children should avoid certain fish that may contain high amounts of the toxin *methylmercury*. This form of mercury can harm the nervous system of the developing fetus, especially during the first trimester of pregnancy. All fish contain some methylmercury, and Table 12.1 on page 422 summarizes the fish consumption guidelines for prepregnant, pregnant, and lactating women.

The caffeine that a pregnant woman drinks in her coffee or soda can be passed on to her baby (as can anything else she consumes). Because the fetus cannot break down the caffeine, it may linger in his body longer than in the mother's. For these reasons, questions have been raised regarding the safety of caffeine consumption during pregnancy. Research studies to date support that caffeine intake of less than 150 milligrams daily, or the amount in 12 ounces (1½ cups) of coffee, doesn't increase the risk of miscarriage or birth defects during pregnancy. However, some studies suggest that intakes greater than 300 milligrams (found in about 3 cups of coffee or 7½ cups of brewed tea) daily, especially if the pregnant woman is also smoking and/or drinking alcohol, may increase the risk of miscarriages.

Some studies also investigate whether caffeine consumption affects a woman's fertility. Research suggests that consuming 500 milligrams or more of caffeine daily

low birth weight baby A baby weighing less than 5½ pounds at birth.

Table 12.1

Fishing for a Healthy Baby

Pregnant and nursing women and women of childbearing age who may become pregnant should follow these guidelines for eating fish:

Do Not Eat	Limit	Enjoy
Shark Swordfish King mackerel Tilefish (Golden bass or Golden snapper)	Albacore (white) tuna to no more than 6 oz weekly Locally caught fish from nearby lakes, rivers, and coastal areas. Check local advisories regarding its safety before consuming it. If no advice is available, eat up to 6 oz weekly. Don't consume any other fish during that week.	Up to 12 oz weekly of fish with low levels of methylmercury, such as: Canned light tuna Cod Catfish Crab Pollack Salmon Scallops Shrimp

Table 12.2

A Jolt of Caffeine

Beverage	Caffeine (mg)
Coffee (8 oz)	
Brewed, drip	85
Brewed, decaffeinated	3
Espresso (1 oz)	40
Tea (8 oz)	
Brewed	40
Iced	25
Soft drinks (8 oz)	24
"Energy drinks" (8 oz)	80
Hot cocoa (8 oz)	6
Chocolate milk (8 oz)	5
Milk chocolate (1 oz)	6

Source: National Toxicology Program, Department of Health and Human Services, www.cerhr.niehs.nih .gov; the International Food Information Council (IFIC), www.ific.org.

Almost 2,300 infants died from SIDS in 2002, which is actually a marked decrease from 25 years ago.

may delay conception.[9] Though the mechanism of how caffeine affects fertility is unknown, to be safe, women who are trying to get pregnant should consume less than 300 milligrams of caffeine per day, and women who are already pregnant should limit their intake to no more than 150 milligrams per day. This means limiting the coffee, tea, and soda to a cup or two a day—or better yet, switching to decaffeinated versions of these drinks. See Table 12.2 for other common sources of caffeine in the diet.

Avoid Cigarettes, Alcohol, Botanical Supplements, and Illicit Drugs

When a pregnant woman smokes, drinks alcohol, takes herbs, and/or consumes drugs, her baby is smoking, drinking, and consuming these substances right along with her.

Cigarette smoking increases the risk of infertility, making conception more difficult.[10] When a smoker does conceive, her infant will weigh a half pound less, on average, than infants of nonsmokers and will be at an increased risk of being born prematurely or dying. Prenatal exposure to smoke can increase the risk of **sudden infant death syndrome** (SIDS) and may stunt the infant's growth and reduce future intellectual and behavioral performance.[11] Though there are thousands of substances in cigarettes and cigarette smoke that can harm the fetus, carbon monoxide and nicotine are particularly dangerous because they reduce the amount of oxygen that reaches the baby, thus intensifying adverse effects.

Pregnant women who smoke often weigh less and gain less weight during pregnancy than nonsmokers, which can also contribute to a low birth weight baby. Whereas these women do not necessarily consume fewer calories, they may have an increased metabolic rate due to smoking. The higher metabolic rate of the pregnant smoker burns calories before the baby can use them. This robs the baby of the calories needed to develop properly and contributes to a lower birth weight.[12]

Even secondhand smoke can affect the health of a mom-to-be and her infant. Exposure to passive smoke can affect the infant's ability to grow properly.[13] Thus, pregnant women and new mothers should avoid work, home, or social environments where they are exposed to secondhand smoke.

sudden infant death syndrome (SIDS) The unexplained death of an infant less than one year of age.

As you read in Chapter 9, drinking alcohol during pregnancy can lead to fetal alcohol spectrum disorders (FASD) in the baby. Children exposed to even low levels of alcohol during pregnancy can be born with learning and behavioral disabilities. Because there is no known safe level of alcohol consumption, pregnant women need to abstain completely to eliminate the chance of having a baby with these disorders. Also, because alcohol can affect a baby within weeks of conception, before a woman is aware that she is pregnant, the Surgeon General has recommended that all women who may become pregnant abstain from alcohol.[14]

Whereas many pregnant women won't even consider taking over-the-counter drugs without clearance from their health care provider, they often don't have the same level of caution when it comes to taking botanical products. **Botanicals** are plants (including herbs) or parts of a plant that are believed to have medicinal effects. Because these products are perceived to be "all natural," people often assume they can take them without risk. Many people even consider them safer than over-the-counter drugs. In fact, this isn't always true, and in some cases, botanicals can be harmful or even dangerous.

Blue cohosh, for example, is an herb that is sometimes used to induce labor, but has been associated with seizures, strokes, and heart attacks in newborns.[15,16] In addition to blue cohosh, other supplements, such as juniper, pennyroyal, goldenseal, and thuja, as well as teas such as raspberry tea, may also cause contractions of the uterus, which can lead to a miscarriage or premature labor.

Green tea, believed by many to be healthy due to its antioxidant content, contains a compound that inhibits folic acid, and may therefore increase risk of neural tube defects.[17] Pregnant women should avoid green tea for this reason. In fact, the American Academy of Pediatrics recommends that pregnant women limit herbal teas in general to two 8-ounce cups daily and choose teas contained in filter bags (rather than loose-leaf).[18]

There have been few research studies conducted on the safety and effectiveness of botanical products during pregnancy. Pregnant women should assume that all herbs and botanical supplements are unsafe and should always check with their health care provider before consuming them.

Smoking marijuana can reduce fertility in both males and females. When used during pregnancy, illicit drugs can increase the risk of miscarriage, preterm labor, a low birth weight baby, and birth defects, which means that the estimated 4.5 percent of pregnant women who use marijuana, cocaine, Ecstasy, and heroin are putting their unborn children at major risk.[19] After birth, the baby may experience drug withdrawal symptoms, such as excessive crying, trembling, and seizures, as well as long-term health problems such as heart defects and behavioral and learning problems.

Women who use these substances should speak with their health care provider about how to stop their habits. They can also visit the National Drug and Alcohol Treatment Referral Routing Service at www.niaaa.nih.gov or phone 1-800-662-HELP (4357).

The Take-Home Message Good nutrition and healthy lifestyle habits are important for both men and women before conception. Smoking, alcohol abuse, and obesity are associated with decreased production and function of sperm. Conception is easier for women when they are at a healthy weight. Women should consume adequate amounts of folic acid prior to getting pregnant and continue to take it during pregnancy. Women should also avoid consuming fish that may contain high amounts of methylmercury, and consume caffeine only in moderation. Smoking, drinking alcohol, and taking herbs and recreational drugs should be avoided.

Smoking during pregnancy can seriously harm the fetus.

As with smoking, drinking alcohol during pregnancy exposes the fetus to potentially toxic substances.

botanicals A part of a plant, such as its root, that is believed to have medicinal or therapeutic attributes. Herbs are considered botanicals.

In the First Trimester: Women Need to Eat When Food May Not Be Appetizing and Practice Food Safety

By the end of the first trimester, the fetus has gone through several developmental milestones. The liver is already forming red blood cells, the heart is pumping blood, the limbs are taking shape, and the brain is growing rapidly. In fact, the head is much larger than the body at this point, to accommodate that developing brain. With all this activity taking place, the fetus still weighs just a half ounce and measures about three inches long. It has a *lot* more growing to do before being born.

During this period, the mother's body is also changing rapidly. She's beginning to notice some breast tenderness, and may start to experience several "side effects" of pregnancy, such as a newly heightened sense of taste or smell, and seemingly random food cravings. She may also have some nausea.

Morning Sickness and Cravings

One of the biggest myths of pregnancy is that morning sickness ends in the morning. Ask any of the 80 percent of women who experience nausea and vomiting during pregnancy and many will tell you that they wished their symptoms ended by noon. Morning sickness is so common that women and health care professionals often use it as an initial sign of possible pregnancy.[20]

Morning sickness usually begins during the first trimester and ends by the twentieth week of pregnancy, although about 10 percent of women experience it longer.[21] The causes of morning sickness are unknown, but fluctuating hormone levels, particularly the increase in estrogen, may play a role.[22] Estrogen heightens a woman's perception of odors (experts sometimes refer to this as the "radar nose" of pregnancy), which leads to nausea and can trigger vomiting.[23] The presence of *Helicobacter pylori* bacteria in the digestive tract has also been associated with morning sickness.[24]

Though there are no known dietary deficiencies that cause, or diet changes that can prevent, morning sickness, some women find relief in eating small, frequent meals that are high in carbohydrates such as pasta, rice, and crackers, and avoiding an empty stomach. Salty foods such as potato chips combined with sour and tart beverages such as lemonade have also been shown to help.[25] Vitamin B_6 may also reduce the nausea and vomiting. Because there is an upper level for vitamin B_6 intake, pregnant women should consult their health care professional before increasing it.

Ginger has also been shown to help, which explains why some pregnant women find relief in drinking ginger ale. However, ginger root may inhibit a specific enzyme in the body, causing potentially adverse effects including interfering with blood clotting.[26] As with vitamin B_6, pregnant women should not consume ginger supplements or extracts without first consulting their health care provider.

Though morning sickness is uncomfortable, it usually does not harm the health of the woman or her fetus. However, in rare cases (less than 1 percent of pregnancies) women experience severe morning sickness with vomiting called **hyperemesis gravidarum** (*hyper* = overstimulated, *emesis* = vomiting, *gravida* = pregnant). This condition can cause serious complications, such as dehydration, electrolyte imbalances, and weight loss. These women often have to be hospitalized for treatment.

While some pregnant women have an aversion to certain foods, such as coffee, tea, or fried or spicy foods, other women can have cravings for specific foods. Chocolate, citrus fruits, pickles, chips, and ice cream are foods that women commonly want when they are pregnant.[27] Sometimes women even crave and consume nonfood substances.

hyperemesis gravidarum Excessive vomiting during pregnancy that can lead to dehydration and loss of electrolytes.

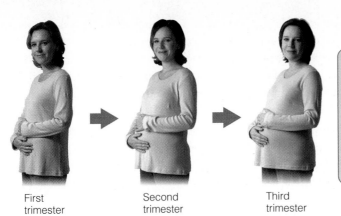

Total weight gain
~30 lbs

- Maternal fat stores (~7 lbs)
- Uterus and breast (4 lbs)
- Blood (3–4 lbs)
- Fetus (~7 lbs)
- Placenta, amniotic fluid, and other fluids (~8 lbs)

First trimester

Second trimester

Third trimester

Figure 12.3 Components of Weight Gain during Pregnancy
Healthy-weight women gain 25 to 35 pounds, on average, during pregnancy.

Pica is the abnormal, compulsive intake of nonedible items such as laundry starch, burnt matches, cornstarch, clay, dirt, paint chips, and/or baking soda. (Women also sometimes crave ice or ice chips.) Pica is more common in African American women and those with a family history of this type of eating. Pica has been associated with low blood levels of iron, which has led to the theory that these women are seeking out nonfood substances that contain this mineral.[28] However, other research suggests that pica causes the iron deficiency seen in these women.[29] Consuming nonfood substances can lead to the ingestion of toxic compounds such as lead that could perpetuate lead poisoning and other ill effects in both the mother and the baby.[30]

Goals for Adequate Weight Gain

Healthy women gain, on average, 27.5 pounds during pregnancy.[31] Not coincidentally, this is the approximate amount of weight that is needed to support the growth of the baby (Figure 12.3). Because a woman's prepregnancy weight can impact the health of the growing baby, women at a healthy weight (with a BMI between 19.8 and 26) should gain 25 to 35 pounds, whereas underweight or overweight women have slightly different goals (Table 12.3). These recommendations are based on the balance between the baby's and the mother's health. This weight gain provides for adequate growth so that the baby will healthfully weigh about 6.5 to 8.5 pounds, yet not increase the risk of complications during delivery or cause excess weight gain for the mother.[32] Gaining excess weight will make it more difficult to lose the weight once the baby is born and increases the likelihood of the mom remaining overweight many years after delivery.[33]

Because pregnant women typically gain only about two pounds in the first trimester, they do not yet need an increased amount of calories. However, a pregnant woman does have an increased need for certain nutrients immediately after conception. The fact that she needs more of some nutrients, but not more calories, creates a potential dietary dilemma.

Dietary Considerations

In the first trimester, a pregnant woman needs up to 50 percent more folate, zinc, and iron than before she was pregnant. Her needs for other nutrients either don't increase or increase only slightly. However, though her other nutrient needs haven't yet increased, a pregnant woman's diet shouldn't fall short of any nutrients, particularly calcium. How does a mom-to-be increase her intake of folate, zinc, and iron and meet her calcium and other nutrient needs without taking in more calories? She has to carefully choose nutrient-dense foods and will probably need a prenatal supplement.

If a woman is conscientious about taking folic acid prior to conception and continues to take a supplement and/or consume folic acid–fortified foods, she should be

Table 12.3

Recommended Weight Gain during Pregnancy

Body Mass Index (BMI)	Recommended Weight Gain (in Pounds)
<19.8	28–40
19.8 to 26	25–35
>26–29	15–25
>29	at least 15

Source: Institute of Medicine, *Nutrition during Pregnancy, Part 1: Weight Gain* (Washington, D.C.: National Academies Press; 1990); L. Kaiser and L. Allen, Position of the American Dietetic Association: Nutrition and Lifestyle for a Healthy Pregnancy Outcome, *Journal of the American Dietetic Association* 102 (2002): 1479–1490.

pica Eating nonfood substances such as dirt and clay.

able to meet her increased needs for this vitamin. Foods high in folate include green leafy vegetables, citrus fruits and juices, and whole-grain products.

Her increased iron needs are not as easy to meet. Even though a woman loses less iron during pregnancy because she's not menstruating, and she absorbs up to three times more iron from foods than before she was pregnant, she still needs to increase her dietary intake for several reasons. She needs extra iron to make additional red blood cells, which increase her oxygen-carrying capacity and will help replace the blood lost during delivery. A woman also needs extra iron to prevent anemia, a condition associated with premature delivery and an increased risk of dying for both mother and baby.[34] Finally, iron is essential for fetal growth and development, and for the growth of the placenta.[35]

Whereas meat, fish, poultry, and enriched grains supply iron, the amount recommended during pregnancy is unlikely to be met from food alone, so a supplement is needed.[36] Many women are prescribed a prenatal supplement to help meet their iron and other increased nutrient needs.

Because iron can interfere with the absorption of other minerals, if a woman is taking more than 30 milligrams of iron daily, she should also take 15 milligrams of zinc and 2 milligrams of copper to prevent a deficiency of these other minerals.[37] Zinc is needed in protein metabolism and in the synthesis of DNA so that cells can replicate and differentiate. Copper, as part of enzymes, is needed in the production of energy, the synthesis of connective tissues, and in the transport and utilization of iron.

Other nutrients are also of concern during pregnancy, especially if the mother is a vegetarian or vegan. Pregnant women, especially vegetarians, should be mindful about meeting their need for linolenic acid, an essential fatty acid found in nuts, soybeans, and canola oil. Essential fatty acids are needed in the development of cell membranes and so are important in the formation of new tissues, particularly those of the central nervous system.[38] Vegans who don't consume any animal products need to make sure that they are getting a reliable source of vitamin B_{12}. Recall from Chapter 8 that vegans also have higher zinc and iron needs even when they aren't pregnant, so a supplement will also ensure that they meet their needs for these minerals.

A pregnant woman will absorb more calcium during pregnancy to offset the amount of calcium needed by the growing fetus, but she still needs to meet her daily needs to preserve bone mass and to prevent osteoporosis later in life. Currently, more than half of women of childbearing age in the United States fall short of the MyPyramid-recommended servings from the dairy and the fruit and vegetable groups, putting them at risk of not meeting many nutrient needs, including calcium.[39]

One way to ensure adequate calcium intake during pregnancy is to drink nutrient-dense milk as the beverage of choice, rather than nutritionally empty sodas. Regular sodas contain calories and sugar and not much else, and so are not a good choice for women during this nutritionally critical period. Even though diet sodas usually don't contain calories, as they are likely to contain sugar substitutes, these beverages lack important nutrients. The vitamin D, calcium, and protein in milk are needed by both the mother and growing baby and are absent in diet beverages. Note: The consumption of products that contain the sugar substitutes aspartame (Equal), sucralose (Splenda), acesulfame-K (Sunett), and saccharin (Sweet 'N Low) during pregnancy has been deemed safe when consumed within the FDA's level of acceptable daily intake.[40]

While it's important that pregnant women meet their nutrient needs, it is equally important that they not consume too much of some nutrients. Too much vitamin A can be toxic and increase the risk of birth defects, especially when taken during the first trimester (see Chapter 7). Women who take a supplement should consume no more

Daily average over one week for a 2,000 calorie diet

Grains	Vegetables	Fruits	Oils	Milk	Meat and Beans
6 oz eq	2.5 cups	2 cups	6 tsp	3 cups	5.5 oz eq

Nutrient	Average Daily Recommended Intake Based on MyPyramid	Recommended DRI for Nonpregnant Women Age 19–50 Years	Recommended Nutrient Intake During Pregnancy
Protein	98 g	46 g	71 g
Carbohydrates	264 g	130 g	175 g (minimum)
Linoleic acid	21 g	12 g	13 g
Alpha-linolenic acid	1.1 g	1.1 g	1.4 g
Dietary folate equivalents	558 mcg	400 mcg	600 mcg*
Thiamin	1.9 mg	1.1 mg	1.4 mg
Riboflavin	2.5 mg	1.1 mg	1.4 mg
Niacin equivalents	24 mg	14 mg	18 mg
Vitamin B_6	2.9 mg	1.3–1.5 mg	1.9 mg
Vitamin B_{12}	18.4 mg	2.4 mg	2.6 mg
Vitamin C	190 mg	75 mg	85 mg
Vitamin E	18.9 mg	15 mg	15 mg
Vitamin A	1,430 mcg	700 mcg	770 mcg
Calcium	1,389 mg	1,000 mcg	1,000 mcg
Magnesium	432 mg	310–320 mg	350–360 mg
Copper	1.9 mg	0.9 mg	1.0 mg
Iron	21 mg	18 mg	27 mg†
Phosphorus	1,830 mg	700 mg	700 mg
Zinc	14 mg	8 mg	11 mg
Calories	**~2,000**	**2,000–2,200‡**	**§**

* Supplemented and/or fortified foods are recommended.
† A supplement is recommended.
‡ Varies depending upon activity level and weight.
§ Doesn't increase until second and third trimester.

than 5,000 IU (1,500 micrograms) of preformed vitamin A daily, which is 100 percent of the Daily Value (DV) listed on the label. Figure 12.4 summarizes the nutrient needs of pregnant women and compares these to a well-balanced diet. As you can see, a balanced diet can meet the majority of a pregnant woman's nutrient needs.

Foodborne Illness

During pregnancy, a woman's immune system is weakened and the fetus's immune system is undeveloped, both of which set the stage for potential difficulties in fighting off pathogens that can cross the placenta. The bacteria *Listeria monocytogenes*, for example, may cause miscarriages, premature labor, low birth weight, developmental problems, and even infant death.

Some foods, like raw meats and fish, are more likely to carry pathogens and need to be handled with care or avoided during pregnancy. Sushi or sashimi, for example, contain raw fish, and are more likely to contain parasites or bacteria. Pregnant women should also avoid undercooked meat, fish, or poultry; unpasteurized milk, cheese, and juices; and raw sprouts (bacteria migrate into immature sprout seeds and can grow to dangerous levels). You will learn more about foodborne pathogens, especially *Listeria monocytogenes*, and how to safeguard your foods in Chapter 14.

Food that may carry pathogens, such as sushi or sashimi, should be avoided by pregnant women for their own safety and the safety of their fetus.

The Take-Home Message A pregnancy is divided into trimesters. During the first trimester, the fertilized egg develops into an embryo and eventually into a fetus. Many women experience morning sickness and cravings during this trimester. Women should gain from 25 to 35 pounds during pregnancy, depending upon their prepregnancy weight. The needs for many nutrients increase during pregnancy, but other than iron, most can be met with a balanced diet. For pregnant women to obtain the iron they need, a supplement is often prescribed. Pregnant women should avoid excess amounts of preformed vitamin A and use sugar substitutes in moderation. They also need to avoid foods that may contain pathogens.

> 1 whole-wheat English muffin
> 2 tbs peanut butter
> + 5 baby carrots
> 340 calories

The extra calorie and nutrient needs of the second and third trimesters can be met with nutrient-dense diet additions.

In the Second Trimester: Healthy Weight Gain and Calorie Intake Are Important

For many pregnant women, the nausea and fatigue of the first trimester subside during the second trimester, and their appetite begins to increase. The baby is growing rapidly, and the mother's body is changing to accommodate this growth (see Figure 12.3). Blood cells are forming in the baby's bone marrow, its body grows bigger than the head, the ears become prominent, the eyes blink, and the lips suck. The fetus is just under 2 pounds and about 13 inches long by the end of this trimester.

The mother's body is also changing as her amniotic fluid and blood volume increase, her breasts get larger, and she stores more fat. During this period of growth, the mother needs to focus on consuming adequate calories and nutrients, exercise, if possible, and be aware of potential complications.

Consume Adequate Calories, Carbohydrate, and Protein

During the second and third trimesters, the mother's calorie needs increase, and she should gain slightly less than a pound per week until delivery. She needs to consume an additional 340 calories daily during the second trimester. This is the equivalent of adding two servings from the grain group, and a serving from each of the meat and vegetable groups. A whole-wheat english muffin topped with peanut butter and a few baby carrots, fit these requirements rather nutritiously, as do many other meal combinations. This combination of food groups also provides plenty of essential fatty acids, carbohydrates, fiber, zinc, iron, and protein—the nutrients that a woman needs more of during pregnancy.

Pregnant women need a minimum of 175 grams of carbohydrates per day (versus 130 grams for nonpregnant women) to cover the amount of glucose needed for both the developing brain and the energy needs of the fetus, and to prevent ketosis. (Ketosis was discussed in Chapter 4). This amount is far exceeded in a typical balanced diet.

A pregnant woman's protein needs also increase by about 35 percent, to about 71 grams daily, during the second and third trimesters. As you can see from Figure 12.4, women typically meet this higher protein demand by eating a balanced diet.

The Importance of Exercise

Daily exercise during pregnancy can help improve sleep, lower the risk of hypertension and diabetes, prevent backaches, help relieve constipation, shorten labor, and allow women to return more quickly to their prepregnancy weight after delivery. Exercise can also help provide an emotional boost by reducing stress, depression, and anxiety.[41] The American College of Obstetricians and Gynecologists recommends 30 minutes

Walking is one form of exercise that is safe for both mother and baby.

or more of moderate exercise on most, if not all, days of the week, as long as the woman doesn't have any medical issues or complications.[42] Pregnant women should check with their health care provider before exercising to see if it is appropriate.

Low-impact activities such as walking, swimming, and stationary cycling are best because they pose less risk of injury for both mother and baby. In contrast, high-impact activities, such as downhill skiing and basketball, could injure the baby and cause joint injuries for the mother (Table 12.4). Exercising moms-to-be should take special care to avoid a significant increase in their body core temperature, and to drink plenty of fluids to avoid dehydration.[43]

Potential Complications: Gestational Diabetes and Hypertension

Sometimes a pregnant woman develops high blood glucose levels during her pregnancy and is diagnosed with **gestational diabetes** (gestation = pregnancy). This type of diabetes occurs in about 7 percent of pregnancies in the United States and manifests itself after approximately the twentieth week.[44] A pregnant woman should be tested for gestational diabetes during her second trimester.

Though the cause of gestational diabetes is still unknown, hormones from the placenta appear to lead to insulin resistance in the mother, which in turn causes hyperglycemia. This elevated blood glucose crosses the placenta, stimulating the baby's pancreas to make more insulin, which leads to the storage of excess glucose as fat and can result in **macrosomia** (*macro* = large, *somia* = body), or a large baby.[45] A larger than normal baby can increase the risk of injury to the baby's shoulders during delivery or of having to have a cesarean delivery.[46]

Gestational diabetes also increases the risk of the baby developing **jaundice,** breathing problems, and birth defects.[47] Because the baby is producing extra insulin during pregnancy, this hormone is elevated after birth, causing a rapid drop in blood glucose levels, which can cause hypoglycemia.[48]

Although this type of diabetes usually doesn't continue after the baby is born, women with gestational diabetes and their babies are at higher risk of developing type 2 diabetes, as well as hypertension and being overweight, later on in life.[49]

Certain factors can increase a woman's risk for gestational diabetes:

- Being overweight
- Being over 25 years old
- Having a history of higher-than-normal blood glucose levels
- Having a family history of diabetes
- Being of Hispanic, African American, Native American, or Pacific Islander descent
- Having previously given birth to a very large baby or a stillborn baby
- Having had gestational diabetes in the past

According to the National Institute of Child Health and Human Development, if a woman has two or more of these risk factors, she is at high risk for developing gestational diabetes. If she has one risk factor, she is at an average risk, whereas if she doesn't have any of these, she is at low risk.[50] Eating healthily, maintaining a healthy weight, and exercising regularly can help reduce the risk of developing diabetes during pregnancy.

Hypertension (high blood pressure) during pregnancy can damage the woman's kidneys and other organs and increase the risk of low birth weight and premature delivery.[51] It occurs in about 8 percent of pregnancies in the United States.[52] Though some women have hypertension prior to conceiving, others develop it during their pregnancy.

Table 12.4
Safe and Unsafe Exercises during Pregnancy

Safe Activities	Unsafe Activities (Contact Sports and High-Impact Activities)
Walking	Hockey (field and ice)
Stationary cycling	Basketball
Low-impact aerobics	Football
Swimming	Soccer
Dancing	Gymnastics
	Horseback riding
	Skating
	Skiing (snow and water)
	Vigorous racquet sport
	Weight lifting

Source: T. Wang, and B. Apgar, Recommendations for Sports Activities during Pregnancy, *American Family Physician* 57 (1998): 1846–1856.

gestational diabetes Diabetes that occurs in women during pregnancy.

macrosomia A large baby, weighing more than 8 pounds, 13 oz.

jaundice A yellowish coloring of the skin due to the presence of bile pigments in the blood.

Exercising While Pregnant

Consult your health care provider before exercising.

Begin slowly to avoid excessive fatigue and shortness of breath.

Exercise in the early morning or evening to avoid becoming overheated.

Drink plenty of fluids to stay hydrated.

Report any problems or unusual symptoms such as chest pains, contractions, dizziness, headaches, calf swelling, blurred vision, vaginal discharge or bleeding, and/or abdominal pain immediately to your health care provider.

Source: Adapted from The National Women's Health Information Center, U.S. Department of Health and Human Services, "Healthy Pregnancy: Have a Fit Pregnancy," 2006.

pregnancy-induced hypertension A category of hypertension that includes **gestational hypertension, preeclampsia,** and **eclampsia.** Gestational hypertension occurs in pregnancy in a woman without prior history of high blood pressure. Preeclampsia occurs when hypertension, severe edema, and protein loss occur. Eclampsia can result in seizures and can be extremely dangerous for both the mother and the baby.

Pregnancy-induced hypertension includes **gestational hypertension, preeclampsia,** and **eclampsia,** each progressively more medically serious. Gestational hypertension is more likely to occur halfway through pregnancy and be a sign of preeclampsia. Preeclampsia (also known as toxemia) occurs when the pregnant woman has hypertension and severe edema, and her urine contains protein, which is a signal of damage to her kidneys.[53] Note: Though some swelling or edema in a woman's feet and ankles is normal during pregnancy, the dramatic edema seen in preeclampsia is visible in her face and hands and can cause weight gain of more than 2 pounds a week.[54]

The cause of preeclampsia is not known, but is dangerous to the baby because less oxygen- and nutrient-rich blood is reaching the placenta.[55] Women who have hypertension prior to pregnancy or develop it during pregnancy, are overweight, under the age of 20 or over the age of 40, are carrying more than one baby, or have diabetes are at higher risk of developing preeclampsia.[56] If left untreated, preeclampsia can lead to eclampsia, which can cause seizures in the mother and is a major cause of death of women during pregnancy.[57]

The only cure for preeclampsia and eclampsia is to deliver the baby. However, delivery too early (before 32 weeks) is unsafe for the baby. Women are often confined to bed rest, managed with medications, and even hospitalized to treat preeclampsia until the baby can be safely born.[58] Calcium supplements had been postulated to prevent preeclampsia, but research doesn't support that it reduces the risk, especially if the mother's diet is adequate in this mineral.[59] Some research suggests that antioxidants, specifically vitamins C and E, may reduce the risk, but more research is needed.[60]

The Take-Home Message Pregnant women need to consume an additional 340 calories daily during the second trimester. A varied selection of nutrient-dense foods will easily meet increased calorie needs. Exercise can provide numerous benefits during pregnancy. Some women develop gestational diabetes and pregnancy-induced high blood pressure and need to be closely monitored by a health care professional.

In the Third Trimester: Eating Frequent Small Meals and a High-Fiber Diet Can Help with Heartburn and Constipation

By the end of the last trimester, a pregnant woman should be taking in an extra 450 calories daily and continue gaining about 1 pound per week (adding a banana to the english muffin, peanut butter, and carrot snack will increase this to about 450 calories). She is likely to have a harder time getting around due to her expanding body. Climbing stairs may literally take her breath away and finding a comfortable sleeping position could take some maneuvering. At the end of the third trimester, the baby will weigh approximately 7 pounds.

As the growing baby exerts pressure on the mother's intestines and stomach, she may experience heartburn. Hormonal changes may also slow the movement of food through the GI tract, and increase the likelihood of stomach contents refluxing back into the esophagus, also causing heartburn. To minimize heartburn, pregnant women should eat frequent, small meals rather than fewer, larger meals, and avoid foods that may irritate the esophagus, such as spicy or highly seasoned foods. They also shouldn't lie down after meals, and they should elevate their heads during sleep to minimize reflux.[61]

Constipation is also very common near the end of pregnancy. The slower movement of food through the GI tract, coupled with a tendency for less physical activity due to the awkward distribution of the woman's body weight, reduces regularity and causes a more stagnant stool. The high amount of iron in prenatal supplements can also contribute to constipation.[62] Adding more fiber-rich foods such as bran cereals, beans, whole grains, fruits, and vegetables, along with plenty of fluids, can help keep things moving along and prevent constipation.

The Take-Home Message During the third trimester, a woman needs an additional 450 calories per day and should continue gaining about a pound per week. Heartburn and constipation commonly occur during the third trimester. Eating smaller meals and increasing the fiber in the diet can help.

NUTRITION IN THE REAL WORLD

eLearn
Virtual Stages of Pregnancy

For a summary of the developments during each stage of pregnancy, visit www.4woman.org/pregnancy/pregnancy/stages/text.cfm.

What Special Concerns Might Younger or Older Mothers-to-Be Face?

Pregnancy and childbirth place demands on the body of a mother-to-be no matter what her age, but women who become pregnant during their teenage years face particular challenges. Women over the age of 35 also face some additional challenges.

Because a teenage girl's body is still growing, she has higher nutrient needs than does an adult woman. In addition, teenage girls, like many adolescents, are more likely to eat on the run, skip meals, eat less-nutrient-dense snacks, and consume inadequate amounts of whole grains, fruits, vegetables, and lean dairy products. Add this unbalanced diet to the increased needs of pregnancy, and these young girls are likely falling short of many of their nutrient requirements, especially iron, folic acid, calcium, and potentially even calories.

Teenage mothers are also more likely to develop pregnancy-induced hypertension and deliver premature and low birth weight babies, putting the baby at risk for health problems. They are more likely to engage in unhealthy lifestyle habits such as smoking, drinking alcohol, and taking illicit drugs, all of which can compromise the baby's health.[63]

Over 400,000 babies are born to young girls annually.[64] To help reduce the incidences of children having children, the National Campaign to Prevent Teen Pregnancy, a nonprofit organization, has set a goal to reduce the rate of teen pregnancy by one-third between 2006 and 2015. More information on this effort can be found at its website at www.teenpregnancy.org.

Women who delay pregnancy until their 30s or beyond, as many now do (in fact, the number of births for women over age 35 has risen 40 percent since 1990), may also face additional challenges.[65] Fertility typically begins to decline in women starting in their early 30s, so conception may take longer. Women are not only at higher risk of having diabetes and high blood pressure after the age of 35, but also are at a higher risk of developing these conditions during pregnancy.

Older mothers should try to achieve a healthy body weight prior to conception, avoid smoking, eat a balanced diet before and during pregnancy, and consume adequate amounts of folic acid. As with all pregnant women, they should limit their caffeine intake and avoid alcohol and illicit drugs.

The Take-Home Message Teens who become pregnant are at higher risk of developing hypertension and delivering a premature and low birth weight baby. Because a teen is still growing, she will likely have a hard time meeting both her nutrient needs and her baby's unless she is diligent about eating a well-balanced diet. Women over age 35 may have a harder time conceiving and are at higher risk for high blood pressure and diabetes during pregnancy.

Regardless of her age, as her due date draws near an expectant mother needs to decide how to nourish her newborn after delivery—should she breast-feed or use formula? Let's look at both of these options next.

What Is Breast-Feeding and Why Is It Beneficial?

A woman who has just given birth will begin a period of **lactation,** that is, her body will produce milk to nourish her new infant. Milk production is stimulated by the infant's suckling at the mother's nipple. Signals sent from the nipple to the hypothalamus in the mother's brain prompt the pituitary gland to release two hormones: prolactin and oxytocin. Prolactin causes milk to be produced in the breast, while oxytocin causes the milk to be released, or **let down,** so the infant can receive it through the nipple (see Figure 12.5).[66]

The old adage "breast is best" when it comes to nourishing an infant is still true. Through **breast-feeding,** or nursing, mothers provide food that is uniquely tailored to meet their infant's nutritional needs in an easily digestible form. Breast-feeding also provides many other advantages for both the mother and the baby.

Breast-Feeding Provides Physical, Emotional, and Financial Benefits for Mothers

Breast-feeding provides short- and long-term benefits for both mother and child. During infancy, breast-feeding can be cheaper, safer, and more convenient than bottle-feeding. The long-term health and emotional benefits can last for years after infancy.

Breast-Feeding Helps with Pregnancy Recovery and Reduces the Risk of Some Chronic Diseases

In addition to stimulating the release of breast milk, the hormone oxytocin stimulates contractions in the uterus, which helps the organ return to its prepregnancy size and shape. Breast-feeding also reduces blood loss in the mother after delivery.[67] Breast-feeding may help some women return to their prepregnancy weight and manage their postpregnancy weight.

Breast-feeding, especially if it is done exclusively (not combining it with formula-feeding), can also help delay the return of the menstrual cycle, which may decrease fertility. However, this does not mean that women who breast-feed their newborns should assume they won't get pregnant. They still need to take precautions if they wish to avoid pregnancy.

lactation The production of milk in a woman's body after childbirth, and the period during which it occurs. The baby receives the milk through breast-feeding.

let-down The release of milk from the mother's breast to feed the baby.

breast-feeding The act of feeding an infant or child milk from a woman's breast.

Women in their 20s who breast-feed for up to two years may reduce the risk of breast and ovarian cancer. Breast-feeding has also been shown to reduce the risk of hip fractures later in life, increase bone density, and reduce the risk of type 2 diabetes.[68]

Breast Milk Is Less Expensive and More Convenient than Formula

A new mother who opts to buy formula rather than breast-feed her baby will spend an estimated $1,200 for the first year's worth of powdered formula (more if she buys the ready-to-feed variety). The costs associated with breast-feeding, in contrast, are primarily for buying the extra food a woman needs to eat to produce her infant's milk, and cost in at about $300 for the first year.[69] In other words, making breast milk is about 75 percent cheaper than buying powdered formula.

There are other costs associated with formula-feeding beyond the price of the product. For instance, an estimated $2 million is spent yearly to produce, package, and ship formula throughout the United States. There are also environmental costs of dealing with the 550 million formula cans and 800,000 pounds of paper packaging and waste that are disposed of in landfills each year, as well as costs associated with the energy needed to properly clean the feeding bottles.[70] For the family, the environment, and society as a whole, breast-feeding is cheaper than formula-feeding.

Feeding from the breast is more convenient than bottle-feeding because the milk is always sterile and at the right temperature, and there isn't any need to prepare bottles. The mother also doesn't need to prepare the milk before feeding, and she has less cleanup to do afterwards.

Breast-Feeding Promotes Bonding

The close interaction between mother and child during nursing promotes a unique bonding experience. The physical contact helps the baby feel safe, secure, and emotionally attached to the mother.[71] Breast-feeding may also play a role in reducing incidences of infants being abandoned by their mothers.[72]

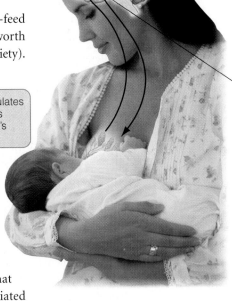

Hypothalamus

2 Hypothalamus stimulates the release of prolactin and oxytocin

1 Sucking stimulates nerve that sends signal to mother's hypothalamus

Pituitary

3 Prolactin triggers milk production and oxytocin triggers the let-down response

Figure 12.5 The Let-Down Response

Breast-Feeding Provides Nutritional and Health Benefits for Infants

There are over 200 compounds in breast milk that benefit infants. Numerous research studies have indicated that breast-feeding provides nutritional and health advantages that can last years beyond the feeding.[73] It is one of the most important strategies for improving an infant's long-term health.

Breast Milk Is Best for an Infant's Unique Nutrition Needs

The nutritional composition of breast milk changes as the infant grows. Right after birth, a new mother produces a carotenoid-rich, yellowish fluid called **colostrum** that has little fat but a lot of protein, vitamin A, and minerals. Colostrum also contains antibodies that help protect the infant from infections, particularly in the digestive tract.

colostrum The fluid that is expressed from the mother's breast after birth and before the development of breast milk.

Four to seven days later, actual breast milk begins to flow. Breast milk is high in lactose, fat, and B vitamins, and lower in fat-soluble vitamins, sodium, and other minerals. These nutrients are proportionally balanced to enhance their absorption.[74] Breast milk is low in protein so as not to stress the infant's immature kidneys with excessive amounts of nitrogen waste products. The protein is also mostly in the form of alpha-lactalbumin, which is easier for the infant to digest.[75] The nutrient composition of breast milk continues to change as the baby grows and his or her needs change.[76] By the time the infant has breast-fed for six months, the mother's milk will contain less protein than it did during the first month.[77]

Breast-Feeding Protects Against Infections, Allergies, and Chronic Diseases and May Enhance Brain Development

Breast milk provides the infant with a disease-fighting boost until the baby's own immune system matures. Research supports that breast-feeding decreases the risk and severity of diarrhea and other intestinal disorders, respiratory infections, meningitis, ear infections, and urinary tract infections.[78]

One protein in breast milk, lactoferrin, protects the infant against bacteria, viruses, fungi, and inflammation by binding with iron, and making it unavailable to the bacteria that need it to flourish.[79] Lactoferrin also inhibits the ability of bacteria to stick to the walls of the intestines. Bacteria must adhere to the intestinal wall to flourish.

Breast milk provides other beneficial compounds, such as antioxidants, hormones, enzymes, and growth factors that play a role in the development of the infant and protect the baby from pathogens, inflammation, diseases, and allergies.[80] Some research suggests that breast milk may also protect against SIDS, asthma, leukemia, heart disease, and diabetes mellitus.[81]

Breast-feeding, especially if continued beyond six months, may help reduce the risk of childhood obesity. The reason for this isn't clear, but could be associated with the tendency of breast-fed infants to gain less weight during the first year of life than formula-fed infants. The lower weight gain may be due to breast-fed infants having more control over when they start and stop eating than their bottle-fed counterparts.[82] Babies at the breast will rely on their internal cues to eat until they are full, and then stop eating. Bottle-fed babies, in contrast, may find their internal cues overruled as the parent or caregiver feeds them until the bottle is empty.[83] This relationship, whereby the caregiver controls how much food is consumed, rather than relying on the child's internal cues, could lead to chronic overfeeding.[84]

Lastly, breast milk may help infants with their intellectual development. Breast milk is rich in two unsaturated fatty acids, docosahexaenoic acid (DHA) and arachidonic acid (AA), which are important for the development of the central nervous system, particularly the brain (see Chapter 5). Research suggests that breast-fed infants may have greater cognitive function, measured by IQ and academic success in school, than formula-fed babies, which may be due in part to these two fatty acids.[85] DHA and AA have been added to some infant formulas.

Because of all of these benefits, the American Academy of Pediatrics (AAP) and the American Dietetic Association (ADA) recommend that women exclusively breast-feed for the first six months and then use a combination of appropriate foods and breast-feeding during at least the first year. Currently, over 70 percent of American

Women can express breast milk using a breast pump and store the milk in the refrigerator or freezer for later use.

Breast-Feeding at Work Can Work

For many women, the decision to breast-feed their infants is an easy one. The bigger challenge is how to juggle breast-feeding with returning to work or school.

Many women feel uncomfortable about breast-feeding outside the home, especially at their place of employment. Consider that about 50 percent of working mothers have babies that are one year of age or younger, and you can see that this reluctance is a big issue.[1] The hesitation isn't just one-sided: Research shows that most companies don't offer support for working mothers, even though employer support for breast-feeding can extend the duration that a mother nurses her baby, which would benefit both mothers and babies.[2] The reality is that many women have to choose between breast-feeding and a paycheck.

But this may be slowly changing. In 1998, the state of Minnesota mandated that its companies aid and support breast-feeding moms. From 1998 to 2002, the percentage of women still breast-feeding at 6 months more than doubled within the state.[3] Currently, 10 states in the United States have laws about breast-feeding in the workplace.[4]

Worksite support is not only healthy for the infant but, in many ways, healthy for the corporate bottom line. Because breast-fed infants are sick less often than formula-fed babies, annual health care costs are approximately $400 lower for breast-fed than for non-breast-fed babies.[5] Employees who are able to breast-feed are also happier, have improved productivity, and show greater loyalty to the employer. In fact, a company's commitment to supporting breast-feeding women can be used as a recruitment tool when seeking new workers. It is estimated that each $1 invested in a corporate breast-feeding program saves the company $3.[6]

Women who return to work while lactating need only minimal worksite resources to accommodate their breast-feeding. First, they need adequate break times throughout the day and access to a private, comfortable room with an electrical outlet in order to pump their breast milk. They also need a sink in which to wash their hands and the pumping equipment, and a refrigerator for storing the milk.[7]

Some companies, such as Johnson & Johnson, have gone beyond these minimum requirements and initiated a company-wide breast-feeding program called Nurture Space. Employees who are new mothers, or their spouses or partners, receive a lactation education kit that includes an instructional DVD, a breast-feeding guide, and other educational materials. They also receive a discount on a portable breast pump and free telephone consultations with a certified lactation consultant. At many Johnson & Johnson corporate locations there are Nurture Space rooms where breast-feeding mothers can comfortably express their milk during the work day.

Johnson & Johnson is committed to this program because there are many benefits to supporting nursing mothers upon their return to work. Breast-fed babies have fewer allergies and illnesses. Working mothers enjoy greater peace of mind and job satisfaction when they can choose to continue to nurse. The company then benefits from fewer absences, faster return-to-work rates, lower health care costs, and improved productivity, loyalty, and corporate image.

---

women initiate breast-feeding when their infants are born, which is close to the goal set for the nation in *Healthy People 2010*.[86] However, only 35 percent still breast-feed their infants at six months and only 17 percent continue until the baby is one year of age.[87] This falls short of the nation's goal for 50 percent of infants to be breast-feeding at six months and at least 25 percent to remain nursing at age one.[88]

The breast-fed infant doesn't always have to consume breast milk directly from the breast. Milk can be pumped, or expressed, with a breast pump, refrigerated, and fed to the baby in a bottle by another caregiver at another time. This allows the mother to work outside the home or enjoy a few hours "off duty." The feature box "Breast-Feeding at Work Can Work" addresses the dilemma of moms who want to breast-feed but who want or have to return to work.

> **Breast milk should be stored in the back of the freezer, where there is less temperature fluctuation and it is less likely to defrost. Premature defrosting increases the risk of harmful bacteria multiplying.**

Expressed breast milk needs to be used within 24 hours or it can be stored in the freezer for three to six months. Kathy, the college student you read about in the beginning of the chapter, can pump and express her milk before she leaves for class. She can refrigerate the milk so that her baby can be fed while she is on campus.

The Take-Home Message Breast-feeding provides numerous benefits for women and babies. It can help mothers return to their prepregnancy weight and reduce the risk of certain cancers, osteoporosis, and type 2 diabetes. Breast-feeding is the least expensive and most convenient way to nourish an infant, and helps the mother and baby to bond. Human milk is rich in nutrients, antibodies, and other compounds that can protect the baby against infections, allergies, and chronic diseases and may enhance the child's cognitive development. Women are advised to breast-feed exclusively for the first six months, and then breast-feed to supplement solid food for the first year.

What Are the Best Dietary and Lifestyle Habits for a Breast-Feeding Mother?

During the first six months of breast-feeding, the mother produces about three-quarters of a quart of breast milk daily and a little over half a quart daily in the second six months of feeding. During this period, her body needs additional amounts of fluid and nutrients.

To meet her increased fluid needs, a breast-feeding woman should drink about 13 cups of water and beverages daily. She also needs 500 extra calories daily during the first six months of lactating. However, not all of these calories have to come from the diet. Approximately 170 calories are mobilized daily from fat that was stored during pregnancy. Therefore, only 330 extra calories need to come from her foods. This use of fat stores allows for a potential weight loss of about 2 pounds a month.

During the second six months of breast-feeding, fewer calories are available from stored body fat, so a lactating woman needs to consume about 400 extra calories daily to meet her needs.[89] Interestingly, these amounts of extra calories are very similar to the needs of pregnant women during the second and third trimesters. Although a breast-feeding woman's dietary carbohydrate, as well as some vitamin and mineral, requirements increase slightly, a well-balanced diet similar to the one she consumed during pregnancy will meet her needs. Lactating women who are vegans should make sure that they consume adequate amounts of vitamin B_{12} and zinc.

Anything that goes into a breast-feeding mother's body can potentially pass into her breast milk, and ultimately to her baby. Illicit drugs, such as cocaine, heroin, and marijuana, for example, can be transferred to a breast-fed infant and cause harm. Methylmercury, which a mother can overconsume if she doesn't avoid certain fish, can also be harmful, so nursing mothers should adhere to the FDA's guidelines about fish to minimize the infant's exposure (Table 12.1).

Caffeine should be limited to two to three cups daily because it can interfere with the baby's sleep and cause crankiness. Alcohol can not only appear in breast milk, it can inhibit milk production, so should be avoided by women who are nursing. Finally, inhaling tobacco smoke is associated with a decrease in milk production and smaller weight gains in the baby, and nicotine can be passed on to the baby in breast milk, so nursing women should not smoke.[90]

Breast milk can also reflect the foods a mother eats, and babies can become fussy if the mother has consumed certain spicy or gassy foods. The mother can stop eating the food, wait a few days, and then try it again in her diet. If the infant reacts the same way, it's best to stop eating that food while nursing.

The Take-Home Message A mother needs to consume an extra 330 calories daily during the first six months of lactation and an extra 400 calories daily during the second six months. She needs to increase her fluid and nutrient intake to help her body produce breast milk. Anything a woman consumes can be passed on to her baby in breast milk, so nursing mothers should avoid all illicit drugs, caffeine, alcohol, and smoking.

When Is Formula a Healthy Alternative to Breast Milk?

If the infant isn't going to be breast-fed, the only other healthy option is formula. For some women, the choice is a personal preference. For others, breast-feeding may not be possible due to illness or other circumstances, and formula-feeding is necessary.

Some Women May Not Be Able to Breast-Feed

Women who are infected with HIV (human immunodeficiency virus), the virus that causes AIDS (acquired immune deficiency syndrome), should not breast-feed, as this virus can be transmitted to the child through breast milk. Women who have AIDS, human T-cell leukemia, active tuberculosis, are receiving chemotherapy and/or radiation, or use illegal drugs should also not breast-feed for the same reason. (Note: For HIV-infected women living in countries where there is inadequate food, an unsafe food supply, and/or frequent incidences of nutritional deficiencies and infectious diseases, the benefits of providing the infant with nutrient- and immune-rich breast milk may outweigh the risks of HIV infection for the baby.[91])

An infant born with a genetic disorder called galactosemia can't metabolize lactose and shouldn't be breast-fed.[92] Lastly, any woman taking prescribed medications should check with her health care provider to ensure that they are safe to consume while breast-feeding.

Formula Can Be a Healthy Alternative to Breast-Feeding

The best alternative to breast-feeding is to feed an infant with a commercially made formula. Cow's milk cannot be used, as it won't meet the nutritional needs of the baby. It contains too much protein, mainly in the form of casein, which is difficult for the infant to digest.[93] Cow's milk, even whole milk, is also too low in fat and linoleic acid, and too high in sodium and potassium.[94] Also, the iron in cow's milk is poorly absorbed, and to make matters worse, cow's milk can cause intestinal blood loss in infants, which will cause iron loss and, possibly, anemia.[95] Feeding infants cow's milk can also increase their risk of developing an allergy to cow's milk.[96]

Infant formula is developed to be as similar as possible to breast milk, so formula-fed infants can grow and develop quite normally. The FDA regulates all infant formulas sold in the United States and has set specific requirements for the nutrients that the formula must contain.

Infant formula is available in several forms and varies in cost and ingredients. Infant formula is highly regulated by the FDA, so any formula on the market in the United States can be considered safe.

Formula is typically made from cow's milk that has been altered to improve its nutrient content and digestibility. Soy protein–based formulas are free of cow's protein and lactose and can be used for infants who can't tolerate cow milk protein–based formula or who are vegetarians. **Hypoallergenic infant formulas** are available for infants who can't consume cow's milk or soy formulas. The AAP recommends that all formula-fed infants consume iron-fortified formulas to reduce the risk of iron deficiency during infancy.[97]

Formula can be purchased as powder, as a concentrated liquid, or in ready-to-use forms. Powdered formula is the cheapest and the ready-to-use form tends to be the most expensive. Care should be taken to mix the powdered or concentrated liquid with the correct amount of water so the formula will not be too diluted or too concentrated.

If the infant doesn't finish the bottle, the formula should be discarded, rather than saved for another feeding. The bacteria in the infant's mouth can contaminate the formula and multiply to levels that could be harmful even if the formula is reheated. Constant reheating of the formula can also destroy some of the heat-sensitive nutrients.[98] Also, formula should not be left out at room temperature for more than two hours, as bacteria can multiply to unhealthy levels.

The Take-Home Message If a woman doesn't breast-feed, formula is the only other healthy option. Cow's milk should not be given before age 1, as it is too high in protein and some minerals and too low in fat. Powdered and concentrated formulas need to be mixed carefully so they are not too diluted or concentrated for the baby's digestive system.

What Are the Nutrient Needs of an Infant and Why Are They so High?

Whereas parents and caregivers can be confident that breast milk and commercial formulas are meeting their infants' unique nutritional needs, they would benefit from knowing exactly what those nutrient needs are, and what causes them to be so high. Let's explore these topics next.

Infants Grow at an Accelerated Rate

During a child's **infancy,** or first year of life, he experiences a tremendous amount of growth. In fact, an infant doubles his birth weight by about 6 months of age, and triples it by the age of 12 months. Length will double around the end of the first year as well. Let's try to imagine the physical growth of an infant in adult terms. On January first, you weigh 100 pounds. Around the month of June, you have grown to 200 pounds. By New Year's Eve, you would weigh 300 pounds! You would have to eat an enormous amount of food every day to actually make this happen. But for an infant, this is a normal growth rate.

Infants are doing much more than just getting heavier and longer. Intellectual and social development are also under way. As time goes by, infant communication skills go beyond crying, and at around three months of age a baby usually starts to smile.

hypoallergenic infant formulas Specially developed formulas for infants who have food allergies and cannot tolerate regular formula.

infancy The age range from birth to 12 months.

Preferences also become clearer: for particular people (such as the mom), for specific activities (getting kisses or being held), and for certain foods (such as mashed bananas).[99]

An infant should reach certain stages of physical development within a distinct time frame. If an infant is not growing in the expected fashion, this may be a sign that something is wrong. Parents, caregivers, and health care providers need to be alert to infants who miss the mark, and then look more deeply into the situation. The child may not be receiving sufficient nutrition. Perhaps an infant has a poor appetite, and the new mom has no idea that the child should be eating more frequently. Maybe an infant is having some digestive problems, and the new day care provider does not mention the frequency of dirty diapers.

Of course, optimal infant nutrition is sometimes hindered by circumstance. In less developed countries where poverty is the norm and food is scarce, problems such as protein-energy malnutrition (see Chapter 6) are common. Even in developed countries, such as the United States, there are problems with poor infant nutrition that may affect growth. For example, iron-deficiency anemia (see Chapter 8) is sometimes seen in infants when caregivers substitute juice or cow's milk for breast milk or formula.[100] Or, if a breast-fed infant does not begin consuming iron in solid foods by around 6 months, his or her iron storage is depleted, paving the way for anemia.

> Newborn babies may eat
> as often as 12 times a day!

Monitoring Infant Growth

An infant who does not receive adequate nutrition (whether in terms of quantity or quality) may have difficulty reaching developmental **milestones** (Figure 12.6). Think of these as developmental checkpoints, which can be physical, social, or intellectual. While most parents do not know the specific nutrient needs of their infant, it's important that the infant attains the specific milestones at the appropriate time. This assures them that they are providing the right amount and type of nourishment.

If a child doesn't reach the appropriate milestones, he or she may eventually develop a condition called failure to thrive (FTT). A child with FTT is delayed in physical growth or size or does not gain enough weight. Poor appetite, an unbalanced diet, or a

Figure 12.6 Foods for Baby's First Year
During the first year after birth, an infant's diet will progress from breast milk or formula only to age-appropriate versions of family meals.

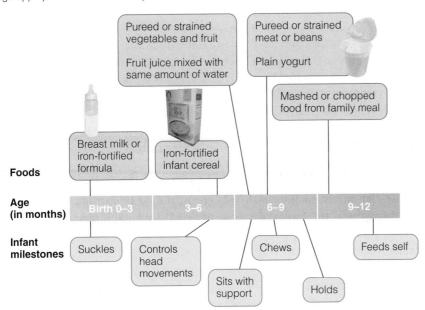

milestones Objectives or significant events that occur during development.

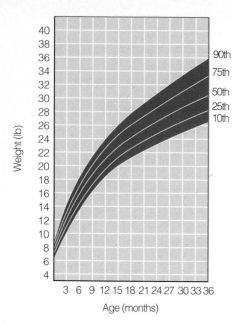

Figure 12.7 Growth Chart
Growth charts can help determine if a child is growing at a healthy rate for his or her age.

medical problem that has not yet been diagnosed can all be causes of FTT. Sometimes, FTT results from inappropriate care or neglect. Caregivers and health care providers need to be aware of the signs of this condition and watch for those signs in their children and patients.

In addition to milestones, parents and health care providers can use **growth charts** to track physical development progress. Typically, measures of head circumference, length, weight, and weight for length are used to assess growth. These measures are taken at each "well-check" visit to the health care provider, about once a month for the first year.

The information obtained from the measurements is plotted on the growth chart, placing the child into a **percentile.** Percentiles rank the infant with regard to other infants of the same age in a reference group. For example, a four-month-old who is in the 25th percentile for weight for age weighs less than 75 percent of the four-month-olds and weighs the same as or more than 25 percent (see Figure 12.7).[101]

Infants Have Specific Calorie, Iron, and Other Nutrient Needs

Though one size does not fit all, when it comes to feeding infants there are certain guidelines to follow in order for them to meet their nutrient needs. For example, an average of 108 calories per kilogram (kg) of body weight is recommended for the first six months of life.[102] Again, imagine a similar proportion of calories at that scale for an adult who weighs 150 pounds (68 kg)—it would work out to 7,344 (68 kg × 108) calories. That's the equivalent of 13 large chocolate milkshakes!

Carbohydrate, protein, and fat needs all change with age. Infants 0 to 6 months should consume 60 grams of carbohydrate per day, which increases to 95 grams daily at 7 to 12 months. Infants need 9.1 grams of protein per day during the first six months of life, which increases to 11 grams daily in the second six months. (Note: The DRIs for infants are listed in the inside front cover of this textbook.) Fat should not be limited at this stage of the life cycle, as this practice could negatively impact growth. In fact, healthy babies should never be put on weight-loss diets, as this can severely impact their physical or mental development.

There are three nutrients that must be added to an infant's diet: vitamin K, vitamin D, and iron. As you recall from Chapter 7, all infants should receive an injection of vitamin K to ensure that their blood will clot. This is necessary because infants are born with a sterile gut, and vitamin K is partially produced from intestinal bacteria.[103]

The amount of vitamin D in breast milk is not enough to prevent rickets, so infants should also receive 200 IU of vitamin D drops daily between the ages of 3 and 12 months. Once they reach age 1, they can drink vitamin D-fortified milk at meals. If vitamin D-fortified formula is introduced before age 1, vitamin D supplementation isn't necessary. Even though vitamin D can be obtained through exposure of the infant's skin to sunlight, this isn't recommended because it can cause sunburns and increases the risk of skin cancer.[104]

Iron-rich foods, such as enriched cereals, should be introduced at around 6 months, as the infant's stores of iron are depleted at about this time. Premature infants, who were born early and thus have lower iron stores, may need iron supplementation before 6 months.[105]

Since vitamin B_{12} is naturally found only in animal foods a supplementation may also be recommended if the infant is being breast-fed by a strict vegan mother.

growth charts Series of percentile curves that illustrate the distribution of selected body measurements in U.S. children.

percentile The most commonly used clinical indicator to assess the size and growth patterns of children in the United States. An individual child is ranked according to the percentage of the reference population he equals or exceeds.

Supplements for Baby?

Beyond the vitamin K and vitamin D supplementation discussed in this chapter, do babies need additional supplements? The short answer is "probably not." Let's take a look at the risks and benefits of providing supplements or fortified foods to infants.

There are situations in which supplementation is absolutely necessary, such as for infants and toddlers with feeding or digestive problems.[8] However, many healthy children who are given supplements don't fall into this category. Rather, their caregivers seem to give supplements "to be safe."

The National Institutes of Health's Office of Dietary Supplements found that multivitamin use is fairly common for infants and toddlers. The Feeding Infants and Toddlers Study (FITS) of 2002 found that supplement use was more common among children who were first born, and also those who were characterized as "picky eater[s]." The majority of the reported supplement users (91 percent) received a regular vitamin and mineral supplement. The most common type used was a multivitamin and mineral combination. Early use (prior to six months of age) was even more frequent when the annual income of the household was higher, and when the mother's educational level was higher.

Is there a potential downside to supplements being given to infants? Researchers are seeking further information on the possible link between multivitamin use in infancy and higher risk of food allergies and asthma.[9] Other concerns emerged from the FITS data. Almost all toddlers who were reported to use supplements had intakes above the upper level for vitamin A. Many of the infants and toddlers who used supplements had usual intakes of zinc above the upper level. This was also true for several toddlers (one in five) for folate.

In some cases, infants had high levels of nutrients even when no supplements were taken. Vitamin A, zinc, and folate are frequently used to fortify commonly consumed foods, such as juices. Although overconsumption of nutrients from enriched and fortified foods can happen, it's actually rare for toxicity to result from food consumption alone. In most cases, it results from high doses of supplements. For example, iron-fortified formulas or foods such as pureed steak generally do not result in iron toxicity (discussed in Chapter 13). The potential for toxicity would be more likely if a child was being given large doses of an iron pill or liquid supplement.

To ensure that they don't give their children too much of a given nutrient, parents and caregivers should be made aware that food alone is often sufficient to fulfill nutrient requirements, and that certain foods may be unintentionally providing supplementation.[10] The FITS concluded that families should rely on food rather than supplements to provide adequate nutrition. The data showed that healthy infants and toddlers can "readily obtain required levels of nutrients" from food without the need for supplements.

If the child's water supply is nonfluoridated or if bottled water is used for mixing formula, a fluoride supplement may also be necessary.[106] See the feature box "Supplements for Baby?" for more information on supplements for infants.

Water (or, more correctly, fluid) needs generally are met with breast milk or formula. Extra fluid is only necessary in hot climates or to replenish stores following episodes of diarrhea, fever, or vomiting when the body loses fluid and electrolytes. Even in these circumstances extra fluid should still be limited, as filling up on water might keep the baby from being hungry for needed, nutrient-rich breast milk or formula.[107]

"Colic" involves an infant's chronic, inconsolable crying, often for long periods of time. Though the cause of colic is not known, some possible nutrition-related contributors include an immature digestive tract, cow's milk allergies or intolerance, food backup into the esophagus, increased intestinal gas, or the breast-feeding mother's diet.

The Take-Home Message Infants grow at a dramatic rate during the first year of life. Caregivers and health care providers can monitor infant growth by making sure the child achieves appropriate developmental milestones and by using growth charts. Nutrient needs during the first year of life are substantial, and supplements may be needed in some circumstances.

When Are Solid Foods Safe?

Often, proud parents can hardly wait to show off how their baby is eating "real food." It is an exciting time, because eating **solid foods** represents maturing skills in the baby. Typically, solid foods are introduced around 6 months of age.[108] However, parents should not suddenly decide to serve their baby steak! The infant must be nutritionally, physiologically, and physically ready to eat solid foods. Let's take a look at what we mean by this.

Solid Foods May Be Introduced Once Certain Milestones Are Met

First, the infant needs to be nutritionally ready for solid foods. At about 6 months old, an infant has depleted his/her stored iron and will need to begin consuming it in foods. Also, common sense tells us that as babies get bigger in size, they need more nutrients. Thus, an older, larger infant has higher nutrient needs than a younger, smaller one. Though breast milk can technically still provide most nutrients, introducing solid foods will further meet the infant's needs and help him develop feeding skills.

The infant also needs to be physiologically ready; that is, his body systems need to be able to process solid foods. At birth, and in early infancy, the GI tract and organs such as the kidneys cannot process solid foods. Introducing solid foods too early can increase a child's risk of allergic reactions to common allergy-causing foods (see the feature box on page 444, "A Taste Could Be Dangerous: Food Allergies").

These next questions are very specific to the individual child. Is the infant physically ready? Has he or she met the necessary developmental milestones? To determine this, caretakers need to answer the following questions:

- Has the **tongue-thrust reflex** faded? This is a reflex infants have to protect against choking. The tongue automatically pushes outward when a substance is placed on it. The reflex fades around 4 to 6 months of age.
- Does the infant have head and neck control? Without control, the infant is at greater risk for choking on solids.
- Have the infant's swallowing skills matured enough?
- Is the infant able to sit with support?
- Does the infant have the ability to turn his or her head to indicate "I'm full!"?

All of the above should be answered with a "Yes" to know that it is safe and realistic to begin offering solid foods. If not, parents and caregivers would be wise to wait until the infant does develop these skills.[109]

Solid Foods Should Be Introduced Gradually

solid foods Foods other than breast milk or formula given to an infant, usually around 6 months of age.

tongue-thrust reflex A forceful protrusion of the tongue in response to an oral stimulus, such as a spoon.

Once an infant is ready for solids, foods should be introduced gradually to make sure the child isn't allergic or intolerant. The best suggestion is to introduce only one new food per week.[110] Parents and caregivers should be mindful of how the infant reacts to new foods. If he develops hives or a rash, or starts sneezing or vomiting, the food may be the culprit. The least allergy-causing food—rice cereal—is a great first food. It is best offered to the infant when it is heavily diluted with breast milk or formula so there is a familiar taste mixed in with the new taste. This will promote the infant's acceptance of the new food. Whole milk shouldn't be given to an infant until after one year of age.

After several days to a week of feeding the infant rice cereal (assuming there has been no negative reaction), a suggested next step is to proceed with other single-grain cereals, such as barley or oats. Once all of these have been fed to the infant without difficulty, then multigrain cereals (rice, barley, and oats) can be offered.

The next step is to offer pureed vegetables, so that the infant will become familiar with the more bitter taste of these foods; then fruits in the same manner; then meats. All of these foods should be introduced one at a time. Phasing in solid foods should take place over a period of several months. The food should initially be served pureed; eventually it can be served not pureed, but cooked so that the texture is soft, as the infant's chewing and swallowing skills are sharpened with practice. Rather than deciding that the infant does not like sweet potatoes because he or she spits it out upon the first taste, parents and caregivers should offer a given food more than once, over several days, to give the infant opportunity to accept the food.[111]

Many motivated parents wonder if they should try making homemade baby food. This is an admirable idea, and certainly gives the child exposure to fresh, unprocessed meals. However, many store-bought baby foods are of high quality and comparable to homemade. The choice is really up to the parent or caregiver. One benefit of homemade food that everyone might agree upon is the financial savings—there are no added costs for fancy packaging and labels. (See "Two Points of View" at the end of this chapter for more on this topic.)

Figure 12.6 on page 439 illustrates suggested foods for a baby's first year of life.

Some Foods Are Dangerous and Should Be Avoided

In spite of all the new skills an infant develops during the first year, becoming stronger, smarter, and more independent, parents and caregivers still need to "baby the baby" when it comes to eating. Many foods are just not appropriate for a baby. For example, some foods, like hot dog rounds or raw carrot slices, present a choking hazard and need to be cut into very small pieces or avoided altogether. Because infants have few teeth, foods should be soft textured so they do not require excessive chewing, and ideally should easily "melt" in the mouth, like a cracker. No matter what they are eating, infants should always be supervised.

Parents and caregivers should also avoid feeding common allergens, such as chocolate, fish, and strawberries, to infants. Reactions may range from a very mild tingling sensation in the mouth or swelling of the tongue and the throat to difficulty breathing, hives, vomiting, abdominal cramps, diarrhea, a drop in blood pressure, and loss of consciousness or death. Waiting a few months until the infant's digestive system has matured is a smart way to keep the infant safe.[112] Other common allergens, like egg whites, cow's milk, and peanut butter, should not be offered before the child is a year old.

Some foods are so dangerous as to be potentially fatal. Honey has been known to carry *Clostridium botulinum*, which can lead to a fatal disease called **botulism.** Though some cultures and families have used honey-dipped pacifiers to calm infants for generations, this is a dangerous practice and should never be done. Infants with botulism become lethargic, feed poorly, and suffer from constipation. They will have a weak

botulism A rare but serious paralytic illness caused by the bacterium *Clostridium botulinum*. Infant botulism is caused by consuming the spores of the bacteria, which then grow in the intestines and release toxin. It can be fatal.

A Taste Could Be Dangerous: Food Allergies

One-year-old Adam was playing in the sandbox at the neighborhood playground, when his babysitter pulled a peanut butter cookie from her backpack. She broke off a small bite of the cookie and handed it to Adam, knowing that he must be hungry for his afternoon snack.

After a minute of chewing, Adam started to wheeze and have difficulty breathing. Then he vomited. The sitter quickly used her cell phone to call for emergency help. She gave the rest of the cookie to one of the paramedics who rushed Adam to the hospital. Unbeknownst to the sitter, Adam was allergic to peanuts.

A **food allergy** is an abnormal physical reaction of the immune system in response to the consumption of a particular food allergen. **Food allergens** are proteins that are not broken down during cooking or by the gastric juices and enzymes in the body during digestion. Because they are not degraded, they enter the body

food allergy An abnormal reaction by the immune system to a particular food.

food allergens Proteins that are not broken down by cooking or digestion and enter the body intact, causing an adverse reaction by the immune system.

mast cells Cells in connective tissue to which antibodies attach, setting the stage for potential future allergic reactions.

anaphylactic reactions Severe, life-threatening reactions that cause constriction of the airways in the lungs, which inhibits the ability to breathe.

food intolerance Adverse reaction to a food that does not involve an immune response. Lactose intolerance is one example.

intact, and can cause an adverse reaction by the immune system if the allergen is perceived as a foreign invader.

A food allergy reaction occurs in two stages, the "sensitization stage" followed by the actual response or "allergic reaction stage." In the first stage (see the figure on the next page) the food allergens don't produce a reaction but rather sensitize or introduce themselves to the person's immune system. In response to the initial introduction of the food allergens, the immune system creates an army of antibodies that enter the blood. The antibodies attach to **mast cells,** setting the stage for a potential future allergic reaction.

The second stage, the reaction stage, occurs when a person eats the food allergens for the second and subsequent times. After they are consumed, the food allergens come in contact with the mast cells. The mast cells release chemicals such as histamine. These chemicals trigger reactions in the body. The areas in the body that manifest a food allergy reaction are the areas where mast cells are prevalent. In very sensitive individuals, a minute exposure of a food allergen—$\frac{1}{44,000}$ of a peanut, for example—can trigger an allergic reaction.[11]

Reactions can appear as quickly as a few minutes after eating the food. In fact, an itchiness in the mouth may occur as soon as the food touches the tongue. After the food reaches the stomach and begins to be digested, vomiting and/or diarrhea may result. When they enter the blood, the food allergens can cause a drop in blood pressure. When the allergens are near the skin, hives can develop, and as the allergens make their way to the lungs, asthma can ensue.[12]

Individuals with allergies, or their caretakers, often carry a syringe injector of epinephrine (adrenaline) to be self-administered in severe reactions and help treat these symptoms. Epinephrine con-

stricts blood vessels, relaxes the muscles in the lungs to help with breathing, and decreases swelling and hives.

Eggs, milk, and peanuts are the most common sources of food allergens in children. In adults, shellfish, peanuts, tree nuts, fish, wheat, soy, and eggs are the most common sources of food allergens. These foods together cause 90 percent of all reactions to food allergens. Some children will outgrow their reactions to milk, and up to 20 percent of them will outgrow a peanut allergy.[13] In contrast, adults are rarely able to rid themselves of a food allergy once it is established.

In the United States, food allergies are the cause of 2,000 admittances to the hospital, approximately 30,000 **anaphylactic** (*ana* = without, no, *phylaxis* = protection) **reactions** (severe, life-threatening allergic reactions), and almost 200 deaths annually.[14] An anaphylactic reaction can cause vomiting and constriction or narrowing of the airways in the lungs, which inhibits breathing.

The symptoms of a **food intolerance,** meanwhile, may mimic a food allergy, but they are different responses. A food intolerance does not involve the immune system. Recall from Chapter 4 that one common food intolerance, lactose intolerance, is caused by inadequate amounts of the enzyme lactase in the body.

The FDA requires that virtually all food ingredients be listed on the food label, and that the food label state whether the product contains protein from any of the major foods known to cause an allergic reaction: milk, egg, fish, shellfish, tree nuts, peanuts, soybeans, or wheat.[15]

The FDA is continually working with food manufacturers and consumer groups to improve public education on food allergies and the seriousness of anaphylactic reactions, in particular, for the most common sources of food allergies.[16]

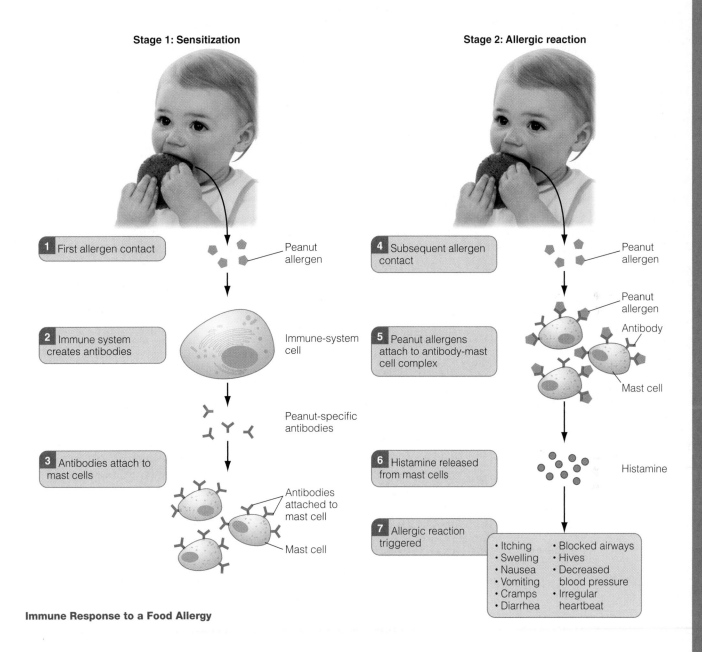

Stage 1: Sensitization

1 First allergen contact

Peanut allergen

2 Immune system creates antibodies

Immune-system cell

Peanut-specific antibodies

3 Antibodies attach to mast cells

Antibodies attached to mast cell

Mast cell

Immune Response to a Food Allergy

Stage 2: Allergic reaction

4 Subsequent allergen contact

Peanut allergen

Peanut allergen

Antibody

5 Peanut allergens attach to antibody-mast cell complex

Mast cell

6 Histamine released from mast cells

Histamine

7 Allergic reaction triggered

- Itching
- Swelling
- Nausea
- Vomiting
- Cramps
- Diarrhea
- Blocked airways
- Hives
- Decreased blood pressure
- Irregular heartbeat

cry and poor muscle tone. Untreated symptoms may cause paralysis of the arms, legs, trunk, and respiratory muscles. The resulting respiratory failure is what makes this food potentially deadly. Older children and adults can consume honey without these concerns as they have adequate amounts of intestinal microorganisms that compete with botulism and inhibit its growth in the intestines.[113]

Herbal tea may also pose a risk to infants. Even though the label says "natural," that does not always mean it is safe, because herbal remedies are not regulated. Many herbs are not well researched, and the effectiveness and potential dangers are not always known.

Parents and caregivers also need to think before adding seasonings such as salt, sugar, and butter to their infants' foods. Restaurants, processed foods, and our own habits have taught us to think that food only tastes "right" if it is salty, sweet, or buttery. Infants do not care if something is bland, and there is no nutritional benefit to enhancing the taste of foods with additional flavors. At this stage of the life cycle, infants can learn to find the natural flavors in whole foods to be satisfying, without added sugar or salt.

As stated earlier, infants should never be put on weight-loss diets. It is difficult to say if low-calorie diets are dangerous, because conducting studies on infants to see if such diets cause harm would be unethical. However, infants are growing and need calories containing plenty of protein, fat, and carbohydrate to support that growth. Restricting calories or nutrients can result in impeded growth and/or development.

What about all those benefits of fiber the experts tell us about? Do babies need "roughage" to keep them "regular" like adults? Though fiber is useful for many reasons, too much can actually be harmful to an infant because it can pull nutrients through the GI tract before they have a chance to be absorbed. As the infant gets older, more fiber is suitable.

Beverages, such as apple juice, are a popular component of infant diets. In fact, 100 percent juice is considered one of the major sources of infants' calories.[114] Although juice can provide some nutrients, it also may provide so many calories that the infant will prefer to drink rather than to eat food, displacing necessary nutrients.

Overabundance of breast milk and formula is not always suitable, either. This is important at the end of the first year, as the infant will likely be learning to use solid food to obtain calories, rather than relying on milk or formula. If an infant spends too much time drinking, he may not be interested in the foods that will help expand his feeding skills. Of course, breast milk or formula will still be the primary source of calories, and some parents and caregivers prefer not to start solid foods until after the first year.

The Take-Home Message An infant must be physically, physiologically, and nutritionally ready before being introduced to solid foods. Solid foods should be introduced gradually and cautiously. Parents and caregivers must educate themselves about foods that are appropriate and those that are not in order to keep the infant safe and healthy.

Putting It All Together

Pregnancy, lactation, and infancy are periods of the life cycle during which women and babies have unique nutrient needs. Fathers also need to consume a healthy diet and avoid certain substances to help produce a healthy baby. Women need to refer to the Dietary Reference Intakes (DRIs), covered in Chapter 2 (and listed on the inside cover

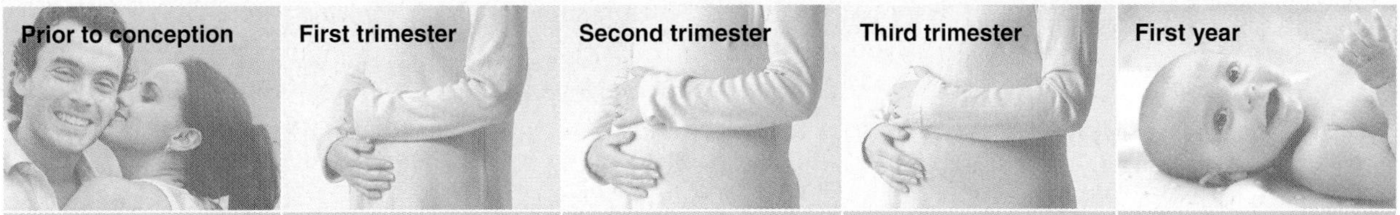

	Prior to conception	First trimester	Second trimester	Third trimester	First year
Father	• Stop smoking • Limit alcohol • Maintain a healthy weight • Consume a balanced diet • Avoid illicit drugs				
Mother	• Consume a balanced diet • Maintain a healthy weight • Add folic acid to diet • Limit caffeine • Avoid certain fish with high levels of methylmercury • Avoid alcohol, herbs, illicit drugs, and smoking • Exercise regularly	• Consume a balanced diet • Continue getting folic acid • Take an iron-rich supplement • Limit caffeine • Avoid too much vitamin A • Avoid foodborne illness • Continue exercising	• Consume a balanced diet with adequate calories for growth • Continue exercising	• Consume a balanced diet with adequate calories for growth • Eat frequent small meals if more comfortable • Choose high fiber foods • Drink plenty of fluids • Continue nonimpact exercises	• Consume a balanced diet with adequate calories and fluids for breastfeeding • Nursing mothers should avoid illicit drugs, smoking, and alcohol • Limit caffeine • Avoid certain fish with high levels of methylmercury
Baby					• Supplement diet with vitamins K and D and sources of iron or iron-fortified foods • Avoid common food allergens, honey, and herbal tea • Consume breast milk or formula as primary source of calories • Do not start drinking cow's milk until after this year • Introduce solid foods gradually and one at a time • Avoid too much fiber and excessive amounts of juice

Figure 12.8 Summary of Nutritional Guidelines
Nutritional guidelines for both parents and infants.

of this text), for pregnancy and lactation to make sure they consume adequate calories, protein, iron, and folate for both their own health and that of their developing baby. Babies have high nutrient and calorie needs during their first year to sustain their rapid growth and development. Figure 12.8 summarizes the nutritional guidelines for both babies and their parents.

The lifestyle habits mentioned in earlier chapters—like smoking and drinking too much alcohol—that have been shown to lead to chronic diseases such as heart disease, cancer, and cirrhosis are also unhealthy during pregnancy and lactation. Both men and women should adopt healthier lifestyles before pregnancy in order to increase the likelihood of having a healthy baby.

Two Points of View

Choosing among Baby Foods

What are the differences between jarred baby food, commercial frozen baby food, and homemade baby food? What are the pros and cons of each? Two experts weigh in.

Amy N. Marlow, MPH, RD, CDN
Dietitian, HAPPYBABY

Richard C. Theuer, PhD
Adjunct Professor in Food Science, North Carolina State University–Raleigh; Adjunct Professor in Nutrition, University of North Carolina–Chapel Hill; Former vice president and CEO, Beech-Nut Nutrition Corp.

Amy Marlow, MPH, RD, CDN, is the consulting dietitian for HAPPYBABY, a company that makes fresh-frozen organic baby meals. Prior to this position, she was a pediatric dietitian at Georgetown University Medical Center in Washington, D.C., and a consultant for a youth development program for underprivileged teens and the National Cancer Institute's 5-A-Day program. She is a published health writer and serves on the board of the New York City affiliate of the American Dietetic Association.

Q: How is commercial frozen baby food prepared?

A: First, we select our ingredients, including ripe fruits, vegetables, grains, and meats. All of our ingredients are organic. In some recipes, we also use some mild herbs and spices, such as coriander or fresh mint. We don't add any salt, sugar, or thickeners; babies don't need those additives. Next, the ingredients are cooked. The fruits and vegetables are gently steamed until soft. The grains, beans, and meats are also gently cooked, using a variety of methods appropriate to each. Once the ingredients are soft enough or fully cooked, we then have to get the food to an appropriate texture for a baby. We often retain the cooking liquid from the cooking process, and use that to thin the food and get it to the right texture. The cooking liquid captures some of the nutrients that leach out during cooking, so using the liquid to thin the food helps restore some of those nutrients. Some fruit and vegetables are also strained to produce an especially smooth texture for younger babies. Once the food is cooked, we use special equipment to flash freeze it in our storage trays. The process cools the food very quickly. The trays look like ice cube trays, and they freeze the foods in 1-ounce portions. The process preserves the flavor, texture, and color of the food.

Q: What are the nutrient differences, if any, between jarred baby foods, commercial frozen baby foods, and homemade baby food?

Richard Theuer, PhD, served as vice president, research and development, for Beech-Nut Nutrition Corporation, a leading U.S. baby food company, for 13 years. He was president and chief executive officer of Beech-Nut from 1986 to 1989. During his tenure with Beech-Nut, Theuer managed formulation changes in the company's Stages brand baby food line, including the removal of added refined sugar and chemically modified starch. Dr. Theuer has PhD and MS degrees in biochemistry from the University of Wisconsin, Madison; a BS degree in chemistry from Saint Peters College, New Jersey; and an MBA from Indiana State University.

Q: How is jarred baby food prepared?

A: The purpose of "baby food"—the pureed and chunky semi-solid foods that parents prepare themselves or purchase ready-made in the supermarket—is to help a baby make the journey from the single-item liquid diet of breast milk (or infant formula if Mom chooses not to breast-feed) to the wide variety of foods that are served at the family table. Thus the ingredients used to make commercial baby foods are the familiar ones that the family eats at the dinner table at home.

The high-quality fruits, vegetables, and other ingredients used in commercial baby foods, whether frozen or in jars, are grown on farms that the baby food manufacturer is familiar with. The prudent manufacturer pretests the soil before certain seeds are planted to make sure it contains no residual contaminants that might taint the produce. The fruits and vegetables in commercial baby food are processed "in season" when the fresh produce is at the peak of quality.

Baby foods are made by combining the peeled, prepared ingredients in a large kettle and cooking them with steam; straining the cooked food; and putting the food into glass jars or plastic containers. Baby foods in glass jars or plastic containers that consumers buy in the "baby food aisle" of the grocery store are "shelf-stable" foods. Achieving

(continued)

(continued)

Choosing among Baby Foods, continued

Amy N. Marlow, MPH, RD, CDN, continued

A: Though jarred, frozen homestyle commercial foods, and homemade foods are all acceptable choices for babies, homemade and commercial frozen baby foods can contain higher levels of nutrients. Studies have shown that homemade and commercial frozen baby foods have more vitamins and minerals than jarred foods. They aren't heated to the high temperatures that jarred foods undergo. High heat during jarring can disrupt the color and flavor and destroy some of the more sensitive vitamins and other nutrients. Homestyle and homemade foods are also consumed more quickly than jarred foods, which are usually shelf-stable for a period of at least a year or more. If the foods are consumed more quickly, the nutrients don't degrade as much over time.

Q: What is the cost difference between commercially prepared jarred and frozen baby food, and what considerations are important when it comes to that difference?

A: Fresh-frozen homestyle baby foods cost about 36 to 41 cents per ounce, compared to jarred foods, which are about 23 to 25 cents per ounce. Both types are more expensive than making your own baby food at home. If you are making homemade baby food, the cost really depends on whether you're using organic ingredients, as well as whether your produce is locally grown or imported. But overall, homemade food is about half the price. Even with the higher cost, buying commercial frozen baby foods may be worthwhile for parents who are pressed for time or can't make homemade baby food for some reason, but still want their child to have the freshest flavors possible, with the least amount of processing and the greatest nutrient density. Most frozen commercial baby foods are organic, so that's also a benefit for parents interested in that focus. Sometimes it's easier to buy baby food that is commercially made but organic when particular organic produce isn't available in your area.

Q: What are the main advantages of commercial frozen baby food over homemade or commercial jarred baby food?

A: The fact that there is greater retention of nutrients in commercial frozen baby food surely is an advantage. Also, parents who make baby food at home have more control over the ingredients when they make their own baby food or use a high-grade homestyle baby food. You can be more confident that your baby is eating foods made from the highest quality ingredients. You can also sometimes choose less conventional ingredients—varieties of produce or mild spices not usually found in conventional foods. If you make your own baby food, or choose a commercial frozen food, you can also feed your baby the same kinds of flavors that

(continued)

Richard C. Theuer, PhD, continued

this state of preservation is done in two ways: pasteurization and sterilization. No chemical preservatives are used in baby foods!

Commercial baby foods made with fruits, fruit juices, and fermented foods are preserved by pasteurization. Heating the food to a temperature just below boiling for a few seconds destroys any pathogenic bacteria.

The manufacturer of commercial "low-acid" foods such as vegetables, meats, and cereals must subject the food to a temperature well above boiling to sterilize the food and destroy any bacteria. The higher temperatures can change the appearance of the food, depending upon how long the food is held at a high temperature. For example, green vegetables can lose their attractive color when sterilized (or even when cooked too long on the stove) and turn olive drab.

Q: What are the nutrient differences, if any, between jarred baby foods, commercial frozen baby foods, and homemade baby food?

A: Most jarred and frozen baby foods are fruit or vegetable foods. Laboratory work funded by the U.S. Department of Agriculture compared the content of 23 nutrients in seven fruits and vegetables prepared fresh, frozen, or jarred/canned. Only small differences were found in most of the 23 nutrients tested. For example, canned and frozen carrots were higher in vitamin A value (actually the content of carotene) than fresh boiled or microwaved carrots. Conversely, fresh boiled carrots contained more vitamin B_6 and manganese than the processed carrots. Canned sweet potatoes contained slightly more vitamin C than frozen sweet potatoes, but both contained less than boiled fresh sweet potatoes. Major variables affecting the nutrient content of fresh fruits and vegetables are the time from harvest to consumption and storage and distribution conditions. The fruits and vegetables used to make commercially frozen or jarred/canned foods have much more tightly controlled histories.

Q: What is the cost difference between commercially prepared jarred and frozen baby food, and what considerations are important when it comes to that difference?

A: Shelf-stable baby foods in 4-ounce glass jars cost about 55 to 90 cents a jar [2007 prices in North Carolina]. Shelf-stable baby foods in 3.5-ounce plastic tubs cost about 65 cents a tub (sold in a two-pack). Frozen baby food brands are no longer in distribution in my local grocery store.

Q: What are the main advantages of commercial frozen baby food over homemade or commercial jarred baby food?

A: Compared to commercial frozen baby food, commercial jarred baby food has a longer shelf life; less demanding

(continued)

Choosing among Baby Foods, continued

Amy N. Marlow, MPH, RD, CDN, continued

you would eat. That introduces your baby to fresh foods early on, when their taste preferences are being formed. If they are exposed to fresh-tasting flavors early, it makes the transition to the family table easier later. The fresher tastes also get babies used to the idea that food should taste fresh, so that they'll be less interested in the tastes of highly processed foods later on. That's important for good nutrition throughout their life, not just when they are babies or toddlers.

Richard C. Theuer, PhD, continued

storage conditions (pantry shelf rather than the freezer); more variety (since more varieties of baby food can be put on the supermarket shelf compared to the amount of space available in the frozen food section); and lower cost. Compared to commercial jarred baby food, commercial frozen baby food has better color, especially of green vegetables; and better flavor due to less cooking time at higher temperatures. Compared to homemade baby food, both commercial frozen baby food and commercial jarred baby food are more convenient and less time consuming to prepare. Historically, parents were cautioned about homemade baby food for two reasons. First, adults may season these foods to their own tastes and add enough salt to raise pediatric concerns. Second, certain vegetables, particularly spinach, beets, and carrots, may contain high levels of nitrates, depending on where the vegetables are grown and how they are harvested. Very young babies are susceptible to high levels of nitrates and nitrites (formed from nitrates); a health condition called methemoglobinemia may result. (A similar problem can occur when using well water high in nitrate to prepare powdered infant formula.)

Be a Nutrition Sleuth

Do You Know How Much Caffeine You Consume?

You probably know that coffee and soda are caffeine culprits, but do you know what other foods contain caffeine? Log on to www.aw-bc.com/blake to find out where else caffeine may be lurking in your diet.

Get Real!

Is Your Diet Adequate in Folic Acid?

Consuming enough folic acid is key for both men and women when they plan to start a family. Log on to www.aw-bc.com/blake and determine if you are meeting your folic acid needs.

The Top Ten Points to Remember

1. Both the father and the mother should make healthy diet and lifestyle changes if needed prior to pregnancy. For healthy sperm, men should stop smoking, abstain from alcohol or drink only in moderation, strive for a healthy body weight, and consume a well-balanced diet with adequate amounts of fruits and vegetables, whole grains, lean meats, dairy foods, and legumes. Women should consume adequate amounts of folic acid prior to conception to reduce the risk of neural tube defects.

2. Women who begin pregnancy at a healthy weight are more likely to conceive more easily, have an uncomplicated pregnancy, and have an easier time nursing their babies. Children born to obese women are at a greater risk for being born larger than normal, having more difficulties breathing, having a slower heart rate, and having an increased risk of both heart defects and certain birth defects. These children are also more likely to develop childhood obesity.

3. Pregnant women should abstain from alcohol, herbs, and illicit drugs, as these can all harm fetal growth and development. They should avoid fish that contain high amounts of methylmercury and consume caffeine only in moderation.

4. To alleviate symptoms of morning sickness, women should eat small, frequent meals that are high in carbohydrates. Salty foods may also help, and tart beverages such as lemonade. Healthy women should gain approximately 25 to 35 pounds during pregnancy. Most of a pregnant woman's increased nutrient needs can be met through a nutrient-dense, balanced diet. A supplement is needed for iron, but care should be taken to avoid consuming too much preformed vitamin A, which can cause birth defects.

5. Awareness of food safety is important, as bacteria such as *Listeria monocytogenes* may cause miscarriages, premature labor, delivery of a low birth weight infant, developmental problems, or even infant death. Pregnant women should handle raw meats and fish with care and avoid consuming raw or undercooked meat, fish, or poultry; unpasteurized milk, cheese, and juices; and raw sprouts. Sugar substitutes can be used in moderation.

Total weight gain ~30 lbs

- Maternal fat stores (~7 lbs)
- Uterus and breast (4 lbs)
- Blood (3–4 lbs)
- Fetus (~7 lbs)
- Placenta, amniotic fluid, and other fluids (~8 lbs)

Third trimester

6. A pregnant woman should consume an additional 340 calories daily during the second trimester and an extra 450 calories daily during the third trimester. This will enable her to gain slightly less than about a pound per week until delivery. Exercise during pregnancy can help improve sleep, lower the risk of hypertension and diabetes, prevent backaches, help relieve constipation, shorten labor, reduce stress and depression, and allow women to return more quickly to their prepregnancy weight after delivery. Low-impact activities such as walking, swimming, and stationary cycling are recommended to prevent injury to both mother and baby.

7. Sometimes a woman develops gestational diabetes and/or hypertension during pregnancy. Gestational diabetes increases the risk of delivering a larger than normal baby who may also be at risk for developing jaundice, breathing problems, and birth defects. Pregnancy-induced hypertension includes gestational hypertension, preeclampsia, and eclampsia, each progressively more medically serious. Gestational hypertension is often a sign of preeclampsia. During preeclampsia, less oxygen- and nutrient-rich blood is reaching the placenta. Eclampsia can cause seizures in the mother and is a major cause of death of women during pregnancy.

8. Breast-feeding is the gold standard for feeding an infant. It provides physical, emotional, convenience, and financial benefits for the mother and nutritional and health benefits for the infant. Breast-feeding mothers need to consume 330 to 400 extra calories daily to produce breast milk. If an infant isn't breast-fed, the only healthy option is formula.

9. An infant doubles his or her birth weight around 6 months of age, and triples it by 12 months. With proper nutrition, an infant should reach certain stages of physical development within a distinct time frame. Poor infant nutrition (whether in quality or quantity) will likely prevent ideal growth and the ability of the child to meet milestones on time. Infants need approximately 108 calories per kilogram of body weight during the first six months of life. All infants should receive a vitamin K injection at birth, and breast-fed infants need vitamin D supplements until one year of age.

Infants older than 6 months need to begin taking in iron through food sources, as their stored iron supply is depleted around this time.

10. Infants need to be nutritionally, physiologically, and physically ready before they begin eating solid foods. Foods should be introduced gradually and one at a time to monitor possible allergies or intolerances. Certain foods can be dangerous and should be avoided. Parents and caregivers should avoid adding heavy seasoning (such as sugar or salt), too much fiber, or fruit juice (which can lead to overconsumption of calories) to their infants' diets.

Test Your Knowledge

1. To prevent neural tube birth defects, a woman should start taking 400 micrograms of folic acid
   a. during the first trimester.
   b. during the second trimester.
   c. at least one month prior to conception and during the early weeks of pregnancy.
   d. during the last trimester.
2. The production and function of sperm in males may decrease because of
   a. antioxidants.
   b. smoking.
   c. obesity.
   d. alcohol abuse.
   e. b, c, and d only.
3. A low birth weight baby is a baby who is born weighing
   a. more than 5½ pounds.
   b. less than 5½ pounds.
   c. more than 6 pounds.
   d. more than 7 pounds.

4. Mary Ellen is pregnant and going out to a seafood restaurant for dinner. She should *not* order
   a. flounder.
   b. shrimp.
   c. grilled swordfish.
   d. lobster.
5. A woman at a healthy weight should gain _____ pounds during pregnancy.
   a. 20 to 30 pounds
   b. 15 to 25 pounds
   c. 50 to 60 pounds
   d. 25 to 35 pounds
6. During pregnancy a woman's need for many nutrients increases. Which mineral requirement is unlikely to be met through her diet alone?
   a. iron
   b. potassium
   c. sodium
   d. calcium
7. During the second trimester of pregnancy, a woman should increase her daily calorie intake by
   a. 450 calories.
   b. 340 calories.
   c. 500 calories.
   d. No increase is needed.
8. Breast-feeding can
   a. help women reduce their risk of breast cancer.
   b. reduce women's risk of type 2 diabetes.
   c. decrease the risk of the baby developing respiratory and ear infections.
   d. do all of the above.
9. Andy is a healthy, bouncing 3 month old baby boy who is being breastfed by his mother. Which of the following nutrients need to be added to his diet?
   a. vitamin D
   b. potassium

c. vitamin C

d. all of the above

10. Six-month-old Cathy is ready to take on solid foods. The first food that should be introduced in her diet is

    a. oatmeal.

    b. iron-fortified cooked rice cereal.

    c. whole milk.

    d. none of the above.

Answers

1. (c) To reduce the risk of these birth defects, folic acid should be consumed prior to conception and continue during the early weeks of pregnancy. Waiting until pregnancy occurs will be too late. Because pregnancy increases the need for this vitamin, the mother should continue to make sure that folate intake is adequate throughout her pregnancy.

2. (e) Smoking, alcohol abuse, and obesity have all been associated with the decreased production and functioning of sperm. Antioxidants, in particular vitamins E and C and carotenoids, may help protect sperm.

3. (b) A baby born weighing less than 5½ pounds is considered a low birth weight baby.

4. (c) The grilled swordfish is off-limits during pregnancy because of its high methylmercury content. However, Mary Ellen can enjoy a nice shrimp cocktail as an appetizer and either the flounder or lobster as an entrée.

5. (d) A woman at a healthy weight should gain 25 to 35 pounds during pregnancy.

6. (a) Because a pregnant woman's increased iron needs cannot be easily met through the diet, she will likely need a supplement. She can get the potassium, sodium, and calcium she needs through a well-balanced diet.

7. (b) A pregnant woman needs 340 extra calories daily during the second trimester to meet her needs. During the third trimester, she needs an extra 450 calories every day. She doesn't need additional daily calories during the first trimester, but does have additional nutrient needs, so she should be sure to eat nutrient-dense foods.

8. (d) Breast-feeding provides health advantages to both the mother and the baby. Breast-feeding reduces the risk of breast cancer and diabetes in the mother and the incidences of respiratory and ear infections in the baby.

9. (a) While breast milk is an ideal food for baby Andy, it doesn't contain enough vitamin D so he should receive daily drops in his diet. He doesn't need to be supplemented with vitamin C or the mineral potassium.

10. (b) Cooked rice cereal is the perfect choice as it is the least likely to cause an allergic reaction. If Cathy tolerates the rice cereal well, oatmeal could be the next grain added to her diet. Milk shouldn't be introduced into Cathy's diet until she turns 1 year of age.

Web Support

■ For more information on breast-feeding, visit the La Leche League International website at www.lalecheleague.org

■ For more food safety guidance for moms-to-be during pregnancy and after the baby is born, visit the FDA's Center for Food Safety and Applied Nutrition website at www.cfsan.fda.gov/~pregnant/pregnant.html

■ For more on infant nutrition, visit the USDA's Food and Nutrition Center website at www.nal.usda.gov/fnic

■ For more information on children and their dietary needs, visit the American Academy of Pediatrics at www.aap.org

■ For more information on food allergies, visit the Food Allergy and Anaphylaxis Network at www.foodallergy.org

■ For more information on dietary supplements, visit the National Institutes of Health Office of Dietary Supplements at http://dietary-supplements.info.nih.gov

13

Life Cycle Nutrition

Toddlers through the Later Years

1. Toddlers and preschoolers are often **too busy** to eat. **T/F**

2. **Iron deficiency** in young children is always caused by eating too much chicken. **T/F**

3. Once a child **refuses** a food, there is no point in offering it again. **T/F**

4. Young children often go on food "**jags.**" **T/F**

5. The rise in **childhood obesity** is due entirely to fast food. **T/F**

6. Lunches served under the National **School Lunch** Program have to follow certain nutritional regulations. **T/F**

7. As long as teens drink **diet soda,** they don't have to worry about negative health effects. **T/F**

8. Older adults don't need as many **calories** daily as they did in their youth. **T/F**

9. **Food insecurity** among elders is a nonissue in the United States. **T/F**

10. **Alcohol abuse** is extremely rare among older adults. **T/F**

Three-year-old Cara has a very busy life. When she gets up in the morning, her mom seats her at the kitchen table to eat a few pieces of banana and some whole-grain cereal, but she usually squirms after just a few bites. Once she's dressed, she spends at least 8 or 9 minutes playing with her dog, Murphy, before running outside to grab her shovel and dig in her sandbox. When she gets bored with shoveling, she shouts for her mom to push her on the swing, or dashes over to investigate an anthill on the sidewalk. Then, she's zipping up to her room in urgent need of her toy trains. By lunchtime, her mom is saying it's time to come to the kitchen and eat, but Cara isn't interested. There's too much to see, do, and explore before she has to lie down for her afternoon nap.

Cara's parents are worried that Cara may be missing some essential nutrients from her diet, but they're not sure how to get their daughter to slow down and eat when she should. Do you have any advice for Cara's mom and dad? What do you think is the best strategy for ensuring that a toddler like Cara gets all the nutrients she needs, without putting her at risk for obesity? In this chapter, we'll explore the answers to these questions, as well as the unique nutrition needs of toddlers, preschoolers, school-aged children, adolescents, and older adults.

Answers

1. True. Between the ages of 1 and 4, small children are extremely active and may forget to eat. Turn to page 457 to find out how to make sure children get the nutrients they need.
2. False. Iron deficiency is often caused by a limited diet that relies too heavily on milk or other iron-poor food sources. Read more about this condition on page 458.
3. False. Parents and caregivers may need to offer foods several times before a child accepts the food. This topic is covered in more detail on page 459.
4. True. Young children often go on food "jags" or may get hooked on a particular food and eat only that item for a while. Learn more about these short-term habits and how to cope with them on page 459.
5. False. Fast food is only part of the problem. Too little exercise and too much screen time also contribute. Read more about the obesity epidemic among children on page 461.
6. True. The school lunch and breakfast programs must meet specific requirements from the USDA. Details are found on page 464.
7. False. Sodas, including diet sodas, are nutritionally empty beverages. Turn to page 468 to find which beverages will help adolescents achieve healthy adult bodies.
8. True. Because a person's metabolism slows naturally with age, older adults need fewer calories than their younger counterparts. Learn more about the altered energy and nutrient needs associated with aging on page 470.
9. False. Financial circumstances or reduced mobility can cause older adults to experience food insecurity. Turn to page 477 to find out how this happens.
10. False. Older adults sometimes turn to alcohol to deal with discomfort, loneliness, or boredom. Find out more on page 480.

What Are the Nutritional Needs and Issues of Young Children?

There are two distinct age categories during early childhood: **toddlers** (1- to 3-year-olds) and **preschoolers** (ages 3 to 5 years). Toddlers and preschoolers are still growing, but their growth rates have slowed significantly, especially compared with those of infants. During the second year of life, the average weight gain is only about 3 to 5 pounds, and the average height or length gain is about 3 to 5 inches a year.[1] As a result of this slowed growth, the nutritional needs and appetites of toddlers diminish, relative to the needs of infants.

Whereas parents spend their child's first year tending to the infant's constant desire for food, they often spend the toddler and preschool years trying to make sure their busy child takes enough time to eat.[2] Toddlers and preschoolers need the same nutrients as older people, but they need them in different amounts due to their lower energy needs (calories per kilogram of body weight), smaller appetites, and smaller stomachs.

As a toddler's appetite diminishes, caregivers may grow concerned that the child isn't eating enough. As long as parents monitor growth and stay alert for anything that seems suspicious (such as changes in the child's energy level; diarrhea; nausea; vomiting; or changes in the quality of the child's hair, skin, or nails), it is likely that the child's food intake will be sufficient.

Because they tend not to eat much food at one sitting, toddlers and preschoolers need to eat frequently in order to keep up with their nutrient needs. This means that they should get many of their calories from small meals and snacks eaten throughout the day.

Young Children Need to Eat Frequent, Small Meals and Nutrient-Dense Foods

Toddlers are extremely active. Just watching them maneuver from activity to activity would exhaust most adults. Because toddlers are always on the go, they need between 1,000 and 1,400 calories per day (see Table 13.1). Since toddlers tend to eat in small quantities, what they eat during their meals and snacks has to be nutrient dense. Meals and snacks should consist of small portions of meat and beans, fruits, vegetables, milk, and whole grains instead of items like chicken nuggets, french fries, sugary drinks, cookies, and crackers.[3] (You can use the MyPyramid For Kids, discussed later in this chapter, for specific numbers of servings for young children.)

Parents must be mindful about portion sizes for young children and avoid pushing children to eat more than they need. One way to help ensure proper portion sizes is to use child-sized plates and cups, which are usually a size more appropriate for the quantity of food that a child can fit into his or her stomach. The rule of thumb is to serve one tablespoon of food at a time per year of age. A two-year-old, for example, would receive two tablespoons of food. Of course, caregivers looking after children with larger or smaller appetites need to tailor portion sizes to each child's individual needs.

Whenever young children are given solid foods it is important that the food does not pose a choking hazard. All foods should be cut into bite-sized pieces. The American Academy of Pediatrics recommends keeping hot dogs, nuts and seeds, chunks of meat or cheese, whole grapes, hard candy, popcorn, chunks of peanut butter, raw vegetables, raisins, and chewing gum away from children younger than age 4.[4] Having the child sit when eating rather than running around will lessen the likelihood of food becoming lodged in the windpipe during a trip or fall. The Table Tips provide some ideas for healthy, toddler-friendly snacks.

Children who attend day care often receive a substantial portion of their daily calories from a day-care provider. Parents should know what is being offered at the day-care site and provide alternative foods for their child if the day-care provider's

Using child-sized dishes at mealtimes can help caregivers monitor portion sizes.

toddlers Children aged 1 to 3 years old.

preschoolers Children aged 3 to 5 years old.

Table 13.1
Calorie Needs for Children and Adolescents

| Age | Gender | Activity Level* | | |
		Sedentary	Moderately Active	Active
2–3 years (toddlers)	Male and Female	1,000	1,000–1,400	1,000–1,400
4–8 years (preschoolers and school aged)	Female	1,200	1,400–1,600	1,400–1,800
4–8 years (preschoolers and school aged)	Male	1,400	1,400–1,600	1,600–2,000
9–13 years (school aged)	Female	1,600	1,600–2,000	1,800–2,200
9–13 years (school aged)	Male	1,800	1,800–2,200	2,000–2,600
14–18 years (adolescent)	Female	1,800	2,000	2,400
14–18 years (adolescent)	Male	2,200	2,400–2,800	2,800–3,200

*These levels are based on Estimated Energy Requirements (EER) from the Institute of Medicine Dietary Reference Intakes Macronutrients Report, 2002, calculated by gender, age, and activity level for reference-sized individuals. "Reference size," as determined by the IOM, is based on median height and weight for ages up to 18 years.

Source: HHS/USDA *Dietary Guidelines for Americans,* 2005.

meals and snacks are insufficient or unhealthy. This is especially important for children who have food allergies or intolerances. Parents should ask day-care providers to alert them of special occasions, such as birthday parties, so they can bring in a treat for their own child if their child is allergic to certain foods. Even if children do not have special dietary concerns, parents have the right to be firm about what their child eats. In some cases, day-care providers may offer menu items or snacks that are superior to what is given at home.

Young Children Need to Consume Enough Calcium and Iron

Toddlers need calcium to develop healthy bones. Children between 1 and 3 years of age should consume 500 milligrams of calcium per day.[5] They can easily meet their needs with two 8-ounce glasses of milk daily as each glass provides 300 milligrams of calcium.

Young children are at particular risk for iron deficiency, which can lead to developmental delays such as diminished mental, motor, and behavioral functioning.[6] Children who suffer iron-deficiency anemia as infants are more likely to have to repeat a grade in school, have reduced math achievement and written expression, and show differences in motor function, spatial memory, and selective recall.[7] A 2004 study investigating iron deficiency in children with attention deficit hyperactivity disorder (ADHD) found that children with the most severe iron deficiencies were also the most inattentive, impulsive, and hyperactive.[8] Iron deficiency is the most common nutrient deficiency among young children. In the United States, an estimated 9 percent of children between the ages of 1 and 2, and 4 percent of children ages 3 to 4, experience iron deficiency.[9] Worldwide, iron deficiency affects about 2 billion people, and young children and their mothers are the most commonly and severely affected.[10]

Often, the culprit behind iron deficiency in children in the United States is an overly milk-heavy diet. If children get too large a percentage of their calories from iron-poor milk, iron-rich foods may be displaced.[11] Parents and caregivers must include good sources of iron, such as lean meats and iron-fortified cereals, in toddlers' diets. The Table Tips list kid-friendly ways to enjoy foods that have plenty of iron.

Although iron deficiency is a real concern, iron toxicity, as well as lead toxicity, can also occur in small children. Iron toxicity is a leading cause of death in children under age 6. Because so little iron is excreted from the body, it can build up to toxic levels in the tissues and organs. Children have died from ingesting as little as 200 milligrams of iron.[12] To protect children from accidental iron poisoning, the FDA requires warning labels on iron-containing drugs and dietary supplements as well as on individual-dose packaging of products with 30 milligrams or more of iron per unit.[13]

Lead toxicity is less common in the United States, but still can be an issue. A study of 3,650 children, aged 9 to 48 months, concluded that iron deficiency is significantly associated with low-level lead poisoning in this age group.[14] Approximately 4 percent of American children have elevated blood lead levels due to consuming paint chips or small pieces of metal, soil, and even water.[15] Children who live in older homes that have lead pipes or faucets are at risk of consuming lead in their drinking water. Inhaling lead dust from paint or swallowing lead can affect any of the body's organs, but the nervous system is most vulnerable. Ingesting lead in high doses can be deadly, and sometimes the most innocent-seeming items can be fatal. In February 2006, a 4-year-old child tragically died after swallowing a metallic charm (off of another child's tennis shoe) that contained lead.[16]

Having kids help in the kitchen is one way to get them excited about trying new foods and eating healthy meals.

Young Children Need to Consume Enough Vitamin D and Fiber

Individuals aged 1 to 8 should consume 5 micrograms (or 200 IU), of vitamin D daily.[17] Vitamin D is found in fortified milk, egg yolk, and certain types of fish. Getting enough vitamin D is important in the prevention of rickets (see Chapter 7). Consuming 2 cups of milk daily will meet a child's daily vitamin D needs. If a child does not get enough vitamin D in the diet, a supplement may be recommended.

The recommended daily intake for fiber is 19 grams for those aged 1 to 3 and 25 grams for 4- to 8-year olds.[18] Like adults, toddlers need fiber to promote bowel regularity and prevent constipation. A balanced diet that contains whole fruits, vegetables, and whole grains can easily meet a young person's daily fiber needs.

Young Children Need Nutrient-Dense Beverages

A toddler's or preschooler's daily fluid recommendations are based on the child's weight. For example, a 7-pound child needs about 2 cups of fluid per day; a 21-pound child needs 5 cups; and a 44-pound child needs 8 cups. Caregivers need to monitor a child's beverage intake and provide water, milk, and possibly some 100 percent juice while avoiding soda and sugary drinks. Drinking too much fluid may result in a lower intake of more nutrient-dense solid foods and important nutrients such as iron (for a child with a milk-heavy diet) or fiber (for a child who gets "fruit" from juice rather than actual whole fruit).

Picky Eating and "Food Jags" Are Common in Small Children

As a young child grows, so should the variety of healthy food choices in his or her diet. If a child's first encounter with cooked peas results in all the peas ending up on the floor, this doesn't mean that peas should be permanently off the menu. Research shows that a child may need to be exposed to a food 10 times or more before accepting it.[19] Parents also should not remove healthy foods, like broccoli or brussels sprouts, from a child's diet because they themselves don't like them. Children will often adapt to the foods made available to them.

According to Ellyn Satter, an expert on child feeding and nutrition, there is a division of responsibility when it comes to control of feeding. The adult is responsible for what the child is offered to eat, as well as when and where the food is offered. The child, however, is responsible for whether he or she eats, and how much.[20] Food and power struggles can occur when adults think that their job is not only to provide the food but also to make sure that the child eats it. Often, parents encourage their children to "clean their plates," even though the children may have indicated that they are finished eating. This is a risky habit that encourages overconsumption of calories, which can ultimately lead to obesity. Children should be allowed to stop eating once they are full.

Small children can sometimes seem to have very narrow food preferences. Parents may think, "My child only eats chicken nuggets and fries," or "She hates vegetables." Though it's true that toddlers often demonstrate **picky eating,** parents should not give up on encouraging them to try and accept new foods.

picky eating Unwillingness to eat unfamiliar foods.

One way to help small children accept a varied diet is to eat a varied diet yourself. Research suggests that adults' vegetable consumption should serve as a "model" for younger diners.[21] That is, adults should load up their own plates with a variety of vegetables, and snack on items like carrot sticks and apple slices between meals, so that children will be more likely to follow suit. Children often mimic adults' behaviors, including the unhealthy ones. A mom who only drinks diet soda for dinner, or a dad who insists that his 3-year-old eat asparagus but never puts it on his own plate, may send confusing messages. Involving children in the food shopping, menu selection, and preparation of meals is another way to encourage them to enjoy a variety of foods.

Whereas picky eating involves not wanting to try new foods, **food jags** are a child's tendency to want to eat only a limited selection of foods. Did your parents ever mention that when you were small, all you wanted to eat was macaroni and cheese or peanut butter? This behavior of getting "stuck" on a small selection of foods is quite common and normal in young children. Luckily, food jags are usually temporary. A child who only wants to eat pretzels and oranges, or refuses to eat anything green, will likely emerge from the phase within a few days or weeks.

If a parent or caregiver senses that the food jag is not going away, then it might be more serious than the natural tendency for a child to assert some independence. At that point, it is helpful to pay careful attention to what the child is eating as well as what he or she is avoiding. Is the child really "eating only goldfish crackers" or is the parent forgetting that the child is also drinking milk and eating green beans and orange slices when they are offered? A parent or caregiver can keep a food diary of everything the child eats and drinks for a few days to help identify any major problems. Sharing concerns (and the food diary) with the child's health care provider and asking for advice may prevent serious nutrient deficiencies in the long run.

In some cases, indulging the food jag may be a means to an end. For example, if a child really does stay stuck on something like pasta, a parent or caregiver can offer a variety of foods within that category (for example, serving different shapes of pasta, and using different accompanying ingredients). Another, braver tactic is to gradually wean the child from a particular food. Parents and caregivers must remember that they have ultimate authority. While this should not be license to have dinner table wars, it does mean that the adult needs to control the situation in a healthy manner for the sake of the child.

Food jags, such as wanting to only eat one food (like macaroni and cheese), or avoiding certain foods, are common among toddlers.

The Take-Home Message
Toddlers grow at a much slower rate than infants, and have reduced appetites. Caregivers need to be sure that toddlers get adequate amounts of calcium, iron, vitamin D, and fiber, and avoid lead. Caregivers also need to monitor a child's beverage intake and provide water, milk, and 100 percent juice while avoiding soda and sugary drinks. Adults should be sure to offer children appropriate portion sizes. Toddlers and preschoolers will stop eating when full and shouldn't be forced to clean their plates. Caregivers should be good role models when it comes to getting children to try new foods. New foods may need to be offered 10 times or more before they are accepted. Food jags are normal and usually temporary.

food jags When a child will only eat the same food meal after meal.

What Are the Nutritional Needs and Issues of School-Aged Children?

School-aged children, usually considered those between the ages of 6 and 10 to 12, still have plenty of growing to do, and the quality of their diet impacts their growth. See Table 13.1 for the range of calorie needs for children in this age group. Gross and fine motor skills become more refined. Due to the routine of school and being away from home, school-aged children do not eat as many times throughout the day as do toddlers and preschoolers.

Although children of school age have developed skills such as tying their own shoes or buckling their own seat belts, there are still several nutrition-related issues that parents and caregivers need to keep in mind. At this point in the life cycle, children are learning habits that they may keep for life, so encouraging a healthy lifestyle is essential. Parents and caregivers should capitalize on their role model status as children are watching and learning from the habits and actions of adults.

School-Aged Children Are Experiencing Higher Rates of Obesity and Diabetes

In recent decades, there has been an increase in overweight and obesity among children in this age group. Over 17 percent of U.S. children and adolescents are currently overweight.[22] The reason for the increase in **childhood obesity** is likely a combination of several factors, including too many calories and too little physical activity.

Children are taking in excess calories from several sources. For instance, they can grab nutritionally empty sugar and calorie-heavy sodas and candy from vending machines, sometimes even in their school's hallway or cafeteria. Excess snacks can add many calories to a child's day, especially if a child has a habit of munching on high-calorie items like chips or soda. The use of sugary sodas and sports beverages among children in the school aged group has increased, and these beverages often replace nutrient-dense milk as well as water that would better provide the fluid they need without the empty calories. While excess sugar and sweets may make weight management a challenge with children, research doesn't support that it negatively affects a child's behavior. The feature box "Does Sugar Cause ADHD?" on the next page discusses this further.

Another key factor for increased calorie intake is that food is everywhere, including in places where it was previously unavailable, such as at gas stations, libraries, and bookshops. Finally, food portions at restaurants and at home are bigger than they used to be.[23]

While children tend to enjoy high-calorie foods and eat them in significant quantities, they often avoid lower calorie, healthy foods like fruits and vegetables. For many school-aged children, high fat french fries and potato chips are their favorite vegetables. Though these foods are technically considered vegetables, they contain too much fat and too many calories to make the grade nutritionally. The consumption of fried potatoes has increased 18 percent in the United States, while vegetable consumption has decreased by over 43 percent.[24]

There are also multiple factors that contribute to the decreased level of physical activity seen in recent years. The combined amount of "screen time" a child spends in

school-aged children Children between the ages of 6 and 10 to 12.

childhood obesity The condition of a child's having too much body weight for his height. Rates of childhood obesity in the United States are increasing.

Does Sugar Cause ADHD?

Many young children are diagnosed with behavior-related conditions such as **attention deficit hyperactivity disorder (ADHD)** (sometimes still called attention deficit disorder, or ADD). ADHD is a condition in which children are inattentive, hyperactive, and impulsive.[1] It generally emerges in early childhood, and those with ADHD have difficulty controlling their behavior. An estimated 3 to 5 percent of children (about 2 million) in the United States have ADHD. Given the common characteristics of the condition, it can be difficult and frustrating to manage. Parents often wonder if dietary factors, like sugar

attention deficit hyperactivity disorder (ADHD) (previously known as attention deficit disorder (ADD)). A condition in which an individual may be easily distracted, have difficulty listening and following directions, difficulty focusing and sustaining attention, difficulty concentrating and staying on task, and/or inconsistent performance in school.

intake or food additives, are responsible for their children's behavior.

Although the myth that sugar contributes to ADHD persists, there isn't any research to support this. In a study, children whose mothers felt they were sugar sensitive were given aspartame as a substitute for sugar. Half of the mothers were told their children were given sugar, half that their children were given aspartame. The mothers who thought their children had received sugar rated them as more hyperactive than the other children and were more critical of their behavior.[2]

Currently, the American Dietetic Association has concluded that sugar doesn't have an effect on behavior or learning. The American Academy of Pediatrics has also confirmed that there is no evidence that ADHD is caused by eating too much sugar, or by food additives, allergies, or immunizations.[3]

With so many children and families affected by ADHD, more theories about the cause of ADHD have emerged in recent years. There have been studies citing a possible connection between cigarette

and alcohol use during pregnancy and increased risk for the child to have ADHD. Other studies have noted a higher risk of ADHD with high levels of lead in the bodies of preschoolers. Attention disorders often run in families, so there are likely to be genetic influences.[4]

With no definitive answers about the root cause, there are a range of treatments for ADHD. Medication, psychotherapy, and behavioral therapies, as well as diet restrictions, are among the many methods used to address the condition. Parents of children with ADHD may want to consult with a dietitian to help their child with nutritional issues, such as underweight due to side effects of certain medications that decrease appetite. Disruptive mealtimes may also be a concern (if untreated). Organizations such as the National Institute of Mental Health (www.nimh.nih.gov) and the American Academy of Child and Adolescent Psychiatry (www.aacap.org/index.ww) provide information for families with children who have ADHD.

front of a television, computer, or playing video games, is significant. Research shows that 8- to 18-year-olds spend more than 3 hours daily watching TV. This amount increases to an average of 4½ hours daily when TV time is combined with videos, DVDs, and movies. Children in the United States also spend slightly more than 1 hour daily on the computer.[25] To make matters worse, children often have TV sets and computers in their bedrooms, likely promoting even more screen time. Screen time should be limited to no more than 2 hours daily.

In addition to their tendency to spend more time in front of TV and computer screens, children are also getting less physical activity while at school and during other parts of their day. More than a third of young people in grades 9 to 12 do not regularly engage in vigorous physical activity. Daily participation in high school physical education classes dropped from 42 percent in 1991 to 29 percent in 1999.[26] Seventy-five percent of "tweens" (preteens) ride in a car for trips of less than a mile, and only 1 percent ride a bike.[27]

To reduce their children's risk of becoming overweight or obese, parents and caregivers need to be sure children receive adequate nutrients without overloading on calories, sugar, and fat, and that they participate in plenty of physical activity. To help prevent children from becoming overweight, the American Academy of Pediatrics recommends that parents and caregivers serve as role models when it comes to healthy eating and offer children healthy snacks such as vegetables, fruits, low-fat dairy products, and whole grains coupled with physical activity.[28]

As children age, outside influences like peers, advertising, and the media can impact their food intake. As early as preschool, peers influence a child. By observing what other children are eating, children may want to try something out of the ordinary. Children often reject healthy meals, such as those provided at school lunch, because the lunches are unpopular with their peers.[29] Portion sizes may also become more affected by environmental influences. Recall from Chapter 10 that portion sizes play an important role in the amount of food and calories consumed at a meal.

One result of increased obesity among children is an associated increase in rates of type 2 diabetes. As you learned in Chapter 4, type 2 diabetes, which used to be seen solely in adulthood, is now being diagnosed in children. Basically, this previously adult-onset disease has now become a childhood-onset disease as well (see Table 4.7 "Red Flags for Type 2 Diabetes in Children and Adolescents" in Chapter 4). As with adults, there is a connection between type 2 diabetes and being overweight.

What can families do to help prevent type 2 diabetes in their children? To start, identify whether the child is at high risk. If a child's father and grandfather have the disease, then paying close attention to the child's health is essential. Decreasing a child's risk factors, such as being overweight or sedentary, ought to be on the "to do" list as well. If a child is diagnosed with type 2 diabetes, early intervention and treatment are a must. The sooner the family learns what the child needs to eat and how to manage all other aspects of the disease, the better off the child will be. In fact, the entire family should consider eating in the same fashion as the child, because managing type 2 diabetes involves moderation, variety, and balance.

Physical activity is also a major part of managing diabetes, and everyone can take part in this as well. Taking a family walk or bike ride after dinner instead of turning on the TV or enjoying weekend games of basketball or tennis, are excellent ways to teach the importance of exercise. The child is more likely to feel supported and succeed with keeping his or her diabetes under control if everyone in the family is educated about what to do to help.

Caregivers also must encourage tooth-friendly dental practices in school-aged children. The potential for tooth decay begins as soon as the teeth start to emerge from the gums. In the year 2000, the Centers for Disease Control and Prevention (CDC) reported that more than half of children aged 5 to 9 had already had at least one cavity or filling.

The American Dental Association recommends that "infants and young children should be provided with a balanced diet in accordance with the *Dietary Guidelines for Americans*." Eating healthy foods makes a difference in the health of teeth. Children's consumption of foods such as juice drinks and soft drinks should be limited, as these may bathe the teeth in sugar and lead to dental caries.[30]

MyPyramid For Kids Can Help Guide Food Choices

Since parents are not nutrition experts, the idea of trying to meet all of the nutrient needs of children can be overwhelming and confusing. Fortunately, a child-friendly (and, therefore, parent-friendly) version of the latest MyPyramid Food Guidance System can help guide their choices (see Figure 13.1 on page 464).

The MyPyramid For Kids slogan is "Eat Right. Exercise. Have Fun." The key messages of this visual guide are:

- Be physically active every day. The child climbing the steps reminds children that physical activity should be done every day.

eLearn
We Can!

Want to learn more about programs that help families battle obesity? Visit www.nhlbi.nih.gov/health/public/heart/obesity/wecan/ to learn about the We Can! program (Ways to Enhance Children's Activity & Nutrition) from the National Institutes of Health, which helps parents and caregivers prevent overweight and obesity in children.

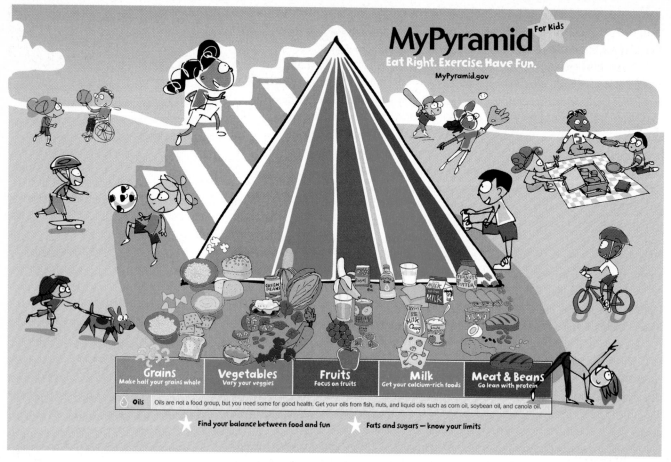

Figure 13.1 MyPyramid For Kids
MyPyramid For Kids is one tool parents and caregivers can use to help plan healthy meals for children.

- Choose healthier foods from each group. Every food group has foods that should be eaten more often than others.
- Eat more of some food groups than others. The size of the color bands suggest how much food should be chosen from each group.
- Eat foods from every food group every day. The different colors of the pyramid represent the five different food groups plus oils.
- Make the right choices for you. MyPyramid.gov gives everyone in the family personal ideas on how to eat better and exercise more.
- Take it one step at a time. Start with one new, good thing a day, and continue to add another new one every day.

Children who have special health-related issues or chronic diseases may not necessarily be able to follow MyPyramid For Kids. For example, children with autism may become especially fixated on specific foods or be reluctant to try new foods. Overcoming these issues generally requires intervention and support from professionals who work with children with special needs, such as a health care provider or a registered dietitian.

School Lunches Contribute to Children's Nutritional Status

The National School Lunch Program (NSLP) provides nutritionally balanced, low-cost or free lunches to more than 28 million children each school day.[31] The NSLP meals are designed meet certain nutrient guidelines including minimum levels for calories, protein, calcium, iron, vitamin A, and vitamin C. There are also maximum levels for the percent of calories from fat and saturated fat (see Table 13.2).

Table 13.2

Minimum Nutrient and Calorie Levels for School Lunches (School Week Averages)

Tips for Packing School Lunches

Nutrients and Energy Allowances	Minimum Requirements			Optional
	Preschool	Grades K–6	Grades 7–12	Grades K–3
Energy allowances (calories)	517	664	825	633
Total fat (g)[†]	17 g*	22 g*	28 g*	21 g*
Saturated fat (g)[‡]	6 g[†]	7 g[†]	9 g[†]	9 g[†]
RDA for protein (g)	7 g	10 g	16 g	9 g
RDA for calcium (mg)	267 mg	286 mg	400 mg	267 mg
RDA for iron (mg)	3.3 mg	3.5 mg	4.5 mg	3.3 mg
RDA for vitamin A (RE)	150 RE	224 RE	300 RE	200 RE
RDA for vitamin C (mg)	14 mg	15 mg	18 mg	15 mg

*Total fat not to exceed 30 percent over a school week.
[†]Saturated fat to be less than 10 percent over a school week.
[‡]Grams of fat will vary depending on the actual level of calories offered.

Source: School Nutrition Association. Available at www.SchoolNutrition.org.

Get children excited about their lunches by having them pick out a fun lunch box or decorate a brown paper bag with stickers.

Involve the child in planning lunches and then shop for the items together.

Make a lunch calendar and go over the specific days the child will eat a school-provided lunch and the days he or she will pack lunch. On packing days, be sure to give the child food options.

Select new foods that the child likes and ask if there are new items he or she wants to try.

Be mindful of what the child is actually eating and what might be left behind or thrown away. If, for example, the apple keeps coming back day after day, it's time to try an orange.

Imagine that you are a school food service director running a school cafeteria. On the one hand, you are running a business. You need to make money for payroll, to keep the ovens heated, to purchase paper goods on which to serve the food, and so forth. On the other hand, you must meet the nutritional requirements set up by the USDA while satisfying your hungry customers who have distinct preferences and dislikes. The USDA donates certain foods, which helps keeps prices down, but you have to stick to the regulations in order to receive these foods. You may also have the competition of nearby fast-food restaurants or vending machines vying for your customer's attention. In order to serve healthy school lunches, the director has to plan a balanced meal, using a variety of food groups, in the right portions, depending on the age of the student. Many times, healthy substitutions can be further made that will improve the quality of the meal (Table 13.3 on page 466).

As you can see, the school food service director has quite a few people to satisfy, and much to consider when deciding what to serve. For some children, the food that they eat at school is the healthiest meal—perhaps the only meal—they eat all day.

If children are not eating the school lunches, it's up to the parents and caregivers to come up with a healthy substitute. Simply giving the child money may lead to a candy bar and soda lunch, which will short change him of about one-third of his nutrition for the day. Rather, it makes nutritional sense for the parent *and* the child to use MyPyramid as a guide to put together a mutually agreeable healthy lunch for the child to take to school. A lunch that the child has helped to plan has a better chance of being eaten. Without the child's input, the "healthy lunch" may end up being swapped for unhealthy foods, or worse, tossed in the trash can. The Table Tips provides some useful ideas to improve the likelihood that a child will eat his packed lunch.

Many school districts are taking measures to ensure that their students eat healthfully during the day, such as offering more fresh fruit in cafeterias, banning soda and snack vending machines, and monitoring students' food choices. Some schools even have gardens that the children tend, and use the produce in their lunch meals.

Table 13.3

What's in a School Lunch?

Item	Elementary Serving Size	Elementary Meal Pattern	Secondary Serving Size	Secondary Meal Pattern	Make It Healthy	Extra Tips
Presidential pizza with ground beef	1 piece	2 oz meat/ meat alternate, 2 grains/breads, ¼ cup fruit/ vegetable	2 pieces	4 oz meat/ meat alternate	Use lowfat cheese, lean beef, whole-wheat flour	Substitute lean turkey for beef; add vegetables as toppings
Green beans	½ cup	½ cup fruit/ vegetable	½ cup	½ cup fruit/ vegetable		Serve fresh, not processed; season with herbs, spices, lemon juice, or salsa
Veggies and dip	½ cup (veggies), 1 tbs (dip)	½ cup fruit/ vegetable	½ cup, (veggies), 1 tbs (dip)	½ cup fruit/ vegetable	Leave edible skins intact	For a dip, use low-fat dressing, seasoned yogurt, or salsa; vary shapes and sizes
Fruit pan dowdy	4 × 2⅖ in piece	1½ grains/ breads, ¼ cup fruit/vegetable	4 × 2⅖ in piece	1½ grains/ breads, ¼ cup fruit/vegetable	Use canned fruit in light syrup or juice	Add whole-wheat flour; reduce sugar
Milk, 1%	8 fl oz	1 milk	8 fl oz	1 milk		

Elementary per Serving: 642 cal., 31.6 g pro., 98 g carb., 7 g fiber, 14.7 g fat, 6.7 g sat. fat, 70 mg chol., 867 mg sod., 5,395 IU vit. A, 19.9 mg vit. C, 621.1 mg ca., 5.6 mg iron

Secondary per Serving: 937 cal., 49.4 g pro., 129.7 g carb., 9.1 g fiber, 25.2 g fat, 11.5 g sat. fat, 112 mg chol., 1,125 mg sod., 6,039 IU vit. A, 33.1 mg vit. C, 866 mg ca., 8.4 mg iron

Total Meal Pattern: 2 oz (elementary) or 4 oz (secondary) meat/meat alternate, 3½ (elementary) or 5½ (secondary) grains/breads, 1½ cups (elementary) or 1¾ cups (secondary) fruit vegetable, 1 milk

Source: www.schoolnutrition.org

The National School Lunch Program provides breakfast and noontime meals for millions of school-aged children.

In addition to serving lunches, some schools also have school breakfast programs. Research has shown that eating breakfast may be associated with healthier body weight in children and adolescents. The habit of skipping breakfast is often seen in children and adolescents who are overweight, with a possible relationship to dieting and disordered eating. Those who miss breakfast are less likely to engage in physical activity. Breakfast can positively benefit cognitive function (especially memory), academic performance, school attendance rates, psychosocial function, and mood.[32] If a child is hungry during the mid morning hours, it will impact his or her learning during this time period.

If children don't have time to eat breakfast at home, and aren't receiving school breakfast, caregivers can still provide quick, nutritious morning meals that can be eaten on the way to school. See the Table Tips on the next page for some on-the-go breakfast ideas.

The Take-Home Message Increasing obesity rates are contributing to rising rates of type 2 diabetes in school-aged children. Parents and caregivers need to be sure children limit their empty-calorie foods and get enough physical activity. MyPyramid For Kids addresses the nutritional needs of school-aged children. School meals provide nourishment for children. For children who refuse to eat school lunches, parents and caregivers need to provide a healthy alternative.

What Are the Nutritional Needs and Issues of Adolescents?

Adolescence is generally the stage of the life cycle between ages 9 and 19. With adolescence come many hormonal, physical, and emotional changes. Among the physical changes are a rapid **growth spurt,** and, for girls, the first menstrual period, or **menarche.** This growth must be supported with appropriate quantities of nutrients, and adequate calories (energy) and protein. Calcium and iron are particularly important at this stage. The greatest concern at this age is the quality of the foods selected in order to support optimal adolescent growth.

The growth spurt of adolescence involves more than just getting taller. While height increases (adolescents attain about 15 percent of their adult height during this stage), weight also increases (they attain about 50 percent of their ideal adult weight). Bones grow significantly. An increase in lean muscle mass and body fat stores are also part of the spurt.

As with younger age groups, rates of overweight and obesity are increasing among adolescents. Results from the 2003–2004 National Health and Nutrition Examination Survey (NHANES) show that the percentage of overweight adolescents aged 12 to 19 increased from 11 to 17 percent.[33]

Adolescent girls who take in too much fat and/or too little fiber may experience menarche earlier than other girls, especially if these young girls are inactive.[34]

Some nutrition-related issues during adolescence may be indirectly caused by the social and emotional growth that is occurring. Adolescents experience a strong desire for independence and individuality. For example, they may have their own money earned through a part-time job as well as their own transportation. Similarly, they will likely want to make their own food choices, which may be less nutritious than what has previously been served at home. Many adolescents exhibit a level of defiance toward authority which may be manifested at the table.

The influence of peers, media, and other nonparent role models also adds fuel to the fire. Teens may see someone on television lose 50 pounds in 30 days, and want to do the same. Or, their favorite celebrities may seem to live on a diet of cigarettes, caffeine, and alcohol. These glamorous individuals with unhealthy habits are not only famous, but likely rich, thin, and attractive—three desirable qualities for most teens, who live for the moment and think the "future" means next weekend. As a result, they willingly adopt damaging habits. Unfortunately, these habits are not only unhealthy but can also contribute to low self-esteem when the outcomes do not meet expectations.

adolescence The developmental period between childhood and early adulthood.

growth spurt A rapid increase in height and weight.

menarche The onset of menstruation.

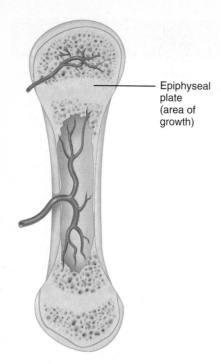

Figure 13.2 Epiphyseal Plate in Long Bone
Adolescent bone growth takes place along the epiphyseal plate. Once the plates close, lengthening of the bone stops.

Epiphyseal plate (area of growth)

Adolescents Need Calcium and Iron for Growth and Development

Whereas several nutrients are essential for healthy growth and maturation in adolescents, calcium and iron are particularly important to ensure optimal bone and muscle growth.

Adolescents Need Calcium for Bone Growth

Since adolescents experience rapid bone growth, inadequate calcium intake can harm this process. Most of the growth occurs in the **epiphyseal plate** (Figure 13.2), the area of tissue near the end of the long bones in children and adolescents. The growth plate determines the future length and shape of the mature bone. At some point during adolescence, bone growth is complete. The plates close and are replaced by solid bone.[35] For this reason, adolescence is the last chance to maximize the potential of the bone, and calcium and vitamin D intakes influence that potential. Inadequate calcium intake is one factor that can lead to low **peak bone mass** and is considered a risk factor for osteoporosis.[36]

A study followed females aged 15 to 18 for seven years and looked at their bone health. Results indicated that subjects' hip and forearm bone density was increased in those who had been given calcium supplements or dairy products rather than a placebo.[37] Another study instructed boys ages 13 to 17 years old to consume an additional three servings per day of either 1 percent milk or unfortified juice. The boys in the milk group had significantly greater increases in bone mineral density than those in the juice group.[38]

Today, inadequate calcium intake among adolescents is common. One reason for this trend is teens' increased preference for sugar-laden soft drinks instead of milk or calcium-fortified soy milk. One study found that about 66 percent of boys and 56 percent of girls between the ages of 12 and 17 drink one or more calorie-containing soft drinks daily.[39] Sodas and other empty-calorie beverages, such as energy drinks and sports drinks, may taste good and be popular with peers, but are missing the calcium that is so crucial for developing bones. While many of these drinks contain a significant number of calories, even noncalorie diet sodas are undesirable because they are likely displacing other nutrient-dense fluids in the diet.

Teen Males and Females Need More Iron for Different Reasons

Adolescents need additional iron to support muscle growth and increased blood volume. Adolescent girls also need more iron to support the onset of menstruation.

Females at this age often have an inadequate iron intake especially if they diet or restrict their food intake. In a large study, iron deficiency was found in over 14 percent of the girls aged 15 to 18 years and 12 percent of the boys aged 11 to 14 years in the United States.[40] Iron deficiency has been shown to exist in both male and female teens of all races and socioeconomic levels.[41] Teens who limit enriched grains, lean meats, and legumes in their diet are running the risk of failing to meet their daily iron needs.

Adolescents Are Sometimes at Risk for Disordered Eating

Teens grapple with trying to fit in and must adjust to new bodies, new thoughts, new situations, and experiences. All of this, along with the typical adolescent feeling of immortality, factors in to the potential for an adolescent to engage in risky tactics to

epiphyseal plate The growth plate of the bone. In puberty, growth in this area leads to increases in height.

peak bone mass The maximum bone mass achieved.

reach a desired weight, and can ultimately lead to disordered eating. Teens can sometimes adopt a variety of unhealthy habits, including eating very little food, using a food substitute, skipping meals, smoking cigarettes, taking diet pills, self-induced vomiting, and/or using laxatives or diuretics. A study found that compared with teens who did not use any weight-control methods, adolescents who engaged in unhealthful behaviors to control their weight exhibited a slightly higher body mass index and a greater risk for being overweight, binge eating, or extreme dieting five years later.[42] In essence, the teen ends up with two problems: The feeling of failure, as well as the health consequences associated with the risky tactic used to try to change his or her weight.

If an eating disorder is not detected or is left untreated, there can be numerous physical and emotional consequences. Because adolescents don't necessarily consider the long-term consequences of their actions, the threat of these consequences may not be enough to prevent disordered eating. Teens who are able to successfully overcome an eating disorder may require the long-term support of a team of professionals dedicated to this area of work.

The Take-Home Message By the life stage of adolescence, a child wants to have authority over food and lifestyle decisions. Peers and media exert a tremendous amount of influence. Calcium and iron intake are particularly important during adolescence to ensure adequate bone and muscle growth. Increased consumption of soft drinks and decreased milk consumption can compromise bone health. Adolescents are sometimes at risk of developing disordered eating patterns due to poor body image, emotional issues, or peer pressure. Because adolescents often live in the "here and now," they may not realize the long-term health consequences of the poor diet and lifestyle habits that they adopt during their teenage years.

What Are the Nutritional Issues of Older Adults?

At about age 50, a person is considered an older adult. Reaching this age wasn't always a given. If you were born in 1900, you would have been lucky to see your fiftieth birthday, as the average **life expectancy** at the time was 47 years. Your relatives born in the 1960s can expect to live to about age 70, while those born in the 1990s are expected to live past age 75.[43] Currently, there are over 50,000 centenarians, people who are 100 years of age or older, living in the United States.[44]

Adults Are Living Longer

What happened in the last 100-plus years to so dramatically increase the average life expectancy? Advances in research and health care, coupled with public health promotion programs, have all contributed to Americans' longer lives. For example, the infectious and deadly diseases of the 1900s, such as tuberculosis, pneumonia, polio, mumps, and measles have been dramatically reduced, if not eradicated, due to better vaccinations and medical care. For decades, ongoing public education campaigns have emphasized a healthy diet and lifestyle to prevent and manage conditions such

life expectancy The number of years that a person will live.

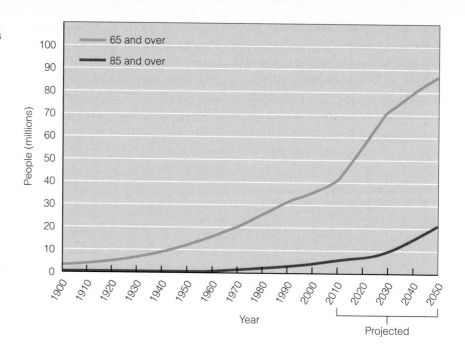

Figure 13.3 Aging of the Baby Boomers
The number of older adults in the United States is expected to increase dramatically over the next several decades.

Source: www.agingstats.gov.

as high blood pressure and blood cholesterol levels before they develop into the more crippling and sometimes deadly stroke and heart disease.

All of these efforts will benefit the generation of "baby boomers" born between 1946 and 1964. Those at the tail end of this group, ages 55 to 64, are expected to be the fastest growing segment of the population over the next decade. The number of individuals 65 years of age and older is projected to increase to over 80 million in 2050. The number of those living beyond the age of 80 will also rise (Figure 13.3).[45]

Good nutrition continues to play a key role in healthful aging. Nutrient needs, and the way the body uses some nutrients, change as you age.[46] Let's look at some of the specific changes that occur during older age.

Older Adults Need Fewer Calories, Not Less Nutrition

Because a person's metabolic rate naturally declines with age, older adults need fewer calories. The decline in their metabolism is a combination of the natural loss of muscle mass (muscle mass requires more energy to be maintained than fat mass) and the tendency for less daily physical activity. This decline amounts to approximately 10 calories a year for men and 7 calories yearly for women.[47] In other words, a man at age 60 needs 300 fewer daily calories—about the amount in a turkey sandwich—than he needed at age 30. Some research has even suggested that at 80 years of age, calorie intake may be reduced by as much as 1,000 calories daily in some men and by 600 calories daily in some women compared to when they were in their 20s.[48]

Though calorie needs may be reduced, the need for many nutrients and phytochemicals isn't. In fact, the requirement for some nutrients actually increases in older adults, making nutrient-dense food selections even more important. Since phytochemicals, especially antioxidants, have possible roles in helping to reduce the risk of certain cancers, heart disease, cataracts, and age-related macular degeneration, foods need to be both nutrient dense and phytochemical dense.

Older Adults Need to Get Enough Fiber and Fluids

Because they are consuming fewer calories, older adults need to eat high-fiber foods, such as whole grains, fruits, and vegetables at each meal. Though their dietary fiber needs actually decrease slightly, over 70 percent of Americans over age 50, on average, are still not meeting their daily needs.[49] Recall from Chapter 4 that fiber may help reduce the risk of diverticulosis, heart disease, type 2 diabetes mellitus, obesity, and certain cancers, which are all more common during the older years. Older adults' requirements for dietary protein, fat, and carbohydrates don't change from their younger years, and research shows that these three nutrient needs can be easily met by a balanced diet.[50]

Consuming adequate amounts of fluid is important, as the kidneys' ability to concentrate urine declines with age, which can lead to dehydration. An older person's thirst mechanism also becomes blunted, further increasing the risk of becoming dehydrated. Certain medications may cause the body to lose water and/or further blunt the thirst mechanism.[51]

Though older adults have the same fluid recommendations as younger people, the fear of frequent trips to the bathroom, especially when they are away from home, often causes them to deliberately consume less fluid. Incidences of urinary incontinence (the loss of the control of the bladder) also increase with age due to prostate problems in men and weakened bladder muscles in many women after pregnancy. This may further reduce the enthusiasm to consume fluids during the day and cause many older people to become dehydrated. Dehydration can also lead to constipation, another common condition in older adults, as the stool becomes hard and compacted in the colon.

Because of the need for nutrient-dense foods, there is little room in an older adult's diet for sugar-laden soft drinks that are high in calories and low in nutrients. Water and milk are better beverages to meet their fluid needs and to avoid dehydration. Table 13.4 on page 472 summarizes these dietary changes.

Older Adults Need to Watch Intake of Vitamins A, D, and B$_{12}$

Though the recommended daily amount of vitamin A doesn't change for those over age 50, there is a concern that too much preformed vitamin A, which is stored in the body, may increase the risk of osteoporosis and fractures (see Chapter 7). Older adults should be cautious when choosing supplements and fortified foods to prevent the overconsumption of preformed vitamin A.[52] The vitamin A precursor, beta-carotene, is not of concern and is actually beneficial because of it's role as an antioxidant in the body.

The skin's ability to make vitamin D from sunlight declines with age. Further, the intestines and kidneys lose some ability to absorb and convert vitamin D into its active form.[53] Because of all these changes, the need for dietary vitamin D doubles at age 50 and triples at age 70. Recall that vitamin D is needed to properly use calcium and phosphorus to strengthen bones, and inadequate amounts of this vitamin can increase the risk of osteoporosis. Older adults need to make sure that they consume vitamin D–fortified dairy products, and many, especially those who have difficulty tolerating lactose as they age, would also benefit from a supplement (Table 13.4).

Since the stomach produces less acidic juice as it ages, up to 30 percent of people over the age of 50 cannot absorb the form of vitamin B$_{12}$ that naturally occurs in

Table 13.4

Dietary Changes Needed As You Age

What Older Adults Need	Why Older Adults Need It	How They Can Get It
More nutrient-dense foods	Lower metabolic rate, which reduces their daily calorie needs	Choose foods in each food group that are low in added sugar and saturated fat.
More fiber	Consumption of fewer daily calories which decreases their fiber intake	Choose whole-wheat bread, whole-grain cereals, brown rice, vegetables, and whole fruit.
More water and nutrient-dense fluids Less sugary, low-nutrient soft drinks	Decreased ability of their kidneys to concentrate urine and blunted thirst mechanism, which can both increase risk of dehydration	Drink low-fat or skim milk and water with and between meals.
More foods high in β-carotene to meet vitamin A needs and less vitamin A supplements and heavily fortified foods	Higher excess amounts of stored preformed vitamin A in the body, which can be unhealthy for bones	Choose carrots, cantaloupe, sweet potatoes, broccoli, and winter squash.
More vitamin D-fortified foods	Decreased ability to make the active form of vitamin D, which decreases the absorption of calcium and phosphorus and increases the risk of osteoporosis	Choose vitamin D-fortified milk, yogurt, and cereals. Add a supplement if needed.
More synthetic form of vitamin B_{12}	Fewer acidic stomach juices, which will lessen the absorption of vitamin B_{12} in foods	Choose vitamin B_{12}-fortified cereals and soy milk. Add a supplement if needed.
More iron-rich foods	Higher prevalence of anemia in aging people	Choose lean meat, fish, and poultry. Enjoy enriched grains and cereals along with vitamin C-rich foods (citrus fruits) to enhance absorption.
More zinc-rich foods	Suppressed immune system and appetite in aging people due to a zinc deficiency	Choose fortified cereals, lean meats, poultry, legumes, and nuts.
More calcium-rich foods	Higher risk of osteoporosis and dietary calcium deficiency	Consume 3 servings of dairy foods daily plus a serving of a calcium-fortified food. Add a supplement if needed.

foods. They can, however, absorb the synthetic variety found in fortified foods and supplements, and these sources should be added to their diet to meet their needs. Vitamin B_{12}, along with adequate amounts of folate and vitamin B_6, may also help lower homocysteine levels. High amounts of homocysteine may increase the risk of heart disease.

Older Adults Need to Be Sure to Get Enough Iron, Zinc, and Calcium

Iron deficiency is not uncommon in older adults, and over 10 percent of adults 65 years of age and older, and over 20 percent of those 85 or older, experience iron-deficiency anemia.[54] Though iron deficiency can occur from intestinal blood loss, an estimated one-third of the anemia in older adults is attributed to inadequate iron consumption alone and/or in combination with diets deficient in folate and vitamin B_{12}.[55] Iron deficiency can lead to fatigue, decreased physical activity, and an impaired immune system. Though women over age 50 need less dietary iron than they did in their younger years (due to menopause, the ending of menstruation), eating iron-rich foods is still important (Table 13.4).

Zinc is also needed for a healthy immune system, in particular in the production of white blood cells that fight infection. Zinc plays a role in the ability to taste and a deficiency can depress one's appetite, affecting a person's desire to eat nutritious foods. About 25 percent of older Americans are not meeting their daily dietary zinc needs, and would benefit from adding more zinc to their diets through foods such as cereals and legumes.[56]

Lastly, the need for calcium increases 20 percent, to 1,200 milligrams daily for those over the age of 50. More than 70 percent of older Americans are falling short of their dietary calcium needs, which increases their risk of weak bones and fractures.[57] An estimated 10 million Americans over age 50 have osteoporosis and another 30 million are at risk of developing it (see Chapter 8).[58] Older adults should consume at least three servings of dairy foods daily, and should add a serving of a calcium-fortified food or a supplement.

The Take-Home Message Life expectancy has increased in the last century due to improved research and health care, as well as dietary and lifestyle changes. Older adults need fewer calories but not less nutrition as they age. Nutrient-dense food selections are important to meet their fiber, fluid, vitamin, mineral, and phytochemical needs.

What Additional Challenges May Older Adults Face?

As adults approach their "leisure years," life should get easier, not harder. However, the physical and emotional changes that accompany older age can make eating and exercising regularly a challenge. Let's look at some of these issues.

Eating Right for Good Health and Disease Prevention

According to the World Health Organization (WHO), the best dietary strategy for aging adults in order to maintain good health and to prevent chronic diseases is to consume a varied, nutrient- and phytochemical-dense, heart-healthy diet.[59] This is the same dietary advice that is recommended in both the *Dietary Guidelines for Americans* and MyPyramid.

The majority of older Americans aren't heeding this advice. When the diets of Americans 65 years of age and older were assessed to see if they were following these guidelines, only 19 percent of those studied had diets that could be rated as "good." More than 65 percent of older Americans were eating diets that needed improvement and 13 percent were consuming diets rated as "poor."[60] In fact, this research showed that less than 30 percent of those studied consumed the recommended servings from

Regular physical activity can help older adults stay physically, mentally, and socially healthy.

the fruit and milk groups, which reduces their dietary sources of phytochemicals, fiber, calcium, and vitamin D. These compounds can help fight certain cancers, heart disease, osteoporosis, cataracts, and age-related macular degeneration. Many older adults have inadequate servings of vegetables and whole grains, limiting dietary sources of zinc, iron, folate, and antioxidants, which can help reduce the risk of diabetes, stroke, certain diseases, and an impaired immune system.[61]

Antioxidants can also help protect the body against free radicals, which damage the brain and lead to the reduced cognitive ability seen in those with Alzheimer's disease and Parkinson's disease.[62] The diets of many older adults have also been shown to be too high in saturated fat, cholesterol, and sodium, increasing their risk of heart disease, hypertension, and stroke.[63]

Eating right is important in every stage of the life cycle, especially in older adults. Table 13.5 summarizes the many diseases and conditions that a healthy diet can affect as you age.

Staying Physically Active in Spite of Physical and Mental Challenges

Joan skis both downhill and cross-country in the winter and has been attending aerobics class six days a week for the last decade—a rather active schedule for a 76-year-old. Robert attends weekly fitness classes and skates in a hockey league three days a week. At age 78, he only skates in nonchecking leagues but admits that collisions are part of the game.

No one is too old to exercise, and physical activity is not a luxury for older adults; it's a necessity. Routine physical activity can help lower the risk of heart disease, colon and breast cancer, diabetes, hypertension, osteoporosis, arthritis, and obesity. It can help maintain healthy bones, muscles, and joints, and reduce anxiety, stress, and depression. Routine exercise improves sleep, flexibility, and range of motion, and can help postpone the decline in cognitive ability that naturally occurs in aging.[64] Elders in good physical shape are also able to live independently longer, reducing the need for assistance with everyday functions.

The number-one physical activity among older Americans is walking. Gardening is second most prevalent, followed by bicycling. Don't know what to get your grandparents for a birthday gift? Consider a pair of walking sneakers.

Despite the many health benefits of being physically active, only 16 percent of those aged 64 to 74 and only 12 percent of those 75 years of age and older engage in at least 30 minutes of moderate activity five days a week. Lifestyle activities such as working in the garden, mowing the lawn, raking leaves, and even dancing will all provide health benefits. Older adults would also benefit from strength training activities such as lifting weights and calisthenics at least twice a week to help maintain muscle strength.[65]

Arthritis

Getting out of bed, trying to open up a jar of mustard, or climbing stairs can all be challenging for anyone with **arthritis** (*arthr* = joint, *itis* = inflammation). Arthritis can cause pain, stiffness, and swelling in joints, muscles, tendons, ligaments, and bones. While there are over 100 types of arthritis, osteoarthritis and rheumatoid arthritis commonly occur in older adults.

Over 20 million Americans suffer with osteoarthritis and more than half of adults age 65 and older have this type of arthritis in at least one joint.[66] Osteoarthritis occurs when the cartilage, which covers the ends of the bones at the joints, wears down, causing the bones to rub together. This constant friction between the bones

arthritis Inflammation in the joints that can cause pain, stiffness, and swelling in joints, muscles, tendons, ligaments, and bones.

Table 13.5

Eating Right to Fight Age-Related Diseases and Conditions

A varied, plant-based diet with plenty of phytochemicals, fiber, and essential nutrients is the best diet defense against the conditions and chronic diseases associated with aging.

Condition/Disease	Disease-Fighting Compounds
Alzheimer's disease Parkinson's disease	Antioxidants, vitamins E and C, and carotenoids (see Chapter 7)
Anemia	Iron Folate Vitamin B_{12} (see Chapters 7 and 8)
Cancer (colon, prostate, breast)	Fiber in whole grains, fruits, vegetables Phytochemicals (phenols, indoles, lycopene, beta-carotene) (see Chapters 2 and 4)
Cataracts, Age-related macular disease	Vitamins C and E Phytochemicals (lycopene, lutein, zeaxanthin) Zinc (see Chapter 7)
Constipation, Diverticulosis	Fiber (see Chapter 4)
Heart disease	Vitamins B_6, B_{12}, and folate Omega-3 fatty acids Soluble fiber Phytochemicals in whole grains (see Chapters 4, 5, and 7)
Hypertension, Stroke	Calcium Magnesium Potassium (see Chapter 8)
Impaired immune response	Iron Zinc Vitamin B_6 (see Chapters 7 and 8)
Obesity	Fiber as part of low-calorie, high-satiety fruits and vegetables (see Chapters 4 and 10)
Osteoporosis	Calcium Vitamins D and K (see Chapter 8)
Type 2 diabetes	Chromium Fiber Phytochemicals (see Chapters 4 and 8)

eLearn
You Can!

Want to learn more about how to help an older relative or friend stay active and healthy? Visit www.aoa.gov/youcan/youcan.asp to find information about how to increase physical activity in older people's lives.

Severe arthritis can make everyday activities, like writing, typing, and handling objects, a challenge.

dementia A disorder of the brain that interferes with a person's memory, learning, and mental stability.

Alzheimer's disease A type of dementia.

causes swelling, loss of motion, and pain. Osteoarthritis commonly occurs in the fingers, neck, lower back, knees, and hips, which can interfere with the normal activities of daily living. Exercises that increase flexibility, keep joints limber, and improve the range of motion can help with osteoarthritis. Losing excess weight will also help relieve some of the stress at the hip and knee joints that bear the weight of the body.[67]

Research has shown that the dietary supplements glucosamine and chondroitin sulfate, which are naturally found in cartilage, may provide some pain relief for some individuals with moderate to severe knee pain due to osteoarthritis. It doesn't appear to help those with mild knee pain.[68] Individuals with osteoarthritis should speak with their health care provider to assess whether they would benefit from using this supplement. For safety's sake, they should also discuss the use of all supplements, including herbs, with a health care provider prior to consuming them. The boxed feature "Drug, Food, and Drug-Herb Interactions" on page 478 discusses the potentially harmful interactions between certain herbs, nutrients, and drugs.

Rheumatoid arthritis, which occurs in about 2 million U.S. adults, is an inflammatory disease of the joints.[69] Research suggests that numerous compounds in a Mediterranean-type diet, which is rich in fish, vegetables, and olive oil, may help protect against and manage rheumatoid arthritis (see Chapter 5). The omega-3 fatty acids in fish have anti-inflammatory effects and may help reduce the stiffness and joint tenderness of rheumatoid arthritis.[70] The current recommendation to eat two fish meals weekly to protect against heart disease may also be helpful to those who suffer with this type of arthritis. Compounds in cooked vegetables have been shown to possibly lower the risk of rheumatoid arthritis, and the fatty acids in olive oil may also help reduce the inflammation.[71]

Routine exercise can help those who suffer from arthritis. Exercise can help reduce joint pain and stiffness, and increase range of motion. It can also build muscles and increase flexibility. Swimming, aquatic exercises, and walking can all help older adults with arthritis.

Alzheimer's Disease

Although it's normal for older adults to experience some cognitive changes, such as taking longer to learn new information, a more serious mental decline can be cause for concern. Some adults begin to forget where they live, become increasingly disoriented, have difficulty speaking, and/or become emotionally unstable. These individuals may be experiencing **dementia,** due to changes in their brain function, which interferes with their ability to remember, speak, and "be themselves." **Alzheimer's disease** is the most common form of dementia in older adults. This irreversible disease slowly damages the brain tissues and can progress over the years to severe brain damage. An estimated 4.5 million Americans have Alzheimer's disease, with approximately 5 percent of adults showing signs of it as early as age 65.[72]

Research suggests that free radicals and inflammation may contribute to the brain damage observed in Alzheimer's disease and that antioxidants, such as vitamins E and C and selenium, may help slow its progression.[73] Studies are currently under way to determine the role these antioxidants may play in preventing Alzheimer's disease or at least helping to slow the loss of cognitive function. A diet adequate in the B vitamins and folate, which may help lower homocysteine levels in the body, could also play a role. A high blood level of homocysteine may damage the blood vessels in the brain, affecting its function.[74] Consuming adequate amounts of these vitamins may help prevent the damage.

Some research suggests that the anti-inflammatory activities of omega-3 fatty acids may reduce the risk of Alzheimer's disease.[75] Studies are also being done to determine whether the herb, ginkgo biloba, which has been purported to improve memory, could play a role in preventing dementia.[76]

Elders with dementia likely need full-time care and shouldn't be allowed to take walks, jogs, or bike rides alone. However, accompanying an elder during any of these activities is a great way for both of you to get some exercise. While those with dementia experience mental deterioration, they should not be allowed to also experience physical deterioration.

Programs such as Meals On Wheels provide hot meals to elderly adults who cannot leave their home.

Economic and Emotional Conditions Can Affect Nutritional Health

Staying physically active and coping with arthritis or Alzheimer's are common challenges that older adults face when it comes to their health. Conditions like food insecurity, depression, grief, or even drug and alcohol abuse may also enter the picture.

Food Insecurity

Between his medical and pharmaceutical costs and basic living expenses, Joe Powers exhausts his entire Social Security check by the twentieth day of each month. For the 10 days until he gets his next check, Joe is relegated to a stark menu of oatmeal and eggs. Though technically he's not starving, his limited diet is depriving him of many basic nutrients.

Joe is not alone. Almost 7 percent of households with elders in the United States experience **food insecurity,** or the routine lack of sufficient food to feed those living there.[77] Research has shown that elders who consistently experience food insecurity have not only more than double the risk of not meeting their daily nutritional needs, but also tend to be in only fair to poor health.[78]

Limited finances aren't always the cause of food insecurity. Some elders may be able to afford food but lack the physical means to obtain it, prepare it, or, because of health issues such as tooth loss, consume it.[79] A quick and easy assessment of an older adult's diet can help screen if he or she is at risk for food insecurity (see the Self-Assessment later in this chapter).

Because America is "the land of plenty," it is unacceptable that older adults should want for food. In 1965, the Older Americans Act was passed to provide support and services to those age 60 and older, including nutritious meals and nutrition education, in order to help them maintain good health, an adequate quality of life, and an acceptable level of independence.[80] **Congregate meals** are one type of available service. These nutritious hot meals are served at specified sites in the community, such as churches and synagogues. This guarantees that older adults receive a nutritious daily meal and provides an opportunity for them to socialize. Often, transportation to these meals is also available.

For those who are homebound, a healthy meal can be delivered to the home.[81] The Meals On Wheels Association of America is the largest organization in the United States providing meals to the homes of older adults who need them.

> There are over 4,500 Meals On Wheels programs serving homebound Americans.

Young people in the community can help make sure the elderly are aware of and take advantage of the numerous services available to them. Consider "adopting" an elder in your neighborhood or a family member and, if need be, help him or her locate these services. Visit First Gov for Seniors at www.seniors.gov to locate these resources.

Depression and Grief

When Laura lost her husband at the age of 78, she stopped cooking a nightly dinner and took to opening a can of chicken soup for most of her evening meals. Her energy level dropped dramatically after his death, and on many days, she didn't even bother to get out of her pajamas. Like many elders who lose a spouse, Laura became depressed.

food insecurity The chronic lack of sufficient food to nutritiously feed oneself.

congregate meals Meals served at churches, synagogues, or other community sites where older adults can receive a nutritious meal and socialize.

Drug, Food, and Drug-Herb Interactions

Seventy-nine-year-old Donald David uses a 7-day plastic pill box to remind him to take his four daily prescriptions. Because Donald takes pills for heart disease, high blood pressure, and diabetes, his local pharmacist works with him to make sure that the drugs do not interact with each other in a way that could harm his health. The pharmacist also reminds Donald that he needs to keep his dietary vitamin K intake at an even keel, as major fluctuations can affect his blood thinner medication, and warns him about taking certain herbs that could also interfere with this drug.

Donald is lucky to have this point person in his life to remind him how drugs, food, and herbs can all interact and produce unhealthy side effects. Some older adults aren't so lucky. About 80 percent of older adults take both prescription and nonprescription medications at the same time, but use more than one pharmacy or order their medications online or through the mail, so they lack this personal guidance.[5]

Food can interact with medications in several ways. For example, it can delay or increase the absorption of a drug. Calcium, for instance, can bind with tetracycline (an antibiotic), decreasing its absorption. For this reason, this drug shouldn't be taken with milk or calcium-fortified foods. In contrast, grapefruit and grapefruit juice will increase the absorption of calcium channel blocking agents, which are a type of medication often used to treat heart disease.[6]

Drugs can also interfere with the metabolism of certain substances in foods.

Potential Side Effects of Selected Herbs and Nutrients

Herb/Nutrient	Purported Use	Potential Side Effects	Drug Interactions
Black cohosh	Reduce hot flashes and other menopausal symptoms	Possible headache and stomach discomfort	May exert estrogen activity and affect breast tissue
Calcium	Prevent osteoporosis	Constipation; calcium deposits in body	Decreases the absorption of tetracycline, thyroid medication, iron, zinc, and magnesium
Dong Quai root	Relieve menopausal symptoms	Excessive bleeding due to blood thinning	Blood-thinning drugs and aspirin. Enhances the blood-thinning actions of vitamin E, garlic, and ginkgo biloba.
Echinacea	Treat the common cold	Skin inflammation in sensitive individuals	May decrease effectiveness of immune-suppressing drugs (cyclosporine, corticosteroids)
Evening primrose oil	Help with chronic fatigue syndrome	Mild stomach and intestinal discomfort; headaches	May interfere with drugs used in epilepsy (phenothiazines)
Fish oil	Reduce the risk of heart disease	Excessive amounts could raise both blood glucose and LDL cholesterol levels, increase the risk of excessive bleeding, and cause a fishy aftertaste in mouth	Blood-thinning drugs and aspirin
Garlic, garlic supplements	Lower blood cholesterol levels	Possible stomach and intestinal discomfort	Blood-thinning drugs and aspirin. Enhances the blood-thinning actions of vitamin E, garlic, and ginkgo biloba.

Sources: A. Fragakis, 2003. *The Health Professional's Guide to Popular Dietary Supplements;* American Botanical Council, *Herb Reference Guide.* Available at www.herbalgram.org/default.asp?c=reference_guide; A. Fugh-Berman, 2000, *The Lancet* 355:134–138; J. Maskalyk, Grapefruit Juice: Potential Drug Interactions. 2002, *Canadian Medical Association Journal* 167:279–280.

The compound tyramine, which is abundant in aged cheese, smoked fish, yogurt, and red wine, is metabolized by an enzyme called monoamine oxidase. Certain medications called monoamine oxidase inhibitors, which may be prescribed to treat depression, prevent tyramine from being properly metabolized. High levels of tyramine in the blood can result in dangerously high blood pressure.

Herbs can also interact with medications. Ginkgo biloba can interfere with blood clotting and shouldn't be consumed with the blood-thinning drug Coumadin, or with aspirin, which also thins the blood. Consuming ginkgo with either or both of these medications can increase the risk of bleeding as well as stroke.[7]

The best way to avoid an interaction is to make sure a health care provider and/or a pharmacist is aware of all the prescribed and over-the-counter medications, herbs, and supplements that are being consumed. See the accompanying table for a list of potential interactions.

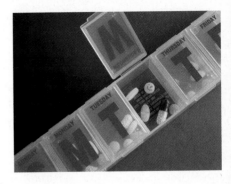

Daily pill containers like this one are often used by the elderly to remind them to take various medications.

Herb/Nutrient	Purported Use	Potential Side Effects	Drug Interactions
Ginkgo biloba	Reduce memory loss, dementia	Possible stomach and intestinal discomfort	Blood-thinning drugs and aspirin. Enhances the blood-thinning actions of vitamin E and garlic.
Ginseng	Reduce fatigue, stress	None known at this time	May interfere with MAO inhibitors, diabetes medication, heart medication (digoxin), blood-thinning drugs, aspirin. Enhances the blood-thinning actions of vitamin E, garlic, and ginkgo biloba.
Grapefruit, grapefruit juice	Source of vitamin C	None known at this time	Potentiates certain heart medications (calcium channel blocking agents), corticosteroids, immuno-suppressants
Kava kava	Reduce anxiety, stress	Possible stomach and intestinal discomfort	Potentiates the effects of alcohol and anti-anxiety medications
St. John's wort	Reduce depression	Excessive amounts may cause an allergic reaction in some individuals	Avoid when taking antidepressants. Can decrease the effect of certain heart medications (digoxin), oral contraceptives, cyclosporine.
Vitamin E	Reduce the risk of heart disease	Excessive amounts can interfere with blood clotting, increasing the risk of hemorrhage	Blood-thinning drugs
Vitamin K	Help blood clot	None known at this time	Blood-thinning drugs

Are You at Nutritional Risk?

Circle the number in the right column for the statements that apply to you (or someone you know if you are taking the assessment for a friend or relative). Add up the circled numbers to determine your score.

I have an illness or condition that has made me change the kind and/or amount of food I eat.	2
I eat fewer than two meals per day.	3
I eat few fruits or vegetables or milk products.	2
I have three or more drinks of beer, liquor, or wine almost every day.	2
I have tooth or mouth problems that make it hard for me to eat.	2
I don't always have enough money to buy food.	4
I eat alone most of the time.	1
I take three or more different prescribed or over-the-counter drugs a day.	1
Without wanting to, I have lost or gained 10 pounds in the last six months.	2
I am not always physically able to shop, cook, and/or feed myself.	2
Total	___

Answer

If your score is

0–2 good! Your diet and lifestyle don't appear to put you at risk of not meeting your nutritional needs.

3–5 you are at moderate nutritional risk. Your local office on aging, senior citizens' center, or health department can help you improve your nutritional health.

6 or over you are at high nutritional risk. Bring this checklist the next time you see your doctor, dietitian, or other qualified health or social service professional. Ask for help to improve your nutritional health.

Source: American Academy of Family Physicians, American Dietetic Association, and National Council on Aging, Inc., 2002. *The Nutrition Screening Initiative* available at http://eatright.org/cps/rde/xchg/ada/hs.xsl/nutrition_nsi_ENU_HTML.htm

Up to 20 percent of older adults can suffer from depression, ranging from mild to major depressive disorders.[82] The loss of significant others and friends as well as chronic pain and concerns about their own health can add to feelings of grief, sadness, and isolation. Depression can interfere with an elder's motivation to eat, be physically active, and socialize—all of which can impact a person's mental and physical health.

Family and friends need to be aware of the changes in elders' eating and lifestyle habits. Younger adults need to help elders reconnect with their communities after a loss and adjust to a new lifestyle. As mentioned, neighbors can "adopt an elder" who may be living alone and coordinate regular visits and delivery of meals. A quick visit by several supportive friends over the course of a month can go a long way to help elders stay healthy.

Alcohol Abuse

Alcohol abuse isn't uncommon among elders, as the bodily changes and emotional swings caused by aging sometimes induce them to turn to alcohol.

As they age, adults become more sensitive to the intoxicating effects of alcohol. This is due in part to the decline of their body water. Individuals with a lower percentage of body water will have a higher blood alcohol concentration (BAC), and thus, feel its effects sooner. Adults' tolerance for alcohol also declines with aging, so the beer that one could manage easily at age 65 may have a narcotic effect at age 75.[83]

Prescription and nonprescription medications, which are commonly taken by those over age 65, can interact with alcohol by intensifying its effects, diminishing the effects of the medication, or both. (On average, people over age 65 are taking two to seven prescription medications daily.[84]) Someone who is taking anticoagulants to reduce the risk of blood clots, for example, may interfere with the drugs' effectiveness if he or she chronically consumes alcohol.[85]

An elderly person's increased alcohol consumption could be a way of self-medicating. Chronic health problems, loss of friends and loved ones, and/or financial stress could make alcohol an appealing sedative to temporarily ease discomfort or depression. As usual, though, consuming alcohol only makes things worse. Heavy drinking can exacerbate depression, which can lead to more drinking.[86] Also, because alcohol impairs one's judgment and interferes with coordination and reaction time, elders who have been drinking are at a higher risk for stumbling, falling, and fracturing bones.

Health care providers sometimes misdiagnose alcohol abuse in elders as the forgetfulness and disorientation associated with "normal aging."[87] Figure 13.4 lists the red flags from the National Institute of Aging that may signal alcohol abuse in an older adult. Because of these numerous potential interactions with alcohol, the National Institute on Alcohol Abuse and Alcoholism recommends that adults over 65 who choose to drink should consume no more than one alcoholic drink daily.[88]

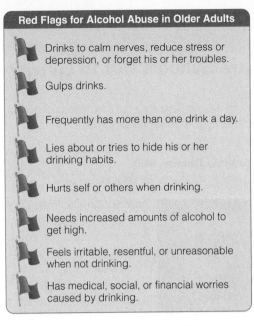

Red Flags for Alcohol Abuse in Older Adults

- Drinks to calm nerves, reduce stress or depression, or forget his or her troubles.
- Gulps drinks.
- Frequently has more than one drink a day.
- Lies about or tries to hide his or her drinking habits.
- Hurts self or others when drinking.
- Needs increased amounts of alcohol to get high.
- Feels irritable, resentful, or unreasonable when not drinking.
- Has medical, social, or financial worries caused by drinking.

Figure 13.4 Red Flags for Alcohol Abuse in Older Adults

Source: National Institute on Aging. Alcohol Use and Abuse. Available at www.niaPublications.org/agepages/alcohol.asp. Accessed May 2006.

The Take-Home Message Older adults should consume a varied, nutrient- and phytochemical-dense diet to meet their needs and help prevent many of the chronic diseases associated with aging. They also benefit from regular physical activity. Arthritis, Alzheimer's disease, food insecurity, depression, and alcohol abuse can challenge the abilities of older adults to maintain healthy diets and lifestyles.

Putting It All Together

We rely on the same general rules for a healthy diet throughout the stages of the life cycle: Eat plenty of nutrient-dense fruits, vegetables, whole grains, lean meats, and low-fat dairy products in order to get adequate amounts of vitamins, minerals, protein, carbohydrates, lipids, and water without overconsuming sugar, salt, or calories. But the specific amounts of nutrients and calories we need during childhood, adolescence, and older age can vary. Fortunately, healthy nutrition habits can last a lifetime, and good habits learned in childhood can lead to a healthy old age.

Two Points of View

Are Schools Out to Lunch?

School lunch programs provide millions of school-aged children with affordable (or free), nutritious meals every year. However, the program has its critics, some of whom contend that the lunches aren't so healthy after all. Who do you think has the stronger argument?

Antonia Demas, PhD
Director, Food Studies Institute

 **Antonia Demas, PhD,** is the founder and director of the Food Studies Institute, a nonprofit organization devoted to improving the health and education of children and their families. She has a doctoral degree from Cornell University in nutrition, education, and anthropology. Her award-winning curriculum, Food Is Elementary, has been taught successfully in more than 800 schools. Dr. Demas has conducted extensive research on school lunch programs, consults throughout the United States and abroad, and trains and certifies teachers as food educators.

Q: Where do most schools obtain the food that goes into typical school lunch programs?

A: Schools obtain food from two primary sources: the USDA commodity program and food distribution companies. There has also been an effort in recent years to obtain foods from local farmers.

The federal commodity program makes surplus commodity goods available to schools for free. In this program, the government contracts with farmers and agrees to buy their surplus food. They make a list of available items for schools to view, and schools that participate in the school lunch program can obtain these foods for free by ordering them in advance through their regional distribution centers. It's a way to help farmers and to make food available to schools so they can operate in the black instead of in the red. The program is also designed to make it affordable to have free breakfast and lunch available for low-income children.

The dual approach has brought problems. Under the commodity program, school lunch services have really gotten into the fast-food approach to cooking. Many schools no longer make things from scratch. For example, when whole turkeys are available, instead of cooking the turkey and slicing it up, school districts will contract with an outside firm to process the whole turkey into turkey nuggets. The idea is to save on labor costs, but it really compromises nutrition by turning whole foods into processed foods. The company that processes these foods is paid and it might make more sense to pay the cafeteria workers more instead. There's a whole list of nutritious commodity foods that have at one time been on the commodity list and are hardly ever

(continued)

Janey Thornton, MS, SNS
President, School Nutrition Association

 **Janey Thornton, MS, SSN** is child nutrition director for Hardin County School District in Elizabethtown, Kentucky. She is credentialed as a school nutrition specialist (SNS), and was elected the 59th president of the School Nutrition Association in July 2006. For almost 25 years, Thornton has served as director of Child Nutrition Programs in Elizabethtown, Kentucky. She has a BS in vocational home economics and a Master's degree in school administration, and is also pursuing a doctoral degree.

Q: Where do most schools obtain the food that goes into typical school lunch programs?

A: We predominantly receive it from three places. The first is the USDA commodity program. There are numerous (180 for the current school year) choices available through USDA, but the choices available to each school would vary from state to state. In most states, you do have a somewhat varied selection of foods to choose from. You can take that commodity food in its raw state, or send it to a manufacturer to have it further processed. Commodity foods make up about 20 percent of the food we use. Those foods have changed a lot. We can get grains, brown rice, fruits, and vegetables—foods that address the nutritional needs we're now looking to fill. We can get low-fat cheese, for instance, and lean meat.

Another 75 to 80 percent of foods are purchased locally. When I say "local," I'm talking about a distributor that would be local, even though they may have national suppliers. We let the distributor know exactly what food we want, and the specifications for those foods. We can get canned fruit that is water packed, for example, instead of packed in heavy syrup. We've worked with distributors and suppliers to create the foods we're looking for. The pizza most of us are buying now has a whole-wheat crust, and low-fat cheese. These companies have worked with us to create products for the school market.

In addition to that, we have fresh produce coming from local produce companies or even local farmers. There are 300 to 400 school districts that are purchasing produce from local growers. That's especially true where you have districts with year-round growing seasons. I live in Kentucky.

(continued)

Are Schools Out to Lunch?, continued

Antonia Demas, PhD, continued

served in schools, such as brown rice, lentils, and bulgur wheat. These foods are high in nutrients and would have positive health impacts on kids.

Schools also obtain foods from food vendors, often the same ones who supply foods to restaurants. Foods from these companies tend to be more processed, such as processed meat, or applesauce instead of apples.

In general, when schools purchase food, they select the items they think the kids will like—a lot of fast-food processed items because these are the foods many kids are most familiar with.

Q: What are the benefits of school lunches?

A: The primary benefit of school lunches is that they feed kids who may not have much else to eat during the school day. The program has been successful in providing calories to children from low-income families for breakfast and lunch. But a lot of those calories aren't nutrient-dense. As a consequence, we're seeing a rise in childhood obesity and diet-related disorders. School lunch programs have the potential of serving a captive audience of 53 million kids every day and therefore being a major influence on public health. The school lunch program is known in the literature as the "school feeding program." That's language I don't like. I'd like to see this changed from the feeding program to the dining program. We need to make good nutrition a part of students' education in the classroom, and use lunches and mealtime to teach them about nutrition and food.

Q: How can school lunches be improved?

A: School lunches need to be integrated with the academic program of the school. While the health connection of school meals has been acknowledged, we've been for the most part ignoring the role that school food plays in student behavior and academic performance. Currently, kids are getting diet-related diseases such as type 2 diabetes and heart disease that were formerly considered adult diseases. We need to look at how school lunches may contribute to those health problems. Behavior issues have escalated, and we're not looking at the underlying causes. Food affects all domains of a child's school experience.

Menus based on processed items are generally lower in nutrients. School lunches need to feature more whole foods. Local foods should be featured because they are fresh and educate students about what's produced in their geographic area so they'll be curious about where food comes from. This is an great educational opportunity to promote food literacy because many students are disconnected to where food comes from and how it is produced. The healthier commodity options are often not selected because of

(continued)

Janey Thornton, MS, SNS, continued

We can get local produce in the summer, but in the fall and winter it's very difficult.

Q: What are the benefits of school lunches?

A: All students in schools can eat lunch, whether they are from high-income or low-income families. There are subsidies that allow low-income children to pay less or eat meals for free.

Obviously, our meals contribute a lot nutritionally to school-aged children. There have been national studies done by USDA, including a recent study, which showed that children who ate meals at school had a better overall nutritional profile than children who did not. The school meals in that study even surpassed the RDAs recommended by the USDA. Children who participated also had lower intake of sugars than children who do not participate.

Children who eat a school lunch are also more likely to have a healthy body weight. Those who don't eat a school lunch are more likely to eat something from home or a vending machine, and some of those choices may be higher in fat or sugar. The program is a real security blanket for many low-income youth who may not have many other food choices outside of school. But this is not only a food assistance program. It helps protect children from excess weight gain, because they are eating well-balanced food instead of junk food. Students who eat school meals are more likely to consume vegetables and more milk products, not only in school but also during a 24-hour period. From their meals at school, they learn how to eat correctly.

Q: How can school lunches be improved?

A: We continue to build on successes we've had in the past, as well as respond to USDA recommendations. We've certainly seen an increase in fresh fruits and vegetables, whole grains, lower fat dairy products, and lean meats. We'd like to see a greater availability of those products to children overall.

We'd like to see continued partnership with industry, so that companies continue to make products that are healthier for children, with lower fat cheeses and other ingredients.

We're also going to continue to conduct taste tests with children so that we develop healthy options that they'll enjoy. We can require good nutrition in our menus until we're blue in the face, but it's not going to do us a bit of good unless the children will eat the meals. It's also important for kids to understand why we're offering what we're offering so that they can make good food choices at home.

Q: How are school lunch programs likely to change in the future?

A: We know that USDA meal pattern requirements will continue to change, and we'll be ready to meet those requirements.

(continued)

Are Schools Out to Lunch?, continued

Antonia Demas, PhD, continued

the perception that kids won't eat them since they are unfamiliar with them and that they are labor intensive to prepare. There also need to be more beverage alternatives to dairy. A lot of minority children are lactose intolerant. Kids need access to water throughout the day so they won't become dehydrated. Students should be able to go to recess before, not after, lunch. They've been sitting all day. If students could get out and run around before eating, they'd be more relaxed at mealtime and focus more on eating.

Q: How are school lunch programs likely to change in the future?

A: There is more public awareness now about what's happened to kids' health and the role that diet plays in disease. School meals are being looked at much more critically than they were before, and there is increased focus on nutrition and providing whole, unprocessed foods as a preventive strategy. But without some real changes to educate kids in a positive way about how food affects health, kids won't want to eat the healthier foods. There needs to be a coordinated program in the classroom, cafeteria, and community to promote food literacy. There needs to a collective voice on the national level to lobby for healthier commodity foods. My research clearly demonstrates that when nutrient-dense foods are introduced in a positive way, kids will incorporate them in their diets. The school meal program could be an effective curricular model for teaching kids about how food is grown and produced. There needs to be a national educational effort to deliberately put food in the curriculum.

I believe food service workers should be part of the educational team and paid as educators. They nourish the minds and bodies of our children and need the classroom teachers to work with them so that students gain positive sensory and educational exposure to health-promoting foods.

Janey Thornton, MS, SNS, continued

We also need to keep a commonsense approach. Children have to understand why they are eating what they're eating, or they aren't going to apply these lessons when choosing foods away from school. We have to talk to them in very simple terms. One area where we're focusing a lot of education is on serving sizes. That's critical for kids. So many children now think 2 cups of rice is a portion size. The serving size of an entrée probably shouldn't be more than a palm of a hand, but they're used to a serving the size of a plate. All foods can fit in a diet. You just need to watch portion size and frequency. There's a lot of re-education to do there.

On the whole, school meals are the best investment we have. Healthy kids are something we need this year, next year, and 30 years from now.

NUTRITION IN THE REAL WORLD

Be a Nutrition Sleuth

Junior Nutrition Sleuth

Do you have a younger sibling or family member who would like to be a nutrition detective and find out what nutrients may be missing in his or her diet? Visit http://exhibits.pacsci.org/ nutrition/ and help this person be a nutrient sleuth by uncovering the missing nutrient in various sample meals!

Get Real!

Blast Off with Good Nutrition and Physical Activity

Visit www.mypyramid.gov/kids/kids_game.html for a fun interactive computer game in which children can learn how to fuel their bodies with good food and a healthy amount of physical activity.

The Top Ten Points to Remember

1. Toddlers and preschoolers grow less rapidly than infants, but need to eat small, frequent, nutrient-dense meals and snacks in order to fuel their busy lifestyles. Young children may be picky eaters and go on food jags, but these behaviors are normal and usually temporary. Caregivers may need to offer new foods up to 10 times before the child accepts it.

2. Iron deficiency is likely with young children who consume large quantities of milk in place of food. Young children need enough calcium, vitamin D, and fiber to ensure healthy bone growth and bowel regularity. Milk, water, and diluted juices are better beverage choices than sweetened, flavored drinks.

3. Obesity and type 2 diabetes are occurring at higher rates in children. Poor dietary choices and not enough exercise are two of the key culprits of this problem. Parents and caregivers must provide healthy foods and encourage physical activity to combat a child's likelihood of developing these conditions.

4. The MyPyramid For Kids provides guidance for planning healthly meals and snacks for children. The National School Lunch Program must meet certain guidelines set by the USDA. Children with packed school lunches should be involved in the planning and preparation of the lunch so they are more likely to eat it.

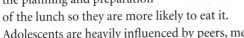

5. Adolescents are heavily influenced by peers, media, and other nonparental role models, which may lead them to adopt unhealthy eating and lifestyle habits, such as skipping meals, choosing unhealthy foods, dieting, or smoking. Because adolescent bones are still growing, teens need to consume enough calcium, and increased soda consumption may interfere with this if it displaces milk in the diet. Iron is also important for growth of lean muscle, and for girls' onset of menstruation. Some teens may be at risk for disordered eating patterns.

6. Metabolism slows with age, so older adults need fewer calories than their younger counterparts. Older adults need to be sure to consume enough fiber, fluid, vitamins D and B_{12}, and the minerals iron, calcium, and zinc. Too much preformed vitamin A, in contrast, may increase an elder's risk of osteoporosis and bone fractures, so should be avoided.

7. Staying physically active is important during the older years, though sometimes this is challenging due to arthritis, Alzheimer's, or other diseases and conditions.

8. Older adults sometimes suffer from food insecurity, due to decreased mobility, financial hardship, or health conditions such as tooth loss. Social programs can help ensure the nourishment of homebound adults by delivering precooked meals. Alcohol abuse is sometimes an issue with older adults.

9. There is no conclusive evidence that sugar causes hyperactivity or ADHD in children. However, some caregivers claim that making certain dietary changes helps their child's behavior.

10. Prescription medications and herbs can reduce or accelerate nutrient absorption, or interact with foods, so those taking drugs or herbs should check with a pharmacist or health care provider to ensure that they don't suffer any unfortunate side effects.

Test Your Knowledge

1. Because they are still growing but have diminished appetites (compared with infants), toddlers and preschoolers should
   a. consume large meals.
   b. consume nutrient-dense foods.
   c. consume foods high in fat.
   d. consume foods high in sugar.
   e. do all of the above.
2. Children living in older homes may be at higher risk for
   a. iron toxicity.
   b. calcium toxicity.
   c. sleep problems.
   d. lead toxicity.
   e. none of these.
3. The key message(s) of MyPyramid For Kids include
   a. Be physically active every day.
   b. Choose healthier foods from each group.
   c. Eat more of some food groups than others.
   d. Eat foods from every food group every day.
   e. all of the above.
4. There appears to be a relationship between the rise in childhood obesity and the increase in
   a. childhood cancers.
   b. ADHD.
   c. type 2 diabetes in children.
   d. childhood cavities.
   e. all of these.
5. The National School Lunch Program must meet strict guidelines set out by
   a. the USDA.
   b. the FDA.
   c. the EPA.
   d. the ROTC.
   e. none of these. There are no mandatory guidelines for school lunches.
6. Which mineral supports healthy bone development and is particularly important during adolescence?
   a. calcium
   b. iron
   c. vitamin D
   d. copper
   e. all of these
7. _____ with ADHD may be on a special diet to control their behaviors.
   a. All children
   b. Some children
   c. Only very young children
   d. Only teens
8. Which of the following two nutrient needs increase with age?
   a. water and lead
   b. calcium and vitamin D
   c. protein and lipids
   d. vitamin K and biotin
9. Which of the following can influence an older adult's ability to consume a nutritious diet?
   a. living on a fixed income
   b. loss of teeth
   c. alcohol abuse
   d. all of the above
   e. a and c only
10. Congregate meals are
    a. meals delivered to the homes of older adults who are homebound.
    b. frozen meals that adults can purchase at the supermarket.
    c. hot meals that are served in the community such as at churches and synagogues.
    d. none of the above.

Answers

1. (b) Toddlers need to eat nutrient-dense foods in order to obtain all the nutrients they need. Their reduced appetites mean they aren't likely to eat large meals, and foods high in fat and sugar may add significant calories without contributing many nutrients.
2. (d) Plumbing and faucets in older homes may contain lead that can leach into a child's drinking water, increasing the risk for lead poisoning. Iron toxicity is a concern in young children, but isn't more likely in children living in older homes.
3. (e) MyPyramid For Kids encourages physical activity and healthy food choices from a variety of food groups for children.
4. (c) Rates of type 2 diabetes among children have risen along with rates of overweight and obesity.
5. (a) The Food and Nutrition Service, part of the USDA, provides guidelines that direct the minimum amounts of some nutrients, and the maximum amounts of calories and saturated fat, that school lunches can contain.
6. (a) Adolescents need adequate amounts of calcium to support their growing bones. Iron is also important during adolescence to support development of lean muscle mass and offset the iron lost by girls as they begin menstruating. Vitamin D is not a mineral, but is also very important for bone growth. Copper is a trace mineral that most people consume in adequate amounts.

7. (b) Though there is no evidence that sugar can impact ADHD in children, some children have benefited from altered or restricted diets.

8. (b) The need for both vitamin D and calcium is increased in older adults. Protein, fat, and water needs don't change with aging. Lead is a toxin and should never be consumed. Vitamin K and biotin are necessary for health, but you don't need them in higher amounts as you age.

9. (d) Older adults who may have a limited income may not be able to purchase adequate amounts of healthy foods to meet their nutrient needs. If they lose their teeth or have other dental problems, they may limit their food choices based on their inability to chew certain foods. An alcohol-heavy diet will not only displace nutritious foods but can increase the risk of falls and injuries.

10. (c) Congregate meals allow older adults in a community to meet and eat hot meals together. Older adults who are homebound can request that a healthy meal be delivered to their home. The supermarket contains a variety of frozen meals that can be purchased by adults of all ages.

Web Support

- For more information on nutrition during the younger years, visit www.cdc.gov/HealthyYouth/nutrition/index.htm
- For more information on children's and teens' health, visit www.kidshealth.org
- For more about ADHD, visit www.nimh.nih.gov
- To learn about practical tools for keeping kids at a healthy weight, visit We Can! at www.nhlbi.nih.gov/health/public/heart/obesity/wecan/index.htm
- For more about the USDA's School Lunch Program, visit www.fns.usda.gov/cnd/lunch
- For more nutrition information for older adults, visit www.cdc.gov/aging/info.htm
- For more information on herbs, visit the National Center for Complementary and Alternative Medicine, National Institutes of Health, at http://nccam.nih.gov

14

Food Safety and Technol

1. Foods that can make you **sick** always smell bad. **T/F**

2. **Hand washing** is a key part of practicing food safety. **T/F**

3. The **temperature** for your refrigerator should be set at 40°F or below. **T/F**

4. Freezing foods kills **bacteria.** **T/F**

5. **Leftovers** that have been stored in the fridge for a week will still be safe to eat. **T/F**

6. As long at the **expiration date** hasn't passed, packaged food is always safe to eat. **T/F**

7. There are no benefits to using **food additives.** **T/F**

8. You can wash **pesticides** off of produce with plain water. **T/F**

9. **Organic** foods can sometimes contain synthetic pesticides. **T/F**

10. **Bioterrorism** is a concern in the United States today. **T/F**

ogy

The summer after his sophomore year in college, 20-year-old Miguel decided to take a backpacking trip through Mexico. He wanted to explore the distinct cultures, spend some time with his cousins, and experience an adventure or two. After a few days of hiking in the Sierra Madre, he made his way south toward Mexico City. One night, he bought a fish taco from a street vendor near the hostel where he was staying. Several hours later, he woke up with horrible cramps. After running to the bathroom and experiencing a painful bout of diar-

rhea, he headed to a local clinic to seek some help.

Can you guess the cause of Miguel's unfortunate illness? Have you heard warnings about traveler's diarrhea and do you know how to avoid it? In this chapter, we'll explore the causes of this and other foodborne illnesses, and find out how they can be prevented. We'll also discuss food additives, pesticides, and the increasingly hot topics of biotechnology and organic foods, and find out the real deal when it comes to their benefits and drawbacks.

Answers

1. False. A food can contain disease-causing bacteria that can make you ill, yet smell perfectly fine. An off smell in food is more likely a sign of *spoilage*. Turn to page 494 to find out more.
2. True. As simple as it sounds, thorough handwashing is one of the best defenses against foodborne illness. The key is to hand wash well. Find out why on page 498.
3. True. To be effective at keeping food safe, the temperature in your refrigerator should be 40°F or below. To find out why, turn to page 501.
4. False. Freezing doesn't kill bacteria but puts them in a dormant state. Find out what happens once the food is thawed on page 501.
5. False. Leftovers should be thrown out if they're not consumed within 3 to 5 days. To find out more about safe food storage, turn to page 501.
6. False. Package dates refer to food quality, not safety. To find out why consuming a food before the expiration date can't guarantee that the item is safe to eat, turn to page 509.
7. False. From keeping bread fresh to enhancing flavors, food additives perform a variety of useful functions in foods. Learn more about specific additives on page 510.
8. True. A good scrub with cold, running water and a vegetable brush can remove pesticide residue, and many germs, from your produce. To find out more, turn to page 518.
9. True. Some synthetic pesticides have been approved for use on organic crops. To find out more about organic foods, turn to page 519.
10. True. There are a couple of ways that the food and water supplies in the United States could be affected by bioterrorism. To learn more, turn to page 524.

What Is Food Safety and Why Is It Important?

Although the United States enjoys one of the safest food supplies in the world, millions of Americans still suffer annually from some type of **foodborne illness.** In fact, foodborne illness causes about 325,000 hospitalizations (and 5,200 deaths) per year.[1] These illnesses often result in distressing gastrointestinal symptoms such as cramps, diarrhea, and vomiting. Efforts to prevent foodborne illnesses have led to extensive **food safety** practices and guidelines. Several government agencies work together to ensure the safety of foods from the farm to the table. Food safety is also the practice of minimizing your risk of contaminating foods as you store and prepare them in your kitchen. There are several strategies consumers can use to make sure the foods they eat and serve are safe. We'll find out more about all of these in this chapter.

What Causes Foodborne Illness and How Can It Make You Sick?

In 1906, an eye-opening book called *The Jungle*, written by a young socialist named Upton Sinclair, shocked the world with its descriptions of the filthy conditions in the meatpacking plants of Chicago.[2] The report, which described rodent droppings and body parts making their way into consumer-bound meat products, so horrified the public that meat sales dropped by half. An enraged President Theodore Roosevelt incited the United States Congress to pass the Meat Inspection Act.[3] The act demanded a continuous inspection of all meat processing plants.[4]

Before long, these food safety precautions resulted in positive effects on the nation's health. By 1920, instances of one foodborne illness, typhoid fever, had declined by about two-thirds, and by the 1950s, it had virtually disappeared in the United States.[5]

Even with stringent regulations in place, however, bouts of foodborne illness still happen. Let's take a look at the causes of foodborne illness.

Foodborne Illnesses Are Often Caused by Pathogens

In order to contract a foodborne illness, you must consume foods or beverages that contain one or more harmful agents. The agents can be disease-causing microbes, also known as **pathogens,** such as viruses, bacteria, and parasites. Pathogens can be found in the stool or droppings of infected humans and/or animals. Drinking water that has been contaminated with infected droppings, or putting anything in the mouth (such as food or your hands) that has been in contact with fecal matter, are common ways to become infected. This route of transmission is known as **fecal-to-oral transmission,** and this is why people should always wash their hands after using the bathroom and before preparing foods. Eating raw or undercooked meat, poultry, and fish from an infected animal can also expose you to pathogens.

Pathogenic viruses and bacteria are the most common causes of foodborne illness in the United States. Parasites are a less common cause. Let's begin with the various viruses that can make you sick.

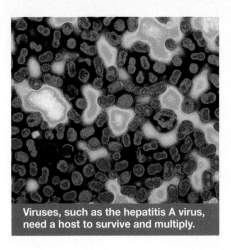

Viruses, such as the hepatitis A virus, need a host to survive and multiply.

Viruses

Viruses must have a living "**host,**" such as a plant or an animal, to survive. If you eat a contaminated plant or animal as food, the pathogen can invade the cells of your stomach and intestinal walls. The virus can then cause your cells' genetic material to start producing more viruses, ultimately leading to illness.[6]

The most common type of virus that causes foodborne illness is the **norovirus.** Noroviruses are named after the original strain of the virus, Norwalk virus, which was the cause of **gastroenteritis** (*gastro* = stomach, *entero* = intestines, *itis* = inflammation), or the "stomach flu," in a school in Norwalk, Ohio, in 1968.[7] (Note: The stomach flu is not the same as influenza (flu), which is a respiratory illness caused by the influenza virus.) About half of all the foodborne illness outbreaks in the United States may be due to noroviruses, making this the single most common cause of foodborne illness (see Table 14.1 on the next page).[8]

Another foodborne virus, hepatitis A, caused a multistate outbreak among young concertgoers in 2003. The concerts were often multiday events at camp grounds that had less than optimal sanitary conditions. The unofficial food vendors were the attendees themselves. Many of the concert attendees traveled from concert to concert. This type of living environment, in which people are living, cooking, and eating in unsanitary conditions, practicing poor hand washing and hygiene, and traveling from state to state, can create a breeding ground for an outbreak. Approximately 300 attendees had to be vaccinated against hepatitis A.[9]

Bacteria

If you were to swab your kitchen sink right now and look at the results under a microscope, you would find that there are about 16 million bacteria living on each square centimeter (less than half an inch) of your sink. Whereas viruses need a host to survive, bacteria can flourish on both living and nonliving surfaces. They live on your computer mouse, keyboard, body, clothing, and in every room of your house. In fact, there are about 600 different types of bacteria on your skin alone.[10] The majority of bacteria around you are harmless, and some are even essential, such as the ones in your

foodborne illness Sickness caused by consuming contaminated food or beverages. Also known as foodborne disease or food poisoning.

food safety Guidelines and procedures that help keep foods free from contaminants and safe to eat.

pathogens Collective term for disease-causing microorganisms (microbes). Pathogens include viruses, bacteria, and parasites and are the most common source of foodborne illness.

fecal-to-oral transmission The spread of pathogens by putting something in the mouth that has been in contact with infected stool. Poor hygiene, such as not washing hands after using the bathroom, can be a cause of this contamination.

virus A microscopic organism that can infect a host and cause illness.

host A living plant or animal (including a human) that harbors a virus, allowing it to survive and reproduce.

noroviruses The most common type of virus that causes foodborne illness. They can cause gastroenteritis, or the "stomach flu." Also known as Norwalk-like viruses.

gastroenteritis Inflammation of the stomach and intestines.

Table 14.1

Pathogens that Cause Foodborne Illness

Microbe	Where You Find It	How You Can Get It	What You May Experience
Viruses			
Noroviruses	In the stool or vomit of infected individuals	Fecal-to-oral transmission; eating ready-to-eat foods or drinking liquids contaminated by an infected person; eating contaminated shellfish; touching contaminated objects and then putting hands in mouth	Watery diarrhea, nausea, vomiting, flulike symptoms; possible fever Can appear 24–48 hours after onset and last 24–60 hours Typically not serious
Hepatitis A	In the stool of infected individuals	Fecal-to-oral transmission; eating raw produce irrigated with contaminated water; eating raw or undercooked foods that have not been properly reheated; drinking contaminated water	Diarrhea, dark urine, jaundice, flulike symptoms that can appear 30 days after incubation Can last 2 weeks to 3 months
Bacteria			
Campylobacter jejuni	Intestinal tracts of animals and birds, raw milk, untreated water, and sewage	Drinking contaminated water or raw milk, and eating raw or undercooked meat, poultry, or shellfish	Fever, headache, and muscle pain followed by diarrhea (sometimes bloody), abdominal pain, and nausea Appears 2 to 5 days after eating; may last 7 to 10 days Guillain-Barré syndrome may occur
Clostridium botulinum	Widely distributed in nature in soil, water, on plants, and in the intestinal tracts of animals and fish. Grows only in environments with little or no oxygen.	Eating improperly canned foods, garlic in oil, vacuum-packaged and tightly wrapped food	Bacteria produce a toxin that causes illness by affecting the nervous system. Symptoms usually appear after 18 to 36 hours. May experience double vision, droopy eyelids, trouble speaking and swallowing, and difficulty breathing. Fatal in 3 to 10 days if not treated.
Clostridium perfringens	Soil, dust, sewage, and intestinal tracts of animals and humans. Grows only in little or no oxygen.	Called "the cafeteria germ" because many outbreaks result from eating food left for long periods in steam tables or at room temperature. Bacteria are destroyed by cooking, but some spores may survive.	Bacteria produce toxin that causes illness. Diarrhea and gas pains may appear 8 to 24 hours after eating; usually last about 1 day, but less severe symptoms may persist for 1 to 2 weeks.
Escherichia coli O157:H7	Intestinal tracts of some mammals, raw milk, unchlorinated water; one of several strains of *E. coli* that can cause human illness.	Drinking contaminated water, unpasteurized apple juice or cider, or raw milk, or eating raw or rare ground beef or uncooked fruits and vegetables	Diarrhea or bloody diarrhea, abdominal cramps, nausea, and weakness Can begin 2 to 5 days after food is eaten, lasting about 8 days Small children and elderly adults may develop hemolytic uremic syndrome (HUS) that causes acute kidney failure. A similar illness, thrombotic thrombocytopenic purpura (TTP), may occur in adults.

Table 14.1 continued

Pathogens that Cause Foodborne Illness

Microbe	Where You Find It	How You Can Get It	What You May Experience
Bacteria, continued			
Enterotoxigenic *Escherichia coli* (major cause of traveler's diarrhea)	Intestinal tracts of some mammals and unpasteurized dairy products. More common in developing countries.	Fecal-to-oral transmission. Consuming stool-contaminated water and foods from unsanitary water supplies and food establishments.	Diarrhea, nausea, vomiting, stomach cramping, bloating, fever, and weakness
Listeria monocytogenes	Intestinal tracts of humans and animals, milk, soil, leafy vegetables; can grow slowly at refrigerator temperatures	Eating ready-to-eat foods such as hot dogs, luncheon meats, cold cuts, fermented or dry sausage, other deli-style meat and poultry, or soft cheeses; drinking unpasteurized milk	Fever, chills, headache, backache, sometimes upset stomach, abdominal pain and diarrhea; may take up to 3 weeks to become ill; may later develop more serious illness in high-risk individuals
Salmonella (over 2,300 types)	Intestinal tracts and feces of animals; *Salmonella enteritidis* in eggs	Eating raw or undercooked eggs, poultry, and meat, raw milk and dairy products, and seafood. Can also be spread by infected food handlers.	Stomach pain, diarrhea, nausea, chills, fever, and headache usually appear 8 to 72 hours after eating. May last 1 to 2 days.
Shigella (over 30 types)	Human intestinal tract; rarely found in other animals	Fecal-to-oral transmission by consuming contaminated food and water. Most outbreaks result from eating food, especially salads, prepared and handled by workers with poor personal hygiene.	Disease referred to as "shigellosis" or bacillary dysentery. Diarrhea containing blood and mucus, fever, abdominal cramps, chills, and vomiting begins 12 to 50 hours from ingestion of bacteria; can last a few days to 2 weeks.
Staphylococcus aureus	On humans (skin, infected cuts, pimples, noses, and throats)	Consuming foods that were contaminated by being improperly handled. Bacteria multiply rapidly at room temperature.	Bacteria produce a toxin that causes illness. Severe nausea, abdominal cramps, vomiting, and diarrhea occur 1 to 6 hours after eating; recovery within 2 to 3 days, longer if severe dehydration occurs.
Parasites			
Crytosporidium parvum	In the intestines of humans and animals	Fecal-to-oral transmission. Drinking contaminated water, eating contaminated vegetables and fruits.	Stomach pains, diarrhea, cramps, fever, and vomiting
Cyclospora cayatenensis	Human stool	Fecal-to-oral transmission. Drinking contaminated water, eating contaminated produce.	Diarrhea, flatulence, stomach cramps, vomiting, fatigue
Giardia lamblia	In the intestines of humans and animals	Fecal-to-oral transmission. Drinking contaminated water, eating contaminated produce.	Diarrhea, stomach pains, flatulence
Trichinella spiralis	In undercooked or raw meats containing *Trichinella* worms	Raw or undercooked contaminated meat, usually pork or game meats	Nausea, vomiting, diarrhea, fever, aching joints and muscles

Source: Centers for Disease Control and Prevention (CDC). 2004. Diagnosis and Management of Foodborne Illness: A Primer for Physicians; CDC. Norovirus: Food Handlers; CDC. 2003. Viral Hepatitis A; CDC. 2004. Travelers' Diarrhea; MMWR Recommendations and Reports 50 (January 2001): 1–69; CDC. 2004. Parasitic Disease Information. All available at www.cdc.gov. Food Safety and Inspection Service. 2006. Foodborne Illness: What Consumers Need to Know; Food Safety and Inspection Service. 2001. Parasites and Foodborne Illness. Both available at www.fsis.usda.gov.

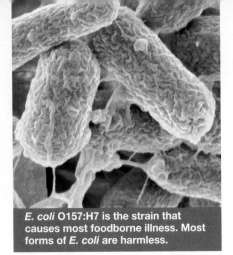

E. coli O157:H7 is the strain that causes most foodborne illness. Most forms of E. coli are harmless.

intestine that synthesize biotin and vitamin K. Bacteria are also used to make some of the foods we most enjoy, like yogurt, cheese, and buttermilk.

A few bacteria are harmful, however, and can cause food spoilage or illness. The bacteria that cause food spoilage are not the same as those that cause foodborne illness. Food spoilage bacteria cause the deterioration of the quality of food. For example, a carton of sour milk and that forgotten Chinese takeout in the back of your refrigerator have gone "bad" because of food spoilage bacteria. Though most individuals will not become seriously ill after eating spoiled foods, these items can cause nausea and shouldn't be eaten. (Luckily, the less-than-pleasant odor of sour milk or spoiled food usually leads to it being thrown away.) In contrast to spoiled foods, contaminated foods that contain bacterial pathogens may look and smell perfectly fine.

The most common bacteria that cause foodborne illness are *Campylobacter, Escherichia coli (E. coli)* O157:H7, and *Salmonella* (see Table 14.1). Another bacterium, *Listeria monocytogenes*, a less prevalent cause of foodborne illness, is still of concern for individuals most likely to get foodborne illness, especially pregnant women and newborns (see the feature box, "The Lowdown on *Listeria*," on page 496).

Campylobacter is one of the most common causes of bacteria-related diarrhea. Over a million people are infected annually with the *Campylobacter jejuni* species, the most prevalent variety, in the United States. It is found mostly in contaminated water, raw milk, and raw meat products. Some individuals may develop a rare nerve disease, called **Guillain-Barré syndrome,** after contracting a *Campylobacter* infection, which causes a person's immune system to attack its own nerves and results in temporary paralysis.[11]

Reptiles (lizards, snakes, and turtles) often carry *Salmonella*. You should always wash your hands after touching a reptile, and keep reptiles away from small children.

The bacterium *E. coli* that is in your intestinal tract helps to make vitamin K. This is not the same as *E. coli* O157:H7, the pathogen that can cause foodborne illness.

Though most strains of *E. coli* are harmless, *E. coli* O157:H7 is estimated to cause more than 70,000 cases of foodborne illness and 60 deaths in the United States annually. Contaminated ground beef has been the culprit behind most cases of foodborne illness caused by *E. coli* O157:H7. Because bacteria live in the gastrointestinal tract of healthy cattle, they can easily come into contact with the meat of the animal during the slaughtering process and then get mixed in when making ground beef. Proper cooking can destroy these bacteria. In people at highest risk for foodborne illness, *E. coli* O157:H7 can cause **hemolytic uremic syndrome** (*hemo* = blood, *lyti* = destroyed, *uremic* = too much urea in blood), which results in the destruction of red blood cells and damage and eventual failure of the kidneys.[12]

Another type of *E. coli*, called enterotoxigenic (*entero* = intestines, *toxi* = toxin, *genic* = forming) *E. coli*, is a common cause of **traveler's diarrhea.** Each year, up to 50 percent of international travelers, like Miguel from the beginning of the chapter, have their trips interrupted by unpleasant intestinal side effects. Traveler's diarrhea is primarily caused by consuming contaminated food or water. People visiting countries where proper sanitation is in question, including some developing countries in Latin America, Africa, the Middle East, and Asia, are at a higher risk of contracting it.[13] See the Table Tips for suggestions on how to avoid traveler's diarrhea.

There are several types of *Salmonella* bacteria. *Salmonella enteritidis* is one of the most common varieties found in the United States. An estimated 40,000 incidences of *Salmonella*-related foodborne illness occur annually, and about 600 individuals die yearly due to this bacterium.[14] *S. enteritidis* is most commonly found in raw eggs, so foods that contain raw eggs, such as the dressing on homemade Caesar salad, raw cookie dough, or cake batter, can potentially cause illness.

Guillain-Barré syndrome A condition that can result from a *Campylobacter* infection. It causes the immune system to attack its own nerves and can lead to paralysis for several weeks.

hemolytic uremic syndrome A rare condition that can be caused by *E. coli* O157:H7 and results in the destruction of red blood cells and kidney failure. Very young children and the elderly are at a higher risk of developing this syndrome.

traveler's diarrhea A common pathogen-induced intestinal disorder experienced by some travelers who visit areas with unsanitary conditions.

Parasites

Parasites are microscopic animals that, like viruses, take their nourishment from hosts. They can be found in food and water and are often transmitted through the fecal-to-oral route.[15] The most common parasitic illness outbreaks in the United States have been caused by just a few types: *Crytosporidium parvum*, *Cyclospora cayatenensis*, *Giardia lamblia*, and *Trichinella spiralis*.[16]

Both *Crytosporidium parvum* and *Cyclospora cayatenensis* can be found in contaminated water or food sources, while *Giardia lamblia* is one of the most common sources of waterborne illness. *Trichinella spiralis* (see photo below) is an intestinal worm whose larvae (hatched eggs) can travel from the digestive tract to the muscles of the body. *Trichinella spiralis* is typically transmitted by eating undercooked or raw meats, such as pork. See Table 14.1 for a summary of these parasites and the foodborne illnesses they cause.

Chemical Agents and Toxins Can Also Cause Illness

Foodborne illnesses can also be caused by **toxins** and chemical agents that occur naturally in foods, such as those found in poisonous mushrooms and some fish. Chemical agents, such as antibiotics and pesticides that are intentionally added to foods, can also cause foodborne illness. We'll discuss specific toxins and chemicals later in the chapter.

Some People Are at Higher Risk for Foodborne Illness

Some individuals are at greater risk of developing foodborne illness than others. Older adults, young children, and those with a compromised immune system are more susceptible to the ill effects of foodborne illness.

In older adults, the age-related deterioration of the immune system increases the risk for foodborne illness. Also, because less gastric juice is produced in the stomach as you age, fewer foodborne pathogens are destroyed during digestion, resulting in greater risk of gastrointestinal infections and their complications. In fact, the elderly are at higher risk of dying of gastroenteritis, which is a severe complication of foodborne illness.[17]

Young children, because of their underdeveloped immune systems, are also more vulnerable to foodborne illness. Children are also smaller and weigh less than adults so can become sickened by exposure to a smaller quantity of pathogens. About a third of the $6.9 billion spent on medical costs and lost job productivity associated with foodborne disease is due to illnesses that occur in children under 10 years of age.[18]

Any condition that weakens a person's immune system can increase his or her risk of contracting foodborne illness.

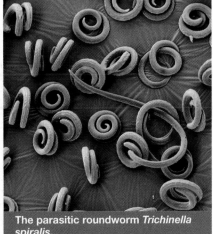

The parasitic roundworm *Trichinella spiralis*.

Table Tips

Don't Let Bad Bugs Ruin Your Trip

If you are traveling abroad, look up the country you're visiting on the Centers for Disease Control's (CDC) National Center for Infectious Diseases Travelers' Health Destination website at www.cdc.gov/travel/destinat.htm to find out about any *specific* health advisories for that area.

Do not eat raw or undercooked meat or seafood.

Do not consume raw fruits and vegetables unless you peel them. Thoroughly cooked fruits and vegetables should be safe to eat.

Do not consume foods or beverages from street vendors or restaurants that appear to be unsanitary.

Do not drink tap water or use ice made from tap water unless it has been boiled first or treated with iodine or chlorine. Bottled water should be safe.

Do not consume unpasteurized milk or other unpasteurized dairy foods.

Source: Centers for Disease Control Division of Bacterial and Mycotic Diseases. Updated 2004. Travelers' Diarrhea. Available at www.cdc.gov/ncidod/dbmd/diseaseinfo/travelersdiarrhea_g.htm.

parasites Organisms that live on or in another organism. Parasites obtain their nourishment from their hosts.

toxins Poisons that can be produced by living organisms.

The Lowdown on *Listeria*

Listeriosis, the illness caused by the bacterium *Listeria monocytogenes,* seriously affects approximately 2,500 individuals annually, with pregnant women being 20 times more likely than other people to become infected. *Listeria* can reach the fetus through the placenta, be transmitted to the newborn, and lead to severe illness, premature delivery, miscarriage, and stillbirth. Older adults and those with a weakened immune system are also at risk for becoming very sick or even dying.

Animals can harbor *Listeria,* which leads to contamination of meat and dairy foods. Pasteurization will kill *Listeria,* so unpasteurized soft cheeses, such as Camembert, Brie, and blue cheeses, carry a higher risk of containing *Listeria*. Compared to hard cheeses such as Parmesan, these soft cheeses are less acidic and contain more moisture, two conditions that enhance bacterial growth. Even though cooking can also destroy *Listeria,* the lower cooking temperature used during the processing of soft cheeses isn't high enough to destroy this bacterium.

Because contamination can occur after processing, many outbreaks have been associated with foods such as hot dogs, deli-style luncheon meats, Brie cheese, salami, and paté. *Listeria* can also continue to multiply at refrigerated temperatures.

The following tips can help pregnant women and other higher risk individuals reduce their likelihood of contracting *Listeria:*

- Reheat ready-to-eat luncheon meats, cold cuts, fermented and dry sausage, deli-style meat and poultry products, and hot dogs until they are steamy hot to kill any existing bacteria before you eat them.
- Wash your hands with hot, soapy water after touching these types of ready-to-eat foods, or any foods, for that matter. Thoroughly wash cutting boards, dishes, and utensils to avoid cross contamination.
- Avoid soft cheeses such as feta, Brie, Camembert, blue-veined (blue) cheese, and Mexican-style cheeses unless they are made with pasteurized milk.

(Read the ingredients list to see if pasteurized milk was used.) You can safely eat hard cheeses, semi-soft cheese such as mozzarella, pasteurized processed cheeses, cream cheese, and cottage cheese.

- Avoid unpasteurized milk and foods made from unpasteurized milk.
- Avoid refrigerated smoked seafood such as smoked salmon (lox or nova style), trout, whitefish, cod, tuna, or mackerel unless they are used in an entrée such as in a heated casserole. You can safely eat canned fish and shelf-stable smoked seafood.
- Avoid refrigerated paté or meat spreads. You can safely eat canned or shelf-stable varieties.
- Eat precooked or ready-to-eat perishable items before the expiration date on the food label.

Source: Centers for Disease Control. 2005. Listeriosis. Available at www.cdc.gov/ncidod/dbmd/diseaseinfo/listeriosis_g.htm; USDA. Listeriosis and Pregnancy: What Is Your Risk? Safe Food Handling for a Healthy Pregnancy. 2001. Available at www.fsis.usda.gov/Fact_Sheets/Listeriosis_and_Pregnancy_What_is_Your_Risk/index.asp.

People with a higher risk of contracting foodborne illness should avoid eating raw seafoods such as oysters and clams, sashimi (raw fish served with condiments), and ceviche (raw fish in citrus juices such as lime). Sushi that includes raw seafood should also be avoided.

This applies to individuals with HIV, AIDS, cancer, and diabetes.[19] The hormonal shifts seen during pregnancy can affect a pregnant woman's immune system, making her more vulnerable to certain foodborne illnesses such as listeriosis (see "The Lowdown on *Listeria*" box).

Individuals in institutional settings (such as nursing homes, hospitals, and schools), where groups of people eat foods from the same source, are also at higher risk of foodborne illness. Improper handling of foods and poor hygiene practices of food service workers are often the cause of foodborne disease outbreaks in institutional settings. Luckily, there are many ways to reduce your risk of contracting such an illness.

The Take-Home Message Foodborne illness is caused by consuming pathogens in contaminated food or drinks. Viruses and bacteria are the most common causes in the United States, though parasites can also cause some foodborne illness. Natural toxins and chemical agents can also cause illness. Certain populations, including the elderly, children, and those with compromised immune systems, are at higher risk of contracting foodborne illness.

What Can You Do to Prevent Foodborne Illness?

One way to prevent foodborne illness is to keep the pathogens that cause it from flourishing in your foods. Bacteria, for instance, thrive and multiply under conditions that provide (1) nutrients, (2) moisture, (3) a proper pH (see Chapter 6), (4) the correct temperature, and (5) some time.[20] Protein- and nutrient-rich animal foods, such as raw and undercooked meat, poultry, seafood, eggs, and unpasteurized milk, are the most common havens for bacterial growth.

Bacteria thrive in moist environments, such as in raw chicken that is sitting in its juices. Dry foods, such as uncooked rice and cereals, do not support bacterial growth until they are hydrated with a liquid. However, these foods can be contaminated by infected utensils or hands. For example, if a person with infected hands rummages through your box of bran flakes, the bacteria could survive on the cereal, and once you eat it, could multiply in your moist intestines and make you sick. Bacteria don't thrive in acidic foods such as citrus fruits, but can flourish in less acidic foods such as meat, fish, and poultry that have a higher pH. Bacteria multiply most abundantly between the temperatures of about 40°F and 140°F. At body temperature, or 98.6°F, bacteria can divide and double within 30 minutes, and multiply to millions in about 12 hours.[21] Perishable food, such as raw meat, left at room temperature for an extended period can become a feast for bacterial growth. Figure 14.1 summarizes the conditions that enable bacteria to thrive.

There are several steps you can take when handling food to destroy bacteria and other pathogens and thereby reduce your risk of foodborne illness. The main thing is to learn and consistently practice proper food handling and storage strategies. The "4 Cs"

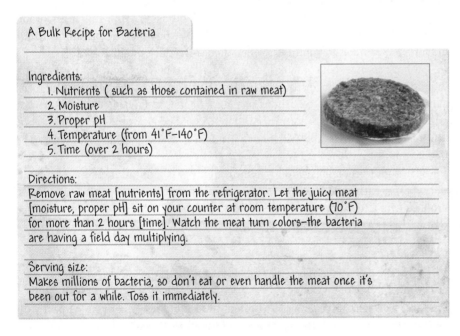

A Bulk Recipe for Bacteria

Ingredients:
1. Nutrients (such as those contained in raw meat)
2. Moisture
3. Proper pH
4. Temperature (from 41°F–140°F)
5. Time (over 2 hours)

Directions:
Remove raw meat [nutrients] from the refrigerator. Let the juicy meat [moisture, proper pH] sit on your counter at room temperature (70°F) for more than 2 hours [time]. Watch the meat turn colors–the bacteria are having a field day multiplying.

Serving size:
Makes millions of bacteria, so don't eat or even handle the meat once it's been out for a while. Toss it immediately.

Figure 14.1 A Bulk Recipe for Bacteria

Figure 14.2 Fight BAC!
The Fight BAC! symbol sums up the four Cs of keeping food safe in your kitchen: clean, combat cross contamination (separate meats from ready-to-eat foods), cook thoroughly, and chill to a cold enough temperature.

One study involving over 300 school-aged children found that those who washed their hands four times a day had almost 25 percent fewer sick days due to respiratory illnesses and more than 50 percent fewer sick days due to stomachaches.

Your countertop sponge may very well be the most contaminated item in your kitchen. Food scraps, moisture, and room temperature can lead to a thriving bacterial colony on this common cleaning item.

cross contaminate The transfer of pathogens from a food, utensil, cutting board, kitchen surface, and/or hands to another food.

of food safety—cleaning, combating cross contamination, cooking, and chilling—help you practice these strategies (Figure 14.2). Let's look at each of these four steps individually.

Clean Your Hands and Produce

You were probably taught as a child to wash your hands before eating, and guess what? Your parents were right! Hand washing is one of the most important strategies for preventing foodborne illness. In fact, if everyone practiced proper handwashing techniques, the incidences of foodborne illness could decrease by about half.[22] Washing your hands *thoroughly* is just as important as washing your hands regularly, and this is where many people fall short. In a study conducted at Utah State University, over 100 participants were videotaped to observe their food handling practices. After reviewing the video, the researchers found that only 2 percent of the participants had washed their hands correctly; that is, with hot soapy water and plenty of agitation (rubbing your hands together). Just rinsing hands in water, or using cold water instead of hot, will not be as effective. Though hot tap water isn't hot enough to kill microbes, it will do a better job than cold water of removing dirt, oil, and germs from your hands. The researchers also found that the average time the participants spent washing their hands was a mere 7 seconds, rather than the recommended minimum of 20 seconds.[23]

In addition to your hands, anything that touches your food, such as knives, utensils, and countertops, should be thoroughly cleaned between each use. Cutting boards should be placed in the dishwasher or scrubbed with hot soapy water and rinsed after each use. Nonporous cutting boards made of plastic, marble, and tempered glass are typically easier to keep clean than the more porous wood cutting boards or wooden surfaces. Cracks in a cutting board can become a hideaway for microbes, so try to keep only unbroken boards on hand. You can routinely sanitize your cutting board by flooding it in your sink in a solution of one teaspoon bleach in one quart of water. Let the board sit in the sanitizing liquid for a few minutes to kill the microbes, then rinse it thoroughly.

A moist sponge that contains food scraps and has been left at room temperature is an ideal environment for bacteria. In fact, household kitchen sponges and dishcloths have been shown to harbor more fecal bacteria than toilet seats.[24] Consequently, sponges and dishcloths need to be washed often in the hot cycle of your washing machine, preferably with bleach in addition to the soap. Sponges can also be put in your dishwasher.

Fruits and vegetables should be thoroughly washed under cold running tap water before eating. This will help remove any dirt or microbes on their surfaces. Produce with a firm surface can be scrubbed with a vegetable brush. The Table Tips summarizes the cleaning strategies you should apply when preparing food.

Combat Cross Contamination

Produce, especially if it's going to be eaten raw, should never come in contact with raw meat, poultry, or fish during the food preparation process. If these items do come in contact, they could **cross contaminate** each other, meaning that microbes from one could move to the other and vice versa. Microbe-containing raw meat, poultry, and fish should be kept separate from ready-to-eat foods during food preparation, and stored separately in your refrigerator. You should even keep these products apart on the trip home from the grocery store.

Marinades that are used to tenderize and flavor meats, poultry, or fish shouldn't be used as a serving sauce unless they have been boiled for several minutes to kill any pathogens. A better bet would be to discard the used marinade and create a fresh batch to use as the sauce.

The knife and cutting board used to cut and prepare the raw meat, poultry, or fish shouldn't be used to slice the vegetables or bread unless both have been thoroughly cleaned. Your best bet is to use separate cutting boards for meat and nonmeat foods to avoid cross contamination. Keep one board for slicing raw meats, poultry, and fish, and use another one for cutting fresh produce, breads, rolls, and other ready-to-eat foods. All plates and bowls that have contained raw meats, poultry, and fish should be thoroughly washed before using them again. For example, at a barbecue, the plate that held the raw hamburgers should *never* be used to serve the cooked burgers unless it has been thoroughly washed between each use.

Soiled dishtowels shouldn't be used to dry clean dishes or utensils. A towel that was used to wipe up raw meat juices or your hands can transfer those microbes to your clean dishes or utensils. You could easily coat those clean surfaces with a layer of germs. Figure 14.3 provides more ways to combat cross contamination when you prepare food.

Cook Foods Thoroughly

Though you may assume that brown meat is cooked meat, this is often not the case. Look at the two hamburger patties in the photo on the next page. Which one do you think looks safe to eat? The answer may surprise you. The patty on the right looks as

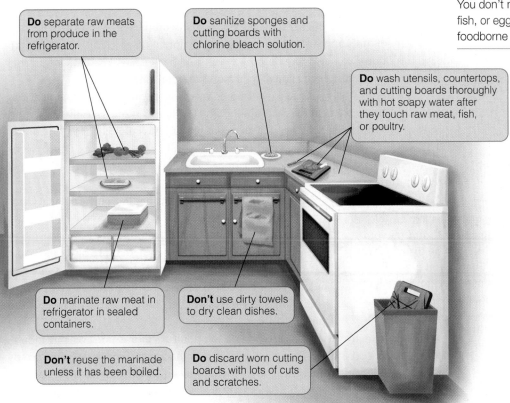

Do separate raw meats from produce in the refrigerator.

Do sanitize sponges and cutting boards with chlorine bleach solution.

Do wash utensils, countertops, and cutting boards thoroughly with hot soapy water after they touch raw meat, fish, or poultry.

Do marinate raw meat in refrigerator in sealed containers.

Don't use dirty towels to dry clean dishes.

Don't reuse the marinade unless it has been boiled.

Do discard worn cutting boards with lots of cuts and scratches.

Figure 14.3 The Do's and Don'ts of Cross Contamination

A hamburger needs to reach an internal temperature of 160°F to ensure that all foodborne pathogens are killed. Can you tell which of these two hamburgers is safe to eat? (If you answered "a," you're right!)

Figure 14.4 Food Thermometers
There are several types of food thermometers you can use to tell if your food is safe to eat. The thermometer should be inserted at least ½ inch deep into the food. It should be washed thoroughly after each use, before it is inserted back into the food.

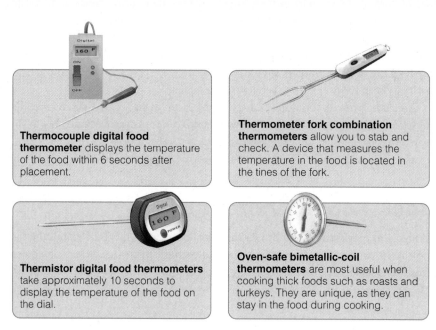

Thermocouple digital food thermometer displays the temperature of the food within 6 seconds after placement.

Thermometer fork combination thermometers allow you to stab and check. A device that measures the temperature in the food is located in the tines of the fork.

Thermistor digital food thermometers take approximately 10 seconds to display the temperature of the food on the dial.

Oven-safe bimetallic-coil thermometers are most useful when cooking thick foods such as roasts and turkeys. They are unique, as they can stay in the food during cooking.

though it is more thoroughly cooked than the patty on the left, but it's actually not. Meat can not only appear to lose its pink color before it is safe to eat, but some lean varieties of beef can also remain pink even though they have reached an internal temperature of 160°F, high enough to kill any potential pathogens.

The color of beef is largely determined by **myoglobin,** a protein that provides the purplish-red pigment in meat (and poultry). Whereas meat typically turns from pink to brown during cooking, if it starts out brown, this color change won't occur. Thus, the burger could look "done" when it may still be raw in places. Research has shown that hamburgers can look "well done" while only having reached an internal temperature of approximately 135°F.[25]

Packaging materials like zip-close bags, egg cartons, and takeout containers should be thrown away after use. Even if you clean them, pathogens can cling to these items and contaminate other foods.

Poultry can also remain pink after thorough cooking. Gases in your oven can cause a chemical reaction in the poultry that will give the meat a pink tinge. Because younger birds have thin skins, the gases can react with their flesh more easily and make the meat look pinker than that of older birds. Also, if nitrates and nitrites are added as a preservative, these can give poultry a pink tinge (see the discussion of food additives later in the chapter).[26]

With so many variables in fresh meat and poultry, color is not a reliable indicator that food is safe to eat. The only way to determine if your food has reached an appropriate internal temperature, high enough to kill pathogens, is to use a food thermometer. Figure 14.4 shows several types of food thermometers you can use when cooking.

myoglobin A protein that provides the purplish-red color in meat and poultry.

When it comes to foodborne pathogens, always remember that though eating raw meats, poultry, and fish can make you *ill*, cooking will *kill* the pathogens. Table 14.2 provides a list of the internal temperatures that your foods should reach to ensure that they are safe to eat.

Chill Foods at a Low Enough Temperature

Just as cooking foods to a high enough temperature to kill pathogens is essential, chilling foods at a low enough temperature to inhibit their growth is also important. Foodborne bacteria multiply most rapidly in temperatures between 40°F and 140°F (or 5°C to 60°C), a range known as the "**danger zone.**" To keep foods out of the danger zone, make sure that you keep hot foods *hot*, above 140°F, and cold foods *cold*, 40°F or below (Figure 14.5). In other words, the lasagna on a buffet table should be sitting on a hot plate or other heat source that keeps its temperature above 140°F, while the potato salad should be sitting on ice that will keep it chilled and at 40°F or below at all times.

Cold temperatures will slow down microbes' ability to multiply to dangerous levels. (The only exception to this is *Listeria*, which can multiply in temperatures at 40°F and below). Because of this, the temperature in your refrigerator should be set at or below 40°F. The only way to know if the temperature in your refrigerator or freezer is low enough is to use a thermometer. Fewer than 65 percent of Americans use a refrigerator thermometer, so it's not surprising that slightly more than 20 percent of their refrigerators aren't cold enough to keep foods safe.[27]

The temperature for the freezer should be set at 0°F or below. Food will stay safe in the freezer indefinitely, though its quality may deteriorate. (For example, freezer burn may occur if frozen food is not tightly wrapped and gets exposed to air. Freezer burn causes food to dry out and taste less pleasant, but it isn't harmful.) Most microbes become dormant and are unable to multiply when they are frozen, but they aren't destroyed. In fact, once the frozen foods are defrosted, the microbes can "thaw out" and thrive if given the proper conditions.

Perishables such as raw meat and poultry shouldn't be left out at room temperature (a temperature within the danger zone) for more than two hours. In temperatures above 90°F, foods shouldn't be left out for more than one hour.[28] Leftovers should be refrigerated within two hours of being served. Large roasts and pots of soup or stews should be divided into smaller batches in order to cool down more quickly in the refrigerator. If these items have been left in the danger zone for too long or have been mishandled, bacteria can not only grow but can also produce toxins that are heat resistant. These toxins won't be destroyed even if the food is cooked to a proper internal temperature, and could make you sick if consumed.[29]

Even stored at a proper temperature, foods shouldn't remain in the refrigerator for more than a few days. The rule of thumb is that leftovers can be in the refrigerator at 40°F or below for no more than four days. Here's an easy way to remember

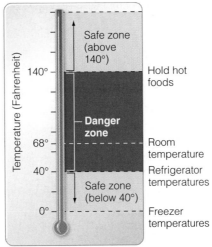

Figure 14.5 The Danger Zone
Bacteria multiply rapidly in the "danger zone," between temperatures of 41°F and 140°F.

Table 14.2
Cook It Until It's Done!

If You Are Cooking (Food)	The Food Thermometer Should Reach (°F)*
Ground Meat and Meat Mixtures	
Beef, pork, veal, lamb	160
Turkey, chicken	165
Fresh Beef, Veal, Lamb	
Medium	160
Well Done	170
Poultry	
Chicken, turkey, whole or parts	165
Duck and goose	165
Fresh Pork	
Medium	160
Well done	170
Ham, raw	160
Ham, precooked (to reheat)	140
Eggs and Egg Dishes	
Eggs	Cook until yolk and white are firm
Egg dishes	160
Leftovers and Casseroles	165

*The thermometer should be placed in the thickest part of the food item.

Source: USDA Food Safety and Inspection Service. Use a Food Thermometer. Available at www.fsis.usda.gov/Fact_Sheets/Use_a_Food_Thermometer/index.asp

danger zone The range of temperatures between 40°F and 140°F at which foodborne bacteria will multiply most rapidly. Room temperature falls within the danger zone.

eLearn

Click your way through this interactive quiz to test your food safety smarts in the kitchen: www.homefoodsafety.org/pages/tips/quiz/index.jsp.

Table 14.3
Keeping It Cool!

Follow these guidelines to keep your perishable foods safe

Product	Storage Time After Purchase*	
For Raw Foods		
Poultry	1 or 2 days	
Beef, veal, pork, and lamb	3 to 5 days	
Ground meat and ground poultry	1 or 2 days	
Fresh variety meats (liver, tongue, brain, kidneys, heart, intestines)	1 or 2 days	
Cured ham, cook-before-eating	5 to 7 days	
Sausage from pork, beef or turkey, uncooked	1 or 2 days	
Eggs	3 to 5 weeks	

Product	Unopened, After Purchase*	After Opening*
For Processed Product Sealed at Plant		
Cooked poultry	3 to 4 days	3 to 4 days
Cooked sausage	3 to 4 days	3 to 4 days
Sausage, hard/dry, shelf-stable	6 weeks/pantry	3 weeks
Corned beef, uncooked, in pouch with pickling juices	5 to 7 days	3 to 4 days
Vacuum-packed dinners, commercial brand with USDA seal	2 weeks	3 to 4 days
Bacon	2 weeks	1 week
Hot dogs	2 weeks	1 week
Luncheon meat	2 weeks	3 to 5 days
Ham, fully cooked, whole	7 days	3 days
Ham, canned, labeled "keep refrigerated"	9 months	3 to 4 days
Ham, canned, shelf-stable	2 years/pantry	3 to 5 days
Canned meat and poultry, shelf-stable	2 to 5 years/pantry	3 to 4 days
Leftovers		3 to 4 days

* Based on refrigerator home storage (at 41°F or below).

Source: Food Safety and Inspection Service. 2005. Keep Foods Safe! Food Safety Basics. Available at www.fsis.usda.gov/Fact_Sheets/Keep_Food_Safe_Food_Safety_Basics/index.asp.

Raw eggs and other perishables such as milk should not be stored on your refrigerator door. The frequent opening and closing of the door makes it the most likely to have temperature swings. Store your perishables in the back of the refrigerator, where it's colder and the temperature is more constant.

---

this: After *four* days in the refrigerator, leftovers are ready *for* the disposal. Raw meats and poultry can be kept for a maximum of two days in the refrigerator. Table 14.3 provides a listing of the storage times for various foods. If you are unsure about the safety of a food, remember this: *When in doubt, throw it out.*

Now that you've read about how cleaning, cooking, chilling, and avoiding cross contamination can help keep your foods safe, think about how many of these strategies you use in your own kitchen. The Self-Assessment on page 503 will help you identify areas in which you may need to improve your food safety habits.

How Do Your Food Safety Habits Stack Up?

Take the following quiz to find out.

How Often Do You	Always	Sometimes	Never
Wash your hands before preparing food?			
Scrub your fruits and vegetables under cold, running water before eating them?			
Use an insulated pouch with an ice pack to carry your perishable lunches and snacks, such as meat-filled sandwiches and/or yogurt and cheese?			
Wash your hands after using the bathroom?			
Throw out refrigerated leftovers after four days?			
Chop raw vegetables on a clean chopping board rather than the one you just used for raw meat, fish, or poultry?			
Use a thermometer to determine if the meat or poultry is done cooking?			

Answer

If you answered "Always" to all of the above, you are a food safety superstar. If you didn't, there's more you can do to reduce your chances of contracting a foodborne illness. This chapter will help!

The Take-Home Message Proper food handling and storage strategies, particularly cleaning, combating cross contamination, cooking, and chilling, can help reduce your risk of foodborne illness. Anything that comes in contact with your foods, including your hands, should be thoroughly washed. You should always wash produce before eating it, and separate raw meats, poultry, and fish, plus any utensils that touch them, from ready-to-eat foods to prevent cross contamination. A food thermometer is the only accurate way to tell if your cooked food is safe to eat. Perishables should be properly and promptly chilled to minimize the growth of bacteria.

Who Protects Your Food and How Do They Do It?

Foods don't originate in the grocery store. Whether in a bag, box, or bin, every food you buy starts life on a farm. Keeping food safe from the time it's harvested until you buy it is the responsibility of farmers, food manufacturers, and several government agencies. In this section, we'll look at the regulations, food preservation techniques, product dating, and irradiation that are done during various steps between the farm and the table. We'll start by looking at the government agencies that keep an eye on the food supply.

Mad Cow Disease

Charlene Singh was 13 years old when she moved from the United Kingdom to sunny Florida in 1992. Nine years later, Charlene suddenly started to be forgetful and depressed. Baffled about her condition, her doctor referred her to a psychologist for help. Within a few weeks, Charlene had problems walking and difficulty dressing. She started to have involuntary movements in her muscles and dreadful incontinence. She visited her local hospital emergency room, and the medical staff concluded that she was suffering from panic attacks. She was sent home with a prescription for antianxiety medication.

In late January 2002, a frustrated Charlene and her mother went to England in search of answers. During the 3 months of extensive medical evaluations that followed, Charlene's memory loss and other neurological symptoms became progressively worse. She couldn't remember routine numbers such as her phone number and couldn't perform simple mathematical problems. She fell often. She became confused, began to hallucinate, and started having difficulties communicating with her mother.

Charlene was referred to a neurologist who had a hunch, which unfortunately turned out to be correct. Charlene had been exposed to **bovine spongiform encephalopathy (BSE),** also known as **mad cow disease.** BSE is a slow, degenerative, and deadly disease that attacks the central nervous system of cattle. Individuals who are exposed to BSE by eating beef from infected cattle also experience neurological damage and symptoms. Because the symptoms don't appear until 9 to 21 years after exposure, Charlene was probably exposed to BSE as a small child in the UK. By September 2002, Charlene had been confined to her bed. She could no longer communicate with her mother and because of her dramatic weight loss, she needed to have a feeding tube surgically implanted. Tragically, Charlene died in 2004.[1]

Bovine spongiform encephalopathy is caused by an unusual protein called a **prion.** Cattle can become infected by consuming feed that is contaminated with BSE.[2] Meat and bone meal given to young calves and cattle that was rendered from contaminated tissues, such as the brain or spinal cord of infected bovines, may have played a role in the outbreak of BSE that occurred in the United Kingdom in the early 1980s.[3] The outbreak also may have been caused by feeding cattle meat and bone meal made from sheep infested with **scrapie,** a prion disease related to BSE.[4] In January 1993, the outbreak peaked in the United Kingdom, when approximately 1,000 new cases of BSE were

bovine spongiform encephalopathy (BSE) A slow, degenerative, and deadly disease that attacks the central nervous system of cattle. Also known as **mad cow disease.**

prion Cellular proteins. An abnormal prion protein is the cause of mad cow disease.

scrapie A prion disease found in sheep that is related to the BSE observed in cattle.

Several Government Agencies Police the Food Supply

Today, several federal agencies share responsibility for food safety in the United States.[30] Table 14.4 lists these agencies and summarizes the roles they each play in safeguarding your foods. This shared responsibility has paid off. There was a 16 percent decline in foodborne illness from 1996 to 2002.[31] Much of this decline can be attributed to the **Food Safety Initiative (FSI),** which was begun in 1997. The FSI coordinates the research, inspection, outbreak response, and educational activities of the various government agencies. The goal of the FSI is to make sure that government agencies work collaboratively.[32]

One program is FoodNet, a combined effort among the Centers for Disease Control and Prevention (CDC), the United States Department of Agriculture (USDA), the Food and Drug Administration (FDA), and other health departments to conduct ongoing active monitoring of specific foodborne illnesses when they arise in the United States. Improved reporting and monitoring systems, as well as outbreak investigations, have helped to quickly identify and trace the causes of foodborne illness.

Food Safety Initiative (FSI) Coordinates the research, surveillance, inspection, outbreak response, and educational activities of the various government agencies that work together to safeguard food.

reported weekly in cows.[5] By the end of November 2003, more than 180,000 cases of BSE were confirmed, involving more than 35,000 different herds in the United Kingdom. Other countries, including the Republic of Ireland, France, Portugal, Holland, and Switzerland, have also been affected by BSE.[6]

The contaminant that causes BSE in animals is thought to cause a similar disease, called **variant Creutzfeldt-Jakob Disease (vCJD),** in humans. Currently, there are approximately 150 cases of documented vCJD in people throughout the world.[7]

Although no one has acquired vCJD from cattle in the United States, a cow that tested positive for BSE was slaughtered in a meat plant in the state of Washington in 2003. Trace-back investigations confirmed that this BSE-infected cow was imported from Canada. A recall was made of all the meat plant's production for that day, and the affected animal's herd was quarantined. Because all the tissues related to the central nervous system of the cattle slaughtered at the Washington meat plant were removed from the plant, any meat that left the plant

for human consumption did not contain these at-risk components. Consequently, the USDA was confident that the recalled beef products posed essentially no risk to the public.[8]

Since the late 1980s, the United States has taken specific steps to protect the public against beef contaminated with BSE. First and foremost, **ruminant animals** such as cattle and sheep, meat and meat products from ruminant animals, and animal feed that contains animal protein derived from countries that are at risk for BSE can no longer be imported into the United States. Also, feed for ruminant animals that is sold in North America is banned from containing any ruminant protein. This type of feed has been identified as a major route of BSE transmission. (The BSE-affected cow that was identified in the state of Washington was born before this feed ban was enforced.)[9]

Since the BSE incident in Washington, additional precautions have been implemented in the United States to ensure a safe food supply. The CDC has improved its ability to investigate potential cases of vCJD through enhanced coordination of state and local health departments. The

National Institutes of Health (NIH) has more than doubled its budget to allow for greater spending in the area of BSE and vCJD research.[10] Sick or lame cattle and specific tissues of the cattle, such as the small intestines and spinal cord tissue, which have the greatest risk of containing the BSE agent, are also banned from the food supply. And lastly, techniques previously used when slaughtering the cattle and separating the meat, which likely increased the potential for the animal's meat to become contaminated, have been prohibited.[11]

variant Creutzfeldt-Jakob Disease (vCJD) A degenerative, fatal nerve disease in humans believed to be caused after exposure to BSE.

ruminant animals Animals, such as cows, that have four chambers in their stomachs for digesting coarse food such as plants. These foods are softened in the first chamber into balls of cud. The cud is then regurgitated, chewed and swallowed again, and passed on into the other chambers.

Table 14.4

Who's Policing the Food Supply?

Agency	Responsible For
USDA Food Safety and Inspection Service (FSIS)	Ensuring safe and accurately labeled meat, poultry, and eggs
Food and Drug Administration (FDA)	Ensuring the safety of all other foods besides meat, poultry, and eggs
Environmental Protection Agency (EPA)	Protecting you and the environment from harmful pesticides
Animal and Plant Health Inspection Service (APHIS)	Protecting against plant and animal pests and disease

Source: Food and Drug Administration and the U.S. Department of Agriculture. 2000. A Description of the U.S. Food Safety System. Available at www.fsis.usda.gov/OA/codex/system.htm.

PulseNet, another foodborne disease watchdog, is a network of government and public health laboratories that specializes in detecting foodborne diseases using **DNA fingerprinting.** Finding similar strains of a bacterium in both a person and a food suggests a common source and potential connection.[33] Once these patterns are determined, they are entered into an electronic database at a local or state health department, which maintains an ongoing collection of DNA fingerprints. These patterns

DNA fingerprinting A technique in which bacterial DNA "gene patterns" (or "fingerprints") are detected and analyzed to distinguish between different strains of a bacterium.

are also sent to the CDC's central computer. If similar patterns emerge at the same time in different states, this could indicate a potential outbreak. Once a suspicious foodborne illness outbreak is reported, several government agencies work together to contain the disease.

The *E. coli* outbreak in spinach that occurred in the fall of 2006 is one example of how these multiple agencies work together to identify and contain an outbreak. First, the CDC alerted the FDA of an outbreak of illness due to *E. coli* O157:H7 that spanned 26 states in the United States. PulseNet used DNA fingerprinting to determine that the strain of *E. coli* was the same in all those infected. The suspected food was bagged raw spinach grown in California. The CDC issued an official health alert about the outbreak, and the FDA advised consumers to stop eating raw spinach. Before it was over, more than 200 people were infected, and more than half of them were hospitalized. Three individuals died and 31 developed hemolytic uremic syndrome from the outbreak. However, the swift, coordinated action of these federal and state agencies helped curtail the outbreak and kept it from being much worse.[34]

Investigators from the FDA, CDC, and USDA worked with the state of California to conclude that the infected spinach came from one grower and most likely occurred because of cross contamination of infected water and animals with the produce in the field. The same strain of *E. coli* was found in a nearby stream and in the feces of cattle on a neighboring farm.

The FDA and USDA have also adopted a food safety program called Hazard Analysis and Critical Control Points (HACCP) (pronounced "hassip") that is used to identify and control foodborne hazards that may occur in all the stages of the food production process.[35] HACCP procedures are in place for food manufacturers and transporters to help safeguard food. Manufacturers also apply food preservation techniques to some foods to make them safer when you buy them. These techniques will be discussed in the next section.

Once the food arrives at retail and food service establishments such as grocery stores and restaurants, these outlets use the Food Code, a reference document published by the FDA. The Food Code provides practical, science-based guidance, including HACCP guidelines, and provisions to help purveyors minimize foodborne illness.[36] The Partnership for Food Safety Education (PFSE) is a program designed to educate the public about safe food handling after purchase.

From the farmer to the consumer, everyone involved in the production and preparation of food plays a role in making sure the food we eat is safe. The **farm-to-table continuum** is a visual tool that shows how farmers, food manufacturers, transporters of food, retailers, and you, the consumer, can help ensure a safe food supply. Figure 14.6 shows the steps in this continuum.

In addition to government efforts to help prevent foodborne illness, food manufacturers also work to safeguard food. Food processing, preservation techniques, and irradiation help destroy contaminants and/or maintain a food's color and freshness, and product dating can help you know when a food is past its prime and needs to be tossed.

farm-to-table continuum
Illustrates the roles that farmers, food manufacturers, food transporters, retailers, and consumers play in ensuring that the food supply, from the farm to the plate, remains safe.

food preservation The treatment of foods to reduce deterioration and spoilage, and help prevent the multiplication of pathogens that can cause foodborne illness.

Food Manufacturers Use Preservation Techniques to Destroy Contaminants

One way to control foodborne hazards is to use **food preservation** methods. Pickling (adding an acidic substance such as vinegar to the food), salting, drying, heating, freezing, and newer techniques such as irradiation and the use of food additive chemicals are all methods of food preservation. You use some of these yourself when you cook

1 Farm: Use good agricultural practices. Farmers grow, harvest, sort, pack, and store their crops in ways that help reduce food safety hazards.

2 Processing: Monitor at critical control points. During processing, HACCP measures are implemented.

3 Transportation: Use clean vehicles and maintain the proper temperature. Food is kept at a proper temperature during transportation to reduce the growth of foodborne microbes.

4 Retail: Follow the Food Code guidelines. Retail outlets, including restaurants, grocery stores, and institutions (such as hospitals) use the Food Code guidelines to reduce the risk of foodborne illness.

5 Consumer: Always follow the four Cs of food safety (clean, combat cross-contamination, cook, chill). The consumer uses the four Cs to reduce the risk of foodborne illness.

(apply heat to) or freeze (apply cold to) foods. Pickling, drying, and canning (a form of heating) have been in use for centuries, though today they're more often done by food manufacturers than home cooks.

Pasteurization is a technique that involves heating foods and liquids to a high enough temperature to kill pathogens. The process kills *E. coli* O157:H7 as well as other bacteria. In addition to dairy foods, most juices (about 98 percent) consumed in

pasteurization The process of heating liquids or food at high temperatures to destroy foodborne pathogens.

the United State are pasteurized. Juices that aren't pasteurized must display a warning on the label.[37]

Pasteurizing milk and dairy foods improves their quality and helps them stay fresh longer. Though raw (unpasteurized) milk and cheese are sometimes touted as being more healthful, this is an unfounded claim and can be dangerous, as raw milk can contain *Salmonella, E. coli* O157:H7, and *Listeria monocytogenes.*

Canning goes a step beyond pasteurization by packing food in airtight containers after heating it to a temperature high enough to kill most bacteria. Though this preserves the safety of most foods, botulism is one illness that can still result from canned foods. The bacterium *Clostridium botulinum* can survive environments without air, such as sealed cans, and creates **spores** that are not destroyed at normal cooking temperatures (see Table 14.2). A temperature higher than boiling (212°F) is needed to kill these spores.[38] **Retort canning** has eliminated botulism from commercially canned foods. Because of the success of retort canning, the very rare cases of botulism typically result from products that have been home canned.

Many people were initially resistant to the processes of pasteurization and canning because they thought the techniques would promote the use of inferior ingredients. The federal government helped address such fears by putting formal food grading processes in place to reassure consumers that only quality foods would be used. Both of these preservation methods are now widely used and generally regarded as effective to thwart foodborne illness.

Two newer preservation methods used to keep foods fresh are MAP and HPP. **Modified atmosphere packaging (MAP)** is a process during which the manufacturer changes the composition of the air surrounding the food in a package. Usually, the amount of oxygen is reduced, which delays the decay of the fruits and vegetables. MAP is used in foods such as packaged fruits and vegetables to extend their shelf life and preserve their quality.[39] **High-pressure processing (HPP)** is a newer method in which foods are exposed to pulses of high pressure, which destroys microorganisms. If bacterial spores are present on the food, heat may also need to be applied along with the HPP. Foods such as jams, fruit juices, fish, vacuum-packed meat products, fruits, and vegetables can be treated with HPP.[40]

There is another method of food preservation used by manufacturers and growers to keep food safe: food irradiation.

Irradiation

After foods have been packaged by a manufacturer, they may undergo **irradiation,** at either the manufacturing plant or another facility. During this process, foods are subjected to a radiant energy source within a protective, shielded chamber called an **irradiator.** Most of the energy passes through the food and the packaging without leaving any residue behind.[41] This level of energy damages the DNA of the harmful organisms, either killing them all or greatly reducing their numbers, thus reducing the risk of foodborne disease.[42]

Foods that have been irradiated are not radioactive and don't undergo any harmful or dangerous chemical changes.[43] The temperature of the food isn't significantly raised during irradiation, which helps prevent nutrient losses. In fact, heat pasteurization, canning, and drying often destroy more nutrients, such as certain vitamins, than does irradiation.[44]

Irradiation destroys bacteria such as *Campylobacter, E. coli* O157:H7, and *Salmonella* and helps control insects and parasites.[45] It does not destroy viruses, such as norovirus and hepatitis A, however, because the higher radiation levels needed to destroy the DNA of these smaller microbes have not yet been approved by the FDA.

canning The process of heating food to a temperature high enough to kill bacteria and then packing the food in airtight containers.

spores Hardy reproductive structures that are produced by certain bacteria. Some bacterial spores can survive boiling temperature (212°F).

retort canning The process of subjecting already-canned foods to an additional high-temperature heat source to destroy potential pathogens.

modified atmosphere packaging (MAP) A food preservation technique that changes the composition of the air surrounding the food in a package to extend its shelf life.

high-pressure processing (HPP) A method used to pasteurize foods by exposing the items to pulses of high pressure, which destroys the microorganisms that are present.

irradiation A process in which foods are placed in a shielded chamber, called an **irradiator,** and subjected to a radiant energy source. This kills specific pathogens in food by breaking up the cells' DNA.

closed or **"coded" dating** Refers to the packing numbers that are decodable only by manufacturers and are often found on nonperishable, shelf-stable foods.

open dating Typically found on perishable items such as meat, poultry, eggs, and dairy foods; must contain a calendar date.

Irradiation can also stop the ripening process in some fruits and vegetables and reduce the number of food spoilage bacteria. Irradiated strawberries can last up to three weeks before spoiling, whereas nonirradiated strawberries typically stay fresh for three to five days.[46]

Food irradiation has been studied and tested for more than 50 years and remains the most researched food-related technology ever approved in the United States.[47] Irradiation has been used for years to sterilize surgical instruments and implants. Hospitals have used irradiation to destroy disease-promoting microbes in foods served to patients with cancer and others who have weakened immune systems.

Foods that are irradiated must bear the "radura" logo, along with the phrase "treated by irradiation" or "treated with radiation" on the package (Figure 14.7). If a product such as sausage contains irradiated meat or poultry, it must be listed as "irradiated pork" or "irradiated chicken" on the food label.[48] A label is not required if a minor ingredient, such as a spice, has been irradiated and used in the product.

Some foods can't be irradiated, as their quality will be altered. Egg whites tend to become milky and liquid, fatty meats may develop an odor, and grapefruits can get soft and mushy after irradiation. Foods that are currently approved for irradiation in the United States include:[49]

- Fruits and vegetables
- Herbs and spices
- Fresh meat, pork, and poultry
- Wheat flour
- White potatoes

Though irradiation has many advantages, it doesn't guarantee that a food is safe, and some foods should still not be eaten raw, even if they have been irradiated. Steak tartare (a dish that contains raw ground beef) isn't a safe menu option even if it is made with irradiated ground beef, because the beef could be recontaminated after irradiation. Proper food handling, preparation, and—especially—cooking techniques must still be used for foods that have been irradiated.

Once foods are preserved as appropriate, many manufacturers stamp them with a food product dating code. A date on a product can help you determine if it's fresh, or if it will still be fresh by the time you consume it. Let's look at the specifics of food product dating.

Product Dating Can Help You Determine Peak Quality

Although food product dating isn't federally mandated, except for infant formula and some baby foods, more than 20 states in the United States require some form of food product dating. There are two types of food product dating: closed dating and open dating. **Closed** (or **"coded"**) **dating** refers to the packing numbers used by manufacturers that are often found on nonperishable, shelf-stable foods, such as cans of soup and fruit (see photo). This type of dating is used by the manufacturer to keep track of product inventory, rotate stock, and identify products that may need to be recalled.[50]

Open dating is typically found on perishable items such as meat, poultry, eggs, and dairy foods and is more useful for the consumer. Open dating must contain a calendar date, which includes at least a month and day. (If the product is shelf-stable or

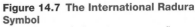

a Closed food product dating

b Open food product dating

(a) Closed food product dating refers to the coded packing numbers that you often see on nonperishable foods such as canned soups. **(b)** Open food product dating must contain a calendar date and is used on perishable food items along with information on how to use the date.

frozen and a calendar date is used, the year must also be included in the date.) You can use open dating to help you decide when to buy and consume a product while it is at its peak quality. Note: This date does not refer to food safety, but to the *quality* of the food. For example, a carton of yogurt that has been mishandled and not refrigerated for several hours may be unsafe to eat even though the date on the container hasn't passed.

When open dating is used, there must be a phrase next to the date that tells you how to interpret it. If there is "Sell By" next to the date, you should purchase the product on or before that date. If there is "Best if Used By" or "Use By" next to it, this refers to the date by which you should consume the product in order to enjoy it at its best.[51] If you don't plan to consume a product by its Use By date, you can freeze it; once frozen, the Use By date doesn't apply.

In addition to preservation techniques, irradiation, and product dating, food manufacturers sometimes use food additives to enhance the safety, but more often the quality, of foods.

What Are Food Additives and How Are They Used?

One of the earliest **food additives** was salt, which our ancestors quickly discovered did a great job of preserving meat and fish through a long winter. Later came spices, and today, when you get to the last heel of your bread loaf without encountering mold, you're enjoying the benefits of additives and/or preservatives that the bread manufacturer included in the bread's production process.

Preserving freshness is a common aim of today's additives; they are also used for many other reasons.[52] For example, food additives can help maintain a product's consistency. Gums are added to thicken yogurts, and lecithin, as you learned in Chapter 5, is added as an emulsifier in some salad dressings. Additives can also be used to enhance a product's nutrition content, such as when refined grains are enriched with added B vitamins and iron. Additives are also used to prevent food spoilage that can create an off taste or off color in a product. The antioxidants vitamin E, butylated hydroxyanisole (BHA), and butylated hydroxytoluene (BHT) are added to cereals and oils to prevent rancidity. Vitamin C is often added to cut fruit to prevent premature browning, and caramel coloring can add color to baked goods. Table 14.5 provides a list of commonly used additives and their functions in your foods.

When a food additive is intentionally added to a food, as we've been discussing, its purpose is to improve the quality of the product. However, food additives are sometimes unintentionally added to a food. For example, very small amounts of substances from the packaging of the food may inadvertently end up in the food. For this reason, manufacturers must ensure that packing substances aren't harmful to the consumer.

The use of food additives is strictly regulated by the FDA. The Federal Food, Drug and Cosmetic Act of 1938 gave the FDA authority to regulate food and food ingredients. The 1958 Food Additives Amendment further mandated that manufacturers document a food additive's safety and obtain FDA approval before using it in a food.[53]

Two categories of food additives were exempted from this amendment. Substances that were known to be safe before 1958 were given **prior-sanctioned** status. For example, because **nitrates** were used to preserve meats before 1958, they have prior-sanctioned status, but *only* for their use in meats. They can't be used in other

food additives Substances added to food that affect its quality, flavor, freshness, and/or safety.

prior-sanctioned Having previous approval.

nitrates (nitrites) Substances that can be added to foods to function as a preservative and to give meats such as hot dogs and luncheon meats a pink color.

Table 14.5

Commonly Used Food Additives

Additive(s)	Function(s)	Where You'll Find Them
Alginates, carrageenan, glyceride, guar gum, lecithin, mono- and diglycerides, methyl cellulose, pectin, sodium aluminosilicate	Impart/maintain desired consistency	Baked goods, cake mixes, coconut, ice cream, processed cheese, salad dressings, table salt
Ascorbic acid (vitamin C), calcium carbonate, folic acid, thiamine (B_1), iron, niacin, pyridoxine (B_6), riboflavin (B_2), vitamins A and D, zinc oxide	Improve/maintain nutritive value	Biscuits, bread, breakfast cereals, desserts, flour, gelatin, iodized margarine, milk, pasta, salt
Ascorbic acid, benzoates, butylated hydroxyanisole (BHA), butylated hydroxytoluene (BHT), citric acid, propionic acid and its salts, sodium nitrite	Maintain palatability and wholesomeness	Bread, cake mixes, cheese, crackers, frozen and dried fruit, lard, margarine, meat, potato chips
Citric acid, fumaric acid, lactic acid, phosphoric acid, sodium bicarbonate, tartrates, yeast	Produce light texture and control acidity/alkalinity	Butter, cakes, cookies, chocolates, crackers, quick breads, soft drinks
Annatto, aspartame, caramel, cloves, FD&C red No. 40, FD&C blue No. 1, fructose, ginger, limonene, MSG, saccharin, turmeric	Enhance flavor or provide desired color	Baked goods, cheeses, confections, gum, spice cake, gingerbread, jams, soft drinks, soup, yogurt

Source: FDA. Food Additives. 2001. Available at www.cfsan.fda.gov/~lrd/foodaddi.html.

foods, such as vegetables, without FDA approval.[54] Substances that are **"generally recognized as safe" (GRAS),** such as salt, sugar, spices, and vitamins, either have a long history of being safe to consume or have extensive research documenting that they are safe to eat.[55]

The FDA continually monitors both prior-sanctioned additives and those with GRAS status to ensure that current research continues to support their safety. If an additive is suddenly called into question, the FDA can prohibit its use or require that the food manufacturer conduct additional studies to ensure its safety.[56]

Even with these safeguards in place, some additives, such as MSG (monosodium glutamate) and sulfites, may cause unwanted effects in some people, and should be avoided by those who are sensitive to them. Let's look a little closer at MSG and sulfites.

MSG is a Common Flavor Enhancer

MSG doesn't have a strong taste of its own, but is often used as a flavor enhancer. You may find MSG in canned vegetables and soups, and you can buy it in a form that is similar in texture to salt. Because of its long history of safe use, MSG has GRAS status. However, the FDA has received numerous consumer complaints that it can cause symptoms such as headaches and nausea, and there are more serious concerns that it can contribute to Alzheimer's disease, brain tumors, and nerve cell damage.[57]

After an extensive review, the FDA confirmed that MSG is safe to consume in the amounts typically used in processed foods and cooking. Some people seem to be sensitive to MSG, however, and may experience short-term reactions after consuming it, especially if they consume more than 3 grams at one time.[58] (A typical meal that contains MSG has less than 0.5 grams.) These reactions, which are called the **MSG symptom complex,** can include numbness, burning sensation, facial pressure or tightness, chest pain, rapid heartbeat, and drowsiness. Also, individuals with severe or poorly controlled asthma may have difficulty breathing after consuming MSG. Because of this, the FDA requires that all foods containing MSG declare this ingredient on the food label.

GRAS (generally recognized as safe) A substance that has GRAS status is believed to be safe to consume based on a long history of use by humans or a substantial amount of research that documents its safety.

monosodium glutamate (MSG) A flavor enhancer.

MSG symptom complex A series of reactions such as numbness, burning sensation, facial pressure or tightness, chest pain, rapid heartbeat, and drowsiness that can occur in some individuals after consuming MSG.

Sulfites Are Used as Preservatives

Sulfites are used as preservatives to help prevent some foods from turning brown and to inhibit the growth of microbes.[59] Sulfites are often found in dried fruits and vegetables, packaged and prepared potatoes, wine, beer, bottled lemon and lime juice, and pickled foods.[60]

Individuals who are sensitive to sulfites may experience symptoms ranging from chest tightness, difficulty breathing, and hives to the more serious and potentially fatal anaphylactic shock (see Chapter 12). Studies suggest that the sulfur dioxide in the sulfites appears to cause these symptoms.[61] Those who tend to be more sensitive to sulfites include people who suffer from asthma, those who are taking steroids, and those who have extremely sensitive airways.

To protect those who are sulfite sensitive, the FDA has prohibited the use of sulfites on fruits and vegetables that are served raw, such as in a salad bar, or are advertised as "fresh." As with MSG, packaged foods must declare added sulfites in the ingredients listing on the label. If a product contains ingredients with sulfites, such as sulfited raisins in a muffin mix, then sulfites must be declared on the food label. Food sold in bulk, such as sulfited dried fruit, must display the ingredients on a sign near the food.[62]

The Take-Home Message Food additives are often used by manufacturers to preserve foods, enhance their color or flavor, or add to their nutrient content. Some additives, such as MSG and sulfites, may cause unpleasant symptoms in sensitive individuals, but all additives are strictly regulated by the FDA.

What Are Toxins and Chemical Agents?

In addition to pathogens, naturally occurring toxins can contaminate foods, and chemicals can accumulate in foods. Chemicals such as hormones, antibiotics, and pesticides are intentionally given to livestock and used in agriculture.[63] In this section we'll discuss these toxins and some of the chemical agents. Pesticides will be covered in the next section.

Toxins Occur Naturally

Toxins frequently occur in nature to help a plant or animal fend off predators or capture its meals. In many cases, toxins in food animals exist in amounts too small to harm humans, but there are instances in which the toxins found in plant and animal foods can make a person ill, or worse. Let's take a closer look at some of these scenarios.

Marine Toxins

Although there are numerous reasons to include fish and seafood in your diet (recall their omega-3 fatty acid and low saturated fat content from Chapter 5), you should be aware of the risks involved. Some seafood, such as some of the raw fish used in sushi, can contain pathogens, and some can harbor naturally occurring **marine toxins.** Thorough cooking will kill many harmful bacteria and viruses found in seafood, but it won't destroy any of the marine toxins.

Spoiled finfish, such as tuna and mackerel, can cause **scombrotoxic fish poisoning,** in which the spoilage bacteria break down proteins in the fish and generate histamine.

sulfites Preservatives used to help prevent foods from turning brown and to inhibit the growth of microbes. Often used in wine and dried fruit products.

marine toxins Chemicals that occur naturally and contaminate some fish.

scombrotoxic fish poisoning A condition caused by consuming spoiled fish that contain large amounts of histamines. Also referred to as histamine fish poisoning.

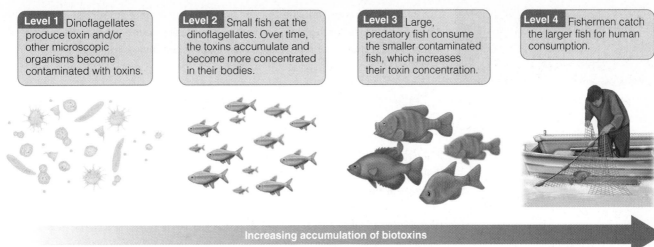

Level 1 Dinoflagellates produce toxin and/or other microscopic organisms become contaminated with toxins.

Level 2 Small fish eat the dinoflagellates. Over time, the toxins accumulate and become more concentrated in their bodies.

Level 3 Large, predatory fish consume the smaller contaminated fish, which increases their toxin concentration.

Level 4 Fishermen catch the larger fish for human consumption.

Increasing accumulation of biotoxins

Figure 14.8 Bioaccumulation of Toxins

Other by-products are created that block the breakdown of histamine. Consuming fish that contain large amounts of histamine can cause symptoms such as diarrhea, flushing, and sweating and vomiting within 2 minutes to 2 hours.[64]

Eating large, predatory reef fish, such as barracuda and grouper, can sometimes result in **ciguatera poisoning,** which is caused by ciguatoxins. These toxins originate in microscopic sea organisms called **dinoflagellates,** which are then eaten by small tropical fish. As larger fish eat the smaller fish, the toxins **bioaccumulate** and become more concentrated in the larger fish.[65] Figure 14.8 shows how these toxins can accumulate in the food chain. In addition to experiencing various gastrointestinal discomforts, individuals infected with ciguatera may have temperature sensation reversal in their mouth when they eat.[66] To them, ice cream feels hot and hot coffee feels cold.

Certain shellfish, such as mussels, clams, scallops, oysters, crabs, and lobsters, that typically live in the coastal waters of New England and the Pacific states can be contaminated with **neurotoxins** (*neuro* = nerve, *toxin* = toxic). Neurotoxins are also produced by dinoflagellates, and the particular reddish-brown-colored dinoflagellates that contain them can become so abundant that the ocean appears to have red streaks, also known as "red tides." Eating contaminated shellfish can lead to **paralytic shellfish poisoning.** Symptoms include mild numbness or tingling in the face, arms, and legs, as well as headaches and dizziness. Muscle paralysis, inability to breathe, and death could result, in severe cases.[67]

Toxins in Other Foods

Many plant foods naturally contain toxins in small amounts, so though they're generally safe to eat, consuming them in very large amounts could be harmful. Potatoes that have been exposed to light and turned green, for example, contain increased amounts of solanine, a toxin that can cause fever, diarrhea, paralysis, and shock. (Luckily, peeling potatoes usually removes the green layer and the potato can be safely eaten. If it tastes bitter, however, throw it out.) Wild lima beans contain high amounts of cyanogenic glycosides, which can be converted to the poison, cyanide. (The variety of lima beans sold commercially have minimal, nonthreatening amounts of this substance, so are safe to eat.) Cassava also contains cyanogenic glycosides and has been known to cause cyanide poisoning in people who eat large amounts of this root vegetable. Raw soybeans contain amylase inhibitors, which are inactivated when cooked or fermented.[68]

ciguatera poisoning A condition caused by marine toxins produced by **dinoflagellates** (microscopic sea organisms). Small fish eat dinoflagellates and larger fish consume the small fish. The toxins then bioaccumulate in the fish.

bioaccumulate When a substance or chemical builds up in an organism over time, so that the concentration of the chemical is higher than would be found naturally in the environment.

neurotoxins A toxin that affects the nerves and can cause symptoms including mild numbness or tingling in the face, arms, and legs as well as headaches and dizziness. Severe cases could result in death.

paralytic shellfish poisoning A condition caused by a reddish-brown-colored dinoflagellate that contains **neurotoxins.**

Table Tips

Ways to Avoid Toxins and Chemical Agents in Your Foods

Keep fish, especially finfish, such as fresh tuna, mackerel, grouper, and mahi mahi, chilled in the refrigerator to prevent spoilage and the formation of histamine toxins.

Never consume finfish or shellfish that is sold as bait, as these do not meet food safety regulations.

Observe all fish consumption advisories. To learn if an advisory is in place for the fish in your area, visit the EPA's Fish and Wildlife Consumption website at www.epa.gov/waterscience/fish/states.htm.

If you fish recreationally, you should always check with the local or state health department for specific advice based on the local waters to avoid eating PCB-containing fish.

Eat a variety of different types of fish to minimize the exposure to a particular toxin.

Source: Centers for Disease Control and Prevention. 2002. Marine Toxins. Available at www.cdc.gov/ncidod/dbmd/diseaseinfo/marinetoxins_g.htm; Agency for Toxic Substances and Disease Registry. Updated 2003. ToxFAQ for Polychlorinated Biphenyls (PCBs). Available at www.atsdr.cdc.gov/tfacts17.html; Environmental Protection Agency Persistent Bioaccumulative and Toxin (PBT) Chemical Program. www.epa.gov/pbt/pbtsandyou.htm.

Other foods contain toxins that are harmful even in trace amounts, and so should be avoided altogether. Certain wild mushrooms, for example, are poisonous; they contain toxins that can cause nausea, vomiting, liver damage, and death.

Chemicals Are Sometimes Due to Pollution

One man's trash can become another man's dilemma. Although industrial and households chemicals have useful purposes in manufacturing and in maintaining your home, if traces of these substances end up in the food supply, they could affect your health.

Polychlorinated Biphenyls (PCBs) and Methylmercury

Polychlorinated biphenyls (PCBs) are chemicals that occur in the food supply due to industrial pollution. A few decades ago, the chemicals were used as coolants and lubricants because they are good insulators and don't burn easily. They were banned in 1977 due to concerns about their toxicity.[69]

PCBs have been shown to cause cancer and have other adverse effects in animals, and they may also be **carcinogenic** (*carcino* = cancer, *genic* = forming) in humans. Adults exposed to large amounts of PCBs may develop acne and rashes. Newborns and developing fetuses are at particularly high risk from the adverse effects of PCBs, as their enzyme systems, which help metabolize and get rid of PCBs in the body, aren't fully developed. Also, because young children are smaller, exposure to PCBs will have a proportionately greater effect on them than would the same level of exposure in adults.[70]

Although PCBs are no longer manufactured in the United States, they can still make their way into the environment through hazardous waste sites, the burning of commercial or municipal wastes, and the improper disposal of consumer products, such as old television sets and electrical fixtures and devices.[71] PCBs have been shown to contaminate the sediments in rivers and lakes. Because PCBs don't break down over time, they bioaccumulate in small organisms and fish. PCBs are the major chemical risk associated with eating fish.[72]

The EPA is working to lower the amount of PCBs in the environment, and the FDA routinely monitors PCB levels in our foods.[73] As a consumer, make sure you adhere to any fish consumption advisories in your area. The Table Tips provide the EPA website where you can easily find these current advisories, as well as tips to minimize your exposure to toxins and chemical agents in foods.

Recall from Chapter 5 that mercury occurs in nature, but is also a by-product of industrial pollution. An airborne form of mercury can accumulate on the surface of streams and oceans and be transformed by the bacteria in the water into the toxic form of methylmercury. As fish either absorb the methylmercury from the water or eat smaller fish that contain methylmercury, they can bioaccumulate the substance to high levels.

Some Chemicals Are Used Intentionally to Enhance the Food Supply

Chemicals are sometimes used to improve the health or output of food-producing animals. Two chemicals commonly used for this purpose are growth hormone and antibiotics.

polychlorinated biphenyls (PCBs) Synthetic chemicals that have been shown to cause cancer and other adverse effects on the immune, reproductive, nervous, and endocrine systems in animals. PCBs may cause cancer in humans.

carcinogenic A substance thought to cause cancer.

Growth Hormone

Scientists and dairy farmers have known for years that cows injected with the naturally occurring bovine **growth hormone,** also known as bovine somatotropin, produce more milk. Cows injected with a synthetic version of the hormone, **recombinant bovine somatotropin (rbST),** can produce up to 25 percent more milk than untreated cows.[74] Though consumer groups and Health Canada (the FDA equivalent in Canada) have questioned the long-term safety of rbST, the FDA's extensive review of rbST has found no evidence that it poses any long-term health threat to humans.[75]

Other steroid hormones are sometimes used to increase the amount of weight that cattle gain and the amount of meat that they produce. The FDA has approved the use of these hormones in beef cattle, as they have been shown to be safe at their approved level of use and not a health concern to consumers.[76]

Antibiotics

Antibiotics are used in food-producing animals for three purposes: (1) to treat animals that are sick; (2) to preventively treat animals that may be at risk for being sick (for example, if one animal becomes ill, the entire herd may be given antibiotics); and (3) to promote growth. When antibiotics are used for the first two purposes, they are used for a relatively short period of time. This isn't true when antibiotics are used for the third purpose. Low-dose antibiotics are routinely put in animal feed, because animals that consume this feed gain more weight than animals fed antibiotic-free feed.[77]

Pathogenic bacteria such as *Campylobacter, E. coli* O157:H7, and *Salmonella* are commonly found in the gastrointestinal tracts of animals without making them sick. However, when animals are chronically given antibiotics, this can result in **antibiotic-resistant bacteria** strains in their intestinal tracts. If someone contracts a foodborne illness from this animal food source, treatment with the same antibiotic that was used in the feed, which killed the bacteria in the past, may no longer be effective.

For example, in the late 1980s, the antibiotic fluoroquinolone was successfully used to treat *Campylobacter*, which is commonly found in chickens. In 1995, this antibiotic began to be used regularly in poultry. Shortly after, doctors began seeing patients with *Campylobacter*-induced foodborne illness whose infections were resistant to treatments with fluoroquinolone.[78]

The chronic intake of antibiotics can also cause the "overgrowth" of other bacteria in the animal that can evade the effects of the antibiotic. These surviving bacteria can flourish and multiply to high levels. Treatment with typical antibiotics to control these surviving, resistant bacteria may be unsuccessful, perpetuating the need for a higher dose of medication and/or a longer treatment period.

Pesticides Are Widely Used in Agriculture

You have probably been handling **pesticides** for years. If you use disinfectant to control the mold in your shower, bug spray to ward off flesh biters on muggy summer nights, or a flea collar to keep your pet itch free, you're making use of chemicals that destroy or mitigate pests. These chemicals are collectively known as pesticides. Different types of pesticides are used to destroy pests that threaten or impact the food supply.

Types of Pesticides

There are several different types of pests that can diminish or destroy crop yields, including insects, weeds, microorganisms (bacteria, viruses), fungi (mold), and rodents (rats and mice). Pesticides used to kill weeds are called **herbicides,** while those used on microorganisms are **antimicrobials. Fungicides** are used to destroy mold.

growth hormone A hormone that is essential for normal growth and development in humans and animals.

recombinant bovine somatotropin (rbST) A synthetically made hormone identical to a cow's natural growth hormone, somatotropin, that stimulates milk production. Also known as rbGH (recombinant bovine growth hormone).

antibiotics Drugs that kill or slow the growth of bacteria.

antibiotic-resistant bacteria Bacteria that have developed a resistance to an antibiotic such that they are no longer affected by antibiotic medication.

pesticides Substances that kill or repel pests such as insects, weeds, microorganisms, rodents, or fungi.

herbicides Substances that are used to kill and control weeds.

antimicrobials Substances or a combination of substances, such as disinfectants and sanitizers, that control the spread of bacteria and viruses on nonliving surfaces or objects.

fungicides Chemicals used to kill mold.

Farmers use pesticides on food crops to diminish the damage from pests.

Pesticides can be either man made or natural. **Synthetic pesticides** are chemically made, whereas naturally derived pesticides, called **biopesticides,** use materials from animals, plants, bacteria, and some minerals.[79] Biopesticides are typically less toxic than chemical pesticides.

Of the numerous synthetic pesticides currently being used, **organophosphates** make up about half of all the insecticides used in the United States.[80] Organophosphates are used on fruits, nuts, vegetables, corn, wheat, and other crops, as well as commercial and residential lawns and plants. They are also used to help control mosquitoes and termites.[81] These pesticides affect the nervous systems of the pests they destroy. The EPA has recently reviewed the safety of organophosphates and concluded that they do not pose a health risk based on current human exposure in food and water.[82]

Antimicrobials such as disinfectants and sanitizers are typically man made, and destroy or curtail the spread of microorganisms on nonliving surfaces or objects, such as walls, countertops, and floors.[83] Sanitizers are often used in addition to washing with soap and water in food processing plants and in restaurants. Although waterless, alcohol-based hand gels are now a popular alternative to hand washing, they are not effective against foodborne pathogens, and should not replace hand washing during food preparation.[84]

Unlike synthetic pesticides, biopesticides only curtail a specific pest, and thus are not harmful to birds and other animals that may come into contact with them.[85] For example, baking soda (sodium bicarbonate) can be diluted with water and sprayed on plants to inhibit the growth of fungi without any known risk to humans.[86] Insect **sex pheromones** can be used in agriculture to interfere with the mating of pests. Scented extracts from plants can also be used to lure and then trap insects.[87]

Pesticides Help Promote Abundant Crop Production

Pesticides can be extremely helpful in preventing the growth of harmful fungi, controlling damaging insects, and stopping rampant weeds from contaminating crops with their natural toxin. By using pesticides on agricultural crops, food plants can flourish and produce a hearty bounty. This enables farmers to offer affordable crops to the market.[88] The consumer then benefits by being able to buy a variety of nutrient-dense foods.

A year-long study in 1998 on the role of pesticides in U.S. agriculture concluded that a variety of pesticide technologies, including chemical methods, can be used to produce safe, productive, and profitable crops.[89]

The Risks of Pesticides

The problem with synthetic pesticides is that because they are strong chemicals, they can cause unintended harm to animals, the environment, and even humans. Research has shown that some pesticides, depending upon their level of toxicity and how much is consumed, may cause serious health problems, such as cancer, birth defects, and nerve damage.[90]

Healthy People 2010 has advocated a reduction in the use of certain potentially dangerous pesticides. In addition, the American Medical Association has urged the U.S. government to improve public education, workplace training, science-based research, and the ongoing surveillance of pesticide usage.[91] To prevent potential harm to consumers, pesticide use is heavily regulated in the United States.

synthetic pesticides Man made, chemically based substances, such as organophosphate pesticides, used to control pests.

biopesticides Substances derived from natural materials such as animals, plants, bacteria, and certain minerals to control pests.

organophosphates A group of synthetic pesticides that adversely affect the nervous systems of pests. They are currently being re-reviewed by the EPA to ensure their safety.

sex pheromones Naturally occurring chemicals secreted by one organism to attract another, used as a biopesticide to control pests by interfering with their mating.

Regulating Pesticides: Who's Watching the Crops?

The EPA evaluates all food pesticides to ensure that they can be used with "a reasonable certainty of no harm." This human health **risk assessment** is a four-step process: hazard identification, dose-response assessment, exposure assessment, and risk characterization.

The first step of this risk assessment, hazard identification, identifies the potential hazards or ill effects that may develop after exposure to a specific pesticide. Tests are often performed on laboratory animals, looking at a wide range of side effects, from eye and skin irritations to more serious health effects such as cancer. Because "the dose makes the poison," the second step, dose-response assessment, determines the dose at which these ill effects occur in animals and then uses this information to identify a potentially equal dose in humans. The third step, exposure assessment, determines all the ways that a person could typically be exposed to that specific pesticide. Exposure could occur orally when you eat food or drink water. Exposure could also occur if you inhale a pesticide or absorb it through your skin when you are using household disinfectants or gardening pesticides around your home. (If you work with pesticides, that's a different level of exposure that is assessed separately.) The fourth and last step, risk characterization, uses the information obtained in the first three steps to determine the pesticide's overall risk.[92]

Because there are potential differences between the effects of a pesticide on animals and its effect on humans, as well as differences among humans, the EPA builds in a margin of safety when determining the health risk. An extra tenfold safety factor is added (unless there is evidence that a lesser margin of safety is adequate) to protect the most vulnerable groups, such as infants and children, who could be exposed to the pesticide.[93] Thus, much effort goes into ensuring that the foods you eat are safe, yet affordable, in order for you to reap their health benefits and minimize any known risks.

In addition to the EPA, the USDA and the FDA are also involved in regulating pesticides. Once the EPA approves pesticides for their specific usages, regulates how much of the pesticide can be used, and establishes their **acceptable tolerance levels,** the tolerances are enforced by the USDA for meat, poultry, and eggs and by the FDA for all other foods.[94]

Alternatives to Pesticides

Rather than pesticides, some growers use an approach called **integrated pest management (IPM)** to manage pests in their crops. The goal of this approach is to use the most economical methods to control pests while causing the least risk of harm to the consumer, the crops, or the environment. Growers using the IPM approach monitor their crops. They use other preventive measures, such as rotating crops and choosing pest-resistant strains of crops, to reduce the likelihood of attracting pests.[95] When these measures aren't adequate to control pests, nonsynthetic alternatives, such as biopesticides or the introduction of natural predators (specific insects that eat the unwanted pests), may be used to curtail an infestation. If all these methods don't control the spread of the pests, targeted spraying of synthetic pesticides is then considered.

Foods grown using IPM methods typically aren't labeled, so the consumer can't easily spot them in the supermarket.[96] Currently, about 70 percent of the crops in the United States are grown using some form of IPM.[97]

risk assessment The process of determining the potential human health risks posed by exposure to substances such as pesticides.

acceptable tolerance levels The maximum amount of pesticide residue that is allowed in or on foods.

integrated pest management (IPM) Alternative to pesticides that uses the most economical and the least harmful methods of pest control to minimize risk to consumers, crops, and the environment.

Figure 14.9 Reducing Pesticides in Your Foods

Wash: Thoroughly wash and scrub all fresh fruits and vegetables with a vegetable brush with sturdy surfaces under running water to dislodge bacteria and some of the pesticide residue. Running water is more effective for this purpose than soaking the fruit and vegetables.

Peel and trim: Peeling fruits and vegetables and tossing the outer leaves of leafy vegetables helps reduce pesticides. Trimming the visible fat from meat and the fatty skin from poultry and fish helps reduce some of the pesticide residue that remains in the fatty tissue of the animal.

Eat a variety of foods: Eating a variety of foods reduces your chances of being overexposed to any particular pesticide.

You Can Minimize Pesticides in Your Diet

Washing your fruits and vegetables with clean, running water and a vegetable brush can remove up to 81 percent of pesticide residue, according to one study by the University of California. This study also found that there wasn't any significant difference in the amount of residue removed when the fruit was washed with plain water or with a commercial produce wash.[98] (Note: Because of the strict pesticide guidelines in place in the United States, the amount of pesticide residue found on all the fruits studied was below the EPA acceptable tolerance level, even *before* the researchers washed it.) Peeling the skin from fruits and removing the outer layers of some vegetables can also help remove pesticide residues. Eating a variety of produce will also minimize the consumption of any one type of pesticide. Note that people who eat more fruit and vegetables, and therefore potentially increase their exposure to pesticides, still typically have a lower risk of cancer than those who eat fewer fruits and vegetables.[99] See Figure 14.9 for a summary of strategies you can use to minimize pesticides in your diet.

The Take-Home Message Toxins can occur naturally in foods and can cause harm to humans. Marine toxins can occur in certain varieties of spoiled fish and bioaccumulate in fish who feed on toxin-containing sea organisms. Chemicals can also occur in the food supply as a result of environmental contamination. Polychlorinated biphenyls (PCBs) and methylmercury have been shown to bioaccumulate in fish. Growth hormone can be given to dairy cows to increase milk production. Animal feed containing low doses of antibiotics has been used to increase the growth of cattle, poultry, and pigs. Chronic antibiotic exposure in animals can lead to antibiotic-resistant strains of bacteria.

Pesticides are used to destroy or mitigate pests; they are regulated in the United States by several government agencies. You can minimize your exposure to plant pesticides by washing your produce under running tap water before consuming it.

What Is Organic and How Do You Find Organic Foods?

Organic farming involves growing crops without the use of *some* synthetic pesticides, synthetic fertilizers, bioengineering (this will be discussed in the next section), or irradiation. Similarly, only antibiotic-free or growth hormone–free animals can be used to produce organic meat, poultry, eggs, and dairy foods.[100] The popularity of organic foods has recently soared. By 2025, the market for organic foods in the United States is projected to reach over $50 billion annually, compared with $12 billion in 2004.[101]

This growing interest in organic foods prompted the USDA to develop National Organic Standards (NOS) in 2002. Before these NOS were in place, over 50 organizations and state agencies had their own (different) sets of organic standards and guidelines.[102] The NOS implemented under the USDA's National Organic Program provide specific criteria that food producers must meet during production, handling, and processing to label their products "organic." As a result of these standards, you can be confident that if the food is labeled as organic, it was produced and handled using specific guidelines and certified by a USDA-accredited inspector.[103]

Contrary to popular belief, organic foods are not necessarily free of all pesticides. Organically grown crops may come into contact with chemicals due to drift from wind and rainwater. Also, though organic farmers use IPM, and grow more disease- and pest-resistant plants, sometimes synthetic pesticides and biopesticides may still be needed. The National Organic Program has created the National List of Allowed and Prohibited Substances that identifies substances that can and cannot be used in organic crop production. According to the list, several synthetic pesticides, such as insecticidal soaps, are allowed, while some natural substances, such as ash from the burning of manure, cannot be used in organic farming.[104]

The USDA hasn't found that organic foods are safer or nutritionally superior to those grown in a conventional manner.[105] The National Organic Trade Association confirms that there currently isn't conclusive evidence that organic foods are more nutritious than conventionally grown foods.[106] Organic foods may also cost more than those that are conventionally grown.

You can identify organically produced foods in your supermarket by looking for the USDA Organic Seal (Figure 14.10). Foods that display this seal or otherwise state that they are organic must contain at least 95 percent organic ingredients. However, organic food producers can choose whether or not to display this seal, so it may not be on all such products. There are other label claims and standards for foods that are 100 percent organic, or that use organic ingredients. See Table 14.6 on page 520 for the standards that organic label claims must meet.

Figure 14.10 The USDA Organic Seal
Foods that are labeled or advertised with the USDA Organic seal must contain at least 95 percent organic ingredients.

The Take-Home Message Organic foods are grown without the use of some synthetic pesticides, synthetic fertilizers, bioengineering, or irradiation. The National Organic Standards provide specific criteria and guidelines for the production, handling, processing, and labeling of organic foods, as well as mandatory certification by an accredited inspector. Organic foods may cost more than conventionally grown foods, and there is no conclusive evidence that they are more nutritious than conventionally grown foods.

organic Being free of chemical-based pesticides, synthetic fertilizers, irradiation, and bioengineering. A USDA-accredited certifying inspector must certify organic foods.

Table 14.6 Various Levels of Organic

If the label ▶
says "Organic" and/or displays the USDA Organic seal
Then: The food contains at least 95 percent organic ingredients.

▲ If the label
says "100% Organic"
Then: The food must be composed entirely of organic ingredients. Note: These foods cannot contain sulfites and must declare the certifying agent. The USDA Organic seal may be displayed.

◀ If the label
Makes no organic claims
Then: The food contains less than 70 percent organic ingredients.

◀ If the label
says "Made with Organic Ingredients"
Then: The food contains at least 70 percent organic ingredients.

biotechnology The application of biological techniques to living cells, which alters their genetic makeup.

plant breeding A type of biotechnology in which two plants are crossbred to produce offspring with desired traits from both.

genetically modified A cell that has its genetic makeup altered.

genetic engineering (GE) A biological technique that isolates and manipulates the genes of organisms to produce a targeted, modified product.

genetically modified organisms (GMOs) Organisms that have been genetically engineered to contain both original and foreign genes.

What Is Biotechnology and Why Is It Used?

Humans have been using **biotechnology** by selectively breeding plants and animals for generations. The fresh apples that you eat today look nothing like their small, sour Asian ancestors. Because apples have been intentionally grown (or cultivated) by humans for thousands of years, apple farmers have had plenty of time to crossbreed different versions of the tree to produce more desirable offspring. For example, if one tree produced large, fleshy apples with thinner skins, and another produced smaller, sour apples with thicker skins, an ancient apple farmer might have bred the two in the hope of producing a tree with large, fleshy, hardy fruit. This process is a form of **plant breeding.**

Historically, farmers have crossbred plants by trial and error, hoping for the best results and using the best offspring to further breed more desirable plants. In the last two centuries, however, as scientists understood more about the workings of DNA and how to manipulate it, the process has become faster and more controlled. Today, farmers routinely use selectively bred, **genetically modified** plants to create bigger and better produce and disease-resistant crops, and to increase crop yields in the United States. In fact, you would be hard pressed to find many fruits and vegetables today that aren't a product of plant breeding.[107]

The apples of today are larger and sweeter than their ancestors, thanks to hundreds of years of selective breeding.

Genetic Engineering Is the Latest Form of Biotechnology

Today's versions of biotechnology include new techniques, such as **genetic engineering (GE),** to alter the genetic makeup of an organism. In genetic engineering, or bioengineering, the exact gene or genes from the DNA of a plant cell are isolated and inserted into the DNA of another cell to create the genetically modified product (Figure 14.11).

As mentioned briefly in the section on growth hormone, this cutting and splicing of genes into the DNA of another cell is called recombinant DNA (rDNA) technology. Organisms that have been genetically engineered to contain both original and foreign genes are called **genetically modified organisms (GMOs).** These GMOs are used to grow genetically engineered (GE) plants that produce GE foods.

Genetically engineered (GE) crops were first grown over a decade ago, and in 2003, 100 million acres of GE crops, including corn, cotton, canola, and soybeans, were cultivated on U.S. soil.[108]

Genetic Engineering Can Produce More and Better Foods

Proponents of GE products believe that these can be good for the environment, help feed countries that have an inadequate food supply, improve the quality and quantity of foods available all year round, and create new uses for plants in industries such as pharmaceuticals and manufacturing.

The original purpose of GE plants was to reduce the amount of pesticides used on food crops.[109] For example, the bacterium *Bacillus thuringiensis* (*Bt*), which is found naturally in soil, produces a toxin that is poisonous to certain pests but not to humans or animals. When the gene for this toxin is inserted into a crop plant, the plant becomes resistant to these pests.[110] Some corn crops in the United States contain the *Bt* gene, which makes them resistant to some insect pests (see photo). Over 20 percent of the acreages of both corn and cotton in the United States in 1998 were planted with this type of genetically engineered, *Bt* gene–containing crop.[111]

First-generation GE products were also created to improve a crop's tolerance to herbicides. With an herbicide-resistant version of a desired crop, a farmer can spray herbicide over a field to kill a variety of weeds without harming the crop.[112] According to the USDA, approximately 75 percent of soybeans have been genetically modified to be herbicide resistant.[113]

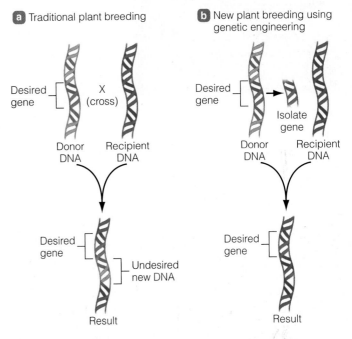

a Traditional plant breeding

Desired gene — Donor DNA

X (cross)

Recipient DNA

Desired gene — Result — Undesired new DNA

b New plant breeding using genetic engineering

Desired gene — Donor DNA

Isolate gene

Recipient DNA

Desired gene — Result

Figure 14.11 Plant Breeding versus Genetic Engineering
(a) Traditional plant breeding involved crossing two plants of the same species in order to produce DNA with more desirable traits. The process was imprecise, however, and achieving the desired result could take years. **(b)** Today, genetic engineering allows scientists to precisely manipulate the DNA from plants and impart desirable qualities from one plant to its offspring much more quickly.

Bt corn has been genetically engineered to be resistant to the corn borer.

"Golden" rice is rich in both beta-carotene and iron, and is a product of genetic engineering.

The second-generation GE products were designed to provide consumers with added nutritional value as well as other attributes, such as increasing the crop's shelf life.[114] For example, "golden" rice contains foreign gene segments that encode the rice grain to make beta-carotene and to stockpile extra iron (see photo). This "super" rice, if planted by farmers and accepted by consumers in Southeast Asia, could help eliminate the epidemic of vitamin A and iron deficiency in children there.[115] Genetically modified, high oleic acid soybean oil is less prone to becoming rancid, and thus is more stable when used for frying foods.

Third-generation GE products hold promise in the pharmaceutical, environmental, and industrial arenas. In fact, the first GE product created for commercial use was human insulin (needed by diabetics) produced by genetically engineered *E. coli*.[116] In addition to bacteria, plants can be genetically modified to create substances with numerous medical uses, such as vaccines, antibiotics, anti-clotting drugs, hormones, and substitutes for certain blood substances.[117] Scientists are currently experimenting with the concept of "growing" vaccines for measles, hepatitis B, and Norwalk virus in produce.[118] Imagine how much easier it would be to give the measles vaccine to a small child in a spoonful of pureed fruit rather than a pointy needle!

Some People Have Concerns about GE Foods

Some opponents of GE products fear that biotechnology can cause everything from harm to monarch butterflies to creation of "Frankenstein" foods. A study at Cornell University in the late 1990s raised concerns that when milkweed leaves, which are the sole diet of monarch caterpillars, were heavily dusted with pollen from *Bt* corn, and then *exclusively* fed to monarch butterfly caterpillars, many of them died. Critics of this finding said that this experiment didn't mimic a "real-life" setting. Most milkweed doesn't grow close enough to cornfields to collect significant amounts of corn pollen, especially since this heavy pollen typically doesn't travel far from its place of origin. Hence, it is unlikely that monarch caterpillars would feed primarily on milkweed that contains such an enormous amount of GE corn pollen.[119] After conducting extensive research coordinated by the USDA, researchers concluded that the monarch butterflies' exposure to GE corn pollen in a natural setting is minimal and so is not likely to be dangerous to these butterflies.[120]

If you are concerned about Franken-foods, you should know that the risk of an abnormal plant is smaller in GE foods than in foods cultivated through plant breeding. In fact, because genetic engineering involves precise cutting and splicing of specific genes, its end products are less likely to have undesirable traits.

Genetic engineering is also more tightly regulated than any other technology, so there are safeguards in place to halt or prevent undesirable outcomes, such as the introduction of a known food allergen into a GE product.[121]

Other concerns have arisen about the production of plant toxins, changes in the nutrient content and substances in foods, and the production of unsafe animal feed. Table 14.7 lists the safeguards that are in place to address these issues.

GE Foods Are Highly Regulated in the United States

GE foods in the United States are regulated by the same three government agencies that regulate pesticides: the FDA, USDA, and EPA. The FDA ensures that GE foods are safe to eat. The USDA ensures that the plants are safe to grow, while the EPA makes

Table 14.7
Concerns and Regulations for GE Foods

Concern	FDA Regulation
Undesirable genetic modification	To avoid the creation of undesirable products, all genes used must not have prior evidence of encoding any harmful substances. The genes must also be stably inserted into the plant in order to avoid any rearranging of genetic information that would produce an undesirable substance.
Introduction of allergens	GE foods must be monitored for food allergens. Protein encoded from common allergen food sources (such as milk, eggs, fish, tree nuts, and legumes) should be presumed to be allergens and should be labeled as such on the GE food.
Excessive level of toxins	GE foods should not contain natural toxins at levels that are higher than those found naturally in plants.
Changes in nutrients	All GE foods should be monitored to assess unintentional changes in the nutrient levels in the plants and their ability to be utilized in the human body as compared with their conventional counterparts.
Creation of new substances	If the genes that are introduced into plants encode substances that are different in structure and function than those normally found in foods, these substances would need to be approved by the FDA, as would any other food additive. However, if these substances are GRAS or "substantially equivalent" to substances that already exist in foods, they do not need the FDA's premarket approval.
Unsafe animal feeds	Because a single plant may be the predominant food source in an animal feed, all GE animal feeds must meet the same strict safety standards that are in place for food that is grown for humans.

Source: FDA. Policy for Food Developed by Biotechnology. Available at http://vm.cfsan.fda.gov/~lrd/bioeme.htm; J.H. Maryanski. 1997. Bioengineered Foods: Will They Cause Allergic Reactions? Center for Food Safety and Applied Nutrition. Available at www.cfsan.fda.gov/~dms/pubalrgy.html.

certain that the gene for any pesticide, such as that for *Bt* toxin, inserted into a plant is safe and won't hurt the environment. Though these agencies work together to ensure the safety of GE foods, the FDA has the overall authority to remove any GE food that doesn't meet the same high safety standards that are set for its conventionally grown equivalent.[122]

The FDA must review and approve all GE products before they are allowed on the market. As part of this process, the FDA mandates that the developers of GE foods test to ensure the safety of those foods. After the testing is completed, the developer must send the FDA a summary of the information pertaining to the product. If the FDA is satisfied with all the documentation and all the follow-up questions are answered, the food is considered safe and will be allowed to enter the market.

More than 50 GE foods, including canola oil, corn, cottonseed oil, potatoes, soybeans, squash, and tomatoes, have been evaluated by the FDA and are considered as safe as their conventional counterparts.[123] Your supermarket shelf is likely littered with foods with GE ingredients.

There is no labeling requirement for GE foods, and you have probably eaten them without being aware of it. The FDA has concluded that because there isn't any scientific evidence that GE foods differ from their conventionally grown counterparts, labeling isn't warranted.[124] This position is shared by the American Medical Association and the Society of Toxicology.[125] Canada follows the United States in this regard. Mandatory labeling of GE foods is required in Europe, Japan, Australia, and New Zealand.[126]

The FDA has created guidelines to assist companies that want to voluntarily label their products as free of GE ingredients. The manufacturers must be able to verify that these claims are not only accurate and credible, but also cannot be misleading to the consumer.[127]

The public seems to be warming up to GE foods because of their health benefits and improved quality. In a survey of approximately 1,000 American adults conducted in January 2004, almost 60 percent felt that biotechnology would benefit themselves and their families in the future. Interestingly, over 60 percent of the consumers surveyed said that food safety issues, such as food handling/preparation, packaging, or disease/contamination, were their primary concern, compared with the mere 1 percent who identified biotechnology as their top worry. The majority also stated that they would be likely to use GE produce that was modified to protect against insect damage, required less pesticide application during growing, or had improved taste or freshness.[128]

The Take-Home Message Both plant breeding and genetic engineering are types of biotechnology that alter the genetic makeup of an organism's cells to create a new plant with more desirable traits. Genetically engineered crops can be developed to be pest resistant, and to provide additional nutrients and enhanced flavor and quality. GE products are heavily regulated to minimize undesirable genetic modifications, toxic substances, and nutrient changes in food, as well as potential food allergens and the creation of unsafe feed for animals. Labeling is not mandatory for GE foods.

What Is Bioterrorism and How Can You Protect Yourself?

Food and water supplies are potential targets for **bioterrorism.** Agents such as the bacterium that causes anthrax and the virus that causes smallpox are examples of possible bioterrorist weapons. Until recently, scenarios of human-caused outbreaks of these diseases were thought to exist only in Hollywood movies. Today, Americans face the real threat of someone using plant or animal food supplies, or drinking water sources, to cause harm.[129]

Food can be the primary agent of bioterrorism by being contaminated with a biological or chemical toxin. In fact, the CDC lists several foodborne pathogens, such as botulism, *Salmonella, E. coli* O157:H7, and *Shigella* as potential bioterrorism agents.[130]

Food and water can also be used as secondary agents of bioterrorism by disrupting the availability of adequate safe amounts of these necessities and by limiting the fuel needed to safely cook and refrigerate perishable foods. Several years ago, London police arrested individuals involved in a plot to add poison to the food served at a British military base, and in Jerusalem, people were arrested for planning to poison customers at a local restaurant.[131] Tainted foods, or even the threat of such contamination, could cause a mandatory or self-imposed avoidance of a particular category of food and/or eating establishment and contribute to social disarray.[132]

To combat these threats, governmental agencies have made bioterrorism a national priority. Under the direction of the Department of Homeland Security, numerous local, state, and federal agencies such as the Federal Emergency Management Agency (FEMA), FDA, and USDA work together at each stage of the food continuum—from the farm to the table—to protect your foods.

bioterrorism The use of a biological or chemical agent to frighten, threaten, coerce, injure, and/or kill individuals.

As a consumer, you also play an important role in **food biosecurity.** Earlier in this chapter, you learned strategies to minimize the risk of foodborne illness through proper food preparation and storage techniques. There are also strategies that you can employ if you should come into contact with suspicious-looking food items. Although **food tampering** is rare in the United States, a watchful consumer can spot it and avoid it. The Table Tips lists tips you can use to identify tampered food items and where to report suspicious items if you find them.

The Take-Home Message Food and water can be primary agents of bioterrorism by being contaminated with a biological or chemical toxin. These necessities can also be used as secondary agents if a terrorist act disrupts their availability, or limits access to the fuel needed to safely cook and refrigerate perishable foods. If you come into contact with a tampered food, you should report the suspicious items to the appropriate authorities.

Putting It All Together

You have access to one of the safest food supplies in the world. This means that you can confidently obtain all of your nutrients—carbohydrates, protein, fats, vitamins, minerals, and water—as well as other important dietary components from your foods for good health. Guidelines and strategies are in place to help everyone, from the farmer to you, the consumer, keep the foods that you eat safe. With everyone working together, you are afforded the opportunity to choose a healthy diet from a wide variety of safe foods to meet your daily nutrient needs.

food biosecurity Protecting the food supply from bioterrorist attacks.

food tampering The deliberate contamination of a food to cause harm.

Two Points of View

Can Organic Go Large Scale?

As organic foods become more popular, more supermarket and discount chains are offering them in their stores. Does the buying and selling of organic foods on a national scale defeat the purpose of their being organic? What does "organic" mean to most people? Let's pose these questions to two experts in the field.

Bob Scowcroft
Cofounder and Executive Director,
Organic Farming Research Foundation

Mark Kastel
Cofounder and Director, Organic Integrity Project,
The Cornucopia Institute

Bob Scowcroft leads the Organic Farming Research Foundation, based in Santa Cruz, California. The nonprofit group's mission is to sponsor research related to organic farming practices, to disseminate research results to organic farmers and to growers interested in adopting organic production

(continued)

Mark Kastel is cofounder of The Cornucopia Institute, a progressive farm policy research group based in Wisconsin. His professional experience includes political consulting and lobbying on behalf of family farm groups and business development work benefiting family-scale farmers. Kastel played a key

(continued)

Can Organic Go Large Scale?, continued

Bob Scowcroft, continued

systems, and to educate the public and decision makers about organic farming issues.

Q: What is the definition of "organic" and how is organic food regulated?

A: There is a definition I really like from the early days of putting together the organic regulations. It says what organic farming is, not just what it isn't. It says that an organic production system is one that avoids or excludes the use of synthetically compounded fertilizers, pesticides, growth-regulating hormones, and livestock feed additives. It also says, to the maximum extent feasible, that organic farming systems rely on alternative growing methods, such as crop rotation, mechanical cultivation, and biological pest control to maintain soil production, supply plant nutrients, and control pests.

The USDA is responsible for enforcing national organic standards, but that has not always taken place to our satisfaction. Many states have their own organic regulations as well, and some have had more enforcement. In California, we've had over 40 enforcement actions against violators.

Within North America there are 9,000 to 10,000 farmers who are certified organic or about to be, and state, local, and independent inspectors who have the will and the way to stop people if they're in violation. I am less confident that organic standards are met by organic imports from overseas. A real issue right now is China. How can we ensure that standards are being followed and enforced?

Q: Why are organic foods becoming more popular, and how has this affected their availability?

A: The primary reason is the concern around conventional foods, whether it's from food scares or what I call food realities. That has led to huge growth in demand and supply. Right now (as of 2006), organic is about 2.5 percent of the food economy. It's predicted to be about 6 to 8 percent of the food economy in 2008. Total sales of organic foods in the United States were about $14.5 billion in 2005, and in 2008 the predictions say about $40 billion. A lot of that growth has been in traditional supermarkets, and now the "big-box" stores (like Wal-Mart) and big food brands are getting involved too.

Some in the organic world aren't comfortable with that kind of growth and organic becoming big business. But there's a positive side of this too. There's also growth in small cooperative farms and farmer's markets, and lots of new interest in buying local. There's a lot of cool stuff happening at the small-farm, family-farm level. Restaurants have really been at the forefront of this. In Santa Cruz, where we are, you're hard pressed to go into a restaurant and not hear what organic farmer they buy from.

(continued)

Mark Kastel, continued

role in a number of cooperative ventures designed to empower farmers in the marketplace. He has also been a certified organic grower.

Q: What is the definition of "organic" and how is organic food regulated?

A: Since 2002, when the USDA finally implemented the Organic Food Production Act, there has been only one legal definition for organic food in the United States. No one can legally produce food to a lower standard. There is also a prohibition against saying you're producing food to a higher standard. Growers are prohibited from adopting standards that are higher than those of the USDA.

Unfortunately, there is debate over the interpretation of the standards. Large corporate agribusiness concerns have now invested in organics. They have a legion of lobbyists in Washington. Why wouldn't the USDA look the other way while some of these large concerns are cutting corners? Interpretation and lack of enforcement are definitely hot topics right now.

A premier issue for us right now is industrial dairy farms producing organic milk. Some of these farms have 8,000 to 10,000 animals or more in feedlot-like conditions. This is contradictory to the intent and spirit of the law.

Q: Why are organic foods becoming more popular, and how has this affected their availability?

A: There are two reasons for the growing popularity. The first is that multiple food scares have woken up a lot of consumers who are really interested in providing healthy, safe food for their families. Whether it's the relationship between antibiotic use in livestock and resistant bacteria, pathogens in our environment and food supply, toxic and carcinogenic chemical residue on our food, or hormones not thoroughly tested on humans, consumers have a wide list of concerns almost universally addressed by organic production.

The other reason is that people who are living an increasingly frenzied lifestyle are finding additional meaning in their lives through a connection to food. That connection has historically been an important part of the human race. In almost every religious tradition there is reference to food and the way it connects us to the earth. It's only since the Industrial Revolution that most of our population is disconnected from food production. And only in the last 75 years has it moved away from being a local enterprise, with food shipped from far away, all wrapped in plastic. Organic food is an opportunity not only to protect your family from harmful substances or provide for them an improved level of nutrition, but to also restore this connection.

Q: Is it possible to grow and distribute truly organic foods on a national scale? Why or why not?

(continued)

Bob Scowcroft, continued

Q: Is it possible to grow and distribute truly organic foods on a national scale? Why or why not?

A: It's possible, but it's complex. It depends on how well something ships, and its shelf life. That's why you see some produce—nuts, apples, bagged salads—available that way. In other cases, the infrastructure just isn't there. That's the case with lots of meat and poultry. To get truly national distribution, you need regional distribution networks that are certified organic, you need larger producers to feed into those networks, and you need products that ship well.

Scale was already an issue when we drafted the organic rules. Some people were very upset about organic farms of 100 acres. We couldn't really envision where this has gone now. I do see what's critically unsustainable about a large-scale system. The energy to get food shipped long distances won't be cheap much longer. And no one should have any illusions about what it's like to do business with the big-box stores.

Still, I'm struck by how many people are saying, "This is bad." We should not forget hundreds of thousands of pounds of agricultural chemicals are *not* being used because of the large shifts to organic production. For us, bringing organic to the masses trumped the other issues. We want everyone to be able to eat certified organic foods.

Q: How will the landscape of organic foods change in the future?

A: I think it will be tumultuously positive. Sadly, there are more food safety issues out there, and those will mean another big push to organic. Some people in the organic movement will have questions about that growth. So there will be more "big organic," and more small organic too. When people see an organic big-brand cookie they say, "I didn't think that's what organic was—I thought it was maple sugar straight out of a tree." But growth of both will continue. You'll still get the maple sugar, but you'll also see more big-brand organic cookies.

Mark Kastel, continued

A: From a technical standpoint, the answer is "Yes." The definition of organic is about the production method. And in some cases, large-scale might be appropriate. If almonds or macadamia nuts can only be grown in one environment, you're going to need a wider distribution.

But it's not organic to concentrate livestock on a factory farm in Colorado and ship their food—grain, hay, soybeans—in from around the world from hundreds of sources. From a philosophical standpoint, shipping that feed isn't organic and then shipping the milk all over the country isn't organic. It breaks the connection. You're sending the milk to Maine and Vermont and Wisconsin, where there are plenty of local farmers who could supply it, and you're undercutting them on price to boot. There's supposed to be this intrinsic relationship between the livestock and the land, and the livestock and the people. This all gets broken when you do it from a distance. A farm like that might be certified organic, but it's certainly not a sustainable system.

Q: How will the landscape of organic foods change in the future?

A: More and more people are finding meaning between their food and the land. They start with their concerns over health and safety of food, like maybe their milk. Then they start to read labels on their food and pay attention to where it comes from. Now we have over 3,000 farmer's markets around the country. Food scares, like the nationwide *E. coli* spinach recall this year (2006), have also really upped the interest in farmer's markets and local food.

Changes are also coming in how organic food is sold. Half of all organic food is now sold in traditional supermarkets. The jury is out whether this extreme growth we're experiencing is going to be good or bad for organics. If the integrity can be maintained, consumers and farmers win. It will create more and more opportunity on a local and regional level for people to connect with their food and each other. But if we allow organic food to be "Wal-Mart'ed," we all lose. We'll lose that connection and quality will undoubtedly suffer. When just a handful of corporations control our food supply, farmers always suffer. The organic movement began with farmers farming in an ecologically responsible manner and consumers willing to pay them a fair price. For organic to survive, we have to preserve that.

NUTRITION IN THE REAL WORLD

Be a Nutrition Sleuth

What's Wrong with This Picture?

Can you spot the food safety hazards in an online kitchen? Go to www.aw-bc.com/blake to find out.

Get Real!

Real Food Safety Decisions

Now that you've read about how you can minimize exposure to foodborne illness, let's put your newfound knowledge to the test. Go to www.aw-bc.com/blake to test your food safety savvy in five real-world scenarios.

The Top Ten Points to Remember

1. Pathogens (viruses, bacteria, and parasites) are the primary causes of foodborne illness. Noroviruses are the single largest cause of foodborne illness. The most common bacteria that cause foodborne illness are *Campylobacter, E. coli* O157:H7, and *Salmonella*. Bacteria multiply rapidly in a protein- and nutrient-rich, moist, nonacidic, and warm environment.

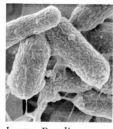

2. Older adults, young children, pregnant women, and those with liver disease or a compromised immune system are at a higher risk for foodborne illness.

3. Animal foods, such as raw and undercooked meat, poultry, seafood, eggs, and unpasteurized milk and cheese, are the most common havens for bacterial growth. Proper food handling techniques during four critical steps—cleaning, combating cross contamination, cooking, and chilling—can help reduce your risk of foodborne illness.

4. Through the coordinated effort of the Food Safety Initiative, numerous United States government agencies work together to safeguard America's food supply against foodborne illness. Everyone, from the farmer to the consumer, plays an important role in food safety. Food irradiation exposes a food item to a radiant energy source that kills or greatly reduces some pathogens.

5. Food additives are used as preservatives, antioxidants, flavoring, coloring, and leavening agents; to maintain a food's consistency; and to add nutrients. The FDA must approve most additives before they can be used in foods, and all additives must be listed on the food label. Some additives are exempted from obtaining FDA approval by having attained GRAS or prior-sanctioned status based on their long history of being safely consumed.

6. In addition to pathogens, toxins and chemical agents can also cause foodborne illness. Naturally occurring toxins and chemical agents include marine toxins and polychlorinated biphenyls. Chemical agents, such as antibiotics and pesticides, are often used by farmers to boost food production and may be found in foods.

7. Pesticides are substances that help crop plants flourish by killing or repelling damaging pests. Pesticides are heavily regulated in the United States. Natural biopesticides and antimicrobials are less toxic than synthetic pesticides, such as organophosphates. Integrated pest management is used by many farmers and is designed to use the most economical methods to control pests with the least risk of harm to the consumer, the crops, and the environment. With this method, pesticides are used only on an as-needed basis. Washing all fresh fruits and vegetables, peeling fruits and vegetables, and discarding the outer leaves of leafy vegetables can help reduce the amount of pesticides left on your foods.

8. Organic foods are grown without the use of some synthetic pesticides, synthetic fertilizers, bioengineering, and irradiation. Organic foods may still come into contact with pesticides from nearby crops. Some synthetic pesticides have been approved for use in organic farming. All foods advertised as "organic" must meet specific standards and be certified by a USDA-accredited inspector.

9. Biotechnology is the application of biological techniques to alter the genetic makeup of living cells in order to create a desired trait in an organism. Plant breeding and genetic engineering are types of biotechnology. Plant breeding has evolved over the years to create disease-resistant crops and increase the yield of crops. Genetic engineering is a more precise technique in which a specific gene or genes are inserted into the DNA of another cell to create a genetically modified product. This technique is called recombinant DNA (rDNA) technology. Genetic engineering

improves crop yields, reduces the need for pesticides, and may have other environmental, industrial, and biological benefits. Concerns about GE include that it may cause harm to some plant and animal species, or cause unforeseen harm to humans through altered food products. To protect the consumer, genetically engineered foods are heavily regulated in the United States.

10. Because food and water are basic necessities, they are targets for bioterrorism. The Department of Home-land Security coordinates the efforts of numerous local, state, and federal agencies to protect the United States, which includes safeguarding your food and water sup-ply. A watchful consumer can play a key role in fight-ing bioterrorism by reporting suspicious food items to the proper authorities.

Test Your Knowledge

1. Which of the following is *not* a potential cause of food-borne illness?
   a. parasites
   b. viruses
   c. bacteria
   d. food additives
   e. naturally occurring chemicals and toxins

2. Which group is at greatest risk of contracting a foodborne illness?
   a. a 70-year-old grandmother, a 2-year-old toddler, and a teenage boy
   b. a 35-year-old basketball coach, a 70-year-old grand-mother, and a 45-year-old professor
   c. a 70-year-old grandmother, a 2-year-old toddler, and a middle-aged woman who has diabetes
   d. a 45-year-old professor, a middle-aged woman who has diabetes, and a teenage boy

3. Bacteria need a "host"—a living plant or animal—to survive.
   a. True
   b. False

4. Foodborne pathogens cause the quality of a food, such as its taste, to deteriorate.
   a. True
   b. False

5. For bacteria to multiply, they need nutrients, moisture, the correct temperature, and
   a. sunlight and the proper pH.
   b. the proper pH and plenty of time.
   c. heat and plenty of time.
   d. water and heat.
   e. water and sunlight.

6. The danger zone is the temperature at which bacteria will multiply most rapidly. The temperature range of the dan-ger zone is
   a. 40°F to 140°F.
   b. 45°F to 140°F.
   c. 40°F to 145°F.
   d. 50°F to 150°F.
   e. 50°F to 140°F.

7. There are four critical steps in the food handling process that you need to take to help prevent foodborne illness. These four steps are
   a. cutting, cleaning, chopping, and chilling.
   b. cleaning, combating cross contamination, cutting, and chilling.
   c. clearing, combating cross contamination, cutting, and chilling.
   d. cleaning, combating cross contamination, cooking, and chilling.
   e. cooking, combating cross contamination, cutting, and chilling.

8. Though most bacteria will grow more slowly in a refriger-ator set at 40°F and below, one of the following does not. Which one?
   a. *E. coli* O157:H7
   b. *Salmonella*
   c. Norwalk virus
   d. *Campylobacter*
   e. *Listeria*

9. You are in the supermarket shopping for cereal and find a package of raisin bran that has the USDA Organic seal on its label. You can be assured that this cereal is made with
   a. at least 95 percent organic ingredients.
   b. 70 percent organic ingredients.
   c. 60 percent organic ingredients.
   d. 50 percent organic ingredients.

10. The process of applying biological techniques to a living cell in order to alter its DNA and create a desired trait is called
   a. biology.
   b. biotechnology.
   c. bioterrorism.
   d. biochemistry.

Answers

1. (d) Parasites, viruses, bacteria, and naturally occurring toxins and chemicals can cause foodborne illness. Food additives do not. In fact, they are either approved by the FDA prior to their use or have GRAS or prior-sanctioned status based on a history of safe consumption.

2. (c) Older adults, young children, and individuals with a compromised immune system, such as those with diabetes,

are at a higher risk of contracting foodborne illness. A healthy teenager and a professor (even a tired one around exam time) aren't at an increased risk for foodborne disease.

3. (b) False. Bacteria can grow or multiply on any living or nonliving surface or object.

4. (b) False. Food spoilage bacteria, not foodborne pathogens, cause your food to go "bad," or deteriorate in quality. Foodborne pathogens can be in a food without affecting its taste or quality. Consequently, you should never taste foods that you suspect may be contaminated with foodborne pathogens. Even a small amount of a contaminated food might be enough to make you ill.

5. (b) In addition to nutrients, moisture, and the correct temperature, bacteria also need the proper pH and plenty of time (2 hours or more) to multiply to potentially dangerous levels. Sunlight isn't needed and high heat can actually destroy bacteria. Water is an additional source of moisture.

6. (a) The danger zone is 40°F to 140°F.

7. (d) To prevent foodborne illness, it's important to employ proper food handling strategies when cleaning, combating cross contamination, cooking, and chilling the foods in your meal.

8. (e) The bacterium *Listeria* can multiply at refrigerator temperatures of 40°F or below. *Salmonella* and

Campylobacter bacteria will not. Norwalk virus is a virus, not a bacterium.

9. (a) Only foods made with at least 95 percent organic ingredients can display the USDA Organic seal. If a product is made with at least 70 percent organic ingredients, an organic statement can be made, but the seal cannot be displayed.

10. (b) Biotechnology, through either plant breeding or bioengineering, can alter a cell's genetic makeup to create a desirable trait and genetically modified product. Biology is the study of living organisms. Bioterrorism is the use of biological or chemical agents to frighten, threaten, coerce, injure, and/or kill individuals. Biochemistry studies the chemistry and mechanisms in living cells.

Web Support

- For food safety education, visit www.fightbac.org/main.cfm
- For foodborne illness fact sheets, visit www.fsis.usda.gov/ fact_sheets/Foodborne_Illness_&_Disease_Fact_Sheets/ index.asp
- For more information on organic foods, visit www.ams .usda.gov/nop/indexIE.htm
- For information on biotechnology, visit www.cfsan.fda .gov/~lrd/biotechm.html

15

Hunger at Home and Abroad

1. **Food insecurity** is a nonissue in the United States. **T/F**

2. There is not enough **food** produced in the world to feed everyone. **T/F**

3. Hunger and starvation in the developing world are primarily due to **poverty.** **T/F**

4. People who are obese don't experience **food** insecurity. **T/F**

5. Children are at higher **risk** for hunger than are healthy adults. **T/F**

6. **Elders** who are financially secure can still be at higher risk for hunger. **T/F**

7. Consuming inadequate **nutrients** won't affect mental development. **T/F**

8. Agricultural advances are helping to increase **food production.** **T/F**

9. **Fortifying** foods is an effective strategy to ensure that some populations receive adequate nutrients. **T/F**

10. There is nothing you can do to help **eradicate hunger.** **T/F**

Anna is in her early 30s, single, and has a four-year-old son named Greg. She is going back to school to become a nurse, and attends classes at her local community college during the morning and early afternoon four days a week. To support herself and her son, she works part-time at a local restaurant every evening. Anna has permission to eat one daily meal at the restaurant at a reasonable cost. With her limited income and time constraints, Anna finds herself frequently unable to buy enough food, or prepare nutritious meals, for her and her son to eat.

Greg, meanwhile, is at day care during the day and spends his evenings with his grandmother. Greg's noon meal at the day-care center is well-balanced and nutritious, but his evening intake usually consists of snacks, like potato chips, dips, sodas, and sweets, that his grandmother eats. Greg doesn't eat anything nourishing while he is at his grandmother's house because Anna cannot afford to bring his meals to her mother's. Anna doesn't want to complain about her mother's food habits. Naturally, she is thankful for the free child care.

Do you think Anna is compromising her and her son's nutritional health? What suggestions would you make to Anna to help improve her situation? In this chapter, we'll explore the conditions of hunger and malnutrition, their causes and effects, and steps you can take to help the hungry in your own community, and around the world.

Answers

1. False. Despite living in a wealthy nation, many people in the United States grapple with food insecurity. Turn to page 535 to find out why.
2. False. The world's agricultural producers grow enough food to nourish every man, woman, and child on the planet. The challenge is distributing their products evenly. Learn more on page 535.
3. True. Poverty does play a significant role in hunger around the world. Additional factors like war, overpopulation, and disease can also impact people's access to sufficient food. Find out more on page 535.
4. False. An overweight or obese individual can also be experiencing a chronic shortage of food. To learn more, turn to page 538.
5. True. Children are dependent on the adults around them for adequate food, and therefore are more susceptible to hunger. Children are also more prone to long-term consequences of nutrient deficiencies. Find out more on page 544.
6. True. Older adults may have sufficient funds for food, but may experience hunger due to mobility issues or emotional problems. Learn more on page 545.
7. False. Poor nutrition impacts *both* physical and mental development. Turn to page 546 to learn more.
8. True. Advances in biotechnology and agricultural processes are increasing the amount of food grown per acre of farmland. Find out more on page 548.
9. True. Fortifying foods can provide numerous nutrients that some populations wouldn't otherwise obtain. Learn which foods are being fortified on page 550.
10. False. You can help the hungry in your own backyard by volunteering your time or making a donation to your local food bank. Learn more on page 551.

What Is Hunger and Why Does It Exist?

Being in a state of **hunger** can mean different things to different people, depending on their circumstances. For example, the Ruthford family may live in the United States and experience hunger when Mr. or Mrs. Ruthford suddenly loses a job and has difficulty finding new employment. If the Ruthfords do not receive a supplemental income during this period (such as unemployment insurance), then their lack of income is likely to lead to the household's not being able to buy sufficient food. Meanwhile, the Jonnuni family living in central Africa may experience chronic hunger that leads to malnutrition after being displaced from their home by civil war. Their having to move leads to loss of livelihood and thus an unstable income, again ultimately resulting in lack of sufficient funds to buy food. We'll discuss all of these circumstances in more depth later in this chapter.

Some people may not experience full-fledged hunger, but may periodically deal with **food insecurity,** which is the chronic inability to secure adequate amounts of nutritious food to meet one's needs (Figure 15.1). We talked in an earlier chapter about how decreased mobility and inadequate financial resources sometimes result in food

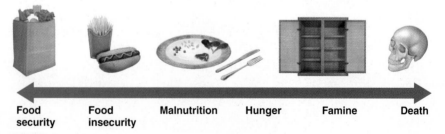

| Food security | Food insecurity | Malnutrition | Hunger | Famine | Death |

Figure 15.1 Spectrum of Hunger, Malnutrition, and Food Insecurity
Food insecurity and hunger are points along the continuum between being food secure and dying from starvation.

A Look at the Numbers:
The State of Hunger Around the World

Hunger is not a local or regional problem, but a global problem. Around the world:

- More than 1.3 billion people live below the international poverty line, earning less than $1.00/day.[1]

- About 1 billion people regularly drink contaminated water.[2]
- More than 840 million people in the world have difficulty obtaining adequate, nutritious food for themselves and their families.[3]

- More than 40 percent of the women in the developing world are anemic, and about 25 percent of the children have insufficient vitamin A reserves.[4]
- Three percent of the world's population is classified as famished.[5]

insecurity among the elderly. Other populations also experience inconsistent access to food due to financial or other circumstances.[1] If a low-income family has to decide between paying the rent and buying groceries, the rent usually comes first. (Figure 15.1).

In 2004, the USDA found that almost 12 percent of households in the United States were food insecure because of a lack of resources. This represented approximately one out of every eight households, or about 13.5 million families. From this group, about one-third, or 4.4 million households, experienced such a severe form of food insecurity that they were classified as "hungry."[2] To put these statistics in perspective, consider this: The combined populations of Nebraska, Kansas, Iowa, Minnesota, and Montana represent approximately 13.5 million people.[3] Because the USDA numbers reflected households, not just individuals, the total number of people affected is even higher.

Worldwide, the 2004 numbers of food insecure people were even more substantial. Over 2 billion people (one-third of the world population) suffered from the consequences of food shortage and nutrient deficiency.[4]

Enough food is available to provide at least 4.3 pounds of food per person per day worldwide.

Hunger and food insecurity exist despite the fact that current global food production exceeds the needs of the population. This sobering reality tells us that adequate agricultural production is not enough to solve the problem. Food distribution and development of human capital must also be improved.[5]

Hunger exists in every country around the world. In the United States, which is a **developed country,** hunger most frequently results from individual economic hardship and poverty. In **developing** and **underdeveloped** countries (see Figure 15.2), poverty is also a factor, but situations such as war, civil unrest, and famine can also come into play.

More people live in developing and underdeveloped countries than in developed countries. Of a global population of 6.5 billion people, approximately 1 billion live in the 50 countries, such as the United States, Canada, Western European nations, and Australia, that are considered the developed world. The other 5.5 billion live in underdeveloped countries, where they have a lower standard of living and lack most goods and services compared with people in developed nations or in countries in transition (such as the former Soviet republics) where daily life is improving.[6] See the boxed feature "A Look at the Numbers: The State of Hunger Around the World."

hunger The physical need for food.

food insecurity The inability to satisfy basic food needs due to lack of financial resources or other problems.

developed country Advanced in industrial capability, technological sophistication, and economic productivity.

developing country Having a relatively low level of industrial capability, technological sophistication, or economic productivity.

underdeveloped country Having a low level of economic productivity and technological sophistication within the contemporary range of possibility.

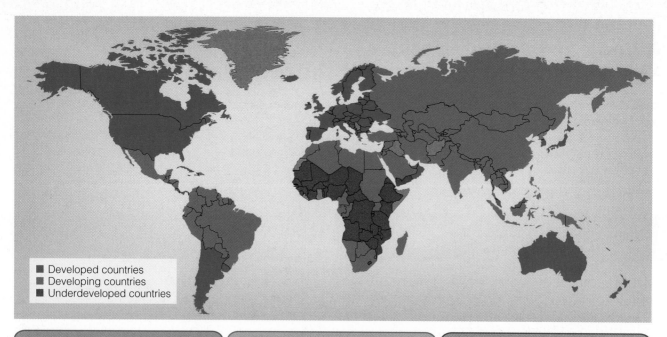

Examples of developed countries	Examples of developing countries	Examples of underdeveloped countries
United States	China	Ethiopia
Canada	India	Sudan
Japan	Mexico	Angola
Australia	Brazil	Haiti
New Zealand	Mongolia	Sierra Leone
Most Western European nations	Saudi Arabia	Yemen

Figure 15.2 Developed, Developing, and Underdeveloped Countries Around the World
Hunger is a global problem. In developed countries, such as the United States, Canada, and the countries of Western Europe, people often experience hunger due to disability, periods of unemployment, and poverty. In underdeveloped countries, like many in central Africa, war, civil conflict, and natural disasters can lead to chronic hunger.

Source: United Nations Development Programme. 2006. *United Nations Human Development Report.* New York: Palgrave Macmillan.

Thanks to agricultural advances, the world's farmers can grow plenty of food. However, distribution problems and other factors keep some people from getting enough to stave off hunger.

The Take-Home Message Hunger is the physical discomfort caused by lack of food. Food insecurity is the lack of access to enough food to live an active, healthy life. Hunger and food insecurity are experienced by people in the United States and around the world. More of the world's population lives in underdeveloped or developing countries than in developed countries.

What Causes Hunger?

We've mentioned poverty and civil war as being causes of hunger for some households. In addition to these, numerous other factors can lead to food insecurity and hunger. Let's take a look at some of the specific causes in the United States, and then in other countries around the world.

Domestic Hunger Is Often Caused by Poverty, Illness, or Lack of Opportunity

People are sometimes surprised to learn that hunger and food insecurity exist in their own communities. Because the United States is the wealthiest country in the world, it seems unlikely that some of its citizens would be unable to visit a local grocery store and purchase a supply of meats and vegetables, or dine out at a local restaurant. However, hunger in the United States is a very real problem, and it is often due to a combination of factors, including poverty and illness (Figure 15.3 on page 538). You may even be at risk for hunger yourself. The Self-Assessment will help you understand your situation.

Poverty

About 12 percent of the United States population lives at or below the **poverty** level, including 16.7 million children.[7] Poverty levels in the United States are defined according to strict guidelines. For a married couple, or a single mother with a child, poverty means a household income below $13,200 per year. A family of four would be impoverished with an income below $20,000.[8]

Factors that lead to poverty include unemployment, lack of resources needed to obtain and keep a job (such as an automobile, a working telephone, and stable address), overpopulation, and poor financial choices. Whatever the cause, poverty is often difficult to overcome. Lack of education or training, poor health, limited or no access to credit, and other obstacles can lock someone into circumstances with few prospects. You may have struggled with money problems and/or unemployment yourself at one time or another. What did you do? Where did you go for assistance?

According to the U.S. Census Bureau, those at the greatest risk of being food insecure and experiencing poverty are people living in households with these life situations[9]:

- Household is headed by a single woman
- Household members are in a minority group
- Household income is below the poverty level
- There are children in the household
- Household is located in the inner city

These circumstances contribute to poverty because they contribute to additional life disadvantages and employment barriers, such as increased exposure to crime, and fewer employment opportunities. Complicated or expensive child-care arrangements add additional stress and can drain an already-tight budget. Single mothers may feel "trapped" with very few employment options or the freedom to explore additional career paths because of obligations to their children. Anna, the single mom you read about at the beginning of the chapter, has a less-than-ideal child-care arrangement but can't afford to change the situation because of her limited employment options. Single mothers with dependent children are more likely to experience times without adequate amounts of food than are families headed by a married couple.[10]

In today's competitive work environment, people without job skills, like Anna, can also have a harder time securing employment than those who are highly educated or who have more specialized skills. Consequently, it's not surprising that an individual's education level affects food insecurity—those without a high school diploma are more than twice as likely to experience food insecurity as are those who have graduated from high school. Even people with good education and employment may experience hunger if they are laid off, are unemployed for an extended period, or are unable to relocate for a job.[11]

poverty Lacking the means to provide for material or comfort needs.

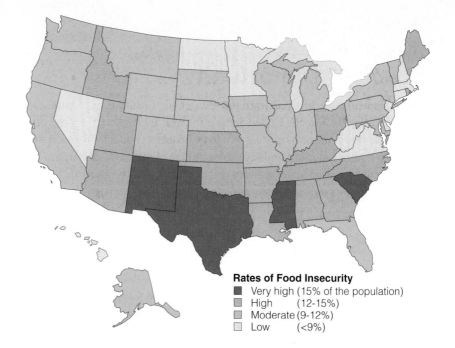

Figure 15.3 Hunger in the United States
Though some areas of the United States have higher rates of food insecurity and/or hunger, these conditions can happen anywhere.

Source: Household Food Security in the United States. 2005. Available at www.ers.usda.gov/Publications/err29.

Rates of Food Insecurity
■ Very high (15% of the population)
■ High   (12-15%)
■ Moderate (9-12%)
□ Low   (<9%)

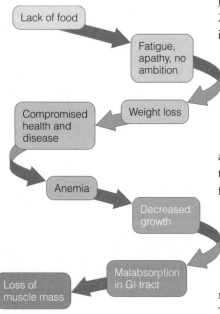

Figure 15.4 Downward Spiral of Poverty and Hunger
Lack of food can lead to numerous other symptoms that compound the problem of hunger.

Lack of food → Fatigue, apathy, no ambition → Weight loss → Compromised health and disease → Anemia → Decreased growth → Malabsorption in GI tract → Loss of muscle mass

"working poor" Individuals or families who are steadily employed but still experience poverty due to low wages or high dependent expenses.

Additionally, people can sometimes be steadily employed in a low-wage full-time job, seasonal jobs, or in several part-time jobs, and still experience hunger. In fact, in 2003, about 7.4 million individuals were classified among the "**working poor.**" That is, they spent at least 27 weeks of the year fully employed, or looking for employment, yet still had incomes below the poverty line.[12] In these households, once the monthly expenses are paid, there is often too little money available to adequately feed everyone. Such individuals may be living "paycheck to paycheck," and an unexpected expense, such as an illness, a hospital stay, or a costly auto repair, can force them and their families to choose between paying the bills or buying food.

Once people fall into poverty and hunger, it can be extremely difficult to get ahead again. Lack of food can lead to physical problems that interfere with a person's ability to earn an adequate income, which leads to continued poverty and lack of adequate food (Figure 15.4).

Some minority groups are at increased risk for poverty and food insecurity. For example, whereas the overall poverty rate for 2005 in the United States was 12 percent for all races, poverty among both African Americans and Hispanics was over 20 percent.[13]

Obesity among those who are food insecure is common. Consider Maria, a mother of two school-aged children, who falls into the "working poor" category. Though she works full-time at a fast-food restaurant in Boston, she has difficulty making ends meet, especially during the winter months, when the cost of heating her one-bedroom apartment cuts into her monthly food budget. Maria eats breakfast and lunch at her job. She purposely fills up on french fries before she leaves work so that she can skip dinner without feeling hungry. With one less mouth to feed at supper, she can stretch her limited household food budget to feed her children and husband. Would it surprise you to learn that Maria is obese? Studies have shown that adults in situations similar to Maria's are at risk for being overweight.[14]

People in these situations often shop for "volume" rather than "value." For example, though fruit punch is nutritionally inferior to orange juice, it is about half the price (Table 15.1). For those living on a limited budget, filling their cupboards with food, even if it is less nutrient-dense food, takes precedence over choosing foods with nutritional value. Table 15.1 illustrates how less nutritious foods can be less expensive,

Table 15.1

Comparing Two Shopping Lists

(Sample prices from one Boston supermarket, 2004)

Meal	Low-Cost Shopping List	Cost	Healthy Shopping List	Cost
Breakfast	Frozen waffles (10)	$1.19	Cereal (10 oz)	$2.69
	Syrup (12 fl oz)	$1.89	Skim milk (1 gallon)	$2.79
	Fruit punch (1 gallon)	$2.78	Orange juice (1 gallon)	$5.32
Snack	Potato chips (1 lb)	$2.46	All natural popcorn (1 lb)	$5.31
Lunch	Bologna (1 lb)	$2.18	Solid white tuna (1 lb)	$3.44
	White bread (1 lb)	$0.68	Whole-wheat bread (1 lb)	$1.73
Dinner	Pasta sauce with meat (1 lb)	$1.16	Chicken breast (1 lb)	$3.29
	Pasta (1 lb)	$0.79	Broccoli (1 lb)	$1.19
Dessert	Ice cream (½ gallon)	$2.39	Strawberries (2 lbs)	$6.98
Total		**$15.52**		**$32.74**

Source: www.projectbread.org/site/DocServer/TheLinkBetweenHungerAndObesity_2004.pdf?docID=104.

and therefore more appealing, to those with severe financial constraints. As you have learned from previous chapters, a diet high in empty calories can increase the risk of obesity as well as malnutrition.

Chronic Disease, Disability, or Mental Illness

Adults who are chronically ill or disabled are less likely to earn a steady income, and therefore, are at risk of having a poor diet. Nutritionally compromised individuals tend to be less productive at work and at increased risk for further illnesses. They may also be unable to obtain proper medical care to improve their health. Missing a day at work to routinely visit a physician due to a chronic illness can significantly reduce a week's paycheck, and thus available funds for food. Many individuals are caught in a vicious cycle of working today so they can eat tomorrow because they don't have the luxury of planning beyond the next day.

Drug and alcohol abuse are also common causes of poverty and hunger, and in extreme situations, **homelessness.** An estimated 85 percent of all homeless men and women in urban areas either abuse alcohol and/or drugs, have a mental illness, or have a combination of these conditions. For these reasons, these individuals will find it difficult to find and keep steady employment and feed themselves. Current estimates predict that 12 million people, or 6.5 percent of all U.S. adults, will experience episodes of homelessness sometime during their lives.[15] Many of these adults bring their children with them into homelessness, and families with children make up about 43 percent of the current homeless population. Fortunately, many individuals find help quickly and reconnect with society within 6 months.

Mental illness is another common cause of poverty, malnutrition, and hunger in the United States. Many mentally ill people, often including the homeless, are difficult to reach, counsel, or help. They may be forced to rely on charity, church meals, or public assistance programs for most of their food. People who suffer from mental illness, such as anxiety disorders, phobias, depression, paranoia, schizophrenia, or some eating disorders, can lose interest in eating or have decreased access to cooking facilities. Depression among mothers, particularly those in low-income families, has been associated with food insecurity in households.[16] Children living in these homes are more likely to be forced to routinely go without food or to routinely rely on unhealthy foods, such as from fast-food restaurants.

In the United States, poor single parents and their children can experience food insecurity due to unemployment, low wages, or other circumstances that lead to financial hardship.

homelessness The state of being homeless. Individuals in this situation are either "crashing" with friends or family members, or residing on the street or in their automobiles.

Global Hunger Is Often Caused by Inequality, Political Conflict, Crop Failure, or Population Overgrowth

Like hunger in the United States, hunger in underdeveloped and developing countries is often caused by a complex set of circumstances. In addition to poverty, situations of war or political unrest, agricultural challenges, or weather disasters can impact food availability and increase food security for large numbers of people, particularly in Asian and African nations (Figure 15.5). As we take a closer look at some of these specific causes of global hunger, think about how these situations compare to the causes of hunger in the United States.

Discrimination and Inequality

Various forms of discrimination, including racial, gender, or ethnic discrimination, contribute to reduced employment, lower educational achievement, and fewer business opportunities in some cultures.[17] The elderly and the disabled may also lack the ability to protect their own interests. Other vulnerable groups include refugees, orphans, migrant workers, and individuals who are illiterate.

> Eighty percent of people who experience hunger around the world make their living from the land, and 50 percent are actually farmers.

In many countries, such as Sudan, Afghanistan, Angola, and Ethiopia, discrimination exists at both the national and local levels. For example, at the national level, control over land and other assets is often inequitable. Paradoxically, there is only a weak relationship between increased crop yield and improved food security. A plentiful crop primarily benefits the landowner, not the farm laborer.[18] To help the farm laborer, either food costs must decrease substantially or the worker's income must increase before food security can be improved.

Figure 15.5 Number and Proportion of Undernourished People
Many developing and underdeveloped nations have high rates of food insecurity.

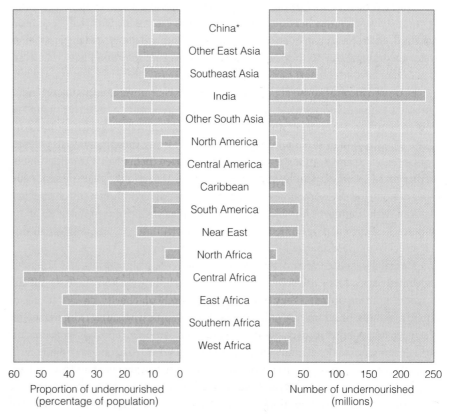

*Including Taiwan Province of China

At the local or household level, access to food is also compromised. In some cultures and within some families, food intake is influenced by factors including gender, control of income, education, birth order, and age.[19]

Gender inequity is a serious problem worldwide. A significant amount of the inequity is due to educational disparity between boys and girls. For example, in sub-Saharan Africa the ratio of boys' to girls' enrollment in primary and secondary schools is eight to one. Accordingly, two-thirds of the almost 900 million illiterate adults in the world are women. Women involved with agriculture produce 50 percent of the world's food, yet they earn only 10 percent of the world's income, and they own less than 1 percent of the world's land. Worldwide, 70 percent of the 1.2 billion individuals who live in extreme poverty are female.[20] In some places, being a woman means being less educated and more likely to experience poverty and hunger.

Political Sanctions and Armed Conflicts

Political **sanctions** and agricultural embargoes create food shortages by decreasing access to agricultural supplies, fuel, or crops. Shortages of these crucial items are more likely to hurt the average citizen than affect government authorities.[21]

Sanctions may be used by one government to postpone or replace military action and force political change on another. Other goals include restoring democracy, condemning the abuse of human rights, and punishing groups that protect terrorists or international criminals. Although the goals of the sanctions are noble, the outcomes often harm innocent people. The sanctions affect "the poor, not the powerful."[22] Higher prices for fuel, food, and other essentials may deprive average citizens of life necessities. Sanctions also contribute to a failing economy by decreasing household income.[23] If the imposed sanction decreases the demand for certain products by blocking their import by other countries, the manufacturers of these products and their workers will experience a drop-off in business, and thus decreased flow of income.

War, armed conflict, and civil unrest cause hunger because of the disruption to agriculture, food distribution, and normal community activities. During the past 15 years, the world has experienced an unprecedented increase in regional conflicts. Examples of this include ethnic grievances, terrorism, and internal struggles for resources in countries such as Angola, Colombia, Ethiopia, Rwanda, Somalia, and Sudan. During wars and regional conflicts, government money is often diverted from nutrition programs and food distribution efforts and redirected toward weapons and military support. Conflicts have caused increases in hunger and overwhelmed the humanitarian safety network. Political turbulence can compromise food distribution programs.[24]

Conflicting political parties and splinter groups have been known to use hunger as a weapon to overpower their enemies.[25] Between 1992 and 2003, wars were a leading cause of hunger, creating more than 35 percent of all food emergencies worldwide. Food emergencies are, increasingly, being imposed by leaders on their own citizens.[26]

Many hunger relief programs work to provide food aid to needy nations. However, successfully delivering the food to those who need it is often challenging.

Crop Failure, Natural Disasters, and Wasteful Agricultural Practices

Natural disasters such as drought, floods, crop diseases, and insects can occur in any country, on any continent. However, the impact of natural disasters is much greater on underdeveloped countries than on developed countries. There are several reasons for this, including the population's inability to relocate away from disaster-prone areas and the inability to make their homes and farms less vulnerable to destructive weather forces. Additionally, the local economy and infrastructure tends to be unstable in underdeveloped areas, so a natural disaster can quickly become devastating.[27]

Drought is the leading cause of severe food shortages in developing and underdeveloped countries. Because of water's essential role in growing crops, water and food security are closely linked. Lack of water is a major cause of **famine** and undernutrition.

sanctions Boycotts or trade embargoes used by one country or international group to apply political pressure on another.

famine A severe shortage of food caused by crop destruction due to weather problems or poor agricultural practices so that the food supply is destroyed or severely diminished. This can also be caused by pestilence and/or war.

This is particularly true in rural areas where people depend on agriculture for both food and income. Similarly, animals require water for their existence. Lack of water forces the animal owners to slaughter part of their herd or sell animals at "distress sales."

In contrast, floods and excessive rain can also destroy food crops, and are major causes of food shortage. For example, in India, more than 70 percent of the annual rainfall occurs during the three months of monsoon season. Farmers contend with water scarcity most of the year and later crop failure due to monsoon rains.[28]

Approximately 33 percent of the world's food supply is destroyed each year by insects.[29] A good example of how destructive insects can be was the locust infestation of 2004, in which locusts devastated pastures and crops in the northern regions of Africa.

The economy of many developing countries is based on agriculture. Therefore, growth in this area is important for economic prosperity.[30] When the population expands and food is in short supply, desperate decisions are often made concerning rangeland, water, forest management, and agricultural production. These choices often threaten the limited resources even more. In particular, any activity that threatens the water supply ultimately hinders food production, decreases rural income, and compromises nutritional well-being.[31] Depletion of natural resources is detrimental because it ultimately reduces the amount of food that can be produced. Specific agricultural practices such as improper land plowing, overgrazing of livestock, aggressive timber harvesting, and misuse of fertilizers, pesticides, and water may increase the yield in the short term, but inhibit production in the long term.[32] Thus, a long-term investment in preserving natural resources could help reduce poverty and hunger.

Irrigation is not a new practice. Evidence shows that Mesopotamians were irrigating crops as early as 5400 BC.

The proper use of irrigation can increase crop yield by 100 to 400 percent. Surprisingly, only 17 percent of the world's land is irrigated, yet this small amount disproportionately produces 40 percent of the world's food.[33] In addition to increased crop yield, irrigation has at least three other favorable outcomes: increased farm income, decreased hunger, and enhanced land values.

Population Overgrowth

The human population is growing by more than 80 million people per year, and the projected world population for 2020 is 7.7 billion people.[34] By 2050, the United Nations estimates, the world population will reach 8 to 12 billion people. Most of this growth is occurring in developing and underdeveloped countries. Whenever rapid population growth occurs in areas that are strained for food production, the resulting **overpopulation** can take a toll on the local people's nutritional status.

One factor contributing to overpopulation is the tendency of many families in the developing world to give birth to multiple children. Because the infant and child death rate is so high, many children do not live to reach adulthood. Therefore, the parents have more children to ensure that some of their offspring will survive to their adolescent years. Several family members are needed to help generate income and support the older family members later in life.[35] This tendency contributes to poverty because the economy cannot sustain the rapid population growth.

The Take-Home Message Causes of hunger in the United States include poverty, unemployment, and illness. Food insecurity and hunger are particularly prevalent in households headed by a single mother, minorities, the poor, those living in inner cities, and among those with unstable or seasonal professions. Causes of hunger in other parts of the world also include poverty, as well as discrimination, political sanctions and conflicts, poor agricultural practices, and overpopulation.

overpopulation When a region has more people than its natural resources can support.

What Are the Effects of Hunger?

The effects of hunger can range from the relatively mild and reversible to the dire and irreversible. Human beings, whether they live in the United States or western Africa, will show symptoms of nutrient deficiencies and emaciation if they go too long without specific vitamins, minerals, or other nutrients. At the extreme, hunger and malnutrition can lead to starvation and death (see Figure 15.1).

Whenever the body experiences fasting, famine, serious disease, or severe malnutrition, it attempts to conserve energy and preserve body tissues. Over an extended period of time, however, the body breaks down its own tissue as a source of energy. This results in the deterioration of internal organs and muscle mass, and the reduction of stored fat. In prolonged starvation, adults can lose up to 50 percent of their body weight. The greatest amount of deterioration occurs in the intestinal tract and the liver. The loss is moderate in the heart and kidneys, and the least damage occurs in the brain and nervous system.[36]

Let's look at some individual effects of chronic malnutrition. We'll begin with the populations most likely to be affected.

Some Populations Are at Higher Risk

Infants, children, and pregnant and lactating women are at higher risk for malnutrition than are healthy adults. Malnourished women are more likely to be ill, have smaller babies, and die at a younger age. Additionally, whenever infant and child mortality rates are high, birth rates are high, which perpetuates the cycle of malnutrition and death.[37]

Pregnant and Lactating Women

As you know from Chapter 12, nutrient requirements increase during pregnancy and lactation. Adequate nutrition during pregnancy greatly enhances the likelihood of having a healthy, full-term, normal-weight infant. Additionally, a healthy pregnancy increases the chances of experiencing successful lactation.

Pregnant women need extra calories and nutrients—in particular, protein, vitamins, and minerals—to support a healthy pregnancy. In general, during the first six months of a pregnancy, most of the extra calories are used to nourish the mother and support her development and fat reserves. During the last three months of a pregnancy, most of the extra calories are needed by the growing infant to supply the infant's reserves of protein, fat, and various micronutrients.[38] Improperly nourished pregnant women often deliver malnourished infants.

Because human milk is the ideal nourishment for infants, women in developing countries are encouraged to breast-feed their babies for optimal nutrition and health. The global recommendation is for women to nurse their babies for the first six months and to continue nursing with supplemental foods into the second year of life.[39] One exception to this is women who are HIV positive, many of whom live in underdeveloped countries. Mothers with HIV risk passing along the virus to their infants through breast milk, and therefore may be encouraged to use formula or a noninfected wet nurse instead of nursing. However, because many HIV-positive women live in poverty and can't afford these alternatives, they may still choose to breast-feed their children. In these cases, the benefits of providing the nutrients in the breast milk outweigh the risks of passing the HIV infection on to the baby.

Infants and Children

Infants are vulnerable to malnutrition because they are growing rapidly, they have high nutrient requirements (per unit of body weight), and they may be cared for by mothers who are malnourished themselves. Because they are dependent on their caregivers to give them adequate breast milk, formula, or foods, they are particularly vulnerable to neglect.

Most mothers can produce enough human milk to support a baby through the first six months. After the age of 6 months, the infant is at increased risk for malnutrition because he starts to need solid food in addition to breast milk. As an infant transitions from an all-breast-milk diet to a diet of breast milk plus solid foods, he may be at risk for improper weaning, which can lead to diminished growth during the first year of life, and the potential for severe malnutrition during the second year of life.[40] Some infants are not given enough food to wean successfully; others do not receive sufficient human milk; and other babies are given foods that are inappropriate because they are too high in protein or difficult to chew.[41]

The risk of malnutrition continues from infancy into early childhood. The two primary reasons that children in this age group experience malnutrition are food shortages within the family and chronic disease. For example, children who are ill have poor appetites and thus their normal hunger sensations are diminished. In some individuals, the problem is worsened by maldigestion and malabsorption, which further increase the loss of nutrients.

Over 40 million people in the world have HIV/AIDS, including 1.5 million children under age 15. Most of these children are born to mothers with HIV or obtain the virus during infancy (via childbirth or human milk intake). In addition, an estimated 13 million children worldwide have become orphaned by AIDS, especially in sub-Saharan Africa and Asia. This situation increases the likelihood of a child's being malnourished.[42] The loss of one or both parents leads to decreased family income, increased incidence of becoming an orphan, and the inability to care for other family members.

The Ill and the Elderly

People who are chronically ill may have malabsorption problems that worsen their nutritional status. Liver and kidney disease can impair the body's ability to process and use some nutrients. Some cancer patients, and most people with AIDS, experience anorexia, which further complicates their treatment and their ability to eat.[43]

As you recall from Chapter 13, older adults need fewer calories as they age due to a decrease in their metabolism and, often, their activity level. However, they have higher requirements for many minerals and vitamins. Older people may be at risk for malnutrition because of a decreased sense of taste and smell, immobility, malabsorption, or chronic illnesses. In particular, some elders, even though they may be food secure, suffer from depression, apathy, or physical difficulties that make moving around a challenge.[44] In addition, loneliness, isolation, missing teeth, confusion, or disinterest in cooking and eating alone also contribute to malnutrition. Many elderly people in developing countries are undernourished, thin, and anemic.

Now that we've discussed who might be at highest risk of malnutrition, let's take a look at the impact an inadequate diet can have on the body.

Impaired Growth and Development

When children do not receive the nutrients they need to grow and to develop properly, they are likely to experience both physical and mental problems, including insufficient weight gain, improper muscle development, lowered resistance to infection,

growth stunting, and impaired brain development (Figure 15.6).[45] Their bodies attempt to compensate for a lack of food by decreasing physical and intellectual growth. Children are more likely to show behavioral, emotional, and academic problems if they come from families that experience hunger and food insufficiency rather than families that do not report hunger experiences.[46] In particular, long-term undernutrition is associated with increased anxiety, irritability, attention problems, and increased prevalence of school absence and tardiness rates.[47]

If hunger persists or occurs at early, crucial times of brain development, cognitive development is impaired.[48] This could result in permanent lower intelligence and hindered learning ability. As a result, malnourished children may have a difficult time completing their basic elementary education. This is particularly unfortunate because school attendance has a measurable impact on earning ability later in life. Research demonstrates that underweight and malnourished children complete fewer years of school compared with well-nourished children.[49]

Even if the children are healthy enough to regularly attend school, hunger and malnutrition impair learning ability. For example, iron deficiency is associated with reduced attention span and decreased memory capacity.[50] Malnourished children also seem to be fatigued, inattentive, and unresponsive to their learning environment. An isolated child who does not respond to or interact with others tends to be neglected by peers, teachers, and adult caregivers.

Globally, an estimated 225 million children experience height stunting because of deficiencies in protein and other nutrients. About 33 percent of children under 5 years of age living in developing countries are physically stunted (decreased height for age), and about 27 percent of these children between 3 and 5 years old are physically **wasted** (decreased weight for age).[51] Growth stunting has also been associated with long-term detrimental effects on physical work capacity and fertility.[52]

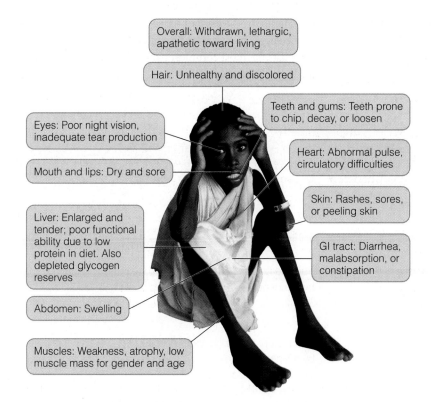

Figure 15.6 Process of Starvation
As hunger persists, physical symptoms set in and lead to further complications.

Overall: Withdrawn, lethargic, apathetic toward living

Hair: Unhealthy and discolored

Eyes: Poor night vision, inadequate tear production

Teeth and gums: Teeth prone to chip, decay, or loosen

Mouth and lips: Dry and sore

Heart: Abnormal pulse, circulatory difficulties

Liver: Enlarged and tender; poor functional ability due to low protein in diet. Also depleted glycogen reserves

Skin: Rashes, sores, or peeling skin

GI tract: Diarrhea, malabsorption, or constipation

Abdomen: Swelling

Muscles: Weakness, atrophy, low muscle mass for gender and age

growth stunting Primarily manifested in early childhood and includes malnutrition during fetal development. Once growth stunting occurs, it is usually permanent. It can affect the vital body organs and cause premature death.

wasting A condition caused by extremely low energy intake from too little food and too little energy. It is sometimes referred to as acute malnutrition. Infections, high energy use, or nutrient loss can cause wasting.

Impaired Immunity and Disease

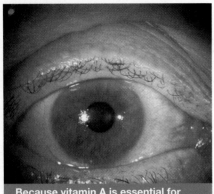

Because vitamin A is essential for vision, a lack of vitamin A causes between 250,000 and 500,000 children to lose their vision each year. Approximately 100 million to 140 million children have depleted vitamin A reserves.

A malnourished individual has a weakened immune system, which increases his or her vulnerability to various infections. Fever, parasitic disease, pneumonia, measles, and malaria are examples of conditions that occur because of weakened immune systems and chronic malnutrition.

The World Health Organization estimates that 60 percent of all childhood deaths in developing countries are associated with chronic hunger and malnutrition. Many of the deaths can be attributed to one of the following five causes or a combination thereof.[53]

1. Diarrhea
2. Acute respiratory infection
3. Measles
4. Malaria
5. Malnutrition

Diarrhea—caused by viruses, parasites, and other harmful microorganisms—can result in severe dehydration (loss of fluids and electrolytes). More than 2 million children die each year from severe dehydration caused by diarrhea. Contaminated water worsens the situation. An ill, malnourished child lacks the physical strength and nutrient reserves to survive a severe case of diarrhea, dehydration, and electrolyte imbalance.[54]

Acute respiratory infection is caused by either viruses or bacteria in the respiratory tract. Pneumonia is the most serious respiratory infection and can be successfully treated with oral antibiotics. Children experiencing measles or malnutrition are especially vulnerable to respiratory problems.[55] Malaria is caused by a parasite-infected mosquito. Table 15.2 summarizes the ramifications of these illnesses.

Vitamin and mineral deficiencies and their resulting diseases are serious concerns for people living in developing countries and in the United States. For example, more than 2 billion people, or greater than one-third of the world's population, live with vitamin A, iron, or iodine deficiency. These micronutrient deficiencies are referred to as "hidden hunger." Table 15.3 lists the most common vitamin and mineral deficiencies observed in those who are malnourished.

Table 15.2
Common Illnesses in Malnourished Children

Disease/Condition	Cause	Effect
Diarrhea	Pathogenic infections	Severe dehydration
Acute respiratory infection	Virus or bacteria	Pneumonia, bronchitis, colds, fast breathing, coughing, and fever
Malaria	Parasite (transmitted by a mosquito)	Flu, weakness, sweating, shivering, shaking, nausea, liver failure, infected red blood cells, kidney failure or bleeding in the kidneys
Measles	Respiratory illness caused by a highly contagious virus, from air-borne droplets (coughing/sneezing)	Pneumonia, brain inflammation, infection, diarrhea, and seizures

Table 15.3

Most Common Vitamin and Mineral Deficiencies Among the Malnourished

Vitamin or Mineral	Effects	Incidence
Vitamin A	Eye disease; blindness	Vitamin A deficiency is the leading cause of preventable blindness in children in developing countries.
Iron	Iron-deficiency anemia	Extremely common worldwide. Anemia is most common among 7- to 12-month-old infants; toddlers and young children (<8 years of age); women of reproductive age; and anyone who has lost large amounts of blood.
Iodine	Goiter, cretinism	Up to 790 million people (13% of the world's population) have some form of iodine deficiency, goiter, or mental impairment caused by lack of iodine.
B vitamins (folic acid, B_{12})	Folic acid: macrocytic anemia	Folic acid deficiency is common among women of reproductive age; individuals with limited diets and reduced vegetable consumption; individuals who abuse alcohol; and obese individuals.
	Vitamin B_{12}: pernicious anemia	B_{12} deficiency is common among elderly men and women (>50 years of age); African-American adults; individuals who have malabsorption syndromes; and persons who practice extreme vegetarianism.

Source: World Health Organization. 1991. Micronutrient Deficiencies. Available at www.who.int/nutrition/topics/micronutrients/en/index.html.

Increased Rates of Infant and Child Mortality

As mentioned, malnutrition is part of a vicious cycle that passes hunger from one generation to the next. Unfortunately, many young women experience undernutrition during their own infancy and childhood. Girls who were low birth weight babies or were undernourished and ill during the first five years of their life may be physically stunted and less able to support a healthy pregnancy when they become adults. The infants born to malnourished women are more likely to be malnourished, experience chronic illness, and have an increased risk of premature death. Premature babies who do reach adulthood are more likely to have malnourished children of their own. Approximately 12 million children younger than 5 years of age die each year in developing countries from preventable causes, such as diarrhea, measles, and malaria mentioned above. Malnutrition is linked to more than half of these childhood deaths.[56]

The Take-Home Message If malnutrition occurs during adulthood, the body will try to conserve nutrients and preserve its own organs, but eventually there could be irreversible organ damage. Pregnant and lactating women, infants and children, and the ill and elderly are particularly vulnerable to the effects of malnutrition. Physical effects of malnutrition include stunted growth, impaired mental development and immunity, and higher likelihood of disease. Other mental effects include anxiety, irritability, and attention problems. Vitamin and mineral deficiency diseases can occur, and the impairment of the immune system increases vulnerability to infectious disease.

How Can We Eradicate Hunger?

Everyone—from children to adults—can help eradicate hunger.

Global hunger harms all of us. When citizens of your community experience hunger, you are likely to see increased disease incidence, low ambition, poverty, and general apathy among the individuals affected. Additionally, from a humanitarian perspective, the painful physical symptoms of hunger are unacceptable when you consider that there is a surplus of food grown each year.

At the local level, individuals, families, churches, and community relief agencies seek out and assist people who have insufficient resources. From providing free food and meals to education and job training, there are numerous ways such organizations can help alleviate hunger. Similarly, corporations and governments can help solve the hunger problem by providing food aid and creating economic opportunity for people who want to improve their life's position. See the feature box "Food Assistance Programs in the United States" for examples of programs that help combat hunger in the United States.

In addition to the human (person-to-person) help provided by people and organizations, technology is also playing a role in alleviating malnutrition. As research and development provide new ways to pack more nutrition into food crops, hunger may be reduced. Enriched crops will ultimately benefit hungry people by providing some of the common nutrients (iron, vitamin A, and iodine) that are in low supply in current crops.

Biotechnology, Better Land Management, and Proper Sanitation

Agriculture plays an important role in the economy and food security of most developing countries. In countries where more than 34 percent of the population is undernourished, almost 70 percent of the people rely on agriculture for their employment.[57] If the producers (land workers and landowners) prosper, the community prospers. For example, when crops are sold, the money generated travels through the community and benefits everyone when goods are traded for services. Thus, agricultural economic growth in rural areas has the potential to have a significant effect on decreasing poverty and hunger.

The latest developments in biotechnology are already helping to reduce hunger in some areas, and new advances are likely to help even more. Some of the most successful new biotechnologies enhance agricultural productivity and improve human nutrition at an affordable cost.

As mentioned in Chapter 14, biotechnology can create crops with increased yields and pest resistance. Some staple crops, such as corn and rice, can be bioengineered to contain nutrients or precursors, like the beta-carotene in "golden rice," to help alleviate common deficiencies. Biotechnology can also improve the quality of plant foods by improving the taste or shelf life of fruits and vegetables.

Better land management, appropriate crop selection, and biotechnology can all help eliminate hunger.

Proper land management and appropriate crop selection can also help increase agricultural production. For example, productive land is frequently used for nonconsumable crops, such as tobacco or flowers, for sale to industrialized nations. Raising edible, nutritious plants such as high-protein beans, vegetables, grains, seeds, nuts,

Food Assistance Programs in the United States

In 2003, the USDA spent over $41.5 billion on numerous food assistance programs to feed Americans in need. Some of the main programs are reviewed below.

- The federally subsidized Food Stamp Program services more than 26 million people.[6] Individuals who are eligible for food stamps can use coupons to purchase specified foods, such as fruit, vegetables, cereals, meats, and dairy products at their local authorized supermarket. (Items such as alcohol, tobacco products, and household items are not covered.) When added to the monthly household income of a needy family, food stamps can help reduce child poverty by an estimated 20 percent or more in the United States.[7]
- The Women, Infants, and Children (WIC) Nutrition Program provides nutritious food to at-risk women and children to supplement their diets. The program also emphasizes nutrition education and offers referrals to health care professionals.
- Under the National School Lunch Program, over 16 million school children receive free or reduced-price lunches each year. A subsidized breakfast is sometimes also available at schools.
- The Summer Food Service Program is a federal program that combines a meal or feeding program with a summer activity program for children. It is available to communities based on income criteria.
- The Child and Adult Care Food Program provides nutritious meals to low-income children and senior adults who receive day care or adult care outside the home. There are income guidelines and specific menu requirements for program participation.
- Congregate meals for the elderly and Meals On Wheels are two programs for the elderly (recall you read about these in Chapter 13) that provide meals at a community site or delivered to the home.
- Additional programs are available for low-income American Indians or for individuals living on a reservation or members of a federally recognized tribe. Some communities also have special feeding or church programs for new immigrants, guest workers, or children of immigrants. College towns often sponsor special programs for international students and their families.

---

or fruit instead of planting export crops like tea, coffee, and cocoa, or raising animal feed for livestock, would help eliminate hunger.[58]

Food security and land access are directly related, even if the land is not irrigated or of the highest quality. Landownership of even a few acres provides incentive for improved land decisions regarding irrigation, crop rotation, land fallowing (plowed, but unplanted, land), and appropriate soil management.[59] Landownership is part of a long-term solution to a very complex problem. However, in the short term, remarkable progress is being made by providing access to land for women and their families for the purpose of growing food and planting gardens.

Most people think providing food is the primary means of reducing hunger, but safe water is equally important. The World Health Organization estimates that 88 percent of all diarrheal illnesses in the world are attributable to inadequate water or sanitation.[60] More than 2.6 billion people (40 percent of the world's population) lack basic sanitation facilities, and over 1 billion people drink unsafe water.[61] The consequences of unsanitary conditions are enormous. Thousands of children become ill or die each month from dehydration-related diseases, and adult workers are less productive when they are ill themselves or caring for family members. Entire communities are often at risk for health problems from drinking contaminated water.

Some innovative solutions are being proposed to alleviate the world's water problems. For example, in some African villages, solar energy is used to thermally purify

Access to clean drinking water is just as important as adequate nutrition for human health.

the water supply. Water is poured into plastic jugs, then the jugs are placed on black-covered roofs and allowed to heat for several hours. If the temperature of the water exceeds 50°C (122°F), it becomes safe to drink. The heat from solar radiation effectively destroys common water-borne bacteria such as cholera, typhoid, and dysentery.[62] This example of technology is available, inexpensive, and accessible in many countries with a warm climate.

Other water sanitation solutions are more complex. They include chlorination of water, irrigation technology, river diversion projects, piped water systems, and the presence of community wells. Sustained economic development for a country or a community depends on a reliable, sanitary water supply.

Fortification of Foods Can Ensure Adequate Intake of Some Nutrients

Food fortification can help alleviate micronutrient deficiencies. Because they are the most commonly deficient, iodine, iron, and vitamin A are the three nutrients most often added to foods. For food fortification to work, the foods chosen to carry these extra nutrients must be a staple in the community's food supply (and therefore eaten often) and consistently available. The food should also be shelf stable and affordable. Rice, cereals, flours, salt, and even sugar are examples of foods that can be successfully fortified.

Because food fortification is inexpensive, yet enormously beneficial, fortification programs are being developed and implemented worldwide. Countries from China and Vietnam to South Africa and Morocco are fortifying foods such as salt, flour, oil, sugar, and soy sauce with iron, iodine, and vitamin A.[63]

Education Is Key

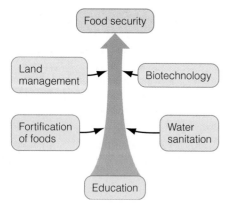

Figure 15.7 Factors in Food Security

Education plays an important role in ensuring food security (see Figure 15.7). Educated people are more likely to have increased economic and career opportunities, and less likely to fall into the trap of poverty. Literacy and education also build self-esteem and self-confidence, two qualities that help people overcome life's challenges.

Education also reduces poverty in other ways. For example, one study found that societies with a more educated population enjoyed:[64]

- Higher earning potential
- Improved sanitation
- More small businesses/rural enterprises
- Lower rates of infant mortality and improved child welfare
- Higher likelihood of technological advancement

The curriculum and format for international education are somewhat different in the developing world than in the developed world. International education ought to focus on literacy, technical knowledge, agricultural skills, horticulture, health education, and the development of natural resources. Agricultural education and increased agricultural production in developing countries help create jobs, which increases income, which then lifts people out of poverty.[65]

Meanwhile, education in the developed world should focus on land management, biotechnology, improved crop yields, boosting nutrient levels within crops, and continued development of drought-resistant and insect-repelling plants.

Hunger among Us (and How You Can Help!)

Food insecurity may be closer than you think. In fact, you may have friends, relatives, or neighbors who've experienced hunger sometime in their lives.

Here's a true account of one young man's experience with hunger.

I grew up poor. My mother, who was single, worked two jobs to support us AND pay her way through college. I was never hungry then, but when I got to college I realized how little wiggle room there can be in a food budget!

It was my first week at LSU in Baton Rouge. We started classes a few days before Labor Day weekend, then got a four-day break before classes really went into full swing the following Monday.

I was enrolled in the 3-squares-a-day university meal plan, but the program was run Monday through Friday only. The dining halls weren't open until after the Labor Day weekend anyway. My mom had given me as much money as she could spare at the time, $20.00. Since I did not have cooking facilities at the dormitory, I was forced to go "out" to eat, and pay for the public transportation to get to places to eat, for the first 3 days of class.

Then the worst happened. My mother was going to pick me up on Friday evening to bring me back home to New Orleans for the weekend. But Friday morning her car got stolen. She had to spend all of her money on the insurance deductible, and didn't have any extra to get me a bus ticket home.

food pantry Community food assistance locations where food is provided to needy individuals and families.

emergency kitchen A kitchen or a commercial food service that prepares for natural disasters, emergencies, or terrorist attacks.

I was stuck on campus, and everyone I knew there had already left for the extended weekend. I had no money, no job to earn money, no food, and the dining halls were closed.

I lived on Celestial Seasonings herbal tea and Ovaltine (made with water, and appropriated from my roommate) for 4 days. I was a wreck because I was so hungry. I couldn't concentrate on anything, I had no patience at all, and I lost over 10 pounds, which I really could not afford to lose since I weighed about 115 pounds at the time.

The good part is that this situation was only temporary for me. I skipped my first class on Monday morning to go eat a mammoth breakfast at the dining hall. But this sort of catch-22 situation can, and does, happen to people everywhere. For most, it isn't a temporary situation at all.

You'd think that this would never happen to someone like me—I'm a middle-class college student. It certainly opened my eyes to what numerous Americans have to face every day. It also made me understand the problems my mother was facing when she was in nursing school when I was little and couldn't chip in at all.

I would have gone to a food bank if I had known about them then. Please, PLEASE volunteer your time at your local shelters, and donate food and money whenever you are able to. The next person that has to go to a food bank might be me, or you!

In addition to the many food assistance programs available, people occasionally also use a **food pantry** or **emergency kitchen** to supplement the various food assistance programs.

America's Second Harvest, the largest hunger-relief organization in the United States, was started to help individuals who are routinely without food. The mission of this organization is to eradicate hunger and ensure that no American goes to bed hungry. America's Second Harvest not only distributes 1.8 billion pounds of excess and donated food and grocery items annually, but it also works to increase public awareness of hunger as well as being an advocate for those who are hungry.

America's Second Harvest has over 200 food banks and a food rescue organization that serves every county in the United States. These food banks collect surplus food from national food companies and other large donors and stores it in a centralized location. Volunteers travel to these food banks and gather and transport these donated foods to local food pantries. Volunteers and workers at a food rescue organization "rescue" prepared food, such as ready-to-eat surplus items from banquets, company and college cafeterias, and restaurants, that would otherwise go to waste. Sometimes food rescue centers are located in the same building as food banks.

When it comes to fighting hunger in America, everyone needs to pitch in. You can help your needy neighbors in three ways: give funds, give food, and/or give time. Funds can be donated online at www.secondharvest.org. Every dollar donated can provide up to four bags of groceries for an individual in need. You can also donate food by hosting a food drive. Finally, you can volunteer your time by helping out in your local community, perhaps tutoring children at a local Kids Cafe, repackaging donated food, stocking shelves at a local food pantry, or transporting food to the hungry.

To find out where you can help, visit the America's Second Harvest website and search for opportunities using the Volunteer Match service (www.secondharvest.org).

The Take-Home Message Eradicating hunger benefits everyone, and local charities and community groups, including faith-based organizations, as well as corporations and governments, can provide aid and organize programs to alleviate hunger. Biotechnology and food fortification are two strategies that work to provide healthier, hardier food crops with additional nutrients. Education of the world's population is also important, along with proper land management and proper crop selection.

Putting It All Together

You've spent most of this course learning about the nutrients you consume in foods and how they work in your body. For most Americans, food choice involves selecting nutrient-dense foods from a variety of food groups that provide sufficient amounts of protein, carbohydrate, fat, vitamins, minerals, and water, without overloading on calories, unhealthy fats, salt, and sugar.

For many individuals worldwide, choosing healthy foods takes a back seat to securing food in the first place. For particularly vulnerable populations, including the poor, children, the sick and elderly, and citizens of impoverished or war-torn areas, having access to enough food and clean water is the most important challenge to overcome.

Two Points of View

Why Does Hunger Exist in the United States?

The United States is among the wealthiest countries in the world, yet millions of Americans experience hunger every day. How can this happen, and what is being done to alleviate the situation? Two experts weigh in.

Jay Bhattacharya, MD, PhD
Assistant Professor of Medicine, Stanford University

Jay Bhattacharya, MD, PhD, serves as a faculty member at Stanford University's Center for Health Policy. In addition to his studies in medicine, Bhattacharya has taught economics. His research focuses on the constraints that vulnerable populations face in making health-related decisions, including decisions about food and nutrition. He recently examined the summer/winter differences in nutritional outcomes for low-income American families.

Q: What is the current state of hunger in the United States? Where is it most prevalent and why?

A: Frankly, malnutrition causing serious medical conditions like kwashiorkor or scurvy is rare or nonexistent in the United

James Weill, JD
President, Food Research and Action Center

Jim Weill, JD, has been president of the Washington, D.C.-based Food Research and Action Center (FRAC) since February 1998. FRAC is a major research, public policy advocacy, and training center that serves an anti-hunger network of hundreds of state and local organizations. Weill has devoted his professional career to issues of hunger, economic security, income support programs, health insurance, and the legal rights of children and the poor.

Q: What is the current state of hunger in the United States? Where is it most prevalent and why?

A: There is far too much hunger in this country, particularly given the wealth that we have. The level of hunger—what

Jay Bhattacharya, MD, PhD, continued

States. There are, nevertheless, a substantial number of American households—about 11 to 12 percent of all households—who report being food insecure, which means that family members have concerns about the adequacy of their food supply. For about 4 percent of all American households, food insecurity results in the occasional or regular physical sensation of hunger. Food insecurity is most prevalent in the South and in regions where poverty rates are highest.

Within those overall numbers, however, noteworthy distinctions exist between different groups. In one study, we found important differences in patterns of poverty, food insecurity, and nutritional quality by race and ethnicity. Poverty appears to have more negative effects on diet quality and nutrient levels among black and Hispanic children than among white children. In contrast, among adults 18 to 64, the effects of poverty are most pronounced for whites and blacks, while food insecurity is associated with poverty in all three groups.

Q: Has the situation improved or worsened in the last 20 years, and why?

A: The best evidence from nationally representative surveys suggests that, like poverty rates, rates of food insecurity have remained roughly flat over the past 20 years.

Q: What is the biggest factor that leaves the United States—the richest country in the world—still grappling with hunger among some of its citizens?

A: Among families that are food insecure, feelings of hunger are most likely when family budgets are constrained by other basic needs, such as when heating bills rise during unexpectedly cold winters. One of my recent research projects, published in the *American Journal of Public Health*, looked at this seasonal issue. My colleagues and I found evidence that poor American families respond to unusually cold weather by spending more on fuel, while spending less on food. This is confirmed by other data sources, which indicate poor families consume fewer calories in winter relative to the rest of the year. Government policies and market changes that permit these families to smooth consumption over such shocks would reduce food insecurity.

A second situation leading to food insecurity involves the timing of food stamp distributions, which typically happens once a month. Instances of food insecurity are most common during the week before a new food stamp distribution. More frequent distributions of food stamps would reduce food insecurity caused by this mechanism.

Q: What can the average person do to improve the state of hunger in the United States?

A: Soup kitchens and other charitable organizations that feed the poor play an important role in reducing food insecurity. Volunteering or otherwise supporting their work would be a constructive way to reduce hunger in the United States.

James Weill, JD, continued

the government calls "food insecurity"— is shocking. According to government figures, we had 38 million people who faced a constant struggle with hunger in 2004. That includes 14 million children.

Hunger tends to be more prevalent when unemployment is high, wages are low, and living costs are higher than wages. It's higher in rural areas and cities, but suburban rates are also too high. The areas with high rates of hunger tend to run from D.C. down the East Coast, across the South and Southwest to the West Coast, and then up the West Coast to Washington state.

Q: Has the situation improved or worsened in the last 20 years, and why?

A: A more significant time frame would be the last 35 years. The situation has improved over that time period. Beginning about 35 years ago, the country focused on hunger in a very intensive bipartisan way. Republicans and Democrats got together and created the food stamp program, the WIC program, and other programs that had a dramatic effect in lowering the hunger numbers. Then those improvements plateaued, and for the last 20 years things haven't gotten consistently better. In the last five years, it's gotten a little worse, with rates going up every year.

One area where we have seen an improvement is with seniors. Two generations ago, seniors were much more likely to be hungry than other people. We've strengthened benefit programs for seniors, and now they are much less likely to be hungry than other people.

Q: What is the biggest factor that leaves the United States—the richest country in the world—still grappling with hunger among some of its citizens?

A: There are two important factors. For the bottom third of the nation, the wages people get at work are too low to support their families. Those wages are not only low, but also getting lower. As of May 2007, the minimum wage hasn't been increased for inflation in nearly a decade. If you earn the minimum wage, because of inflation you earn 20 percent less than you did a decade ago. People aren't getting paid enough at work.

People who aren't earning enough in wages need other kinds of help from the government, like food stamps. But those supports aren't strong enough to lift them out of hunger. And unlike virtually every other wealthy democracy, we're not providing help that lets women work and raise children at the same time, like subsidized child care. That also makes it likely that people won't have enough to live on even though they're working.

Q: What can the average person do to improve the state of hunger in the United States?

A: It's both a public and a private effort. You can support federal and state policies that push up wages for the lowest

(continued)

James Weill, JD, continued

paid workers, increase school meals, increase the number of people getting food stamps, and similar programs. The second thing the average person can do is to support emergency food providers in their community—food banks and soup kitchens. But the private food bank network, while it does great work, cannot do this job alone. The government has to do the lion's share of the work, and it has to do a better job.

Just realizing that there is this widespread struggle against hunger in this country is important. Nutrition students, who may one day work with the poor and hungry in their professions, can weave such awareness into the work they do.

NUTRITION IN THE REAL WORLD

Be a Nutrition Sleuth

The State of Food Insecurity in the United States

Do you know which U.S. states experience the highest rates of hunger and food insecurity? Go to www.aw-bc.com/blake and complete the Nutrition Sleuth activity to find out!

NUTRITION IN THE REAL WORLD

Get Real!

Making Good Decisions to Stay Food Secure

Would you know what to do in a situation where you faced a few days (or more) of being food insecure? Consider the scenarios in the Get Real! activity at www.aw-bc.com/blake and put your nutrition knowledge to work.

The Top Ten Points to Remember

1. Food security is the access by all people at all times to enough food for an active, healthy life. Food insecurity is the inability to secure adequate amounts of nutritious foods to meet one's need

due to lack of available resources. Malnutrition is the state of being under- or overnourished, and hunger leads to undernutrition. Despite abundant food production, many people in the United States and around the world suffer from chronic hunger and malnutrition.

2. Causes of hunger in the United States include poverty, disease or disability, lack of education, and inadequate wages. Mental illness and/or drug and alcohol abuse sometimes lead to homelessness, which in turn often

results in hunger. Individuals who are employed but still fall below the poverty line are sometimes referred to as the "working poor."

3. Political sanctions, armed conflicts, crop failure, wasteful agricultural practices, and overpopulation factor into rates of hunger in many countries. When a country's economy is dependent on agriculture, natural disasters such as drought, floods, diseases, and insect infestations can have a dire impact on food production and levels of hunger.

4. Less than one-sixth of the world's population lives in developed nations that have a high standard of living. Many of the world's residents live in developing or underdeveloped countries and have access to fewer resources. Overpopulation in developing and underdeveloped countries can strain limited food resources.

5. Populations at increased risk of food insecurity and hunger include pregnant and lactating women, infants and children, the ill, and the elderly.

6. Effects of chronic hunger include stunted growth, wasting, impaired immune function, infections, anemia, and nutrient deficiencies. A nutrient deficiency can lead to serious, permanent health damage in both children and adults.

7. Biotechnology and food forti-fication are helling to reduce hunger worldwide by providing larger and more nutrient-dense food crops. Iron, iodine, and vitamin A deficiencies are sometimes labeled as causes of "hidden hunger" because they are less visible than protein or energy deficits. Because deficiencies of these three nutrients are most common, these are the nutrients most often used to fortify foods.

8. Community and faith-based organizations can help end hunger by providing free food and meals and assistance programs to help people overcome poverty and hunger. Corporations and governments can invest in biotechnologies and education programs that provide more nutrient-dense foods and increase economic opportunity.

9. Food assistance programs such as the Food Stamp program, WIC, and the National School Lunch program, among others, provide assistance to those who experience food insecurity in the United States.

10. Local and national organizations, such as America's Second Harvest, provide opportunities and food for those in their communities who are food insecure.

Test Your Knowledge

1. Hunger exists because
   a. there is not enough food produced in the world to feed everyone adequately.
   b. food distribution is uneven, and some people do not have access to enough food.
   c. some people choose not to eat.
   d. None of the above are true.

2. What causes famine?
   a. poverty
   b. lack of education and economic opportunity
   c. war, natural disaster, or civil unrest
   d. using inappropriate farm machinery

3. In which of the following countries does hunger not exist?
   a. the United States and Canada
   b. Brazil and Argentina
   c. France and Germany
   d. Somalia and Ethiopia
   e. none of the above

4. What is the name of the common condition whereby vitamin A, iron, or iodine are consistently deficient in the diet?
   a. concealed concern
   b. hidden hunger
   c. dangerous dilemma
   d. neglected nutrition

5. Which of the following groups are especially vulnerable to illness because of immature immune systems?
   a. infants and young children
   b. adolescents
   c. adult men
   d. adult women

6. Which of the following is a nutritional risk factor for elderly people?
   a. increased metabolic rate
   b. rapid cell growth and turnover
   c. decreased sense of taste and smell
   d. increased energy needs

7. Which of the following is an example of biotechnology being used to help alleviate malnutrition?
   a. fortification of staple food crops
   b. breeding better looking tomatoes
   c. irrigating crops
   d. cloning sheep

8. Who are the "working poor"?
   a. all individuals classified as low income by the United States Department of Labor
   b. all individuals who fall outside the middle-class range of income

c. individuals who are employed but have incomes that fall below the poverty line

d. all minimum wage workers

9. Which nutrients are most likely to be used to fortify food?

   a. vitamins D, E, and K

   b. sodium, potassium, and chloride

   c. magnesium, phosphorus, and sulfur

   d. iron, iodine, and vitamin A

10. Which of the following programs helps decrease hunger in the United States?

    a. Meals On Wheels

    b. soup kitchens

    c. America's Second Harvest

    d. the National School Lunch program

    e. all of the above

Answers

1. (b) Although there is enough food produced to feed everyone in the world, the distribution of the world's food supply is uneven, and people in some parts of the world do not have access to, or cannot afford, adequate food. Everyone needs to eat to survive.

2. (c) Famine is an extreme situation in which food crops cannot be produced because of war, civil unrest, or a natural disaster. Poverty and lack of education are factors that can lead to individual hunger, but don't generally cause crop failure.

3. (e) Whereas the developed nations of North America (the United States and Canada) and Western Europe have a higher standard of living and lower rates of hunger, many people in these countries are still poor, hungry, and/or malnourished. Citizens of the developing countries of South America and the underdeveloped countries of Africa are more likely to be poor and experience hunger.

4. (b) Hidden hunger refers to vitamin A, iron, or iodine deficiency. This condition impacts over 2 billion people in the world.

5. (a) Infants and young children have immature immune systems. Adolescents and adults have stronger (mature), better functioning immune systems.

6. (c) Elderly people sometimes lose interest in food or have a diminished appetite because they cannot enjoy food's smells or tastes. Elderly people have a decreased basal metabolic rate and experience slower cell growth and decreased energy requirements.

7. (a) Fortifying staple foods such as corn and rice is an example of a biotechnological technique that can help reduce malnutrition. Biotechnology is also used to improve the look and hardiness of produce, but this isn't necessarily a nutritional advantage. Crop irrigation has been used for centuries to improve agricultural production but is not considered a method of biotechnology. Cloning food animals is not presently a common practice.

8. (c) The working poor includes individuals who are employed 27 or more weeks of each year, yet still have incomes below the official poverty line.

9. (d) Iron, iodine, and vitamin A are frequently used to fortify food because deficiencies of them are linked to many common and serious illnesses. Many of the other nutrients listed are important, but are not generally incorporated into food fortification programs.

10. (e) While soup kitchens, Meals On Wheels, America's Second Harvest, and the National School Lunch program are funded and run by different groups (including the government and private organizations), they all exist for the same purpose: to help alleviate hunger and food insecurity in the United States.

Web Support

- For more on the state of hunger in the United States and around the world, visit the Bread for the World Institute at www.bread.org
- To learn more about one organization that is fighting global poverty, visit CARE at www.care.org
- To find out how the Food and Agriculture Organization of the United Nations leads international efforts to defeat hunger, visit www.fao.org
- To learn more about the efforts of the Global Health Council, visit the National Council for International Health website at www.ncih.org
- To learn more about an international children's group, visit the UNICEF website at www.unicef.org
- For more about the World Health Organization, visit www.who.org
- To learn more about how biotechnology is improving food production in developing countries, visit www.sustaintech.org

Appendices

Appendix A Nutrient Values of Foods

The following table of nutrient values is taken from the MyDietAnalysis diet analysis software that is available with this text.* The foods in the table are just a fraction of the foods provided in the software. When using the software, you can quickly find foods shown here by entering the MyDietAnalysis code in the search field. Values are obtained from the USDA Nutrient Database for Standard Reference, Release 18. A "0" indicates that nutrient value is determined to be zero; a blank space indicates that nutrient information is not available.

Ener = energy (kilocalories); *Prot* = protein; *Carb* = carbohydrate; Fiber = dietary fiber; *Fat* = total fat; *Mono* = mono-unsaturated fat; *Poly* = polyunsaturated fat; *Sat* = saturated fat; *Chol* = cholesterol; *Calc* = calcium; *Iron* = iron; *Mag* = magnesium; *Phos* = phosphorus; *Sodi* = sodium; *Zinc* = zinc; *Vit A* = vitamin A; *Vit C* = vitamin C; *Thia* = thiamin; *Ribo* = riboflavin; *Niac* = niacin; *Vit B6* = vitamin B$_6$; *Vit B12* = vitamin B$_{12}$; *Vit E* = vitamin E; *Fol* = folate; *Alc* = alcohol.

MDA Code	Food Name	Amt	Wt (g)	Ener (kcal)	Prot (g)	Carb (g)	Fiber (g)	Fat (g)	Mono (g)	Poly (g)
	BEVERAGES									
	Alcoholic									
22831	Beer	12 fl. oz	360	157	1	13		0	0	0
34067	Beer, dark	12 fl. oz	355.5	150	1	13		0	0	0
34053	Beer, light	12 fl. oz	352.9	105	1	5	0	0	0	0
22606	Beer, non	12 fl. oz	352.9	73	1	14	0	0	0	0
22849	Beer, pale ale	12 fl. oz	360.2	179	2	17		0	0	0
22545	Daiquiri, frozen, from	1 ea	36	101	0	26	0	0	0	0
22514	Gin, 80 proof	1 fl. oz	27.8	64	0	0	0	0	0	0
22544	Liqueur, coffee,	1 fl. oz	34.8	107	0	11	0	0	0	0
34085	Martini, prepared from recipe	1 fl. oz	28.2	69	0	1	0	0	0	0
22593	Rum, 80 proof	1 fl. oz	27.8	64	0	0	0	0	0	0
22515	Tequila, 80 proof	1 fl. oz	27.8	64	0	0	0	0	0	0
22594	Vodka, 80 proof	1 fl. oz	27.8	64	0	0	0	0	0	0
22670	Whiskey, 80 proof	1 fl. oz	27.8	64	0	0	0	0	0	0
34084	Wine, cooking	1 tsp	4.9	2	0	0	0	0	0	0
22884	Wine, red, Cabernet Sauvignon	1 fl. oz	29	24	0	1		0	0	0
22876	Wine, red, Pinot Noir	1 fl. oz	29.4	24	0	1		0	0	0
22676	Wine, sake/saki, Japanese	1 fl. oz	29.1	39	0	1	0	0	0	0
22861	Wine, white, Sauvignon Blanc	1 fl. oz	29.3	24	0	1		0	0	0
	Coffee									
20012	Coffee, brewed	1 cup	237	2	0	0	0	0	0	0
20686	Coffee, decaffeinated, brewed	1 cup	236.8	0	0	0	0	0	0	0
20439	Coffee, espresso	1 cup	237	5	0	0	0	0	0	0.2
20972	Coffee, espresso, decaffeinated	1 cup	237	0	0	0	0	0	0	0.2
20091	Coffee, from instant powder, decaffeinated	1 cup	179	4	0	1	0	0	0	0
20023	Coffee, from instant powder	1 cup	238.4	5	0	1	0	0	0	0
20402	Coffee, from mix, French vanilla, sugar & fat free	1 ea	7	25	0	5	0	0		
	Dairy Mixed Drinks and Mixes									
44	Carob flavor, dry mix, prepared w/milk	1 cup	256	192	8	22	1	8	2	0.5
85	Chocolate milk, prepared w/syrup	1 cup	282	254	9	36	1	8	2.1	0.5
46	Hot cocoa, w/aspartame, sodium, vitamin A, prepared w/water	1 cup	256	74	3	14	1	1	0.2	0

*This food composition table has been prepared for Pearson Education, Inc., and is copyrighted by ESHA Research in Salem, Oregon—the developer of the MyDietAnalysis software program.

Contents of Appendix A

Sat (g)	Chol (mg)	Calc (mg)	Iron (mg)	Mag (mg)	Phos (mg)	Pota (mg)	Sodi (mg)	Zinc (mg)	Vit A (RAE)	Vit C (mg)	Thia (mg)	Ribo (mg)	Niac (mg)	Vit B6 (mg)	Vit B12 (µg)	Vit E (mg)	Fol (µg)	Alc (g)
0							9								0			14.3
0							34											17.06
0		11				59	11				0.04	0.04	1.41					14.12
0		19				54	10				0.04	0.07	1.41					1.78
0							9								0			14.7
0		3	0.13	1.1	7	34	123	0.1	0	3.2	0.01	0.01	0	0	0	0	0	0
0		0	0.01	0	1	1	0	0	0	0	0	0	0	0	0	0	0	9.29
0		0	0.02	1	2	10	3	0	0	0	0	0	0.05	0	0	0	0	9.05
0	0	0	0.01	0.6	1	5	1	0	0	0	0	0	0.01	0	0	0	0	9.56
0		0	0.03	0	1	1	0	0	0	0	0	0	0	0	0	0	0	9.29
0		0	0.01	0	1	1	0	0	0	0	0	0	0	0	0	0	0	9.29
0		0	0	0	1	0	0	0	0	0	0	0	0	0	0	0	0	9.29
0		0	0.01	0	1	1	0	0	0	0	0	0	0	0	0	0	0	9.29
0	0	0	0.02	0.5	1	4	31	0	0	0	0	0	0	0	0	0	0	0.16
0																		3.04
0																		3.06
0	0	1	0.03	1.7	2	7	1	0	0	0	0	0	0	0	0	0	0	4.69
0																		3.08
0	0	5	0.02	7.1	7	116	5	0	0	0	0.03	0.18	0.45	0	0	0	4.7	0
0	0	5	0.12	11.8	2	128	5	0	0	0	0	0	0.53	0	0	0	0	0
0.2	0	5	0.31	189.6	17	273	33	0.1	0	0.5	0	0.42	12.34	0	0	0	2.4	0
0.2	0	5	0.31	189.6	17	273	33	0.1	0	0.5	0	0.42	12.34	0	0	0	2.4	0
0	0	5	0.11	9	7	82	4	0	0	0	0	0.03	0.5	0	0	0	0	0
0	0	10	0.1	7.2	7	72	5	0	0	0	0	0	0.56	0	0	0	0	0
0.1	0	4	0.06		16	72	65		0	0								0
4.6	26	251	0.64	25.6	205	335	118	0.9	69	0	0.11	0.45	0.35	0.1	1.08	0.1	12.8	0
4.7	25	251	0.9	50.8	254	409	133	1.2	70	0	0.11	0.47	0.39	0.09	1.07	0.1	14.1	0
0	0	120	1	43.5	179	540	228	0.7	36	0.3	0.05	0.28	0.22	0.06	0.33	0.1	2.6	0

MDA Code	Food Name	Amt	Wt (g)	Ener (kcal)	Prot (g)	Carb (g)	Fiber (g)	Fat (g)	Mono (g)	Poly (g)
195	Hot cocoa, rich chocolate, w/o add sugar, dry pkt	1 ea	15	55	4	8	1	0	0.1	0
172	Hot cocoa, rich chocolate, dry pkt	1 ea	28	112	1	24	1	1	0.3	0.3
21	Hot cocoa, homemade w/milk	1 cup	250	192	9	27	2	6	1.7	0.1
48	Hot cocoa, prep from dry mix with water	1 cup	274.7	151	2	32	1	2	0.5	0
166	Hot cocoa, w/marshmallows, from dry packet	1 ea	28	112	1	24	1	1	0.3	0.4
39	Chocolate flavor, dry mix, prepared w/milk	1 cup	266	226	9	32	1	9	2.2	0.5
34	Chocolate malted milk powder, no added nutrients, prepared w/milk	1 cup	265	225	9	30	1	9	2.2	0.6
29	Natural malt powder, no added nutrients, prepared w/milk	1 cup	265	233	10	27	0	10	2.4	0.7
41	Strawberry flavor, dry mix, prepared w/milk	1 cup	266	234	8	33	0	8	2.4	0.3
	Fruit and Vegetable Beverages and Juices									
2096	Apple cider, from powder, low calorie, with vitamin C	1 cup	240	2	0	1	0	0	0	0
71080	Apple juice, canned or bottled, unsweetened	1 ea	262	123	0	31	0	0	0	0.1
3010	Apple juice, from frozen concentrate, unsweetened	1 cup	239	112	0	28	0	0	0	0.1
3015	Apricot nectar, canned	1 cup	251	141	1	36	2	0	0.1	0
72092	Blackberry juice, canned	0.5 cup	120	46	0	9	0	1	0.1	0.4
20277	Capri Sun All Natural Juice Drink, Fruit Punch	1 ea	210	99	0	26	0	0	0	0
5226	Carrot juice, canned	1 cup	236	94	2	22	2	0	0	0.2
20042	Clam and tomato juice, canned	1 ea	166.1	80	1	18	1	0	0	0
3042	Cranberry juice cocktail	1 cup	252.8	137	0	34	0	0	0	0.1
20115	Cranberry juice cocktail, from frozen concentrate	1 cup	249.6	137	0	35	0	0	0	0
3275	Cranberry-grape drink, bottled	1 cup	244.8	137	0	34	0	0	0	0.1
20024	Fruit punch, canned	1 cup	248	117	0	30	0	0	0	0
20035	Fruit punch, from frozen concentrate	1 cup	247.2	114	0	29	0	0	0	0
20101	Grape drink, canned	1 cup	250.4	153	0	39	0	0	0	0
3165	Grapefruit juice, canned, sweetened	1 cup	250	115	1	28	0	0	0	0.1
3052	Grapefruit juice, canned, unsweetened	1 cup	247	94	1	22	0	0	0	0.1
3053	Grapefruit juice, from frozen concentrate, unsweetened	1 cup	247	101	1	24	0	0	0	0.1
20330	Kool-Aid, sugar free, cherry	1 ea	9.6	28	1	8		0		
20687	Kool-Aid, sugar sweetened, tropical punch	1 ea	17	64	0	16	0	0	0	0
3068	Lemon juice, fresh	1 Tbs	15.2	4	0	1	0	0	0	0
20045	Lemonade flavor drink, from dry mix	1 cup	266	112	0	29	0	0	0	0
20047	Lemonade w/aspartame, low kcal, from dry mix	1 cup	236.8	5	0	1	0	0	0	0
20117	Lemonade, pink, from frozen concentrate	1 cup	247.2	99	0	26	0	0	0	0
20000	Lemonade, white, from frozen concentrate	1 cup	248	131	0	34	0	0	0	0
3072	Lime juice, fresh	1 Tbs	15.4	4	0	1	0	0	0	0
20002	Limeade, from frozen concentrate	1 cup	247.2	104	0	26	0	0	0	0
20070	Orange drink, canned	1 cup	248	122	0	31	0	0	0	0
20004	Orange flavor drink, from dry mix	1 cup	248	122	0	31	0	0	0	0
71108	Orange juice, canned, unsweetened	1 ea	263	110	2	26	1	0	0.1	0.1
3090	Orange juice, fresh	1 cup	248	112	2	26	0	0	0.1	0.1
3091	Orange juice, from frozen concentrate, unsweetened	1 cup	249	112	2	27	0	0	0	0
3170	Orange-grapefruit juice, canned, unsweetened	1 cup	247	106	1	25	0	0	0	0
3095	Papaya nectar, canned	1 cup	250	142	0	36	2	0	0.1	0.1
3200	Passion fruit juice, purple, fresh	1 cup	247	126	1	34	0	0	0	0.1
3101	Peach nectar, canned	1 cup	249	134	1	35	1	0	0	0
20059	Pineapple & grapefruit juice drink, canned	1 cup	250.4	118	1	29	0	0	0	0.1
20025	Pineapple & orange juice drink, canned	1 cup	250.4	125	3	30	0	0	0	0
3120	Pineapple juice, canned, unsweetened	1 cup	250	132	1	32	1	0	0	0.1
3128	Prune juice, canned	1 cup	256	182	2	45	3	0	0.1	0
20340	Tang, from dry mix	2 Tbs	25	92	0	25	0	0	0	0
3140	Tangerine juice, canned, sweetened	1 cup	249	124	1	30	0	0	0	0.1

Sat (g)	Chol (mg)	Calc (mg)	Iron (mg)	Mag (mg)	Phos (mg)	Pota (mg)	Sodi (mg)	Zinc (mg)	Vit A (RAE)	Vit C (mg)	Thia (mg)	Ribo (mg)	Niac (mg)	Vit B6 (mg)	Vit B12 (µg)	Vit E (mg)	Fol (µg)	Alc (g)
0.2	3	123	0.39	27	135	288	142	0.6	0	0.4	0.06	0.22	0.18	0.05	0.45	0	5.8	0
0.3	2	40	0.28	27.4	71	194	102	0.4	0	0	0.03	0.12	0.16	0.03	0.1	0	2	0
3.6	20	262	1.2	57.5	262	492	110	1.6	128	0.5	0.1	0.45	0.33	0.1	1.05	0.1	12.5	0
0.9	3	60	0.47	33	118	269	195	0.6	2	0.5	0.04	0.21	0.22	0.04	0.49	0.2	0	0
0.4	2	41	0.24	16.2	58	142	96	0.2	0	0	0.03	0.12	0.1	0.03	0.12	0	1.1	0
4.9	24	253	0.8	47.9	234	458	154	1.3	70	0.3	0.11	0.48	0.38	0.09	1.06	0.2	13.3	0
5	26	260	0.56	39.8	241	456	159	1.1	70	0.3	0.14	0.49	0.69	0.12	1.11	0.2	23.8	0
5.4	32	310	0.24	45	281	485	209	1.1	87	0.5	0.21	0.64	1.38	0.17	1.22	0.3	21.2	0
5.1	32	293	0.21	31.9	229	370	128	0.9	69	2.4	0.09	0.42	0.22	0.1	0.88	0.3	13.3	0
0	0	26	0.07	2.4	29	0	34	0.1	0	60	0	0	0	0	0	0	0	0
0	0	18	0.97	7.9	18	312	8	0.1	0	2.4	0.06	0.04	0.26	0.08	0	0	0	0
0	0	14	0.62	12	17	301	17	0.1	0	1.4	0.01	0.04	0.09	0.08	0	0	0	0
0	0	18	0.95	12.6	23	286	8	0.2	166	1.5	0.02	0.04	0.65	0.06	0	0.8	2.5	0
0	0	14	0.58	25.2	14	162	1	0.5	10	13.6	0.01	0.02	0.54	0.03	0	1.1	12	0
0	0	2	0.06		2	25	21			2.7								0
0.1	0	57	1.09	33	99	689	68	0.4	2256	20.1	0.22	0.13	0.91	0.51	0	2.7	9.4	0
0	0	13	0.25	8.3	18	148	601	0.1	12	8.3	0.03	0.02	0.38	0.1	0.05	0.2	13.3	0
0	0	8	0.25	2.5	3	35	5	0.1	1	106.9	0	0	0.1	0	0	0.6	0	0
0	0	12	0.22	5	2	35	7	0.1	2	24.7	0.02	0.02	0.03	0.03	0	0	0	0
0.1	0	20	0.02	7.3	10	59	7	0.1	1	78.3	0.02	0.04	0.29	0.07	0	0	2.4	0
0	0	20	0.22	7.4	7	77	94	0	5	73.4	0.01	0.06	0.05	0.03	0	0	2.5	0
0	0	10	0.22	4.9	2	32	10	0	1	108.3	0.02	0.03	0.05	0.01	0	0	2.5	0
0	0	130	0.18	2.5	0	30	40	0.3	0	78.6	0	0.01	0.03	0.01	0	0	0	0
0	0	20	0.9	25	28	405	5	0.1	1	67.2	0.1	0.06	0.8	0.05	0	0.1	25	0
0	0	17	0.49	24.7	27	378	2	0.2	1	72.1	0.1	0.05	0.57	0.05	0	0.1	24.7	0
0	0	20	0.35	27.2	35	336	2	0.1	1	83.2	0.1	0.05	0.54	0.11	0	0.1	9.9	0
		0	0			0	41			53.8						0		0
0	0	28	0.01		13	0	2		0	6								0
0	0	1	0	0.9	1	19	0	0	0	7	0	0	0.02	0.01	0	0	2	0
0	0	29	0.05	2.7	3	3	19	0.1	0	34	0	0	0	0	0	0	0	0
0	0	52	0.09	2.4	24	0	5	0	0	5.9	0	0	0	0	0	0	0	0
0	0	7	0.4	4.9	5	37	7	0.1	0	9.6	0.01	0.05	0.04	0.01	0	0	4.9	0
0	0	10	0.52	5	7	50	7	0.1	0	12.9	0.02	0.07	0.05	0.02	0	0	2.5	0
0	0	2	0.01	1.2	2	18	0	0	0	4.6	0	0	0.02	0.01	0	0	1.5	0
0	0	7	0.02	2.5	2	22	5	0	0	5.9	0	0.01	0.02	0.01	0	0	2.5	0
0	0	12	0.1	5	2	45	7	0	2	142.1	0	0	0.03	0	0	0	5	0
0	0	126	0.02	2.5	47	60	10	0	191	73.2	0	0.22	2.54	0.25	0	0	0	0
0	0	21	1.16	28.9	37	460	5	0.2	24	90.5	0.16	0.07	0.83	0.23	0	0.5	47.3	0
0.1	0	27	0.5	27.3	42	496	2	0.1	25	124	0.22	0.07	0.99	0.1	0	0.1	74.4	0
0	0	22	0.25	24.9	40	473	2	0.1	12	96.9	0.2	0.04	0.5	0.11	0	0.5	109.6	0
0	0	20	1.14	24.7	35	390	7	0.2	15	71.9	0.14	0.07	0.83	0.06	0	0.3	34.6	0
0.1	0	25	0.85	7.5	0	78	12	0.4	45	7.5	0.02	0.01	0.38	0.02	0	0.6	5	0
0	0	10	0.59	42	32	687	15	0.1	89	73.6	0	0.32	3.61	0.12	0	0	17.3	0
0	0	12	0.47	10	15	100	17	0.2	32	13.2	0.01	0.03	0.72	0.02	0	0.7	2.5	0
0	0	18	0.78	15	15	153	35	0.2	0	115.2	0.08	0.04	0.67	0.11	0	0	22.5	0
0	0	13	0.68	15	10	115	8	0.2	3	56.3	0.08	0.05	0.52	0.12	0	0.1	22.5	0
0	0	32	0.78	30	20	325	5	0.3	1	25	0.14	0.05	0.5	0.25	0	0	45	0
0	0	31	3.02	35.8	64	707	10	0.5	0	10.5	0.04	0.18	2.01	0.56	0	0.3	0	0
0	0	92	0.02	0	42	48	2	0		60	0	0.17	2	0.2	0	2	0	0
0	0	45	0.5	19.9	35	443	2	0.1	32	54.8	0.15	0.05	0.25	0.08	0	0.4	12.4	0

MDA Code	Food Name	Amt	Wt (g)	Ener (kcal)	Prot (g)	Carb (g)	Fiber (g)	Fat (g)	Mono (g)	Poly (g)
5397	Tomato juice, canned w/o salt	1 cup	243	41	2	10	1	0	0	0.1
20849	Vegetable and fruit, mixed juice drink	4 oz	113.4	33	0	8	0	0	0	0
20080	Vegetable juice cocktail, canned	1 cup	242	46	2	11	2	0	0	0.1
	Soft Drinks									
20006	Club soda	1 cup	236.8	0	0	0	0	0	0	0
20685	Low-calorie cola, with aspartame, caffeine free	12 fl. oz	355.2	4	0	1	0	0	0	0
20843	Cola, with higher caffeine	12 fl. oz	370	152	0	39	0	0	0	0
20028	Cream soda	1 cup	247.2	126	0	33	0	0	0	0
20008	Ginger ale	1 cup	244	83	0	21	0	0	0	0
20031	Grape soft drink	1 cup	248	107	0	28	0	0	0	0
20032	Lemon-lime soft drink	1 cup	245.6	98	0	25	0	0	0	0
20027	Pepper-type soft drink	1 cup	245.6	101	0	26	0	0	0	0
20009	Root beer	1 cup	246.4	101	0	26	0	0	0	0
	Tea									
20436	Iced tea, lemon flavor	1 cup	240	86	0	22	0	0	0.1	0
20040	Instant tea mix w/lemon flavor, w/saccharin	1 cup	236.8	5	0	1	0	0	0	0
20014	Tea, brewed	1 cup	236.8	2	0	1	0	0	0	0
444	Tea, decaffeinated, brewed	1 cup	236.8	2	0	1	0	0	0	0
20118	Tea, chamomile, brewed	1 cup	236.8	2	0	0	0	0	0	0
20036	Tea, herbal (not chamomile) brewed	1 cup	236.8	2	0	0	0	0	0	0
	Other									
20983	Bean beverage	1 cup	230	78	6	13	0	0	0	0
17	Eggnog	1 cup	254	343	10	34	0	19	5.7	0.9
20440	Rice milk, original	1 cup	244.8	120	0	25	0	2	1.3	0.3
20033	Soy milk	1 cup	245	127	11	12	3	5	0.9	1.9
21070	Soy milk, plain, lite	1 cup	245	90	4	15	2	2	0.5	1
21064	Soy milk, vanilla	1 cup	245	190	11	25	5	5	1	3
20041	Water, tap	1 cup	236.6	0	0	0	0	0	0	0
20076	Wine, nonalcoholic	4 fl-oz	116	7	1	1	0	0	0	0
	BREAKFAST CEREALS									
61211	100% bran (wheat bran & barley)	0.33 cup	29	83	4	23	8	1	0.1	0.3
40095	All-Bran/Kellogg	0.5 cup	30	78	4	22	9	1	0.2	0.6
40295	Apple Cinnamon Cheerios/Gen Mills	0.75 cup	30	118	2	25	1	2	0.7	0.4
40097	Apple Cinnamon Squares Mini-Wheats/Kellogg	0.75 cup	55	182	4	44	5	1	0.3	0.5
40098	Apple Jacks/Kellogg	1 cup	30	117	1	27	1	1	0.2	0.3
40394	Basic 4/Gen Mills	1 cup	55	202	4	42	3	3	1	1.1
40259	Bran Flakes/Kraft, Post	0.75 cup	30	96	3	24	5	1		
40032	Cap'n Crunch/Quaker	0.75 cup	27	108	1	23	1	2	0.3	0.2
40297	Cheerios/Gen Mills	1 cup	30	111	4	22	4	2	0.6	0.7
40414	Cinnamon Grahams/Gen Mills	0.75 cup	30	113	2	26	1	1	0.3	0.3
40126	Cinnamon Toast Crunch/Gen Mills	0.75 cup	30	127	2	24	1	3	1.5	1
40102	Cocoa Krispies/Kellogg	0.75 cup	31	118	2	27	1	1	0.1	0.1
40425	Cocoa Puffs/Gen Mills	1 cup	30	117	1	26	1	1	0.5	0.2
40325	Corn Chex/Gen Mills	1 cup	30	112	2	26	1	0	0.1	0.1
40195	Corn Flakes/Kellogg	1 cup	28	101	2	24	1	0	0	0.1
40089	Corn Grits, instant, plain, prepared/Quaker	1 ea	137	93	2	21	1	0	0	0.1
92416	Corn grits, white, regular/quick, enriched, prepared w/salt	1 cup	242	143	3	31	1	0	0.1	0.2
40206	Corn Pops/Kellogg	1 cup	31	117	1	28	0	0	0.1	0.1
40205	Cracklin' Oat Bran/Kellogg	0.75 cup	55	221	4	39	7	8	2.6	1.6
40179	Cream of Rice, prepared w/salt	1 cup	244	127	2	28	0	0	0.1	0.1

Sat (g)	Chol (mg)	Calc (mg)	Iron (mg)	Mag (mg)	Phos (mg)	Pota (mg)	Sodi (mg)	Zinc (mg)	Vit A (RAE)	Vit C (mg)	Thia (mg)	Ribo (mg)	Niac (mg)	Vit B6 (mg)	Vit B12 (µg)	Vit E (mg)	Fol (µg)	Alc (g)
0	0	24	1.04	26.7	44	556	24	0.4	56	44.5	0.11	0.08	1.64	0.27	0	0.8	48.6	0
0	0	3	0.05	1.1	2	22	24	0	118	36.9	0	0	0.02	0.01	0	1.8	0	0
0	0	27	1.02	26.6	41	467	653	0.5	189	67	0.1	0.07	1.76	0.34	0	0.8	50.8	0
0	0	12	0.02	2.4	0	5	50	0.2	0	0	0	0	0	0	0	0	0	0
0	0	11	0.07	0	36	25	14	0	0	0	0.02	0.08	0	0	0	0	0	0
0	0	7	0.07	0	41	11	15	0	0	0	0	0	0	0	0	0	0	0
0	0	12	0.12	2.5	0	2	30	0.2	0	0	0	0	0	0	0	0	0	0
0	0	7	0.44	2.4	0	2	17	0.1	0	0	0	0	0	0	0	0	0	0
0	0	7	0.2	2.5	0	2	37	0.2	0	0	0	0	0	0	0	0	0	0
0	0	5	0.27	2.5	0	2	22	0.1	0	0	0	0	0.04	0	0	0	0	0
0.2	0	7	0.1	0	27	2	25	0.1	0	0	0	0	0	0	0	0	0	0
0	0	12	0.12	2.5	0	2	32	0.2	0	0	0	0	0	0	0	0	0	0
0.1		7	0	2.4	86	46	50	0.1										0
0	0	7	0.12	2.4	2	31	9	0	0	0	0	0	0.05	0	0	0	0	0
0	0	0	0.05	7.1	2	88	7	0	0	0	0	0.03	0	0	0	0	11.8	0
0	0	0	0.05	7.1	2	88	7	0	0	0	0	0.03	0	0	0	0	11.8	0
0	0	5	0.19	2.4	0	21	2	0.1	2	0	0.02	0.01	0	0	0	0	2.4	0
0	0	5	0.19	2.4	0	21	2	0.1	0	0	0.02	0.01	0	0	0	0	2.4	0
0	0	39	2.88	110.4	212	775	5	0.9	0	0	0.35	0.23	1.43	0.23	0	0.6	138	0
11.3	150	330	0.51	48.3	277	419	137	1.2	116	3.8	0.09	0.48	0.27	0.13	1.14	0.5	2.5	0
0.2	0	20	0.2	9.8	34	69	86	0.2	0	1.2	0.08	0.01	1.91	0.04	0	1.8	90.6	0
0.6	0	93	2.7	61.2	135	304	135	1.1	76	0	0.15	0.12	0.71	0.24	2.99	3.3	39.2	0
0		300	1.44	32	150	160	90			0		0.42						0
0.5		300	2.7	60	250	370	85			0		0.42						0
0	0	5	0	2.4	0	0	5	0	0	0	0	0	0	0	0	0	0	0
0	0	10	0.46	11.6	17	102	8	0.1	0	0	0	0.01	0.12	0.02	0	0	1.2	0
0.1	0	22	8.1	80.6	236	275	121	3.7	225	0	0.37	0.43	5	0.5	0	0.7	100	0
0.2	0	117	5.28	108.6	345	306	73	3.7	158	6	0.68	0.81	4.44	3.6	5.64	0.4	393	0
0.3	0	100	4.5	20.1	65	58	120	3.8	150	6	0.38	0.43	5.01	0.5	1.5	0.2	200.1	0
0.2	0	21	16.23	48.4	154	166	20	1.5	0	0	0.38	0.44	5.01	0.49	1.49	0.3	110	0
0.1	0	8	4.17	16.5	38	36	142	1.5	40	13.8	0.51	0.39	4.62	0.45	1.38	0	93	0
0.4	0	196	3.52	40.2	232	155	316	3	118	0	0.3	0.34	3.9	0.39	1.15	0.6	78.6	0
0.1	0	17	8.1	64.2	152	185	220	1.5		0	0.38	0.43	5	0.5	1.5		99.9	0
0.4	0	4	5.16	15.1	45	54	202	4.3	2	0	0.43	0.48	5.71	0.57	0	0.2	420.1	0
0.4	0	122	10.32	39.3	132	209	213	4.6	150	6	0.54	0.5	5.76	0.66	1.43	0.1	200.1	0
0.2	0	100	4.5	8.1	20	44	237	3.8	150	6	0.38	0.43	5.01	0.5	1.5	0.1	99.9	0
0.5	0	100	4.5	8.1	80	43	206	3.8	150	6	0.38	0.43	5.01	0.5	1.5	0.3	99.9	0
0.6	0	5	6.88	11.8	32	61	197	1.5	153	15	0.46	0.7	4.96	1.02	2.15	0.1	197.5	0
0.2	0	100	4.5	8.1	20	50	171	3.8	0	6	0.38	0.43	5.01	0.5	1.5	0.1	99.9	0
0.1	0	100	9	8.4	22	25	288	3.8	137	6	0.38	0.43	5.01	0.5	1.5	0.1	200.1	0
0.1	0	1	8.12	2.5	10	22	202	0.1	128	6.2	0.6	0.74	6.83	0.96	2.65	0	134.4	0
0	0	8	7.96	9.6	29	38	288	0.2	0	0	0.16	0.19	2.21	0.05	0	0	46.6	0
0.1	0	7	1.45	12.1	27	51	540	0.2	0	0	0.2	0.13	1.75	0.05	0	0	79.9	0
0.1	0	5	1.92	2.2	10	26	120	1.5	143	6	0.37	0.43	4.99	0.5	1.52	0	102	0
3.4	0	33	2.04	67.6	179	248	170	1.7	252	17.6	0.44	0.49	5.67	0.56	1.7	0.5	112.8	0
0	0	7	0.49	7.3	41	49	422	0.4	0	0	0	0	0.98	0.07	0	0	7.3	0

MDA Code	Food Name	Amt	Wt (g)	Ener (kcal)	Prot (g)	Carb (g)	Fiber (g)	Fat (g)	Mono (g)	Poly (g)
40182	Cream of Wheat, instant, prepared w/salt	1 cup	241	149	4	32	1	1	0.1	0.3
40104	Crispix/Kellogg	1 cup	29	109	2	25	0	0	0.1	0.1
40184	Farina, enriched, prepared w/salt	1 cup	233	112	3	24	1	0	0	0.1
40130	Fiber One/Gen Mills	0.5 cup	30	59	2	24	14	1	0.1	0.4
40218	Froot Loops/Kellogg	1 cup	30	118	2	26	1	1	0.1	0.2
40217	Frosted Flakes/Kellogg	0.75 cup	31	114	1	28	1	0	0	0.1
11916	Frosted Mini-Wheats, bite size/Kellogg	1 cup	55	189	6	45	6	1	0.1	0.6
40048	Granola (oats & wheat germ) homemade	0.5 cup	61	299	9	32	5	15	4.7	6.5
40277	Grape-Nuts/Kraft, Post	0.5 cup	58	208	6	47	5	1	0.2	0.7
40292	Honey Bunches of Oats Honey Roasted/Kraft, Post	0.75 cup	30	118	2	25	1	2		
40108	Just Right w/crunchy nuggets/Kellogg	1 cup	55	204	4	46	3	1	0.3	1
40010	Kix/Gen Mills	1.33 cup	30	113	2	26	1	1	0.2	0.2
40011	Life, Plain/Quaker	0.75 cup	32	120	3	25	2	1	0.5	0.5
40197	Low-Fat Granola with Raisins/Kellogg	0.66 cup	55	201	4	44	3	3	1.3	0.5
40300	Lucky Charms/Gen Mills	1 cup	30	114	2	25	2	1	0.3	0.3
40186	Maltex, prepared w/salt	1 cup	249	189	6	39	2	1	0.1	0.4
38659	Nutri-Grain, wheat	1 oz	28.4	102	2	24	2	0	0	0.1
40434	Oat Bran Cereal/Quaker	1.25 cup	57	212	7	43	6	3	0.9	1.2
40430	Oatmeal Squares/Quaker	1 cup	56	212	6	44	4	2	0.8	1
40073	Oatmeal, instant, w/apple & cinnamon, prepared/Quaker	1 ea	149	130	3	26	3	1	0.5	0.4
40018	Puffed Rice/Quaker	1 cup	14	54	1	12	0	0	0	0
40242	Puffed wheat, fortified	1 cup	12	44	2	10	1	0	0	0.1
40209	Raisin Bran/Kellogg	1 cup	61	195	5	47	7	2	0.3	0.9
40343	Reese's Peanut Butter Puffs/Gen Mills	0.75 cup	30	128	2	23	0	3	1.2	0.9
40333	Rice Chex	1.25 cup	31	117	2	27	0	0	0.1	0.1
40210	Rice Krispies/Kellogg	1.25 cup	33	128	2	28	0	0	0.1	0.1
60887	Shredded Wheat, large biscuit	2 ea	37.8	127	4	30	5	1	0.1	0.5
60879	Smart Start/Kellogg	1 cup	50	182	4	43	3	1	0.1	0.4
40211	Special K/Kellogg	1 cup	31	117	7	22	1	0	0.1	0.2
40066	Sweet Crunch/Quisp/Quisp	1 cup	27	109	1	23	1	2	0.3	0.2
40361	Toasted Oatmeal Cereal, Honey Nut/Quaker	1 cup	49	192	4	38	3	4	1.7	1
40413	Toasty O's/Malt-o-Meal	1 cup	30	121	4	22	3	2	0.6	0.7
40382	Total Raisin Bran/Gen Mills	1 cup	55	171	4	41	5	1	0.1	0.5
40021	Total/Gen Mills	0.75 cup	30	97	3	22	3	1	0.1	0.3
40306	Trix/Gen Mills	1 cup	30	117	1	27	1	1	0.6	0.3
40335	Wheat Chex/Gen Mills	1 cup	30	104	3	24	3	1	0.1	0.2
40307	Wheaties/Gen Mills	1 cup	30	106	3	24	3	1	0.3	0.3

DAIRY AND CHEESE

See Fats and Oils for butter.

Dairy

7	Buttermilk, lowfat, cultured	1 cup	245	98	8	12	0	2	0.6	0.1
500	Cream, half & half	2 tbsp	30	39	1	1	0	3	1	0.1
11953	Kefir, peach	1 cup	225	200	7	23	1	7		
218	Milk, 2%, w/added vitamins A & D	1 cup	245	130	8	13	0	5		
21109	Milk, chocolate, reduced fat, w/added calcium	1 cup	250	195	7	30	2	5	1.1	0.2
19	Milk,1% fat, chocolate	1 cup	250	158	8	26	1	2	0.8	0.1
11	Milk, condensed, sweetend, canned	2 tbsp	38.2	123	3	21	0	3	0.9	0.1
23	Milk, goat	1 cup	244	168	9	11	0	10	2.7	0.4
22	Milk, human breast	1 cup	246	172	3	17	0	11	4.1	1.2

Sat (g)	Chol (mg)	Calc (mg)	Iron (mg)	Mag (mg)	Phos (mg)	Pota (mg)	Sodi (mg)	Zinc (mg)	Vit A (RAE)	Vit C (mg)	Thia (mg)	Ribo (mg)	Niac (mg)	Vit B6 (mg)	Vit B12 (µg)	Vit E (mg)	Fol (µg)	Alc (g)
0.1	0	154	11.95	14.5	43	48	364	0.4	559	0	0.56	0.51	7.45	0.74	0	0	149.4	0
0.1	0	4	9.61	7	28	33	222	2.3	262	8.8	1.27	1.25	8.47	0.98	2.09	0	200.1	0
0	0	9	1.16	4.7	28	30	767	0.2	0	0	0.14	0.1	1.14	0.02	0	0	79.2	0
0.1	0	100	4.5	60	150	232	129	3.8	0	6	0.38	0.43	5.01	0.5	1.5	0.2	99.9	0
0.5	0	4	6.12	9.9	34	36	150	5.7	140	14.1	0.68	0.58	7.26	1.1	2.12	0.1	105.6	0
0	0	2	4.5	2.5	11	23	148	0.1	160	6.2	0.37	0.46	5.02	0.5	1.55	0	101.4	0
0.2	0	18	15.4	64.9	162	190	4	1.8	0	0	0.41	0.46	5.39	0.54	1.62	0	107.8	0
2.8	0	48	2.59	106.8	279	328	13	2.5	1	0.7	0.45	0.18	1.29	0.19	0	3.6	50.6	0
0.2	0	20	16.2	58	139	178	354	1.2		0	0.38	0.42	5	0.5	1.5		99.8	0
0.2	0	6	8.1	16.5	48	52	193	0.3		0	0.38	0.43	5	0.5	1.5		99.9	0
0.1	0	14	16.23	34.1	106	121	338	0.9	376	0	0.38	0.44	5.01	0.49	1.49	1.5	102.3	0
0.2	0	150	8.1	8.1	40	35	267	3.8	152	6.3	0.38	0.43	5.01	0.5	1.5	0.1	200.1	0
0.3	0	112	8.95	30.7	133	91	164	4.1	1	0	0.4	0.47	5.5	0.55	0	0.2	416	0
0.6	0	23	1.65	41.2	129	165	135	3.5	206	3.3	0.35	0.38	4.57	1.81	5.5	3.1	369.6	0
0.2	0	100	4.5	15.9	60	57	203	3.8	150	6	0.38	0.43	5.01	0.5	1.5	0.1	200.1	0
0.2	0	22	1.79	57.3	177	266	189	1.9	0	0	0.26	0.1	2.37	0.08	0	1.1	29.9	0
0.1	0	8	0.8	22.2	106	77	193	3.7	0	15.1	0.37	0.43	5	0.51	1.51	7.5	100.3	0
0.5	0	109	17.07	95.8	295	250	207	4	165	6.6	0.41	0.47	5.49	0.55	0	1.4	420.1	0
0.5	0	113	17.07	65.5	206	205	269	4.2	167	6.4	0.39	0.48	5.63	0.55	0	1	439.6	0
0.2	0	110	3.84	28.3	94	109	165	0.6	322	0.3	0.29	0.35	4.07	0.43	0	0.1	84.9	0
0	0	1	0.4	4.2	17	16	1	0.2	0	0	0.06	0.04	0.49	0	0	0	21.6	0
0	0	3	3.8	17.4	43	42	0	0.3	0	0	0.31	0.22	4.24	0.02	0	0	3.8	0
0.3	0	29	4.64	83	259	372	362	1.5	155	0.4	0.39	0.44	5.18	0.52	1.55	0.5	103.7	0
0.6	0	100	4.5	15.9	20	42	166	3.8	144	6	0.38	0.43	5.01	0.5	1.5	0.4	99.9	0
0.1	0	103	9.3	9.3	35	30	292	3.9	155	6.2	0.39	0.44	5.18	0.52	1.55	0	206.8	0
0.1	0	3	2	8.2	33	36	314	0.4	169	7.8	0.73	0.74	7.58	1.08	2.01	0	151.1	0
0.2	0	19	1.12	50.3	140	142	2	1.1	0	3.8	0.1	0.05	1.98	0.44	0	0	16.3	0
0.2	0	17	18	24	80	90	275	15.1	376	15	1.55	1.7	20	2	6	13.5	402.5	0
0.1	0	9	8.37	19.2	68	61	224	0.9	230	21	0.53	0.59	7.13	1.98	6.04	4.7	399.9	0
0.4	0	3	4.96	14.8	45	51	200	4.1	11	2.9	0.41	0.47	5.51	0.55	0	0.2	420.1	0
0.5	0	133	6.81	60.3	166	181	216	5.4	216	1.5	0.59	0.67	7.18	0.72	0	1.8	436.6	0
0.4	0	122	9.81	35.7	112	95	269	4.4	65	6.2	0.47	0.6	5.7	0.72	1.84	0.2	156	0
0.2	0	1000	17.99	40.2	100	354	239	15	150	0	1.5	1.7	20.02	2	5.99	13.5	399.8	0
0.2	0	1104	22.35	39.3	89	103	192	17.5	150	60	2.11	2.42	26.43	2.82	6.42	13.5	477	0
0.2	0	100	4.5	3.6	20	17	194	3.8	150	6	0.38	0.43	5.01	0.5	1.5	0.6	99.9	0
0.1	0	60	8.7	24	90	112	267	2.4	90	3.6	0.22	0.26	3	0.3	0.9	0.2	240	0
0.2	0	0	8.1	32.1	100	111	218	7.5	150	6	0.75	0.85	9.99	1	3	0.2	200.1	0
1.3	10	284	0.12	27	218	370	257	1	17	2.4	0.08	0.38	0.14	0.08	0.54	0.1	12.2	0
2.1	11	32	0.02	3	28	39	12	0.2	29	0.3	0.01	0.04	0.02	0.01	0.1	0.1	0.9	0
6		250	0				110			3.6								0
3		250	0				125			1.2		0.45						0
2.9		485	0.6	35	190	308	165	1	160	0	0.11	1.41	0.41	0.06	0.83	0.1	5	0
1.5	8	288	0.6	32.5	258	425	152	1	146	2.2	0.09	0.41	0.32	0.1	0.85	0	12.5	0
2.1	13	108	0.07	9.9	97	142	49	0.4	28	1	0.03	0.16	0.08	0.02	0.17	0.1	4.2	0
6.5	27	327	0.12	34.2	271	498	122	0.7	139	3.2	0.12	0.34	0.68	0.11	0.17	0.2	2.4	0
4.9	34	79	0.07	7.4	34	125	42	0.4	150	12.3	0.03	0.09	0.44	0.03	0.12	0.2	12.3	0

MDA Code	Food Name	Amt	Wt (g)	Ener (kcal)	Prot (g)	Carb (g)	Fiber (g)	Fat (g)	Mono (g)	Poly (g)
134	Milk, evaporated, w/added vitamin A, canned	2 tbsp	31.5	42	2	3	0	2	0.7	0.1
10	Milk, evaporated, nonfat/skim, canned	2 tbsp	32	25	2	4	0	0	0	0
68	Milk, nonfat, dry w/added vitamin A	0.5 cup	60	217	22	31	0	0	0.1	0
6	Milk, nonfat/skim, w/added vitamin A	1 cup	245	83	8	12	0	0	0.1	0
1	Milk, whole, 3.25%	1 cup	244	146	8	11	0	8	2	0.5
20	Milk, whole, chocolate	1 cup	250	208	8	26	2	8	2.5	0.3
2834	Yogurt, blueberry, fruit on the bottom	1 ea	227	220	9	41	1	2		
2315	Yogurt, blueberry, low fat	1 ea	113	110	3	23	0	1		
72636	Yogurt, blueberry, nonfat	1 ea	227	120	7	21	0	0	0	0
72639	Yogurt, creamy vanilla, nonfat	1 ea	227	120	7	21	0	0	0	0
2001	Yogurt, fruit variety, low fat	1 cup	245	250	11	47	0	3	0.7	0.1
72088	Yogurt, fruit variety, nonfat	1 cup	245	230	11	47	0	0	0.1	0
	Cheese									
1287	American, nonfat slices	1 pce	21.3	32	5	2	0	0		
47855	Blue, 1" cube	1 ea	17.3	61	4	0	0	5	1.3	0.1
47859	Brie, 1" cube	1 ea	17	57	4	0	0	5	1.4	0.1
47861	Camembert, 1" cube	1 ea	17	51	3	0	0	4	1.2	0.1
48333	Cheddar or American, pasteurized processed, fat-free	1 ea	16	24	4	2	0	0	0	0
1440	Cheese, fondue	2 tbsp	26.9	62	4	1	0	4	1	0.1
48288	Cheese food, imitation	1 oz	28.4	40	6	2	0	0	0.1	0
48313	Cheese spread, cream cheese base	1 tbsp	15	44	1	1	0	4	1.2	0.2
13349	Cheez Whiz cheese sauce/Kraft	2 tbsp	33	91	4	3	0	7		
47940	Colby, low fat, 1" cube	1 ea	17.3	30	4	0	0	1	0.4	0
1013	Cottage cheese, creamed, large curd, not packed	0.5 cup	105	108	13	3	0	5	1.3	0.1
1014	Cottage cheese, 2% fat	0.5 cup	113	102	16	4	0	2	0.6	0.1
47867	Cottage cheese, nonfat, small curd, dry	0.5 cup	113	96	20	2	0	0	0.1	0
1015	Cream cheese	2 tbsp	29	101	2	1	0	10	2.9	0.4
1452	Cream cheese, fat free	2 tbsp	29	28	4	2	0	0	0.1	0
1016	Feta, crumbled	0.25 cup	37.5	99	5	2	0	8	1.7	0.2
47874	Fontina, slice, 1oz	1 ea	28.4	110	7	0	0	9	2.5	0.5
1054	Gouda	1 oz	28.4	101	7	1	0	8	2.2	0.2
1442	Mexican, queso anejo, crumbled	0.25 cup	33	123	7	2	0	10	2.8	0.3
47885	Monterey jack, slice	1 ea	28.4	106	7	0	0	9	2.5	0.3
47887	Mozzarella, whole milk, slice	1 ea	34	102	8	1	0	8	2.2	0.3
47892	Muenster, slice	1 ea	28.4	105	7	0	0	9	2.5	0.2
1075	Parmesan, grated	1 tbsp	5	22	2	0	0	1	0.4	0.1
47900	Provolone, slice	1 ea	28.4	100	7	1	0	8	2.1	0.2
1024	Ricotta, part skim	0.25 cup	62	86	7	3	0	5	1.4	0.2
1064	Ricotta, whole milk	0.25 cup	62	108	7	2	0	8	2.2	0.2
	EGGS AND EGG SUBSTITUTES									
19524	Egg substitute, frozen	0.25 cup	60	96	7	2	0	7	1.5	3.7
19525	Egg substitute, liquid	0.25 cup	62.8	53	8	0	0	2	0.6	1
19526	Egg substitute, powdered	1 oz	28.4	126	16	6	0	4	1.5	0.5
19506	Egg, white, raw	1 ea	33.4	17	4	0	0	0	0	0
19509	Egg, whole, fried	1 ea	46	92	6	0	0	7	2.9	1.2
19515	Egg, whole, hard boiled	1 ea	37	57	5	0	0	4	1.5	0.5
19521	Egg, whole, poached	1 ea	37	54	5	0	0	4	1.4	0.5
19516	Egg, whole, scrambled	1 ea	61	101	7	1	0	7	2.9	1.3
19508	Egg, yolk, raw, fresh	1 ea	16.6	53	3	1	0	4	1.9	0.7

Sat (g)	Chol (mg)	Calc (mg)	Iron (mg)	Mag (mg)	Phos (mg)	Pota (mg)	Sodi (mg)	Zinc (mg)	Vit A (RAE)	Vit C (mg)	Thia (mg)	Ribo (mg)	Niac (mg)	Vit B6 (mg)	Vit B12 (µg)	Vit E (mg)	Fol (µg)	Alc (g)
1.4	9	82	0.06	7.6	64	95	33	0.2	35	0.6	0.01	0.1	0.06	0.02	0.05	0.1	2.5	0
0	1	93	0.09	8.6	62	106	37	0.3	38	0.4	0.01	0.1	0.06	0.02	0.08	0	2.9	0
0.3	12	754	0.19	66	581	1076	321	2.4	392	4.1	0.25	0.93	0.57	0.22	2.42	0	30	0
0.1	5	306	0.07	27	247	382	103	1	149	0	0.11	0.45	0.23	0.09	1.3	0	12.2	0
4.6	24	276	0.07	24.4	222	349	98	1	69	0	0.11	0.45	0.26	0.09	1.07	0.1	12.2	0
5.3	30	280	0.6	32.5	252	418	150	1	66	2.2	0.09	0.41	0.31	0.1	0.83	0.1	12.5	0
1		300	0			440	210		0	0								0
0.5		100	0				50		0	0								0
0		350	0	16	200	320	110		0	0		0.25						0
0		350	0	16	200	320	110		0	0		0.25						0
1.7	35	372	0.17	36.8	292	478	142	1.8	25	1.7	0.09	0.44	0.23	0.1	1.15	0	22	0
0.3	5	372	0.17	36.8	292	475	142	1.8	6	1.7	0.1	0.44	0.25	0.1	1.15	0.1	22	0
0.1	3	152	0.01		197	50	276	0.5		0		0.06						0
3.2	13	91	0.05	4	67	44	241	0.5	34	0	0.01	0.07	0.18	0.03	0.21	0	6.2	0
3	17	31	0.08	3.4	32	26	107	0.4	30	0	0.01	0.09	0.06	0.04	0.28	0	11	0
2.6	12	66	0.06	3.4	59	32	143	0.4	41	0	0	0.08	0.11	0.04	0.22	0	10.5	0
0.1	2	110	0.04	5.8	150	46	244	0.5	70	0	0.01	0.08	0.03	0.01	0.18	0	4.3	0
2.3	12	128	0.1	6.2	82	28	36	0.5	29	0	0.01	0.05	0.05	0.01	0.22	0.1	2.2	0.08
0.2	2	157	0.26	9.9	142	95	352	0.9	3	0	0.01	0.14	0.04	0.04	0.35	0	2.3	0
2.7	14	11	0.17	0.9	14	17	101	0.1	51	0	0	0.03	0.14	0.01	0.06	0.1	1.8	0
4.3	25	118	0.06		266	79	541	0.5		0.1		0.08						0
0.8	4	72	0.07	2.8	84	11	106	0.3	10	0	0	0.04	0.01	0.01	0.08	0	1.9	0
3	16	63	0.15	5.2	139	88	425	0.4	46	0	0.02	0.17	0.13	0.07	0.65	0	12.6	0
1.4	9	78	0.18	6.8	171	108	459	0.5	24	0	0.03	0.21	0.16	0.09	0.8	0	14.7	0
0.3	8	36	0.26	4.5	118	36	15	0.5	10	0	0.03	0.16	0.18	0.09	0.94	0	17	0
6.4	32	23	0.35	1.7	30	35	86	0.2	106	0	0	0.06	0.03	0.01	0.12	0.1	3.8	0
0.3	2	54	0.05	4.1	126	47	158	0.3	81	0	0.01	0.05	0.05	0.01	0.16	0	10.7	0
5.6	33	185	0.24	7.1	126	23	418	1.1	47	0	0.06	0.32	0.37	0.16	0.63	0.1	12	0
5.5	33	156	0.07	4	98	18	227	1	74	0	0.01	0.06	0.04	0.02	0.48	0.1	1.7	0
5	32	199	0.07	8.2	155	34	233	1.1	47	0	0.01	0.09	0.02	0.02	0.44	0.1	6	0
6.3	35	224	0.16	9.2	147	29	373	1	18	0	0.01	0.07	0.01	0.02	0.46	0.1	0.3	0
5.4	25	212	0.2	7.7	126	23	152	0.9	56	0	0	0.11	0.03	0.02	0.24	0.1	5.1	0
4.5	27	172	0.15	6.8	120	26	213	1	61	0	0.01	0.1	0.04	0.01	0.78	0.1	2.4	0
5.4	27	204	0.12	7.7	133	38	178	0.8	85	0	0	0.09	0.03	0.02	0.42	0.1	3.4	0
0.9	4	55	0.04	1.9	36	6	76	0.2	6	0	0	0.02	0.01	0	0.11	0	0.5	0
4.9	20	215	0.15	8	141	39	249	0.9	67	0	0.01	0.09	0.04	0.02	0.41	0.1	2.8	0
3.1	19	169	0.27	9.3	113	78	78	0.8	66	0	0.01	0.11	0.05	0.01	0.18	0	8.1	0
5.1	32	128	0.24	6.8	98	65	52	0.7	74	0	0.01	0.12	0.06	0.03	0.21	0.1	7.4	0
1.2	1	44	1.19	9	43	128	119	0.6	7	0.3	0.07	0.23	0.08	0.08	0.2	1	9.6	0
0.4	1	33	1.32	5.7	76	207	111	0.8	11	0	0.07	0.19	0.07	0	0.19	0.2	9.4	0
1.1	162	93	0.9	18.5	136	211	227	0.5	105	0.2	0.06	0.5	0.16	0.04	1	0.4	35.5	0
0	0	2	0.03	3.7	5	54	55	0	0	0	0	0.15	0.04	0	0.03	0	1.3	0
2	210	27	0.91	6	96	68	94	0.6	91	0	0.03	0.24	0.04	0.07	0.64	0.6	23.5	0
1.2	157	18	0.44	3.7	64	47	46	0.4	63	0	0.02	0.19	0.02	0.04	0.41	0.4	16.3	0
1.1	156	20	0.68	4.4	70	49	109	0.4	51	0	0.03	0.18	0.03	0.05	0.47	0.4	17.4	0
2.2	215	43	0.73	7.3	104	84	171	0.6	87	0.1	0.03	0.27	0.05	0.07	0.47	0.5	18.3	0
1.6	205	21	0.45	0.8	65	18	8	0.4	63	0	0.03	0.09	0	0.06	0.32	0.4	24.2	0

MDA Code	Food Name	Amt	Wt (g)	Ener (kcal)	Prot (g)	Carb (g)	Fiber (g)	Fat (g)	Mono (g)	Poly (g)
	FRUIT									
3512	Apples, golden delicious, fresh	1 ea	138	59	0	17	2	0	0	0
71079	Apple w/skin, raw	1 cup	125	65	0	17	3	0	0	0.1
3004	Apple, peeled, raw, medium	1 cup	110	53	0	14	1	0	0	0
3148	Apple, slices, sweetened, canned, drained	0.5 cup	102	68	0	17	2	0	0	0.1
3331	Applesauce, canned, sweetened w/added Vit C	0.5 cup	127.5	97	0	25	2	0	0	0.1
3330	Applesauce, canned, unsweetened w/added Vit C	1 cup	244	105	0	28	3	0	0	0
72101	Apricots, canned, heavy syrup, drained	1 cup	182	151	1	39	5	0	0.1	0
3155	Apricot, frozen, sweetened	0.5 cup	121	119	1	30	3	0	0.1	0
3333	Apricot, peeled, canned in water	0.5 cup	113.5	25	1	6	1	0	0	0
3657	Apricot, raw	1 cup	165	79	2	18	3	1	0.3	0.1
3210	Avocado, California, peeled, raw	1 ea	173	289	3	15	12	27	17	3.1
71082	Banana, peeled, raw	1 ea	81	72	1	19	2	0	0	0.1
3026	Blackberries, raw	0.5 cup	72	31	1	7	4	0	0	0.2
3033	Boysenberries, canned in heavy syrup	0.5 cup	128	113	1	29	3	0	0	0.1
3663	Breadfruit, fresh	1 cup	220	227	2	60	11	1	0.1	0.1
71768	Carambola (starfruit) raw	1 ea	70	22	1	5	2	0	0	0.1
72094	Cherries, maraschino, canned, drained	1 ea	4	7	0	2	0	0	0	0
3403	Cherries, sour, red, canned in heavy syrup	0.5 cup	128	116	1	30	1	0	0	0
3159	Cherries, sour, red, frozen, unsweetened	0.5 cup	77.5	36	1	9	1	0	0.1	0.1
3035	Cherries, sour/tart, red, canned in water	0.5 cup	122	44	1	11	1	0	0	0
3038	Cherries, sweet, canned in heavy syrup	1 cup	253	210	2	54	4	0	0.1	0.1
72103	Cherries, sweet, canned, heavy syrup, drained	1 cup	184	153	1	39	5	0	0.1	0.1
3336	Cherries, sweet, canned in juice	0.5 cup	125	68	1	17	2	0	0	0
71731	Chinese gooseberries, fresh, w/o skin	1 ea	91	56	1	13	3	0	0	0.3
72093	Cranberries, dried, sweetened	0.33 cup	40	123	0	33	2	1	0.1	0.3
3673	Cranberries, raw	1 cup	110	51	0	13	5	0	0	0.1
27019	Cranberry-orange relish, canned	0.25 cup	68.8	122	0	32	0	0	0	0
4900	Currants, red or white, raw	0.25 cup	28	16	0	4	1	0	0	0
3192	Currants, Zante, dried	0.25 cup	36	102	1	27	2	0	0	0.1
3044	Dates, Deglet Noor	5 ea	41.5	117	1	31	3	0	0	0
72111	Dates, medjool	1 ea	24	66	0	18	2	0		
3975	Durian, fresh or frozen	1 ea	602	885	9	163	23	32		
5611	Eggplant, pickled	1 cup	136	67	1	13	3	1	0.1	0.4
3677	Figs, raw	1 ea	40	30	0	8	1	0	0	0.1
3045	Fruit cocktail canned in heavy syrup	1 cup	248	181	1	47	2	0	0	0.1
3164	Fruit cocktail canned in juice	1 cup	237	109	1	28	2	0	0	0
3414	Fruit salad canned in heavy syrup	1 cup	255	186	1	49	3	0	0	0.1
44023	Fruit salad canned in juice	0.5 cup	124.5	62	1	16	1	0	0	0
3203	Gooseberries, raw	0.5 cup	75	33	1	8	3	0	0	0.2
3342	Grapefruit, canned in juice	0.5 cup	124.5	46	1	11	0	0	0	0
71976	Grapefruit, fresh	0.5 ea	154	60	1	16	6	0	0	0
3055	Grapes, Thompson seedless, fresh	0.5 cup	80	55	1	14	1	0	0	0
3634	Guava, raw	0.5 cup	82.5	56	2	12	4	1	0.1	0.3
71732	Kiwifruit (Chinese gooseberry) peeled, raw	1 ea	76	46	1	11	2	0	0	0.2
3252	Kumquat, raw	1 ea	19	13	0	3	1	0	0	0
71979	Lemon, fresh	1 ea	58	15	0	5	1	0	0	0
3071	Limes, peeled, fresh	1 ea	67	20	0	7	2	0	0	0
71743	Lychee (Litchi) shelled, dried	1 ea	2.5	7	0	2	0	0	0	0
71927	Mango, dried	0.33 cup	40	140	0	34	1	0	0	0
3221	Mango, raw	0.5 ea	103.5	67	1	18	2	0	0.1	0.1

Sat (g)	Chol (mg)	Calc (mg)	Iron (mg)	Mag (mg)	Phos (mg)	Pota (mg)	Sodi (mg)	Zinc (mg)	Vit A (RAE)	Vit C (mg)	Thia (mg)	Ribo (mg)	Niac (mg)	Vit B6 (mg)	Vit B12 (µg)	Vit E (mg)	Fol (µg)	Alc (g)
0		4	0.28	5.5		104	3	0.1	2	6.9	0.03	0.01	0.14		0			0
0	0	8	0.15	6.2	14	134	1	0	4	5.7	0.02	0.03	0.11	0.05	0	0.2	3.8	0
0	0	6	0.08	4.4	12	99	0	0.1	2	4.4	0.02	0.03	0.1	0.04	0	0.1	0	0
0.1	0	4	0.23	2	5	69	3	0	3	0.4	0.01	0.01	0.07	0.04	0	0.2	0	0
0	0	5	0.45	3.8	9	78	36	0.1	1	2.2	0.02	0.04	0.24	0.03	0	0.1	1.3	0
0	0	7	0.29	7.3	17	183	5	0.1	2	51.7	0.03	0.06	0.46	0.06	0	0.1	2.4	0
0	0	18	0.55	12.7	24	260	7	0.2	266	5.6	0.04	0.04	0.68	0.1	0	1.6	3.6	0
0	0	12	1.09	10.9	23	277	5	0.1	102	10.9	0.02	0.05	0.97	0.07	0	1.1	2.4	0
0	0	9	0.61	10.2	18	175	12	0.1	103	2	0.02	0.03	0.5	0.06	0	1	2.3	0
0	0	21	0.64	16.5	38	427	2	0.3	158	16.5	0.05	0.07	0.99	0.09	0	1.5	14.8	0
3.7	0	22	1.06	50.2	93	877	14	1.2	12	15.2	0.13	0.25	3.31	0.5	0	3.4	154	0
0.1	0	4	0.21	21.9	18	290	1	0.1	2	7	0.03	0.06	0.54	0.3	0	0.1	16.2	0
0	0	21	0.45	14.4	16	117	1	0.4	8	15.1	0.01	0.02	0.47	0.02	0	0.8	18	0
0	0	23	0.55	14.1	13	115	4	0.2	3	7.9	0.03	0.04	0.29	0.05	0	0.9	43.5	0
0.1	0	37	1.19	55	66	1078	4	0.3	0	63.8	0.24	0.07	1.98	0.22	0	0.2	31	0
0	0	2	0.06	7	8	93	1	0.1	2	24.1	0.01	0.01	0.26	0.01	0	0.1	8.4	0
0	0	2	0.02	0.2	0	1	0	0	0	0	0	0	0	0	0	0	0	0
0	0	13	1.66	7.7	13	119	9	0.1	46	2.6	0.02	0.05	0.22	0.06	0	0.3	10.2	0
0.1	0	10	0.41	7	12	96	1	0.1	34	1.3	0.03	0.03	0.11	0.05	0	0	3.9	0
0	0	13	1.67	7.3	12	120	9	0.1	46	2.6	0.02	0.05	0.22	0.05	0	0.3	9.8	0
0.1	0	23	0.89	22.8	46	367	8	0.3	20	9.1	0.05	0.1	1	0.08	0	0.6	10.1	0
0.1	0	18	0.64	16.6	37	272	6	0.2	22	6.6	0.04	0.08	0.73	0.06	0	0.4	9.2	0
0	0	18	0.72	15	28	164	4	0.1	8	3.1	0.02	0.03	0.51	0.04	0	0.3	5	0
0	7	31	0.28	15.5	31	284	3	0.1	4	84.4	0.02	0.02	0.31	0.06	0	1.3	23	0
0	0	4	0.21	2	3	16	1	0	0	0.1	0	0.01	0.4	0.02	0	0.4	0	0
0	0	9	0.28	6.6	14	94	2	0.1	3	14.6	0.01	0.02	0.11	0.06	0	1.3	1.1	0
0	0	8	0.14	2.8	6	26	22	0.1	3	12.4	0.02	0.01	0.07	0.02	0	0	2.1	0
0	0	9	0.28	3.6	12	77	0	0.1	1	11.5	0.01	0.01	0.03	0.02	0	0	2.2	0
0	0	31	1.17	14.8	45	321	3	0.2	1	1.7	0.06	0.05	0.58	0.11	0	0	3.6	0
0	0	16	0.42	17.8	26	272	1	0.1	0	0.2	0.02	0.03	0.53	0.07	0	0	7.9	0
	0	15	0.22	13	15	167	0	0.1	2	0	0.01	0.01	0.39	0.06			3.6	
		36	2.59	180.6	235	2625	12	1.7	12	119	2.25	1.2	6.47	1.9	0		217	0
0.2	0	34	1.05	8.2	12	16	2277	0.3	4	0	0.07	0.1	0.9	0.19	0	0	27.2	0
0	0	14	0.15	6.8	6	93	0	0.1	3	0.8	0.02	0.02	0.16	0.05	0	0	2.4	0
0	0	15	0.72	12.4	27	218	15	0.2	25	4.7	0.04	0.05	0.93	0.12	0	1	7.4	0
0	0	19	0.5	16.6	33	225	9	0.2	36	6.4	0.03	0.04	0.96	0.12	0	0.9	7.1	0
0	0	15	0.71	12.8	23	204	15	0.2	64	6.1	0.04	0.05	0.88	0.08	0	1	7.6	0
0	0	14	0.31	10	17	144	6	0.2	37	4.1	0.01	0.02	0.44	0.03	0	0.7	3.7	0
0	0	19	0.23	7.5	20	148	1	0.1	11	20.8	0.03	0.03	0.23	0.06	0	0.3	4.5	0
0	0	19	0.26	13.7	15	210	9	0.1	0	42.2	0.04	0.02	0.31	0.02	0	0.1	11.2	0
0		20	0				0		38	66					0			0
0	4	8	0.29	5.6	16	153	2	0.1	2	8.6	0.06	0.06	0.15	0.07	0	0.2	1.6	0
0.2	0	15	0.21	18.2	33	344	2	0.2	26	188.3	0.06	0.03	0.89	0.09	0	0.6	40.4	0
0	0	26	0.24	12.9	26	237	2	0.1	3	70.5	0.02	0.02	0.26	0.05	0	1.1	19	0
0	0	12	0.16	3.8	4	35	2	0	3	8.3	0.01	0.02	0.08	0.01	0	0	3.2	0
0		20	0				5		0	24					0			0
0	3	22	0.4	4	12	68	1	0.1	1	19.5	0.02	0.01	0.13	0.03	0	0.1	5.4	0
0	0	1	0.04	1	5	28	0	0	0	4.6	0	0.01	0.08	0	0	0	0.3	0
0		80	0.36			10	20		25	1.2					0			0
0.1	0	10	0.13	9.3	11	161	2	0	39	28.7	0.06	0.06	0.6	0.14	0	1.2	14.5	0

MDA Code	Food Name	Amt	Wt (g)	Ener (kcal)	Prot (g)	Carb (g)	Fiber (g)	Fat (g)	Mono (g)	Poly (g)
3167	Melon balls (cantaloupe & honeydew) frozen	0.5 cup	86.5	29	1	7	1	0	0	0.1
3642	Melon, cantaloupe, fresh, wedge	1 pce	69	23	1	6	1	0	0	0.1
4488	Melon, casaba, raw	1 pce	164	46	2	11	1	0	0	0.1
3644	Melon, honeydew, fresh	1 ea	1280	461	7	116	10	2	0	0.8
3168	Mixed fruit (prune, apricot & pear) dried	1 oz	28.4	69	1	18	2	0	0.1	0
3216	Nectarine, raw	1 cup	138	61	1	15	2	0	0.1	0.2
27011	Olives, black, pitted, canned	1 ea	3.2	4	0	0	0	0	0.3	0
3228	Orange, California navel, fresh	1 ea	140	69	1	18	3	0	0	0
3230	Orange, Florida, fresh	1 ea	151	69	1	17	4	0	0.1	0.1
3085	Orange, fresh	1 ea	184	86	2	22	4	0	0	0
71990	Orange, mandarin, fresh	1 ea	109	50	1	15	3	0		
3721	Papayas, raw	1 ea	152	59	1	15	3	0	0.1	0
3098	Peach, canned in heavy syrup	1 cup	262	194	1	52	3	0	0.1	0.1
57481	Peach, frozen, sweetened	1 cup	250	235	2	60	4	0	0.1	0.2
3726	Peach, peeled, raw	1 ea	79	31	1	8	1	0	0.1	0.1
3106	Pear, d'anjou, fresh	1 ea	209	121	1	32	6	0	0.1	0.1
3106	Pear, raw	1 ea	209	121	1	32	6	0	0.1	0.1
3194	Persimmon, native, raw	1 ea	25	32	0	8	0	0		
72113	Pineapple, fresh, slice	1 pce	84	38	0	10		0		
3748	Plantain, peeled, cooked	1 cup	200	232	2	62	5	0	0	0.1
3121	Plum, fresh	1 ea	66	30	0	8	1	0	0.1	0
3197	Pomegranates, peeled, raw	1 ea	154	105	1	26	1	0	0.1	0.1
3761	Pummelo, peeled, raw	1 cup	190	72	1	18	2	0		
3263	Quinces, peeled, raw	1 ea	92	52	0	14	2	0	0	0
3766	Raisins, seedless	50 ea	26	78	1	21	1	0	0	0
9758	Raisins, seedless, golden	0.25 cup	40	130	1	31	2	0	0	0
71987	Raspberries, fresh	1 cup	125	50	1	17	8	0	0	0
3133	Rhubarb, frozen, cooked w/sugar	0.5 cup	120	139	0	37	2	0	0	0
3767	Rhubarb, raw	1 ea	51	11	0	2	1	0	0	0.1
3354	Strawberries, frozen, whole, sweetened	0.5 cup	127.5	99	1	27	2	0	0	0.1
3135	Strawberries, halves/slices, raw	1 cup	166	53	1	13	3	0	0.1	0.3
3792	Tamarind, raw	1 cup	120	287	3	75	6	1	0.2	0.1
3717	Tangerine, fresh	1 ea	98	52	1	13	2	0	0.1	0.1
3143	Watermelon, fresh, slice	1 pce	286	86	2	22	1	0	0.1	0.1

GRAIN PRODUCTS, GRAINS, AND FLOURS

Breads, Rolls, Bread Crumbs, and Croutons

MDA Code	Food Name	Amt	Wt (g)	Ener (kcal)	Prot (g)	Carb (g)	Fiber (g)	Fat (g)	Mono (g)	Poly (g)
71170	Bagel, cinnamon-raisin	1 ea	26	71	3	14	1	0	0	0.2
71167	Bagel, egg	1 ea	26	72	3	14	1	1	0.1	0.2
42744	Bagel, blueberry	1 ea	102	264	11	53	2	2	0.4	0.5
71176	Bagel, oatbran	1 ea	26	66	3	14	1	0	0.1	0.1
71152	Bagel, plain/onion/poppy/sesame, enriched	1 ea	26	67	3	13	1	0	0.1	0.2
42039	Banana bread, homemade w/margarine, slice	1 pce	60	196	3	33	1	6	2.7	1.9
42433	Biscuit, w/butter	1 ea	82	280	5	27	0	17		
47709	Biscuit, buttermilk, refrigerated dough	1 ea	64	154	5	30		1	0.6	0.3
42111	Biscuit, mixed grain, refrigerated dough	1 ea	44	116	3	21		2	1.3	0.4
71192	Biscuit, Plain or Buttermilk, refrig dough, baked, reduced fat	1 ea	21	63	2	12	0	1	0.6	0.2
42004	Bread crumbs, dry, plain, grated	1 tbsp	6.8	27	1	5	0	0	0.1	0.1
42144	Bread crumbs, dry, grated, seasoned	1 tbsp	7.5	29	1	5	0	0	0.1	0.2
49144	Bread, crusty Italian w/garlic	1 pce	50	186	4	21		10	3.9	1.8
42090	Bread, egg, slice	1 pce	40	113	4	19	1	2	0.9	0.4

Sat (g)	Chol (mg)	Calc (mg)	Iron (mg)	Mag (mg)	Phos (mg)	Pota (mg)	Sodi (mg)	Zinc (mg)	Vit A (RAE)	Vit C (mg)	Thia (mg)	Ribo (mg)	Niac (mg)	Vit B6 (mg)	Vit B12 (µg)	Vit E (mg)	Fol (µg)	Alc (g)
0.1	0	9	0.25	12.1	10	242	27	0.1	77	5.4	0.14	0.02	0.55	0.09	0	0.1	22.5	0
0	5	6	0.14	8.3	10	184	11	0.1	117	25.3	0.03	0.01	0.51	0.05	0	0	15	0
0	0	18	0.56	18	8	298	15	0.1	0	35.8	0.02	0.05	0.38	0.27	0	0.1	13.1	0
0.5		77	2.18	128	141	2918	230	1.2	38	230	0.49	0.15	5.35	1.13	0	0.3	243	0
0	0	11	0.77	11.1	22	226	5	0.1	35	1.1	0.01	0.04	0.55	0.05	0	0.2	1.1	0
0	0	8	0.39	12.4	36	277	0	0.2	23	7.5	0.05	0.04	1.55	0.03	0	1.1	6.9	0
0	0	3	0.11	0.1	0	0	28	0	1	0	0	0	0	0	0	0.1	0	0
0	12	60	0.18	15.4	32	232	1	0.1	17	82.7	0.1	0.07	0.6	0.11	0	0.2	48	0
0		65	0.14	15.1	18	255	0	0.1	17	68	0.15	0.06	0.6	0.08	0	0.3	26	0
0		74	0.18	18.4	26	333	0	0.1	20	97.9	0.16	0.07	0.52	0.11	0	0.3	55	0
0		40	0				0		0	30					0			0
0.1	0	36	0.15	15.2	8	391	5	0.1	84	93.9	0.04	0.05	0.51	0.03	0	1.1	57.8	0
0	0	8	0.71	13.1	29	241	16	0.2	45	7.3	0.03	0.06	1.61	0.05	0	1.3	7.9	0
0	0	8	0.93	12.5	28	325	15	0.1	35	235.5	0.03	0.09	1.63	0.04	0	1.6	7.5	0
0	0	5	0.2	7.1	16	150	0	0.1	13	5.2	0.02	0.02	0.64	0.02	0	0.6	3.2	0
0	11	19	0.36	14.6	23	249	2	0.2	2	8.8	0.03	0.05	0.33	0.06	0	0.3	15	0
0	0	19	0.36	14.6	23	249	2	0.2	2	8.8	0.03	0.05	0.33	0.06	0	0.3	14.6	0
	0	7	0.62		6	78	0			16.5					0	0.2	2	0
	5	11	0.21	10.1	8	105	1	0.1	3	14.2	0.07	0.02	0.39	0.09			9.2	
0.1	0	4	1.16	64	56	930	10	0.3	90	21.8	0.09	0.1	1.51	0.48	0	0.3	52	0
0		4	0.11	4.6	11	104	0	0.1	11	6.3	0.02	0.02	0.28	0.02	0	0.2	3.3	0
0.1	0	5	0.46	4.6	12	399	5	0.2	8	9.4	0.05	0.05	0.46	0.16	0	0.9	9.2	0
	0	8	0.21	11.4	32	410	2	0.2	1	115.9	0.06	0.05	0.42	0.07	0	0.2	49.4	0
0	0	10	0.64	7.4	16	181	4	0	2	13.8	0.02	0.03	0.18	0.04	0	0.5	2.8	0
0	0	13	0.49	8.3	26	195	3	0.1	0	0.6	0.03	0.03	0.2	0.05	0	0	1.3	0
0		20	1.08				10		0	0								0
0		20	0.36				0		0	24					0			0
0	0	174	0.25	14.4	10	115	1	0.1	5	4	0.02	0.03	0.24	0.02	0	0.3	6	0
0	0	44	0.11	6.1	7	147	2	0.1	3	4.1	0.01	0.02	0.15	0.01	0	0.2	3.6	0
0	0	14	0.6	7.6	15	125	1	0.1	1	50.4	0.02	0.1	0.37	0.04	0	0.3	5.1	0
0	0	27	0.7	21.6	40	254	2	0.2	2	97.6	0.04	0.04	0.64	0.08	0	0.5	39.8	0
0.3	0	89	3.36	110.4	136	754	34	0.1	2	4.2	0.51	0.18	2.33	0.08	0	0.1	16.8	0
0	10	36	0.15	11.8	20	163	2	0.1	33	26.2	0.06	0.04	0.37	0.08	0	0.2	16	0
0	12	20	0.69	28.6	31	320	3	0.3	80	23.2	0.09	0.06	0.51	0.13	0	0.1	8.6	0
0.1	0	5	0.99	7.3	26	38	84	0.3	6	0.2	0.1	0.07	0.8	0.02	0	0.1	28.9	0
0.1	6	3	1.03	6.5	22	18	131	0.2	9	0.2	0.14	0.06	0.9	0.02	0.04	0	22.9	0
0.3	0	57	1.84			158	427		0	0	0.27	0.2	4.08	0.06	0		75.5	0
0	0	3	0.8	8.1	29	30	132	0.2	0	0.1	0.09	0.09	0.77	0.01	0	0.1	25.5	0
0.1	0	23	1.57	5.7	23	20	116	0.5	0	0.3	0.16	0.07	1.03	0.02	0	0	37.7	0
1.3	26	13	0.84	8.4	35	80	181	0.2	64	1	0.1	0.12	0.87	0.09	0.06	1.1	19.8	0
4	0	40	0			130	780			0	0.23	0.14	3					0
0.3			1.55				547											0
0.6	0	7	1.21	13.2	104	201	295	0.3	0	0	0.17	0.09	1.5	0.03	0	0.4	36.5	0
0.3	0	4	0.65	3.6	98	39	305	0.1	0	0	0.09	0.05	0.72	0.01	0	0	17.4	0
0.1	0	12	0.33	2.9	11	13	50	0.1	0	0	0.07	0.03	0.45	0.01	0.02	0	7.3	0
0.1	0	14	0.37	3.4	13	17	132	0.1	1	0.2	0.07	0.03	0.46	0.01	0	0	8.9	0
2.4	6		1.18				200											0
0.6	20	37	1.22	7.6	42	46	197	0.3	25	0	0.18	0.17	1.94	0.03	0.04	0.1	42	0

MDA Code	Food Name	Amt	Wt (g)	Ener (kcal)	Prot (g)	Carb (g)	Fiber (g)	Fat (g)	Mono (g)	Poly (g)
70964	Bread, garlic, frozen/Campione	1 pce	28	101	2	12	1	5		
42119	Bread, Irish soda, homemade, prepared from recipe	1 pce	28	81	2	16	1	1	0.6	0.4
42069	Bread, oatbran	1 pce	30	71	3	12	1	1	0.5	0.5
42076	Bread, oatbran, reduced kcal	1 pce	23	46	2	9	3	1	0.2	0.4
42136	Bread, wheat bran	1 pce	36	89	3	17	1	1	0.6	0.2
42599	Bread, wheat germ	1 pce	28	73	3	14	1	1	0.4	0.2
42095	Bread, wheat, reduced kcal	1 pce	23	46	2	10	3	1	0.1	0.2
71247	Bread, white, commercially prepared, crumbs/cubes/slices	1 pce	9	24	1	5	0	0	0.1	0.1
42084	Bread, white, reduced kcal	1 pce	23	48	2	10	2	1	0.2	0.1
71259	Bread sticks, plain	1 ea	5	21	1	3	0	0	0.2	0.2
26561	Buns, hamburger, Wonder	1 ea	43	117	3	22	1	2	0.4	0.9
42021	Hamburger/hot dog bun, plain	1 ea	43	120	4	21	1	2	0.5	0.8
71364	Hamburger/hot dog bun, whole wheat	1 ea	43	114	4	22	3	2	0.5	0.9
42115	Cornbread, prepared from dry mix	1 pce	60	188	4	29	1	6	3.1	0.7
49012	Cornbread, hushpuppies, homemade	1 ea	22	74	2	10	1	3	0.7	1.6
42016	Croutons, plain, dry	0.25 cup	7.5	31	1	6	0	0	0.2	0.1
71302	Croutons, seasoned, fast food pkg	1 ea	10	46	1	6	0	2	0.9	0.2
71227	Pita bread, white, enriched	1 ea	28	77	3	16	1	0	0	0.1
71228	Pita bread, whole wheat	1 ea	28	74	3	15	2	1	0.1	0.3
42159	Roll, dinner, egg	1 ea	35	107	3	18	1	2	1	0.4
71368	Roll, dinner, plain, homemade w/reduced fat (2%) milk	1 ea	43	136	4	23	1	3	1.2	0.9
42161	Roll, French	1 ea	38	105	3	19	1	2	0.7	0.3
71056	Roll, hard/kaiser	1 ea	57	167	6	30	1	2	0.6	1
42297	Tortilla, corn, w/o salt, ready to cook	1 ea	26	58	1	12	1	1	0.2	0.3
90645	Taco shell, baked	1 ea	5	23	0	3	0	1	0.4	0.4
	Crackers									
71277	Cheese cracker, bite size	1 cup	62	312	6	36	1	16	7.5	1.5
71451	Cheez-its/Goldfish crackers, low sodium	55 pce	33	166	3	19	1	8	3.9	0.8
43532	Crispbread, rye	1 ea	10	37	1	8	2	0	0	0.1
43510	Matzo, whole wheat	1 oz	28.4	100	4	22	3	0	0.1	0.2
71284	Melba Toast Rounds, plain	1 cup	30	117	4	23	2	1	0.2	0.4
71032	Melba Toast, rye or pumpernickel	6 ea	30	117	3	23	2	1	0.3	0.4
43507	Oyster/soda/soup crackers	1 cup	45	193	4	32	1	5	3.2	0.6
70963	Ritz crackers/Nabisco	5 ea	16	79	1	10	0	4	2.8	0.3
43540	Rusk Toast	3 ea	30	122	4	22	1	2	0.8	0.7
43587	Saltine crackers, original premium/Nabisco	5 ea	14	59	2	10	0	1	0.8	0.2
43664	Saltine crackers, fat-free, low-sodium	6 ea	30	118	3	25	1	0	0	0.2
43659	Saltine/oyster/soda/soup crackers, low salt	1 cup	45	195	4	32	1	5	2.9	0.8
43545	Sandwich crackers, cheese filled	4 ea	28	134	3	17	1	6	3.2	0.7
43501	Sandwich crackers, cheese w/peanut butter filling	4 ea	28	139	3	16	1	7	3.6	1.4
43546	Sandwich crackers, peanut butter filled	4 ea	28	138	3	16	1	7	3.9	1.3
44677	Snackwell Wheat Cracker/Nabisco	1 ea	15	62	1	12	1	2		
43581	Wheat Thins, baked/Nabisco	16 ea	29	136	2	20	1	6	2	0.4
43508	Whole wheat cracker	4 ea	32	142	3	22	3	6	1.9	2.1
43570	Whole wheat, low-sodium cracker	7 ea	28	124	2	19	3	5	1.6	1.8
	Muffins and Baked Goods									
71035	English muffin, granola	1 ea	66	155	6	31	2	1	0.5	0.4
42723	English muffin, plain	1 ea	57	132	5	26		1	0.2	0.4
42060	English muffin, sourdough, enriched	1 ea	57	129	5	25	2	1	0.2	0.3
42153	English muffin, wheat	1 ea	57	127	5	26	3	1	0.2	0.5
62916	Muffin, blueberry, commercially prepared	1 ea	11	30	1	5	0	1	0.2	0.3

Sat (g)	Chol (mg)	Calc (mg)	Iron (mg)	Mag (mg)	Phos (mg)	Pota (mg)	Sodi (mg)	Zinc (mg)	Vit A (RAE)	Vit C (mg)	Thia (mg)	Ribo (mg)	Niac (mg)	Vit B6 (mg)	Vit B12 (µg)	Vit E (mg)	Fol (µg)	Alc (g)
0.8			0.3				154											0
0.3	5	23	0.75	6.4	32	74	111	0.2	13	0.2	0.08	0.08	0.67	0.02	0.01	0.3	13.2	0
0.2	0	20	0.94	10.5	42	44	122	0.3	1	0	0.15	0.1	1.45	0.02	0	0.1	24.3	0
0.1	0	13	0.72	12.6	32	23	81	0.2	0	0	0.08	0.05	0.87	0.02	0	0.1	18.6	0
0.3	0	27	1.11	29.2	67	82	175	0.5	0	0	0.14	0.1	1.58	0.06	0	0.1	37.8	0
0.2	0	25	0.97	7.8	34	71	155	0.3	0	0.1	0.1	0.1	1.26	0.02	0.02	0.1	33	0
0.1	0	18	0.68	9	23	28	118	0.3	0	0	0.1	0.07	0.89	0.03	0	0.1	20.9	0
0.1	0	14	0.34	2.1	9	9	61	0.1	0	0	0.04	0.03	0.39	0.01	0	0	10	0
0.1	0	22	0.73	5.3	28	17	104	0.3	0	0.1	0.09	0.07	0.84	0.01	0.06	0	21.8	0
0.1	0	1	0.21	1.6	6	6	33	0	0	0	0.03	0.03	0.26	0	0	0.1	8.1	0
0.4		37	0.95				256											0
0.5	0	59	1.43	9	27	40	206	0.3	0	0	0.17	0.14	1.79	0.03	0.09	0	47.7	0
0.4	0	46	1.04	36.6	96	117	206	0.9	0	0	0.11	0.07	1.58	0.08	0	0.4	12.9	0
1.6	37	44	1.14	12	226	77	467	0.4	26	0.1	0.15	0.16	1.23	0.06	0.1	0.7	33	0
0.5	10	61	0.67	5.3	42	32	147	0.1	9	0	0.08	0.07	0.61	0.02	0.04	0.3	19.6	0
0.1	0	6	0.31	2.3	9	9	52	0.1	0	0	0.05	0.02	0.41	0	0	0	9.9	0
0.5	1	10	0.28	4.2	14	18	124	0.1	1	0	0.05	0.04	0.46	0.01	0.01	0	10.5	0
0	0	24	0.73	7.3	27	34	150	0.2	0	0	0.17	0.09	1.3	0.01	0	0.1	30	0
0.1	0	4	0.86	19.3	50	48	149	0.4	0	0	0.09	0.02	0.8	0.07	0	0.2	9.8	0
0.6	18	21	1.23	8.8	35	36	191	0.4	2	0	0.18	0.18	1.15	0.02	0.08	0.1	64.4	0
0.8	15	26	1.27	8.2	54	65	178	0.3	37	0.1	0.17	0.18	1.48	0.03	0.06	0.4	38.7	0
0.4	0	35	1.03	7.6	32	43	231	0.3	0	0	0.2	0.11	1.65	0.01	0	0.1	42.9	0
0.3	0	54	1.87	15.4	57	62	310	0.5	0	0	0.27	0.19	2.42	0.02	0	0.2	54.2	0
0.1	0	46	0.36	16.9	82	40	3	0.2	0	0	0.03	0.02	0.39	0.06	0	0	29.6	0
0.2	0	8	0.12	5.2	12	9	18	0.1	0	0	0.01	0	0.07	0.01	0	0.1	6.6	0
5.8	8	94	2.96	22.3	135	90	617	0.7	18	0	0.35	0.27	2.9	0.34	0.29	0	94.2	0
3.2	4	50	1.57	11.9	72	35	151	0.4	6	0	0.19	0.14	1.54	0.18	0.15	0.1	29.4	0
0	0	3	0.24	7.8	27	32	26	0.2	0	0	0.02	0.01	0.1	0.02	0	0.1	4.7	0
0.1	0	7	1.32	38.1	87	90	1	0.7	0	0	0.1	0.08	1.54	0.05	0		9.9	0
0.1	0	28	1.11	17.7	59	61	249	0.6	0	0	0.12	0.08	1.23	0.03	0	0.1	37.2	0
0.1	0	23	1.1	11.7	55	58	270	0.4	0	0	0.14	0.09	1.42	0.03	0	0.2	25.5	0
0.7	0	31	2.54	9.9	45	69	482	0.4	0	0	0.04	0.2	2.36	0.04	0	0.4	62.6	0
0.6	0	24	0.65	3.2	48	15	124	0.2	0	0	0.04	0.05	0.61	0.01	0		9.6	0
0.4	23	8	0.82	10.8	46	74	76	0.3	4	0	0.12	0.12	1.39	0.01	0.05	0.2	26.1	0
0.3	0	27	0.73	2.9	14	14	178		0	0	0.05	0.06	0.61	0.01			11.8	0
0.1	0	7	2.32	7.8	34	34	191	0.3	0	0	0.16	0.18	1.71	0.03	0	0	37.2	0
1.3	0	54	2.43	12.2	47	326	286	0.3	0	0	0.25	0.21	2.36	0.02	0	0.1	55.8	0
1.7	1	72	0.67	10.1	114	120	392	0.2	5	0	0.12	0.19	1.05	0.01	0.03	0.1	28	0
1.2	0	14	0.76	15.7	75	61	199	0.3	0	0	0.15	0.08	1.63	0.04	0.08	0.7	26.3	0
1.4	0	23	0.78	15.4	77	60	201	0.3	0	0	0.14	0.08	1.71	0.04	0	0.6	24.1	0
		22	0.59	6.9	50	28	150	0.3	0	0	0.04	0.06				0		0
0.9	0	23	1.07	15.1	60	56	168		0	0	0.09	0.09	1.16	0.03			12.2	0
1.1	0	16	0.99	31.7	94	95	211	0.7	0	0	0.06	0.03	1.45	0.06	0	0.3	9	0
1	0	14	0.86	27.7	83	83	69	0.6	0	0	0.06	0.03	1.27	0.05	0	0.2	7.8	0
0.2	0	129	1.99	27.1	53	103	275	0.9	0	0	0.28	0.21	2.36	0.03	0	0	52.8	0
0.2		76	1.7				210		0	0.1		0.21				1	82.6	0
0.4	0	93	2.28	13.7	52	62	242	0.6	0	1	0.27	0.14	2.32	0.03	0.02	0.2	53.6	0
0.2	0	101	1.64	21.1	61	106	218	0.6	0	0	0.25	0.17	1.91	0.05	0	0.3	36.5	0
0.2	3	6	0.18	1.8	22	14	49	0.1	3	0.1	0.02	0.01	0.12	0	0.06	0.1	8.1	0

MDA Code	Food Name	Amt	Wt (g)	Ener (kcal)	Prot (g)	Carb (g)	Fiber (g)	Fat (g)	Mono (g)	Poly (g)
44521	Muffin, corn, commercially prepared	1 ea	57	174	3	29	2	5	1.2	1.8
44514	Muffin, oatbran	1 ea	57	154	4	28	3	4	1	2.4
44518	Toaster muffin, blueberry	1 ea	33	103	2	18	1	3	0.7	1.8
44522	Toaster muffin, corn	1 ea	33	114	2	19	1	4	0.9	2.1
	Noodles and Pasta									
66103	Angel hair pasta, dry	1 ea	56	201	7	41	2	1	0.2	0.8
91313	Bow tie pasta, enriched, dry	1.5 cup	56	204	8	42	2	1		
38048	Chow mein noodles, dry	1 cup	45	237	4	26	2	14	3.5	7.8
38047	Egg noodles, enriched, cooked	0.5 cup	80	110	4	20	1	2	0.5	0.4
38251	Egg noodles, enriched, cooked w/salt	0.5 cup	80	110	4	20	1	2	0.5	0.4
91316	Elbow pasta, enriched, dry	0.5 cup	56	204	8	42	2	1		
38356	Fettuccine noodles, frozen	70 g	70	200	8	38	2	2		
91293	Fettuccine noodles, spinach, enriched, dry	1.33 cup	56	202	8	40	2	1	0.1	0.6
38102	Macaroni noodles, enriched, cooked	1 cup	140	221	8	43	3	1	0.2	0.4
38110	Macaroni noodles, whole wheat, cooked	1 cup	140	174	7	37	4	1	0.1	0.3
66121	Pasta shells, small, wheat free, low protein, dry	2 oz	56.7	194	0	48	0	0		
92830	Penne pasta, dry	0.25 ea	57	210	7	41	1	1	0	0
38067	Ramen noodles, cooked	0.5 cup	113.5	77	2	10	1	3	0.6	1.7
38551	Rice noodles, cooked	0.5 cup	88	96	1	22	1	0	0	0
38094	Soba noodles, cooked from dry	1 cup	114	113	6	24	1	0	0	0
38118	Spaghetti noodles, enriched, cooked	0.5 cup	70	111	4	22	1	1	0.1	0.2
38066	Spaghetti noodles, spinach, cooked	1 cup	140	182	6	37	5	1	0.1	0.4
38274	Spaghetti noodles, unenrich, cooked w/salt	0.5 cup	70	110	4	21	1	1	0.1	0.2
38060	Spaghetti, whole wheat, cooked	1 cup	140	174	7	37	6	1	0.1	0.3
	Flours									
38071	Arrowroot flour	0.25 cup	32	114	0	28	1	0	0	0
38548	Barley flour or meal	0.25 cup	37	128	4	28	4	1	0.1	0.3
38053	Buckwheat flour, whole groat	0.25 cup	30	100	4	21	3	1	0.3	0.3
38005	Corn flour, masa, enriched	0.25 cup	28.5	104	3	22	3	1	0.3	0.5
7565	Soy flour, full fat, stirred, raw	0.25 cup	21	92	7	7	2	4	1	2.4
38087	Triticale flour, whole grain	0.25 cup	32.5	110	4	24	5	1	0.1	0.3
38033	Wheat, white, all-purpose flours, self-rising, enriched	0.25 cup	31.2	110	3	23	1	0	0	0.1
38277	Wheat, white, bread flours, enriched	0.25 cup	34.2	123	4	25	1	1	0	0.2
38032	Whole wheat flour, whole grain	0.25 cup	30	102	4	22	4	1	0.1	0.2
	Grains									
38003	Barley, pearled, cooked	0.5 cup	78.5	97	2	22	3	0	0	0.2
38028	Bulgar, cooked	1 cup	182	151	6	34	8	0	0.1	0.2
38252	Corn, white, dry	0.25 cup	41.5	151	4	31		2	0.5	0.9
38279	Corn, yellow, dry	0.25 cup	41.5	151	4	31	3	2	0.5	0.9
38183	Cornmeal, white, degermed, enriched	0.25 cup	34.5	126	3	27	3	1	0.1	0.2
38004	Cornmeal, yellow, degermed, enriched	0.25 cup	34.5	126	3	27	3	1	0.1	0.2
38076	Couscous, cooked	0.5 cup	78.5	88	3	18	1	0	0	0.1
5470	Hominy, yellow, canned	0.5 cup	80	58	1	11	2	1	0.2	0.3
38052	Millet, cooked	0.5 cup	87	104	3	21	1	1	0.2	0.4
38078	Oat bran, cooked	0.5 cup	109.5	44	4	13	3	1	0.3	0.4
38080	Oats	0.25 cup	39	152	7	26	4	3	0.8	1
38010	Rice, brown, long grain, cooked	1 cup	195	216	5	45	4	2	0.6	0.6
38082	Rice, brown, medium grain, cooked	0.5 cup	97.5	109	2	23	2	1	0.3	0.3
38083	Rice, white, glutinous, cooked	1 cup	174	169	4	37	2	0	0.1	0.1
38256	Rice, white, long grain, enriched, cooked w/salt	1 cup	158	205	4	45	1	0	0.1	0.1
38019	Rice, white, long grain, instant, enriched, cooked	1 cup	165	193	4	41	1	1	0.1	0

Sat (g)	Chol (mg)	Calc (mg)	Iron (mg)	Mag (mg)	Phos (mg)	Pota (mg)	Sodi (mg)	Zinc (mg)	Vit A (RAE)	Vit C (mg)	Thia (mg)	Ribo (mg)	Niac (mg)	Vit B6 (mg)	Vit B12 (µg)	Vit E (mog)	Fol (µg)	Alc (g)
0.8	15	42	1.6	18.2	162	39	297	0.3	30	0	0.16	0.19	1.16	0.05	0.05	0.5	45.6	0
0.6	0	36	2.39	89.5	214	289	224	1	0	0	0.15	0.05	0.24	0.09	0.01	0.4	50.7	0
0.5	2	4	0.17	4	19	27	158	0.1	31	0	0.08	0.1	0.67	0.01	0.01	0.3	21.4	0
0.6	4	6	0.49	4.6	50	30	142	0.1	6	0	0.1	0.12	0.76	0.02	0.01	0.5	18.8	0
0.3		12	1.61	26.3	90	105	3	0.7	0	0	0.49	0.21	3.34	0.07	0		0.1	111	0
0.2		10	1.8	30.1	79	81	3	0.6	0	0	0.45	0.25	3				120	0
2	0	9	2.13	23.4	72	54	198	0.6	0	0	0.26	0.19	2.68	0.05	0	1.6	40.5	0
0.3	23	10	1.18	16.8	61	30	4	0.5	5	0	0.23	0.11	1.66	0.04	0.07	0.1	67.2	0
0.3		10	1.18	16.8	61	30	132	0.5	5	0	0.23	0.11	1.66	0.04	0.07	0.1	67	0
0.2		10	1.8	30.1	79	81	3	0.6	0	0	0.45	0.25	3				120	0
0		0	0				140		0	0								0
0.3		78	1.8	43.7	117	203	16	0.8	7	0	0.45	0.25	3					0
0.2		10	1.86	25.2	81	63	1	0.7	0	0	0.38	0.19	2.36	0.07	0	0.1	102	0
0.1		21	1.48	42	125	62	4	1.1	0	0	0.15	0.06	0.99	0.11	0	0.4	7	0
0		3	0.68			52			0	0.5								0
0		0	0.72				0		0	0								0
0.8		7	0.2	5.2	12	25	401	0.1	1	0	0.01	0.01	0.13	0.01	0	1.2	1.6	0
0	0	4	0.12	2.6	18	4	17	0.2	0	0	0.02	0	0.06	0.01	0		2.6	0
0	0	5	0.55	10.3	28	40	68	0.1	0	0	0.11	0.03	0.58	0.05	0		8	0
0.1	4	5	0.93	12.6	41	32	1	0.4	0	0	0.19	0.1	1.18	0.03	0	0	51	0
0.1		42	1.46	86.8	151	81	20	1.5	11	0	0.14	0.14	2.14	0.13	0	0	17	0
0.1		5	0.35	12.6	41	32	90	0.4	0	0	0.01	0.01	0.28	0.03	0	0	4.9	0
0.1	0	21	1.48	42	125	62	4	1.1	0	0	0.15	0.06	0.99	0.11	0	0.4	7	0
0	0	13	0.11	1	2	4	1	0	0	0	0	0	0	0	0		2.2	0
0.1	0	12	0.99	35.5	110	114	1	0.7	0	0	0.14	0.04	2.32	0.15	0	0.2	3	0
0.2	0	12	1.22	75.3	101	173	3	0.9	0	0	0.13	0.06	1.85	0.17	0	0.1	16.2	0
0.2	0	40	2.05	31.4	64	85	1	0.5	0	0	0.41	0.21	2.81	0.11	0	0	66.4	0
0.6	0	43	1.34	90.1	104	528	3	0.8	1	0	0.12	0.24	0.91	0.1	0	0.4	72.4	0
0.1	0	11	0.84	49.7	104	151	1	0.9	0	0	0.12	0.04	0.93	0.13	0	0.3	24	0
0	0	105	1.46	5.9	186	39	396	0.2	0	0	0.21	0.13	1.82	0.02	0	0	61.2	0
0.1	0	5	1.51	8.6	33	34	1	0.3	0	0	0.28	0.18	2.58	0.01	0	0.1	62.6	0
0.1	0	10	1.16	41.4	104	122	2	0.9	0	0	0.13	0.06	1.91	0.1	0	0.2	13.2	0
0.1	0	9	1.04	17.3	42	73	2	0.6	0	0	0.07	0.05	1.62	0.09	0	0	12.6	0
0.1	0	18	1.75	58.2	73	124	9	1	0	0	0.1	0.05	1.82	0.15	0	0	32.8	0
0.3	0	3	1.12	52.7	87	119	15	0.9	0	0	0.16	0.08	1.51	0.26	0	0.2		0
0.3	0	3	1.12	52.7	87	119	15	0.9	5	0	0.16	0.08	1.51	0.26	0	0.2	7.9	0
0.1	0	2	1.42	13.8	29	56	1	0.2	0	0	0.25	0.14	1.74	0.09	0	0.1	80.4	0
0.1	0	2	1.42	13.8	29	56	1	0.2	4	0	0.25	0.14	1.74	0.09	0	0.1	80.4	0
0	0	6	0.3	6.3	17	46	4	0.2	0	0	0.05	0.02	0.77	0.04	0	0.1	11.8	0
0.1	0	8	0.5	12.8	28	7	168	0.8	5	0	0	0	0.03	0	0	0.1	0.8	0
0.1	0	3	0.55	38.3	87	54	2	0.8	0	0	0.09	0.07	1.16	0.09	0	0	16.5	0
0.2	0	11	0.96	43.8	130	101	1	0.6	0	0	0.18	0.04	0.16	0.03	0	0.1	6.6	0
0.5	0	21	1.84	69	204	167	1	1.5	0	0	0.3	0.05	0.37	0.05	0	0.3	21.8	0
0.4	0	20	0.82	83.8	162	84	10	1.2	0	0	0.19	0.05	2.98	0.28	0	0.1	7.8	0
0.2	0	10	0.52	42.9	75	77	1	0.6	0	0	0.1	0.01	1.3	0.15	0	0.2	3.9	0
0.1	0	3	0.24	8.7	14	17	9	0.7	0	0	0.03	0.02	0.5	0.05	0	0.1	1.7	0
0.1	0	16	1.9	19	68	55	604	0.8	0	0	0.26	0.02	2.33	0.15	0	0.1	91.6	0
0	0	13	2.92	8.2	61	15	7	0.8	0	0	0.12	0.01	2.87	0.08	0	0	115.5	0

MDA Code	Food Name	Amt	Wt (g)	Ener (kcal)	Prot (g)	Carb (g)	Fiber (g)	Fat (g)	Mono (g)	Poly (g)
38097	Rice, white, medium grain, cooked	0.5 cup	93	121	2	27	0	0	0.1	0.1
38054	Semolina, enriched	0.25 cup	41.8	150	5	30	2	0	0.1	0.2
38085	Sorghum, whole grain	0.5 cup	96	325	11	72	6	3	1	1.3
38034	Tapioca, pearl, dry	0.25 cup	38	136	0	34	0	0	0	0
38025	Wheat germ, crude	0.25 cup	28.8	104	7	15	4	3	0.4	1.7
38068	Wheat, sprouted	0.25 cup	27	53	2	11	0	0	0	0.2
	Pancakes, French Toast, and Waffles									
42155	French Toast, frozen	1 pce	59	126	4	19	1	4	1.2	0.7
42156	French Toast, homemade w/reduced fat (2%) milk	1 pce	65	149	5	16	1	7	2.9	1.7
45192	Pancake/waffle, buttermilk/Eggo/Kellogg	1 ea	42.5	99	3	16	0	3	1.2	0.9
45118	Pancakes, blueberry, homemade	1 ea	77	171	5	22	1	7	1.8	3.2
45121	Pancakes, buttermilk, homemade	1 ea	77	175	5	22	1	7	1.8	3.5
45117	Pancakes, plain, homemade	1 ea	77	175	5	22	1	7	1.9	3.4
45199	Pancakes, plain/buttermilk, frozen	1 ea	36	81	2	14	1	2	0.7	0.4
45193	Waffle, low fat, homestyle, frozen	1 ea	35	83	2	15	0	1	0.4	0.4
45003	Waffle, plain, homemade	1 ea	75	218	6	25	1	11	2.6	5.1
45197	Waffle, plain/buttermilk, frozen, ready-to-heat	1 ea	35	100	2	15	1	3	1.8	0.8
	MEAT AND MEAT SUBSTITUTES									
	Beef									
10093	Beef, average of all cuts, lean & fat (1/4" trim) cooked	3 oz	85.1	260	22	0	0	18	7.8	0.7
10705	Beef, average of all cuts, lean (1/4" trim) cooked	3 oz	85.1	184	25	0	0	8	3.5	0.3
10108	Beef brisket, whole, lean & fat (1/4" trim) braised	3 oz	85.1	328	20	0	0	27	11.8	1
10035	Beef breakfast strip, cured & cooked	3 ea	34	153	11	0	0	12	5.7	0.5
58239	Beef, brisket, flat half, 1/8" trim, select, braised	3 oz	85.1	238	25	0	0	15	6.4	0.5
58051	Beef, chuck, clod roast, trimmed to 1/4" fat, all grades, roasted	3 oz	85.1	206	21	0	0	13	6	0.5
58104	Beef, chuck, clod steak, trimmed to 1/4" fat, all grades, braised	3 oz	85.1	231	22	0	0	15	6.8	0.6
58099	Beef, chuck, tender steak, trimmed to 0" fat, all grades, broiled	3 oz	85.1	136	22	0	0	5	2.3	0.3
58083	Beef, chuck, top blade, trimmed to 0" fat, USDA choice, broiled	3 oz	85.1	193	22	0	0	11	5.3	0.4
10264	Beef, cured, thin sliced	5 pce	21	37	6	1	0	1	0.4	0
10009	Beef, cured, dried, sliced	5 pce	21	32	7	1	0	0	0.2	0
10034	Beef kidney, simmered	3 oz	85.1	134	23	0	0	4	0.6	0.7
10010	Beef liver, pan fried	3 oz	85.1	149	23	4	0	4	0.6	0.8
10624	Beef, short ribs, braised, choice, 1/4" trim	3 oz	85.1	401	18	0	0	36	16.1	1.3
10011	Beef tongue, simmered	3 oz	85.1	242	16	0	0	19	8.6	0.6
10018	Beef tripe, raw	4 oz	113.4	96	14	0	0	4	1.7	0.2
10133	Beef, whole rib, roasted, 1/4" trim	3 oz	85.1	305	19	0	0	25	10.6	0.9
10008	Corned beef brisket, canned	3 oz	85.1	213	23	0	0	13	5.1	0.5
57710	Corned beef hash, canned	1 cup	236	387	21	22	3	24	12.4	0.7
93273	Corned beef hash, canned, with potato	3 oz	85.1	140	7	8	1	9	4.5	0.3
58129	Ground beef (hamburger), 25% fat, cooked, pan-browned	3 oz	85.1	236	22	0	0	15	7.1	0.4
58124	Ground beef (hamburger), 20% fat, cooked, pan-browned	3 oz	85.1	231	23	0	0	15	6.5	0.4
58119	Ground beef (hamburger), 15% fat, cooked, pan-browned	3 oz	85.1	218	24	0	0	13	5.6	0.4
58114	Ground beef (hamburger), 10% fat, cooked, pan-browned	3 oz	85.1	196	24	0	0	10	4.3	0.4
58109	Ground beef (hamburger), 5% fat, cooked, pan-browned	3 oz	85.1	164	25	0	0	6	2.7	0.3
10791	Porterhouse steak, lean & fat (1/4" trim) broiled	3 oz	85.1	280	19	0	0	22	9.8	0.9
11487	Porterhouse steak, lean & fat (1/8" trim) broiled	3 oz	85.1	253	20	0	0	19	8.2	0.7
58257	Rib eye steak, small end (ribs 10–12), 0" trim, broiled	3 oz	85.1	210	23	0	0	13	5.1	0.5
58324	Rib steak, 1/8" trim, broiled	3 oz	85.1	172	24	0	0	8	3.1	0.3
57709	Roast beef hash, canned	1 cup	236	385	21	23	4	24	11.3	0.6
58094	Skirt steak, trimmed to 0" fat, broiled	3 oz	85.1	187	22	0	0	10	5.2	0.4

Sat (g)	Chol (mg)	Calc (mg)	Iron (mg)	Mag (mg)	Phos (mg)	Pota (mg)	Sodi (mg)	Zinc (mg)	Vit A (RAE)	Vit C (mg)	Thia (mg)	Ribo (mg)	Niac (mg)	Vit B6 (mg)	Vit B12 (µg)	Vit E (mg)	Fol (µg)	Alc (g)
0.1	0	3	1.39	12.1	34	27	0	0.4	0	0	0.16	0.01	1.71	0.05	0	0	53.9	0
0.1	0	7	1.82	19.6	57	78	0	0.4	0	0	0.34	0.24	2.5	0.04	0	0.1	76.5	0
0.4	0	27	4.22		276	336	6		0	0	0.23	0.14	2.81		0	0.1		0
0	0	8	0.6	0.4	3	4	0	0	0	0	0	0	0	0	0	0	1.5	0
0.5	0	11	1.8	68.8	242	257	3	3.5	0	0	0.54	0.14	1.96	0.37	0	4	80.9	0
0.1	0	8	0.58	22.1	54	46	4	0.4	0	0.7	0.06	0.04	0.83	0.07	0	0	10.3	0
0.9	48	63	1.3	10	82	79	292	0.5	32	0.2	0.16	0.22	1.61	0.29	0.99	0.4	30.7	0
1.8	75	65	1.09	11	76	87	311	0.4	81	0.2	0.13	0.21	1.06	0.05	0.2	0.7	28	0
0.6	5	15	1.32	7.6	145	44	225	0.3		0.6	0.11	0.12	1.47	0.15	0.44	0	22.1	0
1.5	43	159	1.32	12.3	116	106	317	0.4	38	1.7	0.15	0.21	1.17	0.04	0.15		27.7	0
1.4	45	121	1.31	11.6	107	112	402	0.5	23	0.3	0.16	0.22	1.21	0.03	0.14	1.1	29.3	0
1.6	45	169	1.39	12.3	122	102	338	0.4	42	0.2	0.15	0.22	1.21	0.04	0.17	0.7	29.3	0
0.3	6	26	0.79	5	105	45	182	0.1	23	0.1	0.12	0.18	1.05	0.05	0.03	0.1	25.6	0
0.3	9	20	1.95	23.8	28	50	155			0	0.31	0.26	2.59	0.16	0.55		27	0
2.1	52	191	1.73	14.2	142	119	383	0.5	49	0.3	0.2	0.26	1.55	0.04	0.19	1.7	34.5	0
0.5	5	108	1.96	8	126	44	223	0.2	133	0	0.22	0.22	2.65	0.31	1.03	0.4	23.8	0
7.3	75	9	2.23	18.7	173	266	53	5	0	0	0.07	0.18	3.1	0.28	2.08	0.2	6	0
3.2	73	8	2.54	22.1	198	306	57	5.9	0	0	0.09	0.2	3.51	0.31	2.25	0.1	6.8	0
10.5	80	7	1.91	15.3	159	197	52	4.3	0	0	0.05	0.15	2.55	0.2	1.94	0.2	5.1	0
4.9	40	3	1.07	9.2	80	140	766	2.2	0	0	0.03	0.09	2.2	0.11	1.17	0.1	2.7	0
5.9	60	14	2.04	16.2	153	202	42	5.9	0	0	0.05	0.13	3.55	0.24	1.63	0.4	7.7	0
4.9	64	7	2.39	17	167	287	57	4.9	0	0	0.07	0.19	2.73	0.22	2.41	0.1	7.7	0
5.7	80	8	2.83	16.2	176	220	49	5.8	0	0	0.06	0.19	2.43	0.21	2.33	0.1	6.8	0
1.6	54	7	2.49	19.6	193	249	60	6.7	0	0	0.09	0.2	3.09	0.27	2.88	0.1	6.8	0
3.5	49	6	2.36	20.4	183	255	58	7.5	0	0	0.09	0.19	3.08	0.27	2.88	0.2	6.8	0
0.3	9	2	0.57	4	35	90	302	0.8	0	0	0.02	0.04	1.11	0.07	0.54	0	2.3	0
0.2	17	1	0.61	4.6	41	61	586	0.8	0	0	0.01	0.05	0.69	0.05	0.5	0	1.7	0
0.9	609	16	4.94	10.2	259	115	80	2.4	0	0	0.14	2.53	3.34	0.33	21.19	0.1	70.6	0
1.3	324	5	5.25	18.7	413	299	66	4.5	6590	0.6	0.15	2.91	14.87	0.87	70.74	0.4	221.3	0
15.1	80	10	1.97	12.8	138	191	43	4.2	0	0	0.04	0.13	2.09	0.19	2.23	0.2	4.3	0
6.9	112	4	2.22	12.8	123	157	55	3.5	0	1.1	0.02	0.25	2.97	0.13	2.66	0.3	6	0
1.5	138	78	0.67	14.7	73	76	110	1.6	0	0	0	0.07	1	0.02	1.58	0.1	5.7	0
10	71	9	1.99	17	149	256	54	4.6	0	0	0.06	0.14	2.9	0.2	2.16	0.2	6	0
5.3	73	10	1.77	11.9	94	116	856	3	0	0	0.02	0.13	2.07	0.11	1.38	0.1	7.7	0
10.2	76	45	2.36	30.7		406	1003	3.3	0	2.1								0
3.7	27	16	0.85	11.1	48	146	362	1.2	0	0.8	0.06	0.04	1.34	0.2	0.35	0	6	0
6	76	29	2.24	18.7	182	301	79	5.3	0	0	0.04	0.16	4.55	0.37	2.5	0.4	10.2	0
5.6	76	24	2.37	19.6	192	323	77	5.4	0	0	0.04	0.16	4.96	0.36	2.43	0.4	9.4	0
5	77	19	2.49	21.3	203	346	76	5.6	0	0	0.04	0.16	5.38	0.36	2.37	0.4	8.5	0
4	76	14	2.62	23	213	368	74	5.8	0	0	0.04	0.16	5.79	0.36	2.31	0.4	6.8	0
2.9	76	8	2.75	23.8	224	391	72	6	0	0	0.04	0.17	6.2	0.36	2.25	0.3	6	0
8.7	61	7	2.28	17	151	217	53	3.5	0	0	0.08	0.18	3.28	0.28	1.8	0.2	6	0
7.2	60	7	2.33	19.6	159	273	54	3.9	0	0	0.09	0.19	3.46	0.3	1.83	0.2	6	0
4.9	94	17	1.49	19.6	180	289	48	4.2	0	0	0.06	0.11	6.18	0.49	1.36	0.4	6.8	0
2.9	72	14	1.63	20.4	186	300	49	4.5	0	0	0.06	0.12	7.1	0.5	1.51	0.4	7.7	0
9.9	73	42	2.36	33		432	793	3.3	0	1.9								0
4	51	9	2.36	20.4	196	246	64	6.2	0	0	0.08	0.16	3.19	0.27	3.17	0.1	6	0

MDA Code	Food Name	Amt	Wt (g)	Ener (kcal)	Prot (g)	Carb (g)	Fiber (g)	Fat (g)	Mono (g)	Poly (g)
58069	Skirt steak, outside, trimmed to 0" fat, broiled	3 oz	85.1	198	21	0	0	12	6.3	0.5
58328	Strip steak, top loin, 1/8" trim, broiled	3 oz	85.1	171	25	0	0	7	2.9	0.3
10805	T-Bone steak, lean & fat (1/4" trim) broiled	3 oz	85.1	260	20	0	0	19	8.6	0.7
11491	T-Bone steak, lean & fat (1/8" trim) broiled	3 oz	85.1	238	21	0	0	17	7.3	0.6
58299	Top round steak, lean, 1/8" trim, broiled	3 oz	85.1	151	27	0	0	4	1.7	0.2
58098	Tri-tip roast, loin, broiled, 0" trim	3 oz	85.1	226	26	0	0	13	6.6	0.5
58258	Tri-tip roast, sirloin, roasted, 0" trim	3 oz	85.1	177	22	0	0	9	4.7	0.3
11550	Veal tongue, braised	3 oz	85.1	172	22	0	0	9	3.9	0.3
11531	Veal, average of all cuts, cooked	3 oz	85.1	197	26	0	0	10	3.7	0.7
11530	Veal, ground, broiled, 8% fat	3 oz	85.1	146	21	0	0	6	2.4	0.5
	Chicken									
81185	Chicken breast, fat-free, mesquite flavor, sliced	2 pce	42	34	7	1	0	0	0.1	0
81186	Chicken breast, oven-roasted, fat-free, sliced	2 pce	42	33	7	1	0	0	0.1	0
15013	Chicken breast, w/skin, batter fried	3 oz	85.1	221	21	8	0	11	4.6	2.6
15057	Chicken breast, w/o skin, fried	3 oz	85.1	159	28	0	0	4	1.5	0.9
15113	Chicken, dark meat, w/skin, batter fried	3 oz	85.1	254	19	8	0	16	6.5	3.8
15080	Chicken, dark meat, w/skin, roasted	3 oz	85.1	215	22	0	0	13	5.3	3
15026	Chicken, dark meat, w/o skin, fried	3 oz	85.1	203	25	2	0	10	3.7	2.4
15030	Chicken drumstick, w/skin, batter fried	3 oz	85.1	228	19	7	0	13	5.5	3.2
15042	Chicken drumstick, w/o skin, fried	3 oz	85.1	166	24	0	0	7	2.5	1.7
58216	Chicken, feet, boiled	1 oz	28.4	61	6	0	0	4	1.6	0.8
15105	Chicken giblets, chopped, fried	1 cup	145	402	47	6	0	20	6.4	4.9
15106	Chicken giblets, chopped, simmered	1 cup	145	229	39	1	0	7	1.4	1.2
15025	Chicken gizzard, average, chopped, simmered	3 oz	85.1	124	26	0	0	2	0.4	0.3
15151	Chicken, leg, w/skin, batter fried	3 oz	85.1	232	19	7	0	14	5.6	3.3
81432	Chicken, leg, w/o skin, fried	1 ea	94	196	27	1	0	9	3.2	2.1
15111	Chicken, light meat, w/skin, batter fried	3 oz	85.1	236	20	8	0	13	5.4	3.1
15077	Chicken, light meat, w/skin, roasted	3 oz	85.1	189	25	0	0	9	3.6	2
15031	Chicken, light meat, w/o skin, fried	3 oz	85.1	163	28	0	0	5	1.7	1.1
15072	Chicken, whole, w/skin, batter fried	3 oz	85.1	246	19	8	0	15	6	3.5
15214	Chicken, whole, w/o skin, fried	3 oz	85.1	186	26	1	0	8	2.9	1.8
15000	Chicken, whole, w/o skin, roasted	3 oz	85.1	162	25	0	0	6	2.3	1.4
15036	Chicken, thigh, w/skin, batter fried	3 oz	85.1	236	18	8	0	14	5.7	3.3
15011	Chicken, thigh, w/o skin, fried	3 oz	85.1	186	24	1	0	9	3.3	2.1
15095	Chicken, whole, w/giblet & neck, batter fried	3 oz	85.1	248	19	8	0	15	6.1	3.5
15094	Chicken, whole, w/giblet & neck, raw	4 oz	113.4	242	21	0	0	17	6.9	3.6
15097	Chicken, whole, w/giblet & neck, roasted	3 oz	85.1	199	23	0	0	11	4.4	2.5
15034	Chicken, wing, w/skin, batter fried	3 oz	85.1	276	17	9	0	19	7.6	4.3
15048	Chicken, wing, w/o skin, fried	3 oz	85.1	180	26	0	0	8	2.6	1.8
15059	Chicken, wing, w/o skin, roasted	3 oz	85.1	173	26	0	0	7	2.2	1.5
	Turkey									
13125	Turkey bacon	1 oz	28.4	71	4	0	0	6	2.1	1.3
51151	Turkey bacon, cooked	1 oz	28.4	108	8	1	0	8	3.1	1.9
16073	Turkey giblets, simmered	1 cup	145	289	30	1	0	17	7.2	1.8
51098	Turkey patty, breaded, fried	1 ea	42	119	6	7	0	8	3.1	2
16308	Turkey roast, light & dark meat, no bone, seasoned	1 cup	135	209	29	4	0	8	1.6	2.2
16110	Turkey breast w/skin, roasted	3 oz	85.1	130	25	0	0	3	1	0.6
16038	Turkey breast, no skin, roasted	3 oz	85.1	115	26	0	0	1	0.1	0.2
16101	Turkey, dark meat w/skin, roasted	3 oz	85.1	155	24	0	0	6	1.9	1.6
16099	Turkey, light meat w/skin, roasted	3 oz	85.1	140	24	0	0	4	1.4	0.9
16003	Turkey, ground, cooked	1 ea	82	193	22	0	0	11	4	2.6

Sat (g)	Chol (mg)	Calc (mg)	Iron (mg)	Mag (mg)	Phos (mg)	Pota (mg)	Sodi (mg)	Zinc (mg)	Vit A (RAE)	Vit C (mg)	Thia (mg)	Ribo (mg)	Niac (mg)	Vit B6 (mg)	Vit B12 (µg)	Vit E (mog)	Fol (µg)	Alc (g)
5.1	49	9	2.26	21.3	188	334	80	4.9	0	0	0.1	0.17	3.69	0.42	3.66	0.1	6.8	0
2.7	67	14	1.68	21.3	192	308	51	4.7	0	0	0.07	0.13	7.32	0.52	1.55	0.3	8.5	0
7.6	55	6	2.63	18.7	157	240	57	3.7	0	0	0.08	0.18	3.37	0.29	1.81	0.2	6	0
6.4	53	7	2.41	20.4	164	286	56	4	0	0	0.09	0.19	3.52	0.3	1.85	0.2	6	0
1.4	52	6	2.26	18.7	176	230	37	4.7	0	0	0.06	0.15	4.63	0.35	1.38	0.3	9.4	0
4.9	58	10	3.1	22.1	226	372	61	6	0	0	0.11	0.24	3.6	0.38	2.41	0.1	8.5	0
3.5	71	16	1.41	18.7	171	275	45	4	0	0	0.06	0.11	5.9	0.46	1.3	0.3	6.8	0
3.7	203	8	1.78	15.3	141	138	54	3.8	0	5.1	0.06	0.3	1.25	0.13	4.51	2.1	7.7	0
3.6	97	19	0.98	22.1	203	277	74	4.1	0	0	0.05	0.27	6.78	0.26	1.34	0.3	12.8	0
2.6	88	14	0.84	20.4	185	287	71	3.3	0	0	0.06	0.23	6.83	0.33	1.08	0.1	9.4	0
0.1	15	2	0.13	15.1	108	133	437	0.3	0	0	0.01	0.01	1.15	0.05	0.03	0	0.4	0
0.1	15	3	0.13	3.8	25	28	457	0.1	0	0	0.01	0.01	1.44	0.06	0.04	0	0.4	0
3	72	17	1.06	20.4	157	171	234	0.8	17	0	0.1	0.12	8.96	0.37	0.26	0.9	12.8	0
1.1	77	14	0.97	26.4	209	235	67	0.9	6	0	0.07	0.11	12.58	0.54	0.31	0.4	3.4	0
4.2	76	18	1.23	17	123	157	251	1.8	26	0	0.1	0.19	4.77	0.21	0.23	1	15.3	0
3.7	77	13	1.16	18.7	143	187	74	2.1	51	0	0.06	0.18	5.41	0.26	0.25	0.5	6	0
2.7	82	15	1.27	21.3	159	215	83	2.5	20	0	0.08	0.21	6.02	0.31	0.28	0.5	7.7	0
3.5	73	14	1.15	17	125	158	229	2	22	0	0.1	0.18	4.34	0.23	0.24	1	15.3	0
1.8	80	10	1.12	20.4	158	212	82	2.7	15	0	0.07	0.2	5.23	0.33	0.3	0.4	7.7	0
1.1	24	25	0.26	1.4	24	9	19	0.2	9	0	0.02	0.06	0.11	0	0.13	0.1	24.4	0
5.5	647	26	14.96	36.2	415	478	164	9.1	5194	12.6	0.14	2.21	15.93	0.88	19.3	3.6	549.6	0
1.9	641	20	10.21	20.3	419	325	97	6.1	2542	18.1	0.21	1.53	9.61	0.58	13.69	0.7	372.6	0
0.6	315	14	2.71	2.6	161	152	48	3.8	0	0	0.02	0.18	2.66	0.06	0.89	0.2	4.3	0
3.6	77	15	1.19	17	129	161	237	1.8	23	0	0.1	0.19	4.62	0.23	0.24	1	15.3	0
2.3	93	12	1.32	23.5	181	239	90	2.8	19	0	0.08	0.23	6.29	0.37	0.32		8.5	0
3.5	71	17	1.07	18.7	143	157	244	0.9	20	0	0.1	0.13	7.79	0.33	0.24	0.9	13.6	0
2.6	71	13	0.97	21.3	170	193	64	1	28	0	0.05	0.1	9.48	0.44	0.27	0.3	2.6	0
1.3	77	14	0.97	24.7	197	224	69	1.1	8	0	0.06	0.11	11.37	0.54	0.31	0.3	3.4	0
3.9	74	18	1.17	17.9	132	157	248	1.4	24	0	0.1	0.16	5.99	0.26	0.24	1.1	15.3	0
2.1	80	14	1.15	23	174	219	77	1.9	15	0	0.07	0.17	8.22	0.41	0.29	0.4	6	0
1.7	76	13	1.03	21.3	166	207	73	1.8	14	0	0.06	0.15	7.81	0.4	0.28	0.2	5.1	0
3.8	79	15	1.23	17.9	132	163	245	1.7	25	0	0.1	0.19	4.86	0.22	0.24	1	16.2	0
2.4	87	11	1.24	22.1	169	220	81	2.4	18	0	0.07	0.22	6.06	0.32	0.28	0.5	7.7	0
4	88	18	1.52	17.9	134	162	242	1.6	154	0.3	0.1	0.21	6.03	0.27	0.71	1.1	27.2	0
4.8	102	12	1.49	22.7	169	214	79	1.7	263	2.9	0.07	0.21	7.53	0.39	1.26	0.4	34	0
3.1	91	13	1.41	19.6	155	180	67	1.8	163	0.4	0.05	0.19	6.73	0.32	0.8	0.3	24.7	0
5	67	17	1.1	13.6	103	117	272	1.2	29	0	0.09	0.13	4.48	0.26	0.21	0.9	15.3	0
2.1	71	13	0.97	17.9	140	177	77	1.8	15	0	0.04	0.11	6.16	0.5	0.29	0.3	3.4	0
1.9	72	14	0.99	17.9	141	179	78	1.8	15	0	0.04	0.11	6.22	0.5	0.29	0.2	3.4	0
1.5	26	11	0.41	5.4	57	59	344	0.7	0	0							2.3	0
2.4	28	3	0.6	8.2	131	112	649	0.9	0	0	0.02	0.07	1	0.09	0.1	0.3	2.6	0
5.7	419	9	11.18	26.1	335	392	93	4.5	15569	19.9	0.04	2.18	10.15	0.84	48.21	0.1	485.8	0
2	26	6	0.92	6.3	113	116	336	0.6	5	0	0.04	0.08	0.97	0.08	0.09	0.5	11.8	0
2.6	72	7	2.2	29.7	329	402	918	3.4	0	0	0.06	0.22	8.47	0.36	2.05	0.5	6.8	0
0.7	77	13	1.34	23.8	184	237	45	1.5	0	0	0.03	0.11	5.92	0.43	0.31	0.2	5.1	0
0.2	71	10	1.3	24.7	191	248	44	1.5	0	0	0.04	0.11	6.38	0.48	0.33	0.1	5.1	0
1.8	100	23	1.98	19.6	162	202	65	3.3	0	0	0.04	0.2	2.85	0.28	0.31	0.7	7.7	0
1.1	81	15	1.37	22.1	174	223	49	1.8	0	0	0.03	0.12	5.34	0.42	0.31	0.1	5.1	0
2.8	84	20	1.58	19.7	161	221	88	2.3	0	0	0.04	0.14	3.95	0.32	0.27	0.3	5.7	0

MDA Code	Food Name	Amt	Wt (g)	Ener (kcal)	Prot (g)	Carb (g)	Fiber (g)	Fat (g)	Mono (g)	Poly (g)
	Lamb									
40422	Lamb, Australian, loin, lean, broiled 1/8" trim	3 oz	85.1	163	23	0	0	7	3	0.3
13604	Lamb, average of all cuts (1/4" trim) cooked	3 oz	85.1	250	21	0	0	18	7.5	1.3
13616	Lamb, average of all cuts, lean (1/4" trim) cooked	3 oz	85.1	175	24	0	0	8	3.5	0.5
13669	Lamb, ground, cooked	3 oz	85.1	241	21	0	0	17	7.1	1.2
13522	Lamb, kabob meat, lean, broiled, 1/4" trim	3 oz	85.1	158	24	0	0	6	2.5	0.6
	Pork									
12000	Bacon, broiled, pan-fried, or roasted	3 pce	19	103	7	0	0	8	3.5	0.9
28143	Canadian bacon	1 ea	56	68	9	1		3	1.4	0.3
12212	Ham, cured, boneless, extra lean (5% fat) roasted	1 cup	140	203	29	2	0	8	3.7	0.8
12211	Ham, cured, boneless, regular fat (11% fat) roasted	1 cup	140	249	32	0	0	13	6.2	2
12309	Pork, average of retail cuts, cooked	3 oz	85.1	232	23	0	0	15	6.5	1.2
12097	Pork, ribs, backribs, roasted	3 oz	85.1	315	21	0	0	25	11.5	2
58237	Pork, stomach, cooked	3 oz	85.1	134	18	0	0	6	1.8	0.6
12099	Pork, ground, cooked	3 oz	85.1	253	22	0	0	18	7.9	1.6
12178	Pork, pigs feet, simmered	3 oz	85.1	197	19	0	0	14	6.8	1.3
	Game Meats									
51147	Dove, whole, cooked	3 oz	85.1	186	20	0	0	11	4.6	2.3
16063	Duck, liver, raw, domesticated	1 ea	44	60	8	2	0	2	0.3	0.3
40567	Deer loin, lean, 1" steak, broiled	3 oz	85.1	128	26	0	0	2	0.3	0.1
14009	Bison, roasted	3 oz	85.1	122	24	0	0	2	0.8	0.2
15240	Cornish game hen w/skin, roasted	3 oz	85.1	221	19	0	0	15	6.8	3.1
15242	Cornish game hen, no skin, roasted	3 oz	85.1	114	20	0	0	3	1.1	0.8
16020	Duck breast, wild, no skin, raw	4 oz	113.4	139	23	0	0	5	1.4	0.7
16019	Duck, whole, wild, raw	4 oz	113.4	239	20	0	0	17	7.7	2.3
16048	Goose liver pate/pate de fois gras, smoked, canned	1 tbsp	13	60	1	1	0	6	3.3	0.1
51149	Quail, whole, cooked	3 oz	85.1	199	21	0	0	12	4.2	3
16013	Quail, whole, raw	4 oz	113.4	218	22	0	0	14	4.7	3.4
14004	Rabbit, roasted	3 oz	85.1	168	25	0	0	7	1.8	1.3
51111	Squab/pigeon, whole, raw	4 oz	113.4	333	21	0	0	27	11	3.5
	Lunchmeats									
13103	Beef, chopped smoked & cured, slice, 1 oz	1 pce	28.4	38	6	1	0	1	0.5	0.1
13335	Beef, smoked, sliced	1 pce	71	99	14	0	0	5	2.6	0.2
13000	Beef, thin slices	1 oz	28.4	42	5	0	0	2	0.9	0.1
57871	Salami, beerwurst, beef, 2-3/4" × 1/16" slice	1 pce	6	17	1	0	0	1	0.6	0.1
58275	Bologna, beef and pork, low fat	1 ea	14	32	2	0	0	3	1.3	0.2
58280	Bologna, beef, low fat	1 ea	28	57	3	1	0	4	1.8	0.1
58212	Bologna, beef, reduced sod, thin slice	1 pce	14	44	2	0	0	4	1.9	0.1
13157	Chicken breast, oven roasted deluxe	1 oz	28.4	29	5	1	0	1	0.2	0.1
90737	Chicken salad, lunchmeat spread	1 ea	118	171	6	12		11	3.5	4.2
13306	Corned beef, cooked, chopped, pressed	1 ea	71	101	14	1	0	5	2.6	0.2
13264	Ham, slices, regular (11% fat)	1 cup	135	220	22	5	2	12	5.9	1.1
13206	Lunchmeat loaf, old fashioned	1 pce	28	65	4	2	0	5	2.2	0.7
13049	Lunchmeat loaf, olive w/ pork	1 pce	28.4	67	3	3	0	5	2.2	0.5
13337	Pastrami, cooked, smoked, chopped, pressed	1 oz	28.4	40	6	0	0	2	0.9	0.1
13101	Pastrami, beef, cured	1 oz	28.4	41	6	0	0	2	0.6	0.1
13020	Pastrami, turkey	2 pce	56.7	70	9	2	0	2	0.8	0.6
13215	Salami, beef, cotto	1 oz	28.4	59	4	1	0	4	2	0.2
11913	Spam, pork with ham, minced, canned	1 ea	56.7	176	8	2	0	15	7.8	1.7
13123	Turkey bologna	1 oz	28.4	52	3	1	0	4	1.5	1
16160	Turkey breast slice	1 pce	21	22	4	1	0	0	0.1	0.1

Sat (g)	Chol (mg)	Calc (mg)	Iron (mg)	Mag (mg)	Phos (mg)	Pota (mg)	Sodi (mg)	Zinc (mg)	Vit A (RAE)	Vit C (mg)	Thia (mg)	Ribo (mg)	Niac (mg)	Vit B6 (mg)	Vit B12 (µg)	Vit E (fog)	Fol (µg)	Alc (g)
3.1		18	1.86	22.1	187	289	68	3			0.15	0.28	6.94	0.44	1.71			0
7.5	83	14	1.6	19.6	160	264	61	3.8	0	0	0.09	0.21	5.67	0.11	2.17	0.1	15.3	0
2.9	78	13	1.74	22.1	179	293	65	4.5	0	0	0.09	0.24	5.38	0.14	2.22	0.2	19.6	0
6.9		19	1.52	20.4	171	288	69	4	0	0	0.09	0.21	5.7	0.12	2.22	0.2	16	0
2.2		11	1.99	26.4	191	285	65	4.9	0	0	0.09	0.26	5.63	0.12	2.58	0.2	20	0
2.6	21	2	0.27	6.3	101	107	439	0.7	2	0	0.08	0.05	2.11	0.07	0.23	0.1	0.4	0
1	27	3	0.5	10.6		156	569	1	0	0.8								0
2.5	74	11	2.07	19.6	274	402	1684	4	0	0	1.06	0.28	5.63	0.56	0.91	0.4	4.2	0
4.4	83	11	1.88	30.8	393	573	2100	3.5	0	0	1.02	0.46	8.61	0.43	0.98	0.4	4.2	0
5.3	77	21	0.94	20.4	197	301	53	2.5	2	0.3	0.66	0.28	4.19	0.34	0.66	0.2	5.1	0
9.4	100	38	1.17	17.9	166	268	86	2.9	3	0.3	0.36	0.17	3.02	0.26	0.54	0.4	2.6	0
2.5	269	13	1.05	12.8	110	72	34	2.5	0	0	0.03	0.16	1.17	0.02	0.41	0.1	2.6	0
6.6	80	19	1.1	20.4	192	308	62	2.7	2	0.6	0.6	0.19	3.58	0.33	0.46	0.2	5.1	0
3.7	91	0	0.83	4.3	70	28	62	0.9	0	0	0.01	0.05	0.5	0.03	0.35	0.1	1.7	0
3.2	99	14	5.03	22.1	283	218	49	3.3	24	2.5	0.24	0.3	6.47	0.49	0.35	0.1	5.1	0
0.6	227	5	13.43	10.6	118	101	62	1.4	5273	2	0.25	0.39	2.86	0.33	23.76	0.6	324.7	0
0.7	67	5	3.48	25.5	236	339	49	3.1	0	0	0.24	0.44	9.15	0.64	1.56	0.5	7.7	0
0.8	70	7	2.91	22.1	178	307	49	3.1	0	0	0.09	0.23	3.16	0.34	2.43	0.3	6.8	0
4.3	111	11	0.77	15.3	124	208	54	1.3	27	0.4	0.06	0.17	5.02	0.26	0.24	0.3	1.7	0
0.8	90	11	0.66	16.2	127	213	54	1.3	17	0.5	0.06	0.19	5.34	0.3	0.26	0.2	1.7	0
1.5	87	3	5.11	24.9	211	304	65	0.8	18	7	0.47	0.35	3.91	0.71	0.86	0.3	28.4	0
5.7	91	6	4.72	22.7	191	282	64	0.9	29	5.9	0.4	0.31	3.76	0.6	0.74	0.8	23.8	0
1.9	20	9	0.72	1.7	26	18	91	0.1	130	0.3	0.01	0.04	0.33	0.01	1.22	0.2	7.8	0
3.4	73	13	3.77	18.7	237	184	44	2.6	60	2	0.19	0.26	6.74	0.53	0.31	0.6	5.1	0
3.8	86	15	4.5	26.1	312	245	60	2.7	83	6.9	0.28	0.29	8.55	0.68	0.49	0.8	9.1	0
2	70	16	1.93	17.9	224	326	40	1.9	0	0	0.08	0.18	7.17	0.4	7.06	0.7	9.4	0
9.6	108	14	4.01	24.9	281	226	61	2.5	83	5.9	0.24	0.25	6.86	0.46	0.45	0.1	6.8	0
0.5	13	2	0.81	6	51	107	357	1.1	0	0	0.02	0.05	1.3	0.1	0.49		2.3	0
1.8	48	10	1.6			239	1016				0.06	0.17	2.74					0
0.8	20	3	0.59	5.4	48	122	401	1.1	0	0	0.02	0.05	1.21	0.1	0.73	0.1	3.1	0
0.5	4	2	0.1	1.1	8	15	44	0.1	0	0	0.01	0.01	0.18	0.01	0.07	0	0.3	0
1	5	2	0.09	1.7	25	22	155	0.2	0	0	0.02	0.02	0.36	0.03	0.18	0	0.7	0
1.5	12	3	0.28	3.4	50	41	330	0.5	0	0.3	0.01	0.03	0.7	0.04	0.39	0.1	1.4	0
1.6	8	2	0.2	1.4	11	22	95	0.3	0	0	0.01	0.02	0.37	0.03	0.2	0	0.7	0
0.2	14	2	0.33	6.8	76	75	337	0.2	0	0								0
2.3	31						552		0									0
2	46	12	1.7			250	953				0.06	0.17	2.98					0
4	77	32	1.38	29.7	207	387	1760	1.8	0	5.4	0.85	0.24	3.92	0.44	0.57	0.1	9.4	0
1.6	17	32	0.37	6.4	58	82	332	0.5	0	0								0
1.7	11	31	0.15	5.4	36	84	421	0.4	17	0	0.08	0.07	0.52	0.07	0.36	0.1	0.6	0
0.9	18	5	0.7			104	300				0.03	0.07	1.16					0
0.8	19	3	0.63	5.4	50	67	251	1.4	9	0.4	0.02	0.05	1.21	0.08	0.52	0.1	2	0
0.7	39	6	2.38	7.9	113	196	556	1.2	2	9.1	0.03	0.14	2	0.15	0.14	0.1	2.8	0
1.9	24	2	0.77	4.8	64	59	372	0.6		0								0
5.6	40	8	0.51	7.9		130	776	1	0	0.5							1.7	0
1.1	19	35	0.47	6.2	56	43	306	0.5	0	0							1.7	0
0.1	9	2	0.3	4.4	34	63	213	0.3	2	1.2	0.03	0.07	0.02	0.03	0.02	0	0.8	0

MDA Code	Food Name	Amt	Wt (g)	Ener (kcal)	Prot (g)	Carb (g)	Fiber (g)	Fat (g)	Mono (g)	Poly (g)
57889	Turkey ham, cured	1 ea	227	286	40	5	0	11	4.3	3
58279	Turkey ham, sliced, extra lean, prepackaged or deli-sliced	1 cup	138	163	27	2	0	5	1.2	1.6
13144	Turkey salami	1 ea	28	41	4	0	0	3	0.9	0.7
	Sausage									
58009	Bacon and beef sticks	2 oz	56.7	293	16	0	0	25	12.4	2.4
58230	Beef sausage, fresh, cooked	2 oz	56.7	188	10	0	0	16	7.2	0.5
58228	Beef sausage, precooked	2 oz	56.7	230	9	0	0	21	9.3	0.6
13077	Blood sausage	1 pce	25	95	4	0	0	9	4	0.9
13079	Bratwurst, pork, cooked	1 ea	85	283	12	2	0	25	12.5	2.2
58012	Bratwurst, pork, beef and turkey, lite, smoked	3 oz	85.1	158	12	1	0	12	6.1	0.7
13070	Chorizo, pork & beef	1 ea	60	273	14	1	0	23	11	2.1
13190	Frank, beef, bun length	1 ea	57	185	6	2	0	17	8.3	0.5
13250	Frank, beef, fat free	1 ea	50	39	7	3	0	0	0.1	0
13191	Frank, beef	1 ea	45	147	5	1	0	14	6.6	0.6
13129	Frank, turkey & chicken	1 ea	45	85	5	2	0	6	2.5	1.4
57877	Frankfurter, beef	1 ea	45	148	5	2	0	13	6.4	0.5
58027	Frankfurter, beef, heated	1 ea	52	170	6	2	0	15	7.4	0.6
13260	Frankfurter, chicken	1 ea	45	116	6	3	0	9	3.8	1.8
13012	Frankfurter, turkey	1 ea	45	102	6	1	0	8	2.5	2.2
57890	Italian sausage, pork, cooked	1 ea	83	286	16	4	0	23	9.9	2.7
13043	Kielbasa, pork, beef & nonfat dry milk	1 pce	26	81	3	1	0	7	3.4	0.8
58020	Kielbasa, Polish sausage, smoked	3 oz	85.1	192	11	3	0	15	7	2
13044	Knockwurst/knackwurst	1 ea	68	209	8	2	0	19	8.7	2
13019	Liver sausage (Liverwurst)	1 pce	18	59	3	0	0	5	2.4	0.5
13021	Pepperoni sausage	1 pce	5.5	26	1	0	0	2	1	0.1
13022	Polish sausage, pork	1 ea	227	740	32	4	0	65	30.7	7
13185	Pork sausage links, cooked	2 ea	48	165	8	0	0	15	7.1	1.8
13180	Sausage, Braunschweiger liver sausage, sliced	1 pce	28	93	4	1	0	8	4.2	1
58227	Sausage, pork, precooked	3 oz	85	321	12	0	0	30	12.9	4.1
13184	Smokie links sausage	1 ea	43	130	5	1	0	12	5.7	1.2
13200	Summer sausage/Thuringer Cervalat	2 ea	46	140	7	0	0	12	5.6	1
58007	Turkey sausage, breakfast links, mild	2 ea	56	132	9	1	0	10	2.8	1.8
58219	Turkey, pork, and beef sausage, low fat, smoked	2 oz	56	57	4	6	0	1	0.6	0.2
	Meat Substitutes									
27044	Bacon bits, meatless	1 tbsp	7	33	2	2	1	2	0.4	0.9
7509	Bacon substitute, vegetarian, strips	3 ea	15	46	2	1	0	4	1.1	2.3
7558	Beef substitute, vegetarian fillets	1 ea	85	246	20	8	5	15	3.7	7.9
7561	Beef substitute, vegetarian patties	1 ea	56	110	12	4	3	5	1.2	2.6
62359	Breakfast patties, vegetarian	1 ea	38	79	10	4	2	3	0.7	1.3
91055	Burger patty, vegetarian	1 ea	85	91	14	8	4	1	0.3	0.2
7725	Burger crumbles, vegetarian	0.5 cup	55	116	11	3	3	6	2.3	2.5
7547	Chicken, meatless	1 cup	168	376	40	6	6	21	4.6	12.2
7722	Garden patties, frozen/Worthington, Morningstar	1 ea	67	119	11	10	4	4	1.1	2.2
7674	Harvest burger, original flavor, vegetable protein patty	1 ea	90	138	18	7	6	4	2.1	0.3
90626	Sausage, vegetarian, meatless	1 ea	28	72	5	3	1	5	1.3	2.6
7554	Soyburger	1 ea	70	125	13	9	3	4	0.8	1.6
7726	Spicy Black Bean Burger/Worthington, Morningstar	1 ea	78	115	12	15	5	1	0.2	0.4
	NUTS AND SEEDS									
4642	Beechnuts, dried	2 oz	56.7	327	4	19	2	28	12.4	11.4
4757	Butternuts, dried	1 ea	3	18	1	0	0	2	0.3	1.3

Sat (g)	Chol (mg)	Calc (mg)	Iron (mg)	Mag (mg)	Phos (mg)	Pota (mg)	Sodi (mg)	Zinc (mg)	Vit A (RAE)	Vit C (mg)	Thia (mg)	Ribo (mg)	Niac (mg)	Vit B6 (mg)	Vit B12 (µg)	Vit E (mog)	Fol (µg)	Alc (g)
3.5	163	18	5.31	49.9	667	651	2529	5.9	16	0	0.07	0.34	4.81	0.47	0.52	1.5	15.9	0
1.8	92	7	1.86	27.6	420	413	1432	3.3	0	0	0.07	0.34	4.87	0.32	0.36	0.5	8.3	0
0.8	21	11	0.35	6.2	74	60	281	0.6	0	0								0
9.1	58	8	1.05	9.6	81	218	805	1.8	0	0	0.34	0.16	2.76	0.28	1.08	0.2	1.1	0
6.2	46	6	0.89	7.9	80	146	370	2.5	7	0	0.03	0.09	2.04	0.18	1.14	0.1	1.7	0
8.6	47	9	0.87	7.4	105	133	516	1.7	14	0.4	0.02	0.07	1.82	0.11	1.15	0.3	2.8	0
3.3	30	2	1.6	2	6	10	170	0.3	0	0	0.02	0.03	0.3	0.01	0.25	0	1.2	0
8.6	63	24	0.45	17.8	191	220	719	2.1	2	0	0.53	0.22	3.94	0.35	0.68	0	2.6	0
4.1	48	12	0.8	11.9	112	209	836	2.3	0	0	0.08	0.14	1.57	0.18	1.36	0	4.3	0
8.6	53	5	0.95	10.8	90	239	741	2	0	0	0.38	0.18	3.08	0.32	1.2	0.1	1.2	0
7.1	34	7	0.89	8.6	60	90	584	1.3	0	0							6.3	0
0.1	15	10	0.98	9.5	64	234	464	1.2	0	0								0
5.6	25	4	0.6	5.8	63	58	461	1	0	0	0.02	0.05	1.03	0.03	0.73		2.7	0
1.7	41	59	0.98	10.4	66	72	511	0.8	0	0								0
5.3	24	6	0.68	6.3	72	70	513	1.1	0	0	0.02	0.07	1.07	0.04	0.77	0.1	2.2	0
5.9	29	6	0.81	7.3	89	76	600	1.2	0		0.02	0.07	1.22	0.05	0.86	0.1	3.6	0
2.5	45	43	0.9	4.5	48	38	616	0.5	18	0	0.03	0.05	1.39	0.14	0.11	0.1	1.8	0
2.7	48	48	0.83	6.3	60	81	642	1.4	0	0	0.02	0.08	1.86	0.1	0.13	0.3	3.6	0
7.9	47	17	1.19	14.9	141	252	1002	2	8	0.1	0.52	0.19	3.46	0.27	1.08	0.2	4.2	0
2.6	17	11	0.38	4.2	38	70	280	0.5	0	0	0.06	0.06	0.75	0.05	0.42	0.1	1.3	0
5.3	60		1.06				1021		0	12.6								0
6.9	41	7	0.45	7.5	67	135	632	1.1	0	0	0.23	0.1	1.86	0.12	0.8	0.4	1.4	0
1.9	28	5	1.15	2.2	41	31	155	0.4	1495	0	0.05	0.19	0.77	0.03	2.42	0.1	5.4	0
0.9	6	1	0.08	1	10	17	98	0.2		0	0.03	0.01	0.3	0.02	0.09	0	0.3	0
23.4	159	27	3.27	31.8	309	538	1989	4.4	0	2.3	1.14	0.34	7.82	0.43	2.22	0.5	4.5	0
5.1	37	8	0.83	8.6	76	114	401	1.2	0	0								0
3	50	3	2.94	3.9	56	57	325	1	1322	2.5	0.06	0.45	2.57	0.09	5.26	0	13.2	0
9.9	63	116	0.78	11	234	261	639	1.3	16	0.6	0.18	0.13	3.44	0.13	0.6	0.5	0.8	0
4	27	4	0.5	7.3	103	77	433	0.9	0	0								0
4.9	39	4	1.03	6.9	60	105	658	1		0	0.11	0.13	2.02	0.14	1.73		2.3	0
4.4	34	18	0.6	14	104	110	328	1.2	0	17	0.04	0.1	2.06	0.21	0.24	0.2	4.5	0
0.5	12	6	1.23	9	41	136	446	0.7	0	1.1	0.07	0.04	0.87	0.06	0.16	0.1	3.4	0
0.3	0	7	0.05	6.6	15	10	124	0.1	0	0.1	0.04	0	0.11	0.01	0.08	0.5	8.9	0
0.7	0	3	0.36	2.8	10	26	220	0.1	1	0	0.66	0.07	1.13	0.07	0	1	6.3	0
2.4	0	81	1.7	19.6	382	510	416	1.2	0	0	0.94	0.76	10.2	1.27	3.57	2.9	86.7	0
0.8	0	16	1.18	10.1	193	101	308	1	0	0	0.5	0.34	5.6	0.67	1.34	1	43.7	0
0.5	1	18	1.92	1.1	106	102	259	0.4	0	0	5.38	0.13	1.84	0.19	1.5	0.3		0
0.1	0	87	2.9	16.2	181	434	382	0.7	0	0	0.26	0.55	4.11	0.2	0	0	245.6	0
1.6	0	40	3.2	1.1	87	89	238	0.8	0	0	4.96	0.18	1.49	0.27	2.18	0.3		0
3.1	0	59	5.49	28.6	563	91	1191	1.2	0	0	1.15	0.41	2.44	1.18	3.66	4.5	127.7	0
0.5	1	48	1.21	29.5	124	180	382	0.6	134	0	6.47	0.1	0	0	0	0.5	59	0
1	0	102	3.85	70.2	225	432	411	8.1	0	0	0.31	0.2	6.3	0.39	0	1.6	21.6	0
0.8	0	18	1.04	10.1	63	65	249	0.4	0	0	0.66	0.11	3.13	0.23	0	0.6	7.3	0
0.5	0	20	1.47	12.6	241	126	385	1.3	0	0	0.63	0.42	7	0.84	0	1.2	54.6	0
0.2	1	56	1.84	43.7	150	269	499	0.9		0	8.06	0.14	0	0.21	0.07	0.4		0
3.2	0	1	1.39	0	0	577	22	0.2	0	8.8	0.17	0.21	0.5	0.39	0		64.1	0
0	0	2	0.12	7.1	13	13	0	0.1	0	0.1	0.01	0	0.03	0.02	0	0.1	2	0

MDA Code	Food Name	Amt	Wt (g)	Ener (kcal)	Prot (g)	Carb (g)	Fiber (g)	Fat (g)	Mono (g)	Poly (g)
63195	Cashew nuts, raw	2 oz	56.7	314	10	17	2	25	13.5	4.4
4519	Cashews, dry roasted w/salt	0.25 cup	34.2	196	5	11	1	16	9.3	2.7
4645	Chestnuts, Chinese, dried	1 oz	28.4	103	2	23	1	1	0.3	0.1
63429	Filberts nuts, dry roasted, unsalted	1 oz	28	181	4	5	3	17	13.1	2.4
63081	Flax seeds/linseeds, whole	1 tbsp	11.2	60	2	3	3	5	0.8	3.2
4728	Macadamia nuts, dry roasted, unsalted	1 cup	134	962	10	18	11	102	79.4	2
4592	Mixed nuts, w/peanuts, dry roasted, salted	0.25 cup	34.2	203	6	9	3	18	10.7	3.7
4626	Peanut butter, chunky w/salt	2 tbsp	32	188	8	7	3	16	7.9	4.7
4756	Peanuts, dry roasted w/o salt	30 ea	30	176	7	6	2	15	7.4	4.7
4696	Peanuts, raw	0.25 cup	36.5	207	9	6	3	18	8.9	5.7
4540	Pistachio nuts, dry roasted, salted	0.25 cup	32	182	7	9	3	15	7.7	4.4
4565	Pumpkin seeds/squash kernels, roasted w/o salt	0.25 cup	56.8	296	19	8	2	24	7.4	10.9
4523	Sesame seeds, whole, dried	0.25 cup	36	206	6	8	4	18	6.8	7.8
4551	Sunflower kernels, dry roast w/o salt	0.25 cup	32	186	6	8	4	16	3	10.5
	SEAFOOD									
50710	Fish broth	1 cup	244	39	5	1	0	1	0.3	0.4
7549	Fish sticks, meatless	1 ea	28	81	6	3	2	5	1.2	2.6
19041	Abalone, fried	3 oz	85.1	161	17	9	0	6	2.3	1.4
17029	Bass, freshwater, cooked w/dry heat	3 oz	85.1	124	21	0	0	4	1.6	1.2
17104	Bass, striped, cooked w/dry heat	3 oz	85.1	106	19	0	0	3	0.7	0.9
17032	Carp, raw	4 oz	113.4	144	20	0	0	6	2.6	1.6
17088	Catfish, channel, breaded & fried	3 oz	85.1	195	15	7	1	11	4.8	2.8
17179	Catfish, channel, farmed, cooked w/dry heat	3 oz	85.1	129	16	0	0	7	3.5	1.2
17035	Caviar, black/red, granular	1 tbsp	16	40	4	1	0	3	0.7	1.2
19002	Clams, canned, drained	3 oz	85.1	126	22	4	0	2	0.1	0.5
71140	Clams, raw	4 oz	113.4	84	14	3	0	1	0.1	0.3
17037	Cod, Atlantic, baked/broiled (dry heat)	3 oz	85.1	89	19	0	0	1	0.1	0.2
17107	Cod, Pacific, cooked w/dry heat	3 oz	85.1	89	20	0	0	1	0.1	0.3
72116	Conch, baked/broiled	3 oz	85.1	111	22	1	0	1	0.3	0.2
19036	Crab, Alaskan King, boiled/steamed	3 oz	85.1	83	16	0	0	1	0.2	0.5
19037	Crab, Alaskan King, imitation surimi	3 oz	85.1	87	10	9	0	1	0.2	0.6
71722	Crayfish, farmed, cooked w/moist heat	3 oz	85.1	74	15	0	0	1	0.2	0.4
17289	Eel, baked or broiled (dry heat)	3 oz	85.1	201	20	0	0	13	7.8	1
17090	Haddock, baked or broiled (dry heat)	3 oz	85.1	95	21	0	0	1	0.1	0.3
17291	Halibut, Atlantic & Pacific, baked or broiled (dry heat)	3 oz	85.1	119	23	0	0	3	0.8	0.8
17111	Halibut, Greenland, cooked w/dry heat	3 oz	85.1	203	16	0	0	15	9.1	1.5
17047	Herring, Atlantic, baked or broiled (dry heat)	3 oz	85.1	173	20	0	0	10	4.1	2.3
17112	Herring, Pacific, cooked w/dry heat	3 oz	85.1	213	18	0	0	15	7.5	2.6
17049	Mackerel, Atlantic, baked or broiled (dry heat)	3 oz	85.1	223	20	0	0	15	6	3.7
17115	Mackerel, king, cooked w/dry heat	3 oz	85.1	114	22	0	0	2	0.8	0.5
19044	Shellfish, Mussel, Blue, boiled/steamed	3 oz	85.1	146	20	6	0	4	0.9	1
17093	Ocean Perch, Atlantic, baked or broiled (dry heat)	3 oz	85.1	103	20	0	0	2	0.7	0.5
19048	Octopus, common, cooked w/moist heat	3 oz	85.1	140	25	4	0	2	0.3	0.4
19089	Oyster, Eastern, farmed, raw	4 oz	113.4	67	6	6	0	2	0.2	0.7
17094	Perch, baked or broiled (dry heat)	3 oz	85.1	100	21	0	0	1	0.2	0.4
17095	Pike, Northern, baked or broiled (dry heat)	3 oz	85.1	96	21	0	0	1	0.2	0.2
17118	Pike, Walleye, cooked w/dry heat	3 oz	85.1	101	21	0	0	1	0.3	0.5
17096	Pollock, Walleye, baked or broiled	3 oz	85.1	96	20	0	0	1	0.1	0.4
17073	Pompano, Florida, baked or broiled (dry heat)	3 oz	85.1	180	20	0	0	10	2.8	1.2
17074	Rockfish, Pacific, baked or broiled (dry heat)	3 oz	85.1	103	20	0	0	2	0.4	0.5

Sat (g)	Chol (mg)	Calc (mg)	Iron (mg)	Mag (mg)	Phos (mg)	Pota (mg)	Sodi (mg)	Zinc (mg)	Vit A (RAE)	Vit C (mg)	Thia (mg)	Ribo (mg)	Niac (mg)	Vit B6 (mg)	Vit B12 (µg)	Vit E (mog)	Fol (µg)	Alc (g)
4.4	0	21	3.79	165.6	336	374	7	3.3	0	0.3	0.24	0.03	0.6	0.24	0	0.5	14.2	0
3.1	0	15	2.05	88.9	168	193	219	1.9	0	0	0.07	0.07	0.48	0.09	0	0.3	23.6	0
0.1	0	8	0.65	38.9	44	206	1	0.4	5	16.6	0.07	0.08	0.37	0.19	0	0.3	31.2	0
1.3	0	34	1.23	48.4	87	211	0	0.7	1	1.1	0.09	0.03	0.57	0.17	0	4.3	24.6	0
0.4	0	29	0.64	43.9	72	91	3	0.5	0	0.1	0.18	0.02	0.34	0.05	0	0	9.7	0
16	0	94	3.55	158.1	265	486	5	1.7	0	0.9	0.95	0.12	3.05	0.48	0	0.8	13.4	0
2.4	0	24	1.27	77	149	204	229	1.3	0	0.1	0.07	0.07	1.61	0.1	0	3.7	17.1	0
2.6	0	14	0.61	51.2	102	238	156	0.9	0	0	0.03	0.04	4.38	0.13	0	2	29.4	0
2.1	0	16	0.68	52.8	107	197	2	1	0	0	0.13	0.03	4.06	0.08	0	2.1	43.5	0
2.5	0	34	1.67	61.3	137	257	7	1.2	0	0	0.23	0.05	4.4	0.13	0	3	87.6	0
1.8	0	35	1.34	38.4	155	333	130	0.7	4	0.7	0.27	0.05	0.46	0.41	0	0.6	16	0
4.5	0	24	8.49	303.3	666	458	10	4.2	11	1	0.12	0.18	0.99	0.05	0	0	32.4	0
2.5	0	351	5.24	126.4	226	168	4	2.8	0	0	0.28	0.09	1.63	0.28	0	0.1	34.9	0
1.7	0	22	1.22	41.3	370	272	1	1.7	0	0.4	0.03	0.08	2.25	0.26	0	8.4	75.8	0
0.3	0	73	0.51	2.4	73	210	776	0.2	2	0	0	0.07	3.34	0.02	0.24	0.4	9.8	0
0.8	0	27	0.56	6.4	126	168	137	0.4	0	0	0.31	0.25	3.36	0.42	1.18	1.1	28.6	0
1.4	80	31	3.23	47.7	185	242	503	0.8	2	1.5	0.19	0.11	1.62	0.13	0.59	5.1	11.9	0
0.9	74	88	1.63	32.3	218	388	77	0.7	30	1.8	0.07	0.08	1.3	0.12	1.97	0.6	14.5	0
0.6	88	16	0.92	43.4	216	279	75	0.4	26	0	0.1	0.03	2.18	0.29	3.75	0.5	8.5	0
1.2	75	46	1.41	32.9	471	378	56	1.7	10	1.8	0.13	0.06	1.86	0.22	1.74	0.7	17	0
2.8	69	37	1.22	23	184	289	238	0.7	7	0	0.06	0.11	1.94	0.16	1.62	1.1	25.5	0
1.5	54	8	0.7	22.1	208	273	68	0.9	13	0.7	0.36	0.06	2.14	0.14	2.38	1.1	6	0
0.6	94	44	1.9	48	57	29	240	0.2	90	0	0.03	0.1	0.02	0.05	3.2	1.1	8	0
0.2	57	78	23.79	15.3	288	534	95	2.3	154	18.8	0.13	0.36	2.85	0.09	84.16	0.5	24.7	0
0.1	39	52	15.85	10.2	192	356	64	1.6	102	14.7	0.09	0.24	2	0.07	56.06	0.4	18.1	0
0.1	47	12	0.42	35.7	117	208	66	0.5	12	0.9	0.07	0.07	2.14	0.24	0.89	0.7	6.8	0
0.1	40	8	0.28	26.4	190	440	77	0.4	9	2.6	0.02	0.04	2.11	0.39	0.89	0.3	6.8	0
0.3	55	83	1.2	202.5	185	139	130	1.5	6	0	0.05	0.07	0.89	0.05	4.47	5.4	152.3	0
0.1	45	50	0.65	53.6	238	223	912	6.5	8	6.5	0.05	0.05	1.14	0.15	9.79	0.8	43.4	0
0.2	17	11	0.33	36.6	240	77	716	0.3	17	0	0.03	0.02	0.15	0.03	1.36	0.1	1.7	0
0.2	117	43	0.94	28.1	205	203	83	1.3	13	0.4	0.04	0.07	1.42	0.11	2.64	0.8	9.4	0
2.6	137	22	0.54	22.1	236	297	55	1.8	968	1.5	0.16	0.04	3.82	0.07	2.46	4.3	14.5	0
0.1	63	36	1.15	42.5	205	340	74	0.4	16	0	0.03	0.04	3.94	0.29	1.18	0.4	11.1	0
0.4	35	51	0.91	91.1	243	490	59	0.5	46	0	0.06	0.08	6.06	0.34	1.17	0.9	11.9	0
2.6	50	3	0.72	28.1	179	293	88	0.4	15	0	0.06	0.09	1.64	0.41	0.82	1.1	0.9	0
2.2	66	63	1.2	34.9	258	357	98	1.1	31	0.6	0.1	0.25	3.51	0.3	11.18	1.2	10.2	0
3.6	84	90	1.23	34.9	248	461	81	0.6	30	0	0.06	0.22	2.4	0.44	8.19	1.1	5.1	0
3.6	64	13	1.34	82.5	237	341	71	0.8	46	0.3	0.14	0.35	5.83	0.39	16.17	1.6	1.7	0
0.4	58	34	1.94	34.9	271	475	173	0.6	214	1.4	0.1	0.49	8.9	0.43	15.32	1.5	7.7	0
0.7	48	28	5.72	31.5	243	228	314	2.3	77	11.6	0.26	0.36	2.55	0.09	20.42	1.2	64.7	0
0.3	46	117	1	33.2	236	298	82	0.5	12	0.7	0.11	0.11	2.07	0.23	0.98	1.4	8.5	0
0.4	82	90	8.12	51.1	237	536	391	2.9	77	6.8	0.05	0.06	3.22	0.55	30.64	1	20.4	0
0.5	28	50	6.55	37.4	105	141	202	43	9	5.3	0.12	0.07	1.44	0.07	18.37	0.8	20.4	0
0.2	98	87	0.99	32.3	219	293	67	1.2	9	1.4	0.07	0.1	1.62	0.12	1.87	1.3	5.1	0
0.1	43	62	0.6	34	240	282	42	0.7	20	3.2	0.06	0.07	2.38	0.11	1.96	0.2	14.5	0
0.3	94	120	1.42	32.3	229	425	55	0.7	20	0	0.27	0.17	2.38	0.12	1.97	0.2	14.5	0
0.2	82	5	0.24	62.1	410	329	99	0.5	21	0	0.06	0.06	1.4	0.06	3.57	0.7	3.4	0
3.8	54	37	0.57	26.4	290	541	65	0.6	31	0	0.58	0.13	3.23	0.2	1.02	0.2	14.5	0
0.4	37	10	0.45	28.9	194	443	66	0.5	60	0	0.04	0.07	3.34	0.23	1.02	1.3	8.5	0

MDA Code	Food Name	Amt	Wt (g)	Ener (kcal)	Prot (g)	Carb (g)	Fiber (g)	Fat (g)	Mono (g)	Poly (g)
17120	Roe, cooked w/dry heat	3 oz	85.1	174	24	2	0	7	1.8	2.9
17121	Roughy, Orange, cooked w/dry heat	3 oz	85.1	89	19	0	0	1	0.4	0.2
17181	Salmon, Atlantic, farmed, cooked w/dry heat	3 oz	85.1	175	19	0	0	11	3.8	3.8
17123	Salmon, Atlantic, wild, cooked w/dry heat	3 oz	85.1	155	22	0	0	7	2.3	2.8
17099	Salmon, Sockeye, baked or broiled (dry heat)	3 oz	85.1	184	23	0	0	9	4.5	2.1
17086	Sea bass, baked or broiled (dry heat)	3 oz	85.1	106	20	0	0	2	0.5	0.8
17023	Sea trout, cooked w/dry heat	3 oz	85.1	113	18	0	0	4	1	0.8
17076	Shark, battered, fried	3 oz	85.1	194	16	5	0	12	5.1	3.1
17100	Smelt, Rainbow, baked or broiled (dry heat)	3 oz	85.1	106	19	0	0	3	0.7	1
17022	Snapper, baked or broiled (dry heat)	3 oz	85.1	109	22	0	0	1	0.3	0.5
71707	Squid, fried	3 oz	85.1	149	15	7	0	6	2.3	1.8
71139	Sturgeon, baked or broiled	3 oz	85.1	115	18	0	0	4	2.1	0.8
17079	Sturgeon, smoked	3 oz	85.1	147	27	0	0	4	2	0.4
17066	Swordfish, baked or broiled (dry heat)	3 oz	85.1	132	22	0	0	4	1.7	1
17185	Trout, Rainbow, farmed, cooked w/dry heat	3 oz	85.1	144	21	0	0	6	1.8	2
17082	Trout, Rainbow, wild, cooked w/dry heat	3 oz	85.1	128	20	0	0	5	1.5	1.6
56007	Tuna salad, lunchmeat spread	2 tbsp	25.6	48	4	2	0	2	0.7	1.1
17101	Tuna, Bluefin, baked or broiled (dry heat)	3 oz	85.1	157	25	0	0	5	1.7	1.6
17177	Tuna, Yellowfin, fresh, cooked w/dry heat	3 oz	85.1	118	26	0	0	1	0.2	0.3
17151	White tuna, canned in H20, drained	3 oz	85.1	109	20	0	0	3	0.7	0.9
17083	White tuna, canned in oil, drained	3 oz	85.1	158	23	0	0	7	2.8	2.5
17162	Fish, Whitefish, cooked w/dry heat	3 oz	85.1	146	21	0	0	6	2.2	2.3
17164	Fish, Yellowtail, cooked w/dry heat	3 oz	85.1	159	25	0	0	6		

VEGETABLES AND LEGUMES
Beans

MDA Code	Food Name	Amt	Wt (g)	Ener (kcal)	Prot (g)	Carb (g)	Fiber (g)	Fat (g)	Mono (g)	Poly (g)
92132	Baked beans, canned, no salt added	1 cup	253	266	12	52	14	1	0.1	0.4
7038	Baked beans, plain or vegetarian, canned	1 cup	254	239	12	54	10	1	0.2	0.3
56101	Baked beans w/franks, canned	0.5 cup	129.5	184	9	20	9	9	3.7	1.1
5197	Bean sprouts, mung, canned, drained	1 cup	125	15	2	3	1	0	0	0
7012	Black beans, boiled w/o salt	1 cup	172	227	15	41	15	1	0.1	0.4
92152	Chili beans, barbeque, ranch style, cooked	1 cup	253	245	13	43	11	3	0.2	1.4
9574	Cowpeas (blackeyed peas), immature seeds, boiled w/salt, drained	1 cup	165	160	5	34	8	1	0.1	0.3
90018	Cowpeas, cooked w/salt	1 cup	171	198	13	35	11	1	0.1	0.4
7057	Cowpeas, w/pork, canned	0.5 cup	120	100	3	20	4	2	0.8	0.3
9583	Fava beans (broadbeans), boiled w/salt	1 cup	170	187	13	33	9	1	0.1	0.3
7913	Fava beans, in pod, raw	1 cup	126	111	10	22		1	0.1	0.4
7081	Hummus, garbanzo or chick pea spread, homemade	1 tbsp	15.4	27	1	3	1	1	0.8	0.3
7087	Kidney beans, canned	1 cup	256	210	13	37	11	2	0.6	0.4
7047	Kidney beans, red, boiled w/o salt	1 cup	177	225	15	40	13	1	0.1	0.5
7006	Lentils, boiled w/o salt	1 cup	198	230	18	40	16	1	0.1	0.3
90021	Lima beans (baby), boiled w/salt	1 cup	182	229	15	42	14	1	0.1	0.3
7010	Lima beans (large) boiled w/o salt	1 cup	188	216	15	39	13	1	0.1	0.3
7011	Lima beans (large), canned	1 cup	241	190	12	36	12	0	0	0.2
5850	Lima beans, (baby), immature seeds, frozen, boiled w/salt, drained	0.5 cup	90	94	6	18	5	0	0	0.1
7219	Mung beans, boiled w/o salt	1 cup	202	212	14	39	15	1	0.1	0.3
7217	Mung beans, raw	1 cup	207	718	49	130	34	2	0.3	0.8
7022	Navy beans, boiled w/o salt	1 cup	182	255	15	47	19	1	0.2	0.6
7122	Navy beans, canned	1 cup	262	296	20	54	13	1	0.1	0.5
7051	Pinto beans, canned	1 cup	240	206	12	37	11	2	0.4	0.7
5854	Pinto beans, immature seeds, boiled w/salt, drained	3 oz	85.1	138	8	26	7	0	0	0.2

Sat (g)	Chol (mg)	Calc (mg)	Iron (mg)	Mag (mg)	Phos (mg)	Pota (mg)	Sodi (mg)	Zinc (mg)	Vit A (RAE)	Vit C (mg)	Thia (mg)	Ribo (mg)	Niac (mg)	Vit B6 (mg)	Vit B12 (µg)	Vit E (mg)	Fol (µg)	Alc (g)
1.6	408	24	0.66	22.1	438	241	100	1.1	77	14	0.24	0.81	1.87	0.16	9.82	7.2	78.3	0
0	68	9	0.96	15.3	87	154	59	0.3	20	0	0.04	0.05	1.55	0.06	0.4	1.6	4.3	0
2.1	54	13	0.29	25.5	214	327	52	0.4	13	3.1	0.29	0.11	6.85	0.55	2.38	0.8	28.9	0
1.1	60	13	0.88	31.5	218	534	48	0.7	11	0	0.23	0.41	8.58	0.8	2.6	1.1	24.7	0
1.6	74	6	0.47	26.4	235	319	56	0.4	54	0	0.18	0.15	5.68	0.19	4.94	1.1	4.3	0
0.6	45	11	0.31	45.1	211	279	74	0.4	54	0	0.11	0.13	1.62	0.39	0.26	0.5	5.1	0
1.1	90	19	0.3	34	273	372	63	0.5	30	0	0.06	0.18	2.49	0.39	2.94	0.2	5.1	0
2.7	50	43	0.94	36.6	165	132	104	0.4	46	0	0.06	0.08	2.37	0.26	1.03	0.9	12.8	0
0.5	77	66	0.98	32.3	251	317	66	1.8	14	0	0.01	0.12	1.5	0.14	3.38	0.5	4.3	0
0.3	40	34	0.2	31.5	171	444	49	0.4	30	1.4	0.05	0	0.29	0.39	2.98	0.5	5.1	0
1.6	221	33	0.86	32.3	214	237	260	1.5	9	3.6	0.05	0.39	2.21	0.05	1.05	1.6	11.9	0
1	66	14	0.77	38.3	231	310	59	0.5	224	0	0.07	0.08	8.6	0.2	2.13	0.5	14.5	0
0.9	68	14	0.79	40	239	323	629	0.5	238	0	0.08	0.08	9.45	0.23	2.47	0.4	17	0
1.2	43	5	0.89	28.9	287	314	98	1.3	35	0.9	0.04	0.1	10.03	0.32	1.72	0.5	1.7	0
1.8	58	73	0.28	27.2	226	375	36	0.4	73	2.8	0.2	0.07	7.48	0.34	4.23	0	20.4	0
1.4	59	73	0.32	26.4	229	381	48	0.4	13	1.7	0.13	0.08	4.91	0.29	5.36	0.4	16.2	0
0.4	3	4	0.26	4.9	46	46	103	0.1	6	0.6	0.01	0.02	1.72	0.02	0.31	0.2	2	0
1.4	42	9	1.11	54.5	277	275	43	0.7	644	0	0.24	0.26	8.97	0.45	9.26	1.1	1.7	0
0.3	49	18	0.8	54.5	208	484	40	0.6	17	0.9	0.43	0.05	10.16	0.88	0.51	0.5	1.7	0
0.7	36	12	0.83	28.1	185	202	321	0.4	5	0	0.01	0.04	4.93	0.18	1	0.7	1.7	0
1.1	26	3	0.55	28.9	227	283	337	0.4	4	0	0.01	0.07	9.95	0.37	1.87	2	4.3	0
1	66	28	0.4	35.7	294	346	55	1.1	33	0	0.15	0.13	3.27	0.29	0.82	0.2	14.5	0
	60	25	0.54	32.3	171	458	43	0.6	26	2.5	0.15	0.04	7.42	0.16	1.06	0.2	3.4	0
0.3	0	126	0.73	81	263	749	3	3.5	13	7.8	0.38	0.15	1.09	0.33	0	1.3	60.7	0
0.2	0	86	3	66	183	551	856	4.2	13	0	0.24	0.1	1.09	0.21	0	0.4	30.5	0
3	8	62	2.24	36.3	135	304	557	2.4	5	3	0.08	0.07	1.17	0.06	0.44	0.6	38.8	0
0	0	18	0.54	11.2	40	34	175	0.4	1	0.4	0.04	0.09	0.27	0.04	0	0	12.5	0
0.2	0	46	3.61	120.4	241	611	2	1.9	1	0	0.42	0.1	0.87	0.12	0	0.1	256.3	0
0.4	0	78	4.71	113.8	390	1138	1834	5.1	3	4.3	0.1	0.38	0.91	0.68	0.03	0.5	65.8	0
0.2	0	211	1.85	85.8	84	690	396	1.7	66	3.6	0.17	0.24	2.31	0.11	0	0.4	209.6	0
0.2	0	41	4.29	90.6	267	475	410	2.2	2	0.7	0.35	0.09	0.85	0.17	0	0.5	355.7	0
0.7	8	20	1.7	51.6	115	214	420	1.2	0	0.2	0.08	0.06	0.52	0.05	0	0.6	61.2	0
0.1	0	61	2.55	73.1	212	456	410	1.7	2	0.5	0.16	0.15	1.21	0.12	0	0	176.8	0
0.1	0	47	1.95	41.6	163	418	32	1.3	21	4.7	0.17	0.37	2.83	0.13	0		186.5	0
0.2	0	8	0.24	4.5	17	27	37	0.2	0	1.2	0.01	0.01	0.06	0.06	0	0.1	9.1	0
0.2	0	87	3	69.1	230	607	758	1.2	0	3.1	0.3	0.13	1.05	0.19	0	0.1	92.2	0
0.1	0	50	5.2	79.6	251	713	4	1.9	0	2.1	0.28	0.1	1.02	0.21	0	1.5	230.1	0
0.1	0	38	6.59	71.3	356	731	4	2.5	1	3	0.33	0.14	2.1	0.35	0	0.2	358.4	0
0.2	0	53	4.37	96.5	231	730	435	1.9	0	0	0.29	0.1	1.2	0.14	0	0.3	273	0
0.2	0	32	4.49	80.8	209	955	4	1.8	0	0	0.3	0.1	0.79	0.3	0	0.3	156	0
0.1	0	51	4.36	94	178	530	810	1.6	0	0	0.13	0.08	0.63	0.22	0	0.2	120.5	0
0.1	0	25	1.76	50.4	101	370	238	0.5	7	5.2	0.06	0.05	0.69	0.1	0	0.6	14.4	0
0.2	0	55	2.83	97	200	537	4	1.7	2	2	0.33	0.12	1.17	0.14	0	0.3	321.2	0
0.7	0	273	13.95	391.2	760	2579	31	5.5	12	9.9	1.29	0.48	4.66	0.79	0	1.1	1293.8	0
0.1	0	126	4.3	96.5	262	708	0	1.9	0	1.6	0.43	0.12	1.18	0.25	0	0	254.8	0
0.3	0	123	4.85	123.1	351	755	1174	2	0	1.8	0.37	0.14	1.28	0.27	0	2	162.4	0
0.4	0	103	3.5	64.8	221	583	706	1.7	0	2.2	0.24	0.15	0.7	0.18	0	1.4	144	0
0	0	44	2.31	46	85	550	271	0.6	0	0.6	0.23	0.09	0.54	0.17	0	0.3	28.9	0

MDA Code	Food Name	Amt	Wt (g)	Ener (kcal)	Prot (g)	Carb (g)	Fiber (g)	Fat (g)	Mono (g)	Poly (g)
5856	Snap green beans, boiled w/salt, drained	1 cup	125	44	2	10	4	0	0	0.2
6748	Snap green beans, raw	10 ea	55	17	1	4	2	0	0	0
5857	Snap yellow beans, boiled w/salt, drained	1 cup	125	44	2	10	4	0	0	0.2
5320	Snap yellow beans, raw	0.5 cup	55	17	1	4	2	0	0	0
90026	Split peas, boiled w/salt	0.5 cup	98	116	8	21	8	0	0.1	0.2
7053	White beans, boiled w/o salt	1 cup	179	249	17	45	11	1	0.1	0.3
7054	White beans, canned	1 cup	262	307	19	57	13	1	0.1	0.3
7052	Yellow beans, boiled w/o salt	1 cup	177	255	16	45	18	2	0.2	0.8
	Fresh Vegetables									
90542	Arrowroot, raw	1 ea	33	21	1	4	0	0	0	0
9577	Artichokes (globe or French) boiled w/salt, drained	1 ea	20	10	1	2	1	0	0	0
5723	Artichokes (globe or French) frozen	3 oz	85.1	32	2	7	3	0	0	0.2
6033	Arugula/roquette, raw	1 cup	20	5	1	1	0	0	0	0.1
5841	Asparagus, boiled w/salt, drained	0.5 cup	90	20	2	4	2	0	0	0.1
90406	Asparagus, raw	10 ea	35	7	1	1	1	0	0	0
6949	Bamboo shoots, boiled w/salt, drained	1 cup	120	13	2	2	1	0	0	0.1
6737	Bamboo shoots, raw	1 cup	151	41	4	8	3	0	0	0.2
5863	Beet greens, boiled w/salt, drained	1 cup	144	39	4	8	4	0	0.1	0.1
5312	Beet greens, raw	0.5 cup	19	4	0	1	1	0	0	0
5862	Beets, boiled w/salt, drained	0.5 cup	85	37	1	8	2	0	0	0.1
6755	Beets, canned, drained	1 cup	170	53	2	12	3	0	0	0.1
5573	Beets, peeled, raw	0.5 cup	68	29	1	7	2	0	0	0
5558	Broccoli stalks, raw	1 ea	114	32	3	6	4	0	0	0.2
6091	Broccoli, boiled w/salt, chopped, drained	0.5 cup	78	22	2	4	3	0	0	0.1
7909	Broccoli, Chinese, cooked	1 cup	88	19	1	3	2	1	0	0.3
9542	Broccoli raab, cooked	3 oz	85.1	28	3	3	2	0	0	0.1
9541	Broccoli raab, raw	3 oz	85.1	19	3	2	2	0	0	0.1
5870	Brussels sprouts, boiled w/salt, drained	0.5 cup	78	32	2	7	2	0	0	0.2
5036	Cabbage, raw	1 cup	70	17	1	4	2	0	0	0
5878	Cabbage, boiled w/salt, drained	0.5 cup	75	16	1	3	1	0	0	0.1
5608	Cabbage, Japanese style, fresh, pickled	0.5 cup	75	22	1	4	2	0	0	0
5609	Cabbage, mustard, salted	1 cup	128	36	1	7	4	0	0	0.1
9591	Cabbage, Pak-Choi (Chinese) boiled w/salt, drained	0.5 cup	85	10	1	2	1	0	0	0.1
5040	Cabbage, Pe-Tsai (Chinese) raw	1 cup	76	12	1	2	1	0	0	0.1
5880	Cabbage, red, boiled w/salt, drained	0.5 cup	75	22	1	5	2	0	0	0
5042	Cabbage, red, raw	0.5 cup	35	11	1	3	1	0	0	0
9550	Carrot, dehydrated	1 tbsp	4.6	16	0	4	1	0	0	0
90605	Carrots, baby, raw	1 ea	15	5	0	1	0	0	0	0
5887	Carrots, boiled w/salt, drained	0.5 cup	78	27	1	6	2	0	0	0.1
5199	Carrots, canned, drained	0.5 cup	73	18	0	4	1	0	0	0.1
5045	Carrots, chopped/grated, raw	1 ea	72	30	1	7	2	0	0	0.1
9197	Cassava (Yucca) raw	1 cup	206	330	3	78	4	1	0.2	0.1
5049	Cauliflower, raw	0.5 cup	50	12	1	3	1	0	0	0
5891	Cauliflower, boiled w/salt, drained	0.5 cup	62	14	1	3	2	0	0	0.1
5894	Celery, boiled w/salt, drained	0.5 cup	75	14	1	3	1	0	0	0.1
90436	Celery, raw	1 ea	17	2	0	1	0	0	0	0
9212	Chard, Swiss, boiled w/salt, drained	0.5 cup	87.5	18	2	4	2	0	0	0
9160	Chicory, Witloof (Belgian endive) raw	0.5 cup	45	8	0	2	1	0	0	0
6093	Collards, boiled w/salt, drained	1 cup	190	49	4	9	5	1	0	0.3
5060	Collards, raw	1 cup	36	11	1	2	1	0	0	0.1
6801	Corn ears, yellow, sweet, raw	1 ea	73	63	2	14	2	1	0.3	0.4

Sat (g)	Chol (mg)	Calc (mg)	Iron (mg)	Mag (mg)	Phos (mg)	Pota (mg)	Sodi (mg)	Zinc (mg)	Vit A (RAE)	Vit C (mg)	Thia (mg)	Ribo (mg)	Niac (mg)	Vit B6 (mg)	Vit B12 (µg)	Vit E (mg)	Fol (µg)	Alc (g)
0.1	0	55	0.81	22.5	36	182	299	0.3	44	12.1	0.09	0.12	0.77	0.07	0	0.6	41.2	0
0	0	20	0.57	13.8	21	115	3	0.1	19	9	0.05	0.06	0.41	0.04	0	0.2	20.4	0
0.1	0	58	1.6	31.2	49	374	299	0.5	5	12.1	0.09	0.12	0.77	0.07	0	0.6	41.2	0
0	0	20	0.57	13.8	21	115	3	0.1	3	9	0.05	0.06	0.41	0.04	0	0.1	20.4	0
0.1	0	14	1.26	35.3	97	355	233	1	0	0.4	0.19	0.05	0.87	0.05	0	0	63.7	0
0.2	0	161	6.62	112.8	202	1004	11	2.5	0	0	0.21	0.08	0.25	0.17	0	1.7	145	0
0.2	0	191	7.83	133.6	238	1189	13	2.9	0	0	0.25	0.1	0.3	0.2	0	0.5	170.3	0
0.5	0	110	4.39	131	324	575	9	1.9	0	3.2	0.33	0.18	1.25	0.23	0	0.9	143.4	0
0	0	2	0.73	8.2	32	150	9	0.2	0	0.6	0.05	0.02	0.56	0.09	0		111.5	0
0	0	9	0.26	12	17	71	66	0.1	2	2	0.01	0.01	0.2	0.02	0	0	10.2	0
0.1	0	16	0.43	23	49	211	40	0.3	7	4.5	0.05	0.12	0.73	0.07	0	0.1	107.2	0
0	0	32	0.29	9.4	10	74	5	0.1	24	3	0.01	0.02	0.06	0.01	0	0.1	19.4	0
0.1	0	21	0.82	12.6	49	202	216	0.5	45	6.9	0.15	0.13	0.98	0.07	0	1.4	134.1	0
0	0	8	0.75	4.9	18	71	1	0.2	13	2	0.05	0.05	0.34	0.03	0	0.4	18.2	0
0.1	0	14	0.29	3.6	24	640	288	0.6	0	0	0.02	0.06	0.36	0.12	0	0.8	2.4	0
0.1	0	20	0.76	4.5	89	805	6	1.7	2	6	0.23	0.11	0.91	0.36	0	1.5	10.6	0
0	0	164	2.74	97.9	59	1309	687	0.7	552	35.9	0.17	0.42	0.72	0.19	0	2.6	20.2	0
0	0	22	0.49	13.3	8	145	43	0.1	60	5.7	0.02	0.04	0.08	0.02	0	0.3	2.8	0
0	0	14	0.67	19.6	32	259	242	0.3	2	3.1	0.02	0.03	0.28	0.06	0	0	68	0
0	0	26	3.09	28.9	29	252	330	0.4	2	7	0.02	0.07	0.27	0.1	0	0.1	51	0
0	0	11	0.54	15.6	27	221	53	0.2	1	3.3	0.02	0.03	0.23	0.05	0	0	74.1	0
0.1	0	55	1	28.5	75	370	31	0.5	23	106.2	0.07	0.14	0.73	0.18	0	0.5	80.9	0
0	0	31	0.52	16.4	52	229	204	0.4	76	32.8	0.05	0.1	0.43	0.16	0	1.1	84.2	0
0.1	0	88	0.49	15.8	36	230	6	0.3	72	24.8	0.08	0.13	0.38	0.06	0	0.4	87.1	0
0	0	100	1.08	23	70	292	48	0.5	193	31.5	0.14	0.12	1.71	0.19		2.2	60.4	0
0	0	92	1.82	18.7	62	167	28	0.7	111	17.2	0.14	0.11	1.04	0.15	0	1.4	70.6	0
0.1	0	28	0.94	15.6	44	247	200	0.3	30	48.4	0.08	0.06	0.47	0.14	0	0.3	46.8	0
0	0	33	0.41	10.5	16	172	13	0.1	6	22.5	0.04	0.03	0.21	0.07	0	0.1	30.1	0
0	0	23	0.13	6	11	73	191	0.1	5	15.1	0.04	0.04	0.21	0.08	0	0.1	15	0
0	0	36	0.37	9	32	640	208	0.2	7	0.5	0	0.03	0.14	0.08	0	0.1	31.5	0
0	0	86	0.9	19.2	35	315	918	0.4	63	0	0.05	0.12	0.92	0.38	0	0	92.2	0
0	0	79	0.88	9.4	25	315	230	0.1	180	22.1	0.03	0.05	0.36	0.14	0	0.1	34.8	0
0	0	59	0.24	9.9	22	181	7	0.2	12	20.5	0.03	0.04	0.3	0.18	0	0.1	60	0
0	0	32	0.5	12.8	25	196	21	0.2	2	8.1	0.05	0.04	0.29	0.17	0	0.1	18	0
0	0	16	0.28	5.6	10	85	9	0.1	20	20	0.02	0.02	0.15	0.07	0	0	6.3	0
0	0	10	0.18	5.4	16	117	13	0.1	249	0.7	0.02	0.02	0.3	0.05	0	0.3	2.5	0
0	0	5	0.13	1.5	4	36	12	0	104	1.3	0	0.01	0.08	0.02	0	0.1	5	0
0	0	23	0.27	7.8	23	183	236	0.2	659	2.8	0.05	0.03	0.5	0.12	0	0.8	1.6	0
0	0	18	0.47	5.8	18	131	177	0.2	407	2	0.01	0.02	0.4	0.08	0	0.5	6.6	0
0	0	24	0.22	8.6	25	230	50	0.2	605	4.2	0.05	0.04	0.71	0.1	0	0.5	13.7	0
0.2	0	33	0.56	43.3	56	558	29	0.7	2	42.4	0.18	0.1	1.76	0.18	0	0.4	55.6	0
0	0	11	0.22	7.5	22	152	15	0.1	0	23.2	0.03	0.03	0.26	0.11	0	0	28.5	0
0	0	10	0.2	5.6	20	88	150	0.1	1	27.5	0.03	0.03	0.25	0.11	0	0	27.3	0
0	0	32	0.31	9	19	213	245	0.1	22	4.6	0.03	0.04	0.24	0.06	0	0.3	16.5	0
0	0	7	0.03	1.9	4	44	14	0	4	0.5	0	0.01	0.05	0.01	0	0	6.1	0
0	0	51	1.98	75.2	29	480	363	0.3	268	15.8	0.03	0.08	0.32	0.07	0	1.7	7.9	0
0	0	9	0.11	4.5	12	95	1	0.1	0	1.3	0.03	0.01	0.07	0.02	0		16.6	0
0.1	0	266	2.2	38	57	220	479	0.4	771	34.6	0.08	0.2	1.09	0.24	0	1.7	176.7	0
0	0	52	0.07	3.2	4	61	7	0	120	12.7	0.02	0.05	0.27	0.06	0	0.8	59.8	0
0.1	0	1	0.38	27	65	197	11	0.3	7	5	0.15	0.04	1.24	0.04	0	0.1	33.6	0

MDA Code	Food Name	Amt	Wt (g)	Ener (kcal)	Prot (g)	Carb (g)	Fiber (g)	Fat (g)	Mono (g)	Poly (g)
7202	Corn, white, sweet, ears, raw	1 ea	73	63	2	14	2	1	0.3	0.4
5900	Corn, yellow, sweet, boiled w/salt, drained	0.5 cup	82	89	3	21	2	1	0.3	0.5
5373	Cress, garden, raw	20 ea	20	6	1	1	0	0	0	0
5241	Dandelion greens, raw	1 cup	55	25	1	5	2	0	0	0.2
5908	Eggplant (brinjal) boiled w/salt, drained	1 cup	99	35	1	9	2	0	0	0.1
5202	Endive (escarole) raw	0.5 cup	25	4	0	1	1	0	0	0
5450	Fennel bulb, raw	0.5 cup	43.5	13	1	3	1	0		
7270	Hearts of palm, canned	0.5 cup	73	20	2	3	2	0	0.1	0.1
9182	Jicama, raw, slices	1 cup	120	46	1	11	6	0	0	0.1
5915	Kale, boiled w/salt, drained	0.5 cup	65	18	1	4	1	0	0	0.1
9191	Kale, raw	1 cup	67	34	2	7	1	0	0	0.2
5918	Kohlrabi, boiled w/salt, drained	1 cup	165	48	3	11	2	0	0	0.1
5078	Kohlrabi, peeled, raw	0.5 cup	67.5	18	1	4	2	0	0	0
5205	Leeks (bulb & lower leaves) raw	0.5 cup	44.5	27	1	6	1	0	0	0.1
5920	Leeks (bulb & lower leaves) boiled w/salt, drained	1 ea	124	38	1	9	1	0	0	0.1
90445	Lettuce, butterhead leaves, raw	1 pce	5	1	0	0	0	0	0	0
5089	Lettuce, cos/romaine, raw	2 pce	20	3	0	1	0	0	0	0
5087	Lettuce, looseleaf, raw	2 pce	20	3	0	1	0	0	0	0
9545	Lettuce, red leaf, raw	1 cup	28	4	0	1	0	0		
7949	Mushroom, oyster, raw	1 ea	15	5	1	1	0	0	0	0
5926	Mushroom, shiitake, boiled w/salt, drained	1 cup	145	81	2	21	3	0	0.1	0
51069	Mushrooms, brown, Italian, or crimini, raw	2 ea	28	6	1	1	0	0	0	0
90457	Mushrooms, canned, caps/slices, drained	8 ea	47	12	1	2	1	0	0	0.1
51067	Mushrooms, portobello, raw	1 oz	28	7	1	1	0	0	0	0
5927	Mustard greens, boiled w/salt, drained	0.5 cup	70	10	2	1	1	0	0.1	0
5207	Mustard greens, raw	1 cup	56	15	2	3	2	0	0.1	0
6971	Okra, boiled w/salt, drained	0.5 cup	80	18	1	4	2	0	0	0
90182	Okra, raw	8 ea	95	29	2	7	3	0	0	0
6074	Onions, boiled w/salt, chopped, drained	0.5 cup	105	46	1	11	1	0	0	0.1
90472	Onions, chopped, raw	1 ea	70	29	1	7	1	0	0	0
90487	Onions, spring (tops & bulb) chopped, raw	1 ea	5	2	0	0	0	0	0	0
9548	Onions, sweet, raw	1 oz	28	9	0	2	0	0		
9547	Onions, young green, tops only	1 tbsp	6	2	0	0	0	0	0	0
5936	Parsnip, boiled w/salt, drained	0.5 cup	78	63	1	15	3	0	0.1	0
5211	Parsnip, peeled, raw	0.5 cup	66.5	50	1	12	3	0	0.1	0
5281	Peas & carrots, canned, regular pack, solids & liquid	0.5 cup	127.5	48	3	11	3	0	0	0.2
6096	Peas w/edible pod-snow/sugar, boiled w/salt, drained	1 cup	160	67	5	11	4	0	0	0.2
6836	Peas w/edible pod-snow/sugar, raw	1 cup	98	41	3	7	3	0	0	0.1
5938	Peas, green, boiled w/salt, drained	0.5 cup	80	67	4	13	4	0	0	0.1
5116	Peas, green, raw	1 cup	145	117	8	21	7	1	0.1	0.3
9611	Peppers, green chili, canned	0.5 cup	69.5	15	1	3	1	0	0	0.1
7932	Peppers, jalapeno, raw	1 cup	90	27	1	5	2	1	0	0.3
9632	Peppers, serrano, raw	1 cup	105	34	2	7	4	0	0	0.2
90493	Peppers, sweet green, chopped/sliced, raw	10 pce	27	5	0	1	0	0	0	0
9549	Peppers, sweet, green, sauteed	1 oz	28	36	0	1	1	3	0.7	1.7
6990	Pepper, sweet red, raw	1 ea	10	3	0	1	0	0	0	0
9551	Peppers, sweet, red, sauteed	1 oz	28	41	0	2	1	4	0.7	1.8
9300	Pepper, sweet yellow, raw	1 ea	119	32	1	8	1	0	0	0.1
90589	Pickles, sweet, spear	1 ea	20	23	0	6	0	0	0	0
92209	Pickles, bread and butter	1 ea	8	6	0	2	0	0	0	0
5228	Pimiento, canned	20 pce	20	5	0	1	0	0	0	0

Sat (g)	Chol (mg)	Calc (mg)	Iron (mg)	Mag (mg)	Phos (mg)	Pota (mg)	Sodi (mg)	Zinc (mg)	Vit A (RAE)	Vit C (mg)	Thia (mg)	Ribo (mg)	Niac (mg)	Vit B6 (mg)	Vit B12 (µg)	Vit E (mg)	Fol (µg)	Alc (g)
0.1	0	1	0.38	27	65	197	11	0.3	0	5	0.15	0.04	1.24	0.04	0	0.1	33.6	0
0.2	0	2	0.5	26.2	84	204	207	0.4	11	5.1	0.18	0.06	1.32	0.05	0	0.1	37.7	0
0	0	16	0.26	7.6	15	121	3	0	69	13.8	0.02	0.05	0.2	0.05	0	0.1	16	0
0.1	0	103	1.7	19.8	36	218	42	0.2	136	19.2	0.1	0.14	0.44	0.14	0	2.6	14.8	0
0	0	6	0.25	10.9	15	122	237	0.1	2	1.3	0.08	0.02	0.59	0.09	0	0.4	13.9	0
0	0	13	0.21	3.8	7	78	6	0.2	27	1.6	0.02	0.02	0.1	0	0	0.1	35.5	0
	0	21	0.32	7.4	22	180	23	0.1	3	5.2	0	0.01	0.28	0.02	0		11.7	0
0.1	0	42	2.28	27.7	47	129	311	0.8	0	5.8	0.01	0.04	0.32	0.02	0		28.5	0
0	0	14	0.72	14.4	22	180	5	0.2	1	24.2	0.02	0.03	0.24	0.05	0	0.6	14.4	0
0	0	47	0.58	11.7	18	148	168	0.2	443	26.6	0.03	0.05	0.32	0.09	0	0.6	8.4	0
0.1	0	90	1.14	22.8	38	299	29	0.3	515	80.4	0.07	0.09	0.67	0.18	0	0.5	19.4	0
0	0	41	0.66	31.4	74	561	424	0.5	3	89.1	0.07	0.03	0.64	0.25	0	0.9	19.8	0
0	0	16	0.27	12.8	31	236	14	0	1	41.8	0.03	0.01	0.27	0.1	0	0.3	10.8	0
0	0	26	0.93	12.5	16	80	9	0.1	37	5.3	0.03	0.01	0.18	0.1	0	0.4	28.5	0
0	0	37	1.36	17.4	21	108	305	0.1	2	5.2	0.03	0.02	0.25	0.14	0	0.8	29.8	0
0	0	2	0.06	0.6	2	12	0	0	8	0.2	0	0	0.02	0	0	0	3.6	0
0	0	7	0.19	2.8	6	49	2	0	58	4.8	0.01	0.01	0.06	0.01	0	0	27.2	0
0	0	7	0.17	2.6	6	39	6	0	74	3.6	0.01	0.02	0.08	0.02	0	0.1	7.6	0
	0	9	0.34	3.4	8	52	7	0.1	105	1	0.02	0.02	0.09	0.03	0		10.1	0
0	0	0	0.2	2.7	18	63	3	0.1	0	0	0.02	0.05	0.74	0.02	0	0	4	0
0.1	0	4	0.64	20.3	42	170	348	1.9	0	0.4	0.05	0.25	2.17	0.23	0	0	30.4	0
0	0	5	0.11	2.5	34	125	2	0.3	0	0	0.03	0.14	1.06	0.03	0.03	0	3.9	0
0	0	5	0.37	7	31	61	200	0.3	0	0	0.04	0.01	0.75	0.03	0	0	5.6	0
0	0	2	0.17	3.1	36	136	2	0.2	0	0	0.02	0.13	1.26	0.03	0.01	0	6.2	0
0	0	52	0.49	10.5	29	141	176	0.1	221	17.7	0.03	0.04	0.3	0.07	0	0.8	51.1	0
0	0	58	0.82	17.9	24	198	14	0.1	294	39.2	0.04	0.06	0.45	0.1	0	1.1	104.7	0
0	0	62	0.22	28.8	26	108	193	0.3	11	13	0.11	0.04	0.7	0.15	0	0.2	36.8	0
0	0	77	0.76	54.2	60	288	8	0.6	18	20	0.19	0.06	0.95	0.2	0	0.3	83.6	0
0	0	23	0.25	11.6	37	174	251	0.2	0	5.5	0.04	0.02	0.17	0.14	0	0	15.8	0
0	0	15	0.13	7	19	101	2	0.1	0	4.5	0.03	0.02	0.06	0.1	0	0	13.3	0
0	0	4	0.07	1	2	14	1	0	2	0.9	0	0	0.03	0	0	0	3.2	0
	0	6	0.07	2.5	8	33	2	0	0	1.3	0.01	0.01	0.04	0.04		0	6.4	0
0	0	4	0.12	1.2	2	16	0	0	12	2.7	0	0.01	0.01	0	0	0	0.8	0
0	0	29	0.45	22.6	54	286	192	0.2	0	10.1	0.06	0.04	0.56	0.07	0	0.8	45.2	0
0	0	24	0.39	19.3	47	249	7	0.4	0	11.3	0.06	0.03	0.47	0.06	0	1	44.6	0
0.1	0	29	0.96	17.8	59	128	332	0.7	368	8.4	0.09	0.07	0.74	0.11	0	0.2	23	0
0.1	0	67	3.15	41.6	88	384	384	0.6	83	76.6	0.2	0.12	0.86	0.23	0	0.6	46.4	0
0	0	42	2.04	23.5	52	196	4	0.3	53	58.8	0.15	0.08	0.59	0.16	0	0.4	41.2	0
0	0	22	1.23	31.2	94	217	191	1	32	11.4	0.21	0.12	1.62	0.17	0	0.1	50.4	0
0.1	0	36	2.13	47.8	157	354	7	1.8	55	58	0.39	0.19	3.03	0.25	0	0.2	94.2	0
0	0	25	0.92	2.8	8	79	276	0.1	4	23.8	0.01	0.02	0.44	0.08	0		37.5	0
0.1	0	9	0.63	17.1	28	194	1	0.2	36	39.9	0.13	0.05	1.01	0.46	0	0.4	42.3	0
0.1	0	12	0.9	23.1	42	320	10	0.3	49	47.1	0.06	0.09	1.61	0.53	0	0.7	24.2	0
0	0	3	0.09	2.7	5	47	1	0	5	21.7	0.02	0.01	0.13	0.06	0	0.1	3	0
0.4	0	2	0.08	2.2	4	38	5	0	4	49.6	0.01	0.01	0.16	0.05	0	0.4	0.6	0
0	0	1	0.04	1.2	3	21	0	0	16	19	0.01	0.01	0.1	0.03	0	0.2	1.8	0
0.5	0	2	0.13	3.4	6	54	6	0	39	45.6	0.02	0.03	0.27	0.1	0	0.9	0.6	0
0	0	13	0.55	14.3	29	252	2	0.2	12	218.4	0.03	0.03	1.06	0.2	0	0.8	30.9	0
0	0	1	0.12	0.8	2	6	188	0	8	0.2	0	0.01	0.03	0	0	0.1	0.2	0
0	0	3	0.03	0.2	2	16	54	0	1	0.7	0	0	0	0	0	0	0.3	0
0	0	1	0.34	1.2	3	32	3	0	27	17	0	0.01	0.12	0.04	0	0.1	1.2	0

MDA Code	Food Name	Amt	Wt (g)	Ener (kcal)	Prot (g)	Carb (g)	Fiber (g)	Fat (g)	Mono (g)	Poly (g)
9251	Potatoes, red, flesh and skin, baked	1 ea	138	123	3	27	2	0	0	0.1
9245	Potatoes, russet, flesh and skin, baked	1 ea	138	134	4	30	3	0	0	0.1
90564	Potato, boiled w/o skin & w/salt	1 ea	299.6	258	5	60	6	0	0	0.1
5950	Potato, skin only, baked w/salt	1 ea	58	115	2	27	5	0	0	0
5964	Pumpkin, canned w/salt	0.5 cup	122.5	42	1	10	4	0	0	0
9203	Radicchio, raw	1 cup	40	9	1	2	0	0	0	0
90505	Radish, slices, raw	10 ea	20	3	0	1	0	0	0	0
5969	Rutabaga, boiled w/salt, drained	0.5 cup	120	47	2	10	2	0	0	0.1
90508	Sauerkraut, canned, solids & liquid	0.5 cup	71	13	1	3	2	0	0	0
6859	Seaweed, kelp, raw	0.5 cup	40	17	1	4	1	0	0	0
5260	Seaweed, spirulina, dried	0.5 cup	59.5	173	34	14	2	5	0.4	1.2
5427	Shallots, peeled, raw	1 tbsp	10	7	0	2	0	0	0	0
56076	Spinach egg souffle, homemade	1 cup	136	233	11	8	1	18	4.1	0.8
5972	Spinach, boiled w/salt, drained	0.5 cup	90	21	3	3	2	0	0	0.1
5149	Spinach, canned, drained	0.5 cup	107	25	3	4	3	1	0	0.2
5146	Spinach, raw	1 cup	30	7	1	1	1	0	0	0
5982	Squash, acorn, peeled, baked w/salt	0.5 cup	102.5	57	1	15	5	0	0	0.1
5984	Squash, butternut, baked w/salt	0.5 cup	102.5	41	1	11	3	0	0	0
6922	Squash, spaghetti, baked or boiled w/salt, drained	0.5 cup	77.5	21	1	5	1	0	0	0.1
5975	Squash, summer, all varieties, boiled w/salt, drained	0.5 cup	90	18	1	4	1	0	0	0.1
5981	Squash, winter, all varieties, baked w/salt	0.5 cup	102.5	40	1	9	3	1	0	0.3
90525	Squash, zucchini w/akin, slices, raw	1 ea	118	19	1	4	1	0	0	0.1
6921	Squash, zucchini w/skin, boiled w/salt, drained	0.5 cup	120	19	1	5	2	0	0	0
5989	Succotash (corn & lima beans) boiled w/salt, drained	0.5 cup	96	107	5	23	5	1	0.1	0.4
6924	Sweet potato, baked in skin w/salt	0.5 cup	100	90	2	21	3	0	0	0.1
5555	Sweet potato, canned w/syrup, drained	1 cup	196	212	3	50	6	1	0	0.3
9221	Taro, cooked w/salt	0.5 cup	66	94	0	23	3	0	0	0
5445	Tomatillos, raw	1 ea	34	11	0	2	1	0	0.1	0.1
5476	Tomato puree, canned w/salt	0.5 cup	125	48	2	11	2	0	0	0.1
5180	Tomato sauce, canned	0.5 cup	122.5	39	2	9	2	0	0	0.1
5474	Tomato, red, canned, stewed	0.5 cup	127.5	33	1	8	1	0	0	0.1
6887	Tomato, red, canned, whole	1 ea	190	32	2	7	2	0	0	0.1
90532	Tomato, red, ripe, whole, raw	1 pce	15	3	0	1	0	0	0	0
5447	Tomato, Sun-dried	10 pce	20	52	3	11	2	1	0.1	0.2
9299	Tomato, yellow, raw	1 ea	17	3	0	1	0	0	0	0
6004	Turnip greens, boiled w/salt, drained	0.5 cup	72	14	1	3	3	0	0	0.1
6002	Turnip, boiled w/salt, drained	0.5 cup	115	25	1	6	2	0	0	0
7955	Wasabi root, raw	1 ea	169	184	8	40	13	1		
5388	Waterchestnut, Chinese, canned, solids & liquid	4 ea	28	14	0	3	1	0	0	0
5223	Watercress, raw	10 ea	25	3	1	0	0	0	0	0
6010	Yam, boiled or baked w/salt	0.5 cup	68	79	1	19	3	0	0	0
5306	Yam, peeled, raw	0.5 cup	75	88	1	21	3	0	0	0.1
	Soy and Soy Products									
7503	Miso	1 tbsp	17.2	34	2	5	1	1	0.2	0.6
7508	Natto	1 cup	175	371	31	25	9	19	4.3	10.9
7564	Tempeh	0.5 cup	83	160	15	8		9	2.5	3.2
7015	Soybeans, cooked	1 cup	172	298	29	17	10	15	3.4	8.7
7014	Soybeans, dry	0.25 cup	46.5	193	17	14	4	9	2	5.2
4707	Soybeans, roasted & salted	0.25 cup	43	203	15	14	8	11	2.4	6.2
7585	Soymeal, defatted, raw	0.5 cup	61	207	27	24		1	0.2	0.6
71584	Soy yogurt, peach	1 ea	170.1	170	4	32	1	2		

Sat (g)	Chol (mg)	Calc (mg)	Iron (mg)	Mag (mg)	Phos (mg)	Pota (mg)	Sodi (mg)	Zinc (mg)	Vit A (RAE)	Vit C (mg)	Thia (mg)	Ribo (mg)	Niac (mg)	Vit B6 (mg)	Vit B12 (µg)	Vit E (mg)	Fol (µg)	Alc (g)
0	0	12	0.97	38.6	99	752	11	0.6	1	17.4	0.1	0.07	2.2	0.29	0	0.1	37.3	0
0	0	25	1.48	41.4	98	759	11	0.5	1	17.8	0.09	0.07	1.86	0.49	0	0.1	15.2	0
0.1	0	24	0.93	59.9	120	983	722	0.8	0	22.2	0.29	0.06	3.93	0.81	0	0	27	0
0	0	20	4.08	24.9	59	332	149	0.3	1	7.8	0.07	0.06	1.78	0.36	0	0	12.8	0
0.2	0	32	1.7	28.2	43	252	295	0.2	953	5.1	0.03	0.07	0.45	0.07	0	1.3	14.7	0
0	0	8	0.23	5.2	16	121	9	0.2	0	3.2	0.01	0.01	0.1	0.02	0	0.9	24	0
0	0	5	0.07	2	4	47	8	0.1	0	3	0	0.01	0.05	0.01	0	0	5	0
0	0	58	0.64	27.6	67	391	305	0.4	0	22.6	0.1	0.05	0.86	0.12	0	0.4	18	0
0	0	21	1.04	9.2	14	121	469	0.1	1	10.4	0.01	0.02	0.1	0.09	0	0.1	17	0
0.1	0	67	1.14	48.4	17	36	93	0.5	2	1.2	0.02	0.06	0.19	0	0	0.3	72	0
1.6	0	71	16.96	116	70	811	624	1.2	17	6	1.42	2.18	7.63	0.22	0	3	55.9	0
0	0	4	0.12	2.1	6	33	1	0	6	0.8	0.01	0	0.02	0.03	0	0	3.4	0
8.3	160	224	1.62	40.8	192	318	770	1.2	326	9.9	0.11	0.36	0.66	0.13	0.53	1.3	99.3	0
0	0	122	3.21	78.3	50	419	275	0.7	472	8.8	0.09	0.21	0.44	0.22	0	1.9	131.4	0
0.1	0	136	2.46	81.3	47	370	29	0.5	524	15.3	0.02	0.15	0.42	0.11	0	2.1	104.9	0
0	0	30	0.81	23.7	15	167	24	0.2	141	8.4	0.02	0.06	0.22	0.06	0	0.6	58.2	0
0	0	45	0.95	44.1	46	448	246	0.2	22	11.1	0.17	0.01	0.9	0.2	0	0.1	19.5	0
0	0	42	0.62	29.7	28	291	246	0.1	572	15.5	0.07	0.02	0.99	0.13	0	1.3	19.5	0
0	0	16	0.26	8.5	11	91	197	0.2	5	2.7	0.03	0.02	0.63	0.02	0	0.1	6.2	0
0.1	0	24	0.32	21.6	35	173	213	0.4	10	5	0.04	0.04	0.46	0.06	0	0.1	18	0
0.1	0	14	0.34	8.2	20	448	243	0.3	268	9.8	0.09	0.02	0.72	0.07	0	0.1	28.7	0
0	0	18	0.41	20.1	45	309	12	0.3	12	20.1	0.06	0.17	0.57	0.26	0	0.1	34.2	0
0	0	16	0.42	26.4	48	304	287	0.2	67	5.5	0.05	0.05	0.51	0.09	0	0.1	20.4	0
0.1	0	16	1.46	50.9	112	394	243	0.6	14	7.9	0.16	0.09	1.27	0.11	0	0.3	31.7	0
0.1	0	38	0.69	27	54	475	246	0.3	961	19.6	0.11	0.11	1.49	0.29	0	0.7	6	0
0.1	0	33	1.86	23.5	49	378	76	0.3	898	21.2	0.05	0.07	0.67	0.12	0	2.3	15.7	0
0	0	12	0.48	19.8	50	319	166	0.2	3	3.3	0.07	0.02	0.34	0.22	0	1.9	12.5	0
0	0	2	0.21	6.8	13	91	0	0.1	2	4	0.01	0.01	0.63	0.02	0	0.1	2.4	0
0	0	22	2.22	28.8	50	549	499	0.5	32	13.3	0.03	0.1	1.83	0.16	0	2.5	13.8	0
0	0	16	1.25	19.6	32	405	642	0.2	21	8.6	0.03	0.08	1.19	0.12	0	2.5	11	0
0	0	43	1.7	15.3	26	264	282	0.2	11	10.1	0.06	0.04	0.91	0.02	0	1.1	6.4	0
0	0	59	1.84	20.9	36	357	243	0.3	11	17.1	0.09	0.09	1.4	0.17	0	1.3	15.2	0
0	0	2	0.04	1.6	4	36	1	0	6	1.9	0.01	0	0.09	0.01	0	0.1	2.2	0
0.1	0	22	1.82	38.8	71	685	419	0.4	9	7.8	0.11	0.1	1.81	0.07	0	0	13.6	0
0	0	2	0.08	2	6	44	4	0	0	1.5	0.01	0.01	0.2	0.01	0		5.1	0
0	0	99	0.58	15.8	21	146	191	0.1	274	19.7	0.03	0.05	0.3	0.13	0	1.4	85	0
0	0	25	0.25	9.2	22	155	329	0.2	0	13.3	0.03	0.03	0.34	0.08	0	0	10.4	0
	0	216	1.74	116.6	135	960	29	2.7	3	70.8	0.22	0.19	1.26	0.46	0		30.4	0
0	0	1	0.24	1.4	5	33	2	0.1	0	0.4	0	0.01	0.1	0.04	0	0.1	1.7	0
0	0	30	0.05	5.2	15	82	10	0	59	10.8	0.02	0.03	0.05	0.03	0	0.2	2.2	0
0	0	10	0.35	12.2	33	456	166	0.1	4	8.2	0.06	0.02	0.38	0.16	0	0.3	10.9	0
0	0	13	0.41	15.8	41	612	7	0.2	5	12.8	0.08	0.02	0.41	0.22	0	0.3	17.2	0
0.2	0	10	0.43	8.3	27	36	641	0.4	1	0	0.02	0.04	0.16	0.03	0.01	0	3.3	0
2.8	0	380	15.05	201.2	304	1276	12	5.3	0	22.8	0.28	0.33	0	0.23	0	0	14	0
1.8	0	92	2.24	67.2	221	342	7	0.9	0	0	0.06	0.3	2.19	0.18	0.07	0	19.9	0
2.2	0	175	8.84	147.9	421	886	2	2	1	2.9	0.27	0.49	0.69	0.4	0	0.6	92.9	0
1.3	0	129	7.3	130.2	327	836	1	2.3	0	2.8	0.41	0.4	0.75	0.18	0	0.4	174.4	0
1.6	0	59	1.68	62.4	156	632	70	1.4	4	0.9	0.04	0.06	0.61	0.09	0	0.4	90.7	0
0.2	0	149	8.36	186.7	428	1519	2	3.1	1	0	0.42	0.15	1.58	0.35	0		184.8	0
0		500	0				20			0								0

MDA Code	Food Name	Amt	Wt (g)	Ener (kcal)	Prot (g)	Carb (g)	Fiber (g)	Fat (g)	Mono (g)	Poly (g)
7542	Tofu, firm, silken, 1" slice	3 oz	85.1	53	6	2	0	2	0.5	1.3
7799	Tofu, firm, silken, light, 1" slice	3 oz	85.1	31	5	1	0	1	0.1	0.4
7541	Tofu, soft, silken, 1" slice	3 oz	85.1	47	4	2	0	2	0.4	1.3
7546	Tofu yogurt	1 cup	262	246	9	42	1	5	1	2.7
	MEALS AND DISHES									
	Homemade									
57482	Coleslaw, homemade	0.5 cup	60	41	1	7	1	2	0.4	0.8
56102	Falafel, patty, 2-1/4"	1 ea	17	57	2	5		3	1.7	0.7
53125	Mole poblano, homemade	2 tbsp	30.3	50	1	4	1	3	1.5	0.9
56005	Potato salad, homemade	0.5 cup	125	179	3	14	2	10	3.1	4.7
5786	Potato, au gratin, homemade w/butter	1 cup	245	323	12	28	4	19	5.3	0.7
92216	Tortellini with cheese filling	1 cup	108	332	15	51	2	8	2.2	0.5
	Packaged or Canned Meals or Dishes									
57705	Alfredo egg noodles in a creamy sauce, from dry mix	1 ea	124	518	19	77		15	4.8	1.5
90098	Beef ravioli in tomato & meat sauce, canned entree/Chef Boyardee	1 ea	244	229	8	37	4	5	2	0.2
25279	Beefaroni, macaroni w/beef in tomato sauce, canned entree/ Chef Boyardee	1 ea	212.6	185	8	31	3	3	1.3	0.3
56976	Chicken & dumplings, canned/Sweet Sue	1 cup	240	218	15	23	3	7	3	1.6
57658	Chili con carne w/beans, canned entree	1 cup	222	269	16	25	9	12	4.8	0.9
56001	Chili w/beans, canned	1 cup	256	287	15	30	11	14	6	0.9
57700	Chili w/o beans, canned entree/Hormel	1 cup	236	194	17	18	3	7	2.2	0.8
57703	Chili, vegetarian chili w/beans, canned entree/Hormel	1 cup	247	205	12	38	10	1	0.1	0.4
50317	Chili, vegetarian w/beans, canned entree/Nestle Chef-Mate	1 cup	253	412	18	29	11	25	10.7	1.4
6247	Creamed spinach/Stouffer	0.5 cup	125	169	3	9	2	13	2.8	4.5
90738	Hamburger Helper, cheeseburger macaroni	1.5 oz	42.5	168	5	27		4		
57068	Macaroni and cheese, unprepared/Kraft	1 ea	70	259	11	48	1	3		
90103	Mini beef ravioli in tomato & meat sauce, canned entree/Chef Boyardee	1 ea	252	239	9	41	3	5	2	0.2
47708	Spaghetti & meatballs in tomato sauce, canned entree/Chef Boyardee	1 ea	240	250	9	34	2	9	3.7	0.4
70959	Spinach au gratin/The Budget Gourmet	1 ea	155	222	7	11	2	17		
57484	Scalloped potatoes, from mix, prepared w/water, whole milk & butter	1 ea	822	764	17	105	9	35	10	1.6
42147	Stuffing, corn, dry mix, prepared	0.5 cup	100	179	3	22	3	9	3.9	2.7
42037	Stuffing, plain, dry mix, prepared	0.5 cup	100	178	3	22	3	9	3.8	2.6
57701	Turkey chili w/beans, canned entree/Hormel	1 cup	247	203	19	26	6	3	0.4	1.2
90739	Whole-wheat macaroni and cheese dinner, dry mix/Hodgson Mill	1 ea	70	263	10	48	5	3		
	Frozen Meals or Dishes									
83053	Chicken cacciatore	1 ea	354	266	22	36	5	4	2.4	0.6
70958	Stir fry, rice & vegetables, w/soy sauce/Hanover	1 cup	137	130	5	27	2	0		
16220	BBQ glazed chicken & sauce w/mixed vegetables/Weight Watchers	1 ea	209	217	19	26		4	1.6	1.1
70943	Beef & bean burrito/Las Campanas	1 ea	114	296	9	38	1	12	5.5	0.8
70961	Beef & bean chimichanga/Fiesta Cafe	1 ea	227	422	24	56	6	12	3.9	3.5
70948	Beef enchiladas & tamales, beans & rice/Patio	1 ea	376	508	14	68	8	20	7.7	2.7
11112	Beef macaroni/Healthy Choice	1 ea	226.8	200	13	32	4	2	1.1	0.3
70893	Beef pot pie, frozen	1 ea	198	449	13	44	2	24	9.7	2.7
83051	Beef pot roast w/whipped potatoes/Lean Cuisine Homestyle	1 ea	255	207	17	22	4	5	2.3	0.8
70935	Beef sirloin salisbury steak w/red skinned potatoes/Budget Gourmet	1 ea	311	261	18	34	7	6	1.8	0.9
83027	Beef stir fry kit/Orienta	1 ea	405	433	26	71		5		
57474	Beef stroganoff and noodles/Marie Callender	1 ea	368	600	30	59	4	27	12	4
56915	Broccoli in cheese-flavored sauce, frozen/GreenGiant	0.5 cup	84	56	2	7		2	0.8	0.2
16195	Chicken & vegetables/Lean Cuisine	1 ea	297	252	19	32	5	6	2.1	1.4
15965	Chicken a l'Orange w/broccoli & rice/Lean Cuisine	1 ea	255	268	24	39		2	0.5	0.4

Sat (g)	Chol (mg)	Calc (mg)	Iron (mg)	Mag (mg)	Phos (mg)	Pota (mg)	Sodi (mg)	Zinc (mg)	Vit A (RAE)	Vit C (mg)	Thia (mg)	Ribo (mg)	Niac (mg)	Vit B6 (mg)	Vit B12 (µg)	Vit E (mg)	Fol (µg)	Alc (g)
0.3	0	27	0.88	23	77	165	31	0.5	0	0	0.09	0.03	0.21	0.01	0	0.2		0
0.1	0	31	0.64	8.5	69	54	72	0.3	0	0	0.03	0.02	0.09	0	0	0.1		0
0.3	0	26	0.7	24.7	53	153	4	0.4	0	0	0.09	0.03	0.26	0.01	0	0.2		0
0.7	0	309	2.78	104.8	100	123	92	0.8	5	6.6	0.16	0.05	0.63	0.05	0	0.8	15.7	0
0.2	5	27	0.35	6	19	109	14	0.1	32	19.6	0.04	0.04	0.16	0.08	0	0.1	16.2	0
0.4	0	9	0.58	13.9	33	99	50	0.3	0	0.3	0.02	0.03	0.18	0.02	0	0.2	15.8	0
	0	7	0.56	9.7	25	99	41	0.1	45	0	0.01	0	0.5	0.08	0.01	0.4	8.5	0
1.8	85	24	0.81	18.8	65	318	661	0.4	40	12.5	0.1	0.07	1.11	0.18	0	2.3	8.8	0
11.6	56	292	1.57	49	277	970	1061	1.7	157	24.3	0.16	0.28	2.43	0.43	0	0.5	27	0
3.9	45	164	1.62	22.7	229	96	372	1.1	41	0	0.34	0.33	2.91	0.05	0.17	0.2	79.9	0
5.7	139	157	3.74				2195											0
2.5	15	20	2.42			354	1174			0.2								0
1.2	17	17	1.51				802			0.4								0
1.8	36		2.57				946		0									0
3.9	29	84	5.79	64.4	215	608	941	2.3		3.1	0.12	0.22	2.16	0.28	1.44	0.3	57.7	0
6	44	120	8.78	115.2	394	934	1336	5.1	44	4.4	0.12	0.27	0.92	0.34	0	1.5	58.9	0
2.2	35	50	2.6	37.8		349	970	2.6		0								0
0.1	0	96	3.46	81.5		803	778	1.7		1.2								0
10.9	56	89	4.83	45.5	167	511	1171	3.9		0.8	0.11	0.2	3.48	0.23	1.44	1.2		0
3.7	16	141	1.06			245	335			5.9					0			0
1.2	4						863											0
1.3	10	92	2.56	40	265	296	561			0.4	0.67	0.41	4.54				65.1	0
1.8	18	23	2.42				1197			0.3								0
3.9	22	17	1.78				941			1								0
7.6	42	243	1.95				654			27.1								0
21.6	90	296	3.12	115.1	460	1669	2803	2.1	288	27.1	0.16	0.46	8.46	0.35	0	1.2	82.2	0
1.8	0	26	0.94	13	34	62	455	0.2	78	0.8	0.12	0.09	1.25	0.04	0.01	0.9	97	0
1.7	0	32	1.09	12	42	74	543	0.3	118	0	0.14	0.11	1.48	0.04	0.01	1.4	39	0
0.7	35	116	3.46	69.2		682	1198	2.7		1.5								0
1	6	80	1.83				428											0
1	32	53	2.23		255	750	552											0
							636			16.3								0
1	48		1.09				405		0	21.5								0
4.2	13		3.11				579		0									0
2.2	36		6.81				804		0	5.9								0
6.8	26	241	2.86				1812		30	4.9								0
0.6	14	43	2.56	34	127	345	420	1.2	52	54.9	0.26	0.15	2.94	0.18	0.11	1.6	99.8	0
8.5	38						737		51									0
1.3	38						495		48									0
2	44		3.05				494		72	51								0
							1584			25.1								0
11.1	70	70	1.8				1141			0								0
0.4		45	0.54				403			29.7								0
1	24	104	1.34			648	582			14.6								0
0.4	46	20	0.36			430	360	1		18.1								0

MDA Code	Food Name	Amt	Wt (g)	Ener (kcal)	Prot (g)	Carb (g)	Fiber (g)	Fat (g)	Mono (g)	Poly (g)
83052	Chicken alfredo w/fettucini & vegetables/Stouffer's Lunch Express	1 ea	272	373	19	33	4	18	6.3	2.4
70945	Chicken cordon bleu, filled w/cheese & ham/Barber Food	1 ea	168	344	26	15		20	8.2	3.2
16198	Chicken enchilada & Mexican rice/Stouffers	1 ea	283	376	12	48	5	15	4.4	3.7
83028	Chicken fajita kit/Tyson	1 ea	107	129	8	17		3	1.3	0.6
70931	Chicken mesquite w/BBQ sauce, corn medley & potatoes au gratin/ Tyson	1 ea	255	321	18	45	4	8	2.7	0.5
70899	Chicken pot pie, frozen entree	1 ea	217	484	13	43	2	29	12.5	4.5
16266	Chicken teriyaki w/rice, mixed vegetables w/butter sauce & apple cherry compote	1 ea	312	268	17	37	3	6	2.2	0.5
70582	Cosmic chicken nuggets w/macaroni & cheese, corn, chocolate pudding	1 ea	257	524	18	53	3	27	10.7	6
16930	Country roast turkey w/mushrooms in brown gravy & rice pilaf/ Healthy Choice	1 ea	240	223	19	28	3	4	1.8	0.9
15974	Escalloped chicken & noodles/Stouffer's	1 ea	283	419	17	31		25	7	12.3
90565	French fries, frozen, oven heated, w/salt	10 ea	50	100	2	16	2	4	2.4	0.4
16310	French recipe chicken breast, vegetables & potatoes in red wine sauce/Budget	1 ea	255	178	23	9	6	6	2.7	0.5
70950	Gravy & sliced beef, mashed potatoes & carrots/Freezer Queen	1 ea	255	207	15	26	4	5	1.2	1.7
56738	Homestyle stuffed cabbage w/meat in tomato sauce & whipped potatoes/Stouffer's	1 ea	269	199	12	26	6	6	2.4	0.7
70917	Hot Pockets, beef & cheddar, frozen	1 ea	142	403	16	39		20	6.7	1.2
70918	Hot Pockets, croissant pocket w/chicken, broccoli, & cheddar, frozen	1 ea	128	301	11	39	1	11	4.4	1.7
70434	Italian sausage lasagna/Budget Gourmet	1 ea	298	456	21	40	3	24	9.8	2
56757	Lasagna w/meat sauce/Stouffer's	1 ea	215	277	19	26	3	11	3.5	0.6
70921	Lean Pockets, glazed chicken supreme stuffed, frozen	1 ea	128	233	10	34		6	2.5	1
11029	Macaroni & beef in tomato sauce/Lean Cuisine	1 ea	283	249	14	37	3	5	2.1	0.7
5587	Mashed potatoes, from granules w/milk, prep w/water & margarine	0.5 cup	105	122	2	17	1	5	2.1	1.4
11107	Meat loaf w/tomato sauce, mashed potatoes & carrots in seasoned sauce/Banquet Hearty Ones	1 ea	453	612	29	34	6	40	17.3	7.2
6999	Mixed vegetables, frozen, boiled w/salt, drained	1 ea	275	165	8	36	12	0	0	0.2
90491	Onion rings, breaded, par fried, from frozen, oven heated	1 cup	48	195	3	18	1	13	5.2	2.5
1746	Original fried chicken meal w/mashed potatoes & corn/Banquet	1 ea	228	470	21	35	2	27	15.4	2.4
70898	Pizza, pepperoni, frozen	1 ea	146	432	16	42	3	22	10	3.4
70949	Roasted chicken w/garlic sauce, pasta & vegetable medley/Tyson	1 ea	255	214	17	22	4	7	2.3	2.1
81146	Sandwich, sausage w/biscuit, frozen/Jimmy Dean	1 ea	48	192	5	12	1	14		
70895	Scrambled eggs & sausage w/hash browns	1 ea	177	361	13	17	1	27	12.7	3.6
56762	Stuffed green peppers, w/tomato sauce/Stouffer's	0.5 ea	219.5	189	8	21	5	8	3.8	0.5
56703	Spaghetti w/meat sauce/Lean Cuisine	1 ea	326	313	14	51	6	6	2.3	1.3
70960	Spaghetti w/meatballs & pomodoro sauce, low fat/Michelina's	1 ea	284	312	14	49	6	7	2.6	1.1
11099	Swedish meatballs w/pasta/Lean Cuisine	1 ea	258	276	22	31	3	7	2.3	1
70892	Turkey pot pie, frozen	1 ea	397	699	26	70	4	35	13.7	5.5
16306	Turkey w/gravy, frozen	1 ea	141.8	95	8	7	0	4	1.4	0.7
70936	Turkey w/gravy & dressing w/broccoli/Marie Callender	1 ea	397	504	31	52		19	8.2	1.7
	SNACK FOODS AND GRANOLA BARS									
3307	Banana chips	1 oz	28.4	147	1	17	2	10	0.6	0.2
10051	Beef jerky	1 ea	19.8	81	7	2	0	5	2.2	0.2
10052	Beef, snack stick, smoked	1 ea	19.8	109	4	1		10	4.1	0.9
63331	Breakfast bars, oats, sugar, raisins, coconut	1 ea	43	200	4	29	1	8	0.8	0.7
53227	Cereal bar, mixed berry	1 ea	37	137	2	27	1	3	1.8	0.4
61251	Cheese puffs and twists, corn based, low fat	1 oz	28.4	123	2	21	3	3	1	1.6
44032	Chex snack mix	1 cup	42.5	181	5	28	2	7	3.9	1.1

Sat (g)	Chol (mg)	Calc (mg)	Iron (mg)	Mag (mg)	Phos (mg)	Pota (mg)	Sodi (mg)	Zinc (mg)	Vit A (RAE)	Vit C (mg)	Thia (mg)	Ribo (mg)	Niac (mg)	Vit B6 (mg)	Vit B12 (µg)	Vit E (mg)	Fol (µg)	Alc (g)
7	57	147					588			24.2								0
5.7	81	144					754											0
3.4	25	255	0.76			473	1002			15.3								0
0.8	13						350			10.4								0
2.6	26						793			0								0
9.7	41	33	2.06	23.9	119	256	857	1	256	1.5	0.25	0.36	4.13	0.2	0.15	3.8	41.2	0
3	44	37	1.09		225	424	602			12.2								0
6.6	49	206	2.85				974	0										0
1.2	26	22	1.03				437											0
6	76	116	1.13			329	1211	0		0								0
0.6	0	4	0.62	11	41	209	133	0.2	0	5.1	0.06	0.01	1.04	0.15	0	0.1	6	0
1.4	26						864		115									0
1.3	31						648		530									0
1.7	24	105	1.08			459	412		0	53								0
8.8	53	337	2.93				906		0									0
3.4	37		3.8				652			6.3								0
8.2	48	316	2.68				903											0
4.7	41	230	1.17			412	735		0	2.6								0
1.9	23	122					562		38									0
1.6	23	40	2.18			639	563			157.3								0
1.3	2	36	0.21	21	67	165	180	0.3	49	6.8	0.09	0.09	0.91	0.17	0.11	0.5	8.4	0
15.5	113	77	3.94				1943			7.7								0
0.1	0	69	2.25	60.5	140	465	745	1.3	588	8.8	0.2	0.33	2.34	0.2	0	1.2	52.2	0
4.1	0	15	0.81	9.1	39	62	180	0.2	5	0.7	0.13	0.07	1.73	0.04	0	0.3	31.7	0
9.2	89	39	1.37				1500		0	1.4								0
7.1	22	220	3.52	35	302	289	902	2.2	0	2.8	0.33	0.34	3.61	0.14	0.83	1.6	68.6	0
1.3	28		1.56				467											0
4.3	16	38	0.79				441											0
7.3	283		1.66				772		0									0
2.7	22	20	1.08			370	577		0	86.5								0
1.4	13	80	2.12			580	610			34.9	0.3	0.34	4					0
2.2	14		2.93				1011		26	8.8								0
2.4	46	206	2.06	43.9	206	599	562	3.7	0	0	0.59	0.52	4.98	0.31	1.01	0.3	31.9	0
11.4	64		3.97				1390		349									0
1.2	26	20	1.32	11.3	115	86	786	1	18	0	0.03	0.18	2.55	0.14	0.34	0.5	5.7	0
9.1	79	131	4.37				2037			23.8								0
8.2	0	5	0.35	21.6	16	152	2	0.2	1	1.8	0.02	0	0.2	0.07	0	0.1	4	0
2.1	10	4	1.07	10.1	81	118	438	1.6	0	0	0.03	0.03	0.34	0.04	0.2	0.1	26.5	0
4.1	26	13	0.67	4.2	36	51	293	0.5	3	1.3	0.03	0.09	0.9	0.04	0.2	0.1	0	0
5.5	0	26	1.37	43.4	119	140	120	0.7	3	0.4	0.12	0.05	0.75	0.15	0	0.4	34.8	0
0.6	0	14	1.81	9.6	36	70	110	1.5		0	0.37	0.41	5	0.52	0	0	40	0
0.6	0	101	0.36	11.6	101	81	365	0.6	12	6.1	0.15	0.17	2.03	0.2	0.61	1.2	27.5	0
2.4	0	15	10.5	26.8	79	114	432	0.9	3	20.2	0.66	0.21	7.16	0.66	5.27	0.1	21.2	0

MDA Code	Food Name	Amt	Wt (g)	Ener (kcal)	Prot (g)	Carb (g)	Fiber (g)	Fat (g)	Mono (g)	Poly (g)
44034	Corn Nuts, BBQ flavor	1 oz	28.4	124	3	20	2	4	2.1	0.9
44031	Corn Nuts, plain	1 oz	28.4	127	2	20	2	4	2.7	0.9
44212	Fruit leather, bar	1 ea	23	81	0	18	1	1	0.1	0
11594	Fruit leather, berry, w/vitamin C	2 ea	28	104	0	24		1	0.5	0
44214	Fruit leather, pieces, 0.75 oz pkg	1 ea	21.3	76	0	18	0	1	0.3	0.1
23404	Fruit leather, roll, large	1 ea	21	78	0	18	0	1	0.3	0.1
23103	Granola bar, hard, peanut butter	1 ea	23.6	114	2	15	1	6	1.7	2.9
23059	Granola bar, hard, plain	1 ea	24.5	115	2	16	1	5	1.1	3
23101	Granola bar, hard, w/chocolate chips	1 ea	23.6	103	2	17	1	4	0.6	0.3
23096	Granola bar, soft, chocolate chip, milk chocolate cover	1 ea	35.4	165	2	23	1	9	2.8	0.6
23107	Granola bar, soft, nut & raisin	1 ea	28.4	129	2	18	2	6	1.2	1.6
23104	Granola bar, soft, plain	1 ea	28.4	126	2	19	1	5	1.1	1.5
44036	Oriental mix, rice-based	1 oz	28.4	144	5	15	4	7	2.8	3
44022	Popcorn cakes	1 ea	10	38	1	8	0	0	0.1	0.1
44012	Popcorn, air-popped	1 cup	8	31	1	6	1	0	0.1	0.2
44014	Popcorn, caramel coated, no peanuts	1 oz	28.4	122	1	22	1	4	0.8	1.3
44038	Popcorn, cheese flavor	1 cup	11	58	1	6	1	4	1.1	1.7
44066	Popcorn, microwave, low fat and sodium	1 cup	8	34	1	6	1	1	0.3	0.3
44013	Popcorn, oil-popped, yellow corn	1 cup	11	60	1	6	1	4	0.9	2
61252	Popcorn, sugar syrup/caramel, fat-free	1 cup	37.3	142	1	34	1	1	0.1	0.2
12080	Pork skins, plain	1 oz	28	153	17	0	0	9	4.1	1
61249	Potato chips, fat-free, made with olestra	1 oz	28	74	2	17	1	0	0.1	0.1
44043	Potato chips, light	1 oz	28.4	134	2	19	2	6	1.4	3.1
44076	Potato chips, plain, no salt	1 oz	28.4	152	2	15	1	10	2.8	3.5
5437	Potato chips, sour cream & onion	1 oz	28.4	151	2	15	1	10	1.7	4.9
61257	Potato chips, without salt, reduced fat	1 oz	28.4	138	2	19	2	6	1.4	3.1
44015	Pretzels, hard	5 pce	30	114	3	24	1	1	0.3	0.3
44079	Pretzels, hard, unsalted, w/enriched flour	10 ea	60	229	5	48	2	2	0.8	0.7
61182	Pretzels, soft	1 ea	115	389	9	80	2	4	1.2	1.1
44053	Rice cake, brown rice & sesame seed	2 ea	18	71	1	15	1	1	0.2	0.2
44021	Rice cake, brown rice, plain, salted	1 ea	9	35	1	7	0	0	0.1	0.1
44020	Taro chips	1 oz	28.4	141	1	19	2	7	1.3	3.7
44058	Trail mix, regular	0.25 cup	37.5	173	5	17	2	11	4.7	3.6
44059	Trail mix, regular, chocolate chip, salted nuts & seeds	0.25 cup	36.2	175	5	16	2	12	4.9	4.1
	SOUPS									
92160	Bean and ham, canned, reduced sodium, prepared with water or ready-to-serve	0.5 cup	128	95	5	17	5	1	0.5	0.3
50151	Bean w/bacon, from dehydrated mix, made w/water	1 cup	265	106	5	16	9	2	0.9	0.2
92192	Beef and mushroom, low sodium, chunk style	1 cup	251	173	11	24	1	6	1	0.2
50398	Beef barley, canned/Progresso Healthy Classics	1 cup	241	142	11	20	3	2	0.7	0.3
50198	Beef mushroom, canned, made w/water	1 cup	244	73	6	6	0	3	1.2	0.1
57659	Beef stew, canned entree	1 ea	232	220	11	16	3	12	5.5	0.5
50155	Cauliflower, from dehydrated mix, made w/water	1 cup	256.1	69	3	11		2	0.7	0.6
50077	Chicken gumbo, canned, made w/water	1 cup	244	56	3	8	2	1	0.7	0.3
50080	Chicken mushroom, canned, made w/water	1 cup	244	132	4	9	0	9	4	2.3
50081	Chicken noodle, chunky, canned	1 cup	240	175	13	17	4	6	2.7	1.5
50085	Chicken rice, chunky, ready to eat, canned	1 cup	240	127	12	13	1	3	1.4	0.7
50088	Chicken vegetable, chunky, canned	1 cup	240	166	12	19	0	5	2.2	1
90238	Chicken, chunky, canned	1 cup	240	170	12	17	1	6	2.8	1.3
50402	Cream of broccoli, canned, ready to eat/Progresso Healthy Classics	1 cup	244	88	2	13	2	3	0.9	0.6

Sat (g)	Chol (mg)	Calc (mg)	Iron (mg)	Mag (mg)	Phos (mg)	Pota (mg)	Sodi (mg)	Zinc (mg)	Vit A (RAE)	Vit C (mg)	Thia (mg)	Ribo (mg)	Niac (mg)	Vit B6 (mg)	Vit B12 (µg)	Vit E (mg)	Fol (µg)	Alc (g)
0.7	0	5	0.48	31	80	81	277	0.5	5	0.1	0.1	0.04	0.43	0.05	0	0.3	0	0
0.7	0	3	0.47	32.1	78	79	156	0.5	0	0	0.01	0.04	0.48	0.07	0	0.6	0	0
0.9	0	7	0.18	5.1	13	32	18	0	1	16.1	0.01	0.01	0.02	0.07	0	0.1	0.9	0
0.3	0						89			33.6								0
0.1	0	4	0.16	3	5	35	86	0	1	11.9	0.01	0.02	0.02	0.06	0	0.1	0.9	0
0.1	0	7	0.21	4.2	7	62	67	0	1	25.2	0.02	0	0.02	0.06	0	0.1	0.4	0
0.8	0	10	0.57	13	33	69	67	0.3	0	0	0.05	0.02	0.46	0.02	0	0.3	4.2	0
0.6	0	15	0.72	23.8	68	82	72	0.5	2	0.2	0.06	0.03	0.39	0.02	0	0.3	5.6	0
2.7	0	18	0.72	17	48	59	81	0.5	0	0	0.04	0.02	0.13	0.01	0	0.2	3.1	0
5	2	36	0.82	23.4	70	111	71	0.5	2	0	0.03	0.09	0.25	0.04	0.2	0.4	9.2	0
2.7	0	24	0.62	25.8	68	111	72	0.5	0	0	0.05	0.05	0.74	0.03	0.07	0.3	8.5	0
2.1	0	30	0.73	21	65	92	79	0.4	0	0	0.08	0.05	0.15	0.03	0.11	0.3	6.8	0
1.1	0	15	0.69	33.5	74	93	117	0.8	0	0.1	0.09	0.04	0.88	0.02	0	1.6	10.8	0
0	0	1	0.19	15.9	28	33	29	0.4	0	0	0.01	0.02	0.6	0.02	0	0	1.8	0
0.1	0	1	0.26	11.5	29	26	1	0.2	1	0	0.01	0.01	0.18	0.01	0	0	2.5	0
1	1	12	0.49	9.9	24	31	59	0.2	1	0	0.02	0.02	0.62	0.01	0	0.3	1.4	0
0.7	1	12	0.25	10	40	29	98	0.2	4	0.1	0.01	0.03	0.16	0.03	0.06	0	1.2	0
0.1	0	1	0.18	12.1	21	19	39	0.3	1	0	0.03	0.01	0.17	0.01	0	0.4	1.4	0
0.6	0	0	0.21	8.9	23	21	1		1	0	0.01	0.01	0.13	0.01	0	0.6	1.9	0
0.1	0	7	0.3	10.1	21	41	107	0.2	1	0	0.01		0.13	0.02	0		1.5	0
3.2	27	8	0.25	3.1	24	36	515	0.2	3	0.1	0.03	0.08	0.43	0.01	0.18	0.1	0	0
0	0	10	0.42	23	46	361	183	0.3	0	8.3	0.1	0.02	1.29	0.51	0	0	8.4	0
1.2	0	6	0.38	25.3	55	495	140	0	0	7.3	0.06	0.08	1.99	0.19	0	1.6	7.7	0
3.1	0	7	0.46	19	47	362	2	0.3	0	8.8	0.05	0.06	1.09	0.19	0	2.6	12.8	0
2.5	2	20	0.45	21	50	378	177	0.3	4	10.6	0.05	0.06	1.14	0.19	0.28	1.4	17.6	0
1.2	0	6	0.38	25.3	55	495	2	0.3	0	7.3	0.06	0.08	1.99	0.19	0	1.6	2.8	0
0.1	0	5	1.56	8.7	34	44	407	0.4	0	0	0.14	0.1	1.54	0.01	0	0.1	55.8	0
0.4	0	22	2.59	21	68	88	173	0.5	0	0	0.28	0.37	3.15	0.07	0	0.2	102.6	0
0.8	3	26	4.51	24.2	91	101	1615	1.1	0	0	0.47	0.33	4.91	0.02	0	0.6	27.6	0
0.1	0	2	0.28	24.5	68	52	41	0.5	0	0.5	0.01	0.02	1.3	0.03	0	0	3.2	0
0.1	0	1	0.13	11.8	32	26	29	0.3	0	0	0.01	0.01	0.7	0.01	0	0.1	1.9	0
1.8	0	17	0.34	23.9	37	214	97	0.1	2	1.4	0.05	0.01	0.15	0.12	0	3.2	5.7	0
2.1	0	29	1.14	59.2	129	257	86	1.2	0	0.5	0.17	0.07	1.77	0.11	0	1.3	26.6	0
2.2	1	39	1.23	58.3	140	235	44	1.1	1	0.5	0.15	0.08	1.59	0.09	0	3.9	23.5	0
0.3	3	49	1.31	24.3	17	202	239	0.7	45	1.4	0.07	0.04	0.41	0.06	0.04	0.5	37.1	0
1	3	56	1.32	29.2	90	326	928	0.7	3	1.1	0.05	0.27	0.4	0.03	0.03	0.6	8	0
4.1	15	33	2.43	5	126	351	63	2.8	246	7.5	0.1	0.28	2.84	0.15	0.65	0.6	12.6	0
0.7	19	29	1.86	31.3	118	366	470	1.5		3.6	0.13	0.13	2.92	0.19	0.36	0.3	24.1	0
1.5	7	5	0.88	9.8	34	154	942	1.5	0	4.6	0.04	0.06	0.95	0.05		0.2		9.8	0
5.2	37	28	1.65	32.5	128	404	947	1.9	193	10.2	0.17	0.14	2.86	0.3	0.86	0.3	25.5	0
0.3	0	10	0.51	2.6	51	105	843	0.3		2.6	0.08	0.08	0.51	0.03	0.18		2.6	0
0.3	5	24	0.9	4.9	24	76	954	0.4	7	4.9	0.02	0.05	0.66	0.06	0.02	0.4	4.9	0
2.4	10	29	0.88	9.8	27	154	942	1	56	0	0.02	0.11	1.63	0.05	0.05	1.2	0	0
1.4	19	24	1.44	9.6	72	108	850	1	67	0	0.07	0.17	4.32	0.05	0.31	0.3	38.4	0
1	12	34	1.87	9.6	72	108	888	1	293	3.8	0.02	0.1	4.1	0.05	0.31	0.6	4.8	0
1.4	17	26	1.46	9.6	106	367	1068	2.2	300	5.5	0.04	0.17	3.29	0.1	0.24	0.1	12	0
1.9	29	24	1.66	7.2	108	168	850	1	65	1.2	0.08	0.17	4.22	0.05	0.24	0.3	4.8	0
0.7	5	41	1.22	14.6	39	161	578	0.3		5.9	0.03	0.06	0.32	0.07	0	0.4	29.3	0

MDA Code	Food Name	Amt	Wt (g)	Ener (kcal)	Prot (g)	Carb (g)	Fiber (g)	Fat (g)	Mono (g)	Poly (g)
50016	Cream of celery, canned, made w/water	1 cup	244	90	2	9	1	6	1.3	2.5
50049	Cream of mushroom, canned, made w/water	1 cup	244	129	2	9	0	9	1.7	4.2
50197	Cream of potato, canned, made w/water	1 cup	244	73	2	11	0	2	0.6	0.4
50697	Cup Of Noodles, ramen, chicken flavor, dry/Nissin	1 ea	64	296	6	37		14		
50050	Green pea, canned, made w/water	1 cup	250	165	9	27	5	3	1	0.4
50021	Manhattan clam chowder, canned, made w/water	1 cup	244	78	2	12	1	2	0.4	1.3
50009	Minestrone, canned, made w/water	1 cup	241	82	4	11	1	3	0.7	1.1
92163	Ramen noodle, any flavor, dehydrated, dry	0.5 cup	38	172	4	25	1	6	2.4	1
50690	Shark fin, restaurant-prepared	1 cup	216	99	7	8	0	4	1.3	0.7
50025	Split pea w/ham, canned, made w/water	1 cup	253	190	10	28	2	4	1.8	0.6
50689	Stock, fish, homemade	1 cup	233	40	5	0	0	2	0.5	0.3
50043	Tomato vegetable, from dry mix, made w/water	1 cup	253	56	2	10	1	1	0.3	0.1
50028	Tomato, canned, made w/water	1 cup	244	85	2	17	0	2	0.4	1
50014	Vegetable beef, canned, made w/water	1 cup	244	78	6	10	0	2	0.8	0.1
92189	Vegetable chicken, low sodium	1 cup	241	166	12	21	1	5	2.2	1
7559	Vegetarian stew	1 cup	247	304	42	17	3	7	1.8	3.8
50013	Vegetarian vegetable, canned, made w/water	1 cup	241	72	2	12	0	2	0.8	0.7

BABY FOODS

MDA Code	Food Name	Amt	Wt (g)	Ener (kcal)	Prot (g)	Carb (g)	Fiber (g)	Fat (g)	Mono (g)	Poly (g)
61234	Infant cereal, brown rice, inst	1 tbsp	3.7	15	0	3	0	0	0	0
60619	Infant cereal, rice, dry	1 tbsp	2.5	10	0	2	0	0	0	0.1
60844	Infant cookie, banana/Gerber	1 ea	8	34	1	6	0	1		
60419	Infant dessert, apricot tapioca/Heinz	6.25 tbsp	100	66	0	16	0	0		
60192	Infant dessert, vanilla custard pudding/Gerber	1 ea	170	163	4	31		3		
60778	Infant dinner, beef & carrots, straind/Heinz	1 ea	113.4	64	4	4	2	4		
60871	Infant dinner, broccoli chicken, strained	1 ea	113.4	48	4	4	3	2	0.6	0.4
60793	Infant vegetable, peas, strained/Heinz	1 ea	113.4	65	5	11	4	0		
62354	Infant formula, lactofree, w/iron	0.125 cup	30.5	19	0	2	0	1	0.4	0.2
60135	Infant formula, low iron/Similac	1 fl. oz	31	20	0	2	0	1	0.4	0.2
60299	Infant formula, soy, w/iron/ Isomil	1 fl. oz	30.5	20	0	2	0	1	0.4	0.3
62586	Toddler formula, soy, prepared from powder	1 fl. oz	30.5	20	1	2	0	1	0.3	0.2

DESSERTS, CANDIES, AND PASTRIES
Brownies and Fudge

MDA Code	Food Name	Amt	Wt (g)	Ener (kcal)	Prot (g)	Carb (g)	Fiber (g)	Fat (g)	Mono (g)	Poly (g)
62904	Brownie, commercially prepared, square, lrg, 2-3/4" × 7/8"	1 ea	56	227	3	36	1	9	5	1.3
47019	Brownie, homemade, 2" square	1 ea	24	112	1	12	1	7	2.6	2.3
23127	Fudge, chocolate marshmallow, w/nuts, prep f/recipe	1 pce	22	104	1	15	0	5	1.2	0.9
23026	Fudge, chocolate, w/nuts, prep f/recipe	1 pce	19	88	1	13	0	4	0.7	1.4
23025	Fudge, chocolate, prep f/recipe	1 pce	17	70	0	13	0	2	0.5	0

Cakes, Pies, and Donuts

MDA Code	Food Name	Amt	Wt (g)	Ener (kcal)	Prot (g)	Carb (g)	Fiber (g)	Fat (g)	Mono (g)	Poly (g)
46062	Cake, chocolate, homemade, w/o icing	1 pce	95	340	5	51	2	14	5.7	2.6
42721	Cake, Ding Dongs, w/cream filling/Hostess	1 ea	80	368	3	45	2	19	4	1.2
46000	Cake, gingerbread, homemade	1 pce	74	263	3	36	1	12	5.3	3.1
46092	Coffee cake, cheese 1/6 of 16 oz	1 pce	76	258	5	34	1	12	5.4	1.3
46096	Coffee cake, creme filled, w/chocolate frosting 1/6 of 19 oz	1 pce	90	298	4	48	2	10	5.1	1.3
46001	Cake, sponge, commercially prepared	1 pce	38	110	2	23	0	1	0.4	0.2
46003	Cake, white w/coconut icing, homemade	1 pce	112	399	5	71	1	12	4.1	2.4
46085	Cake, white, homemade, w/o icing	1 pce	74	264	4	42	1	9	3.9	2.3
46091	Cake, yellow, homemade, w/o icing	1 pce	68	245	4	36	0	10	4.2	2.4
49001	Cheesecake, no bake mix, prep	1 pce	99	271	5	35	2	13	4.5	0.8
46426	Cupcake, chocolate, w/frosting, low fat	1 ea	43	131	2	29	2	2	0.8	0.2

Sat (g)	Chol (mg)	Calc (mg)	Iron (mg)	Mag (mg)	Phos (mg)	Pota (mg)	Sodi (mg)	Zinc (mg)	Vit A (RAE)	Vit C (mg)	Thia (mg)	Ribo (mg)	Niac (mg)	Vit B6 (mg)	Vit B12 (µg)	Vit E (mg)	Fol (µg)	Alc (g)
1.4	15	39	0.63	7.3	37	122	949	0.1	56	0.2	0.03	0.05	0.33	0.01	0.24	0.9	2.4	0
2.4	2	46	0.51	4.9	49	100	881	0.6	15	1	0.05	0.09	0.72	0.01	0.05	1	4.9	0
1.2	5	20	0.49	2.4	46	137	1000	0.6	71	0	0.03	0.04	0.54	0.04	0.05	0	2.4	0
6.3		2.18					1434		20									0
1.4	0	28	1.95	40	125	190	918	1.7	10	1.7	0.11	0.07	1.24	0.05	0	0.4	2.5	0
0.4	2	27	1.63	12.2	41	188	578	1	56	3.9	0.03	0.04	0.82	0.1	4.05	0.3	9.8	0
0.6	2	34	0.92	7.2	55	313	911	0.7	118	1.2	0.05	0.04	0.94	0.1	0	0.1	36.2	0
2.9	0	6	1.62	9.1	41	46	441	0.2	0	0	0.25	0.17	2.05	0.02	0	0.8	55.9	0
1.1	4	22	2.03	15.1	45	114	1082	1.8	0	0.2	0.06	0.08	1.06	0.06	0.41	6.9	19.4	0
1.8	8	23	2.28	48.1	213	400	1007	1.3	23	1.5	0.15	0.08	1.47	0.07	0.25	0.2	2.5	0
0.5	2	7	0.02	16.3	130	336	363	0.1	5	0.2	0.08	0.18	2.76	0.09	1.61	0.4	4.7	0
0.4	0	8	0.63	20.2	30	104	1146	0.2	10	6.1	0.06	0.05	0.79	0.05	0	0.4	10.1	0
0.4	0	12	1.76	7.3	34	264	695	0.2	24	66.4	0.09	0.05	1.42	0.11	0	2.3	14.6	0
0.9	5	17	1.12	4.9	41	173	791	1.5	95	2.4	0.04	0.05	1.03	0.08	0.32	0.4	9.8	0
1.4	17	27	1.47	9.6	106	369	84	2.2	333	5.5	0.05	0.17	3.3	0.1	0.24	0.7	43.4	0
1.2	0	77	3.21	313.7	543	296	988	2.7	116	0	1.73	1.48	29.64	2.72	5.43	1.2	254.4	0
0.3	0	22	1.08	7.2	34	210	822	0.5	116	1.4	0.05	0.05	0.92	0.06	0	0.4	9.6	0
0		2	1.76	1	10	14	0	0	0	0	0.03	0.01	0.59	0.04	0	0	0.6	0
0		21	1.19	5.2	15	10	1	0	0	0.1	0.07	0.06	0.78	0.01	0	0.1	0.6	0
0.2		120	3	2.8	14	33	1	2.4	122	0.1	0.03	0.03	1.35	0.02		2		0
0		9	0.25		6	63	9	0		61.6	0.02	0.01	0.14	0.01				0
		95	0.51	9.9	114	112	42	0.7			0.03	0.15	0.12	0.05				0
		27	0.54		39	164	16			0.3	0.02	0.05	0.83	0.08				0
0.5		46	0.65	13.6	67	192	22	0.7	26	21.5	0.02	0.1	0.88	0.1	0.01	1	51	0
0.1		22	1		78	136	2		23	0	0.11	0.09	1.35					0
0.5		16	0.36	1.5	11	22	6	0.2	18	2.4	0.02	0.03	0.2	0.01	0.06	0.3	3.4	0
0.4	3	16	0.04	1.2	9	21	5	0.2	18	1.8	0.02	0.03	0.21	0.01	0.05	0.4	3.1	0
0.4	2	21	0.36	1.5	15	22	9	0.1	18	1.8	0.01	0.02	0.27	0.01	0.09	0.4	3	0
0.4	0	39	0.4	2.1	26	24	7	0.2	18	2.4	0.02	0.02	0.2	0.01	0.06	0.3	3.4	0
2.4	10	16	1.26	17.4	57	83	175	0.4	11	0	0.14	0.12	0.96	0.02	0.04	0.1	26.3	0
1.8	18	14	0.44	12.7	32	42	82	0.2	42	0.1	0.03	0.05	0.24	0.02	0.04	0.7	7	0
2.2	5	11	0.25	10.1	19	37	21	0.2	17	0.1	0.01	0.02	0.06	0.01	0.01	0.2	1.8	0
1.1	2	10	0.37	10.4	21	34	8	0.3	7	0	0.01	0.02	0.06	0.02	0.01	0	3	0
1	2	8	0.3	6.1	12	22	8	0.2	7	0	0	0.01	0.03		0.02	0	0.7	0
5.2	55	57	1.53	30.4	101	133	299	0.7	38	0.2	0.13	0.2	1.08	0.04	0.15	1.5	25.6	0
11	14	3	1.84				241											0
3.1	24	53	2.13	51.8	40	325	242	0.3	10	0.1	0.14	0.12	1.29	0.14	0.04	1.8	24.4	0
4.1	65	45	0.49	11.4	77	220	258	0.4	65	0.1	0.08	0.1	0.52	0.04	0.26	1.2	29.6	0
2.5	62	34	0.46	13.5	68	70	291	0.4	33	0.1	0.07	0.07	0.76	0.04	0.18	1.6	36.9	0
0.3	39	27	1.03	4.2	52	38	93	0.2	17	0	0.09	0.1	0.73	0.02	0.09	0.1	17.9	0
4.4	1	101	1.3	13.4	78	111	318	0.4	14	0.1	0.14	0.21	1.19	0.03	0.07	0.1	34.7	0
2.4	1	96	1.12	8.9	69	70	242	0.2	11	0.1	0.14	0.18	1.13	0.02	0.06	0.1	28.1	0
2.7	37	99	1.12	8.2	80	62	233	0.3	27	0.1	0.12	0.16	0.99	0.02	0.11	0.8	23.1	0
6.6	29	170	0.47	18.8	232	209	376	0.5	95	0.5	0.12	0.26	0.49	0.05	0.31	1.1	29.7	0
0.5	0	15	0.66	10.8	79	96	178	0.2	0	0	0.02	0.06	0.31	0	0	0.8	6.4	0

MDA Code	Food Name	Amt	Wt (g)	Ener (kcal)	Prot (g)	Carb (g)	Fiber (g)	Fat (g)	Mono (g)	Poly (g)
46011	Cupcake, snack, chocolate, w/frosting & cream filling	1 ea	50	188	2	30	0	7	2.8	2.6
71338	Doughnut, cake, chocolate, glazed/sugared, 3-3/4"	1 ea	60	250	3	34	1	12	6.8	1.5
71337	Doughnut, cake, w/chocolate icing, lrg, 3-1/2"	1 ea	57	270	3	27	1	18	10	2.2
45525	Doughnut, cake, glazed/sugared, med, 3"	1 ea	45	192	2	23	1	10	5.7	1.3
71335	Doughnut, cake, holes	1 ea	14	59	1	7	0	3	1.3	1.1
45527	Doughnut, French crullers, glazed, 3"	1 ea	41	169	1	24	1	8	4.3	0.9
45563	Doughnut, creme filled, 3-1/2" oval	1 ea	85	307	5	26	1	21	10.3	2.6
48044	Pumpkin pie mix, canned	0.5 cup	135	140	1	36	11	0	0	0
	Candy									
51150	Candied fruit	1 oz	28.4	91	0	23	0	0	0	0
23074	Candies, hard, dietetic or low-calorie (sorbitol)	1 pce	3	11	0	3	0	0	0	0
4148	Candy, Bit O Honey, Nestle	6 pce	40	160	1	32	0	3	0.8	0.2
23115	Candy, butterscotch	5 pce	30	117	0	27	0	1	0.3	0
23015	Candy, caramels	1 pce	10.1	39	0	8	0	1	0.2	0.4
92202	Candy, chocolate covered, caramel with nuts	1 ea	14	66	1	8	1	3	1.3	0.8
90671	Candy, Jellybeans	10 ea	28.4	106	0	27	0	0	0	0
90690	Candy, M&M's Peanut Chocolate	1 ea	47.3	244	4	29	2	12	5.2	2
90691	Candy, M&M's Plain Chocolate	1 ea	42	207	2	30	1	9	1.5	0.2
92212	Candy, milk chocolate coated coffee beans	1 oz	28.4	146	2	18	2	7	1.7	0.2
23419	Candy, milk chocolate coated peanuts	10 pce	40	208	5	20	2	13	5.2	1.7
23022	Candy, milk chocolate coated raisins	1.5 oz	42.5	166	2	29	2	6	2	0.2
90682	Candy, milk chocolate w/almonds	1 ea	43.9	231	4	23	3	15	5.9	1
92201	Candy, nougat	1 ea	14	56	0	13	0	0	0	0
23081	Candy, peanut brittle, homemade	1.5 oz	42.5	207	3	30	1	8	3.4	1.9
90698	Candy, Rolo, caramels in milk chocolate, 1.74 oz roll	1 ea	49.3	234	3	33	0	10	1	0.1
23142	Candy, Sesame crunch	20 pce	35	181	4	18	3	12	4.4	5.1
90702	Candy, Starburst, fruit chews, 16 oz pkg	1 oz	28.4	112	0	24	0	2	1	0.9
92198	Candy, strawberry twists, 8 oz pkg	4 pce	45	158	1	36	0	1		
90661	Candy, York Peppermint Patty	1 ea	17	65	0	14	0	1	0.1	0
91509	Candy bar, milk chocolate, w/almonds, bites	17 pce	39	214	4	20	1	14	5.6	0.9
90681	Candy bar, milk chocolate, mini	1 ea	7	37	1	4	0	2	0.9	0.1
90685	Candy bar, milk chocolate w/rice cereal	1 ea	10	50	1	6	0	3	0.9	0.1
23145	Candy bar, sweet chocolate, 1.45 oz bar	1 ea	41.1	208	2	24	2	14	4.6	0.4
90704	Candy bar, 3 Musketeers, 0.8 oz bar	1 ea	22.7	94	1	17	0	3	1	0.1
23405	Candy bar, Almond Joy, fun size, 0.7 oz	1 ea	19.8	95	1	12	1	5	1	0.2
90679	Candy bar, Baby Ruth, 2.28 oz bar	1 ea	64.6	300	5	40	2	16	4.2	2.1
90653	Candy bar, Butterfinger, 1.6 oz bar	1 ea	45.4	216	3	33	1	9	0	0
23116	Candy bar, Caramello, 1.6 oz bar	1 ea	45.4	210	3	29	1	10	2.4	0.3
23060	Candy bar, Kit Kat, 1.5 oz bar	1 ea	42.5	220	3	27	0	11	2.5	0.4
23061	Candy bar, Krackel, 1.5 oz bar	1 ea	42.5	218	3	27	1	11	2.7	0.2
23037	Candy bar, Mars almond, 1.76 oz bar	1 ea	50	234	4	31	1	12	5.3	2
90688	Candy bar, Milky Way, 2.05 oz bar	1 ea	58.1	246	3	42	1	9	3.5	0.3
23062	Candy bar, Mr. Goodbar, 1.75 oz bar	1 ea	49.6	267	5	27	2	16	4.1	2.2
23135	Candy bar, Oh Henry!, 2 oz bar	1 ea	56.7	262	4	37	1	13	3.8	1.5
23036	Candy bar, Skor, toffee bar, 1.4 oz bar	1 ea	39.7	212	1	25	1	13	3.7	0.5
23057	Candy bar, Special Dark, sweet chocolate, 1.45 oz bar	1 ea	41.1	218	2	24	3	13	2.1	0.2
23149	Candy bar, Twix, caramel, 2 oz bar	1 ea	56.7	283	3	37	1	14	7.6	0.5
90712	Chewing gum	10 pce	16	40	0	11	0	0	0	0
	Cookies									
47026	Animal crackers/Arrowroot/Tea Biscuits	10 ea	12.5	56	1	9	0	2	1	0.2
90636	Chocolate chip cookie, commercially prepared 3.5" to 4"	1 ea	40	196	2	26	1	10	5.3	0.5

Sat (g)	Chol (mg)	Calc (mg)	Iron (mg)	Mag (mg)	Phos (mg)	Pota (mg)	Sodi (mg)	Zinc (mg)	Vit A (RAE)	Vit C (mg)	Thia (mg)	Ribo (mg)	Niac (mg)	Vit B6 (mg)	Vit B12 (µg)	Vit E (mg)	Fol (µg)	Alc (g)
1.4	8	36	1.68	20.5	46	61	212	0.3	2	0	0.11	0.15	1.21	0.01	0.03	1.1	20	0
3.1	34	128	1.36	20.4	97	64	204	0.3	7	0.1	0.03	0.04	0.28	0.02	0.06	0.1	27	0
4.6	35	20	1.4	22.8	115	112	245	0.3	4	0.1	0.07	0.06	0.74	0.03	0.14	0.2	26.8	0
2.7	14	27	0.48	7.6	53	46	181	0.2	1	0	0.1	0.09	0.68	0.01	0.11	0.4	20.7	0
0.5	5	6	0.27	2.8	38	18	76	0.1	5	0	0.03	0.03	0.26	0.01	0.04	0.3	7.3	0
1.9	5	11	0.99	4.9	50	32	141	0.1	1	0	0.07	0.09	0.87	0.01	0.02	0.1	17.2	0
4.6	20	21	1.56	17	65	68	263	0.7	10	0	0.29	0.13	1.91	0.06	0.12	0.2	59.5	0
0.1	0	50	1.43	21.6	61	186	281	0.4	560	4.7	0.02	0.16	0.5	0.21	0	1.1	47.2	0
0	0	5	0.05	1.1	1	16	28	0	0	0	0	0	0	0	0	0	0	0
0	0	0	0	0	0	0	0	0	0	0	0	0	0	0	0	0	0	0
2	0	20	0.12	2.8	18	50	120	0.1	0	0	0	0.1	0.02	0.01	0.08	0.4	1.2	0
0.6	3	1	0	0	0	1	117	0	8	0	0	0	0	0	0	0	0	0
0.3	1	14	0.01	1.7	12	22	25	0	1	0	0.01	0.03	0.01	0.01	0.03	0	0.4	0
0.7	0	11	0.24	11.3	23	62	3	0.3	6	0.2	0.01	0.02	0.67	0.02	0	0.2	12.9	0
0	0	1	0.04	0.6	1	11	14	0	0	0	0	0	0	0	0	0	0	0
4.9	4	48	0.54	35.9	110	164	23	1.1	12	0.2	0.05	0.07	1.93	0.04	0.08	1.2	18	0
5.5	6	44	0.47	14.3	48	85	26	0.5	11	0.2	0.03	0.07	0.09	0.01	0.14	0.5	2.5	0
3.5	6	48	0.65	18.2	53	117	20	0.5	12	0	0.03	0.09	0.09	0.01	0.15	0.5	2.8	0
5.8	4	42	0.52	38.4	85	201	16	1	14	0	0.05	0.07	1.7	0.08	0.18	1.4	3.2	0
3.7	1	37	0.73	19.1	61	218	15	0.3	10	0.1	0.04	0.07	0.17	0.03	0.08	0.4	3	0
7.5	8	98	0.72	39.5	116	195	32	0.6	19	0.1	0.03	0.19	0.33	0.02	0.14	2	6.1	0
0.2	0	4	0.08	4.5	8	15	5	0.1	0	0	0.02	0.07	0	0		0.4	0.7	0
1.8	5	11	0.52	17.8	45	71	189	0.4	17	0	0.06	0.02	1.12	0.03	0	1.1	19.6	0
7.2	6	71	0.21	0	35	93	93	0	17	0.4	0.01	0.06	0.02	0	0.16	0.5	0	0
1.6	0	229	1.49	87.8	148	113	58	1.3	0	0	0.19	0.06	1.3	0.19	0	0.1	18.2	0
0.4	0	1	0.04	0.3	2	1	16	0	0	15	0	0	0	0	0	0.2	0	0
0	0	0	0.23				129		0	0								0
0.7	0	2	0.16	10.7	0	19	5	0.1		0	0.01	0.02	0.14	0		0		0
6.8	7	86	0.58	23	89	184	29	0.5		0.7	0.03	0.15	0.24	0.03		0.2	6.2	0
1	2	13	0.16	4.4	15	26	6	0.1	3	0	0.01	0.02	0.03	0	0.04	0.1	0.8	0
1.6	2	17	0.08	4.9	19	34	14	0.1	6	0	0.01	0.03	0.05	0.01	0.06	0.2	1.5	0
8.3	0	10	1.13	46.4	60	119	7	0.6	0	0	0.01	0.1	0.28	0.02	0	0.1	1.2	0
1.5	2	19	0.17	6.6	21	30	44	0.1	3	0.1	0.01	0.03	0.05	0	0.04	0.2	0	0
3.5	1	13	0.25	13.1	22	50	28	0.2		0.1	0.01	0.03	0.09	0.01	0.02	0		0
7.9	1	29	0.45	47.2	89	230	138	0.8	2	0.1	0.06	0.05	1.79	0.04	0.03	1.2	20	0
4.5	0	16	0.35	24.5	52	107	97	0.4	0		0.06	0.03	1.61	0.04	0.02	0.9	17.3	0
5.8	12	97	0.49	19.1	68	155	55	0.4		0.8	0.02	0.18	0.52	0.02	0.29	0.1		0
7.6	5	53	0.42	15.7	57	98	23	0	10	0	0.05	0.09	0.21	0.01	0.24	0.1	6	0
6.8	5	67	0.45	5.5	52	138	83	0.2		0.3	0.02	0.08	0.11	0.02	0.25	0	2.6	0
3.6	8	84	0.55	36	117	162	85	0.6	8	0.3	0.02	0.16	0.47	0.03	0.18	3.9	4.5	0
4.5	8	76	0.44	19.8	84	140	139	0.4	11	0.6	0.02	0.13	0.2	0.03	0.19	0.7	3.5	0
7	5	55	0.69	23.3	81	195	20	0.5	17	0.4	0.07	0.07	1.71	0.03	0.16	1.6	18.8	0
3.8	5	46	0.35	28.9	79	184	131	0.7	6	0.1	0.01	0.09	1.59	0.05	0.11	1.2	24.9	0
7.5	21	52	0.23	4	24	61	126	0.1		0.2	0.01	0.04	0.05	0.01	0.11	0	1.2	0
7.9	2	12	0.88	12.7	21	206	2	0		0	0	0	0	0	0	0.1	0	0
5	3	51	0.46	14.2	49	88	109	0.5	15	0.2	0.08	0.1	0.63	0.01	0.12	1	14.7	0
0	0	0	0	0	0	0	0	0	0	0	0	0	0	0	0	0	0	0
0.4	0	5	0.34	2.2	14	12	49	0.1	0	0	0.04	0.04	0.43	0	0.01	0	12.9	0
3.1	0	14	1.43	19.2	46	59	119	0.3	0	0	0.1	0.09	0.96	0.02	0	0.6	25.2	0

MDA Code	Food Name	Amt	Wt (g)	Ener (kcal)	Prot (g)	Carb (g)	Fiber (g)	Fat (g)	Mono (g)	Poly (g)
47037	Chocolate chip cookie, homemade w/butter, 2-1/4"	2 ea	32	156	2	19	1	9	2.6	1.5
47032	Chocolate chip cookie, lower fat, commercially prepared	3 ea	30	136	2	22	1	5	1.8	1.4
47001	Chocolate chip cookie, soft, commercially prepared	2 ea	30	137	1	18	1	7	3.9	1
43527	Chocolate coated graham crackers, 2-1/2" square	2 ea	28	136	2	19	1	6	2.2	0.3
47006	Chocolate sandwich cookie, creme filled	3 ea	30	140	2	21	1	6	3.2	0.7
71272	Cinnamon graham crackers, small rectangle pieces	4 ea	14	59	1	11	0	1	0.6	0.5
47042	Coconut macaroons, homemade, 2"	1 ea	24	97	1	17	0	3	0.1	0
62905	Fig bar, 2 oz	1 ea	56.7	197	2	40	3	4	1.7	1.6
47043	Fortune cookie	3 ea	24	91	1	20	0	1	0.3	0.1
90638	Gingersnap, lrg, 3-1/2" to 4"	1 ea	32	133	2	25	1	3	1.7	0.4
45787	Little Debbie Nutty Bars, chocolate covered wafers w/peanut butter	1 ea	57	312	5	31		19		
90639	Molasses cookie, 3-1/2" to 4"	1 ea	32	138	2	24	0	4	2.3	0.6
47706	Molasses cookies/Archway Home Style	1 ea	26	103	1	18	0	3	1.1	0.2
90640	Oatmeal cookie, commercially prepared, 3-1/2" to 4"	1 ea	25	112	2	17	1	5	2.5	0.6
47003	Oatmeal raisin cookie, homemade, 2-5/8"	1 ea	15	65	1	10	0	2	1	0.8
47010	Peanut butter cookie, homemade, 3"	1 ea	20	95	2	12	0	5	2.2	1.4
47549	Peanut butter cookies/Archway Home Style	1 ea	21	101	2	12	1	5	2.1	0.9
47059	Peanut butter sandwich cookie	2 ea	28	134	2	18	1	6	3.1	1.1
47062	Shortbread pecan cookie, commercially prepared, 2"	2 ea	28	152	1	16	1	9	5.2	1.2
47007	Shortbread plain cookie, commercially prepared, 1-5/8" square	4 ea	32	161	2	21	1	8	4.3	1
47559	Sugar cookies/Archway Home Style	1 ea	24	98	1	17	0	3	1.1	0.2
47690	Sugar cookies, fat-free/Archway Home Style	1 ea	20	71	1	17	0	0	0	0.1
62907	Sugar cookie, refrigerated dough, baked	1 ea	23	111	1	15	0	5	3	0.7
90642	Sugar wafer cookie, creme filled, 2-1/2" × 3/4" × 1/4"	1 ea	3.5	18	0	2	0	1	0.4	0.3
90643	Vanilla sandwich cookie, creme filled, 3-1/8" × 1-1/4"	2 ea	30	145	1	22	0	6	2.5	2.3
47072	Vanilla wafer	4 ea	24	114	1	17	0	5	2.7	0.6
	Custards and Puddings									
2622	Custard, egg, prepared from dry mix w/2% milk	0.5 cup	133	148	5	23	0	4	1.1	0.3
2613	Custard, egg, prepared from dry mix w/whole milk	0.5 cup	133	161	5	23	0	5	1.6	0.3
57896	Flan (Caramel Custard) dry mix	1 ea	21	73	0	19	0	0	0	0
2632	Pudding, banana, ready to eat	1 ea	141.8	180	3	30	0	5	2.2	1.9
57894	Pudding, chocolate, ready to eat	1 ea	113.4	158	3	26	1	5	1.9	1.6
2612	Pudding, vanilla, ready-to-eat	1 ea	113.4	147	3	25	0	4	1.7	0.5
2764	Pudding, JELL-O fat-free pudding snacks, vanilla	1 ea	113	104	2	23	0	0	0	0
2757	Pudding, JELL-O fat-free sugar-free instant, vanilla, powder	1 ea	8	26	0	6	0	0		
2651	Rice pudding, ready-to-eat	1 ea	141.8	231	3	31	0	11	4.6	4
57902	Tapioca pudding, ready-to-eat	1 ea	113.4	135	2	22	0	4	2.6	0.4
	Ice Cream and Frozen Desserts									
71819	Frozen yogurts, chocolate, nonfat	1 cup	186	199	8	37	2	1	0.4	0.1
72124	Frozen yogurts, flavors other than chocolate	1 cup	174	221	5	38	0	6	1.7	0.2
49111	Ice cream cone, cake or wafer	1 ea	29	121	2	23	1	2	0.5	0.9
49014	Ice cream cone, sugar, rolled	1 ea	10	40	1	8	0	0	0.1	0.1
52152	Ice cream bar, vanilla w/dark chocolate coating	1 ea	50	166	2	12		12		
2010	Ice cream, light, vanilla, soft serve	0.5 cup	88	111	4	19	0	2	0.7	0.1
90723	Ice popsicle	1 ea	59	47	0	11	0	0	0	0
	Pastries									
45788	Apple turnover, frozen, ready to bake	1 ea	89	284	4	31	2	16	8.6	0.8
42264	Cinnamon rolls w/icing, refrigerated dough/Pillsbury	1 ea	44	150	2	24		5	2.7	0.3
45675	Cream Puff/Eclair Shell, homemade	1 ea	48	174	4	11	0	12	5.3	3.5
71299	Croissant, butter	1 ea	67	272	5	31	2	14	3.7	0.7
71301	Croissant, cheese	1 ea	67	277	6	31	2	14	4.4	1.6

Sat (g)	Chol (mg)	Calc (mg)	Iron (mg)	Mag (mg)	Phos (mg)	Pota (mg)	Sodi (mg)	Zinc (mg)	Vit A (RAE)	Vit C (mg)	Thia (mg)	Ribo (mg)	Niac (mg)	Vit B6 (mg)	Vit B12 (µg)	Vit E (mg)	Fol (µg)	Alc (g)
4.5	22	12	0.79	17.6	32	71	109	0.3	44	0.1	0.06	0.06	0.44	0.03	0.03	0.3	10.6	0
1.1	0	6	0.92	8.4	25	37	113	0.2		0	0.09	0.08	0.83	0.08	0	0.5	21	0
2.2	0	4	0.72	10.5	15	28	98	0.1		0	0.03	0.06	0.49	0.05	0	0.9	11.7	0
3.7	0	16	1	16.2	38	59	81	0.3	1	0	0.04	0.06	0.61	0.02	0	0.1	5.6	0
1.1	0	6	1.18	14.4	28	56	145	0.3		0	0.05	0.04	0.8	0	0.01	0.5	15.9	0
0.2	0	3	0.52	4.2	15	19	85	0.1	0	0	0.03	0.04	0.58	0.01	0	0	6.4	0
2.7	0	2	0.18	5	10	37	59	0.2	0	0	0	0.03	0.03	0.02	0.01	0	1	0
0.6	0	36	1.64	15.3	35	117	198	0.2	5	0.2	0.09	0.12	1.06	0.04	0.05	0.4	19.8	0
0.2	0	3	0.35	1.7	8	10	66	0	0	0	0.04	0.03	0.44	0	0	0	15.8	0
0.8	0	25	2.05	15.7	27	111	209	0.2	0	0	0.06	0.09	1.04	0.03	0	0.3	27.8	0
3.6							127			1.1								0
1	0	24	2.06	16.6	30	111	147	0.1	0	0	0.11	0.08	0.97	0.03	0	0	28.5	0
0.7	8	9	1.14			29	144			0	0.07	0.06	0.66					0
1.1	0	9	0.64	8.2	34	36	96	0.2	1	0.1	0.07	0.06	0.56	0.02	0	0.1	14.8	0
0.5	5	15	0.4	6.3	24	36	81	0.1	21	0.1	0.04	0.02	0.19	0.01	0.01	0.4	4.5	0
0.9	6	8	0.45	7.8	23	46	104	0.2	27	0	0.04	0.04	0.7	0.02	0.02	0.8	11	0
1.1	8	7	0.57			44	85			0	0.05	0.04	0.92					0
1.4	0	15	0.73	13.7	53	54	103	0.3	0	0	0.09	0.07	1.05	0.04	0.06	0.5	17.1	0
2.3	9	8	0.68	5	24	20	79	0.2	0	0	0.08	0.06	0.69	0.01	0	1.1	17.6	0
2	6	11	0.88	5.4	35	32	146	0.2	6	0	0.11	0.11	1.07	0.03	0.03	0.1	22.4	0
0.8	5	7	0.53			20	162			0	0.07	0.06	0.59					0
0.1	0	3	0.44			12	80		0	0	0.06	0.04	0.5				15.2	0
1.4	7	21	0.42	1.8	43	37	108	0.1	3	0	0.04	0.03	0.55	0.01	0.02	0	16.1	0
0.1	0	1	0.07	0.4	2	2	5	0	0	0	0	0.01	0.09	0	0	0.1	1.8	0
0.9	0	8	0.66	4.2	22	27	105	0.1	0	0	0.08	0.07	0.81	0.01	0	0.5	15	0
1.2	0	6	0.53	2.9	15	26	73	0.1		0	0.09	0.05	0.71	0.01	0.01	0.3	10.3	0
1.8	64	193	0.47	25.3	184	298	118	0.7	81	1.1	0.07	0.28	0.17	0.09	0.6	0.3	12	0
2.8	70	190	0.47	25.3	181	294	117	0.7	49	1.1	0.07	0.28	0.17	0.09	0.59	0.1	12	0
0	0	5	0.02	0	0	32	91	0	0	0	0	0	0	0	0	0	0	0
0.8	0	121	0.18	11.3	98	156	278	0.4	9	0.7	0.03	0.21	0.23	0.03	0.26	0	2.8	0
0.8	3	102	0.58	23.8	91	204	146	0.5	12	2	0.03	0.18	0.39	0.03	0	0.3	3.4	0
1.7	8	100	0.15	9.1	77	128	153	0.3	7	0	0.02	0.16	0.29	0.01	0.11	0	0	0
0.2	2	86	0.05		115	123	241			0.3								0
0	0	12	0.01		189	2	332			0	0							0
1.7	1	74	0.43	11.3	96	85	121	0.7	35	0.7	0.03	0.1	0.23	0.04	0.3	2	4.3	0
1.1	1	95	0.26	9.1	90	109	180	0.3	0	0.8	0.02	0.11	0.35	0.02	0.24	0.3	3.4	0
0.9	7	296	0.07	74.4	240	631	151	0.9	4	1.3	0.07	0.33	0.37	0.07	0.91	0.1	22.3	0
4	23	174	0.8	17.4	155	271	110	0.5	85	1.2	0.07	0.31	0.12	0.07	0.12	0.2	7	0
0.4	0	7	1.04	7.5	28	32	41	0.2	0	0	0.07	0.1	1.28	0.01	0	0.2	50.2	0
0.1	0	4	0.44	3.1	10	14	32	0.1	0	0	0.05	0.04	0.51	0.01	0	0	14	0
7.2	14	60					34											0
1.4	11	138	0.05	12.3	106	194	62	0.5	26	0.8	0.05	0.17	0.1	0.04	0.44	0.1	4.4	0
0	0	0	0.32	0.6	0	9	4	0.1	0	0.4	0	0	0	0	0	0	0	0
4			1.22				176				0							0
1.2							334											0
2.7	94	17	0.97	5.8	57	47	267	0.4	133	0	0.1	0.17	0.75	0.04	0.19	1.3	25.4	0
7.8	45	25	1.36	10.7	70	79	498	0.5	138	0.1	0.26	0.16	1.47	0.04	0.11	0.6	59	0
7.1	38	36	1.44	16.1	87	88	372	0.6	137	0.1	0.35	0.22	1.45	0.05	0.21	1	49.6	0

MDA Code	Food Name	Amt	Wt (g)	Ener (kcal)	Prot (g)	Carb (g)	Fiber (g)	Fat (g)	Mono (g)	Poly (g)
45572	Danish, cheese	1 ea	71	266	6	26	1	16	8	1.8
71330	Danish, cinnamon nut	1 pce	53.2	229	4	24	1	13	7.3	2.3
70913	Pie crust, cookie type nilla wafer, ready to use	1 ea	28	144	1	18	0	8	5.2	0.4
49015	Strudel, apple	1 pce	71	195	2	29	2	8	2.3	3.8
42164	Sweet roll, cheese	1 ea	66	238	5	29	1	12	6	1.3
42166	Sweet roll, cinnamon, frosted, baked from refrigerated dough	1 ea	30	109	2	17	1	4	2.2	0.5
71367	Sweet roll, cinnamon raisin, commercial, large	1 ea	83	309	5	42	2	14	4	6.2
45683	Toaster pastry, brown sugar-cinnamon	1 ea	50	206	3	34	0	7	4	0.9
45593	Toaster pastry, Pop Tart, apple-cinnamon/Kellogg	1 ea	52	205	2	37	1	5	3.1	1.4
45763	Toaster pastry, Pop Tart, frosted apple cinnamon, low fat/Kellogg	1 ea	52	191	2	40	1	3	1.5	0.8
45768	Toaster pastry, Pop Tart, frosted chocolate fudge, low fat/Kellogg	1 ea	52	190	3	40	1	3	1.2	0.9
45601	Toaster pastry, Pop Tart, frosted chocolate fudge/Kellogg	1 ea	52	201	3	37	1	5	2.7	1.1
	Toppings and Frostings									
23000	Apple butter	1 tbsp	18	31	0	8	0	0	0	0
23070	Caramel topping	2 tbsp	41	103	1	27	0	0	0	0
23014	Chocolate syrup, fudge-type	2 tbsp	38	133	2	24	1	3	1.5	0.1
46039	Frosting, cream cheese flavor	1 oz	28.4	118	0	19	0	5	1.1	1.7
54334	Hazelnut-chocolate flavored spread	1 oz	28	151	2	17	2	8	4.6	1.9
23164	Strawberry topping	2 tbsp	42.5	108	0	28	0	0	0	0
510	Whipped cream topping, pressurized	2 tbsp	7.5	19	0	1	0	2	0.5	0.1
514	Whipped dessert topping, nondairy, pressurized can	2 tbsp	8.8	23	0	1	0	2	0.2	0
508	Whipped dessert topping, nondairy, semisolid, frozen	2 tbsp	9.4	30	0	2	0	2	0.2	0
54387	Whipped topping, frozen, low fat	2 tbsp	9.4	21	0	2	0	1	0.1	0
	FATS AND OILS									
44469	Butter, light, stick, with salt	1 tbsp	13	65	0	0	0	7	2.1	0.3
44470	Butter, light, stick, without salt	1 tbsp	13	65	0	0	0	7	2.1	0.3
44952	Butter, salted	1 tbsp	14	100	0	0	0	11		
90210	Butter, unsalted	1 tbsp	14	100	0	0	0	11	2.9	0.4
90209	Butter, whipped (with salt)	1 tbsp	9.4	67	0	0	0	8	2.2	0.3
8003	Fat, bacon grease	1 tsp	4.3	39	0	0	0	4	1.9	0.5
8005	Fat, chicken	1 tbsp	12.8	115	0	0	0	13	5.7	2.7
8107	Fat, lard	1 tbsp	12.8	115	0	0	0	13	5.8	1.4
8135	Margarine & butter, blend, w/60% corn oil & 40% butter	1 tbsp	14.2	102	0	0	0	11	4.7	2.3
44476	Margarine, regular, 80% fat, with salt	1 tbsp	14.2	102	0	0	0	11	5.1	4
8067	Oil, fish, cod liver	1 tbsp	13.6	123	0	0	0	14	6.4	3.1
8084	Oil, vegetable, canola	1 tbsp	14	124	0	0	0	14	8.2	4.1
8008	Oil, olive, salad or cooking	1 tbsp	13.5	119	0	0	0	14	9.8	1.4
8111	Oil, safflower, salad or cooking, greater than 70% oleic	1 tbsp	13.6	120	0	0	0	14	10.2	2
8027	Oil, sesame, salad or cooking	1 tbsp	13.6	120	0	0	0	14	5.4	5.7
44483	Shortening, household	1 tbsp	12.8	113	0	0	0	13	5.7	4
8007	Shortening, soy hydrogenated & cottonseed hydrogenated	1 tbsp	12.8	113	0	0	0	13	5.7	3.3
	CONDIMENTS, SAUCES, AND SYRUPS									
53382	Barbecue sauce, hickory smoke	2 tbsp	34	39	0	9	0	0		
1708	Barbecue sauce, original	2 tbsp	36	63	0	15		0		
27001	Catsup	1 ea	6	6	0	2	0	0	0	0
53523	Cheese sauce, ready-to-eat	0.25 cup	63	110	4	4	0	8	2.4	1.6
54388	Cream substitute, powdered, light	1 tbsp	5.9	25	0	4	0	1	0.7	0
63334	Dietetic syrup	1 tbsp	15	6	0	7	0	0	0	0
53636	Enchilada sauce	0.25 cup	60.3	20	0	3	0	1		

Sat (g)	Chol (mg)	Calc (mg)	Iron (mg)	Mag (mg)	Phos (mg)	Pota (mg)	Sodi (mg)	Zinc (mg)	Vit A (RAE)	Vit C (mg)	Thia (mg)	Ribo (mg)	Niac (mg)	Vit B6 (mg)	Vit B12 (µg)	Vit E (mg)	Fol (µg)	Alc (g)
4.8	11	25	1.14	10.6	77	70	320	0.5	25	0.1	0.13	0.18	1.42	0.03	0.12	0.2	42.6	0
3.1	24	50	0.96	17	59	51	193	0.5	5	0.9	0.12	0.13	1.22	0.06	0.11	0.4	44.2	0
1.4	3	11	0.5	2.2	23	19	63	0.1			0.05	0.05	0.7	0.01	0.03		8.4	0
1.5	4	11	0.3	6.4	23	106	191	0.1	5	1.2	0.03	0.02	0.23	0.03	0.16	1	19.9	0
4	50	78	0.5	12.5	65	90	236	0.4		0.1	0.1	0.09	0.55	0.05	0.2	1.3	28.4	0
1	0	10	0.8	3.6	104	19	250	0.1		0.1	0.12	0.07	1.09	0.01	0.02	0.5	16.5	0
2.6	55	60	1.33	14.1	63	92	318	0.5	51	1.7	0.27	0.22	1.98	0.09	0.12	1.7	59.8	0
1.8	0	17	2.02	12	66	57	212	0.3	148	0.1	0.19	0.29	2.29	0.21	0.11	0.9	14.5	0
0.9	0	12	1.82	5.7	28	47	174	0.3		0	0.15	0.17	1.98	0.2	0	0	41.6	0
0.6	0	6	1.82	4.7	21	28	206	0.2		0	0.16	0.16	1.98	0.21	0	0	52	0
0.5	0	14	1.82	14.6	40	62	249	0.3		0	0.16	0.16	1.98	0.21	0	0	52	0
1	0	20	1.82	15.1	44	82	203	0.3		0	0.16	0.16	1.98	0.21	0	0	52	0
0	0	3	0.06	0.9	1	16	3	0	0	0.2	0	0	0.01	0.01	0	0	0.2	0
0	0	22	0.08	2.9	19	34	143	0.1	11	0.1	0	0.04	0.02	0.01	0.04	0	0.8	0
1.5	1	38	0.6	24.3	64	171	131	0.3	2	0	0.03	0.11	0.14	0.03	0.11	0.9	1.9	0
1.3	0	1	0.05	0.6	1	10	54	0	0	0	0	0	0	0	0	1.2	0	0
1.5	0	30	1.23	17.9	43	114	11	0.3	0	0	0.03	0.05	0.12	0.02	0.08	1.4	3.9	0
0	0	3	0.12	1.7	2	22	9	0	0	5.8	0	0.01	0.07	0.01	0	0	2.6	0
1	6	8	0	0.8	7	11	10	0	14	0	0	0.01	0	0	0.02	0	0.2	0
1.7	0	0	0	0.1	2	2	5	0	0	0	0	0	0	0	0	0.1	0	0
2	0	1	0.01	0.2	1	2	2	0	1	0	0	0	0	0	0	0.1	0	0
1.1	0	7	0.01	0.7	7	9	7	0	0	0	0	0.01	0.01	0	0.02	0	0.3	0
4.5	14	6	0.14	0.6	4	9	58	0	60	0	0	0.01	0	0	0.02	0.2	0.1	0
4.5	14	6	0.14	0.6	4	9	5	0	60	0	0	0.01	0	0	0.02	0.2	0.1	0
7		0	0				75			0								0
7.2	30	3	0	0.3	3	3	2	0	96	0	0	0	0.01	0	0.02	0.3	0.4	0
4.7	21	2	0.02	0.2	2	2	78	0	64	0	0	0	0	0	0.01	0.2	0.3	0
1.7	4	0	0	0	0	0	6	0	0	0	0	0	0	0	0	0	0	0
3.8	11	0	0	0	0	0	0	0	0	0	0	0	0	0	0	0.3	0	0
5	12	0	0	0	0	0	0	0	0	0	0	0	0	0	0	0.1	0	0
4		4	0.01	0.3	3	5	127	0	116	0	0	0	0	0	0.01	0.6	0.3	0
1.8	0	4	0	0.3	3	5	153	0	116	0	0	0	0	0	0.01	0.7	0.1	0
3.1	78	0	0	0	0	0	0	0	4080	0	0	0	0	0	0	0.4	0	0
1	0	0	0	0	0	0	0	0	0	0	0	0	0	0	0	2.4	0	0
1.9	0	0	0.08	0	0	0	0	0	0	0	0	0	0	0	0	1.9	0	0
0.8	0	0	0	0	0	0	0	0	0	0	0	0	0	0	0	4.6	0	0
1.9	0	0	0	0	0	0	0	0	0	0	0	0	0	0	0	0.2	0	0
2.6	0	0	0	0	0	0	0	0	0	0	0	0	0	0	0	0.1	0	0
3.2	0	0	0	0	0	0	0	0	0	0	0	0	0	0	0	0.1	0	0
0	0	5	0.21		3	28	418			0.1								0
							302											0
0	0	1	0.03	1.1	2	23	67	0	3	0.9	0	0.03	0.09	0.01	0	0.1	0.6	0
3.8	18	116	0.13	5.7	99	19	522	0.6	50	0.3	0	0.07	0.02	0.01	0.09	0.2	2.5	0
0.2	0	0	0	0	8	53	14	0	0	0	0	0	0	0	0	0	0.1	0
0	0	0	0	0	0	0	3	0	0	0	0	0	0	0	0	0	0	0
	0	7	0.07				397		70	2.7								0

MDA Code	Food Name	Amt	Wt (g)	Ener (kcal)	Prot (g)	Carb (g)	Fiber (g)	Fat (g)	Mono (g)	Poly (g)
53474	Fish sauce	2 tbsp	36	13	2	1	0	0	0	0
50939	Gravy, brown, homestyle, canned	0.25 cup	60	25	1	3		1	0.3	0
53472	Hoisin sauce	2 tbsp	32	70	1	14	1	1	0.3	0.5
9533	Hollandaise sauce, with butterfat, dehydrated, prepared with water	1 ea	204	188	4	11	1	16	4.7	0.7
27004	Horseradish	1 tsp	5	2	0	1	0	0	0	0
92174	Hot sauce, chili, from immature green peppers, canned	1 tbsp	15	3	0	1	0	0	0	0
92173	Hot sauce, chili, from mature red peppers, canned	1 tbsp	15	3	0	1	0	0	0.1	0
23003	Jelly	1 tbsp	19	51	0	13	0	0	0	0
25002	Maple syrup	1 tbsp	20	52	0	13	0	0	0	0
23005	Marmalade, orange	1 tbsp	20	49	0	13	0	0	0	0
44697	Mayonnaise, light	1 tbsp	15	49	0	1	0	5	1.2	2.7
8145	Mayonnaise, safflower / soybean oil	1 tbsp	13.8	99	0	0	0	11	1.8	7.6
8502	Miracle Whip, light/Kraft	1 tbsp	16	37	0	2	0	3		
435	Mustard, yellow	1 tsp	5	3	0	0	0	0	0.1	0
53656	Nacho cheese sauce with jalapeno pepper, medium	0.25 cup	71.6	122	1	7	0	10	4.5	1.8
53473	Oyster sauce	2 tbsp	8	4	0	1	0	0	0	0
23042	Pancake syrup	1 tbsp	20	47	0	12	0	0	0	0
23172	Pancake syrup, reduced-kcal	1 tbsp	15	25	0	7	0	0	0	0
23090	Pancake syrup w/butter	1 tbsp	19.7	58	0	15	0	0	0.1	0
53650	Pasta sauce, smooth, traditional, jar/Ragu	0.5 cup	125	80	2	12	3	3	0.5	1.3
53524	Pasta sauce, spaghetti/marinara	0.5 cup	125	92	2	14	1	3	1	1.2
53470	Pepper or hot sauce	1 tsp	4.7	1	0	0	0	0	0	0
53461	Plum sauce	2 tbsp	38.1	70	0	16	0	0	0.1	0.2
92229	Preserves	1 tbsp	20	56	0	14	0	0	0	0
90594	Relish, pickle, sweet	1 ea	10	13	0	4	0	0	0	0
53651	Salsa, chili, chunky, canned	2 tbsp	30	9	0	2	0	0		
53642	Salsa, green chili, mild	2 tbsp	30.5	8	0	1	0	0		
53638	Salsa, green, Jalapena	2 tbsp	30.2	10	0	1	0	0		
53637	Salsa, red, Jalapena	2 tbsp	30.5	12	0	2	0	0		
90280	Salsa, packet	1 ea	8.9	2	0	1	0	0	0	0
53646	Salsa picante, mild	2 tbsp	30.5	8	0	1	0	0		
26014	Salt, table	0.25 tsp	1.5	0	0	0	0	0	0	0
504	Sour cream, cultured	2 tbsp	28.8	62	1	1	0	6	1.7	0.2
54383	Sour cream, fat free	1 oz	28	21	1	4	0	0	0	0
505	Sour cream, imitation, cultured	2 tbsp	28.8	60	1	2	0	6	0.2	0
54381	Sour cream, light	1 oz	28	38	1	2	0	3	0.9	0.1
515	Sour cream, reduced fat, cultured	2 tbsp	30	40	1	1	0	4	1	0.1
516	Sour dressing, non-butterfat, cultured, filled cream-type	1 tbsp	14.7	26	0	1	0	2	0.3	0.1
53063	Soy sauce	1 tbsp	18	11	2	1	0	0	0	0
90035	Soy sauce, low sodium	1 tbsp	18	10	1	2	0	0	0	0
53357	Sweet and sour sauce, ready-to-eat	2 tbsp	33	40	0	8	0	1	0.2	0.4
91056	Taco sauce, green, medium	1 tbsp	15.1	5	0	1	0	0		
53652	Taco sauce, red, mild	1 Tbs	15.7	7	0	1	0	0		
4655	Tahini made w/roasted & toasted kernels	1 tbsp	15	89	3	3	1	8	3	3.5
53004	Teriyaki sauce	1 tbsp	18	15	1	3	0	0	0	0
53468	White sauce, medium, homemade	1 cup	250	368	10	23	1	27	11.1	7.2
53099	Worcestershire sauce	1 tbsp	17	11	0	3	0	0	0	0
27175	Yeast extract spread	1 tsp	6	9	2	1	0	0	0	0
	Salad Dressing									
44497	1000 Island, fat-free	1 tbsp	16	21	0	5	1	0	0.1	0.1
8024	1000 Island, regular	1 tbsp	15.6	58	0	2	0	5	1.2	2.8

Sat (g)	Chol (mg)	Calc (mg)	Iron (mg)	Mag (mg)	Phos (mg)	Pota (mg)	Sodi (mg)	Zinc (mg)	Vit A (RAE)	Vit C (mg)	Thia (mg)	Ribo (mg)	Niac (mg)	Vit B6 (mg)	Vit B12 (µg)	Vit E (mg)	Fol (µg)	Alc (g)
0	0	15	0.28	63	3	104	2779	0.1	1	0.2	0	0.02	0.83	0.14	0.17	0	18.4	0
0.3	2						352											0
0.2	1	10	0.32	7.7	12	38	517	0.1	0	0.1	0	0.07	0.37	0.02	0	0.1	7.4	0
9.1	41	98	0.71	6.1	100	98	1232	0.6	120	0.2	0.04	0.14	0.04	0.41	0.61	0.6	10.2	0
0	0	3	0.02	1.4	2	12	16	0	0	1.2	0	0	0.02	0	0	0	2.8	0
0	0	1	0.06	1.8	2	85	4	0	4	10.2	0	0	0.1	0.02	0	0.1	1.8	0
0	0	1	0.08	1.8	2	85	4	0	3	4.5	0	0.01	0.09	0.02	0	0.1	1.6	0
0	0	1	0.04	1.1	1	10	6	0	0	0.2	0	0	0.01	0	0	0	0.4	0
0	0	13	0.24	2.8	0	41	2	0.8	0	0	0	0	0.01	0	0	0	0	0
0	0	8	0.03	0.4	1	7	11	0	1	1	0	0.01	0.01	0	0	0	1.8	0
0.8	5	1	0.05	0.3	5	6	101	0	3	0	0	0	0	0	0	0.5	0.6	0
1.2	8	2	0.07	0.1	4	5	78	0	12	0	0	0	0	0.08	0.04	3	1.1	0
0.5	4	1	0.03		2	4	131			0						0.1		0
0	0	4	0.09	1.9	4	8	56	0	0	0.1	0	0	0.02	0	0	0	0.4	0
2.7	4	64	0.86				548			1.1								0
0	0	3	0.01	0.3	2	4	219	0	0	0	0	0.01	0.12	0	0.03	0	1.2	0
0	0	1	0.01	0.4	2	3	16	0	0	0	0	0	0	0	0	0	0	0
0	0	0	0	0	6	0	30	0	0	0	0	0	0	0	0	0	0	0
0.2	1	0	0.02	0.4	2	1	19	0	3	0	0	0	0	0	0	0	0	0
0.4	0		1.02				756		32									0
0.4	0	34	1.06	26.2	45	470	601	0.7	34	3.9	0.03	0.08	4.9	0.22	0	2.5	13.8	0
0	0	0	0.02	0.2	1	7	124	0	0	3.5	0	0	0.01	0.01	0	0	0.3	0
0.1	0	5	0.54	4.6	8	99	205	0.1	1	0.2	0.01	0.03	0.39	0.03	0	0.1	2.3	0
0	0	4	0.1	0.8	4	15	6	0	0	1.8	0	0.02	0.01	0	0	0	2.2	0
0	0	0	0.09	0.5	1	2	81	0	4	0.1	0	0	0.02	0	0	0	0.1	0
		4	0.01				148		3	3.2								0
		5	0.28				175		7	4.1								0
	0	5	0.12				181		4	3.6								0
		6	0.05				149		43	9.8								0
0	0	2	0.04	1.3	3	26	53	0	1	0.2	0	0	0.01	0.02	0	0.1	0.4	0
	0	5	0.03				182		6	1.9								0
0	0	0	0	0	0	0	581	0	0	0	0	0	0	0	0	0	0	0
3.8	13	33	0.02	3.2	24	41	15	0.1	51	0.3	0.01	0.04	0.02	0	0.09	0.2	3.2	0
0	3	35	0	2.8	27	36	39	0.1	20	0	0.01	0.04	0.02	0.01	0.08	0	3.1	0
5.1	0	1	0.11	1.7	13	46	29	0.3	0	0	0	0	0	0	0	0.2	0	0
1.8	10	39	0.02	2.8	20	59	20	0.1	25	0.3	0.01	0.03	0.02	0.01	0.12	0.1	3.1	0
2.2	12	31	0.02	3	28	39	12	0.2	31	0.3	0.01	0.04	0.02	0	0.09	0.1	3.3	0
2	1	17	0	1.5	13	24	7	0.1	0	0.1	0.01	0.02	0.01	0	0.05	0.2	1.8	0
0	0	4	0.43	7.2	23	38	1005	0.1	0	0	0.01	0.03	0.71	0.04	0	0	3.2	0
0	0	3	0.36	6.1	20	32	600	0.1	0	0	0.01	0.02	0.6	0.03	0	0	2.9	0
0.1	0	6	0.28	2.3	3	22	116	0		0	0.01	0	0.07	0.01	0	0.1	0.7	0
	0	1	0.01				96		1	0.7								0
	0	3	0.03				103		13	2.8								0
1.1	0	64	1.34	14.2	110	62	17	0.7	0	0	0.18	0.07	0.82	0.02	0	0	14.7	0
0	0	4	0.31	11	28	40	690	0	0	0	0.01	0.01	0.23	0.02	0	0	3.6	0
7.1	18	295	0.83	35	245	390	885	1	225	2	0.17	0.46	1.01	0.1	0.7	0.7	20	0
0	0	18	0.9	2.2	10	136	167	0	1	2.2	0.01	0.02	0.12	0	0	0	1.4	0
0	0	5	0.22	10.8	6	156	216	0.1	0	0	0.58	0.86	5.82	0.08	0.03	0	60.6	0
0	1	2	0.04	0.6	0	20	117	0	0	0	0.04	0.01	0.04	0	0	0.1	1.9	0
0.8	4	3	0.18	1.2	4	17	135	0	2	0	0.23	0.01	0.07	0	0	0.6	0	0

MDA Code	Food Name	Amt	Wt (g)	Ener (kcal)	Prot (g)	Carb (g)	Fiber (g)	Fat (g)	Mono (g)	Poly (g)
8013	Blue/Roquefort cheese, regular	2 tbsp	30.6	154	1	2	0	16	3.8	8.5
92511	Caesar	2 tbsp	30	150	1	1	0	16		
44467	French, fat-free	1 tbsp	16	21	0	5	0	0	0	0
8255	French, low fat, no salt, diet (5kcal/tsp)	1 tbsp	16.3	38	0	5	0	2	1	0.8
90232	French, regular	1 tbsp	12.3	56	0	2	0	6	1	2.6
92510	Italian	2 tbsp	30	140	0	2	0	15		
44498	Italian, fat-free	1 tbsp	14	7	0	1	0	0	0	0
44499	Ranch, fat-free	1 oz	28.4	34	0	8	0	1	0.1	0.2
44696	Ranch, reduced fat	1 tbsp	15	33	0	2	0	3	0.8	0.7
8022	Russian	1 tbsp	15.3	54	0	5	0	4	0.9	2.3
8144	Sesame seed	2 tbsp	30.6	136	1	3	0	14	3.6	7.7
8035	Vinegar & oil, homemade	2 tbsp	31.2	140	0	1	0	16	4.6	7.5
	SPICES, FLAVORS, AND SEASONINGS									
26000	Allspice, ground	1 tbsp	1.9	5	0	1	0	0	0	0
26106	Anise seed	1 tbsp	2.1	7	0	1	0	0	0.2	0.1
26001	Basil, ground	1 tbsp	1.4	4	0	1	1	0	0	0
26107	Bay leaf, crumbled	1 tbsp	0.6	2	0	0	0	0	0	0
9518	Celery flakes, dried	0.5 oz	14.2	45	2	9	4	0	0.1	0.1
26040	Celery seed	1 tsp	2	8	0	1	0	1	0.3	0.1
26002	Chili powder	1 tsp	2.6	8	0	1	1	0	0.1	0.2
26003	Cinnamon, ground	1 tsp	2.3	6	0	2	1	0	0	0
26019	Cloves, ground	1 tsp	2.1	7	0	1	1	0	0	0.1
26041	Coriander seed	1 tsp	1.8	5	0	1	1	0	0.2	0
26036	Cumin seed	1 tsp	2.1	8	0	1	0	0	0.3	0.1
26004	Curry powder	1 tsp	2	6	0	1	1	0	0.1	0.1
26109	Dill seed	1 tsp	2.1	6	0	1	0	0	0.2	0
26105	Fennel seed	1 tsp	2	7	0	1	1	0	0.2	0
26007	Garlic powder	1 tsp	2.8	9	0	2	0	0	0	0
26023	Ginger, ground	1 tsp	1.8	6	0	1	0	0	0	0
90442	Ginger root, peeled, raw	1 tsp	2	2	0	0	0	0	0	0
3067	Lemon peel, fresh	1 tbsp	6	3	0	1	1	0	0	0
26110	Mustard seed, yellow	1 tsp	3.3	15	1	1	0	1	0.7	0.2
26026	Nutmeg, ground	1 tsp	2.2	12	0	1	0	1	0.1	0
26008	Onion powder	1 tsp	2.1	7	0	2	0	0	0	0
26010	Paprika	1 tsp	2.1	6	0	1	1	0	0	0.2
26035	Parsley, dried	1 tsp	0.3	1	0	0	0	0	0	0
90212	Pepper, black	1 ea	0.1	0	0	0	0	0	0	0
26015	Poppy seed	1 tsp	2.8	15	1	1	0	1	0.2	0.9
26030	Rosemary, dried	1 tsp	1.2	4	0	1	1	0	0	0
26111	Saffron	1 tsp	0.7	2	0	0	0	0	0	0
26033	Thyme, ground	1 tsp	1.4	4	0	1	1	0	0	0
26034	Turmeric, ground	1 tsp	2.2	8	0	1	0	0	0	0
26624	Vanilla extract	1 tsp	4.3	12	0	1	0	0	0	0
	BAKING INGREDIENTS									
28001	Baker's yeast, active	1 ea	7	21	3	3	1	0	0.2	0
28003	Baking soda	1 tsp	4.6	0	0	0	0	0	0	0
25005	Brown sugar, packed	1 tsp	4.6	17	0	4	0	0	0	0
23010	Chocolate, baking, unsweetened, square	1 ea	28.4	142	4	8	5	15	4.6	0.4
23418	Chocolate, baking, Mexican, squares	1 ea	20	85	1	15	1	3	1	0.2

Sat (g)	Chol (mg)	Calc (mg)	Iron (mg)	Mag (mg)	Phos (mg)	Pota (mg)	Sodi (mg)	Zinc (mg)	Vit A (RAE)	Vit C (mg)	Thia (mg)	Ribo (mg)	Niac (mg)	Vit B6 (mg)	Vit B12 (µg)	Vit E (mg)	Fol (µg)	Alc (g)
3	5	25	0.06	0	23	11	335	0.1	21	0.6	0	0.03	0.03	0.01	0.08	1.8	8.6	0
3		0	0.36				280		0	0								0
0	0	1	0.09	0.5	0	13	128	0	1	0	0	0	0.02	0	0	0	2.2	0
0.2	0	2	0.14	1.3	3	17	5	0	4	0	0	0.01	0.08	0.01	0	0.5	0.3	0
0.7	0	3	0.1	0.6	2	8	103	0	3	0	0	0.01	0.02	0	0.02	0.6	0	0
2.5	0	0	0				360	0	0									0
0	0	4	0.06	0.7	15	14	158	0.1	1	0.1	0	0.01	0.02	0	0.04	0.1	1.7	0
0.1	2	14	0.3	2.3	32	32	214	0.1	0	0	0.01	0.01	0	0.01	0	0.1	1.7	0
0.2	3	19	0.13	0.9	29	20	140	0.1	3	0.1	0	0	0	0	0	0.2	0.6	0
0.6	0	3	0.11	1.5	3	26	144	0	7	0.7	0	0.01	0.09	0.01	0	0.5	0.8	0
1.9	0	6	0.18	0	11	48	306	0	1	0	0	0	0	0	0	1.5	0	0
2.8	0	0	0	0	0	2	0	0	0	0	0	0	0	0	0	1.4	0	0
0	0	13	0.13	2.6	2	20	1	0	1	0.7	0	0	0.05	0	0	0	0.7	0
0	0	14	0.78	3.6	9	30	0	0.1	0	0.4	0.01	0.01	0.06	0.01	0	0	0.2	0
0	0	30	0.59	5.9	7	48	0	0.1	7	0.9	0	0	0.1	0.03	0	0.1	3.8	0
0	0	5	0.26	0.7	1	3	0	0	2	0.3	0	0	0.01	0.01	0	0	1.1	0
0.1	0	83	1.11	27.8	57	623	204	0.4	14	12.3	0.06	0.07	0.66	0.07	0	0.8	15.2	0
0	0	35	0.9	8.8	11	28	3	0.1	0	0.3	0.01	0.01	0.06	0.02	0	0	0.2	0
0.1	0	7	0.37	4.4	8	50	26	0.1	39	1.7	0.01	0.02	0.21	0.1	0	0.8	2.6	0
0	0	28	0.88	1.3	1	11	1	0	0	0.7	0	0	0.03	0.01	0	0	0.7	0
0.1	0	14	0.18	5.5	2	23	5	0	1	1.7	0	0.01	0.03	0.01	0	0.2	2	0
0	0	13	0.29	5.9	7	23	1	0.1	0	0.4	0	0.01	0.04		0		0	0
0	0	20	1.39	7.7	10	38	4	0.1	1	0.2	0.01	0.01	0.1	0.01	0	0.1	0.2	0
0	0	10	0.59	5.1	7	31	1	0.1	1	0.2	0.01	0.01	0.07	0.02	0	0.4	3.1	0
0	0	32	0.34	5.4	6	25	0	0.1	0	0.4	0.01	0.01	0.06	0.01	0	0	0.2	0
0	0	24	0.37	7.7	10	34	2	0.1	0	0.4	0.01	0.01	0.12	0.01	0			0
0	0	2	0.08	1.6	12	31	1	0.1	0	0.5	0.01	0	0.02	0.08	0	0	0.1	0
0	0	2	0.21	3.3	3	24	1	0.1	0	0.1	0	0	0.09	0.02	0	0.3	0.7	0
0	0	0	0.01	0.9	1	8	0	0	0	0.1	0	0	0.02	0	0	0	0.2	0
0	0	8	0.05	0.9	1	10	0	0	0	7.7	0	0	0.02	0.01	0	0	0.8	0
0	0	17	0.33	9.8	28	23	0	0.2	0	0.1	0.02	0.01	0.26	0.01	0	0.1	2.5	0
0.6	0	4	0.07	4	5	8	0	0	0	0.1	0.01	0	0.03	0	0	0	1.7	0
0	0	8	0.05	2.6	7	20	1	0	0	0.3	0.01	0	0.01	0.03	0	0	3.5	0
0	0	4	0.5	3.9	7	49	1	0.1	55	1.5	0.01	0.04	0.32	0.08	0	0.6	2.2	0
0	0	4	0.29	0.7	1	11	1	0	2	0.4	0	0	0.02	0	0	0	0.5	0
0	0	0	0.03	0.2	0	1	0	0	0	0	0	0	0	0	0	0	0	0
0.1	0	41	0.26	9.3	24	20	1	0.3	0	0.1	0.02	0	0.03	0.01	0	0	1.6	0
0.1	0	15	0.35	2.6	1	11	1	0	2	0.7	0.01	0.01	0.01	0.02	0	0	3.7	0
0	0	1	0.08	1.8	2	12	1	0	0	0.6	0	0	0.01	0.01	0	0	0.7	0
0	0	26	1.73	3.1	3	11	1	0.1	3	0.7	0.01	0.01	0.07	0.01	0	0.1	3.8	0
0.1	0	4	0.91	4.2	6	56	1	0.1	0	0.6	0	0.01	0.11	0.04	0	0.1	0.9	0
0	0	0	0.01	0.5	0	6	0	0	0	0	0	0	0.02	0	0	0	0	1.48
0	0	4	1.16	6.9	90	140	4	0.4	0	0	0.17	0.38	2.78	0.11	0	0	163.8	0
0	0	0	0	0	0	0	1259	0	0	0	0	0	0	0	0	0	0	0
0	0	4	0.09	1.3	1	16	2	0	0	0	0	0	0	0	0	0	0	0
9.2	0	29	4.94	92.9	114	236	7	2.7	0	0	0.04	0.03	0.38	0.01	0	0.1	8	0
1.7	0	7	0.44	19	28	79	1	0.3	0	0	0.01	0.02	0.37	0.01	0	0.1	1	0

MDA Code	Food Name	Amt	Wt (g)	Ener (kcal)	Prot (g)	Carb (g)	Fiber (g)	Fat (g)	Mono (g)	Poly (g)
90657	Chocolate chips, semisweet	0.25 cup	43.2	207	2	27	3	13	4.3	0.4
4649	Coconut cream, canned	1 tbsp	18.5	36	0	2	0	3	0.1	0
4527	Coconut water	1 cup	240	46	2	9	3	0	0	0
4574	Coconut, sweetened, flakes, dried	2 tbsp	9.2	44	0	4	0	3	0.1	0
4510	Coconut, unsweetened, dried	2 tbsp	9.2	61	1	2	1	6	0.3	0.1
25203	Corn syrup, hi-fructose	1 tbsp	19.4	55	0	15	0	0	0	0
25000	Corn syrup, light	1 tbsp	20.5	58	0	16	0	0	0	0
26017	Cream of tartar	1 tsp	3	8	0	2	0	0	0	0
23052	Gelatin, prep from dry mix w/water	0.5 cup	135	84	2	19	0	0	0	0
23360	Gelatin, strawberry, sugar free, low cal, dry mix	1 ea	2.5	8	1	0	0	0		
25006	Granulated white sugar	1 tsp	4.2	16	0	4	0	0	0	0
25001	Honey, strained/extracted	1 tbsp	21.2	64	0	17	0	0	0	0
25202	Maple sugar	1 tsp	3	11	0	3	0	0	0	0
25003	Molasses	1 tbsp	20.5	59	0	15	0	0	0	0
25111	Sorghum syrup	1 tbsp	21	61	0	16	0	0	0	0
27007	Vinegar, cider	1 tbsp	15	3	0	0	0	0	0	0
92153	Vinegar, distilled	1 tbsp	17	3	0	0	0	0	0	0
92129	Wheat gluten, vital	1 oz	28.4	105	21	4	0	1	0	0.2
	FAST FOOD									
	Generic Fast Food									
6178	Baked potato, topped w/cheese & bacon	1 ea	299	451	18	44		26	9.7	4.8
6177	Baked potato, topped w/cheese sauce	1 ea	296	474	15	47		29	10.7	6
6181	Baked potato, topped w/sour cream & chives	1 ea	302	393	7	50		22	7.9	3.3
66025	Burrito w/beans	1 ea	108.5	224	7	36	4	7	2.4	0.6
56629	Burrito w/beans & cheese	1 ea	93	189	8	27		6	1.2	0.9
66023	Burrito w/beans, cheese & beef	1 ea	101.5	165	7	20	2	7	2.2	0.5
66024	Burrito w/beef	1 ea	110	262	13	29	1	10	3.7	0.4
56600	Biscuit w/egg sandwich	1 ea	136	373	12	32	1	22	9.1	6.4
56601	Biscuit w/egg & bacon sandwich	1 ea	150	458	17	29	1	31	13.4	7.5
56602	Biscuit w/egg & ham sandwich	1 ea	192	461	20	35	1	27	11	7.7
66028	Biscuit w/egg & sausage sandwich	1 ea	180	581	19	41	1	39	16.4	4.4
66029	Biscuit w/egg, cheese & bacon sandwich	1 ea	144	477	16	33	0	31	14.2	3.5
56604	Biscuit w/ham sandwich	1 ea	113	386	13	44	1	18	4.8	1
66030	Biscuit w/sausage sandwich	1 ea	124	485	12	40	1	32	12.8	3
66013	Cheeseburger, double, condiments & vegetables	1 ea	166	417	21	35		21	7.8	2.7
66016	Cheeseburger, double, plain	1 ea	155	457	28	22		28	11	1.9
56651	Cheeseburger, large, one meat patty w/bacon & condiments	1 ea	195	608	32	37		37	14.5	2.7
56649	Cheeseburger, large, one meat patty w/condiments & vegetables	1 ea	219	563	28	38		33	12.6	2
15063	Chicken, breaded, fried, dark meat (drumstick or thigh)	3 oz	85.1	248	17	9	1	15	6.3	3.6
15064	Chicken, breaded, fried, light meat (breast or wing)	3 oz	85.1	258	19	10	1	15	6.4	3.5
56656	Chicken filet w/cheese	1 ea	228	632	29	42		39	13.7	9.9
56000	Chicken filet, plain	1 ea	182	515	24	39		29	10.4	8.4
50312	Chili con carne	1 cup	253	256	25	22		8	3.4	0.5
56635	Chimichanga w/beef & cheese	1 ea	183	443	20	39		23	9.4	0.7
19110	Clams (shellfish) breaded, fried	3 oz	85.1	334	9	29		20	8.5	5
5461	Cole slaw	0.75 cup	99	147	1	13		11	2.4	6.4
6175	Corn on the cob w/butter	1 ea	146	155	4	32		3	1	0.6
56606	Croissant w/egg & cheese sandwich	1 ea	127	368	13	24		25	7.5	1.4
56607	Croissant w/egg, cheese & bacon sandwich	1 ea	129	413	16	24		28	9.2	1.8

Sat (g)	Chol (mg)	Calc (mg)	Iron (mg)	Mag (mg)	Phos (mg)	Pota (mg)	Sodi (mg)	Zinc (mg)	Vit A (RAE)	Vit C (mg)	Thia (mg)	Ribo (mg)	Niac (mg)	Vit B6 (mg)	Vit B12 (µg)	Vit E (mg)	Fol (µg)	Alc (g)
7.7	0	14	1.35	49.7	57	158	5	0.7	0	0	0.02	0.04	0.18	0.02	0	0.1	5.6	0
2.9	0	0	0.09	3.1	4	19	9	0.1	0	0.3	0	0.01	0.01	0.01	0	0	2.6	0
0.4	0	58	0.7	60	48	600	252	0.2	0	5.8	0.07	0.14	0.19	0.08	0	0	7.2	0
2.6	0	1	0.17	4.4	9	29	24	0.2	0	0	0	0.03	0.02	0	0		0.7	0
5.3	0	2	0.31	8.3	19	50	3	0.2	0	0.1	0.01	0.01	0.06	0.03	0	0	0.8	0
0	0	0	0.01	0	0	0	0	0	0	0	0	0	0	0	0	0	0	0
0	0	3	0	0.2	0	0	13	0.1	0	0	0.01	0	0	0	0	0	0	0
0	0	0	0.11	0.1	0	495	2	0	0	0	0	0	0	0	0	0	0	0
0	0	4	0.03	1.4	30	1	101	0	0	0	0.01	0	0	0	0		1.4	0
0	0	1	0.03		34	0	57		0	0								0
0	0	0	0	0	0	0	0	0	0	0	0	0	0	0	0	0	0	0
0	0	1	0.09	0.4	1	11	1	0	0	0.1	0	0.01	0.03	0.01	0	0	0.4	0
0	0	3	0.05	0.6	0	8	0	0.2	0	0	0	0	0	0	0	0	0	0
0	0	42	0.97	49.6	6	300	8	0.1	0	0	0.01	0	0.19	0.14	0	0	0	0
0	0	32	0.8	21	12	210	2	0.1	0	0	0.02	0.03	0.02	0.14	0	0	0	0
0	0	1	0.03	0.8	1	11	1	0	0	0	0	0	0	0	0	0	0	0
0	0	1	0.01	0.2	1	0	0	0	0	0	0	0	0	0	0	0	0	0
0.1	0	40	1.48	7.1	74	28	8	0.2	0	0	0	0	0	0	0	0	0	0
10.1	30	308	3.14	68.8	347	1178	972	2.2	188	28.7	0.27	0.24	3.98	0.75	0.33		29.9	0
10.6	18	311	3.02	65.1	320	1166	382	1.9	252	26	0.24	0.21	3.34	0.71	0.18		26.6	0
10	24	106	3.11	69.5	184	1383	181	0.9	266	33.8	0.27	0.18	3.71	0.79	0.21		33.2	0
3.4	2	56	2.26	43.4	49	327	493	0.8	9	1	0.31	0.3	2.03	0.15	0.54	0.9	43.4	0
3.4	14	107	1.13	40	90	248	583	0.8	49	0.8	0.11	0.35	1.79	0.12	0.45		37.2	0
3.6	62	65	1.87	25.4	70	205	495	1.2	75	2.5	0.15	0.36	1.93	0.11	0.55	0.4	37.6	0
5.2	32	42	3.05	40.7	87	370	746	2.4	7	0.6	0.12	0.46	3.22	0.15	0.98	0.6	64.9	0
4.7	245	82	2.9	19	388	238	891	1	180	0.1	0.3	0.49	2.15	0.11	0.63	3.3	57.1	0
8	352	189	3.74	24	238	250	999	1.6	107	2.7	0.14	0.23	2.4	0.14	1.03	2	60	0
5.9	300	221	4.55	30.7	317	319	1382	2.2	236	0	0.67	0.6	2	0.27	1.19	2.3	65.3	0
15	302	155	3.96	25.2	490	320	1141	2.2	160	0	0.5	0.45	3.6	0.2	1.37	2.8	64.8	0
11.4	261	164	2.55	20.2	459	230	1260	1.5	190	1.6	0.3	0.43	2.3	0.1	1.05	1.4	53.3	0
11.4	25	160	2.72	22.6	554	197	1433	1.6	31	0.1	0.51	0.32	3.48	0.14	0.03	1.7	38.4	0
14.2	35	128	2.58	19.8	446	198	1071	1.6	13	0.1	0.4	0.29	3.27	0.11	0.51	1.4	45.9	0
8.7	60	171	3.42	29.9	242	335	1051	3.5	71	1.7	0.35	0.28	8.05	0.18	1.93		61.4	0
13	110	232	3.41	32.6	374	308	636	5	99	0	0.25	0.37	6.01	0.25	2.31	1.2	68.2	0
16.2	111	162	4.74	44.8	400	332	1043	6.8	82	2.1	0.31	0.41	6.63	0.31	2.34		85.8	0
15	88	206	4.66	43.8	311	445	1108	4.6	140	7.9	0.39	0.46	7.38	0.28	2.56	1.2	81	0
4.1	95	20	0.92	21.3	138	256	434	1.9	38	0	0.08	0.25	4.14	0.19	0.48	0.8	14.5	0
4.1	77	31	0.77	19.6	160	295	509	0.8	30	0	0.08	0.15	6.25	0.3	0.35	0.8	15.3	0
12.4	78	258	3.63	43.3	406	333	1238	2.9	164	3	0.41	0.46	9.07	0.41	0.46		109.4	0
8.5	60	60	4.68	34.6	233	353	957	1.9	31	8.9	0.33	0.24	6.81	0.2	0.38		100.1	0
3.4	134	68	5.19	45.5	197	691	1007	3.6	83	1.5	0.13	1.14	2.48	0.33	1.14	1.6	45.5	0
11.2	51	238	3.84	60.4	187	203	957	3.4	132	2.7	0.38	0.86	4.67	0.22	1.3		91.5	0
4.9	65	15	2.26	23	176	197	617	1.2	27	0	0.15	0.2	2.12	0.03	0.82		31.5	0
1.6	5	34	0.72	8.9	36	177	267	0.2	36	8.3	0.04	0.03	0.08	0.11	0.18	4	38.6	0
1.6	6	4	0.88	40.9	108	359	29	0.9	34	6.9	0.25	0.1	2.18	0.32	0		43.8	0
14.1	216	244	2.2	21.6	348	174	551	1.8	277	0.1	0.19	0.38	1.51	0.1	0.77		47	0
15.4	215	151	2.19	23.2	276	201	889	1.9	142	2.2	0.35	0.34	2.19	0.12	0.86		45.2	0

MDA Code	Food Name	Amt	Wt (g)	Ener (kcal)	Prot (g)	Carb (g)	Fiber (g)	Fat (g)	Mono (g)	Poly (g)
56608	Croissant w/egg, cheese & ham sandwich	1 ea	152	474	19	24		34	11.4	2.4
45588	Danish pastry, cheese	1 ea	91	353	6	29		25	15.6	2.4
45513	Danish pastry, fruit	1 ea	94	335	5	45		16	10.1	1.6
66021	Enchilada w/cheese	1 ea	163	319	10	29		19	6.3	0.8
66022	Enchilada w/cheese & beef	1 ea	192	323	12	30		18	6.1	1.4
66020	Enchirito w/cheese, beef & beans	1 ea	193	344	18	34		16	6.5	0.3
42064	English muffin w/butter	1 ea	63	189	5	30	2	6	1.5	1.3
66031	English muffin w/cheese & sausage sandwich	1 ea	115	393	15	29	1	24	10.1	2.7
66032	English muffin w/egg, cheese & Canadian bacon sandwich	1 ea	146	308	18	28	2	13	5	1.7
66010	Fish sandwich w/tartar sauce	1 ea	158	431	17	41	0	23	7.7	8.2
66011	Fish sandwich w/tartar sauce & cheese	1 ea	183	523	21	48	0	29	8.9	9.4
90736	French fries fried in vegetable oil, medium	1 ea	134	427	5	50	5	23	13.3	4
42354	French toast sticks	5 pce	141	513	8	58	3	29	12.6	9.9
42353	French toast w/butter	2 pce	135	356	10	36	0	19	7.1	2.4
56638	Frijoles (beans) w/cheese	0.5 cup	83.5	113	6	14		4	1.3	0.3
56664	Ham & cheese sandwich	1 ea	146	352	21	33		15	6.7	1.4
56665	Ham, egg & cheese sandwich	1 ea	143	347	19	31		16	5.7	1.7
69150	Hamburger, large, one meat patty w/condiments	1 ea	171.5	425	23	37	2	21	9.3	1.6
56662	Hamburger, large, double, w/condiments & vegetables	1 ea	226	540	34	40		27	10.3	2.8
56661	Hamburger, large, one meat patty w/condiments & vegetables	1 ea	218	512	26	40		27	11.4	2.2
56659	Hamburger, one patty w/condiments & vegetables	1 ea	110	279	13	27		13	5.3	2.6
66007	Hamburger, plain	1 ea	90	274	12	31		12	5.5	0.9
5463	Hash browns	0.5 cup	72	151	2	16		9	3.9	0.5
56667	Hot dog w/chili, plain	1 ea	114	296	14	31		13	6.6	1.2
56668	Hot dog w/corn flour coating, corn dog	1 ea	175	460	17	56		19	9.1	3.5
66004	Hot dog, plain	1 ea	98	242	10	18		15	6.9	1.7
56666	Hush puppies	5 pce	78	257	5	35	3	12	7.8	0.4
2032	Ice cream sundae, hot fudge	1 ea	158	284	6	48	0	9	2.3	0.8
6185	Mashed potatoes	0.5 cup	121	100	3	20		1	0.4	0.4
90214	Mayonnaise, soybean oil packet	1 ea	10	72	0	0	0	8	2	4.3
56639	Nachos w/cheese	7 pce	113	346	9	36		19	8	2.2
56641	Nachos w/cheese, beans, ground beef & peppers	7 pce	225	502	17	49		27	9.7	5
6176	Onion rings, breaded, fried	8 pce	78.1	259	3	29		15	6.3	0.6
19109	Oysters (shellfish) battered/breaded, fried	3 oz	85.1	226	8	24	0	11	4.2	2.8
45122	Pancakes w/butter & syrup	1 ea	116	260	4	45	1	7	2.6	1
6173	Potato salad	1/3 cup	95	108	1	13		6	1.6	2.9
56619	Pizza w/pepperoni 12" or 1/8	1 pce	108	275	15	30		11	4.8	1.8
56669	Roast beef sandwich w/cheese	1 ea	176	473	32	45		18	3.7	3.5
66003	Roast beef sandwich, plain	1 ea	139	346	22	33		14	6.8	1.7
56643	Taco salad	1.5 cup	198	279	13	24		15	5.2	1.7
56644	Taco salad w/chili con carne	1.5 cup	261	290	17	27		13	4.5	1.5
19115	Shrimp (shellfish) breaded, fried	4 ea	93.7	260	11	23		14	9.9	0.4
56670	Steak sandwich	1 ea	204	459	30	52		14	5.3	3.3
56671	Submarine sandwich, cold cuts	1 ea	228	456	22	51	2	19	8.2	2.3
56673	Submarine sandwich, tuna salad	1 ea	256	584	30	55		28	13.4	7.3
57531	Taco	1 ea	171	369	21	27		21	6.6	1
66017	Tostada w/beans & cheese	1 ea	144	223	10	27		10	3.1	0.7
56645	Tostada w/beef & cheese	1 ea	163	315	19	23		16	3.3	1
71129	Shake, chocolate 12 fl. oz	1 ea	249.6	317	8	51	5	9	2.7	0.3
71132	Shake, vanilla, 12 fl. oz	1 ea	249.6	369	8	49	2	16	4.5	0.8

Sat (g)	Chol (mg)	Calc (mg)	Iron (mg)	Mag (mg)	Phos (mg)	Pota (mg)	Sodi (mg)	Zinc (mg)	Vit A (RAE)	Vit C (mg)	Thia (mg)	Ribo (mg)	Niac (mg)	Vit B6 (mg)	Vit B12 (µg)	Vit E (mg)	Fol (µg)	Alc (g)
17.5	213	144	2.13	25.8	336	272	1081	2.2	131	11.4	0.52	0.3	3.19	0.23	1		45.6	0
5.1	20	70	1.85	15.5	80	116	319	0.6	45	2.6	0.26	0.21	2.55	0.05	0.23		54.6	0
3.3	19	22	1.4	14.1	69	110	333	0.5	25	1.6	0.29	0.21	1.8	0.06	0.24	0.8	31	0
10.6	44	324	1.32	50.5	134	240	784	2.5	99	1	0.08	0.42	1.91	0.39	0.75	1.5	65.2	0
9	40	228	3.07	82.6	167	574	1319	2.7	98	1.3	0.1	0.4	2.52	0.27	1.02	1.5	67.2	0
7.9	50	218	2.39	71.4	224	560	1251	2.8	89	4.6	0.17	0.69	2.99	0.21	1.62	1.5	94.6	0
2.4	13	103	1.59	13.2	85	69	386	0.4	32	0.8	0.25	0.32	2.61	0.04	0.02	0.1	56.7	0
9.9	59	168	2.25	24.2	186	215	1036	1.7	101	1.3	0.7	0.25	4.14	0.15	0.68	1.3	66.7	0
5	250	161	2.6	24.8	288	212	777	1.7	188	1.9	0.53	0.48	3.55	0.16	0.72	0.6	73	0
5.2	55	84	2.61	33.2	212	340	615	1	33	2.8	0.33	0.22	3.4	0.11	1.07	0.9	85.3	0
8.1	68	185	3.5	36.6	311	353	939	1.2	130	2.7	0.46	0.42	4.23	0.11	1.08	1.8	91.5	0
5.3	0	17	1.84	45.6	185	737	260	1	0	3.6	0.23	0.09	3.35	0.51	0	1	40.2	0
4.7	75	78	2.96	26.8	123	127	499	0.9	0	0	0.23	0.25	2.96	0.25	0.07	2.3	197.4	0
7.7	116	73	1.89	16.2	146	177	513	0.6	136	0.1	0.58	0.5	3.92	0.05	0.36		72.9	0
2	18	94	1.12	42.6	88	302	441	0.9	18	0.8	0.07	0.17	0.74	0.1	0.34		55.9	0
6.4	58	130	3.24	16.1	152	291	771	1.4	96	2.8	0.31	0.48	2.69	0.2	0.54	0.3	75.9	0
7.4	246	212	3.1	25.7	346	210	1005	2	166	2.7	0.43	0.56	4.2	0.16	1.23	0.6	75.8	0
7.9	70	134	4.13	34.3	213	394	729	4.8	5	2.6	0.34	0.28	6.54	0.25	2.57	0	61.7	0
10.5	122	102	5.85	49.7	314	570	791	5.7	5	1.1	0.36	0.38	7.57	0.54	4.07		76.8	0
10.4	87	96	4.93	43.6	233	480	824	4.9	24	2.6	0.41	0.37	7.28	0.33	2.38	1.2	82.8	0
4.1	26	63	2.63	22	124	227	504	2.1	4	1.6	0.23	0.2	3.68	0.12	0.88	0.8	51.7	0
4.1	35	63	2.4	18.9	103	145	387	2	0	0	0.33	0.27	3.72	0.06	0.89	0.5	53.1	0
4.3	9	7	0.48	15.8	69	267	290	0.2	1	5.5	0.08	0.01	1.07	0.17	0.01	0.1	7.9	0
4.9	51	19	3.28	10.3	192	166	480	0.8	3	2.7	0.22	0.4	3.74	0.05	0.3		73	0
5.2	79	102	6.18	17.5	166	262	973	1.3	60	0	0.28	0.7	4.17	0.09	0.44	0.7	103.2	0
5.1	44	24	2.31	12.7	97	143	670	2	0	0.1	0.24	0.27	3.65	0.05	0.51	0.3	48	0
2.7	135	69	1.43	16.4	190	188	965	0.4	9	0	0	0.02	2.03	0.1	0.17		57.7	0
5	21	207	0.58	33.2	228	395	182	0.9	58	2.4	0.06	0.3	1.07	0.13	0.65	0.7	9.5	0
0.6	2	25	0.57	21.8	67	356	275	0.4	13	0.5	0.11	0.06	1.45	0.28	0.06		9.7	0
1.2	4	2	0.05	0.1	3	3	57	0	8	0	0	0	0	0.06	0.03	0.5	0.8	0
7.8	18	272	1.28	55.4	276	172	816	1.8	149	1.2	0.19	0.37	1.54	0.2	0.82		10.2	0
11	18	340	2.45	85.5	342	398	1588	3.2	385	4.3	0.2	0.61	2.95	0.36	0.9		33.8	0
6.5	13	69	0.8	14.8	81	122	405	0.3	1	0.5	0.08	0.09	0.87	0.05	0.12	0.3	51.5	0
2.8	66	17	2.73	14.5	120	111	414	9.6	66	2.6	0.19	0.21	2.71	0.02	0.62		18.7	0
2.9	29	64	1.31	24.4	238	125	552	0.5	41	1.7	0.2	0.28	1.69	0.06	0.12	0.7	25.5	0
1	57	13	0.69	7.6	53	256	312	0.2	28	1	0.07	0.1	0.26	0.14	0.11		23.8	0
3.4	22	98	1.43	13	114	232	406	0.8	80	2.5	0.21	0.36	4.63	0.09	0.28		56.2	0
9	77	183	5.05	40.5	401	345	1633	5.4	58	0	0.39	0.46	5.9	0.33	2.06		63.4	0
3.6	51	54	4.23	30.6	239	316	792	3.4	11	2.1	0.38	0.31	5.87	0.26	1.22	0.2	57	0
6.8	44	192	2.28	51.5	143	416	762	2.7	71	3.6	0.1	0.36	2.46	0.22	0.63		83.2	0
6	5	245	2.66	52.2	154	392	885	3.3	258	3.4	0.16	0.5	2.53	0.52	0.73		91.4	0
3.1	114	48	1.69	22.5	197	105	826	0.7	21	0	0.12	0.52	0	0.04	0.08		57.2	0
3.8	73	92	5.16	49	298	524	798	4.5	20	5.5	0.41	0.37	7.3	0.37	1.57		89.8	0
6.8	36	189	2.51	68.4	287	394	1651	2.6	71	12.3	1	0.8	5.49	0.14	1.09		86.6	0
5.3	49	74	2.64	79.4	220	335	1293	1.9	46	3.6	0.46	0.33	11.34	0.23	1.61		102.4	0
11.4	56	221	2.41	70.1	203	474	802	3.9	108	2.2	0.15	0.44	3.21	0.24	1.04	1.9	68.4	0
5.4	30	210	1.89	59	117	403	543	1.9	45	1.3	0.1	0.33	1.32	0.16	0.69	1.2	43.2	0
10.4	41	217	2.87	63.6	179	572	896	3.7	51	2.6	0.1	0.55	3.15	0.23	1.17		75	0
5.8	32	282	0.77	42.4	255	499	242	1	65	1	0.14	0.61	0.4	0.12	0.85	0.3	12.5	0
9.9	57	287	1.15	32.4	245	414	202	1.4	227	0	0.06	1.65	0.53	0.15	0.55	0.6	0	0

MDA Code	Food Name	Amt	Wt (g)	Ener (kcal)	Prot (g)	Carb (g)	Fiber (g)	Fat (g)	Mono (g)	Poly (g)
	Arby's									
6429	Baked potato broccoli cheddar cheese	1 ea	384	540	12	71	7	24		
9011	Chicken, finger, 4 pack	1 ea	192	640	31	42	0	38		
8987	French fries, curly, large serving	1 ea	198	619	8	78	6	30		
9006	French fries, large serving	1 ea	212.6	562	6	79	6	24		
9008	Mozzarella sticks	1 ea	137	470	18	34	2	29		
8998	Salad, caesar & grilled chicken	1 ea	338	230	33	8	3	8		
8988	Sandwich, beef melt, w/cheddar	1 ea	150	320	16	36	2	14		
69055	Sandwich, beef, philly & swiss cheese, submarine	1 ea	311	670	36	46	4	40		
9014	Sandwich, breakfast, bacon, w/sourdough	1 ea	144	420	16	66	3	10		
69046	Sandwich, chicken, grilled, deluxe	1 ea	252	450	29	37	2	22		
9001	Sandwich, chicken, grilled, light	1 ea	174	280	29	30	3	5		
69043	Sandwich, French dip, submarine	1 ea	285	410	28	43	2	16		
8991	Sandwich, ham swiss, hot, submarine	1 ea	278	530	29	45	3	27		
56336	Sandwich, roast beef, regular	1 ea	157	330	21	35	2	14		
53256	Sauce, Arbys, packet	1 ea	14	15	0	4	0	0	0	0
9018	Sauce, barbecue, dipping	1 serving	28.4	40	0	10	0	0	0	0
	Source: Arby's									
	Burger King									
56352	Cheeseburger	1 ea	133	380	19	32	4	20	7.6	2
56355	Cheeseburger, Whopper	1 ea	316	790	35	53	3	48	16	12
56357	Cheeseburger, Whopper, double	1 ea	399	1061	58	54	6	68	25.1	11.9
9087	Chicken tenders, 4 piece serving	1 ea	62	179	11	11	1	10	5.9	1.3
9065	French fries, large serving	1 ea	160	530	6	64	5	28	17.7	1.8
56351	Hamburger	1 ea	121	333	17	33	2	15	6.4	1.5
56354	Hamburger, Whopper	1 ea	291	678	31	54	5	37	13.6	9.9
9071	Hash browns, rounds, large serving	1 ea	128	390	3	38	4	25		
2127	Milk shake, chocolate, medium	1 ea	397	440	13	80	4	8		
2129	Milk shake, vanilla, medium	1 ea	397	667	13	76	0	35	9.8	1.7
9041	Onion rings, large	1 ea	137	480	7	60	5	23		
69071	Sandwich, breakfast, bacon egg cheese, w/biscuit	1 ea	189	692	27	51	1	61		
57002	Sandwich, Chicken Broiler	1 ea	258	550	30	52	3	25		
9084	Sandwich, croissant, w/sausage & cheese	1 ea	107	410	14	24	1	29		
	Source: Burger King Corporation									
	Chik-Fil-A									
69185	Chicken breast fillet, chargrilled	1 ea	79	100	20	1	0	2		
15263	Chicken, nuggets, 8 piece serving	1 ea	113	260	26	12	1	12		
15262	Chick-N-Strips, 4 piece serving	1 ea	108	250	25	12	0	11		
52138	Cole slaw, small	1 ea	105	210	1	14	2	17		
48214	Pie, lemon, slice	1 pce	113	320	7	51	3	10		
52134	Salad, garden w/chargrilled chicken	1 ea	278	180	23	8	3	6		
52137	Salad, side	1 ea	164	80	5	6	2	5		
69155	Sandwich, chicken salad, w/whole wheat	1 ea	153	350	20	32	5	15		
69189	Sandwich, chicken, deluxe	1 ea	208	420	28	39	2	16		
69176	Sauce, honey mustard, dipping, pkt	1 ea	28	45	0	10	0	0	0	0
69182	Wrap, chicken, spicy	1 ea	225	390	31	51	3	7		
	Source: Chik-Fil-A									
	Dairy Queen									
56372	Cheeseburger, double, homestyle	1 ea	219	540	35	30	2	31		
72142	Frozen dessert, banana split, large	1 ea	527	810	17	134	2	23		
71693	Frozen dessert, Brownie Earthquake	1 ea	304	740	10	112	0	27		

Sat (g)	Chol (mg)	Calc (mg)	Iron (mg)	Mag (mg)	Phos (mg)	Pota (mg)	Sodi (mg)	Zinc (mg)	Vit A (RAE)	Vit C (mg)	Thia (mg)	Ribo (mg)	Niac (mg)	Vit B6 (mg)	Vit B12 (µg)	Vit E (mg)	Fol (µg)	Alc (g)
12	50	250	3.6			1643	680			72	0.1	0.19	3.4		0			0
8	70	20	2.7				1590			0								0
7	0	0	2.87			1445	1537	1.2	0	23.9	0.12	0.14	3.99		0			0
6.6	0	0	1.35				1069			28.1								0
14	60	400	0.72				1330			1.2								0
3.5	80	200	1.8				920			42								0
6	45	80	2.7				850			0								0
16	75	300	2.7			646	1850	5.9		9	0.45	0.72	13.89					0
2.5	10	80	2.16				960			0								0
4	110	60	2.7			722	1050			1.2	0.34	0.32	14.9					0
1.5	55	80	1.8				1170			0								0
9	45	80	4.5			679	1200			1.2	0.36	0.88	15.55					0
8	110	300	2.7				1860			2.4								0
7	45	60	3.6	16.2	122	427	890	3.8	0	0								0
0	0	0	0			28	180			1.2								0
0	0	0	0.36				351			2.4								0
9.1	60	124	3.32	31.9	190	237	801	3.2		0.3	0.4	0.32	4.52	0.12		0.1		
18.3	114	259	6.32	56.9	357	534	1431	5.1		0.6	0.67	0.63	8.09	0.23		0.3	161.2	
27.9	188	311	21.15	75.8	511	754	1544	14		0.8	1.07	0.84	11.97	0.45		0.2	107.7	
2.6	32	9	0.38	15.5	141	163	447	0.4		0.4	0.08	0.07	4.64	0.22		0.5	4.3	
7		14	2.06	48	229	757	728	1.8		1.1	0.28	0.05	3.75	0.28		1.2		
6.1	42	62	3.05	29	144	220	551	2.6		0.2	0.4	0.27	4.78	0.12		0	77.4	
12.4	87	113	12.72	52.4	262	492	911	8.2		0.6	0.63	0.51	8.36	0.26		0.4	136.8	
7	0	0	0.72				760		0	1.2								0
5	35	350	1.8				270			0								0
21.2	123	413	1.67	47.6	385	607	397	2.7		0	0	0.71	0.36	0.12	1.43	1.3		
6	0	150	0				690		0	0								0
18.6	253	200	3.59				2130			0								0
5	105	60	3.6				1110			6								0
11	40	100	1.8				830			0								0
0	60	0	0.36				690		0	0								0
2.5	70	40	1.08				1090		0	0								0
2.5	70	40	1.08				570		0	0								0
2.5	20	40	0.36				180			27								0
3.5	110	150	0				220			4.8								0
3	70	150	0.36				730			6								0
2.5	15	150	0				110			4.8								0
3	65	150	1.8				880		0	0								0
3.5	60	100	2.7				1300			2.4								0
0	0	0	0				150		0	0								0
3.5	70	200	3.6				1150			4.8								0
16	115	250	4.5				1130			3.6								0
15	70	600	2.7				360			12								0
16	50	250	1.8				350			0								0

MDA Code	Food Name	Amt	Wt (g)	Ener (kcal)	Prot (g)	Carb (g)	Fiber (g)	Fat (g)	Mono (g)	Poly (g)
72139	Frozen dessert, chocolate cookie dough, large	1 ea	560	1320	21	193	0	52		
72134	Frozen dessert, chocolate sundae, large	1 ea	333	580	11	100	1	15		
72138	Frozen dessert, oreo, large	1 ea	500	1010	19	148	2	37		
72135	Frozen dessert, strawberry sundae, large	1 ea	333	500	10	83	1	15		
72137	Frozen dessert, Triple Chocolate Utopia	1 ea	284	770	12	96	5	39		
2222	Ice cream cone, chocolate, medium	1 ea	198	340	8	53	0	11		
2136	Ice cream cone, dipped, medium	1 ea	220	490	8	59	1	24		
2143	Ice cream cone, vanilla, medium	1 ea	213	355	9	57	0	10		
2134	Ice cream sandwich	1 ea	85	200	4	31	1	6		
72129	Milk shake, chocolate malt, large	1 ea	836	1320	29	222	2	35		
	Source: International Dairy Queen, Inc.									
	Domino's Pizza									
91365	Breadsticks	1 ea	37.2	116	3	18	1	4		
91369	Chicken, buffalo wings	1 ea	24.9	50	6	2	0	2		
56386	Pizza, cheese, hand tossed, 12"	2 pce	159	375	15	55	3	11		
91356	Pizza, deluxe feast, hand tossed, 12"	2 pce	200.8	465	20	57	3	18		
91358	Pizza, meatzza feast, hand tossed, 12"	2 pce	216.2	560	26	57	3	26		
91361	Pizza, pepperoni feast, hand tossed, 12"	2 pce	196.1	534	24	56	3	25		
91357	Pizza, veggie feast, hand tossed, 12"	2 pce	203.2	439	19	57	4	16		
	Source: Domino's Pizza Incorporated									
	Hardee's									
9295	Apple turnover	1 ea	91	270	4	38		12		
42330	Biscuit, cinnamon 'n raisin	1 ea	75	250	2	42		8		
15201	Chicken, wing, serving	1 ea	66	200	10	23	0	8		
9278	Chili dog	1 ea	160	451	15	24	2	32		
9284	Chicken, strips, 5 pce serving	1 ea	92	201	18	13	0	8		
9277	Hamburger, Monster	1 ea	278	949	53	35	2	67		
9275	Hamburger, Six Dollar	1 ea	353	911	41	50	2	61		
2247	Ice cream cone, twist	1 ea	118	180	4	34		2		
6147	French fries, large serving	1 ea	150	440	5	59	0	21		
9281	Sandwich, chicken, bbq, grilled	1 ea	171	268	24	34	2	3		
56423	Sandwich, fish, Fisherman's Fillet	1 ea	221	530	25	45		28		
	Source: Hardee's Food Systems, Inc.									
	Jack In the Box									
56437	Cheeseburger, Jumbo Jack	1 ea	296	640	31	44	2	38		
62547	Cheeseburger w/bacon, ultimate	1 ea	302	1020	58	37	1	71		
57014	Chicken teriyaki bowl	1 ea	502	670	26	128	3	4		
56445	Egg roll, small, 3 piece serving	1 ea	170	440	15	40	4	24		
62558	French toast sticks, serving	1 ea	120	420	7	53	2	20		
56433	Hamburger	1 ea	104	250	12	30	2	9		
62560	Milk shake, cappuccino, medium	1 ea	419	630	11	80	0	29		
2964	Milk shake, oreo cookie, medium	1 ea	419	740	13	91	2	36		
2165	Milk shake, vanilla, medium	1 ea	332	610	12	73	0	31		
56446	Onion rings, serving	1 ea	120	450	7	50	3	25		
6425	French fries, curly, seasoned	1 ea	125	410	6	45	4	23		
6150	French fries, regular serving	1 ea	113	350	4	46	3	16		
62551	Potato wedges, bacon cheddar	1 ea	268	750	20	55	0	50		
8368	Salad dressing, blue cheese, packet	1 ea	57	210	1	11	0	15		
8449	Salad dressing, Italian, low cal	1 ea	57	25	0	2	0	2		
52088	Salad, garden w/chicken	1 ea	253	200	23	8	3	9		
56441	Sandwich, chicken fajita pita	1 ea	230	320	24	34	3	10		

Sat (g)	Chol (mg)	Calc (mg)	Iron (mg)	Mag (mg)	Phos (mg)	Pota (mg)	Sodi (mg)	Zinc (mg)	Vit A (RAE)	Vit C (mg)	Thia (mg)	Ribo (mg)	Niac (mg)	Vit B6 (mg)	Vit B12 (µg)	Vit E (mg)	Fol (µg)	Alc (g)
26	90	600	4.5				670			2.4								0
10	45	350	1.8				260			1.2								0
18	70	600	4.5				770			2.4								0
9	45	400	1.8				230			18								0
17	55	300	1.8				390			1.2								0
7	30	250	1.8				160			1.2								0
13	30	250	1.8				190			2.4								0
6.5	32	269	1.94				172			2.6								0
3	10	80	1.08				140			0								0
22	110	900	3.6				670			4.8								0
0.8	0	6	0.87				152			0.1								0
0.6	26	6	0.32				175			0.1								0
4.8	23	187	2.99				776			0								0
7.7	40	199	3.56				1063			1.4								0
11.4	64	282	3.72				1463			0.1								0
10.9	57	279	3.4				1349			0.1								0
7.1	34	279	3.44				987			1.3								0
4	0						250											0
2	0						350											0
2	30						740											0
12	55						1238											0
1.7	25						736											0
25	185						1573											0
27	137						1584											0
1	10						120											0
3	0						520											0
1	60						697											0
7	75						1280											0
15	105	250	4.5			530	1340			9								0
26	210	300	7.2			630	1740			0.6								0
1	15	100	4.5			620	1730			24								0
6	30	80	4.5			500	1020			12								0
4	5	100	0.72			160	420		0	0								0
3.5	30	100	3.6			155	610		0	0								0
17	90	350	0			710	320			0								0
19	95	400	0.36			730	490			0								0
18	95	400	0			730	320			0								0
5	0	40	2.7			150	780			18								0
5	0	40	1.8			630	1010		15	0					0			0
4	0	10	0.72			590	710		0	6								0
16	45	300	0.72			1085	1510			3.6								0
2.5	25	20	0			40	750		0	0								0
0	0	10	0			40	670		0	0								0
4	65	200	0.72			560	420			12								0
4.5	55	200	2.7			410	850			15								0

MDA Code	Food Name	Amt	Wt (g)	Ener (kcal)	Prot (g)	Carb (g)	Fiber (g)	Fat (g)	Mono (g)	Poly (g)
56431	Sandwich, croissant w/sausage	1 ea	181	660	20	37	0	48		
56377	Taco	1 ea	90	170	7	12	2	10		
	Source: Jack In the Box									
	Kentucky Fried Chicken									
42331	Biscuit, buttermilk	1 ea	57	190	2	23	0	10		
15169	Chicken breast, extra crispy	1 ea	162	460	34	19	0	28		
15185	Chicken breast, hot & spicy	1 ea	179	460	33	20	0	27		
15163	Chicken breast, original recipe	1 ea	161	380	40	11	0	19		
81292	Chicken breast, original recipe, w/o skin or brd	1 ea	108	140	29	0	0	3		
81293	Chicken drumstick, original recipe	1 ea	59	140	14	4	0	8		
15166	Chicken thigh, original recipe	1 ea	126	360	22	12	0	25		
416	Chicken wing, pieces, honey bbq	6 ea	157	540	25	36	1	33		
56451	Cole slaw, svg	1 ea	130	190	1	22	3	11		
9535	Corn, cob, small	1 ea	82	76	3	13	4	2		
2897	Dessert, strawberry shortcake, Lil Bucket	1 ea	99	200	2	34	0	6		
56681	Macaroni & cheese	1 ea	287	130	5	15	1	6		
56453	Mashed potatoes, w/gravy	1 ea	136	130	2	18	1	4		
45166	Pie, pecan, Colonel's Pies, slice	1 pce	95	370	4	55	2	15		
81090	Pot pie, chicken, chunky	1 ea	423	770	29	70	5	40		
56454	Potato salad	1 ea	128	180	2	22	1	9		
49148	Sandwich, chicken, honey bbq flavor, w/sauce	1 ea	147	300	21	41	4	6		
81301	Sandwich, chicken, tender roasted, w/o sauce	1 ea	177	260	31	23	1	5		
81093	Sandwich, chicken, tender roasted, w/sauce	1 ea	196	390	31	24	1	19		
81302	Sandwich, chicken, Twister	1 ea	252	670	27	55	3	38		
	Source: Kentucky Fried Chicken/Yum! Brands, Inc.									
	Long John Silver's									
91388	Cheesesticks, breaded & fried	3 ea	45	140	4	12	1	8		
91390	Clam chowder	1 ea	227	220	9	23	1	10		
56477	Cornbread, hush puppies	1 ea	23	60	1	9	1	2		
56461	Fish, batter dipped, regular	1 pce	92	230	11	16	0	13		
92415	Fish, cod, baked	1 ea	100.7	120	21	0	0	4		
91392	Sandwich, fish, batter dipped, ultimate	1 ea	199	500	20	48	3	25		
92290	Shrimp, battered, 4 piece serving	1 ea	65.8	197	7	14	0	13		
92292	Shrimp, crunchy, breaded, fried, basket	1 ea	114	340	12	32	2	19		
	Source: Long John Silver's/Yum! Brands, Inc.									
	McDonald's									
81465	Breakfast, big, w/eggs sausage hashbrowns biscuit	1 ea	266	732	28	47	3	50	22.6	6.5
56675	Burrito, sausage, breakfast	1 ea	113	296	13	24	1	17	6.5	2.4
69010	Cheeseburger, Big Mac	1 ea	219	563	26	44	4	33	7.6	0.7
81458	Cheeseburger, double	1 ea	173	458	26	34	1	26	8.6	0.8
69012	Cheeseburger, Quarter Pounder	1 ea	199	513	29	40	3	28	9.2	0.9
49152	Chicken McNuggets, 6 piece serving	6 pce	100	264	16	16	0	15	6.2	5
42334	Croutons	1 ea	12	50	1	9	1	1		
42335	Danish, apple	1 ea	105	340	5	47	2	15		
72902	Dessert, apple dipper, w/low-fat caramel sauce	1 ea	89	99	0	23		1	0.2	0
81440	French fries, large	1 ea	171	525	6	68	7	27	11.7	7.1
1747	Frozen dessert, McFlurry, Butterfinger	1 ea	348	620	16	90	1	22		
2171	Frozen dessert, hot fudge sundae	1 ea	179	333	7	54	1	11	1.9	0.4
69008	Hamburger	1 ea	105	265	13	32	1	10	3.3	0.2
69011	Hamburger, Quarter Pounder	1 ea	171	417	24	38	3	20	7.2	0.5
6155	Hash browns	1 ea	53	136	1	13	2	9	3.9	2.2

Sat (g)	Chol (mg)	Calc (mg)	Iron (mg)	Mag (mg)	Phos (mg)	Pota (mg)	Sodi (mg)	Zinc (mg)	Vit A (RAE)	Vit C (mg)	Thia (mg)	Ribo (mg)	Niac (mg)	Vit B6 (mg)	Vit B12 (µg)	Vit E (mg)	Fol (µg)	Alc (g)
15	240	100	1.8			160	860			0								0
3.5	15	100	1.08	40.4	168	235	390	1.4		0.2								0
2	0	0	0.72				580	0		0								0
8	135	0	1.44				1230	0		0								0
8	130	0	1.14				1450	0		0								0
6	145	0	1.8				1150	0		0								0
1	95	0	0.72				410	0		0								0
2	75	0	0.72				440	0		0								0
7	165	0	1.14				1060	0		0								0
7	150	60	2.7				1130			4.8								0
2	5	40	0				300			24								0
0.5	0	30	0.55				5	0		3								0
4	20	20	0				110	0		0								0
2	5	100	0.72				610			24								0
1	0	0	0.36				380			2.4								0
2.5	40	0	1.44				190			0								0
15	115	0	3.6				1680			0								0
1.5	5	0	0.36				470	0		6								0
1.5	50	60	2.7				640			2.4								0
1.5	65	40	1.8				690	0		0								0
4	70	40	1.8				810	0		0								0
7	60	150	2.7				1650			4.8								0
2	10	100	0.72				320			0								0
4	25	150	0.72				810			0								0
0.5	0	20	0.36				200	0		0								0
4	30	20	1.8				700	0		4.8								0
1	90	20	0.72				240			0								0
8	50	150	3.6				1310			9								0
4.1	64	23	0.83				579	0		2.8								0
5	105	500	1.8				720	0		0								0
13.3	471	133	5.05	39.9	692	548	1460	2.6		1.6	0.62	0.96	6.1	0.46	1.54	3.1	196.8	
6.1	173	203	1.84	19.2	247	155	763	1.3	97	0.9	0.18	0.33	1.92	0.41	0.61	0.2	70.1	
8.3	79	254	4.38	43.8	267	396	1007	4.2		0.9	0.39	0.46	7.41	0.37	1.93	0.1	100.7	0
10.5	83	277	3.68	34.6	280	375	1137	4.2		0.7	0.28	0.43	6.68		2.04		77.8	
11.2	94	287	4.18	43.8	320	436	1152	5.2		1.6	0.33	0.7	7.66	0.19	2.51	0.4	101.5	0
3.3	39	14	0.78	22	332	251	699	0.6		1	0.16	0.11	7.4	0.4	0.33		28	
0	0	20	0.36	3.9	18	26	105	0.1	0	0.2	0.08	0.05	0.57	0.02	0.02		5.1	0
3	20	60	1.44		0	113	340			15	0.3	0.17	2					0
0.4	3	57	0.1				36	0.1	11	188.3	0.02	0.03	0	0.01	0	0.1	0	
4.8	0	27	1.76	54.7	226	958	332	0.8	0	8.4	0.56	0.06	4.72	0.89		3.5	102.6	0
14	70	450	0.36				260			2.4								0
6.4	23	249	1.49	34	229	440	168	1	145		0.08	0.4	0.27	0.09	0.98	0.3		0
3.1	28	127	2.77	21	112	213	532	2		0.6	0.26	0.25	4.77	0.1	0.87	0.1	67.2	0
6.9	67	144	4.12	37.6	212	388	730	4.6		1.5	0.31	0.59	7.61	0.25	2.19	0.1	95.8	0
1.6	0	10	0.4	11.1	57	207	289	0.2	0	1.6	0.06	0.01	1.19	0.13		1	20.1	

MDA Code	Food Name	Amt	Wt (g)	Ener (kcal)	Prot (g)	Carb (g)	Fiber (g)	Fat (g)	Mono (g)	Poly (g)
72913	Milk shake, chocolate, triple thick, large	1 ea	713	1162	26	199	1	32	8	1.5
81453	Pancakes, hotcakes, w/2 pats margarine & syrup	1 ea	221	601	9	102	2	18	1.9	4.6
81154	Parfait, fruit n' yogurt, w/o granola	1 ea	142	128	4	25	1	2	0	0
48136	Pie, apple	1 ea	77	249	2	34	2	12	7.1	0.8
69218	Salad, bacon ranch, w/crispy chicken	1 ea	316	335	27	23	3	18	5.5	3.6
608	Salad, caesar, w/chicken, shaker	1 ea	163	100	17	3	2	2		
61674	Salad, Calif cobb, w/grilled chicken	1 ea	325	260	33	11	4	11	4.1	1.3
57764	Salad, chef, shaker	1 ea	206	150	17	5	2	8		
61667	Salad, fruit & walnut	1 ea	264	312	5	44		13	2.1	8.5
81466	Sandwich, breakfast, McGriddle, w/bacon egg cheese	1 ea	168	450	20	44	1	22	8.1	3
69013	Sandwich, Filet O Fish	1 ea	141	400	15	40	1	20	4.3	7
81456	Sandwich, Filet-O-Fish, w/o tartar sauce	1 ea	123	289	15	40	1	11	2.2	1.8
53176	Sauce, barbecue, packet	1 ea	28	46	0	10	0	0	0.1	0.1
53177	Sauce, sweet & sour, packet	1 ea	28	48	0	11	0	0	0.1	0.1
12230	Sausage, pork, serving	1 ea	43	170	6	0	0	16		
42747	Sweet roll, cinnamon	1 ea	105	418	8	56	2	19	9.5	3

Source: McDonald's Nutrition Information Center

Pizza Hut

MDA Code	Food Name	Amt	Wt (g)	Ener (kcal)	Prot (g)	Carb (g)	Fiber (g)	Fat (g)	Mono (g)	Poly (g)
92497	Breadsticks, cheese, svg	1 ea	67	200	7	21	1	10		
92526	Dessert, pizza, cherry, slice	1 pce	102	240	4	47	1	4		
92519	Pasta Bake, primavera w/chicken	1 ea	540	1050	52	97	6	50		
57394	Pizza, beef, med, 12"	1 pce	91	230	11	21	2	11		
56489	Pizza, cheese, med, 12"	1 pce	96	260	11	30	2	10	2.8	1.8
56481	Pizza, cheese, pan, med, 12"	1 pce	100	280	12	30	2	13	3.2	2.8
57781	Pizza, chicken supreme, med, 12"	1 pce	120	230	14	30	2	6		
830	Pizza, super supreme, med, 12"	1 pce	127	309	14	33	3	14	5	2.2
92483	Pizza, green pepper onion & tomato, mediuim, 12"	1 pce	104	150	6	24	2	4		
92482	Pizza, ham pine & tomato, med, 12"	1 pce	99	160	8	24	2	4		
57810	Pizza, Meat Lover's, med, 12"	1 pce	169	450	21	43	3	21		
56486	Pizza, pepperoni, med, 12"	1 pce	77	210	10	21	1	10		
57811	Pizza, Veggie Lover's, med, 12"	1 pce	172	360	16	45	3	14		

Source: Pizza Hut/Yum! Brands, Inc.

Subway

MDA Code	Food Name	Amt	Wt (g)	Ener (kcal)	Prot (g)	Carb (g)	Fiber (g)	Fat (g)	Mono (g)	Poly (g)
47658	Cookie, chocolate chip, M&M's	1 ea	45	220	2	30	1	10		
52119	Salad, chicken, breast, roasted	1 ea	303	140	16	12	3	3		
52115	Salad, club	1 ea	322	150	17	12	3	4		
52118	Salad, tuna, w/light mayonnaise	1 ea	314	240	13	10	3	16		
52113	Salad, veggie delite	1 ea	233	50	2	9	3	1		
91761	Sandwich, chicken, teriyaki, w/sweet onion, w/white bread, 6"	1 ea	269	380	26	59	4	5		
69117	Sandwich, club, w/white bread, 6"	1 ea	255	320	24	46	4	6		
69113	Sandwich, cold cut trio, w/white bread, 6"	1 ea	257	440	21	47	4	21		
91763	Sandwich, ham, w/honey mustard, w/white bread, 6"	1 ea	232	310	18	52	4	5		
69139	Sandwich, Italian BMT, w/white bread, 6"	1 ea	248	480	23	46	4	24		
69129	Sandwich, meatball, w/white bread, 6"	1 ea	287	530	24	53	6	26		
69103	Sandwich, roast beef, deli style	1 ea	151	220	13	35	3	4		
69143	Sandwich, tuna, w/light mayonnaise, w/white bread, 6"	1 ea	255	450	20	46	4	22		
69101	Sandwich, turkey, deli style	1 ea	151	220	13	36	3	4		
69109	Sandwich, veggie delite, w/white bread, 6"	1 ea	166	230	9	44	4	3		
91778	Soup, chicken noodle, roasted	1 cup	240	90	7	7	1	4		
91791	Soup, cream of broccoli	1 cup	240	130	5	15	2	6		
91783	Soup, minestrone	1 cup	240	70	3	11	2	1		

Sat (g)	Chol (mg)	Calc (mg)	Iron (mg)	Mag (mg)	Phos (mg)	Pota (mg)	Sodi (mg)	Zinc (mg)	Vit A (RAE)	Vit C (mg)	Thia (mg)	Ribo (mg)	Niac (mg)	Vit B6 (mg)	Vit B12 (µg)	Vit E (mg)	Fol (µg)	Alc (g)
16.4	100	870	3.85	114.1	749	1611	506	3.6	649		0.28	1.53	0.94	0.36	3.85	0	7.1	
1.8	20	126	2.83	28.7	391	276	625	0.6		0	0.45	0.4	3.24	0.11	0.02		143.6	
0	7	124	0.51	17	101	234	54	0.4		20.6	0.05	0.17	0.27			0.28	15.6	
3.1		15	1.53	5.4	28	49	153	0.2		24.9	0.23	0.16	2.03	0.04		1.5	87	
5.3	66	149	2.02				1030			31	0.18	0.24	8.3		0.41		154.8	
1.5	40	100	1.08				240			12								0
4.9	146	143	2.31				1063			31.5	0.14	0.3	11.86				149.5	
3.5	95	150	1.44				740			15								0
1.8	5	172	0.9	34.3	129		84	0.7		383.6	0.1	0.15	0.27	0.25	0.16		13.2	
7.3	247	183	2.77				1258			3	0.21	0.51	2.22				89	
3.7	39	164	2.07	28.2	166	247	633	0.7		0	0.36	0.26	3.4	0.06	1.03	1.6	70.5	0
2.1	31	159	2	28.3	161	237	520	0.7		0	0.35	0.25	3.41		0.98		70.1	
0		3	0.11	3.6	8	55	255	0	3	0	0.01	0.01	0.19	0.02		0.3	2.2	
0		2	0.18	1.7	4	28	156	0	2	0.3	0.05	0.01	0.11	0.01		0.2	0	
5	35	7	0.36	6.6	59	102	290	0.8	0	0	0.18	0.06	1.7	0.09	0.35	0.3		0
4.7	61	60	1.81	20	109	147	397	0.9	132	0	0.32	0.28	2.53	0.11		1.9	108.2	
3.5	15	100	3.6				340			0								0
0.5	0	20	1.08				250			6								0
12	75	800	5.4				2760			6								0
5	25	150	1.8				710			3.6								0
4.8	23	201	1.87	21.1	239	166	658	1.6	71	0	0.25	0.25	3.16	0.11	0.67	0.7		
5.2	21	208	1.86	21	241	168	624	1.6	74	0	0.24	0.25	3.91	0.11	0.64	1.1		
3	25	150	1.8				550			6								0
5.8	25	164	2.54	29.2	254	296	875	1.8	46	0	0.34	0.31	4.55	0.19	0.79	1		
1.5	10	80	1.44				360			21								0
2	15	80	1.44				470			12								0
10	55	250	2.7				1250			9								0
4.5	25	150	1.44				550			2.4								0
7	35	250	2.7				980			9								0
4	15	0	1.08				105	0		0								0
1	45	40	1.08				800			30								0
1.5	35	40	18				1110			30								0
4	40	100	1.08				880			30								0
0	0	40	1.08				310			30								0
1.5	50	80	3.6				1100			27								0
2	35	60	5.4				1300			21								0
7	55	150	5.4				1680			24								0
1.5	25	60	3.6				1260			24								0
9	55	150	3.6				1900			24								0
10	55	150	5.4				1360			27								0
2	15	60	5.4				660			12								0
6	40	15	3.6				1190			24								0
1.5	15	60	3.6				730			12								0
1	0	60	3.6				510			21								0
1	20	20	0				1180			3.6								0
0	10	150	0				860			12								0
0	10	40	0				1030			6								0

MDA Code	Food Name	Amt	Wt (g)	Ener (kcal)	Prot (g)	Carb (g)	Fiber (g)	Fat (g)	Mono (g)	Poly (g)
91788	Soup, rice, brown & wild, w/chicken	1 cup	240	190	6	17	2	11		
	Source: Subway International									
	Taco Bell									
92107	Border Bowl, chicken, zesty	1 ea	417	730	23	65	12	42		
56519	Burrito, bean	1 ea	198	404	16	55	8	14	5.9	1.7
56522	Burrito, beef, supreme	1 ea	248	469	20	52	8	20	8.1	2
57668	Burrito, chicken, fiesta	1 ea	184	370	18	48	3	12		
56691	Burrito, seven layer	1 ea	283	530	18	67	10	22		
92113	Burrito, steak, grilled, Stuft	1 ea	325	680	31	76	8	28		
92118	Chalupa, beef, nacho cheese	1 ea	153	380	12	33	3	22		
92120	Chalupa, chicken, Baja	1 ea	153	400	17	30	2	24		
92122	Chalupa, steak, supreme	1 ea	153	370	15	29	2	22		
45585	Dessert, cinnamon twists, svg	1 ea	35	160	1	28	0	5		
57666	Gordita, beef, Baja	1 ea	153	350	14	31	4	19		
57669	Gordita, chicken, Baja	1 ea	153	320	17	29	2	15		
57662	Gordita, steak, Baja	1 ea	153	320	15	29	2	16		
56530	Guacamole, svg	1 ea	21	35	0	2	1	3		
38561	Mexican rice, svg	1 ea	131	210	6	23	3	10		
56534	Nachos, BellGrande, svg	1 ea	308	780	20	80	12	43		
56536	Pintos & cheese, svg	1 ea	128	180	10	20	6	7		
56531	Pizza, Mexican	1 ea	216	550	21	46	7	31		
57689	Quesadilla, chicken	1 ea	184	540	28	40	3	30		
92098	Salsa, fiesta, svg	1 ea	21	5	0	1		0	0	0
53186	Sauce, border, hot, pkt	1 ea	11	4	0	0	0	0	0	0
92105	Southwest steak bowl	1 ea	443	700	30	73	13	32		
56524	Taco, beef	1 ea	78	184	8	14	3	11	4.2	1.6
57671	Taco, Double Decker, supreme	1 ea	191	380	15	40	6	18		
56693	Taco, soft, steak, grilled	1 ea	127	286	15	22	2	15	5	4.4
56537	Taco salad, w/salsa & shell	1 ea	533	906	36	80	16	49	21.2	4
56528	Tostada	1 ea	170	250	11	29	7	10		
	Source: Taco Bell/Yum! Brands, Inc.									
	Wendy's									
56579	Baked potato w/bacon & cheese	1 ea	380	580	18	79	7	22		
56582	Baked potato, w/sour cream & chives	1 ea	312	370	7	73	7	6		
81445	Cheeseburger, classic single	1 ea	236	522	35	34	3	27	10.4	3.3
56571	Cheeseburger, w/bacon, jr	1 ea	165	380	20	34	2	19		
15176	Chicken nuggets, 5 piece serving	1 ea	75	250	12	12	1	17	8.5	4.3
50311	Chili, small	1 ea	227	200	17	21	5	6		
6169	French fries, Biggie	1 ea	159	507	6	63	6	26	13.5	5.9
2177	Frozen dessert, Frosty, medium	1 ea	298	393	10	70	10	8	2.1	0.3
56574	Hamburger, Big Bacon Classic	1 ea	282	570	34	46	3	29		
56566	Hamburger, classic single	1 ea	218	464	28	37	3	23	8.9	3.4
8457	Salad dressing, blue cheese, packet	1 ea	71	290	2	3	0	30		
8461	Salad dressing, French, fat free, packet	1 ea	71	90	0	21	1	0	0	0
71595	Salad dressing, oriental sesame, packet	1 ea	71	280	2	21	0	21		
81444	Sandwich, chicken fillet, homestyle	1 ea	230	492	32	50	3	19	6.7	7.1
81443	Sandwich, chicken, Ultimate Grill	1 ea	225	403	33	42	2	11	3.3	4.1
52080	Salad, caesar, w/o dressing, side	1 ea	99	70	7	2	1	4		
71592	Salad, chicken mandarin, w/o dressing	1 ea	348	150	20	17	3	2		
52083	Salad, garden, w/o dressing, side	1 ea	167	35	2	7	3	0	0	0
	Source: Wendy's Foods International									

Sat (g)	Chol (mg)	Calc (mg)	Iron (mg)	Mag (mg)	Phos (mg)	Pota (mg)	Sodi (mg)	Zinc (mg)	Vit A (RAE)	Vit C (mg)	Thia (mg)	Ribo (mg)	Niac (mg)	Vit B6 (mg)	Vit B12 (µg)	Vit E (mg)	Fol (µg)	Alc (g)
4.5	20	300	0				990			24								0
9	45	150	3.6				1640			9								0
4.8	18	232	4.57	61.4	337	533	1216	1.7	6		0.4	0.3	3.39	0.24	0	1	99	
7.6	40	231	5.6	62	337	608	1424	2.6	10		0.38	0.37	4.33	0.26	1.24	1.1	111.6	
3.5	30	200	2.7				1090			3.6								0
8	25	300	3.6				1360			4.8								0
8	55	300	4.5				1940			3.6								0
7	20	100	1.44				740			6								0
6	40	100	1.08				690			3.6								0
8	35	100	1.44				520			3.6								0
1	0	0	0.36				150		0	0								0
5	30	150	2.7				750			4.8								0
3.5	40	100	1.8				690			3.6								0
4	30	100	1.8				680			3.6								0
0	0	0	0				100		0	0								0
4	15	100	1.8				740			4.8								0
13	35	200	2.7				1300			6								0
3.5	15	150	1.08				700			3.6								0
11	45	350	3.6				1030			6								0
13	80	500	1.8				1380			2.4								0
0	0	0	0				60	5		2.4								0
0	0	0	0				102			0								0
8	55	200	6.3				2050			9								0
3.6	24	62	1.47	25.7	139	168	349	1.7	3		0.07	0.15	1.5	0.11	0.75	0.5	14.8	
8	40	150	2.7				820			4.8								0
4.3	39	149	2.82	26.7	197	232	700	2.7	1		0.39	0.25	3.78	0.11	1.22	0.5	47	
15.9	101	506	9.43	143.9	549	1221	1935	6.2	16		0.8	0.56	8.02	0.55	2.13	2.9	229.2	
4	15	150	1.44				710			4.8								0
6	40	200	3.6			1410	950			42								0
4	15	60	3.6			1230	40			36								0
12.3	90	177	5.52	44.8	297	441	1123	6.1		1.2	0.61	0.6	7.53	0.25	3.63			
7	55	150	3.6			320	890			9								0
3.7	38	18	0.56	18	215	177	509	0.5		1	0.06	0.09	4.53	0.19	0.25			
2.5	35	80	1.8			470	870			2.4								0
5.1		24	3.07	54.1	218	914	273	0.8		8.1	0.28	0.1	3.95	0.62			27	
4.9	48	381	3.1	59.6	334	551	292	1.3		0	0.18	2.15	1.04	0	1.76			
12	100	200	5.4			580	1460			15								0
8	76	74	5.95	39.2	225	425	861	5.4		1.1	0.6	0.45	7.03	0.25	3.16			
6	45	60	1.08			25	870			0								0
0	0	0	0.72			10	240		0	0								0
3	0	20	0.72			40	620		0	0								0
3.7	71	53	3.45	55.2	370	524	922	1.4		0.7	0.68	0.3	7.59	0.43	0.76			
2.3	90	56	3.49	54	378	497	961	1.3		2.5	0.88	0.58	9.36	0.32	0.74			
2	15	150	1.08			280	250			21								0
0	10	60	1.8			420	650			30								0
0	0	40	0.72			350	20		350	18								0

Appendix B Calculations and Conversions

Calculation and Conversion Aids

Commonly Used Metric Units

millimeter (mm): one-thousandth of a meter (0.001)
centimeter (cm): one-hundredth of a meter (0.01)
kilometer (km): one-thousand times a meter (1000)
kilogram (kg): one-thousand times a gram (1000)
milligram (mg): one-thousandth of a gram (0.001)
microgram (μg): one-millionth of a gram (0.000001)
milliliter (ml): one-thousandth of a liter (0.001)

International Units

Some vitamin supplements may report vitamin content as International Units (IU).

To convert IU to:

- Micrograms of vitamin D (cholecalciferol), divide the IU value by 40 or multiply by 0.025.
- Milligrams of vitamin E (alpha-tocopherol), divide the IU value by 1.5 if vitamin E is from natural sources. Divide the IU value by 2.22 if vitamin E is from synthetic sources.
- Vitamin A: 1 IU = 0.3 μg retinol or 3.6 μg beta-carotene

Retinol Activity Equivalents

Retinol Activity Equivalents (RAE) are a standardized unit of measure for vitamin A. RAE account for the various differences in bioavailability from sources of vitamin A. Many supplements will report vitamin A content in IU, as shown above, or Retinol Equivalents (RE).

1 RAE = 1 μg retinol
　　　　12 μg beta-carotene
　　　　24 μg other vitamin A carotenoids

To calculate RAE from the RE value of vitamin carotenoids in foods, divide RE by 2.

For vitamin A supplements and foods fortified with vitamin A, 1 RE = 1 RAE.

Folate

Folate is measured as Dietary Folate Equivalents (DFE). DFE account for the different factors affecting bioavailability of folate sources.

1 DFE = 1 μg food folate
　　　　0.6 μg folate from fortified foods
　　　　0.5 μg folate supplement taken on an empty stomach
　　　　0.6 μg folate as a supplement consumed with a meal

To convert micrograms of synthetic folate, such as that found in supplements or fortified foods, to DFE:

$$\text{μg synthetic folate} \times 1.7 = \text{μg DFE}$$

For naturally occurring food folate, such as spinach, each microgram of folate equals 1 microgram DFE:

$$\text{μg folate} = \text{μg DFE}$$

Conversion Factors

Use the following table to convert U.S. measurements to metric equivalents:

Original Unit	Multiply by	To Get
ounces avdp	28.3495	grams
ounces	0.0625	pounds
pounds	0.4536	kilograms
pounds	16	ounces
grams	0.0353	ounces
grams	0.002205	pounds
kilograms	2.2046	pounds
liters	1.8162	pints (dry)
liters	2.1134	pints (liquid)
liters	0.9081	quarts (dry)
liters	1.0567	quarts (liquid)
liters	0.2642	gallons (U.S.)
pints (dry)	0.5506	liters
pints (liquid)	0.4732	liters
quarts (dry)	1.1012	liters
quarts (liquid)	0.9463	liters
gallons (U.S.)	3.7853	liters
millimeters	0.0394	inches
centimeters	0.3937	inches
centimeters	0.03281	feet
inches	25.4000	millimeters
inches	2.5400	centimeters
inches	0.0254	meters
feet	0.3048	meters
meters	3.2808	feet
meters	1.0936	yards
cubic feet	0.0283	cubic meters
cubic meters	35.3145	cubic feet
cubic meters	1.3079	cubic yards
cubic yards	0.7646	cubic meters

Length: U.S. and Metric Equivalents

¼ inch = 0.6 centimeters
1 inch = 2.5 centimeters
1 foot = 0.3048 meter
　　　　30.48 centimeters
1 yard = 0.91144 meter
1 millimeter = 0.03937 inch
1 centimeter = 0.3937 inch
1 decimeter = 3.937 inches
1 meter = 39.37 inches
　　　　1.094 yards
1 micrometer = 0.00003937 inch

Weights and Measures

Food Measurement Equivalencies from U.S. to Metric

Capacity

⅕ teaspoon = 1 milliliter
¼ teaspoon = 1.25 milliliters
½ teaspoon = 2.5 milliliters
1 teaspoon = 5 milliliters
1 tablespoon = 15 milliliters
1 fluid ounce = 28.4 milliliters
¼ cup = 60 milliliters
⅓ cup = 80 milliliters
½ cup = 120 milliliters
1 cup = 225 milliliters
1 pint (2 cups) = 473 milliliters
1 quart (4 cups) = 0.95 liter
1 liter (1.06 quarts) = 1,000 milliliters
1 gallon (4 quarts) = 3.84 liters

Weight

0.035 ounce = 1 gram
1 ounce = 28 grams
¼ pound (4 ounces) = 114 grams
1 pound (16 ounces) = 454 grams
2.2 pounds (35 ounces) = 1 kilogram

U.S. Food Measurement Equivalents

3 teaspoons = 1 tablespoon
½ tablespoon = 1½ teaspoons
2 tablespoons = ⅛ cup
4 tablespoons = ¼ cup
5 tablespoons + 1 teaspoon = ⅓ up
8 tablespoons = ½ cup
10 tablespoons + 2 teaspoons = ⅔ cup
12 tablespoons = ¾ cup
16 tablespoons = 1 cup
2 cups = 1 pint
4 cups = 1 quart
2 pints = 1 quart
4 quarts = 1 gallon

Volumes and Capacities

1 cup = 8 fluid ounces
½ liquid pint
1 milliliter = 0.061 cubic inches
1 liter = 1.057 liquid quarts
0.908 dry quart
61.024 cubic inches
1 U.S. gallon = 231 cubic inches
3.785 liters
0.833 British gallon
128 U.S. fluid ounces

1 British Imperial gallon = 277.42 cubic inches
1.201 U.S. gallons
4.546 liters
160 British fluid ounces
1 U.S. ounce, liquid or fluid = 1.805 cubic inches
29.574 milliliters
1.041 British fluid ounces
1 pint, dry = 33.600 cubic inches
0.551 liter
1 pint, liquid = 28.875 cubic inches
0.473 liter
1 U.S. quart, dry = 67.201 cubic inches
1.101 liters
1 U.S. quart, liquid = 57.75 cubic inches
0.946 liter
1 British quart = 69.354 cubic inches
1.032 U.S. quarts, dry
1.201 U.S. quarts, liquid

Energy Units

1 kilocalorie (kcal) = 4.2 kilojoules
1 millijoule (MJ) = 240 kilocalories
1 kilojoule (kJ) = 0.24 kcal
1 gram carbohydrate = 4 kcal
1 gram fat = 9 kcal
1 gram protein = 4 kcal

Temperature Standards

	°Fahrenheit	°Celsius
Body temperature	98.6°	37°
Comfortable room temperature	65–75°	18–24°
Boiling point of water	212°	100°
Freezing point of water	32°	0°

Temperature Scales

To Convert Fahrenheit to Celsius:

$[(°F − 32) × 5]/9$

1. Subtract 32 from °F
2. Multiply (°F − 32) by 5, then divide by 9

To Convert Celsius to Fahrenheit:

$[(°C × 9)/5] + 32$

1. Multiply °C by 9, then divide by 5
2. Add 32 to (°C × 9/5)

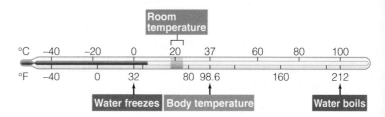

The "Exchange Lists for Meal Planning" group foods together according to their carbohydrate, protein, and fat composition. There are three main groups: the Carbohydrate Group, the Meat and Meat Substitutes Group, and the Fat Group. As you will see in the charts on the following pages, the Carbohydrate Group contains starchy foods such as bread and other grain products, as well as fruit, milk, and vegetables; the Meat and Meat Substitutes Group includes meat, fish, poultry, eggs, luncheon meats, and legumes; and the Fat Group contains oils, nuts, and other spreads. Also note that two of these main groups (specifically, the Carbohydrate Group and the Meat and Meat Substitutes Group) also contain subgroups.

Specific portion sizes are provided for each of the foods within each group. This ensures that all the foods in each subgroup contain relatively the same amount of carbohydrates, protein, and fats, and thus, will have a similar amount of calories per serving. Because any food within a food subgroup will have similar amounts of these nutrients, they can be exchanged or swapped with each other at meals and snacks. This flexible meal plan is a useful tool to help individuals, such as those with diabetes and/or those who want to lose weight, better control the amount of nutrient and calories at all meals and snacks. A diet with a set amount of nutrients, such as carbohydrates and calories, can help individuals with diabetes better control their blood glucose levels and calories throughout the day. Calorie control is important for those who are trying to improve or manage their body weight.

The following chart shows the amount of nutrients in one serving from each of the three main groups.

Group/List	Carbohydrate (grams)	Protein (grams)	Fat (grams)	Calories
Carbohydrate Group				
Starch	15	3	0–1	80
Fruit	15	—	—	60
Milk				
Fat-free, low-fat	12	8	0–3	90
Reduced-fat	12	8	5	120
Whole	12	8	8	150
Other carbohydrates	15	varies	varies	varies
Nonstarchy vegetables	5	2	—	25
Meat and Meat Substitutes Group				
Very lean	—	7	0–1	35
Lean	—	7	3	55
Medium-fat	—	7	5	75
High-fat	—	7	8	100
Fat Group				
	—	—	5	45

The charts on the following pages show the exchange lists for each of the subgroups shown above (i.e., Starch, Fruit, Milk, etc.).

Starch List

Food	Serving Size
Bread	
Bagel, 4 oz	¼ (1 oz)
Bread, white, whole-wheat, pumpernickel, rye	1 slice (1 oz)
English muffin	½
Hot dog bun or hamburger bun	½
Pancake, 4″ across, ¼″ thick	1
Pita, 6″ across	½
Roll, plain, small	1 (1 oz)
Tortilla, flour, 6″ across	1
Cereals and Grains	
Bran cereals	½ cup
Bulgur	½ cup
Cereals, cooked	½ cup
Cereals, unsweetened, ready-to-eat	¾ cup
Couscous	⅓ cup
Oats	½ cup
Pasta	⅓ cup
Puffed cereal	1½ cup
Rice, white or brown	⅓ cup
Shredded Wheat	½ cup
Sugar-frosted cereal	½ cup
Starchy Vegetables	
Baked beans	⅓ cup
Corn	½ cup
Peas, green	½ cup

Source: © American Dietetic Association. Used with permission.

Food	Serving Size
Potato, mashed	½ cup
Squash, winter (acorn, butternut, pumpkin)	1 cup
Yam, sweet potato, plain	½ cup
Crackers and Snacks	
Animal crackers	8
Graham crackers, 2½″ square	3
Popcorn (popped, no fat added or low-fat microwave)	3 cups
Pretzels	¾ oz
Rice cakes, 4″ across	2
Saltine-type crackers	6
Snack chips, fat-free or baked (tortilla, potato)	15–20 (¾ oz)
Whole-wheat crackers, no fat added	2–5 (¾ oz)
Beans, Peas, and Lentils	
(Count as 1 starch exchange, plus 1 very lean meat exchange)	
Beans and peas (garbanzo, pinto, kidney, white, split, black-eyed)	½ cup
Lima beans	⅔ cup
Starchy Foods Prepared with Fat	
(Count as 1 starch exchange plus 1 fat exchange)	
Biscuit, 2½″ across	1
Crackers, round butter type	6
Croutons	1 cup
French-fried potatoes (oven-baked) (see also the fast foods list)	1 cup (2 oz)
Muffin, 5 oz	⅕ (1 oz)
Popcorn, microwaved	3 cups

Fruit List

Food	Serving Size
Apples, unpeeled, small	1 (4 oz)
Applesauce, unsweetened	½ cup
Apricots, dried	8 halves
Banana, small	1 (4 oz)
Blueberries	⅓ cup
Cantaloupe, small or 1 cup cubes	⅓ melon (11 oz)
Cherries, sweet, fresh	12 (3 oz)
Dates	3
Figs, dried	1½
Grapefruit, large	½ (11 oz)
Grapes, small	17 (3 oz)
Honeydew melon or 1 cup cubes	1 slice (10 oz)
Kiwi	1 (3½ oz)
Mango, small	½ (5½ oz) or ½ cup
Orange, small	1 (6½ oz)
Peach, medium, fresh	1 (4 oz)
Pear, large, fresh	½ (4 oz)

Food	Serving Size
Pineapple, fresh	¾ cup
Plums, small	2 (5 oz)
Raisins	2 tbsp
Raspberries	1 cup
Strawberries	1¼ cup whole berries
Watermelon	1 slice (13½ oz) or 1¼ cup cubes
Fruit Juice, Unsweetened	
Apple juice/cider	½ cup
Cranberry juice cocktail	⅓ cup
Cranberry juice cocktail, reduced-calorie	1 cup
Fruit juice blends, 100% juice	⅓ cup
Grape juice	⅓ cup
Grapefruit juice	½ cup
Orange juice	½ cup
Pineapple juice	½ cup

Milk List

Food	Serving Size	Food	Serving Size
Fat-Free and Low-Fat Milk		**Reduced-Fat Milk**	
(0–3 g fat per serving)		*(5 g fat per serving)*	
Fat-free milk	1 cup	2% milk	1 cup
½% milk	1 cup	Soy milk	1 cup
1% milk	1 cup	**Whole Milk**	
Buttermilk, low-fat or fat-free	1 cup	*(8 g fat per serving)*	
Soy milk, low-fat or fat-free	1 cup	Whole milk	1 cup
Yogurt, plain, fat-free	6 oz	Yogurt, plain (made from whole milk)	8 oz
Yogurt, fat-free, flavored, sweetened with nonnutritive sweetener and fructose	1 cup		

Other Carbohydrates List

These carbohydrate-rich foods can be substituted for a starch, fruit, or milk choice.

Food	Serving Size	Exchanges per Serving
Angel food cake, unfrosted	1/12 cake (about 2 oz)	2 carbohydrates
Brownies, small, unfrosted	2″ square (about 1 oz)	1 carbohydrate, 1 fat
Cake, frosted	2″ square (about 2 oz)	2 carbohydrates, 1 fat
Cookie or sandwich cookie with creme filling	2 small (about ⅔ oz)	1 carbohydrate, 1 fat
Cranberry sauce, jellied	¼ cup	1½ carbohydrates
Doughnut, plain cake	1 medium, (1½ oz)	1½ carbohydrates, 2 fats
Energy, sport, or breakfast bar	1 bar (2 oz)	2 carbohydrates, 1 fat
Fruit juice bars, frozen, 100% juice	1 bar (3 oz)	1 carbohydrate
Granola or snack bar, regular or low-fat	1 bar (1 oz)	1½ carbohydrates
Ice cream	½ cup	1 carbohydrate, 2 fats
Ice cream, light	½ cup	1 carbohydrate, 1 fat
Milk, chocolate, whole	1 cup	2 carbohydrates, 1 fat
Pudding, regular (made with reduced-fat milk)	½ cup	2 carbohydrates
Pudding, sugar-free, or sugar-free and fat-free (made with fat-free milk)	½ cup	1 carbohydrate
Sherbet, sorbet	½ cup	2 carbohydrates
Sports drink	8 oz (1 cup)	1 carbohydrate
Yogurt, frozen, fat-free	⅓ cup	1 carbohydrate
Yogurt, frozen, fat-free, no sugar added	½ cup	1 carbohydrate, 0–1 fat

Vegetable List

Serving size = ½ c cooked vegetables or vegetable juice or 1 c raw vegetables

Asparagus
Beans (green, wax, Italian)
Broccoli
Brussels sprouts
Cabbage
Carrots
Cauliflower
Celery
Cucumber
Eggplant
Mushrooms
Okra
Onions
Pea pods
Peppers (all varieties)
Radishes
Salad greens (endive, escarole, lettuce, romaine, spinach)
Spinach
Summer squash
Tomato
Tomatoes, canned
Tomato sauce*
Tomato/vegetable juice*
Zucchini

= 400 mg or more sodium per exchange.

Meat and Meat Substitutes List

Food	Serving Size
Very Lean Meat and Substitutes	
Poultry: Chicken or turkey (white meat, no skin)	1 oz
Fish: Fresh or frozen cod, flounder, haddock, halibut, trout, lox (smoked salmon)*; tuna, fresh or canned in water	1 oz
Shellfish: Clams, crab, lobster, scallops, shrimp, imitation shellfish	1 oz
Cheese with 1 g fat/oz:	
Fat-free or low-fat cottage cheese	¼ cup
Fat-free cheese	1 oz
Other:	
Processed sandwich meats with 1 g fat/oz (such as deli thin, shaved meats, chipped beef*, turkey ham)	1 oz
Egg whites	2
Hot dogs with 1 g fat/oz*	1 oz
Sausage with 1 g fat/oz.	1 oz
Count as one very lean meat and one starch exchange:	
Beans, peas, lentils (cooked)	½ cup
Lean Meat and Substitutes	
Beef: USDA Select or Choice grades of lean beef trimmed of fat (round, sirloin); tenderloin; roast; steak; ground round	1 oz
Pork: Lean pork (fresh ham); canned, cured, or boiled ham; Canadian bacon*; tenderloin, center loin chop	1 oz
Lamb: Roast, chop, leg	1 oz
Veal: Lean chop, roast	1 oz
Poultry: Chicken, turkey (dark meat, no skin), chicken white meat (with skin)	1 oz
Fish:	
Oysters	6 medium
Salmon (fresh or canned), catfish	1 oz
Tuna (canned in oil, drained)	1 oz
Cheese:	
4.5% fat cottage cheese	¼ cup
Grated Parmesan	2 tbsp
Cheeses with 3 g fat/oz	1 oz

Food	Serving Size
Other:	
Hot dogs with 3 g fat/oz*	1½ oz
Processed sandwich meat with 3 g fat/oz (turkey, pastrami, or kielbasa)	1 oz
Medium-Fat Meat and Substitutes	
Beef: Most beef products (ground beef, meatloaf, corned beef, short ribs, Prime grades of meat trimmed of fat, such as prime rib)	1 oz
Pork: Top loin, chop, cutlet	1 oz
Lamb: Rib roast, ground	1 oz
Veal: Cutlet (ground or cubed, unbreaded)	1 oz
Poultry: Chicken dark meat (with skin), ground turkey or ground chicken, fried chicken (with skin)	1 oz
Fish: Any fried fish product	1 oz
Cheese with 5 g fat/oz:	
Feta	1 oz
Mozzarella	1 oz
Ricotta	¼ cup (2 oz)
Other:	
Egg (high in cholesterol, limit to 3/week)	1
Sausage with 5 g fat/oz	1 oz
Tempeh	¼ cup
Tofu	4 oz or ½ cup
High-Fat Meat and Substitutes	
Pork: Spareribs, ground pork, pork sausage	1 oz
Cheese: All regular cheeses (American* cheddar, Monterey Jack, Swiss)	1 oz
Other:	
Processed sandwich meats with 8 g fat/oz (bologna, salami)	1 oz
Sausage (bratwurst, Italian, knockwurst, Polish, smoked)	1 oz
Hot dog (turkey or chicken)*	1 (10/lb)
Bacon	3 slices
Peanut butter (contains unsaturated fat)	1 tbsp
Count as one high-fat meat plus one fat exchange:	
Hot dog (beef, pork, or combination)*	1 (10/lb)

*= 400 mg or more of sodium per serving.

Fat List

Food	Serving Size
Monounsaturated Fats	
Avocado, medium	2 tbsp (1 oz)
Oil (canola, olive, peanut)	1 tsp
Olives, ripe (black)	8 large
Olives, green, stuffed*	10 large
Almonds, cashews	6 nuts
Peanuts	10 nuts
Pecans	4 halves
Peanut butter, smooth or crunchy	½ tbsp
Sesame seeds	1 tbsp
Polyunsaturated Fats	
Margarine, stick, tub, or squeeze	1 tsp
Margarine, lower-fat (30 to 50% vegetable oil)	1 tbsp
Mayonnaise, regular	1 tsp
Mayonnaise, reduced-fat	1 tbsp
Nuts, walnuts, English	4 halves
Oil (corn, safflower, soybean)	1 tsp
Salad dressing, regular*	1 tbsp
Salad dressing, reduced-fat	2 tbsp
Seeds, pumpkin, sunflower	1 tbsp
Saturated Fats	
Bacon, cooked	1 slice (20 slices/lb)
Butter, stick	1 tsp
Butter, whipped	2 tsp
Butter, reduced-fat	1 tbsp
Cream, half and half	2 tbsp
Cream cheese, regular	1 tbsp (½ oz)
Cream cheese, reduced-fat	1½ tbsp (¾ oz)
Sour cream, regular	2 tbsp
Sour cream, reduced-fat	3 tbsp

*= 400 mg or more sodium per exchange.

Free Foods List

A free food *is any food that contains less than 20 calories or less than 5 grams of carbohydrate per serving. Free foods should be limited to three servings per day.*

Fat-Free or Reduced-Fat Foods
Cream cheese, fat-free	1 tbsp (½ oz)
Creamers, nondairy, liquid	1 tbsp
Mayonnaise, fat-free	1 tbsp
Mayonnaise, reduced-fat	1 tsp
Margarine, spread, fat-free	4 tbsp
Nonstick cooking spray	
Salad dressing, fat-free or low-fat	1 tbsp
Sour cream, fat-free, reduced-fat	1 tbsp

Sugar-Free Foods
Candy, hard, sugar-free	1 candy
Gelatin dessert, sugar-free	
Gum, sugar-free	
Jam or jelly, light	2 tsp
Syrup, sugar-free	2 tbsp

Drinks
Bouillon, broth, consommé*
Bouillon or broth, low-sodium
Carbonated or mineral water
Club soda
Cocoa powder, unsweetened . . . . 1 tbsp
Coffee
Diet soft drinks, sugar-free
Drink mixes, sugar-free
Tea
Tonic water, sugar-free

Condiments
Catsup	1 tbsp
Horseradish	
Lemon juice	
Lime juice	
Mustard	
Salsa	¼ cup
Soy sauce, regular or light*	1 tbsp
Taco sauce	1 tbsp
Vinegar	
Yogurt	2 tbsp

*= 400 mg or more sodium per choice.

Combination Foods List

Food	Serving Size	Exchanges per Serving
Entrées		
Tuna noodle casserole, lasagna, spaghetti with meatballs, chili with beans, macaroni and cheese*	1 cup (8 oz)	2 carbohydrates, 2 medium-fat meats
Tuna or chicken salad	½ cup (3½ oz)	½ carbohydrate, 2 lean meats, 1 fat
Frozen Entrées		
Dinner-type meal*	generally 14–17 oz	3 carbohydrates, 3 medium-fat meats, 3 fats
Meatless burger, soy based	3 oz	½ carbohydrate, 2 lean meats
Meatless burger, vegetable and starch based	3 oz	1 carbohydrate, 1 lean meat
Pizza, cheese, thin crust* (5 oz)	¼ of 12" (6 oz)	2 carbohydrates, 2 medium-fat meats
Pizza, meat topping, thin crust* (5 oz)	¼ of 12" (6 oz)	2 carbohydrates, 2 medium-fat meats, 1½ fats
Entrée with less than 340 calories*	about 8–11 oz	2–3 carbohydrates, 1–2 lean meats
Soups		
Bean*	1 cup	1 carbohydrate, 1 very lean meat
Cream (made with water)*	1 cup (8 oz)	1 carbohydrate, 1 fat
Split pea (made with water)*	½ cup (4 oz)	1 carbohydrate
Tomato (made with water)*	1 cup (8 oz)	1 carbohydrate
Vegetable beef, chicken noodle, or other broth-type*	1 cup (8 oz)	1 carbohydrate

*= 400 mg or more sodium per exchange.

Fast Foods List[a]

Food	Serving Size	Exchanges per Serving
Burrito with beef*	1 (5–7 oz)	3 carbohydrates, 1 medium-fat meat, 1 fat
Chicken nuggets*	6	1 carbohydrate, 2 medium-fat meats, 1 fat
Chicken breast and wing, breaded and fried*	1 each	1 carbohydrate, 4 medium-fat meats, 2 fats
Chicken sandwich, grilled*	1	2 carbohydrates, 3 very lean meats
Chicken wings, hot*	6 (5 oz)	1 carbohydrate, 3 medium-fat meats, 4 fats
Fish sandwich/tartar sauce*	1	3 carbohydrates, 1 medium-fat meat, 3 fats
French fries, thin	20–25	2 carbohydrates, 2 fats
Hamburger, regular	1	2 carbohydrates, 2 medium-fat meats
Hamburger, large*	1	2 carbohydrates, 3 medium-fat meats, 1 fat
Hot dog with bun*	1	1 carbohydrate, 1 high-fat meat, 1 fat
Individual pan pizza*	1	5 carbohydrates, 3 medium-fat meats, 3 fats
Pizza, cheese, thin crust*	¼ of 12" (about 6 oz)	2½ carbohydrates, 2 medium-fat meats, 1½ fats
Pizza, meat, thin crust*	¼ of 12" (about 6 oz)	2½ carbohydrates, 2 medium-fat meats, 2 fats
Soft serve cone	1 medium	2 carbohydrates, 1 fat
Submarine sandwich*	1 (6")	3 carbohydrates, 1 vegetable, 2 medium-fat meats, 1 fat
Taco, hard shell*	1 (6 oz)	2 carbohydrates, 2 medium-fat meats, 2 fats
Taco, soft shell*	1 (3 oz)	1 carbohydrate, 1 medium-fat meat, 1 fat

*= 400 mg or more sodium per exchange.
[a]Ask at your fast-food restaurant for nutrition information about your favorite fast foods or check Web sites.

The following charts show a possible distribution of exchanges for an individual consuming 2,000 calories. This set amount of exchanges can help you plan meals and snacks for a day, such as shown in the "One Day Sample Meal Plan."

Daily Meal Pattern

Targets:
Total kcal = 2,000/day

	Percent of Kcal	Amount in Grams
Carbohydrate	50–55	250–275
Protein	15–20	75–100
Fat	27–30	60–67

Exchange	Number of Exchanges	Protein (g)	Fat (g)	Carbohydrate (g)
Milk, low-fat	3	24	9	36
Fruit	4	0	0	60
Vegetable	6	12	0	30
Starch/Bread/Cereal	9	27	0	135
Meat, lean	6	42	18	0
Fat	6	0	30	0
Total		105	57	261
Total kcals	1,977	420	513	1,044
% kcals		21	26	53

Distributiuon of Exchanges at Meals and Snacks

Exchanges	Total Number	Breakfast	AM Snack	Lunch	PM Snack	Dinner	Night Snack
Milk	3	1	1	0	0	1	0
Fruit	4	1	1	1	0	0	1
Vegetable	6	0	0	2	1	3	0
Starch/Bread/ Cereal	9	2	1	2	2	2	0
Meat	6	0	0	3	0	3	0
Fat	6	2	0	2	1	1	0
Total	34	6	3	10	4	10	1
Total carbohydrate (g)	261	57	42	55	35	57	15
% Total Carb.		22	16	21	13	22	6

One Day Sample Meal Plan

Breakfast
1% milk
 (8 oz glass) . . . . . . 1 milk exchange
Honeydew melon
 (1 cup cubes) . . . . 1 fruit exchange
Whole-wheat English
 muffin (1) . . . . 2 starch exchanges
Peanut butter
 (1 tbsp) . . . . 2 fat exchanges

Morning Snack
Low-fat plain yogurt
 (6 oz) . . . . 1 milk exchange
Strawberries (1¼ cup whole
 berries) . . . . 1 fruit exchange
Low-fat granola
 (¼ cup) . . . . 1 starch exchange

Lunch
2 slices whole-wheat
 bread . . . . 2 starch exchanges
Canned light tuna
 (3 oz) . . . . 3 meat exchanges
Reduced-fat mayonnaise
 (1 tbsp) . . . . 1 fat exchange
Small tossed salad (1 c romain lettuce, 1 c raw
 veggies) . . . . 2 vegetable exchanges
Reduced-fat Italian dressing
 (2 tbsp) . . . . 1 fat exchange
Apple (1 small). . . . . 1 fruit exchange
Unsweetened
 ice tea. . . . . Free food

Afternoon Snack
Baby carrots
 (1 cup raw) . . . . . . 1 vegetable exchange
4 whole-wheat crackers,
 no fat added . . . . . 1 starch exchange
Hummus (⅓ cup) . . . 1 starch exchange
 1 fat exchange

Dinner
1% milk
 (8 oz glass) . . . . . . 1 milk exchange
3 oz grilled chicken
 breast . . . . 3 meat exchanges
⅔ c rice pilaf (prepared with reduced-fat
 butter) . . . . 2 starch exchanges
 1 fat exchange
¾ c steamed
 broccoli. . . . . 1½ vegetable exchanges
1½ c baby salad
 greens . . . . 1½ vegetable exchanges
Low-fat salad dressing
 (1 tbsp) . . . . Free food

Night Snack
Reduced-calorie cranberry juice
 cocktail (8 oz) . . . 1 fruit exchange

Appendix D Organizations and Resources

Academic Journals

International Journal of Sport Nutrition and Exercise Metabolism
Human Kinetics
P.O. Box 5076
Champaign, IL 61825-5076
(800) 747-4457
www.humankinetics.com/IJSNEM

Journal of Nutrition
A. Catharine Ross, Editor
Department of Nutrition
Pennsylvania State University
126-S Henderson Building
University Park, PA 16802-6504
(814) 865-4721
www.nutrition.org

Nutrition Research
Elsevier: Journals Customer Service
6277 Sea Harbor Drive
Orlando, FL 32887
(877) 839-7126
www.journals.elsevierhealth.com/periodicals/NTR

Nutrition
Elsevier: Journals Customer Service
6277 Sea Harbor Drive
Orlando, FL 32887
(877) 839-7126
www.journals.elsevierhealth.com/periodicals/NUT

Nutrition Reviews
International Life Sciences Institute
Subscription Office
P.O. Box 830430
Birmingham, AL 35283
(800) 633-4931
www.ingentaconnect.com/content/ilsi/nure

Obesity Research
North American Association for the Study of Obesity (NAASO)
8630 Fenton Street, Suite 918
Silver Spring, MD 20910
(301) 563-6526
www.obesityresearch.org

International Journal of Obesity
Journal of the International Association for the Study of Obesity
Nature Publishing Group
The Macmillan Building
4 Crinan Street
London N1 9XW
United Kingdom
www.nature.com/ijo

Journal of the American Medical Association
American Medical Association
P.O. Box 10946
Chicago, IL 60610-0946
(800) 262-2350
http://jama.ama-assn.org

New England Journal of Medicine
10 Shattuck Street
Boston, MA 02115-6094
(617) 734-9800
http://content.nejm.org/

American Journal of Clinical Nutrition
The American Journal of Clinical Nutrition
9650 Rockville Pike
Bethesda, MD 20814-3998
(301) 634-7038
www.ajcn.org

Journal of the American Dietetic Association
Elsevier: Health Sciences Division
Subscription Customer Service
6277 Sea Harbor Drive
Orlando, FL 32887
(800) 654-2452
www.adajournal.org

Aging

Administration on Aging
U.S. Health & Human Services
200 Independence Avenue, SW
Washington, DC 20201
(877) 696-6775
www.aoa.gov

American Association of Retired Persons (AARP)
601 E. Street, NW
Washington, DC 20049
(888) 687-2277
www.aarp.org

Health and Age
Sponsored by the Novartis Foundation for Gerontology & The Web-Based Health Education Foundation
Robert Griffith, MD
Executive Director
573 Vista de la Ciudad
Santa Fe, NM 87501
www.healthandage.com

National Council on the Aging
300 D Street, SW, Suite 801
Washington, DC 20024
(202) 479-1200
www.ncoa.org

International Osteoporosis Foundation
5 Rue Perdtemps
1260 Nyon
Switzerland
41 22 994 01 00
www.osteofound.org

National Institute on Aging
Building 31, Room 5C27
31 Center Drive, MSC 2292
Bethesda, MD 20892
(301) 496-1752
www.nia.nih.gov

Osteoporosis and Related Bone Diseases National Resource Center
2 AMS Circle
Bethesda, MD 20892-3676
(800) 624-BONE
www.osteo.org

American Geriatrics Society
The Empire State Building
350 Fifth Avenue, Suite 801
New York, NY 10118
(212) 308-1414
www.americangeriatrics.org

National Osteoporosis Foundation
1232 22nd Street, NW
Washington, DC 20037-1292
(202) 223-2226
www.nof.org/

Alcohol and Drug Abuse

National Institute on Drug Abuse
6001 Executive Boulevard, Room 5213
Bethesda, MD 20892-9561
(301) 443-1124
www.nida.nih.gov

National Institute on Alcohol Abuse and Alcoholism
5635 Fishers Lane, MSC 9304
Bethesda, MD 20892-9304
www.niaaa.nih.gov

Alcoholics Anonymous
Grand Central Station
P.O. Box 459
New York, NY 10163
www.alcoholics-anonymous.org

Narcotics Anonymous
P.O. Box 9999
Van Nuys, California 91409
(818) 773-9999
www.na.org

National Council on Alcoholism and Drug Dependence
20 Exchange Place, Suite 2902
New York, NY 10005
(212) 269-7797
www.ncadd.org

National Clearinghouse for Alcohol and Drug Information
11420 Rockville Pike
Rockville, MD 20852
(800) 729-6686
http://ncadi.samhsa.gov

Canadian Government

Health Canada
A.L. 0900C2
Ottawa, ON K1A 0K9
(613) 957-2991
www.hc-sc.gc.ca/english

National Institute of Nutrition
408 Queen Street, 3rd Floor
Ottawa, ON K1R 5A7
(613) 235-3355
www.nin.ca/public_html/index.html

Agricultural and Agri-Food Canada
Public Information Request Service
Sir John Carling Building
930 Carling Avenue
Ottawa, ON K1A 0C5
(613) 759-1000
www.arg.gc.ca

Bureau of Nutritional Sciences
Sir Frederick G. Banting Research Centre
Tunney's Pasture (2203A)
Ottawa, ON K1A 0L2
(613) 957-0352
www.hc-sc.gc.ca/food-aliment/ns-sc/e_nutrition.html

Canadian Food Inspection Agency
59 Camelot Drive
Ottawa, ON K1A 0Y9
(613) 225-2342
www.inspection.gc.ca/english/toce.shtml

Canadian Institute for Health Information
CIHI Ottawa
377 Dalhousie Street, Suite 200
Ottawa, ON K1N 9N8
(613) 241-7860
www.cihi.ca

Canadian Public Health Association
1565 Carling Avenue, Suite 400
Ottawa, ON K1Z 8R1
(613) 725-3769
www.cpha.ca

Canadian Nutrition and Professional Organizations

Dietitians of Canada, Canadian Dietetic Association
480 University Avenue, Suite 604
Toronto, ON M5G 1V2
(416) 596-0857
www.dietitians.ca

Canadian Diabetes Association
National Life Building
1400-522 University Avenue
Toronto, ON M5G 2R5
(800) 226-8464
www.diabetes.ca

National Eating Disorder Information Centre
CW 1-211, 200 Elizabeth Street
Toronto, ON M5G 2C4
(866) NEDIC-20
www.nedic.ca

Canadian Pediatric Society
100-2204 Walkley Road
Ottawa, ON K1G 4G8
(613) 526-9397
www.cps.ca

Disordered Eating/ Eating Disorders

American Psychiatric Association
1000 Wilson Boulevard, Suite 1825
Arlington, VA 22209
(703) 907-7300
www.psych.org

Harvard Eating Disorders Center
WACC 725
15 Parkman Street
Boston, MA 02114
(617) 236-7766
www.hedc.org

National Institute of Mental Health
Office of Communications
6001 Executive Boulevard, Room 8184, MSC 9663
Bethesda, MD 20892
(866) 615-6464
www.nimh.nih.gov

National Association of Anorexia Nervosa and Associated Disorders (ANAD)
P.O. Box 7
Highland Park, IL 60035
(847) 831-3438
www.anad.org

National Eating Disorders Association
603 Stewart Street, Suite 803
Seattle, WA 98101
(206) 382-3587
www.nationaleatingdisorders.org

Eating Disorder Referral and Information Center
2923 Sandy Pointe, Suite 6
Del Mar, CA 92014
(858) 792-7463
www.edreferral.com

Anorexia Nervosa and Related Eating Disorders, Inc. (ANRED)
E-mail: jarinor@rio.com
www.anred.com

Overeaters Anonymous
P.O. Box 44020
Rio Rancho, NM 87174
(505) 891-2664
www.oa.org

Exercise, Physical Activity, and Sports

American College of Sports Medicine (ACSM)
P.O. Box 1440
Indianapolis, IN 46206-1440
(317) 637-9200
www.acsm.org

American Physical Therapy Association (APTA)
1111 North Fairfax Street
Alexandria, VA 22314
(800) 999-APTA
www.apta.org

Gatorade Sports Science Institute (GSSI)
617 West Main Street
Barrington, IL 60010
(800) 616-GSSI
www.gssiweb.com

National Coalition for Promoting Physical Activity (NCPPA)
1010 Massachusetts Avenue, Suite 350
Washington, DC 20001
(202) 454-7518
www.ncppa.org

Sports, Wellness, Eating Disorder and Cardiovascular Nutritionists (SCAN)
P.O. Box 60820
Colorado Springs, CO 80960
(719) 635-6005
www.scandpg.org

President's Council on Physical Fitness and Sports
Department W
200 Independence Avenue, SW
Room 738-H
Washington, DC 20201-0004
(202) 690-9000
www.fitness.gov

American Council on Exercise
4851 Paramount Drive
San Diego, CA 92123
(858) 279-8227
www.acefitness.org

The International Association for Fitness Professionals (IDEA)
10455 Pacific Center Court
San Diego, CA 92121
(800) 999-4332, ext. 7
www.ideafit.com

Food Safety

Food Marketing Institute
655 15th Street, NW
Washington, DC 20005
(202) 452-8444
www.fmi.org

Agency for Toxic Substances and Disease Registry (ATSDR)
ORO Washington Office
Ariel Rios Building
1200 Pennsylvania Avenue, NW
M/C 5204G
Washington, DC 20460
(888) 422-8737
www.atsdr.cdc.gov

Food Allergy and Anaphylaxis Network
11781 Lee Jackson Highway, Suite 160
Fairfax, VA 22033-3309
(800) 929-4040
www.foodallergy.org

Foodsafety.gov
www.foodsafety.gov

The USDA Food Safety and Inspection Service
Food Safety and Inspection Service
United States Department of Agriculture
Washington, DC 20250
www.fsis.usda.gov

Consumer Reports
Web Site Customer Relations Department
101 Truman Avenue
Yonkers, NY 10703
www.consumerreports.org

Center for Science in the Public Interest: Food Safety
1875 Connecticut Avenue, NW
Washington, DC 20009
(202) 332-9110
www.cspinet.org/foodsafety/index.html

Center for Food Safety and Applied Nutrition
5100 Paint Branch Parkway
College Park, MD 20740
(888) SAFEFOOD
www.cfsan.fda.gov

Food Safety Project
Dan Henroid, MS, RD, CFSP
HRIM Extension Specialist and Website Coordinator
Hotel, Restaurant and Institution Management
9e MacKay Hall
Iowa State University
Ames, IA 50011
(515) 294-3527
www.extension.iastate.edu/foodsafety

Organic Consumers Association
6101 Cliff Estate Road
Little Marais, MN 55614
(218) 226-4164
www.organicconsumers.org

Infancy and Childhood

Administration for Children and Families
370 L'Enfant Promenade, SW
Washington, DC 20447
www.acf.dhhs.gov

The American Academy of Pediatrics
141 Northwest Point Boulevard
Elk Grove Village, IL 60007
(847) 434-4000
www.aap.org

Kidshealth: The Nemours Foundation
1600 Rockland Road
Wilmington, DE 19803
(302) 651-4046
www.kidshealth.org

National Center for Education in Maternal and Child Health
Georgetown University
Box 571272
Washington, DC 20057
(202) 784-9770
www.ncemch.org

Birth Defects Research for Children, Inc.
930 Woodcock Road, Suite 225
Orlando, FL 32803
(407) 895-0802
www.birthdefects.org

USDA/ARS Children's Nutrition Research Center at Baylor College of Medicine
1100 Bates Street
Houston, TX 77030
www.kidsnutrition.org

Centers for Disease Control—Healthy Youth
www.cdc.gov/healthyyouth

International Agencies

UNICEF
3 United Nations Plaza
New York, NY 10017
(212) 326-7000
www.unicef.org

World Health Organization
Avenue Appia 20
1211 Geneva 27
Switzerland
41 22 791 21 11
www.who.int/en

The Stockholm Convention on Persistent Organic Pollutants
11–13 Chemin des Anémones
1219 Châtelaine
Geneva, Switzerland
41 22 917 8191
www.pops.int

Food and Agricultural Organization of the United Nations
Viale delle Terme di Caracalla
00100 Rome, Italy
39 06 57051
www.fao.org

International Food Information Council
1100 Connecticut Avenue, NW
Suite 430
Washington, DC 20036
(202) 296-6540
www.ific.org

Pregnancy and Lactation

San Diego County Breastfeeding Coalition
c/o Children's Hospital and Health Center
3020 Children's Way, MC 5073
San Diego, CA 92123
(800) 371-MILK
www.breastfeeding.org

National Alliance for Breastfeeding Advocacy
Barbara Heiser, Executive Director
9684 Oak Hill Drive
Ellicott City, MD 21042-6321
OR
Marsha Walker, Executive Director
254 Conant Road
Weston, MA 02493-1756
www.naba-breastfeeding.org

American College of Obstetricians and Gynecologists
409 12th Street, SW, P.O. Box 96920
Washington, DC 20090
www.acog.org

La Leche League
1400 N. Meacham Road
Schaumburg, IL 60173
(847) 519-7730
www.lalecheleague.org

National Organization on Fetal Alcohol Syndrome
900 17th Street, NW
Suite 910
Washington, DC 20006
(800) 66 NOFAS
www.nofas.org

March of Dimes Birth Defects Foundation
1275 Mamaroneck Avenue
White Plains, NY 10605
(888) 663-4637
http://modimes.org

Professional Nutrition Organizations

North American Association for the Study of Obesity (NAASO)
8630 Fenton Street, Suite 918
Silver Spring, MD 20910
(301) 563-6526
www.naaso.org

American Dental Association
211 East Chicago Avenue
Chicago, IL 60611-2678
(312) 440-2500
www.ada.org

American Heart Association
National Center
7272 Greenville Avenue
Dallas, TX 75231
(800) 242-8721
www.americanheart.org

American Dietetic Association (ADA)
120 South Riverside Plaza, Suite 2000
Chicago, IL 60606-6995
(800) 877-1600
www.eatright.org

The American Society for Nutrition (ASN)
9650 Rockville Pike, Suite L-4500
Bethesda, MD 20814-3998
(301) 634-7050
www.nutrition.org

The Society for Nutrition Education
7150 Winton Drive, Suite 300
Indianapolis, IN 46268
(800) 235-6690
www.sne.org

American College of Nutrition
300 S. Duncan Avenue, Suite 225
Clearwater, FL 33755
(727) 446-6086
www.amcollnutr.org

American Obesity Association
1250 24th Street, NW, Suite 300
Washington, DC 20037
(800) 98-OBESE
www.obesity.org

American Council on Science and Health
1995 Broadway
Second Floor
New York, NY 10023
(212) 362-7044
www.acsh.org

American Diabetes Association
ATTN: National Call Center
1701 North Beauregard Street
Alexandria, VA 22311
(800) 342-2383
www.diabetes.org

Institute of Food Technologies
525 W. Van Buren, Suite 1000
Chicago, IL 60607
(312) 782-8424
www.ift.org

ILSI Human Nutrition Institute
One Thomas Circle, Ninth Floor
Washington, DC 20005
(202) 659-0524
http://hni.ilsi.org

Trade Organizations

American Meat Institute
1700 North Moore Street
Suite 1600
Arlington, VA 22209
(703) 841-2400
www.meatami.com

National Dairy Council
10255 W. Higgins Road, Suite 900
Rosemont, IL 60018
(312) 240-2880
www.nationaldairycouncil.org

United Fresh Fruit and Vegetable Association
1901 Pennsylvania Ave., NW, Suite 1100
Washington, DC 20006
(202) 303-3400
www.uffva.org

U.S.A. Rice Federation
4301 North Fairfax Drive, Suite 425
Arlington, VA 22203
(703) 236-2300
www.usarice.com

U.S. Government

The USDA National Organic Program
Agricultural Marketing Service
USDA-AMS-TMP-NOP
Room 4008-South Building
1400 Independence Avenue, SW
Washington, DC 20250-0020
(202) 720-3252
www.ams.usda.gov

U.S. Department of Health and Human Services
200 Independence Avenue, SW
Washington, DC 20201
(877) 696-6775
www.hhs.gov

Food and Drug Administration (FDA)
5600 Fishers Lane
Rockville, MD 20857
(888) 463-6332
www.fda.gov

Environmental Protection Agency
Ariel Rios Building
1200 Pennsylvania Avenue, NW
Washington, DC 20460
(202) 272-0167
www.epa.gov

Federal Trade Commission
600 Pennsylvania Avenue, NW
Washington, DC 20580
(202) 326-2222
www.ftc.gov

Partnership for Healthy Weight Management
www.consumer.gov/weightloss

Office of Dietary Supplements
National Institutes of Health
6100 Executive Boulevard, Room 3B01, MSC 7517
Bethesda, MD 20892
(301) 435-2920
http://dietary-supplements.info.nih.gov

Nutrient Data Laboratory Homepage
Beltsville Human Nutrition Center
10300 Baltimore Avenue
Building 307-C, Room 117
BARC-East
Beltsville, MD 20705
(301) 504-8157
www.nal.usda.gov/fnic/foodcomp

National Digestive Disease Clearinghouse
2 Information Way
Bethesda, MD 20892-3570
(800) 891-5389
http://digestive.niddk.nih.gov

The National Cancer Institute
NCI Public Inquiries Office
Suite 3036A
6116 Executive Boulevard, MSC 8322
Bethesda, MD 20892-8322
(800) 4-CANCER
www.cancer.gov

The National Eye Institute
31 Center Drive, MSC 2510
Bethesda, MD 20892-2510
(301) 496-5248
www.nei.nih.gov

The National Heart, Lung, and Blood Institute
Building 31, Room 5A52
31 Center Drive, MSC 2486
Bethesda, MD 20892
(301) 592-8573
www.nhlbi.nih.gov/index.htm

Institute of Diabetes and Digestive and Kidney Diseases
Office of Communications and Public Liaison
NIDDK, NIH, Building 31, Room 9A04
Center Drive, MSC 2560
Bethesda, MD 20892
(301) 496-4000
www.niddk.nih.gov

National Center for Complementary and Alternative Medicine
NCCAM Clearinghouse
P.O. Box 7923
Gaithersburg, MD 20898
(888) 644-6226
http://nccam.nih.gov

U.S. Department of Agriculture (USDA)
1400 Independence Avenue, SW
Washington, DC 20250
(202) 720-2791
www.usda.gov

Centers for Disease Control and Prevention (CDC)
1600 Clifton Road
Atlanta, GA 30333
(404) 639-3311 / Public Inquiries: (800) 311-3435
www.cdc.gov

National Institutes of Health (NIH)
9000 Rockville Pike
Bethesda, MD 20892
(301) 496-4000
www.nih.gov

Food and Nutrition Information Center
Agricultural Research Service, USDA
National Agricultural Library, Room 105
10301 Baltimore Avenue
Beltsville, MD 20705-2351
(301) 504-5719
www.nal.usda.gov/fnic

National Institute of Allergy and Infectious Diseases
NIAID Office of Communications and Public Liaison
6610 Rockledge Drive, MSC 6612
Bethesda, MD 20892
(301) 496-5717
www.niaid.nih.gov

Weight and Health Management

The Vegetarian Resource Group
P.O. Box 1463, Dept. IN
Baltimore, MD 21203
(410) 366-VEGE
www.vrg.org

American Obesity Association
1250 24th Street, NW
Suite 300
Washington, DC 20037
(202) 776-7711
www.obesity.org

Anemia Lifeline
(888) 722-4407
www.anemia.com

The Arc
(301) 565-3842
E-mail: info@thearc.org
www.thearc.org

Bottled Water Web
P.O. Box 5658
Santa Barbara, CA 93150
(805) 879-1564
www.bottledwaterweb.com

The Food and Nutrition Board
Institute of Medicine
500 Fifth Street, NW
Washington, DC 20001
(202) 334-2352
www.iom.edu/board.asp?id-3788

The Calorie Control Council
www.caloriecontrol.org

TOPS (Take Off Pounds Sensibly)
4575 South Fifth Street
P.O. Box 07360
Milwaukee, WI 53207
(800) 932-8677
www.tops.org

Shape Up America!
15009 Native Dancer Road
N. Potomac, MD 20878
(240) 631-6533
www.shapeup.org

World Hunger

Center on Hunger, Poverty, and Nutrition Policy
Tufts University
Medford, MA 02155
(617) 627-3020
www.tufts.edu/nutrition

Freedom from Hunger
1644 DaVinci Court
Davis, CA 95616
(800) 708-2555
www.freefromhunger.org

Oxfam International
1112 16th Street, NW, Suite 600
Washington, DC 20036
(202) 496-1170
www.oxfam.org

WorldWatch Institute
1776 Massachusetts Avenue, NW
Washington, DC 20036
(202) 452-1999
www.worldwatch.org

The Hunger Project
15 East 26th Street
New York, NY 10010
(212) 251-9100
www.thp.org

U.S. Agency for International Development
Information Center
Ronald Reagan Building
Washington, DC 20523
(202) 712-0000
www.usaid.gov

America's Second Harvest
35 E. Wacker Drive #2000
Chicago, IL 60601
www.secondharvest.org

Glossary

A

α-tocopherol See alpha-tocopherol.

absorption The process by which digested nutrients move into the tissues where they can be transported and used by the body's cells.

Acceptable Macronutrient Distribution Range (AMDR) A healthy range of intakes for the energy-containing nutrients—carbohydrates, proteins, and fats—in your diet designed to meet your nutrient needs and help reduce the risk of chronic diseases.

acceptable tolerance levels The maximum amount of pesticide residue that is allowed in or on foods.

acetaldehyde An intermediary by-product of the breakdown of ethanol in the liver.

acid group The COOH group that is part of every amino acid.

acromegaly A condition caused by excess growth hormone in which tissues, bones, and internal organs grow abnormally large.

acute dehydration Dehydration starting after a short period of time.

added sugars Sugars that are added to processed foods and sweets.

adenosine triphosphate (ATP) A compound that is broken down to produce energy for working muscles and other tissues.

Adequate Intake (AI) The *approximate* amount of a nutrient that groups of similar individuals are consuming to maintain good health.

ADH See antidiuretic hormone.

ADHD See attention deficit hyperactivity disorder.

adolescence The developmental period between childhood and early adulthood.

aerobic With oxygen.

age-related macular degeneration (AMD) A disease that affects the macula of the retina, causing blurry vision.

AI See Adequate Intake.

alcohol A chemical class of substances that contain ethanol, methanol, and isopropanol. Ethanol is often referred to as "alcohol."

alcohol abuse The continuation of alcohol consumption even though this behavior has created social, legal, and/or health problems.

alcohol dehydrogenase One of the alcohol-metabolizing enzymes in the body.

alcohol dependence See alcoholism.

alcohol hepatitis Stage 2 of alcohol liver disease; due to chronic inflammation.

alcohol liver disease A degenerative liver condition that occurs in three stages: (1) fatty liver, (2) alcohol hepatitis, and (3) cirrhosis.

alcohol poisoning When the BAC rises to such an extreme level that a person's central nervous system is affected and his or her breathing and heart rate are interrupted.

alcohol tolerance When the body adjusts to long-term alcohol use by becoming less sensitive to the alcohol. More alcohol needs to be consumed in order to get the same effect.

alcoholism Also referred to as **alcohol dependence,** a chronic disease with genetic, psychological, and environmental components. Alcoholics crave alcohol, can't control their intake, and develop a higher tolerance for it. Alcoholics also exhibit a dependency on alcohol, as abstaining from drinking will cause withdrawal symptoms.

alpha-linolenic acid A polyunsaturated essential fatty acid; part of the omega-3 fatty acid family.

alpha-tocopherol (α-tocopherol) The most active form of vitamin E.

Alzheimer's disease A type of dementia.

AMD See age-related macular degeneration.

AMDR See Acceptable Macronutrient Distribution Range.

amenorrhea Absence of menstruation.

amine group The nitrogen-containing part (NH_2) of an amino acid.

amino acid pools A limited supply of amino acids stored in your blood and cells and used to build new proteins.

amino acid profile The composition of amino acids in a protein.

amino acids The building blocks of protein. Amino acids contain carbon, hydrogen, oxygen, and nitrogen. All amino acids are composed of an acid group, an amine group, and a unique side chain.

anacephaly A type of birth defect caused by the improper developing of the neural tube, which forms a baby's spine, brain and skull.

anaerobic Without oxygen.

anaphylactic reactions Severe, life-threatening reactions that cause constriction of the airways in the lungs, which inhibits the ability to breathe.

anemia A condition caused by low levels of red blood cells and hemoglobin, the oxygen-carrying protein compound in the blood. Fatigue is often a symptom of anemia.

antibiotic-resistant bacteria Bacteria that have developed a resistance to an antibiotic such that they are no longer affected by antibiotic medication.

antibiotics Drugs that kill or slow the growth of bacteria.

antibodies Proteins made by your body to bind to and neutralize foreign invaders, such as harmful bacteria, fungi, and viruses, as part of the body's immune response.

anticoagulant A substance that can interfere with blood clotting

antidiuretic hormone (ADH) A hormone that directs the kidneys to concentrate and reduce the volume of urine produced in order to reduce water loss from the body.

antimicrobials Substances or a combination of substances, such as disinfectants and sanitizers, that control the spread of bacteria and viruses on nonliving surfaces or objects.

antioxidants Substances that neutralize harmful oxygen-containing free radicals that can cause cell damage. Vitamins A, C, and E and beta-carotene are antioxidants.

anus See rectum.

appetite The psychological desire to eat or drink.

arthritis Inflammation in the joints that can cause pain, stiffness, and swelling in joints, muscles, tendons, ligaments, and bones.

ascorbic acid Another term for water-soluble, **vitamin C.**

atherosclerosis Narrowing of the coronary arteries due to buildup of debris along the artery walls.

ATP See adenosine triphosphate.

attention deficit hyperactivity disorder (ADHD) (previously known as attention deficit disorder (ADD)). A condition in which an individual may be easily distracted, have difficulty listening and following directions, difficulty focusing and sustaining attention, difficulty concentrating and staying on task, and/or inconsistent performance in school.

B

baby bottle tooth decay The decay of baby teeth in children due to continual exposure to fermentable sugary liquids.

BAC See blood alcohol concentration.

basal metabolism The amount of energy the body expends to meet its basic physiological needs. Also referred to as **basal metabolism rate (BMR).**

basal metabolism rate (BMR) See basal metabolism.

behavior modification Changing behaviors to improve health. Identifying and altering eating patterns that contribute to weight gain or impede weight loss is behavior modification.

beriberi A condition caused by a deficiency of thiamin that can cause confusion, loss of muscle, and nerve damage.

bile A greenish yellow fluid made in the liver and concentrated and stored in the gallbladder. It helps emulsify fat and prepare it for digestion.

binge drinking The consumption of 5 or more alcoholic drinks by men, or 4 or more drinks by women, in a very short time.

bioaccumulate When a substance or chemical builds up in an organism over time, so that the concentration of the chemical is higher than would be found naturally in the environment.

bioavailability The degree to which a nutrient from foods is available for absorption by the body.

biopesticides Substances derived from natural materials such as animals, plants, bacteria, and certain minerals to control pests.

biotechnology The application of biological techniques to living cells, which alters their genetic makeup.

bioterrorism The use of a biological or chemical agent to frighten, threaten, coerce, injure, and/or kill individuals.

blackouts Periods of time when an intoxicated person cannot recall part or all of an event.

bleaching The breakdown of the rhodopsin and iodopsin due to its absorption of light.

blood alcohol concentration (BAC) The measurement of the amount of alcohol in your blood. BAC is measured in grams of alcohol per deciliter of blood, usually expressed as a percentage.

BMD See bone mineral density.

BMI See body mass index.

BMR See basal metabolism rate.

body composition The relative proportion of muscle, fat, water, and other tissues in the body.

body mass index (BMI) A calculation of your weight in relationship to your height. A BMI between 18.5 and 24.9 is considered healthy.

bolus Chewed mass of food.

bone mineral density (BMD) The amount of minerals, in particular calcium, per volume in an individual's bone. The denser the bones, the stronger the bones.

botanicals A part of a plant, such as its root, that is believed to have medicinal or therapeutic attributes. Herbs are considered botanicals.

botulism A rare but serious paralytic illness caused by the bacterium *Clostridium botulinum*. Infant botulism is caused by consuming the spores of the bacteria, which then grow in the intestines and release toxin. It can be fatal.

bovine spongiform encephalopathy (BSE) A slow, degenerative, and deadly disease that attacks the central nervous system of cattle. Also known as **mad cow disease.**

breast-feeding The act of feeding an infant or child milk from a woman's breast.

BSE See bovine spongiform encephalopathy.

buffers Substances that help maintain the proper pH in a solution by attracting or donating hydrogen ions.

C

canning The process of heating food to a temperature high enough to kill bacteria and then packing the food in airtight containers.

carbohydrate loading A diet and training strategy that maximizes glycogen stores in the body before an endurance event.

carcinogenic A substance thought to cause cancer.

cardiorespiratory endurance The body's ability to sustain prolonged exercise.

carnitine A vitamin-like substance needed to properly utilize fat.

carotenodermia A discoloring of the skin due to an excessive amount of the yellow-reddish carotenoids stored in fat tissues.

carpal tunnel syndrome A painful condition caused by an irritated nerve that extends down the arm into the hand; numbness can occur.

catalysts Substances that aid and speed up reactions in your body without being changed, damaged, or used up in the process.

cataract A common eye disorder that occurs when the lens of the eye becomes cloudy.

celiac disease An illness of the small intestine that involves the inability to digest the protein gluten.

cell differentiation The process that distinguishes a cell's features and determines what type of cell it ultimately becomes in your body.

cellulite A non-medical term that refers to fat cells under the skin that give it a ripplelike appearance. Contrary to popular belief, cellulite is no different from other fat in the body.

central obesity An excess storage of visceral fat in the abdominal area, which increases the risk of heart disease, diabetes, and hypertension.

chemical digestion Breaking down food with enzymes or digestive juices.

childhood obesity The condition of a child's having too much body weight for his height. Rates of childhood obesity in the United States are increasing.

chlorophyll The green pigment in plants that absorbs energy from sunlight to begin the process of photosynthesis.

cholecystokinin A hormone released when the stomach is distended. It is associated with the feeling of satiation.

choline A vitamin-like substance needed for healthy cells and nerves.

chronic dehydration Dehydration over a long period of time.

chylomicron A type of lipoprotein that carries digested fat and other lipids through the lymph system into the blood.

chyme A liquid combination of partially digested food, water, HCl, and digestive enzymes.

ciguatera poisoning A condition caused by marine toxins produced by **dinoflagellates** (microscopic sea organisms). Small fish eat dinoflagellates and larger fish consume the small fish. The toxins then bioaccumulate in the fish.

cirrhosis Stage 3 of alcohol liver disease in which liver cells die, causing severe scarring.

closed or **"coded" dating** Refers to the packing numbers that are decodable only by manufacturers and are often found on nonperishable, shelf-stable foods.

clotting factors Substances in the blood that cause your blood to clot. Vitamin K helps synthesize some of these factors.

coagulation The thickening of a liquid into a solid mass; clotting.

coenzymes Substances needed by enzymes to perform many chemical reactions in your body. Many vitamins act as coenzymes.

collagen A ropelike, fibrous protein that is the most abundant protein in your body.

colostrum The fluid that is expressed from the mother's breast after birth and before the development of breast milk.

complemented proteins Incomplete proteins that are combined with modest amounts of animal or soy proteins or with other plant proteins that are rich in the limiting amino acids to create a complete protein.

complete protein A protein that provides all the essential amino acids that your body needs, along with some nonessential amino acids. Soy protein and protein from animal sources, in general, are complete.

complex carbohydrates A category of carbohydrates that contain many sugar units combined. A polysaccharide is a complex carbohydrate.

conception The moment when a sperm fertilizes an egg.

cones The light absorbing cells, along with rods, in the retina that contain the photopigment or protein, iodopsin.

congeners Compounds in alcohol that enhance the taste but may contribute to hangover symptoms.

congregate meals Meals served at churches, synagogues, or other community sites where older adults can receive a nutritious meal and socialize.

connective tissues The most abundant tissue in the body. Made up primarily of collagen, it supports and connects body parts as well as providing protection and insulation.

consensus The opinion of a group of experts based on a collection of information.

constipation Difficulty in passing stools.

control group The group given a placebo.

creatine phosphate A compound stored in the muscles that is broken down to replenish ATP stores.

Cretinism (congenital hypothyroidism) A condition caused by a severe iodine deficiency and hypothyroidism resulting in abnormal sexual development, mental retardation, and dwarfism.

cross contaminate The transfer of pathogens from a food, utensil, cutting board, kitchen surface, and/or hands to another food.

D

Daily Values (DVs) Ballpark reference levels used only on the food label.

danger zone The range of temperatures between 40°F and 140°F at which foodborne bacteria will multiply most rapidly. Room temperature falls within the danger zone.

dehydration Loss of water in the body as a result of inadequate fluid intake or excess fluid loss, such as through sweating.

dementia A disorder of the brain that interferes with a person's memory, learning, and mental stability.

denatured The alteration of a protein's shape, which changes the structure and function of the protein.

dental caries The decay or erosion of your teeth.

deoxyribonucleic acid (DNA) Contains the genetic instructions needed to develop and direct the activities of your body.

dermatitis Inflammation or irritation of the skin

developed country Advanced in industrial capability, technological sophistication, and economic productivity.

developing country Having a relatively low level of industrial capability, technological sophistication, or economic productivity.

DFE See dietary folate equivalents.

DHA See docosahexaenoic acid.

diabetes mellitus A medical condition whereby an individual either doesn't have enough insulin or is resistant to the insulin available. This will cause the blood glucose level to rise. Diabetes mellitus is often called diabetes.

diarrhea Frequent, loose, watery stools.

diastolic pressure The pressure of your blood against the artery walls when the heart is at rest between beats.

dietary fiber Nondigestible polysaccharides found in foods.

dietary folate equivalents (DFE) The adjusted amount of folate in a food after correcting for the higher absorbability of folic acid compared to folate.

Dietary Guidelines for Americans 2005 Guidelines published in 2005 that provide dietary and lifestyle advice to healthy individuals over the age of 2 to maintain good health and prevent chronic diseases.

Dietary Reference Intakes (DRIs) Reference values for the essential nutrients needed to maintain good health, to prevent chronic diseases, and to avoid unhealthy excesses.

digestibility A food's capacity to be broken down so that it can be absorbed.

digestive process The breakdown of foods into absorbable components using mechanical and chemical means.

diglyceride A glycerol with only two attached fatty acids.

dinoflagellates See ciguatera poisoning.

dipepide Two bonded amino acids.

disaccharides Two sugar units combined. There are three disaccharides: sucrose, lactose, and maltose.

discretionary calorie allowance Calories left over in the diet once all nutrient needs have been met from the basic food groups.

disordered eating Abnormal and potentially harmful eating behaviors that do not meet specific criteria for anorexia nervosa or bulimia nervosa.

distillation The evaporation and then collection of a liquid by condensation. Liquors are made using distillation.

diuretics Substances such as alcohol and some medications that cause the body to lose water.

diverticula Small bulges at weak spots in the colon wall.

diverticulitis Infection of the diverticula.

diverticulosis The existence of diverticula in the lining of your intestine.

DNA fingerprinting A technique in which bacterial DNA "gene patterns" (or "fingerprints") are detected and analyzed to distinguish between different strains of a bacterium.

DNA (deoxyribonucleic acid) The blueprint in cells that stores all genetic information. DNA remains in the nucleus of the cell and directs the synthesis of proteins.

double-blind placebo-controlled study When the scientists in a research experiment can't distinguish between the treatment given to the subjects and don't know which group of subjects received which treatment.

DRIs See Dietary Reference Intakes.

duration The length of time of performing an activity.

DVs See Daily Values.

dysphagia Difficult swallowing.

E

EAR See Estimated Average Requirement.

eating disorders The term used to describe psychological illnesses that involve specific abnormal eating behaviors: anorexia nervosa (self-starvation) and bulimia nervosa (bingeing and purging).

eclampsia See pregnancy-induced hpertension.

edema The accumulation of excess water in the spaces surrounding your cells, which causes swelling of the body tissue.

EER See estimated energy requirement.

eicosanoids Hormonelike substances in the body. Prostaglandins, thromboxanes, and leukotrienes are all eicosanoids.

eicosapentaenoic acid (EPA) and **docosahexaenoic acid (DHA)** Two omega-3 fatty acids that are heart healthy. Fatty fish such as salmon are good sources.

electrolytes Charged ions that conduct an electrical current in a solvent such as water. Sodium, potassium, and chloride are examples of electrolytes in the body. Vomiting and diarrhea cause the loss of electrolytes from your body.

electron The negatively charged particles in an atom, which is the smallest unit of all matter. Electrons determine how atoms interact with one another.

embryo Term that refers to a fertilized egg during the third through the eighth week of pregnancy. After the eighth week, the developing baby is called a fetus.

emergency kitchen A kitchen or a commercial food service that prepares for natural disasters, emergencies, or terrorist attacks.

empty calories Calories that come with little nutrition. Jelly beans are an example of a food that provides lots of calories from sugar but few nutrients.

emulsifier A compound that keeps two incompatible substances, such as oil and water, mixed together.

endotoxin A damaging product produced by intestinal bacteria that travels in the blood to the liver and initiates the release of cytokines that damage liver cells, leading to scarring.

energy balance The state at which energy (calorie) intake and energy (calorie) output in the body are equal.

energy gap The difference between the number of calories needed to maintain weight before and after weight loss.

enzymes Substances that produce chemical changes or catalyze chemical reactions.

EPA See eicosapentaenoic acid.

epidemiological research Research that looks at populations of people; it is often observational.

epiglottis Flap of tissue that protects the trachea while swallowing.

epiphyseal plate The growth plate of the bone. In puberty, growth in this area leads to increases in height.

ergogenic aid A substance, such as a dietary supplement, used to enhance athletic performance.

esophagus Tube that extends from the throat to the stomach.

essential amino acids The 9 amino acids that the body cannot synthesize; they must be obtained through dietary sources.

essential fatty acids The two polyunsaturated fatty acids that the body cannot make and therefore must be eaten in foods: linoleic acid and alpha-linolenic acid.

Estimated Average Requirement (EAR) The average amount of a nutrient that is known to meet the needs of 50 percent of the individuals in a similar age and gender group.

estimated energy requirement (EER) The average calorie intake that is estimated to maintain energy balance based on a person's gender, age, height, body weight, and level of physical activity.

estrogen The hormone responsible for female sex characteristics.

ethanol The type of alcohol in alcoholic beverages such as wine, beer, and liquor.

Exchange Lists for Meal Planning A grouping of foods, in specific portions, according to their carbohydrate, protein, and fat composition to ensure that each food in the group contributes a similar amount of calories per serving.

exercise Any type of structured or planned physical activity.

experimental group The group given a specific treatment.

experimental research Research involving at least two groups of subjects.

extracellular fluid compartment The fluid located outside your cells. Interstitial fluids and fluids in the blood are extracellular fluids.

extreme obesity Having a BMI > 40.

F

famine A severe shortage of food caused by crop destruction due to weather problems or poor agricultural practices so that the food supply is destroyed or severely diminished. This can also be caused by pestilence and/or war.

farm-to-table continuum Illustrates the roles that farmers, food manufacturers, food transporters, retailers, and consumers play in ensuring that the food supply, from the farm to the plate, remains safe.

FASDs See fetal alcohol spectrum disorders.

fat See triglyceride.

fat substitutes Substances that replace added fat in foods by providing the creamy properties of fat for fewer calories and fewer total fat grams.

fatty acid The most basic unit of triglyercides and phospholipids.

fatty liver Stage 1 of alcohol liver disease.

fecal-to-oral transmission The spread of pathogens by putting something in the mouth that has been in contact with infected stool. Poor hygiene, such as not washing hands after using the bathroom, can be a cause of this contamination.

feces See stool.

fermentation The process by which yeast converts sugars in grains or fruits into ethanol and carbon dioxide, resulting in an alcoholic beverage.

fetal alcohol spectrum disorders (FASDs) A range of conditions that can occur in children who are exposed to alcohol in utero. Fetal alcohol syndrome (FAS) is the most severe of the FASDs; children with FAS will display physical, mental, and behavioral abnormalities.

fetus A developing embryo that is at least eight weeks old.

fiber The portion of plant foods that isn't digested in the small intestine.

flavonoids A food pigment that acts as an antioxidant in many fruits, vegetables, tea, and wine that may help reduce the risk of chronic diseases.

flexibility The joints' ability to move freely through a full and normal range of motion.

fluid balance The equal distribution of water throughout your body and within and between cells.

fluorosis A condition whereby the teeth become mottled (pitted) and develop white patches or stains on the surface due to excessive consumption of fluoride.

flushing A reddish coloring of the face, arms, and chest that can result from consuming too much niacin.

folate A B vitamin that is also called folic acid.

folic acid A B vitamin that is also called folate.

food additives Substances added to food that affect its quality, flavor, freshness, and/or safety.

food allergens Proteins that are not broken down by cooking or digestion and enter the body intact, causing an adverse reaction by the immune system.

food allergy An abnormal reaction by the immune system to a particular food.

food biosecurity Protecting the food supply from bioterrorist attacks.

food guidance systems Visual diagrams that provide a variety of food recommendations to help a person create a well-balanced diet.

food insecurity The inability to satisfy basic food needs due to lack of financial resources or other problems.

food intolerance Adverse reaction to a food that does not involve an immune response. Lactose intolerance is one example.

food jags When a child will only eat the same food meal after meal.

food pantry Community food assistance locations where food is provided to needy individuals and families.

food preservation The treatment of foods to reduce deterioration and spoilage, and help prevent the multiplication of pathogens that can cause foodborne illness.

food safety Guidelines and procedures that help keep foods free from contaminants and safe to eat.

Food Safety Initiative (FSI) Coordinates the research, surveillance, inspection, outbreak response, and educational activities of the various government agencies that work together to safeguard food.

food tampering The deliberate contamination of a food to cause harm.

foodborne illness Sickness caused by consuming contaminated food or beverages. Also known as foodborne disease or food poisoning.

fortified foods Foods with added nutrients.

free radicals Unstable oxygen-containing molecules that can damage the cells of the body and possibly contribute to the increased risk of chronic diseases.

fructose The sweetest of all the monosaccharides; also known as fruit sugar.

FSI See Food Safety Initiative.

functional fiber The nondigestible polysaccharides that are added to foods because of a specific desired effect on human health.

functional foods Foods that have a positive effect on health beyond providing basic nutrients.

fungicides Chemicals used to kill mold.

G

galactose A monosaccharide that links with glucose to create the sugar found in dairy foods.

gallstones Small, hard, crystalline structures formed in the gallbladder or bile duct due to abnormally thick bile.

gastric banding A type of gastric surgery that uses a silicon band to reduce the size of the stomach so that less food is needed to feel full.

gastric bypass surgeries Surgical procedures that reduce the functional volume of the stomach so that less food is eaten. Such surgeries are sometimes used to treat extreme obesity.

gastrin A digestive hormone produced in the stomach that stimulates digestive activities and increases motility and emptying.

gastritis Inflammation of the stomach.

gastroenteritis Formal term for "stomach flu." Caused by virus or bacteria and results in inflammation of the stomach and/or intestines.

gastroenteritis Inflammation of the stomach and intestines.

gastroesophageal reflux disease (GERD) See heartburn.

gastrointestinal (GI) tract Referring to the organs of the digestive tract. It extends from the mouth to the anus.

GE See genetic engineering.

gene A DNA segment that codes for a specific protein.

gene expression The processing of genetic information to create a specific protein.

gene-environment interaction The interaction of both genetics and the environment that increases the risk of obesity in some people.

generally recognized as safe (GRAS) See GRAS.

genetically modified A cell that has its genetic makeup altered.

genetically modified organisms (GMOs) Organisms that have been genetically engineered to contain both original and foreign genes.

genetic engineering (GE) A biological technique that isolates and manipulates the genes of organisms to produce a targeted, modified product.

GERD See gastroesophageal reflux disease.

gestational diabetes Diabetes that occurs in women during pregnancy.

gestational hypertension See pregnancy-induced hpertension.

ghrelin A hormone produced mainly in the stomach that increases hunger.

GI See gastrointestinal tract.

glucagon The hormone that directs glycogenolysis and gluconeogenesis to increase glucose in the blood. Glucagon is produced in and released from the pancreas.

gluconeogenesis The creation of glucose from noncarbohydrate sources, predominantly protein.

glucose The most abundant sugar in foods and the energy source for your body.

glycerol The three-carbon backbone of a triglyceride.

glycogen The storage form of glucose in humans and animals.

glycogenesis The process of converting excess glucose into glycogen in your liver and muscle.

glycogenolysis The breakdown of glycogen to release glucose.

GMOs See genetically modified organisms.

goiter An enlarged thyroid gland due to an iodine deficiency.

gradual improvement Making small changes over time in order to realize long-term results.

GRAS (generally recognized as safe) A substance that has GRAS status is believed to be safe to consume based on a long history of use by humans or a substantial amount of research that documents its safety.

growth charts Series of percentile curves that illustrate the distribution of selected body measurements in U.S. children.

growth hormone A hormone that is essential for normal growth and development in humans and animals.

growth spurt A rapid increase in height and weight.

growth stunting Primarily manifested in early childhood and includes malnutrition during fetal development. Once growth stunting occurs, it is usually permanent. It can affect the vital body organs and cause premature death.

Guillain-Barré syndrome A condition that can result from a *Campylobacter* infection. It causes the immune system to attack its own nerves and can lead to paralysis for several weeks.

H

hangover A collective term for the unpleasant symptoms, such as a headache and dizziness, that occur after drinking an excessive amount of alcohol.

HCl See hydrochloric acid.

HDL See high-density lipoprotein.

health claims Claims on the label that describe a relationship between a food or dietary compound and a disease or health-related condition.

Healthy People 2010 A set of disease prevention and health promotion objectives for Americans to meet during the first decade of the new millennium.

healthy weight A body weight in relationship to your height that doesn't increase the risk of developing any weight-related health problems or diseases.

heart attack Permanent damage to the heart muscle that results from a sudden lack of oxygen-rich blood.

heartburn A burning sensation originating in the esophagus. Heartburn is usually caused by the reflux of gastric contents from the stomach into the esophagus. Chronic heartburn can lead to **gastroesophageal reflux disease (GERD).**

hemochromatosis A genetic disorder that causes iron overload in the body and can damage various organs.

hemoglobin The oxygen-carrying transport protein in your red blood cells.

hemolytic uremic syndrome A rare condition that can be caused by *E. coli* O157:H7 and results in the destruction of red blood cells and kidney failure. Very young children and the elderly are at a higher risk of developing this syndrome.

hemorrhage Severe bleeding

herbicides Substances that are used to kill and control weeds.

high-density lipoprotein (HDL) A lipoprotein that removes cholesterol from the tissues and delivers it to the liver to be used as part of bile and/or to be excreted from the body. Because of this, it is known as the good cholesterol carrier.

high-pressure processing (HPP) A method used to pasteurize foods by exposing the items to pulses of high pressure, which destroys the microorganisms that are present.

homelessness The state of being homeless. Individuals in this situation are either "crashing" with friends or family members, or residing on the street or in their automobiles.

hormones Chemical messengers in your body that initiate or direct specific actions. Insulin, glucagon, and estrogen are examples of hormones in your body.

host A living plant or animal (including a human) that harbors a virus, allowing it to survive and reproduce.

HPP See high-pressure processing.

Human Genome Project A project sponsored by the United States government to determine the complete set and sequencing of DNA in your cells and identify all human genes.

hunger The physical need for food.

hydrochloric acid (HCl) A powerful acid made in the stomach that has digestive functions. It also helps to kill microorganisms and lowers the pH in the stomach.

hydrogenation Adding hydrogen to an unsaturated fatty acid to make it more saturated and solid at room temperature.

hydrophobic Having an aversion to water.

hypercalcemia The condition of having an excessive amount of calcium in the blood.

hyperemesis gravidarum Excessive vomiting during pregnancy that can lead to dehydration and loss of electrolytes.

hyperkalemia Too much potassium in the blood.

hyperphosphatemia Too much phosphate in the blood.

hypertension High blood pressure.

hypervitaminosis A A condition caused by storage of an excessive amount of vitamin A in the body.

hypervitaminosis D An accumulation of dangerous levels of vitamin D in the body.

hypoallergenic infant formulas Specially developed formulas for infants who have food allergies and cannot tolerate regular formula.

hypoglycemia A blood glucose level that drops to lower than 70 mg/dl. Hunger, shakiness, dizziness, perspiration, and light-headedness are some signs of hypoglycemia.

hypokalemia Too little potassium in the blood

hyponatremia A condition of too little sodium in the blood.

hypotension Low blood pressure.

hypothesis An idea generated by scientists based on their observations.

I

IBS See irritable bowel syndrome.

ileocecal sphincter Gateway between the end of the small intestine and the beginning of the large intestine. The sphincter prevents backflow of fecal contents from the large intestine into the small intestine.

immunity The state of having built up antibodies to a particular foreign substance so that when particles of the substance enter the body, they are destroyed by the antibodies.

impaired glucose intolerance A condition whereby a fasting blood glucose level is higher than normal (> 100 mg/dl), but not high enough (≤ 126 mg/dl) to be classified as having diabetes mellitus. Also called prediabetes.

incomplete protein A protein that is low in one or more of the essential amino acids. Protein from plant sources tend to be incomplete.

infancy The age range from birth to 12 months.

inorganic Compounds that do not contain carbon and are not formed by living things.

inositol A substance synthesized in your body that helps to keep your cells and their membranes healthy.

insensible water loss The water that is lost from the body daily through routine respiration and evaporation off the skin.

insoluble fiber A type of fiber that doesn't dissolve in water or fermented by intestinal bacteria.

insulin The hormone that directs the glucose from your blood into your cells. Insulin is produced in and released from the pancreas.

insulin resistance The inability of the cells to respond to insulin.

integrated pest management (IPM) Alternative to pesticides that uses the most economical and the least harmful methods of pest control to minimize risk to consumers, crops, and the environment.

intensity The level of difficulty of an activity.

international units (IU) The method of measuring vitamin A that is used on food and dietary supplement labels.

interstitial fluids Fluids located between cells.

intracellular fluid compartment The fluid located inside your cells.

intrinsic factor A protein produced in the stomach that binds with vitamin B_{12} in the intestinal tract so that the vitamin can be absorbed in the intestine.

iodopsin A photopigment in the cones of the retina. Vitamin A is a component of this pigment.

IPM See integrated pest management.

iron-deficiency anemia An anemia caused by decreased levels of hemoglobin in the blood, which diminishes the delivery of oxygen through the body.

irradiation A process in which foods are placed in a shielded chamber, called an **irradiator,** and subjected to a radiant energy source. This kills specific pathogens in food by breaking up the cells' DNA.

irradiator See irradiation.

irritable bowel syndrome (IBS) A functional disorder that involves changes in colon rhythm.

isoflavones Naturally occurring phytoestrogens, or weak plant estrogens, which function in a similar fashion to the hormone estrogen in the human body.

IU See international units.

J

jaundice A yellowish coloring of the skin due to the presence of bile pigments in the blood.

K

Keshan disease A rare disease due to a deficiency of selenium, which damages the heart.

ketoacidosis The buildup of ketone bodies to dangerous levels, which can result in coma or death.

ketone bodies The by-products of the incomplete breakdown of fat.

ketosis The condition of increased ketone bodies in the blood.

kidney stones A hard mass or stone typically composed of calcium oxalate that occurs in the kidneys and could stop the flow of urine from the body.

kilocalories The measurement of energy in foods.

kwashiorkor A state of PEM where there is a severe deficiency of dietary protein.

L

laboratory experiment A scientific experiment conducted in a laboratory. Some laboratory experiments involve animals.

lactation The production of milk in a woman's body after childbirth, and the period during which it occurs. The baby receives the milk through breast-feeding.

lactic acid A by-product of rapid glucose metabolism.

lactose A disaccharide composed of glucose and galactose; also known as milk sugar.

lactose intolerant When maldigestion of lactose results in symptoms such as nausea, cramps, bloating, flatulence, and diarrhea.

lactose maldigestion The inability to digest lactose in foods due to low levels of the enzyme lactase.

lanugo Very fine, soft hair on the face and arms of people with anorexia nervosa.

large intestine Final organ of the GI tract. It consists of the cecum, appendix, colons, and rectum.

LD See licensed dietitian.

LDL See low-density lipoprotein.

lean body mass The body mass once the fat mass has been subtracted. It contains mostly muscle but also organs and fluids. Lean body mass is the metabolically active tissue in the body.

leptin A hormone produced in fat tissue that helps regulate body fat by signaling the reduction of food intake in the brain and interfering with the storage of fat in the cells.

LES See lower esophageal sphincter.

let-down The release of milk from the mother's breast to feed the baby.

licensed dietitian (LD) An individual who has met specified educational and experience criteria deemed by a state licensing board necessary to be considered an expert in the field of nutrition. An RD would meet all the qualifications to be an LD.

life expectancy The number of years that a person will live.

limiting amino acid The amino acid that is in the shortest supply in an incomplete protein.

linoleic acid A polyunsaturated essential fatty acid; part of the omega-6 fatty acid family.

lipid A category of carbon, hydrogen, and oxygen compounds that are insoluble in water.

lipoic acid A vitamin-like substance in your body needed in energy production; it may also act as an antioxidant.

lipoproteins Capsule-shaped transport carriers that enable fat and cholesterol to travel through the lymph and blood.

liposuction The surgical removal of subcutaneous fat with a penlike instrument. Usually performed on the abdomen, hips, and thighs, and/or other areas of the body.

liver The largest gland of the body. The liver aids in digestive activity and is responsible for the metabolism of nutrients, detoxification of alcohol, and some nutrient storage.

low birth weight baby A baby weighing less than 5½ pounds at birth.

low-density lipoprotein (LDL) A lipoprotein that deposits cholesterol in the walls of the arteries. Because this can lead to heart disease, LDL is referred to as the bad cholesterol carrier.

lower esophogeal sphincter (LES) A circular band of muscle between the esophagus and stomach that opens and closes to allow food to enter the stomach.

lumen The interior of the digestive tract, through which food passes.

lymph Watery fluid that circulates through the body in lymph vessels and eventually enters the blood.

M

macrocytes Mature but abnormal red blood cells.

macrocytic anemia A condition caused by the inability of red blood cells to form properly due to a folate deficiency.

macronutrients The energy-containing essential nutrients that you need in higher amounts: carbohydrates, lipids (fats), and proteins.

macrosomia A large baby, weighing more than 8 pounds, 13 oz.

mad cow disease See bovine spongiform encephalopathy (BSE).

major minerals Minerals needed from your diet and in your body in amounts greater than 100 milligrams per day. These include sodium, chloride, potassium, calcium, phosphorus, magnesium, and sulfur.

malnourished The long-term outcome of consuming a diet that doesn't meet nutrient needs.

maltose A disaccharide composed of two glucose units joined together.

MAP See modified atmosphere packaging.

marasmus A state of PEM where there is a severe deficiency of calories that perpetuates wasting; also called starvation.

marine toxins Chemicals that occur naturally and contaminate some fish.

mast cells Cells in connective tissue to which antibodies attach, setting the stage for potential future allergic reactions.

mechanical digestion Breaking food down through chewing and grinding, or moving it through the GI tract with peristalsis.

medical nutrition therapy The integration of nutrition counseling and dietary changes based on an individual's medical and health needs to treat a patient's medical condition.

megaloblasts Large, immature red cells that develop due to a folate deficiency. These can develop into macrocytes.

menaquinone A form of vitamin K made by bacteria in your intestinal tract.

menarche The onset of menstruation.

MEOS See microsomal ethanol-oxidizing system.

messenger RNA (mRNA) A type of RNA that copies the genetic information encoded in DNA and carries it out of the nucleus of the cell to synthesize the protein.

metabolism The numerous reactions that occur within the cell. The calories in foods are converted to energy in the cells of the body.

micelles Small transport carriers in the intestine that enable fatty acids and other compounds to be absorbed.

micronutrients Essential nutrients you need in smaller amounts: vitamins and minerals.

microsomal ethanol-oxidizing system (MEOS) The other major enzyme system in the liver that metabolizes alcohol.

microvilli See villi.

milestones Objectives or significant events that occur during development.

minerals Inorganic elements essential to the nutrition of humans.

moderate alcohol consumption Consuming no more than one alcoholic drink daily for adult women and no more than two drinks daily for men.

moderation Consuming reasonable but not excessive amounts of foods.

modified atmosphere packaging (MAP) A food preservation technique that changes the composition of the air surrounding the food in a package to extend its shelf life.

monoglyceride A glycerol with only one attached fatty acid.

monosaccharides One sugar unit. There are three monosaccharides: glucose, fructose, and galactose.

monosodium glutamate (MSG) A flavor enhancer.

monounsaturated fatty acid (MUFA) A fatty acid that has one double bond.

mRNA See messenger RNA.

MSG See monosodium glutamate.

MSG symptom complex A series of reactions such as numbness, burning sensation, facial pressure or tightness, chest pain, rapid heartbeat, and drowsiness that can occur in some individuals after consuming MSG.

mucus Viscous, slippery secretions found in saliva.

MUFA See monounsaturated fatty acid.

muscle endurance The ability of the muscle to produce prolonged effort.

muscle strength The greatest amount of force exerted by the muscle at one time.

myoglobin The protein that transports and stores oxygen in your muscles. It provides the purplish-red color in meat and poultry.

MyPyramid A food guidance system that illustrates the recommendations in the *Dietary Guidelines for Americans 2005* and the Dietary Reference Intakes (DRIs) nutrient goals.

N

naturally occurring sugars Sugars such as fructose and lactose that are found naturally in fruit and dairy foods.

NE See niacin equivalents.

NEAT See nonexercise-associated thermogenesis.

negative energy balance The state whereby you expend more energy than you consume. Over time, this results in weight loss.

neural tube defects Birth defects, including anencephaly and spina bifida, caused by the improper developing of the neural tube, which forms a baby's spine, brain and skull.

neurotoxins A toxin that affects the nerves and can cause symptoms including mild numbness or tingling in the face, arms, and legs as well as headaches and dizziness. Severe cases could result in death.

niacin equivalents (NE) Since niacin can be derived from the amino acid, tryptophan, in addition to occurring naturally in food, it is measured in NE. (60 milligrams (mg) of typtophan is equal to 1 mg of niacin or 1 mg NE.)

nicotinamide A B vitamin that is also known as niacin, nictonic acid or vitamin B_3.

nicotinic acid A B vitamin that is also known as niacin, nicotinamide or vitamin B_3.

night blindness The inability to adjust one's eyesight from daylight to dark due to a vitamin A deficiency in the diet.

nitrates (nitrites) Substances that can be added to foods to function as a preservative and to give meats such as hot dogs and luncheon meats a pink color.

nonessential amino acids The 11 amino acids that the body can synthesize.

nonexercise-associated thermogenesis (NEAT) The energy expenditure that occurs during nonexercise movements, such as fidgeting, standing, and chewing gum.

normal blood pressure Less than 120 mm Hg (systolic—the top number) and less than 80 mm Hg (diastolic—the bottom number). Referred to as 120/80.

noroviruses The most common type of virus that causes foodborne illness. They can cause gastroenteritis, or the "stomach flu." Also known as Norwalk-like viruses.

nutrient content claims Claims on the label that describe the level or amount of a nutrient in a food product.

nutrient density The amount of nutrients per calorie in a given food. Nutrient-dense foods provide more nutrients per calorie than less nutrient-dense foods.

nutrients Compounds in foods that sustain your body processes. There are six classes of nutrients: carbohydrates, fats (lipids), proteins, vitamins, minerals, and water.

nutrition The science that studies how the nutrients and compounds in foods that you eat nourish and affect your body functions and health.

Nutrition Facts panel The area on the food label that provides a uniform listing of specific nutrients obtained in one serving of the food.

nutritional genomics A field of study that researches the relationship between nutrition and genomics (the study of genes and gene expression).

nutritionist A generic term with no recognized legal or professional meaning. Some people may call themselves nutritionists without having any credible training in nutrition.

O

obesity Having an unhealthy amount of body fat.

observational research Research that involves looking at factors in two or more groups of subjects to see if there is a relationship to certain outcomes.

oils Lipids that are liquid at room temperature.

open dating Typically found on perishable items such as meat, poultry, eggs, and dairy foods; must contain a calendar date.

organic Being free of chemical-based pesticides, synthetic fertilizers, irradiation, and bioengineering. A USDA-accredited certifying inspector must certify organic foods.

organophosphates A group of synthetic pesticides that adversely affect the nervous systems of pests. They are currently being re-reviewed by the EPA to ensure their safety.

osmosis The movement of a solvent, such as water, from an area of lower concentration of solutes across a membrane to an area of higher concentration of solutes. Osmosis balances the concentration of solutes between the compartments.

osteocalcin A protein in bone that binds with calcium.

osteomalacia The adult equivalent to rickets, which can cause muscle weakness and bone pain.

osteopenia Low bone mass.

osteoporosis A condition whereby the bones are less dense and weaken, which increases the risk of fractures.

overnutrition A state of excess nutrients and calories in the diet.

overpopulation When a region has more people than its natural resources can support.

overweight Carrying extra weight on your body in relation to your height.

oxidation The process during which oxygen combines with other molecules.

oxidative stress A condition whereby the production of harmful free radicals overwhelms the ability of the body's natural defense system to keep them at bay.

P

pancreas Accessory organ for digestion that produces hormones and enzymes. It's connected to the duodenum via the bile duct.

paralytic shellfish poisoning A condition caused by a reddish-brown-colored dinoflagellate that contains neurotoxins (nerve toxins).

parasites Organisms that live on or in another organism. Parasites obtain their nourishment from their hosts.

parathyroid hormone A hormone that causes the release of calcium from bone so that adequate amounts of this mineral in maintained in the blood.

pasteurization The process of heating liquids or food at high temperatures to destroy foodborne pathogens.

pathogens Collective term for disease-causing microorganisms (microbes). Pathogens include viruses, bacteria, and parasites and are the most common source of foodborne illness.

PCBs See polychlorinated biphenyls.

PDCAAS See protein digestibility corrected amino acid score.

peak bone mass The genetically determined maximum amount of bone mass an individual can build up.

peer-reviewed journal A research journal in which fellow scientists (peers) review studies to assess if they are accurate and sound before they are published.

pellagra A condition caused by a niacin deficiency; symptoms include dermatitis or the inflammation or irritation of the skin, dementia or memory loss, and diarrhea.

PEM See protein-energy malnutrition.

pendular movement A constrictive wave that involves both forward and reverse movements of chyme and enhances nutrient absorption.

pepsin A digestive enzyme produced in the stomach that breaks down protein.

peptic ulcers Sores, erosions, or breaks in the mucosal lining of the stomach.

peptide bonds The bonds that connect amino acids, created when the acid group of one amino acid is joined with the nitrogen-containing amine group of another amino acid.

percentile The most commonly used clinical indicator to assess the size and growth patterns of children in the United States. An individual child is ranked according to the percentage of the reference population he equals or exceeds.

peristalsis The forward, rhythmic motion that moves food through the digestive system. Peristalsis is a form of mechanical digestion because it influences motion, but it does not add chemical secretions.

pernicious anemia A rare condition that leads to anemia and nerve damage due to vitamin B_{12} deficiency in the absence of intrinsic factor.

pesticides Substances that kill or repel pests such as insects, weeds, microorganisms, rodents, or fungi.

pharynx The throat. Passageway for the respiratory (air) and digestive tracts (food and beverages).

phospholipids Lipids made up of two fatty acids and a phosphorus-containing group attached to a glycerol backbone.

photosynthesis A process by which green plants create carbohydrates using the energy from sunlight.

phylloquinone The primary form of vitamin K in your diet; found in plants.

physical activity Voluntary movement that results in energy expenditure (burning calories).

phytochemicals Naturally occurring substances in fruits, vegetables, and whole grains that protect against certain chronic diseases. Beta-carotene is a phytochemical.

phytosterols Naturally occurring sterols found in plants. Phytosterols lower LDL cholesterol levels by competing with cholesterol for absorption in the intestinal tract.

pica Eating nonfood substances such as dirt and clay.

picky eating Unwillingness to eat familiar foods.

placebo A sugar pill that has no impact on the individual's health when ingested.

placenta The site of common tissue between the mother and growing embryo. The placenta is attached to the fetus with the **umbilical cord.**

plant breeding A type of biotechnology in which two plants are crossbred to produce offspring with desired traits from both.

plaque The hardened buildup of cholesterol-laden foam cells, platelets, cellular waste products, and calcium in the arteries that results in atherosclerosis.

PMS See premenstrual syndrome.

polychlorinated biphenyls (PCBs) Synthetic chemicals that have been shown to cause cancer and other adverse effects on the immune, reproductive, nervous, and endocrine systems in animals. PCBs may cause cancer in humans.

polyneuritis An inflammation and numbness of the nerves which can be caused by consuming too much thiamin.

polysaccharides Many sugar units combined. Starch, glycogen, and fiber are all polysaccharides.

polyunsaturated fatty acid (PUFA) A fatty acid with two or more double bonds.

positive energy balance The state whereby you store more energy than you expend. Over time, this results in weight gain.

poverty Lacking the means to provide for material or comfort needs.

precursors Substances that precede a step or reaction. A precursor is a substance that is converted to another substance in your body.

preeclampsia See pregnancy-induced hpertension.

preformed vitamin A The collective name for retinol, retinal, and retinoic acid, which is the form that is used in your body. Preformed vitamin A is found only in foods from animal sources.

pregnancy-induced hypertension A category of hypertension that includes **gestational hypertension, preeclampsia, and eclampsia.** Gestational hypertension occurs in pregnancy in a woman without prior history of high blood pressure. Preeclampsia occurs when hypertension, severe edema, and protein loss occur. Eclampsia can result in seizures and can be extremely dangerous for both the mother and the baby.

premenstrual syndrome (PMS) Symptoms such as mood swings, anxiety and fatigue, some women experience prior to menstruation.

preschoolers Children aged 3 to 5 years old.

prion Cellular proteins. An abnormal prion protein is the cause of mad cow disease.

prior-sanctioned Having previous approval.

proportionality The relationship of one entity to another. Grains, fruits, and vegetables should be consumed in a higher proportion to oils and meats in the diet.

protein digestibility corrected amino acid score (PDCAAS) A score measured as a percentage that takes into account both digestibility and amino acid profile and gives a good indication of the quality of a protein.

protein quality The measure of a protein's digestibility and how its amino acid pattern compares with your body's needs. Proteins that are more easily digested and have a complete set of amino acids are of higher quality.

protein turnover The continual process of degrading and synthesizing protein. When the daily amount of degraded protein is equivalent to the amount that is synthesized, you are in protein balance.

protein-energy malnutrition (PEM) A lack of sufficient dietary protein and/or calories.

proteins Compounds in your body that consist of numerous amino acids and are found in all living cells.

protein-sparing modified fast See very-low-calorie diet.

provitamin A carotenoids Compounds that can be converted to vitamin A in your body.

public health nutritionist An individual who may have an undergraduate degree in nutrition but isn't an RD.

PUFA See polyunsaturated fatty acid.

pyloric sphincter Sphincter in the bottom of the stomach that separates the pylorus from the duodenum of the small intestine.

pyridoxal, pyridoxamine Forms of vitamin B_6.

pyridoxine The major form of B_6 in plant foods, supplements, and fortified foods.

Q

quackery The promotion and selling of health products and services of questionable validity. A quack is a person who promotes these products and services in order to make money.

R

RAE See retinol activity equivalents.

rancidity The decomposition, or spoiling, of fats through oxidation.

rate of perceived exertion (RPE) A subjective measure of the intensity level of an activity using a numerical scale.

rbGH See recombinant bovine somatotropin.

rbST See recombinant bovine somatotropin.

RD See registered dietitian.

RDA See Recommended Dietary Allowance.

recombinant bovine somatotropin (rbST) A synthetically made hormone identical to a cow's natural growth hormone, somatotropin, that stimulates milk production. Also known as rbGH (recombinant bovine growth hormone).

Recommended Dietary Allowance (RDA) The average amount of a nutrient that meets the needs of nearly all individuals (97 to 98 percent) in a similar age and gender group. The RDA is higher than the EAR.

rectum The lowest part of the large intestine, continuous with the sigmoid colon and the **anus**.

registered dietitian (RD) A health professional who has completed at least a bachelor's degree in an accredited university or college in the United States, completed a supervised practice, and passed an exam administered by the American Dietetic Association (ADA).

remineralization The repairing of teeth by adding back the minerals lost during tooth decay. Your saliva can help remineralize teeth.

repetitions of maximum (RM) The maximum amount of weight that can be lifted for a specified number of repetitions.

retinal A form of vitamin A

retinoic acid Another form of vitamin A.

retinoids The family of vitamins, which include **retinol, retinal,** and **retinoic acid** as well as synthetically made vitamin-A like compounds.

retinol The predominate form of vitamin A in foods and in the body.

retinol activity equivalents (RAE) The preferred way to measure the amount of vitamin A in foods as it converts both retinoids and provitamin A carotenoids into one measurement.

retort canning The process of subjecting already-canned foods to an additional high-temperature heat source to destroy potential pathogens.

rhodopsin The photopigment in the rods of the retina. Vitamin A is a component of this pigment.

rickets A condition in children caused by the deficiency of vitamin D that can cause abnormal growth and soft bones. Bowed legs are a common symptom.

risk assessment The process of determining the potential human health risks posed by exposure to substances such as pesticides.

RM See repetitions of maximum.

RNA A molecule that carries out the orders of DNA.

rods The light absorbing cells in the retina that contain the photopigment or protein, rhodopsin

RPE See rate of perceived exertion.

ruminant animals Animals, such as cows, that have four chambers in their stomachs for digesting coarse food such as plants. These foods are softened in the first chamber into balls of cud. The cud is then regurgitated, chewed and swallowed again, and passed on into the other chambers.

S

saliva Watery fluid secreted by the salivary glands in the mouth. Saliva moistens food and makes it easier to swallow.

sanctions Boycotts or trade embargoes used by one country or international group to apply political pressure on another.

satiation The feeling during eating that determines how long and how much you eat.

satiety The sensation that you feel when you have had enough to eat. It determines how long you will go between meals and/or snacks.

saturated fats Fats that contain mostly saturated fatty acids.

saturated fatty acid A fatty acid that has all of its carbons bound with hydrogen.

school-aged children Children between the ages of 6 and 10 to 12.

scientific method A stepwise process used by scientists to generate sound research findings.

scombrotoxic fish poisoning A condition caused by consuming spoiled fish that contain large amounts of histamines. Also referred to as histamine fish poisoning.

scrapie A prion disease found in sheep that is related to the BSE observed in cattle.

scurvy A condition caused by a deficiency of vitamin C that can cause bleeding gums, loss of teeth, and skin lesions or wounds.

segmentation A "sloshing" motion that thoroughly mixes chyme with the chemical secretions of the intestine.

selenosis Excessive amounts of selenium in the body.

sex pheromones Naturally occurring chemicals secreted by one organism to attract another, used as a biopesticide to control pests by interfering with their mating.

sickle-cell anemia A blood disorder caused by a genetic defect in the development of hemoglobin. Sickle-cell anemia causes the red blood cells to distort into a sickle shape and can damage organs and tissues.

side chain The side group of an amino acid that provides it with its unique qualities.

SIDS See sudden infant death syndrome.

simple carbohydrates A category of carbohydrates that contain a single sugar unit or two sugar units combined. Monosaccharides and disaccharides are simple carbohydrates.

small intestine Comprised of the duodenum, jejunum, and ileum. The longest part of the GI tract. Most of the digestion and absorption of food occurs in the small intestine.

sodium sensitivity A more pronounced blood pressure response in an individual when sodium is consumed in the diet.

solid foods Foods other than breast milk or formula given to an infant, usually around 4 to 6 months of age.

soluble fiber A type of fiber that dissolves in water and is fermented by intestinal bacteria. Many soluble fibers are viscous and have gummy or thickening properties.

solvent A liquid that acts as a medium in which substances dissolve. Water is considered the universal solvent.

spina bifida A neural tube birth defect due to the incomplete development of the brain and/or spinal cord.

spores Hardy reproductive structures that are produced by certain bacteria. Some bacterial spores can survive boiling temperature (212° F).

starch The storage form of glucose in plants.

sterol A lipid that contains four connecting rings of carbon and hydrogen.

stomach Digestive organ that holds food after it's moved down the esophagus and before it is propelled into the small intestine.

stool (feces) Waste products that are stored in the large intestine and then excreted from the body. Stool consists mostly of bacteria, sloughed-off gastrointestinal cells, inorganic matter, water, unabsorbed nutrients, food residue, undigested fibers, fatty acids, mucus, and remnants of digestive fluids.

stroke A condition caused by a lack of oxygen to the brain that could result in paralysis and possibly death.

stroke volume The amount of blood pumped by the heart with each heart beat.

structure/function claims Claims on the label that describe how a nutrient or dietary compound affects the structure or function of the human body.

stunting Restricted growth due to malnutrition.

subcutaneous fat The fat located under the skin and between the muscles.

sucrose A dissacharide composed of glucose and fructose. Also known as table sugar.

sudden infant death syndrome (SIDS) The unexplained death of an infant less than one year of age.

sugar substitutes Alternatives to table sugar that sweeten foods for fewer calories.

sulfites Preservatives used to help prevent foods from turning brown and to inhibit the growth of microbes. Often used in wine and dried fruit products.

synthetic pesticides Man made, chemically based substances, such as organophosphate pesticides, used to control pests.

systolic pressure The force of your blood against the artery walls when your heart beats.

T

TEF See thermic effect of food.

thermic effect of food (TEF) The amount of calories the body uses to digest, absorb, and process food.

thermogenesis The production of heat in body cells.

thirst The physical need for water.

thirst mechanism Various bodily reactions caused by dehydration that signal you to drink fluids.

toddlers Children aged 1 to 3 years old.

Tolerable Upper Intake Level (UL) The highest amount of a nutrient that can be consumed daily without harm in a similar age and group of individuals.

tongue-thrust reflex A forceful protrusion of the tongue in response to an oral stimulus, such as a spoon.

toxicity The level at which exposure to a substance becomes harmful.

toxins Poisons that can be produced by living organisms.

trace minerals Minerals needed from your diet and in your body in small amounts, less than 20 milligrams daily. These include iron, zinc, selenium, fluoride, chromium, copper, manganese, and molybdenum.

trans fat Substance that contains mostly *trans* **fatty acids,** which result from the hydrogenating of an unsaturated fatty acid, causing a reconfiguring of some of its double bonds. A small amount of *trans* fatty acids occur naturally in animal foods.

trans fatty acids See *trans* fat.

transfer RNA (tRNA) A type of RNA that collects the amino acids within the cell that are needed to make a specific protein.

transport proteins Proteins that carry lipids (fat and cholesterol), oxygen, waste products, and vitamins through your blood to your various organs and tissues. Proteins can also act as channels through which some substances enter your cells.

traveler's diarrhea A common pathogen-induced intestinal disorder experienced by some travelers who visit areas with unsanitary conditions.

triglyceride Three fatty acids that are attached to a glycerol backbone. Also known as fat.

trimesters The three time periods of pregnancy.

tripeptide Three bonded amino acids.

tRNA See transfer RNA.

tryptophan An amino acid that can be converted in the body to niacin.

U

ultraviolet (UV) rays Rays of light energy from the sun that allow vitamin D synthesis in the body.

umbilical cord See placenta.

underdeveloped country Having a low level of economic productivity and technological sophistication within the contemporary range of possibility.

undernutrition A state of inadequate nutrition whereby a person's nutrient and/or calorie needs aren't met through the diet.

underweight Weighing too little for your height.

unsaturated fats Fats that contain mostly unsaturated fatty acids.

unsaturated fatty acid A fatty acid that has one or more double bonds between carbons.

urea A nitrogen-containing waste product that is excreted in your urine.

U.S. Pharmacopeia (USP) A nonprofit organization that sets purity and reliability standards for dietary supplements.

UL See Tolerable Upper Intake Level

V

variant Creutzfeldt-Jakob Disease (vCJD) A degenerative, fatal nerve disease in humans believed to be caused after exposure to BSE.

variety Consuming different food groups and foods within each group.

vCJD See variant Creutzfeldt-Jakob Disease.

vegetarian A person who doesn't eat meat, fish, or poultry or (sometimes) foods made from these animal sources.

very low-calorie diet or **protein-sparing modified fast** A diet of fewer than 800 calories per day and high in protein. These diets are very low in or devoid of carbohydrates and have a minimal amount of fat.

very low-density lipoprotein (VLDL) A lipoprotein that delivers fat made in the liver to the tissues. VLDL remnants are converted into LDLs.

villi Projections on the walls of the small intestine that increase the surface area over which nutrients can be absorbed. Villi are in turn covered with **microvilli,** which increase the surface area even more.

virus A microscopic organism that can infect a host and cause illness.

visceral fat The fat stored in the abdominal area.

vitamin C See ascorbic acid.

vitamins Essential nutrients that your body needs in small amounts to grow, reproduce, and maintain good health.

VLDL See very low-density lipoprotein.

W

warfarin An anti-clotting medication.

wasting A condition caused by extremely low energy intake from too little food and too little energy. It is sometimes referred to as acute malnutrition. Infections, high energy use, or nutrient loss can cause wasting.

water balance The state whereby an equal amount of water is lost and replenished daily in the body.

weight cycling The repeated gain and loss of body weight.

weight management Maintaining your weight within a healthy range.

weight training Exercising with weights to build, strengthen, and tone muscle to improve or maintain overall fitness; also called resistance training.

Wernicke-Korsakoff syndrome A brain disorder caused by a thiamin deficiency, which can lead to mental confusion and memory loss, vision impairment, low blood pressure, uncontrolled movement of the arms and legs, and coma.

"working poor" Individuals or families who are steadily employed but still experience poverty due to low wages or high dependent expenses.

X

xerophthalmia An eye condition that causes dryness and damage to the cornea due to a prolonged vitamin A deficiency in the body.

Z

zoochemicals Compounds in animal food products that are beneficial to human health. Omega-3 fatty acids are an example of zoochemicals.

zygote Term that refers to a fertilized egg for the first two weeks after conception.

References

Chapter 1

1. Glanz, K., M. Basil, E. Maibach, J. Goldberg, and D. Snyder. 1998. Why Americans Eat What They Do: Taste, Nutrition, Cost, Convenience, and Weight Control Concerns as Influences on Food Consumption. *Journal of the American Dietetic Association* 98: 1118–1126.
2. National Turkey Federation. 2004. Turkey Facts and Trivia. Available at www.eatturkey.com/consumer/history/history.html. Accessed February 2006.
3. Freeland-Graves, J., and S. Nitzke. 2002. Total Diet Approach to Communicating Food and Nutrition Information. *Journal of the American Dietetic Association* 102: 100–108.
4. Coomes, S. Pizza Marketplace. Personal communication. February 2006.
5. Mintel International Group. 2005. Cinemas and Movie Theaters-United States, Mintel Reports-USA, Leisure-USA. Available at www.reports.mintel.com. Accessed March 2006.
6. Gallo, A. 1999. Food Advertising in the United States. In America's Eating Habits: Changes and Consequences. Economic Research Service. Agriculture Information Bulletin No. AIB750. Available at www.ers.usda.gov/Publications/aib750. Accessed March 2006.
7. Story, M., and S. French. 2004. Food Advertising and Marketing Directed at Children and Adolescents in the U.S. *International Journal of Behavioral Nutrition and Physical Activity* 1: 1–17.
8. Blisard, N. 1999. Advertising and How We Eat: The Case of Dairy Products. In America's Eating Habits: Changes and Consequences. Economic Research Service. Agriculture Information Bulletin No. AIB750. Available at www.ers.usda.gov/Publications/aib750.
9. Freeland-Graves and Nitzke. Total Diet Approach.
10. Specialty Coffee Association. 2006. Retail in the USA 2004–2007. Available at www.scaa.org. Accessed March 2006.
11. Economic Research Service. 2005. Table 12 in Food CPI, Prices and Expenditure Tables: Food Expenditure Table. Available at www.ers.usda.gov/Briefing/CPIFoodAndExpenditures/Data/table12.htm. Accessed February 2006.
12. Mintel International Group. 2004. Breakfast Foods: The Consumer-US, Mintel Reports-USA, Food and Food Service-USA. Available at www.reports.mintel.com. Accessed February 2006.
13. Debusk, R., C. Fogarty, J. Ordovas, and K. Kornman. 2005. Nutrition Genomics in Practice: Where Do We Begin? *Journal of the American Dietetic Association* 105: 589–598.
14. Mashfegh, A. L., J. Goldman, and L. Cleveland. 2005. What We Eat in America, NHANES 2001–2002; Usual Nutrient Intakes from Food Compared to Dietary Reference Intakes. U.S. Department of Agriculture, Agricultural Research Service.
15. Centers for Disease Control. 2005. Overweight and Obesity: Obesity Trends. Available at www.cdc.gov. Accessed February 2006.
16. Healthy People 2010. 2000. Health Finder: Nutrition and Overweight. Available at www.healthypeople.gov. Accessed March 2006.
17. Krane, D. 2005. Number of "Cyberchondriacs"—U.S. Adults Who Go Online for Health Information—Increases to Estimated 117 Million. HarrisInteractive Healthcare Research. Available at www.harrisinteractive.com. Accessed March 2006.
18. National Center for Complementary and Alternative Medicine. 10 Things to Know About Evaluating Medical Resources on the Web. Updated 2006. Available at www.nccam.nih.gov. Accessed March 2006.

Chapter 2

1. Institute of Medicine. 2003. Dietary Reference Intakes: Applications in Dietary Planning. Washington, D.C.: The National Academies Press.
2. Davis, C., and E. Saltos. 1999. Chapter 2: Dietary Recommendations and How They Have Changed Over Time. In E. Frazo, ed., *America's Eating Habits: Changes and Consequences*. Agriculture Information Bulletin No. AIB750. Available at www.ers.usda.gov/publications/aib750. Accessed September 2005.
3. Lee, P. R. 1978. Nutrition Policy: From Neglect and Uncertainty to Debate and Action. *Journal of the American Dietetics Association* 72: 581–588.

4. U.S. Department of Agriculture. 2005. *2005 Report of the Dietary Guidelines Advisory Committee*. Available at www.health.gov/dietaryguidelines/dga2005/report. Accessed February 2005.
5. Ibid.
6. Painter, J., J. Rah, and Y. Lee. 2002. Comparison of International Food Guide Pictorial Representations. *Journal of the American Dietetic Association* 102: 483–489.
7. U.S. Department of Agriculture. 2005. The New Look and Messages of USDA's MyPyramid: Background. Available at www.mypyramid.gov/global_nav/media_backgrounder.html. Accessed June 2005.
8. Center for Food Safety and Applied Nutrition. 1999. A Food Labeling Guide. Available at www.cfsan.fda.gov/~dms/flg-toc.html. Accessed May 2005.
9. Kurtzweil, P. 1993. Good Reading for Good Eating. *FDA Consumer Magazine*. Available at www.fda.gov/fdac/special/foodlabel/goodread.html. Accessed May 2005.
10. Center for Food Safety and Applied Nutrition. A Food Labeling Guide.
11. U.S. Food and Drug Administration. Food Labeling: Guidelines for Voluntary Nutrition Labeling of Raw Fruits, Vegetables and Fish; Identification of the 20 Most Frequently Consumed Raw Fruits, Vegetables, and Fish. *Federal Register* (March 20, 2002) 67: 12918–12937. Available at www.cfsan.fda.gov/~lrd/fr05404a.html. Accessed September 2005.
12. Food Safety and Inspection Service. 2001. Nutrition Labeling Proposed for Raw Meat and Poultry Products. Available at www.fsis.usda.gov/oa/background/nutrlabel.htm. Accessed June 2005.
13. Center for Food Safety and Applied Nutrition. 2004. How to Understand and Use the Nutrition Facts Label. Available at www.cfsan.fda.gov/~acrobat/foodlab.pdf. Accessed June 2005.
14. Ibid.
15. Farley, D. 1993. Look for "Legit" Health Claims on Foods. *FDA Consumer Magazine*, 21–28.
16. Center for Food Safety and Applied Nutrition. 2003. Claims That Can Be Made for Conventional Foods and Dietary Supplements. Available at www.cfsan.fda.gov/~dms/hclaims.html. Accessed June 2005.
17. Hasler, C. M., A. S. Bloch, C. A. Thomson, E. Enrione, and C. Manning. 2004. Position of the American Dietetic Association: Functional Foods. *Journal of the American Dietetic Association* 104: 814–826.
18. Institute of Food Technologists. 2005. Expert Report on Functional Foods: Opportunities and Challenges, Executive Summary. Available at www.ift.org/cms/?pid=1001247. Accessed June 2005.

Feature Box References

1. Hasler, C. M., A. S. Bloch, C. A. Thomson, E. Enrione, and C. Manning. 2004. Position of the American Dietetic Association: Functional Foods. *Journal of the American Dietetic Association* 104: 814–826. The International Food Information Council. 2004. Background on Functional Foods. Available at www.ific.org. Accessed June 2005.
2. Hasler, C. M. 2002. Functional Foods: Benefits, Concerns and Challenges: A Position Paper from the American Council on Science and Health. *Journal of Nutrition* 132: 3772–3781. The International Food Information Council. 2002. The Consumer View on Functional Foods: Yesterday and Today. Food Insight. Available at www.ific.org/foodinsight/2002/mj/funcfdsfi302.cfm?renderforprint=1. Accessed June 2005. The International Food Information Council. 2002. Functional Foods: Attitudinal Research (2002). Available at www.ific.org/research/funcfoodsres02.cfm?renderforprint=1. Accessed June 2005.
3. Clydesdale, F. 2004. Functional Foods: Opportunities and Challenges. IFT Expert Panel Report, Executive Summary. Available at www.ift.org/pdfs/expert/ff/Executive-Summary.pdf. Accessed June 2005. Hasler, C. M. 2000. The Changing Face of Functional Foods. *Journal of the American College of Nutrition* 19: 499S–506S.
4. Hasler, et al. Position of the American Dietetic Association.
5. Institute of Food Technologists. 2005. Expert Report on Functional Foods: Opportunities and Challenges, Executive Summary. Available at www.ift.org/cms/?pid=1001247. Accessed June 2005.

Chapter 3

1. Mennella, J. A., and G. K. Beauchamp. 1994. Early Flavor Experiences: When Do They Start? *Nutrition Today* 29 (5): 25.
2. De Roos, K. B. 1997. How Lipids Influence Food Flavor. *Food Technology* 51 (5): 60–62.
3. Bodyfelt, F. W., J. Tobias, and G. M. Trout. 1988. *The Sensory Evaluation of Dairy Products.* New York: Van Nostrand Reinhold.
4. Nagodawithana, T. 1994. Flavor Enhancers: Their Probable Mode of Action. *Food Technology* 48 (4): 79–85.
5. De Roos. How Lipids Influence Food Flavor.
6. Mahan, K., and S. Escott-Stump. 2004. *Krause's Food, Nutrition, and Diet Therapy.* 11th ed. Philadelphia: Saunders.
7. Ibid.
8. Marieb, E. N. *Human Anatomy and Physiology.* 7th ed. San Francisco, CA: Benjamin Cummings.
9. Ganong, W. F. 1977. *Review of Medical Physiology.* 8th ed. Los Altos, CA: Lange Medical Publications.
10. Mahan. *Krause's Food, Nutrition, and Diet Therapy.*
11. Gropper, S. S., J. L. Smith, and J. L. Groff. 2005. *Advanced Nutrition and Human Metabolism.* 4th ed. Belmont, CA: Thomson Wadsworth.
12. Tortora, G. J., and N. P. Anagnostakos. 1990. *Principles of Anatomy and Physiology.* 6th ed. New York: Harper & Row Publishers.
13. Hole, J. W. 1984. *Human Anatomy and Physiology.* 3rd ed. Dubuque, IA: WC Brown Publishers.
14. Guyton, A. C. 1981. *Textbook of Medical Physiology.* 6th ed. Philadelphia: Saunders.
15. Ganong. *Review of Medical Physiology.*
16. Gropper. *Advanced Nutrition and Human Metabolism.*
17. Guyton. *Textbook of Medical Physiology.*
18. Mahan. *Krause's Food, Nutrition, and Diet Therapy.*
19. Gropper. *Advanced Nutrition and Human Metabolism.*
20. Marieb. *Human Anatomy and Physiology.*
21. Gropper. *Advanced Nutrition and Human Metabolism.*
22. U.S. Department of Health and Human Services. Oral Health. Available at www.4woman.gov/faq/oral_health.htm. Accessed June 2006.
23. Ibid.
24. Nelson, J. K., K. E. Moxness, M. D. Jensen, and C. F. Gastineau. 1994. *Mayo Clinic Diet Manual.* 7th ed. St. Louis: Mosby.
25. American Cancer Society. www.cancer.org.
26. Nelson et al. *Mayo Clinic Diet Manual.*
27. Anderson, D. M. 2002. *Mosby's Medical, Nursing and Allied Health Dictionary.* 6th ed. St. Louis: Mosby.
28. Mahan. *Krause's Food, Nutrition, and Diet Therapy.*
29. Nelson et al. *Mayo Clinic Diet Manual.*

Chapter 4

1. Painter, J., J. Rah, and Y. Lee. 2002. Comparison of International Food Guide Pictorial Representations. *Journal of the American Dietetic Association* 102: 483–489; Gifford, K. D. The Asian Diet Pyramid. *Oldways Preservation and Exchange Trust.* Available at www.oldwayspt.org. Accessed March 2003.
2. Johnson, M. 2003. *Human Biology: Concepts and Current Issues.* 2nd ed. San Francisco: Benjamin Cummings.
3. McBean, L., and G. Miller. 1998. Allaying Fears and Fallacies About Lactose Intolerance. *Journal of the American Dietetic Association* 98: 671–676; Suarez, M. D., D. Savaiano, and M. Levitt. 1995. A Comparison of Symptoms After the Consumption of Milk or Lactose-Hydrolyzed Milk by People with Self-Reported Severe Lactose Intolerance. *New England Journal of Medicine* 333: 1–4.
4. Suarez. A Comparison of Symptoms; Johnson, A., J. Semenya, M. Buchowski, C. Enownwu, and N. Scrimshaw. 1993. Correlation of Lactose Maldigestion, Lactose Intolerance, and Milk Intolerance. *American Journal of Clinical Nutrition* 57: 399–401.
5. Putnam, J., J. Allshouse, and L. Kantor. 2002. U.S. Per Capita Food Supply Trends: More Calories, Refined Carbohydrates, and Fats. Economic Research Service, *Food Review* 25: 2–15.
6. National Digestive Diseases Information Clearinghouse. May 2002. Lactose Intolerance. National Institutes of Health Publication No. 02-2751.
7. McBean. Allaying Fears and Fallacies.
8. Suarez, F., and M. Levitt. 1996. Abdominal Symptoms and Lactose: The Discrepancy Between Patients' Claims and the Results of Blinded Trials. *American Journal of Clinical Nutrition* 64: 251–252; Suarez, F. L., D. Savaiano, P. Arbisi, and M. Levitt. 1997. Tolerance to the Daily Ingestion of Two Cups of Milk by Individuals Claiming Lactose Intolerance. *American Journal of Clinical Nutrition* 65: 1502–1506.

9. Suarez. Tolerance to the Daily Ingestion; Dehkordi, N., D. R. Rao, A. P. Warren, and C. B. Chawan. 1995. Lactose Malabsorption as Influenced by Chocolate Milk, Skim Milk, Sucrose, Whole Milk, and Lactic Cultures. *Journal of the American Dietetic Association* 95: 484–486.
10. Johnson, A., J. Semenya, M. Buchowski, C. Enwonwu, and N. Scrimshaw 1993. Adaptation of Lactose Maldigesters to Continued Milk Intakes. *American Journal of Clinical Nutrition* 58: 879–881.
11. Lee, C., and C. Hardy. 1989. Cocoa Feeding and Human Lactose Intolerance. *American Journal of Clinical Nutrition* 49: 840–844; Hertzler, S., B. Huynh, and D. Savaiano. 1996. How Much Lactose Is Low Lactose? *Journal of the American Dietetic Association* 96: 243–246.
12. Institute of Medicine. *Dietary Reference Intakes for Energy, Carbohydrate, Fiber, Fat, Fatty Acids, Cholesterol, Protein, and Amino Acids.* 2002. Washington, D.C.: The National Academies Press.
13. Ibid.
14. Lin, B., and R. Morrison. 2002. Higher Fruit Consumption Linked with Lower Body Mass Index. Economic Research Service, *FoodReview* 25: 28–32.
15. Putnam. U.S. Per Capita Food Supply Trends.
16. Position of the American Dietetic Association: Use of Nutritive and Nonnutritive Sweeteners. 1998. *Journal of the American Dietetic Association* 98: 580–587.
17. Howard, B., and J. Wylie-Rosett. 2002. Sugar and Cardiovascular Disease: A Statement for Healthcare Professionals from the Committee on Nutrition of the Council on Nutrition, Physical Activity, and Metabolism of the American Heart Association. *Circulation* 106: 523–527.
18. American Dietetic Association: Use of Nutritive and Nonnutritive Sweeteners.
19. Institute of Medicine. *Dietary Reference Intakes for Energy.*
20. World Health Organization and the Food and Agricultural Organization. 2003. Report of the Joint WHO/FAO Expert Consultation on Diet, Nutrition and the Prevention of Chronic Diseases. www.who.int.
21. Putnam. U.S. Per Capita Food Supply Trends.
22. American Dietetic Association: Use of Nutritive and Nonnutritive Sweeteners.
23. Calorie Control Council. Reduced Calorie Sweeteners: Hydrogenated Starch Hydrolysates. Available at www.caloriecontrol.org. Accessed March 2003.
24. Report on Carcinogens, 2000. 9th ed.; U.S. Department of Health and Human Services. Public Health Service, National Toxicology Program.
25. Ajinomoto USA, Inc. The History of Aspartame. Available at www.aspartame.net/media/history.html. Accessed April 2003.
26. Council on Scientific Affairs. 1985. Aspartame: Review of Safety Issues. *Journal of the American Medical Association* 254: 400–402.
27. American Diabetes Association. 2003. Evidence-Based Nutrition Principles and Recommendations for the Treatment and Prevention of Diabetes and Related Complications. *Diabetes Care* 26: S51–S61; Hattan, D. G. 2002. Aspartame Limits. *FDA Consumer Magazine.* Available at www.cfsan.fda.gov. Accessed April 2003.
28. European Commission, Scientific Committee on Food. December 2002. Opinion of the Scientific Committee on Food: Update on the Safety of Aspartame. Available at www.europa.eu.int. Accessed March 2003.
29. National Institutes of Health. 2000. Report of the NIH Consensus Development Conference on Phenylketonuria (PKU): Screening and Management. Available at www.nichd.nih.gov. Accessed May 2003.
30. The NutraSweet Company. Neotame: A Scientific Overview. Available at www.neotame.com. Accessed March 2003.
31. National Digestive Diseases Information Clearinghouse. May 2000. Constipation. National Institutes of Health Publication No. 95-2754. Available at www.niddk.nih.gov. Accessed April 2003.
32. Ibid.
33. National Digestive Diseases Information Clearinghouse. January 2002. Diverticulosis and Diverticulitis. National Institutes of Health Publication No. 02-1163. Available at www.niddk.nih.gov. Accessed April 2003.
34. Miller, W., M. Niederpruem, J. Wallace, and A. Lindeman. 1994. Dietary Fat, Sugar, and Fiber Predict Body Fat Content. *Journal of the American Dietetic Association* 94: 612–615; Appley, P., M. Thorogood, J. Mann, and T. Key. 1998. Low Body Mass Index in Non-Meat Eaters: The Possible Roles of Animal Fat, Dietary Fibre and Alcohol. *International Journal of Obesity-Related Metabolic Disorders* 22: 454–460.
35. Pietinen, P., E. Rimm, P. Korhonen, A. Hartman, W. Willett, D. Albanes, and J. Virtamo. 1996. Intake of Dietary Fiber and Risk of Coronary Heart Disease in a Cohort of Finnish Men: The Alpha-Tocopherol, Beta-Carotene Cancer Prevention Study. *Circulation* 94: 2720–2727; Rimm, E., A. Ascherio, E. Giovannucci, D. Spiegelman, M. Stampfer, and W. Willett. 1996. Vegetable, Fruit, and Cereal Fiber Intake and Risk of Coronary Heart Disease Among Men. *Journal of the American Medical Association* 275: 447–451.

36. Wolk, A., J. Manson, M. Stampfer, G. Colditz, F. Hu, F. Speizer, C. Hennekens, and W. Willett. 1999. Long-Term Intake of Dietary Fiber and Decreased Risk of Coronary Heart Disease among Women. *Journal of the American Medical Association* 281: 1998–2004.

37. Chandalia, M., A. Garg, D. Lutjohann, K. von Bergmann, S. Grundy, and L. Brinkley. 2000. Beneficial Effects of High Fiber Intake in Patients with Type 2 Diabetes Mellitus. *New England Journal of Medicine* 342: 1392–1398; Vuksan, V., D. Jenkins, P. Spadafora, J. Sievenpiper, R. Owen, E. Vidgen, F. Brighenti, R. Josse, L. Leiter, and C. Bruce-Thompson. 1999. Konjac-Mannan (glucomannan) Improves Glycemia and Other Associated Risk Factors for Coronary Heart Disease in Type 2 Diabetes: A Randomized Controlled Metabolic Trial. *Diabetes Care* 22: 913–919; Anderson, J., L. Allgood, J. Turner, P. Oeltgen, and B. Daggy. 1999. Effects of Psyllium on Glucose and Serum Lipid Responses in Men with Type 2 Diabetes and Hypercholesterolemia. *American Journal of Clinical Nutrition* 70: 466–473.

38. Marlett, J., M. McBurney, and J. Slavin. 2002. Position of the American Dietetic Association: Health Implications of Dietary Fiber. *Journal of the American Dietetic Association* 102: 993–1000.

39. Institute of Medicine. *Dietary Reference Intakes for Energy*.

40. National Cancer Institute. 2003. Prevention of Colorectal Cancer. Available at www.cancer.gov. Accessed May 2003.

41. Bingham, S., N. Day, R. Luben, P. Ferrari, N. Slimani, T. Norat, et al. 2003. Dietary Fiber in Food and Protection Against Colorectal Cancer in the European Prospective Investigation into Cancer and Nutrition (EPIC): An Observation Study. *The Lancet* 361: 1496–1501; Ferguson, L., and P. Harris. 2003. The Dietary Fiber Debate: More Food for Thought. *The Lancet* 361: 1487–1488.

42. Ibid.

43. National Digestive Diseases Information Clearinghouse. September 2002. Diabetes Overview. National Institutes of Health Publication No. 06-3873. Available at www.niddk.nih.gov. Accessed January 2007.

44. American Diabetes Association. 2002. The Prevention or Delay of Type 2 Diabetes. *Diabetes Care* 25: 742–749.

45. National Digestive Diseases Information Clearinghouse. Diabetes Overview.

46. Ibid.

47. Ibid.

48. Centers for Disease Control and Prevention. 2002. Diabetes: Disabling, Deadly, and on the Rise. Accessed March 2003.

49. American Diabetes Association. 2003. Tests of Glycemia in Diabetes. *Diabetes Care* 26: S106–S108; National Diabetes Information Clearinghouse. October 2001. Diabetes Control and Complications Trial (DCCT). National Institutes of Health Publication No. 02-3874. Available at www.niddk.nih.gov. Accessed April 2003.

50. American Diabetes Association. Evidence-Based Nutrition Principles and Recommendations.

51. Sheard, N., N. Clark, J. Brand-Miller, M. Franz, F. Pi-Sunyer, E. Mayer-Davis, K. Kulkarni, and P. Geil. 2004. Dietary Carbohydrate (Amount and Type) in the Prevention and Management of Diabetes. *Diabetes Care* 27: 2266–2271.

52. Ludwig, D. 2002. The Glycemic Index: Physiological Mechanisms Relating to Obesity, Diabetes, and Cardiovascular Disease. *Journal of the American Medical Association* 287: 2414–2423.

53. Roberts, S. 2000. High-Glycemic Index Foods, Hunger, and Obesity: Is There a Connection? *Nutrition Reviews* 58: 163–169; Foster-Powell, K., and J. Brand-Miller. 1995. International Tables of Glycemic Index. *American Journal of Clinical Nutrition* 62: 871S–893S.

54. American Diabetes Association. Evidence-Based Nutrition Principles and Recommendations.

55. Centers for Disease Control and Prevention. Diabetes: Disabling, Deadly, and on the Rise.

56. American Diabetes Association Position Statement. 2003. Screening for Type 2 Diabetes. *Diabetes Care* 26: S21–S24.

57. National Digestive Diseases Information Clearinghouse. Diabetes Overview; Centers for Disease Control and Prevention. Diabetes: Disabling, Deadly, and on the Rise.

58. Centers for Disease Control and Prevention. Prevalence of Overweight among Children and Adolescents: United States, 1999–2000. National Center for Health Statistics. Available at: www.cdc.gov. Accessed March 2003.

59. American Diabetes Association. 2004. Type 2 Diabetes in the Young: The Evolving Epidemic. *Diabetes Care* 27: 1798–1811.

60. Diabetes Prevention Program Research Group. 2002. Reduction in the Incidence of Type 2 Diabetes with Lifestyle Intervention or Metformin. *New England Journal of Medicine* 346: 393–403.

61. National Digestive Diseases Information Clearinghouse. March 2003. Hypoglycemia. National Institutes of Health Publication No. 03-3926.

Feature Box References

1. Putnam, J., J. Allshouse, and L. Kantor. 2002. U.S. Per Capita Food Supply Trends: More Calories, Refined Carbohydrates, and Fats. Economic Research Service, *Food Review* 25: 2–15.

2. Slavin, J., D. Jacobs, L. Marquart, and K. Wiemer. 2001. The Role of Whole Grains in Disease Prevention. *Journal of the American Dietetic Association* 101: 780–785.

3. Jacobs, D., K. Meyer, L. Kushi, and A. Folsom. 1999. Is Whole Grain Intake Associated with Reduced Total and Cause-Specific Death Rates in Older Women? The Iowa Women's Health Study. *American Journal of Public Health* 89: 322–329; Liu, S., J. Manson, M. Stampfer, K. Rexrode, F. Hu, E. Rimm, and W. Willett. 2000. Whole Grain Consumption and Risk of Ischemic Stroke in Women. *Journal of the American Medical Association* 284: 1534–1540.

4. Jorge, S., A. Ascherio, E. Rimm, G. Colditz, D. Spiegelman, D. Jenkins, M. Stampfer, A. Wing, and W. Willett. 1997. Dietary Fiber, Glycemic Load, and Risk of NIDDM in Men. *Diabetes Care* 20: 545–550; Salmeron, J., J. Manson, M. Stampfer, G. Colditz, A. Wing, and W. Willett. 1997. Dietary Fiber, Glycemic Load, and Risk of Non-Insulin-Dependent Diabetes Mellitus in Women. *Journal of the American Medical Association* 277: 472–477; Meyer, K., L. Kushi, D. Jacobs, J. Slavin, T. Seller, and A. Folsom. 2000. Carbohydrates, Dietary Fiber, and Incident Type 2 Diabetes in Older Women. *American Journal of Clinical Nutrition* 71: 921–930.

5. Slavin. The Role of Whole Grains.

6. U. S. Department of Health and Human Services. November 2000. *Healthy People 2010*. With Understanding and Improving Health and Objectives for Improving Health. 2 vols. Washington, D.C.: U. S. Government Printing Office.

7. Burt, A., and P. Satishchandra. 2001. Sugar Consumption and Caries Risk: A Systematic Review. *Journal of Dental Education* 65: 1017–1023.

8. NIH Consenus Statement. 2001. Diagnosis and Management of Dental Caries Throughout Life. Available at www.concensus.nih.gov. Accessed March 2003.

9. Heller, K., B. Burt, and S. Ekund. 2001. Sugared Soda Consumption and Dental Caries in the United States. *Journal of Dental Research* 80, no. 10: 1949–1953; American Dental Association. 2002. Diet and Tooth Decay. *Journal of the American Dental Association* 133: 527; Joint Report of the American Dental Association Council on Access, Prevention and Interprofessional Relations and the Council on Scientific Affairs to the House of Delegates. 2001. Response to Resolution 73H-200. American Dental Association, 1–10. Available at: www.ada.org. Accessed May 2003.

10. Moynihan, P. 2002. Dietary Advice in Dental Practice. *British Dental Journal* 193: 563–568.

11. American Dental Association. 2003. Early Childhood Tooth Decay. Available at www.ada.org. Accessed May 2003.

12. Moynihan, P., S. Ferrier, and G. Jenkins. 1999. Eating Cheese: Does It Reduce Caries? *British Dental Journal* 187: 664–667; Kashket, S., and D. DePaola. 2002. Cheese Consumption and the Development and Progression of Dental Caries. *Nutrition Reviews* 60: 97–103.

13. Mandel, I. 1996. Caries Prevention: Current Strategies, New Directions. *Journal of the American Dental Association* 127: 1477–1488.

Chapter 5

1. Institute of Medicine. 2002. *Dietary Reference Intakes for Energy, Carbohydrate, Fiber, Fat, Fatty Acids, Cholesterol, Protein, and Amino Acids.* Washington, D.C.: The National Academies Press.

2. Kris-Etherton, P. M., W. S. Harris, and L. J. Appel. 2002. Fish Consumption, Fish Oil, Omega-3 Fatty Acids, and Cardiovascular Disease. *Circulation* 106: 2747–2757.

3. Stephen, A. M., and N. J. Wald. 1990. Trends in Individual Consumption of Dietary Fat in the United States, 1920–1984. *American Journal of Clinical Nutrition* 52: 457–469; Agriculture Research Service. 2000. Pyramid Servings Intakes by Children and Adults: 1994–1996, 1998. ARS Community Nutrition Research Group. Available at www.barc.usda.gov/bhnrc/cnrg. Accessed August 2003.

4. Chanmugam, P., J. F. Guthrie, S. Cecilio, J. F. Morton, P. Basiotis, and R. Anand. 2003. Did Fat Intake in the United States Really Decline between 1989–1991 and 1994–1996? *Journal of the American Dietetic Association* 103: 867–872.

5. Institute of Medicine. 2002. *Dietary Reference Intakes for Energy, Carbohydrate, Fiber, Fat, Fatty Acids, Cholesterol, Protein, and Amino Acids.* Washington, D.C.: The National Academies Press.

6. Ibid.

7. Ibid.

8. U.S. Department of Agriculture. 2000. Nutrition and Your Health: Dietary Guidelines for Americans. Home and Garden Bulletin No. 232.

9. Allison, D. B., S. K. Egan, L. M. Barraj, C. Caughman, M. Infante, and J. T. Heimbach. 1999. Estimated Intakes of *Trans* Fatty and Other Fatty Acids in the U.S. Population. *Journal of the American Dietetic Association* 99: 166–174.

10. Center for Food Safety and Applied Nutrition. July 9, 2003. Questions and Answers About *Trans* Fat Nutrition Labeling. CFSAN Office of Nutritional Products, Labeling and Dietary Supplements. Available at www.cfsan.fda .gov/~dams/qatrans2.html. Accessed July 2003.

11. Ibid.

12. Calorie Control Council. Fat Replacers: Food Ingredients for Healthy Eating. Available at www.caloriedcontrol.org/fatreprint.html. Accessed August 2003.

13. Mattes, R. D. 1998. Fat Replacers. *Journal of the American Dietetic Association* 98: 463–468.

14. Ibid.

15. Mattes. Fat Replacers; Wylie-Rosett, J. 2002. Fat Substitutes and Health: An Advisory from the Nutrition Committee of the American Heart Association. *Circulation* 105: 2800–2804.

16. Segal, M. Updated 1998. Fat Substitutes: A Taste of the Future? *FDA Consumer*. Available at www.vm.cfsan.fda.gov~lrd/fats.html. Accessed August 2003.

17. Ibid.

18. Mattes. Fat Replacers.

19. Ibid.

20. Sandler, R. S., N. L. Zorich, T. G. Filloon, H. B. Wiseman, D. J. Lietz, M. H. Brock, M. G. Royer, and R. K. Miday. 1999. Gastrointestinal Symptoms in 3,181 Volunteers Ingesting Snack Foods Containing Olestra or Trigylcerides: A 6-Week Randomized, Placebo-Controlled Trial. *Annals of Internal Medicine* 130: 253–261; Cheskin, L. J., R. Miday, N. Zorich, and T. Filloon. 1998. Gastrointestinal Symptoms Following Consumption of Olestra or Regular Triglyceride Potato Chips: A Controlled Comparison. *Journal of the American Medical Association* 279: 150–152.

21. Sandler, R. S., N. L. Zorich, T. G. Filloon, H. B. Wiseman, D. J. Lietz, M. H. Brock, M. G. Royer, and R. K. Miday. 1999. Gastrointestinal Symptoms in 3,181 Volunteers Ingesting Snack Foods Containing Olestra or Trigylcerides: A 6-Week Randomized, Placebo-Controlled Trial. *Annals of Internal Medicine* 130: 253–261.

22. U.S. Food and Drug Administration. 2003. FDA Changes Labeling Requirement for Olestra. FDA Talk Paper. Available at www.fda.gov/bbs/ topics/ANSWERS/2003/ANA01245.html. Accessed August 2003.

23. Patterson, R. E., A. R. Kristal, J. C. Peters, M. L. Neuhouser, C. L. Rock, L. J. Cheskin, D. Neumark-Sztainer, and M. D. Thornquist. 2000. Changes in Diet, Weight, and Serum Lipid Levels Associated with Olestra Consumption. *Archives of Internal Medicine* 160: 2600–2604.

24. Heart Disease and Stroke Statistics—2003 Update. December 2002. The American Heart Association. www.aha.org. Accessed July 2003.

25. American Heart Association. Atherosclerosis. www.aha.org. Accessed July 2003.

26. National Cholesterol Education Program. May 2001. High Blood Cholesterol: What You Need to Know. National Institutes of Health, National Heart, Lung, and Blood Institute. NIH Publication No. 01-3290. Available at www.nhlbi.nih.gov/health/public/heart/chol/hbc_what.htm. Accessed July 2003.

27. Sandmaier, M. Revised 2003. The Healthy Heart Handbook for Women. National Institutes of Health, National Heart, Lung, and Blood Institute. NIH Publicaiton No. 03-2720.

28. National Cholesterol Education Program. May 2001. High Blood Cholesterol: What You Need to Know. National Institutes of Health, National Heart, Lung, and Blood Institute. NIH Publication No. 01-3290. Available at www.nhlbi.nih.gov/health/public/heart/chol/hbc_what.htm. Accessed July 2003.

29. Heart Disease and Stroke Statistics—2003 Update. December 2002. The American Heart Association. www.aha.org. Accessed July 2003.

30. National Heart, Lung, and Blood Institute. Quitting Smoking. Available at www.nhlbi.nih.gov/hbp/prevent/q_smoke/Q_smoke.htm. Accessed July 2003.

31. Pace, B., C. L. Lynn, and R. M. Glass. 2001. Alcohol Use and Heart Disease. *Journal of the American Medical Association*. Vol. 285, no. 15.

32. Sandmaier, M. Revised 2003. The Healthy Heart Handbook for Women. National Institutes of Health, National Heart, Lung, and Blood Institute. NIH Publication No. 03-2720.

33. National Cholesterol Education Program. May 2001. Detection, Evaluation, and Treatment of High Blood Cholesterol in Adults (Adult Treatment Panel III). National Institutes of Health Publication No. 01-3290; Grundy, S. A., N. Abate, and M. Chandalia. 2002. Diet Composition and the Metabolic Syndrome: What Is the Optimal Fat Intake? *American Journal of Medicine* 113 (9B): 25S–29S.

34. National Cholesterol Education Program. May 2001. Detection, Evaluation, and Treatment of High Blood Cholesterol in Adults (Adult Treatment Panel III). National Institutes of Health Publication No. 01-670.

35. Institute of Medicine. 2002. *Dietary Reference Intakes for Energy, Carbohydrate, Fiber, Fat, Fatty Acids, Cholesterol, Protein, and Amino Acids.* Washington, D.C.: The National Academies Press.

36. Center for Food Safety and Applied Nutrition. July 9, 2003. Questions and Answers About *Trans* Fat Nutrition Labeling. CFSAN Office of Nutritional Products, Labeling and Dietary Supplements. Available at www.cfsan.fda .gov/~dams/qatrans2.html. Accessed July 2003.

37. Krauss, R. M., H. B. Eckel, and committee. 2000. 2000 AHA Dietary Guidelines. Revision 2000: A Statement for Healthcare Professionals from the Nutrition Committee of the American Heart Association. *Circulation* 102: 2296–2311.

38. U.S. Department of Agriculture. 2000. Nutrition and Your Health: Dietary Guidelines for Americans. *Home and Garden Bulletin* No. 232; Krauss. 2000 AHA Dietary Guidelines; Howell, W. H., D. J. McNamara, M. A. Tosca, B. T. Smith, and J. A. Gaines. 1997. Plasma Lipid and Lipoprotein Responses to Dietary Fat and Cholesterol: A Meta-Analysis. *American Journal of Clinical Nutrition* 65: 1747–1764.

39. Institute of Medicine. 2002. *Dietary Reference Intakes for Energy, Carbohydrate, Fiber, Fat, Fatty Acids, Cholesterol, Protein, and Amino Acids.* Washington, D.C.: The National Academies Press.

40. Krauss. 2000 AHA Dietary Guidelines. Hu, F. B., M. J. Stampfer, E. B. Rimm, J. E. Manson, A. Ascherio, G. Colditz, B. Rosner, D. Spiegelman, F. E. Speizer, F. M. Sacks, C. H. Hennekens, and W. C. Willett. 1999. A Prospective Study of Egg Consumption and Risk of Cardiovascular Disease in Men and Women. *Journal of the American Medical Association* 281: 1387–1394.

41. Kramhout, D., E. B. Bosschieter, and C. Coulander. 1985. The Inverse Relation between Fish Consumption and 20-Year Mortality from Coronary Heart Disease. *New England Journal of Medicine* 312: 1205–1209.

42. Institute of Medicine. *Dietary Reference Intakes for Energy, Carbohydrate, Fiber, Fat, Fatty Acids, Cholesterol, Protein, and Amino Acids.* 2002. Washington, D.C.: The National Academies Press; Kris-Etherton, P. M., W. S. Harris, and L. J. Appel. 2002. Fish Consumption, Fish Oil, Omega-3 Fatty Acids, and Cardiovascular Disease. *Circulation* 106: 2747–2757.

43. Daviglus, M. L., J. Stamler, A. J. Orencia, A. R. Dyer, K. Liu, P. H. Greenland, M. K. Walsh, D. Morris, and R. B. Shekelle. 1997. Fish Consumption and the 30-Year Risk of Fatal Myocardial Infaction. *New England Journal of Medicine* 336: 1046–1053; Albert, C. M., C. H. Hennekens, C. J. O'Donnell, U. A. Ajani, V. J. Carey, W. C. Willette, J. N. Ruskin, and J. E. Manson. 1998. Fish Consumption and Sudden Cardiac Death. *Journal of the American Medical Association* 279: 23–28.

44. Kris-Etherton, P. M., W. S. Harris, and L. J. Appel. 2002. Fish Consumption, Fish Oil, Omega-3 Fatty Acids, and Cardiovascular Disease. *Circulation* 106: 2747–2757.

45. Ibid.

46. Kris-Etherton, P. M., W. S. Harris, and L. J. Appel. 2002. Fish Consumption, Fish Oil, Omega-3 Fatty Acids, and Cardiovascular Disease. *Circulation* 106: 2747–2757; Center for Food Safety and Applied Nutrition. October 2000. Letter Regarding Dietary Supplement Health Claim for Omega-3 Fatty Acids and Coronary Heart Disease. Docket No. 91N-0103. Available at http://vm.cfsan.fda.gov/~dms/ds-ltr11.html. Accessed July 2003.

47. Center for Food Safety and Applied Nutrition. October 2000. Letter Regarding Dietary Supplement Health Claim for Omega-3 Fatty Acids and Coronary Heart Disease. Docket No. 91N-0103. Available at http://vm .cfsan.fda.gov/~dms/ds-ltr11.html. Accessed July 2003.

48. Kris-Etherton, P. M., D. S. Taylor, S. Yu-Poth, P. Huth, K. Moriarty, V. Fishell, R. L. Hargrove, G. Zhao, and T. D. Etherton. 2000. Polyunsaturated Fatty Acids in the Food Chain in the United States. *American Journal of Clinical Nutrition* 71: 179S–188S.

49. Brown, L., B. Rosner, W. Willett, and F. Sacks. 1999. Cholesterol-Lowering Effects of Dietary Fiber: A Meta-Analysis. *American Journal of Clinical Nutrition* 69: 30–42.

50. National Cholesterol Education Program. May 2001. Detection, Evaluation, and Treatment of High Blood Cholesterol in Adults (Adult Treatment Panel III). National Institutes of Health Publication No. 01-3290.

51. Anderson, J., B. Johnstone, and M. Cook-Newell. 1995. Meta-Analysis of the Effects of Soy Protein Intake on Serum Lipids. *New England Journal of Medicine* 333: 276–282.

52. Law, M. 2000. Plant Sterol and Stanol Margarines and Health. *British Medical Journal* 320: 861–864.

53. Food and Drug Administration. September 2000. FDA Authorizes New Coronary Heart Disease Health Claim for Plant Sterol and Plant Stanol

Esters. FDA Talk Paper. Available at www.cfsan.fda.gov/~lrd/tpstero.html. Accessed July 2003.

54. Miettinen, T. A., P. Puska, H. Gylling, H. Vanhanen, and E. Vartiainen. 1995. Reduction of Serum Cholesterol with Sitostanol-Ester Margarine in a Mildly Hypercholesterolemic Population. *New England Journal of Medicine* 333: 1308–1312.

55. Tribble, D. L. 1999. AHA Science Advisory. Antioxidant Consumption and Risk of Coronary Heart Disease: Emphasis on Vitamin C, Vitamin E, and β-Carotene. *Circulation* 99: 591–595.

56. Hu, F. B., M. J. Stampfer, J. E. Manson, E. B. Rimm, G. A. Colditz, B. A. Rosner, F. E. Speizer, C. H. Hennekens, and W. C. Willett. 1998. Frequent Nut Consumption and Risk of Coronary Heart Disease in Women: Prospective Cohort Study. *British Medical Journal* 317: 1341–1345.

57. Lino, M., K. Marcoe, J. M. Dinkins, H. Hiza, and R. Anand. 2000. The Role of Nuts in a Healthy Diet. Nutrition Insights. USDA Center for Nutrition Policy and Promotion. Available at www.usda.gov/cnpp/Insights. Accessed August 2003; Sabate, J., G. E. Fraser, K. Burke, S. Knutsen, H. Bennett, and K. Lindsted. 1993. Effects of Walnuts on Serum Lipid Levels and Blood Pressure in Normal Men. *New England Journal of Medicine* 328: 603–607; Hu, F. B., M. J. Stampfer, J. E. Manson, E. B. Rimm, G. A. Colditz, B. A. Rosner, F. E. Speizer, C. H. Hennekens, and W. C. Willett. 1998. Frequent Nut Consumption and Risk of Coronary Heart Disease in Women: Prospective Cohort Study. *British Medical Journal* 317: 1341–1345.

58. Feldman, E. B. 2002. LSRO Report: The Scientific Evidence of a Beneficial Health Relationship between Walnuts and Coronary Heart Disease. *Journal of Nutrition* 132: 1062S–1101S; Center for Food Safety and Applied Nutrition. 2003. Qualified Health Claims: Letter of Enforcement Discretion–Nuts and Coronary Heart Disease. Available at www.cfsan.fda/gov/~dms/qhcnuts2.html. Accessed August 2003.

59. Howard, B. V., and D. Kritchevsky. 1997. Phytochemcials and Cardiovascular Disease. *Circulation* 95: 2591; Warshafsky, S., R. Kamer, and S. Sivak. 1993. Effect of Garlic on Total Serum Cholesterol: A Meta-Analysis. *Annals of Internal Medicine* 119: 599–605.

60. Ibid.; Spigelski, D., and P. J. Jones. 2001. Efficacy of Garlic Supplementation in Lowering Serum Cholesterol Levels. *Nutrition Reviews* 59: 236–244.

61. Hertog, M. G. L., E. J. M. Feskens, P. C. H. Hollman, M. B. Katan, and D. Kromhout. 1993. Dietary Antioxidant Flavonoids and Risk of Coronary Heart Disease: The Zutphen Elderly Study. *The Lancet* 342: 1007–1011.

62. Mukamal, K. J., M. Maclure, J. E. Muffer, J. B. Sherwood, and M. A. Mittleman. 2002. Tea Consumption and Mortality After Acute Myocardial Infarction. *Circulation* 105: 2476–2481.

63. National Cholesterol Education Program. May 2001. Detection, Evaluation, and Treatment of High Blood Cholesterol in Adults (Adult Treatment Panel III). National Institutes of Health Publication No. 01-3290.

64. Thompson, P. D., D. Buchner, I. Pina, G. Balady, M. A. Williams, B. H. Marcus, K. Berra, S. N. Blair, F. Costa, B. Franklin, G. F. Fletcher, N. F. Gordon, R. P. Pate, B. J. Rodriguez, A. K. Yancey, and N. K. Wenger. 2003. AHA Scientific Statement. Exercise and Physical Activity in the Prevention and Treatment of Atherosclerotic Cardiovascular Disease. A Statement from the Council on Clinical Cardiology (Subcommittee on Exercise, Rehabilitation, and Prevention) and the Council on Nutrition, Physical Activity, and Metabolism (Subcommittee on Physical Activity). *Circulation* 107: 3109–3116.

65. World Health Organization and the Food and Agricultural Organization. 2003. Report of the Joint WHO/FAO Expert Consultation on Diet, Nutrition and the Prevention of Chronic Diseases. www.who.int.

66. Rimm, E., A. Klatsky, D. Grobbee, and M. J. Stampfer. 1996. Review of Moderate Alcohol Consumption and Reduced Risk of Coronary Heart Disease: Is the Effect Due to Beer, Wine or Spirits? *British Medical Journal* 312: 731–736.

67. Goldberg, I. J., L. Mosca, M. R. Piano, and E. A. Fisher. 2001. Wine and Your Heart: A Science Advisory for Healthcare Professionals from the Nutrition Committee, Council on Epidemiology and Prevention, and Council on Cardiovascular Nursing of the American Heart Association. *Circulation* 103: 472–475.

68. Rimm, E., and R. C. Ellison. 1995. Alcohol in the Mediterranean Diet. *American Journal of Clinical Nutrition* 61: 1378S–1382S.

69. Mukamal, K. J., K. M. Conigrave, M. A. Mittleman, C. A. Camaro, M. J. Stampfer, W. C. Willett, and E. B. Rimm. 2003. Roles of Drinking Pattern and Type of Alcohol Consumed in Coronary Heart Disease in Men. *New England Journal of Medicine* 348:109–118.

70. Jenkins, D. J., C. W. Kendal, A. Marchie, D. A. Faulkner, J. M. Wong, R. de Souza, A. Emam, T. L. Parker, E. Vidgen, K. G. Lapsley, E. A. Trautwein, R. G. Josse, L. A. Leiter, and P. W. Connelly. 2003. Effects of a Dietary Portfolio of Cholesterol-Lowering Foods vs. Lovastatin on Serum Lipids and C-Reactive Protein. *Journal of the American Medical Association* 290: 502–510.

71. Anderson, J. W. 2003. Diet First, Then Medication of Hypercholesterolemia. *Journal of the American Medical Association* 290: 531–533.

72. Institute of Medicine. *Dietary Reference Intakes for Energy, Carbohydrate, Fiber, Fat, Fatty Acids, Cholesterol, Protein, and Amino Acids.* 2002. Washington, D.C.: The National Academies Press.

73. Ibid.

74. U.S. Department of Agriculture. 2000. Nutrition and Your Health: Dietary Guidelines for Americans. *Home and Garden Bulletin* No. 232.

Feature Box References

1. Helsing, E. 1995. Traditional Diets and Disease Patterns of the Mediterranean, circa 1960. *American Journal of Clinical Nutrition* 61: 1329S–1337S.

2. Trichopoulou, A. N., T. Costacou, C. Bamia, and D. Trichopoulos. 2003. Adherence to a Mediterranean Diet and Survival in a Greek Population. *New England Journal of Medicine* 348: 2599–2608; de Lorgeril, M., P. Salen, J. L. Martin, I. Monjaud, J. Delaye, and N. Mamelle. 1999. Mediterranean Diet, Traditional Risk Factors, and the Rate of Cardiovascular Complications After Myocardial Infarction: Final Report of the Lyon Diet Heart Study. *Circulation* 99: 779–785; Kris-Etherton, P., R. H. Eckel, B. V. Howard, S. St. Jeor, T. L. Bazzarre. 2001. Lyon Diet Heart Study. Benefits of a Mediterranean-Style, National Cholesterol Education Program/American Heart Association Step I Dietary Pattern on Cardiovascular Disease Circulation 103: 1823–1825.

3. Willett, W. C., F. Sacks, A. N. Trichopoulou, G. Drescher, A. Ferro-Luzzi, E. Helsing, and D. Trichopoulos. 1995. Mediterranean Diet Pyramid: A Cultural Model for Healthy Eating. *American Journal of Clinical Nutrition* 61: 1402S–1406S.

4. Ibid.

5. de Lorgeril, M., P. Salen, J. L. Martin, I. Monjaud, J. Delaye, and N. Mamelle. 1999. Mediterranean Diet, Traditional Risk Factors, and the Rate of Cardiovascular Complications After Myocardial Infarction: Final Report of the Lyon Diet Heart Study. *Circulation* 99: 779–785.

6. Willett. Mediterranean Diet Pyramid; Nestle, M. 1995. Mediterranean Diets: Historical and Research Overview. *American Journal of Clinical Nutrition* 61: 1313S–1320S.

7. Nestle, M. 1995. Mediterranean Diets: Historical and Research Overview. *American Journal of Clinical Nutrition* 61: 1313S–1320S.

8. Ibid.

9. Keys, A. 1995. Mediterranean Diet and Public Health: Personal Reflections. *American Journal of Clinical Nutrition* 61: 1321S–1323S.

10. Food and Drug Administration. April 2003. FDA's Advisory on Methylmercury in Fish. Available at www.fda.gov/bbs/topics/ANSWERS/2003/ANS01209.html. Accessed July 2003; Food and Drug Administration. Revised May 1995. Mercury in Fish: Cause for Concern? *FDA Consumer Magazine.* Available at www.fda.gov/fdac/reprints/mercury.html. Accessed July 2003.

11. Center for Food Safety and Applied Nutrition. March 2001. An Important Message for Pregnant Women and Women of Childbearing Age Who May Become Pregnant about the Risks of Mercury in Fish. Available at www.cfsan.fda.gov/~acrobat/hgadv1.pdf. Accessed July 2003.

12. Food and Drug Administration. FDA's Advisory on Methylmercury in Fish; Food and Drug Administration. Revised May 1995. Mercury in Fish: Cause for Concern?

13. Environmental Protection Agency. Updated January 2003. Consumption Advice: EPA National Advice on Mercury in Freshwater Fish For Women Who Are or May Become Pregnant, Nursing Mothers, and Young Children. Available at www.epa.gov/waterscience/fishadvice/advice.html. Accessed July 2003.

Chapter 6

1. Johnson, M. D. 2003. *Human Biology: Concepts and Current Issues.* 2nd ed. San Francisco: Benjamin Cummings.

2. Institute of Medicine, National Academy of Sciences. 2002. *Dietary Reference Intakes for Energy, Carbohydrate, Fiber, Fat, Fatty Acids, Cholesterol, Protein, and Amino Acids.* Washington, DC: The National Academies Press.

3. Bennion, M. 1980. *The Science of Food.* New York: Harper & Row.

4. Food Safety and Inspection Service, U.S. Department of Agriculture. 1999. *Poultry: Basting, Brining, and Marinating.* Available at www.fsis.usda.gov/OA/pubs/bastebrine.htm. Accessed May 2004.

5. Institute of Medicine. *Dietary Reference Intakes for Energy.*

6. National Human Genome Research Institute. 2004. *Learning about Sickle Cell Disease.* Available at www.genome.gov. Accessed June 2004; National Institutes of Health. Genes and Disease, Sickle Cell Anemia. Available at www.ncbi.nlm.nih.gov/disease/sickle.html. Accessed June 2004.

7. Marieb, E. N. 2004. *Human Anatomy and Physiology.* 6th ed. San Francisco: Benjamin Cummings.

8. Murray, R. K., D. K. Granner, P. A. Mayes, and V. W. Rodwell. 2000. *Harper's Illustrated Biochemistry.* 26th ed. New York: Lange Medical Books/McGraw-Hill.

9. National Institute of Allergy and Infectious Diseases, National Institutes of Health. 2004. *Food Allergy and Intolerances.* Available at www.niaid.nih.gov/factsheets/food.htm. Accessed May 2004.

10. Stipanuk, M. 2000. *Biochemical and Physiological Aspects of Human Nutrition.* Philadelphia: W. B. Saunders Company.

11. Institute of Medicine. Dietary Reference Intakes for Energy.

12. American Dietetic Association, Dietitians of Canada, and the American College of Sports Medicine. 2000. Nutrition and Athletic Performance. *Journal of the American Dietetics Association* 100: 1543–1556; Eschbach, L. C. October–December 2002. *Nutrition: Protein and Creatine: Some Basic Facts.* American College of Sports Medicine, Fit Society Page. Available at www.acsm.org/health%2Bfitness/fit_society.htm. Accessed June 2004; Gibala, M. J., K. Tipton, and M. Hargreaves. 2000. *Amino Acids, Proteins, and Exercise Performance.* Gatorade Sports Science Institute, Sports Science Exchange Roundtable 42. Available at www.gssiweb.com. Accessed June 2004; Kleiner, S. M. Summer 2002. *Nutrition: Eating for Strength and Power.* American College of Sports Medicine, Fit Society Page. Available at www.acsm.org/health%2Bfitness/fit_society.htm. Accessed June 2004.

13. Institute of Medicine. *Dietary Reference Intakes for Energy.*

14. Allen, L. H., E. A. Oddoye, and S. Margen. 1979. Protein-induced Calciuria: A Longer-term Study. *American Journal of Clinical Nutrition* 32: 741–749; Lemann, J. 1999. Relationship between Urinary Calcium and Net Acid Excretion as Determined by Dietary Protein and Potassium: A Review. *Nephron* 81: 1–25; Reddy, S. T., C. Wang, K. Sahaee, L. Brinkley, and C. Pak. 2002. Effect of Low-carbohydrate High-protein Diets on Acid-base Balance, Stone-forming Propensity, and Calcium Metabolism. *American Journal of Kidney Diseases* 40: 265–274.

15. Heaney, R. P. 1998. Excess Dietary Protein May Not Adversely Affect Bone. *Journal of Nutrition* 128: 1054–1057.

16. Key, T. J., N. E. Allen, E. A. Spencer, and R. C. Travis. 2002. The Effect of Diet on Risk of Cancer. *The Lancet* 360: 861–868.

17. Promislow, J. H. E., D. Goodman-Gruen, D. J. Slymen, and E. Barrett-Connor. 2002. Protein Consumption and Bone Mineral Density in the Elderly. The Rancho Bernardo Study. *American Journal of Epidemiology* 155: 636–644; Wengreen, H. J., R. G. Munger, N. A. West, D. R. Cutler, C. D. Corcoran, J. Zhang, and N. E. Sassano. 2004. Dietary Protein Intake and Risk of Osteoporotic Hip and Fracture in Elderly Residents of Utah. *Journal of Bone and Mineral Research* 19: 537–545.

18. Institute of Medicine. *Dietary Reference Intakes for Energy.*

19. Shils, M. E., J. A. Olson, M. Shike, and A. C. Ross. 1999. *Modern Nutrition in Health and Disease,* 9th ed. Baltimore: Williams and Wilkens; World Health Organization/Programme of Nutrition. *WHO Global Database on Child Growth and Malnutrition* Introduction. Available at www.who.int/nutgrowthdb/about/introduction/en. Accessed June 2004.

20. Caulfield, L. E, M. de Onis, M. Blossner, and R. E. Black. 2004. Undernutrition as an Underlying Cause of Child Deaths Associated with Diarrhea, Pneumonia, Malaria, and Meals. *American Journal of Clinical Nutrition* 80: 193–198; de Onis, M., M. Blossner, E. Borghi, E. Frongillo, and R. Morris. 2004. Estimates of Global Prevalence of Childhood Underweight in 1990 and 2015. *Journal of the American Medical Association* 291: 2600–2606.

21. Shils. *Modern Nutrition.*

22. Ibid.

23. Ibid.

24. United Nations General Assembly. 2000. UN Resolution A/55/2. Available at www.un.org/millenium/declaration/ares552e.htm. Accessed June 2004; United Nations. 2002. The Millenium Development Goals: How Are We Doing? Available at www.un.org/milleniumgoals. Accessed June 2004.

25. Ginsberg, C., and A. Ostrowski. 2003. *The Market for Vegetarian Foods.* Available at www.vrg.org/nutshell/market.htm. Accessed June 2004. Position of the American Dietetic Association and Dietitians of Canada: Vegetarian Diets. *Journal of the American Dietetic Association* 103: 748–765.

26. Mintel Consumer Intelligence. 2003. *Vegetarian Foods, United States.* Available at www.consumer.mintel.com. Accessed June 2004; The Vegetarian Resource Group. 2003. *How Many Vegetarians Are There?* Available at www.vrg.org/press/2003poll.htm. Accessed June 2004.

27. Burger King Corporation Nutritional Facts. Available at www.burgerking.com/Food/Nutrition/ingredients.aspx. Accessed June 2004; Ginsberg. *Market for Vegetarian Foods.*

28. Appleby, P. N., M. Thorogood, J. Mann, T. J. Key. 1999. The Oxford Vegetarian Study: An Overview. *American Journal of Clinical Nutrition* 70: 525S–531S; Key, T. J., G. E. Fraser, M. Thorogood, P. N. Appleby, B. Beral, G. Reeves, M. L. Burr, J. Chang-Claude, R. Grentzel-Beyme, J. W. Kuzma, J. Mann, and K. McPherson. 1999. Mortality in Vegetarians and Non-vegetarians: Detailed Findings from a Collaborative Analysis of Five Prospective Studies. *American Journal of Clinical Nutrition* 70: 516S–524S.

29. Fraser, G. E. 1999. Associations between Diet and Cancer, Ischemic Heart Disease, and All-cause Mortality in Non-Hispanic White California Seventh-Day Adventists. *American Journal of Clinical Nutrition* 70: 532S–538S.

30. Fraser. Associations between Diet and Cancer; Jenkins, D. J., C. Kendall, A. Marchie, A. L. Jenkins, L. Augustin, D. S. Ludwig, N. D. Barnard, and J. W. Anderson. 2003. Type 2 Diabetes and the Vegetarian Diet. *American Journal of Clinical Nutrition* 78: 610S–616S.

31. Fraser. Association between Diet and Cancer.

Feature Box References

1. Energy Bars, Unwrapped. 2003. *Consumer Reports* (June 2003): 19–21.

2. Soyatech. 2004. *Soyfoods: The U.S. Market 2004 Report.* Available at www.soyatech.com. Accessed July 2004; United Soybean Board. 2003. *Consumer Attitudes about Nutrition.* Available at www.talksoy.com/ConsumerAttitudes/default.htm. Accessed July 2004.

3. Henkel, J. 2000. Soy Health Claims for Soy Protein, Questions about Other Components. *FDA Consumer Magazine.* Available at www.cfsan.fda.gov/~dms/fdsoypr.html. Accessed July 2004.

4. Munro, I. C., M. Harwood, J. J. Hlywka, A. M. Stephen, J. Doull, W. G. Flammn, and H. Adlercrutz. 2003. Soy Isoflavones: A Safety Review. *Nutrition Reviews* 61: 1–33; Vegetarian Nutrition, A Practice Group of the American Dietetics Association. 1999. *Isoflavones.* Available at www.vegetariannutrition.net.

5. Munro. Soy Isoflavones.

6. Anderson, J. W., B. M. Johnstone, and M. E. Cook-Newell. 1995. Meta-analysis of the Effects of Soy Protein Intake on Serum Lipids. *New England Journal of Medicine* 333: 276–282. Henkel, J. Soy: Health Claims for Soy Protein.

7. Messina, M. 1995. Modern Uses for an Ancient Bean: Soyfoods and Disease. *Chemistry and Industry* 11: 412–415; Messina, M. J., V. Persky, K. D. R. Setchell, and S. Barnes. 1994. Soy Intake and Cancer Risk: A Review of the In Vitro and In Vivo Data. *Nutrition and Cancer* 21: 113–131; Messina, M. J. and C. L. Loprinzi, 2001. Soy for Breast Cancer Survivors: A Critical Review of the Literature. *Journal of Nutrition* 131: 3095S–3108S.

8. Shu, X. O., F. Jin, Q. Dai, W. Wen, J. D. Potter, L. H. Kushi, Z. Ruan Y. Gao, and W. Zhenng. 2001. Soyfood Intake during Adolescence and Subsequent Risk of Breast Cancer among Chinese Women. *Cancer Epidemiology, Biomarkers & Prevention* 10: 483–488.

9. American Cancer Society. 2003. *Frequently Asked Questions about Nutrition and Physical Activity.* Available at www.cancer.org. Accessed July 2004; McMichael-Phillips, D. F., C. Harding, M. Morton, S. A. Roberts, A. Howell, C. S. Potten, and N. J. Bundred. 1998. Effects of Soy-Protein Supplementation on Epithelial Proliferation in the Histologically Normal Human Breast. *American Journal of Clinical Nutrition* 68: 1431S–1436S.

Chapter 7

1. Rosenfeld, L. 1997. Vitamine-Vitamin. The Early Years of Discovery. *Clinical Chemistry* 43: 680–685.

2. U.S. Department of Agriculture Food and Nutrition Services. 2002. Chapter 5 in *Building Blocks for Fun and Healthy Meals–A Menu Planner for the Child and Adult Care Food Program.* USDA Team Nutrition Resources. Available at www.fns.usda.gov/tn/Resources/buildingblocks.html. Accessed July 2005.

3. Lee, S. K., and A. A. Kader. 2000. Preharvest and Postharvest Factors Influencing Vitamin C Content of Horticultural Crops. *Postharvest Biology and Technology* 20: 207–220.

4. Pandrangi, S., and L. E. LaBorde. 2004. Retention of Folate, Carotenoid, and Other Quality Characteristics in Commercially Packaged Fresh Spinach. *Journal of Food Science* 69: C702-C707.

5. Institute of Medicine, Food and Nutrition Board. 2001. *Dietary Reference Intakes: Vitamin A, Vitamin K, Arsenic, Boron, Chromium, Copper, Iodine, Iron, Manganese, Molybdenum, Nickel, Silicon, Vanadium, and Zinc.* Washington, DC: The National Academies Press; Ross, A. C. 1999. Vitamin A and Retinoids. In M. E. Shils, J. Olson, M. Shike, A. C. Ross, eds., *Modern Nutrition in Health and Disease.* 9th ed. Baltimore: Williams and Wilkins.

6. Institute of Medicine. *Dietary Reference Intakes: Vitamin A.*

7. Office of Dietary Supplements, National Institutes of Health. 2003. Vitamin A and Caroteneids. Available at http://ods.od.nih.gov/factsheets/vitamina.asp; Ross, A. C. 1993. Vitamin A as Hormone: Recent Advances in Understanding the Actions of Retinol, Retinoic Acid, and Beta Carotene. *Journal of the American Dietetic Association* 93: 1285–1290.

8. Bershad, S. V. 2001. The Modern Age of Acne Therapy: A Review of Current Treatment Options. *Mount Sinai Journal of Medicine* 68: 279–286.

9. Institute of Medicine. *Dietary Reference Intakes: Vitamin A;* Ross. Vitamin A as Hormone.

10. Institute of Medicine. *Dietary Reference Intakes: Vitamin A.*

11. Institute of Medicine, Food and Nutrition Board. 2000. *Dietary Reference Intakes: Vitamin C, Vitamin E, Selenium, and Carotenoids.* Washington, DC: The National Academies Press.

12. Giovannuci, E. 1999. Tomatoes, Tomato-Based Products, Lycopene, and Cancer: Review of the Epidemiologic Literature. *Journal of the National Cancer Institute* 91: 317–331.

13. Institute of Medicine. *Dietary Reference Intakes: Vitamin A;* Office of Dietary Supplements. Vitamin A.

14. Institute of Medicine. *Dietary Reference Intakes: Vitamin A.*

15. Office of Dietary Supplements. Vitamin A.

16. Brinkley, N., and D. Krueger. 2000. Hypervitaminosis A and Bone. *Nutrition Reviews* 58: 138–144; de Souza, P. G., and L. G. Martini. 2004. Vitamin A Supplementation and Risk of Skeletal Fracture. mark, R. Berstrom, L. Holmber, H. Mallmin, A. Wolk, and S. Ljunghall. 1998. Excessive Dietary Intake of Vitamin A Is Associated with Reduced Bone Mineral Density and Increased Risk for Hip Fractures. *Annals of Internal Medicine* 129: 770–778; Office of Dietary Supplements. Vitamin A.

17. Feskanich, D., V. Singh, W. Willett, and G. Colditz. 2002. Vitamin A Intake and Hip Fractures among Postmenopausal Women. *Journal of the American Medical Association* 287: 47–54; Lips, P. 2003. Hypervitaminosis A and Fractures. *New England Journal of Medicine* 348: 347–349; Michaelsson, K., H. Lithell, B. Bvessby, and H. Melhus. 2003. Serum Retinol Levels and the Risk of Fractures. *New England Journal of Medicine* 348: 287–294.

18. Institute of Medicine. *Dietary Reference Intakes: Vitamin C.*

19. The Alpha-Tocopherol, Beta Carotene Cancer Prevention Study Group. 1994. The Effects of Vitamin E and Beta Carotene on the Incidence of Lung Cancer and Other Cancers in Male Smokers. *New England Journal of Medicine* 330: 1029–1035.

20. World Health Organization. 2004. Nutrition, Micronutrient Deficiencies. Available at www.who.int/nut/vad.htm. Accessed September 2004.

21. Mertz, W. 1994. A Balanced Approach to Nutrition for Health: The Need for Biologically Essential Minerals and Vitamins. *Journal of the American Dietetic Association* 94: 1259–1262.

22. Office of Dietary Supplements, National Institutes of Health. 2003. Vitamin E and Carotenoids. Available at http://ods.od.nih.gov/factsheets/vitamine.asp. Accessed November 2004.

23. Young, I. S., and J. V. Woodside. 2001. Antioxidants in Health and Disease. *Journal of Clincial Pathology* 54: 176–186.

24. Office of Dietary Supplements. Vitamin E.

25. Institute of Medicine. *Dietary Reference Intakes: Vitamin C.*

26. Miller, E. R., R. Pastor-Barriso, D. Dalal, R. A. Riemersma, L. J. Appel, and E. Guallar. 2005. Meta-Analysis: High-Dosage Vitamin E Supplementation May Increase All-Cause Mortality. *Annals of Internal Medicine* 142: 37–46.

27. Feskanich, D., P. Weber, W. C. Willet, H. Rockett, S. L. Booth, and G. A. Colditz. 1999. Vitamin K Intake and Hip Fractures in Women: A Prospective Study. *American Journal of Clinical Nutrition* 69: 74–79.

28. Brinkley, N. C., and J. W. Suttie. 1995. Vitamin K Nutrition and Osteoporosis. *Journal of Nutrition* 125: 1812–1821. Institute of Medicine. *Dietary Reference Intakes: Vitamin A.*

29. National Institutes of Health. 2003. Coumadin and Vitamin K. Available at http://ods.od.nih.gov/factsheets/cc/coumadin1.pdf. Accessed March 2005.

30. Institute of Medicine. *Dietary Reference Intakes: Vitamin A.*

31. Institute of Medicine, Food, and Nutrition Board. 1997. *Dietary Reference Intakes for Calcium, Phosphorus, Magnesium, Vitamin D, and Fluoride.* Washington, DC: The National Academies Press.

32. Heaney, R. P. 2003. Long-latency Deficiency Disease: Insights from Calcium and Vitamin D. *American Journal of Clinical Nutrition* 78: 912–919; National Institutes of Health Conference. 2003. Vitamin D and Health in the 21st Century. Available at www.nichd.nih.gov/about/od/prip/index.htm. Accessed October 2004.

33. Chiu, K. C., A. Chu, V. L. W. Go, and M. F. Saad. 2004. Hypovitaminosis D Is Associated with Insulin Resistance and Cell Dysfunction. *American Journal of Clinical Nutrition* 79: 820–825.

34. Newark, H. J., R. P. Heaney, and P. A. Lachance. 2004. Should Calcium and Vitamin D Be Added to the Current Enrichment Program for Cereal-Grain Products. *American Journal of Clinical Nutrition* 80: 264–270.

35. Institute of Medicine. *Dietary Reference Intakes for Calcium.*

36. Ibid.

37. Ibid.

38. National Institutes of Health. 2004. Dietary Supplement Fact Sheet: Vitamin D. Available at http://ods.od.nih.gov/factsheets/vitamind.asp. Accessed October 2004; Wharton, B., and N. Bishop. 2003. Rickets. *The Lancet* 362: 1389–1400.

39. Centers for Disease Control and Prevention. 2001. Severe Malnutrition among Young Children—Georgia, January 1997–June 1999. *Morbidity and Mortality Weekly Report.* Available at www.cdc.gov/mmwr/preview/mmwrhtml/mm5012a3.htm. Accessed October 2004; Gordon, C. M., K. C. DePeter, H. A. Feldman, E. Grace, and S. J. Emans. 2004. Prevalence of Vitamin D Deficiency among Healthy Adolescents. *Archives of Pediatric and Adolescent Medicine* 158: 531–537; Weisberg, P., K. S. Scanlon, R. Li, and M. E. Cogswell. 2004. Nutritional Rickets among Children in the United States: Review of Cases Reported between 1986 and 2003. *American Journal of Clinical Nutrition* 80: 1697S–1705S.

40. Lin, B., and K. Ralston. 2003. *Competitive Foods: Soft Drinks vs. Milk.* Washington, DC: U.S. Department of Agriculture, Economic Research Service. Available at www.ers.usda.gov/publications/fanrr34/fanrr34-7. Accessed October 2004.

41. Gartner, L. M., and F. R. Greer. 2003. Prevention of Rickets and Vitamin D Deficiency: New Guidelines for Vitamin D Intake. *Pediatric* 111: 908–910; Scanlon, K. S. 2001. Vitamin D Expert Panel Meeting. Available at www.cdc.gov/nccdphp/dnpa/nutrition/pdf/Vitamin_D_Expert_Panel_Meeting.pdf. Accessed October 2004.

42. Wharton. Rickets.

43. Agarwal, K. S., M. Z. Mughal, P. Upadhyay, J. L. Berry, E. B. Mawer, and J. M. Puliyel. 2002. The Impact of Atmospheric Pollution on Vitamin D Status of Infants and Toddlers in Delhi, India. *Archives of Disease in Childhood* 87: 111–113.

44. Heaney. Long-Latency Deficiency Disease; Holick, M. F. 1999. Vitamin D. In M. E. Shils, J. Olson, M. Shike, A. C. Ross, eds., *Modern Nutrition in Health and Disease.* 9th ed. Baltimore: Williams and Wilkins.

45. Rosenfeld. Vitamine-Vitamin.

46. Institute of Medicine, Food, and Nutrition Board. 1998. *Dietary Reference Intakes: Thiamin, Riboflavin, Niacin, Vitamin B$_6$, Folate, Vitamin B$_{12}$ Pantothenic Acid, Biotin, and Choline.* Washington, DC: The National Academies Press.

47. National Institute of Neurological Disorders and Stroke (NINDS). 2004. NINDS WernickeKorsakoff Syndrome Information Page. Updated 2004. Available at www.ninds.nih.gov/disorders/wernicke_korsakoff/wernicke-korsakoff.htm. Accessed December 2005.

48. Herreid, E. O., B. Ruskin, G. L. Clark, and T. B. Parks. 1952. Ascorbic Acid and Riboflavin Destruction and Flavor Development in Milk Exposed to the Sun in Amber, Clear, Paper, and Ruby Bottles. *Journal of Dairy Science* 35: 772–778.

49. Institute of Medicine. Dietary Reference Intakes: Thiamin.

50. Ibid.

51. Cervantes-Laurean, D., G. McElvaney, and J. Moss. Niacin. In M. E. Shils, J. Olson, M. Shike, A. C. Ross, eds., *Modern Nutrition in Health and Disease.* 9th ed. Baltimore: Williams and Wilkins.

52. Institute of Medicine. *Dietary Reference Intakes: Thiamin.*

53. Ibid.

54. National Institutes of Health. 2002. Vitamin B$_6$. Available at www.nih.gov. Accessed February 2005.

55. Leklem, J. M. 1999. Vitamin B$_6$. In M. E. Shils, J. Olson, M. Shike, A. C. Ross, eds., *Modern Nutrition in Health and Disease.* 9th ed. Baltimore: Williams and Wilkins.

56. American College of Obstetricians and Gynecologists. 2000. ACOG Practice Bulletin. *Premenstrual Syndrome.* No. 15; National Institute of Neurological Disorders and Stroke, National Institutes of Health. 2002. Carpal Tunnel Syndrome Fact Sheet. Available at www.ninds.nih.gov/disorders/carpal_tunnel/detail_carpal_tunnel.htm. Accessed February 2005; National Women's Health Information Center, U.S. Department of Health and Human Services. 2002. *Premenstrual Syndrome.* Available at www.4woman.gov/faq/pms.htm. Accessed February 2005; Schaumburg, H., J. Kaplan, A. Windebran, N. Vick, S. Rasmus, D. Pleasure, and M. J. Brown. 1983. Sensory Neuropathy from Pyridoxine Abuse. *New England Journal of Medicine* 309: 445–448.

57. Institute of Medicine. *Dietary Reference Intakes: Thiamin;* Office of Dietary Supplements, National Institutes of Health. 2004. Dietary Supplement Fact Sheet: Folate. Available at http://ods.od.nih.gov/factsheets/folate.asp. Accessed February 2005.

58. Centers for Disease Control and Prevention. 2003. Folic Acid Now Fact Sheet. Available at www.cdc.gov/doc.do/id/0900f3ec8000d615. Accessed February 2005.

59. Centers for Disease Control and Prevention. May 7, 2004. Spina Bifida and Anencephaly Before and After Folic Acid Mandate—United States, 1995–1996 and 1999–2000. *Morbidity and Morality Weekly Reports* 17: 362-365. Available at www.cdc.gov/mmwr/preview/mmwrhtml/mm5317a3.htm. Accessed in February 2005; Centers for Disease Control and Prevention. 2003. Information for Health Professional—Recommendations. Available at www.cdc.gov/doc.do/id/0900f3ec800523d6. Accessed February 2005; Centers for Disease Control and Prevention. August 2, 1991.

Effectiveness in Disease and Injury Prevention Use of Folic Acid for Prevention of Spina Bifida and Other Neural Tube Defects: 1983–1991. *Morbidity and Morality Weekly Reports* 40: 513–516. Available at www.cdc.gov/mmwr/preview/vitaminbhtml/00014915.htm. Accessed February 2005.

60. Centers for Disease Control. Folic Acid Now; Institute of Medicine. *Dietary Reference Intakes: Thiamin.*

61. Giovannucci, E., M. J. Stampfer, G. A. Colditz, D. J. Hunter, C. Fuchs, B. A. Rosner, F. E. Speizer, and W. C. Willett. 1998. Multivitamin Use, Folate, and Colon Cancer in Women in the Nurses Health Study. *Annals of Internal Medicine* 129: 517–524.

62. Institute of Medicine. *Dietary Reference Intakes: Thiamin.*

63. Centers for Disease Control. Effectiveness in Disease; Centers for Disease Control. Information for Health Professionals.

64. Institute of Medicine. *Dietary Reference Intakes: Thiamin.*

65. Office of Dietary Supplements, National Institutes of Health. 2004. Dietary Supplement Fact Sheet: Vitamin B_{12}. Available at www.ods.od.nih.gov/factsheets/vitaminb12.asp. Accessed February 2005; Shane, B. 2000. Folic Acid, Vitamin B_{12}, and Vitamin B_6. In M. H. Stipanuk, ed., *Biochemical and Physiological Aspects of Human Nutrition.* Philadelphia: Saunders.

66. Institute of Medicine. *Dietary Reference Intakes: Thiamin;* Office of Dietary Supplements. Fact Sheet: Vitamin B_{12}.

67. Ibid.

68. Ibid.

69. Institute of Medicine. *Dietary Reference Intakes: Vitamin C.*

70. Iqbal, K., A. Khan, M. Khattak. 2004. Biological Significance of Ascorbic Acid (Vitamin C) in Human Health. *Pakistan Journal of Nutrition* 3: 5–13.

71. Ibid.

72. Institute of Medicine. *Dietary Reference Intakes: Vitamin C.*

73. Rosenfeld. Vitamine-Vitamin.

74. Ibid.

75. Glusman, M. 1947. The Syndrome of "Burning Feet" (Nutritional Melagia) as a Manifestation of Nutritional Deficiency. *America Journal of Medicine* 3: 211–223.

76. Sweetmna, L. 2000. Pantothenic Acid and Biotin. In M. H. Stipanuk, ed., *Biochemical and Physiological Aspects of Human Nutrition.* Philadelphia: Saunders.

77. Mock. D. M. 1999. Biotin. In M. E. Shils, J. Olson, M. Shike, A. C. Ross, eds., *Modern Nutrition in Health and Disease.* 9th ed. Baltimore: Williams and Wilkins.

78. Institute of Medicine. *Dietary Reference Intakes: Thiamin;* Zeisel, S. H., K. H. Da Costa, P. D. Franklin, E. A. Alexander, J. T. Lamont, N. F. Sheard, and A. Beiser. 1991. Choline, an Essential Nutrient for Humans. *Federation of American Societies for Experimental Biology* 5: 2093–2098.

79. National Institutes of Health. 2004. Carnitine: The Science Behind a Conditionally Essential Nutrient. Available at http://ods.od.nih.gov/News/Carnitine_Conference_Summary.aspx. Accessed September 2004.

80. Packer, L., E. H. Witt, and H. J. Tritschler. 1994. Alpha-lipoic Acid as a Biological Antioxidant. *Free Radical Biology and Medicine* 19: 227–250.

81. Young. Antioxidants in Health.

82. Dröge, W. 2002. Free Radicals in the Physiological Control of Cell Function. *Physiology Review* 82: 47–95; Traber, M. G. and H. Sies. 1996. Vitamin E in Humans: Demand and Delivery. *Annual Review of Nutrition* 16: 321–347; Young. Antioxidants in Health.

83. National Eye Institute, National Institutes of Health. 2004. Age-Related Macular Degeneration: What You Should Know. Updated June 2004. Available at www.nei.nih.gov/health/maculardegen/armd_facts.asp#1. Accessed September 2004.

84. Age-Related Eye Disease Study Research Group. 2001. A Randomized, Placebo-Controlled, Clinical Trial of High-Dose Supplementation with Vitamins C and E, Beta Carotene, and Zinc for Age-Related Macular Degeneration and Vision Loss: AREDS Report No. 8. *Archives of Ophthalmology* 119: 1417–1436; Brown, L., E. B. Rimm, J. M. Seddon, E. L. Giovannucci., L. Chasan-Tabar, D. Spiegelman, W. C. Willett, and S. E. Hankinson. 1999. A Prospective Study of Carotenoid Intake and Risk of Cataract Extraction in U.S. Men. *American Journal of Clinical Nutrition* 70: 517–524; Chasan-Tabar, L., W. C. Willett, J. M. Seddon, M. J. Stampfer, B. Rosner, G. A. Colditz, F. E. Speizer, and S. E. Hankinson. 1999. A Prospective Study of Carotenoid Intake and Risk of Cataract Extraction in U.S. Women. *American Journal of Clinical Nutrition* 70: 509–516; The National Eye Institute, National Institutes of Health. 2004. The AREDS Formulation and Age-Related Macular Degeneration: Are These High Levels of Antioxidants and Zinc Right for You? Updated June 2004. Available at www.nei.nih.gov/amd/summary.asp. Accessed September 2004.

85. Mares, J. A., T. L. La Rowe, and B. A. Blodi. 2004. Doctor, What Vitamins Should I Take for My Eyes? *Archives of Ophthalmology* 122: 628–635; The National Eye Institute, National Institutes of Health. 2004. Cataract: What

You Should Know. Updated August 2004. Available at www.nei.nih.gov/health/cataract/cataract_facts.asp. Accessed September 2004.

86. Craig, W. J. 1997. Phytochemicals: Guardians of Our Health. *Journal of the American Dietetic Association* 97: S199–S204.

87. Kris-Etherton, P., A. H. Lichtenstein, B. V. Howard, D. Steinberg, J. L. Witztum. 2004. Antioxidant Vitamin Supplements and Cardiovascular Disease. *Circulation* 110: 637–641; U.S. Preventive Services Task Force. 2003. Routine Vitamin Supplementation to Prevent Cancer and Cardiovascular Disease: Recommendations and Rationale. *Annals of Internal Medicine* 139: 51–55.

88. U.S. Department of Agriculture. 2005. *2005 Report of the Dietary Guidelines Advisory Committee on the Dietary Guidelines for Americans.* Available at www.health.gov/dietaryguidelines/dga2005/report. Accessed February 2005.

89. Packaged Facts. The U.S. Market for Fortified Foods: Expanding the Boundaries. Available at www.marketresearch.com.

90. Balluz, L. S., S. M. Kieszak, R. M. Philen, and J. Mulinare. 2000. Vitamin and Mineral Supplement Use in the United States. *Archives of Family Medicine* 9: 258–262; Kaufman, D. W., J. P. Kelly, L. Rosenberg, T. E. Anderson, and A. A. Mitchell. 2002. Recent Patterns of Medication Use in the Ambulatory Adult Population of the United States: The Slone Survey. *Journal of the American Medical Association* 287: 337–344.

91. Hunt, J., and J. Dwyer. 2001. Position of the American Dietetic Association: Food Fortification and Dietary Supplements. *Journal of the American Dietetic Association* 101: 115–125.

92. Food and Drug Administration. 2004. FDA Announces Major Initiatives for Dietary Supplements. Available at www.cfsan.fda.gov/~lrd/fpsupp.html. Accessed March 2005; Food and Drug Administration, Center for Food Safety and Applied Nutrition. 2002. Overview of Dietary Supplements. Available at www.cfsan.fda.gov/~dms/supplmnt.html. Accessed March 2005; National Center for Complementary and Alternative Medicine. 2004. What's in the Bottle? An Introduction to Dietary Supplements. Available at http://nccam.nih.gov/health/supplements.htm. Accessed March 2005.

93. United States Pharmacopoeia. USP's Dietary Supplement Verification Program. Available at www.uspverified.org/index.html. Accessed March 2005.

Feature Box References

1. Chalmers, T. C. 1975. Effects of Ascorbic Acid on the Common Cold. An Evaluation of the Evidence. *American Journal of Medicine* 58: 532–536; Hemila, H., and Z. S. Herman. 1995. Vitamin C and the Common Cold: A Retrospective Analysis of Chalmers' Review. *American College of Nutrition* 14: 116–123; Institute of Medicine, Food, and Nutrition Board. 2001. *Dietary Reference Intakes: Vitamin A, Vitamin K, Arsenic, Boron, Chromium, Copper, Iodine, Iron, Manganese, Molybdenum, Nickel, Silicon, Vanadium, and Zinc.* Washington, DC: National Academy Press; Institute of Medicine, Food, and Nutrition Board. 2000. *Dietary Reference Intakes: Vitamin C, Vitamin E, Selenium, and Carotenoids.* Washington, DC: National Academy Press; Mossad, S. B. 2005. Treatment of the Common Cold. *British Medical Journal* 317: 33–36; National Institute of Allergy and Infectious Diseases, National Institutes of Health. 2004. *The Common Cold.* Available at www.niaid.nih.gov/factsheets/cold.htm. Accessed March 2005; Pauling, L. 1971. The Significance of the Evidence about Ascorbic Acid and the Common Cold. *Proceedings from the National Academy of Science* 68: 2678–2681.

2. Caruso, T. J., and J. M. Gwaltney. 2005. Treatment of the Common Cold with Echinacea: A Structured Review. *Clinical Infectious Diseases* 40: 807–810; Taylor, J. A., W. Weber, L. Standish, H. Quinn, J. Goesling, M. McGann, C. Calabrese. 2003. Efficacy and Safety of Echniacea in Treating Upper Respiratory Tract Infections in Children. *Journal of the American Medical Association* 290: 2824–2830; Turner, R. B., R. Bauer, K. Woelkart, T. C. Haulsey, and D. Gangemie. 2005. An Evaluation of *Echniacea Angustifolia* in Experimental Rhinovirus Infections. *New England Journal of Medicine* 353: 341–348.

3. Centers for Disease Control and Prevention, U.S. Department of Health and Human Services. 2004. Stopping Germs at Home, Work and School. Available at www.cdc.gov/germstopper/home_work_school.htm. Accessed March 2005; Food and Drug Administration Center for Foods Safety and Applied Nutrition, National Science Teachers Association. 2001. Hand Washing. Available at www.cfsan.fda.gov/~dms/a2z-h.html. Accessed March 2005.

4. Appel, L. J., E. R. Miller, S. H. Jee, R. Stolzenberg-Solomon, P. Lin, T. Erlinger, M. R. Nadeau, and J. Selhub. 2000. Effect of Dietary Patterns on Serum Homocysteine: Results of a Randomized Controlled Feeding Study. *Circulation* 102: 852–857; Finklestein, J. D. 2000. Homocysteine: A History in Progress. *Nutrition Reviews* 58: 193–204; Institute of Medicine, Food,

and Nutrition Board. 1998. *Dietary Reference Intakes: Thiamin, Riboflavin, Niacin, Vitamin B$_6$, Folate, Vitamin B$_{12}$ Pantothenic Acid, Biotin, and Choline.* Washington, DC: National Academy Press.

5. Jacques, P. F., J. Selhum, A. G. Bostom, P. W. F. Wilson, and I. H. Rosenberg. 1999. The Effects of Folic Acid Fortification on Plasma Folate and Total Homocysteine Concentrations. *New England Journal of Medicine* 340: 1449–1454; Malinow, M. R., A. G. Bostom, and R. M. Krauss. 1999. Homocyst(e)ine, Diet and Cardiovascular Diseases. A Statement for Health Care Professionals from the Nutrition Committee. *Circulation* 99: 178–182; Miller, J. W. 2000. Does Lowering Plasma Homocysteine Reduce Vascular Disease Risk? *Nutrition Reviews* 59: 241–244.

Chapter 8

1. Grandjean, A., and S. Campbell. 2004 *Hydration: Fluids for Life.* Washington, D.C.: ILSI Press. Available at http://www.ilsi.org. Accessed August 2005; Institute of Medicine. 2004. *Dietary Reference Intakes: Water, Potassium, Sodium, Chloride, and Sulfate.* Washington, D.C.: The National Academies Press. Available at www.nap.edu; Marieb, E. N. 2004. Chemistry comes alive. In *Human Anatomy and Physiology.* 6th ed. San Francisco: Pearson/Benjamin Cummings.

2. Sheng, H. 2000. Body fluids and water balance. In *Biochemical and Physiological Aspects of Human Nutrition.* Philadelphia: W. B. Saunders.

3. Institute of Medicine. *Dietary Reference Intakes: Water.*

4. Grandjean and Campbell. *Hydration: Fluids for Life;* Institute of Medicine. *Dietary Reference Intakes: Water;* Marieb, *Human Anatomy and Physiology.*

5. Marieb. *Human Anatomy and Physiology.*

6. Sheng. Body fluids and water balance.

7. Institute of Medicine. *Dietary Reference Intakes: Water.*

8. Ibid.

9. Casa, D. J., L. E. Armstrong, S. K. Hillman, S. J. Montain, R. C. Reiff, B. S. E. Rich, W. O. Roberts, J. A. Stone. 2000. National Athletic Trainers Association Position Statement: Fluid Replacement for Athletes. *Journal of Athletic Training* 35: 212–224.

10. Institute of Medicine. *Dietary Reference Intakes: Water.*

11. Arnold, D. To the End, Marathon Was at Center of Student's Life. *The Boston Globe,* April 18, 2002; Aucoin, D. Tribute to a Fallen Champion of the Needs of the Afflicted. *The Boston Globe.* October 26, 2002; Noakes, T. D. 2003. Overconsumption of Fluids by Athletes. *British Medical Journal* 327: 113–114; Rosinski, J. Friends Remember Marathoner Who Died. Available at www.remembercynthia.com. Accessed August 2005; Smith, S. Marathon Runner's Death Linked to Excessive Fluid Intake. *The Boston Globe,* August 13, 2002.

12. Grandjean, A. C., K. J. Reimers, and M. E. Buyckx. 2003. Hydration: Issues for the 21st Century. *Nutrition Reviews* 61: 261–271.

13. Grandjean and Campbell. *Hydration: Fluids for Life;* Institute of Medicine. *Dietary Reference Intakes: Water.*

14. Institute of Medicine. *Dietary Reference Intakes: Water.*

15. Grandjean et al. Hydration: Issues for the 21st Century; Institute of Medicine. *Dietary Reference Intakes: Water.*

16. Anderson, J. B. 2004. Minerals. In *Krause's Food, Nutrition and Diet Therapy.* 11th ed. Philadelphia: W. B. Saunders.

17. Institute of Medicine. *Dietary Reference Intakes: Water.*

18. Ibid.

19. Ibid.

20. Sheng. Body fluids and water balance.

21. Institute of Medicine. 1997. *Dietary Reference Intakes: Calcium, Phosphorus, Magnesium, Vitamin D, and Fluoride.* Washington, D.C.: The National Academies Press. Available at www.nap.edu.

22. Institute of Medicine. *Dietary Reference Intakes: Calcium;* Office of Dietary Supplements. Updated 2005. Dietary Supplement Fact Sheet: Calcium. Available at http://ods.od.nih.gov/factsheets/calcium.asp. Accessed October 2005.

23. Institute of Medicine, *Dietary Reference Intakes: Calcium;* Miller, G. D., G. D. DiRienzo, M. E. Reusser, and D. A. McCarron. 2000. Benefits of Dairy Product Consumption on Blood Pressure in Humans: A Summary of the Biomedical Literature. *Journal of the American College of Nutrition* 19: 147S–164S.

24. Baron, J. A., M. Beach, J. S. Mandel, R. U. van Stolk, R. W. Haile, R. S. Sandler, R. Rothstein, R. W. Summers, D. C. Snover, G. J. Beck, J. H. Bond, and E. R. Greenberg. 1999. Calcium Supplements for the Prevention of Colorectal Adenomas. *The New England Journal of Medicine* 340: 101–107; Wu, K., W. C. Willet, C. S. Fuchs, G. A. Colditz, and E. L. Giovannucci. 2002. Calcium Intake and Risk of Colon Cancer in Women and Men. *Journal of the National Cancer Institute* 94: 437–446.

25. National Kidney and Urologic Diseases Information Clearinghouse, National Institute of Diabetes and Digestive and Kidney Diseases, National Institutes of Health. 2004. Kidney and Urologic Diseases Statistics for the United States. Available at http://kidney.niddk.nih.gov/kudiseases/pubs/kustats/index.htm. Accessed October 2005; Reynolds, T. M. 2005. Chemical Pathology Clinical Investigation and Management of Nephrolithiasis, *Journal of Clinical Pathology* 58: 134–140.

26. Borghi, L., R. Schianchi, T. Meschi, A. Guerra, U. Maggiore, and A. Novarini. 2002. Comparison of Two Diets for the Prevention of Recurrent Stones in Idiopathic Hypercalciuria. *New England Journal of Medicine* 346: 77–84; Bushinsky, D. A. 2002. Recurrent Hypercalciuric Nephrolithiasis: Does Diet Help? *New England Journal of Medicine* 346: 124–125; Curhan, G. C., W. C. Willett, E. B. Rimm, and M. J. Stampfer. 1993. A Prospective Study of Dietary Calcium and Other Nutrients and the Risk of Symptomatic Kidney Stones. *New England Journal of Medicine* 328: 838–888.

27. Zemel, M. B., W. Thompson, K. Morris, and P. Campbell. 2004. Calcium and Dairy Acceleration of Weight and Fat Loss During Energy Restriction in Obese Adults. *Obesity Research* 12: 582–590.

28. Parikh, S. J. and J. A. Yanovski. 2003. Calcium Intake and Adiposity. *American Journal of Clinical Nutrition* 77: 281–287.

29. U.S. Department of Agriculture. Results from USDA's 1996 Continuing Survey of Food Intakes by Individuals and 1996 Diet and Health Knowledge Survey, Table Set 6. Available at www.ars.usda.gov/SP2UserFiles/Place/12355000/pdf/Csfii96.PDF. Accessed October 2005.

30. U.S. Department of Agriculture. Pyramid Servings Data: Results from the USDA's 1995 and 1996 Continuing Survey of Food Intakes by Individuals, Table Set 7. Available at www.ars.usda.gov/SP2UserFiles/Place/12355000/pdf/3yr_py.PDF. Accessed October 2005.

31. National Institutes of Health, Osteoporosis and Related Bone Diseases-National Resource Center. 2005. Osteoporosis Overview. Available at www.osteo.org/osteo.html. Accessed October 2005; U.S. Department of Health and Human Services. 2004. *Bone Health and Osteoporosis: A Report of the Surgeon General.* Rockville, MD: U.S. Department of Health and Human Services, Office of the Surgeon General.

32. National Institutes of Health (NIH). 2000. Osteoporosis Prevention, Diagnosis, and Therapy. NIH Consensus Statement Online. Available at http://consensus.nih.gov/2000/2000Osteoporosis111html.htm. Accessed October 2005.

33. National Institutes of Health, Osteoporosis and Related Bone Diseases-National Resource Center. 2005. Calcium Supplements: What to Look For. Available at http://www.niams.nih.gov/bone/hi/calcium_supp.pdf. Accessed October 2005.

34. Institute of Medicine. *Dietary Reference Intakes: Calcium.*

35. Ibid.

36. Office of Dietary Supplements. Updated 2005. Magnesium. Available at http://ods.od.nih.gov. Accessed October 2005.

37. Appel, L. J., T. J. Moore, E. Obarzanek, W. M. Vollmer, L. P. Svetkey, F. M. Sacks, G. A. Bray, T. M. Vogt, J. A. Cutler, M. M. Windhauser, P. Lin, and N. Karanja. 1997. A Clinical Trial of the Effects of Dietary Patterns on Blood Pressure. *New England Journal of Medicine* 336: 1117–1124.

38. Harsha, D. W., P. Lin, E. Obarzanek, N. M. Karanja, T. J. Moore, and B. Caballero. 1999. Dietary Approaches to Stop Hypertension: A Summary of Study Results. *Journal of the American Dietetics Association* 99: S35–S39.

39. American Diabetes Association. 2004. Nutrition Principles and Recommendations in Diabetes. *Diabetes Care* 27: S36; Lopez-Ridaura, R., W. C. Willet, E. B. Rimm, S. Liu, M. J. Stampfer, J. E. Manson, and F. B. Hu. 2004. Magnesium Intake and Risk of Type 2 Diabetes in Men and Women. *Diabetes Care* 27: 134–140.

40. Institute of Medicine, *Dietary Reference Intakes: Calcium.*

41. Institute of Medicine. *Dietary Reference Intakes: Water.*

42. Anderson. Minerals.

43. Institute of Medicine. 2001. *Dietary Reference Intakes: Vitamin A, Vitamin K, Arsenic, Boron, Chromium, Copper, Iodine, Iron, Manganese, Molybdenum, Nickel, Silicon, Vanadium, and Zinc.* Washington, D.C.: The National Academies Press. Available at www.nap.edu.

44. Ibid.

45. Beard, J. 2003. Iron Deficiency Alters Brain Development and Functioning. *Journal of Nutrition* 133: 1468S–1472S; Black, M. M. 2003. Micronutrient Deficiencies and Cognitive Function. *Journal of Nutrition* 133: 3972S–3931S.

46. Institute of Medicine. *Dietary Reference Intakes: Calcium.*

47. Britton, H. C., and C. E. Nossamn. 1986. Iron Content of Food Cooked in Iron Utensils. *Journal of the American Dietetic Association* 86: 897–901.

48. U.S. Food and Drug Administration. 1997. FDA Backgrounder: Preventing Iron Poisoning in Children. Available at www.cfsan.fda.gov/~dms/bgiron.html. Accessed November 2005.

49. Centers for Disease Control and Prevention (CDC). 2005. Iron Overload and Hemochromatosis: Causes and Risk Factors. Available at www.cdc.gov/hemochromatosis/index.htm. Accessed November 2005; CDC. 1998.

Recommendations to Prevent and Control Iron Deficiency in the United States. *Morbidity and Mortality Weekly Report* 47: 1–29; Office of Dietary Supplements. Updated 2005. Dietary Supplement Fact Sheet: Iron. Available at http://ods.od.nih.gov/factsheets/iron.asp. Accessed October 2005.

50. Institute of Medicine. 2001. *Dietary Reference Intakes: Vitamin A;* Turnlund, J. R. 2006. Copper. In Shils, M. E., M. Shike, A. C. Ross, B. Caballero, and R. J. Cousins, eds. *Modern Nutrition in Health and Disease.* 10th ed. Philadelphia: Lippincott Williams and Wilkins; Uaruy, R., M. Olivares, and M. Gonzalez. 1998. Essentiality of Copper in Humans. *American Journal of Clinical Nutrition* 67: 952S–959S.

51. Institute of Medicine. *Dietary Reference Intakes: Vitamin A;* Office of Dietary Supplements. Updated 2002. Zinc. Available at http://ods.od.nih.gov/factsheets/cc/zinc.html. Accessed November 2005.

52. Ibs, K., and L. Rink. 2003. Zinc-altered Immune Function. *Journal of Nutrition* 133: 1452S–1456S; Schwartz, J. R., R. G. Marsh, and Z. D. Draelos. 2005. Zinc and Skin Health: Overview of Physiology and Pharmacology. *Dermatological Surgery* 31: 837–847; Walravens, P. A. 1979. Zinc Metabolism and Its Implications in Clinical Medicine. *Western Journal of Medicine* 130: 133–142.

53. Russell, R. M., M. E. Cox, and N. Solomons. 1983. Zinc and the Special Senses. *Annals of Internal Medicine* 99: 227–239.

54. Farr, B. M., and J. M. Gwaltney. 1987. The Problems of Taste in Placebo Matching: An Evaluation of Zinc Gluconate for the Common Cold. *Journal of Chronic Disease* 40: 875–879.

55. Desbiens, M. A. 2000. Lessons Learned from Attempts to Establish the Blind in Placebo-controlled Trial of Zinc for the Common Cold. *Annals of Internal Medicine* 133: 302–303; Jackson, J. L., E. Lesho, and C. Peterson. 2000. Zinc and the Common Cold: A Meta-analysis Revisited. *Journal of Nutrition* 130: 1512S–1515S; King, J. C., and R. J. Cousins. 2006. Zinc. In Shils et al. *Modern Nutrition in Health and Disease.* 10th ed. Philadelphia: Lippincott Williams and Wilkins; Mossad, S. B., M. L. Macknin, S. V. Medendorp, and P. Mason. 1996. Zinc Gluconate Lozenges for Treating the Common Cold: A Randomized, Double-blind, Placebo-controlled Study. *Annals of Internal Medicine* 125: 81–88; Prasad, A. S., J. T. Fitzgerald, B. Bao, F. W. J. Beck, and P. H. Chandrasekar. 2000. Duration of Symptoms and Plasma Cytokine Levels in Patients with the Common Cold Treated with Zinc Acetate. *Annals of Internal Medicine* 133: 245–252.

56. King and Cousins. Zinc; Walravens. Zinc Metabolism and Its Implications in Clinical Medicine.

57. Combs, G. F. 2005. Current Evidence and Research Needs to Support a Health Claims for Selenium and Cancer Prevention. *Journal of Nutrition* 135: 343–347; Institute of Medicine. 2000. *Dietary Reference Intakes: Vitamin C, Vitamin E, Selenium, and Carotenoids.* Washington, D.C.: The National Academies Press. Available at www.nap.edu.; Office of Dietary Supplements. Updated 2004. Selenium. Available at http://ods.od.nih.gov/factsheets/Selenium_pf.asp. Accessed November 2005.

58. Beck, M. A., O. A. Levander, and O. Handy. 2003. Selenium Deficiency and Viral Infection. *Journal of Nutrition* 133: 1463S–1467S; Li, H., M. J. Stampfer, E. L. Giovannucci, J. S. Morris, W. C. Willett, M. Gaziano, and J. Ma. 2004. A Prospective Study of Plasma Selenium Levels and Prostate Cancer Risk. *Journal of the National Cancer Institute* 96: 696–703; Sunde, R. A. 2000. Selenium. In Stipnauk, M. H. *Biochemical and Physiological Aspects of Human Nutrition.* Philadelphia: W. B. Saunders; Center for Food Safety and Applied Nutrition. 2005. Qualified Health Claims Subject to Enforcement Discretion. Available at www.cfsan.fda.gov/~dms/qhc-sum.html. Accessed November 2005; Wei, W., C. C. Abnet, Y. Qiao, S. M. Dawsey, Z. Dong, X. Sun, J. Fan, E. Q. Gunter, P. R. Taylor, and S. D. Mark. 2004. Prospective Study of Serum Selenium Concentrations and Esophageal and Gastric Cardia Cancer, Heart Disease, Stroke, and Total Death. *American Journal of Nutrition* 79: 80–85.

59. Beck et al. Selenium Deficiency and Viral Infection.

60. American Dental Association. 2005. Fluoridation Facts. Available at www.ada.org/public/topics/fluoride/facts/fluoridation_facts.pdf. Accessed November 2005.

61. Centers for Disease Control and Prevention (CDC). 1999. Achievements in Public Health, 1900–1999: Fluoridation of Drinking Water to Prevent Dental Caries. *Morbidity and Mortality Weekly Report* 48(41): 933–940. Available at www.cdc.gov/mmwr/preview/mmwrhtml/mm4841a1.htm. Accessed November 2005; CDC. Updated 2005. Water Fluoridation: Benefits, Background Information. Available at www.cdc.gov/oralhealth/waterfluoridation/benefits/background.htm. Accessed November 2005. CDC. Updated 2005. Water Fluoridation: Fact Sheets, Benefits. Available at www.cdc.gov/oralhealth/waterfluoridation/fact_sheets/benefits.htm. Accessed November 2005.

62. Institute of Medicine. *Dietary Reference Intakes: Calcium.*

63. Centers for Disease Control and Prevention. Updated 2005. Water Fluoridation. Safety—Enamel Fluorosis. Available at www.cdc.gov/oralhealth/waterfluoridation/safety/enamel_fluorosis.htm. Accessed November 2005.

64. Mertz, W. 1993. Chromium in Human Nutrition: A Review. *Journal of Nutrition* 123: 626–633.

65. Hopkins, L. L., O. Ransome-Kuti, and A. S. Majaj. 1968. Improvement of Impaired Carbohydrate Metabolism by Chromium (III) in Malnourished Infants. *American Journal of Clinical Nutrition* 21: 203–211; Jeejeebhoy, K. N., R. C. Clu, E. B. Marliss, G. R. Greenberg, and A. Bruce-Robertson. 1977. Chromium Deficiency, Glucose Intolerance, and Neuropathy Reversed by Chromium Supplementation in a Patient Receiving Long-term Total Parenteral Nutrition. *American Journal of Clinical Nutrition* 30: 531–538; Mertz, W. 1998. Interaction of Chromium with Insulin: A Progress Report. *Nutrition Reviews* 56: 174–177; Office of Dietary Supplements. Updated 2005. Chromium. Available at http://ods.od.nih.gov/factsheets/Chromium_pf.asp. Accessed November 2005.

66. Cefalu, W. T. and F. B. Hu. 2004. Role of Chromium in Human Health and in Diabetes. *Diabetes Care* 27: 2741–2751; Center for Food Safety and Applied Nutrition. 2005. Qualified Health Claims Subject to Enforcement Discretion: Chromium Picolinate and Insulin Resistance. Available at www.cfsan.fda.gov/~dms/qhccr.html. Accessed November 2005.

67. National Institutes of Health. Chromium.

68. Institute of Medicine. *Dietary Reference Intakes: Vitamin A.*

69. Anderson. Minerals.

70. Freake, H. C. 2000. Iodine. In Stipnauk, M. H. *Biochemical and Physiological Aspects of Human Nutrition.* Philadelphia: W. B. Saunders; Stanbury, J. B., A. E. Ermans, P. Bourdoux, C. Todd, E. Oken, R. Tonglet, T. G. Vidor, L. E. Braverman, and G. Medeiros-Neto. 1998. Iodine-induced Hyperthyroidism: Occurrence and Epidemiology. *Thyroid* 8: 83–100; Institute of Medicine. *Dietary Reference Intakes: Vitamin A.*

71. Ibid.

72. Institute of Medicine. *Dietary Reference Intakes: Vitamin A.*

73. Barceloux, D. G. 1999. Manganese. *Clinical Toxicology* 37: 293–307.

74. Institute of Medicine. *Dietary Reference Intakes: Vitamin A.*

75. Ibid.

Feature Box References

1. U.S. Environmental Protection Agency. 2005. Ground Water and Drinking Water: Frequently Asked Questions. Available at www.epa.gov/safewater/faq/faq.html. Accessed August 2005.

2. Bullers, A. C. 2002. Bottled Water: Better than the Tap? *FDA Consumer Magazine,* Food and Drug Administration. Available at www.fda.gov/fdac/features/2002/402_h2o.html. Accessed August 2005; U.S. Environmental Protection Agency. 2003. Water on Tap: What You Need to Know. Available at www.epa.gov/safewater/wot/index.html. Accessed August 2005.

3. Centers for Disease Control and Prevention. 2005. Oral Health: Water Fluoridation Fact Sheets and States' Statistics 2002. Available at www.cdc.gov/oralhealth/waterfluoridation/fact_sheets/states_stats2002.html. Accessed December 2005.

4. Natural Resources Defense Council. 1999. Bottled Water: Pure Drink or Pure Hype? Available at www.nrdc.org. Accessed August 2005; San Francisco Department of Public Health, Environmental Health Section, and San Francisco Public Utilities Commission. 2004. Bottled Water vs. Tap Water: Making a Healthy Choice. Available at www.dph.sf.ca.us/ehs/phes/publications/water/FactSheets/bottled_water.pdf. Accessed August 2005.

5. Fluoride Recommendations Work Group. 2001. Recommendations for Using Fluoride to Prevent and Control Dental Caries in the United States 50 (RR14): 1–42. Available at www.cdc.gov/mmwr/preview/mmwrhtml/rr5014a1.htm. Accessed November 2005.

6. American Heart Association. 2004. What Is High Blood Pressure? Available at www.americanheart.org. Accessed October 2005.

7. Franklin, S. S., et al. 1997. Hemodynamic Patterns of Age-Related Changes in Blood Pressure. *Circulation* 96: 308–315. Available at www.circ.ahajournals.org/cgi/content/full/96/1/308. Accessed August 2005.

8. Chobanian, A. V., G. L. Bakris, H. R. Black, W. C. Cushman, L. A. Green, J. L. Izzo, D. W. Jones, B. J. Materson, S. Oparil, J. T. Wright, E. J. Roccella, and the National High Blood Pressure Education Program Coordinating Committee. 2003. The Seventh Report of the Joint National Committee on Prevention, Detection, Evaluation, and Treatment of High Blood Pressure. *Journal of the American Medical Association* 289: 2560–2572; National Heart, Lung, and Blood Institute. 2004. High Blood Pressure. Available at www.nhlbi.nih.gov/health/dci/Diseases/Hbp/HBP_WhatIs.html. Accessed September 2005.

9. American Heart Association. 2005. Am I at Risk? Available at www.americanheart.org. Accessed September 2005.

10. U.S. Department of Health and Human Services. Overweight and Obesity: Health Consequences. Available at www.surgeongeneral.gov/topics/

obesity/calltoaction/fact_consequences.htm. Accessed September 2005; National Institutes of Health, National Heart, Lung, and Blood Institute. 2004. The seventh Report of the Joint National Committee on Prevention, Detection, Evaluation, and Treatment of High Blood Pressure (JNC 7). Available at www.nhlbi.nih.gov/guidelines/hypertension/jnc7full.htm. Accessed September 2005; Wharton, S. P., A. Chin, X. Xin, and J. He. 2002. Effect of Aerobic Exercise on Blood Pressure: A Meta-analysis of Randomized Controlled Trials. *Annals of Internal Medicine* 136 (7): 493–503.

11. Xin, X., J. He, M. G. Frontini, L. G. Ogden, O I. Motsamai, and P. K. Whelton. 2001. Effects of Alcohol Reduction on Blood Pressure: A Meta-analysis of Randomized Controlled Trials. *Hypertension* 38: 1112–1117.

12. Harsha, D. W., P. Lin, E. Obarzanek, N. M. Karanja, T. J. Moore, and B. Caballero. 1999. Dietary Approaches to Stop Hypertension: A Summary of Study Results. *Journal of the American Dietetics Association* 99: S35–S39; Kotchen, T.A., and J. M. Kotchen. 2006. Nutrition, Diet, and Hypertension. In M. Shils, M. Shike, A. C. Ross, B. Caballero, and R. J. Cousins, eds., *Modern Nutrition in Health and Disease.* 10th ed. Philadelphia, PA: Lippincott Williams and Wilkins; National Institutes of Health, National Heart, Lung, and Blood Institute. 2002. Primary Prevention of Hypertension: Clinical and Public Health Advisory from the National Blood Pressure Education Program. Available at www.nhlbi.nih.gov/health/prof/heart/hbp/pphbp.pdf. Accessed September 2005.

13. National Institutes of Health, National Heart, Lung, and Blood Institute. 2003. The DASH Eating Plan. Available at www.nhlbi.nih.gov/health/public/heart/hbp/dash. Accessed September 2005.

14. Patlak, M. 2001. Bone Builders: The Discoveries Behind Preventing and Treating Osteoporosis. *The FASEB Journal* 15: 1677.

15. National Institutes of Health, Osteoporosis and Related Bone Diseases-National Resource Center. 2005. Osteoporosis Overview. Available at www.osteo.org/osteo.html. Accessed October 2005; U.S. Department of Health and Human Services 2004. *Bone Health and Osteoporosis: A Report of the Surgeon General.* Washington, D.C.: U.S. Department of Health and Human Services, Office of the Surgeon General.

16. National Institutes of Health, Consensus Development Conference Statement. 2000. Osteoporosis Prevention, Diagnosis, and Therapy. Available at www.consensus.nih.gov/2000/2000Osteoporosis111html.htm. Accessed October 2005.

17. U.S. Department of Health and Human Services. *Bone Health and Osteoporosis.*

18. Office of Dietary Supplements. Updated 2005. Dietary Supplement Fact Sheet: Calcium. Available at http://ods.od.nih.gov/factsheets/calcium.asp. Accessed October 2005; U.S. Department of Health and Human Services. *Bone Health and Osteoporosis.*

19. U.S. Department of Health and Human Services. *Bone Health and Osteoporosis:* Osteoporosis in Postmenopausal Women: Diagnosis and Monitoring Evidence Report/Technology Assessment No. 28. Agency for Healthcare Research and Quality; 2001. Publication No.: 01-E032.

20. Miller, K. K. 2003. Mechanisms by which Nutritional Disorders Cause Reduced Bone Mass in Adults. *Journal of Women's Health* 12:145–150.

21. National Institutes of Health. *Osteoporosis Overview.*

22. U.S. Department of Health and Human Services. Bone Health and Osteoporosis.

23. Ibid.

Chapter 9

1. Distilled Spirits Councils in the United States. 2001. Reporters' Guide to the Distilled Spirits Industry. Available at www.discus.org/mediaroom/guide.htm. Accessed December 2005.

2. Centers for Disease Control and Prevention. 2005. Alcohol and Public Health: General Alcohol Information. Available at www.cdc.gov/alcohol/factsheets/general_information.htm. Accessed January 2006.

3. National Institute on Alcohol Abuse and Alcoholism. 2003. Understanding Alcohol: Investigations into Biology and Behavior. Available at http://science.education.nih.gov/supplements/nih3/alcohol/default.htm. Accessed December 2005.

4. Mandelbaum, D. G. 1965. Alcohol and Culture. *Current Anthropology* 6: 281–288.

5. U.S. Department of Agriculture. 2005. 2005 Report of the Dietary Guidelines Advisory Committee. Available at www.health.gov/dietaryguidelines/dga2005/report/. Accessed January 2006; Goldberg, I. J., L. Mosca, M. R. Piano, and E. A. Fisher. 2001. Wine and Your Heart. A Science Advisory for Healthcare Professionals from the Nutrition Committee, Council on Epidemiology and Prevention, and Council on Cardiovascular Nursing of the American Heart Association. *Circulation* 103: 472–475.

6. Dodd, T. H., and S. Morse. 1994. The Impact of Media Stories Concerning Health Issues on Food Product Sales. *The Journal of Consumer Marketing* 11: 17–24.

7. U.S. Department of Agriculture. 2005 Report; Goldberg et al. Wine and Your Heart.

8. Andreasson, S., P. Allebeck, and A. Romelsjo. 1988. Alcohol and Mortality Among Young Men: Longitudinal Study of Swedish Conscripts. *British Medical Journal* 296: 1021–1025.

9. National Institute on Alcohol Abuse and Alcoholism. 1997. Alcohol Alert: Alcohol Metabolism. Available at www.niaaa.nih.gov/Publications/AlcoholAlerts. Accessed December 2005.

10. Frezza, M., C. diPadova, G. Pozzato, M. Terpin, E. Baraona, and C. S. Leiber. High Blood Alcohol Levels in Women: The Role of Decreased Gastric Alcohol Dehydrogenase Activity and First-Pass Metabolism. *New England Journal of Medicine* 332: 95–99.

11. Jones, A. W., and K. A. Jonsson. 1994. Food-Induced Lowering of Blood-Ethanol Profiles and Increased Rate of Elimination Immediately After a Meal. *Journal of Forensic Sciences* 39: 1084–1093.

12. National Institute on Alcohol Abuse and Alcoholism. Alcohol Alert: Alcohol Metabolism.

13. Ibid.

14. National Institute on Alcohol Abuse and Alcoholism. 1998. Alcohol Alert: Alcohol and Sleep. Available at www.niaaa.nih.gov/Publications/AlcoholAlerts. Accessed December 2005.

15. National Institute on Alcohol Abuse and Alcoholism. Alcohol Alert: Alcohol and Sleep; Roehrs, T., D. Beare, F. Zorick, and T. Roth. 1994. Sleepiness and Ethanol Effects on Simulated Driving. *Alcoholism: Clinical and Experimental Research* 18: 154–158.

16. Swift, R. S., and D. Davidson. 1998. Alcohol Hangover, Mechanisms and Mediators. *Alcohol Health & Research World* 22: 54–60. Available at http://pubs.niaaa.nih.gov/publications/arh22-1/54-60.pdf. Accessed January 2006.

17. Ibid.

18. National Institute on Alcohol Abuse and Alcoholism. Alcohol Alert: Alcohol Metabolism; Swift and Davidson. Alcohol Hangover.

19. Swift and Davidson. Alcohol Hangover; National Institute on Alcohol Abuse and Alcoholism. 1994. Alcohol Alert: Alcohol and Hormones. Available at www.niaaa.nih.gov/Publications/AlcoholAlerts. Accessed December 2005.

20. Ibid.

21. National Institute on Alcohol Abuse and Alcoholism. 2003. State of the Science Report on the Effects of Moderate Drinking. Available at http://pubs.niaaa.nih.gov/publications/ModerateDrinking-03.htm. Accessed January 2003; National Institute on Alcohol Abuse and Alcoholism. Updated 2000. Alcohol Alert: Alcohol and Cancer. Available at http://pubs.niaaa.nih.gov/publications/aa21.htm. Accessed January 2005; National Institute on Alcohol Abuse and Alcoholism. Updated 2000. Alcohol Alert: Alcohol and Tobacco. Available at http://pubs.niaaa.nih.gov/publications/aa21.htm. Accessed June 2006.

22. Lieber, C. S. 2000. Alcohol: Its Metabolism and Interaction with Nutrients. *Annual Review of Nutrition* 20: 394–430.

23. National Institute on Alcohol Abuse and Alcoholism. Alcohol Alert: Alcohol and Cancer; National Institute on Alcohol Abuse and Alcoholism. Alcohol Alert: Alcohol and Tobacco.

24. National Institute on Alcohol Abuse and Alcoholism. Understanding Alcohol.

25. Ibid.

26. Lieber. Alcohol: Its Metabolism.

27. National Institute on Alcohol Abuse and Alcoholism. 2000. Alcohol and the Liver: Research Update. Available at http://pubs.niaaa.nih.gov/publications/aa42.htm. Accessed January 2006.

28. National Institute on Alcohol Abuse and Alcoholism. 2005. Alcohol Alert: Alcohol and the Liver. Available at www.niaaa.nih.gov/Publications/AlcoholAlerts. Accessed January 2006.

29. Centers for Disease Control and Prevention. Alcohol and Public Health.

30. Jones, K., and D. Smith. 1973. Recognition of the Fetal Alcohol Syndrome in Early Infancy. *The Lancet* 2: 999–1001; Bertrand, J., R. L. Floyd, and M. K. Weber. 2005. Guidelines for Identifying and Referring Persons with Fetal Alcohol Syndrome. *Morbidity and Mortality Weekly Report* 54 (RR11): 1–10. Available at www.cdc.gov/mmwr/preview/mmwrhtml/rr5411a1.htm. Accessed January 2006; U.S. Department of Health and Human Services. Substance Abuse and Mental Health Services Administrator. 2005 Fetal Alcohol Spectrum Disorders, The Basics. Available at http://fasdcenter.samhsa.gov/misc/FASDBASICS/FASDTheBasics.pdf. Accessed January 2006.

31. Bertrand et al. Guidelines for Identifying and Referring Persons; Centers for Disease Control and Prevention. 2005. Fetal Alcohol Spectrum Disorders: Frequently Asked Questions. Available at www.cdc.gov/ncbddd/fas/faqs.htm. Accessed January 2006.

32. National Institute on Alcohol Abuse and Alcoholism. Understanding Alcohol.
33. Henao, L. A. July 5, 2005. Obituary. *The Boston Globe.*
34. National Institute on Alcohol Abuse and Alcoholism. Understanding Alcohol.
35. Centers for Disease Control and Prevention. Alcohol and Public Health.
36. National Institute on Alcohol Abuse and Alcoholism. 2004. Alcohol Alert: Alcohol's Damaging Effects on the Brain. Available at http://pubs.niaaa.nih.gov/publications/aa63/aa63.htm. Accessed December 2005; White, A. M., D. W. Jamieson-Drake, and H. S. Swartzwelder. 2002. Prevalence and Correlates of Alcohol-Induced Blackouts Among College Students: Results of an E-Mail Survey. *Journal of American College Health* 51: 117–131.
37. National Institute on Alcohol Abuse and Alcoholism. Publication No. 29 PH 357. Updated 2000. Available at www.niaaa.nih.gov/Publications/AlcoholAlerts/default.htm. Accessed January 2006.
38. National Institute on Alcohol Abuse and Alcoholism. Understanding Alcohol.
39. National Highway Traffic Safety Administration. Traffic Safety Facts: Crash Statistics on Alcohol-Related Fatalities in 2004. Available at www.nrd.nhtsa.dot.gov/pdf/nrd-30/NCSA/RNotes/2005/809904.pdf. Accessed January 2006.
40. Centers for Disease Control and Prevention. Alcohol and Public Health.
41. National Institute on Alcohol Abuse and Alcoholism. 2003. Underage Drinking: A Major Public Health Challenge. Available at www.niaaa.nih.gov/Publications/AlcoholAlerts/default.htm. Accessed January 2006.
42. National Research Council, Institute of Medicine. 2003. *Reducing Underage Drinking: A Collective Responsibility.* Washington, D.C.: The National Academies Press.
43. National Institute on Alcohol Abuse and Alcoholism. Underage Drinking.
44. American Medical Association. 2003. The Minimum Legal Drinking Age: Facts and Fallacies. Available at www.ama-assn.org. Accessed in December 2005.
45. National Institute on Alcohol Abuse and Alcoholism. Underage Drinking.
46. National Institute on Alcohol Abuse and Alcoholism. Underage Drinking.
47. National Institute on Alcohol Abuse and Alcoholism. College Drinking, Changing the Culture; Alcoholism: Getting the Facts. Available at www.collegedrinkingprevention.gov. Accessed January 2006.
48. Alcoholics Anonymous. 2004. Membership Survey. Available at www.aa.org. Accessed January 2006.
49. U.S. Department of Agriculture. 2005 Report.

Feature Box References

1. Austin, E., and S. Hust. 2005. Targeting Adolescents? The Content and Frequency of Alcoholic and Nonalcoholic Beverage Ads in Magazine and Video Formats November 1999–April 2000. *Journal of Health Communications* 10: 769–785.
2. Austin, E., M. Chen, and J. Grube. 2006. How Does Alcohol Advertising Influence Underage Drinking? The Role of Desirability, Identification, and Skepticism. *Journal of Adolescent Health* 38: 376–384.

Chapter 10

1. Manson, J., P. Skerrett, P. Greenland, and T. Van Itallie. 2004. The Escalating Pandemics of Obesity and Sedentary Lifestyle: A Call to Action for Clinicians. *Archives of Internal Medicine* 164: 249–258.
2. IFIC Foundation. 2005. Food for Thought VI, Reporting of Diet, Nutrition, and Food Safety News. Available at www.ific.org/research/fftres.cfm. Accessed July 2006.
3. Mintel Reports: USA, Health and Medical: USA, Health and Wellness: USA. 2005. Commercial Weight Loss Programs–U.S. Available at http://reports.mintel.com/sinatra/reports/display/id=121277/display/id=192441. Accessed June 2006.
4. Weight-control Information Network. 2004. Do You Know the Health Risks of Being Overweight? Available at http://win.niddk.nih.gov/publications/health_risks.htm. Accessed June 2006.
5. National Institutes of Health. 1998. Clinical Guidelines on the Identification, Evaluation, and Treatment of Overweight and Obesity in Adults. Available at www.nhlbi.nih.gov/guidelines/obesity/ob_gdlns.htm. Accessed June 2006.
6. Centers for Disease Control and Prevention. 2006. Overweight and Obesity: Economic Consequences. Available at www.cdc.gov/nccdphp/dnpa/obesity/economic_consequences.htm. Accessed June 2006.
7. National Institutes of Health. Clinical Guidelines on the Identification, Evaluation, and Treatment of Overweight and Obesity in Adults.
8. Ibid.
9. Weight-control Information Network. Do You Know the Health Risks of Being Overweight?; National Institutes of Health. Clinical Guidelines on the Identification, Evaluation, and Treatment of Overweight and Obesity in Adults.
10. Laquatra, I. 2004. Nutrition for Weight Management. In L. Mahan and S. Escott-Stump, eds., *Krause's Food, Nutrition, and Diet Therapy.* 11th ed. Philadelphia: Saunders.
11. Hammond, K. 2004. Dietary and Clinical Assessment. In L. Mahan and S. Escott-Stump, eds., *Krause's Food, Nutrition, and Diet Therapy.* 11th ed. Philadelphia: Saunders.
12. U.S. Department of Health and Human Services. 2002. A Century of Women's Health, 1900–2000. Available at www.4woman.gov/TimeCapsule/century/century.pdf. Accessed July 2006.
13. National Institutes of Health. Clinical Guidelines on the Identification, Evaluation, and Treatment of Overweight and Obesity in Adults.
14. Ibid.
15. Ibid.
16. Ibid.
17. Ibid.
18. Institute of Medicine. 2002. *Dietary Reference Intakes for Energy, Carbohydrate, Fiber, Fat, Fatty Acids, Cholesterol, Protein, and Amino Acids.* Available at www.iom.edu. Accessed June 2006.
19. Hoffer, L. J. 2006. Metabolic Consequences of Starvation. In M. Shils et al., eds., *Modern Nutrition in Health and Disease.* 10th ed. Philadelphia: Lippincott Williams & Wilkins.
20. Mattes, R., J. Hollis, D. Hayes, and A. Stunkard. 2005. Appetite: Measurement and Manipulations Misgivings. *Journal of the American Dietetic Association* 105 (supplement): S87–S97.
21. Smith, G. 2006. Controls of Food Intake. In M. Shils et al., eds., *Modern Nutrition.*
22. Mattes, R. Appetite: Measurement and Manipulations Misgivings.
23. Smith, G. Controls of Food Intake. In M. Shils et al., eds., *Modern Nutrition.*
24. Center for Genomics and Public Health. 2004. Obesity and Current Topics in Genetics. Available at www.cdc.gov/genomics/training/perspectives/obesity.htm#Perspective. Accessed June 2006.
25. Hill, J., V. Catenacci, and H. Wyatt. 2006. Obesity: Etiology. In M. Shils et al., eds., *Modern Nutrition.*
26. Hill, J. Obesity: Etiology. In M. Shils et al., eds., *Modern Nutrition.*
27. Bray, G., and C. Champagne. 2005. Beyond Energy Balance: There Is More to Obesity than Kilocalories. *Journal of the American Dietetic Association* 105 (supplement): S17–S23.
28. Brodsky, I. 2006. Hormones and Growth Factors. In M. Shils et al., eds., *Modern Nutrition.*
29. Hill, J. Obesity.
30. Ibid.
31. Gale, S., T. Van Itallie, and I. Faust. 1981. Effects of Palatable Diets on Body Weight and Adipose Tissue Cellularity in the Adult Obese Female Zucker Rat (fa/fa). *Metabolism* 30: 105–110.
32. Ravussin, E., M. Valencia, J. Esparza, P. Bennett, and L. Schulz. 1994. Effects of a Traditional Lifestyle on Obesity in Pima Indians. *Diabetes Care* 17: 1067–1074; Wang, S., and K. Brownell. 2005. Public Policy and Obesity: The Need to Marry Science with Advocacy. *Psychiatric Clinics of North America* 28: 235–252.
33. Bray, G. Beyond Energy Balance; Loos, R., and T. Rankinen. 2005. Gene-Diet Interactions on Body Weight Changes. *Journal of the American Dietetic Association* 105 (supplement): S29–S34.
34. The Keystone Group. 2006. The Keystone Forums on Away-From-Home Food, Opportunities for Preventing Weight Gain and Obesity. Available at www.keystone.org/spp/documents/Forum_Report_FINAL_5-30-06.pdf. Accessed June 2006.
35. Ibid.
36. Wang. Public Policy and Obesity.
37. The Keystone Group. The Keystone Forums on Away-From-Home Food.
38. Ibid.; Clemens, L., D. Slawson, and R. Klesges. 1999. The Effect of Eating Out on Quality of Diet in Premenopausal Women. *Journal of the American Dietetic Association* 99: 442–444.
39. The Keystone Group. The Keystone Forums on Away-From-Home Food; Meyers, A., A. Stunkard, and M. Coll. 1980. Food Accessibility and Food Choice. *Archives of General Psychiatry* 37: 1133–1135.
40. The Keystone Group. The Keystone Forums on Away-From-Home Food; Rolls, B. 1986. Sensory-Specific Satiety. *Nutrition Reviews* 44: 93–101.
41. Rolls, B. 2003. The Supersizing of America. *Nutrition Today* 38: 42–53.
42. Wansink, B. 1996. Can Package Size Accelerate Usage Volume? *Journal of Marketing* 60: 1–14.
43. Rolls, B., L. Roe, and J. Meengs. 2006. Larger Portion Sizes Lead to a Sustained Increase in Energy Intake over 2 Days. *Journal of the American Dietetic Association* 106: 543–549.
44. Putnam, J., J. Allshouse, and L. Kantor. 2002. U.S. Per Capita Food Supply Trends: More Calories, Refined Carbohydrates, and Fats. Economic Re-

search Service, USDA. *FoodReview* 25: 2–15; French, S., M. Story, and R. Jeffery. 2001. Environmental Influences on Eating and Physical Activity. *Annual Reviews of Public Health* 22: 309–335.

45. French, S. Environmental Influences on Eating.

46. Mummery, W., G. Schofield, R. Steele, E. Eakin, and W. Brown. 2005. Occupational Sitting Time and Overweight and Obesity in Australian Workers. *American Journal of Preventative Medicine* 29: 91–97.

47. French. Environmental Influences on Eating.

48. Wang. Public Policy and Obesity.

49. Lanningham-Foster, L., L. Nysse, and J. Levine. 2003. Labor Saved, Calories Lost: The Energetic Impact of Domestic Labor-Saving Devices. *Obesity Research* 11: 1178–1181.

50. Ibid.

51. Centers for Disease Control and Prevention. 2003. Prevalence of Physical Activity, Including Lifestyle Activities Among Adults—United States, 2000–2001. *Morbidity and Mortality Weekly Report* 52:763–769. Available at www.cdc.gov/mmwr/preview/mmwrhtml/mm5232a2.htm. Accessed June 2006.

52. Centers for Disease Control and Prevention. 2005 Trends in Leisure-Time Physical Inactivity by Age, Sex, and Race/Ethnicity—United States, 1994–2004. *Morbidity and Mortality Weekly Report* 54: 991–994. Available at www.cdc.gov/mmwr/preview/mmwrhtml/mm5439a5.htm. Accessed June 2006.

53. Nielsen Media Research. 2000. Report on Television. Available at www.nielsenmedia.com. Accessed July 2006.

54. Roberts, D., U. Foehr, V. Rideout, and M. Brodie. 1999. Kids & Media@ the New Millennium. The Kaiser Family Foundation. Available at www.kff.org/entmedia/index.cfm. Accessed July 2006.

55. National Institutes of Health. Clinical Guidelines on the Identification, Evaluation, and Treatment of Overweight and Obesity in Adults.

56. Mattes, R. Appetite: Measurement and Manipulations Misgivings; Lissner, L., D. Levitsky, B. Strupp, H. Kalkwarf, and D. Roe. 1987. Dietary Fat and the Regulation of Energy Intake in Human Subjects. *American Journal of Clinical Nutrition* 46: 886–892.

57. Tohill, B., J. Seymour, M. Serdula, L. Kettel-Khan, and B. Rolls. 2004. What Epidemiologic Studies Tell Us about the Relationship between Fruit and Vegetable Consumption and Body Weight. *Nutrition Reviews* 62: 365–374.

58. Rolls, B., E. Bell, and E. Thorwart. 1999. Water Incorporated into a Food but Not Served with a Food Decreases Energy Intake in Lean Women. *American Journal of Clinical Nutrition* 70: 448–455.

59. Burton-Freeman, B. 2000. Dietary Fiber and Energy Regulation. *Journal of Nutrition* 130: 272S–275S.

60. Davis, J., V. Hodges, and B. Gillham. 2006. Normal-Weight Adults Consume More Fiber and Fruit than Their Age- and Height-Matched Overweight/Obese Counterparts. *Journal of the American Dietetic Association* 106: 833–840.

61. Mattes, R. Appetite: Measurement and Manipulations Misgivings.

62. Saries, W., S. Blair, M. van Baak, et al. 2003. How Much Physical Activity Is Enough to Prevent Unhealthy Weight Gain? Outcome of the IASO Stock Conference and Consensus Statement. *Obesity Reviews* 4: 101–114.

63. Keim, N., C. Blanton, and M. Kretsch. 2004. America's Obesity Epidemic: Measuring Physical Activity to Promote an Active Lifestyle. *Journal of the American Dietetic Association* 104: 1398–1409.

64. Jakicic, J., and A. Otto. 2005. Physical Activity Consideration for the Treatment and Prevention of Obesity. *American Journal of Clinical Nutrition* 82: 226S–229S.

65. Shape Up America! Not dated. 10,000 Steps. Available at www.shapeup.org/shape/steps.php. Accessed July 2006.

66. Edwards, J., and H. Meiselman. 2003. Changes in Dietary Habits during the First Year at University. *British Nutrition Foundation Nutrition Bulletin* 28: 21–34.

67. Graham, M., and A. Jones. 2002. Freshman 15: Valid Theory or Harmful Myth? *Journal of American College Health* 50: 171–173.

68. Poston, W., and J. Foreyt. 2000. Successful Management of the Obese Patient. *American Family Physician* 61: 3615–3622.

69. Schlundt, D., J. Hill, T. Sbrocco, J. Pope-Cordle, and T. Sharp. 1992. The Role of Breakfast in the Treatment of Obesity: A Randomized Clinical Trial. *American Journal of Clinical Nutrition* 55: 645–651.

70. Rosenbaum, M., R. Leibel, and J. Hirsch. 1997. Obesity. *New England Journal of Medicine* 337: 396–407.

71. National Institute of Diabetes and Digestive and Kidney Diseases. 2006. Weight Cycling. Available at http://win.niddk.nih.gov/publications/cycling.htm. Accessed July 2006.

72. Rosenbaum, M. Obesity; Klem, M. L., R. R. Wing, M. T. McGuire, H. M. Seagle, and J. O. Hill. 1997. A Descriptive Study of Individuals Successful at Long-Term Maintenance of Substantial Weight Loss. *American Journal of Clinical Nutrition* 66: 239–246.

73. Klem, M. L. A Descriptive Study of Individuals Successful at Long-Term Maintenance of Substantial Weight Loss.

74. Hill, J., H. Wyatt, G. Reed, and J. Peters. 2003. Obesity and the Environment: Where Do We Go from Here? *Science* 299: 853–897.

75. Hill, J., H. Thompson, and H. Wyatt. 2005. Weight Maintenance: What's Missing? *Journal of the American Dietetic Association* 105: S63–S66.

76. U.S. Department of Health and Human Services. 2005. Report of the Dietary Guidelines Advisory Committee on the *Dietary Guidelines for Americans, 2005*. Available at www.health.gov/DietaryGuidelines/dga2005/report. Accessed July 2006.

77. Ibid.

78. National Eating Disorders Association. 2006. Statistics: Eating Disorders and Their Precursors. Available at www.nationaleatingdisorders.org/p.asp?WebPage_ID=286&Profile_ID=41138. Accessed July 2006.

79. Chamorro, R., and Y. Flores-Ortiz. 2000. Acculturation and Disordered Eating Patterns among Mexican American Women. *International Journal of Eating Disorders* 28, no. 1: 125–129; Crago, M., C. M. Shisslak, and L. S. Estes. 1996. Eating Disturbances among American Minority Groups: A Review. *International Journal of Eating Disorders* 19, no. 3: 239–248; Kjelsas, E., C. Bjornstrom, and K. G. Gotestam. 2004. Prevalence of Eating Disorders in Female and Male Adolescents (14–15 Years). *Eating Behaviors* 5, no. 1: 13–25; O'Dea, J., and S. Abraham. 2002. Eating and Exercise Disorders in Young College Men. *Journal of American College Health* 50, no. 6: 273–278.

80. Woodside, D. B., P. E. Garfinkel, E. Lin, P. Goering, A. S. Kaplan, D. S. Goldbloom, and S. H. Kennedy. 2001. Comparisons of Men with Full or Partial Eating Disorders, Men without Eating Disorders, and Women with Eating Disorders in the Community. *American Journal of Psychiatry* 158: 570–574.

81. Birketvedt, G. S., J. Florholmen, J. Sundsfjord, B. Osterud, D. Dinges, W. Bilker, and A. Stunkard. 1999. Behavioral and Neuroendocrine Characteristics of the Night Eating Syndrome. *Journal of the American Medical Association* 282, no. 7: 657–663.

82. Marshall, H. M., K. C. Allison, J. P. O'Reardon, G. Birketvedt, and A. J. Stunkard. 2004. Night Eating Syndrome among Nonobese Persons. *International Journal of Eating Disorders* 35, no. 2: 217–222.

83. Birketvedt, G. S. Behavioral and Neuroendocrine Characteristics of the Night Eating Syndrome.

84. Gluck, M., A. Geliebter, and T. Satov. 2001. Night Eating Syndrome Is Associated with Depression, Low Self-Esteem, Reduced Daytime Hunger, and Less Weight Loss in Obese Outpatients. *Obesity Research* 9: 264–267.

85. Birketvedt, G. S., J. Sundsfjord, and J. R. Florholmen. 2002. Hypothalamic-Pituitary-Adrenal Axis in the Night Eating Syndrome. *American Journal of Physiology–Endocrinology and Metabolism* 282, no. 2: E366–E369.

Feature Box References

1. Stein, K. 2000. High-Protein, Low-Carbohydrate Diets: Do They Work? *Journal of the American Dietetic Association* 100: 760–761.

2. Freedman, M., J. King, and E. Kennedy. 2001. Popular Diets: A Scientific Review. *Obesity Research* 9: 1S–40S.

3. Dansinger, M., J. Gleason, J. Griffith, H. Selker, and E. Schaefer. 2005. Comparison of the Atkins, Ornish, Weight Watchers, and Zone Diets for Weight Loss and Heart Disease Risk Reduction. *Journal of the American Medical Association* 293: 43–53.

4. Yudkin, J., and M. Carey. 1960. The Treatment of Obesity by the "Highfat" Diet: The Inevitability of Calories. *The Lancet* 2: 939–941.

5. Ornish, D. 2004. Was Dr. Atkins Right? *Journal of the American Dietetic Association* 104: 537–542.

6. Denke, M. 2001. Metabolic Effects of High-Protein, Low-Carbohydrate Diets. *The American Journal of Cardiology* 88: 59–61.

7. Ibid.

8. Federal Trade Commission. 2000. Marketers of "The Enforma System" Settle FTC Charges of Deceptive Advertising for Their Weight Loss Products. Available at www.quackwatch.org/02ConsumerProtection/FTCActions/enforma.html. Accessed July 2006.

9. Dwyer, J., D. Allison, and P. Coates. 2005. Dietary Supplements in Weight Reduction. *Journal of the American Dietetic Association* 105: S80–S86; Pittler, M., and E. Ernst. 2004. Dietary Supplements for Body-Weight Reduction: A Systematic Review. *American Journal of Clinical Nutrition* 79: 529–536.

10. Pittler, M. Dietary Supplements for Body-Weight Reduction.

11. Dwyer, J. Dietary Supplements in Weight Reduction.

12. National Heart, Lung, and Blood Institute. 1998. Clinical Guidelines on the Identification, Evaluation, and Treatment of Overweight and Obesity in Adults. Available at www.nhlbi.nih.gov/guidelines/obesity/ob_gdlns.htm. Accessed June 2006.

13. Mariant, M. 2005. Oprah Regrets Her 1988 Liquid Diet. *USA Today* (November). Available at www.usatoday.com/life/people/2005-11-16-oprah-liquid-diet_x.htm. Accessed July 2006.

14. DeWald, T., L. Khaodhiar, M. Donahue, and G. Blackburn. 2006. Pharmacological and Surgical Treatments for Obesity. *American Heart Journal* 151: 604–624.

15. Meadows, M. 2003. Public Health Officials Caution Against Ephedra Use. *FDA Consumer Magazine.* Available at www.fda.gov/fdac/features/2003/303_ephedra.html. Accessed July 2006; Food and Drug Administration. 2004. FDA Issues Regulation Prohibiting Sale of Dietary Supplements Containing Ephedrine Alkaloids and Reiterates Its Advice That Consumers Stop Using These Products. Available at www.cfsan.fda.gov/~lrd/fpephed6.html. Accessed July 2006.

16. Encinosa, W., D. Bernard, C. Steiner, and C. Chen. 2005. Trends: Use and Costs of Bariatric Surgery and Prescription Weight-Loss Medications. *Health Affairs* 24: 1039–1046.

17. Crookes, P. 2006. Surgical Treatment of Morbid Obesity. *Annual Review of Medicine* 57: 243–264.

18. DeWald. Pharmacological and Surgical Treatments for Obesity; Crookes. Surgical Treatment of Morbid Obesity.

Chapter 11

1. Centers for Disease Control and Prevention. 2003. Prevalence of Physical Activity, Including Lifestyle Activities Among Adults—United States, 2000–2001. *Morbidity and Mortality Weekly Report* 52: 764–769.

2. Coyle, E. F., A. R. Coggan, M. K. Hemmert, and J. L. Ivy. 1986. Muscle Glycogen Utilization During Prolonged Strenuous Exercise When Fed Carbohydrate. *Journal of Applied Physiology* 61: 165–172; Hargreaves, M. 2004. Muscle Glycogen and Metabolic Regulation. *Proceedings of the Nutrition Society* 63: 217–220.

3. Costill, D., R. Thomas, R. Roberts, D. Pascoe, C. Lambert, S. Barr, and W. Fink. 1991. Adaptations to Swimming Training: Influence of Training Volume. *Medicine & Science in Sports & Exercise* 23: 371–377; Sherman W., M. Peden, and D. Wright. 1991. Carbohydrate Feedings 1 Hour Before Exercise Improves Cycling Performance. *American Journal of Clinical Nutrition* 54: 866–870.

4. Brooks, G. 2002. Lactate Shuttles in Nature. *Biochemical Society Transactions* 30: 258–264.

5. Romijn, J. A., E. F. Coyle, L. S. Sidossis, A. Gastaldelli, J. F. Horowitz, E. Endert, and R. R. Wolfe. 1993. Regulation of Endogenous Fat and Carbohydrate Metabolism in Relation to Exercise Intensity and Duration. *American Journal of Physiology–Endocrinology and Metabolism* 265: E380–E391.

6. Rosenbloom, C., ed. 2000. *Sports Nutrition: A Guide for the Professional Working with Active People.* 3rd ed. Chicago: The American Dietetic Association, 16.

7. American College of Sports Medicine, American Dietetic Association, and Dietitians of Canada. 2000. Nutrition and Athletic Performance Joint Position Statement. *Medicine & Science in Sports & Exercise* 32: 2130–2145.

8. Ibid.

9. Brownell, K. D., S. N. Steen, and J. H. Wilmore. 1987. Weight Regulation Practices in Athletes: Analysis of Metabolic and Health Effects. *Medicine & Science in Sports & Exercise* 19: 546–556; Horvath, P. J., C. K. Eagen, S. D. Ryer-Calvin, and D. R. Pendergast. 2000. The Effects of Varying Dietary Fat on the Nutrient Intake in Male and Female Runners. *Journal of the American College of Nutrition* 19: 42–51.

10. American College of Sports Medicine, American Dietetic Association, and Dietitians of Canada. Nutrition and Athletic Performance Joint Position Statement.

11. Yaspelkis, B. B., J. G. Patterson, P. A. Anderla, Z. Ding, and J. L. Ivy. 1993. Carbohydrate Supplementation Spares Muscle Glycogen During Variable-Intensity Exercise. *Journal of Applied Physiology* 75: 1477–1485; Coyle, E. F., J. M. Hagberg, B. F. Hurley, W. H. Martin, A. A. Ehsani, and J. O. Holloszy. 1983. Carbohydrate Feeding During Prolonged Strenuous Exercise Can Delay Fatigue. *Journal of Applied Physiology* 55: 230–235.

12. Miller, S. L., K. D. Tipton, D. L. Chinkes, S. E. Wolf, and R. R. Wolfe. 2003. Independent and Combined Effects of Amino Acids and Glucose After Resistance Exercise. *Medicine & Science in Sports & Exercise* 35: 449–455.

13. Koopman, R., D. L. Pannemans, A. E. Jeukendrup, A. P. Gijsen, J. M. Senden, D. Halliday, W. H. Saris, L. J. van Loon, and A. J. Wagenmakers. 2004. Combined Ingestion of Protein and Carbohydrate Improves Protein Balance During Ultra-Endurance Exercise. *American Journal of Physiology–Endocrinology and Metabolism* 287: E712–E720.

14. Ivy, J. L., A. L. Katz, C. L. Cutler, W. M. Sherman, and E. F. Coyle. 1988. Muscle Glycogen Synthesis After Exercise: Effect of Time of Carbohydrate Ingestion. *Journal of Applied Physiology* 64: 1480–1485.

15. Roy, B. D., M. A. Tarnopolsky, J. D. MacDougall, J. Fowles, and K. E. Yarasheski. 1997. Effect of Glucose Supplement Timing on Protein Metabolism After Resistance Training. *Journal of Applied Physiology* 82: 1882–1888.

16. Rasmussen, B. B., K. D. Tipton, S. L. Miller, S. E. Wolf, and R. R. Wolfe. 2000. An Oral Essential Amino Acid-Carbohydrate Supplement Enhances Muscle Protein Anabolism After Resistance Exercise. *Journal of Applied Physiology* 88: 386–392; Zawadzki, K. M., B. B. Yaspelkis, and J. L. Ivy. 1992. Carbohydrate-Protein Complex Increases the Rate of Muscle Glycogen Storage After Exercise. *Journal of Applied Physiology* 72: 1854–1859.

17. Zawadzki. Carbohydrate-Protein Complex; Ivy, J. L., H. W. Goforth, B. M. Damon, T. R. McCauley, E. C. Parsons, and T. B. Price. 2002. Early Postexercise Muscle Glycogen Recovery Is Enhanced with a Carbohydrate-Protein Supplement. *Journal of Applied Physiology* 93: 1337–1344.

18. Karp, J. R., J. D. Johnston, S. Tecklenburg, T. D. Mickleborough, A. D. Fly, and J. M. Stager. 2006. Chocolate Milk as a Post-Exercise Recovery Aid. *International Journal of Sport Nutrition and Exercise Metabolism* 16: 78–91.

19. Krumbach, C. J., D. R. Ellis, and J. A. Driskell. 1999. A Report of Vitamin and Mineral Supplement Use Among University Athletes in a Division I Institution. *International Journal of Sport Nutrition and Exercise Metabolism* 9: 416–425; Herbold, N. H., B. K. Visconti, S. Frates, and L. Bandini. 2004. Traditional and Nontraditional Supplement Use by Collegiate Female Varsity Athletes. *International Journal of Sport Nutrition and Exercise Metabolism* 14: 586–593.

20. Singh, A., F. M. Moses, and P. A. Deuster. 1992. Chronic Multivitamin-Mineral Supplementation Does Not Enhance Physical Performance. *Medicine & Science in Sports & Exercise* 24: 726–732.

21. McAnulty, S. R., L. S. McAnulty, D. C. Nieman, J. D. Morrow, L. A. Shooter, S. Holmes, C. Heward, and D. A. Henson. 2005. Effect of Alpha-Tocopherol Supplementation on Plasma Homocysteine and Oxidative Stress in Highly Trained Athletes Before and After Exhaustive Exercise. *Journal of Nutritional Biochemistry* 16: 530–537; Nieman, D. C., D. A. Henson, S. R. McAnulty, L. S. McAnulty, N. S. Swick, A. C. Utter, D. M. Vinci, S. J. Opiela, and J. D. Morrow. 2002. Influence of Vitamin C Supplementation on Oxidative and Immune Changes After an Ultramarathon. *Journal of Applied Physiology* 92: 1970–1977.

22. Dubnov, G., and N. W. Constantini. 2004. Prevalence of Iron Depletion and Anemia in Top-Level Basketball Players. *International Journal of Sport Nutrition and Exercise Metabolism* 14: 30–37.

23. Gropper, S. S., D. Glessing, K. Dunham, and J. M. Barksdale. 2006. Iron Status of Female Collegiate Athletes Involved in Different Sports. *Biological Trace Element Research* 109: 1–14; Dubnov. Prevalence of Iron Depletion.

24. Klesges, R. C., K. D. Ward, M. L. Shelton, W. B. Applegate, E. D. Cantler, G. M. Palmieri, K. Harmon, and J. Davis. 1996. Changes in Bone Mineral Content in Male Athletes: Mechanisms of Action and Intervention Effects. *Journal of the American Medical Association* 276: 226–230.

25. C. Rosenbloom, *Sports Nutrition: A Guide for the Professional Working with Active People,* 102–104.

26. Wilk, B., and O. Bar-Or. 1996. Effect of Drink Flavor and NaCl on Voluntary Drinking and Hydration in Boys Exercising in the Heat. *Journal of Applied Physiology* 80: 1112–1117.

27. American College of Sports Medicine. 1996. Position Stand on Exercise and Fluid Replacement. 1996. *Medicine and Science in Sports and Exercise* 28: i–vii.

28. von Fraunhofer, J. A., and M. M. Rogers. 2005. Effects of Sports Drinks and Other Beverages on Dental Enamel. *General Dentistry* 53: 28–31.

29. McGee, W. 2005. Caffeine in the Diet. National Institutes of Health Medline Plus Medical Encyclopedia. Available at www.nlm.nih.gov/medlineplus/ency/article/002445.htm.

30. USA Track & Field. Press Release April 19, 2003. USATF Announces Major Change in Hydration Guidelines. Available at www.usatf.org/news/showRelease.asp?article=/news/releases/2003-04-19-2.xml.

31. Greenhaff, P. L., A. Casey, A. H. Short, R. Harris, K. Söderlund, and E. Hultman. 1993. Influence of Oral Creatine Supplementation on Muscle Torque During Repeated Bouts of Maximal Voluntary Exercise in Man. *Clinical Science* 84: 565–571.

32. Vandenberghe, K., M. Goris, P. Van Hecke, M. Van Leemputte, L. Vangerven, and P. Hespel. 1997. Long-Term Creatine Intake Is Beneficial to Muscle Performance During Resistance Training. *Journal of Applied Physiology* 83: 2055–2063; Kreider, R. B., M. Ferreira, M. Wilson, P. Grindstaff, S. Plisk, J. Reinardy, E. Cantler, and A. L. Almada. 1998. Effects of Creatine Supplementation on Body Composition, Strength, and Sprint Performance. *Medicine & Science in Sports & Exercise* 30(1): 73–82.

33. Mayhew, D. L., J. L. Mayhew, and J. S. Ware. 2002. Effects of Long-Term Creatine Supplementation on Liver and Kidney Functions in American College Football Players. *International Journal of Sport Nutrition and Exercise Metabolism* 12: 453–460; Kreider, R. B., C. Melton, C. J. Rasmussen, M. Greenwood, S. Lancaster, E. C. Cantler, P. Milnor, and A. L. Almada.

2003. Long-Term Creatine Supplementation Does Not Significantly Affect Clinical Markers of Health in Athletes. *Molecular and Cellular Biochemistry* 244: 95–104.

34. Pritchard, N. R., and P. A. Kalra. 1998. Renal Dysfunction Accompanying Oral Creatine Supplements. *The Lancet* 351: 1252–1253; Greenhaff, P. 1998. Renal Dysfunction Accompanying Oral Creatine Supplements. *The Lancet* 352: 233–234.

35. Wiles, J. D., S. R. Bird, J. Hopkins, and M. Riley. 1992. Effect of Caffeinated Coffee on Running Speed, Respiratory Factors, Blood Lactate and Perceived Exertion During 1500 M Treadmill Running. *British Journal of Sports Medicine* 26:116–120; Spriet, L. L., D. A. MacLean, D. J. Dyck, E. Hultman, G. Cederblad, and T. E. Graham. 1992. Caffeine Ingestion and Muscle Metabolism During Prolonged Exercise in Humans. *American Journal of Physiology–Endocrinology and Metabolism* 262: E891–E898.

36. Paton, C. D., W. G. Hopkins, and L. Vollebregt. 2001. Little Effect of Caffeine Ingestion on Repeated Sprints in Team-Sport Athletes. *Medicine & Science in Sports & Exercise* 33: 822–825.

37. Crist, D. M., G. T. Peake, P. A. Egan, and D. L. Waters. 1988. Body Composition Responses to Exogenous GH During Training in Highly Conditioned Adults. *Journal of Applied Physiology* 65: 579–584; Foss, M., and S. Keteyian. 1998. *Physiological Basis for Exercise and Sport.* 6th ed. McGraw-Hill: 498.

38. Deyssig, R., H. Frisch, W. Blum, and T. Waldorf. 1993. Effect of Growth Hormone Treatment on Hormonal Parameters, Body Composition, and Strength in Athletes. *Acta Endocrinologica* 128: 313–318; Lange, K., J. Andersen, N. Beyer, F. Isaksson, B. Larsson, A. Rasmussen, A. Juul, J. Bülow, and M. Kjær. 2002. GH Administration Changes Myosin Heavy Chain Isoforms in Skeletal Muscle but Does Not Augment Muscle Strength or Hypertrophy, Either Alone or Combined with Resistance Exercise Training in Healthy Elderly Men. *Journal of Clinical Endocrinology & Metabolism* 87: 513–523.

39. Woodhouse, L. J., S. L. Asa, S. G. Thomas, and S. Ezzat. 1999. Measures of Submaximal Aerobic Performance Evaluate and Predict Functional Response to Growth Hormone (GH) Treatment in GH-Deficient Adults. *Journal of Clinical Endocrinology and Metabolism* 84: 4570–4577.

40. Ekblom, B., and B. Berglund. 1991. Effect of Erythropoietin Administration on Maximal Aerobic Power. *Scandinavian Journal of Medicine and Science in Sports* 1: 88–93.

Feature Box References

1. Tarnopolsky, M. A., S. A. Atkinson, S. M. Phillips, and J. D. MacDougall. 1995. Carbohydrate Loading and Metabolism During Exercise in Men and Women. *Journal of Applied Physiology* 78: 1360–1368.

2. Goforth, W. H., D. Laurent, W. K. Prusaczyk, K. E. Schneider, K. F. Peterson, and G. I. Shulman. 2003. Effects of Depletion Exercise and Light Training on Muscle Glycogen Supercompensation in Men. *American Journal of Physiology Endocrinology and Metabolism* 285: E1304–1311.

3. Houmard, J. A., D. L. Costill, J. B. Mitchell, S. H. Park, R. C. Hickner, and J. N. Roemmich. 1990. Reduced Training Maintains Performance in Distance Runners. *International Journal of Sports Medicine* 11: 46–52.

Table 11.1 References

1. Whelton, S. P., A. Chin, X. Xin, J. He. 2002. Effect of Aerobic Exercise on Blood Pressure: A Meta-Analysis of Randomized, Controlled Trials. *Annals of Internal Medicine* 136: 493–503.

2. Alhassan S., K. A. Reese, J. Mahurin, E. P. Plaisance, B. D. Hilson, J. C. Garner, S. O. Wee, and P. W. Grandjean. 2006. Blood Lipid Responses to Plant Stanol Ester Supplementation and Aerobic Exercise Training. *Metabolism* 55: 541–549.

3. Janssen, I., P. T. Katzmarzyk, R. Ross, A. S. Leon, J. S. Skinner, D. C. Rao, J. H. Wilmore, T. Rankinen, and C. Bouchard. 2004. Fitness Alters the Associations of BMI and Waist Circumference with Total and Abdominal Fat. *Obesity* 12: 525–537.

4. O'Donovan, G., E. M. Kearney, A. M. Nevill, K. Woolf-May, and S. R. Bird. 2005. The Effects of 24 Weeks of Moderate- or High-Intensity Exercise on Insulin Resistance. *European Journal of Applied Physiology* 95: 522–528.

5. Kato, T., T. Terashima, T. Yamashita, Y. Hatanaka, A. Honda, and Y. Umemura. 2006. Effect of Low-Repetition Jump Training on Bone Mineral Density in Young Women. *Journal of Applied Physiology* 100: 839–843; Daly, R. M., D. W. Dunstan, N. Owen, D. Jolley, J. E. Shaw, P. Z. Zimmet. 2005. Does High-Intensity Resistance Training Maintain Bone Mass During Moderate Weight Loss in Older Overweight Adults with Type 2 Diabetes? *Osteoporosis International* 16: 1703–1712; Yung, P. S., Y. M. Lai, P. Y. Tung, H. T. Tsui, C. K. Wong, V. W. Hung, and L. Qin. 2005. Effects of Weight Bearing and Nonweight Bearing Exercises on Bone Properties Using Calcaneal Quantitative Ultrasound. *British Journal of Sports Medicine* 39: 547–551.

6. Karacabey, K., O. Saygin, R. Ozmerdivenli, E. Zorba, A. Godekmerdan, and V. Bulut. 2005. The Effects of Exercise on the Immune System and Stress Hormones in Sportswomen. *Neuroendocrinology Letters* 26: 361–366.

7. Tworoger, S. S., Y. Yasui, M. V. Vitiello, R. S. Schwartz, C. M. Ulrich, E. J. Aiello, M. L. Irwin, D. Bowen, J. D. Potter, and A. McTiernan. 2003. Effects of a Yearlong Moderate-Intensity Exercise and a Stretching Intervention on Sleep Quality in Postmenopausal Women. *Sleep* 26: 830–836.

Chapter 12

1. Wong, W., C. Thomas, J. Merkus, G. Zielhuis, and R. Steegers-Theunissen. 2000. Male Factor Subfertility: Possible Causes and the Impact of Nutritional Factors. *Fertility and Sterility* 73: 435–442; Magnusdottir, E., T. Thorsteinsson, S. Thorsteinsdottir, M. Heimisdottir, and K. Olagsdottir. 2005. Persistent Organochlorines, Sedentary Occupation, Obesity, and Human Male Subfertility. *Human Reproduction* 20: 208–225.

2. Eskenazi, B., S. Kidd, A. Marks, E. Sloter, G. Block, and A. Wyrobek. 2005. Antioxidant Intake Is Associated with Semen Quality in Healthy Men. *Human Reproduction* 20: 1006–1012.

3. Wong. Male Factor Subfertility; Magnusdottir. Persistent Organochlorines, Sedentary Occupation, Obesity, and Human Male Subfertility; Eskenazi. Antioxidant Intake Is Associated with Semen Quality in Healthy Men.

4. Kaiser, L., and L. Allen. 2002. Position of the American Dietetic Association: Nutrition and Lifestyle for a Healthy Pregnancy Outcome. *Journal of the American Dietetic Association* 102: 1479–1490; Norman, R., and A. Clark. 1998. Obesity and Reproductive Disorders. *Reproduction Fertility and Development* 10: 55–63.

5. Ibid.

6. Kaiser. Position of the American Dietetic Association; Galtier-Dereure, F., C. Boegner, and J. Bringer. 2000. Obesity and Pregnancy: Complications and Cost. *American Journal of Clinical Nutrition* 71: 1242S–1248S.

7. Chobanian, A., G. Bakris, H. Black, W. Cushman, L. Green, J. Izzo, D. Jones, B. Materson, S. Oparil, J. Wright, E. Roccella, and the National High Blood Pressure Education Program Coordinating Committee. 2003. Seventh Report of the Joint National Committee on Prevention, Detection, Evaluation, and Treatment of High Blood Pressure. *Hypertension* 42: 1206–1252; Casro, L., and R. Avinoa. 2002. Maternal Obesity and Pregnancy Outcomes. *Current Opinion in Obstetrics and Gynecology* 14: 601–606; Institute of Medicine. 1990. *Nutrition During Pregnancy.* Washington, D.C.: National Academies Press.

8. Kaiser. Position of the American Dietetic Association.

9. Bolumar, F., J. Olsen, M. Rebagliato, L. Bisanti, and the European Study Group on Infertility and Subfecundity. 1997. Caffeine Intake and Delayed Conception: A European Multicenter Study on Infertility and Subfecundity. *American Journal of Epidemiology* 145: 324–334.

10. U.S. Department of Health and Human Services. 2004. *The Health Consequences of Smoking: A Report of the Surgeon General.* Atlanta: Centers for Disease Control and Prevention, National Center for Chronic Disease Prevention and Health Promotion, Office on Smoking and Health.

11. Institute of Medicine. 1990. *Nutrition During Pregnancy;* U.S. Department of Health and Human Services. *The Health Consequences of Smoking.*

12. Institute of Medicine. *Nutrition During Pregnancy.*

13. Kaiser. Position of the American Dietetic Association.

14. U.S. Department of Health and Human Services. 2005. U.S. Surgeon General Advisory on Alcohol Use in Pregnancy. Available at www.cdc.gov/ncbddd/fas/documents/Released%20Advisory.pdf. Accessed April 2005.

15. Finkel, R., and K. Zarlengo. 2004. Blue Cohosh and Perinatal Stroke. *New England Journal of Medicine* 351: 302–303.

16. Marcus, D., and W. Snodgrass. 2005. Do No Harm: Avoidance of Herbal Medicines During Pregnancy. *Obstetrics & Gynecology* 105: 1119–1122; Jones, T., and T. Lawson. 1998. Profound Neonatal Congestive Heart Failure Caused by Maternal Consumption of Blue Cohosh Herbal Medication. *Journal of Pediatrics* 132: 550–552.

17. Correa, A., A. Stolley, and Y. Liu. 2000. Prenatal Tea Consumption and Risk of Anencephaly and Spina Bifida. *Annals of Epidemiology* 10: 476–477; Navarro-Peran, E., J. Cabezas-Herrera, F. Garcia-Canovas, M. Durrant, R. Thorneley, and J. Rodríguez-Lopez. 2005. The Antifolate Activity of Tea Catechins. *Cancer Research* 65: 2059–2064.

18. Mattison, D. Herbal Supplements: Their Safety, a Concern of Health Care Providers. March of Dimes. Available at www.marchofdimes.com. Accessed April 2006; Kleinman, R., ed. 2004. *Pediatic Nutrition Handbook,* 4th ed. Elk Grove Village, IL: American Academy of Pediatrics.

19. Substance Abuse and Mental Health Services Administration. 2005. Results from the 2004 National Survey on Drug Use and Health: National Findings. Available at http://oas.samhsa.gov/nsduh/2k4nsduh/2k4Results/2k4Results.htm. Accessed April 2004.

20. Lacroix, R., E. Eason, and R. Melzack. 2000. Nausea and Vomiting During Pregnancy: A Prospective Study of Its Frequency, Intensity, and Patterns of Change. *American Journal of Obstetrics and Gynecology* 182: 931–937.

21. Quilan, J., and D. Hill. 2003. Nausea and Vomiting of Pregnancy. *American Family Physicians* 68: 121–128; Lacroix. Nausea and Vomiting During Pregnancy.

22. Quilan. Nausea and Vomiting of Pregnancy; Strong, T. 2001. Alternative Therapies of Morning Sickness. *Clinical Obstetrics and Gynecology* 44: 653–660.

23. Erick, M. 1994. Battling Morning (Noon and Night) Sickness. *Journal of the American Dietetic Association* 94: 147–148; Pirisi, A. 2001. Meaning of Morning Sickness Still Unsettled. *The Lancet* 357: 1272.

24. Strong. Alternative Therapies of Morning Sickness.

25. Erick. Battling Morning (Noon and Night) Sickness.

26. Backon, J. 1991. Ginger in Preventing Nausea and Vomiting of Pregnancy: A Caveat Due to Its Thromboxane Synthetase Activity and Effect on Testosterone Binding. *European Journal of Obstetrics & Gynecology and Reproductive Biology* 42: 163–164; Backon, J. 1991. Ginger as an Antiemetic: Possible Side Effects Due to Its Thromboxane Synthetase Activity. *Anaesthesia* 46: 705–706.

27. Kaiser. Position of the American Dietetic Association.

28. Rose, E., J. Porcerelli, and A. Neale. 2000. Pica: Common but Commonly Missed. *Journal of the American Board of Family Practice 2000* 13: 353–358.

29. Kettaneh, A., V. Eclache, O. Fain, C. Sontag, M. Uzan, L. Carbillon, J. Stirnemann, and M. Thomas. 2005. Pica and Food Craving in Patients with Iron-Deficiency Anemia: A Case-Control Study in France. *American Journal of Medicine* 118: 185–188.

30. Kaiser. Position of the American Dietetic Association.

31. Institute of Medicine. *Nutrition During Pregnancy.*

32. Picciano, M. 2003. Pregnancy and Lactation: Physiological Adjustments, Nutritional Requirements and the Role of Dietary Supplements. *Journal of Nutrition* 133: 1997S–2002S.

33. Rooney, B., and C. Schauberger. 2002. Excess Pregnancy Weight Gain and Long-Term Obesity: One Decade Later. *Obstetrics & Gynecology* 100: 245–252.

34. Institute of Medicine. *Nutrition During Pregnancy;* Picciano. Pregnancy and Lactation.

35. Institute of Medicine. *Nutrition During Pregnancy.*

36. Ibid.; Picciano. Pregnancy and Lactation.

37. Kaiser. Position of the American Dietetic Association.

38. Hornstra, G. 2000. Essential Fatty Acids in Mothers and Their Neonates. *American Journal of Clinical Nutrition* 71: 1262S–1269S.

39. Cooke, A., and J. Friday. 2005. CNRG Table Set 3.0: Pyramid Servings Intakes in the United States 1999–2002, 1 day. Community Nutrition Research Group Agricultural Research Service, U.S. Department of Agriculture. Available at www.ba.ars.usda.gov/cnrg. Accessed April 2006.

40. Duffy, V., and M. Sigman-Grant. 2004. Position of the American Dietetic Association: Use of Nutritive and Nonnutritive Sweeteners. *Journal of the American Dietetic Association* 104: 255–275.

41. Wang, T., and B. Apgar. 1998. Exercise During Pregnancy. *American Family Physician* 57: 1846–1856; The National Women's Health Information Center, U.S. Department of Health and Human Services. 2006. Healthy Pregnancy: Have a Fit Pregnancy. Available at www.4woman.org/pregnancy. Accessed April 2006.

42. ACOG Committee Obstetric Practice. 2002. ACOG Committee Opinion No. 267, Exercise During Pregnancy and the Postpartum Period. *Obstetrics and Gynecology* 99: 171–173.

43. Wang. Exercise During Pregnancy.

44. Kaiser. Position of the American Dietetic Association.

45. American Diabetes Association. Gestational Diabetes. Available at www.diabetes.org/gestational-diabetes.jsp. Accessed April 2006.

46. National Institute of Child Health and Human Development. 2004. Will Gestational Diabetes Hurt My Baby? Available at www.nichd.nih.gov/publications/pubs/gdm/GDM2004_section2.pdf. Accessed April 2006.

47. Correa, A., L. Botto, Y. Liu, J. Mulinare, and J. Erickson. 2003. Do Multivitamin Supplements Attenuate the Risk of Diabetes-Associated Birth Defects? *Pediatrics 2003* 111: 1146–1151; National Institute of Child Health and Human Development. Will Gestational Diabetes Hurt My Baby?

48. American Diabetes Association. Gestational Diabetes.

49. National Institute of Child Health and Human Development. Will Gestational Diabetes Hurt My Baby?

50. National Institute of Child Health and Human Development. Updated 2005. Am I at Risk for Gestational Diabetes? Available at www.nichd.nih.gov/publications/pubs_details.cfm?from=&pubs_id=113.

51. Chobanian. Seventh Report of the Joint National Committee on Prevention, Detection, Evaluation, and Treatment of High Blood Pressure; National Heart, Lung, and Blood Institute. High Blood Pressure in Pregnancy. Available at www.nhlbi.nih.gov/health/public/heart/hbp/hbp_preg.htm. Accessed April 2006.

52. Kaiser. Position of the American Dietetic Association; National Heart, Lung, and Blood Institute. High Blood Pressure in Pregnancy.

53. Chobanian. Seventh Report of the Joint National Committee on Prevention, Detection, Evaluation, and Treatment of High Blood Pressure; American Academy of Family Physicians. Update 2005. Preeclampsia. Available at http://familydoctor.org/064.xml. Accessed April 2006.

54. Ibid.; U.S. National Library of Medicine. 2004. Medical Encyclopedia: Eclampsia. Available at www.nlm.nih.gov/medlineplus/ency/article/000899.htm. Accessed April 2006.

55. American Academy of Family Physicians. Preeclampsia.

56. Kaiser. Position of the American Dietetic Association; National Heart, Lung, and Blood Institute. High Blood Pressure in Pregnancy.

57. Ibid.

58. Chobanian. Seventh Report of the Joint National Committee on Prevention, Detection, Evaluation, and Treatment of High Blood Pressure.

59. Solomon, C., and E. Seely. 2004. Preeclampsia: Searching for the Cause. *New England Journal of Medicine* 350: 641–642; Roberts, J., J. Balk, L. Bodnar, J. Belizan, E. Bergel, and A. Martinez. 2003. Nutrient Involvement in Preeclampsia. *Journal of Nutrition* 133: 1684S–1692S.

60. Kaiser. Position of the American Dietetic Association; Roberts. Nutrient Involvement in Preeclampsia.

61. Kaiser. Position of the American Dietetic Association.

62. Ibid.

63. Rees, J., and B. Worthington-Roberts. 1994. Position of the American Dietetic Association: Nutrition Care for Pregnant Adolescents. *Journal of the American Dietetic Association* 94: 449–450.

64. Martin, J., B. Hamilton, P. Sutton, S. Ventura, F. Menacker, and M. Munson. 2005. Births: Final Data for 2003. *National Vital Statistics Reports*, Centers for Disease Control and Prevention. Available at http://www.cdc.gov/nchs/data/nvsr/nvsr54/nvsr54_02.pdf. Accessed April 2006.

65. National Center for Health Statistics. 2006. Final Births for 2004. Available at www.cdc.gov/nchs/products/pubs/pubd/hestats/finalbirths04/finalbirths04.htm. Accessed October 2006.

66. Shabert, J. 2000. Nutrition During Pregnancy and Lactation. In Krause, *Food, Nutrition, & Diet Therapy.* 11th ed. Philadelphia: Saunders.

67. U.S. Department of Health and Human Services (HSS). 2000. HHS Blueprint for Action on Breastfeeding. Available at www.cdc.gov/breastfeeding/pdf/bluprntbk2.pdf. Accessed April 2006.

68. Ibid.

69. U.S. Breastfeeding Committee. 2002. Economic Costs of Breastfeeding. Available at www.usbreastfeeding.org/Issue-Papers/Economics.pdf. Accessed April 2006.

70. Ibid.

71. U.S. Breastfeeding Committee. 2002. Benefits of Breastfeeding. Available at www.usbreastfeeding.org/Issue-Papers/Benefits.pdf. Accessed April 2006.

72. Klaus, M. 1998. Mother and Infant: Early Emotional Ties. *Pediatrics* 102: 1244–1246.

73. Institute of Medicine. 1991. *Nutrition During Lactation.* Washington, D.C.: National Academies Press.

74. James, D., and B. Dobson. 2005. Position of the American Dietetic Association: Promoting and Supporting Breastfeeding. *Journal of the American Dietetic Association* 105: 810–818; Picciano, M., and S. McDonald. 2006. Lactation. In Shils, M. *Modern Nutrition in Health and Disease.* Philadelphia: Lippincott Williams & Wilkins.

75. U.S. Department of Health and Human Services. HHS Blueprint for Action on Breastfeeding; James. Position of the American Dietetic Association: Promoting and Supporting Breastfeeding.

76. Ibid.

77. Allen, J., R. Keler, P. Archer, and M. Neville. 1991. Studies in Human Lactation: Milk Composition and Daily Secretion Rates of Macronutrients in the First Year of Lactation. *American Journal of Clinical Nutrition* 54: 69–80.

78. James. Position of the American Dietetic Association: Promoting and Supporting Breastfeeding.

79. Bidlack, W., and W. Wang. 2006. Designing Functional Foods. In Shils, M. *Modern Nutrition in Health and Disease.* Philadelphia: Lippincott Williams & Wilkins.

80. Picciano. Lactation. In Shils, *Modern Nutrition in Health and Disease.*

81. James. Position of the American Dietetic Association: Promoting and Supporting Breastfeeding; Gartner, L., A. Eidelman, J. Morton, R. Lawrence, A. Naylor, D. O'Hare, and R. Schanler. 2005. Breastfeeding and the Use of Human Milk. *Pediatrics* 115: 496–506.

82. U.S. Department of Health and Human Services. HHS Blueprint for Action on Breastfeeding; Dewey, K. 2003. Is Breastfeeding Protective Against Child Obesity? *Journal of Human Lactation* 19: 9–18.

83. Ibid.; Fisher, J., L. Birch, H. Smiciklas-Wright, and M. Picciano. 2000. Breast-feeding through the First Year Predicts Maternal Control in Feeding and Subsequent Toddler Energy Intakes. *Journal of the American Dietetic Association* 100: 641–646.

84. Ibid.; Grummer-Strawn, L., and Z. Mei. 2004. Does Breastfeeding Protect Against Pediatric Overweight? Analysis of Longitudinal Data from the Centers for Disease Control and Prevention Pediatric Nutrition Surveillance System. *Pediatrics* 113:e81–e86; Krebs, N., M. Jacobson, R. Baker, F. Greer, M. Heyman, T. Jaksic, and F. Lifshitz. 2003. Prevention of Pediatric Overweight and Obesity. *Pediatrics* 112: 424–430.

85. Kaiser. Position of the American Dietetic Association; U.S. Department of Health and Human Services. HHS Blueprint for Action on Breastfeeding; Picciano. Lactation. In Shils. *Modern Nutrition in Health and Disease.* Horwood, L., and D. Fergusson. 1998. Breastfeeding and Later Cognitive Academic Outcomes. *Pediatrics* 101: e1–e9.

86. Centers for Disease Control. 2005. Breastfeeding Data and Statistics: Breastfeeding Practices—Results from the 2004 National Immunization Survey. Available at www.cdc.gov/breastfeeding/data/NIS_data/data_2004 .htm. Accessed May 2006; U.S. Department of Health and Human Services. 2000. *Healthy People 2010,* Maternal, Infant, and Child Health. Available at www.healthypeople.gov/document/HTML/Volume2/16MICH .htm. Accessed April 2006.

87. Centers for Disease Control. Breastfeeding Data and Statistics.

88. James. Position of the American Dietetic Association: Promoting and Supporting Breastfeeding.

89. Institute of Medicine. *Nutrition During Lactation.*

90. Ward, R., B. Bates, W. Benitz, D. Burchfield, J. Ring, J. Walls, and P. Walson. 2001. The Transfer of Drugs and Other Chemicals into Human Milk. American Academy of Pediatrics Committee on Drugs. *Pediatrics* 108: 776–784.

91. U.S. Department of Health and Human Services. HHS Blueprint for Action on Breastfeeding.

92. Ibid.; Gartner, L., 2005. Breastfeeding and the Use of Human Milk. *Pediatrics* 115: 496–506.

93. Udall, J., and R. Suskind. 1999. Cow's Milk versus Formula in Older Infants: Consequences for Human Nutrition. *Acta paediatrica. Supplementum* 430: 61–70.

94. Ibid.; Heird, W., and A. Cooper. 2006. Infancy and Childhood. In Shils, *Modern Nutrition in Health and Disease.* Philadelphia: Lippincott Williams & Wilkins.

95. Ibid.

96. Sarrinen, K., K. Juntunen-Backman, A. Jarvenpaa, P. Kuitunen, L. Lope, M. Renlund, M. Siivola, and E. Savilahti. 1999. Supplementary Feeding in Maternity Hospitals and the Risk of Cow's Milk Allergy: A Prospective Study of 6,209 Infants. *Journal of Allergy and Clinical Immunology* 104: 457–461.

97. Baker, S., W. Cochran, C. Flores, C. Georgieff, M. Jacobson, T. Jaksic, and N. Krebs. 1999. Iron Fortification of Infant Formulas. *Pediatrics* 104: 119–123.

98. Food and Drug Administration. 2005. Food Safety for Moms-to-Be. Once Baby Arrives. www.cfsan.fda.gov/~pregnant/pregnant.html. Accessed May 2006.

99. American Academy of Pediatrics. www.aap.org. Accessed April 2006.

100. D. L. Bogen, A. K. Duggan, G. J. Dover, and M. H. Wilson. 2000. Screening for Iron Deficiency Anemia by Dietary History in a High-Risk Population. *Pediatrics* 105: 1254–1259.

101. National Center for Health Statistics. www.cdc.gov/nchs/about/major/nhanes/growthcharts/background.htm. Accessed April 2006.

102. Institute of Medicine. Food and Nutrition Board. 2002. *Dietary Reference Intakes for Energy, Carbohydrate, Fiber, Fat, Fatty Acids, Cholesterol, Protein, and Amino Acids.* Washington, D.C.: National Academies Press.

103. Gartner. Breastfeeding and the Use of Human Milk.

104. Ibid.

105. Ibid.

106. Institute of Medicine. Food and Nutrition Board. *Dietary Reference Intakes for Energy, Carbohydrate, Fiber, Fat, Fatty Acids, Cholesterol, Protein, and Amino Acids.*

107. American Academy of Pediatrics. www.aap.org. Accessed April 2006; Institute of Medicine. Food and Nutrition Board. *Dietary Reference Intakes for Energy, Carbohydrate, Fiber, Fat, Fatty Acids, Cholesterol, Protein, and Amino Acids.*

108. American Heart Association, S. Gidding, B. Dennison, L. Birch, S. Daniels, M. Gilman, A. Lichtenstein, K. Rattay, J. Steinberger, N. Stettler, and L. Horn. 2006. Dietary Recommendations for Children and Adolescents: A Guide for Practitioners. *Pediatrics* 117: 544–559.

109. Guthrie, H. A. 1966. Effect of Early Feeding of Solid Foods on Nutritive Intake of Infants. *Pediatrics* 38: 879–885; Briley, M., and C. Roberts-Gray, 2005. Position of the American Dietetic Association: Benchmarks for Nutrition Programs in Child Care Settings. *Journal of the American Dietetic Association* 105: 979–986.

110. Ibid.; Butte, N., K. Cobb, J. Dwyer, L. Graney, W. Heird, and K. Rickard. 2004. The Start Healthy Feeding Guidelines for Infants and Toddlers. *Journal of the American Dietetic Association* 104: 442–454.

111. Butte. The Start Healthy Feeding Guidelines for Infants and Toddlers.

112. The Food Allergy and Anaphylaxis Network. www.foodallergy.org. Accessed April 2006.

113. Centers for Disease Control and Prevention. www.cdc.gov/ncidod/dbmd/diseaseinfo/botulism_g.htm. Accessed April 2006.

114. Briefel R., P. Ziegler, T. Novak, and M. Ponza. 2006. Feeding Infants and Toddlers Study: Characteristics and Usual Nutrient Intake of Hispanic and Non-Hispanic Infants and Toddlers. *Journal of the American Dietetic Association* 106 (supplement): S84–S95.

Feature Box References

1. Bureau of Labor Statistics. 2006. Table 6: Employment Status of Mothers with Own Children Under 3 Years Old by Single Year of Age of Youngest Child, and Marital Status, 2004–2005 Annual Averages. Available at www.bls.gov/news.release/famee.t06.htm. Accessed May 2006.

2. Slusser, W., L. Lange, V. Dickson, C. Hawkes, and R. Cohen. 2004. Breast Milk Expression in the Workplace: A Look at Frequency and Time. *Journal of Human Lactation* 20: 164–169.

3. Johnson, M. 2006. Letter to the Editor: Twentieth Anniversary Issue. *Journal of Human Lactation* 22: 14–15.

4. National Conference of State Legislatures. 2006. 50 State Summary of Breastfeeding Laws. Available at www.ncsl.org/programs/health/breast50 .htm. Accessed May 2006.

5. U.S. Breastfeeding Committee. 2002. Workplace Breastfeeding Support. Available at www.usbreastfeeding.org/Issue-Papers/Workplace.pdf. Accessed May 2006.

6. Ibid.

7. Ibid.

8. Briefel, R., C. Hanson, M. K. Fox, T. Novak, and P. Ziegler. 2006. Feeding Infants and Toddlers Study: Do Vitamin and Mineral Supplements Contribute to Nutrient Adequacy or Excess among U.S. Infants and Toddlers? *Journal of the American Dietetic Association* 106 (supplement): S52–S65.

9. Milner, J. D., D. M. Stein, R. McCarter, and R. Y. Moon. 2004. Early Infant Multivitamin Supplementation Is Associated with Increased Risk for Food Allergy and Asthma. *Pediatrics* 114: 27–32.

10. Briefel. Feeding Infants and Toddlers Study: Do Vitamin and Mineral Supplements Contribute to Nutrient Adequacy or Excess among U.S. Infants and Toddlers?

11. National Institute of Allergy and Infectious Diseases. 2004. Food Allergy and Intolerances. Available at www.niaid.nih.gov/factsheets/food.htm. Accessed May 2004.

12. Ibid.

13. Ibid.; The Food Allergy and Anaphylaxis Network. 2004. Common Food Allergens. Available at www.foodallergy.org/allergens.html. Accessed October 2006.

14. Long, A. 2002. The Nuts and Bolts of Peanut Allergy. *New England Journal of Medicine* 346: 1320–1322.

15. Food and Drug Administration. 2006. Food Allergen Labeling and Consumer Protection Act of 2004 (Title II of Public Law 108–282). Report to The Committee on Health, Education, Labor, and Pensions United States Senate and the Committee on Energy and Commerce United States House of Representatives. Available at www.cfsan.fda.gov/~acrobat/alrgrep.pdf. Accessed January 2007.

16. Food and Drug Administration. 2005. Compliance Policy Guide. Section 555.250. Statement of Policy for Labeling and Preventing Cross-Contact of Common Food Allergens. Available at www.fda.gov/ora/compliance _ref/cpg/cpgfod/cpg555-250.htm. Accessed October 2006.

Chapter 13

1. National Center for Health Statistics. 2000. *NCHS Growth Curves for Children 0–19 Years.* U.S. Vital and Health Statistics, Health Resources Administration. Washington, D.C.: U.S. Government Printing Office.

2. American Academy of Pediatrics. Available at www.aap.org. Accessed April 2006.

3. Ziegler, P., C. Hanson, M. Ponza, T. Novak, and K. Hendricks. 2006. Feeding Infants and Toddlers Study: Meal and Snack Intakes of Hispanic and

Non-Hispanic Infants and Toddlers. *Journal of the American Dietetic Association* 106 (supplement).

4. American Academy of Pediatrics. Available at www.aap.org. Accessed April 2006.

5. U.S. Department of Health and Human Services. 2004. *The 2004 Surgeon General's Report on Bone Health and Osteoporosis: What It Means to You.* Washington, D.C.: Office of the Surgeon General.

6. Kazal, L. A., Jr. 2002. Prevention of Iron Deficiency in Infants and Toddlers. *American Family Physician* 66: 1217–1224.

7. Konofal, E. et al. 2004. Iron Deficiency in Children with Attention Deficit/Hyperactivity Disorder. *Archives of Pediatrics & Adolescent Medicine* 158.

8. Ibid.

9. *Healthy People 2010.* Available at www.healthypeople.gov. Accessed October 2006.

10. World Health Organization. 2002. *World Health Report 2002: Reducing Risks, Promoting Healthy Lives.* Geneva, Switzerland: The WHO Press. Available at www.who.int/en.

11. Ziegler. Feeding Infants and Toddlers Study.

12. Corbett, J. V. 1995. Accidental Poisoning with Iron Supplements. *MCN: The American Journal of Maternal Child Nursing* 20: 234.

13. Center for Food Safety and Applied Nutrition. 1998. *Inside FDA.*

14. Wright, R. O., M. W. Shannon, R. J. Wright, and H. Hu. 1999. Association between Iron Deficiency and Low-Level Lead Poisoning in an Urban Primary Care Clinic. *American Journal of Public Health* 89: 1049–1053.

15. Agency for Toxic Substances and Disease Registry. Available at www.atsdr.cdc.gov. Accessed October 2006.

16. Centers for Disease Control and Prevention. 2006. Death of a Child after Ingestion of a Metallic Charm, Minnesota. *Morbidity and Mortality Weekly Report* 55 (Dispatch): 1–2.

17. Institute of Medicine. 2003. *Dietary Reference Intakes for Energy, Carbohydrate, Fiber, Fat, Protein, and Amino Acids.* Washington, D.C.: National Academies Press.

18. Ibid.

19. American Academy of Pediatrics (AAP). Committee on Nutrition. 2003. *Pediatric Nutrition Handbook.* Elk Grove Village, IL: AAP.

20. Satter, E. 2003. *Child of Mine: Feeding with Love and Good Sense.* Boulder, CO: Bull Publishing.

21. Rolls, B. J., D. Engell, and L. L. Birch. 2000. Serving Portion Size Influences 5-Year-Old but Not 3-Year-Old Children's Food Intakes. *Journal of the American Dietetic Association* 100: 232–234.

22. National Center for Health Statistics (NCHS): National Health and Nutrition Examination Survey Data. Hyattsville, MD: U.S. Department of Health and Human Services, Centers for Disease Control and Prevention, 2003–2004. Available at www.cdc.gov/nchs/fastats/overwt.htm. Accessed February 2007.

23. National Institutes of Health. *Obesity Education Initiative.* Available at www.nhlbi.nih.gov/health/public/heart/obesity/wecan. Accessed April 2006.

24. U.S. Department of Agriculture, Agriculture Research Service. 2004. *What We Eat in America.* NHANES 2001–2002. Available at www.ars.usda.gov/ba/bhnrc/fsrg.

25. Henry J. Kaiser Family Foundation. 2005. Generation M: Media in the Lives of 8–18-Year-Olds: Report.

26. U.S. Department of Health and Human Services. 2002. *HHS Promotes Health through Physical Activity.*

27. Centers for Disease Control and Prevention. 2002. *Exploratory Research Report. Life's First Great Crossroad: Tweens Make Choices that Affect their Lives Forever.*

28. American Academy of Pediatrics. Committee on Nutrition. 2003. Prevention of Pediatric Overweight and Obesity. *Pediatrics* 112: 424–430.

29. Samour, P. Q., and K. King, eds. 2005. *Handbook of Pediatric Nutrition.* 3rd ed. Sudbury, MA: Jones and Bartlett Publishers, Inc.

30. American Dental Association. 1997. Position statement on Early Childhood Caries, Resolution 6H-1997.

31. U.S. Department of Agriculture, Food and Nutrition Service. 2005. National School Lunch Program Fact Sheet.

32. Rampersaud, G. C., M. A. Pereira, B. L. Girard, J. Adams, and J. D. Metzl. 2005. Breakfast Habits, Nutritional Status, Body Weight, and Academic Performance in Children and Adolescents. *Journal of the American Dietetic Association* 105.

33. Ogden, C. L., M. D. Carroll, L. R. Curtin, T. A. McDowell, C. J. Tabak, and K. M. Flegal. 2006. Prevalence of Overweight and Obesity in the United States, 1999–2004. *Journal of the American Medical Association* 295: 1549–1555.

34. Meyer, F., J. Moisan, D. Marcoux, et al. 1990. Dietary and Physical Determinants of Menarche. *Epidemiology* 1: 377–381.

35. National Institute of Arthritis and Musculoskeletal and Skin Diseases. 2001. Available at www.niams.nih.gov/hi/topics/growth_plate/growth.htm. Accessed April 2006.

36. Food and Drug Administration. 1993. *Health Claims: Calcium and Osteoporosis.* Available at www.cfsan.fda.gov/~lrd/cf101-72.html. Accessed October 2006.

37. Lanou, A. J., S. E. Berkow, and N. D. Barnard. 2005. Calcium, Dairy Products, and Bone Health in Children and Young Adults: A Reevaluation of the Evidence. *Pediatrics* 115: 736–743.

38. Volek, J. S. et al. 2003. Increasing Fluid Milk Favorably Affects Bone Mineral Density Responses to Resistance Training in Adolescent Boys. *Journal of the American Dietetic Association* 103: 1353–1356.

39. U.S. Department of Agriculture. 1998. *Food and Nutrient Intakes by Children 1994–1996, Table Set 17.* Available at www.ars.usda.gov/Services/docs.htm?docid=7716. Accessed October 2006.

40. Alaimo, K. 1994. *Dietary Intake of Vitamins, Minerals and Fiber of Persons Ages 2 Months and Over in the United States.* Third National Health and Nutrition Examination Survey Phase 1, 1988–1991: Advance Data from Vital and Health Statistics, No. 258. Hyattsville, MD: National Center for Health Statistics.

41. Johnson R. K., D. G. Johnson, M. Q. Wang, H. Smiciklas-Wright, and H. Guthrie. 1994. Characterizing Nutrient Intakes of Adolescents by Sociodemographic Factors. *Journal of Adolescent Health* 15: 149–152.

42. Neumark-Sztainer, D., M. Wall, J. Guo, M. Story, J. Haines, and M. Eisenberg. 2006. Obesity, Disordered Eating, and Eating Disorders in a Longitudinal Study of Adolescents: How Do Dieters Fare Five Years Later? *Journal of the American Dietetic Association* 106.

43. Centers for Disease Control and Prevention. 2006. *Health, United States, 2005, with Chartbook on Trends in the Health of Americans with Special Feature on Adults 55–64 Years.* Available at www.cdc.gov/nchs/hus.htm. Accessed May 2006.

44. He, W., M. Sengupta, V. Velkoff, and K. Debarros. 2005. *65+ in the United States, Current Population Reports.* U.S. Census Bureau. Washington D.C.: U.S. Government Printing Office.

45. Centers for Disease Control and Prevention. 2003. Public Health and Aging: Trends in Aging—United States and Worldwide. *Morbidity and Mortality Weekly Report* 52: 101–106.

46. Bales, C., and C. Ritchie. 2006. The Elderly. In M. Shils, M. Shike, A. Ross, B. Caballero, and R. Cousins. *Modern Nutrition in Health and Disease.* 10th ed. Philadelphia: Lippincott Williams & Wilkins.

47. Institute of Medicine. *Dietary Reference Intakes for Energy.*

48. Kurczmarski, M., and D. Weddle. 2005. Position Paper of the American Dietetic Association: Nutrition across the Spectrum of Aging. *Journal of the American Dietetic Association* 105: 616–633; Wakimoto, P., and G. Block. 2001. Dietary Intake, Dietary Patterns, and Changes with Age: An Epidemiological Perspective. *Journals of Gerontology Series A: Biological Sciences and Medical Sciences* 56A: 65–80.

49. Moshfegh, A., J. Goldman, and L. Cleveland. 2005. What We Eat in America. NHANES 2001–2002: Usual Nutrient Intakes from Food Compared to Dietary Reference Intakes. U.S. Department of Agriculture, Agricultural Research Service.

50. Ibid.

51. Kurczmarski. Position Paper of the American Dietetic Association.

52. Penniston, K., and S. Tanumihardjo. 2003. Vitamin A in Dietary Supplements and Fortified Foods: Too Much of a Good Thing. *Journal of the American Dietetic Association* 103: 1185–1187.

53. Bales. The Elderly.

54. Kurczmarski. Position Paper of the American Dietetic Association; Guaralnik, J., R. Eisenstaedt, L. Ferrucci, H. Klein, and R. Woodman. 2004. Prevalence of Anemia in Persons 65 Years and Older in the United States: Evidence for a High Rate of Unexplained Anemia. *Blood* 104: 2263–2268.

55. Ibid.

56. Institute of Medicine. *Dietary Reference Intakes for Energy.*

57. Cooke, A., and J. Friday. 2005. *Pyramid Servings Intakes in the United States 1999–2002: CNRG Table Set 3.0.* Community Nutrition Research Group, Agricultural Research Service, U.S. Department of Agriculture. Available at www.ba.ars.usda.gov/cnrg. Accessed May 2006.

58. U.S. Department of Health and Human Services. 2004. *Bone Health and Osteoporosis: A Report of the Surgeon General.* Washington, D.C.: Office of the Surgeon General.

59. World Health Organization. 2002. *Keep Fit for Life: Meeting the Nutritional Needs of Older Persons.* Geneva, Switzerland: WHO. Available at www.who.int/nutrition/publications/olderpersons/en/index.html. Accessed May 2006.

60. Juan, W., M. Lino, and P. Basiotis. 2004. Quality of Diet of Older Americans. *Nutrition Insight* 29. Center of Nutrition Policy and Promotion. Available at www.cnpp.usda.gov/insights.html. Accessed May 2006.

61. Cooke. *Pyramid Servings Intakes in the United States 1999–2002.*
62. World Health Organization. *Keep Fit for Life.*
63. Juan. Quality of Diet of Older Americans; Cooke. *Pyramid Servings Intakes in the United States 1999–2002.*
64. World Health Organization. *Keep Fit for Life.*
65. Agency for Healthcare Research and Quality and the Centers for Disease Control and Prevention. 2002. *Physical Activity and Older Americans: Benefits and Strategies.* Available at www.ahrq.gov/ppip/activity.htm. Accessed May 2006.
66. National Institute of Arthritis and Musculoskeletal and Skin Diseases. 2002. *Osteoarthritis.* Available at www.niams.nih.gov/hi/topics/arthritis/oahandout.htm. Accessed May 2006.
67. Ibid.
68. Clegg, D. et al. 2006. Glucosamine, Chondroitin Sulfate, and the Two in Combination for Painful Knee Osteoarthritis. *New England Journal of Medicine* 354: 795–808.
69. National Institute of Arthritis and Musculoskeletal and Skin Diseases. 2004. *Rheumatoid Arthritis.* Available at www.niams.nih.gov/hi/topics/arthritis/rahandout.htm#ra_9. Accessed May 2006.
70. Choi, H. 2005. Dietary Risk Factors for Rheumatic Diseases. *Current Opinion in Rheumatology* 17: 141–146.
71. Linos, A., V. Kaklamani, E. Kaklamani, Y. Koumantaki, E. Giziaki, S. Papzoglou, and C. Mantzoros. 1999. Dietary Factors in Relation to Rheumatoid Arthritis: A Role for Olive Oil and Cooked Vegetables. *American Journal of Clinical Nutrition* 70: 1077–1082.
72. National Institute on Aging. 2006. Alzheimer's Fact Sheet. Available at www.nia.nih.gov/Alzheimers/Publications/adfact.htm. Accessed May 2006.
73. National Institute on Aging. Alzheimer's Fact Sheet; Nourhashemi, F., S. Gillette-Guyonnet, S. Andrieu, A. Ghisolfi, P. Ousset, H. Grandjean, A. Grand, J. Pous, B. Vellas, and J. Albarede. 2000. Alzheimer Disease: Protective Factors. *American Journal of Clinical Nutrition* 71: 643S–649S; Martin, A. 2003. Antioxidant Vitamins E and C and Risk of Alzheimer's Disease. *Nutrition Reviews* 61: 69–79.
74. Nourhashemi. Alzheimer Disease: Protective Factors.
75. Maclean, C., A. Iss, S. Newberry, W. Mojica, S. Morton, R. Garland, L. Hilton, S. Traina, and P. Shekell. 2005. *Effects of Omega-3 Fatty Acids on Cognitive Function with Aging, Dementia, and Neurological Diseases. Summary, Evidence Report/Technology Assessment No. 114.* Agency for Healthcare Research and Quality. Available at www.ahrq.gov/downloads/pub/evidence/pdf/o3cogn/o3cogn.pdf. Accessed May 2006.
76. National Institute on Aging. Alzheimer's Fact Sheet; U.S. Food and Drug Administration. 2003. *Dietary Supplements: Tips for Older Dietary Supplement Users.* Available at www.cfsan.fda.gov/~dms/ds-savv2.html. Accessed May 2006.
77. Nord, M., M. Andrews, and S. Carlson. 2005. *Household Food Security in the United States, 2005.* Economic Research Services. Available at www.ers.usda.gov/publications/err11. Accessed May 2006.
78. Lee, J., and E. Frongillo. 2001. Nutritional and Health Consequences Are Associated with Food Insecurity among U.S. Elderly Persons. *Journal of Nutrition* 131: 1503–1509.
79. Wolfe, W., E. Frongillo, and P. Valois. 2003. Understanding the Experience of Food Insecurity by Elders Suggests Ways to Improve Its Measurement. *Journal of Nutrition* 133: 2762–2769.
80. Administration on Aging. 2006. Older Americans Act. Available at www.aoa.gov/about/legbudg/oaa/legbudg_oaa.asp. Accessed May 2006.
81. Kurczmarski. Position Paper of the American Dietetic Association.
82. U.S. Department of Health and Human Services. 1999. *Mental Health: A Report of the Surgeon General—Executive Summary.* Rockville, MD: U.S. Department of Health and Human Services, Substance Abuse and Mental Health Services Administration, Center for Mental Health Services, National Institutes of Health, National Institute of Mental Health.
83. National Institute on Alcohol Abuse and Alcoholism. *Alcohol and Aging.* Available at http://pubs.niaaa.nih.gov/publications/aa40.htm. Accessed May 2006.
84. National Institute on Aging. 2005. *Alcohol Use and Abuse.* Available at www.niapublications.org/agepages/alcohol.asp. Accessed May 2006.
85. National Institute on Alcohol Abuse and Alcoholism. *Alcohol and Aging.*
86. Administration on Aging. Older Americans Act.
87. National Institute on Aging. *Alcohol Use and Abuse.*
88. National Institute on Alcohol Abuse and Alcoholism. *Alcohol and Aging.*

Feature Box References

1. National Institute of Mental Health. Available at www.nimh.nih.gov/publicat/adhd.cfm. Accessed April 2006.
2. Consensus Development Panel. 1982. *Defined Diets and Childhood Hyperactivity.* National Institutes of Health Consensus Development Conference Summary, Volume 4, no. 3; National Institute of Mental Health. Available at www.nimh.nih.gov/publicat/adhd.cfm. Accessed April 2006.
3. Position of the American Dietetic Association 2004. Use of Nutritive and Nonnutritive Sweeteners. *Journal of the American Dietetic Association* 104.
4. Biederman J., S. V. Faraone, K. Keenan, D. Knee, M. F. Tsuang. 1990. Family-Genetic and Psychosocial Risk Factors in DSM-III Attention Deficit Disorder. *Journal of the American Academy of Child and Adolescent Psychiatry* 29: 526–533.
5. Brown, C. 2000. Overview of Drug Interactions. *U.S. Pharmacist* 25: e1–e16.
6. Maskalyk, J. 2002. Grapefruit Juice: Potential Drug Interactions. *Canadian Medical Association Journal* 167: 279–280.
7. U.S. Food and Drug Administration. 2003. *Dietary Supplements: Tips for Older Dietary Supplement Users.* Available at www.cfsan.fda.gov/~dms/ds-savv2.html. Accessed May 2006.

Chapter 14

1. Centers for Disease Control Division of Bacterial and Mycotic Diseases. 2002. Updated 2003. Foodborne Illness: General Information. Available at www.cdc.gov/ncidod/dbmd/diseaseinfo/foodborneinfections_g.htm. Accessed October 2003.
2. Centers for Disease Control and Prevention. 1999. Safer and Healthier Foods: 1900–1999. *Journal of the American Medical Association* 48: 905–913; Young, J. H. 1981. Updated 1999. The Long Struggle for the 1906 Law. *FDA Consumer Magazine.* Available at www.cfsan.fda.gov/~lrd/history2.html. Accessed December 2006.
3. Young. The Long Struggle for the 1906 Law.
4. Food Safety and Inspection Service. 1999. Origins of the Federal Food Safety System. *Food Safety Educator* 4: 3–4. Available at www.fsis.usda.gov/News_&_Events/food_safety_educator/index.asp. Accessed December 2006.
5. Centers for Disease Control and Prevention. Safer and Healthier Foods.
6. Center for Food Safety and Applied Nutrition. Updated 2002. Food Safety A to Z Reference Guide: Virus. Available at www.cfsan.fda.gov/~dms/a2z-uvw.html#virus. Accessed December 2006.
7. National Center for Infectious Diseases. Updated 2005. Norovirus: Technical Fact Sheet. Available at www.cdc.gov/ncidod/dvrd/revb/gastro/noro-factsheet.pdf. Accessed December 2006.
8. National Center for Infectious Diseases. Updated 2005. Norovirus: Food Handlers. Available at www.cdc.gov/ncidod/dvrd/revb/gastro/noro-foodhandlers.pdf. Accessed December 2006.
9. Centers for Disease Control. September 9, 2003. Public Health Dispatch: Multistate Outbreak of Hepatitis A among Young Adult Concert Attendees, United States, 2003. *Morbidity and Mortality Weekly Report* 52: 844–845. Available at www.cdc.gov/mmwr/preview/mmwrhtml/mm5235a5.htm. Accessed December 2006.
10. Center for Food Safety and Applied Nutrition. Updated 2002. Food Safety A to Z Reference Guide: Bacteria. Available at www.cfsan.fda.gov/~dms/a2z-b.html. Accessed December 2006.
11. Centers for Disease Control Division of Bacterial and Mycotic Diseases. Reviewed 2003. *Campylobacter* Infections. Available at www.cdc.gov/ncidod/dbmd/diseaseinfo/campylobacter_g.htm. Accessed December 2006.
12. Centers for Disease Control Division of Bacterial and Mycotic Diseases. Updated September 2006. *Escherichia coli* O157:H7. Available at www.cdc.gov/ncidod/dbmd/diseaseinfo/escherichiacoli_g.htm. Accessed December 2006.
13. Centers for Disease Control Division of Bacterial and Mycotic Diseases. Updated 2004. Travelers' Diarrhea. Available at www.cdc.gov/ncidod/dbmd/diseaseinfo/travelersdiarrhea_g.htm. Accessed December 2006.
14. Centers for Disease Control Division of Bacterial and Mycotic Diseases. Updated 2006. Salmonellosis. Available at www.cdc.gov/ncidod/dbmd/diseaseinfo/salmonellosis_g.htm. Accessed December 2006.
15. Food Safety and Inspection Service. 2001. Parasites and Foodborne Illness. Available at www.fsis.usda.gov/Fact_Sheets/Parasites_and_Foodborne_Illness/index.asp Access December 2006.
16. Gerald, B. J., and J. E. Perkin. 2003. Position of the American Dietetic Association: Food and Water Safety. *Journal of the American Dietetic Association* 103: 1203–1218.
17. Buzby, J. C. 2003. Older Adults at Risk of Complications from Microbial Foodborne Illness. *Food Review* 25: 30–35.
18. Buzby, J. C. 2002. Children and Microbial Foodborne Illness. *Food Review* 24: 32–37.
19. Gerald. Position of the American Dietetic Association: Food and Water Safety.
20. Center for Food Safety and Applied Nutrition. Food Safety A to Z Reference Guide: Bacteria.
21. Ibid.

22. Center for Food Safety and Applied Nutrition. Updated 2002. Food Safety A to Z Reference Guide: Handwashing. Available at www.cfsan.fda.gov/~dms/a2z-h.html. Accessed December 2006.

23. Food Safety and Inspection Service. 2003. The Food Safety Educator: Thinking Globally, Working Locally. Available at www.fsis.usda.gov/Frame/FrameRedirect.asp?main=http://www.fsis.usda.gov/OA/educator/educator8-1.htm. Accessed December 2006.

24. Ibid.

25. Agriculture Research Service, Food Safety and Inspection Service. 1998. Premature Browning of Cooked Ground Beef. Available at www.fsis.usda.gov/OPHS/prebrown.htm. Accessed December 2006.

26. Food Safety and Inspection Service. Updated 2006. The Color of Meat and Poultry. Available at www.fsis.usda.gov/Fact_Sheets/Color_of_Meat_&_Poultry/index.asp. Accessed December 2006.

27. American Dietetic Association. 2001. Survey Reveals Americans Need a Refrigeration Refresher. Available at www.homefoodsafety.org. Accessed December 2003; Partnership for Food Safety Education. 2006. Fridge Fact Sheet. Available at www.fightbac.org/chill_facts.cfm. Accessed December 2006.

28. Food Safety and Inspection Service. Updated 2006. How Temperatures Affect Food. Available at www.fsis.usda.gov/Fact_Sheets/How_Temperatures_Affect_Food/index.asp. Accessed December 2006.

29. Ibid.

30. Food and Drug Administration and U.S. Department of Agriculture. 2000. A Description of the US Food Safety System. Available at www.fsis.usda.gov/OA/codex/system.htm. Accessed December 2006.

31. Food Safety and Inspection Service. 2003. Enhancing Public Health: Strategies for the Future—2003 FSIS Food Safety Vision. Available at www.fsis.usda.gov/oa/programs/vision071003.htm. Accessed December 2006.

32. Food and Drug Administration and U.S. Department of Agriculture. A description of the US Food Safety System.

33. Centers for Disease Control. Updated 2003. PulseNet: The National Molecular Subtyping Network for Foodborne Disease Surveillance. Available at www.cdc.gov/pulsenet. Accessed December 2006.

34. Bracket, R. 2006. Statement before the Committee on Health, Education, Labor and Pensions, United States Senate. Available at www.fda.gov/ola/2006/foodsafety1115.html. Accessed November 2006; Food and Drug Administration. 2006. Nationwide E. coli O157:H7 Outbreak: Questions and Answers. Available at www.cfsan.fda.gov/~dms/spinacqa.html. Accessed November 2006.

35. Food and Drug Administration. 2001. HACCP: A State-of-the-Art Approach to Food Safety. FDA Backgrounder. Available at www.cfsan.fda.gov/~lrd/bghaccp.html. Accessed December 2006.

36. Food and Drug Administration. Updated 2003. FDA Food Code. Available at www.cfsan.fda.gov/~dms/foodcode.html. Accessed December 2006.

37. Center for Food Safety and Applied Nutrition. 1998. Updated 2001. What Consumers Need to Know abut Juice Safety. Available at www.cfsan.fda.gov/~dms/juicsafe.html. Accessed December 2006.

38. Tauxe, R. B. 2001. Food Safety and Irradiation: Protecting the Public from Foodborne Infections. Centers for Disease Control and Prevention, Emerging Infectious Diseases. Available at www.cdc.gov/ncidod/eid/vol7no3_supp/tauxe.htm#Figure. Accessed December 2006.

39. Center for Food Safety and Applied Nutrition. 2001. Analysis and Evaluation of Preventive Control Measures for the Control and Reduction/Elimination of Microbial Hazards on Fresh and Fresh-Cut Produce. Available at www.cfsan.fda.gov/~comm/ift3-toc.html. Accessed November 2006.

40. Finley, J., D. Deming, and R. Smith. 2006. Food Processing: Nutrition, Safety, and Quality. In Shils, M., M. Shike, A. Ross, B. Caballero, and R. Cousins. Modern Nutrition in Health and Disease. 10th ed. Philadelphia: Lippincott Williams & Wilkins.

41. Tauxe. Food Safety and Irradiation; Emmert, K., V. Duffy, and R. Earl. 2000. Position of the American Dietetic Association: Food Irradiation. Journal of the American Dietetic Association 100: 246–253.

42. Tauxe. Food Safety and Irradiation; Food and Drug Administration. 2000. Food Irradiation: A Safe Measure. Available at www.fda.gov/opacom/catalog/irradbro.html. Accessed December 2006.

43. Food and Drug Administration. Food Irradiation.

44. Tauxe. Food Safety and Irradiation; Emmert. Position of the American Dietetic Association: Food Irradiation.

45. Tauxe. Food Safety and Irradiation; Food and Drug Administration. Food Irradiation.

46. Ibid.

47. Emmert. Position of the American Dietetic Association: Food Irradiation.

48. Food Safety and Inspection Service. 2005. Irradiation of Raw Meat and Poultry: Questions and Answers. Available at www.fsis.usda.gov/Fact_Sheets/Irradiation_and_Food_Safety/index.asp. Accessed December

2006. Food Safety and Inspection Service. Irradiation of Raw Meat and Poultry. Tauxe. Food Safety and Irradiation.

49. Centers for Disease Control and Prevention. 2005. Frequently Asked Questions about Food Irradiation. Available at www.cdc.gov/ncidod/dbmd/diseaseinfo/foodirradiation.htm Accessed December 2006.

50. Lewis, C. 2002. Food Freshness and "Smart" Packaging. FDA Consumer Magazine. Available at www.fda.gov/fdac/features/2002/502_food.html Accessed November 2006.

51. Food Safety and Inspection Service. Updated 2006. Focus On: Food Product Dating. Available at www.fsis.usda.gov/Fact_Sheets/Food_Product_Dating/index.asp. Accessed December 2006.

52. Center for Food Safety and Applied Nutrition. 2001. Food Additives. Available at www.cfsan.fda.gov/~lrd/foodaddi.html. Accessed December 2006.

53. Ibid.

54. Rados, C. 2004. GRAS: Time-Tested and Trusted Food Ingredients. FDA Consumer Magazine. Available at www.fda.gov/fdac/features/2004/204_gras.html. Accessed December 2006.

55. Center for Food Safety and Applied Nutrition. Food Additives.

56. Rados. GRAS.

57. Center for Food Safety and Applied Nutrition. 2003. MSG: A Common Flavor Enhancer. Available at www.cfsan.fda.gov/~dms/fdacmsg.html. Accessed December 2006.

58. Ibid.

59. Center for Food Safety and Applied Nutrition. 2000. Sulfites: An Important Food Safety Issue. Available at www.cfsan.fda.gov/~dms/fssulfit.html. Accessed December 2006.

60. International Food Information Council. 1997. Everything You Need to Know about Asthma and Food. Available at www.ific.org/publications/brochures/asthmabroch.cfm?renderforprint=1. Accessed December 2006.

61. Papazian, R. 1996. Sulfites: Safe for Most, Dangerous for Some. Center for Food Safety and Applied Nutrition. Available at www.fda.gov/fdac/features/096_sulf.html. Accessed December 2006.

62. Center for Food Safety and Applied Nutrition. Sulfites.

63. Gerald. Position of the American Dietetic Association: Food and Water Safety.

64. Centers for Disease Control and Prevention. 2002. Marine Toxins. Available at www.cdc.gov/ncidod/dbmd/diseaseinfo/marinetoxins_g.htm. Accessed December 2006.

65. Ibid. Centers for Disease Control and Prevention. 1998. Ciguatera Fish Poisoning: Texas 1997. Morbidity and Mortality Weekly Report. Available at www.cdc.gov/mmwr/preview/mmwrhtml/00054548.htm. Accessed December 2006.

66. Centers for Disease Control and Prevention. Marine Toxins.

67. U.S. Environmental Protection Agency. Updated 2003. Polychlorinated Biphenyls (PCBs). Available at www.epa.gov/opptintr/pcb/. Accessed December 2006.

68. Taylor, S. 2006. Food Additives, Contaminants, and Natural Toxicants and Their Risk Assessment. In Shils, M., M. Shike, A. Ross, B. Caballero, and R. Cousins. Modern Nutrition in Health and Disease. 10th ed. Philadelphia: Lippincott Williams & Wilkins.

69. U.S. Environmental Protection Agency. Polychlorinated Biphenyls (PCBs).

70. Agency for Toxic Substances and Disease Registry. Updated 2006. ToxFAQ for Polychlorinated Biphenyls (PCBs). Available at www.atsdr.cdc.gov/tfacts17.html. Accessed December 2006.

71. U.S. Environmental Protection Agency. Persistent Bioaccumulative and Toxic (PBT) Chemical Program. Updated 2006. Polychlorinated Biphenyls (PCBs). Available at www.epa.gov/pbt/pubs/pcbs.htm. Accessed December 2006.

72. Ibid.

73. Gerald. Position of the American Dietetic Association: Food and Water Safety; U.S. Environmental Protection Agency, Persistent Bioaccumulative and Toxic (PBT) Chemical Program. Polychlorinated Biphenyls (PCBs).

74. Center for Veterinary Medicine. Report on the Food and Drug Administration's Review of the Safety of Recombinant Bovine Somatotrophin. Available at www.fda.gov/cvm/CVM_Updates/BSTADEUP.html. Accessed December 2006.

75. Center for Veterinary Medicine. 2002. The Use of Steroid Hormones for Growth Promotion in Food-Producing Animals. Available at www.fda.gov/cvm/hormones.htm. Accessed December 2006.

76. Ibid.

77. Centers for Disease Control and Prevention. 2005. Frequently Asked Questions about NARMS. Available at www.cdc.gov/narms/faq_antiresis.htm. Accessed November 2006.

78. Ibid.

79. U.S. Environmental Protection Agency. Updated 2003. About Pesticides: What Is a Pesticide? Available at www.epa.gov/pesticides/about/index.htm#what_pesticide. Accessed December 2006.

80. Ibid.

81. Ibid.

82. U.S. Environmental Protection Agency. 2006. Organophosphate Pesticides (OP) Cumulative Assessment: 2006 Update. Available at www.epa.gov/pesticides/cumulative/2006-op/index.htm. Accessed November 2006.

83. U.S. Environmental Protection Agency. Updated 2006. Pesticides: Topical and Chemical Fact Sheets—Antimicrobial Pesticide Products. Available at www.epa.gov/pesticides/factsheets/antimic.htm. Accessed December 2006.

84. Food and Drug Administration. 2003. Hand Hygiene in Retail and Food Service Establishments. Available at www.cfsan.fda.gov/~comm/handhyg.html. Accessed December 2006.

85. U.S. Environmental Protection Agency. About Pesticides.

86. U.S. Environmental Protection Agency. Updated 2006. Pesticides: Regulating Pesticides—Potassium Bicarbonate (073508) and Sodium Bicarbonate (073505). Available at www.epa.gov/pesticides/biopesticides/ingredients/factsheets/factsheet_073508.htm. Accessed December 2006.

87. U.S. Environmental Protection Agency. About Pesticides.

88. U.S. Environmental Protection Agency, Pesticides and Safety. Updated 2006. Health Problems Pesticides May Pose. Available at www.epa.gov/pesticides/food/risks.htm. Accessed December 2006.

89. Office of Disease Prevention and Health Promotion. 2000. *Healthy People 2010.* Available at www.healthypeople.gov/document/HTML/Volume1/08Environmental.htm. Accessed December 2006.

90. U.S. Environmental Protection Agency, Pesticides and Safety. Health Problems Pesticides May Pose. Office of Disease Prevention and Health Promotion. *Healthy People 2010.*

91. American Medical Association. Updated 2003. Report 4 of the Council on Scientific Affairs (I-94). Available at www.ama-assn.org/ama1/pub/upload/mm/443/csai-94.pdf. Accessed December 2006.

92. U.S. Environmental Protection Agency. Updated 2006. Pesticides: Topical and Chemical Fact Sheets—Assessing Health Risks from Pesticides. Available at www.epa.gov/pesticides/factsheets/riskassess.htm. Accessed December 2006.

93. U.S. Environmental Protection Agency. Updated 2006. Pesticides: Regulating Pesticides—Laws. Available at www.epa.gov/pesticides/regulating/laws.htm. Accessed December 2006.

94. U.S. Environmental Protection Agency. Updated 2006. Pesticides and Food: How the Government Regulates Pesticides. Available at www.epa.gov/pesticides/food/govt.htm. Accessed December 2006; U.S. Environmental Protection Agency. Pesticides: Regulating Pesticides—Laws.

95. U.S. Environmental Protection Agency. Updated 2006. Pesticides: Topical and Chemical Fact Sheets—Integrated Pest Management (IPM) and Food Production. Available at www.epa.gov/pesticides/factsheets/ipm.htm. Accessed December 2006.

96. Ibid.

97. International Food Information Council. 2006. Agriculture and Food Production. Available at www.ific.org/food/agriculture/index.cfm. Accessed December 2006.

98. Krieger, R. I., P. Brutsche-Keiper, H. R. Crosby, and A. D. Krieger. 2003. Reduction of Pesticide Residues of Fruit Using Water Only or Plus Fit Fruit and Vegetable Wash. *Bulletin of Environmental Contamination and Toxicology* 70: 213–218.

99. American Cancer Society. 2000. The Environment and Cancer Risk. Available at www.cancer.org/docroot/NWS/content/NWS_2_1x_The_Environment_and_Cancer_Risk.asp. Accessed December 2006.

100. Agricultural Marketing Service, National Organic Program. 2002. Organic Food Standards and Labels: The Facts. Available at www.ams.usda.gov/nop/Consumers/Consumerhome.html. Accessed December 2006.

101. Organic Trade Association. 2005. The Past, Present and Future of the Organic Industry: A Retrospective of the First 20 Years, a Look at the Current State of the Organic Industry and Forecasting the Next 20 Years. Available at www.ota.com/pics/documents/Forecasting2005.pdf Accessed November 2006.

102. International Food Information Council. 2003. USDA Launches Organic Standards. Available at www.ific.org/foodinsight/2003/mj/organicfi303.cfm. Accessed December 2006.

103. Agricultural Marketing Service, National Organic Program. Organic Food Standards.

104. Agency for Toxic Substances and Disease Registry. ToxFAQ for Polychlorinated Biphenyls (PCBs).

105. Agricultural Marketing Service, National Organic Program. Organic Food Standards.

106. Organic Trade Association. The Past, Present and Future of the Organic Industry.

107. Gregar, J. L. 2000. Biotechnology: Mobilizing Dietitians to Be a Resource. *Journal of the American Dietetic Association* 100: 1306–1308.

108. McCullum, C. 2000. Food Biotechnology in the New Millennium: Promises, Realities, and Challenges. *Journal of the American Dietetic Association* 100: 1311–1315; Bren, L. 2003. Genetic Engineering: The Future of Foods. *FDA Consumer Magazine.* Available at www.fda.gov/fdac/features/2003/603_food.html. Accessed March 2004.

109. McCullum. Food Biotechnology.

110. Gregar. Biotechnology; Thompson, L. 2000. Are Bioengineered Foods Safe? *FDA Consumer Magazine.* Available at www.fda.gov/fdac/features/2000/100_bio.html. Accessed December 2006.

111. Gregar. Biotechnology.

112. Thompson. Are Bioengineered Foods Safe?

113. Shoemaker, R., D. D. Johnson, and E. Golan. 2003. Consumers and the Future of Biotech Foods in the United States. Amber Waves. Available at www.ers.usda.gov/Amberwaves/November03/Features/futureofbiotech.htm. Accessed December 2006.

114. McCullum. Food Biotechnology.

115. Gregar. Biotechnology.

116. American Dietetic Association. 1995. Biotechnology and the Future of Food. *Journal of the American Dietetic Association* 95: 1429–1432.

117. Ibid.

118. Bren. Genetic Engineering: The Future of Foods; Shoemaker. Consumers and the Future of Biotech Foods.

119. U.S. Department of Agriculture. 2007. Q&A: *Bt* Corn and Monarch Butterflies. Available at www.ars.usda.gov/is/br/btcorn/index.html?pf=1. Accessed February 2007.

120. U.S. Department of Agriculture. Q&A: *Bt* Corn and Monarch Butterflies; Jones, L. 1999. Genetically Modified Foods. *British Medical Journal* 318: 581–584.

121. Thompson. Are Bioengineered Foods Safe?; Maryanski, J. H. 1997. Bioengineered Foods: Will They Cause Allergic Reactions? Center for Food Safety and Applied Nutrition. Available at www.cfsan.fda.gov/~dms/pubalrgy.html. Accessed December 2006; American Medical Association. 2005. Report 10 of the Council on Scientific Affairs (I-94). Genetically Modified Crops and Foods. Available at www.ama-assn.org/ama/pub/category/13595.html. Accessed December 2006.

122. Thompson. Are Bioengineered Foods Safe?

123. Formanek, R. 2001. Proposed Rules Issued for Bioengineered Foods. *FDA Consumer Magazine.* Available at www.cfsan.fda.gov/~dms/fdbioen2.html. Accessed March 2004.

124. Thompson. Are Bioengineered Foods Safe?

125. American Medical Association. Report 10 of the Council on Scientific Affairs; Society of Toxicology. 2002. Society of Toxicology Position Paper: The Safety of Genetically Modified Foods Produced through Biotechnology. Available at www.toxicology.org. Accessed December 2006.

126. Thompson. Are Bioengineered Foods Safe?

127. Formanek. Proposed Rules Issued for Bioengineered Foods.

128. International Food Information Council. 2006. Support for Food Biotechnology Stable Despite News on Unrelated Food Safety Issues. Available at www.ific.org/research/biotechres03.cfm. Accessed December 2006.

129. Bruemmer, B. 2003. Food Biosecurity. *Journal of the American Dietetic Association* 203: 687–691.

130. Centers for Disease Control and Prevention. 2003. Food Safety Threats. Available at www.bt.cdc.gov/agent/food/index.asp. Accessed December 2006.

131. Meadows, M. 2004. The FDA and the Fight Against Terrorism. *FDA Consumer Magazine.* Available at www.fda.gov/fdac/features/2004/104_terror.html. Accessed December 2006.

132. Bruemmer. Food Biosecurity.

Feature Box References

1. Centers for Disease Control and Prevention. 2002. Probable Variant Creutzfeldt-Jakob Disease in a U.S. Resident—Florida, 2002. *Morbidity and Mortality Weekly Report.* Available at www.cdc.gov/mmwr/preview/mmwrhtml/mm5141a3.htm. Accessed December 2006.

2. Animal and Plant Health Inspection Service. 2003. Bovine Spongiform Encephalopathy (BSE) Q & As. Available at www.aphis.usda.gov/lpa/issues/bse/bse_trade.html. Accessed December 2006.

3. Animal and Plant Health Inspection Service. Bovine Spongiform Encephalopathy; U.S. Department of Health and Human Services. 2001. Federal Agencies Take Special Precautions to Keep "Mad Cow Disease" Out of the United States. Available at www.hhs.gov/news/press/2001pres/01fsbse.html. Accessed December 2006; Centers for Disease Control and Prevention. 2003. Questions and Answers Regarding Bovine Spongiform Encephalopathy (BSE) and Creutzfeldt-Jakob Disease (CJD). Available at www.cdc.gov/ncidod/dvrd/bse/. Accessed December 2006.

4. Center for Food Safety and Applied Nutrition. 2005. Consumer Questions and Answers about BSE. Available at www.cfsan.fda.gov/~comm/bsefaq .html. Accessed December 2006.

5. Centers for Disease Control and Prevention. Questions and Answers Regarding Bovine Spongiform Encephalopathy (BSE) and Creutzfeldt-Jakob Disease (CJD).

6. Animal and Plant Health Inspection Service. 2003. Bovine Spongiform Encephalopathy.

7. Centers for Disease Control and Prevention. Questions and Answers Regarding Bovine Spongiform Encephalopathy (BSE) and Creutzfeldt-Jakob Disease (CJD).

8. U.S. Department of Agriculture. 2004. Hot Issues: BSE. Available at www.aphis.usda.gov/lpa/issues/bse/bse.html. Accessed December 2006.

9. Ibid.

10. U.S. Department of Health and Human Services. 2001. HHS Launches Expanded Plan to Combat "Mad Cow Disease." Available at www.hhs.gov/ news/press/2001pres/20010823.html. Accessed December 2006.

11. U.S. Department of Agriculture. Hot Issues: BSE.

Chapter 15

1. *Hunger in the United States.* 2005. Available at www.frac.org. Accessed May 2006; U.S. Department of Agriculture Census Bureau Survey. 2004. *Food Security in the United States.* Available at http://ers.usda.gov/Briefing/ FoodSecurity. Accessed May 2006.

2. Ibid.

3. U.S. Census Bureau, Population Division. 2005. State and County Quick Facts. Available at www.census.gov. Accessed December 2006.

4. ADA Reports. 2003. Position of the American Dietetic Association: Addressing World Hunger, Malnutrition, and Food Insecurity. *Journal of the American Dietetic Association* 103: 1046–1057.

5. Ibid.

6. Bread for the World Institute. 2006. Hunger Basics: World Hunger and Hunger Facts. Available at www.bread.org/learn/hunger-basics/. Accessed April 2006; Bread for the World Institute. 2004. Hunger Report 2004: *Are We on Track to End Hunger?* Available at www.bread.org/institute/ hunger_report/index.html.

7. America's Second Harvest. 2005. *Current Hunger and Poverty Statistics.* Available at www.secondharvest.org. Accessed May 2004.

8. U.S. Department of Health and Human Services. 2006. 2006 HHS Poverty Guidelines. *Federal Register* 71: 3848–3849. Available at http://aspe.hhs .gov/poverty/06poverty.shtml.

9. *Hunger in the United States.* 2005. U.S. Department of Agriculture Census Bureau Survey; *Food Security in the United States.*

10. United Nations Association of the United States of America and the Business Council for the United Nations. 2006. Millennium Development Goals—Goal 3: Gender Equity. Available at www.unausa.org. Accessed March 2006.

11. Caliendo, M. A. 1979. *Nutrition and the World Food Crisis.* New York: Macmillan Publishing Company, Inc.

12. U.S. Department of Labor, Bureau of Labor Statistics. 2003. A Profile of the Working Poor. Available at www.bls.gov/cps/cpswp2000.htm. Accessed December 2006.

13. United States Census. Historical Poverty Tables. Available at www.census .gov. Accessed October 2006.

14. ADA Reports. Position of the American Dietetic Association. Hunger.

15. Ibid.

16. Ibid.

17. U.S. Department of Health and Human Services. 2006 HHS Poverty Guidelines.

18. ADA Reports: Position of the American Dietetic Association.

19. Smith, L. C., and L. Haddad. 2000. *Explaining Child Malnutrition in Developing Countries: A Cross-Country Analysis of International Food Policy.* Washington, D.C.: International Food Policy Research Institute.

20. United Nations Association of the United States of America and the Business Council for the United Nations. Millennium Development Goals.

21. United States Census. Historical Poverty Tables.

22. Department of Foreign Affairs and International Trade, Canada. 2002. *Protecting Children from Sanctions.* Available at www.epals.com/ waraffectedchildren/chap11. Accessed March 2006.

23. DeRose, L., E. Messer, and S. Millman. 1998. Conflict as a Cause of Hunger in *Who's Hungry? And How Do We Know? Food Shortage, Poverty, and Deprivation.* Tokyo: United Nations University Press. www.unu.edu/ unupress. Accessed March 2006.

24. ADA Reports: Position of the American Dietetic Association. Addressing World Hunger.

25. Ibid.

26. Food and Agriculture Organization, Global Policy Forum. 2005. *Armed Conflicts a Leading Cause of World Hunger Emergencies.* Available at www.globalpolicy.org/socecon/hunger/oppressive/index.htm. Accessed May 2005.

27. Food and Agriculture Organization. 2005. *The State of Food Insecurity in the World, 2005.* Rome: Food and Agriculture Organization of the United Nations.

28. Food and Agriculture Organization. 2002. *The State of Food Insecurity in the World, 2002.* Rome: Food and Agriculture Organization of the United Nations.

29. Agriculture and Agri-Food Canada. 1997. The Pros and Cons of Pesticides. Available at www.ns.ec.gc.ca/epb/factsheets/pesticides/pro_con .html. Accessed March 2006.

30. ADA Reports. Position of the American Dietetic Association.

31. Food and Agriculture Organization. 2003. *The State of Food Insecurity in the World, 2003.* Rome: Food and Agriculture Organization of the United Nations.

32. ADA Reports. Position of the American Dietetic Association.

33. Food and Agriculture Organization. *The State of Food Insecurity in the World, 2003.*

34. Bread for the World Institute. Hunger Basics; Rosegrant, M. W., and M. A. Sombilia. 1997. Critical Issues Suggested by Trends in Food, Population, and the Environment for the Year 2020. *American Journal of Agricultural Economics* 79: 1467–1471; Brown, L. R., G. Gardner, and B. Halweil. 1999. 16 Impacts of Population Growth. *Futurist* 33: 36–41.

35. Scott, B., E. W. Counts, M. Medora, and C. Woolery. 1998. The Dietitian's Role in Ending World Hunger: As Citizen and Health Professional. *Topics in Clinical Nutrition* 13: 31–45.

36. Beers, M., R. Porter, T. Jones, J. Kaplan, and M. Berkwits, eds. 2006. Starvation. In *The Merck Manual of Diagnosis and Therapy, Section 1—Nutritional Disorders, Chapter 2: Malnutrition Topics.* Available at www.merck .com/mrkshared/mmanual/section1/chapter2/2b.jsp. Accessed April 2006.

37. U.S. Department of Health and Human Services. 2006 HHS Poverty Guidelines.

38. King, F. S., and A. Burgess. 1993. *Nutrition for Developing Countries.* 2nd ed. Oxford, England: Oxford Medical Publications, Oxford University Press.

39. World Health Organization. 2002. The Optimal Duration of Exclusive Breast-Feeding: A Systematic Review. Geneva, Switzerland: World Health Organization.

40. King. *Nutrition for Developing Countries.*

41. Beers, M., R. Porter, T. Jones, J. Kaplan, and M. Berkwits. 2006. Infant Nutrition. *The Merck Manual of Diagnosis and Therapy, Section 19—Pediatrics, Chapter 256: Health Management in Normal Newborns, Infants,* and *Children.* Available at www.merck.com/mrkshared/mmanual/section19/ chapter256/256g.jsp. Accessed April 2006.

42. ADA Reports. Position of the American Dietetic Association.

43. Beers. *The Merck Manual of Diagnosis and Therapy, Section 1—Nutritional Disorders.*

44. U.S. Department of Labor, Bureau of Labor Statistics. A Profile of the Working Poor.

45. SUSTAIN. 2002. Malnutrition Overview. Available at www.sustaintech .org/world.htm. Accessed March 2006.

46. Kleinman, R. E. et al. 1998. Hunger in Children in the United States: Potential Behavioral and Emotional Correlates. *Pediatrics* 101: 3–10.

47. Scanlon, K. S. 1989. (Thesis) Activity and Behavior Changes of Marginally Malnourished Mexican Pre-Schoolers. Storrs, CT: University of Connecticut; Mora, J. O. 1979. Nutritional Supplementation, Early Stimulation, and Child Development. In J. Brozek, ed. *Behavioral Effects of Energy and Protein Deficits.* Bethesda, MD: U.S. Department of Health, Education, and Welfare.

48. Uvin, P. 1994. The State of World Hunger. In P. Uvin, ed. *The Hunger Report, 1993.* Langhorne, PA: Gordon and Breach Science Publishers: 102.

49. U.S. Department of Health and Human Services. 2006 HHS Poverty Guidelines.

50. Food and Agriculture Organization. *The State of Food Insecurity in the World, 2005.*

51. U.S. Department of Health and Human Services. 2006 HHS Poverty Guidelines; United Nations Administrative Committee on Coordination Sub-Committee on Nutrition. 2000. *Fourth Report on the World Situation.* Geneva, Switzerland: ACC/SCN in collaboration with the International Food Policy Research Institute.

52. Martorell, R., J. Rivera, and H. Kaplowitz, 1992a. Consequences of Stunting in Early Childhood for Adult Body Size in Rural Guatemala. *Annales Nestle* 48: 85–92; Martorell, R., J. Rivera, H. Kaplowitz, and E. Pollit, 1992b. Proceeedings of the VIth International Congress of Auxiology. Long-Term Consequences of Growth Retardation during Early Childhood. New York: Elsevier Science Publishers.

53. UNICEF Statistics. 2006. Integrated Management of Childhood Illness (IMCI). Available at www.childinfo.org/eddb/imci/index.htm. Accessed April 2006.

54. U. S. Department of Health and Human Services. 2006 HHS Poverty Guidelines.

55. UNICEF Statistics. IMCI.

56. SUSTAIN. Malnutrition Overview. King. *Nutrition for Developing Countries.* Bread for the World Institute. Hunger Report 2004.

57. Food and Agriculture Organization. *The State of Food Insecurity in the World, 2003.*

58. Ten Population Myths: Exposing the Myths. Available at www.unesco.org. Accessed April 2006. Adapted from F. Lappe, J. Collins. 1998. *World Hunger: Twelve Myths,* 2nd ed. New York: Grove Press.

59. Ibid.

60. BBC News, Africa. 2006. *Using the Sun to Sterilize Water.* Available at http://news.bbc.co.uk/2/hi/africa/4786216.stm. Accessed April 2006.

61. UNICEF. *Water, Environment, and Sanitation.* 2005 Proceedings. Available at www.unicef.org/wes. Accessed April 2006.

62. BBC News, Africa. *Using the Sun to Sterilize Water.*

63. UNICEF Nutrition Section. 1996. The Progress of Nations, 1996. *18 Nations Fortify Foods.* Available at www.unicef.org/pon96/nufortif.htm. Accessed April 2006; Global Alliance for Improved Nutrition. 1996. Why Food Fortification? Available at www.gainhealth.org. Accessed January 2007.

64. Cleland, J. G., and J. K. Van Ginneken. 1988. Maternal Education and Child Survival in Developing Countries: The Search for Pathways of Influence. *Social Science and Medicine* 27: 1357–1368.

65. Bergeson, T. 2006. Office of Washington Superintendent of Public Instruction, Career, and Technical Education Pathways. Agriculture and Science. Available at www.k12.wa.us/CareerTechEd/pathways/Agriculture/ default/aspx. Accessed April 2006; Silent Killer Film. The Unfinished Campaign Against Hunger. 2005. Available at www.silentkillerfilm.org. Accessed April 2006.

Feature Box References

1. World Bank. 1997. World Development Indicators. Washington, D.C.: World Bank; Pinstrup-Anderson, P., R. Pandya-Lorch, and M. W. Rosegrant. 1997. The World Food Situation: Recent Developments, Emerging Issues, and Long-Term Prospects Food Policy Report. Washington, D.C.: The International Food Policy Research Institute.

2. ADA Reports. 2003. Position of the American Dietetic Association: Addressing World Hunger, Malnutrition, and Food Insecurity. *Journal of the American Dietetic Association* 103: 1046–1057.

3. Food and Agriculture Organization. 2002. *The State of Food Insecurity in the World, 2002.* Rome: Food and Agriculture Organization of the United Nations.

4. Food and Agriculture Organization. *The State of Food Insecurity in the World, 2002;* Mason, J. B. et al. 2001. *The Micronutrient Report: Current Progress and Trends in the Control of Vitamin A, Iron, and Iodine Deficiencies.* Ottawa, Ontario: The Micronutrient Initiative.

5. Uvin, P. 1994. The State of World Hunger. In P. Uvin, ed. *The Hunger Report, 1993.* Langhorne, PA: Gordon and Breach Science Publishers: 102.

6. Food and Agriculture Organization. 2000. *The State of Food Insecurity in the World, 2000.* Rome: Food and Agriculture Organization of the United Nations.

7. Department of Foreign Affairs and International Trade, Canada. 2002. *Protecting Children from Sanctions.* Available at www.epals.com/ waraffectedchildren/chap11. Accessed March 2006.

Index

Credits

p. iv, top: Don Smetzer/Alamy; p. iv, bottom: foodfolio/Alamy; p. v: PhotoLink/Getty Images; p. vi, top: Brian Hagiwara/Foodpix/Jupiter Images; p. vi, bottom: Cindy Jones/Foodpix/Jupiter Images; p. vii, top: Foodcollection.com/Getty Images; p. vii, bottom: foodfolio/Alamy; p. viii, top: Pixland/CORBIS; p. viii, bottom: Image Source/Jupiter Images; p. ix: N. Aubrier/age fotostock; p. x: Dennis MacDonald/PhotoEdit; p. xi: Abid Katib/Getty Images; p. xii: Matt Bowman/Foodpix/Jupiter Images; p. xiii: Digital Vision/Getty Images; p. xiv: Author

Chapter 1 Chapter Opener: Envision/CORBIS; p. 4: Kristin Piljay, Pearson Benjamin Cummings; p. 5, top right: Erich Lessing/Art Resource, NY; p. 5, bottom left: Burke/Triolo Productions/Foodpix/Jupiter Images; p. 5, bottom right: foodfolio/Alamy; p. 6, top left: Marc Romanelli/Workbook Stock/Getty Images; p. 7, top left: America's Milk Processors; p. 14: Bruce Ayres/Getty Images; p. 15: top right: Aaron Goodman/*Time* Magazine/Time & Life Pictures/Getty Images; p. 15: bottom right: Biophoto Associates/Photo Researchers; P. 22, left: Margo G. Wootan; p. 22, right: Radley Balko

Chapter 2 Chapter Opener: CORBIS; p. 28: Michael Keller/Index Stock Imagery; p. 29: Don Smetzer/Alamy; p. 32: Dorling Kindersley; p. 33: Brian Hagiwara/Foodpix/Jupiter Images; p. 34: Thomas Firak/Foodpix/Jupiter Images; p. 35: J. Painter, J. Rah, and Y. Lee; p. 36, top: USDA; p. 36, bottom left: Stockbyte Gold/Alamy; p. 39: davies & starr/Getty Images; p. 40: Kristin Piljay, Pearson Benjamin Cummings; p. 42: Richard Megna/Fundamental Photographs; p. 44: James Keyser/Time Life Pictures/Getty Images; p. 55, left: Sheila R. Cohn; p. 55, right: Barbara J. Rolls

Chapter 3 Chapter Opener: Thomas Kruesselmann/zefa/CORBIS; p. 62: BananaStock/age fotostock; p. 63: Stockbyte/CORBIS; p. 64: Mark Thomas/FoodPix/Jupiter Images; p. 66, center: CORBIS; p. 68, top left: Steve Gschmeissner/SPL/Photo Researchers; p. 68, bottom center: Tom Grill/CORBIS; p. 77, top left: Dr. E. Walker/SPL/Photo Researchers; p. 77, top right: C. James Webb/Phototake; p. 78: ISM/Phototake; p. 81, left: James Anderson; p. 81, right: Madelyn Fenstrom

Chapter 4 Chapter Opener: Bryan F. Peterson/CORBIS; p. 88: David Caton/Alamy; p. 94: Virgo Productions/zefa/CORBIS; p. 96: Felicia Martinez/PhotoEdit; p. 99: Cindy Jones/Foodpix/Jupiter Images; p. 100: Royalty-Free/CORBIS; p. 101: PhotoLink/Getty Images; p. 102: Kristin Piljay, Pearson Benjamin Cummings; p. 103: Foodcollection.com/Alamy; p. 104, Figure 4.9a: Hemera Technologies/Alamy; p. 106, Figure 4.11: Michael Newman/PhotoEdit; p. 108, left: Kristin Piljay, Pearson Benjamin Cummings; p. 110: Kristin Piljay, Pearson Benjamin Cummings; p. 112: BSIP/Phototake; p. 113: Coston Stock/Alamy; p. 115: BSIP/Phototake; p. 120: D. Hurst/Alamy; p. 123: davies & starr/Getty Images; p. 124, left: Robert Earl; p. 124, right: Barry M. Popkin

Chapter 5 Chapter Opener: Maximilian Stock Ltd/PhotoCuisine/CORBIS; p. 130: Stockbyte/Getty Images; p. 135, upper right: Colin Young-Wolff/PhotoEdit; p. 136: Comstock Images/Jupiter Images; p. 140, left: Dorling Kindersley; p. 140, right: Image Source/Jupiter Images; p. 141: Royalty-Free/CORBIS; p. 150: Kristin Piljay, Pearson Benjamin Cummings; p. 155: Kristin Piljay, Pearson Benjamin Cummings; p. 160: Matt Bowman/Foodpix/Jupiter Images; p. 161: Comstock/Jupiter Images; p. 166: David O. Carpenter; p. 168: Rachel Epstein/ PhotoEdit

Chapter 6: Chapter Opener: Kelly-Mooney Photography/CORBIS; p. 172: Digital Vision/Getty Images; p. 175: Push/Foodpix/Jupiter Images; p. 176: Virgo/zefa/CORBIS; p. 179: Oliver Meckes/Nicole Ottawa/Photo Researchers; p. 181, top right: Safia Fatimi/Getty Images; p. 181, Figure 6.9: Dr. P. Marazzi/SPL/Photo Researchers; p .183: Dorling Kindersley; p. 184: Lisa Romerein/Foodpix/Jupiter Images; p. 185, top: Charles Gullung/Getty Images; p. 185, middle: Jeff Boyle/Getty Images; p. 185, bottom: Brian Yarvin Photography/Photo Researchers; p. 187: Royalty-Free/CORBIS; p. 193, Figure 6.13: Hartmut Schwarzbach/Peter Arnold; p. 194, Figure 6.14: John Isaac/United Nations; p. 196, top left: Luzia Ellert/StockFood Creative/Getty Images; p. 196, top right: White Wave Foods; p. 196, bottom left: Mark Thomas/Foodpix/Jupiter Images; p. 196, bottom right: Dorling Kindersley; p. 197, top left: Steven Mark Needham/Foodpix/Jupiter Images; p. 197, top right: Kristin Piljay, Pearson Benjamin Cummings; p. 197, bottom left: Dorling Kindersley; p. 197, bottom right: Lisa Romerein/Foodpix/Jupiter Images; p. 203, bottom right: Evan Sklar/Foodpix/Jupiter Images; p. 204, left: Nancy Clark; p. 204, right: Joan Buchbinder

Chapter 7 Chapter Opener: Lluis Real/age footstock; p. 210: Darren Robb/Getty Images; p. 211, top left: James Baigrie/Foodpix/Jupiter Images; p. 211, top right: Photodisc/Getty Images; p. 211, bottom left: Virgo/zefa/CORBIS; p. 212: Mary Ellen Bartley/Foodpix/Jupiter Images; p. 214: Digital Vision/Getty Images; p. 215, top: Royalty-Free/CORBIS; p. 215, bottom: Dr. P. Marazzi/Photo Researchers; p. 216, top: Kathyrn Russell/Foodpix/Jupiter Images; p. 216, bottom: altrendo images/Getty Images; p. 217, top: Envision/CORBIS; p. 217, bottom: Dal Canton Mazzone, *The New England Journal of Medicine*, Vol. 346, p. 821, March 14, 2002; p. 218, top: Dorling Kindersley; p. 218, bottom right: Maurice Nimmo/Frank Lane Picture Agency/CORBIS; p. 219, top right: Brian Hagiwaraj/Foodpix/Jupiter Images; p. 219, bottom left: Rachel Epstein/PhotoEdit; p. 220, top left: Eye of Science/Photo Researchers; p. 220, top right: Hugh Turvey/Photo Researchers; p. 220, bottom left: Cristina Pedrassini/Photo Researchers; p. 220, bottom right: Royalty-Free/CORBIS; p. 221, far right: Royalty-Free/CORBIS; p. 221, left: Lisa Hubbard/Foodpix/Jupiter Images; p. 221, middle top: Dee Breger/Photo Researchers; p. 221, middle bottom: ISM/Phototake; p. 222, top right: Zephyr Photography/Photo Researchers; p. 222, bottom left: Stewart Cohen/Index Stock Imagery; p. 223, top right: Tom Main/Getty Images; p. 223, bottom left: Pearson Education/PH College; p. 224: Biophoto Associates/Photo Researchers; p. 225: Kristin Piljay, Pearson Benjamin Cummings; p. 226, left: Isabelle Rozenbaum/age fotostock; p. 226, top right: Brian Leatart/Foodpix/Jupiter Images; p. 226, bottom right: Leigh Belsch/Foodpix/Jupiter Images; p. 227, top right: David Prince/Foodpix/Jupiter Images; p. 227, bottom left: Leigh Belsch/Foodpix/Jupiter Pictures; p. 228, top right: Johner/Getty Images; p. 228, left: Ralph Morse/Getty Images; p. 228, bottom right: Pornchai Mittongtare/Foodpix/Jupiter Images; p. 229, bottom left: Eisenhut & Mayer/Foodpix/Jupiter Images; p. 229, bottom right: Gibson & Smith/Foodpix/Jupiter Images; p. 230, top: Michael Deuson/Foodpix/Jupiter Images; p. 230, bottom: Lisa Thompson/Foodpix/Jupiter Images; p. 231, top right: Dr. M. A. Ansary/Photo Researchers; p. 231, bottom left: davies & starr/Getty Images; p. 232, top left: CORBIS; p. 232, top right: Photodisc Green/Getty Images; p. 232, bottom right: Anthony-Masterson/Foodpix/Jupiter Images; p. 233, top right: Michael Newman/PhotoEdit; p. 233, bottom left: Cristina Cassinelli/Foodpix/Jupiter Images; p. 234, bottom left: NMSB/Custom Medical Stock Photo; p. 234, bottom right: Dorling Kindersley; p. 235: CORBIS; p. 236, top right: Rick Souders/Foodpix/Jupiter Images; p. 236, bottom left: Dorling Kindersley; p. 236, bottom right: Lew Robertson/Foodpix/Jupiter Images; p. 237, top right: Martin Jacobs/Foodpix/Jupiter Images; p. 237, bottom: Getty Images; p. 238, top right: CORBIS; p. 238, bottom left: Dimitri Vervits/Getty Images; p. 238, middle: SPL/Photo Researchers; p. 238, bottom right: CORBIS; p. 239, top right: St. Mary's Hospital Medical School/Photo Researchers; p. 239, bottom left: Wally Eberhart/Botanica/Jupiter Images; p. 239, bottom middle: CORBIS; p. 240, top right: Photodisc/Getty Images; p. 240, middle right: Chris Everard/Getty Images; p. 240, bottom middle: Robin MacDougall/Foodpix/Jupiter Images; p. 240, bottom right: Lew Robertson/Foodpix/Jupiter Images; p. 241, top right: Dick Clintsman/CORBIS; p. 241, bottom left: Richard Radstone/Getty Images; p. 244: National Eye Institute, National Institutes of Health;

Tolerable Upper Intake Levels (UL[a])

Vitamins

Life-Stage Group	Vitamin A (µg/d)[b]	Vitamin C (mg/d)	Vitamin D (µg/d)	Vitamin E (mg/d)[c,d]	Niacin (mg/d)[d]	Vitamin B_6 (mg/d)	Folate (µg/d)[d]	Choline (g/d)
Infants								
0–6 mo	600	ND[e]	25	ND	ND	ND	ND	ND
7–12 mo	600	ND	25	ND	ND	ND	ND	ND
Children								
1–3 y	600	400	50	200	10	30	300	1.0
4–8 y	900	650	50	300	15	40	400	1.0
Males, Females								
9–13 y	1,700	1,200	50	600	20	60	600	2.0
14–18 y	2,800	1,800	50	800	30	80	800	3.0
19–70 y	3,000	2,000	50	1,000	35	100	1,000	3.5
>70 y	3,000	2,000	50	1,000	35	100	1,000	3.5
Pregnancy								
≤18 y	2,800	1,800	50	800	30	80	800	3.0
19–50 y	3,000	2,000	50	1,000	35	100	1,000	3.5
Lactation								
≤18 y	2,800	1,800	50	800	30	80	800	3.0
19–50 y	3,000	2,000	50	1,000	35	100	1,000	3.5

Elements

Life-Stage Group	Boron (mg/d)	Calcium (g/d)	Copper (µg/d)	Fluoride (mg/d)	Iodine (µg/d)	Iron (mg/d)	Magnesium (mg/d)[f]	Manganese (mg/d)	Molybdenum (µg/d)	Nickel (mg/d)	Phosphorus (g/d)	Selenium (µg/d)	Vanadium (mg/d)[g]	Zinc (mg/d)
Infants														
0–6 mo	ND	ND	ND	0.7	ND	40	ND	ND	ND	ND	ND	45	ND	4
7–12 mo	ND	ND	ND	0.9	ND	40	ND	ND	ND	ND	ND	60	ND	5
Children														
1–3 y	3	2.5	1,000	1.3	200	40	65	2	300	0.2	3	90	ND	7
4–8 y	6	2.5	3,000	2.2	300	40	110	3	600	0.3	3	150	ND	12
Males, Females														
9–13 y	11	2.5	5,000	10	600	40	350	6	1,100	0.6	4	280	ND	23
14–18 y	17	2.5	8,000	10	900	45	350	9	1,700	1.0	4	400	ND	34
19–70 y	20	2.5	10,000	10	1,100	45	350	11	2,000	1.0	4	400	1.8	40
>70 y	20	2.5	10,000	10	1,100	45	350	11	2,000	1.0	3	400	1.8	40
Pregnancy														
≤18 y	17	2.5	8,000	10	900	45	350	9	1,700	1.0	3.5	400	ND	34
19–50 y	20	2.5	10,000	10	1,100	45	350	11	2000	1.0	3.5	400	ND	40
Lactation														
≤18 y	17	2.5	8,000	10	900	45	350	9	1,700	1.0	4	400	ND	34
19–50 y	20	2.5	10,000	10	1,100	45	350	11	2,000	1.0	4	400	ND	40

Source: Adapted from the Dietary Reference Intakes series, National Academies Press. Copyright 1997, 1998, 2000, 2001, by the National Academy of Sciences. These reports may be accessed via www.nap.edu. Courtesy of the National Academies Press, Washington, DC.

[a] UL = The maximum level of daily nutrient intake that is likely to pose no risk of adverse effects. Unless otherwise specified, the UL represents total intake from food, water, and supplements. Due to lack of suitable data, ULs could not be established for vitamin K, thiamin, riboflavin, vitamin B_{12}, pantothenic acid, biotin, or carotenoids. In the absence of ULs, extra caution may be warranted in consuming levels above recommended intakes.

[b] As preformed vitamin A only.

[c] As α-tocopherol; applies to any form of supplemental α-tocopherol.

[d] The ULs for vitamin E, niacin, and folate apply to synthetic forms obtained from supplements, fortified foods, or a combination of the two.

[e] ND = Not determinable due to lack of data of adverse effects in this age group and concern with regard to lack of ability to handle excess amounts. Source of intake should be from food only to prevent high levels of intake.

[f] The ULs for magnesium represent intake from a pharmacological agent only and do not include intake from food and water.

[g] Although vanadium in food has not been shown to cause adverse effects in humans, there is no justification for adding vanadium to food, and vanadium supplements should be used with caution. The UL is based on adverse effects in laboratory animals, and this data could be used to set a UL for adults but not children and adolescents.